D MAP PAGES

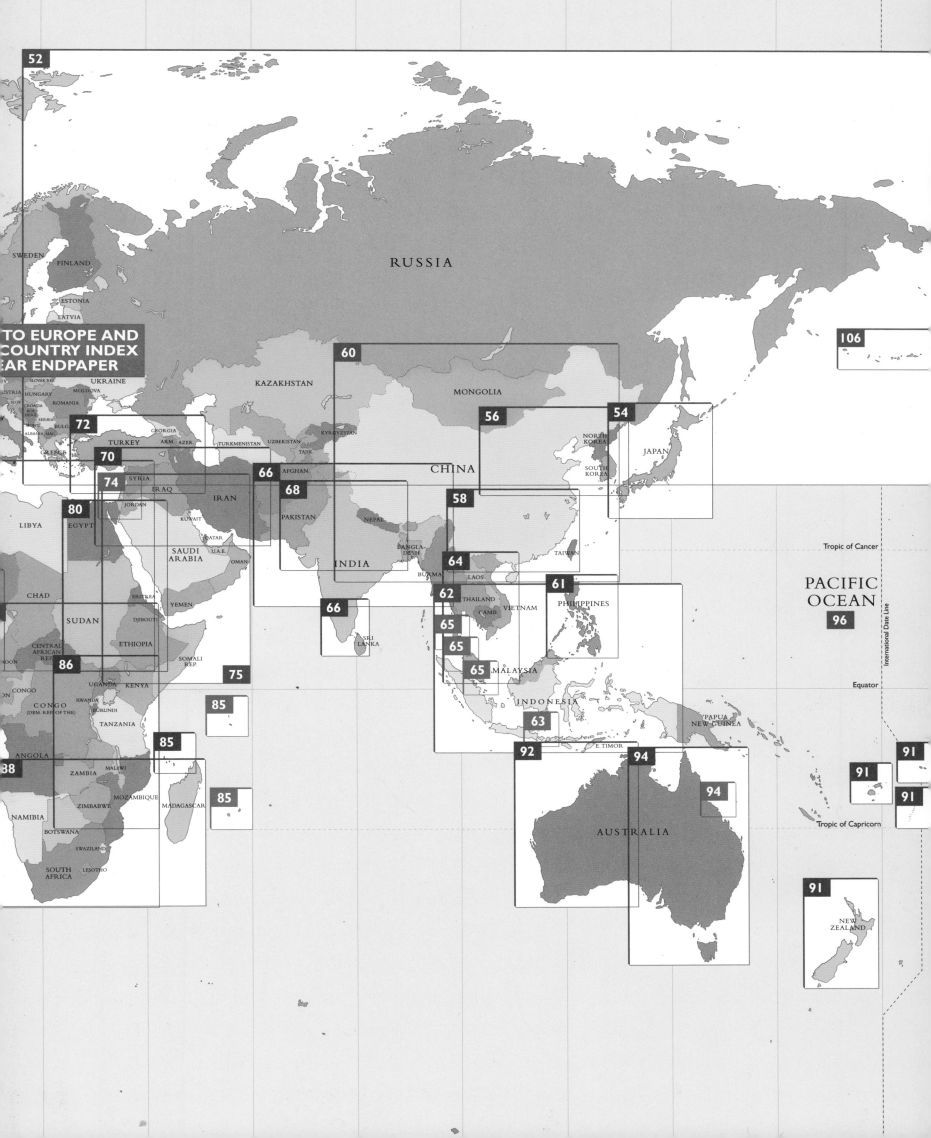

52

SWEDEN
FINLAND
ESTONIA
LATVIA

RUSSIA

TO EUROPE AND
COUNTRY INDEX
EAR ENDPAPER

UKRAINE
AUSTRIA
HUNGARY   MOLDOVA
CROATIA   ROMANIA
BOS.
HERZ.   SERBIA
ALBANIA MAC.   BULG.
GREECE

KAZAKHSTAN

MONGOLIA

106

60

72

GEORGIA
ARM. AZER.

70

TURKEY

74

SYRIA

80

JORDAN

IRAQ

EGYPT

LIBYA

56

54

KYRGYZSTAN

TURKMENISTAN   UZBEKISTAN

NORTH
KOREA

JAPAN

TAJIK.

66

AFGHAN.

68

CHINA

SOUTH
KOREA

58

PAKISTAN

NEPAL

IRAN

SAUDI
ARABIA

KUWAIT

QATAR

U.A.E.

OMAN

BANGLA-
DESH

INDIA

BURMA

64

TAIWAN

Tropic of Cancer

PACIFIC
OCEAN

CHAD

SUDAN

ERITREA

YEMEN

ETHIOPIA

DJIBOUTI

SOMALI
REP.

66

SRI
LANKA

LAOS

62

THAILAND

CAMB.

61

PHILIPPINES

96

65

VIETNAM

65

CENTRAL
AFRICAN
REP.

86

UGANDA   KENYA

RWANDA

65

MALAYSIA

85

International Date Line

Equator

CONGO
(DEM. REP. OF THE)

BURUNDI

TANZANIA

INDONESIA

75

PAPUA
NEW GUINEA

91

91

ANGOLA

88

ZAMBIA

MALAWI

63

E. TIMOR

92

94

91

ZIMBABWE

MOZAMBIQUE

MADAGASCAR

85

85

NAMIBIA

BOTSWANA

SWAZILAND

AUSTRALIA

94

Tropic of Capricorn

SOUTH
AFRICA

LESOTHO

91

NEW
ZEALAND

OXFORD

NEW CONCISE
WORLD
ATLAS

OXFORD

NEW CONCISE
WORLD
ATLAS

SECOND EDITION

THE EARTH IN SPACE
Cartography by Philip's

Text
Keith Lye

Illustrations
Stefan Chabluk

Star Charts
Wil Tirion

PICTURE ACKNOWLEDGEMENTS
Mike Brown 46 (top left), 48 (top left), 50 (top left), 56 (top left), 60 (top left)
Corbis /Ed Eckstein 58 (bottom), /Colin Garratt; Milepost 92 1/2 60 (bottom), /Aaron Horowitz
40 (top left), /Wolfgang Kaehler 37, /Manoocher/Webistan 48 (top right), /Kevin R. Morris 48
(bottom), /Galen Rowell 62 (bottom), /Royalty-Free 36 (top left), 44 (top left), 47, 52 (top left),
54 (top left), 58 (top left), 62 (top left), /Peter Turnley 51, /Nik Wheeler 46 (bottom), /Tim Wright 61
Corbis Saba /Shepard Sherbell 56 (bottom)
Corbis Sygma /Thorne Anderson 63
Michael P. Doukas/USGS/CVO 32 (top left)
Akira Fujii/David Malin Images 27
Getty Images/The Image Bank /Peter Hendrie 36 (top right), /Pete Turner 55
Getty Images/Stone /James Balog 32 (bottom), /Simeone Huber 49, /Gary John Norman 52 (bottom),
/Frank Oberle 41 (top), /Dennis Oda 33, /Donovan Reese 34–5, /Michael Townsend 45
Robert Harding Picture Library /Bill Ross 57, /Adam Woolfitt 59
Images Colour Library Limited 31
NASA 18 (top left), 20 (top left), 22 (top left), 24 (top left), 26 (top left), 26 (bottom), /Jacques
Descloitres, MODIS/GSFC 28 (top left), /ESA, S. Beckwith (STScI) and the HUDF Team 18 (bottom),
/GSFC 24 (top right), /Hubble Heritage Team (STScI/AURA)/R.G. French (Wellesley College)/J. Cuzzi
and J. Lissauer (NASA/Ames Research Center)/L. Dones (SwRI) 25 (bottom left), /JPL 24 (center left),
24 (bottom left), 25 (top left), 25 (center right), /JPL/Univ. Arizona 25 (top left), /JPL/USGS
24 (bottom right), /JSC 38 (top left), 42 (top left), /Hal Pierce/GSFC 40 (top right), /A. Stern (SwRI),
M. Buie (Lowell Observatory)/ESA 25 (bottom right), /Reto Stöckli, Robert Simmon/GSFC 17
NPA Group, Edenbridge, UK 28 (bottom), 29, (top), 29 (bottom), 64
Caroline O'Hara 34 (top left)
Christopher Rayner 30 (top left), 35 (top)
Rex Features /Sipa 50 (bottom)
Science Photo Library /Martin Bond 30 (bottom), /CNES, 1992 Distribution SPOT Image 43 (top),
/Luke Dodd 19, 21, /Earth Satellite Corporation 41 (bottom), /Simon Fraser 54 (bottom), /NASA 38
(bottom), 39, /David Parker 42 (bottom), /Peter Ryan 43 (bottom), /Jerry Schad 20 (bottom)
Still Pictures /François Pierrel 44 (bottom)
Tony Stone Images /Nigel Press 53

Philip's,
a division of Octopus Publishing Group Limited,
2–4 Heron Quays, London E14 4JP

Cartography by Philip's

Published in North America by
Oxford University Press, Inc.
198 Madison Avenue,
New York, NY 10016

www.oup.com/us

OXFORD
UNIVERSITY PRESS   Oxford is a registered trademark of Oxford University Press

Library of Congress Cataloging-in-Publication Data available

ISBN-13 978–0–19–532015–2
ISBN-10 0–19–532015–8

Printing (last digit): 9 8 7 6 5 4 3 2 1

Printed in Hong Kong

USER GUIDE

The reference maps which form the main body of this atlas have been prepared in accordance with the highest standards of international cartography to provide an accurate and detailed representation of the Earth. The scales and projections used have been carefully chosen to give balanced coverage of the world, while emphasizing the most densely populated and economically significant regions. A hallmark of Philip's mapping is the use of hill shading and relief coloring to create a graphic impression of landforms: this makes the maps exceptionally easy to read. However, knowledge of the key features employed in the construction and presentation of the maps will enable the reader to derive the fullest benefit from the atlas.

MAP SEQUENCE

The atlas covers the Earth continent by continent: first Europe; then its land neighbor Asia (mapped north before south, in a clockwise sequence), then Africa, Australia and Oceania, North America, and South America. This is the classic arrangement adopted by most cartographers since the 16th century. For each continent, there are maps at a variety of scales. First, physical relief

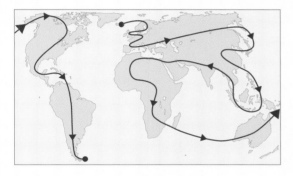

and political maps of the whole continent; then a series of larger-scale maps of the regions within the continent, each followed, where required, by still larger-scale maps of the most important or densely populated areas. The governing principle is that by turning the pages of the atlas, the reader moves steadily from north to south through each continent, with each map overlapping its neighbors.

MAP PRESENTATION

With very few exceptions (for example, for the Arctic and Antarctica), the maps are drawn with north at the top, regardless of whether they are presented upright or sideways on the page. In the borders will be found the map title; a locator diagram showing the area covered; continuation arrows showing the page numbers for maps of adjacent areas; the scale; the projection used; the degrees of latitude and longitude; and the letters and figures used in the index for locating place names and geographical features. Physical relief maps also have a height reference panel identifying the colors used for each layer of contouring.

MAP SYMBOLS

Each map contains a vast amount of detail which can only be conveyed clearly and accurately by the use of symbols. Points and circles of varying sizes locate and identify the relative importance of towns and cities; different styles of type are employed for administrative, geographical and regional place names to aid identification. A variety of pictorial symbols denote landscape features such as glaciers, marshes, and coral reefs, and man-made structures including roads, railroads, airports, canals, and dams. International borders are shown by red lines. Where neighboring countries are in dispute, for example in parts of the Middle East, the maps show the *de facto* boundary between nations, regardless of the legal or historical situation. The symbols are explained on the first page of the *World Maps* section of the atlas.

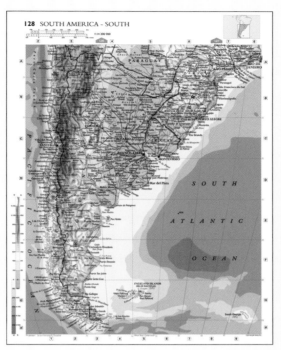

MAP SCALES

1:16 000 000
1 inch = 252 statute miles

The scale of each map is given in the numerical form known as the "representative fraction." The first figure is always one, signifying one unit of distance on the map; the second figure, usually in millions, is the number by which the map unit must be multiplied to give the equivalent distance on the Earth's surface. Calculations can easily be made in centimeters and kilometers, by dividing the Earth units figure by 100 000 (i.e. deleting the last five 0s). Thus 1:1 000 000 means 1 cm = 10 km. The calculation for inches and miles is more laborious, but 1 000 000 divided by 63 360 (the number of inches in a mile) shows that 1:1 000 000 means approximately 1 inch = 16 miles. The table below provides distance equivalents for scales down to 1:50 000 000.

LARGE SCALE		
1:1 000 000	1 cm = 10 km	1 inch = 16 miles
1:2 500 000	1 cm = 25 km	1 inch = 39.5 miles
1:5 000 000	1 cm = 50 km	1 inch = 79 miles
1:6 000 000	1 cm = 60 km	1 inch = 95 miles
1:8 000 000	1 cm = 80 km	1 inch = 126 miles
1:10 000 000	1 cm = 100 km	1 inch = 158 miles
1:15 000 000	1 cm = 150 km	1 inch = 237 miles
1:20 000 000	1 cm = 200 km	1 inch = 316 miles
1:50 000 000	1 cm = 500 km	1 inch = 790 miles
SMALL SCALE		

MEASURING DISTANCES

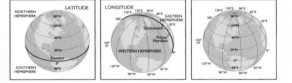

Although each map is accompanied by a scale bar, distances cannot always be measured with confidence because of the distortions involved in portraying the curved surface of the Earth on a flat page. As a general rule, the larger the map scale (that is, the lower the number of Earth units in the representative fraction), the more accurate and reliable will be the distance measured. On small-scale maps such as those of the world and of entire continents, measurement may only be accurate

along the "standard parallels," or central axes, and should not be attempted without considering the map projection.

MAP PROJECTIONS

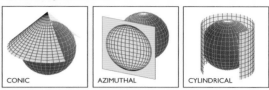

Unlike a globe, no flat map can give a true scale representation of the world in terms of area, shape and position of every region. Each of the numerous systems that have been devised for projecting the curved surface of the Earth on to a flat page involves the sacrifice of accuracy in one or more of these elements. The variations in shape and position of land masses such as Alaska, Greenland, and Australia, for example, can be quite dramatic when different projections are compared. For this atlas, the guiding principle has been to select projections that involve the least distortion of size and distance. The projection used for each map is noted in the border. Most fall into one of three categories – conic, azimuthal, or cylindrical – whose basic concepts are shown above. Each involves plotting the forms of the Earth's surface on a grid of latitude and longitude lines, which may be shown as parallels, curves, or radiating spokes.

LATITUDE AND LONGITUDE

Accurate positioning of individual points on the Earth's surface is made possible by reference to the geometrical system of latitude and longitude. Latitude *parallels* are drawn west–east around the Earth and numbered by degrees north and south of the equator, which is designated 0° of latitude. Longitude *meridians* are drawn north–south and numbered by degrees east and west of the *prime meridian*, 0° of longitude, which passes through Greenwich in England. By referring to these coordinates and their subdivisions of minutes (1/60th of a degree) and seconds (1/60th of a minute), any place on Earth can be located to within a few hundred yards. Latitude and longitude are indicated by blue lines on the maps; they are straight or curved according to the projection employed. Reference to these lines is the easiest way of determining the relative positions of places on different maps, and for plotting compass directions.

NAME FORMS

For ease of reference, both English and local name forms appear in the atlas. Oceans, seas, and countries are shown in English throughout the atlas; country names may be abbreviated to their commonly accepted form (for example, Germany, not The Federal Republic of Germany). Conventional English forms are also used for place names on the smaller-scale maps of the continents. However, local name forms are used on all large-scale and regional maps, with the English form given in brackets only for important cities – the large-scale map of Russia and Central Asia thus shows Moskva (Moscow). For countries which do not use a Roman script, place names have been transcribed according to the systems adopted by the British and US Geographic Names Authorities. For China, the Pin Yin system has been used, with some more widely known forms appearing in brackets, as with Beijing (Peking). Both English and local names appear in the index, the English form being cross-referenced to the local form.

CONTENTS

WORLD STATISTICS

COUNTRIES	10
CITIES	11
CLIMATE	12–13
PHYSICAL DIMENSIONS	14–15
REGIONS IN THE NEWS	16

THE EARTH IN SPACE

THE UNIVERSE	18–19
THE CONSTELLATIONS	20–21
STAR CHARTS	22–23
THE SOLAR SYSTEM	24–25
THE EARTH: TIME AND MOTION	26–27
THE EARTH FROM SPACE	28–29
THE DYNAMIC EARTH	30–31
EARTHQUAKES AND VOLCANOES	32–33
FORCES OF NATURE	34–35
OCEANS AND ICE	36–37
THE EARTH'S ATMOSPHERE	38–39
CLIMATE AND WEATHER	40–41
WATER AND LAND USE	42–43
THE NATURAL WORLD	44–45
THE HUMAN WORLD	46–47
LANGUAGES AND RELIGIONS	48–49
INTERNATIONAL ORGANIZATIONS	50–51
AGRICULTURE	52–53
ENERGY AND MINERALS	54–55
WORLD ECONOMIES	56–57
TRADE AND COMMERCE	58–59
TRAVEL AND COMMUNICATIONS	60–61
THE WORLD TODAY	62–63

WORLD MAPS

MAP SYMBOLS	1
THE WORLD: POLITICAL 1:84 000 000	2–3
ARCTIC OCEAN 1:31 100 000	4
ANTARCTICA 1:31 100 000	5

EUROPE

EUROPE: PHYSICAL 1:17 800 000	6
EUROPE: POLITICAL 1:17 800 000	7

SCANDINAVIA
1:5 300 000
Iceland 1:5 300 000
Færoe Islands 1:5 300 000

8–9

DENMARK AND SOUTHERN SWEDEN
1:2 200 000

10–11

IRELAND
1:1 800 000

12

SCOTLAND
1:1 800 000
Orkney Islands 1:1 800 000
Shetland Islands 1:1 800 000

13

ENGLAND AND WALES
1:1 800 000
Isles of Scilly 1:1 800 000

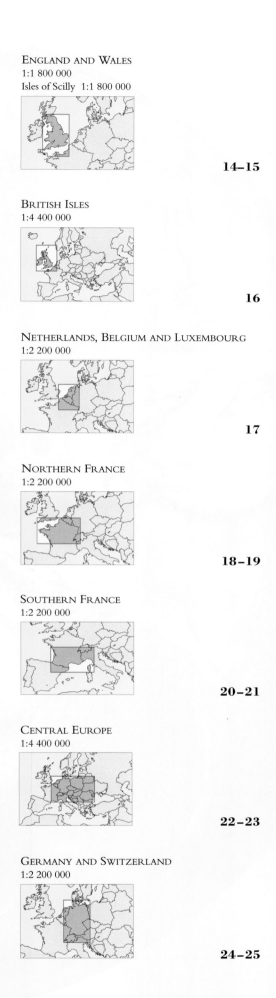

14–15

BRITISH ISLES
1:4 400 000

16

NETHERLANDS, BELGIUM AND LUXEMBOURG
1:2 200 000

17

NORTHERN FRANCE
1:2 200 000

18–19

SOUTHERN FRANCE
1:2 200 000

20–21

CENTRAL EUROPE
1:4 400 000

22–23

GERMANY AND SWITZERLAND
1:2 200 000

24–25

AUSTRIA, CZECH REPUBLIC
   AND SLOVAK REPUBLIC
1:2 200 000

26–27

HUNGARY, ROMANIA AND THE LOWER DANUBE
1:2 200 000

28–29

POLAND AND THE SOUTHERN BALTIC
1:2 200 000

30–31

BALTIC STATES, BELARUS AND UKRAINE
1:4 400 000

32–33

THE VOLGA BASIN AND THE CAUCASUS
1:4 400 000

34–35

WESTERN SPAIN AND PORTUGAL
1:2 200 000

36–37

EASTERN SPAIN
1:2 200 000
Menorca 1:2 200 000

38–39

NORTHERN ITALY, SLOVENIA AND CROATIA
1:2 200 000

40–41

SOUTHERN ITALY
1:2 200 000

42–43

THE BALKANS
1:2 200 000

44–45

SOUTHERN GREECE AND WESTERN TURKEY
1:2 200 000

46–47

THE BALEARICS, THE CANARIES AND MADEIRA
1:900 000 / 1:1 800 000

48

MALTA, CRETE, CORFU, RHODES AND CYPRUS
1:900 000 / 1:1 200 000

49

ASIA

ASIA: PHYSICAL
1:44 400 000   **50**

ASIA: POLITICAL
1:44 400 000   **51**

RUSSIA AND CENTRAL ASIA
1:17 800 000

      52–53

JAPAN
1:4 400 000
Ryukyu Islands 1:4 400 000

      54–55

NORTHERN CHINA AND KOREA
1:5 300 000

      56–57

SOUTHERN CHINA
1:5 300 000

      58–59

CHINA
1:17 800 000

      60

THE PHILIPPINES
1:6 700 000

      61

INDONESIA AND THE PHILIPPINES
1:11 100 000
Java and Madura 1:6 700 000
Bali 1:1 800 000

      62–63

MAINLAND SOUTHEAST ASIA
1:5 300 000
Ko Phuket 1:900 000
Ko Samui 1:900 000
Pinang 1:900 000
Singapore 1:900 000

      64–65

SOUTH ASIA
1:8 900 000

      66–67

NORTHERN INDIA, PAKISTAN AND NEPAL
1:5 300 000
Jammu and Kashmir 1:5 300 000

      68–69

THE MIDDLE EAST
1:6 200 000

      70–71

TURKEY AND TRANSCAUCASIA
1:4 400 000

      72–73

THE NEAR EAST
1:2 200 000

      74

ARABIA AND THE HORN OF AFRICA
1:13 300 000

      75

AFRICA

AFRICA: PHYSICAL
1:37 300 000   **76**

AFRICA: POLITICAL
1: 37 300 000   **77**

NORTHERN AFRICA
1:13 300 000
The Azores 1:13 300 000
Cape Verde Islands 1:11 100 000

      78–79

THE NILE VALLEY
1:7 100 000
The Nile Delta 1:3 600 000

      80–81

WEST AFRICA
1:7 100 000

      82–83

CENTRAL AND SOUTHERN AFRICA
1:13 300 000
Seychelles 1:2 200 000
Réunion 1:2 200 000
Mauritius 1:2 200 000
Comoros 1:7 100 000

      84–85

EAST AFRICA
1:7 100 000

      86–87

SOUTHERN AFRICA
1:7 100 000
Madagascar 1:7 100 000

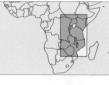

      88–89

Australia and Oceania

Australia and Oceania:
 Physical and Political
1:44 400 000   **90**

New Zealand
1:5 300 000
Fiji 1:5 300 000
Samoan Islands 1:5 300 000
Tonga 1:5 300 000
Tahiti and Moorea 1:1 100 000
    91

Western Australia
1:7 100 000
    92–93

Eastern Australia
1:7 100 000
Whitsunday Islands 1:2 200 000
Tasmania 1:7 100 000
    94–95

Pacific Ocean
1:48 000 000   **96–97**

North America

North America: Physical
1:31 100 000   **98**

North America: Political
1:31 100 000   **99**

Canada
1:13 300 000
    100–101

Western Canada
1:6 200 000
    102–103

Eastern Canada
1:6 200 000
    104–105

United States
1:10 700 000
Hawai'i 1:8 900 000
Alaska 1:26 700 000
    106–107

United States – West
1:6 000 000
    108–109

Central and Southern California
 and Western Washington
1:2 200 000
    110–111

United States Midwest and
 Northeast
1:6 000 000
    112–113

Northeastern United States
1:2 200 000
    114–115

United States – South
1:6 000 000
    116–117

Mexico
1:7 100 000
    118–119

Central America and the West Indies
1:7 100 000
Jamaica 1:2 700 000
Guadeloupe 1:1 800 000
Martinique 1:1 800 000
Puerto Rico 1:2 700 000
Virgin Islands 1:1 800 000
St Lucia 1:890 000
Barbados 1:890 000
    120–121

South America

South America: Physical
1:31 100 000   **122**

South America: Political
1:31 100 000   **123**

South America – North
1:14 200 000
Trinidad and Tobago 1:2 200 000
    124–125

Central South America
1:7 100 000
    126–127

South America – South
1:14 200 000
    128

Index to World Maps
    129–224

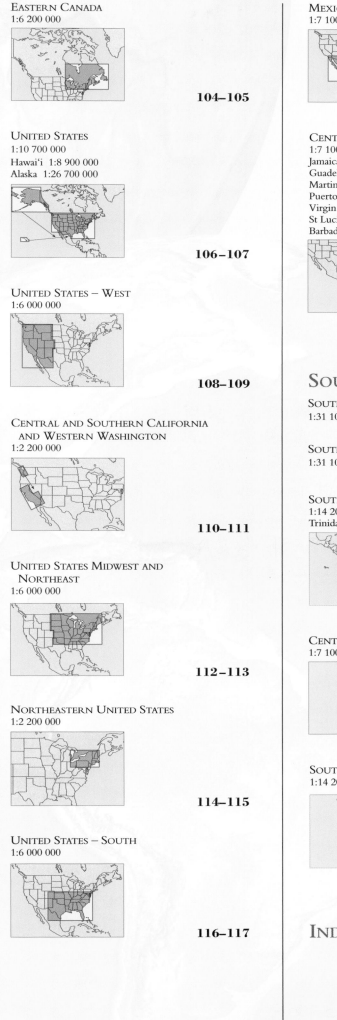

World Statistics: Countries

This alphabetical list includes the principal countries and territories of the world. If a territory is not completely independent, the country it is associated with is named. The area figures give the total area of land, inland water, and ice. The population figures are 2005 estimates where available. The annual income is the Gross Domestic Product per capita in US dollars. The figures are the latest available, usually 2005 estimates.

Country/Territory	Area km² Thousands	Area miles² Thousands	Population Thousands	Capital	Annual Income US $
Afghanistan	652	252	29,929	Kabul	800
Albania	28.7	11.1	3,563	Tirana	4,900
Algeria	2,382	920	32,532	Algiers	7,300
American Samoa (US)	0.20	0.08	58	Pago Pago	8,000
Andorra	0.47	0.18	71	Andorra La Vella	26,800
Angola	1,247	481	11,191	Luanda	2,500
Anguilla (UK)	0.10	0.04	13	The Valley	7,500
Antigua & Barbuda	0.44	0.17	69	St John's	11,000
Argentina	2,780	1,074	39,538	Buenos Aires	13,600
Armenia	29.8	11.5	2,983	Yerevan	5,100
Aruba (Netherlands)	0.19	0.07	72	Oranjestad	28,000
Australia	7,741	2,989	20,090	Canberra	32,000
Austria	83.9	32.4	8,185	Vienna	32,900
Azerbaijan	86.6	33.4	7,912	Baku	4,600
Azores (Portugal)	2.2	0.86	236	Ponta Delgada	15,000
Bahamas	13.9	5.4	302	Nassau	18,800
Bahrain	0.69	0.27	688	Manama	20,500
Bangladesh	144	55.6	144,320	Dhaka	2,100
Barbados	0.43	0.17	279	Bridgetown	17,300
Belarus	208	80.2	10,300	Minsk	7,600
Belgium	30.5	11.8	10,364	Brussels	31,800
Belize	23.0	8.9	279	Belmopan	6,800
Benin	113	43.5	7,460	Porto-Novo	1,200
Bermuda (UK)	0.05	0.02	65	Hamilton	36,000
Bhutan	47.0	18.1	2,232	Thimphu	1,400
Bolivia	1,099	424	8,858	La Paz/Sucre	2,700
Bosnia-Herzegovina	51.2	19.8	4,025	Sarajevo	6,800
Botswana	582	225	1,640	Gaborone	10,100
Brazil	8,514	3,287	186,113	Brasília	8,500
Brunei	5.8	2.2	372	Bandar Seri Begawan	23,600
Bulgaria	111	42.8	7,450	Sofia	9,000
Burkina Faso	274	106	13,925	Ouagadougou	1,200
Burma (= Myanmar)	677	261	42,909	Rangoon/Pyinmana	1,800
Burundi	27.8	10.7	6,371	Bujumbura	700
Cambodia	181	69.9	13,607	Phnom Penh	2,100
Cameroon	475	184	16,380	Yaoundé	2,000
Canada	9,971	3,850	32,805	Ottawa	32,800
Canary Is. (Spain)	7.2	2.8	1,682	Las Palmas/Santa Cruz	19,900
Cape Verde Is.	4.0	1.6	418	Praia	6,200
Cayman Is. (UK)	0.26	0.10	44	George Town	32,300
Central African Republic	623	241	3,800	Bangui	1,200
Chad	1,284	496	9,826	Ndjaména	1,900
Chile	757	292	15,981	Santiago	11,300
China	9,597	3,705	1,306,314	Beijing	6,200
Colombia	1,139	440	42,954	Bogotá	7,100
Comoros	2.2	0.86	671	Moroni	600
Congo	342	132	3,039	Brazzaville	800
Congo (Dem. Rep. of the)	2,345	905	60,086	Kinshasa	800
Cook Is. (NZ)	0.24	0.09	21	Avarua	5,000
Costa Rica	51.1	19.7	4,016	San José	10,000
Croatia	56.5	21.8	4,496	Zagreb	11,600
Cuba	111	42.8	11,347	Havana	3,300
Cyprus	9.3	3.6	780	Nicosia	21,600
Czech Republic	78.9	30.5	10,241	Prague	18,100
Denmark	43.1	16.6	5,432	Copenhagen	33,500
Djibouti	23.2	9.0	477	Djibouti	1,300
Dominica	0.75	0.29	69	Roseau	5,500
Dominican Republic	48.5	18.7	8,950	Santo Domingo	6,500
East Timor	14.9	5.7	1,041	Dili	400
Ecuador	284	109	13,364	Quito	3,900
Egypt	1,001	387	77,506	Cairo	4,400
El Salvador	21.0	8.1	6,705	San Salvador	5,100
Equatorial Guinea	28.1	10.8	536	Malabo	2,700
Eritrea	118	45.4	4,562	Asmara	1,000
Estonia	45.1	17.4	1,333	Tallinn	16,400
Ethiopia	1,104	426	73,053	Addis Ababa	800
Faroe Is. (Denmark)	1.4	0.54	47	Tórshavn	22,000
Fiji	18.3	7.1	893	Suva	6,000
Finland	338	131	5,223	Helsinki	30,300
France	552	213	60,656	Paris	29,900
French Guiana (France)	90.0	34.7	196	Cayenne	8,300
French Polynesia (France)	4.0	1.5	270	Papeete	17,500
Gabon	268	103	1,389	Libreville	5,800
Gambia, The	11.3	4.4	1,593	Banjul	1,900
Gaza Strip (OPT)*	0.36	0.14	1,376	–	600
Georgia	69.7	26.9	4,677	Tbilisi	3,400
Germany	357	138	82,431	Berlin	29,700
Ghana	239	92.1	21,030	Accra	2,500
Gibraltar (UK)	0.006	0.002	28	Gibraltar Town	27,900
Greece	132	50.9	10,668	Athens	22,800
Greenland (Denmark)	2,176	840	56	Nuuk (Godthåb)	20,000
Grenada	0.34	0.13	90	St George's	5,000
Guadeloupe (France)	1.7	0.66	449	Basse-Terre	7,900
Guam (US)	0.55	0.21	169	Agana	21,000
Guatemala	109	42.0	14,655	Guatemala City	4,300
Guinea	246	94.9	9,468	Conakry	2,200
Guinea-Bissau	36.1	13.9	1,416	Bissau	800
Guyana	215	83.0	765	Georgetown	3,900
Haiti	27.8	10.7	8,122	Port-au-Prince	1,600
Honduras	112	43.3	6,975	Tegucigalpa	2,900
Hong Kong (China)	1.1	0.42	6,899	–	36,800
Hungary	93.0	35.9	10,007	Budapest	15,900
Iceland	103	39.8	297	Reykjavik	34,600
India	3,287	1,269	1,080,264	New Delhi	3,400
Indonesia	1,905	735	241,974	Jakarta	3,700
Iran	1,648	636	68,018	Tehran	8,100
Iraq	438	169	26,075	Baghdad	3,400
Ireland	70.3	27.1	4,016	Dublin	34,100
Israel	20.6	8.0	6,277	Jerusalem	22,200
Italy	301	116	58,103	Rome	28,300
Ivory Coast (= Côte d'Ivoire)	322	125	17,298	Yamoussoukro	1,400
Jamaica	11.0	4.2	2,732	Kingston	4,300
Japan	378	146	127,417	Tokyo	30,400
Jordan	89.3	34.5	5,760	Amman	4,800
Kazakhstan	2,725	1,052	15,186	Astana	8,700
Kenya	580	224	33,830	Nairobi	1,200
Kiribati	0.73	0.28	103	Tarawa	800
Korea, North	121	46.5	22,912	Pyŏngyang	1,800
Korea, South	99.3	38.3	48,423	Seoul	20,300
Kuwait	17.8	6.9	2,336	Kuwait City	22,100
Kyrgyzstan	200	77.2	5,146	Bishkek	1,800
Laos	237	91.4	6,217	Vientiane	1,900
Latvia	64.6	24.9	2,290	Riga	12,800

Country/Territory	Area km² Thousands	Area miles² Thousands	Population Thousands	Capital	Annual Income US $
Lebanon	10.4	4.0	3,826	Beirut	5,100
Lesotho	30.4	11.7	1,867	Maseru	3,300
Liberia	111	43.0	3,482	Monrovia	700
Libya	1,760	679	5,766	Tripoli	8,400
Liechtenstein	0.16	0.06	34	Vaduz	25,000
Lithuania	65.2	25.2	3,597	Vilnius	13,700
Luxembourg	2.6	1.0	469	Luxembourg	62,700
Macau (China)	0.02	0.007	449	–	19,400
Macedonia (FYROM)	25.7	9.9	2,045	Skopje	7,400
Madagascar	587	227	18,040	Antananarivo	900
Madeira (Portugal)	0.78	0.30	241	Funchal	22,700
Malawi	118	45.7	12,159	Lilongwe	600
Malaysia	330	127	23,953	Kuala Lumpur/Putrajaya	10,400
Maldives	0.30	0.12	349	Malé	3,900
Mali	1,240	479	12,292	Bamako	1,000
Malta	0.32	0.12	399	Valletta	18,800
Marshall Is.	0.18	0.07	59	Majuro	1,600
Martinique (France)	1.1	0.43	433	Fort-de-France	14,400
Mauritania	1,026	396	3,087	Nouakchott	2,000
Mauritius	2.0	0.79	1,231	Port Louis	13,300
Mayotte (France)	0.37	0.14	194	Mamoundzou	2,600
Mexico	1,958	756	106,203	Mexico City	10,000
Micronesia, Fed. States of	0.70	0.27	108	Palikir	2,000
Moldova	33.9	13.1	4,455	Chişinău	2,100
Monaco	0.001	0.0004	32	Monaco	27,000
Mongolia	1,567	605	2,791	Ulan Bator	2,200
Montserrat (UK)	0.10	0.04	9	Plymouth	3,400
Morocco	447	172	32,726	Rabat	4,300
Mozambique	802	309	19,407	Maputo	1,300
Namibia	824	318	2,031	Windhoek	7,800
Nauru	0.02	0.008	13	Yaren District	5,000
Nepal	147	56.8	27,677	Katmandu	1,500
Netherlands	41.5	16.0	16,407	Amsterdam/The Hague	30,500
Netherlands Antilles (Neths)	0.80	0.31	220	Willemstad	11,400
New Caledonia (France)	18.6	7.2	216	Nouméa	15,000
New Zealand	271	104	4,035	Wellington	24,100
Nicaragua	130	50.2	5,465	Managua	2,800
Niger	1,267	489	11,666	Niamey	900
Nigeria	924	357	128,772	Abuja	1,000
Northern Mariana Is. (US)	0.46	0.18	80	Saipan	12,500
Norway	324	125	4,593	Oslo	42,400
Oman	310	119	3,002	Muscat	13,400
Pakistan	796	307	162,420	Islamabad	2,400
Palau	0.46	0.18	20	Koror	9,000
Panama	75.5	29.2	3,039	Panamá	7,300
Papua New Guinea	463	179	5,545	Port Moresby	2,400
Paraguay	407	157	6,348	Asunción	4,900
Peru	1,285	496	27,926	Lima	6,000
Philippines	300	116	87,857	Manila	5,100
Poland	323	125	38,635	Warsaw	12,700
Portugal	88.8	34.3	10,566	Lisbon	18,400
Puerto Rico (US)	8.9	3.4	3,917	San Juan	18,500
Qatar	11.0	4.2	863	Doha	26,000
Réunion (France)	2.5	0.97	777	St-Denis	6,200
Romania	238	92.0	22,330	Bucharest	8,300
Russia	17,075	6,593	143,420	Moscow	10,700
Rwanda	26.3	10.2	8,441	Kigali	1,300
St Kitts & Nevis	0.26	0.10	39	Basseterre	8,800
St Lucia	0.54	0.21	166	Castries	5,400
St Vincent & Grenadines	0.39	0.15	118	Kingstown	2,900
Samoa	2.8	1.1	177	Apia	5,600
San Marino	0.06	0.02	29	San Marino	34,600
São Tomé & Príncipe	0.96	0.37	187	São Tomé	1,200
Saudi Arabia	2,150	830	26,418	Riyadh	12,900
Senegal	197	76.0	11,127	Dakar	1,800
Serbia & Montenegro†	102	39.4	10,829	Belgrade	2,600
Seychelles	0.46	0.18	81	Victoria	7,800
Sierra Leone	71.7	27.7	6,018	Freetown	800
Singapore	0.68	0.26	4,426	Singapore City	29,700
Slovak Republic	49.0	18.9	5,431	Bratislava	15,700
Slovenia	20.3	7.8	2,011	Ljubljana	20,900
Solomon Is.	28.9	11.2	538	Honiara	1,700
Somalia	638	246	8,592	Mogadishu	600
South Africa	1,221	471	44,344	C. Town/Pretoria/Bloem.	11,900
Spain	498	192	40,341	Madrid	25,100
Sri Lanka	65.6	25.3	20,065	Colombo	4,300
Sudan	2,506	967	40,187	Khartoum	2,100
Suriname	163	63.0	438	Paramaribo	4,700
Swaziland	17.4	6.7	1,174	Mbabane	5,300
Sweden	450	174	9,002	Stockholm	29,600
Switzerland	41.3	15.9	7,489	Bern	35,000
Syria	185	71.5	18,449	Damascus	3,500
Taiwan	36.0	13.9	22,894	Taipei	26,700
Tajikistan	143	55.3	7,164	Dushanbe	1,200
Tanzania	945	365	36,766	Dodoma	700
Thailand	513	198	65,444	Bangkok	8,300
Togo	56.8	21.9	5,682	Lomé	1,600
Tonga	0.65	0.25	112	Nuku'alofa	2,300
Trinidad & Tobago	5.1	2.0	1,089	Port of Spain	12,700
Tunisia	164	63.2	10,075	Tunis	7,600
Turkey	775	299	69,661	Ankara	7,900
Turkmenistan	488	188	4,952	Ashkhabad	5,900
Turks & Caicos Is. (UK)	0.43	0.17	21	Cockburn Town	11,500
Tuvalu	0.03	0.01	12	Fongafale	1,100
Uganda	241	93.1	27,269	Kampala	1,700
Ukraine	604	233	47,425	Kiev	6,800
United Arab Emirates	83.6	32.3	2,563	Abu Dhabi	29,100
United Kingdom	242	93.4	60,441	London	30,900
United States of America	9,629	3,718	295,734	Washington, DC	41,800
Uruguay	175	67.6	3,416	Montevideo	10,000
Uzbekistan	447	173	26,851	Tashkent	1,900
Vanuatu	12.2	4.7	206	Port-Vila	2,900
Vatican City	0.0004	0.0002	1	Vatican City	N/A
Venezuela	912	352	25,375	Caracas	6,400
Vietnam	332	128	83,536	Hanoi	3,000
Virgin Is. (UK)	0.15	0.06	23	Road Town	38,500
Virgin Is. (US)	0.35	0.13	109	Charlotte Amalie	17,200
Wallis & Futuna Is. (France)	0.20	0.08	16	Mata-Utu	3,800
West Bank (OPT)*	5.9	2.3	2,386	–	1,100
Western Sahara	266	103	273	El Aaiún	N/A
Yemen	528	204	20,727	Sana'	800
Zambia	753	291	11,262	Lusaka	900
Zimbabwe	391	151	12,747	Harare	1,900

*OPT = Occupied Palestinian Territory N/A = Not available

† In June 2006, Serbia and Montenegro formally declared their independence and are now separate sovereign states.

World Statistics: Cities

This list shows the principal cities with more than 750,000 inhabitants. The figures are taken from the most recent census or estimate available, usually 2005, and as far as possible are the population of the metropolitan area or urban agglomeration (for example, greater New York, Mexico, or Paris). All the figures are in thousands. Local name forms have been used for the smaller cities (for example, Thessaloniki).

AFGHANISTAN	
Kabul	3,288
ALGERIA	
Algiers	3,260
ANGOLA	
Luanda	2,839
ARGENTINA	
Buenos Aires	13,349
Córdoba	1,592
Rosario	1,312
Mendoza	1,072
San Miguel de Tucumán	837
ARMENIA	
Yerevan	1,066
AUSTRALIA	
Sydney	4,388
Melbourne	3,663
Brisbane	1,769
Perth	1,484
Adelaide	1,137
AUSTRIA	
Vienna	2,190
AZERBAIJAN	
Baku	1,830
BANGLADESH	
Dhaka	12,560
Chittagong	4,171
Khulna	1,497
Rajshahi	1,035
BELARUS	
Minsk	1,709
BELGIUM	
Brussels	964
BOLIVIA	
La Paz	1,533
Santa Cruz	1,352
Cochabamba	797
BRAZIL	
São Paulo	18,333
Rio de Janeiro	11,469
Belo Horizonte	5,304
Pôrto Alegre	3,795
Recife	3,527
Brasília	3,341
Salvador	3,331
Fortaleza	3,261
Curitiba	2,871
Campinas	2,640
Belém	2,097
Goiânia	1,878
Manaus	1,673
Santos	1,634
Vitória	1,602
Maceió	1,137
Natal	1,049
São Luís	982
São José dos Campos	972
João Pessoa	931
Teresina	895
Campo Grande	821
BULGARIA	
Sofia	1,045
BURKINA FASO	
Ouagadougou	870
BURMA (MYANMAR)	
Rangoon	4,082
Mandalay	927
CAMBODIA	
Phnom Penh	1,174
CAMEROON	
Douala	1,980
Yaoundé	1,727
CANADA	
Toronto	5,060
Montréal	3,511
Vancouver	2,125
Ottawa	1,120
Calgary	1,074
Edmonton	1,005
CHILE	
Santiago	5,623
CHINA	
Shanghai	12,665
Beijing	10,849
Tianjin	9,346
Hong Kong	7,182
Wuhan	6,003
Chongqing	4,975
Shenyang	4,916
Guangzhou	3,881
Chengdu	3,478
Xi'an	3,256
Changchun	3,092
Harbin	2,898
Nanjing	2,806
Zibo	2,775
Dalian	2,709
Jinan	2,654
Taiyuan	2,516
Guiyang	2,467
Qingdao	2,431
Zhengzhou	2,250
Zaozhuang	2,189
Handan	2,120
Liupanshui	1,118
Changsha	2,051
Linyi	2,035
Lu'an	2,015
Wanxian	1,963
Hangzhou	1,955
Tianmen	1,948
Jinxi	1,850
Heze	1,847
Lanzhou	1,788
Tangshan	1,773
Xiantao	1,758
Kunming	1,748
Nanchang	1,742
Shijiazhuang	1,733
Yantai	1,707
Yulin	1,691
Yancheng	1,678
Xuzhou	1,662
Luoyang	1,594
Xinghua	1,587
Pingxiang	1,562
Ürümqi	1,562
Zhanjiang	1,562
Tai'an	1,550
Suining, Sichuan	1,520
Yiyang	1,510
Jilin	1,496
Changde	1,483
Wenzhou	1,475
Anshan	1,459
Qiqihar	1,452
Neijiang	1,449
Fushun	1,425
Huainan	1,422
Fuzhou	1,398
Nanning	1,395
Baotou	1,367
Weifang	1,360
Shantou	1,356
Xintai	1,334
Hefei	1,320
Huaian	1,297
Yueyang	1,286
Shenzhen	1,285
Tianshui	1,269
Suqian	1,258
Jingmen	1,228
Yuzhou	1,226
Zaoyang	1,210
Suzhou	1,201
Wuxi	1,192
Ningbo	1,188
Yongzhou	1,182
Mianyang	1,174
Leshan	1,172
Dongguan	1,150
Chifeng	1,140
Xiaoshan	1,130
Yixing	1,129
Zigong	1,123
Daqing	1,117
Datong	1,113
Huzhou	1,102
Jining, Shandong	1,101
Nanchong	1,072
Fuyu	1,068
Liuzhou	1,031
Xinyi, Jiangsu	1,022
Jixi	1,012
Linqing	1,009
Jiamusi	1,006
Hohhot	998
Xianyang	988
Changzhou	976
Zhangjiakou	973
Benxi	967
Xiangxiang	936
Zhangjiagang	936
Xinyu	932
Yichun, Heilongjiang	916
Yichun, Jiangxi	890
Jinzhou	888
Zhaotong	879
Yuyao	876
Anshun	864
Hengyang	853
Xuanzhou	851
Tongliao	847
Huaibei	830
Mudanjiang	827
Jiaxing	817
Kaifeng	810
Fuxin	807
Hunjiang	798
COLOMBIA	
Bogotá	7,594
Medellín	3,236
Cali	2,583
Barranquilla	1,918
Bucaramanga	1,069
Cartagena	1,002
Cúcuta	883
CONGO	
Brazzaville	1,153
CONGO (DEM. REP. OF THE)	
Kinshasa	5,717
Lubumbashi	1,102
Mbuji-Mayi	806
COSTA RICA	
San José	1,145
CROATIA	
Zagreb	1,067
CUBA	
Havana	2,192
CZECH REPUBLIC	
Prague	1,164
DENMARK	
Copenhagen	1,091
DOMINICAN REPUBLIC	
Santo Domingo	2,563
Santiago de los Caballeros	804
ECUADOR	
Guayaquil	2,387
Quito	1,514
EGYPT	
Cairo	11,146
Alexandria	3,760
Shubrâ el Kheima	937
EL SALVADOR	
San Salvador	1,472
ETHIOPIA	
Addis Ababa	2,899
FINLAND	
Helsinki	937
FRANCE	
Paris	9,630
Lyons	1,353
Marseilles	1,290
Lille	991
Nice	889
Toulouse	761
Bordeaux	754
GEORGIA	
Tbilisi	1,406
GERMANY	
Berlin	3,387
Hamburg	1,705
Munich	1,195
Cologne	963
GHANA	
Accra	1,970
Kumasi	862
GREECE	
Athens	3,238
Thessaloniki	824
GUATEMALA	
Guatemala City	3,242
GUINEA	
Conakry	1,465
HAITI	
Port-au-Prince	2,090
HONDURAS	
Tegucigalpa	1,061
HUNGARY	
Budapest	1,670
INDIA	
Mumbai	18,336
Delhi	15,334
Kolkata	14,299
Chennai	6,915
Bangalore	6,532
Hyderabad	6,145
Ahmedabad	5,171
Pune	4,485
Surat	3,671
Kanpur	3,040
Jaipur	2,796
Lucknow	2,589
Nagpur	2,359
Patna	2,066
Indore	1,941
Vadodara	1,686
Bhopal	1,656
Coimbatore	1,628
Ludhiana	1,583
Agra	1,526
Visakhapatnam	1,468
Cochin	1,461
Nashik	1,408
Meerut	1,340
Faridabad	1,330
Varanasi	1,300
Ghaziabad	1,277
Asansol	1,272
Jamshedpur	1,246
Madurai	1,245
Jabalpur	1,234
Rajkot	1,205
Dhanbad	1,195
Amritsar	1,162
Allahabad	1,153
Vijayawada	1,093
Srinagar	1,093
Aurangabad	1,065
Bhilainagar-Durg	1,051
Solapur	1,012
Ranchi	999
Jodhpur	954
Guwahati	941
Gwalior	939
Trivandrum	918
Calicut	917
Tiruchchirapalli	913
Chandigarh	896
Hubli-Dharwad	854
Mysore	851
INDONESIA	
Jakarta	13,194
Bandung	4,020
Surabaya	2,735
Medan	2,109
Palembang	1,675
Ujung Pandang	1,205
Bandar Lampung	915
Malang	898
Tegal	898
Semarang	816
Bogor	761
IRAN	
Tehran	7,352
Mashhad	2,147
Esfahan	1,547
Tabriz	1,396
Karaj	1,235
Shiraz	1,230
Qom	1,045
Ahvaz	967
Bakhtaran	771
IRAQ	
Baghdad	5,910
Mosul	1,236
Basra	1,187
Irbil	840
IRELAND	
Dublin	985
ISRAEL	
Tel Aviv-Yafo	3,025
Haifa	948
ITALY	
Rome	2,649
Milan	1,183
Naples	993
Turin	857
Genoa	803
IVORY COAST	
Abidjan	3,516
JAPAN	
Tokyo	12,064
Yokohama	6,427
Osaka	2,599
Nagoya	2,172
Sapporo	1,922
Kobe	1,493
Kyoto	1,468
Fukuoka	1,341
Kawasaki	1,250
Hiroshima	1,126
Kitakyushu	1,011
Sendai	1,008
Chiba	887
Sakai	792
JORDAN	
Amman	1,292
KAZAKHSTAN	
Almaty	1,103
KENYA	
Nairobi	2,818
KOREA, NORTH	
Pyŏngyang	3,124
Hamhung	821
KOREA, SOUTH	
Seoul	9,888
Pusan	3,830
Inch'on	2,884
Taegu	2,675
Taejŏn	1,522
Kwangju	1,379
Sŏngnam	1,353
Ulsan	1,340
Ansan	984
Puch'on	900
Suwŏn	876
P'ohang	790
KUWAIT	
Kuwait City	879
KYRGYZSTAN	
Bishkek	828
LATVIA	
Riga	719
LEBANON	
Beirut	2,070
LIBYA	
Tripoli	1,733
Benghazi	829
MADAGASCAR	
Antananarivo	1,808
MALAYSIA	
Kuala Lumpur	1,392
MALI	
Bamako	1,379
MEXICO	
Mexico City	19,013
Guadalajara	3,905
Monterrey	3,517
Toluca	1,987
Puebla	1,880
Tijuana	1,570
Ciudad Juárez	1,469
León	1,438
Torreón	1,057
San Luis Potosí	927
Mérida	919
Querétaro	913
Mexicali	840
Culiacán	799
MONGOLIA	
Ulan Bator	842
MOROCCO	
Casablanca	3,743
Rabat	1,859
Fès	1,032
Marrakesh	951
MOZAMBIQUE	
Maputo	1,316
NEPAL	
Katmandu	1,176
NETHERLANDS	
Amsterdam	1,157
Rotterdam	1,112
NEW ZEALAND	
Auckland	1,152
NICARAGUA	
Managua	1,159
NIGER	
Niamey	997
NIGERIA	
Lagos	11,135
Kano	2,884
Ibadan	2,375
Kaduna	1,329
Benin City	1,022
Ogbomosho	959
Port Harcourt	942
NORWAY	
Oslo	808
PAKISTAN	
Karachi	11,819
Lahore	6,373
Faisalabad	2,533
Rawalpindi	1,794
Gujranwala	1,466
Multan	1,459
Hyderabad	1,392
Peshawar	1,255
Islamabad	791
PANAMA	
Panamá	1,173
PARAGUAY	
Asunción	1,750
PERU	
Lima	8,180
PHILIPPINES	
Manila	10,677
Davao	1,326
POLAND	
Warsaw	1,626
Lódz	815
PORTUGAL	
Lisbon	1,977
Porto	1,303
PUERTO RICO	
San Juan	2,357
ROMANIA	
Bucharest	1,764
RUSSIA	
Moscow	10,672
Saint Petersburg	5,315
Novosibirsk	1,425
Nizhniy Novgorod	1,288
Yekaterinburg	1,281
Samara	1,140
Omsk	1,132
Kazan	1,108
Rostov	1,081
Chelyabinsk	1,067
Ufa	1,035
Volgograd	1,016
Perm	1,014
Voronezh	918
Saratov	881
Simbirsk	864
Krasnoyarsk	840
Togliatti	771
SAUDI ARABIA	
Riyadh	5,514
Jedda	3,807
Mecca	1,529
Medina	1,044
Dammam	920
SENEGAL	
Dakar	2,313
SERBIA AND MONTENEGRO	
Belgrade	1,116
SIERRA LEONE	
Freetown	1,007
SINGAPORE	
Singapore City	4,372
SOMALIA	
Mogadishu	1,257
SOUTH AFRICA	
Johannesburg	2,950
Cape Town	2,930
Durban / eThekwini	2,391
Pretoria / Tshwane	1,590
Port Elizabeth	1,006
SPAIN	
Madrid	3,017
Barcelona	1,527
SUDAN	
Khartoum	2,742
SWEDEN	
Stockholm	1,729
Gothenburg	829
SWITZERLAND	
Zürich	984
SYRIA	
Aleppo	2,505
Damascus	2,317
Homs	915
TAIWAN	
Taipei	2,473
Kaohsiung	1,506
T'aichung	1,066
TANZANIA	
Dar es Salaam	2,683
THAILAND	
Bangkok	6,604
TUNISIA	
Tunis	2,063
TURKEY	
Istanbul	8,953
Ankara	3,203
Izmir	2,250
Bursa	1,184
Adana	1,133
Gaziantep	862
Konya	761
UGANDA	
Kampala	1,345
UKRAINE	
Kiev	2,621
Kharkov	1,521
Dnepropetrovsk	1,122
Donetsk	1,065
Odessa	1,027
Zaporozhye	863
Lvov	794
UNITED ARAB EMIRATES	
Abu Dhabi	928
Dubai	886
UNITED KINGDOM	
London	8,089
Birmingham	2,373
Manchester	2,353
Liverpool	852
Glasgow	832
UNITED STATES OF AMERICA	
New York	17,800
Los Angeles	11,789
Chicago	8,308
Philadelphia	5,149
Miami	4,919
Dallas–Fort Worth	4,146
Boston	4,032
Washington	3,934
Detroit	3,903
Houston	3,823
Atlanta	3,500
San Francisco	3,229
Phoenix	2,907
Seattle	2,712
San Diego	2,674
Minneapolis–St Paul	2,389
St Louis	2,078
Baltimore	2,076
Tampa–St Petersburg	2,062
Denver	1,985
Cleveland	1,787
Pittsburgh	1,753
Portland	1,583
San Jose	1,538
San Bernardino	1,507
Cincinnati	1,503
Norfolk–Virginia Beach	1,394
Sacramento	1,393
Kansas City	1,362
San Antonio	1,328
Las Vegas	1,314
Milwaukee	1,309
Indianapolis	1,219
Providence	1,175
Orlando	1,157
Columbus	1,133
New Orleans	1,009
Buffalo	977
Memphis	972
Austin	902
Stamford	889
Salt Lake City	888
Jacksonville	882
Louisville	864
Hartford	852
Richmond	819
Charlotte	759
URUGUAY	
Montevideo	1,353
UZBEKISTAN	
Tashkent	2,160
VENEZUELA	
Caracas	3,276
Valencia	2,330
Maracaibo	2,182
Maracay	1,138
Ciudad Guayana	966
Barquisimeto	923
VIETNAM	
Ho Chi Minh City	5,030
Hanoi	4,147
Haiphong	1,817
YEMEN	
Sana'	1,621
ZAMBIA	
Lusaka	1,450
ZIMBABWE	
Harare	1,527
Bulawayo	824

WORLD STATISTICS: CLIMATE

Rainfall and temperature figures are provided for more than 70 cities around the world. As climate is affected by altitude, the height of each city is shown in meters beneath its name. For each location, the top row of figures shows the total rainfall or snow in millimeters, and the bottom row the average temperature in degrees Celsius; the average annual temperature and total annual rainfall are at the end of the rows. The map opposite shows the city locations.

CITY	JAN.	FEB.	MAR.	APR.	MAY	JUNE	JULY	AUG.	SEPT.	OCT.	NOV.	DEC.	YEAR
EUROPE													
Athens, Greece	62	37	37	23	23	14	6	7	15	51	56	71	402
107 m	10	10	12	16	20	25	28	28	24	20	15	11	18
Berlin, Germany	46	40	33	42	49	65	73	69	48	49	46	43	603
55 m	−1	0	4	9	14	17	19	18	15	9	5	1	9
Istanbul, Turkey	109	92	72	46	38	34	34	30	58	81	103	119	816
14 m	5	6	7	11	16	20	23	23	20	16	12	8	14
Lisbon, Portugal	111	76	109	54	44	16	3	4	33	62	93	103	708
77 m	11	12	14	16	17	20	22	23	21	18	14	12	17
London, UK	54	40	37	37	46	45	57	59	49	57	64	48	593
5 m	4	5	7	9	12	16	18	17	15	11	8	5	11
Málaga, Spain	61	51	62	46	26	5	1	3	29	64	64	62	474
33 m	12	13	16	17	19	29	25	26	23	20	16	13	18
Moscow, Russia	39	38	36	37	53	58	88	71	58	45	47	54	624
156 m	−13	−10	−4	6	13	16	18	17	12	6	−1	−7	4
Odesa, Ukraine	57	62	30	21	34	34	42	37	37	13	35	71	473
64 m	−3	−1	2	9	15	20	22	22	18	12	9	1	10
Paris, France	56	46	35	42	57	54	59	64	55	50	51	50	619
75 m	3	4	8	11	15	18	20	19	17	12	7	4	12
Rome, Italy	71	62	57	51	46	37	15	21	63	99	129	93	744
17 m	8	9	11	14	18	22	25	25	22	17	13	10	16
Shannon, Ireland	94	67	56	53	61	57	77	79	86	86	96	117	929
2 m	5	5	7	9	12	14	16	16	14	11	8	6	10
Stockholm, Sweden	43	30	25	31	34	45	61	76	60	48	53	48	554
44 m	−3	−3	−1	5	10	15	18	17	12	7	3	0	7
ASIA													
Bahrain	8	18	13	8	<3	0	0	0	0	0	18	18	81
5 m	17	18	21	25	29	32	33	34	31	28	24	19	26
Bangkok, Thailand	8	20	36	58	198	160	160	175	305	206	66	5	1,397
2 m	26	28	29	30	29	29	28	28	28	28	26	25	28
Beirut, Lebanon	191	158	94	53	18	3	<3	<3	5	51	132	185	892
34 m	14	14	16	18	22	24	27	28	26	24	19	16	21
Colombo, Sri Lanka	89	69	147	231	371	224	135	109	160	348	315	147	2,365
7 m	26	26	27	28	28	27	27	27	27	27	26	26	27
Harbin, China	6	5	10	23	43	94	112	104	46	33	8	5	488
160 m	−18	−15	−5	6	13	19	22	21	14	4	−6	−16	3
Ho Chi Minh, Vietnam	15	3	13	43	221	330	315	269	335	269	114	56	1,984
9 m	26	27	29	30	29	28	28	28	27	27	27	26	28
Hong Kong, China	33	46	74	137	292	394	381	361	257	114	43	31	2,162
33 m	16	15	18	22	26	28	28	28	27	25	21	18	23

CITY	JAN.	FEB.	MAR.	APR.	MAY	JUNE	JULY	AUG.	SEPT.	OCT.	NOV.	DEC.	YEAR
ASIA (continued)													
Jakarta, Indonesia	300	300	211	147	114	97	64	43	66	112	142	203	1,798
8 m	26	26	27	27	27	27	27	27	27	27	27	26	27
Kabul, Afghanistan	31	36	94	102	20	5	3	3	<3	15	20	10	338
1,815 m	−3	−1	6	13	18	22	25	24	20	14	7	3	12
Karachi, Pakistan	13	10	8	3	3	18	81	41	13	<3	3	5	196
4 m	19	20	24	28	30	31	30	29	28	28	24	20	26
Kazalinsk, Kazakhstan	10	10	13	13	15	5	5	8	8	10	13	15	125
63 m	−12	−11	−3	6	18	23	25	23	16	8	−1	−7	7
Kolkata (Calcutta), India	10	31	36	43	140	297	325	328	252	114	20	5	1,600
6 m	20	22	27	30	30	30	29	29	29	28	23	19	26
Mumbai (Bombay), India	3	3	3	<3	18	485	617	340	264	64	13	3	1,809
11 m	24	24	26	28	30	29	27	27	27	28	27	26	27
New Delhi, India	23	18	13	8	13	74	180	172	117	10	3	10	640
218 m	14	17	23	28	33	34	31	30	29	26	20	15	25
Omsk, Russia	15	8	8	13	31	51	51	51	28	25	18	20	318
85 m	−22	−19	−12	−1	10	16	18	16	10	1	−11	−18	−1
Shanghai, China	48	58	84	94	94	180	147	142	130	71	51	36	1,135
7 m	4	5	9	14	20	24	28	28	23	19	12	7	16
Singapore	252	173	193	188	173	173	170	196	178	208	254	257	2,413
10 m	26	27	28	28	28	28	28	27	27	27	27	27	27
Tehran, Iran	46	38	46	36	13	3	3	3	3	8	20	31	246
1,220 m	2	5	9	16	21	26	30	29	25	18	12	6	17
Tokyo, Japan	48	74	107	135	147	165	142	152	234	208	97	56	1,565
6 m	3	4	7	13	17	21	25	26	23	17	11	6	14
Ulan Bator, Mongolia	<3	<3	3	5	10	28	76	51	23	5	5	3	208
1,325 m	−26	−21	−13	−1	6	14	16	14	8	−1	−13	−22	−3
Verkhoyansk, Russia	5	5	3	5	8	23	28	25	13	8	8	5	134
100 m	−50	−45	−32	−15	0	12	14	9	2	−15	−38	−48	−17
AFRICA													
Addis Ababa, Ethiopia	<3	3	25	135	213	201	206	239	102	28	<3	0	1,151
2,450 m	19	20	20	20	19	18	18	19	21	22	21	20	20
Antananarivo, Madag.	300	279	178	53	18	8	8	10	18	61	135	287	1,356
1,372 m	21	21	21	19	18	15	14	15	17	19	21	21	19
Cairo, Egypt	5	5	5	3	3	<3	0	0	<3	<3	3	5	28
116 m	13	15	18	21	25	28	28	28	26	24	20	15	22
Cape Town, S. Africa	15	8	18	48	79	84	89	66	43	31	18	10	508
17 m	21	21	20	17	14	13	12	13	14	16	18	19	17
Jo'burg, S. Africa	114	109	89	38	25	8	8	8	23	56	107	125	709
1,665 m	20	20	18	16	13	10	11	13	16	18	19	20	16

CITY	JAN.	FEB.	MAR.	APR.	MAY	JUNE	JULY	AUG.	SEPT.	OCT.	NOV.	DEC.	YEAR
AFRICA (continued)													
Khartoum, Sudan	<3	<3	<3	<3	3	8	53	71	18	5	<3	0	158
390 m	24	25	28	31	33	34	32	31	32	32	28	25	29
Kinshasa, Congo (D.R.)	135	145	196	196	158	8	3	3	31	119	221	142	1,354
325 m	26	26	27	27	26	24	23	24	25	26	26	26	25
Lagos, Nigeria	28	46	102	150	269	460	279	64	140	206	69	25	1,836
3 m	27	28	29	28	28	26	26	25	26	26	28	28	27
Lusaka, Zambia	231	191	142	18	3	<3	<3	0	<3	10	91	150	836
1,277 m	21	22	21	21	19	16	16	18	22	24	23	22	21
Monrovia, Liberia	31	56	97	216	516	973	996	373	744	772	236	130	5,138
23 m	26	26	27	27	26	25	24	25	25	25	26	26	26
Nairobi, Kenya	38	64	125	211	158	46	15	23	31	53	109	86	958
820 m	19	19	19	19	18	16	16	16	18	19	18	18	18
Timbuktu, Mali	<3	<3	3	<3	5	23	79	81	38	3	<3	<3	231
301 m	22	24	28	32	34	35	32	30	32	31	28	23	29
Tunis, Tunisia	64	51	41	36	18	8	3	8	33	51	48	61	419
66 m	10	11	13	16	19	23	26	27	25	20	16	11	18
Walvis Bay, Namibia	<3	5	8	3	3	<3	<3	3	<3	<3	<3	<3	23
7 m	19	19	19	18	17	16	15	14	14	15	17	18	18
AUSTRALIA, NEW ZEALAND AND ANTARCTICA													
Alice Springs, Aust.	43	33	28	10	15	13	8	8	8	18	31	38	252
579 m	29	28	25	20	15	12	12	14	18	23	26	28	21
Christchurch, N.Z.	56	43	48	48	66	66	69	48	46	43	48	56	638
10 m	16	16	14	12	9	6	6	7	9	12	14	16	11
Darwin, Australia	386	312	254	97	15	3	<3	3	13	51	119	239	1,491
30 m	29	29	29	29	28	26	25	26	28	29	30	29	28
Mawson, Antarctica	11	30	20	10	44	180	4	40	3	20	0	0	362
14 m	0	-5	-10	-14	-15	-16	-18	-18	-19	-13	-5	-1	-11
Perth, Australia	8	10	20	43	130	180	170	149	86	56	20	13	881
60 m	23	23	22	19	16	14	13	13	15	16	19	22	18
Sydney, Australia	89	102	127	135	127	117	117	76	73	71	73	73	1,181
42 m	22	22	21	18	15	13	12	13	15	18	19	21	17
NORTH AMERICA													
Anchorage, USA	20	18	15	10	13	18	41	66	66	56	25	23	371
40 m	-11	-8	-5	2	7	12	14	13	9	2	-5	-11	2
Chicago, USA	51	51	66	71	86	89	84	81	79	66	61	51	836
251 m	-4	-3	2	9	14	20	23	22	19	12	5	-1	10
Churchill, Canada	15	13	18	23	32	44	46	58	51	43	39	21	402
13 m	-28	-26	-20	-10	-2	6	12	11	5	-2	-12	-22	-7
Edmonton, Canada	25	19	19	22	43	77	89	78	39	17	16	25	466
676 m	-15	-10	-5	4	11	15	17	16	11	6	-4	-10	3
Honolulu, USA	104	66	79	48	25	18	23	28	36	48	64	104	643
12 m	23	18	19	20	22	24	25	26	26	24	22	19	22
Houston, USA	89	76	84	91	119	117	99	99	104	94	89	109	1,171
12 m	12	13	17	21	24	27	28	29	26	22	16	12	21

CITY	JAN.	FEB.	MAR.	APR.	MAY	JUNE	JULY	AUG.	SEPT.	OCT.	NOV.	DEC.	YEAR
NORTH AMERICA (continued)													
Kingston, Jamaica	23	15	23	31	102	89	38	91	99	180	74	36	800
34 m	25	25	25	26	26	28	28	28	27	27	26	26	26
Los Angeles, USA	79	76	71	25	10	3	<3	<3	5	15	31	66	381
95 m	13	14	14	16	17	19	21	22	21	18	16	14	17
Mexico City, Mexico	13	5	10	20	53	119	170	152	130	51	18	8	747
2,309 m	12	13	16	18	19	19	17	18	18	16	14	13	16
Miami, USA	71	53	64	81	173	178	155	160	203	234	71	51	1,516
8 m	20	20	22	23	25	27	28	28	27	25	22	21	24
Montréal, Canada	72	65	74	74	66	82	90	92	88	76	81	87	946
57 m	-10	-9	-3	-6	13	18	21	20	15	9	2	-7	6
New York City, USA	94	97	91	81	81	84	107	109	86	89	76	91	1,092
96 m	-1	-1	3	10	16	20	23	23	21	15	7	2	11
St Louis, USA	58	64	89	97	114	114	89	86	81	74	71	64	1,001
173 m	0	1	7	13	19	24	26	26	22	15	8	2	14
San José, Costa Rica	15	5	20	46	229	241	211	241	305	300	145	41	1,798
1,146 m	19	19	21	21	22	21	21	21	21	20	20	19	20
Vancouver, Canada	154	115	101	60	52	45	32	41	67	114	150	182	1,113
14 m	3	5	6	9	12	15	17	17	14	10	6	4	10
Washington, DC, USA	86	76	91	84	94	99	112	109	94	74	66	79	1,064
22 m	1	2	7	12	18	23	25	24	20	14	8	3	13
SOUTH AMERICA													
Antofagasta, Chile	0	0	0	<3	<3	3	5	3	<3	3	<3	0	13
94 m	21	21	20	18	16	15	14	14	15	16	18	19	17
Buenos Aires, Arg.	79	71	109	89	76	61	56	61	79	86	84	99	950
27 m	23	23	21	17	13	9	10	11	13	15	19	22	16
Lima, Peru	3	<3	<3	<3	5	5	8	8	8	3	3	<3	41
120 m	23	24	24	22	19	17	17	16	17	18	19	21	20
Manaus, Brazil	249	231	262	221	170	84	58	38	46	107	142	203	1,811
44 m	28	28	28	27	28	28	28	28	29	29	29	28	28
Paraná, Brazil	287	236	239	102	13	<3	3	5	28	127	231	310	1,582
260 m	23	23	23	23	23	21	21	22	24	24	24	23	23
Rio de Janeiro, Brazil	125	122	130	107	79	53	41	43	66	79	104	137	1,082
61 m	26	26	25	24	22	21	21	21	22	23	23	25	23

WORLD STATISTICS: PHYSICAL DIMENSIONS

Each topic list is divided into continents and within a continent the items are listed in order of size. The bottom part of many of the lists is selective in order to give examples from as many different countries as possible. The order of the continents is as in the atlas, Europe through to South America. The world top ten are shown in square brackets; in the case of mountains this has not been done because the world top 30 are all in Asia. The figures are rounded as appropriate.

WORLD, CONTINENTS, OCEANS

THE WORLD	km²	miles²	%
The World	509,450,000	196,672,000	–
Land	149,450,000	57,688,000	29.3
Water	360,000,000	138,984,000	70.7
Asia	44,500,000	17,177,000	29.8
Africa	30,302,000	11,697,000	20.3
North America	24,241,000	9,357,000	16.2
South America	17,793,000	6,868,000	11.9
Antarctica	14,100,000	5,443,000	9.4
Europe	9,957,000	3,843,000	6.7
Australia & Oceania	8,557,000	3,303,000	5.7
Pacific Ocean	155,557,000	60,061,000	46.4
Atlantic Ocean	76,762,000	29,638,000	22.9
Indian Ocean	68,556,000	26,470,000	20.4
Southern Ocean	20,327,000	7,848,000	6.1
Arctic Ocean	14,056,000	5,427,000	4.2

SEAS

PACIFIC	km²	miles²
South China Sea	2,974,600	1,148,500
Bering Sea	2,268,000	875,000
Sea of Okhotsk	1,528,000	590,000
East China & Yellow	1,249,000	482,000
Sea of Japan	1,008,000	389,000
Gulf of California	162,000	62,500
Bass Strait	75,000	29,000

ATLANTIC	km²	miles²
Caribbean Sea	2,766,000	1,068,000
Mediterranean Sea	2,516,000	971,000
Gulf of Mexico	1,543,000	596,000
Hudson Bay	1,232,000	476,000
North Sea	575,000	223,000
Black Sea	462,000	178,000
Baltic Sea	422,170	163,000
Gulf of St Lawrence	238,000	92,000

INDIAN	km²	miles²
Red Sea	438,000	169,000
Persian Gulf	239,000	92,000

MOUNTAINS

EUROPE		m	ft
Elbrus	Russia	5,642	18,510
Mont Blanc	France/Italy	4,807	15,771
Monte Rosa	Italy/Switzerland	4,634	15,203
Dom	Switzerland	4,545	14,911
Liskamm	Switzerland	4,527	14,852
Weisshorn	Switzerland	4,505	14,780
Taschorn	Switzerland	4,490	14,730
Matterhorn/Cervino	Italy/Switzerland	4,478	14,691
Mont Maudit	France/Italy	4,465	14,649
Dent Blanche	Switzerland	4,356	14,291
Nadelhorn	Switzerland	4,327	14,196
Grandes Jorasses	France/Italy	4,208	13,806
Jungfrau	Switzerland	4,158	13,642
Barre des Ecrins	France	4,103	13,461
Gran Paradiso	Italy	4,061	13,323
Piz Bernina	Italy/Switzerland	4,049	13,284
Eiger	Switzerland	3,970	13,025
Monte Viso	Italy	3,841	12,602
Grossglockner	Austria	3,797	12,457
Wildspitze	Austria	3,772	12,382
Monte Disgrazia	Italy	3,678	12,066
Mulhacén	Spain	3,478	11,411
Pico de Aneto	Spain	3,404	11,168
Etna	Italy	3,340	10,958
Zugspitze	Germany	2,962	9,718
Musala	Bulgaria	2,925	9,596
Olympus	Greece	2,917	9,570
Triglav	Slovenia	2,863	9,393
Monte Cinto	France (Corsica)	2,710	8,891
Galdhøpiggen	Norway	2,469	8,100
Ben Nevis	UK	1,342	4,403

ASIA		m	ft
Everest	China/Nepal	8,850	29,035
K2 (Godwin Austen)	China/Kashmir	8,611	28,251
Kanchenjunga	India/Nepal	8,598	28,208
Lhotse	China/Nepal	8,516	27,939
Makalu	China/Nepal	8,481	27,824
Cho Oyu	China/Nepal	8,201	26,906
Dhaulagiri	Nepal	8,167	26,795
Manaslu	Nepal	8,156	26,758
Nanga Parbat	Kashmir	8,126	26,660
Annapurna	Nepal	8,078	26,502
Gasherbrum	China/Kashmir	8,068	26,469
Broad Peak	China/Kashmir	8,051	26,414
Xixabangma	China	8,012	26,286
Gayachung Kang	Nepal	7,897	25,909
Himalchuli	Nepal	7,893	25,896
Disteghil Sar	Kashmir	7,885	25,869
Nuptse	Nepal	7,879	25,849
Kangbachen	Nepal	7,858	25,781
Khunyang Chhish	Kashmir	7,852	25,761
Masherbrum	Kashmir	7,821	25,659
Nanda Devi	India	7,817	25,646
Rakaposhi	Kashmir	7,788	25,551
Batura	Kashmir	7,785	25,541
Namche Barwa	China	7,782	25,531
Kamet	India	7,756	25,447
Soltoro Kangri	Kashmir	7,742	25,400
Gurla Mandhata	China	7,728	25,354
Trivor	Pakistan	7,720	25,328
Kongur Shan	China	7,719	25,324
Jannu	Nepal	7,710	25,295
Tirich Mir	Pakistan	7,690	25,229
K'ula Shan	Bhutan/China	7,543	24,747
Pik Imeni Ismail Samani	Tajikistan	7,495	24,590
Demavend	Iran	5,604	18,386
Ararat	Turkey	5,165	16,945
Gunong Kinabalu	Malaysia (Borneo)	4,101	13,455
Yu Shan	Taiwan	3,997	13,113
Fuji-San	Japan	3,776	12,388

AFRICA		m	ft
Kilimanjaro	Tanzania	5,895	19,340
Mt Kenya	Kenya	5,199	17,057
Ruwenzori			
(Margherita)	Uganda/Congo (D.R.)	5,109	16,762
Ras Dashen	Ethiopia	4,620	15,157
Meru	Tanzania	4,565	14,977
Karisimbi	Rwanda/Congo (D.R.)	4,507	14,787
Mt Elgon	Kenya/Uganda	4,321	14,176
Batu	Ethiopia	4,307	14,130
Guna	Ethiopia	4,231	13,882
Toubkal	Morocco	4,165	13,665
Irhil Mgoun	Morocco	4,071	13,356
Mt Cameroun	Cameroon	4,070	13,353
Amba Ferit	Ethiopia	3,875	13,042
Pico del Teide	Spain (Tenerife)	3,718	12,198
Thabana Ntlenyana	Lesotho	3,482	11,424
Emi Koussi	Chad	3,415	11,204
Mt aux Sources	Lesotho/South Africa	3,282	10,768
Mt Piton	Réunion	3,069	10,069

OCEANIA		m	ft
Puncak Jaya	Indonesia	5,029	16,499
Puncak Trikora	Indonesia	4,730	15,518
Puncak Mandala	Indonesia	4,702	15,427
Mt Wilhelm	Papua New Guinea	4,508	14,790
Mauna Kea	USA (Hawai'i)	4,205	13,796
Mauna Loa	USA (Hawai'i)	4,169	13,678
Aoraki Mt Cook	New Zealand	3,753	12,313
Mt Balbi	Solomon Is.	2,439	8,002
Orohena	Tahiti	2,241	7,352
Mt Kosciuszko	Australia	2,230	7,316

NORTH AMERICA		m	ft
Mt McKinley			
(Denali)	USA (Alaska)	6,194	20,321
Mt Logan	Canada	5,959	19,551
Pico de Orizaba	Mexico	5,610	18,405
Mt St Elias	USA/Canada	5,489	18,008
Popocatépetl	Mexico	5,452	17,887

NORTH AMERICA (continued)		m	ft
Mt Foraker	USA (Alaska)	5,304	17,401
Iztaccihuatl	Mexico	5,286	17,343
Lucania	Canada	5,226	17,146
Mt Steele	Canada	5,073	16,644
Mt Bona	USA (Alaska)	5,005	16,420
Mt Blackburn	USA (Alaska)	4,996	16,391
Mt Sanford	USA (Alaska)	4,940	16,207
Mt Wood	Canada	4,848	15,905
Nevado de Toluca	Mexico	4,670	15,321
Mt Fairweather	USA (Alaska)	4,663	15,298
Mt Hunter	USA (Alaska)	4,442	14,573
Mt Whitney	USA	4,418	14,495
Mt Elbert	USA	4,399	14,432
Mt Harvard	USA	4,395	14,419
Mt Rainier	USA	4,392	14,409
Blanca Peak	USA	4,372	14,344
Longs Peak	USA	4,345	14,255
Tajumulco	Guatemala	4,220	13,845
Grand Teton	USA	4,197	13,770
Mt Waddington	Canada	3,994	13,104
Mt Robson	Canada	3,954	12,972
Chirripó Grande	Costa Rica	3,837	12,589
Pico Duarte	Dominican Rep.	3,175	10,417

SOUTH AMERICA		m	ft
Aconcagua	Argentina	6,962	22,841
Bonete	Argentina	6,872	22,546
Ojos del Salado	Argentina/Chile	6,863	22,516
Pissis	Argentina/Chile	6,779	22,241
Mercedario	Argentina/Chile	6,770	22,211
Huascarán	Peru	6,768	22,205
Llullaillaco	Argentina/Chile	6,723	22,057
Nudo de Cachi	Argentina	6,720	22,047
Yerupaja	Peru	6,632	21,758
N. de Tres Cruces	Argentina/Chile	6,620	21,719
Incahuasi	Argentina/Chile	6,601	21,654
Cerro Galan	Argentina	6,600	21,654
Tupungato	Argentina/Chile	6,570	21,555
Sajama	Bolivia	6,520	21,391
Illimani	Bolivia	6,485	21,276
Coropuna	Peru	6,425	21,079
Ausangate	Peru	6,384	20,945
Cerro del Toro	Argentina	6,380	20,932
Siula Grande	Peru	6,356	20,853
Chimborazo	Ecuador	6,267	20,561
Alpamayo	Peru	5,947	19,511
Cotapaxi	Ecuador	5,896	19,344
Pico Cristóbal Colón	Colombia	5,800	19,029
Pico Bolivar	Venezuela	5,007	16,427

ANTARCTICA		m	ft
Vinson Massif		4,897	16,066
Mt Kirkpatrick		4,528	14,855
Mt Markham		4,349	14,268

OCEAN DEPTHS

ATLANTIC OCEAN	m	ft	
Puerto Rico (Milwaukee) Deep	9,220	30,249	[7]
Cayman Trench	7,680	25,197	[10]
Gulf of Mexico	5,203	17,070	
Mediterranean Sea	5,121	16,801	
Black Sea	2,211	7,254	
North Sea	660	2,165	
Baltic Sea	463	1,519	
Hudson Bay	258	846	

INDIAN OCEAN	m	ft	
Java Trench	7,450	24,442	
Red Sea	2,635	8,454	
Persian Gulf	73	239	

PACIFIC OCEAN	m	ft	
Mariana Trench	11,022	36,161	[1]
Tonga Trench	10,882	35,702	[2]
Japan Trench	10,554	34,626	[3]
Kuril Trench	10,542	34,587	[4]
Mindanao Trench	10,497	34,439	[5]
Kermadec Trench	10,047	32,962	[6]

PACIFIC OCEAN (continued)

	m	ft	
Peru–Chile Trench	8,050	26,410	[8]
Aleutian Trench	7,822	25,662	[9]

ARCTIC OCEAN

	m	ft
Molloy Deep	5,608	18,399

SOUTHERN OCEAN

	m	ft
South Sandwich Trench	7,235	23,737

LAND LOWS

		m	ft
Caspian Sea	Europe	−28	−92
Dead Sea	Asia	−418	−1,371
Lake Assal	Africa	−156	−512
Lake Eyre North	Oceania	−16	−52
Death Valley	North America	−86	−282
Valdés Peninsula	South America	−40	−131

RIVERS

EUROPE

		km	miles
Volga	Caspian Sea	3,700	2,300
Danube	Black Sea	2,850	1,770
Ural	Caspian Sea	2,535	1,575
Dnepr (Dnipro)	Black Sea	2,285	1,420
Kama	Volga	2,030	1,260
Don	Black Sea	1,990	1,240
Petchora	Arctic Ocean	1,790	1,110
Oka	Volga	1,480	920
Belaya	Kama	1,420	880
Dnister (Dniester)	Black Sea	1,400	870
Vyatka	Kama	1,370	850
Rhine	North Sea	1,320	820
N. Dvina	Arctic Ocean	1,290	800
Desna	Dnepr (Dnipro)	1,190	740
Elbe	North Sea	1,145	710
Wisla	Baltic Sea	1,090	675
Loire	Atlantic Ocean	1,020	635

ASIA

		km	miles	
Yangtze	Pacific Ocean	6,380	3,960	[3]
Yenisey–Angara	Arctic Ocean	5,550	3,445	[5]
Huang He	Pacific Ocean	5,464	3,395	[6]
Ob–Irtysh	Arctic Ocean	5,410	3,360	[7]
Mekong	Pacific Ocean	4,500	2,795	[9]
Amur	Pacific Ocean	4,442	2,760	[10]
Lena	Arctic Ocean	4,402	2,735	
Irtysh	Ob	4,250	2,640	
Yenisey	Arctic Ocean	4,090	2,540	
Ob	Arctic Ocean	3,680	2,285	
Indus	Indian Ocean	3,100	1,925	
Brahmaputra	Indian Ocean	2,900	1,800	
Syrdarya	Aral Sea	2,860	1,775	
Salween	Indian Ocean	2,800	1,740	
Euphrates	Indian Ocean	2,700	1,675	
Vilyuy	Lena	2,650	1,645	
Kolyma	Arctic Ocean	2,600	1,615	
Amudarya	Aral Sea	2,540	1,575	
Ural	Caspian Sea	2,535	1,575	
Ganges	Indian Ocean	2,510	1,560	
Si Kiang	Pacific Ocean	2,100	1,305	
Irrawaddy	Indian Ocean	2,010	1,250	
Tarim–Yarkand	Lop Nor	2,000	1,240	
Tigris	Indian Ocean	1,900	1,180	

AFRICA

		km	miles	
Nile	Mediterranean	6,670	4,140	[1]
Congo	Atlantic Ocean	4,670	2,900	[8]
Niger	Atlantic Ocean	4,180	2,595	
Zambezi	Indian Ocean	3,540	2,200	
Oubangi/Uele	Congo (D.R.)	2,250	1,400	
Kasai	Congo (D.R.)	1,950	1,210	
Shaballe	Indian Ocean	1,930	1,200	
Orange	Atlantic Ocean	1,860	1,155	
Cubango	Okavango Delta	1,800	1,120	
Limpopo	Indian Ocean	1,770	1,100	
Senegal	Atlantic Ocean	1,640	1,020	
Volta	Atlantic Ocean	1,500	930	

AUSTRALIA

		km	miles
Murray–Darling	Southern Ocean	3,750	2,330
Darling	Murray	3,070	1,905
Murray	Southern Ocean	2,575	1,600
Murrumbidgee	Murray	1,690	1,050

NORTH AMERICA

		km	miles	
Mississippi–Missouri	Gulf of Mexico	5,971	3,710	[4]
Mackenzie	Arctic Ocean	4,240	2,630	
Missouri	Mississippi	4,088	2,540	

NORTH AMERICA (continued)

		km	miles
Mississippi	Gulf of Mexico	3,782	2,350
Yukon	Pacific Ocean	3,185	1,980
Rio Grande	Gulf of Mexico	3,030	1,880
Arkansas	Mississippi	2,340	1,450
Colorado	Pacific Ocean	2,330	1,445
Red	Mississippi	2,040	1,270
Columbia	Pacific Ocean	1,950	1,210
Saskatchewan	Lake Winnipeg	1,940	1,205
Snake	Columbia	1,670	1,040
Churchill	Hudson Bay	1,600	990
Ohio	Mississippi	1,580	980
Brazos	Gulf of Mexico	1,400	870
St Lawrence	Atlantic Ocean	1,170	730

SOUTH AMERICA

		km	miles	
Amazon	Atlantic Ocean	6,450	4,010	[2]
Paraná–Plate	Atlantic Ocean	4,500	2,800	
Purus	Amazon	3,350	2,080	
Madeira	Amazon	3,200	1,990	
São Francisco	Atlantic Ocean	2,900	1,800	
Paraná	Plate	2,800	1,740	
Tocantins	Atlantic Ocean	2,750	1,710	
Orinoco	Atlantic Ocean	2,740	1,700	
Paraguay	Paraná	2,550	1,580	
Pilcomayo	Paraná	2,500	1,550	
Araguaia	Tocantins	2,250	1,400	
Juruá	Amazon	2,000	1,240	
Xingu	Amazon	1,980	1,230	
Ucayali	Amazon	1,900	1,180	
Uruguay	Plate	1,610	1,000	

LAKES

EUROPE

		km²	miles²
Lake Ladoga	Russia	17,700	6,800
Lake Onega	Russia	9,700	3,700
Saimaa system	Finland	8,000	3,100
Vänern	Sweden	5,500	2,100

ASIA

		km²	miles²	
Caspian Sea	Asia	371,000	143,000	[1]
Lake Baikal	Russia	30,500	11,780	[8]
Tonlé Sap	Cambodia	20,000	7,700	
Lake Balqash	Kazakhstan	18,500	7,100	
Aral Sea	Kazakhstan/Uzbekistan	17,160	6,625	
Lake Dongting	China	12,000	4,600	
Lake Ysyk	Kyrgyzstan	6,200	2,400	
Lake Orumiyeh	Iran	5,900	2,300	
Lake Koko	China	5,700	2,200	
Lake Poyang	China	5,000	1,900	
Lake Khanka	China/Russia	4,400	1,700	
Lake Van	Turkey	3,500	1,400	

AFRICA

		km²	miles²	
Lake Victoria	East Africa	68,000	26,300	[3]
Lake Tanganyika	Central Africa	33,000	13,000	[6]
Lake Malawi/Nyasa	East Africa	29,600	11,430	[9]
Lake Chad	Central Africa	25,000	9,700	
Lake Turkana	Ethiopia/Kenya	8,500	3,290	
Lake Volta	Ghana	8,480	3,270	
Lake Bangweulu	Zambia	8,000	3,100	
Lake Rukwa	Tanzania	7,000	2,700	
Lake Mai-Ndombe	Congo (D.R.)	6,500	2,500	
Lake Kariba	Zambia/Zimbabwe	5,300	2,000	
Lake Albert	Uganda/Congo (D.R.)	5,300	2,000	
Lake Nasser	Egypt/Sudan	5,200	2,000	
Lake Mweru	Zambia/Congo (D.R.)	4,900	1,900	
Lake Cabora Bassa	Mozambique	4,500	1,700	
Lake Kyoga	Uganda	4,400	1,700	
Lake Tana	Ethiopia	3,630	1,400	

AUSTRALIA

		km²	miles²
Lake Eyre	Australia	8,900	3,400
Lake Torrens	Australia	5,800	2,200
Lake Gairdner	Australia	4,800	1,900

NORTH AMERICA

		km²	miles²	
Lake Superior	Canada/USA	82,350	31,800	[2]
Lake Huron	Canada/USA	59,600	23,010	[4]
Lake Michigan	USA	58,000	22,400	[5]
Great Bear Lake	Canada	31,800	12,280	[7]
Great Slave Lake	Canada	28,500	11,000	[10]
Lake Erie	Canada/USA	25,700	9,900	
Lake Winnipeg	Canada	24,400	9,400	
Lake Ontario	Canada/USA	19,500	7,500	
Lake Nicaragua	Nicaragua	8,200	3,200	
Lake Athabasca	Canada	8,100	3,100	
Smallwood Reservoir	Canada	6,530	2,520	
Reindeer Lake	Canada	6,400	2,500	
Nettilling Lake	Canada	5,500	2,100	

SOUTH AMERICA

		km²	miles²
Lake Titicaca	Bolivia/Peru	8,300	3,200
Lake Poopo	Bolivia	2,800	1,100

ISLANDS

EUROPE

		km²	miles²	
Great Britain	UK	229,880	88,700	[8]
Iceland	Atlantic Ocean	103,000	39,800	
Ireland	Ireland/UK	84,400	32,600	
Novaya Zemlya (N.)	Russia	48,200	18,600	
W. Spitzbergen	Norway	39,000	15,100	
Novaya Zemlya (S.)	Russia	33,200	12,800	
Sicily	Italy	25,500	9,800	
Sardinia	Italy	24,000	9,300	
N.E. Spitzbergen	Norway	15,000	5,600	
Corsica	France	8,700	3,400	
Crete	Greece	8,350	3,200	
Zealand	Denmark	6,850	2,600	

ASIA

		km²	miles²	
Borneo	Southeast Asia	744,360	287,400	[3]
Sumatra	Indonesia	473,600	182,860	[6]
Honshu	Japan	230,500	88,980	[7]
Sulawesi (Celebes)	Indonesia	189,000	73,000	
Java	Indonesia	126,700	48,900	
Luzon	Philippines	104,700	40,400	
Mindanao	Philippines	101,500	39,200	
Hokkaido	Japan	78,400	30,300	
Sakhalin	Russia	74,060	28,600	
Sri Lanka	Indian Ocean	65,600	25,300	
Taiwan	Pacific Ocean	36,000	13,900	
Kyushu	Japan	35,700	13,800	
Hainan	China	34,000	13,100	
Timor	Indonesia	33,600	13,000	
Shikoku	Japan	18,800	7,300	
Halmahera	Indonesia	18,000	6,900	
Ceram	Indonesia	17,150	6,600	
Sumbawa	Indonesia	15,450	6,000	
Flores	Indonesia	15,200	5,900	
Samar	Philippines	13,100	5,100	
Negros	Philippines	12,700	4,900	
Bangka	Indonesia	12,000	4,600	
Palawan	Philippines	12,000	4,600	
Panay	Philippines	11,500	4,400	
Sumba	Indonesia	11,100	4,300	
Mindoro	Philippines	9,750	3,800	

AFRICA

		km²	miles²	
Madagascar	Indian Ocean	587,040	226,660	[4]
Socotra	Indian Ocean	3,600	1,400	
Réunion	Indian Ocean	2,500	965	
Tenerife	Atlantic Ocean	2,350	900	
Mauritius	Indian Ocean	1,865	720	

OCEANIA

		km²	miles²	
New Guinea	Indonesia/Papua NG	821,030	317,000	[2]
New Zealand (S.)	Pacific Ocean	150,500	58,100	
New Zealand (N.)	Pacific Ocean	114,700	44,300	
Tasmania	Australia	67,800	26,200	
New Britain	Papua New Guinea	37,800	14,600	
New Caledonia	Pacific Ocean	19,100	7,400	
Viti Levu	Fiji	10,500	4,100	
Hawai'i	Pacific Ocean	10,450	4,000	
Bougainville	Papua New Guinea	9,600	3,700	
Guadalcanal	Solomon Is.	6,500	2,500	
Vanua Levu	Fiji	5,550	2,100	
New Ireland	Papua New Guinea	3,200	1,200	

NORTH AMERICA

		km²	miles²	
Greenland	Atlantic Ocean	2,175,600	839,800	[1]
Baffin Is.	Canada	508,000	196,100	[5]
Victoria Is.	Canada	212,200	81,900	[9]
Ellesmere Is.	Canada	212,000	81,800	[10]
Cuba	Caribbean Sea	110,860	42,800	
Newfoundland	Canada	110,680	42,700	
Hispaniola	Dominican Rep./Haiti	76,200	29,400	
Banks Is.	Canada	67,000	25,900	
Devon Is.	Canada	54,500	21,000	
Melville Is.	Canada	42,400	16,400	
Vancouver Is.	Canada	32,150	12,400	
Somerset Is.	Canada	24,300	9,400	
Jamaica	Caribbean Sea	11,400	4,400	
Puerto Rico	Atlantic Ocean	8,900	3,400	
Cape Breton Is.	Canada	4,000	1,500	

SOUTH AMERICA

		km²	miles²
Tierra del Fuego	Argentina/Chile	47,000	18,100
Falkland Is. (East)	Atlantic Ocean	6,800	2,600
South Georgia	Atlantic Ocean	4,200	1,600
Galapagos (Isabela)	Pacific Ocean	2,250	870

WORLD: REGIONS IN THE NEWS

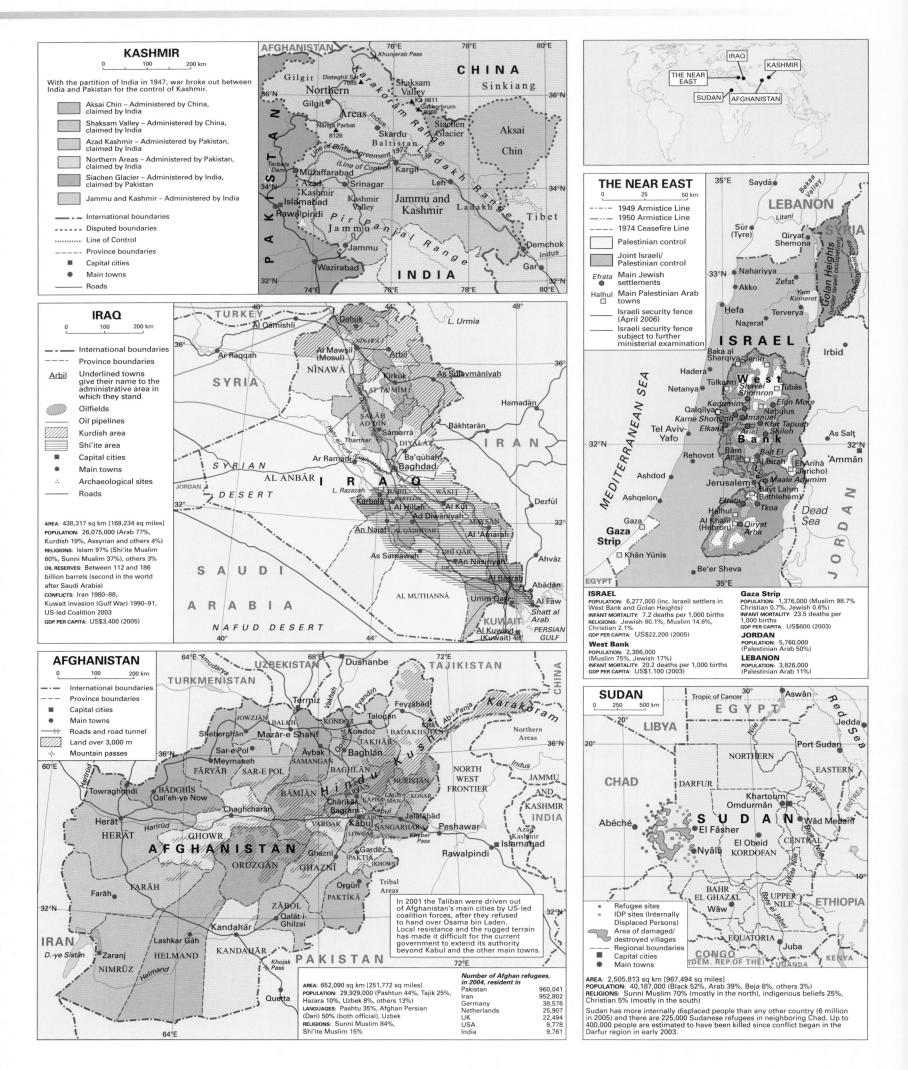

KASHMIR

0   100   200 km

With the partition of India in 1947, war broke out between India and Pakistan for the control of Kashmir.

- Aksai Chin – Administered by China, claimed by India
- Shaksam Valley – Administered by China, claimed by India
- Azad Kashmir – Administered by Pakistan, claimed by India
- Northern Areas – Administered by Pakistan, claimed by India
- Siachen Glacier – Administered by India, claimed by Pakistan
- Jammu and Kashmir – Administered by India

- ─ · ─ International boundaries
- ------ Disputed boundaries
- ········ Line of Control
- ----- Province boundaries
- ■ Capital cities
- ● Main towns
- ─ Roads

THE NEAR EAST

0   25   50 km

- ─ · ─ 1949 Armistice Line
- ─ ·· ─ 1950 Armistice Line
- ---- 1974 Ceasefire Line
- Palestinian control
- Joint Israeli/ Palestinian control
- *Efrata* ● Main Jewish settlements
- Halhul □ Main Palestinian Arab towns
- ─ Israeli security fence (April 2006)
- ─ Israeli security fence subject to further ministerial examination

ISRAEL
POPULATION: 6,277,000 (inc. Israeli settlers in West Bank and Golan Heights)
INFANT MORTALITY: 7.2 deaths per 1,000 births
RELIGIONS: Jewish 80.1%, Muslim 14.6%, Christian 2.1%
GDP PER CAPITA: US$22,200 (2005)

West Bank
POPULATION: 2,386,000
(Muslim 75%, Jewish 17%)
INFANT MORTALITY: 20.2 deaths per 1,000 births
GDP PER CAPITA: US$1,100 (2003)

Gaza Strip
POPULATION: 1,376,000 (Muslim 98.7% Christian 0.7%, Jewish 0.6%)
INFANT MORTALITY: 23.5 deaths per 1,000 births
GDP PER CAPITA: US$600 (2003)

JORDAN
POPULATION: 5,760,000
(Palestinian Arab 50%)

LEBANON
POPULATION: 3,826,000
(Palestinian Arab 11%)

IRAQ

0   100   200 km

- ─ · ─ International boundaries
- ----- Province boundaries
- *Arbīl* Underlined towns give their name to the administrative area in which they stand
- Oilfields
- Oil pipelines
- Kurdish area
- Shi'ite area
- ■ Capital cities
- ● Main towns
- ∴ Archaeological sites
- ─ Roads

AREA: 438,317 sq km [169,234 sq miles]
POPULATION: 26,075,000 (Arab 77%, Kurdish 19%, Assyrian and others 4%)
RELIGIONS: Islam 97% (Shi'ite Muslim 60%, Sunni Muslim 37%), others 3%
OIL RESERVES: Between 112 and 186 billion barrels (second in the world after Saudi Arabia)
CONFLICTS: Iran 1980–88, Kuwait invasion (Gulf War) 1990–91, US-led Coalition 2003
GDP PER CAPITA: US$3,400 (2005)

AFGHANISTAN

0   100   200 km

- ─ · ─ International boundaries
- ----- Province boundaries
- ■ Capital cities
- ● Main towns
- ─)(Roads and road tunnel
- Land over 3,000 m
-)(Mountain passes

In 2001 the Taliban were driven out of Afghanistan's main cities by US-led coalition forces, after they refused to hand over Osama bin Laden. Local resistance and the rugged terrain has made it difficult for the current government to extend its authority beyond Kabul and the other main towns.

AREA: 652,090 sq km [251,772 sq miles]
POPULATION: 29,929,000 (Pashtun 44%, Tajik 25%, Hazara 10%, Uzbek 8%, others 13%)
LANGUAGES: Pashtu 35%, Afghan Persian (Dari) 50% (both official), Uzbek
RELIGIONS: Sunni Muslim 84%, Shi'ite Muslim 15%

Number of Afghan refugees, in 2004, resident in

Pakistan	960,041
Iran	952,802
Germany	38,576
Netherlands	25,907
UK	22,494
USA	9,778
India	9,761

SUDAN

0   250   500 km

- ● Refugee sites
- ● IDP sites (Internally Displaced Persons)
- Area of damaged/ destroyed villages
- ----- Regional boundaries
- ■ Capital cities
- ● Main towns

AREA: 2,505,813 sq km [967,494 sq miles]
POPULATION: 40,187,000 (Black 52%, Arab 39%, Beja 6%, others 3%)
RELIGIONS: Sunni Muslim 70% (mostly in the north), indigenous beliefs 25%, Christian 5% (mostly in the south)

Sudan has more internally displaced people than any other country (6 million in 2005) and there are 225,000 Sudanese refugees in neighboring Chad. Up to 400,000 people are estimated to have been killed since conflict began in the Darfur region in early 2003.

THE EARTH
IN SPACE

THE UNIVERSE

In early 2003, NASA scientists produced an image of the Universe as it was about 380,000 years after its creation. The image was produced by an American satellite called the Wilkinson Microwave Anisotropy Probe (WMAP), which was launched in June 2001.

The probe measures small variations in the cosmic microwave background (CMB) radiation, left over from the creation of the Universe. By measuring the size of hot and cold spots in the CMB, scientists have calculated how far away they are, and this data has enabled them to calculate the age of the Universe. It has also established the proportions of its three ingredients, namely 4% ordinary matter (made up of atoms), 23% of "cold dark matter," whose nature is unknown, and 73% of the mysterious "dark energy," which seems to be accelerating the expansion of space.

▼ *The depths of the Universe*

In this segment of sky, just one-tenth the area of the full Moon, the Hubble Space Telescope recorded an estimated 10,000 galaxies in 2003–4.

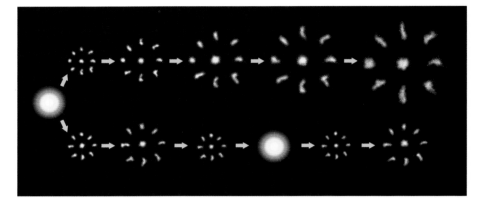

Scientists have established that our Universe was created, or "time" began, about 13.7 billion years ago (disproving earlier estimates that ranged from 8 billion to 24 billion years), that it is flat, and that the first stars did not appear until it was 200 million years old.

THE BIG BANG

Most scientists agree that the Universe was formed by a colossal explosion, called the "Big Bang." In the first millionth of a second after the Big Bang, the Universe expanded from a dimensionless point of infinite mass and

▲ *The end of the Universe*

The diagram shows two theories concerning the fate of the Universe. One theory, top, suggests that the Universe will expand indefinitely, becoming an immense dark graveyard. Another theory, bottom, suggests that the galaxies will fall back until everything is again concentrated in one point in a so-called Big Crunch. This might then be followed by a new Big Bang.

THE NEAREST STARS

The 22 nearest stars, excluding the Sun, with their distance from the Earth in light-years.*

Proxima Centauri	4.2
Alpha Centauri A	4.4
Alpha Centauri B	4.4
Barnard's Star	5.9
Wolf 359	7.8
Lalande 21185	8.3
Sirius A	8.6
Sirius B	8.6
UV Ceti A	8.7
UV Ceti B	8.7
Ross 154	9.7
Ross 248	10.3
Epsilon Eridani	10.5
HD 217987	10.7
Ross 128	10.9
L789-6	11.2
61 Cygni A	11.4
Procyon A	11.4
Procyon B	11.4
61 Cygni B	11.4
HD 173740	11.5
HD 173739	11.7

* *A light-year is about 5,900 billion miles [9,500 billion km].*

density into a fireball about 19 billion miles [30 billion km] across. The Universe has been expanding ever since, as demonstrated in the 1920s by Edwin Hubble, the American astronomer for whom the Hubble Space Telescope, which has also been shedding light on the origins of the Universe, was named.

The temperature at the end of the first second was perhaps 10 billion degrees – far too hot for composite atomic nuclei to exist. As a result, the fireball consisted mainly of radiation mixed with microscopic particles of matter. Almost a million years passed before the Universe was cool enough for atoms to form.

In regions where matter was relatively dense, atoms began, under the influence of gravity, to move together to form protogalaxies – masses of gas separated by empty space. The protogalaxies were dark, because the Universe had cooled. But 200 million years after its creation, stars began to form within the protogalaxies as particles were drawn together. The internal pressure produced as matter condensed created the high temperatures required to cause nuclear fusion. Stars were born and later destroyed. Each generation of stars fed on the debris of extinct ones. Each generation produced larger atoms, increasing the number of different chemical elements.

▲ The Milky Way
This section of the Milky Way is dominated by Sirius, the Dog Star, top center, in the constellation of Canis Major. Sirius is the brightest star in the sky.

THE GALAXIES

At least a billion galaxies are scattered through the Universe, though the discoveries made by the Hubble Space Telescope suggest that there may be far more than once thought, and some estimates are as high as 100 billion. The largest galaxies contain trillions of stars, while small ones contain less than a billion.

Galaxies tend to occur in groups or clusters, while some clusters appear to be grouped in vast superclusters. Our Local Cluster includes the spiral Milky Way galaxy, whose diameter is about 100,000 light-years; one light-year, the distance that light travels in one year, is about 5,900 billion miles [9,500 billion km]. The Milky Way is a huge galaxy, shaped like a disk with a bulge at the center. It is larger, brighter, and more massive than many other known galaxies. It contains about 100 billion stars, which rotate around the center of the galaxy in the same direction as the Sun does.

One medium-sized star in the Milky Way galaxy is the Sun. After its formation, about 5 billion years ago, there was enough leftover matter around it to create the planets, asteroids, moons, and other bodies that together form our Solar System. The Solar System rotates around the center of the Milky Way galaxy approximately every 225 million years.

Stars similar to our Sun are known to have planets orbiting around them. By the start of 2005, over a hundred of these extrasolar planets had been reported, and evidence from the Hubble Space Telescope suggests that the raw materials from which planets are formed is common in dusty disks around many stars. This raises one of the most intriguing questions that has ever faced humanity: if other planets exist in the Universe, are they home to living organisms?

Before the time of Galileo, people thought that the Earth lay at the center of the Universe. But we now know that our Solar System and even the Milky Way galaxy are tiny specks in the Universe as a whole. Perhaps our planet is also not unique in its ability to support intelligent life.

▲ The Home Galaxy
This schematic plan shows that our Solar System is located in one of the spiral arms of the Milky Way galaxy, a little less than 30,000 light-years from its center. The center of the Milky Way galaxy is not visible from Earth. Instead, it is masked by light-absorbing clouds of interstellar dust.

Solar System

THE CONSTELLATIONS

On a clear night, under the best conditions and far away from the glare of city lights, a person in northern Europe can look up and see about 2,500 stars. In a town, however, light pollution can reduce visibility to 200 stars or fewer. Over the whole celestial sphere it is possible to see about 8,500 stars with the naked eye and it is only when you look through a telescope that you begin to realize that the number of stars is countless.

SMALL AND LARGE STARS

Stars come in many sizes. Some, called neutron stars, are compact, with the same mass as the Sun but with diameters of only about 12 miles [20 km]. Larger than neutron stars are the small white dwarfs. Our Sun is a medium-sized star, but many visible stars in the night sky are giants with diameters typically 20 times that of the Sun, or supergiants with diameters from 50 to several hundred times that of the Sun.

Two bright stars in the constellation Orion are Betelgeuse (also known as Alpha Orionis) and Rigel (or Beta Orionis). Betelgeuse is an orange-red supergiant, whose diameter is about

500 times that of the Sun. Rigel is also a supergiant. Its diameter is about 50 times that of the Sun, but its luminosity is estimated to be 40,000 times that of the Sun.

The stars we see in the night sky all belong to our home galaxy, the Milky Way. This name is also used for the faint, silvery band that arches across the sky. This band, a slice through our galaxy, contains an enormous number of stars.

▼ **The Big Dipper**

The Big Dipper, or Plough, or seen above glowing yellow clouds lit by city lights. It is part of a larger group called Ursa Major, one of the best-known constellations of the northern hemisphere. The two bright stars to the lower right of the photograph (Merak and Dubhe) are known as the Pointers because they show the way to the Pole Star.

THE CONSTELLATIONS

The constellations and their English names. Constellations visible from both hemispheres are listed.

Andromeda	Andromeda	Delphinus	Dolphin	Perseus	Perseus
Antlia	Air Pump	Dorado	Swordfish	Phoenix	Phoenix
Apus	Bird of Paradise	Draco	Dragon	Pictor	Easel
Aquarius	Water Carrier	Equuleus	Little Horse	Pisces	Fishes
Aquila	Eagle	Eridanus	River Eridanus	Piscis Austrinus	Southern Fish
Ara	Altar	Fornax	Furnace	Puppis	Ship's Stern
Aries	Ram	Gemini	Twins	Pyxis	Mariner's Compass
Auriga	Charioteer	Grus	Crane	Reticulum	Net
Boötes	Herdsman	Hercules	Hercules	Sagitta	Arrow
Caelum	Chisel	Horologium	Clock	Sagittarius	Archer
Camelopardalis	Giraffe	Hydra	Water Snake	Scorpius	Scorpion
Cancer	Crab	Hydrus	Sea Serpent	Sculptor	Sculptor
Canes Venatici	Hunting Dogs	Indus	Indian	Scutum	Shield
Canis Major	Great Dog	Lacerta	Lizard	Serpens*	Serpent
Canis Minor	Little Dog	Leo	Lion	Sextans	Sextant
Capricornus	Sea Goat	Leo Minor	Little Lion	Taurus	Bull
Carina	Ship's Keel	Lepus	Hare	Telescopium	Telescope
Cassiopeia	Cassiopeia	Libra	Scales	Triangulum	Triangle
Centaurus	Centaur	Lupus	Wolf	Triangulum	Southern
Cepheus	Cepheus	Lynx	Lynx	Australe	Triangle
Cetus	Whale	Lyra	Lyre	Tucana	Toucan
Chamaeleon	Chameleon	Mensa	Table Mountain	Ursa Major	Great Bear
Circinus	Compasses	Microscopium	Microscope	Ursa Minor	Little Bear
Columba	Dove	Monoceros	Unicorn	Vela	Ship's Sails
Coma Berenices	Berenice's Hair	Musca	Fly	Virgo	Virgin
Corona Australis	Southern Crown	Norma	Level	Volans	Flying Fish
Corona Borealis	Northern Crown	Octans	Octant	Vulpecula	Fox
Corvus	Crow	Ophiuchus	Serpent Bearer		
Crater	Cup	Orion	Hunter	** In two halves: Serpens Caput, the*	
Crux	Southern Cross	Pavo	Peacock	*head, and Serpens Cauda, the tail.*	
Cygnus	Swan	Pegasus	Winged Horse		

THE BRIGHTEST STARS

The 15 brightest stars visible from northern Europe. Magnitudes are given to the nearest tenth.

Sirius	−1.4
Arcturus	0.0
Vega	0.0
Capella	0.1
Rigel	0.2
Procyon	0.4
Betelgeuse	0.4
Altair	0.8
Aldebaran	0.9
Spica	1.0
Antares	1.0
Pollux	1.2
Fomalhaut	1.2
Deneb	1.2
Regulus	1.4

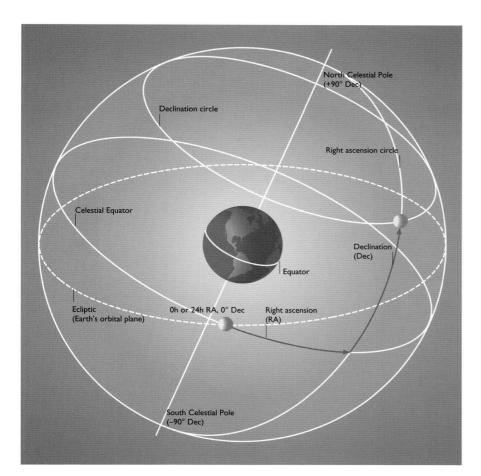

The nucleus of the Milky Way galaxy cannot be seen from Earth. Lying in the direction of the constellation Sagittarius in the southern hemisphere, it is masked by clouds of dust.

THE BRIGHTNESS OF STARS

Astronomers use a scale of magnitudes to measure the brightness of stars. The brightest visible to the naked eye were originally known as first-magnitude stars, ones not so bright were second-magnitude, down to the faintest visible, which were rated as sixth-magnitude. The brighter the star, the lower the magnitude. With the advent of telescopes and the development of accurate instruments for measuring brightnesses, the magnitude scale has been refined and extended. Very bright bodies, such as Sirius, Venus, and the Sun, have negative magnitudes. The nearest star is Proxima Centauri, part of a multiple star system, which is 4.2 light-years away. Proxima Centauri is very faint and has a magnitude of 11.0. Alpha Centauri A, one of the two brighter members of the system, is the nearest visible star to Earth. It has a magnitude of 1.7.

These magnitudes are known as apparent magnitudes – measures of the brightnesses of the stars as they appear to us. These are the magnitudes indicated on the star charts on pages 22–23. But the stars are at very different distances. The star Deneb, in the constellation Cygnus, for example, is 3,200 light-years away. So astronomers also use absolute magnitudes – measures of how bright the stars really are. A star's absolute magnitude is the apparent magnitude it would have if it could be placed 32.6 light-years away. So Deneb, with an apparent magnitude of 1.2, has an absolute magnitude of –8.7.

The brightest star in the night sky is Sirius, the Dog Star, with a magnitude of –1.4. This medium-sized star is 8.6 light-years distant but it gives out about 20 times as much light as the Sun. After the Sun and the Moon, the brightest objects in the sky are the planets Venus, Mars, and Jupiter. For example, Venus has a magnitude of up to –4. The planets have no light of their own, however, and shine only because they reflect the Sun's rays. But while stars have fixed positions, the planets shift nightly in relation to the constellations, following a path called the ecliptic (shown on the star charts overleaf). As they follow their orbits around the Sun, their distances from the Earth vary, and therefore so also do their magnitudes.

While atlas maps record the details of the Earth's surface, star charts are a guide to the heavens. An observer at the equator can see the entire sky over the course of a year, but an observer at one of the poles can see only the stars in a single hemisphere.

STAR CHARTS

Star magnitudes

Apparent visual magnitudes

Magnitudes: −1 0 1 2 3 4 5

⊙ Variable star   ○ Open Cluster
⊕ Globular Cluster   □ Nebula   ◯ Galaxy

The Milky Way is shown in light blue on the chart.

These pages show a star chart for each hemisphere. The northern hemisphere chart is centered on the North Celestial Pole, while the southern hemisphere chart is centered on the South Celestial Pole.

In the northern hemisphere, the North Pole is marked by the star Polaris, or Pole Star. Polaris lies within a degree of the point where an extension of the Earth's axis meets the sky. Polaris appears to be almost stationary, and navigators throughout history have used it as a guide. Unfortunately, the South Celestial Pole has no convenient reference point.

Star charts of the two hemispheres are bounded by the celestial equator, an imaginary line in the sky directly above the terrestrial equator. Astronomical coordinates, which give the location of stars, are normally stated in terms of

▲ *Star chart of the northern hemisphere*

When you look into the sky, the stars seem to be on the inside of a huge dome. This gives astronomers a way of mapping them. This chart shows the sky as it would appear from the North Pole. To use the star chart above, an observer in the northern hemisphere should face south and turn the chart so that the current month appears at the bottom. The chart will then show the constellations on view at about 11 p.m. Greenwich Mean Time. The map should be rotated clockwise 15° for each hour before 11 p.m. and counterclockwise for each hour after 11 p.m.

right ascension (the equivalent of longitude) and declination (the equivalent of latitude). Because the stars appear to rotate around the Earth every 24 hours, right ascension is measured eastward in hours and minutes. Declination is measured in degrees north or south of the celestial equator.

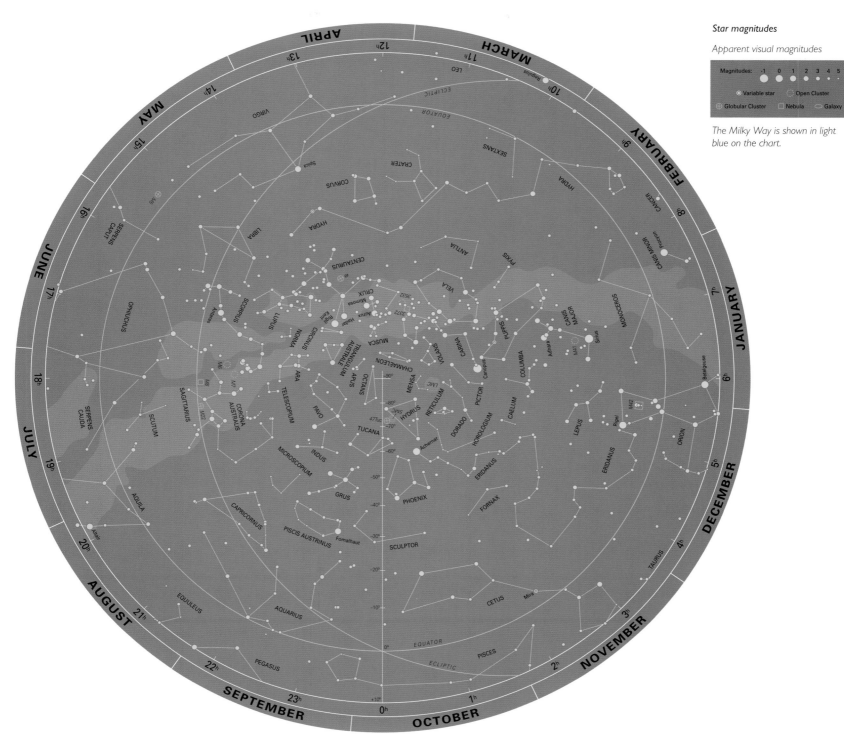

CONSTELLATIONS

Every star belongs to a particular constellation. There are 88 constellations, many of which were named by the ancient Greeks, Romans, and other early peoples after animals and mythological characters, such as Orion and Perseus. More recently, astronomers invented names for constellations seen in the southern hemisphere, in areas not visible from around the Mediterranean Sea.

Some groups of easily recognizable stars form parts of a constellation. For example, seven stars form the shape of the Big Dipper, or Plough, within the constellation Ursa Major. Such groups are called asterisms.

The stars in constellations lie in the same direction in space, but normally at vastly different distances. Hence, there is no real connection

▲ Star chart of the southern hemisphere

Many constellations in the southern hemisphere were named not by the ancients but by later astronomers and thus have modern names. The Large and Small Magellanic Clouds (LMC, SMC) are small "satellite" galaxies of the Milky Way. To use the chart, an observer in the southern hemisphere should face north and turn the chart so that the current month appears at the bottom. The map will then show the constellations on view at about 11 p.m. Greenwich Mean Time. The chart should be rotated clockwise 15° for each hour before 11 p.m. and counterclockwise for each hour after 11 p.m.

between them. The positions of stars seem fixed, but in fact the shapes of the constellations are changing slowly over very long periods of time. This is because the stars have their own "proper motions," which because of the huge distances involved are imperceptible to the naked eye.

THE SOLAR SYSTEM

Our knowledge of the Solar System has increased greatly since the start of the Space Age in 1957, with the launch of the Soviet satellite Sputnik 1. In 2005, US astronomers announced the discovery of what could be a "tenth planet," officially called 2003 UB313, and, unofficially, "Xena." It is a little bigger than Pluto and is the most distant object ever seen in the Solar System, lying about 9 billion miles [14.5 billion km] from the Sun.

Scientists believe that the Solar System was formed from a rotating disk of gas and dust, the remains of a previous generation of stars. About 5 billion years ago, a new star, the Sun, was born, containing 99.8% of the mass of our Solar System. The remaining material makes up the planets and other bodies in the Solar System.

THE PLANETS

Mercury is the closest planet to the Sun and the fastest moving. Space probes have revealed that its surface is covered by craters, and looks much like the Earth's Moon. Mercury is a hostile place, with no significant atmosphere and temperatures ranging between 750°F [400°C] by day and −275°F [−170°C] by night. It seems unlikely that anyone will ever want to visit this planet.

Venus is much the same size as Earth, but it is the hottest of the planets, with temperatures reaching 885°F [475°C], even at night. The reason for this scorching heat is the atmosphere, which consists mainly of carbon dioxide, a gas that traps heat thus creating a greenhouse effect. The density of the atmosphere is about 90 times that of Earth, and dense clouds permanently mask the planet's surface. Active volcanic regions discharging sulfur dioxide may account for the haze of sulfuric-acid droplets in the upper atmosphere. Seen from Earth, Venus is brighter than any other star or planet and is

easy to spot. It is often the first object to be seen in the evening sky and the last to be seen in the morning sky. It can even be seen in daylight.

Earth, seen from space, looks blue (because of the oceans which cover more than 70% of the planet) and white (a result of clouds in the atmosphere). The atmosphere and water make Earth the only planet known to support life. The Earth's hard outer layers, including the crust and the top of the mantle, are divided into rigid plates. Forces inside the Earth move the plates, modifying the landscape, and causing earthquakes and volcanic activity. Weathering and erosion also change the surface.

Mars has many features in common with the Earth, including an atmosphere with clouds and polar caps that partly melt in summer. Scientists once considered that it was the most likely planet on which other life might exist, but the two Viking space probes that went there in the 1970s found only a barren rocky surface, with no trace of water. But, in 2004, two NASA Mars rovers – Spirit and Opportunity – sent back evidence that Mars was once wet and potentially habitable, at least by simple microbes.

PLANETARY DATA

Planet	Mean distance from Sun (million miles)	Mass (Earth=1)	Period of orbit (Earth days/yrs)	Period of rotation (Earth days)	Equatorial diameter (miles)	Average density (water=1)	Surface gravity (Earth=1)	Number of known satellites*
Sun	–	332,946	–	25.38	865,000	1.41	27.9	–
Mercury	36.0	0.06	87.97d	58.65	3,032	5.43	0.38	0
Venus	67.2	0.82	224.7d	243.02	7,521	5.24	0.91	0
Earth	93.0	1.00	365.3d	1.00	7,926	5.52	1.00	1
Mars	141.6	0.11	687.0d	1.029	4,220	3.94	0.38	2
Jupiter	483.7	317.8	11.86y	0.411	88,848	1.33	2.36	63
Saturn	886.6	95.2	29.45y	0.428	74,900	0.69	0.91	56
Uranus	1,784.0	14.5	84.02y	0.720	31,764	1.27	0.89	27
Neptune	2,795.2	17.2	164.8y	0.673	30,776	1.64	1.13	13
Pluto	3,670.2	0.002	247.9y	6.39	1,485	1.8	0.07	3

* Number of known satellites at mid-2006

Asteroids are small, rocky bodies. Most of them orbit the Sun between Mars and Jupiter, but some small ones can approach the Earth. The largest is Ceres, 567 miles [913 km] in diameter. There may be around a million asteroids bigger than 0.6 miles [1 km].

Jupiter, the giant planet, lies beyond Mars and the asteroid belt. Its mass is almost three times as much as all the other planets combined and, because of its size, it shines more brightly than any other planet apart from Venus and, occasionally, Mars. Jupiter is made up mostly of hydrogen and helium, covered by a layer of clouds. Its Great Red Spot is a high-pressure storm. The planet also has a faint ring system. The four largest moons of Jupiter were discovered by Galileo. They are worlds in their own right: Io is the most volcanic body yet discovered; Europa and Ganymede have icy surfaces, perhaps with liquid oceans below; and Callisto has an ancient, cratered terrain. Jupiter made headline news when it was struck by fragments of Comet Shoemaker–Levy 9 in July 1994, creating huge fireballs that caused scars on the planet that remained visible for months after the event.

Saturn is structurally similar to Jupiter but it is best known for its rings. The rings measure about 170,000 miles [270,000 km] across, yet they are no more than a few hundred yards thick. Seen from Earth, the rings seem divided into three main bands of varying brightness, but photographs sent back by space probes showed that they are broken up into thousands of thin ringlets composed of ice particles ranging in size from a snowball to an iceberg. The origin of the rings is still a matter of debate.

Uranus was discovered in 1781 by William Herschel, who first thought it was a comet. It is broadly similar to Jupiter and Saturn in composition, though its distance from the Sun makes its surface even colder. Uranus is circled by thin rings which were discovered in 1977. Unlike the rings of Saturn, the rings of Uranus are black, which explains why they cannot be seen from Earth.

Neptune, named after the mythological sea god, was discovered in 1846 as the result of mathematical predictions made by astronomers to explain irregularities in the orbit of Uranus, its near twin. Little was known about this distant body until Voyager 2 came close to it in 1989. Neptune has thin rings, like those of Uranus. Its atmosphere features blue-green clouds and the occasional prominent dark spot.

Pluto is the smallest planet in the Solar System, even smaller than the Earth's Moon. The American astronomer Clyde Tombaugh discovered Pluto in 1930. Its orbit is odd and it sometimes comes closer to the Sun than Neptune. The Kuiper Belt is a vast region beyond the orbit of Neptune which contains many icy, asteroid-sized objects. Pluto and its principal moon, Charon, are two of the largest objects in the Kuiper Belt.

Comets are small icy bodies that orbit the Sun in highly elliptical orbits. When a comet swings in toward the Sun some of its ice evaporates, and the comet brightens and may become visible from Earth. The best known is Halley's Comet, which takes 76 years to orbit the Sun.

THE EARTH: TIME AND MOTION

The Earth is constantly moving through space like a huge, self-sufficient spaceship. First, with the rest of the Solar System, it moves around the center of the Milky Way galaxy. Second, it rotates around the Sun at a speed of more than 60,000 mph [100,000 km/h], covering a distance of nearly 600 million miles [1,000 million km] in a little over 365 days. The Earth also spins on its axis, an imaginary line joining the North and South Poles, via the center of the Earth, completing one turn in a day. The Earth's movements around the Sun determine our calendar, though accurate observations of the stars made by astronomers

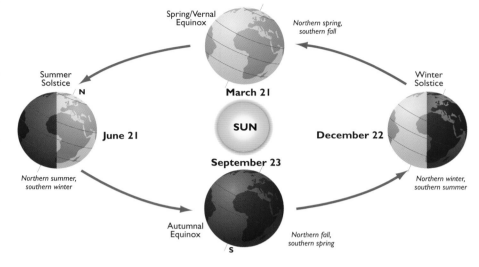

▼ The Earth from the Moon
In 1969, Neil Armstrong and Edwin "Buzz" Aldrin, Jr, were the first people to set foot on the Moon. This photograph of the Earth was taken by the crew of Apollo 11 as they orbited the Moon.

help to keep our clocks in step with the rotation of the Earth around the Sun.

THE CHANGING YEAR

The Earth takes 365 days, 6 hours, 9 minutes and 9.54 seconds to complete one orbit around the Sun. We have a calendar year of 365 days, so allowance has to be made for the extra time over and above the 365 days. This is allowed for by introducing leap years of 366 days. Leap years are generally those, such as 1992 and 1996, which are divisible by four. Century years, however, are not leap years unless they are divisible by 400. Hence, 1700, 1800, and 1900 were not leap years, but the year 2000 was one. Leap years help to make the calendar conform with the solar year.

Because the Earth's axis is tilted by approximately 23½°, the middle latitudes enjoy four distinct seasons. On March 21, the vernal or spring equinox in the northern hemisphere, the Sun is directly overhead at the equator and everywhere on Earth has about 12 hours of daylight and 12 hours of darkness. But as the Earth continues on its journey around the Sun, the northern hemisphere tilts more and more toward the Sun. Finally, on June 21, the Sun is overhead at the Tropic of Cancer (latitude 23½° North). This is the summer solstice in the northern hemisphere.

▲ The Seasons
The approximate 23½° tilt of the Earth's axis remains constant as the Earth orbits around the Sun. As a result, first the northern and then the southern hemispheres lean toward the Sun. Annual variations in the amount of sunlight received in turn by each hemisphere are responsible for the four seasons experienced in the middle latitudes.

▼ Tides
The daily rises and falls of the ocean's waters are caused by the gravitational pull of the Moon and the Sun. The effect is greatest on the hemisphere facing the Moon, causing a "tidal bulge.". The diagram below shows that the Sun, Moon, and Earth are in line when the spring tides occur. This causes the greatest tidal ranges. On the other hand, the neap tides occur when the pull of the Moon and the Sun are opposed. Neap tides, when tidal ranges are at their lowest, occur near the Moon's first and third quarters.

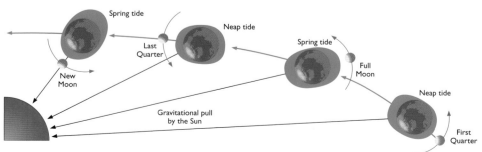

SUN DATA

DIAMETER	865,000 miles
VOLUME	3.388×10^{17} cu miles
VOLUME (EARTH=1)	1.303×10^6
MASS	1.989×10^{30} kg
MASS (EARTH=1)	3.329×10^6
MEAN DENSITY (WATER=1)	1.409
ROTATION PERIOD:	
AT EQUATOR	25.4 days
AT POLES	about 35 days
SURFACE GRAVITY	
(EARTH=1)	28
MAGNITUDE:	
APPARENT	−26.9
ABSOLUTE	+4.71
TEMPERATURE:	
AT SURFACE	9,932°F [5,800 K]
AT CORE	15×10^6 K

MOON DATA

DIAMETER	2,159 miles
MASS (EARTH=1)	0.0123
DENSITY (WATER=1)	3.34
MEAN DISTANCE FROM EARTH	238,856 miles
MAXIMUM DISTANCE (APOGEE)	252,712 miles
MINIMUM DISTANCE (PERIGEE)	221,457 miles
SIDEREAL ROTATION AND REVOLUTION PERIOD	27.322 days
SYNODIC MONTH (NEW MOON TO NEW MOON)	29.531 days
SURFACE GRAVITY (EARTH=1)	0.165
MEAN DAYTIME SURFACE TEMPERATURE	+243°F [390 K]
MEAN NIGHTTIME SURFACE TEMPERATURE	−261°F [110 K]

► *Phases of the Moon*

The Moon rotates more slowly than the Earth, making one complete turn on its axis in just over 27 days. This corresponds to its period of revolution around the Earth and, hence, the same hemisphere always faces us. The interval between one full Moon and the next (and also between new Moons) is about 29½ days, or one lunar month. The apparent changes in the appearance of the Moon are caused by its changing position in relation to the Earth. Like the planets, the Moon produces no light of its own. It shines by reflecting the Sun's rays, varying from a slim crescent to a full circle, and back again.

The overhead Sun then moves south again until, on September 23, the autumnal equinox in the northern hemisphere, the Sun is again overhead at the Equator. The overhead Sun then moves south until, on around December 22, it is overhead at the Tropic of Capricorn. This is the winter solstice in the northern hemisphere, and the summer solstice in the southern, where the seasons are reversed.

At the poles, there are two seasons. During half of the year, one of the poles leans toward the Sun and has continuous sunlight. For the other six months, the pole leans away from the Sun and is in continuous darkness.

Regions around the equator do not have marked seasons. Because the Sun is high in the sky throughout the year, it is always hot or warm. When people talk of seasons in the tropics, they are usually referring to other factors, such as rainy and dry periods.

DAY, NIGHT, AND TIDES

As the Earth rotates on its axis every 24 hours, first one side of the planet and then the other faces the Sun and enjoys daylight, while the opposite side is in darkness.

The length of daylight varies throughout the year. The longest day in the northern hemisphere falls on the summer solstice, June 21, while the longest day in the southern hemisphere is on December 22. At 40° latitude, the length of daylight on the longest day is 14 hours, 30 minutes. At 60° latitude, daylight on that day lasts 18 hours, 30 minutes. On the shortest day, December 22 in the northern hemisphere and June 21 in the southern, daylight hours at 40° latitude total 9 hours and 9 minutes. At latitude 60°, daylight lasts only 5 hours, 30 minutes in the 24-hour period.

Tides are caused by the gravitational pull of the Moon and, to a lesser extent, the Sun on the waters in the world's oceans. Tides occur twice every 24 hours, 50 minutes – one complete orbit of the Moon around the Earth.

▲ *Total eclipse of the Sun*

A total eclipse is caused when the Moon passes between the Sun and the Earth. With the Sun's bright disk completely obscured, the Sun's corona, or outer atmosphere, can be viewed.

The highest tides, the spring tides, occur when the Earth, Moon, and Sun are in a straight line, so that the gravitational pulls of the Moon and Sun are combined. The lowest, or neap, tides occur when the Moon, Earth, and Sun form a right angle. The gravitational pull of the Moon is then opposed by the gravitational pull of the Sun. The greatest tidal ranges occur in the Bay of Fundy in Canada. The greatest mean spring range is 47.5 ft [14.5 m].

The speed at which the Earth is spinning on its axis is gradually slowing down, because of the movement of tides. As a result, experts have calculated that, in about 200 million years, the day will be 25 hours long.

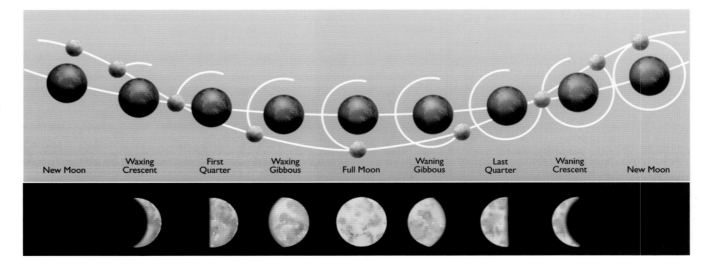

| New Moon | Waxing Crescent | First Quarter | Waxing Gibbous | Full Moon | Waning Gibbous | Last Quarter | Waning Crescent | New Moon |

THE EARTH FROM SPACE

Any last doubts about whether the Earth was round or flat were finally resolved by the appearance of the first photographs of our planet taken at the start of the Space Age. Satellite images also confirmed that map- and globe-makers had correctly worked out the shapes of the continents and the oceans.

More importantly, images of our beautiful, blue, white, and brown planet from space impressed on many people that the Earth and its resources are finite. They made people realize that if we allow our planet to be damaged by such factors as overpopulation, pollution and irresponsible over-use of resources, then its future and the survival of all the living things upon it may be threatened.

VIEWS FROM ABOVE

The first aerial photographs were taken from balloons in the mid-19th century and their importance in military reconnaissance was recognized as early as the 1860s during the American Civil War.

Since the end of World War II, photographs taken by aircraft have been widely used in map-making. The use of air photographs has greatly speeded up the laborious process of mapping land details and they have enabled cartographers to produce maps of the most remote parts of the world.

Aerial photographs have also proved useful because they reveal features that are not visible at ground level. For example, circles that appear on many air photographs do not correspond to visible features on the ground. Many of these mysterious shapes have turned out to be the sites of ancient settlements previously unknown to archaeologists.

IMAGES FROM SPACE

Space probes equipped with cameras and a variety of remote-sensing instruments have sent back images of distant planets and moons. From these images, detailed maps have been produced, rapidly expanding our knowledge of the Solar System.

Images from space are also proving invaluable in the study of the Earth. One of the best known uses of space imagery is the study of the atmosphere. Polar-orbiting weather satellites that circle the Earth, together with geostationary satellites, whose motion is synchronized with the Earth's rotation, now regularly transmit images showing the changing patterns of weather systems from above. Forecasters use these images to track the development and the paths taken by hurricanes, enabling them to issue storm warnings to endangered areas, saving lives and reducing damage to property.

Remote-sensing devices are now monitoring changes in temperatures over the land and sea, while photographs indicate the melting of ice sheets. Such evidence is vital in the study of global warming. Other devices reveal polluted areas, patterns of vegetation growth, and areas suffering deforestation.

In recent years, remote-sensing devices have been used to monitor the damage being done to the ozone layer in the stratosphere, which prevents most of the Sun's harmful ultraviolet radiation from reaching the surface. The discovery of "ozone holes," where the protective layer of ozone is being thinned by chlorofluoro-carbons (CFCs), chemicals used in the manufacture of such things as air conditioners and refrigerators, has enabled governments to take concerted action to save our planet from imminent danger.

▼ *Mount Etna, Sicily*
The most active volcano in Europe, Mount Etna, 10,906 ft [3,323 m] high, is shown here during the 2002–3 eruption, its plume of ash and smoke spreading southward over the Mediterranean, east of Malta.

EARTH DATA	
MAXIMUM DISTANCE FROM SUN (APHELION)	94,508,166 miles
MINIMUM DISTANCE FROM SUN (PERIHELION)	91,403,477 miles
LENGTH OF YEAR — SOLAR TROPICAL (EQUINOX TO EQUINOX)	365.24 days
LENGTH OF YEAR — SIDEREAL (FIXED STAR TO FIXED STAR)	365.26 days
LENGTH OF DAY — MEAN SOLAR DAY	24 hours, 3 minutes, 56 seconds
LENGTH OF DAY — MEAN SIDEREAL DAY	23 hours, 56 minutes, 4 seconds
SUPERFICIAL AREA	197,000,000 sq miles
LAND SURFACE	57,500,000 sq miles (29.2%)
WATER SURFACE	139,500,000 sq miles (70.8%)
EQUATORIAL CIRCUMFERENCE	24,901 miles
POLAR CIRCUMFERENCE	24,860 miles
EQUATORIAL DIAMETER	7,926 miles
POLAR DIAMETER	7,900 miles
EQUATORIAL RADIUS	3,963 miles
POLAR RADIUS	3,950 miles
VOLUME OF THE EARTH	$259,880 \times 10^6$ cu miles
MASS OF THE EARTH	5.97×10^{24} kg

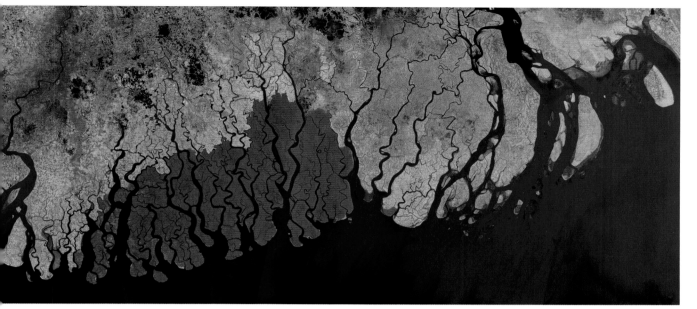

◄ *Ganges Delta, India/Bangladesh*
*Over 186 miles [300 km] wide, this
is the world's largest delta, created by
the River Ganges depositing sediment
it has carried from the Himalayas.
It is extremely vulnerable to frequent
cyclones and tidal surges, but is
densely populated because of the
fertile land. On the western side of
the image is the mouth of the Hugli,
with the elongated city of Kolkata
(Calcutta) showing as dark gray just to
the north. The large red area indicates
the presence of mangrove forests and
swamps, and is divided between the
countries of India and Bangladesh.*

▶ *Imperial Valley, USA/Mexico*
*The Salton Sea is the dark area
at the top left of the image.
It was inadvertently created in
1905 during an attempt to divert
the flow of the Colorado River for
irrigation. It lies 236 ft [72 m]
below sea level and is very saline.
To the south is a large area of
productive land, showing bright
red on this image. The abrupt
color change toward the
bottom of this area marks
the US–Mexico boundary.*

THE DYNAMIC EARTH

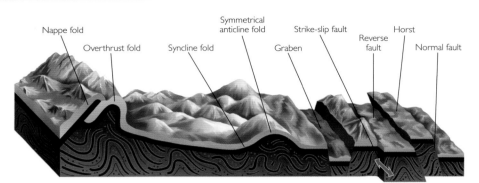

Nappe fold   Overthrust fold   Syncline fold   Symmetrical anticline fold   Graben   Strike-slip fault   Reverse fault   Horst   Normal fault

The Earth was formed about 4.6 billion years [4,600 million years] ago from the ring of gas and dust left over after the formation of the Sun. As the Earth took shape, lighter elements, such as silicon, rose to the surface, while heavy elements, notably iron, sank toward the center.

Gradually, the outer layers cooled to form a hard crust. The crust enclosed the dense mantle which, in turn, surrounded the even denser liquid outer and solid inner core. Around the Earth was an atmosphere, which contained abundant water vapor. When the surface cooled, rainwater began to fill hollows, forming the first lakes and seas. Since that time, our planet has been subject to constant change – the result of powerful internal and external forces that still operate today.

THE HISTORY OF THE EARTH

From their study of rocks, geologists have pieced together the history of our planet and the life forms that evolved upon it. They have dated the oldest known crystals, composed of the mineral zircon, at 4.2 billion years. But the oldest rocks are younger, less than 4 billion years old. This is because older rocks have been recycled or weathered away by natural processes.

The oldest rocks that contain fossils, which are

▼ *Lulworth Cove, southern England*
When undisturbed by earth movements, sedimentary rock strata are generally horizontal. But lateral pressure has squeezed the Jurassic strata at Lulworth Cove into complex folds.

evidence of once-living organisms, are around 3.5 billion years old. But fossils are rare in rocks formed in the first 4 billion years of Earth history. This vast expanse of time is called the Precambrian. This is because it precedes the Cambrian period, at the start of which, about 590 million years ago, life was abundant in the seas.

The Cambrian is the first period in the Paleozoic (or ancient life) era. The Paleozoic era is followed by the Mesozoic (middle life) era, which witnessed the spectacular rise and fall of the dinosaurs, and the Cenozoic (recent life) era, which was dominated by the evolution of mammals. Each of the eras is divided into periods, and the periods in the Cenozoic era, covering the last 65 million years, are further divided into epochs.

THE EARTH'S CHANGING FACE

While life was gradually evolving, the face of the Earth was constantly changing. By piecing together evidence of rock structures and fossils, geologists have demonstrated that around 250 million years ago, all the world's land areas were grouped together in one huge land mass called Pangaea. Around 180 million years ago, the supercontinent Pangaea began to break up. New oceans opened up as the continents began to move toward their present positions.

Evidence of how continents drift came from studies of the ocean floor in the 1950s and 1960s. Scientists discovered that the oceans are young features. By contrast with the continents, no part of the ocean floor is more than 200 million years old. The floors of oceans older than 200 million years have completely vanished.

Studies of long undersea ranges, called ocean ridges, revealed that the youngest rocks occur along their centers, which are the edges of huge plates – rigid blocks of the Earth's lithosphere, which is made up of the crust and the solid upper layer of the mantle. The Earth's lithosphere is split into six large and several smaller plates. The ocean ridges are "constructive" plate margins, because new crustal rock is being

▲ *Mountain building*
Lateral pressure, which occurs when plates collide, squeezes and compresses rocks into folds. Simple symmetrical upfolds are called anticlines, while downfolds are synclines. As the pressure builds up, strata become asymmetrical and they may be tilted over to form recumbent folds. The rocks often crack under the intense pressure and the folds are sheared away and pushed forward over other rocks. These features are called overthrust folds or nappes. Plate movements also create faults along which rocks move upward, downward, and sideways. The diagram shows a downfaulted graben, or rift valley, and an uplifted horst, or block mountain.

formed there from magma that wells up from the mantle as the plates gradually move apart. The deep-ocean trenches are "destructive" plate edges where two plates are pushing against each other. One plate descends beneath the other into the mantle where it is melted. These areas are called "subduction zones."

A third type of plate edge is called a transform fault. Here two plates are moving alongside each other. The best known of these plate edges is the San Andreas fault in California, which separates the Pacific plate from the North American plate.

Slow-moving currents in the partly molten asthenosphere, which underlies the solid lithosphere, are responsible for moving the plates, a process called plate tectonics.

MOUNTAIN BUILDING

The study of plate tectonics has helped geol-

▲ The Himalayas seen from Nepal

The Himalayas are a young fold mountain range formed by a collision between two plates. The earthquakes felt in the region testify that the plate movements are still continuing.

ogists to understand the mechanisms that are responsible for the creation of mountains. Many of the world's greatest ranges were created by the collision of two plates and the bending of the intervening strata into huge loops, or folds. For example, the Himalayas began to rise around 50 million years ago, when a plate supporting India collided with the huge Eurasian plate. Rocks on the floor of the intervening and long-vanished Tethys Sea were squeezed up to form the Himalayan Mountain Range.

Plate movements also create tension that cracks rocks, producing long faults along which rocks move upward, downward, or sideways. Block mountains are formed when blocks of rock are pushed upward along faults. Steep-sided rift valleys are formed when blocks of land sink down between faults. For example, the basin and range region of the southwestern United States has both block mountains and downfaulted basins, such as Death Valley.

▼ Geological time scale

The geological time scale was first constructed by a study of the stratigraphic, or relative, ages of layers of rock. But the absolute ages of rock strata could not be fixed until the discovery of radioactivity in the early 20th century. Some names of periods, such as Cambrian (Latin for Wales), come from places where the rocks were first studied. Others, such as Carboniferous, refer to the nature of the rocks formed during the period. For example, coal seams (containing carbon) were formed from decayed plant matter during the Carboniferous period.

Pre-Cambrian	Lower	Paleozoic (Primary)		Upper			Mesozoic (Secondary)			Cenozoic (Tertiary, Quaternary)						Era
Pre-Cambrian	Cambrian	Ordovician	Silurian	Devonian	Carboniferous	Permian	Triassic	Jurassic	Cretaceous	Paleocene	Eocene	Oligocene	Miocene	Pliocene	Quaternary	System
			CALEDONIAN FOLDING		HERCYNIAN FOLDING							LARAMIDE FOLDING	ALPINE FOLDING			Orogeny
600	550	500	450	400	350	300	250	200	150	100		50				

Millions of years before present

EARTHQUAKES AND VOLCANOES

On October 8, 2005, a massive earthquake occurred along the converging Indian and Eurasian plates in northern Pakistan's Northwest Frontier province and Indian-ruled Kashmir. Measuring 7.6 on the Richter scale, it caused about 87,000 deaths. Thousands were injured and 3 million people were left homeless at the onset of winter. The relief work was hampered by landslides, which blocked the roads leading to remote village communities.

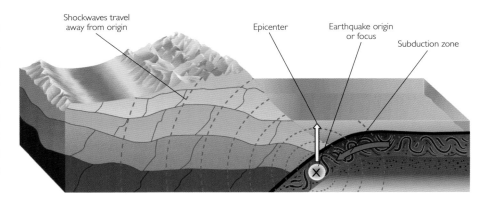

THE RESTLESS EARTH

Earthquakes can occur anywhere, whenever rocks move along faults. But the most severe and most numerous earthquakes occur near the edges of the plates that make up the Earth's lithosphere. Japan, for example, lies in a particularly unstable region above subduction zones, where plates are descending into the Earth's mantle. It lies in a zone encircling the Pacific Ocean, called the "Pacific ring of fire."

Plates do not move smoothly. Their edges are jagged and for most of the time they are locked together. However, pressure gradually builds up until the rocks break and the plates lurch forward, setting off vibrations ranging from slight tremors to terrifying earthquakes. The greater the pressure released, the more destructive the earthquake.

Earthquakes are also common along the ocean trenches where plates are moving apart, but they mostly occur so far from land that they do little damage. Far more destructive are the earthquakes that occur where plates are moving alongside each other. For example, the earthquakes that periodically rock southwestern California are caused by movements along the San Andreas Fault.

The spot where an earthquake originates is called the focus, while the point on the Earth's surface directly above the focus is called the epicenter. Two kinds of waves, P-waves or compressional waves and S-waves or shear waves, travel from the focus to the surface where they make the ground shake. P-waves travel faster than S-waves and the time difference between their arrival at recording stations enables scientists to calculate the distance from a station to the epicenter.

Earthquakes are measured on the Richter scale, which indicates the magnitude of the shock. The most destructive earthquakes are shallow-focus, that is, the focus is within 37 miles [60 km] of the surface. A magnitude of 7.0 is a major earthquake, but lower magnitude 'quakes can cause great damage if their epicenters are close to densely populated areas.

Scientists have been working for years to find effective ways of forecasting earthquakes but

▼ San Andreas Fault, United States
Geologists call the San Andreas fault in southwestern California a transform, or strike-slip, fault. Sudden movements along it cause earthquakes. In 1906, shifts of about 15 ft [4.5 m] occurred near San Francisco, causing a massive earthquake.

▲ Earthquakes in subduction zones
Along subduction zones, one plate is descending beneath another. The plates are locked together until the rocks break and the descending plate lurches forward. From the point where the plate moves – the origin – seismic waves spread through the lithosphere, making the ground shake. The earthquake in Mexico City in 1985 occurred in this way.

NOTABLE EARTHQUAKES
(since 1900)

Year	Location	Mag.
1906	San Francisco, USA	8.3
1906	Valparaiso, Chile	8.6
1908	Messina, Italy	7.5
1915	Avezzano, Italy	7.5
1920	Gansu, China	8.6
1923	Yokohama, Japan	8.3
1927	Nan Shan, China	8.3
1932	Gansu, China	7.6
1934	Bihar, India/Nepal	8.4
1935	Quetta, India†	7.5
1939	Chillan, Chile	8.3
1939	Erzincan, Turkey	7.9
1964	Anchorage, Alaska	8.4
1968	N. E. Iran	7.4
1970	N. Peru	7.7
1976	Guatemala	7.5
1976	Tangshan, China	8.2
1978	Tabas, Iran	7.7
1980	El Asnam, Algeria	7.3
1980	S. Italy	7.2
1985	Mexico City, Mexico	8.1
1988	N. W. Armenia	6.8
1990	N. Iran	7.7
1993	Maharashtra, India	6.4
1994	Los Angeles, USA	6.6
1995	Kobe, Japan	7.2
1995	Sakhalin Is., Russia	7.5
1996	Yunnan, China	7.0
1997	N. E. Iran	7.1
1998	N. Afghanistan	6.1
1998	N. E. Afghanistan	7.0
1999	Izmit, Turkey	7.4
1999	Taipei, Taiwan	7.6
2001	El Salvador	7.7
2001	Gujarat, India	7.7
2002	Baghlan, Afghanistan	6.1
2003	Mexico	7.8
2003	Bam, Iran	6.7
2004	N. Morocco	6.5
2004	Sumatra, Indonesia	9.1
2005	N. Pakistan	7.6
2006	Java, Indonesia	6.4

† *now Pakistan*

with limited success. But in the early 2000s, some scientists claimed that they had successfully forecast eruptions by identifying tremors, called "long-period events." They believe these relatively minor but long-lasting tremors are caused when magma surges up underground passages but fails to reach the surface.

VOLCANIC ERUPTIONS

Most active volcanoes also occur on or near plate edges. Many undersea volcanoes along the ocean ridges are formed from magma that wells up from the asthenosphere to fill the gaps created as the plates, on the opposite sides of the ridges, move apart. Some of these volcanoes reach the surface to form islands. Iceland is a country which straddles the Mid-Atlantic Ocean Ridge. It is gradually becoming wider as magma rises to the surface through faults and vents. Other volcanoes lie alongside subduction zones. The magma that fuels them comes from the melted edges of the descending plates.

A few volcanoes lie far from plate edges. For example, Mauna Loa and Kilauea on Hawai'i are situated near the center of the huge Pacific plate. The molten magma that reaches the surface is created by a source of heat, called a "hot spot," in the Earth's mantle.

Magma is molten rock at temperatures of about 2,012°F to 2,192°F [1,100°C to 1,200°C]. It contains gases and superheated steam. The chemical composition of magma varies. Viscous magma is rich in silica and superheated steam, while runny magma contains less silica and steam. The chemical composition of the magma affects the nature of volcanic eruptions.

Explosive volcanoes contain thick, viscous magma. When they erupt, they usually hurl clouds of ash (shattered fragments of cooled magma) into the air. By contrast, quiet volcanoes emit long streams of runny magma, or lava. However, many volcanoes are intermediate in type, sometimes erupting explosively and sometimes emitting streams of fluid lava. Explosive and intermediate volcanoes usually have a conical shape, while quiet volcanoes are flattened, resembling upturned saucers. They are often called shield volcanoes.

One dangerous type of eruption is called a *nuée ardente*, or "glowing cloud." It occurs when a cloud of intensely hot volcanic gases, dust particles, and superheated steam are exploded sideways from a volcano, often following a violent explosion which hurls ash high into the air. Pyroclastic surges and flows are similar. The clouds sweep downhill, destroying all in their paths. Pyroclastic surges and flows killed many people during the Vesuvius eruption in AD 79. The bodies were later buried by ash falls.

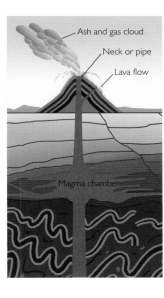

▲ *Cross-section of a volcano*
Volcanoes are vents in the ground, through which magma reaches the surface. The term volcano is also used for the mountains formed from volcanic rocks. Beneath volcanoes are pockets of magma derived from the semimolten asthenosphere in the mantle. The magma rises under pressure through the overlying rocks until it reaches the surface. There it emerges through vents as pyroclasts, ranging in size from large lumps of magma, called volcanic bombs, to fine volcanic ash and dust. In quiet eruptions, streams of liquid lava run down the side of the mountain. Side vents sometimes appear on the flanks of existing volcanoes.

▲ *Kilauea Volcano, Hawai'i*
The volcanic Hawaiian islands in the North Pacific Ocean were formed as the Pacific plate moved over a "hot spot" in the Earth's mantle. Kilauea on Hawai'i emits blazing streams of liquid lava.

FORCES OF NATURE

On December 26, 2004, a sudden movement of the plates beneath the Indian Ocean triggered a magnitude 9.1 earthquake. The 'quake created a tsunami, a fast-moving wave that battered the coasts of southern and southeastern Asia, and was even felt in East Africa. Entire communities were wiped out and the death toll was about 280,000. The worst damage occurred in Indonesia, Thailand, Sri Lanka, and India. Such events remind us of the great forces that operate inside our planet. But other forces are operating continuously, forever changing the landscape.

The chief forces acting on the surface of the Earth are weathering, running water, ice, and winds. The forces of erosion seem to act slowly. One estimate suggests that an average of only 1.4 inches [3.5 cm] of land is removed by natural processes every 1,000 years. But over millions of years, the highest mountains are eroded away.

WEATHERING

Weathering occurs in all parts of the world, but the most effective type of weathering in any area depends on the climate and the nature of the

▼ *Grand Canyon, Arizona, at dusk*
The Grand Canyon in the United States is one of the world's natural wonders. Eroded by the Colorado River and its tributaries, it is up to 1 mile [1.6 km] deep and 18 miles [29 km] wide.

RATES OF EROSION

| | WEATHERING RATE | | |
	SLOW ◄———————————►		FAST
Mineral solubility	low (e.g. quartz)	moderate (e.g. feldspar)	high (e.g. calcite)
Rainfall	low	moderate	heavy
Temperature	cold	temperate	hot
Vegetation	sparse	moderate	lush
Soil cover	bare rock	thin to moderate soil	thick soil

Weathering is the breakdown and decay of rocks in situ. It may be mechanical (physical), chemical, or biological.

rocks. For example, in cold mountain areas, when water freezes in cracks in rocks, the ice occupies 9% more space than the water. This exerts a force which, when repeated over and over again, can split boulders apart. By contrast, in hot deserts, intense heating by day and cooling by night causes the outer layers of rocks to expand and contract until they break up and peel away like layers of an onion. These are examples of what is called mechanical weathering.

Chemical weathering involves chemical reactions in various rocks. These reactions usually involve water. For example, rainwater containing carbon dioxide dissolved from the air or soil is a weak acid that reacts with limestone, wearing out pits, tunnels, and complex networks of caves. Water also combines with some minerals, such as feldspar in granite, to create kaolin, a soft white clay.

▲ *Rates of erosion*
The chart shows that the rates at which weathering takes place depend on the chemistry and hardness of rocks, climatic factors, especially rainfall and temperature, the vegetation, and the nature of the soil cover in any area. The effects of weathering are increased by human action, particularly the removal of vegetation and the exposure of soils to the rain and wind.

RUNNING WATER, ICE, AND WIND

In moist regions, rivers are effective in shaping the land. They transport material worn away by weathering and erode the land. They wear out V-shaped valleys in upland regions, while vigorous meanders widen their middle courses. The work of rivers is at its most spectacular when earth movements lift up flat areas and rejuvenate the rivers, giving them a new erosive power capable of wearing out such features as the Grand Canyon. Rivers also have a constructive role. Some of the world's most fertile regions are deltas and flood plains composed of sediments periodically dumped there by such rivers as the Ganges, Mississippi, and Nile.

▼ *Glaciers*

During Ice Ages, ice spreads over large areas but, during warm periods, the ice retreats. The chart shows that the volume of ice in many glaciers is decreasing, possibly as a result of global warming. Experts estimate that, between 1850 and the early 21st century, more than half of the ice in Alpine glaciers has melted.

ANNUAL FLUCTUATIONS FOR SELECTED GLACIERS

Glacier name and location	Changes in the annual mass balance[†]		
	1970–1	1990–1	2000–2001
Alfotbreen, Norway	+940	+790	−50
Careser, Italy	−650	−1,730	−1,860
Djankuat, Russia	−230	−310	−1,760
Grasubreen, Norway	+470	−520	−30
Gries, Switzerland	−970	−1,480	−902
Hintereisferner, Austria	−600	−1,325	−806
Place, Canada	−343	−990	−690
Sarennes, France	−1,100	−1,360	−1,160
Storglaciaren, Sweden	−190	+170	−115
Ürümqi, China	+102	−706	−1,170
Wolverine, USA	+770	−410	−480

[†] *The annual mass balance is defined as the difference between glacier accumulation and ablation (melting) averaged over the whole glacier. Balances are expressed as water equivalent in millimeters. A "plus" indicates an increase in the depth or length of the glacier; a "minus" indicates a reduction.*

▲ *Juneau Glacier, Alaska*

Like huge conveyor belts, glaciers transport weathered debris from mountain regions. Rocks frozen in the ice give the glaciers teeth, enabling them to wear out typical glaciated land features.

Running water in the form of sea waves and currents shapes coastlines, wearing out caves, natural arches, and stacks. The sea also transports and deposits worn material to form such features as spits and bars.

Glaciers in cold mountain regions flow downhill, gradually deepening valleys and shaping dramatic landscapes. They erode steep-sided U-shaped valleys, into which rivers often plunge in large waterfalls. Other features include cirques, armchair-shaped basins bounded by knife-edged ridges called *arêtes*. When several glacial cirques erode to form radial *arêtes*, pyramidal peaks like the Matterhorn are created. Deposits of moraine, rock material dumped by the glacier, are further evidence that ice once covered large areas.

The work of glaciers, like other agents of erosion, varies with the climate. In recent years, global warming has been making glaciers retreat in many areas, while several of the ice shelves in Antarctica have been breaking up.

Many land features in deserts were formed by running water at a time when the climate was much rainier than it is today. Water erosion also occurs when flash floods are caused by rare thunderstorms. But the chief agent of erosion in dry areas is wind-blown sand, which can strip the paint from cars, and undercut boulders to create mushroom-shaped rocks.

OCEANS AND ICE

In 2005, Tim Barnett of the Scripps Institution of Oceanography presented a paper to the American Association for the Advancement of Science showing that the upper waters of the oceans had markedly warmed up in the last 65 years, dramatic evidence of global warming.

Oceanography is a major science, but, only about 50 years ago, little was known of the dark world beneath the waves. But through the use of modern technology, including echo-sounders, magnetometers, research ships equipped with huge drills, and satellites, many of the oceans' secrets have been unraveled. Scientists have visited the ocean ridges in submersibles. There, they found hot vents, or "black smokers" – chimney-like structures made up of minerals deposited from the hot water. Around them, are swarms of bacteria – the base of a food chain that includes strange creatures, many unknown to science, such as giant worms, eyeless shrimps, and white clams. These discoveries have led some to speculate that the first living organisms on Earth may have evolved in such conditions on ancient ocean floors.

The study of the ocean floor led to the discovery that the oceans are geologically young features – no more than 200 million years old. It also revealed evidence as to how oceans form and continents drift because of the action of plate tectonics.

THE BLUE PLANET

Water covers almost 71% of the Earth's surface, which makes it look blue when viewed from space. Oceanographers recognize five oceans: the Pacific, Atlantic, Indian, Southern (or Antarctic), and Arctic, but they are all interconnected. The average depth of the oceans is 12,238 ft [3,370 m], but they are divided into several zones.

Around most continents are gently sloping continental shelves, which are flooded parts of the continents. The shelves end at the continental slope, at a depth of about 656 ft [200 m]. This slope leads steeply down to the abyss. The deepest parts of the oceans are the trenches, which reach a maximum depth of 36,161 ft [11,022 m] in the Mariana Trench in the western Pacific.

Most marine life is found in the top 200 m [656 ft], where there is sufficient sunlight for plants, called phytoplankton, to grow. Below this zone, life becomes more and more scarce, though no part of the ocean, even at the bottom of the deepest trenches, is completely without living things.

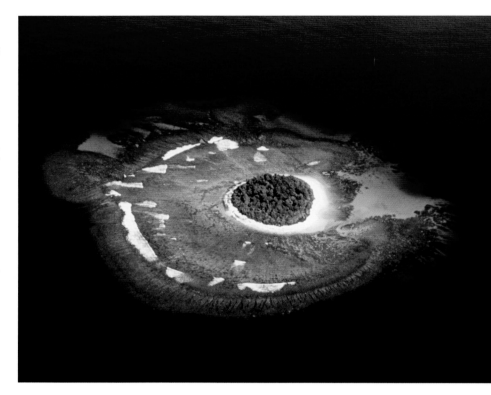

▲ *Vava'u Island, Tonga*
This small coral atoll in northern Tonga consists of a central island covered by rain forest. Low coral reefs washed by the waves surround a shallow central lagoon.

Continental islands, such as the British Isles, are high parts of the continental shelves. For example, until about 7,500 years ago, when the ice sheets formed during the Ice Ages were melting, raising the sea level and filling the North Sea and the Strait of Dover, Britain was linked to mainland Europe.

By contrast, oceanic islands, such as the Hawaiian chain in the North Pacific Ocean, rise from the ocean floor. All oceanic islands are of volcanic origin, although many of them in warm parts of the oceans have sunk and are capped by layers of coral to form ring- or horseshoe-shaped atolls and coral reefs.

OCEAN WATER

The oceans contain about 97% of the world's water. Seawater contains more than 70 dissolved elements, but chloride and sodium make up 85% of the total. Sodium chloride is common salt and it makes seawater salty. The salinity of the oceans is mostly between 3.3–3.7%. Ocean water fed by icebergs or large rivers is less saline than shallow seas in the tropics, where the evaporation rate is high. Seawater is a source of salt but the water is useless for agriculture or drinking unless it is desalinated. However, land areas get a regular

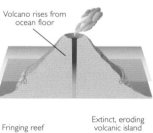

Volcano rises from ocean floor

Fringing reef

Extinct, eroding volcanic island

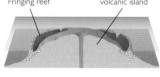

After subsidence, reef covers buried island

Lagoon

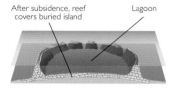

▲ *Development of an atoll*
Some of the volcanoes that rise from the ocean floor reach the surface to form islands. Some of these islands subside and become submerged. As an island sinks, coral starts to grow around the rim of the volcano, building up layer upon layer of limestone deposits to form fringing reefs. Sometimes coral grows on the tip of a central cone to form an island in the middle of the atoll.

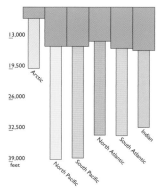

▲ *The ocean depths*

The diagram shows the average depths (in dark blue) and the greatest depths in the four oceans. The North Pacific Ocean contains the world's deepest trenches, including the Mariana Trench, where the deepest manned descent was made by the bathyscaphe Trieste in 1960. It reached a depth of 35,813 ft [10,916 m].

Relative sizes of the world's oceans:

PACIFIC 46.4%   ATLANTIC 22.9%
INDIAN 20.4%   SOUTHERN 6.1%
ARCTIC 4.2%

Since 2000, the International Hydrographic Organization has recognized the existence of five oceans, including the Southern or Antarctic Ocean.

supply of fresh water through the hydrological cycle (see page 42).

The density of seawater depends on its salinity and temperature. Temperatures vary from 28°F [–2°C], the freezing point of seawater at the poles, to around 86°F [30°C] in parts of the tropics. Density differences help to maintain the circulation of the world's oceans, especially deep-sea currents. But the main cause of currents within 1,148 ft [350 m] of the surface is the wind. Because of the Earth's rotation, currents are deflected, creating huge circular motions of surface water – clockwise in the northern hemisphere and counterclockwise in the southern hemisphere.

Ocean currents transport heat from the tropics to the polar regions and thus form part of the heat engine that drives the Earth's climates. Ocean currents have an especially marked effect on coastal climates, such as northwestern Europe. Some scientists are concerned that global warming may radically alter climates by weakening currents, such as the Gulf Stream, which is responsible for the mild winters in northwestern Europe.

ICE SHEETS, ICE CAPS, AND GLACIERS

Of the world's two ice sheets, the largest, covering most of Antarctica, has maximum depths of 15,748 ft [4,800 m]. Its volume is about nine times greater than the Greenland ice sheet. The ice sheets, together with smaller ice caps and glaciers, account for about 2% of the world's

water. However, in many parts of the world, the ice is melting and many scientists think the cause is global warming. In March 2002, the vast Larsen ice shelf bordering the Antarctic peninsula collapsed and broke up into icebergs. Some scientists thought this was evidence of global warming, though some attributed the event to local factors.

Only about 11,000 years ago, during the final phase of the Pleistocene Ice Age, ice covered much of the northern hemisphere. The Ice Age, which began about 1.8 million years ago, was not a continuous period of cold. Instead, it consisted of glacial periods when the ice advanced and warmer interglacial periods when temperatures rose and the ice retreated.

Some scientists believe that we are now living in an interglacial period, and that glacial conditions will recur in the future. Others fear that global warming, caused mainly by pollution, may melt the world's ice, raising sea levels by up to 180 ft [55 m]. Many fertile and densely populated coastal plains, islands, and cities would vanish from the map.

▼ *Icebergs float past the Antarctic Peninsula*

The Antarctic peninsula overlooks the Weddell Sea. The Weddell Sea and the Ross Sea are largely covered by huge ice shelves, which are extensions of the continental ice sheet. Many scientists are concerned that warmer weather is melting the ice sheets. In 2002, parts of the Larsen Ice Shelf, which adjoins the Antarctic Peninsula, collapsed and split up into icebergs.

THE EARTH'S ATMOSPHERE

Since the discovery in 1985 of a thinning of the ozone layer, creating a so-called "ozone hole," over Antarctica, many governments have worked to reduce the emissions of ozone-eating substances, notably the chlorofluorocarbons (CFCs) used in aerosols, refrigeration, air-conditioning, and dry cleaning.

Following forecasts that the ozone layer would rapidly repair itself as a result of controls on these emissions, scientists were surprised in early 1996 when a marked thinning of the ozone layer over the northern hemisphere was recorded. In 2005, scientists reported that the ozone hole over Antarctica was the largest since 2000, while 2005 also saw a marked thinning of the ozone layer over the Arctic region. Scientists predicted that it might take more than 50 years before the ozone layer made a full recovery.

The ozone layer in the stratosphere blocks out most of the dangerous ultraviolet B radiation in the Sun's rays. This radiation causes skin cancer and cataracts, as well as harming plants on the land and plankton in the oceans. The ozone layer is only one way in which the atmosphere protects life on Earth. The atmosphere also provides the air we breathe and the carbon dioxide required by plants. It is also a shield against meteors and it acts as a blanket to prevent heat radiated from the Earth escaping into space.

LAYERS OF AIR

The atmosphere is divided into four main layers. The troposphere at the bottom contains about 85% of the atmosphere's total mass, where most weather conditions occur. The troposphere is about 9 miles [15 km] thick over the equator and 5 miles [8 km] thick at the poles. Temperatures decrease with height by approximately 2°F [1°C] for every 328 ft [100 m]. At the top of the troposphere is a level called the tropopause where temperatures are stable at around –67°F [–55°C]. Above the tropopause is the stratosphere, which contains the ozone layer. Here, at about 30 miles [50 km] above the Earth's surface, temperatures rise to about 32°F [0°C].

The ionosphere extends from the stratopause to about 373 miles [600 km] above the surface. Here temperatures fall up to about 50 miles [80 km], but then rise. The aurorae, which occur in the ionosphere when charged particles

CIRCULATION OF AIR

HIGH PRESSURE
LOW PRESSURE
WARM AIR
COLD AIR
SURFACE WINDS
CLOUDS

▲ The circulation of the atmosphere can be divided into three rotating but interconnected air systems. These systems, or cells, are responsible for redistributing heat from the warm regions to the cold, and back again.

▼ *Moonrise seen from orbit*

This photograph taken by an orbiting Shuttle shows the crescent of the Moon. Silhouetted at the horizon is a dense cloud layer. The reddish-brown band is the tropopause, which separates the blue-white stratosphere from the yellow troposphere.

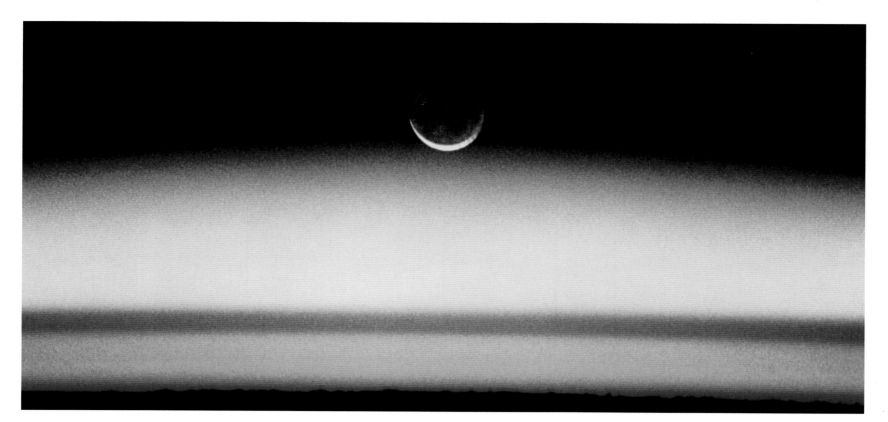

► *Classification of clouds*

*Clouds are classified broadly
into cumuliform, or "heap" clouds,
and stratiform, or "layer" clouds.
Both types occur at all levels.
The highest clouds, composed
of ice crystals, are cirrus,
cirrostratus, and cirrocumulus.
Medium-height clouds include
altostratus, a gray cloud that
often indicates the approach
of a depression, and altocumulus,
a thicker and fluffier version
of cirrocumulus. Low clouds
include stratus, which forms
dull, overcast skies; nimbostratus,
a dark gray layer cloud which
brings almost continuous
rain and snow; cumulus, a
brilliant white heap cloud; and
stratocumulus, a layer cloud
arranged in globular masses
or rolls. Cumulonimbus, a cloud
associated with thunderstorms,
lightning, and heavy rain, often
extends from low to medium
altitudes. It has a flat base,
a fluffy outline, and often an
anvil-shaped top.*

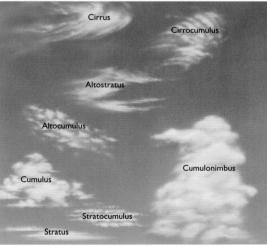

from the Sun interact with the Earth's magnetic field, are strongest near the poles. In the exosphere, the outermost layer, the atmosphere merges into space.

CIRCULATION OF THE ATMOSPHERE

The heating of the Earth is most intense around the equator where the Sun is high in the sky. Here warm, moist air rises in strong currents, creating a zone of low air pressure: the doldrums. The rising air eventually cools and spreads out north and south until it sinks downward around latitudes 30° North and 30° South. The zones of high air pressure caused

▲ *Jetstream from space*

*Jetstreams are strong winds that normally blow near the
tropopause. Cirrus clouds mark the route of the jet stream
in this photograph, which shows the Red Sea, North Africa,
and the Nile valley, which appears as a dark band crossing
the desert.*

by the sinking air are called the "horse latitudes."

From the horse latitudes, trade winds blow back across the surface toward the equator, while westerly winds blow toward the poles. The warm westerlies finally meet the polar easterlies (cold dense air flowing from the poles). The line along which the warm and cold air streams meet is called the polar front. Depressions (or cyclones) are low-air-pressure frontal systems that form along the polar front.

COMPOSITION OF THE ATMOSPHERE

The air in the troposphere is made up mainly of nitrogen (78%) and oxygen (21%). Argon makes up more than 0.9% and there are also minute amounts of carbon dioxide, helium, hydrogen, krypton, methane, ozone, and xenon. The atmosphere also contains water vapor, the gaseous form of water, which, when it condenses around minute specks of dust and salt, forms tiny water droplets or ice crystals. Large masses of water droplets or ice crystals form clouds.

CLIMATE AND WEATHER

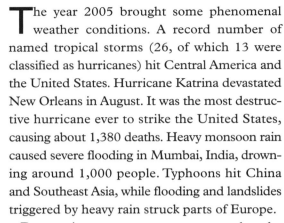

The year 2005 brought some phenomenal weather conditions. A record number of named tropical storms (26, of which 13 were classified as hurricanes) hit Central America and the United States. Hurricane Katrina devastated New Orleans in August. It was the most destructive hurricane ever to strike the United States, causing about 1,380 deaths. Heavy monsoon rain caused severe flooding in Mumbai, India, drowning around 1,000 people. Typhoons hit China and Southeast Asia, while flooding and landslides triggered by heavy rain struck parts of Europe.

Destructive storms occur every year, but the increasing frequency and intensity of extreme weather has led some scientists to wonder whether it might be the result of global warming, and also that the trend toward increasing weather disasters may be irreversible.

Weather is the day-to-day condition of the atmosphere. In some places, the weather is normally stable, but in other areas, especially the middle latitudes, it is highly variable, changing with the passing of a depression. By contrast, climate is the average weather of a place, based on data obtained over a long period.

CLIMATIC FACTORS

Climate depends basically on the unequal heating of the Sun between the equator and the poles. But ocean currents and terrain also affect climate. For example, despite their northerly positions, Norway's ports remain ice-free in winter. This is because of the warming effect of the North Atlantic Drift, an extension of the Gulf Stream which flows across the Atlantic Ocean from the Gulf of Mexico.

▲ *Satellite image of Hurricane Floyd in 1999*
Hurricanes form over warm oceans north and south of the equator. Their movements are tracked by satellites, enabling forecasters to issue advance warnings. North American forecasters identify them with boys' and girls' names.

By contrast, the cold Benguela current which flows up the coast of southwestern Africa cools the coast and causes arid conditions. This is because the cold onshore winds are warmed as they pass over the land. The warm air can hold more water vapor than cold air, giving the winds a drying effect.

The terrain affects climate in several ways. Because temperatures fall with altitude, high-

CLIMATIC REGIONS

Tropical rainy climates
All mean monthly temperatures above 64°F [18°C].

■ RAIN FOREST CLIMATE
□ MONSOON CLIMATE
□ SAVANNA CLIMATE

Dry climates
Low rainfall combined with a wide range of temperatures.

□ STEPPE CLIMATE
□ DESERT CLIMATE

Warm temperate rainy climates
The mean temperature is below 64°F [18°C] but above 26°F [–3°C], and that of the warmest month is over 50°F [10°C].

□ DRY WINTER CLIMATE
■ DRY SUMMER CLIMATE
■ CLIMATE WITH NO DRY SEASON

Cold temperate rainy climates
The mean temperature of the coldest month is below 37°F [3°C] but the warmest month is over 50°F [10°C].

□ DRY WINTER CLIMATE
□ CLIMATE WITH NO DRY SEASON

Polar climates
The temperature of the warmest month is below 50°F [10°C], giving permanently frozen subsoil.

□ TUNDRA CLIMATE
■ POLAR CLIMATE

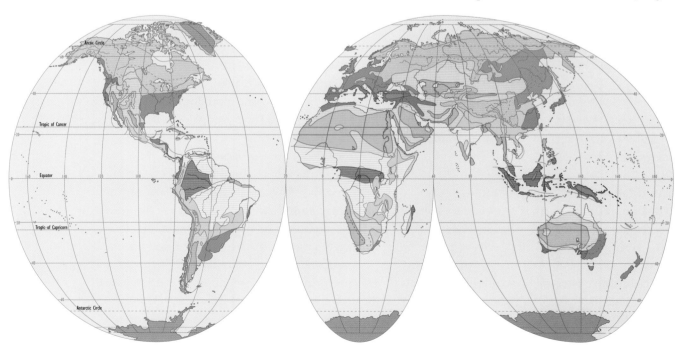

▶ *Floods in St Louis, USA*

The satellite image, right, shows the extent of the floods at St Louis at the confluence of the Mississippi and the Missouri rivers in June and July 1993. The floods occurred when very heavy rainfall raised river levels by up to 46 ft [14 m]. The floods reached their greatest extent between Minneapolis in the north and a point approximately 93 miles [150 km] south of St Louis. In places, the width of the Mississippi increased to nearly 7 miles [11 km], while the Missouri reached widths of 20 miles [32 km]. In all, more than 10,800 sq miles [28,000 sq km] were inundated and hundreds of towns and cities were flooded. Damage to crops was estimated at $8 billion. The US was hit again by flooding in early 1997, when heavy rainfall in North Dakota and Minnesota caused the Red River to flood. The flooding had a catastrophic effect on the city of Grand Forks, which was inundated for months.

▲ *Flood damage in the United States*

In June and July 1993, the Mississippi River basin suffered record floods. The photograph shows a sunken church in Illinois. The flooding along the Mississippi, Missouri, and other rivers caused great damage, amounting to about $12 billion. At least 48 people died in the floods.

CLIMATIC REGIONS

The two major factors that affect climate are temperature and precipitation, including rain and snow. In addition, seasonal variations and other climatic features are also taken into account. Climatic classifications vary because of the weighting given to various features. Yet most classifications are based on five main climatic types: tropical rainy climates; dry climates; warm temperate rainy climates; cold temperate rainy climates; and very cold polar climates. Some classifications also allow for the effect of altitude. The main climatic regions are sub-divided according to seasonal variations and also to the kind of vegetation associated with the climate. With rain throughout the year, rain forest climates differ from monsoon and savanna climates, which have dry seasons, while desert climates differ from steppe climates, which have enough moisture for grasses to grow.

lands are cooler than lowlands at the same latitude. Terrain also affects rainfall. When moist onshore winds pass over mountain ranges, they are chilled as they are forced to rise and the water vapor they contain condenses to form clouds, which bring rain and snow. Beyond the mountains, the air descends and is warmed. These drying winds create rain-shadow (arid) regions on the lee side of mountains.

WATER AND LAND USE

All life on land depends on fresh water. Yet about 80 countries now face acute water shortages. The world demand for fresh water is increasing by about 2.3% a year and this demand will double every 21 years. About a billion people, mainly in developing countries, do not have access to clean drinking water and around 10 million die every year from drinking dirty water. This problem is made worse in many countries by the pollution of rivers and lakes.

UN experts predict that water is becoming the most pressing environmental and development issue facing the world. By 2003, heavily populated regions in 26 countries were suffering serious water shortages. In 20 years, this number will probably rise to 65. Further, the United Nations estimated in 2005 that 1.1 billion people lack sufficient clean water for drinking and bathing. However, experts stress that while individual countries face water crises, there is no global crisis. The chief global problems are the uneven distribution of water and its inefficient and wasteful use.

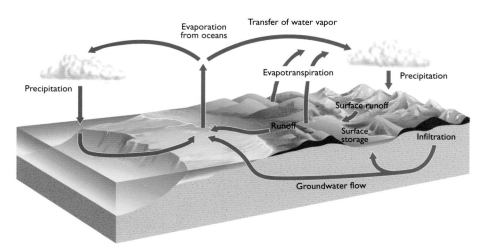

▲ *The hydrological cycle*
The hydrological cycle is responsible for the continuous circulation of water around the planet. Water vapor contains and transports latent heat, or latent energy. When the water vapor condenses back into water (and falls as rain, hail, or snow), the heat is released. When condensation takes place on cold nights, the cooling effect associated with nightfall is offset by the liberation of latent heat.

THE WORLD'S WATER SUPPLY

Of the world's total water supply, 99.4% is in the oceans or frozen in bodies of ice. Most of the rest circulates through the rocks beneath our feet as groundwater. Water in rivers and lakes, in the soil, and in the atmosphere together make up only 0.013% of the world's water.

The freshwater supply on land is dependent on the hydrological, or water, cycle which is driven by the Sun's heat. Water is evaporated from the oceans and carried into the air as invisible water vapor. Although this vapor averages less than 2% of the total mass of the atmosphere, it is the chief component from the standpoint of weather.

When air rises, water vapor condenses into visible water droplets or ice crystals, which eventually fall to earth as rain, snow, sleet, hail, or frost. Some of the precipitation that reaches the ground returns directly to the atmosphere through evaporation or transpiration via plants. Much of the rest of the water flows into the rocks to become groundwater, or across the surface into rivers and, eventually, back to the oceans, so completing the hydrological cycle.

WATER AND AGRICULTURE

In 2005, a US study revealed that about 40% of the world's land is used to grow crops or to graze cattle. The biggest recent changes have occurred in the Amazon basin, where tropical forest is being felled to create land for growing soybeans.

▼ *Hoover Dam, United States*
The Hoover Dam in Arizona controls the Colorado River's flood waters. Its reservoir supplies domestic and irrigation water to the southwest, while a hydroelectric plant produces electricity.

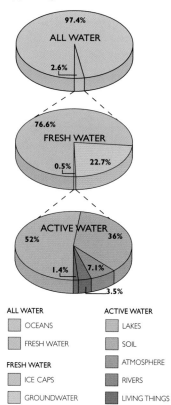

WATER DISTRIBUTION
The distribution of planetary water, by percentage.

97.4%
ALL WATER
2.6%

76.6%
FRESH WATER
0.5%   22.7%

ACTIVE WATER
52%   36%
1.4%   7.1%
3.5%

ALL WATER	ACTIVE WATER
OCEANS	LAKES
FRESH WATER	SOIL
FRESH WATER	ATMOSPHERE
ICE CAPS	RIVERS
GROUNDWATER	LIVING THINGS
ACTIVE WATER	

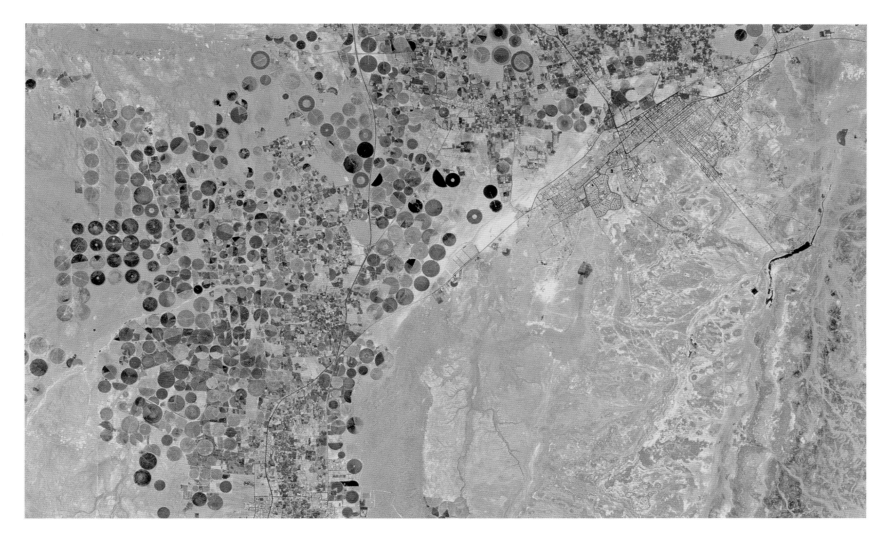

Saudi Arabia is a desert country that gets its water from oases, which tap groundwater supplies, and desalination plants. The sale of oil has enabled the arid countries of southwestern Asia to develop their agriculture. In the above satellite image, vegetation appears as brown and red circles, generated by center-pivot irrigation systems.

▶ *Irrigation boom*

The photograph shows a pivotal irrigation boom used to sprinkle water over a wheat field in Saudi Arabia. Irrigation in hot countries often takes place at night so that water loss through evaporation is reduced. Irrigation techniques vary from place to place. In monsoon areas with abundant water, the fields are often flooded, or the water is led to the crops along straight furrows. Sprinkler irrigation has become important since the 1940s. In other types of irrigation, the water is led through pipes which are on or under the ground. Underground pipes supply water directly to the plant roots and, as a result, water loss through evaporation is minimized.

The study pointed out that the world is running out of fertile land, because large areas are too dry, too cold, or too mountainous for farming. Although the demand for food increases every year, problems arise when attempts are made to increase the area of farmland. The soils and climate of tropical forests or semiarid regions are not ideal for farming and often lead to the deterioration of fragile environments. To increase food supply, farmers must concentrate on making existing agriculture more productive.

To grow crops, farmers need fertile, workable land, an equable climate, and an adequate supply of fresh water. In some areas, the water supply comes directly from rain, but many other regions depend on irrigation.

Irrigation involves water conservation through the building of dams which hold back storage reservoirs. In some areas, irrigation water comes from underground aquifers, layers of permeable and porous rocks through which groundwater percolates. But in many cases, the water in the aquifers has been there for thousands of years, having accumulated at a time when the rainfall was much greater than it is today. As a result, these aquifers are not being renewed and will, one day, dry up.

Other sources of irrigation water are desalination plants, which remove salt from seawater and pump it to farms. This is a highly expensive process and is employed in areas where water supplies are extremely low, such as the island of Malta, or in the oil-rich desert countries around the Persian Gulf, which can afford to build huge desalination plants.

LAND USE BY CONTINENT (2003)

	Forest	Permanent pasture	Permanent crops	Arable	Non-productive
N. & C. America	26.0%	16.4%	0.7%	12.0%	45.0%
S. America	50.5%	26.4%	0.8%	6.1%	16.0%
Europe	46.0%	8.3%	0.8%	12.9%	32.0%
Africa	21.8%	31.1%	0.9%	6.7%	39.5%
Asia	17.8%	35.8%	2.1%	16.4%	28.0%
Oceania	23.3%	47.8%	0.4%	5.9%	23.0%

THE NATURAL WORLD

In 2006, the International Union for the Conservation of Nature released its Red List of 16,118 plant and animal species that are threatened with extinction – more than 500 species than in 2004. Human activities, ranging from habitat destruction to the introduction of alien species from one area to another, are the main causes of this devastating reduction of our planet's biodiversity, which might lead to the loss of unique combinations of genes that could be vital in improving food yields on farms or in the production of drugs to combat disease.

Extinctions of species have occurred through-out Earth's history, but today the extinction rate is estimated to be about 10,000 times the natural average. Some scientists have even compared it with the mass extinction that wiped out the dinosaurs 65 million years ago. However, the main cause of today's high extinction rate is not some natural disaster, such as the impact of an asteroid a few miles across, but it is the result of human actions. In some areas, such as Western Europe, the natural habitats were destroyed long ago. The greatest damage is now

▼ *Rain forest in Rwanda*

Rain forests are the most threatened of the world's biomes. Effective conservation policies must demonstrate to poor local people that they can benefit from the survival of the forests.

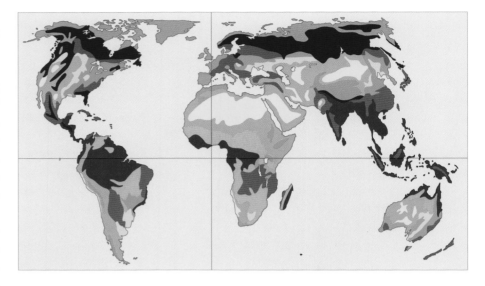

occurring in tropical rain forests, which contain more than half of the world's known species. Even the polar regions are threatened as global warming melts ice sheets and sea ice.

Modern technology has enabled people to live comfortably almost anywhere on Earth. But most plants and many animals are adapted to particular climatic conditions, and they live in association with and dependent on each other. Plant and animal communities that cover large areas are called biomes.

THE WORLD'S BIOMES

The world's biomes are defined mainly by climate and vegetation. They range from the tundra, in polar regions and high mountain regions, to the lush equatorial rain forests.

The Arctic tundra covers large areas in the polar regions of the northern hemisphere. Snow covers the land for more than half of the year and the subsoil, called permafrost, is per-manently frozen. Comparatively few species can survive in this harsh, treeless environment. The main plants are hardy mosses, lichens, grasses, sedges, and low shrubs. However, in summer, the tundra plays an important part in world animal geography, when its growing plants and swarms of insects provide food for migrating animals and birds that arrive from the south.

The tundra of the northern hemisphere merges in the south into a vast region of needle-leaf evergreen forest, called the boreal forest or taiga. Such trees as fir, larch, pine, and spruce are adapted to survive the long, bitterly cold winters of this region, but the number of plant and animal species is again small. South of the boreal forests is a zone of mixed needleleaf evergreens and broadleaf deciduous trees, which shed their leaves in winter. In warmer areas, this

NATURAL VEGETATION

- TUNDRA & MOUNTAIN VEGETATION
- NEEDLELEAF EVERGREEN FOREST
- MIXED NEEDLELEAF EVERGREEN & BROADLEAF DECIDUOUS TREES
- BROADLEAF DECIDUOUS WOODLAND
- MID-LATITUDE GRASSLAND
- EVERGREEN BROADLEAF & DECIDUOUS TREES & SHRUBS
- SEMIDESERT SCRUB
- DESERT
- TROPICAL GRASSLAND (SAVANNA)
- TROPICAL BROADLEAF RAIN FOREST & MONSOON FOREST
- SUBTROPICAL BROADLEAF & NEEDLELEAF FOREST

▲ *The map shows the world's main biomes. The classification is based on the natural "climax" vegetation of regions, a result of the climate and the terrain. But human activities have greatly modified this basic division. For example, the original deciduous forests of Western Europe and the eastern United States have largely disappeared. In recent times, human development of some semiarid areas has turned former dry grasslands into barren desert.*

mixed forest merges into broadleaf deciduous forest, where the number and diversity of plant species is much greater.

Deciduous forests are adapted to temperate, humid regions. Evergreen broadleaf and deciduous trees grow in Mediterranean regions, with their hot, dry summers. But much of the original deciduous forest has been cut down and has given way to scrub and heathland. Grasslands occupy large areas in the middle latitudes, where the rainfall is insufficient to support forest growth. The moister grasslands are often called prairies, while drier areas are called steppe.

▲ *Tundra in subarctic Alaska, United States*
The Denali National Park, Alaska, contains magnificent mountain scenery and tundra vegetation that flourishes during the brief summer. The park is open between June 1 and September 15.

The tropics also contain vast dry areas of semidesert scrub that merges into desert, as well as large areas of tropical savanna, which is grassland, ranging from luxuriant to sparse, with scattered shrubs and trees, whose growth is limited by a marked dry season. Savanna regions support a wide range of animals.

Tropical and subtropical regions contain three types of forest biomes. The tropical rain forest, the world's richest biome measured by its plant and animal species, experiences rain and high temperatures throughout the year. Similar forests occur in monsoon regions, which have a season of very heavy rainfall. They, too, are rich in plant species, though less so than the tropical rain forest. A third type of forest is the subtropical broadleaf and needleleaf forest, found in such places as southeastern China, south-central Africa, and eastern Brazil.

▼ *The net primary production of eight major biomes is expressed in grams of dry organic matter per square meter per year. The tropical rain forests produce the greatest amount of organic material. The tundra and deserts produce the least.*

NET PRIMARY PRODUCTION OF EIGHT MAJOR BIOMES

- ■ TROPICAL RAIN FORESTS
- ■ DECIDUOUS FORESTS
- ■ TROPICAL GRASSLANDS
- ■ CONIFEROUS FORESTS
- ■ MEDITERRANEAN
- ■ TEMPERATE GRASSLANDS
- ■ TUNDRA
- ■ DESERTS

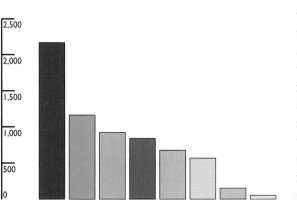

THE HUMAN WORLD

Every minute, the world's population increases by more than 100. Predictions of future growth vary. In 1999, UN demographers stated that the population, which passed the 6 billion mark in October 1999, would reach 8.9 billion. It would level out after 2200, when it would peak at 11 billion. But, in 2004, UN demographers predicted that the world's population would peak at 9.1 billion in 2050 and then could start to decline. However, while some European countries are concerned about declining birth rates, all experts agree that the fastest rates of population increase will occur in developing countries – the places least able to afford the high costs arising from a rapidly growing population.

▼ *Quito, capital city of Ecuador*
In common with world trends, the annual growth rate in the population of Ecuador is declining, while urbanization is increasing rapidly.

Average world population growth rates are expected to decline from 1.6% per year in 1975–2001 to 1.1% in 2001–15. This is partly due to a decline in fertility rates – that is, the number of births to the number of women of child-bearing age – especially in developed countries where, as income has risen, the average size of families has fallen.

Declining fertility rates were also evident in many developing countries. Even Africa shows signs of such change, though its population is expected to triple before it begins to fall. Population growth is also dependent on death rates, which are affected by such factors as famine, disease, and the quality of medical care.

THE POPULATION EXPLOSION

The world's population has grown steadily throughout most of human history, though certain events triggered periods of population growth. The invention of agriculture, around 10,000 years ago, led to great changes in human society. Before then, most people had obtained food by hunting animals and gathering plants. Average life expectancies were probably no more than 20 years and life was hard. However, when farmers began to produce food surpluses, people began to live settled lives. This major milestone in human history led to the development of the first cities and early civilizations.

From an estimated 8 million in 8000 BC, the world population rose to about 300 million by AD 1000. Between 1000 and 1750, the rate of world population increase was around 0.1% per year, but another period of major economic and social change – the Industrial Revolution – began in the late 18th century. The Industrial Revolution led to improvements in farm technology and increases in food production. The world population began to increase quickly as industrialization spread across Europe and into North America. By 1850, it had reached 1.2 billion. The 2 billion mark was passed in the 1920s, and then the population rapidly doubled to 4 billion by the 1970s.

POPULATION FEATURES

Population growth affects the structure of societies. In developing countries with high annual rates of population increase, the large majority of the people are young and soon to become parents themselves. For example, in Kenya, which had until recently an annual rate of population growth of around 4%, about 42% of the population is under 15 years of age, as

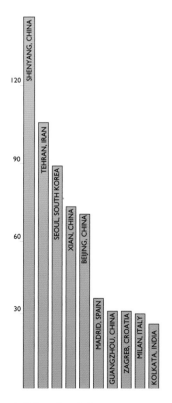

▲ *Urban air pollution*
This diagram of the world's most polluted cities indicates the number of days per year when sulfur dioxide levels exceed the WHO threshhold of 150 micrograms per cubic meter.

compared with 21% in the United States. Most developed countries have a fairly even spread across the age groups.

Such differences are reflected in average life expectancies. In a rich country, such as the USA, the average life expectancy in 2005 was 77 years (74 for men and 80 for women; women live longer, on average, than men). As a result, an increasing proportion of the people are elderly and retired. The reverse applies in many poor countries, where average life expectancies are below 60 years. In the early 21st century, life expectancies were falling in parts of southern Africa because of the spread of HIV and AIDS. However, overall, the world population is aging. In 2003, demographers predicted that the average age of the world's people will rise from 28 to 40 years.

Paralleling the population explosion has been a rapid growth in the number and size of cities. Urban areas contained nearly half the world's people in the early 2000s. This proportion is expected to rise to nearly two-thirds by 2025.

Urbanization occurred first in areas under-

▲ *Hong Kong's business district*

By contrast with the picturesque old streets of Hong Kong, the business district of Hong Kong City, on the northern shore of Hong Kong Island, is a cluster of modern high-rise buildings. The glittering skyscrapers reflect the success of this tiny region, which has one of the strongest economies in Asia.

going the industrialization of their economies, but today it is also a feature of the developing world. In developing countries, people are leaving impoverished rural areas hoping to gain access to the education, health, and other services available in cities. But many cities cannot provide the facilities necessitated by rapid population growth. Slums develop and pollution, crime, and disease become features of everyday life.

The population explosion poses another problem for the entire world. No one knows how many people the world can support or how consumer demand will damage the fragile environments on our planet. The British economist Thomas Malthus argued in the late 18th century that overpopulation would lead to famine and war. But an increase in farm technology in the 19th and 20th centuries, combined with a green revolution, in which scientists developed high-yield crop varieties, has greatly increased food production since Malthus' time.

However, some modern scientists argue that overpopulation may become a problem in the 21st century. They argue that food and water shortages leading to disastrous famines will result unless population growth can be halted. Such people argue in favor of birth-control programs. China, one of the two countries with more than a billion people, introduced a one-child family policy. Its action has slowed the growth of China's huge population.

POPULATION CHANGE

The projected population change for the years 2004–2050.

- OVER 125% POPULATION GAIN
- 100–125% POPULATION GAIN
- 50–100% POPULATION GAIN
- 25–50% POPULATION GAIN
- 0–25% POPULATION GAIN
- LOSS OR NO CHANGE
- NO DATA AVAILABLE

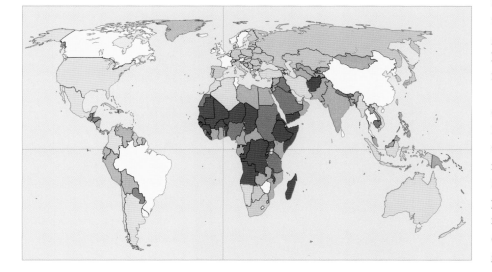

LANGUAGES AND RELIGIONS

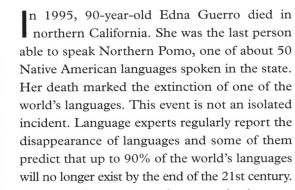

In 1995, 90-year-old Edna Guerro died in northern California. She was the last person able to speak Northern Pomo, one of about 50 Native American languages spoken in the state. Her death marked the extinction of one of the world's languages. This event is not an isolated incident. Language experts regularly report the disappearance of languages and some of them predict that up to 90% of the world's languages will no longer exist by the end of the 21st century.

Improved transport and communications are partly to blame, because they bring people from various cultures into closer and closer contact. Many children no longer speak the language of their parents, preferring instead to learn the language used at their schools. The pressures on children to speak dominant rather than minority languages are often great. In the first part of the 20th century, Native American children were punished if they spoke their native language.

The disappearance of a language represents the extinction of a way of thinking, a unique expression of the experiences and knowledge of a group of people. Language and religion together give people an identity and a sense of belonging. However, there are others who argue that the disappearance of minority languages is a step toward international understanding and economic efficiency.

THE WORLD'S LANGUAGES

Definitions of what is a language or a dialect vary and, hence, estimates of the number of languages spoken around the world range from about 3,000 to 6,000. But whatever the figure, it is clear that the number of languages far exceeds the number of countries.

◀ *The Kaaba, Makkah (Mecca), Saudi Arabia*

Islam is a major world religion. It was first preached by the Prophet Muhammad who was born in Makkah (or Mecca) in Saudi Arabia in about AD 570. Its holiest shrine is the Kaaba, a black, square building in the Great Mosque in Makkah. Every adult Muslim must, if possible, make at least one pilgrimage (or hajj) to Makkah. More than a million Muslims make the pilgrimage every year. The pilgrims walk or run around the Kaaba seven times, praying or reciting verses from the Koran, the sacred book of the Muslims.

RELIGIOUS ADHERENTS

Number of adherents to the world's major religions, in millions (2005).

Christianity	2,100
Roman Catholic	1,050
Protestant	396
Orthodox	240
Anglican	73
Others	341
Islam	1,070
Sunni	940
Shi'ite	120
Others	10
Secular/Atheist/Agnostic/	
Non-religious	1,100
Hinduism	832
Chinese folk	394
Buddhism	329
Ethnic religions	300
New religions	103
Sikhism	23
Judaism	15
Spiritism	12
Baha'i	6
Confucianism	6
Jainism	5
Shintoism	3

◀ *Statues of the Buddha, Wat Yai Chai Mongkol, Thailand*

Buddhism is a major religion in Southeast Asia, Sri Lanka, and Japan. The statues of the Buddha in the photograph are swathed in saffron robes. They surround the main chedi, or Golden Mount Pagoda, at Wat Yai Chai Mongkol, a World Heritage site near the ancient city of Ayutthaya, north of Bangkok.

Countries with only one language tend to be small. For example, in Liechtenstein, everyone speaks German. By contrast, more than 860 languages have been identified in Papua New Guinea, whose population is only about 5.5 million people. Hence, many of its languages are spoken by only small groups of people. In fact, scientists have estimated that about a third of the world's languages are now spoken by less than 1,000 people. By contrast, more than half of the world's population speak just seven languages.

The world's languages are grouped into families. The Indo-European family consists of languages spoken between Europe and the Indian subcontinent. The growth of European empires over the last 300 years led several Indo-European languages, most notably English, French, Portuguese, and Spanish, to spread throughout much of North and South America, Africa, Australia, and New Zealand.

English has become the official language in many countries which together contain more than a quarter of the world's population. It is now a major international language, surpassing in importance Mandarin Chinese, a member of the Sino-Tibetan family, which is the world's leading first language. Without a knowledge of English, businessmen face many problems when conducting international trade, especially with the United States or other English-speaking countries. But proposals that English, French, Russian, or some other language should become a world language seem unlikely to be acceptable to a majority of the world's peoples.

WORLD RELIGIONS

Religion is another fundamental aspect of human culture. It has inspired much of the world's finest architecture, literature, music, and art. It has also helped to shape human cultures since prehistoric times and is responsible for the codes of ethics by which most people live.

The world's major religions were all founded in Asia. Judaism, one of the first faiths to teach that there is only one god, is one of the world's oldest. Founded in southwestern Asia, it influenced the more recent Christianity and Islam, two other monotheistic religions which now have the great-

MOTHER TONGUES
First-language speakers of the major languages, in millions.

- MANDARIN CHINESE 874M
- HINDI 366M
- ENGLISH 341M
- SPANISH 336M
- BENGALI 207M
- PORTUGUESE 176M
- RUSSIAN 167M
- JAPANESE 125M
- GERMAN 100M
- WU CHINESE 77M

OFFICIAL LANGUAGES: % OF WORLD POPULATION

English	27.0%
Chinese	19.0%
Hindi	13.5%
Spanish	5.4%
Russian	5.2%
French	4.2%
Arabic	3.3%
Portuguese	3.0%
Malay	3.0%
Bengali	2.9%
Japanese	2.3%

▶ *Polyglot nations*

The graph shows countries of the world with more than 200 languages. Although it has only about 5.5 million people, Papua New Guinea holds the record for the number of languages spoken.

Brazil (210)
Congo (DR) (220)
Australia (230)
Mexico (240)
Cameroon (275)
India (410)
Nigeria (470)
Indonesia (701)
Papua New Guinea (862)

▲ *The Church of San Giovanni, Dolomites, Italy*
Christianity has done much to shape Western civilization. Christian churches were built as places of worship, but many of them are among the finest achievements of world architecture.

est number of followers. Hinduism, the third leading faith in terms of the numbers of followers, originated in the Indian subcontinent and most Hindus are now found in India. Another major religion, Buddhism, was founded in the subcontinent partly as a reaction to certain aspects of Hinduism. But unlike Hinduism, it has spread from India throughout much of eastern Asia.

Religion and language are powerful creative forces. They are also essential features of nationalism, which gives people a sense of belonging and pride. But nationalism is often also a cause of rivalry and tension. Cultural differences have led to racial hatred, the persecution of minorities, and to war between national groups.

INTERNATIONAL ORGANIZATIONS

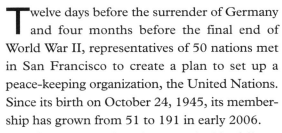

Twelve days before the surrender of Germany and four months before the final end of World War II, representatives of 50 nations met in San Francisco to create a plan to set up a peace-keeping organization, the United Nations. Since its birth on October 24, 1945, its membership has grown from 51 to 191 in early 2006.

Its first 60 years have been marked by failures as well as successes. For example, because of the UN policy of neutrality, the Blue Berets, as UN troops are called, have been sometimes forced to stand by when atrocities have occurred. As a result, the UN Secretary-General, Kofi Annan, announced a reform plan in 2005.

THE WORK OF THE UN

The United Nations has six main organs. They include the General Assembly, where member states meet to discuss issues concerned with peace, security, and development. The Security Council, containing 15 members, is concerned with maintaining world peace. The Secretariat, under the Secretary-General, helps the other organs to do their jobs effectively, while the Economic and Social Council works with specialized agencies to implement policies concerned with such matters as development, education, and health. The International Court of Justice, or World Court, helps to settle disputes between member nations. The sixth organ of the UN, the Trusteeship Council, was designed to bring 11 UN trust territories to independence. Its task has now been completed.

The specialized agencies do much important

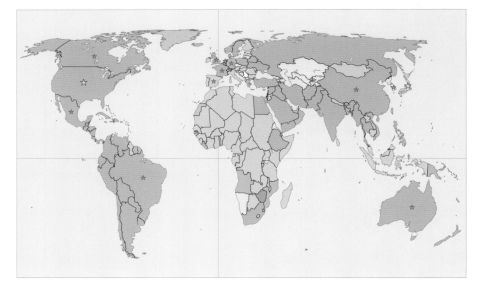

▼ *UN peace-keeping missions*
In the 1990s, a UN peace-keeping mission worked to restore peace to Bosnia-Herzegovina, following the Dayton Peace Accord of 1995. By 2005, hopes of long-term stability were high and refugees were returning home in large numbers.

work. For example, UNICEF (United Nations International Children's Fund) has provided health care and aid for children in many parts of the world. The ILO (International Labor Organization) has improved working conditions in many areas, while the FAO (Food and Agricultural Organization) has worked to improve the production and distribution of food. Among the other agencies are organizations to help refugees, to further human rights, and to control the environment. The latest agency, set up in 1995, is the WTO (World Trade Organization), which took over the work of GATT (General Agreement on Tariffs and Trade).

OTHER ORGANIZATIONS

In a world in which nations have become increasingly interdependent, many other organizations have been set up to deal with a variety of problems. Some, such as NATO (the North Atlantic Treaty Organization), are defense alliances. In the early 1990s, the end of the Cold War suggested that NATO's role might be finished, but the civil war in the former Yugoslavia showed that it still has a role in maintaining peace and security.

Other organizations encourage social and economic cooperation in various regions. Some are NGOs (non-governmental organizations), such as the Red Cross and its Muslim equivalent, the Red Crescent. Other NGOs raise funds to provide aid to countries facing major crises, such as famine.

Some major international organizations aim at economic cooperation and the removal of trade barriers. For example, in 2003, the European Union had 15 members, of which 12 had adopted a single currency, the euro, on January 1, 2001. On May 1, 2004, another ten countries in

MEMBERS OF THE UNITED NATIONS
Year of joining:

- 1940s
- 1950s
- 1960s
- 1970s
- 1980s
- 1990s
- 2000s
- NON–MEMBERS

★ 1% – 10% CONTRIBUTION TO FUNDING
☆ OVER 10% CONTRIBUTION TO FUNDING

INTERNATIONAL AID AND GNI
Aid provided as a percentage of GNI, with total aid in brackets (2003).

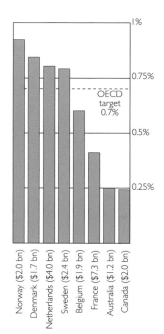

Norway ($2.0 bn)
Denmark ($1.7 bn)
Netherlands ($4.0 bn)
Sweden ($2.4 bn)
Belgium ($1.9 bn)
France ($7.3 bn)
Australia ($1.2 bn)
Canada ($2.0 bn)

OECD target 0.7%
1%
0.75%
0.5%
0.25%

eastern and southern Europe joined the EU, bringing the total membership to 25. Further expansion is anticipated in the next decade.

Other groupings include ASEAN (the Association of Southeast Asian Nations) which aims to reduce trade barriers between its members (Brunei, Burma [Myanmar], Cambodia, Indonesia, Laos, Malaysia, the Philippines, Singapore, Thailand, and Vietnam). APEC (the Asia-Pacific Cooperation Group), founded in 1989, aims to create a free-trade zone between the countries

▲ Refugee camp, Sudan
In the late 20th and early 21st centuries, many people in the Horn of Africa and Sudan were displaced by war. Here, and in other parts of the world, refugees from war depend largely on aid from international organizations and NGOs.

of eastern Asia, North America, Australia, and New Zealand by 2020. Meanwhile, Canada, Mexico, and the United States have formed NAFTA (the North American Free Trade Agreement), while other economic groupings link most of the countries in Latin America. Another grouping with a more limited but important objective is OPEC (the Organization of Oil-Exporting Countries). OPEC works to unify policies concerning trade in oil on the world markets.

Some organizations exist to discuss matters of common interest between groups of nations. The Commonwealth of Nations, for example, grew out of links created by the British Empire. In North and South America, the OAS (Organization of American States) aims to increase understanding in the Western hemisphere. The African Union (formerly the Organization of African Unity) has a similar role in Africa, while the Arab League represents Arab nations.

COUNTRIES OF THE EUROPEAN UNION

Country	Total land area (sq miles)	Total population (2005 est.)	Year of accession to the EU	Country	Total land area (sq miles)	Total population (2005 est.)	Year of accession to the EU
Austria	32,378	8,185,000	1995	Latvia	24,942	2,290,000	2004
Belgium	11,787	10,364,000	1958	Lithuania	25,174	3,597,000	2004
Cyprus	3,572	780,000	2004	Luxembourg	998	469,000	1958
Czech Republic	30,450	10,241,000	2004	Malta	122	399,000	2004
Denmark	16,639	5,432,000	1973	Netherlands	16,033	16,407,000	1958
Estonia	17,413	1,333,000	2004	Poland	124,807	38,635,000	2004
Finland	130,558	5,223,000	1995	Portugal	34,285	10,566,000	1986
France	212,934	60,656,000	1958	Slovak Republic	18,924	5,431,000	2004
Germany	137,846	82,431,000	1958	Slovenia	7,821	2,011,000	2004
Greece	50,949	10,668,000	1981	Spain	192,103	40,341,000	1986
Hungary	35,920	10,007,000	2004	Sweden	173,731	9,002,000	1995
Ireland	27,132	4,016,000	1973	United Kingdom	93,381	60,441,000	1973
Italy	116,339	58,103,000	1958				

AGRICULTURE

Ever since 1798, when the British economist Thomas Robert Malthus published his view that populations would outgrow food supply, leading to famine and war, food production and distribution, and agricultural technology have been subjects of debate. The situation is complicated by the fact that, in rich countries, food is cheaper than ever, yet obesity has been identified as a major health hazard. On the other hand, malnutrition is rife in Africa, where local farmers cannot compete with the flood of subsidized food from the richer nations.

From the 1950s, the "green revolution" greatly increased food production. By using new crop varieties, irrigation, and the extensive use of fertilizers and pesticides, India, once a food importer, became self-sufficient in food.

In the early 2000s, many people placed hopes in the use of genetically modified crops. Sup-

▼ *Rice harvest, Bali, Indonesia*
More than half of the world's people eat rice as their basic food. Rice grows well in tropical and subtropical regions, such as in Indonesia, India, and southeastern China.

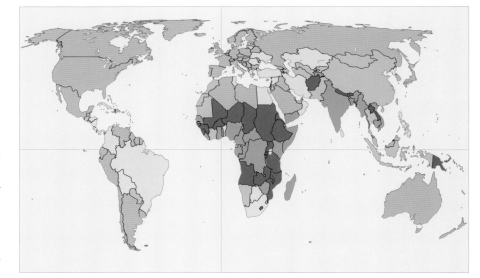

porters argued that GM crops could be one of the greatest advances ever in farming. But critics of GM crops voiced serious environmental and health concerns. The lack of conclusive scientific evidence led to strong consumer resistance in some parts of the world, notably in Western Europe. Even some developing countries were doubtful. For example, in 2004, Angola, a country badly in need of food aid, joined several other southern African countries in rejecting offers of GM foods.

FOOD PRODUCTION

Agriculture, which supplies most of our food, together with materials to make clothes and other products, is the world's most important economic activity. But its relative importance has declined in comparison with manufacturing and service industries. As a result, the end of the 20th century marked the first time for 10,000 years when the vast majority of the people no longer had to depend for their living on growing crops and herding animals.

However, agriculture remains the dominant economic activity in many developing countries in Africa and Asia. For example, in the early 21st century, 80% or more of the people of Bhutan, Burundi, and Rwanda depended on farming for their living.

Many people in developing countries eke out the barest of livings by nomadic herding or shifting cultivation, combined with hunting, fishing and gathering plant foods. A large proportion of farmers live at subsistence level, producing little more than they require to provide the basic needs of their families.

The world's largest food producer and exporter is the United States, although agriculture employs around 1.4% of its total work force.

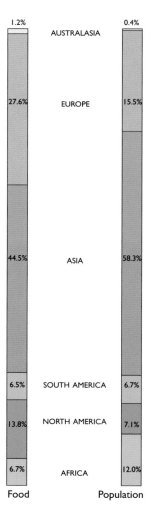

IMPORTANCE OF AGRICULTURE
Agricultural work force as a percentage of the total work force (2003).

A comparison of world food production and population by continent.

▲ *Landsat image of the Nile delta, Egypt*

*Most Egyptians live in the Nile valley and on its delta.
Because much of the silt carried by the Nile now ends up
on the floor of Lake Nasser, upstream of the Aswan Dam,
the delta is now retreating and seawater is seeping inland.
This eventuality was not foreseen when the Aswan High
Dam was built in the 1960s.*

The high production of the United States is explained by its use of scientific methods and mechanization, which are features of agriculture throughout the developed world.

INTENSIVE OR ORGANIC FARMING

In the early 21st century, some people were beginning to question the dependence of farmers on chemical fertilizers and pesticides. Many people became concerned that the widespread use of chemicals was seriously polluting and damaging the environment.

Others objected to the intensive farming of animals to raise production and lower prices. For example, the suggestion in Britain in 1996 that BSE, or "mad cow disease," might be passed on to people causing CJD (Creuzfeldt-Jakob Disease) caused widespread alarm. Such factors, combined with the debate about the safety issues surrounding GM foods, have caused much concern.

Some farmers have returned to organic farming, which is based on animal-welfare principles and the banning of chemical fertilizers and pesticides. Organic foods are more expensive to produce than those produced by intensive farming, but an increasing number of consumers are demanding them.

WHEAT

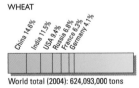

World total (2004): 624,093,000 tons

RICE

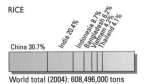

World total (2004): 608,496,000 tons

CASSAVA

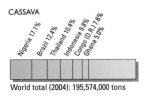

World total (2004): 195,574,000 tons

ENERGY AND MINERALS

In August 2004, a serious accident occurred when a pipe carrying superheated steam exploded at Mihama nuclear power plant, 50 miles [80 km] north of Kyoto, Japan. Four people were killed and seven injured. No nuclear contamination occurred, but the accident further weakened public confidence in the industry. Nuclear power provides about 17% of the world's electricity, though concerns about safety and high costs cloud its future. But, while some nations are committed to phasing out nuclear energy, others are considering further development of nuclear power plants, as the reserves of fuels, which cause global warming, start to run low.

FOSSIL FUELS

Huge amounts of energy are needed for heating, generating electricity, and for transport. In the

early years of the Industrial Revolution, coal, formed from organic matter buried beneath the Earth's surface, was the leading source of energy. It remains important as a raw material in the manufacture of drugs and other products, and also as a fuel, despite the fact that burning coal causes air pollution and gives off carbon dioxide, an important greenhouse gas.

However, oil and natural gas, which came into wide use in the 20th century, are cheaper to produce and easier to handle than coal, while, kilogram for kilogram, they give out more heat. Oil is especially important in moving transport, supplying about 97% of the fuel required.

In the 1990s, proven reserves of oil were sufficient to supply the world, at current rates of production, for 43 years, while supplies of natural gas stood at about 66 years. Coal reserves are more abundant and known reserves would last 200 years at present rates of use. Although these figures must be regarded with caution, because they do not allow for future discoveries, it is clear that fossil fuel reserves will one day run out.

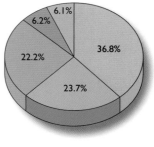

WORLD ENERGY CONSUMPTION

- OIL
- GAS
- COAL
- HYDRO
- NUCLEAR

▲ *The diagram shows the proportion of world energy consumption in 2004 by form. Total energy consumption was 10,224 million tonnes of oil equivalent. Wood, peat and animal wastes, plus renewable forms, such as wind power, are locally important but they comprise only 0.8% of the total.*

▼ *Wind farms in California, United States*

Wind farms using giant turbines can produce electricity at a lower cost than conventional power stations. But in many areas, winds are too light or too strong for wind farms to be effective.

SELECTED MINERAL PRODUCTION STATISTICS
(percentage of world total output, 2003)

Bauxite		Diamonds	
Australia	35.9%	Australia	20.7%
Brazil	11.9%	Botswana	20.2%
Guinea	11.0%	Congo (D.R.)	19.3%
Jamaica	8.7%	Russia	16.0%
China	7.1%	S. Africa	8.4%
Gold		**Iron ore**	
S. Africa	14.8%	China	21.1%
Australia	11.2%	Brazil	18.9%
USA	11.0%	Australia	17.2%
China	8.3%	India	9.7%
Russia	6.8%	Russia	7.4%
Manganese		**Zinc**	
China	23.2%	China	19.6%
S. Africa	14.4%	Australia	16.1%
Ukraine	11.1%	Peru	14.9%
Brazil	11.1%	Canada	8.6%
Australia	10.3%	USA	8.0%

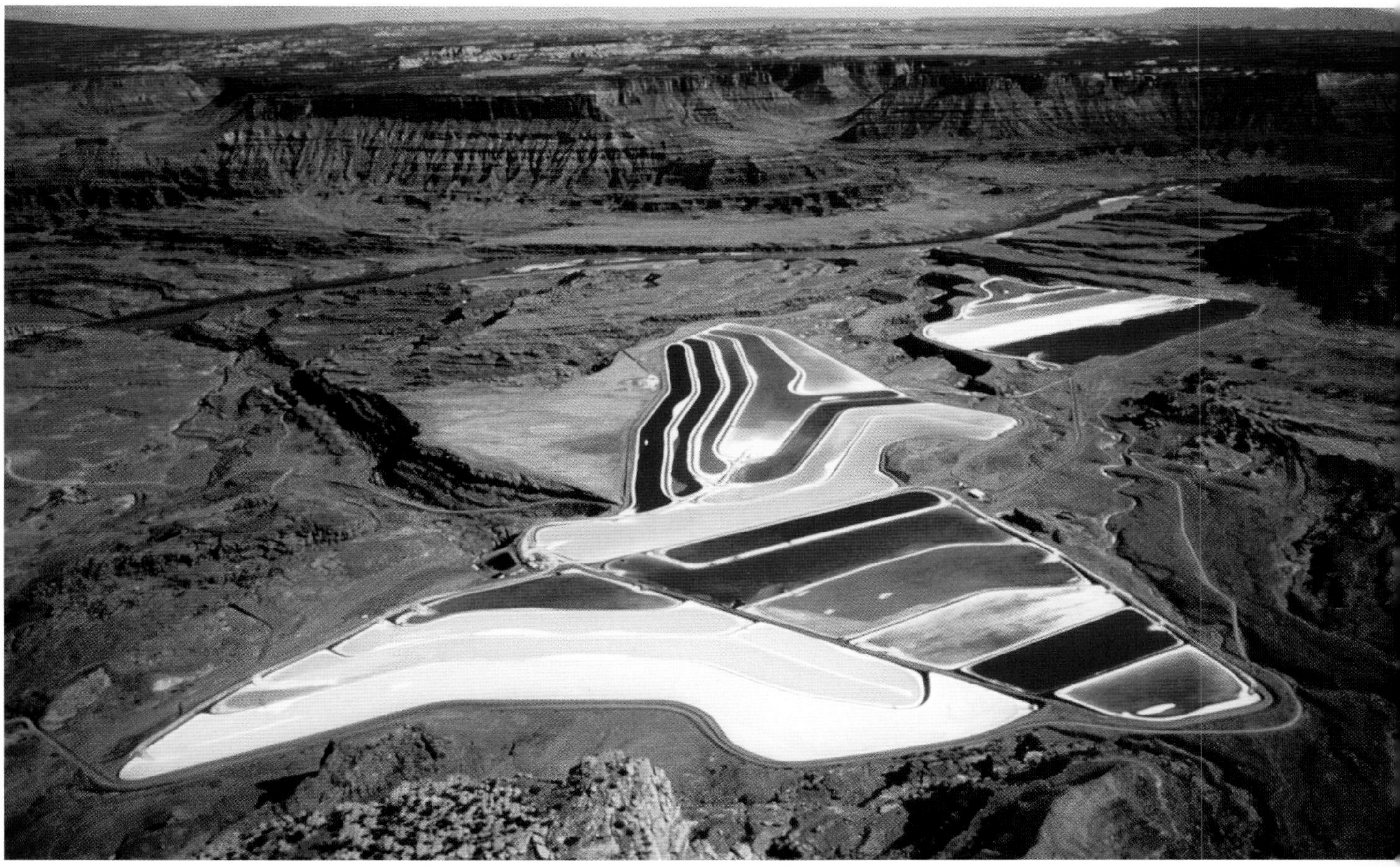

▲ *Potash mines in Utah, United States*
Potash is a mineral used mainly to make fertilizers. Much of it comes from mines where deposits formed when ancient seas dried up are exploited. Potash is also extracted from salt lakes.

Alternative Energy

Other sources of energy are therefore required. Besides nuclear energy, the main alternative to fossil fuels is water power. The costs of building dams and hydroelectric power stations are high, though hydroelectric production is comparatively cheap. But the creation of reservoirs uproots people and destroys natural habitats. Water power is also suitable only in areas with plenty of rivers and steep slopes, such as Norway.

In Brazil, alcohol made from sugar has been used to fuel cars. Initially, this government-backed policy met with success. However, it proved to be expensive and the production of ethanol-fueled cars was halted until Brazil struck a deal with Germany in the early 2000s. Battery-run electric cars have been developed in the United States, but regular and time-consuming recharging is a major drawback.

Other forms of energy, which are renewable and cleaner than fossil fuels, are winds, sea waves, the rise and fall of tides, and geothermal power. While renewable energy sources are attractive, some experts doubt whether they can provide sufficient energy on their own.

Minerals for Industry

In addition to energy, manufacturing industries need raw materials, including minerals, and these natural resources, like fossil fuels, are being used in such huge quantities that some experts have predicted shortages of some of them before long.

Manufacturers depend on supplies of about 80 minerals. Some, such as bauxite (aluminum ore) and iron, are abundant, but others are scarce or are found only in deposits that are uneconomical to mine. Many experts advocate a policy of recycling scrap metal, including aluminum, chromium, copper, lead, nickel, and zinc. This practice would reduce pollution and conserve the energy required for extracting and refining mineral ores.

▼ MINERAL DISTRIBUTION
The map shows the richest sources of the most important minerals. Major mineral locations are named. Undersea deposits, most of which are considered inaccessible, are not shown.

- GOLD
- SILVER
- DIAMONDS
- TUNGSTEN
- IRON ORE
- NICKEL
- CHROME
- MANGANESE
- COBALT
- MOLYBDENUM
- COPPER
- LEAD
- BAUXITE
- TIN
- ZINC
- MERCURY

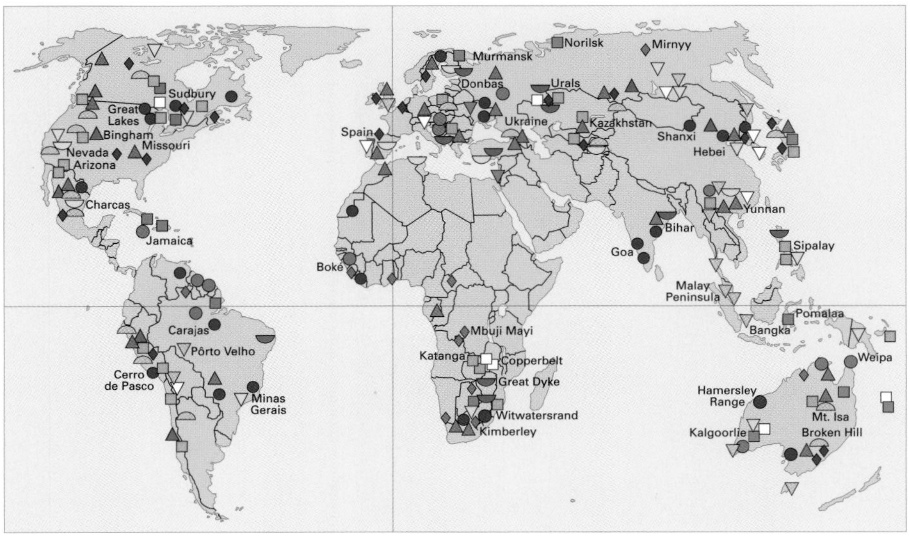

WORLD ECONOMIES

In 2004, Ethiopia had a per capita GNI (Gross National Income) of US$110, as compared with Norway, whose per capita GNI stood at $52,030, according to the World Bank. These figures indicate the vast gap between the economies and standards of living of the two countries.

The GNI includes the GDP (Gross Domestic Product), which consists of the total output of goods and services in a country in a given year, plus net exports – that is, the value of goods and services sold abroad less the value of foreign goods and services used in the country in the same year. The GNI divided by the population gives a country's GNI per capita. In low-income developing countries, agriculture makes a high contribution to the GNI. For example, in Ethiopia, 40% of the country's GDP came from agriculture. On the other hand, industry was small-scale and contributed only 13% of the GDP. By comparison, in high-income economies, the percentage contribution of manufacturing far exceeds that of agriculture.

▼ *Hard-disk assembly factory*

The manufacture of computer equipment and computer software is a fairly new industrial phenomenon. In Asia, high-tech industries have developed quickly, helping relatively poor developing countries to achieve rapid economic growth.

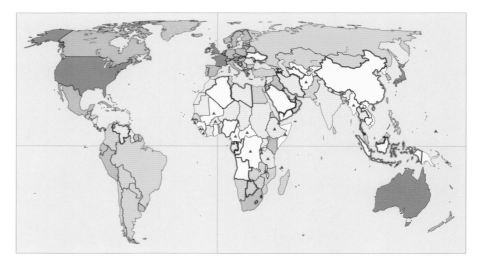

INDUSTRIALIZATION

The Industrial Revolution began in Britain in the late 18th century. Before that time, most people worked on farms. But with the Industrial Revolution came factories, using machines that could manufacture goods much faster and more cheaply than those made by cottage industries that already existed.

The Industrial Revolution soon spread to several countries in mainland Europe and the United States and, by the late 19th century, it had reached Canada, Japan, and Russia. At first, industrial development was based on such areas as coalfields or ironfields. But in the 20th

IMPORTANCE OF THE SERVICE INDUSTRY
Percentage of total GDP from the service sector (2003).

- OVER 70%
- 60–70%
- 50–60%
- 40–50%
- UNDER 40%
- NO DATA AVAILABLE
- OVER 40% OF TOTAL GDP FROM THE INDUSTRIAL SECTOR
- ▲ OVER 40% OF TOTAL GDP FROM THE AGRICULTURAL SECTOR

GROSS NATIONAL INCOME PER CAPITA IN US$ (2004)		
1	Luxembourg	$56,230
2	Switzerland	$52,030
3	Norway	$48,230
4	United States	$41,400
5	Denmark	$40,650
6	Iceland	$38,620
7	Japan	$37,180
8	Sweden	$35,770
9	Ireland	$34,280
10	United Kingdom	$33,940
11	Finland	$32,790
12	Austria	$32,300
13	Netherlands	$31,700
14	Belgium	$31,030
15	Germany	$30,120
16	France	$30,090
17	Canada	$28,390
18	Australia	$26,900
19	Italy	$26,120
20	Singapore	$24,220

century, the use of oil, which is easy to transport along pipelines, made it possible for industries to be set up anywhere.

Some nations, such as Switzerland, became industrialized even though they lacked natural resources. They depended instead on the specialized skills of their workers. This same pattern applies today. Some countries with rich natural resources, such as Mexico (with a per capita GNI in 2004 of US$6,770), lag far behind Japan ($37,180) and Cyprus ($17,580), which lack resources and have to import many of the materials they need to sustain their manufacturing industries.

THE WORK FORCE
Percentage of men and women over 15 years old in employment, selected countries.

■ MEN
□ WOMEN

SERVICE INDUSTRIES

Experts often refer to high-income countries as industrial economies. But manufacturing employs only one in six workers in the United States, one in five in Britain, and one in three in Germany and Japan.

▲ *New cars awaiting transportation, Los Angeles, USA*
Cars are the most important single manufactured item in world trade, followed by vehicle parts and engines. The world's leading car producers are Japan, the United States, Germany, and France.

In most developed economies, the percentage of manufacturing jobs has fallen in recent years, while jobs in service industries have risen. For example, in Britain, the proportion of jobs in manufacturing fell from 37% in 1970 to 12.8% in 2003, while jobs in the service sector rose from just under 50% to 78.6%. While change in Britain was especially rapid, similar changes were taking place in most industrial economies. Service industries now account for well over half the jobs in the generally prosperous countries that made up the OECD (Organization for Economic Cooperation and Development). Instead of being called the "industrial" economies, these countries might be better named the "service" economies.

Service industries offer a wide range of jobs and many of them require high educational qualifications. These include finance, insurance, and high-tech industries, such as computer programing, entertainment, and telecommunications. Service industries also include marketing and advertising, which are essential if the cars and television sets made by manufacturers are to be sold. Another valuable service industry is tourism; in some countries, such as the Gambia, it is the major foreign-exchange earner. Trade in services plays a crucial part in world economies. Service industries now account for more than a fifth of world trade.

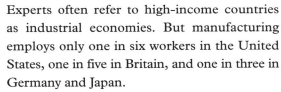

TRADE AND COMMERCE

The establishment of the WTO (World Trade Organization) on January 1, 1995, was the latest step in the long history of world trade. The WTO was set up by the eighth round of negotiations, popularly called the "Uruguay round," conducted by the General Agreement on Tariffs and Trade (GATT). This treaty was signed by representatives of 125 governments in April 1994. The membership reached 149 when Saudi Arabia joined in November 2005.

GATT was first established in 1948. Its initial aim was to produce a charter to create a body called the International Trade Organization. This body never came into being. Instead, GATT, acting as an *ad hoc* agency, pioneered a series of agreements aimed at liberalizing world trade by reducing tariffs on imports and other obstacles to free trade.

▼ *New York City Stock Exchange, United States*
Stock exchanges, where stocks and shares are sold and bought, are important in channeling savings and investments to companies and governments. The world's largest stock exchange is in Tokyo, Japan.

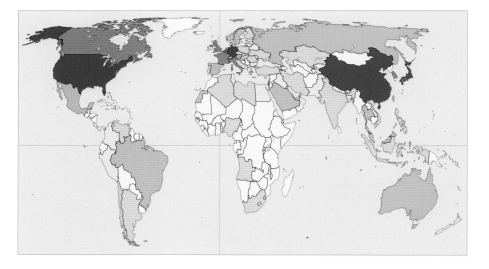

GATT's objectives were based on the belief that international trade creates wealth. Trade occurs because the world's resources are not distributed evenly between countries, and, in theory, free trade means that every country should concentrate on what it can do best and purchase from others goods and services that they can supply more cheaply. In practice, however, free trade may cause unemployment when imported goods are cheaper than those produced within the country.

Trade is sometimes an important factor in world politics, especially when trade sanctions are applied against countries whose actions incur the disapproval of the international community. For example, in the 1990s, worldwide trade sanctions were imposed on Serbia because of its involvement in the civil war in Bosnia-Herzegovina.

WORLD TRADE
Percentage share of total world exports by value (2005).
- OVER 5%
- 2.5–5%
- 1–2.5%
- 0.25–1%
- 0.1–0.25%
- UNDER 0.1%
- NO DATA AVAILABLE

The world's leading trading nations, according to the combined value of their exports and imports, are the United States, Germany, Japan, France, and the United Kingdom.

CHANGING TRADE PATTERNS

The early 16th century, when Europeans began to divide the world into huge empires, opened up a new era in international trade. By the 19th century, the colonial powers, who were among the first industrial powers, promoted trade with their colonies, from which they obtained unprocessed raw materials, such as food, natural fibers, minerals, and timber. In return, they shipped clothes, shoes, and other cheap items to the colonies.

From the late 19th century until the early 1950s, primary products dominated world trade, with oil becoming the leading item in the latter part of this period. Many developing countries still depend heavily on the export of one or two primary products, such as coffee or iron ore, but overall the proportion of primary products in world trade has fallen since the 1950s. Today the most important elements

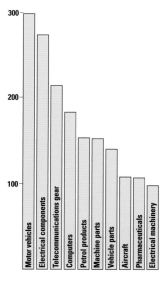

TRADED PRODUCTS
The diagram shows major manufactures traded by value in billions of US$. Manufactures in total comprise 74% of the world's total trade, the value of which was $7,294 billion in 2003.

in world trade are manufactures and semi-manufactures, exchanged mainly between the industrialized nations.

THE WORLD'S MARKETS

Private companies conduct most of world trade, but government policies affect it. Governments which believe that certain industries are strategic, or essential for the country's future, may impose tariffs on imports, or import quotas to limit the volume of imports, if they are thought to be undercutting the domestic industries.

For example, the United States has argued that

▲ *Rotterdam, Netherlands*

World trade depends on transport. Rotterdam, the world's largest port, serves not only the Netherlands, but also industrial areas in parts of Germany, France, and Switzerland.

Japan has greater access to its markets than the United States has to Japan's. This might have led the United States to resort to protectionism, but instead the United States remains committed to free trade despite occasional disputes.

Other problems in international trade occur when governments give subsidies to its producers, who can then export products at low prices. Another difficulty, called "dumping," occurs when products are sold at below the market price in order to gain a market share. One of the aims of the newly-created WTO is the phasing out of government subsidies for agricultural products, though the world's poorest countries will be exempt from many of the WTO's most severe regulations.

Governments are also concerned about the volume of imports and exports, and most countries keep records of international transactions. When the total value of goods and services imported exceeds the value of goods and services exported, then the country has a deficit in its balance of payments. Large deficits can weaken a country's economy.

DEPENDENCE ON TRADE

Value of exports as a percentage of GDP (2005).

- OVER 50% GDP FROM EXPORTS
- 25–50% GDP FROM EXPORTS
- 10–25% GDP FROM EXPORTS
- 5–10% GDP FROM EXPORTS
- UNDER 5% GDP FROM EXPORTS
- NO DATA AVAILABLE

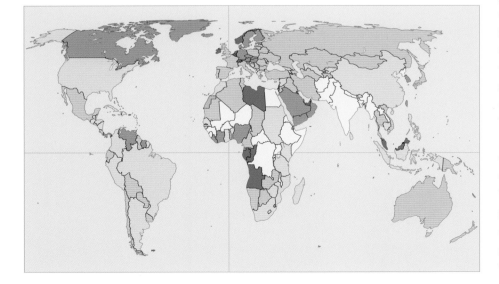

TRAVEL AND COMMUNICATIONS

By the early 21st century, millions of people were linked to an "information super-highway" called the Internet. Equipped with a personal computer, an electricity supply, a telephone and a modem, people are able to communicate with others all over the world. People can now send messages by e-mail (electronic mail), they can engage in electronic discussions, contacting people with similar interests, and engage in "chat lines," which are the latest equivalent of telephone conferences.

These new developments are likely to affect the working lives of people everywhere, enabling them to work at home whilst having many of the facilities that are available in an office. The Internet is part of an ongoing and astonishingly rapid evolution in the fields of communications and transport.

TRANSPORT

Around 200 years ago, most people never traveled far from their birthplace, but today we are much more mobile. Cars and buses now provide convenient forms of transport for many millions of people, huge ships transport massive cargoes around the world, and jet airliners, some traveling faster than the speed of sound, can transport high-value goods as well as vacationers to almost any part of the world.

Land transport of freight has developed greatly since the start of the Industrial Revolution.

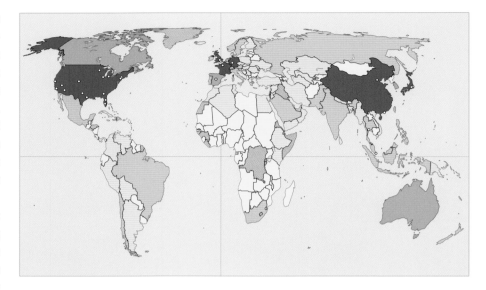

▼ *Eurostar travel*

High-speed Eurostar services connect London to Paris and Brussels via the $15 billion Channel Tunnel, linking the UK to mainland Europe. Only ten years after the tunnel opened in 1994, Eurostar carried about 7.3 million passengers per year.

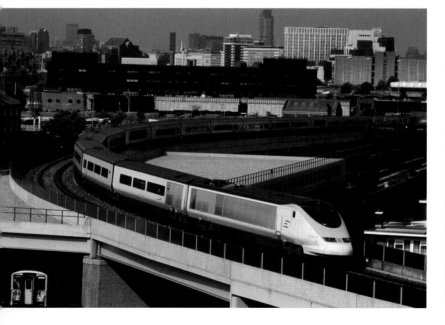

Canals, which became important in the 18th century, could not compete with rail transport in the 19th century. Rail transport remains important, but, during the 20th century, it suffered from competition with road transport, which is cheaper and has the advantage of carrying materials and goods from door to door.

Road transport causes pollution and the burning of fuels creates greenhouse gases that contribute to global warming. Yet privately owned cars are now the leading form of passenger traffic in developed nations, especially for journeys of less than around 250 miles [400 km]. Car owners do not have to suffer the inconvenience of waiting for public transport, such as buses, though they often have to endure traffic jams at peak travel times.

Ocean passenger traffic is now modest, but ships carry the bulk of international trade. Huge oil tankers and bulk grain carriers now ply the oceans with their cargoes, while container ships carry mixed cargoes. Containers are boxes built to international standards that contain cargo. Containers are easy to handle, and so they

AIR TRAVEL – PASSENGER KILOMETERS* FLOWN *(2002)*.

- ▪ OVER 100,000 MILLION
- ▪ 50,000–100,000 MILLION
- ▫ 10,000–50,000 MILLION
- ▫ 1,000–10,000 MILLION
- ▫ UNDER 1,000 MILLION
- ▪ NO DATA AVAILABLE

- ○ MAJOR AIRPORTS (HANDLING OVER 30 MILLION PASSENGERS)

* Passenger kilometers are the number of passengers (both international and domestic) multiplied by the distance flown by each passenger from the airport of origin.

SELECTED NEWSPAPER CIRCULATION FIGURES (2005)

France		**Russia**	
Le Monde	372,000	Argumenty i Fakty	2,900,000
Le Figaro	341,000	Pravda	674,000
		Izvestia	241,000
Germany			
Bild	3,970,000	**Spain**	
Süddeutsche Zeitung	442,000	El Pais	578,000
India		**United Kingdom**	
The Times of India	2,600,000	The Sun	3,000,000
The Hindustan Times	1,857,000	Daily Mail	2,293,000
		Daily Mirror	1,544,000
Italy		The Daily Telegraph	852,000
Corriere della Sera	674,000	Daily Express	788,000
La Repubblica	623,000		
La Stampa	332,000	**United States**	
		USA Today	2,613,000
Japan		The Wall Street Journal	2,070,000
Yomiuri Shimbun	10,110,000	The New York Times	1,681,000
Asahi Shimbun	8,260,000	Los Angeles Times	1,254,000

TOP TOURIST DESTINATIONS

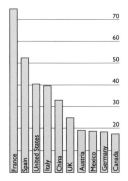

International tourist arrivals in millions (2003)

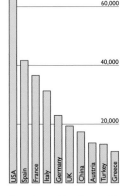

Countries receiving the most from overseas tourism, US$ million (2003).

reduce shipping costs, speed up deliveries, and cut losses caused by breakages. Most large ports now have the facilities to handle containers.

Air transport is suitable for carrying goods that are expensive, light and compact, or perishable. However, because of the high costs of air freight, it is most suitable for carrying passengers along long-distance routes around the world. Through air travel, international tourism has become a major industry, despite anxieties about aircraft pollution that contributes to global warming.

COMMUNICATIONS

After humans first began to communicate by using the spoken word, the next great stage in the development of communications was the invention of writing around 5,500 years ago.

The invention of movable type in the mid-15th century led to the mass production of books and, in the early 17th century, the first newspapers. Newspapers now play an important part in the mass communication of information, although today radio and, even more important, television have led to a decline in the circulation of newspapers in many parts of the world.

The most recent developments have occurred in the field of electronics. Artificial communications satellites now circle the planet, relaying radio, television, telegraph, and telephone signals. This enables people to watch events on the far side of the globe as they are happening. Electronic equipment is also used in many other ways, such as in navigation systems used in air,

▲ *Commercial jet airliners, Washington, DC, United States*
Air travel has transformed world tourism. However, the terrorist attacks by suicide bombers on the United States on September 11, 2001, led to greater security checks at airports. Falls in passenger numbers were another consequence of the hijackings.

sea, and space, and also in modern weaponry, as shown vividly in the television coverage of Middle Eastern conflicts in the 21st century.

THE AGE OF COMPUTERS

One of the most remarkable applications of electronics is in the field of computers. Computers are now making a huge contribution to communications. They are able to process data at incredibly high speeds and can store vast quantities of information. For example, the work of weather forecasters has been greatly improved now that computers can process the enormous amount of data required for a single weather forecast. They also have many other applications in such fields as business, government, science, and medicine.

Through the Internet, computers provide a free interchange of news and views around the world. But the dangers of misuse, such as the exchange of pornographic images, have led to calls for censorship. Censorship, however, is a blunt weapon, which can be used by authoritarian governments to suppress the free exchange of information that the new information superhighway makes possible.

THE WORLD TODAY

The early years of the 20th century witnessed the exploration of Antarctica, the last uncharted continent. Today, less than 100 years later, tourists are able to take cruises to the icy southern continent, while almost no part of the globe is inaccessible to the determined traveler. Improved transport and images from space have made our world seem smaller.

A DIVIDED WORLD

Between the end of World War II in 1945 and the late 1980s, the world was divided, politically and economically, into three main groups: the developed countries or Western democracies, with their free enterprise or mixed economies; the centrally planned or Communist countries; and the developing countries or Third World.

This division became obsolete when the former Soviet Union and its old European allies, together with the "special economic zones" in eastern China, began the transition from centrally planned to free enterprise economies. This left the world divided into two broad camps: the prosperous developed countries and the poorer developing countries. The simplest way of distinguishing between the groups is with reference to their per capita GNIs (Gross National Incomes).

The World Bank divides the developing countries into three main groups. At the bottom are the low-income economies, including India and most of sub-Saharan Africa. In 2004, the population of this group totaled more than

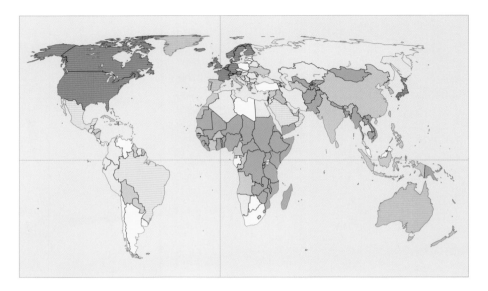

2 billion people. However, the average per capita Gross National Income was only US$510, with some as low as $100. Two other groups, with a combined population of around 3 billion people, are the lower-middle-income economies, with an average per capita GNI of $1,580, and the upper-middle-income economies with an average per capita GNI of $4,770. The high-income economies, with around 1 billion people, have an average (and rising) per capita GNI of $33,040.

ECONOMIC AND SOCIAL CONTRASTS

Economic differences are coupled with other factors, such as rates of population growth. For example, around the turn of the century, the low- and middle-income economies had a high population growth rate of 1.7%, while the growth rate in high-income economies was about 0.1%. In high-income economies, youths made up only 18% of the population and people over 65, 14%.

Stark contrasts exist worldwide in the quality of life. Generally, the people in Western Europe

GROSS NATIONAL INCOME PER CAPITA
The value of total income divided by the population (2003).

- OVER 400% OF WORLD AVERAGE
- 200–400% OF WORLD AVERAGE
- 100–200% OF WORLD AVERAGE
- 50–100% OF WORLD AVERAGE
- 25–50% OF WORLD AVERAGE
- 10–25% OF WORLD AVERAGE
- UNDER 10% OF WORLD AVERAGE
- NO DATA AVAILABLE

RICHEST COUNTRIES (GNI PER CAPITA, 2004)

Luxembourg	US$56,230
Switzerland	US$52,030
Norway	US$48,230
United States	US$41,400
Denmark	US$40,650

POOREST COUNTRIES (GNI PER CAPITA, 2004)

Burundi	US$90
Liberia	US$110
Ethiopia	US$110
Congo (Dem. Rep.)	US$120
Guinea-Bissau	US$160

▼ *East African tourism*
Improved transport, including the use of four-wheel drive vehicles, has led to a boom in tourism in many developing regions, such as East Africa. But terrorist incidents may slow down the development of tourism in some areas.

and North America are better fed, healthier, and have more cars and better homes than the people in low- and middle-income economies.

In 2006, the World Health Organization stated that, due partly to AIDS and partly to poverty, average life expectancy at birth in Zimbabwe had fallen to 37 years for men and 34 years for women. By contrast, the average life expectancy in Japan was 82 years. Illiteracy rates in low-income economies are also substantially lower for women than for men, whereas, in high-income countries, illiteracy is rare for both sexes.

FUTURE DEVELOPMENT

In the last 50 years, despite all the aid supplied to developing countries, much of the world still suffers from poverty and economic backwardness. Some countries are even poorer now than they were a generation ago.

However, several factors suggest that poor countries may find progress easier in the 21st century. For example, technology is now more readily transferable between countries, while improved transport and communications make it easier for countries to take part in the world economy. But industrial development could lead to an increase in global pollution. Hence, any strategy for global economic expansion must also take account of environmental factors.

▲ *Operation Enduring Freedom, Afghanistan*
A joint patrol of US Marines and Army soldiers is seen here patroling through the village of Cem, Afghanistan, some 6 miles [10 km] from the airport near Kandahar, in January 2002.

A WORLD IN CONFLICT

The end of the Cold War held out hopes of a new world order. But ethnic, religious, and other rivalries have subsequently led to appalling violence in places as diverse as the Balkan peninsula, Israel and the Palestinian territories, and Rwanda–Burundi. Then, on September 11, 2001, the attack on those symbols of the economic and military might of the United States – the World Trade Center and the Pentagon Building – demonstrated that nowhere on Earth is safe from attack by extremists prepared to sacrifice their lives in pursuit of their aims.

The danger posed by terrorist groups, such as al Qaida, or by rogue states, possibly in possession of nuclear or biological weapons, has forced many countries into new alliances to combat the terrorists and the governments that give them shelter. Many people also recognize a pressing need to correct the wrongs, real or perceived, that lead people to acts of martyrdom or murderous destruction, while simultaneously tackling the problems of world poverty.

▲ *Years of life expectancy at birth, selected countries (2006).*
The chart shows the contrasting range of average life expectancies at birth for a range of countries, including both low-income and high-income economies. Generally, improved health services are raising life expectancies. On average, women live longer than men, even in the poorer developing countries.

Cape Town sits to the bottom left of this image, with
the Cape Peninsula running southeast to the Cape of
Good Hope. Inland from the fertile coastal plain, where
most of South Africa's wine is produced, is the rugged
interior of the Great Karoo where parallel mountain
ranges are dissected by river valleys.

WORLD MAPS

SETTLEMENTS

■ **PARIS**   ◉ Rotterdam   ◉ Livorno   ◉ Brugge   ◎ Exeter   ○ Torremolinos   ○ Oberammergau   ○ Thira

Settlement symbols and type styles vary according to the scale of each map and indicate the importance
of towns on the map rather than specific population figures

● Vaduz   Capital cities have red infills   ∴   Ruins or archaeological sites

⬠   Urban agglomerations   ᵕ   Wells in desert

ADMINISTRATION

———— International boundaries   ············· Internal boundaries   **PERU**   Country names

— — — · International boundaries   ⬡ National parks   KENT   Administrative
      (undefined or disputed)   area names

International boundaries show the *de facto* situation where there are rival claims to territory

---

COMMUNICATIONS

———— Motorways, freeways   ———— Principal railways   ᴸᴴᴿ ✈ Principal airports
    and expressways

———— Principal roads   – – – – Railways   ⊕   Other airports
               under construction

———— Other roads   ———— Other railways   ·········· Principal canals

+--·-+ Road tunnels   +--·-+ Railway tunnels   ≍   Passes

PHYSICAL FEATURES

〜〜 Perennial streams   ⬭ Intermittent lakes   ▲ 8850   Elevations in metres

– – – Intermittent streams   Swamps and marshes   ▼ 8500   Sea depths in metres

⬮ Perennial lakes   Permanent ice   *1134*   Height of lake surface
             and glaciers   above sea level in metres

ELEVATION AND DEPTH TINTS

| Height of land above sea level | | | | | | | | | Land below sea level | | Depth of sea | |

in metres | 6000 | 4000 | 3000 | 2000 | 1500 | 1000 | 400 | 200 | 0 |

                                    6000 | 12 000 | 15 000 | 18 000 | 24 000   in feet

in feet | 18 000 | 12 000 | 9000 | 6000 | 4500 | 3000 | 1200 | 600 |

                                 0 | 200 | 2000 | 4000 | 5000 | 6000 | 8000   in metres

Some of the maps have different contours to highlight and clarify the principal relief features

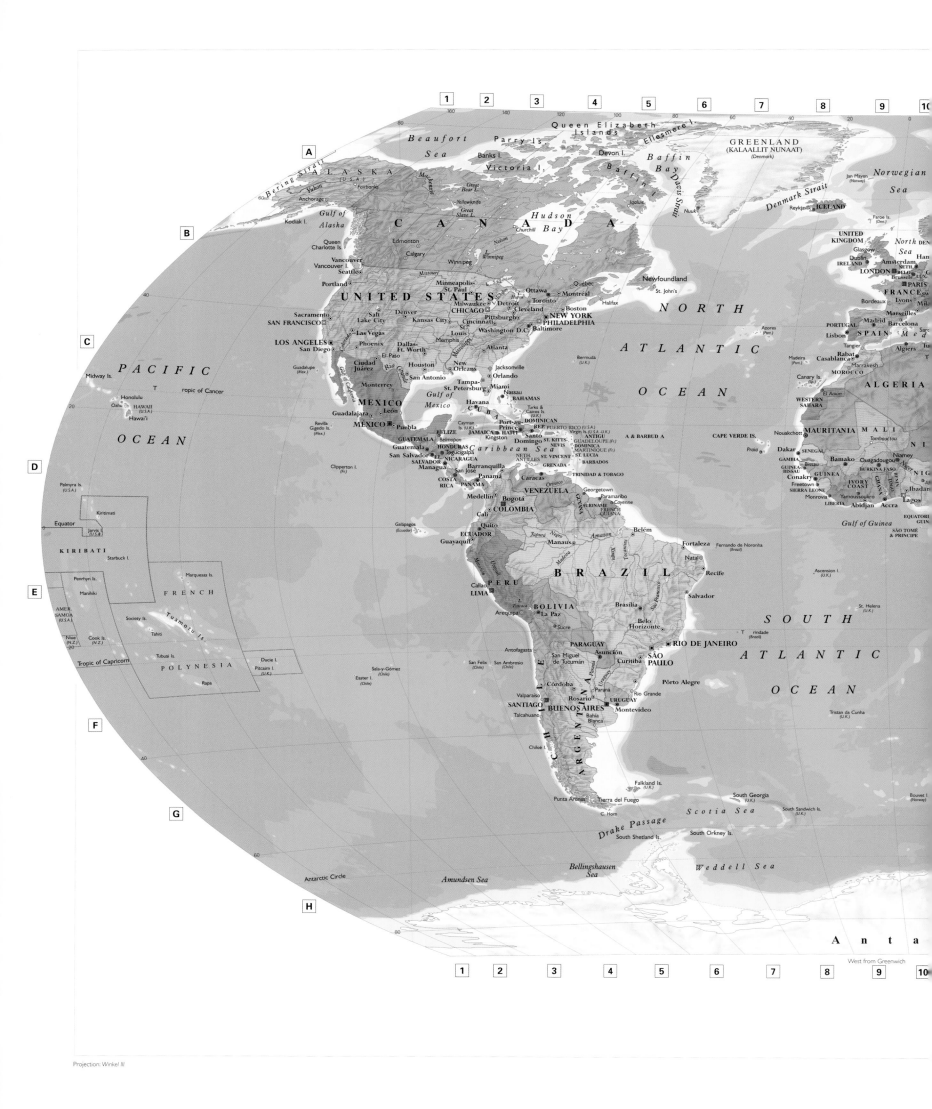

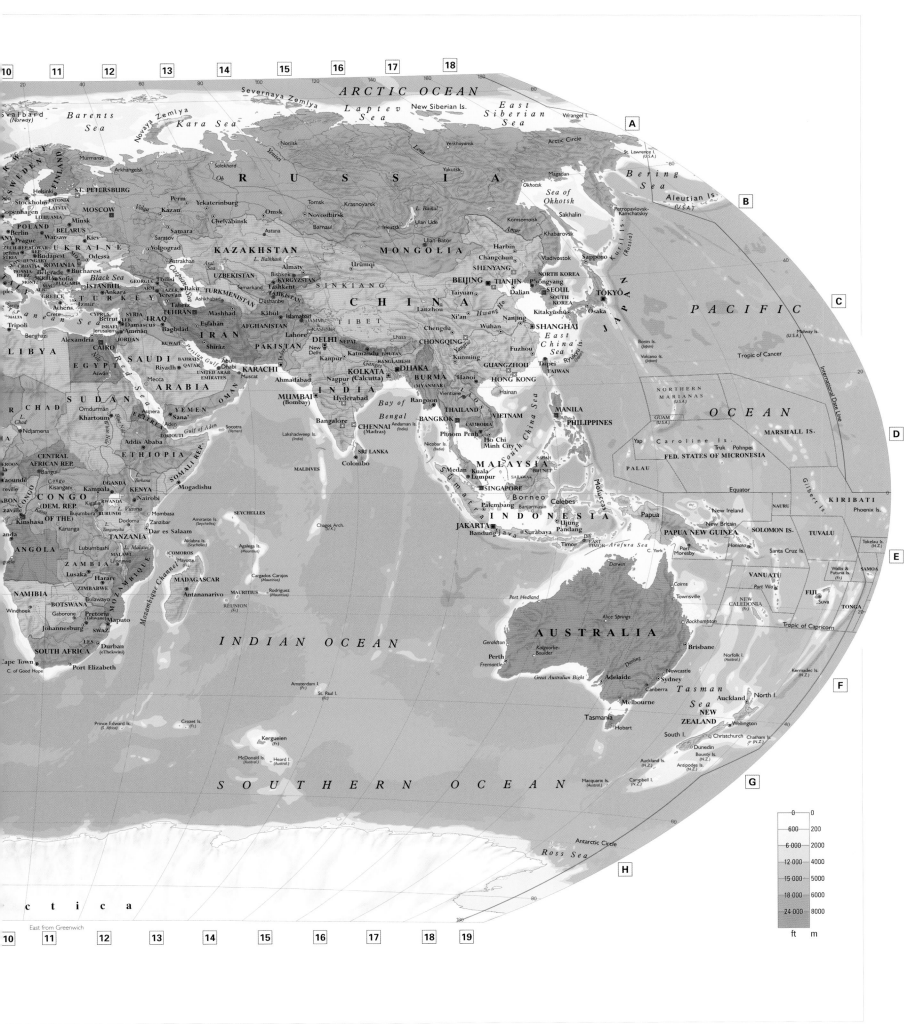

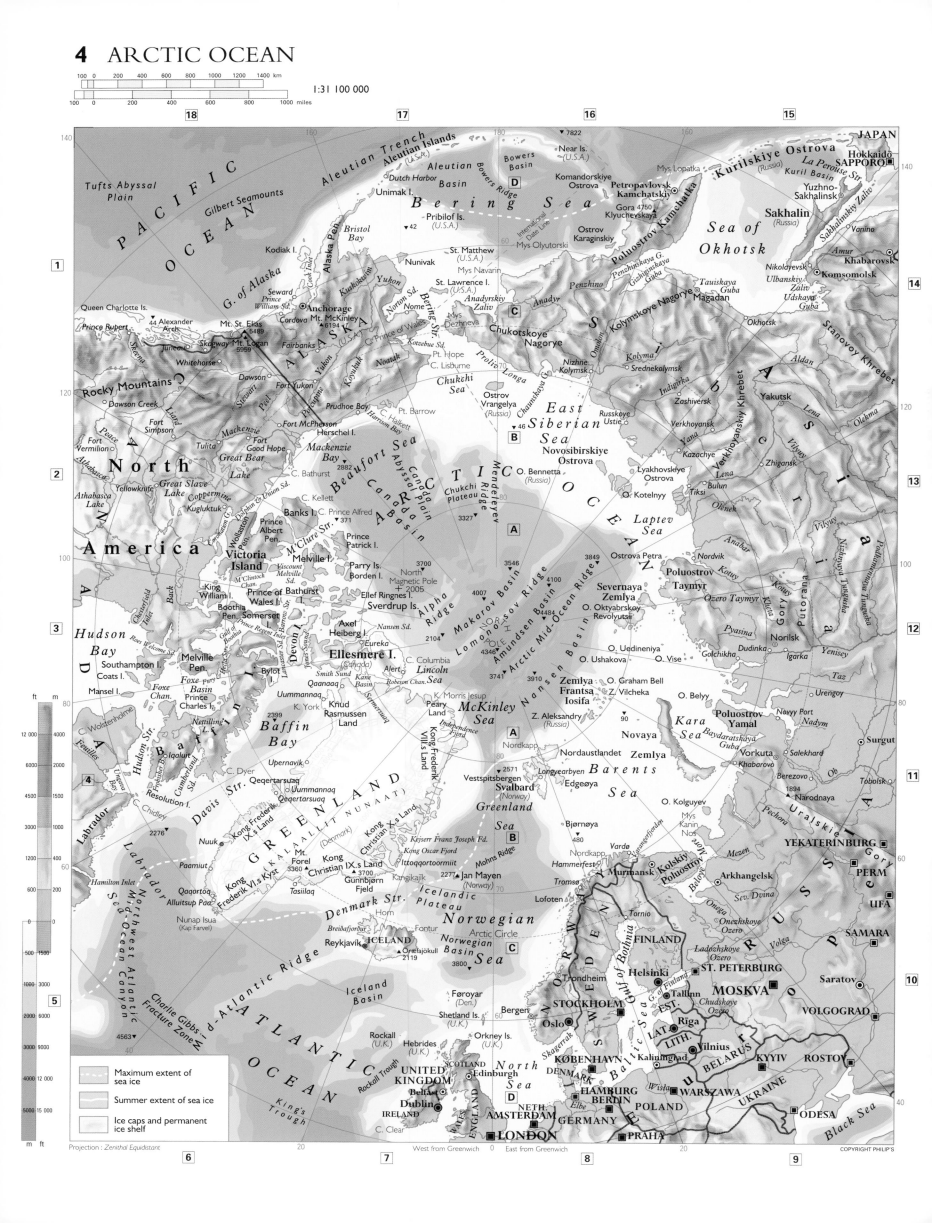

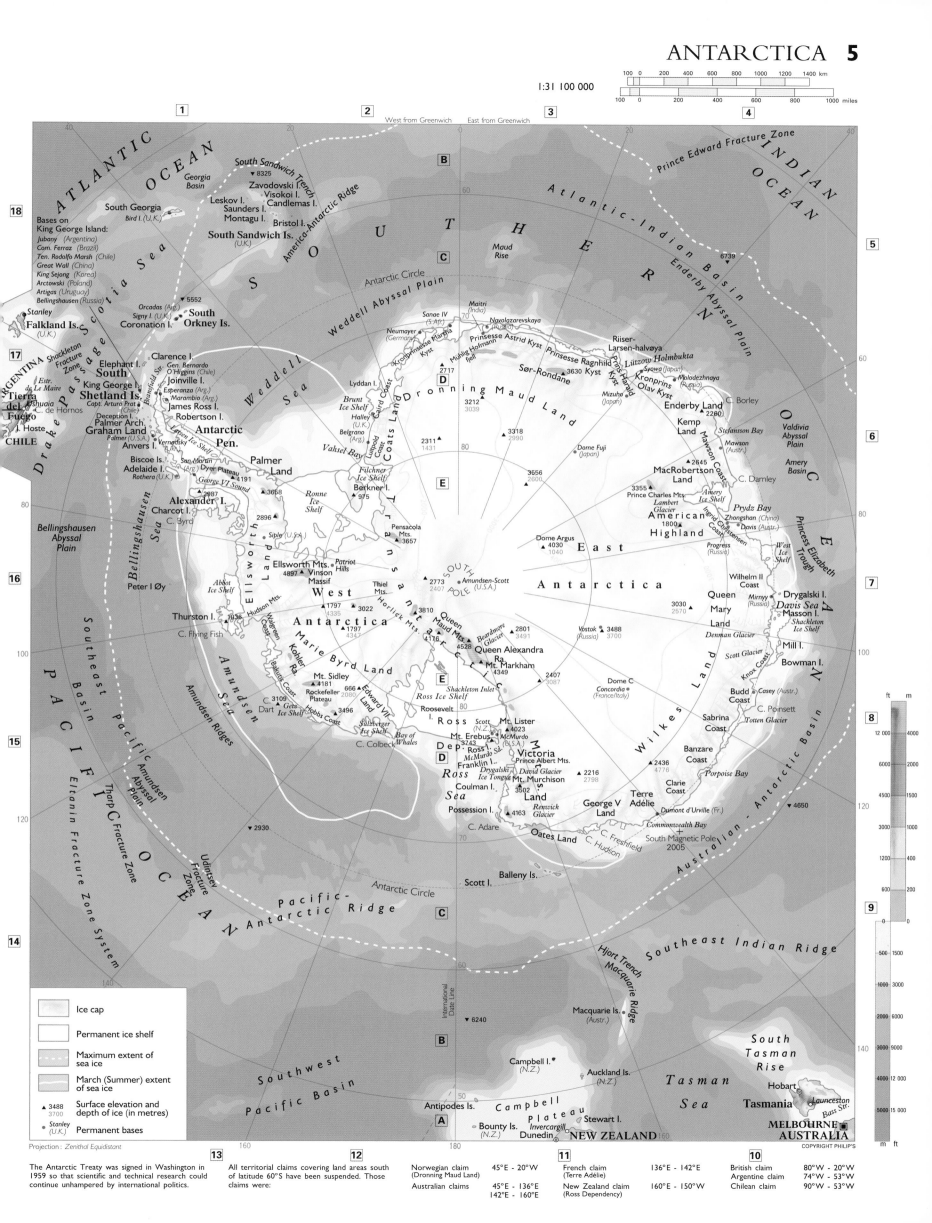

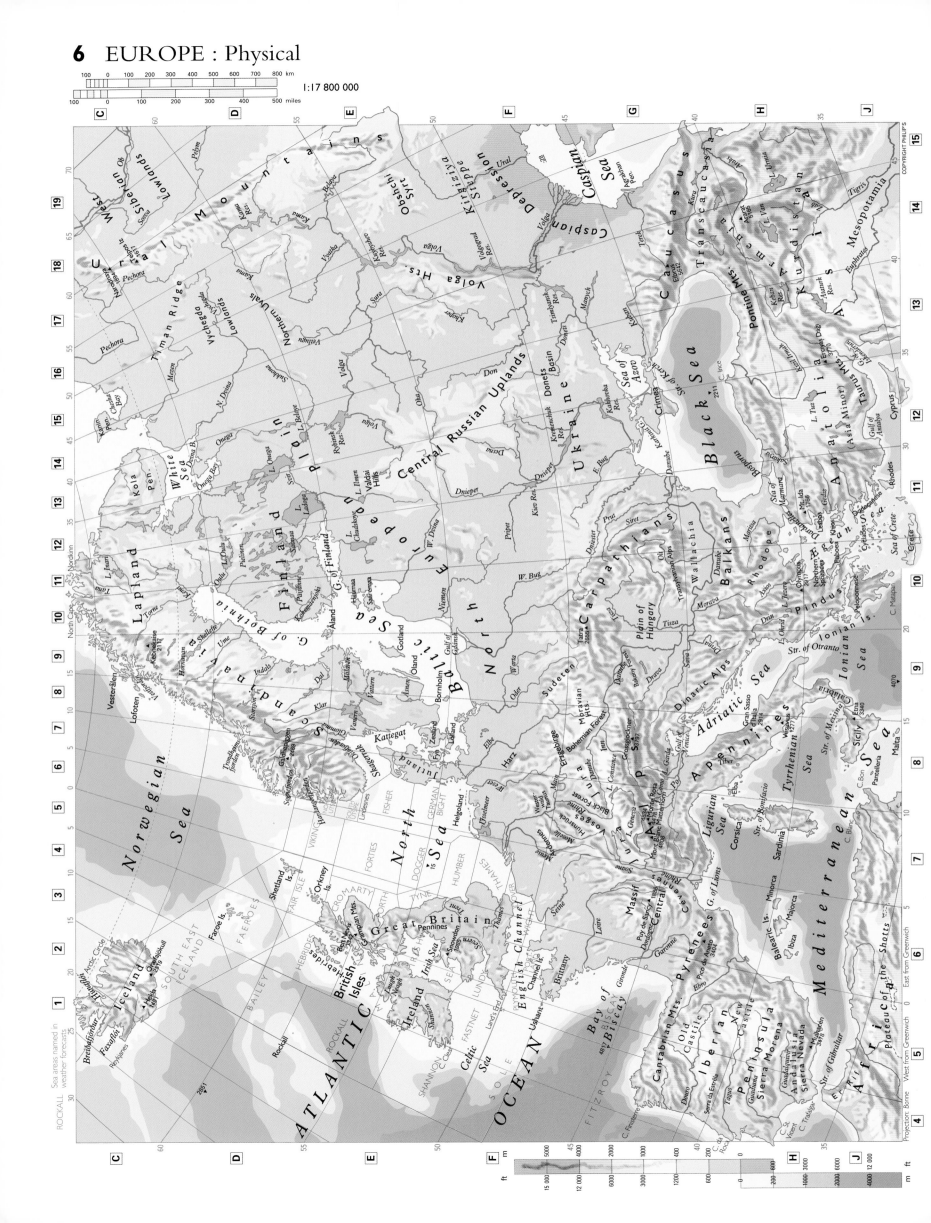

1:17 800 000

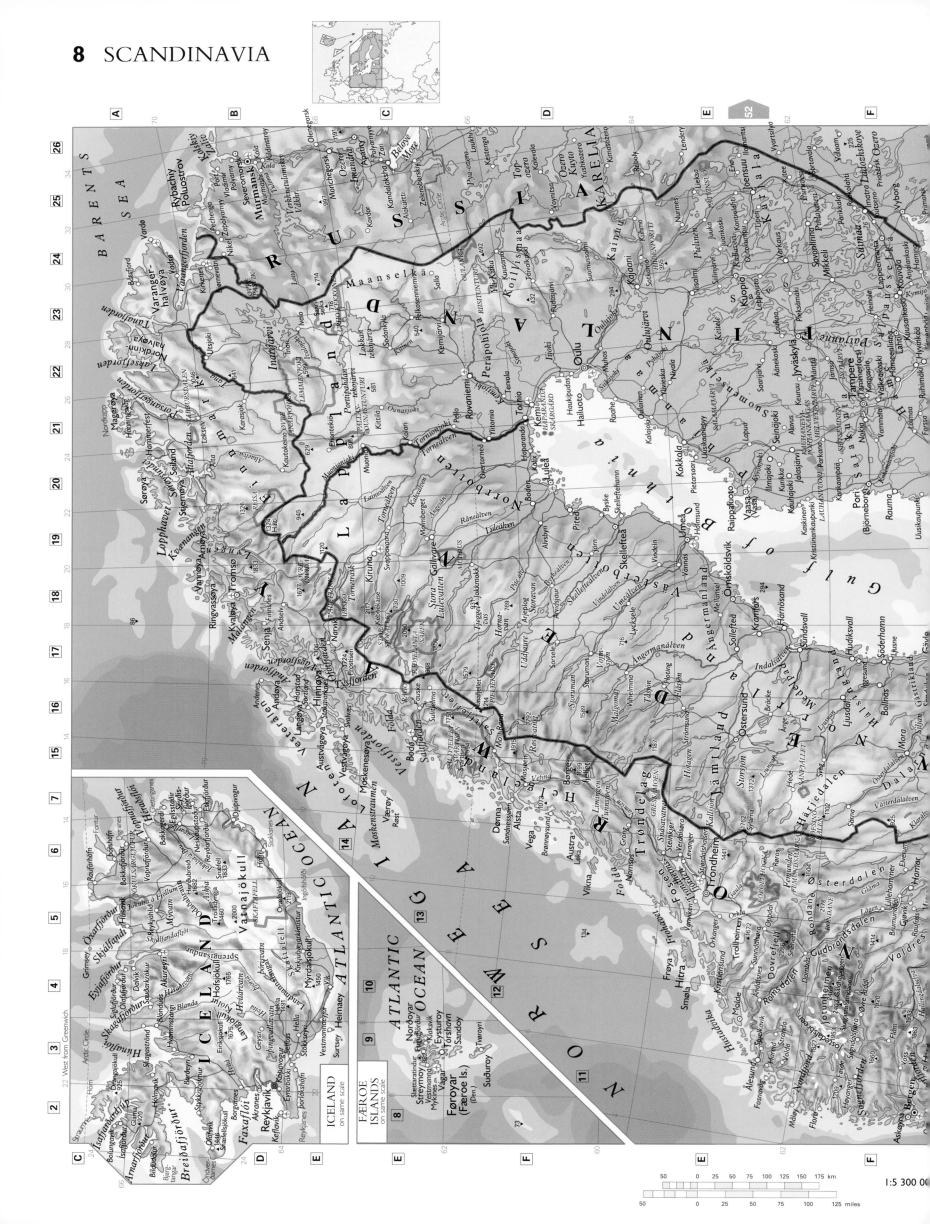

ICELAND
on same scale

FÆROE
ISLANDS
on same scale

1:5 300 000

50 0 25 50 75 100 125 150 175 km

50 0 25 50 75 100 125 miles

Projection: Conical with two standard parallels

East from Greenwich

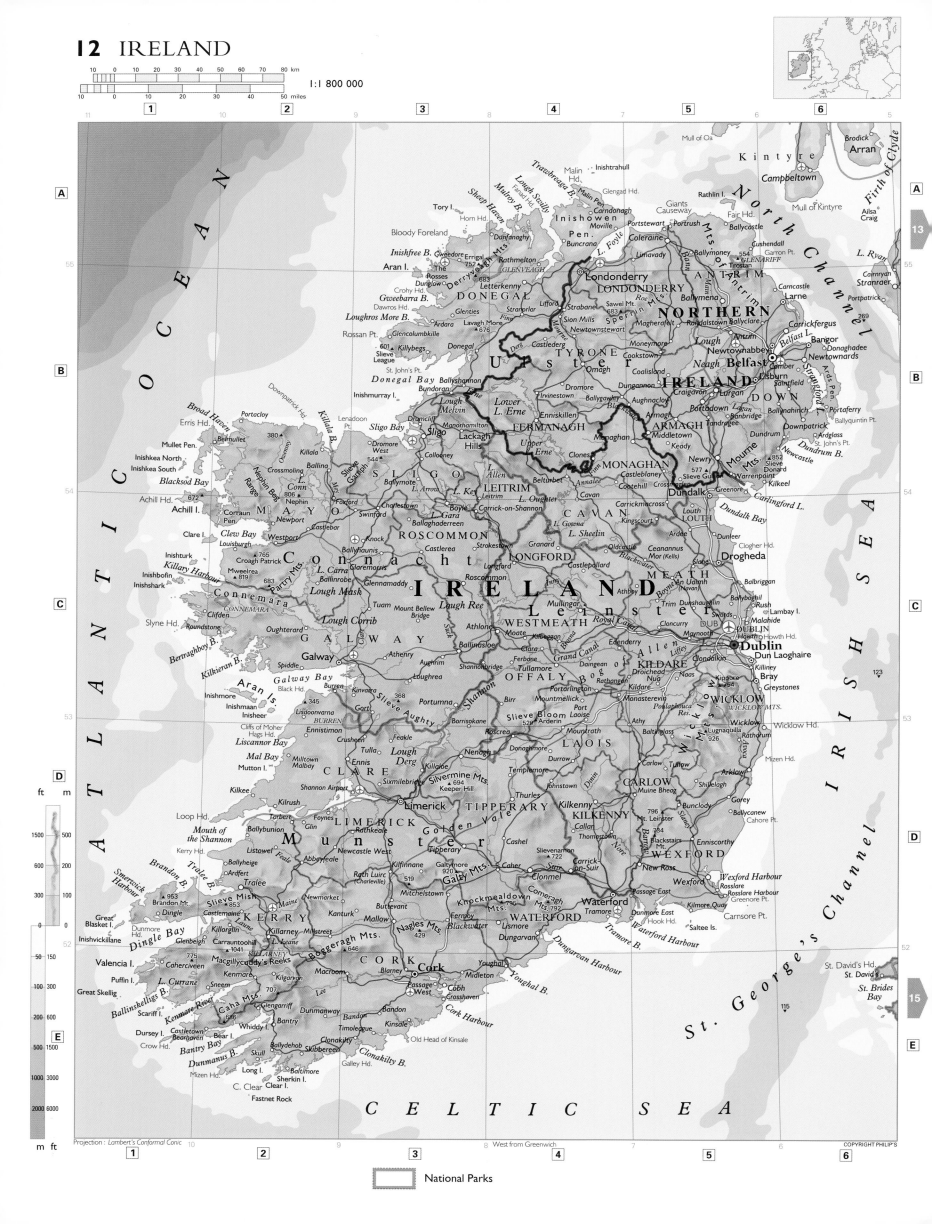

1:1 800 000

10 0 10 20 30 40 50 60 70 80 km
10 0 10 20 30 40 50 miles

Key to Scottish unitary authorities on map
1 CITY OF ABERDEEN
2 DUNDEE CITY
3 WEST DUNBARTONSHIRE
4 EAST DUNBARTONSHIRE
5 CITY OF GLASGOW
6 INVERCLYDE
7 RENFREWSHIRE
8 EAST RENFREWSHIRE
9 NORTH LANARKSHIRE
10 FALKIRK
11 CLACKMANNANSHIRE
12 WEST LOTHIAN
13 CITY OF EDINBURGH
14 MIDLOTHIAN

ORKNEY IS.
on same scale

SHETLAND IS.
on same scale

National Parks and Forest Parks in Scotland

Projection : Lambert's Conformal Conic

West from Greenwich

COPYRIGHT PHILIP'S

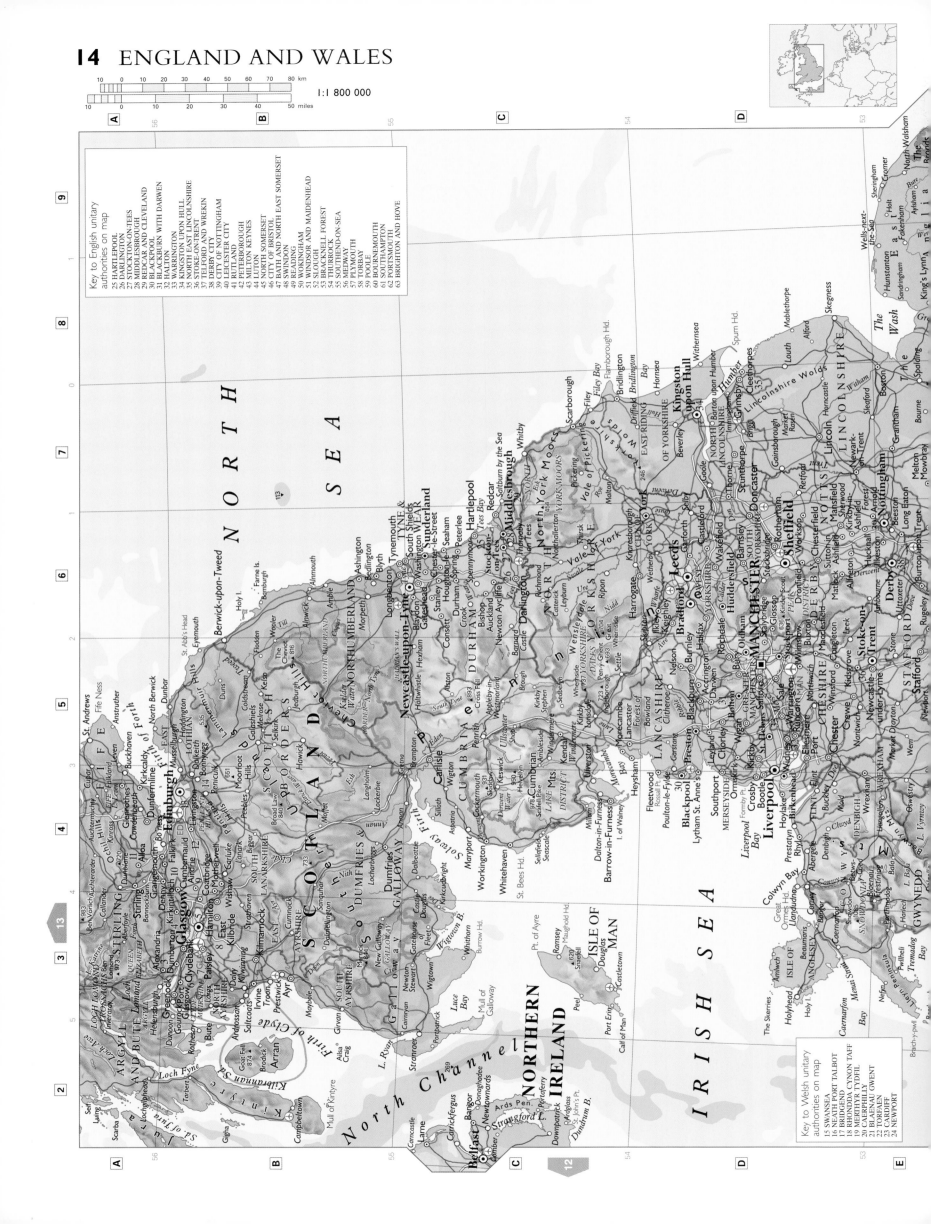

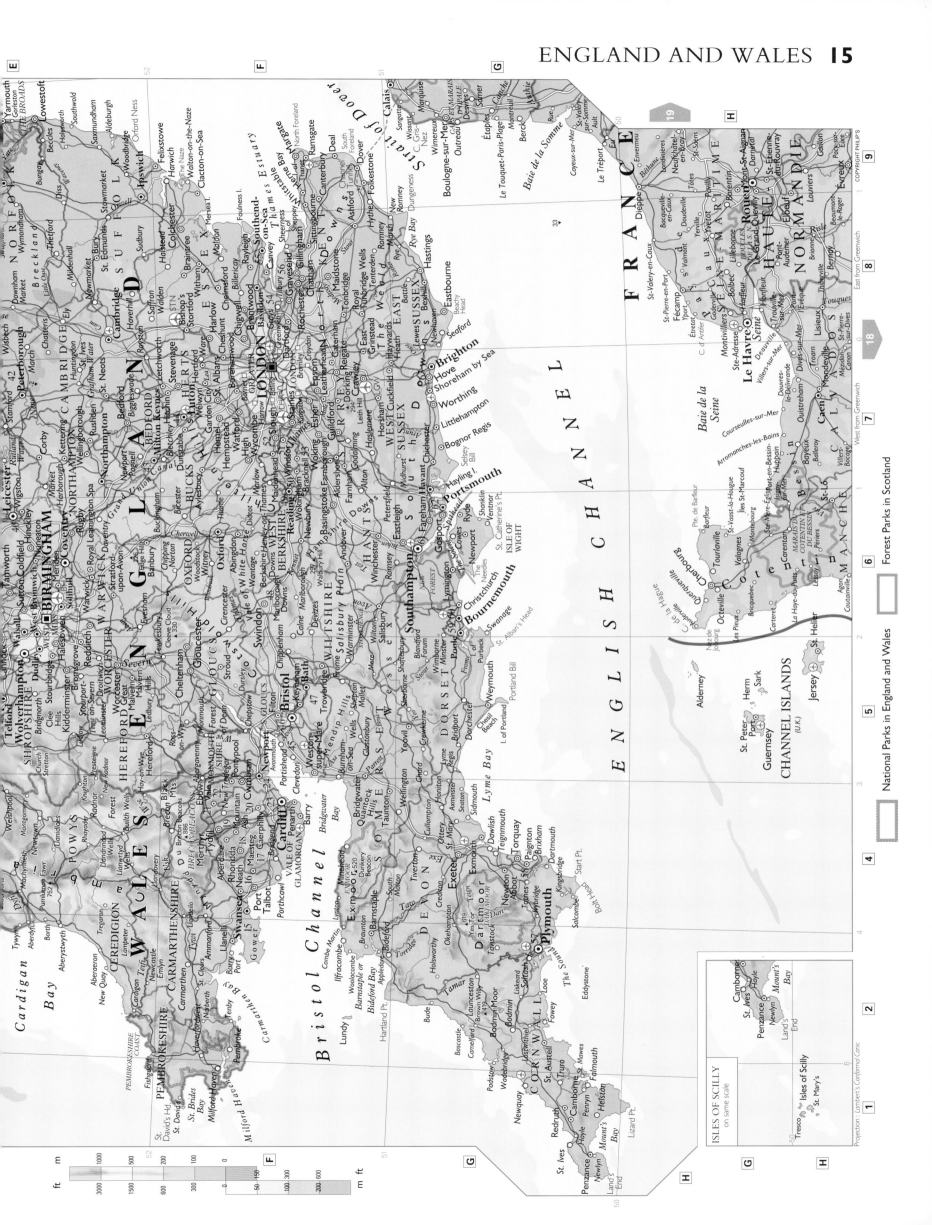

50   0   25 50 75 100 125 150 175 km

1:4 400 000

50   0   25   50   75   100   125 miles

Projection: Conical with two standard parallels

East from Greenwich
COPYRIGHT PHILIP'S

West from Greenwich

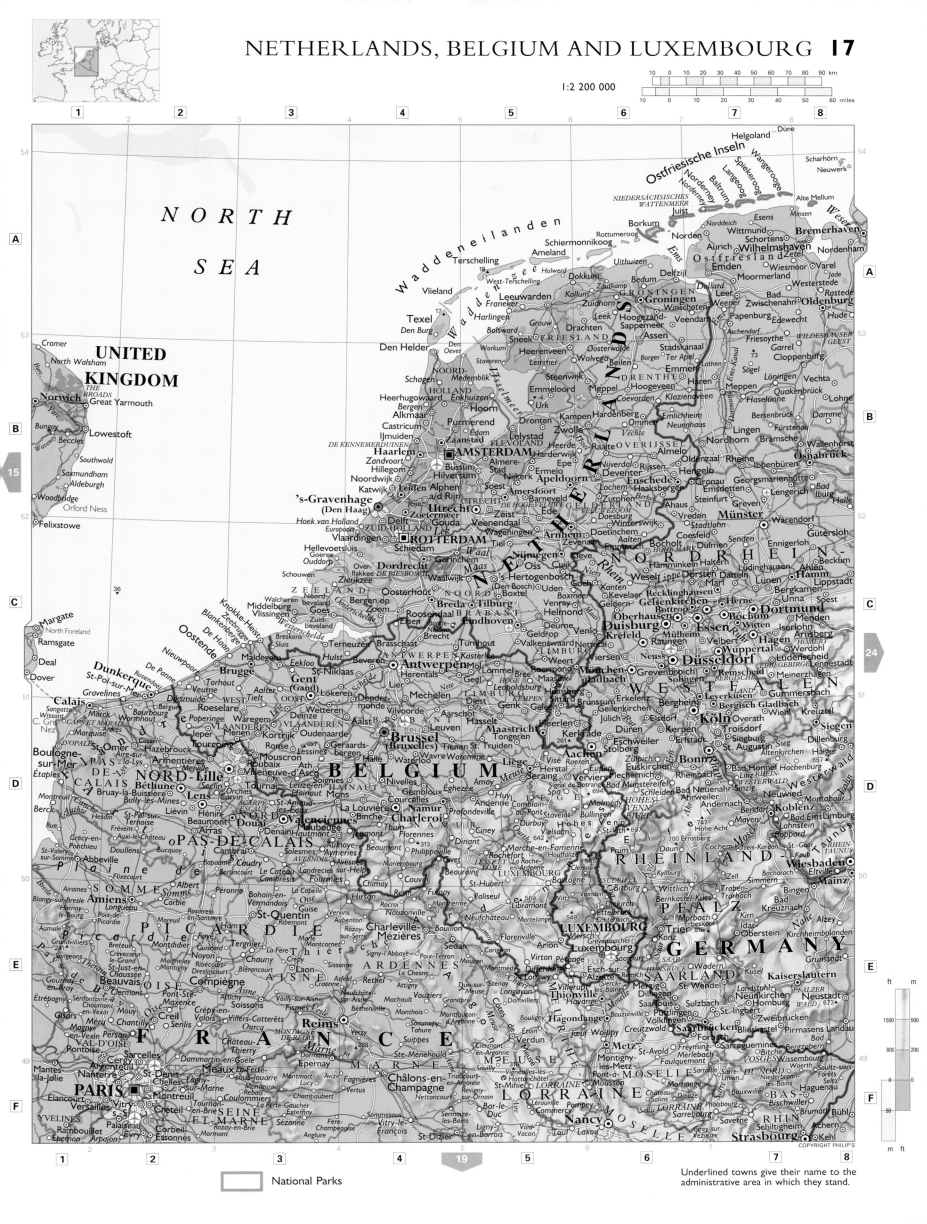

1:2 200 000

NORTH SEA

UNITED KINGDOM

NETHERLANDS

BELGIUM

LUXEMBOURG

GERMANY

FRANCE

National Parks

Underlined towns give their name to the administrative area in which they stand.

COPYRIGHT PHILIP'S

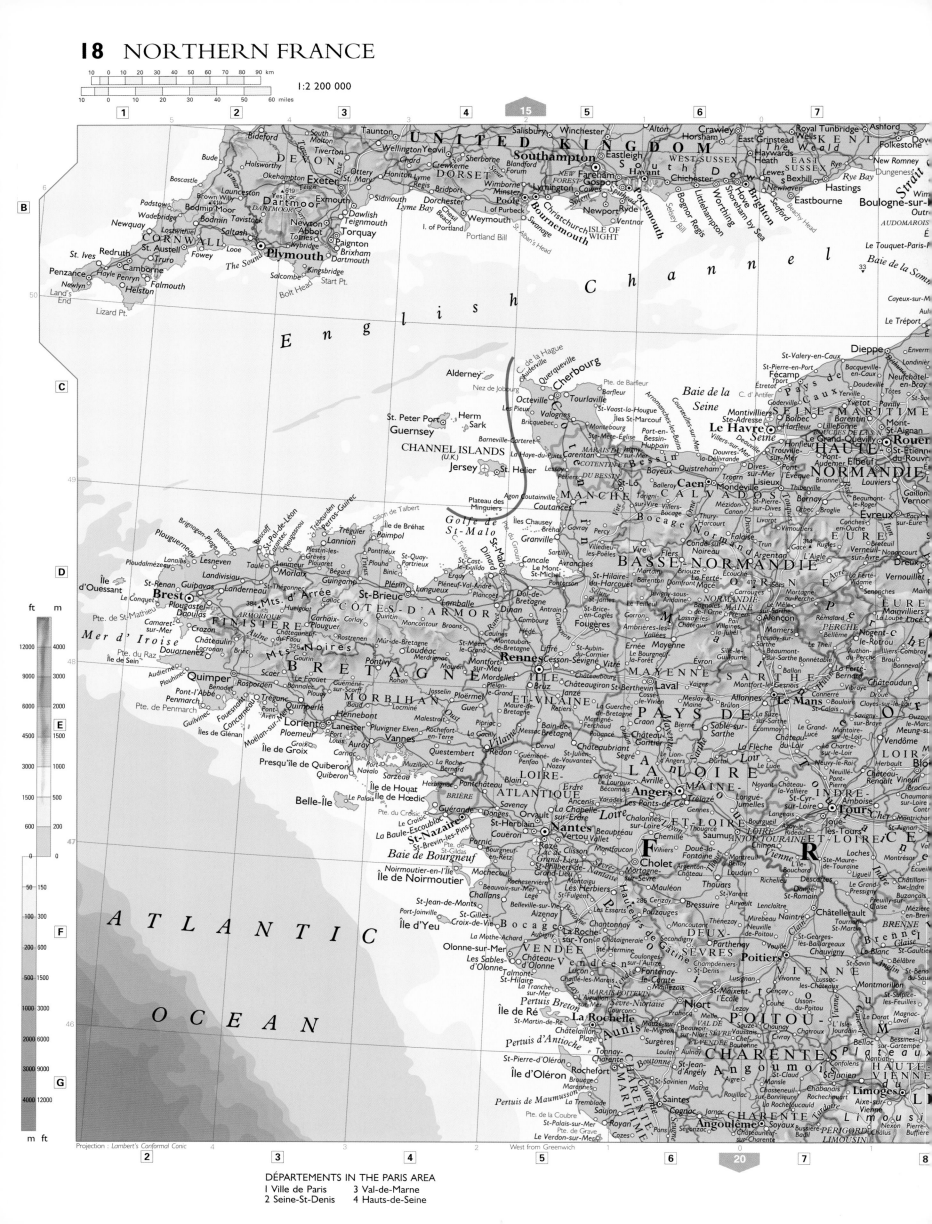

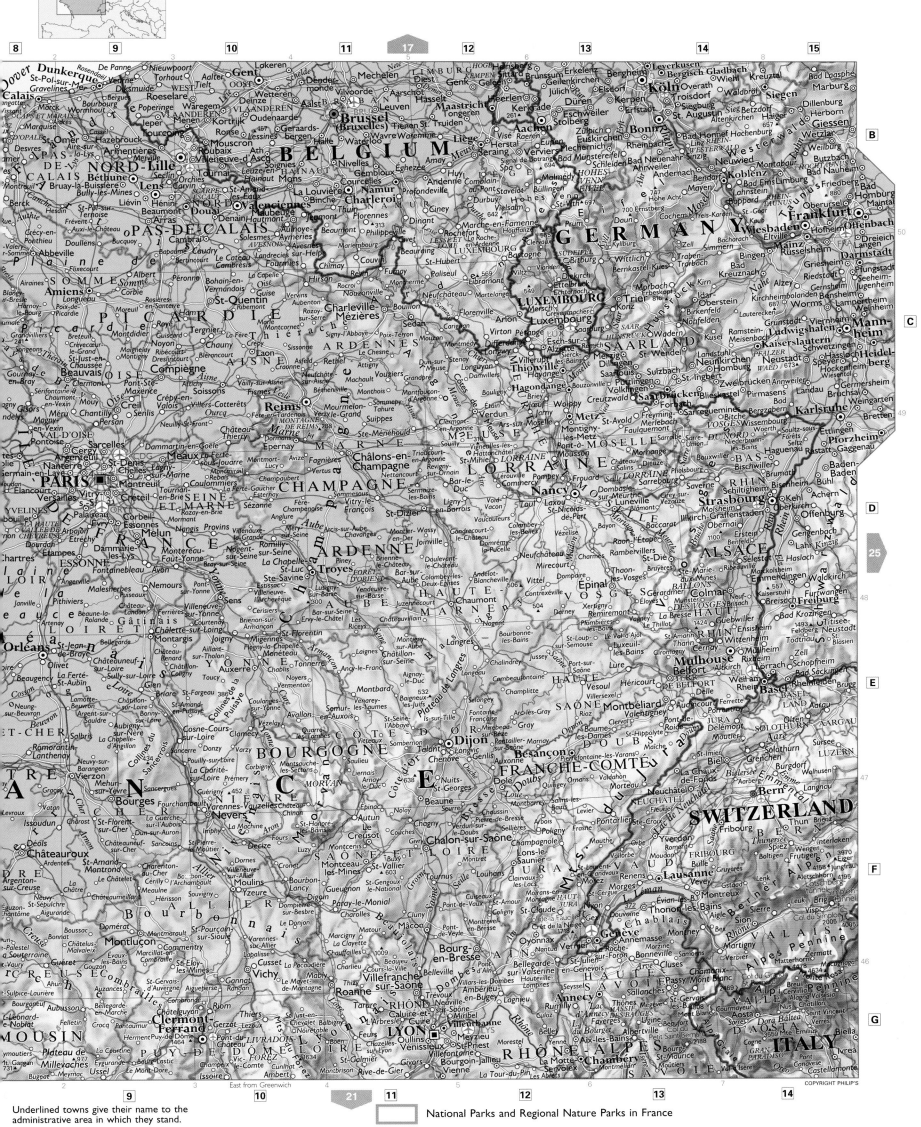

Underlined towns give their name to the administrative area in which they stand.

National Parks and Regional Nature Parks in France

COPYRIGHT PHILIP'S

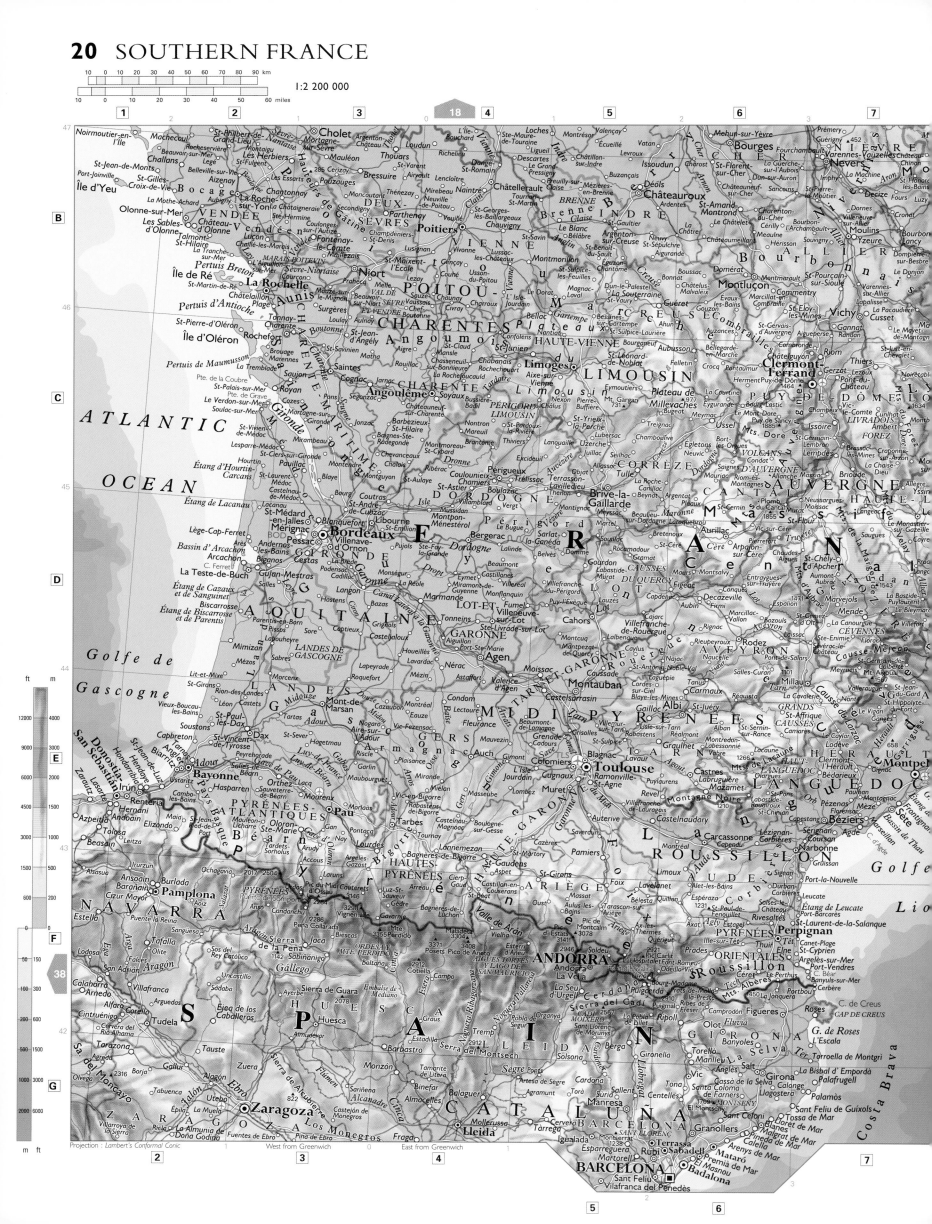

National Parks and Regional Nature Parks in France

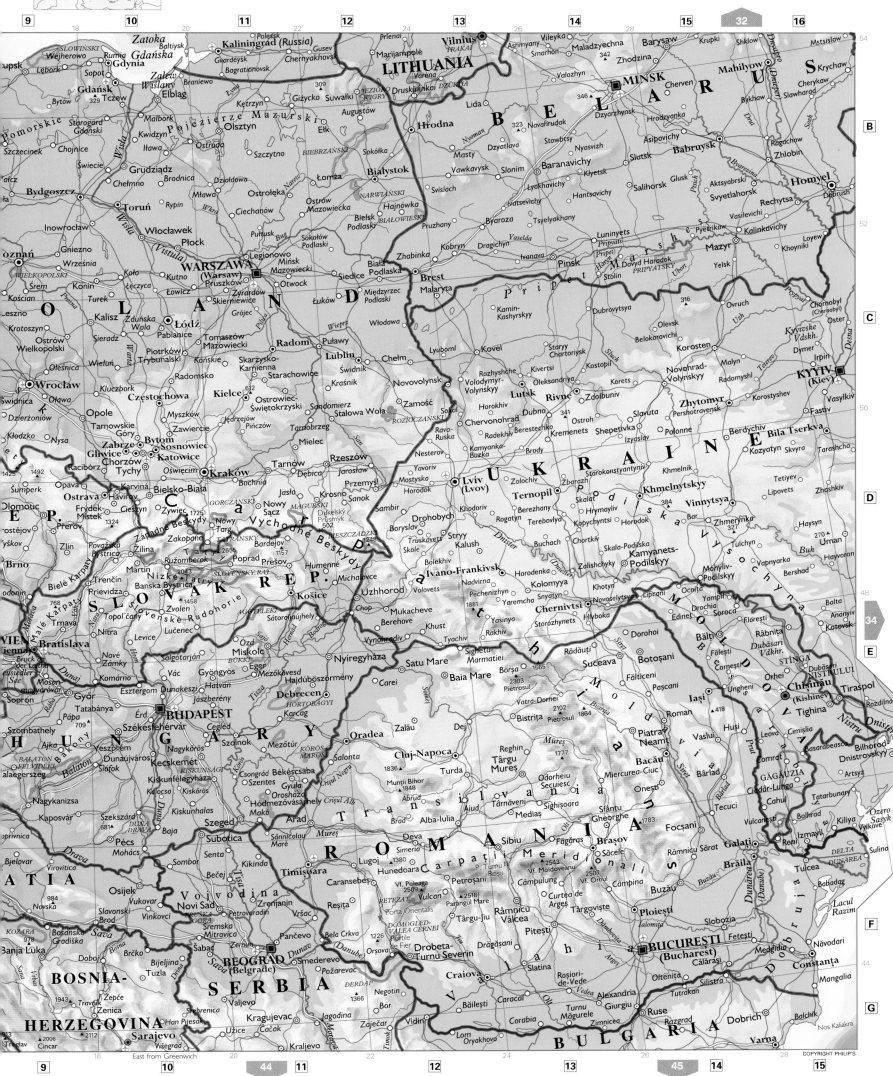

SŁOWIŃSKI
Zatoka Baltiysk
Wejherowo Rumia Gdańska Kaliningrad (Russia) Gusev
upsk Lębork Sopot Gdynia Gvardeysk Chernyakhovsk Prienai Vilnius Ašmyany Smarhon Maladzyechna Barysaw Krupki Shklow Dnyapro Mstsislaw
Gdańsk Zalew Braniewo Bagrationovsk Marijampolė TRAKAI Vileyka Zhodzina Krychaw
Bytów Tczew Wiślany Elbląg Lyna Druskininkai DZŪKIJA LITHUANIA Valozhyn MINSK Cherven Byelaaz Cherykaw
ałcz Szczecinek Chojnice Malbork Giżycko Suwałki JEZIORO WIGRY Lida Navahrudak Hrodzyanka Asipovichy Slawharad
Grudziądz Kwidzyn Iława Olsztyn Pojezierze Mazurski Ełk Augustów Nyoman Dzyarzhynsk Rahachow Zhlobin
Starogard Malbork Ostróda Szczytno Hrodna Masty Vawkavysk Slonim Baranavichy Kletsk Slutsk Salihorsk Glusk Aktsyabrski Svyetlahorsk Homyel
Bydgoszcz Gdański Brodnica Działdowo BIEBRZAŃSKI Białystok Lyakhavichy Hantsavichy Dobrush
Toruń Chełmno Rypin Mława Narew Łomża Svisloch Pruzhany Byaroza Rechytsa
Inowrocław Włocławek Ciechanów Ostrołęka Ostrów NARWIAŃSKI Hajnówka BIAŁOWIESKI Kobryn Ivanava Pinsk Luninyets Pietrikaw Kalinkavichy
oznań Gniezno Września Płock Pułtusk Bug Sokołów Podlaski Bielsk Podlaski Dragichyn Pripyat M Davyd Haradok Mazyr Loyew
WIELKOPOLSKI Śrem Konin Koło Kutno WARSZAWA Legionowo Mińsk Mazowiecki Siedlce Biała Podlaska Brest Malaryta Zhabinka Yaselda Stólin PRIPYATSKY Uborts Yelsk Khoyniki
Kościan Turek Łęczyca Łowicz (Warsaw) Pruszków Otwock Łuków Międzyrzec Podlaski Kamin- Kashyrskyy Pripet Dubrovytsya Ovruch Chornobyl (Chernobyl)
OLA Kalisz Sieradz Zduńska Wola Łódź Pabianice Skierniewice Grójec Pilica Radzyń Podlaski Włodawa Lyuboml Kovel Staryy Chartoryysk Olevsk Belokorovichi Uzh Korosten Irpin Dymer
Ostrów Wielkopolski Piotrków Trybunalski Tomaszów Mazowiecki Radom Puławy Chełm Novovolynsk Volodymyr- Volynskyy Rozhyshche Kivertsi Kostopil Novohrad- Volynskyy Malyn Teteriv KYYIV (Kiev)
Wrocław Wieluń Radomsko Kańsk Wieprz Kraśnik Lublin Zamość Sokal Horokhiv Lutsk Rivne Zdolbuniv Slavuta Pershotravensk Korostyshev Vasylkiv
świdnica Oleśnica Oława Kluczbork Częstochowa Kielce 612 Ostrowiec- Świętokrzyski Stalowa Wola ROZTOCZAŃSKI Chervonohrad Dubno 341 Ostroh Polonne Berdychiv Bila Tserkva Fastiv
Dzierżoniów Opole Myszków Jędrzejów Pińczów Tarnobrzeg Rava- Ruska Radekhiv Berestechko Izyaslav Zhytomyr Kozyatyn Skvyra Tarashcha
Kłodzko Nysa Tarnowskie Góry Zawiercie Mielec Nesterov Kamyanka- Buzka Brody Kremenets Shepetivka Pershotravensk
et Zabrze Bytom Sosnowiec Rzeszów Yavoriv Mostyska UKRAINE Zolochiv Zbarazh Khmelnytskyy Vinnytsya Zhmerynka 327 Zhashkiv
Racibórz Gliwice Chorzów Katowice Tarnów Dębica Przemyśl Horodok Lviv (Lvov) Ternopil Skalat Starokonstyantyniv Khmelnik Lipovets
Šumperk Opava Tychy Oświęcim Kraków Bochnia Jarosław Mostyska Horodok Berezhany Hrymayliv Bar Zhmerynka 270 Uman
Olomouc Ostrava Havířov Bielsko-Biała GORCZAŃSKI Nowy Sącz Jasło Krosno Sanok Sambir Drohobych Khodoriv Rogatyn Terebovlya Kopychyntsi Horodok Skala-Podilska Vapnyarka Hayvoron Bershad
yškov Přerov Frýdek- Mistek Cieszyn Żywiec Zakopane MAGURSKI BIESZCZADZKI Borslav Stryy Kalush Buchach Chortkiv Zalishchyky Mohyliv- Podilskyy Bershad
Zlín Povážská Bystrica Żilina Nowy Targ TATRANSKY Poprad Prešov Humenné Skole Bolekhiv Dnister Kamyanets- Podilskyy
Brno odonín Bielé Karpaty Trenčín Martin Nízke Tatry SLOVENSKÝ RAJ Bardejov Michalovce Ivano-Frankivsk Nadvirna Kolomyya Khotyn Chernivtsi Novoselytsya Lipcani Yampil Ananyiv Balta
Malé Karpaty Prievidza Banská Bystrica Zvolen AGGTELEKI Košice Uzhhorod Volovets Pechenizhyn Yaremcha Snyatyn Storozhynets Hlyboka Drochia Soroca Kotovsk
VIEN ienna Bratislava Nové Zámky Slovenské Rudohorie Lučenec Chop Mukacheve Berehove Khust Rakhiv Yasinya Sighetu- Marmatiei Rădăuţi Edinet Bălţi Dubăsari Vdkhr. Ananyiv
Bruck an der Leitha See Nitra Levice Salgótarján Ózd Miskolc Sátoraljaújhely Vynohradiv Tyachiv Siret Dorohoi Suceava Fălticeni Orhei Chişinău (Kishinev) Tiraspol Rozdilna
Moson- magyaróvár Győr Komárno Vác Gyöngyös Eger BÜKKI Nyíregyháza Satu Mare Baia Mare Borşa 1565 Vatra- Dornei Botoşani Ungheni Iaşi Tighina Dnister
Sopron Esztergom Dunakeszi Jászberény Hatvan Mezőkövesd Hajdúböszörmény Carei Pietrosul 2303 Piatra Neamţ Vaslui Huşi Comrat Basarabeasca
Szombathely Tatabánya 709 BUDAPEST Székesfehérvár Cegléd Szolnok HORTOBÁGYI Debrecen Karcag Zalău Dej Bistriţa Pietrosul 1864 2102 Roman Bârlad GĂGĂUZIA Ciadâr-Lunga Artsyz
Pápa Veszprém BAKONY Dunaújváros Nagykőrös Mezőtúr KÖRÖS MAROS Oradea Cluj-Napoca Mureş Reghin Târgu Mureş 1777 Bacău 418 Tecuci Cahul Bolhrad
BALATON- FELVIDÉKI Balaton Siófok Kecskemét Kiskunfélegyháza KISKUNSÁGI Salonta Turda Odorheiu Secuiesc Onesti Bârlad Vulcaneşti Reni Izmayil Kiliya
alaegerszeg Ajka Nagykanizsa Kaposvár DUNA Szekszárd 681 Pécs Kalocsa Kiskőrös Kiskunhalas Csongrád Szentes Békéscsaba Gyula Oroszháza 1836 Munţii Bihor 1848 Aiud Alba-Iulia Mediaş Sighişoara Sfântu Gheorghe 1783 Miercurea-Ciuc Focşani Bârlad Galaţi Sulina
DRÁVA Mohács Hódmezővásárhely Makó Arad Crişul Alb Deva Brad Simeria Sibiu Făgăraş Braşov Săcele Râmnicu Sărat DELTA DUNAREA
oprivnica Pécs Baja Szeged Sânnicolau Mare Mureş Lugoj Hunedoara 2543 2509 Carpaţii Meridionali Câmpulung Vf. Omul 2507 Buzău Brăila Tulcea Babadag
ATIA Bjelovar Virovitica Osijek Subotica Senta Kikinda Timişoara Caransebeş Reşiţa Petroşani P. Turnu Roşu Vf. Moldoveanu Câmpina Târgovişte Ploieşti Lacul Razim
Slavonski Brod Vukovar Vinkovci Voivodina Novi Sad Zrenjanin Vršac Bela Crkva RETEZAT Vulcan Parângul Mare 2518 Curtea de Argeş Ialomiţa Slobozia
984 FRUŠKA GORA Sremska Mitrovica Sombor Bečej Vf. Peleaga 2509 Porta Orientalis DOMOGLED- VALEA CERNEI Râmnicu Vâlcea Piteşti Dâmboviţa BUCUREŞTI (Bucharest) Călăraşi Constanţa
Bosanski Brod Doboj Brčko Bijeljina Tuzla Šabac Beograd (Belgrade) Smederevo 1226 de Fier Drobeta- Turnu Severin Orşova Drăgăşani Slatina Olt Oltenita Feteşti Medgidia
KOZARA BOSNIA- Banja Luka Srebrenica Valjevo Pančevo ĐERDAP Craiova Roşiori- de-Vede Giurgiu Ruse Silistra Mangalia
1943 Travnik Zenica Užice Čačak Kragujevac Jagodina 1366 Bor Negotin Vidin Băileşti Caracal Vedea Turnu Măgurele Zimnicea Corabia Razgrad Dobrich Nos Kaliakra
HERZEGOVINA 2112 SERBIA Višegrad Han Pijesak Kraljevo Zaječar Timok Lom Oryakhovo BULGARIA Varna Balchik
Sarajevo Cincar 2006 Troglav Kladovo

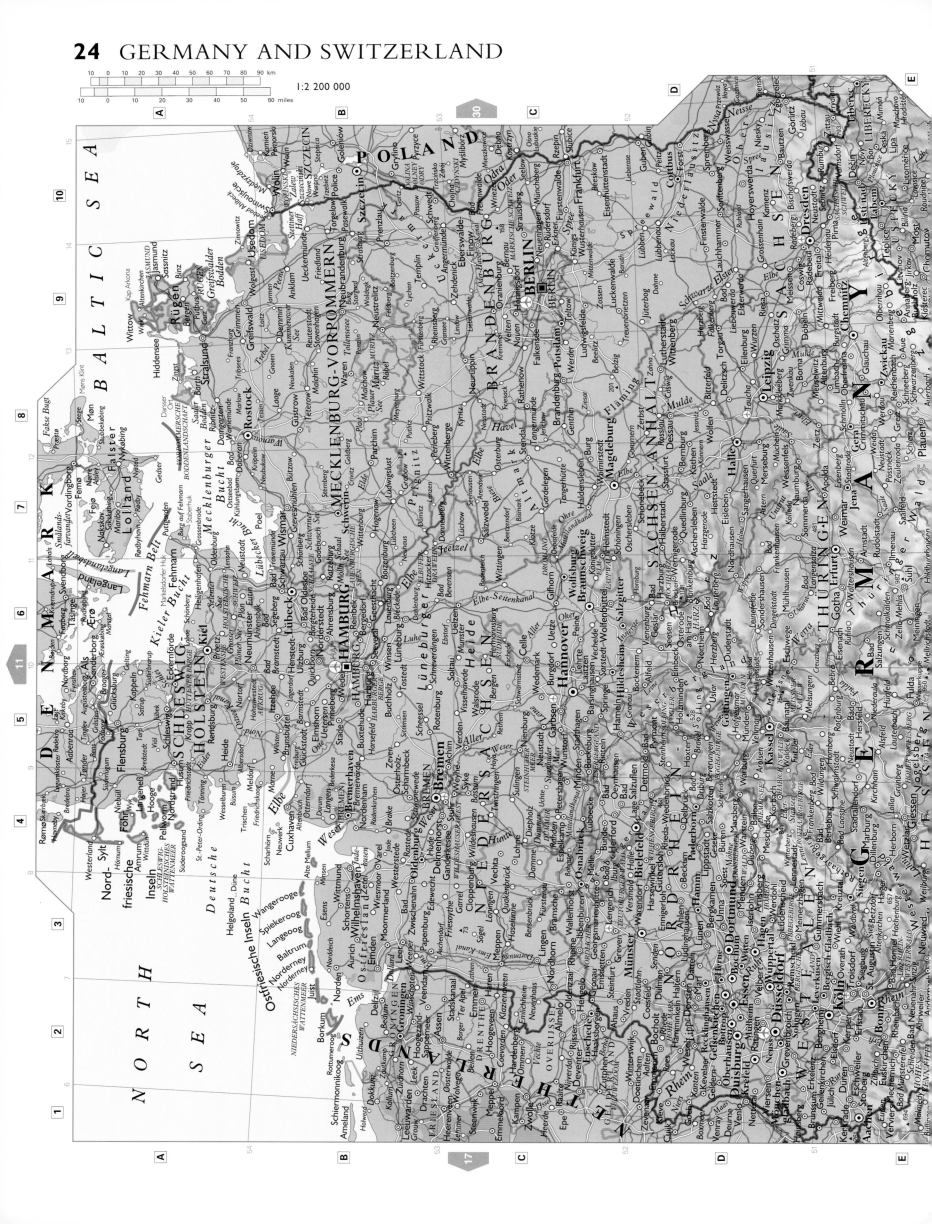

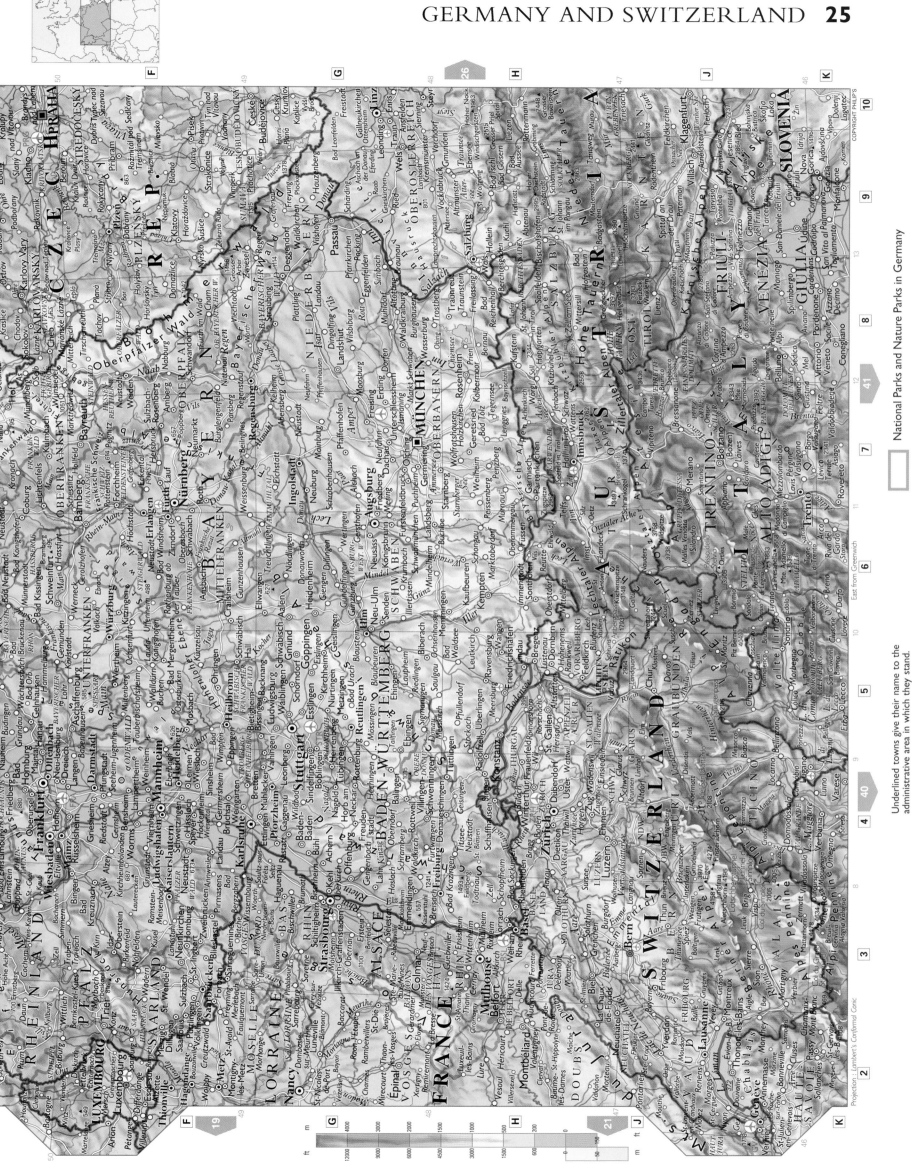

National Parks and Nature Parks in Germany

Underlined towns give their name to the administrative area in which they stand.

East from Greenwich

Projection : Lambert's Conformal Conic

1:2 200 000

Projection : Lambert's Conformal Conic

Underlined towns give their name to the administrative area in which they stand.

National Parks

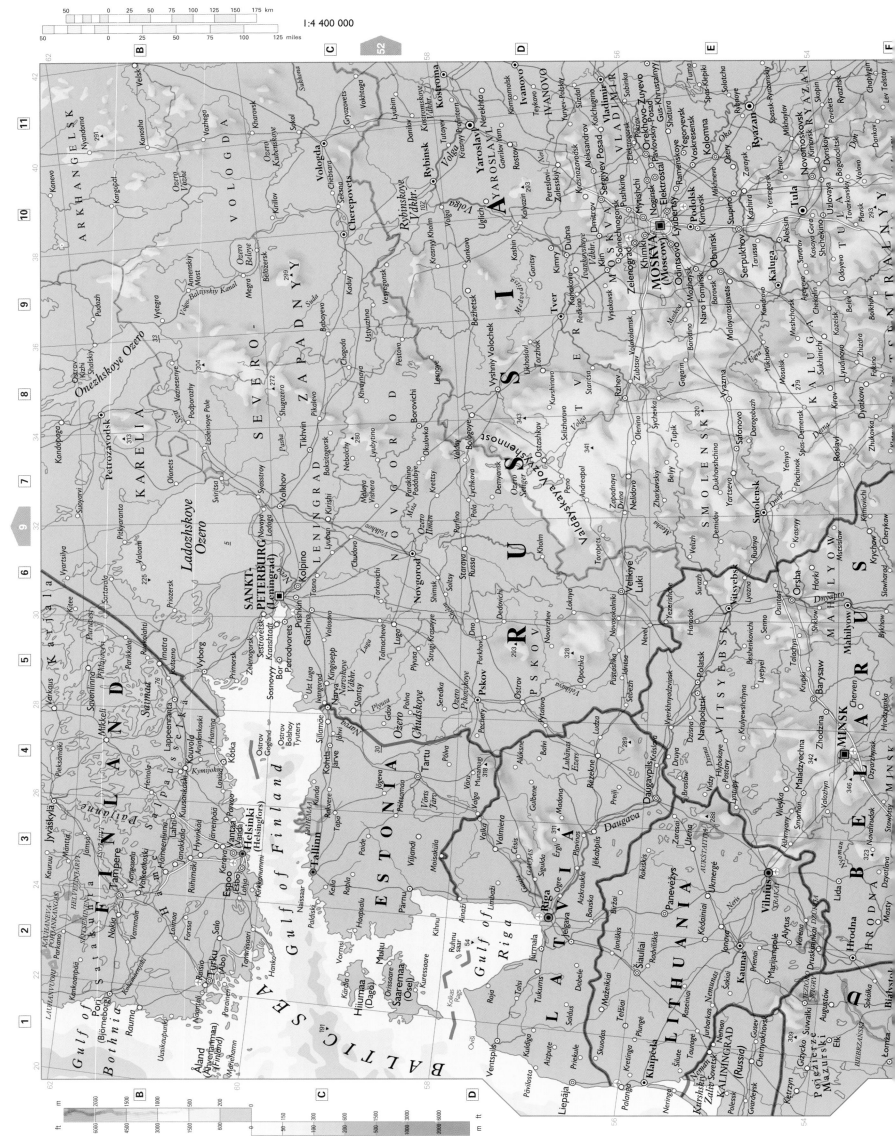

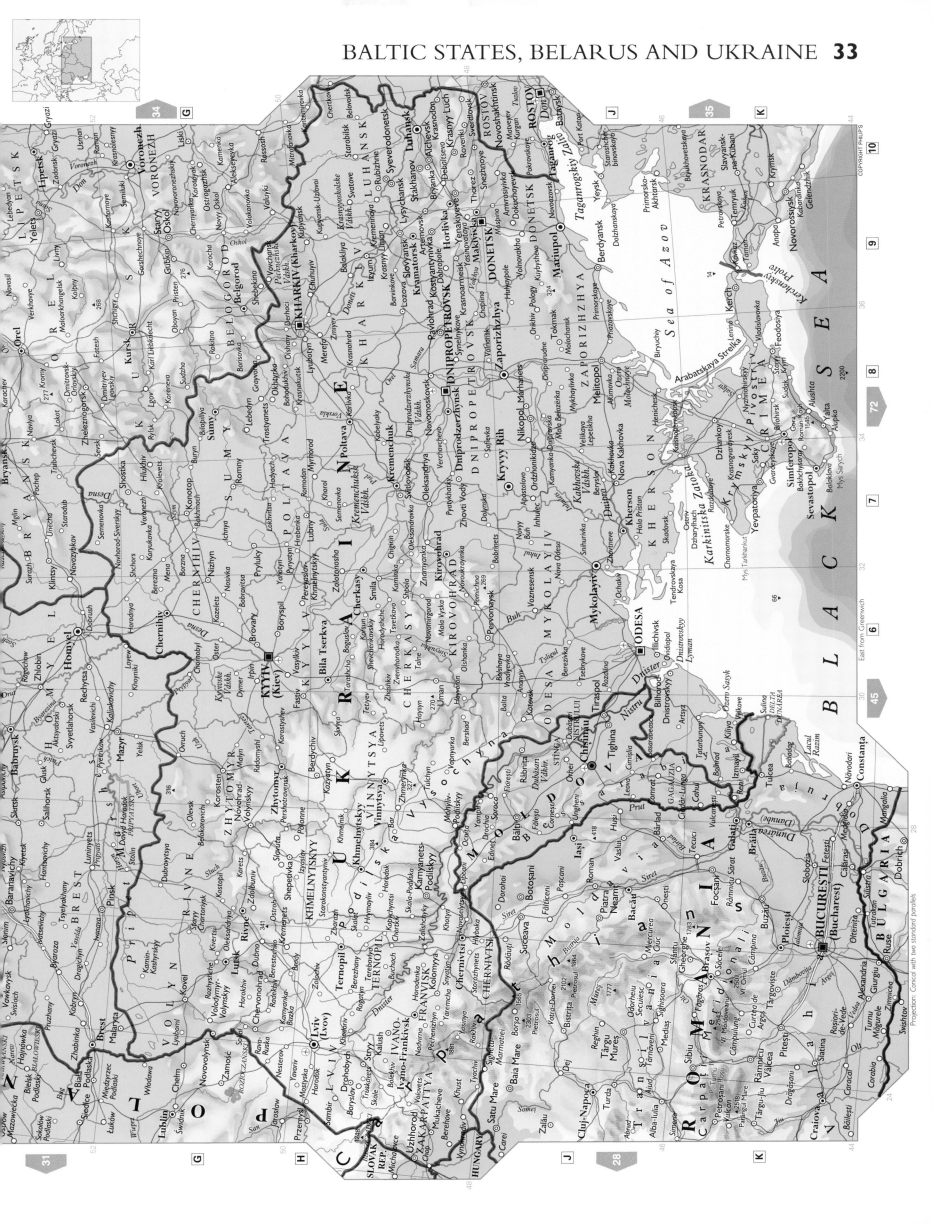

Projection Conical with two standard parallels

East from Greenwich

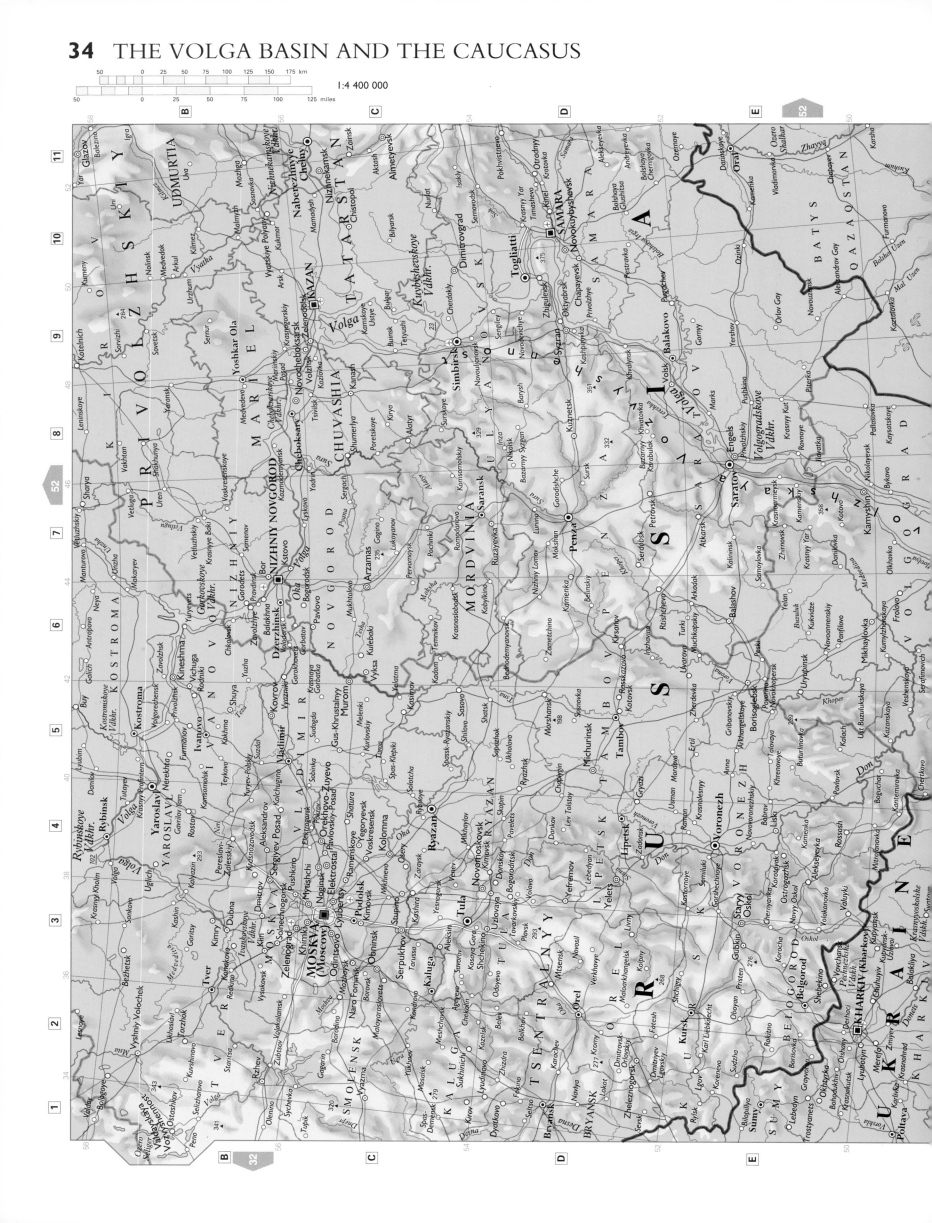

1:4 400 000

50   0   25   50   75   100   125   150   175 km
50   0   25   50   75   100   125 miles

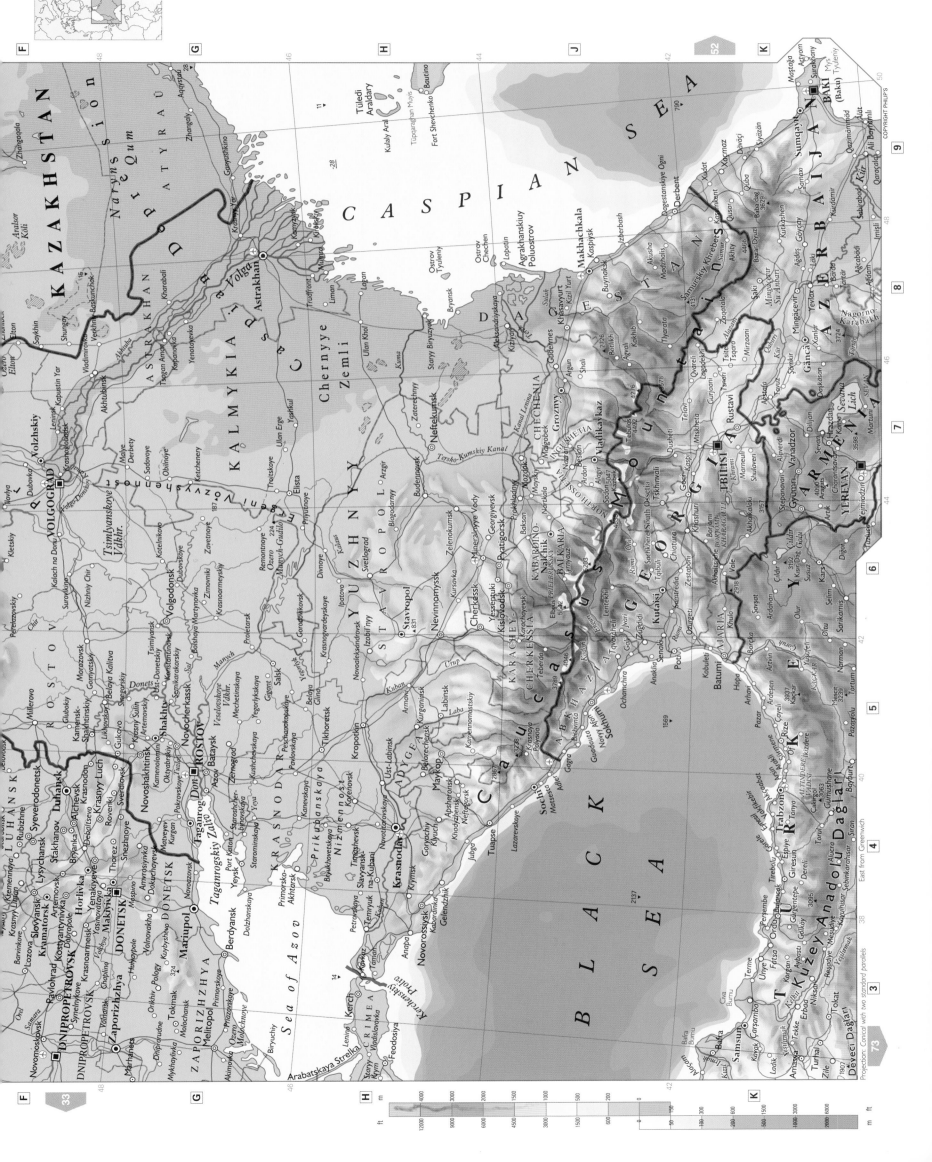

Projection: Conical with two standard parallels

1:2 200 000

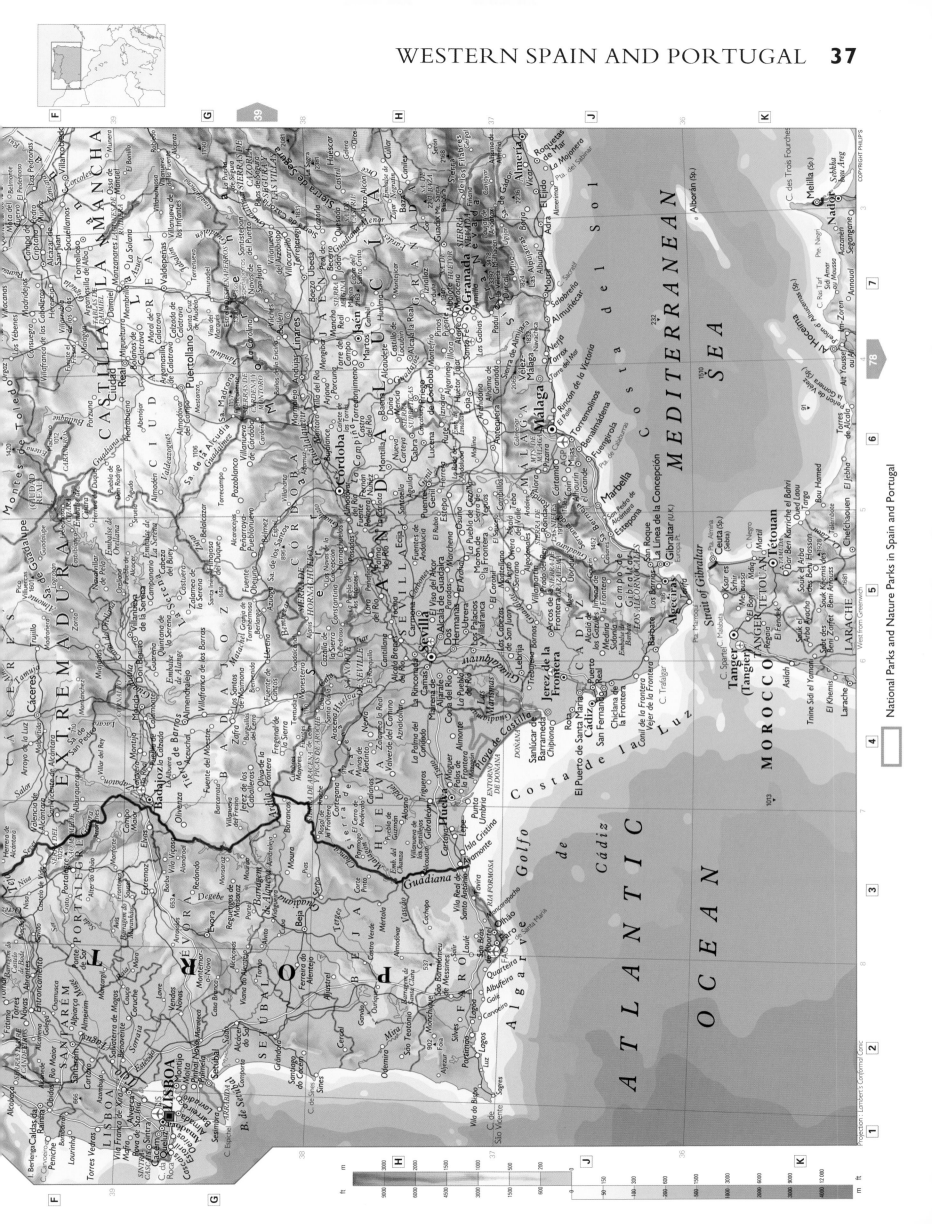

10 0 10 20 30 40 50 60 70 80 90 km

1:2 200 000

10 0 10 20 30 40 50 60 miles

National Parks and Nature Parks in Spain

Projection : Lambert's Conformal Conic

1:2 200 000

Underlined towns give their name to the administrative area in which they stand.

Administrative divisions in Croatia:

Brodsko-Posavska   4 Medimurska   8 Virovitičko-Podravska
Koprivničko-Križevačka 6 Požeško-Slavonska   10 Zagreba čka
Krapinsko-Zagorska   7 Varaždinska

National Parks and Nature Parks in Italy

Inter-entity boundaries as agreed
at the 1995 Dayton Peace Agreement

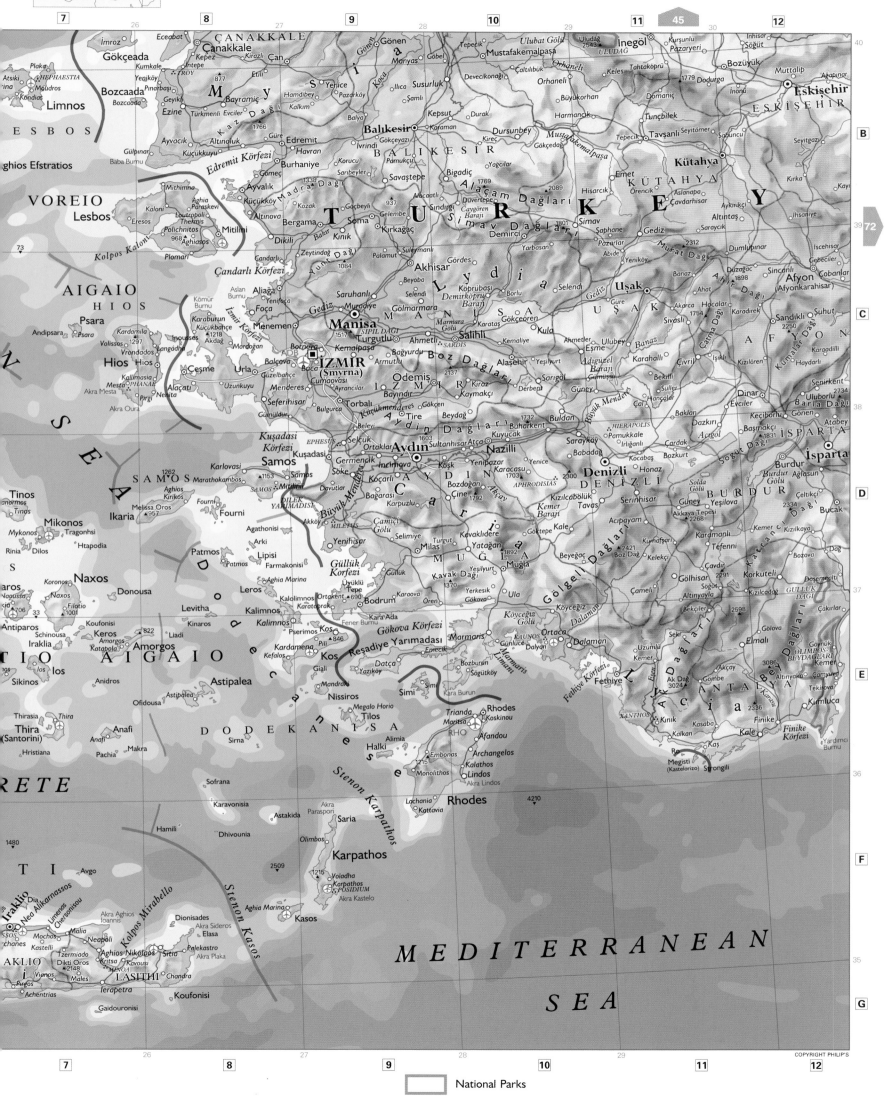

National Parks

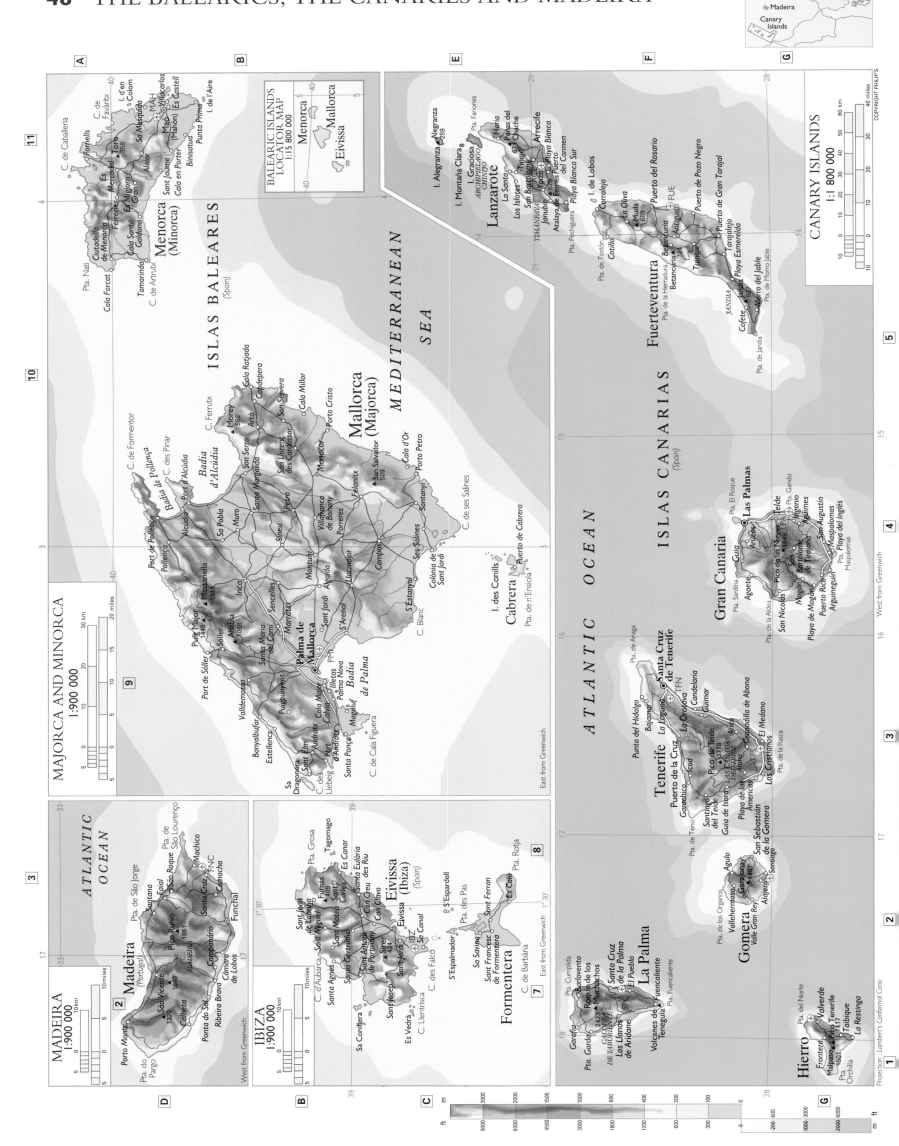

Madeira

Canary Islands

Balearic Islands

A **B** **E** **F** **G**

11

10

4

3

2

BALEARIC ISLANDS
LOCATOR MAP
1:15 800 000

Menorca

Mallorca

Eivissa

ISLAS BALEARES
(Spain)

Menorca
(Minorca)

Pta. Nati
C. de Cavalleria
Fornells
I. d'en Colom
MAH
Villacarlos
Es Castell
Ciutadella de Menorca
Ferreries
Es Mercadal
Toro
358
Sa Mesquida
Mao (Mahón)
Cala Santa Goldana
Es Migjorn Gran
Alaior
Sant Jaume
Cala en Porter
Binisafua
Punta Prima
I. de l'Aire
Cala Forcat
Tamarinda
C. de Artrutx

ISLAS CANARIAS
(Spain)

CANARY ISLANDS
1:1 800 000

I. Alegranza
Alegranza 259
Pta. Fariones
I. Montaña Clara
I. Graciosa
ARCHIPIÉLAGO CHINIJO
La Santa
Haria
Peñas del Chache 617
Arrecife
TIMANFAYA
Yaiza
Tinajo
Los Islotes
San Bartolomé
Playa Blanca
Puerto del Carmen
Janubio
Atalaya de Femés
I. de Lobos
Pta. Pechiguera
Corralejo
Pta. de Tostón
Cotillo
La Oliva
Puerto del Rosario
FUE
Betancuria
Muda 659
Antigua
Tarajalejo
Tuineje
Betancuria 724
Puerto de Pozo Negro
Puerto de Gran Tarajal
JANDÍA
Cofete
Morro del Jable
807
Playa Esmeralda
Morro Jable
Pta. de Jandía

Lanzarote

Fuerteventura

MEDITERRANEAN SEA

**Mallorca
(Majorca)**

Cala Ratjada
Cala Mesquida
Cala Millor
Son Servera
San Lorenç des Cardassar
Artà
Morey 562
Cala Millor
Porto Cristo
Cala d'Or
Porto Petro
C. Ferrutx
C. de Formentor
C. des Pinar
C. de Pollença
Port de Pollença
Pollença
Badia de Pollença
Port d'Alcúdia
Alcúdia
Badia d'Alcúdia
Massanella 1348
Sa Pobla
Santa Margalida
Muro
Inca
Petra
Sineu
Manacor
San Salvador 509
Felanitx
Villafranca de Bonany
Porreres
Santanyí
Santa María del Camí
Sencelles
Algaida
Sant Jordi
Llucmajor
Campos
Ses Salines
C. de ses Salines
Colonia de Sant Jordi
C. des Salines
Puig Major 1445
Sóller
Port de Sóller
Alfàbia 1068
Valldemossa
Banyalbufar
Estellencs
Puigpunyent
Marratxí
Palma de Mallorca
PMI
Badia de Palma de Palma
S'Arenal
S'Estanyol
S'Estanyol
Palma Nova
Illetes
Cala Major
Calvià
Magaluf
Santa Ponça
Port d'Andratx
Andratx
Sant Elm
Sa Dragonera
C. des Llebeig
Santa Ponça
C. de Cala Figuera

Cabrera
I. des Conills
C. Blanc
Puerto de Cabrera
Cabrera de Cabrera
Pta. de n'Ensiola

ATLANTIC OCEAN

ISLAS CANARIAS
(Spain)

Gran Canaria

Pta. El Roque
Las Palmas
Arucas
Telde
Guía
Pta. Sardina
Pico de las Nieves 1949
Ingenio
Gando
Agaete
San Nicolás
Mogán
Bartolomé de Tirajana
Aguimes
San Agustín
Maspalomas
Pta. de la Aldea
Puerto Rico
Playa de Mogán
Arguineguín
Playa del Inglés
Maspalomas

Tenerife

Pta. de Teno
Pta. de Anaga
Punta del Hidalgo
La Laguna
Santa Cruz de Tenerife
TFN
Puerto de la Cruz
La Orotava
Candelaria
Icod
Pico de Teide 3718
Güímar
LAS CAÑADAS
Arico
Bajamar
Santiago del Teide
Guía de Isora
Granadilla de Abona
Playa de las Américas
Arona
El Médano
Los Cristianos
Pta. de la Rasca

Gomera
Pta. de los Organos
Vallehermoso
Agulo
Valle Gran Rey
Garajonay 1487
San Sebastián de la Gomera
Alojera
Santiago

1:1 800 000
0 10 20 30 40 50 60 km
0 10 20 30 40 miles
COPYRIGHT PHILIP'S

West from Greenwich
29
14
15
16
17
28

5

4

3

2

1

D

B

C

G

MAJORCA AND MINORCA
1:900 000
5 0 5 10 15 20 25 30 km
5 0 5 10 15 20 miles

9

ATLANTIC OCEAN

Madeira
(Portugal)

Pta. de São Lourenço
Pta. de São Jorge
Santana
Faial
São Roque
Machico
Santa Cruz
São Vicente 1320
Pico Ruivo 1861
FNC
Caniço
Funchal
Câmara de Lobos
Campanário
Ribeira Brava
Ponta do Sol
Porto Moniz
Pta. do Pargo
Calheta
Pta. da Cruz

MADEIRA
1:900 000
5 0 5 10 km
0 5 10 miles

2

West from Greenwich
17
33

3

Ibiza

C. d'Aubarca
Pta. Grosa
Tagomago
Santa Agnès
Es Canar
Sant Miguel
Santa Eulària
Sant Joan de Labritja
Sant Mateu
Sant Carles
Sant Rafel
Santa Gertrudis
Can Clavo
Can Creu des Riu
**Eivissa
(Ibiza)**
(Spain)
Sant Antoni de Portmany
Sant Josep
Eivissa
IBZ
Sa Canal
Sant Jordi
424
Sa Conillera
Es Vedrà
S'Espardell
S'Espalmador
Pta. des Pas
Sant Ferran
Es Caló
Pta. Rotja
Formentera
Sant Francesc de Formentera
Sa Savina
C. de Barbària
C. des Falcó
S'Espalmador
Pta. de sa Barbària

IBIZA
1:900 000
5 0 5 10 km
0 5 10 miles

7

8

East from Greenwich
39
1° 30'

B

La Palma
Pta. Cumplida
Barlovento
Roque de los Muchachos 2423
Santa Cruz de la Palma
SPC
El Pueblo
Los Llanos de Aridane
CALDERA DE TABURIENTE
Volcanes de Fuencaliente
Teneguía
Pta. Fuencaliente

Hierro
Garafía
Pta. Gorda
Pta. del Norte
Frontera
Valverde
Malpaso 1501
Pico de Tenerife 1417
Taibique
La Restinga
Pta. Orchilla

East from Greenwich
18
28

Projection: Lambert's Conformal Conic

m ft
3000 9000
2000 6000
1500 4500
1000 3000
600 1800
400 1200
200 600
100 300
0 0

m ft
4000 12000
3000 9000
1500 4500
1000 3000
600 1800
400 1200
200 600
0 0

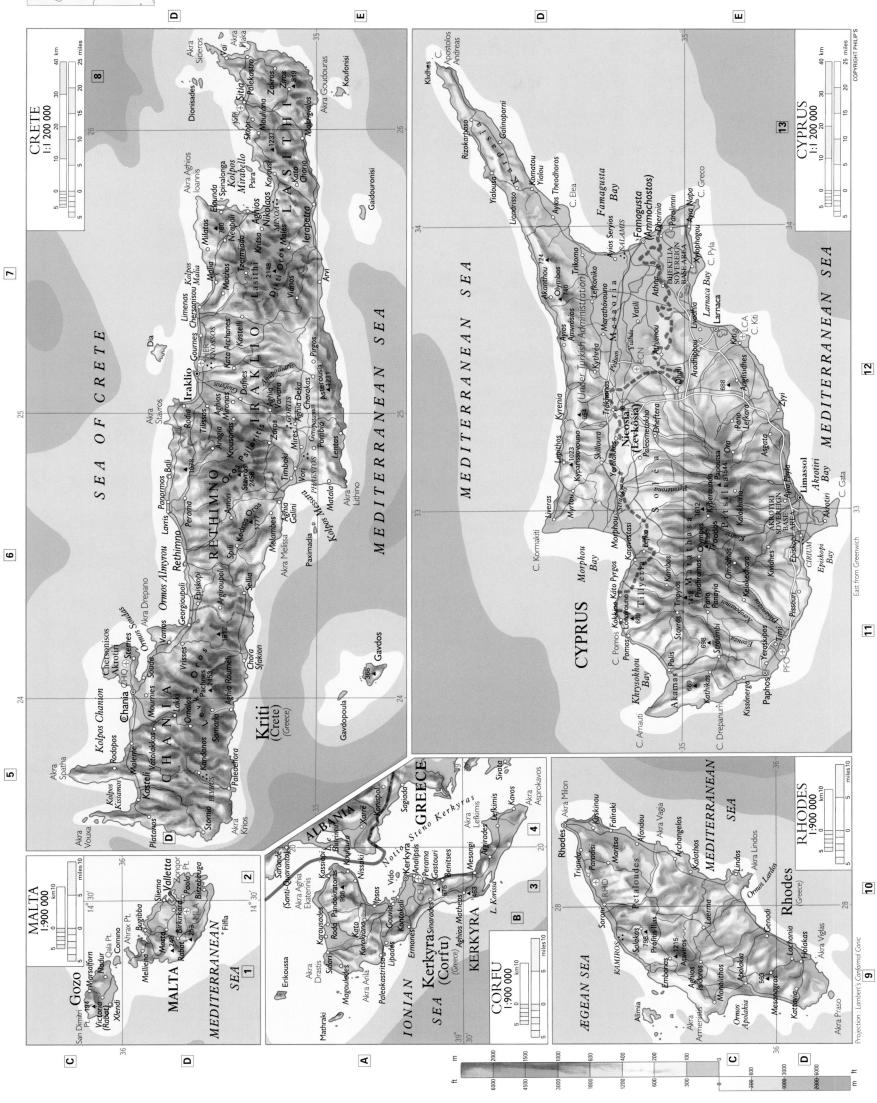

CRETE
1:1 200 000

40 km
25 miles
30
20
10
15
5
5

8

Akra
Sideros
Akra
Plaka

Vai
Palekastro
Sitia
Moulliana
Zakros
Zros
▲419

Dionisades
Skopi
1237

Kolpos
Akra Gaidouras

Akra Agios
Ioannis
Elounda
Spinalonga
Kolpos
Mirabello
Psira

L A S I T H I

Koufonisi

Milatos
760
Agios
Neapoli
Kritsa
Nikolaos
Kato
Chorio

Malia
Mochos
Tzermiado
Lasithi
Ierapetra

Chersonisou Malia
Dikti Oros Males
Limenas
2148

Arvi

HER
KNOSSOS
Kata Archanes
Anopodiaris

Gournes
Pirgos

Dia
Iraklio
Rodia
Agios
Mirona
Agia
Varvara
Asterousia
▲1231

SEA OF CRETE

Akra
Stavros
GORTIS
Agia
Deka

Dofnes
Grobounas
Pombia
Vori

Stavros
I R A K L I O
Zaros
Psiloritis
2456

Anogia
Kousounas

Tilissos

R E T H I M N O

Mires
PHESTOS
Lentas

Timboki

Panormos
Beli

Akra
Matala
Akra
Lithino

Kolpos Mesara

Perama
Melambes
Agia
Galini

Lavris
Kedros
1777
Oros

Paximadia

Rethimno
Spil
Amari
Oros

Georgioupoli
Argiroupoli
Sella

Episkopi

M E D I T E R R A N E A N   S E A

Ormos Almyrou
Akra Drepano

7

Kolpos Chanion

Chersonisos
Akrotiri
Stavros
Sternes
1612

Vamos

Souda

Mournies
Vrisses

C H A N I A
Levka Oros
2453

Chania
Laki

Ornalos
Kandanos

Akra
Spatha

Kasteli

Rodopos

Platanos
Stomio

Vatolakkos
Samaria
Agia Roumeli

Kolpos
Kissamos

Malerne

Akra
Vouxa

Akra
Krios

Chora
Sfakion

6

Gavdos

366

Kriti
(Crete)
(Greece)

Gavdopoula

Akra Praso

5

Gaidouronisi

MALTA
1:900 000

10 miles
5
km

2

San Dimitri
Pt.
194

GOZO

Victoria
(Rabat)
Xlendi

Marsalforn
Nadur
Qala Pt.

Melliena
Comino

Ahrax Pt.
Bugibba
Mosta
240
Mgarr
253
Rabat
MLA

Sliema
Valletta
Paola
Birzebbuga
Zonqor

MALTA

14° 30′

Filfla

M E D I T E R R A N E A N   S E A

1

GREECE

ALBANIA

Corfu
39°

Sagiada
Sivota

Kerkyra
Komispol
Akra
Lefkimis
Kavos

Santi-Quaranta
(Sarandë)

Agia Aghia
Ekaterinis

Kassiopi
Koufaki

Xarra
Steno Kerkyras

Notio

Akra
Asprokavos

Vido
Perama
Gastouri
Benitses

Kerkyra
Analipsis

Rodd
996

Koulouri
Kato
Korakiana
Gouvia
Kontokoli

Pandokratoras
676

1463

CFU

Mesongi

Kastelani
Mathews
Agios

Paleokastritsa

Ermones
Sinarades

Lipades

Magoulades

Akra
Arila

Akra
Drastis

Sidari

Karousades

Erikoussa

Mathraki

L. Korissa

KERKYRA

Kerkyra
(Corfu)
(Greece)

CORFU
1:900 000

10 miles
5
km

3

4

I O N I A N   S E A

CYPRUS
1:1 200 000

40 km
25 miles
30
20
10
15
5
5

COPYRIGHT PHILIPS

13

Klidhes C.

Apostolos
Andreas

Rizokarpaso

Galinoporni

Yialousa
Komatou
Yialou

Liandrisso
C. Elea

Ayios Theodhoros

Akanthou
724
Trikomo
Lefkoniko

Ayios Seryios

Olymbos
740

Athna

Famagusta
Bay

Famagusta
(Ammochostos)

DHEKELIA
SOVEREIGN
BASE AREA

Dherinia
Paralimni

C. Greco
Ayia Napa

Marathovouno

Kythrea

Xylophagou
C. Pyla

Vatili

ECN
Petoms

Larnaca Bay

Lefkara

M E S A O R I A

Yialia

Larnaca

Aradhippou

Kyrenia

Lapithos
1023
Kyparissovouno

Ayios

Skilloura
Paleometokho

Dhali

LCA
C. Kiti

Nicosia
(Levkosia)
554

Athienou

688

Myrtou

Yerolakkos

Kokkinotrimithia
(Under Turkish Administration)
Peristerona

C. Kormakiti

Morphou
Bay

Lapithos

Kato Pyrgos

Morphou

Kalokhorio

Kophinou
Zyyi

M E D I T E R R A N E A N   S E A

12

Liveras

Solea

Pedhieos

Asgata

C. Pomos
Kokkina
Pomos

Troodos
1951

Kalokhorio

Kakopetria
1612

Karavostasi
Lefka

Tillyria

Pano
Panayia

M a l a t h i a s
1418
Olympos

Peristerona

Kokkinorotsos

Papoutsa
1544

AKROTIRI
SOVEREIGN
BASE AREA

Limassol

CYPRUS

Kambos

Tripylos
660

Stavros
Podhirlavnos

Pano
Platres
Omodhos
Kilani

Pano
Lefkara

Kalokedhara

Akrotiri
Bay

Akrotiri

C. Gata

Khrysokhou
Bay

Akamas

Polis
659

Stroumbi
698

Kathikas
689

Yeroskipos

Timi

Kyperounda

Kyvides

Episkopi
Bay

CIRIUM
Episkopi
Passouri

C. Arnauti

C. Pomos

Paphos

PFO

Lemba

C. Drepanum

11

M E D I T E R R A N E A N   S E A

East from Greenwich

RHODES
1:900 000

10 miles
5
km

10

Rhodes
Akra Milon

Trianda
Koskinou

Paradisi
Faliraki

Soroni
Maritsa

RHO
Afandou

Petaloudes
Archangelos

Kalathos

KAMIROS
Akra Vagia

Soldaks
Akra Vigla

Profitis Ilias
798

1215

Kamiros

Akra Lindos

Lindos

Lerma

Ormos Lindos

Embonas

Genadi

Agios
Isidoros
563

Apolakia
Lachania

Monolithos
Holakas

Alimia

Kattavia

Mesanagros

Ormos
Apolakia

Akra
Armenisti

Akra Praso

Rhodes
(Greece)

9

A E G E A N   S E A

M E D I T E R R A N E A N
S E A

Projection: Lambert's Conformal Conic

m ft
6000 2000
4500 1500
3000 1000
1800 600
1200 400
600   200
300   100
0   0
200   600
1600 3000
2000 6000
ft m

1:44 400 000

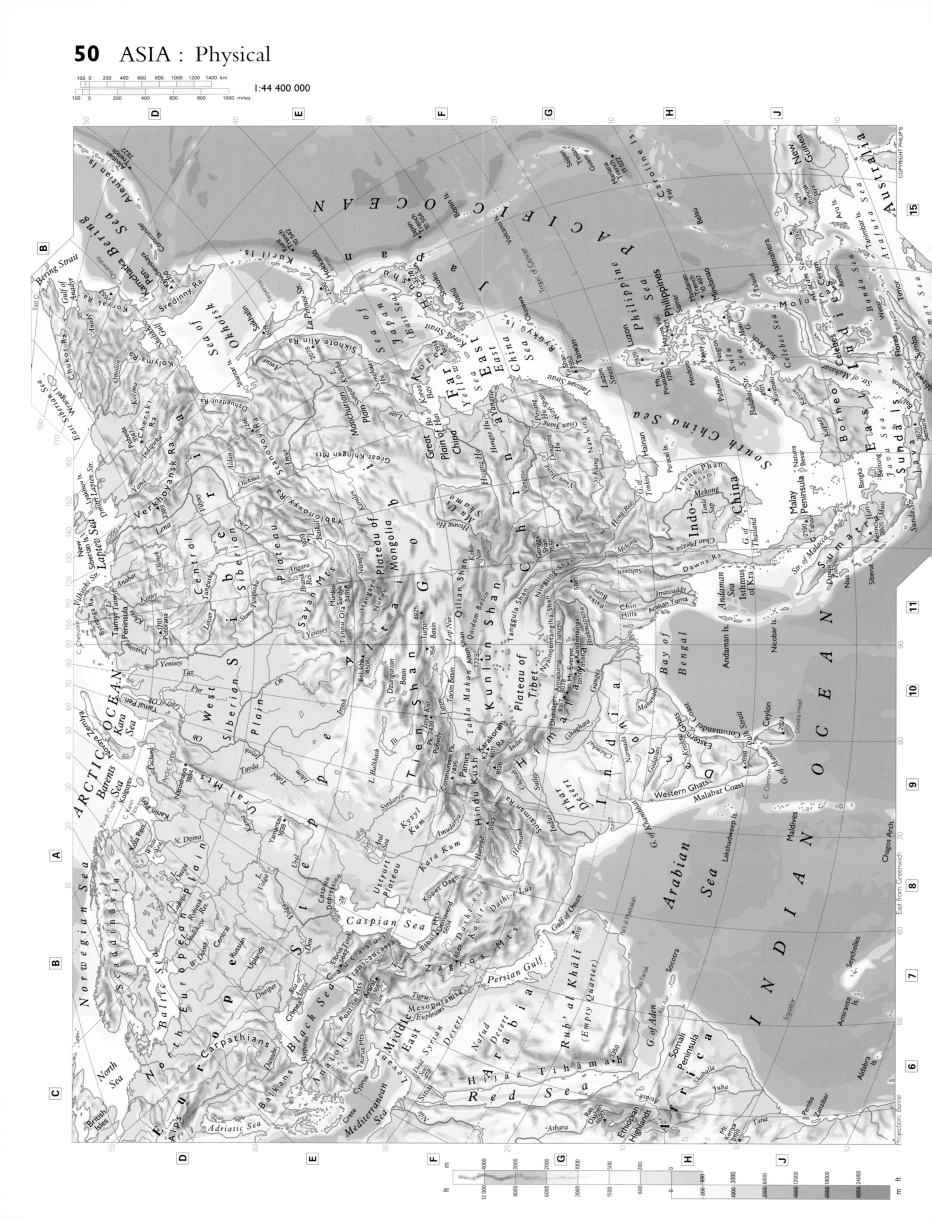

COPYRIGHT PHILIPS

Projection: Bonne

1:44 400 000

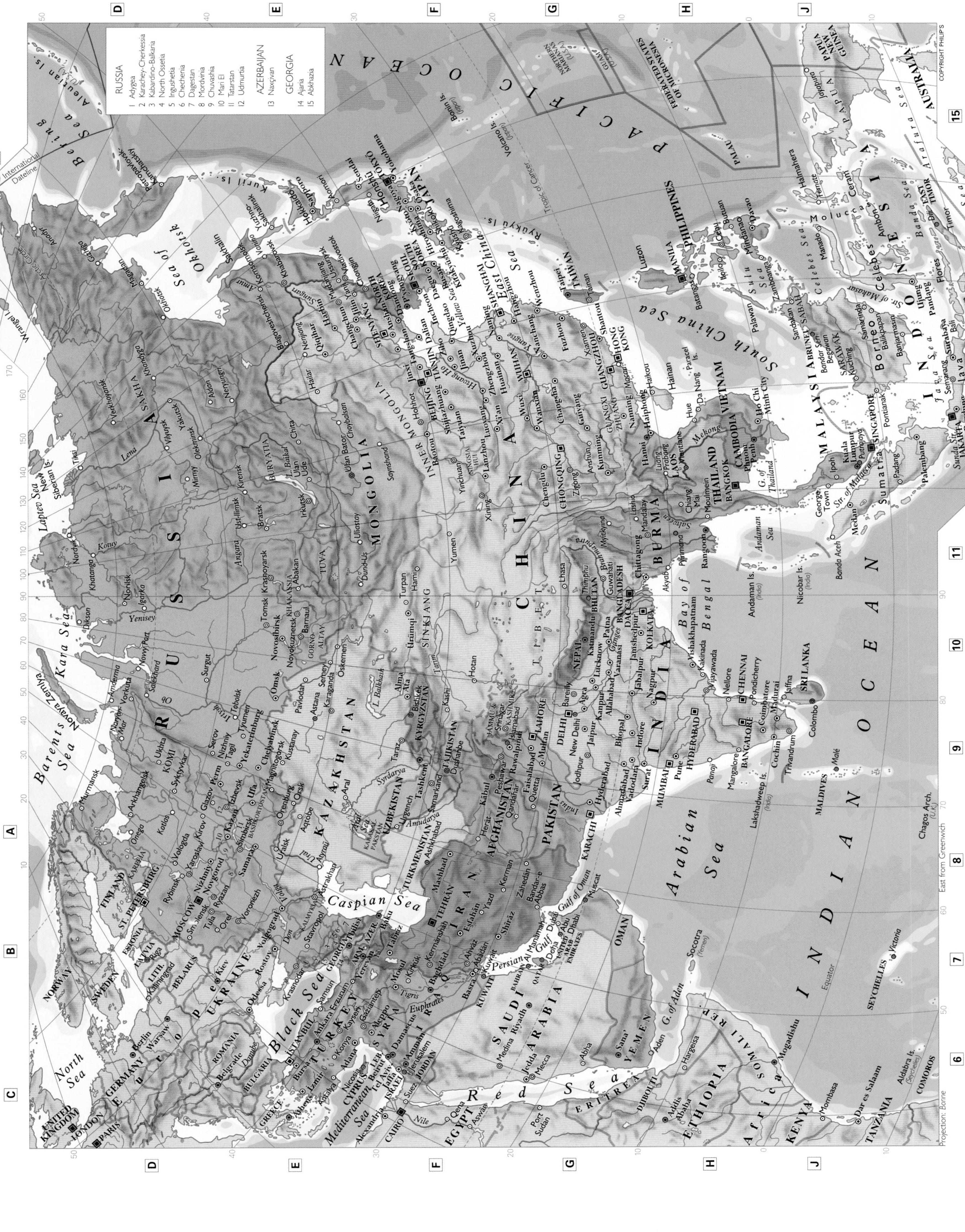

100 0 200 400 600 800 1000 1200 1400 km
100 0 200 400 600 800 1000 miles

RUSSIA
1 Adygea
2 Karachey-Cherkessia
3 Kabardino-Balkaria
4 North Ossetia
5 Ingushetia
6 Chechenia
7 Dagestan
8 Mordvinia
9 Chuvashia
10 Mari El
11 Tatarstan
12 Udmurtia

AZERBAIJAN
13 Naxçivan

GEORGIA
14 Ajaria
15 Abkhazia

PACIFIC OCEAN

INDIAN OCEAN

R U S S I A

C H I N A

MONGOLIA

INDIA

KAZAKHSTAN

SAUDI ARABIA

IRAN

INDONESIA

AUSTRALIA

Projection: Bonne

1:17 800 000

RUSSIA
1 Adygea
2 Karachey-Cherkessia
3 Kabardino-Balkaria
4 North Ossetia
5 Ingushetia
6 Chechenia
7 Dagestan
8 Mordvinia
9 Chuvashia
10 Mari El
11 Tatarstan
12 Udmurtia
13 Khakassia

AZERBAIJAN
14 Naxçivan

GEORGIA	UKRAINE
15 Ajaria	17 Crimea
16 Abkhazia	

Projection: Conical Orthomorphic with two standard parallels

East from Greenwich

50 0 25 50 75 100 125 150 175 km
50 0 25 50 75 100 125 miles
1:4 400 000

SEA OF OKHOTSK

Sakhalin (Russia)

La Perouse Strait (Sōya-Kaikyō)

Ostrov Moneron (Russia)

HOKKAIDŌ

SAPPORO

TOHOKU

SENDAI

Honshū

CHŪBU

RUSSIA

CHINA

HEILONG-JIANG

JILIN

Lake Khanka

Vladivostok

Ussuriysk

Nakhodka

NORTH KOREA

SEA OF JAPAN (EAST SEA)

Yamato Rise

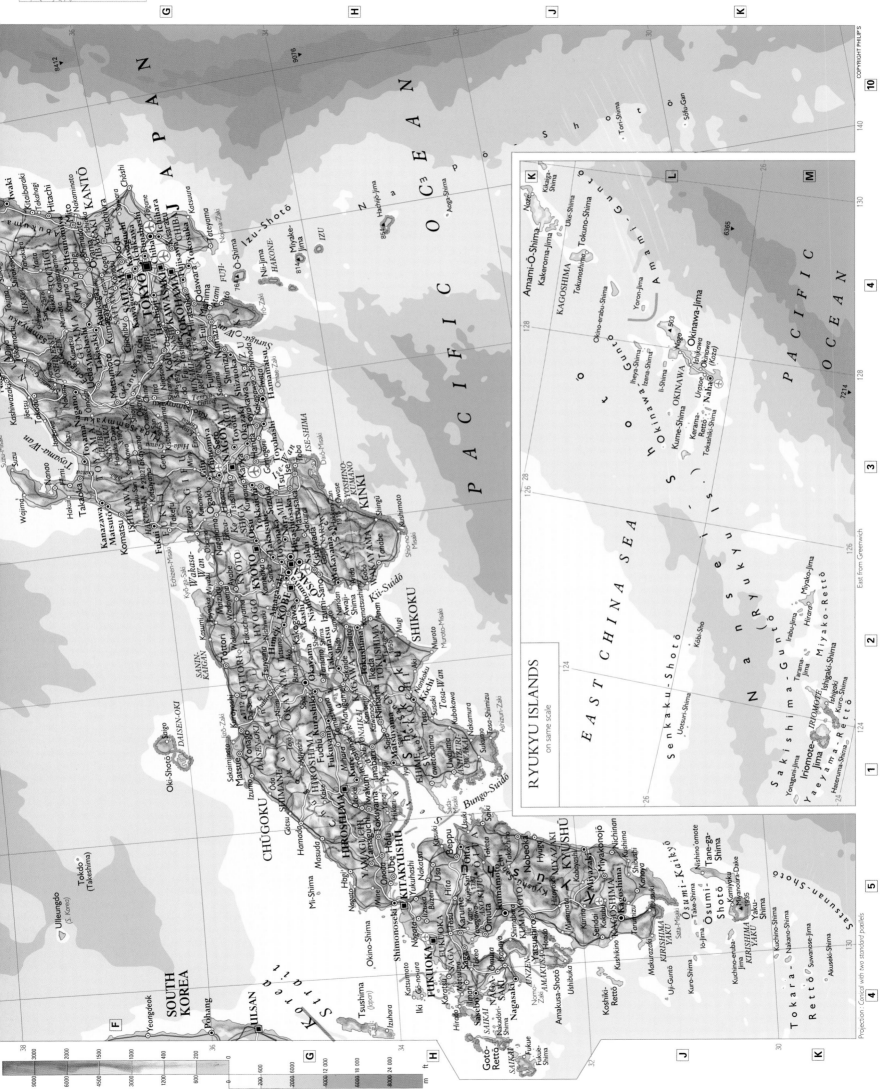

G   H   J   K

K   L   M

10

▼8412

▼9076

J   A   P   A   N

KANTŌ

TOKYO

YOKOHAMA

KAWASAKI

CHIBA

IZU

FUJI

HAKONE

Izu-Shotō

▼814 Miyake-Jima

76 Ō-Shima

Nii-Jima

Hachijō-Jima

▼85

Aoga-Shima

P A C I F I C   O C E A N

Tori-Shima

Sōfu-Gan

▼ō

s h

t

140

RYUKYU ISLANDS
on same scale

Amami-Ō-Shima

Kakeroma-Jima

Uke-Shima

Tokuno-Shima

Kikaiga-Shima

KAGOSHIMA

Okino-erabu-Shima

Yoron-Jima

Iheya-Shima

Izena-Shima

Ii-Shima ▼503

Nago

OKINAWA

Okinawa-Jima

Urasoe Ishikawa

Kume-Jima

Kerama-Rettō

Tokashiki-Shima

Naha

Okinawa (Koza)

E A S T   C H I N A   S E A

Senkaku-Shotō

Uotsuri-Shima

Kōbi-Shō

Sakishima-Gunto

Tarama-Jima

Irabu-Jima

Miyako-Jima

Miyako-Rettō

IRIOMOTE

Iriomote-Jima

Ishigaki-Shima

Kuro-Shima

Yaeyama-Rettō

Yonaguni-Jima

Haterumajima

N a n s e i   I s l s   (R Y U K Y U)

N   a   n   s   e   i   g   u   n   t   ō

O k i n a w a - G u n t ō

A m a m i - G u n t ō

▼6365

▼7214

P A C I F I C   O C E A N

K   4

K   3

K   2

K   1

L   4

M   4

East from Greenwich

124   126   128   130

SOUTH KOREA

Yeongdeok

Pohang

ULSAN

Ulleungdo (S. Korea)

Tokdo (Takeshima)

K o r e a   S t r a i t

Tsushima (Japan)

Iki

Izuhara

FUKUOKA

KITAKYUSHU

SAGA

OITA

NAGASAKI

KUMAMOTO

MIYAZAKI

KAGOSHIMA

K Y U S H U

UNZEN

ASO

KIRISHIMA-YAKU

Amakusa-Shotō

Gotō-Rettō

Fukue-Shima

SAIKAI

Nagasaki

Sasebo

Hirado

Saiki

Ōsumi-Shotō

Ōsumi-Kaikyō

Tane-ga-Shima

Yaku-Shima

Tanegashima

Tokara-Rettō

Suwanose-Jima

Akuseki-Shima

Nakano-Shima

Kuchino-Shima

Kuchino-erabu-Jima

Io-Jima

Kuro-Shima

Uji-Guntō

Nishino-omote

Kōshiki-Rettō

Satsunan-Shotō

CHŪGOKU

SHIKOKU

HIROSHIMA

OKAYAMA

KŌCHI

TOKUSHIMA

EHIME

KAGAWA

Matsuyama

Tosa-Wan

Bungo-Suidō

Kii-Suidō

OSAKA

KYOTO

KŌBE

HYOGO

NAGOYA

GIFU

NAGANO

KINKI

CHŪBU

KANAZAWA

FUKUI

WAKAYAMA

MIE

SHIGA

NARA

ISE-SHIMA

Ise-Wan

Suruga S

DAISEN-OKI

Oki-Shotō

SANIN-KAIGAN

SAN'IN

SHIMANE

TOTTORI

Matsue

Tottori

Tsu

30   32   34   36

G   5

H   4

J   5

K   5

F   G   H

Projection: Conical with two standard parallels

9000 6000 4500 3000 2000 1500 1000 400 200 0

ft 24 000 18 000 12 000 6000 2000 600 200 0 m

ft 9000 6000 4500 3000 2000 1500 1000 400 200 0

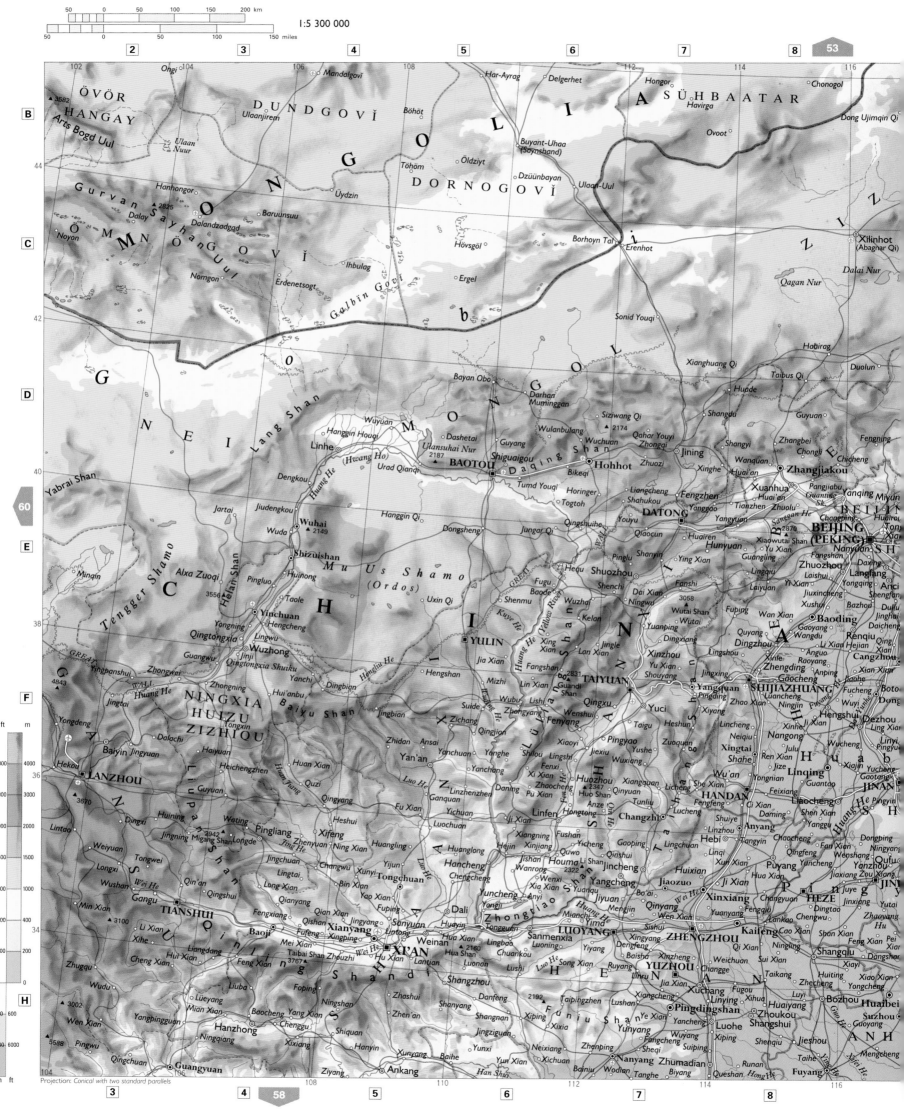

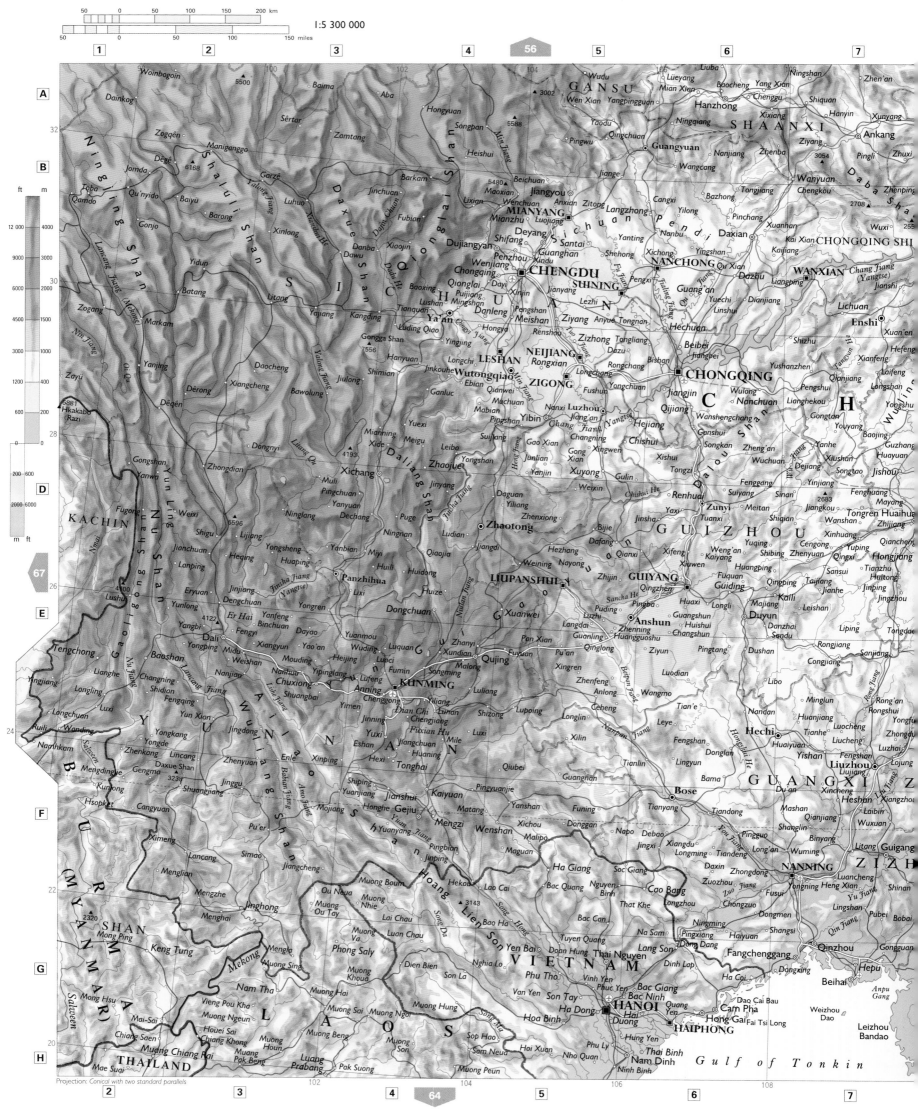

Projection: Conical with two standard parallels

1:5 300 000

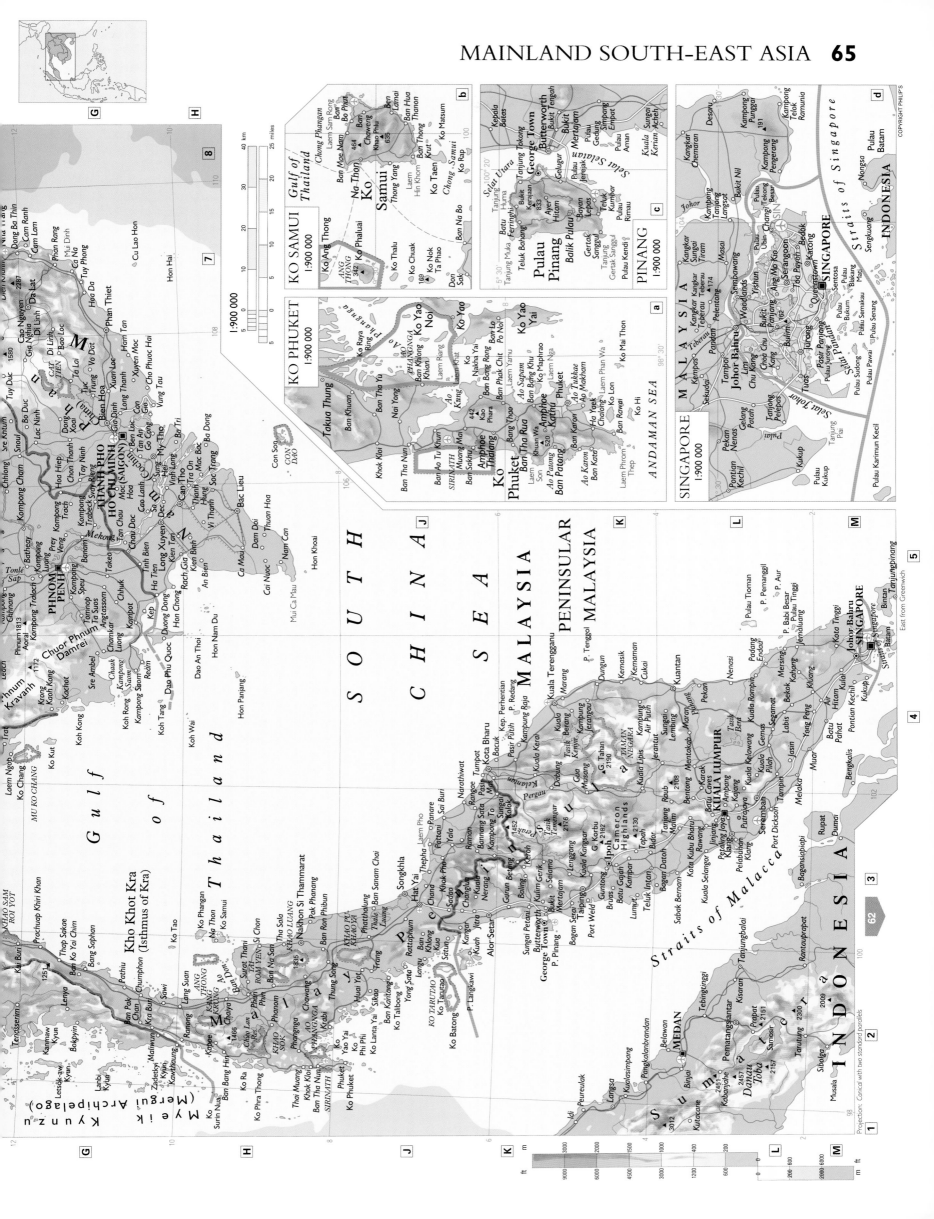

G H 8 7

b

KO SAMUI
1:900 000

Gulf of
Thailand

Chong Phangan
Ban Mae Nam
Ban Bo Phut
Ban
Chaweng
Ko
Samui
Ban Hua
Thanon
Ban Thong
Na Thon
Thong Yang
Laem
Hin Khom
Ko Taen
Chong Samui
Ko Rap
Ko Matsum

KO SAMUI
1:900 000

Ko Ang Thong
ANG
THONG
Ko Phaluai
Ko Thalu
Ko Chuak
Ko Nok
Ta Phao
Don
Sak

a

KO PHUKET
1:900 000

Takua Thung
Ko Raya
Yai
Ko Yao
Noi
Ko Yao
Yai
AO
PHANGNGA
Ban Khlong
Khian
Laem Riang
Ko Maphrao
Laem Nga
Ban Thao
Ko Yao
SIRINATH
Son
Ban Bang Rong
Ban Lo
Po Nol
Ban Tha Rua
Amphoe
Kathu
Ban Tha Nun
Ban A Tu Khun
Nai Yong
Ban Sakhu
Ban Bang Khu
Ao Bang Thao
Ao Supam
Ban Phok Chit
Ko
Phuket
Phara
520
442
Kao
Amphoe
Thalang
Ban Khian
Nakha Yai
Ko Maikhao
Laem
Phan Wa
Ko Mai Thon
Muang Mai
Ban Karon
Ao Makham
Ko Lon
Ao Patong
Laem
Chalong
Ban Rawai
Ko Hi
Ko Karon
Ban Kata
Ha Yaek
Ao Tukbae
Laem Phrom
Thep

ANDAMAN SEA

George Town
Butterworth
Bukit Tengah
Kepala
Batas
Simpang
Empat
Pulau Pinang
Balik Pulau
833
Bukit
Kerajan
Ayer
Hitam
Bayan
Lepas
Teluk
Kumbar
Pulau
Rimau
Batu
Ferringhi
Tanjung
Huma
Tanjung Muka
Teluk Bahang
Gertak
Sanggul
Tanjung
Gertak Sanggul

Pulau
Pinang
1:900 000

c

PINANG
1:900 000

Kuala
Kerian
Sungai
Acheh
Gedung
Gelugar
Pulau
Jerejak
Selat Utara

d

Desaru
Kampong
Punggai
Kampong
Telok
Kampong
Ramunia
191
Kampong
Pengerang
Pulau
Batam
Nongsa

INDONESIA

Straits of Singapore

SINGAPORE
1:900 000

MALAYSIA
Kangkar
Chemaran
Kangkar
Sungai
Tiram
Masai
Johor Bahru
Kampong
Tanjung
Langsat
Pulau
Ubin
Pulau
Tekong Besar
Changi
Ang Mo Kio
Bedok
Katong
SINGAPORE
Serangoon
Yishun
Woodlands
Sembawang
Toa Payoh
Pasir Panjang
Jurong
Queenstown
Sentosa
Pulau
Blakang
Mati
174
162
Bukit
Panjang
Bulim
Choa Chu
Kang
Tampoi
Kempas
Sekudai
Pontian
Kechil
Pulau
Kukup
Tanjong
Pelepas
Tanjung
Piai
Pulau
Pawai
Pulau
Senang
Pulau
Semakau
Pulau
Sudong
Selat Johor
Johor

SINGAPORE
Singapore
Johor Bahru
Straits
Bintan
Batam

East from Greenwich

G H

J
H

Ko Phuket
SIRINATH
Phuket
Ko Yao Yai
Phi Phi
Ko Yao Noi
PHANGNGA
Phangnga
Krabi
KHAO
SOK
1466
Ban Tha Nun
Thai Muang
Ko Lanta Yai
Ko Jum
Sikao
Trang
Huai Yot
Thung Song
Ban Na San
Phunphin
Surat Thani
Ban Don
TAI
ROM YEN
Chaiya
Phanom
1835
AO BAN
DON
KRUNG
ANG
THONG
Ko Samui
Ko Phangan
Ko Tao
Bang Saphan
Chumphon
Lang Suan
Chaiya
Lamphu
Phato

G

KHAO SAM
ROI YOT
Prachuap Khiri Khan
Kui Buri
Thap Sakae
Bang Saphan
1251
Ban Ko Yai Chim
Ban Bang Hin
Kra Buri
Ban Pak
Chan
Pathiu
Ranong
Kapoe
Takua Pa
La-un
Kraburi
Khuraburi
Khao Lak

M
Myeik
(Mergui Archipelago)
Kyunzu
Lenya
Tenasserim
Lenya
Kanmaw
Kyun
Letsok-aw
Kyun
Lanbi
Kyun
Zadetkyi
Kyun
Maliwun
Bokpyin
Kawthaung
Surin Nua
Ko Ra
Ko Phra Thong
Ko Surin

SOUTH

CHINA

SEA

MALAYSIA

PENINSULAR MALAYSIA

Kota Bharu
Pasir Mas
Tumpat
Sungai Kolok
Tak Bai
Tumpat
Kep. Perhentian
P. Redang
Kuala Terengganu
Marang
Dungun
Kemasik
Kemaman
Cukai
Kuantan
Pekan
Kuala Rompin
Endau
Mersing
P. Tenggol
P. Tioman
P. Pemanggil
P. Aur
P. Babi Besar
Pulau Tinggi
SINGAPORE
Johor Bahru
Kota Tinggi
Jemaluang
Kluang
Batu Pahat
Yong Peng
Muar
Melaka
Segamat
Labis
Gemas
Tampin
Seremban
Port Dickson
KUALA LUMPUR
Kajang
Klang
Petaling Jaya
Putrajaya
Ampang
Batu Caves
2183
Genting
Raub
Bentong
2108
TAMAN
NEGARA
2190
G. Tahan
Kuala Lipis
Jerantut
Kuala Krai
Gua
Musang
2176
Temangan
Grik
G. Korbu
2183
Cameron
Highlands
2130
Ipoh
Kuala Kangsar
Taiping
Lumut
Teluk Intan
Bidor
Tapah
Kampar
Gopeng
Sungkai
Kuala Lumpur
Selama
Bagan Datoh
Sabak Bernam
Kuala Selangor
Teluk Intan
Tanjong
Malim
Gurun
Kulim Gerik
Kroh
Betong
Kampong Raman
1452
Yala
Pattani
Bannang Sata
Raman
Kolok
Sungai
Padang Sara
Baling
Kuala Nerang
Changlun
Kangar
Jitra
Alor Setar
Kedah
Kuala
Kangar
Sadao
Hat Yai
Songkhla
Pattani
Thepha
Khok Pho
Chana
Sai Buri
Narathiwat
Panare
Rangae

KHAO LUANG
1835
KHAO PU
KHAO YA
Phatthalung
Ban Sanam Chai
Thale
Luang
Pak Phanang
Nakhon Si Thammarat
Ron Phibun
Phatthalung
Trang
Kantang
Ban Kantang
Ko Talibong
Ko Batong
KO TARUTAO
Ko Tarutao
P. Langkawi
Kuah
Ban Khlong
Satun
Kua
Gulf

of

Thailand

Ko Samui
Ko Phangan
Ko Tao

Straits of Malacca

INDONESIA

Sumatera
Danau
Toba
3012
2457
3009
2151
2151
2300
Medan
Musala
Sibolga
Kabanjahe
Kutacane
Belawan
Binjai
Pangkalanbrandan
Tebingtinggi
Pematangsiantar
Kisaran
Tanjungbalai
Rantauprapat
Bagansiapiapi
Dumai
Rupat
Bengkalis
Pekanbaru
Bukittinggi
Langsa
Kualasimpang
Idi
Peureulak
Kuala Tadu

J 6
K 5
L 4
M 3
2
1

m ft
9000
4500
3000
1500
600
200
0
0
200
2000
6000
ft m

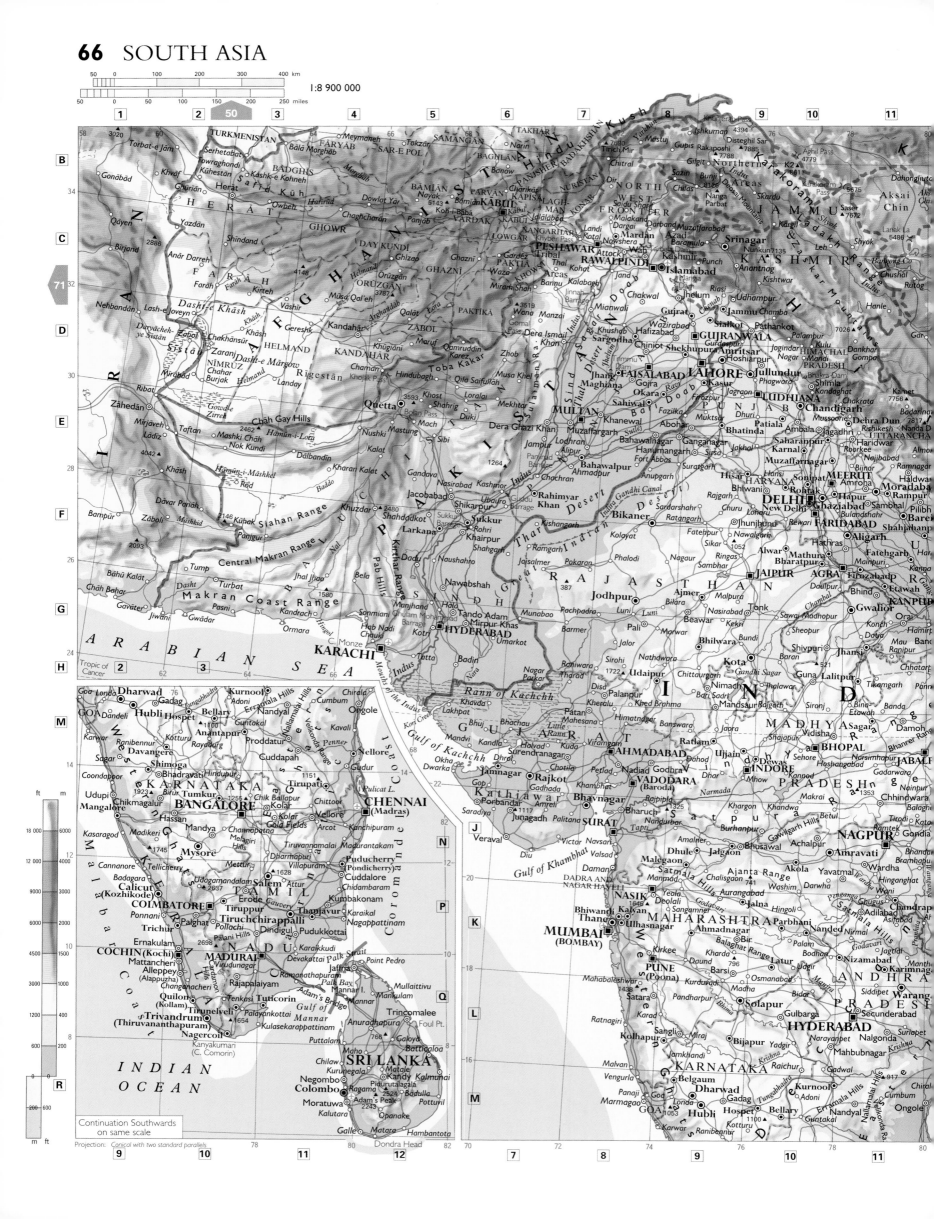

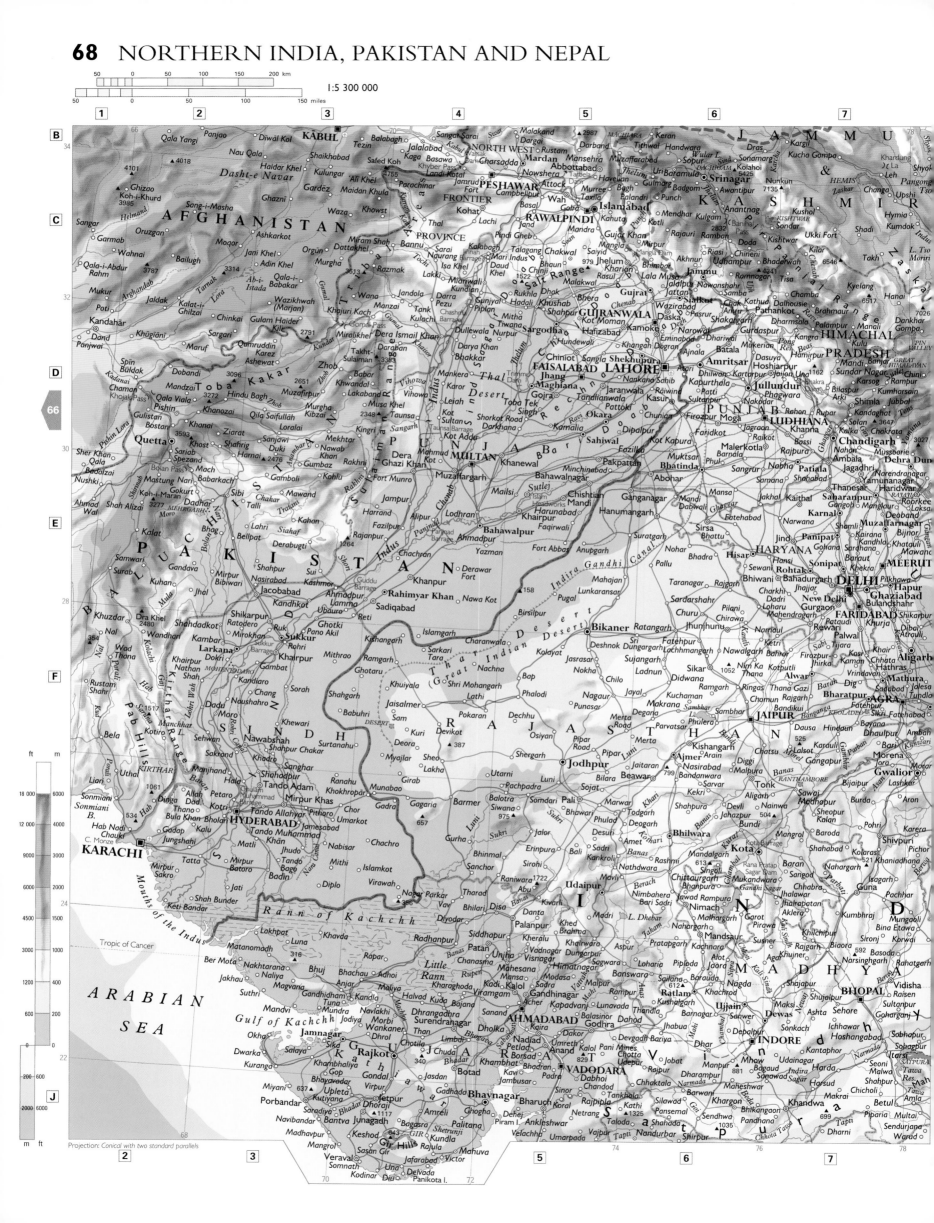

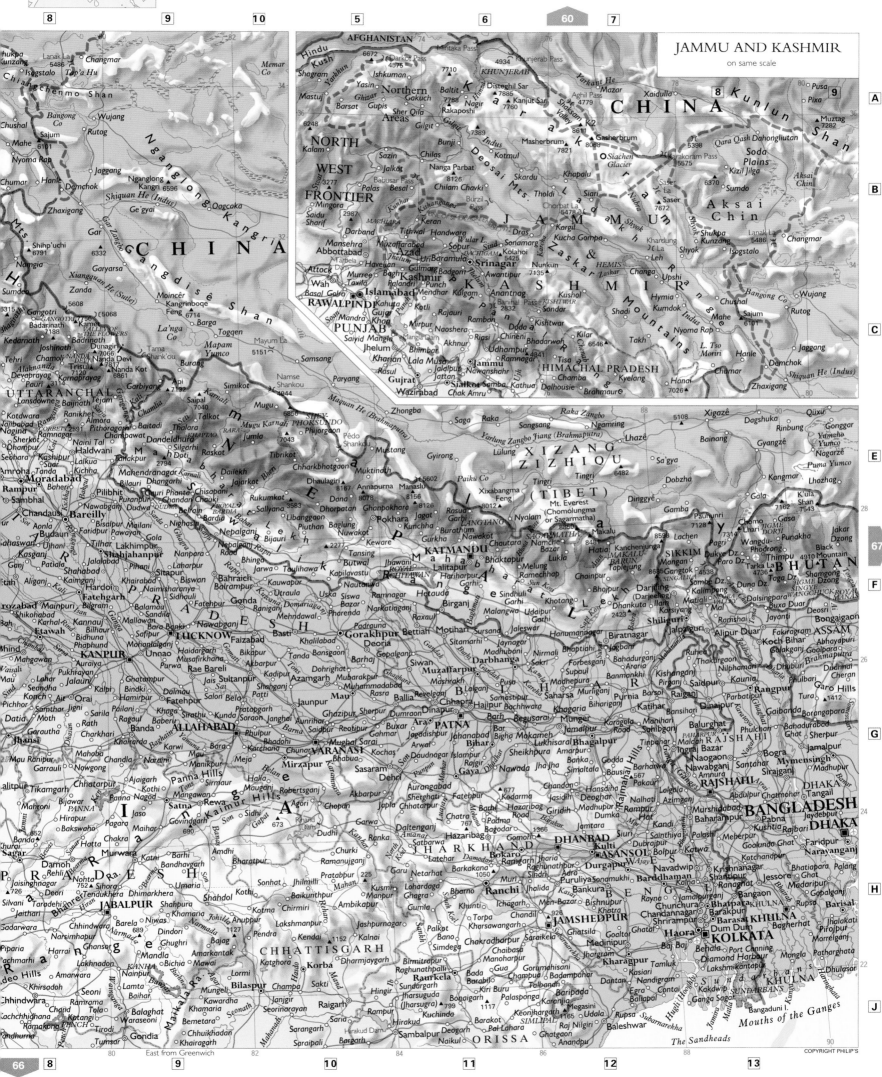

JAMMU AND KASHMIR
on same scale

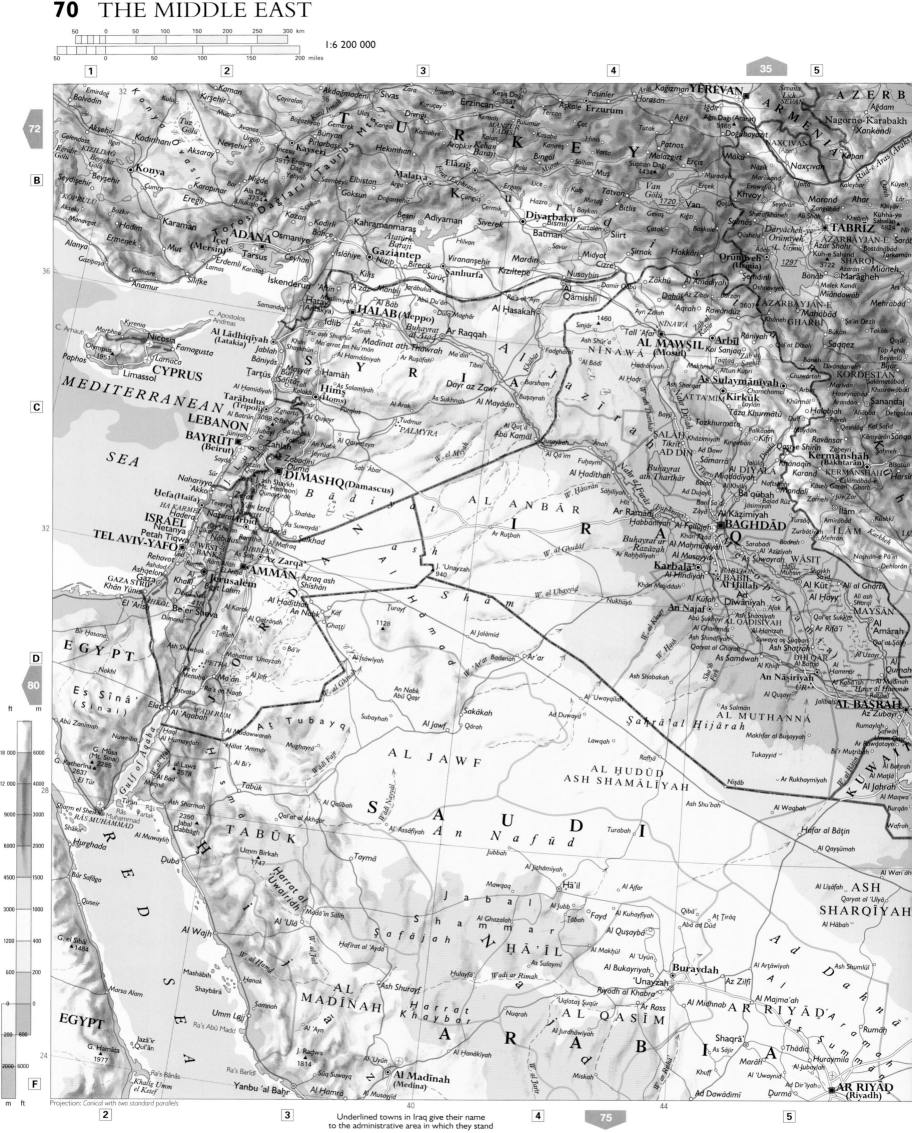

50 0   100 150 200 250   300 km

1:6 200 000

50   50   100   150   200 miles

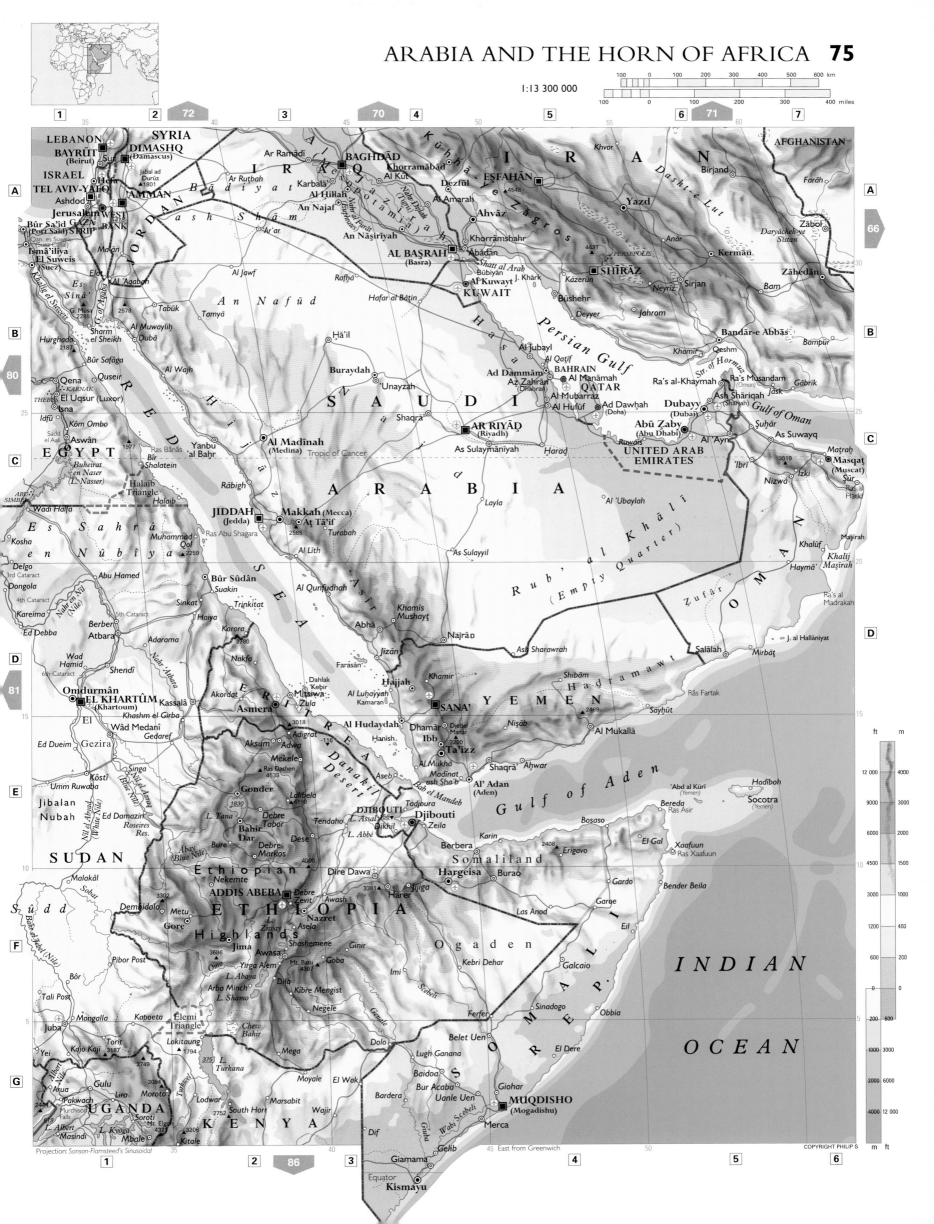

1:37 300 000

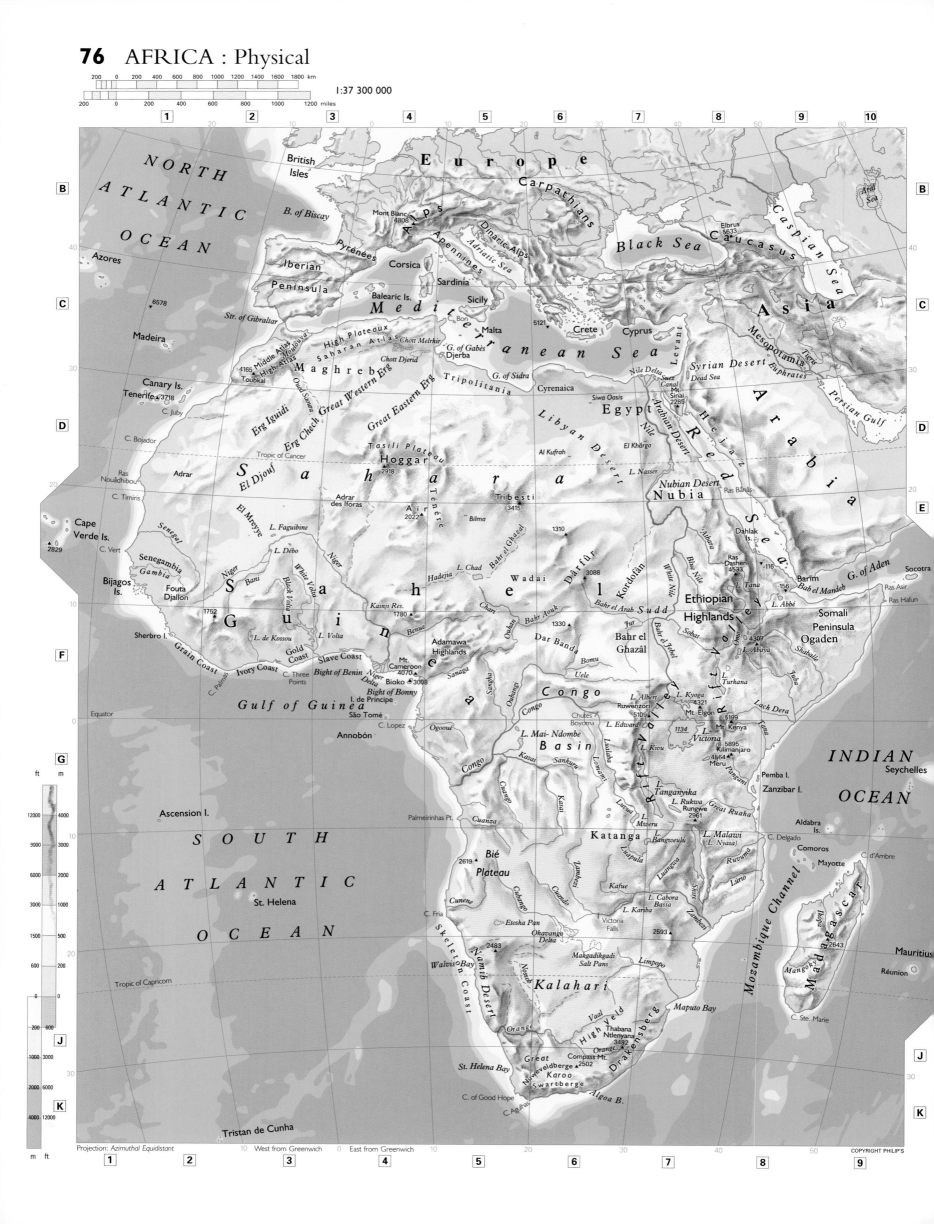

NORTH ATLANTIC OCEAN

Europe

British Isles

B. of Biscay

Azores

Iberian Peninsula

Pyrénées

Mont Blanc 4808

Alps

Apennines

Dinaric Alps

Adriatic Sea

Carpathians

Black Sea

Caucasus

Elbrus 5633

Caspian Sea

Aral Sea

Asia

Madeira

6578

Str. of Gibraltar

Balearic Is.

Corsica

Sardinia

Sicily

C. Bon

Malta

5121

Crete

Cyprus

Mediterranean Sea

Levant

Mesopotamia

Tigris

Euphrates

Canary Is.
Tenerife 3718

C. Juby

C. Bojador

Middle Atlas
High Atlas
Moulouya
4165
Toubkal

High Plateaux
Saharan Atlas

Maghreb

Chott Melrhir

Chott Djerid

G. of Gabès
Djerba

G. of Sidra

Tripolitania

Cyrenaica

Siwa Oasis

Syrian Desert

Dead Sea

Nile Delta
Suez Canal
Mt. Sinai 2285

Egypt

Arabian Desert

Red Sea

Hejaz

Arabia

Persian Gulf

Ras Nouâdhibou

C. Timiris

Adrar

El Djouf

Sahara

Erg Iguidi
Oued Saoura
Erg Chech
Great Western Erg

Great Eastern Erg

Tasili Plateau

Hoggar
2918

Adrar des Iforas

Tropic of Cancer

Libyan Desert

Al Kufrah

El Khârga

L. Nasser

Ras Banâs

Nubia

Nubian Desert

Cape Verde Is.
2829

C. Vert

El Mreyye

Senegal

L. Faguibine

Niger

Aïr
2022

Ténéré

Bilma

Tibesti
3415

1310

Dahlak Is.

Ras Dashen 4533

–116

Barim
Bab el Mandeb

G. of Aden

Socotra

Ras Asir

Bijagos Is.

Senegambia

Gambia

Fouta Djallon

L. Débo

Bani

White Volta

Niger

Hadejia

L. Chad

Bahr el Ghazal

Wadai

Dârfûr
3088

Kordofan

White Nile

Blue Nile

L. Tana

Albara

Ethiopian Highlands

Ras Hafun

Somali Peninsula
Ogaden

Sherbro I.

1752

Grain Coast

L. de Kossou

Black Volta

Kainji Res.
1780

L. Volta

Gold Coast

Ivory Coast

C. Palmas

C. Three Points

Slave Coast

Bight of Benin

Benue

Adamawa Highlands

Chari

Bahr el Arab

Bahr Aouk
1330

Ouham

Dar Banda

Bomu

Bahr el Ghazâl

Jur

Bahr el Jebel

Sobat

Sudd

Omo

4307

L. Abaya

Shabelle

Juba

Lach Dera

Guinea

Mt. Cameroon 4070

Bioko 3008

Bight of Bonny

I. de Principe

São Tomé

C. Lopez

Niger Delta

Gulf of Guinea

Sanaga

Sangha

Ogooué

Ubangi

Congo

Uele

Congo Basin

L. Mai-Ndombe

Kasai

Lualaba

Lomami

L. Edward

L. Kivu

L. Albert
Ruwenzori
5109

L. Kyoga

Mt. Elgon
4321

1134

L. Victoria

Mt. Kenya
5199

5895
Kilimanjaro
4564
Meru

Ituri

Tana

L. Turkana

Equator

Annobón

INDIAN OCEAN

Seychelles

Ascension I.

SOUTH ATLANTIC OCEAN

St. Helena

Palmeirinhas Pt.

Cuanza

Kwango

Cuango

Kasai

Sankuru

Congo

Katanga

L. Mweru

L. Bangweulu

L. Tanganyika

L. Rukwa
Rungwe 2961

Great Ruaha

Pemba I.

Zanzibar I.

Luapula

Luangwa

Lúrio

Ruvuma

C. Delgado

Comoros

Mayotte

C. d'Ambre

Aldabra Is.

10

Bié Plateau
2619

Kafue

Zambezi

Cubango

Cuito

Cuando

L. Malawi
(L. Nyasa)

Shire

Cunene

C. Fria

Etosha Pan

Okavango Delta

Makgadikgadi Salt Pans

Victoria Falls

L. Cabora Bassa

L. Kariba

Zambezi
2593

Mtwirikwi

Thaba Tseka

Madagascar

Tsiafajavona
2643

Mangoky

Mauritius

Réunion

Tropic of Capricorn

20

Walvis Bay

Namib Desert

Nosob

2483

Kalahari

Makgadikgadi Salt Pans

Limpopo

Maputo Bay

Mozambique Channel

C. Ste. Marie

Skeleton Coast

Orange

Vaal

High Veld

Thabana Ntlenyana 3482

Orange

Great Karoo

Nuweveldberge

Compass Mt. 2502

Drakensberg

Algoa B.

St. Helena Bay

Swartberge

C. of Good Hope

C. Agulhas

Tristan de Cunha

ft   m
12000 4000
9000   3000
6000   2000
3000   1000
1500   500
600   200
0   0
200   600
1000   3000
2000   6000
4000   12000
m   ft

1:37 300 000

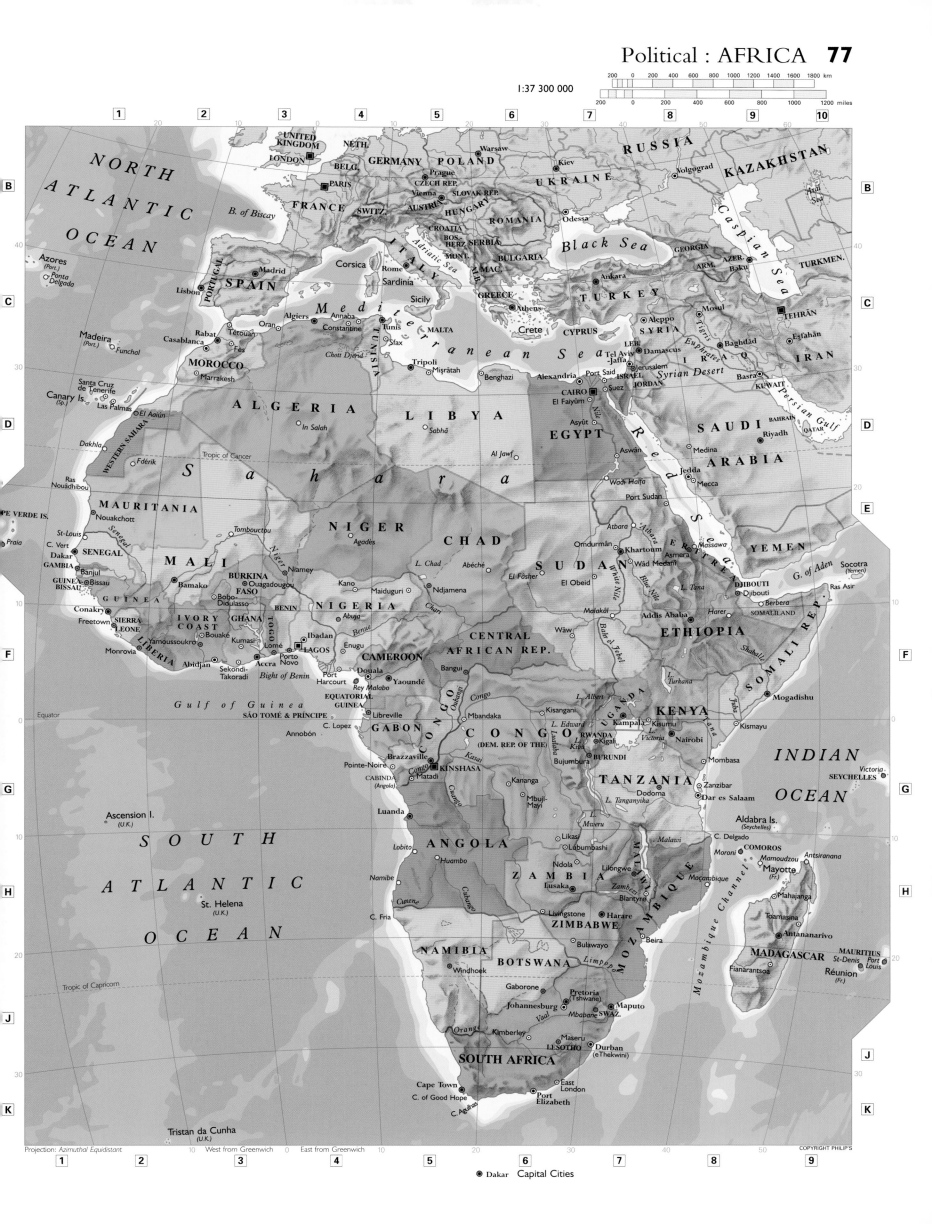

● Dakar   Capital Cities

Projection: Azimuthal Equidistant

West from Greenwich East from Greenwich

COPYRIGHT PHILIP'S

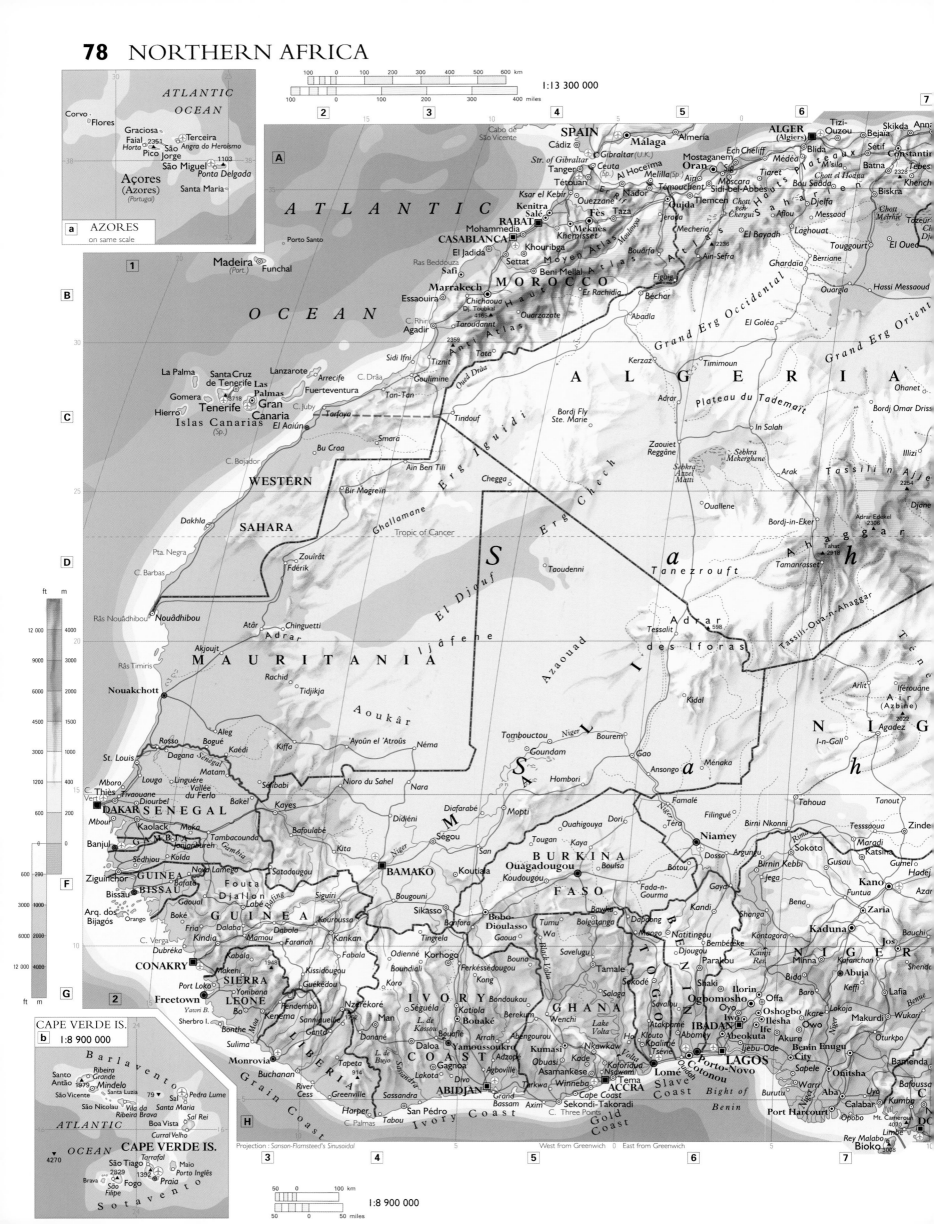

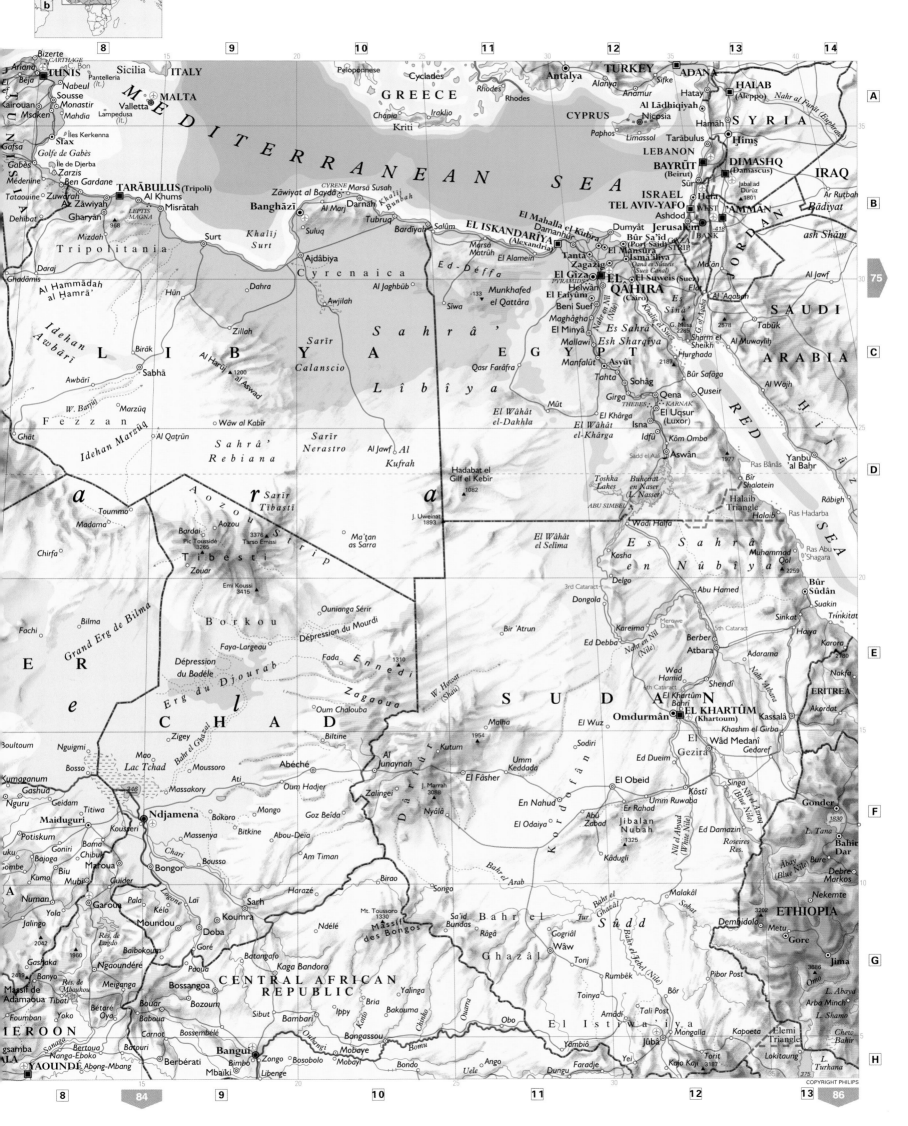

1:7 100 000

50 0 50 100 150 200 250 300 km
50 0 50 100 150 200 miles

THE NILE DELTA
1:3 600 000

MEDITERRANEAN SEA

Bûr Saʿid (Port Said)
Dumyât
El Manzala
El Mansûra
Ismâʿîlîya
El Suweis (Suez)
EL QÂHIRA (Cairo)
El Gîza
Imbâbâ
EL ISKANDARÎYA (Alexandria)
Rashîd (Rosetta)
Damanhûr
Kafr el Dauwâr
Tanta
El Mahalla el Kubra
Shibîn el Kôm
Zagazig
Benha
Shubrâ el Kheima
Helwân
El Faiyûm
Beni Suef

SAUDI ARABIA

Tropic of Cancer

Makkah (Mecca)
Al Madînah (Medina)
JIDDAH (Jedda)

Bûr Sûdân (Port Sudan)

RED SEA
BAHR EL AHMAR

HALAIB TRIANGLE

Buheirat en Naser (Lake Nasser)

Aswân

Es Sahrâ en Nûbîya (Nubian Desert)

AN NÎL

EL WÂHÂT EL KHÂRGA

Es Sahrâ el Gharbîya (Western Desert)

Munkafad el Qattâra (Qattâra Depression)

Ed-Deffa (Libyan Plateau)

E G Y P T

L i b y a

S a h r â

SHAMÂL

ESH SHAMÂLÎYA

L I B Y A

JORDAN
ISRAEL
AMMÂN
Jerusalem (Al Quds)
TEL AVIV-YÂFÔ
GAZA STRIP
Gaza
Sinai
ES Sînâ

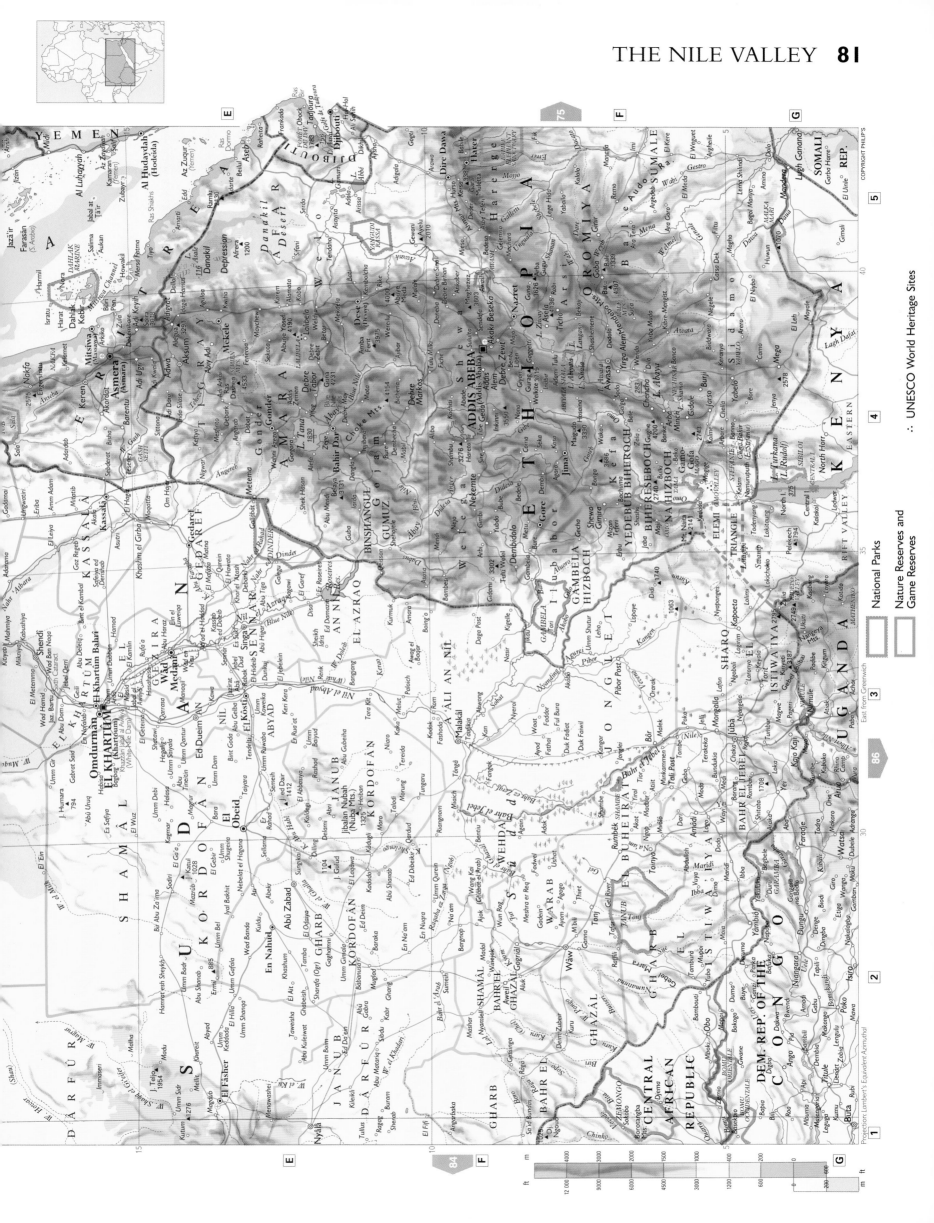

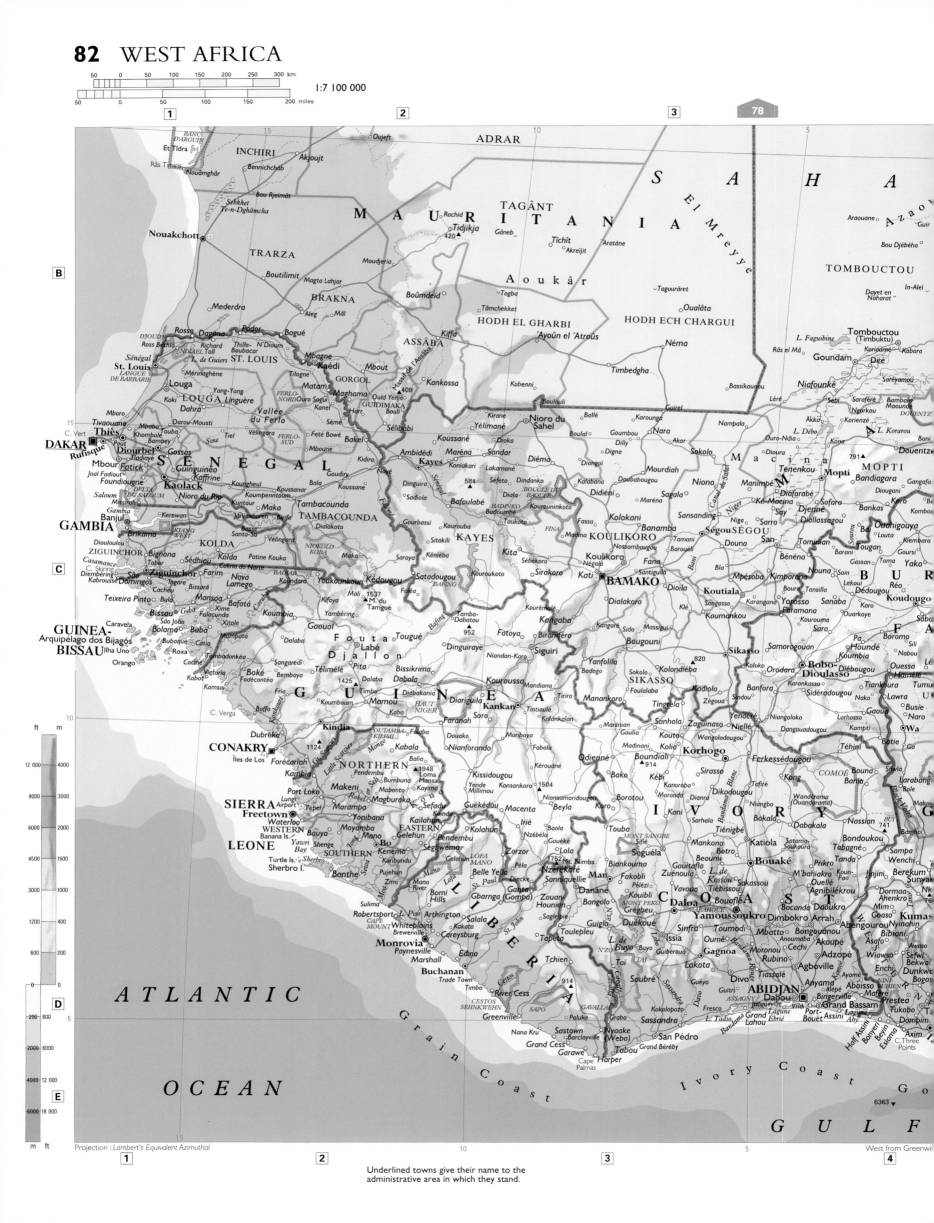

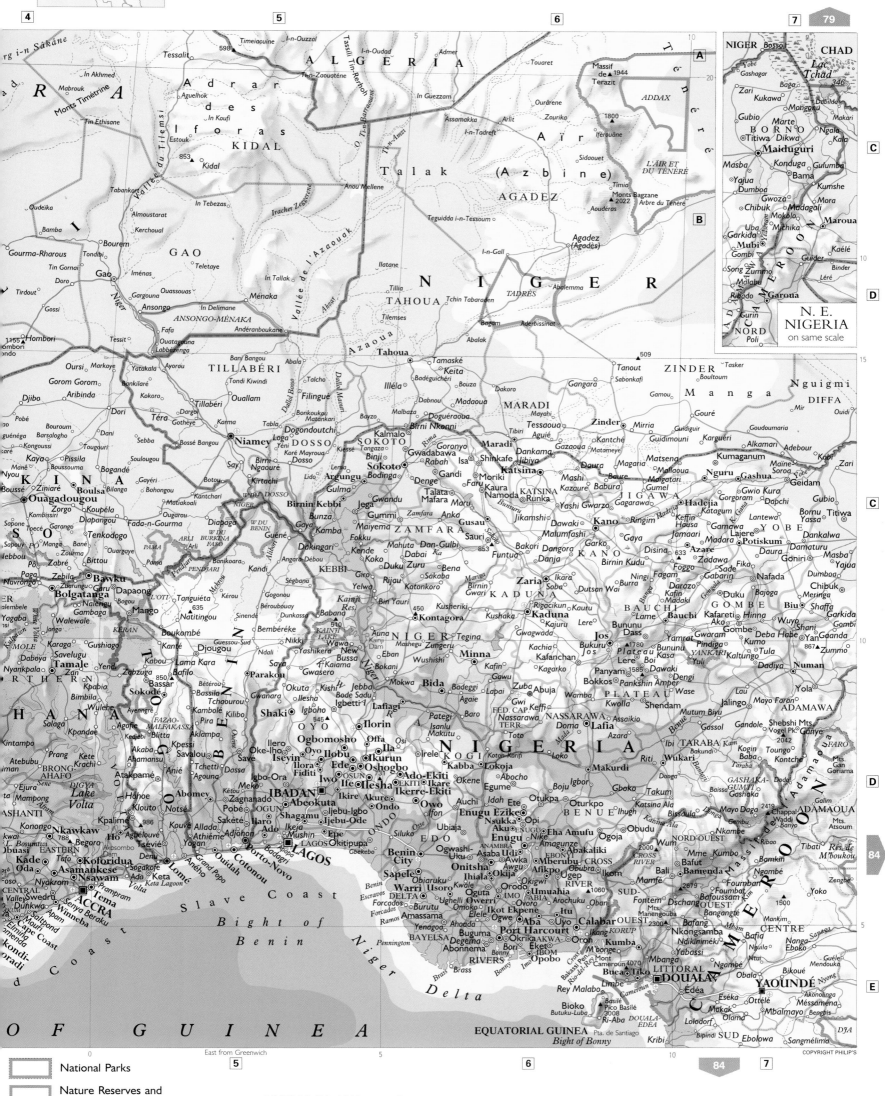

National Parks

Nature Reserves and Game Reserves

∴ UNESCO World Heritage Sites

East from Greenwich

COPYRIGHT PHILIP'S

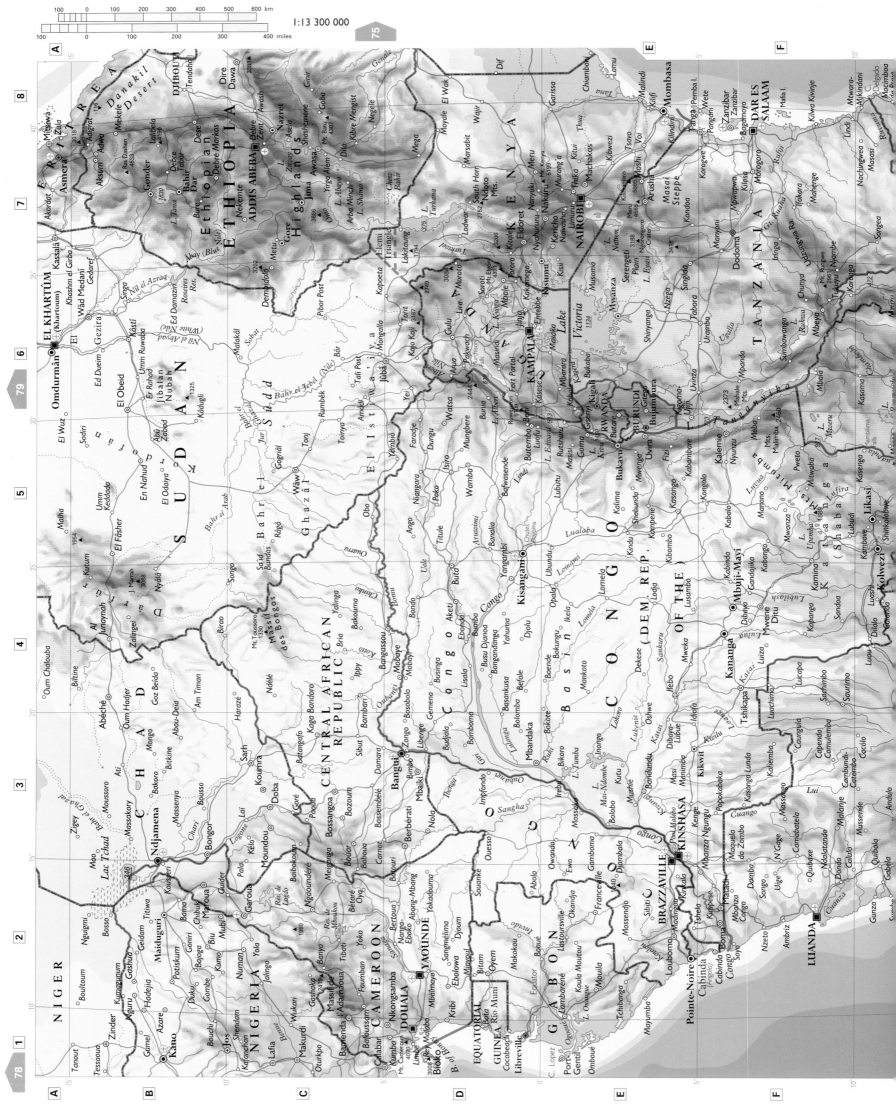

1:13 300 000

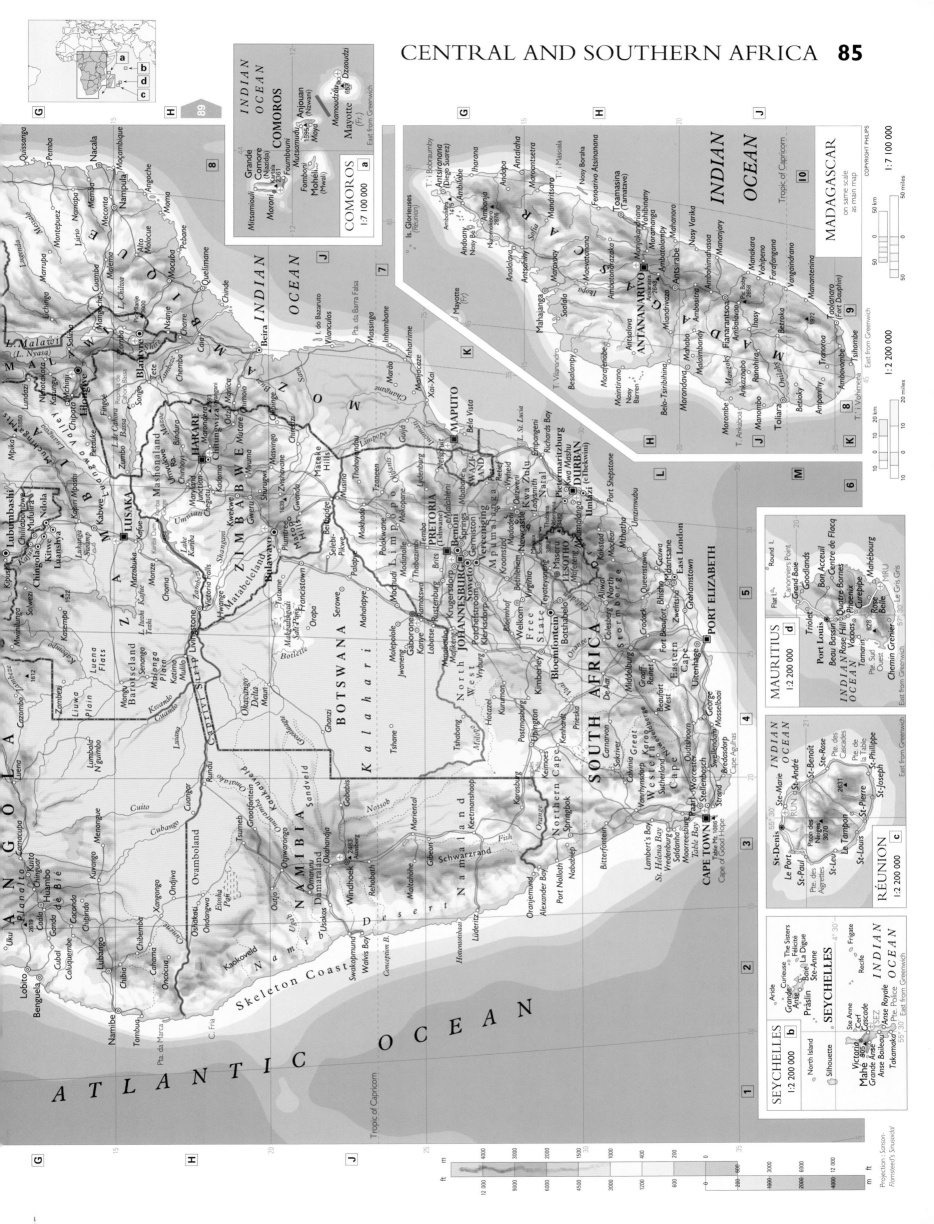

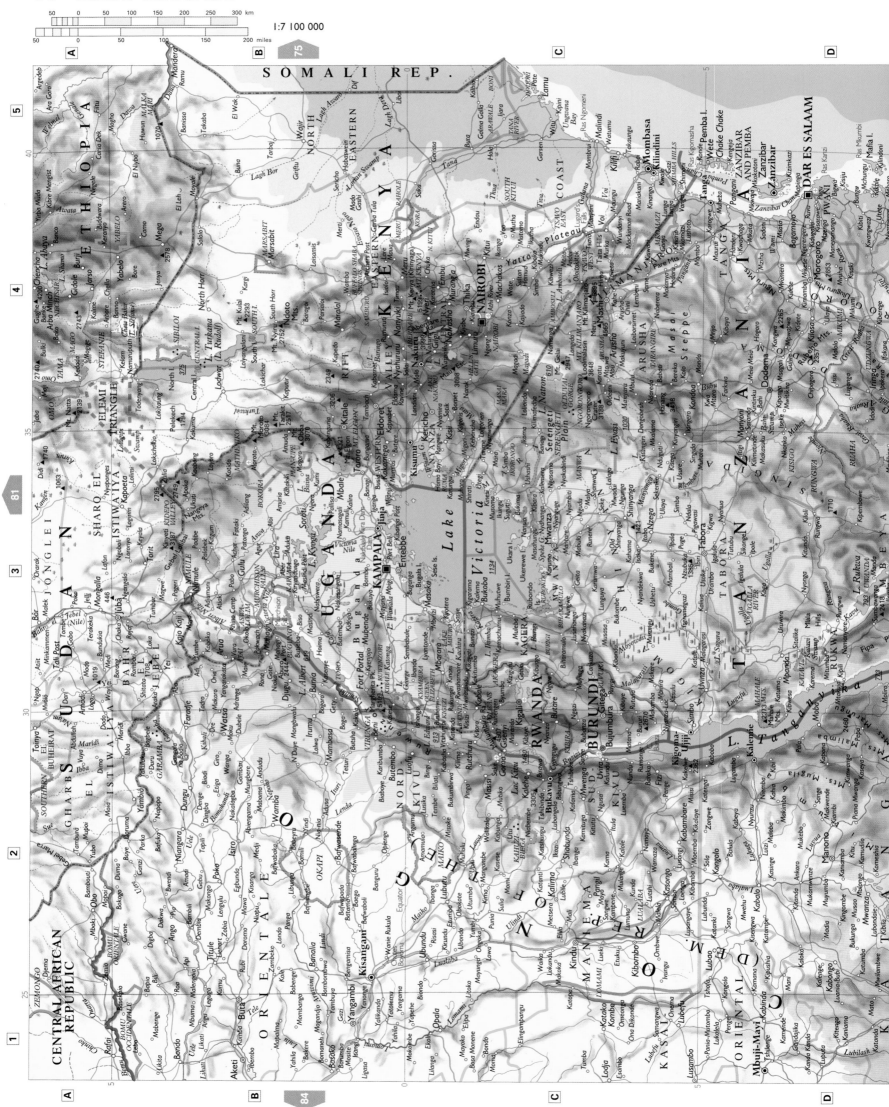

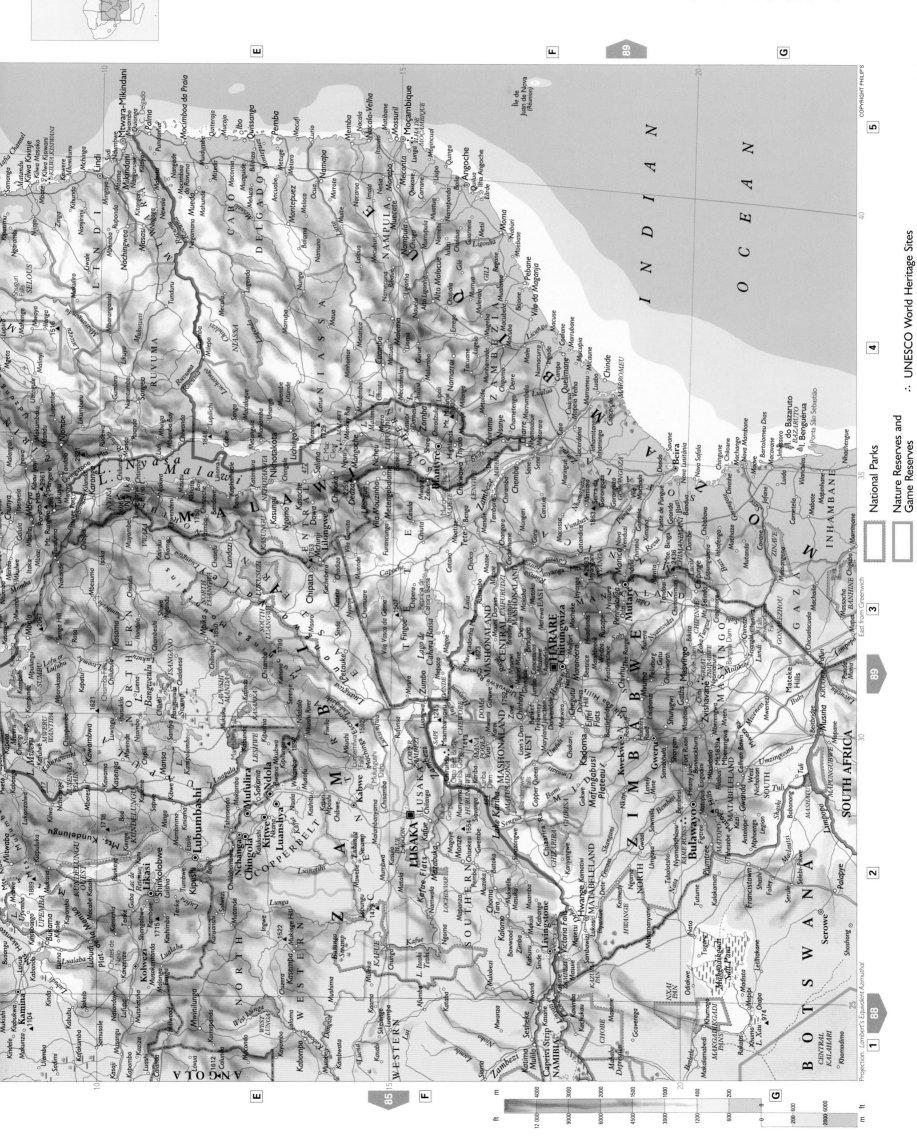

National Parks

Nature Reserves and
Game Reserves

∴ UNESCO World Heritage Sites

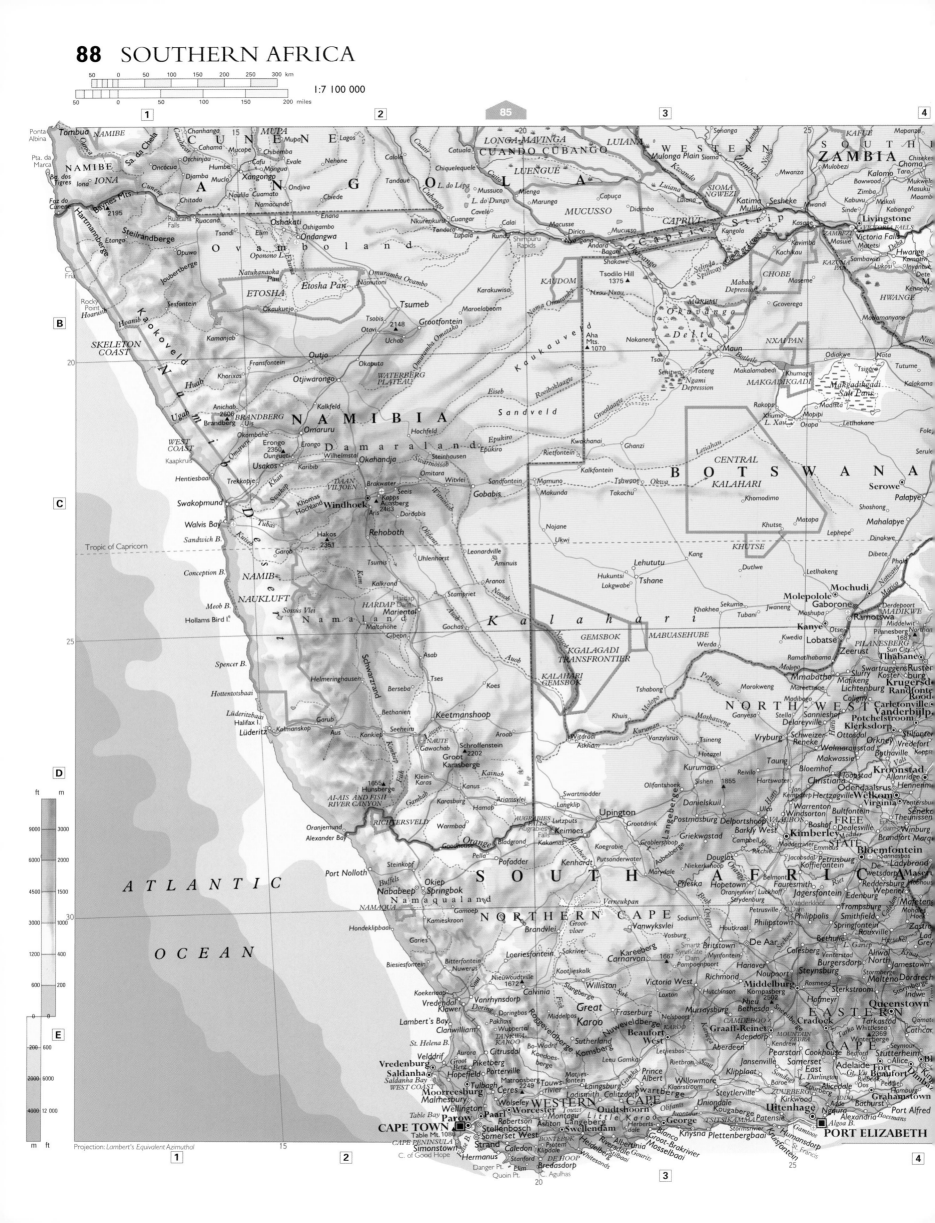

50 0 50 100 150 200 250 300 km

1:7 100 000

50 0 50 100 150 200 miles

1   **2**   85   **3**   **4**

Ponta Albina
Pta. da Marca
Tombua NAMIBE
Bq. dos Tigres
Iona IONA

NAMIBE

Rocky Point
Hoarusib

SKELETON COAST

A N G O L A

C U N E N E

MUPA

CUANDO CUBANGO

LONGA-MAVINGA

LUIANA

WESTERN

SOUTH

ZAMBIA

KAFUE

Livingstone
VICTORIA FALLS
Victoria Falls
ZAMBEZI

CAPRIVI Strip

B

NAMIBIA

ETOSHA

Etosha Pan

Ovamboland

Tsumeb

Grootfontein

KAUDOM

Tsodilo Hill

CHOBE

HWANGE

OKavango Delta

Maun

NXAI PAN

20

MAKGADIKGADI

Makgadikgadi Salt Pans

C

Swakopmund

Walvis Bay

Sandwich B.

Windhoek

Rehoboth

BOTSWANA

CENTRAL KALAHARI

Serowe
Palapye

Mahalapye

Tropic of Capricorn

NAMIB

NAUKLUFT

Namaland

HARDAP Dam
Mariental

Kalahari

KHUTSE

Molepolole
Mochudi
Gaborone
MADIKWE
Ramotswa
Kanye
Lobatse
Zeerust
PILANESBERG
Sun City

25

Lüderitz

Keetmanshoop

GEMSBOK
KGALAGADI TRANSFRONTIER
KALAHARI GEMSBOK

NORTH-WEST

Mmabatho
Mafikeng
Lichtenburg
Klerksdorp

Carletonville
Vanderbijlp
Randfont
Roods

D

Oranjemund
Alexander Bay

AI-AIS AND FISH RIVER CANYON

RICHTERSVELD

Upington

Kuruman

Vryburg

Kimberley

Bloemfontein

FREE STATE

Welkom
Virginia

Kroonstad
Allanridge
Hennen

Winbur

Port Nolloth

SOUTH AFRICA

E

ATLANTIC

OCEAN

Nababeep
Okiep
Springbok
Namaqualand

NAMAQUA

NORTHERN CAPE

De Aar

Colesberg

Bethulie

30

Calvinia

Victoria West

Richmond

Hanover

Noupoort

Middelburg

Steynsburg

Burgersdorp

Aliwal North

Jamestown

Queenstown

Great Karoo

Beaufort West

Graaff-Reinet
Cradock

EASTERN CAPE

Vredenburg
Saldanha

CAPE TOWN

WESTERN CAPE

Worcester

Oudtshoorn

Little Karoo

George

Mossel Bay

PORT ELIZABETH

Algoa B.

CAPE PENINSULA
Table Mt. 1086
CAPE OF GOOD HOPE
C. of Good Hope
C. Agulhas

ft m

9000 3000

6000 2000

4500 1500

3000 1000

400

1200

600

200

0

200 600

2000 6000

4000 12 000

m ft

Projection: Lambert's Equivalent Azimuthal

National Parks

Nature Reserves and
Game Reserves

∴ UNESCO World Heritage Sites

MADAGASCAR

on same scale

INDIAN

OCEAN

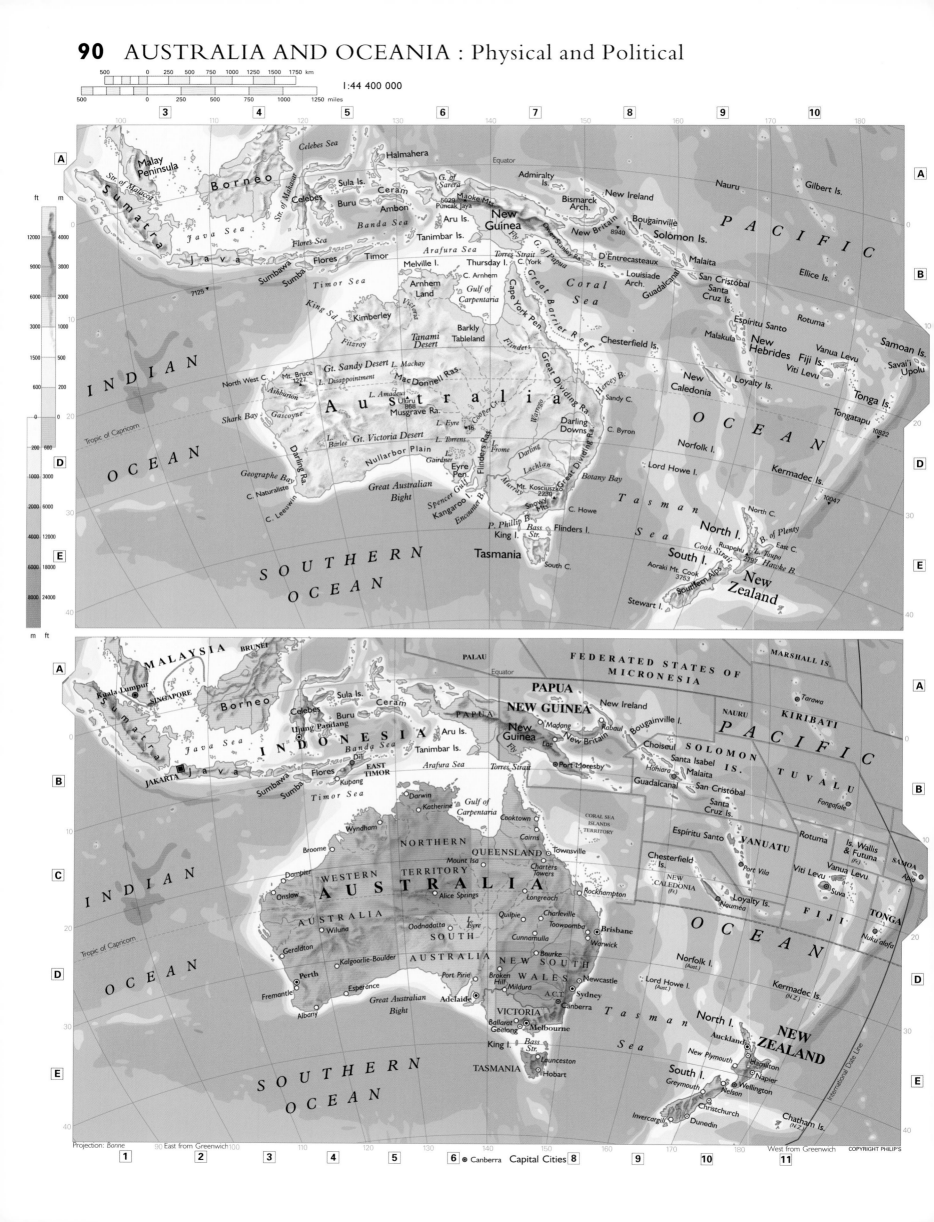

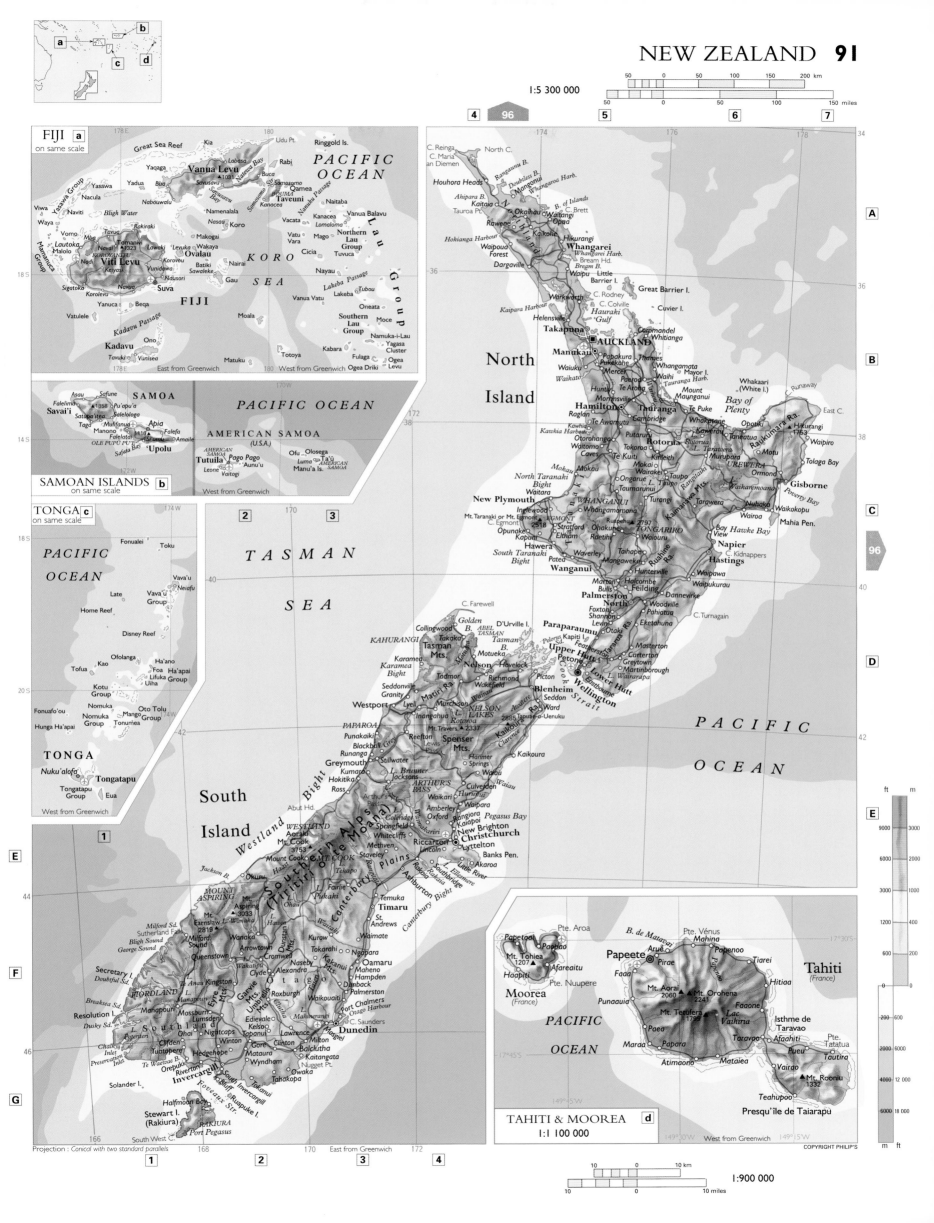

1:7 100 000

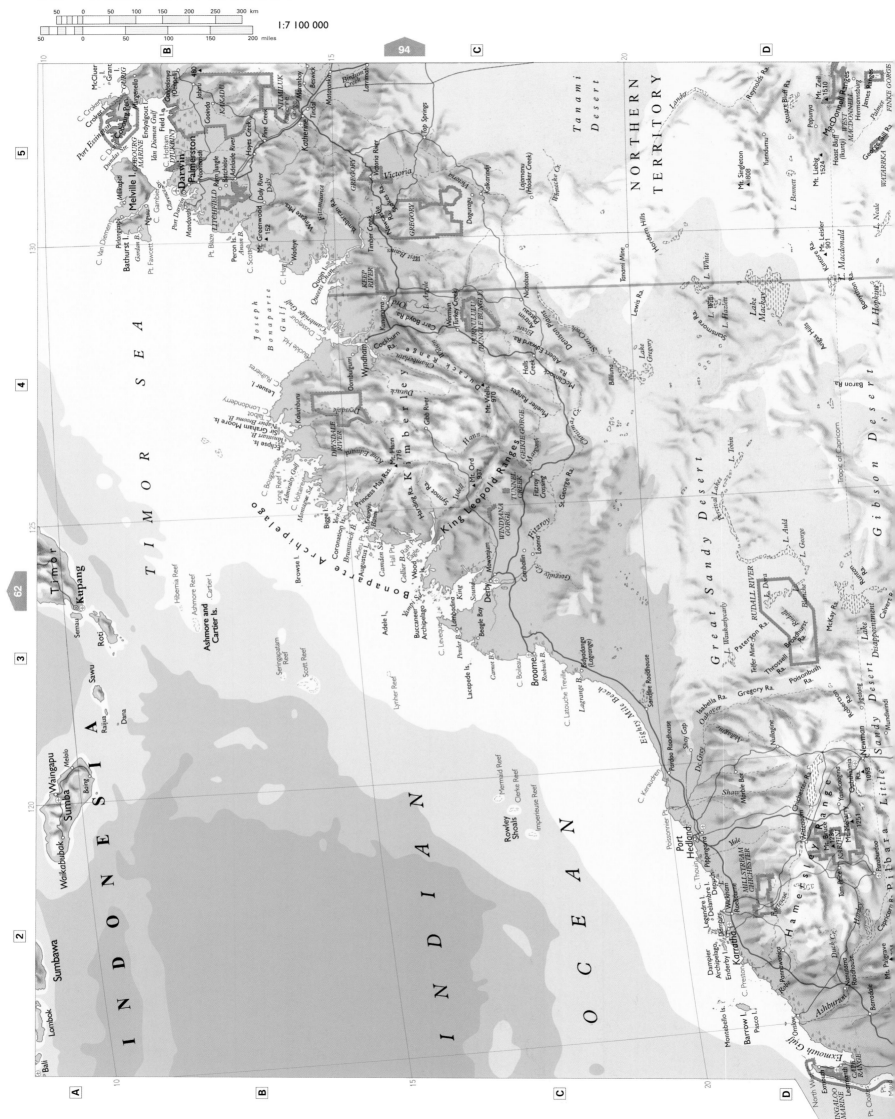

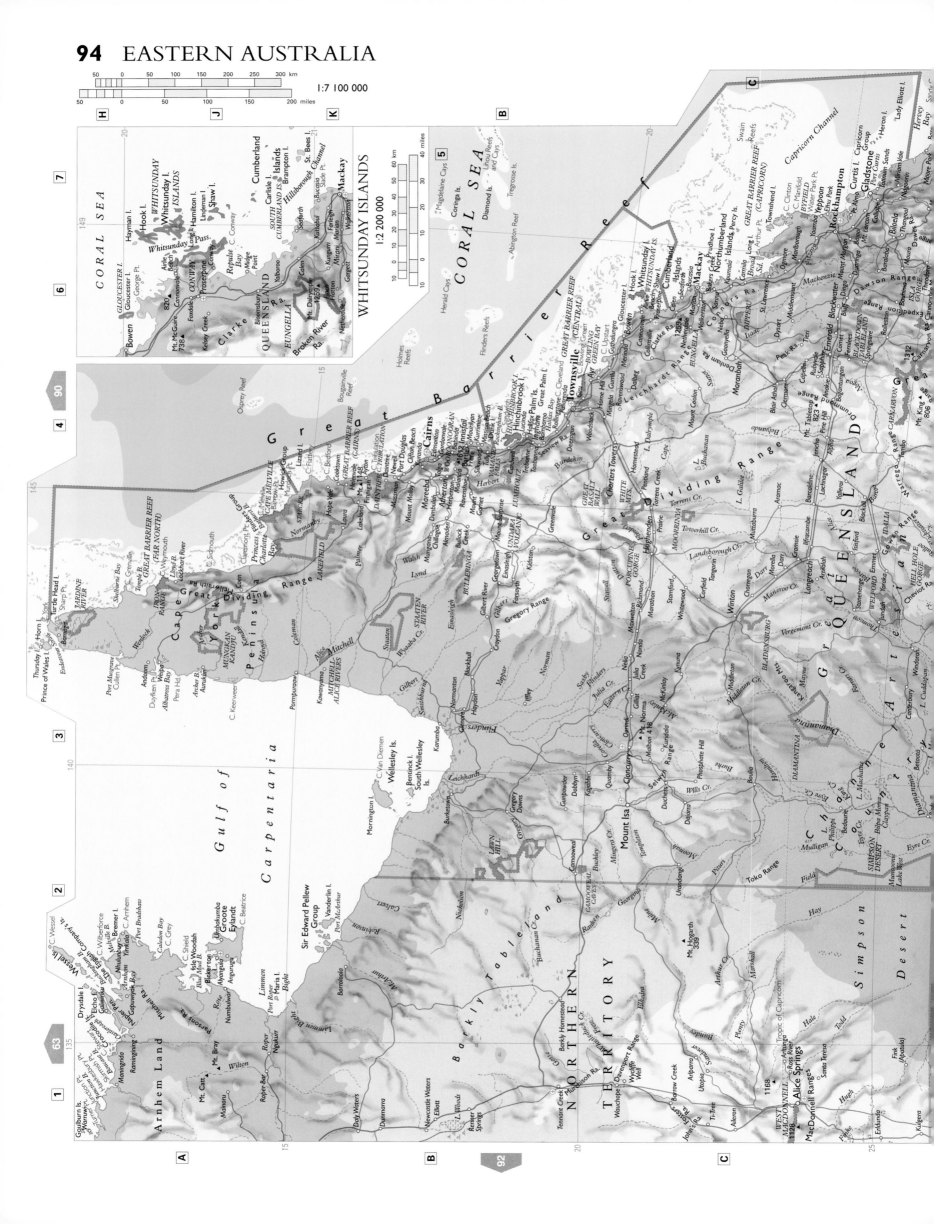

Equatorial Scale 1:48 000 000

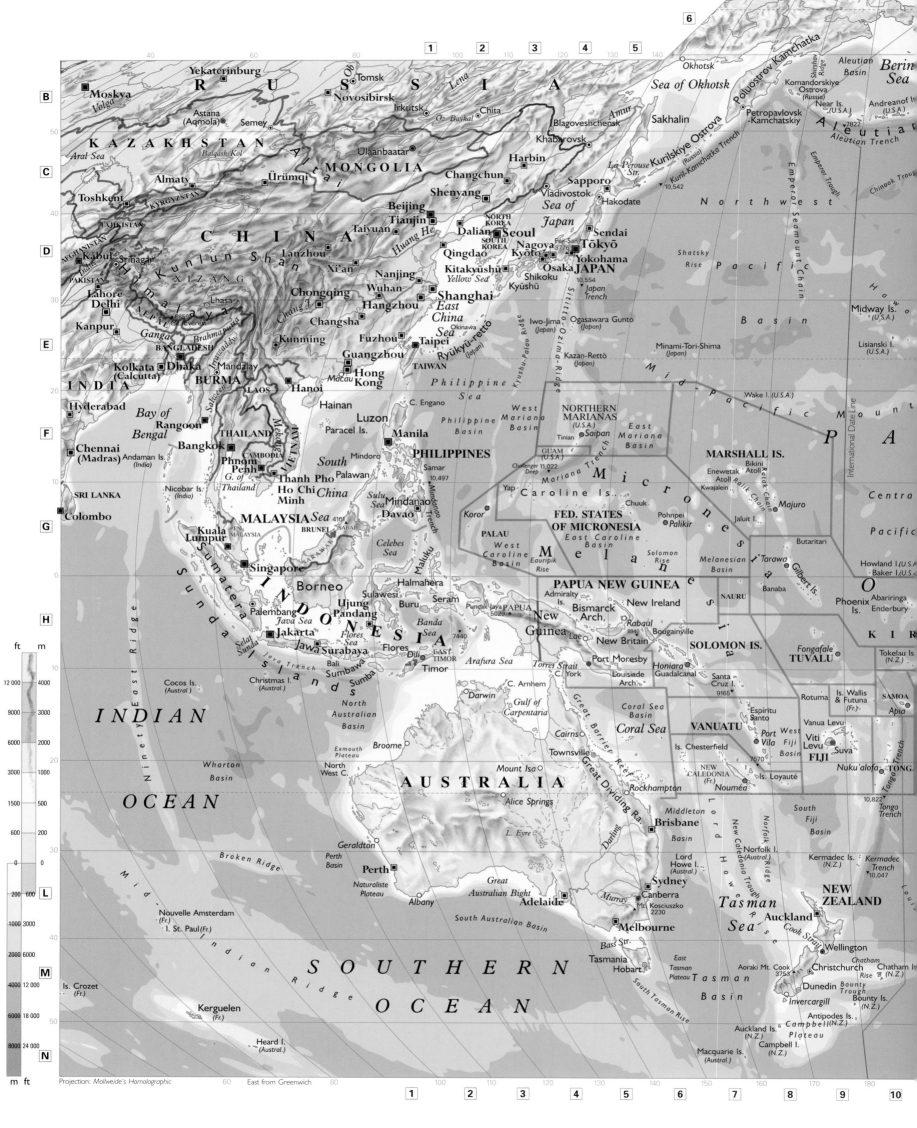

Projection: Mollweide's Homolographic   East from Greenwich

11 160 **12** 150 **13** 140 **14** 130

Arctic Circle

15

ALASKA
(U.S.A.)
Anchorage ⊙

5959

16 120 **17** 110 **18** 100 **19** 90 **20** 80 70 60 50 40 30 20

R
O
C
K
Y

C A N A D A

Newfoundland

B

Bristol Bay
Gulf of Alaska
Prince of Wales I.
(U.S.A.) Prince Rupert
Queen Charlotte Is.
(Canada)

Juneau ⊙

Edmonton ⊙

L. Winnipeg

St. Lawrence

N O R T H

Is. (U.S.A.)

Vancouver
Vancouver I. Victoria
Seattle

Calgary
Regina

Winnipeg ⊙

Québec
Montréal
Ottawa
L. Superior
Minneapolis L. Huron Toronto
L. Michigan Detroit Buffalo L. Ontario
Boston

St. John's

50

C

Tufts
Abyssal
Plain

Portland

Boise

Snake

Missouri

N o r t h e a s t

Mendocino Fracture Zone C. Mendocino

Salt Lake
City

Denver

Minneapolis
Chicago
Pittsburgh

New York
Philadelphia
Baltimore
Washington D.C.

A T L A N T I C

40

D

Sacramento
San Francisco

6741

Murray Fracture Zone

4418

Kansas City

St. Louis

Cincinnati

Memphis

Atlanta

C. Hatteras

Bermuda
(U.K.)

P a c i f i c

U N I T E D   S T A T E S

Oklahoma City

Dallas

Los Angeles
San Diego

Phoenix

Ciudad
Juárez

Houston

San Antonio

New
Orleans

Jacksonville

Tampa

S a r g a s s o   S e a

30

E

Guadalupe
(Mex.)

Molokai Fracture Zone

M
E
X

Gulf of Mexico
Monterrey

Miami
BAHAMAS

O C E A N

Tropic of Cancer

B a s i n

C. San Lucas

La Habana

West Indies

Honolulu
Kauai Maui
Oahu HAWAIIAN IS.
(U.S.A.)
4205
Hilo Hawaii

Guadalajara

Mexico
5619
Puebla

Mérida

Canal de Yucatán

CUBA

9200

HAITI
JAMAICA
Kingston

DOMINICAN REP.
PUERTO
RICO
(U.S.A.)

Leeward
Is.

20

F

Johnston I.
(U.S.A.)

C
I
F
I
C

Clarion Fracture Zone Is. Revilla Gigedo
(Mex.)

Acapulco

6662
GUATEMALA
Guatemala
San Salvador
EL SALVADOR

HONDURAS
NICARAGUA
Managua

Caribbean Sea

Middle America Trench
Guatemala
Basin

Barranquilla
San José

Maracaibo

BARBADOS

Windward Is.

Caracas

10

G

N o r t h   W e s t   C h r i s t m a s   R i d g e

Palmyra Is.
(U.S.A.)

I. Clipperton
(Fr.)

Clipperton Fracture Zone

COSTA
RICA
Colón Panamá
PANAMA

I. del Coco
(Costa Rica)

Cocos Ridge

Panama
Basin

Medellín

I. de Malpelo
(Colombia)

Cali

Bogotá

VENEZUELA

Orinoco

Teraina
Tabuaeran
Kiritimati

O C E A N

Line Islands

COLOMBIA

Equator

Galápagos Fracture Zone

Galápagos
(Ecuador)

Carnegie Ridge

Quito
ECUADOR

0

Jarvis I.
(U.S.A.)

Guayaquil

Iquitos

BRAZIL

H

KIRIBATI

Malden I.
Starbuck I.

Amazonas

C. Paliñas

Swains I.
AMER.
SAMOA
(U.S.A.)

Manihiki
Pukapuka

Manihiki
Plateau

Nuku Hiva Îs. Marquises
Hiva Oa

Marquesas Fracture Zone

Yupanqui
Basin

Galápagos Rise

Trujillo

6369

PERU

10

J

Vostok I.
Caroline I.
(Millennium I.)
Flint I.

Mendaña
Fracture
Zone

Lima

Cuzco

Nevada Ancohuma
6550

Suwarrow Is.

Austral
Seamount
Chain

Îs. de la
Société
Bora Bora
Huahine
Raiatea Tahiti
Papeete

Rangiroa

Îs. Tuamotu

P e r u   B a s i n

Nazca Ridge

Arequipa
Peru–
Arica

L. Titicaca
6866

La Paz
BOLIVIA

20

Niue
(N.Z.)

Cook Is.
(N.Z.)
Aitutaki

Atiu
Rarotonga
Mangaia

Îs. Gambier
Mururoa

Îs. Tubuai

East Pacific Rise

Oeno I.
Henderson I.
Pitcairn I. Ducie I.
(U.K.)

Rapa

Tropic of Capricorn

FRENCH POLYNESIA

Sala y Gómez Ridge

Iquique
Chile

Antofagasta

Trench

8050

PARAGUAY

Asunción

K

Tuamotu Ridge

Easter Fracture Zone

Sala-y-Gómez

I. de Pascua
(Chile)

San Félix
(Chile)

San Ambrosio
(Chile)

San Miguel
de Tucumán

30

FRACTURE

Roggeveen
Basin

Arch. de
Juan Fernández
(Chile)

Chile Rise

Córdoba

Aconcagua
6962

Porto
Alegre

L

S o u t h w e s t

Challenger Fracture Zone

Valparaíso
Santiago
Concepción

Rosario
Buenos
Aires

URUGUAY
Montevideo
Río de la Plata

P a c i f i c

Pacific–Antarctic East Pacific Rise Ridge

ARGENTINA

40

M

B a s i n

Menard Fracture
Zone

SOUTH

ATLANTIC

Chile Ridge

6212 OCEAN

50

N

Punta Arenas
C. de Hornos
Est. de Magallanes
Tierra del Fuego

Falkland Is.
(U.K.)

South Georgia
(U.K.)

S o u t h e a s t
Pacific Basin

Drake Passage

West from Greenwich

COPYRIGHT PHILIP'S

11 160 **12** 150 **13** 140 **14** 130 **15** 120 **16** 110 **17** 100 **18** 90 **19** 80 **20** 70 60 40

100 0 200 400 600 800 1000 1200 1400 km

1:31 100 000

100 0 200 400 600 800 1000 miles

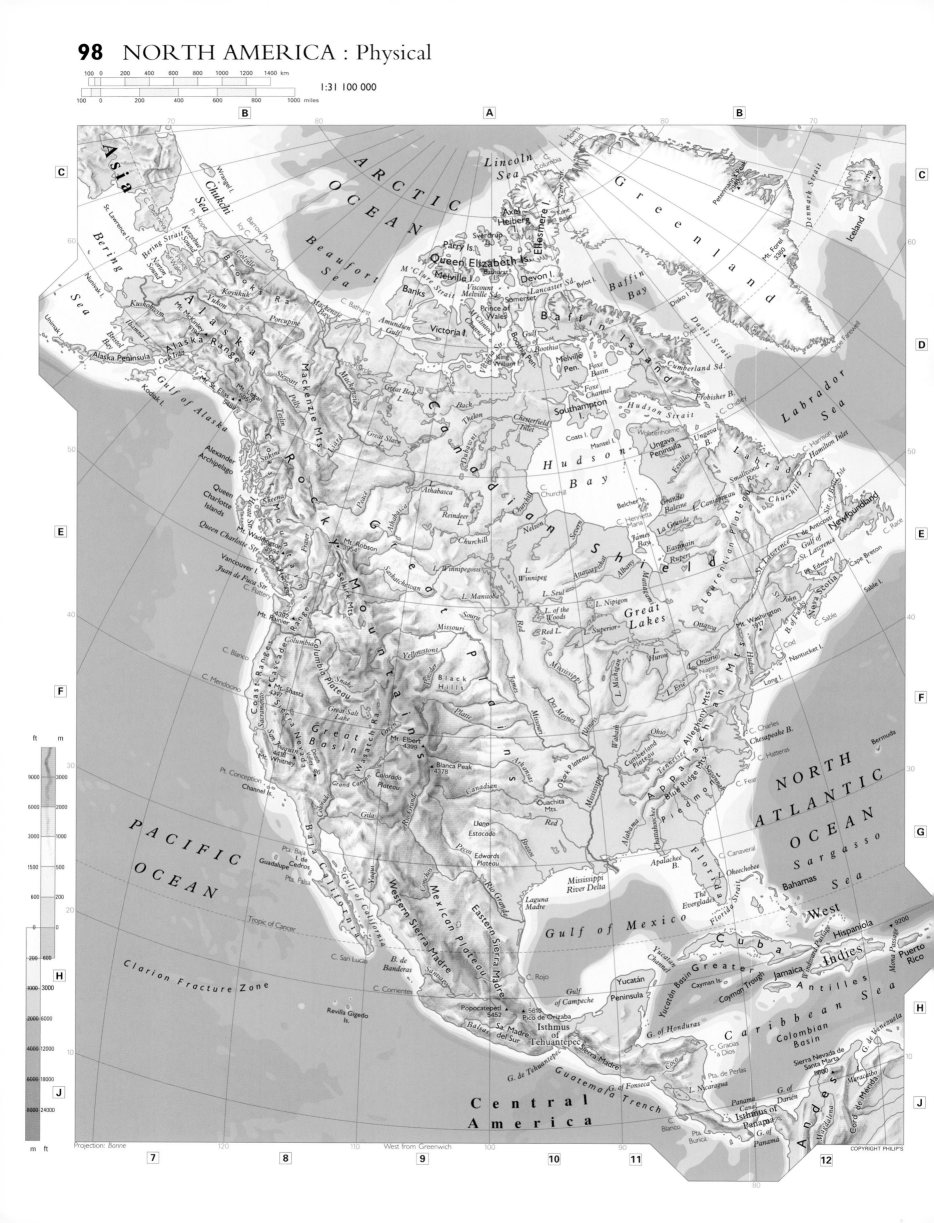

Projection: Bonne

West from Greenwich

COPYRIGHT PHILIP'S

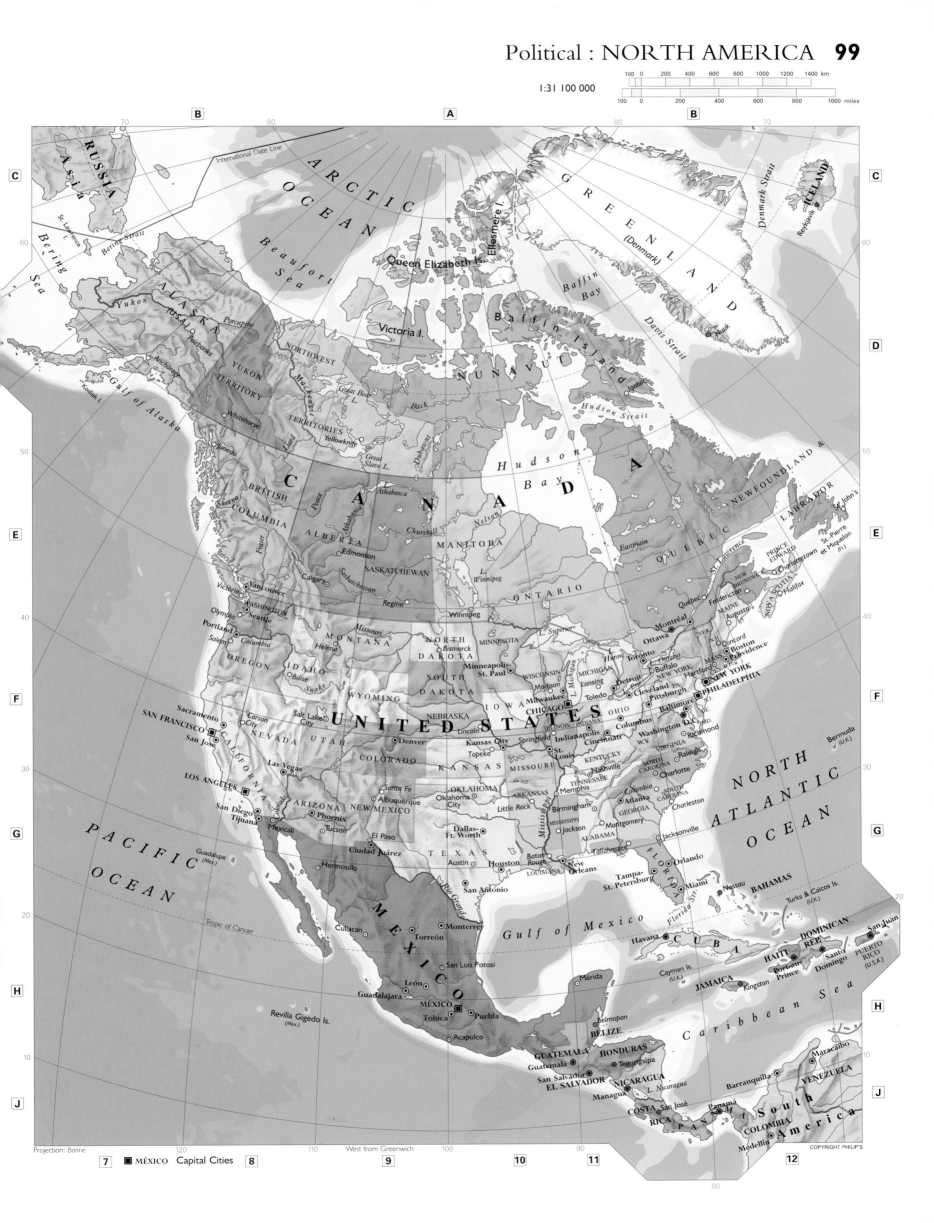

1:31 100 000

100 0 200 400 600 800 1000 1200 1400 km
100 0 200 400 600 800 1000 miles

C
A S I A
RUSSIA

ARCTIC OCEAN

International Date Line

GREENLAND

Denmark Strait

ICELAND

Reykjavík

C

Bering Strait

St. Lawrence I.

Bering Sea

Beaufort Sea

Queen Elizabeth Is.

Ellesmere I.

(Denmark)

Baffin Bay

Nuuk

D

Yukon

ALASKA (USA)

Fairbanks

Anchorage

Porcupine

Victoria I.

NUNAVUT

Baffin Island

Davis Strait

Kodiak I.

Gulf of Alaska

Whitehorse

YUKON TERRITORY

Arctic Circle

Great Bear L.

Mackenzie

NORTHWEST

Juneau

NORTHWEST TERRITORIES

Yellowknife

Liard

Great Slave L.

Dubawnt

Back

Hudson Strait

Iqaluit

E

BRITISH COLUMBIA

Skeena

Fraser

Peace

Athabasca

Athabasca

C A N A D A

Churchill

Nelson

Hudson Bay

Eastmain

QUÉBEC

NEWFOUNDLAND &

LABRADOR

St. John's

St-Pierre et Miquelon (Fr.)

E

Victoria

Vancouver

Calgary

ALBERTA

Edmonton

SASKATCHEWAN

Saskatchewan

MANITOBA

L. Winnipeg

ONTARIO

St. Lawrence

Québec

Fredericton

NEW BRUNSWICK

PRINCE EDWARD

Charlottetown

MAINE

Augusta

NOVA SCOTIA

Halifax

WASHINGTON

Olympia

Seattle

Regina

Winnipeg

L. Superior

Ottawa

Montréal

VER.

N.H.

Concord

Boston MASS.

40

Portland

Salem

OREGON

Columbia

MONTANA

Helena

IDAHO

Boise

Snake

Missouri

NORTH DAKOTA

Bismarck

SOUTH DAKOTA

WYOMING

MINNESOTA

Minneapolis-St. Paul

WISCONSIN

Madison

MICHIGAN

L. Michigan

L. Huron

Lansing

Detroit

Toronto

L. Erie

L. Ontario

Buffalo

NEW YORK

Cleveland

Hartford

Providence

R.I.

CONN.

NEW YORK

Pittsburgh

PA.

PHILADELPHIA

F

Sacramento

Carson City

Salt Lake City

Denver

MILWAUKEE

CHICAGO

ILLINOIS

IOWA

NEBRASKA

Lincoln

INDIANA

OHIO

Columbus

Cincinnati

Toledo

W.VA.

Baltimore

Washington D.C.

Richmond

VIRGINIA

MD.

DEL.

N.J.

F

San Francisco

San Jose

NEVADA

UTAH

U N I T E D   S T A T E S

COLORADO

Kansas City

Topeka

KANSAS

MISSOURI

St. Louis

Springfield

Indianapolis

KENTUCKY

Nashville

TENNESSEE

NORTH CAROLINA

Raleigh

Charlotte

Bermuda (U.K.)

30

Las Vegas

Santa Fe

CALIFORNIA

LOS ANGELES

ARIZONA

NEW MEXICO

Albuquerque

Oklahoma City

OKLAHOMA

ARKANSAS

Little Rock

Memphis

Mississippi

Birmingham

ALABAMA

Montgomery

GEORGIA

Atlanta

Columbia

SOUTH CAROLINA

Charleston

NORTH ATLANTIC OCEAN

San Diego

Tijuana

Mexicali

Colorado

Phoenix

Tucson

El Paso

Ciudad Juárez

T E X A S

Dallas-Ft. Worth

Mississippi

Jackson

Jacksonville

Tallahassee

FLORIDA

Orlando

G

PACIFIC

Guadalupe (Mex.)

Hermosillo

Rio Grande

Austin

Houston

Baton Rouge

LOUISIANA

New Orleans

Tampa-St. Petersburg

Miami

Nassau

BAHAMAS

Turks & Caicos Is. (U.K.)

20

OCEAN

Tropic of Cancer

Culiacán

M E X I C O

Torreón

San Antonio

San Luis Potosí

Monterrey

Gulf of Mexico

Havana

CUBA

Florida Str.

Cayman Is. (U.K.)

JAMAICA

Kingston

Port-au-Prince

HAITI

DOMINICAN REP.

Santo Domingo

PUERTO RICO (U.S.A.)

San Juan

H

León

Guadalajara

MÉXICO

Toluca

Puebla

Mérida

Belmopan

BELIZE

Caribbean Sea

Maracaibo

H

Revilla Gigedo Is. (Mex.)

Acapulco

GUATEMALA

Guatemala

San Salvador

EL SALVADOR

HONDURAS

Tegucigalpa

NICARAGUA

L. Nicaragua

Managua

Barranquilla

VENEZUELA

J

COSTA RICA

San José

PANAMÁ

COLOMBIA

South America

Medellín

J

Projection: Bonne

West from Greenwich

COPYRIGHT PHILIP'S

7   ■MÉXICO Capital Cities   8   9   10   11   12

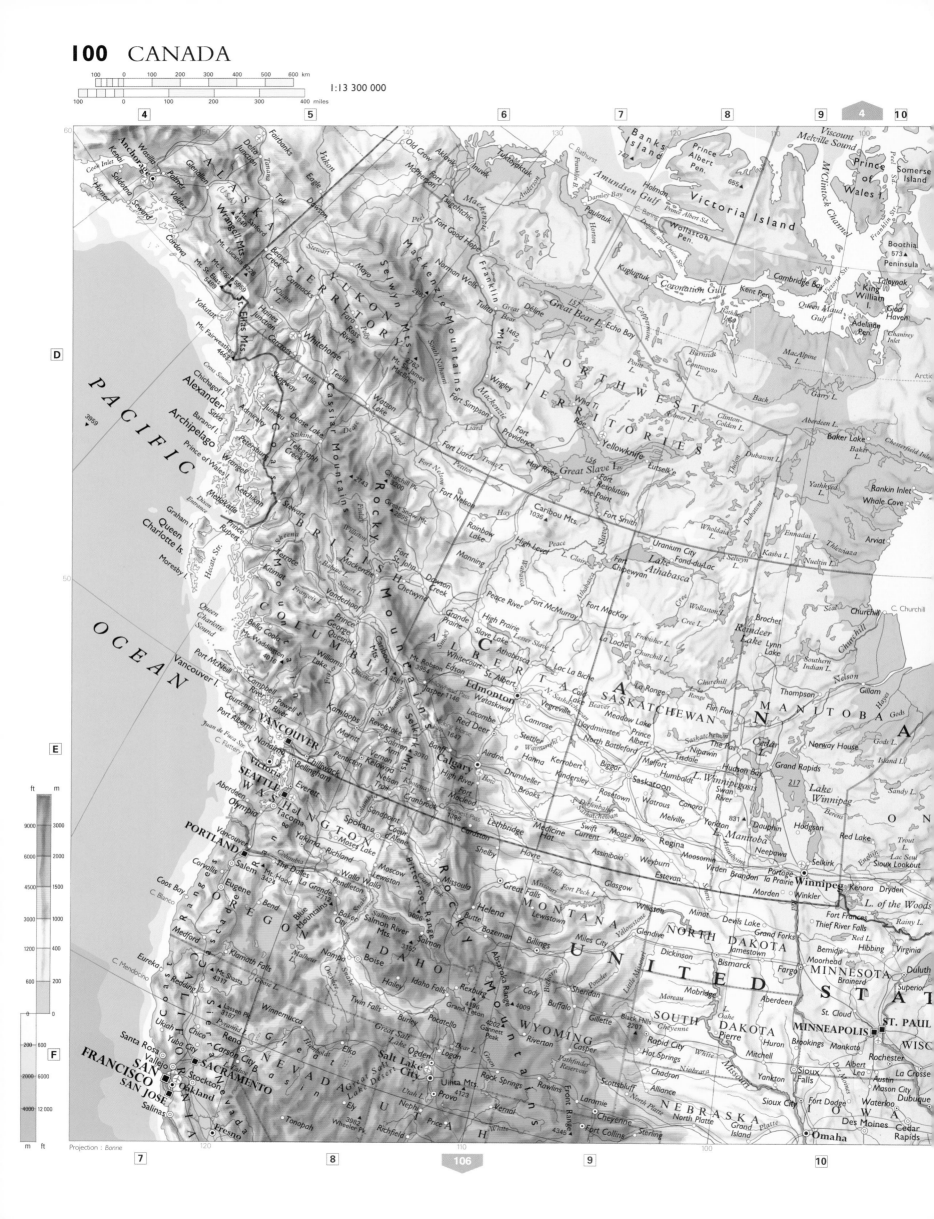

NORTHERN CANADA
continuation northwards on same
scale as main map

ARCTIC OCEAN

Devon I.
Lancaster Sound

Baffin Bay

Arctic Bay Nanisivik
Brodeur
Peninsula
Gulf of Boothia

Simpson Pen.
Melville
Peninsula

Kugaaruk

Rae Isthmus
Repulse Bay
Circle

Chesterfield Inlet

Southampton I.
Coral Harbour
Bell Pen.

Foxe
Basin

Foxe Channel

Cape Dorset

Salisbury I.
Nottingham I.
Coats I.

Mansel I.

Hudson Strait

Ivujivik Salluit

Hudson Bay

Sleeper Is.
King George Is.
Bakers Dozen Is.
Sanikiluaq
Belcher Is.
Kuujjuarapik

C. Tatnam

Peawanuck
Winisk

James Bay
Akimiski I.

Attawapiskat
Fort Albany
Moosonee

Big Trout L.

ATLANTIC OCEAN

Labrador Sea

MILWAUKEE
CHICAGO DETROIT
CLEVELAND

TORONTO
Hamilton
Buffalo

MONTRÉAL
OTTAWA

NEW YORK
BOSTON
PROVIDENCE

West from Greenwich

COPYRIGHT PHILIP'S

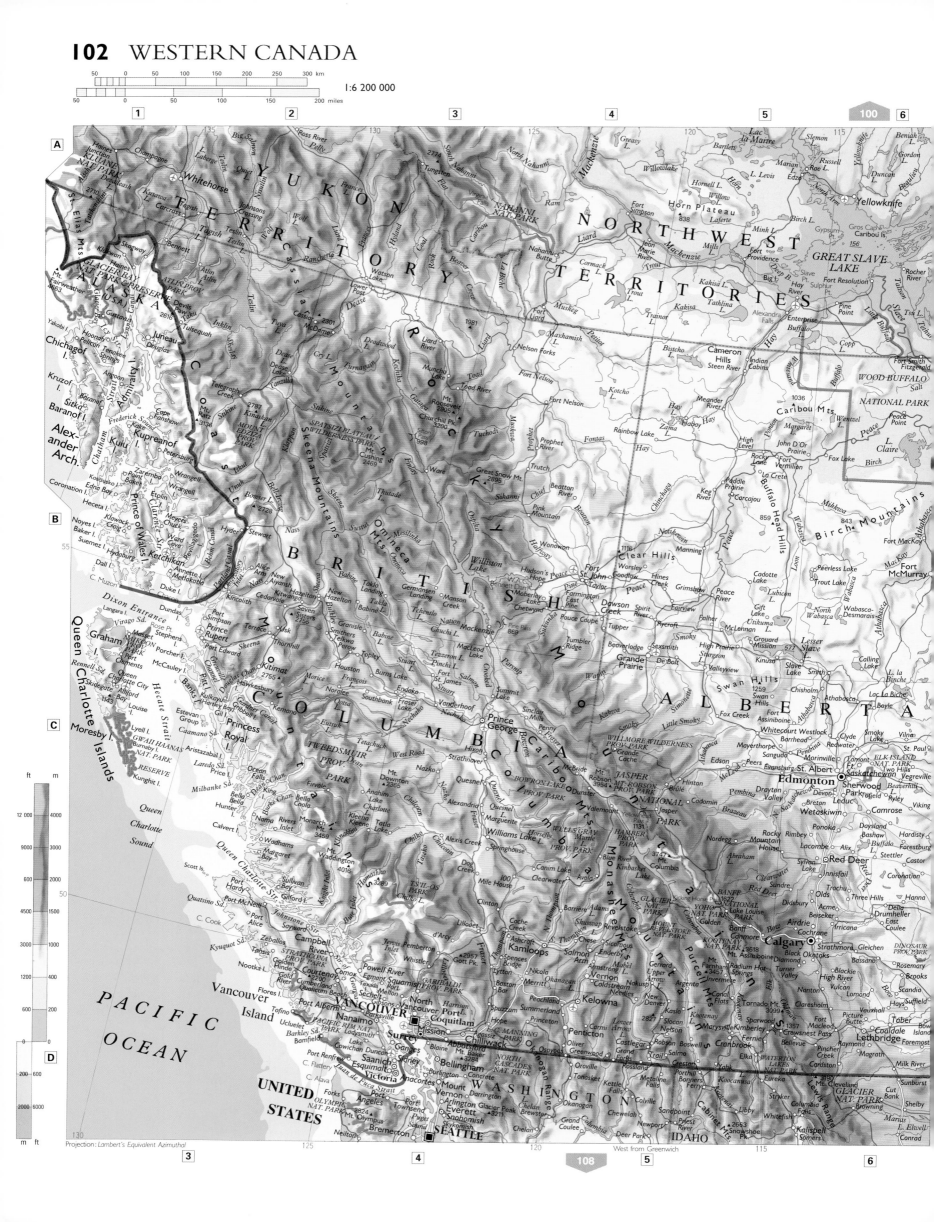

1:6 200 000

50   0   50   100   150   200   250   300 km

50   0   50   100   150   200 miles

| 1 | 2 | 3 | 4 | 5 | 100 | 6 |

YUKON TERRITORY

NORTHWEST TERRITORIES

GREAT SLAVE LAKE

ALASKA (U.S.A.)

Whitehorse

Yellowknife

WOOD BUFFALO NATIONAL PARK

KLUANE NAT. PARK

Horn Plateau

Juneau

Mt. Fairweather

GLACIER BAY NAT. PARK & PRESERVE

Chichagof I.

Kruzof I.

Sitka

Baranof I.

Alex- ander Arch.

Kuiu

Kupreanof I.

Admiralty I.

NAHANNI NAT. PARK

Fort Nelson

Fort Liard

Hay River

Fort Smith

Fort McMurray

BRITISH COLUMBIA

ALBERTA

Caribou Mts.

Birch Mountains

Prince Rupert

Queen Charlotte Islands

Graham I.

Moresby Islands

GWAII HAANAS NAT. PARK RESERVE

Dixon Entrance

Hecate Strait

Ketchikan

Prince George

Grande Prairie

Williston Lake

Fort St. John

Dawson Creek

Peace River

Lesser Slave Lake

Edmonton

St. Albert

Saskatchewan

Sherwood Park

Leduc

Camrose

PACIFIC OCEAN

Queen Charlotte Sound

TWEEDSMUIR PROV. PARK

WELLS GRAY PROV. PARK

JASPER NATIONAL PARK

MOUNT ROBSON PROV. PARK

Williams Lake

Quesnel

Prince George

Red Deer

Vancouver Island

Campbell River

Courtenay

Comox

Powell River

Nanaimo

VANCOUVER

Coquitlam

Surrey

Victoria

GARIBALDI PROV. PARK

Whistler

Kamloops

Vernon

Kelowna

Penticton

Revelstoke

GLACIER NAT. PARK

YOHO NAT. PARK

BANFF NATIONAL PARK

Lake Louise

Banff

Canmore

Calgary

Cochrane

Red Deer

Rocky Mountain House

MANNING PROV. PARK

Hope

Chilliwack

Mission

Abbotsford

KOOTENAY NAT. PARK

Cranbrook

Fernie

Lethbridge

WATERTON LAKES NAT. PARK

UNITED STATES

WASHINGTON

IDAHO

Bellingham

Mount Vernon

Everett

SEATTLE

Bremerton

OLYMPIC NAT. PARK

NORTH CASCADES NAT. PARK

GLACIER NAT. PARK

Kalispell

PACIFIC RIM NAT. PARK

| 3 | 4 | 108 | 5 | 6 |

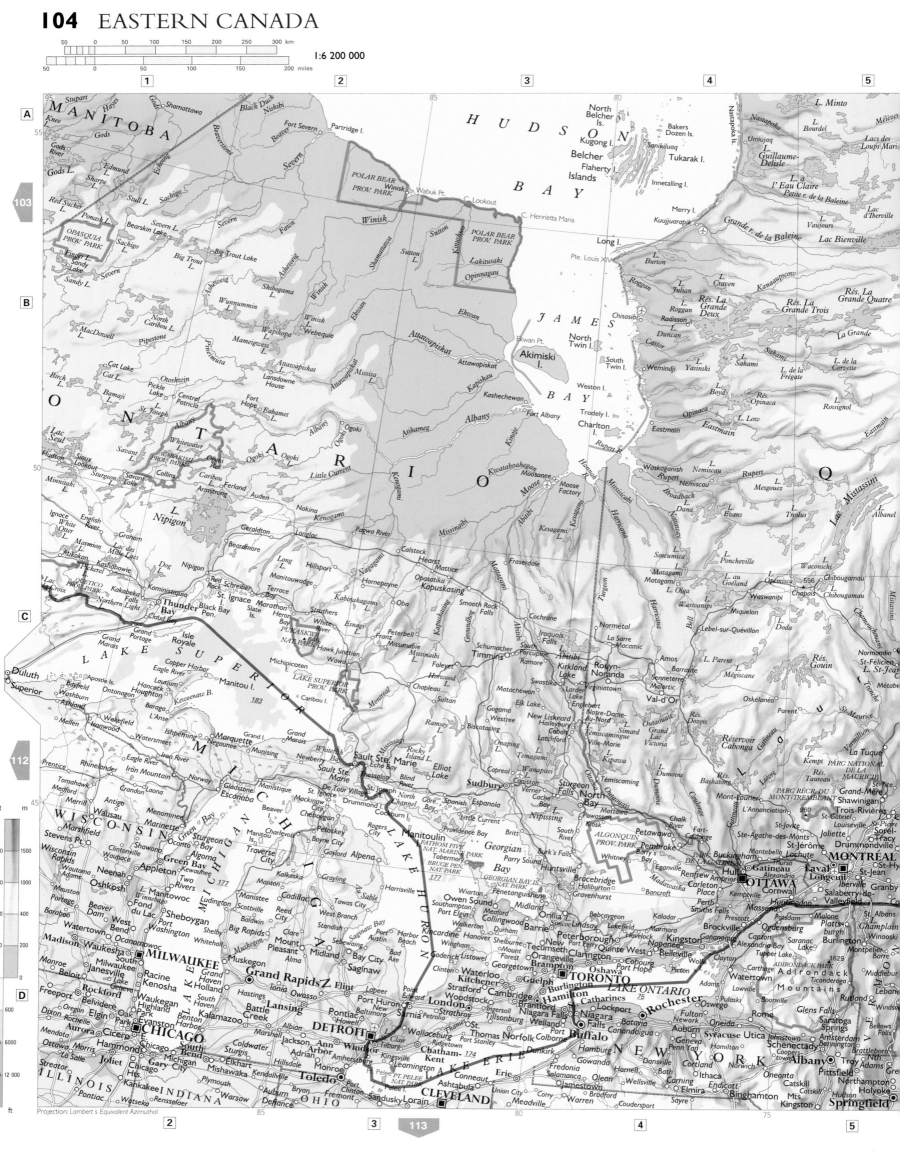

1:6 200 000

Projection: Lambert's Equivalent Azimuthal

L A B R A D O R

S E A

B

NEWFOUNDLAND &

LABRADOR

Newfoundland

GULF OF

ST. LAWRENCE

Cabot Strait

ST-PIERRE
et MIQUELON
(France)

PRINCE EDWARD
ISLAND

NEW

BRUNSWICK

Cape Breton
Island

N O V A   S C O T I A

MAINE

A T L A N T I C

Bay of Fundy

O C E A N

Sable I.
(Nova Scotia)

NEW HAMPSHIRE

UNITED

STATES

West from Greenwich

COPYRIGHT PHILIP'S

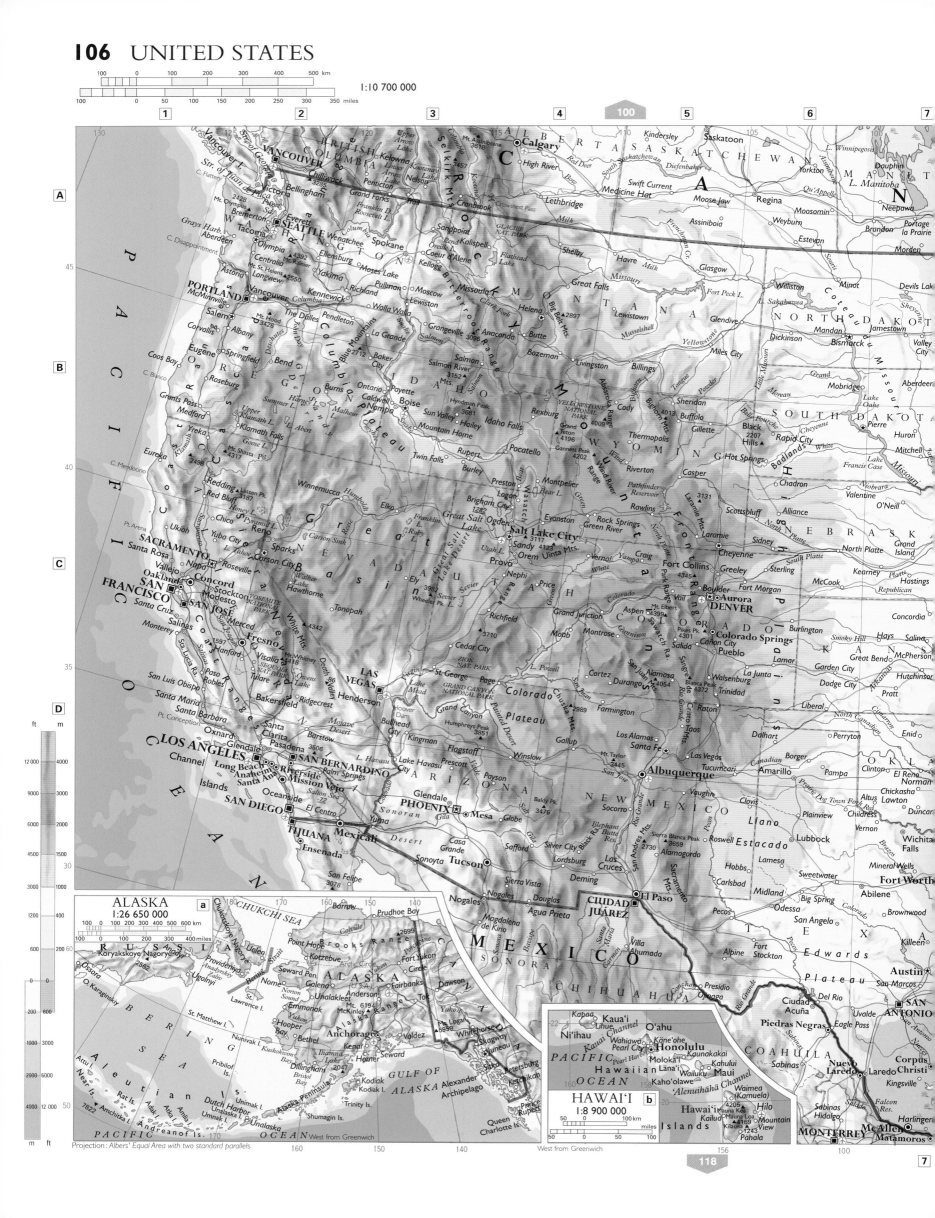

Tallahassee ⊛   U.S. State capitals

1:6 250 000

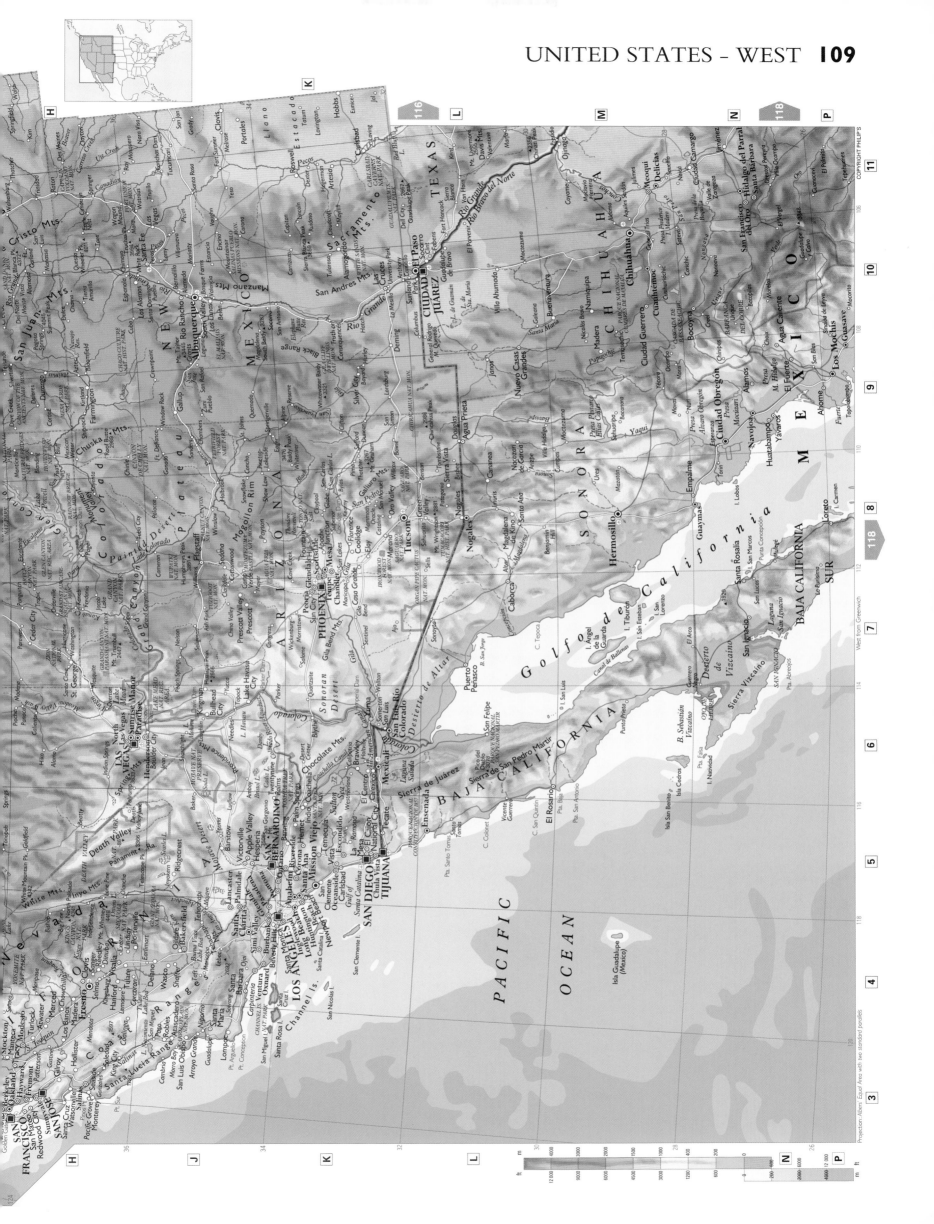

Projection: Albers Equal Area with two standard parallels

1:2 200 000

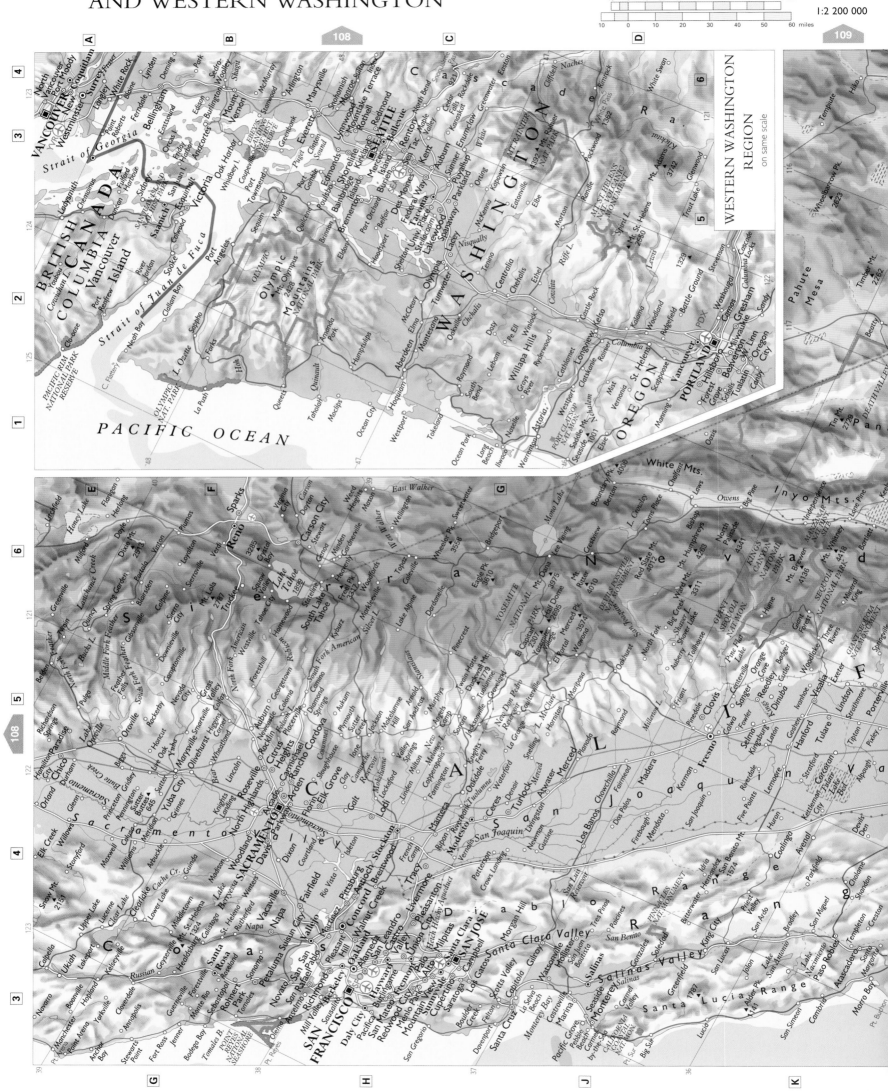

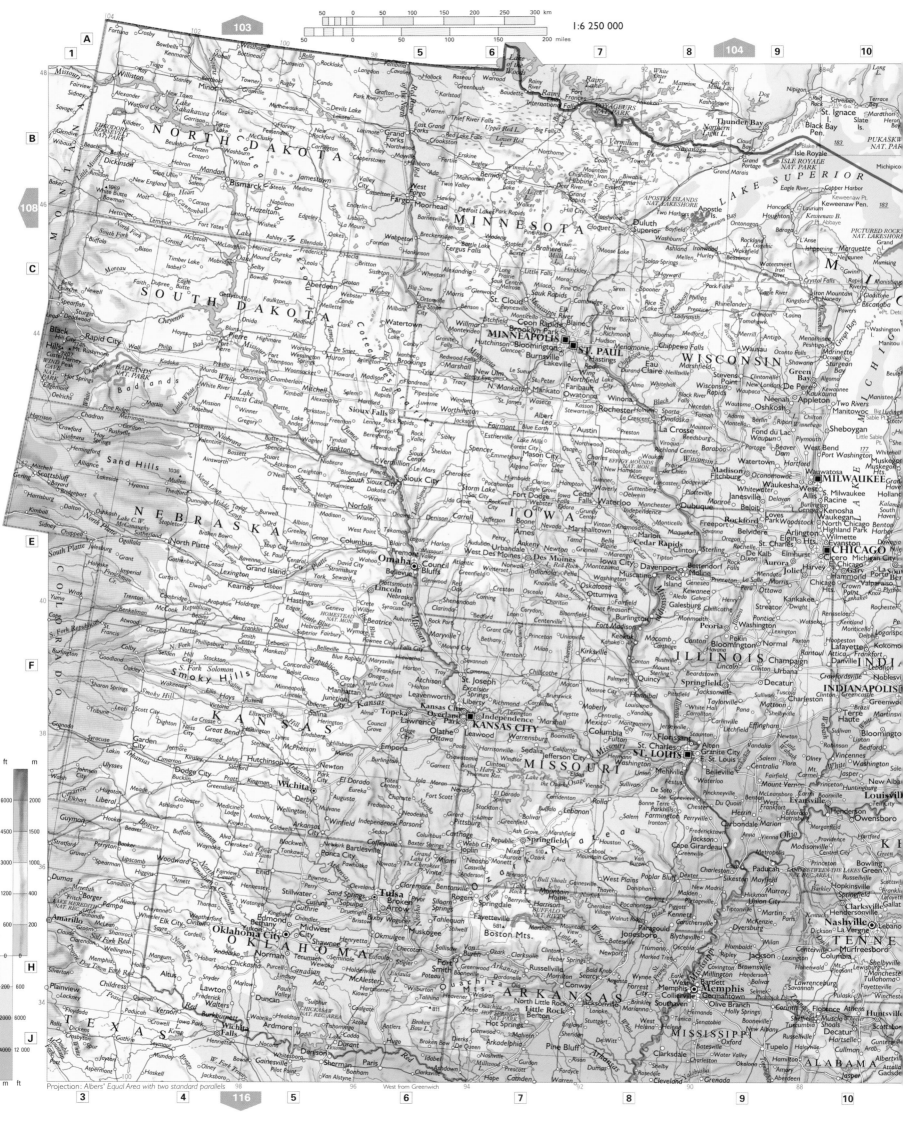

50 0 50 100 150 200 250 300 km

1:6 250 000

50 0 50 100 150

200 miles

Projection: Albers' Equal Area with two standard parallels

West from Greenwich

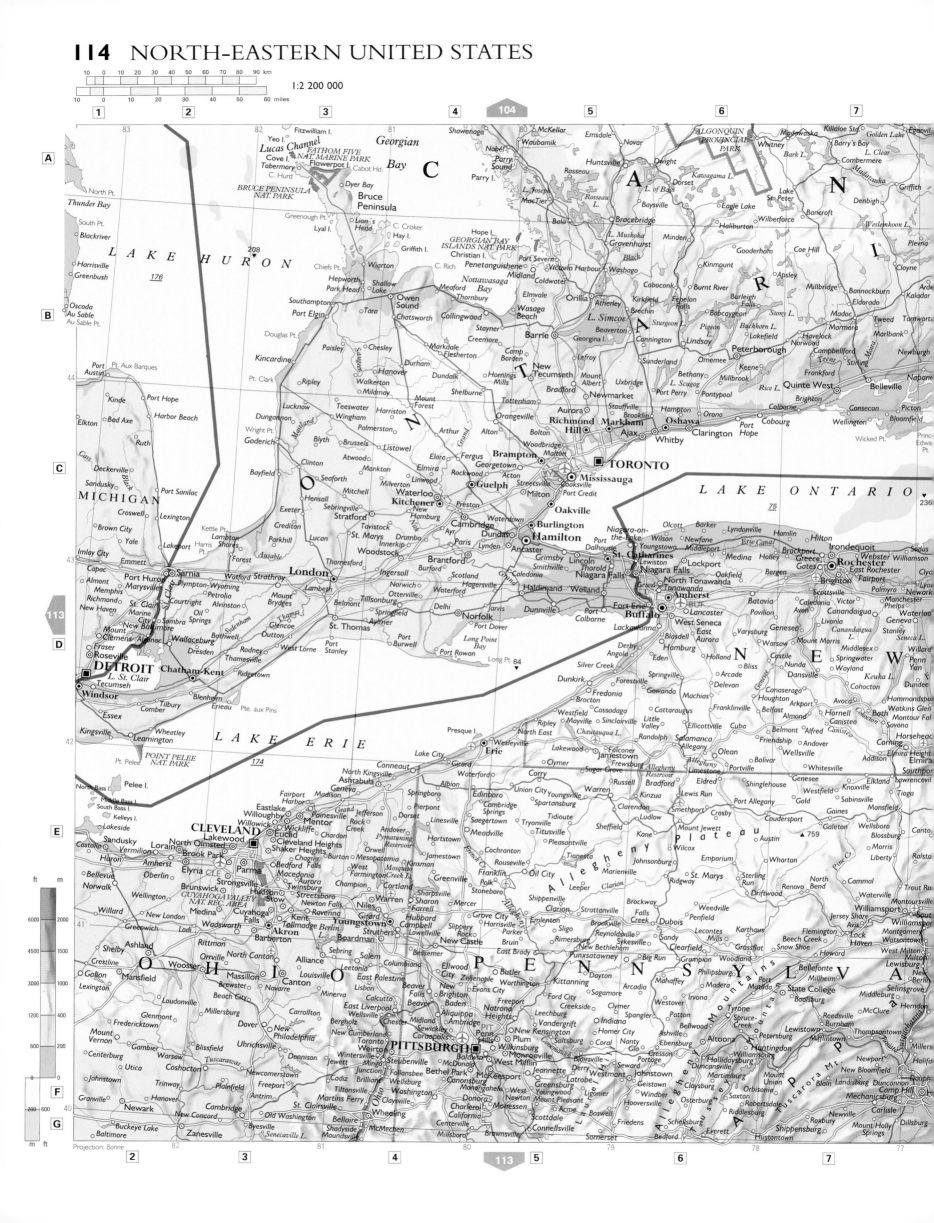

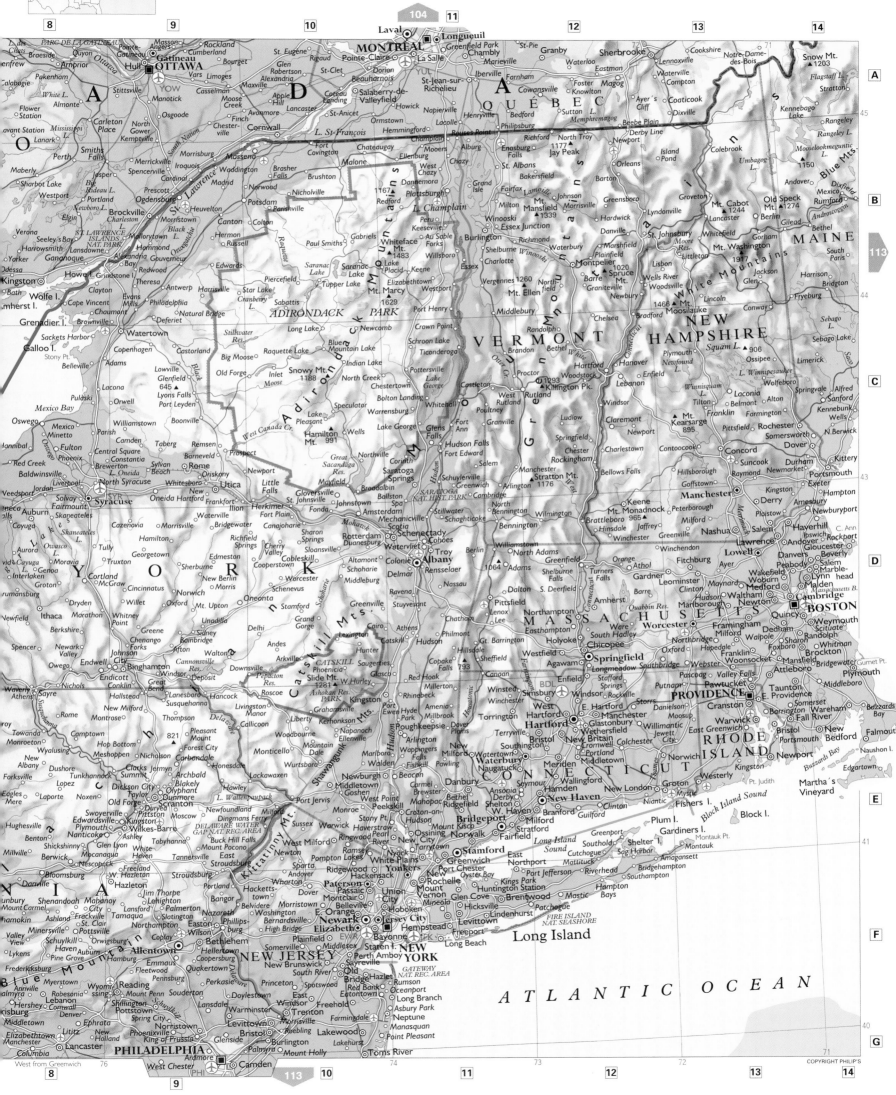

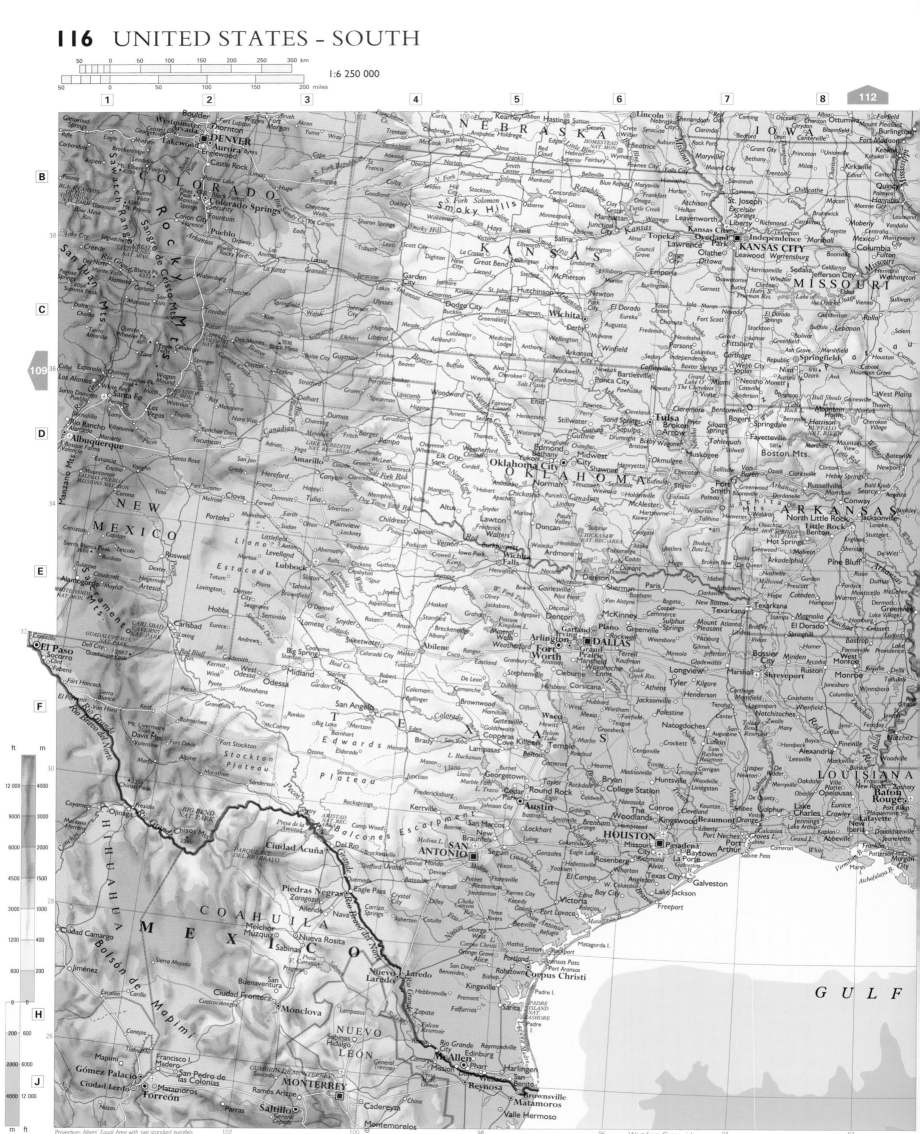

50 0 50 100 150 200 250 300 km

1:6 250 000

50 0 50 100 150 200 miles

Projection: Albers' Equal Area with two standard parallels

West from Greenwich

118

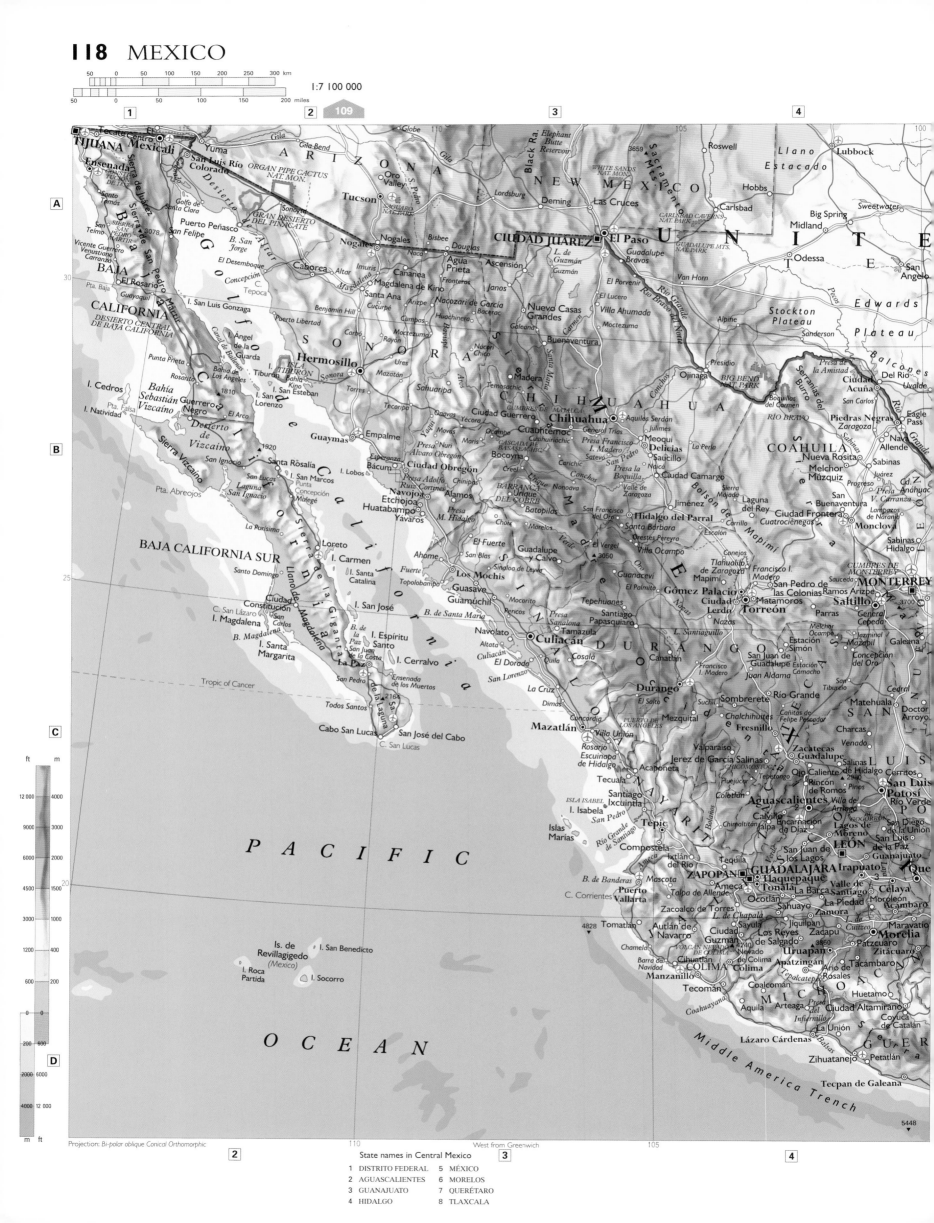

117

5   6   7   8

A

Wichita
Falls   Denison   Paris   95   Red   Hope
Sherman   Greenville
Denton   Texarkana   El Dorado   Camden   Greenville   Tuscaloosa   Opelika
DALLAS   Marshall   ARKANSAS   Monroe   Vicksburg   Meridian   Phenix City   Columbus
Fort Worth   Longview   MISSISSIPPI   Montgomery   Cordele   McRae
Ranger   Cleburne   Tyler   Shreveport   Jackson   Selma   Troy   Americus   GEORGIA
Abilene   Hillsboro   Corsicana   Natchez   Laurel   Hattiesburg   Dothan   Tifton   Waycross   Valdosta

B

GULF OF MEXICO

C

Tropic of Cancer

Banco
Campeche

CUBA

D

Golfo
de
Campeche

CAMPECHE

YUCATÁN

QUINTANA
ROO

BELIZE

E

GUATEMALA

HONDURAS

Tehuantepec

COPYRIGHT PHILIP'S

120

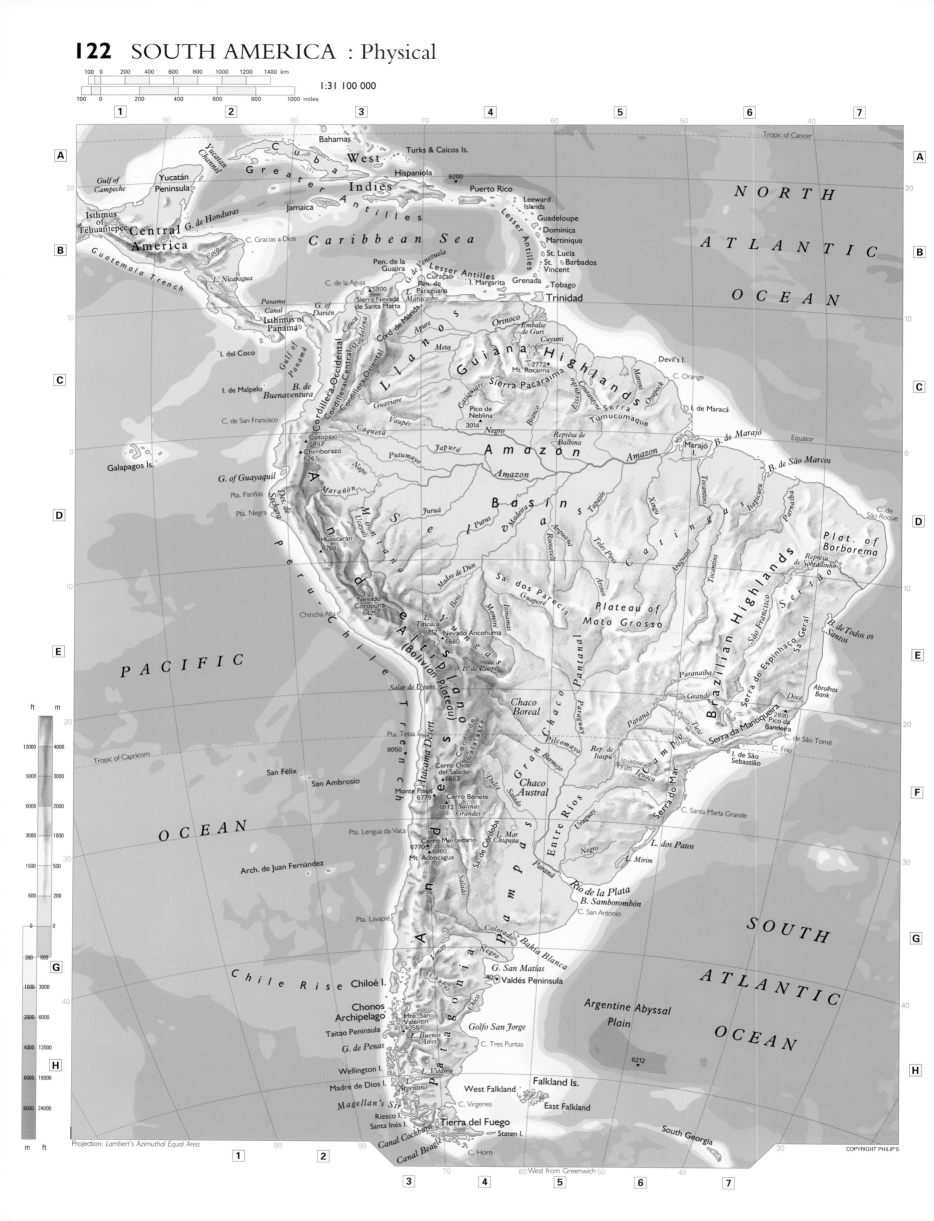

1:31 100 000

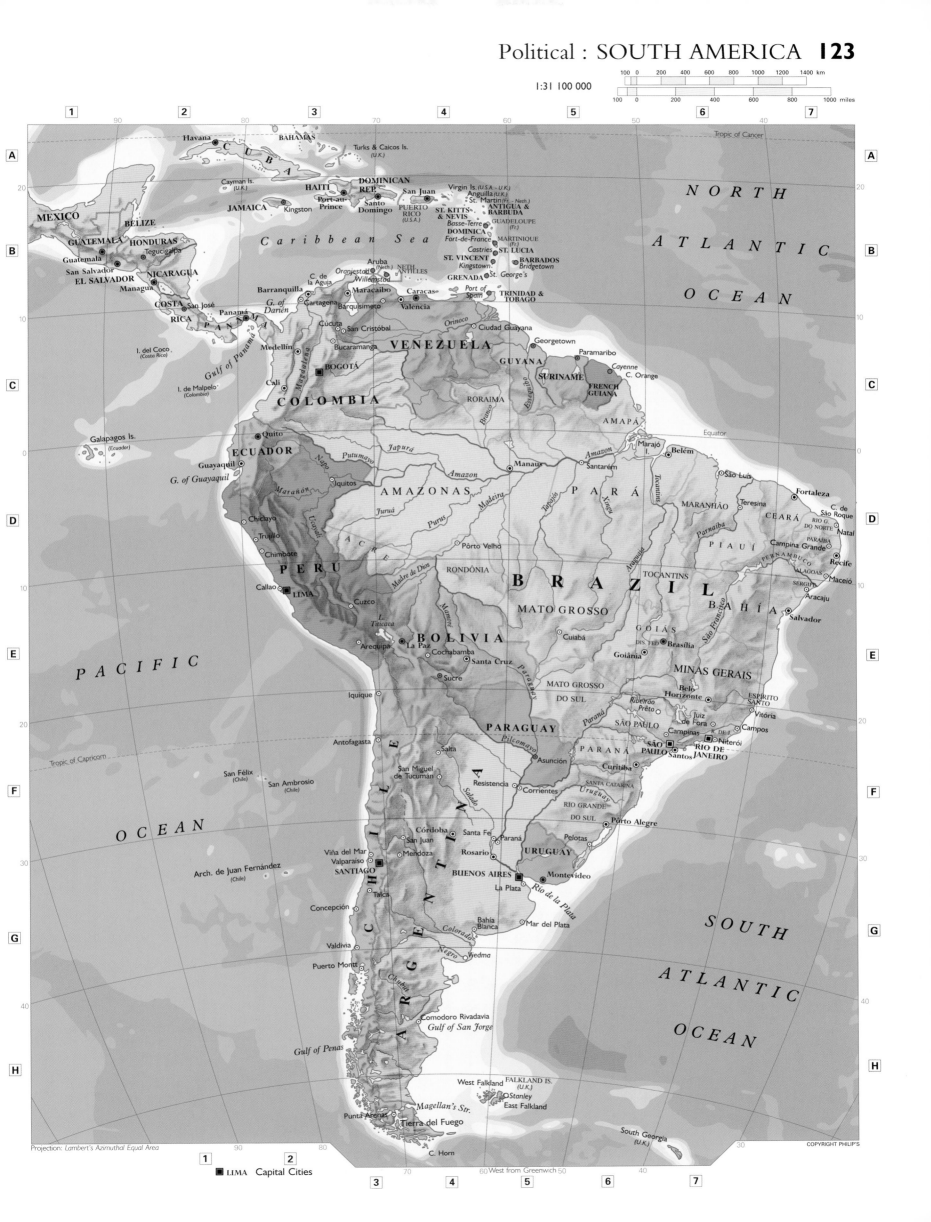

Projection: Lambert's Azimuthal Equal Area

COPYRIGHT PHILIP'S

Tropic of Cancer

NORTH

ATLANTIC

OCEAN

Caribbean Sea

MEXICO

BELIZE

GUATEMALA HONDURAS
Guatemala Tegucigalpa
San Salvador
EL SALVADOR NICARAGUA
Managua
COSTA San José
RICA Panamá
PANAMÁ

Havana
CUBA
BAHAMAS

Cayman Is.
(U.K.)

JAMAICA Kingston

HAITI DOMINICAN
Port-au- REP.
Prince Santo San Juan
Domingo PUERTO
RICO
(U.S.A.)

Turks & Caicos Is.
(U.K.)

Virgin Is. (U.S.A.-U.K.)
Anguilla (U.K.)
St. Martin (Fr.-Neth.)
ANTIGUA &
BARBUDA
ST. KITTS
& NEVIS Basse-Terre
DOMINICA GUADELOUPE
Fort-de-France (Fr.)
MARTINIQUE
Castries (Fr.)
ST. VINCENT ST. LUCIA
Kingstown BARBADOS
GRENADA Bridgetown
St. George's
TRINIDAD &
TOBAGO

I. del Coco
(Costa Rica)

I. de Malpelo
(Colombia)

Galapagos Is.
(Ecuador)

C. de
la Aguja
Barranquilla
Cartagena
Barquisimeto
Maracaibo
G. of
Darién
Cúcuta San Cristóbal
Medellín Bucaramanga
BOGOTÁ
Cali
COLOMBIA

Caracas
Valencia
Aruba
(Neth.)
Oranjestad NETH.
Willemstad ANTILLES
Port of
Spain

Orinoco
Ciudad Guayana
VENEZUELA

Georgetown
GUYANA Paramaribo
SURINAME Cayenne
FRENCH C. Orange
GUIANA
RORAIMA
Essequibo
Branco
AMAPÁ

Quito
ECUADOR
Guayaquil
G. of Guayaquil

Napo
Putumayo
Marañon
Iquitos
Ucayali
PERU
Chiclayo
Trujillo
Chimbote
Callao LIMA
Cuzco
L.
Titicaca
Arequipa

Japurá
Amazon
Juruá
Purus
ACRE
Madre de Dios
Mamoré

Equator

Amazon Manaus
Santarém
AMAZONAS

Madeira
Tapajós
Xingu
PARÁ

Marajó
I.
Belém
São Luís

Tocantins

MARANHÃO

Teresina

São Francisco
Fortaleza
C. de
São Roque
CEARÁ Natal
RIO G.
DO NORTE
PIAUÍ Campina Grande PARAÍBA
PERNAMBUCO Recife
ALAGOAS Maceió
SERGIPE
Aracaju
BAHÍA Salvador

RONDÔNIA
Pôrto Velho

BRAZIL
MATO GROSSO
Cuiabá

TOCANTINS
GOIÁS DIS. FED.
Brasília
Goiânia

BOLIVIA
La Paz Cochabamba
Sucre Santa Cruz

MINAS GERAIS
Belo
Horizonte
ESPÍRITO
SANTO
Ribeirão Vitória
Prêto
Juiz Campos
de Fora
Campinas R. DE J.
Niterói
SÃO PAULO RIO DE
JANEIRO
São Santos
Paulo

PACIFIC

OCEAN

Iquique

Antofagasta

Tropic of Capricorn

San Félix
(Chile)
San Ambrosio
(Chile)

Arch. de Juan Fernández
(Chile)

Salta

San Miguel
de Tucumán

Córdoba
San Juan
Viña del Mar
Valparaíso Mendoza
SANTIAGO

Talca

Concepción

Valdivia

Puerto Montt

MATO GROSSO
DO SUL

PARAGUAY

Asunción

Pilcomayo
Salado
Paraguay
Paraná

Resistencia
Corrientes

Santa Fe
Paraná
Rosario

Buenos Aires

La Plata

Bahía
Blanca

Mar del Plata

Colorado

Negro

Viedma

PARANÁ Curitiba
SANTA CATARINA
Uruguay Pôrto Alegre
RIO GRANDE
DO SUL
Pelotas

URUGUAY
Montevideo
Río de la Plata

ARGENTINA

CHILE

SOUTH

ATLANTIC

OCEAN

Comodoro Rivadavia
Gulf of San Jorge

Chubut

Gulf of Penas

Magellan's Str.
Punta Arenas
Tierra del Fuego
C. Horn

West Falkland FALKLAND IS.
(U.K.)
Stanley
East Falkland

South Georgia
(U.K.)

West from Greenwich

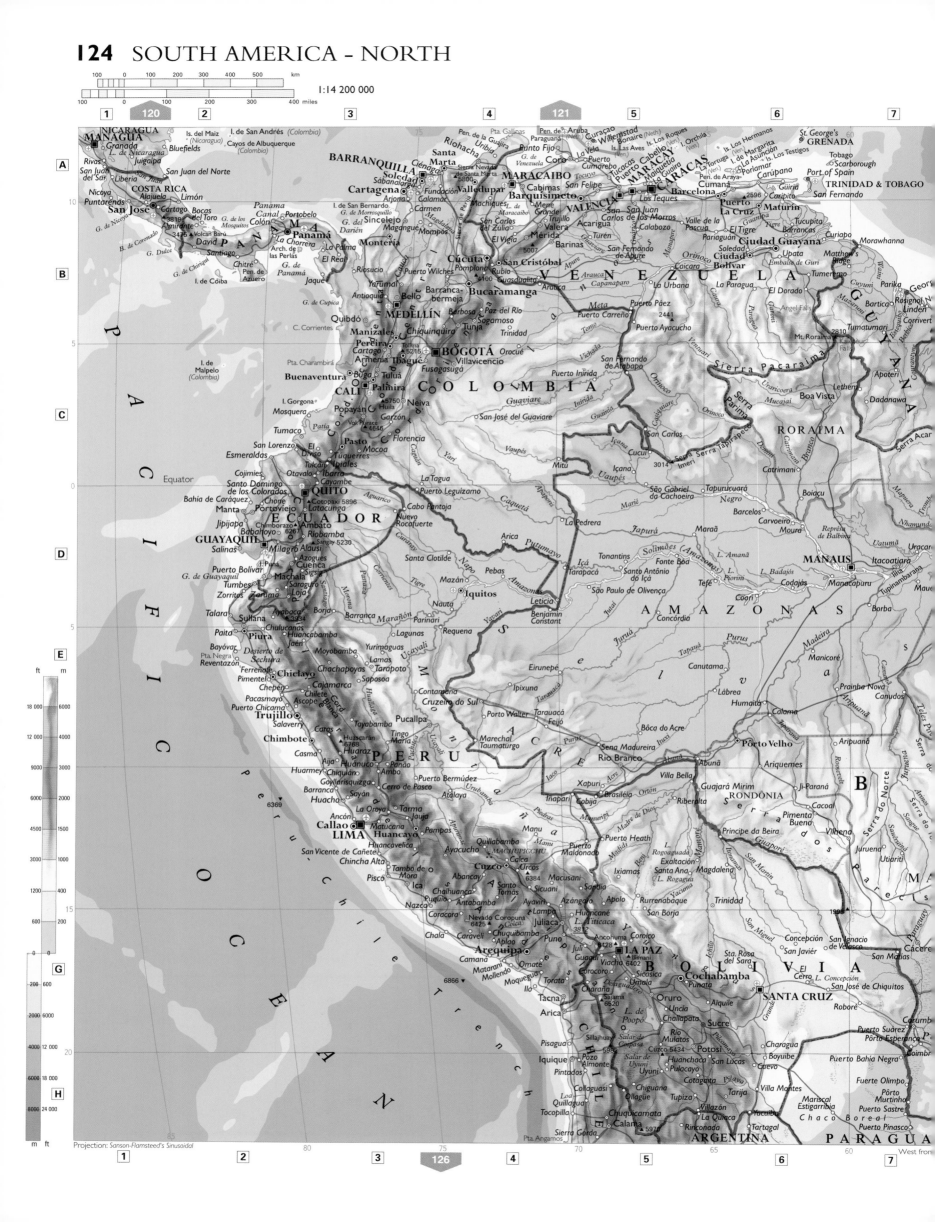

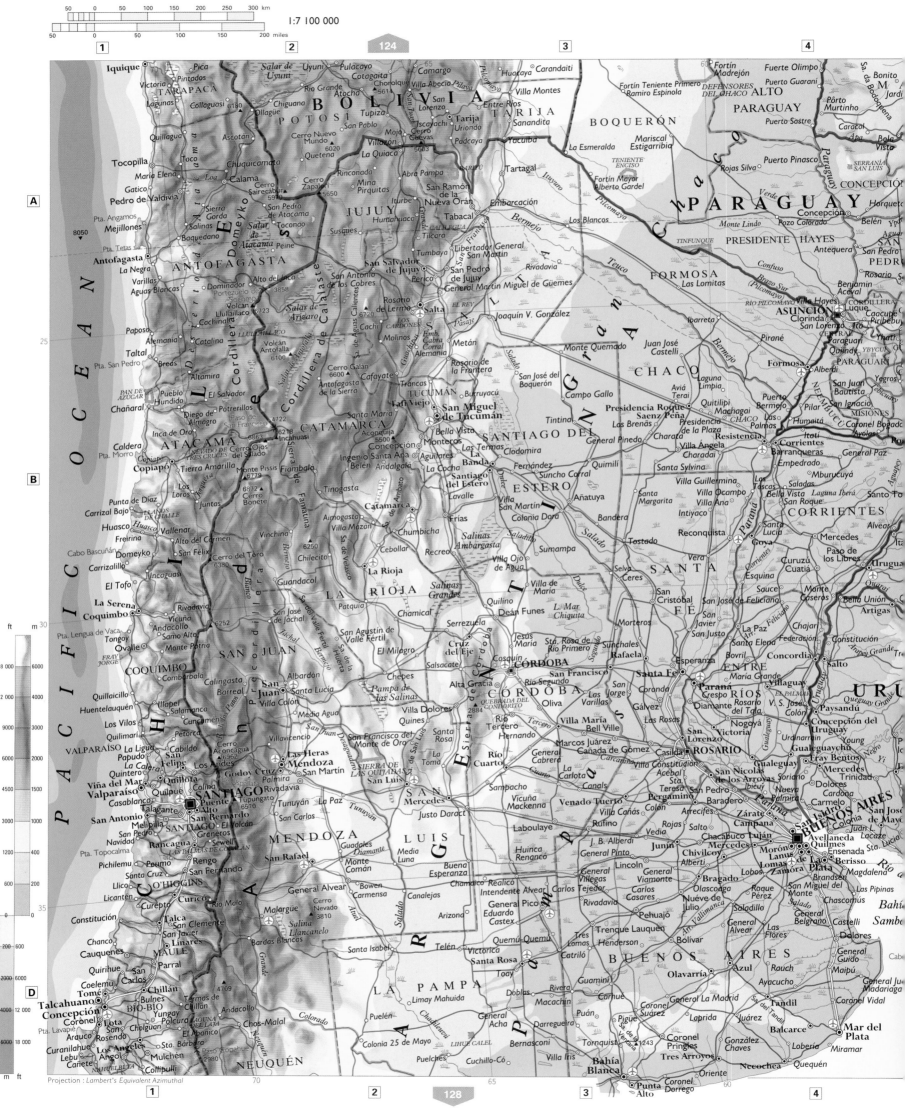

1:7 100 000

Projection : Lambert's Equivalent Azimuthal

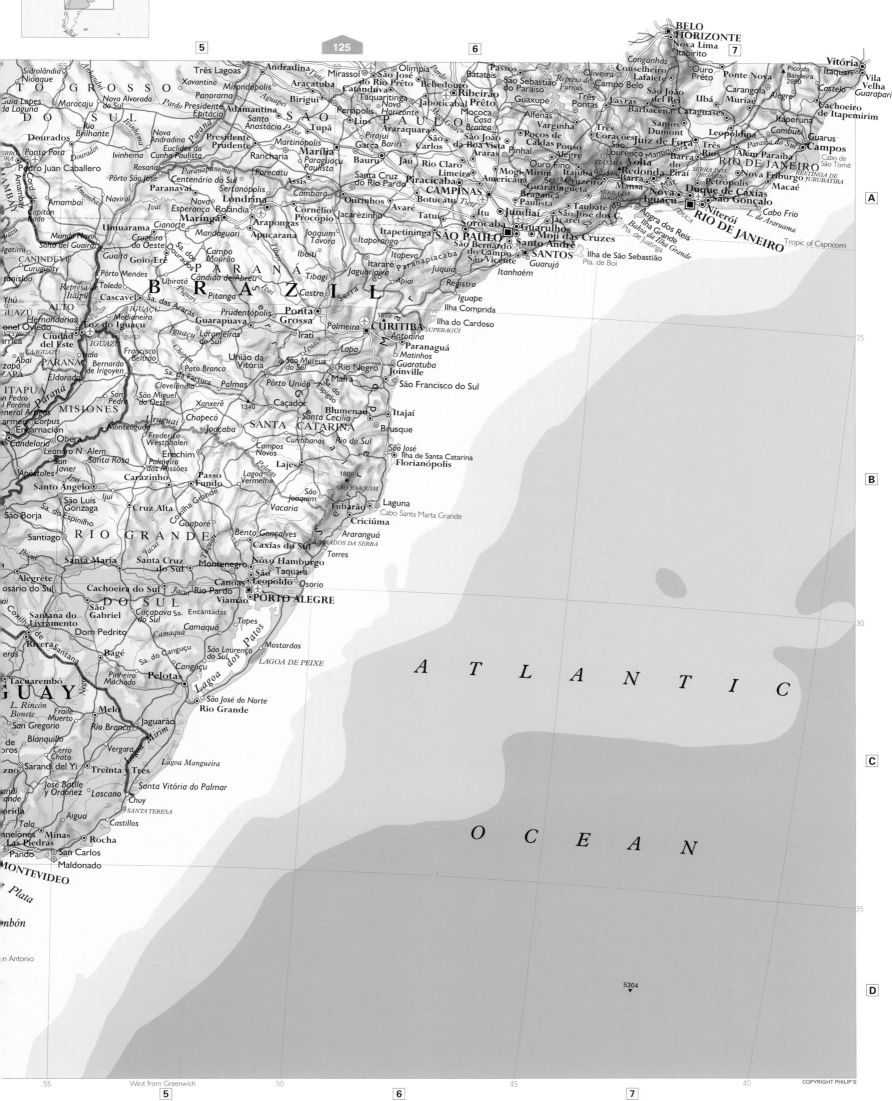

5 125 6 7

BELO HORIZONTE
Nova Lima
Itabirito

Sidrolândia
Nioaque
TO GROSSO
Guia Lopes
da Laguna
Maracaju
Nova Alvorada
Dourados
Rio
Brilhante
DO SUL
Ponta Porã
Pedro Juan Caballero
Amambaí

Três Lagoas
Xavantina
Mirandópolis
Panorama
Presidente
Epitácio
Adamantina
Nova Andradina
Euclides da
Cunha Paulista
Ivinhema
Presidente
Prudente
Rancharia
Rosana
Porecatu
Paranavaí
Nova
Esperança
Rolândia

Andradina
Araçatuba
Catanduva
Birigui
Tupã
SÃO
Marília
Paraguaçu
Paulista
Assis
Londrina
Maringá
Apucarana
Arapongas

Mirassol
São José
do Rio Prêto
Taquaritinga
Lins
Bauru
Garça
Bariri
Jaú
PAULO
Araraquara
São
Carlos
Rio Claro
Piracicaba
CAMPINAS

Olímpia
Bebedouro
Jaboticabal
Novo
Horizonte
Pirajuí
Avaré

Passos
Batatais
Ribeirão
Prêto
Mocóca
Casa
Branca
Mogi
Guaçu
Americana
Botucatu

Oliveira
Campo Belo
Guaxupé
Alfenas
Poços de
Caldas
Ouro Fino
Pinhal
Itu
Sorocaba

Congonhas
Conselheiro
Ouro
Prêto
Lavras
Varginha
Pouso
Alegre
Mogi-
Mirim

Ponte Nova
São João
del Rei
Três
Corações
Juiz de Fora
Cruzeiro
Volta
Redonda
Barra
Mansa

Vitória
Itaquaí
Vila
Velha
Guarapari
Carangola
Ubá
Muriaé
Barbacena
Cataguases
Leopoldina
Além Paraíba
Três
Rios
Nova Friburgo

Tropic of Capricorn

ATLANTIC

OCEAN

5304

PORTO ALEGRE

MONTEVIDEO

West from Greenwich   COPYRIGHT PHILIP'S

5 6 7

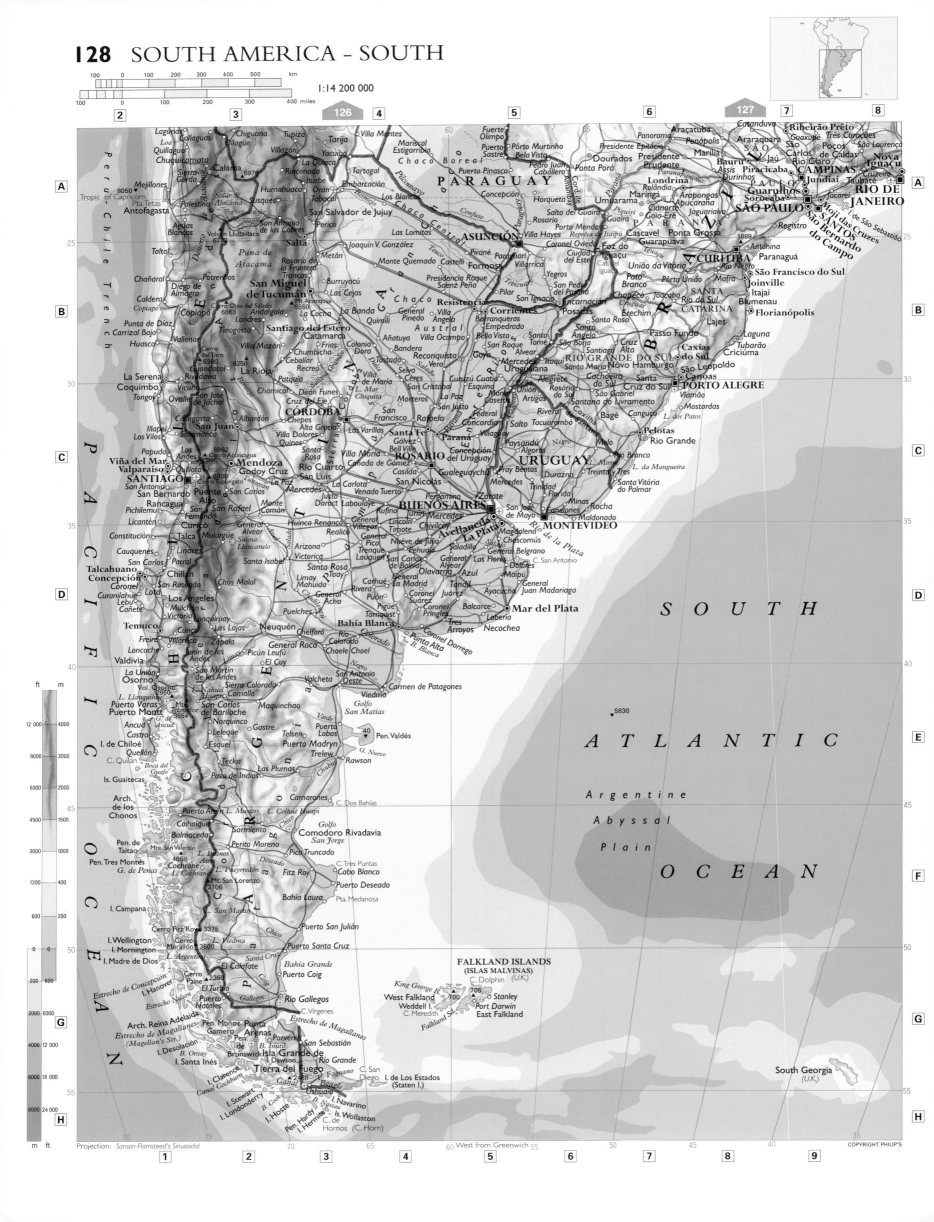

1:14 200 000

km
miles

SOUTH

ATLANTIC

Argentine

Abyssal

Plain

OCEAN

PARAGUAY

ASUNCIÓN

BRASIL

CURITIBA

RIO DE JANEIRO

SÃO PAULO

CAMPINAS

SANTOS

PORTO ALEGRE

CÓRDOBA

ROSARIO

URUGUAY

SANTIAGO

MENDOZA

BUENOS AIRES

MONTEVIDEO

Mar del Plata

Bahía Blanca

FALKLAND ISLANDS
(ISLAS MALVINAS)
(U.K.)

West Falkland
Weddell I.
C. Meredith

Stanley
Port Darwin
East Falkland

South Georgia
(U.K.)

Tropic of Capricorn

PACIFIC OCEAN

Projection: Sanson-Flamsteed's Sinusoidal

West from Greenwich

COPYRIGHT PHILIP'S

INDEX TO WORLD MAPS

How to use the index

The index contains the names of all the principal places and features shown on the World Maps. Each name is followed by an additional entry in italics giving the country or region within which it is located. The alphabetical order of names composed of two or more words is governed primarily by the first word and then by the second. This is an example of the rule:

Miquelon *St-P. &M.* **105** C8
Mir *Niger* **83** C7
Mīr Kūh *Iran* **71** E8
Mīr Shahdād *Iran* **71** E8
Mira *Italy* **41** C9

Physical features composed of a proper name (Erie) and a description (Lake) are positioned alphabetically by the proper name. The description is positioned after the proper name and is usually abbreviated:

Erie, L. *N. Amer.* **114** D4

Where a description forms part of a settlement or administrative name however, it is always written in full and put in its true alphabetic position:

Mount Morris *U.S.A.* **114** D7

Names beginning with M' and Mc are indexed as if they were spelled Mac. Names beginning St. are alphabetised under Saint, but Sankt, Sint, Sant', Santa and San are all spelt in full and are alphabetised accordingly. If the same place name occurs two or more times in the index and all are in the same country, each is followed by the name of the administrative subdivision in which it is located. For example:

Jackson *Ky., U.S.A.* **113** G12
Jackson *Mich., U.S.A.* **113** D11
Jackson *Minn., U.S.A.* **112** D6

The number in bold type which follows each name in the index refers to the number of the map page where that feature or place will be found. This is usually the largest scale at which the place or feature appears.

The letter and figure which are in bold type immediately after the page number give the grid square on the map page, within which the feature is situated. The letter represents the latitude and the figure the longitude. A lower case letter immediately after the page number refers to an inset map on that page.

In some cases the feature itself may fall within the specified square, while the name is outside. This is usually the case only with features which are larger than a grid square.

Rivers are indexed to their mouths or confluences, and carry the symbol ➤ after their names. The following symbols are also used in the index: ■ country, ☑ overseas territory or dependency, ☐ first order administrative area, △ national park, ◠ other park (provincial park, nature reserve or game reserve), ✈ (LHR) principal airport (and location identifier).

How to pronounce place names

English-speaking people usually have no difficulty in reading and pronouncing correctly English place names. However, foreign place name pronunciations may present many problems. Such problems can be minimised by following some simple rules. However, these rules cannot be applied to all situations, and there will be many exceptions.

1. In general, stress each syllable equally, unless your experience suggests otherwise.
2. Pronounce the letter 'a' as a broad 'a' as in 'arm'.
3. Pronounce the letter 'e' as a short 'e' as in 'elm'.
4. Pronounce the letter 'i' as a cross between a short 'i' and long 'e', as the two 'i's in 'California'.
5. Pronounce the letter 'o' as an intermediate 'o' as in 'soft'.
6. Pronounce the letter 'u' as an intermediate 'u' as in 'sure'.
7. Pronounce consonants hard, except in the Romance-language areas where 'g's are likely to be pronounced softly like 'j' in 'jam'; 'j' itself may be pronounced as 'y'; and 'x's may be pronounced as 'h'.
8. For names in mainland China, pronounce 'q' like the 'ch' in 'chin', 'x' like the 'sh' in 'she', 'zh' like the 'j' in 'jam', and 'z' as if it were spelled 'dz'. In general pronounce 'a' as in 'father', 'e' as in 'but', 'i' as in 'keep', 'o' as in 'or', and 'u' as in 'rule'.

Moreover, English has no diacritical marks (accent and pronunciation signs), although some languages do. The following is a brief and general guide to the pronunciation of those most frequently used in the principal Western European languages.

		Pronunciation as in
French	é	day and shows that the e is to be pronounced; e.g. Orléans.
	è	mare
	î	used over any vowel and does not affect pronunciation; shows contraction of the name, usually omission of 's' following a vowel.
	ç	's' before 'a', 'o' and 'u'.
	ë, ï, ü	over 'e', 'i' and 'u' when they are used with another vowel and shows that each is to be pronounced.
German	ä	fate
	ö	fur
	ü	no English equivalent; like French 'tu'
Italian	à, é	over vowels and indicates stress.
Portuguese	ã, õ	vowels pronounced nasally.
	ç	boss
	á	shows stress
	ô	shows that a vowel has an 'i' or 'u' sound combined with it.
Spanish	ñ	canyon
	ü	pronounced as w and separately from adjoining vowels.
	á	usually indicates that this is a stressed vowel.

Abbreviations

A.C.T. – Australian Capital Territory
A.R. – Autonomous Region
Afghan. – Afghanistan
Afr. – Africa
Ala. – Alabama
Alta. – Alberta
Amer. – America(n)
Arch. – Archipelago
Ariz. – Arizona
Ark. – Arkansas
Atl. Oc. – Atlantic Ocean
B. – Baie, Bahía, Bay, Bucht, Bugt
B.C. – British Columbia
Bangla. – Bangladesh
Barr. – Barrage
Bos.-H. – Bosnia-Herzegovina
C. – Cabo, Cap, Cape, Coast
C.A.R. – Central African Republic
C. Prov. – Cape Province
Calif. – California
Cat. – Catarata
Cent. – Central
Chan. – Channel
Colo. – Colorado
Conn. – Connecticut
Cord. – Cordillera
Cr. – Creek
Czech. – Czech Republic
D.C. – District of Columbia
Del. – Delaware
Dem. – Democratic
Dep. – Dependency
Des. – Desert
Dét. – Détroit
Dist. – District
Dj. – Djebel
Domin. – Dominica
Dom. Rep. – Dominican Republic
E. – East

E. Salv. – El Salvador
Eq. Guin. – Equatorial Guinea
Est. – Estrecho
Falk. Is. – Falkland Is.
Fd. – Fjord
Fla. – Florida
Fr. – French
G. – Golfe, Golfo, Gulf, Guba, Gebel
Ga. – Georgia
Gt. – Great, Greater
Guinea-Biss. – Guinea-Bissau
H.K. – Hong Kong
H.P. – Himachal Pradesh
Hants. – Hampshire
Harb. – Harbor, Harbour
Hd. – Head
Hts. – Heights
I.(s). – Île, Ilha, Insel, Isla, Island, Isle
Ill. – Illinois
Ind. – Indiana
Ind. Oc. – Indian Ocean
Ivory C. – Ivory Coast
J. – Jabal, Jebel
Jaz. – Jazīrah
Junc. – Junction
K. – Kap, Kapp
Kans. – Kansas
Kep. – Kepulauan
Ky. – Kentucky
L. – Lac, Lacul, Lago, Lagoa, Lake, Limni, Loch, Lough
La. – Louisiana
Ld. – Land
Liech. – Liechtenstein
Lux. – Luxembourg
Mad. P. – Madhya Pradesh
Madag. – Madagascar
Man. – Manitoba

Mass. – Massachusetts
Md. – Maryland
Me. – Maine
Medit. S. – Mediterranean Sea
Mich. – Michigan
Minn. – Minnesota
Miss. – Mississippi
Mo. – Missouri
Mont. – Montana
Mozam. – Mozambique
Mt.(s) – Mont, Montaña, Mountain
Mte. – Monte
Mti. – Monti
N. – Nord, Norte, North, Northern, Nouveau
N.B. – New Brunswick
N.C. – North Carolina
N. Cal. – New Caledonia
N. Dak. – North Dakota
N.H. – New Hampshire
N.I. – North Island
N.J. – New Jersey
N. Mex. – New Mexico
N.S. – Nova Scotia
N.S.W. – New South Wales
N.W.T. – North West Territory
N.Y. – New York
N.Z. – New Zealand
Nac. – Nacional
Nat. – National
Nebr. – Nebraska
Neths. – Netherlands
Nev. – Nevada
Nfld. & L. – Newfoundland and Labrador
Nic. – Nicaragua
O. – Oued, Ouadi
Occ. – Occidentale
Okla. – Oklahoma

Ont. – Ontario
Or. – Orientale
Oreg. – Oregon
Os. – Ostrov
Oz. – Ozero
P. – Pass, Passo, Pasul, Pulau
P.E.I. – Prince Edward Island
Pa. – Pennsylvania
Pac. Oc. – Pacific Ocean
Papua N.G. – Papua New Guinea
Pass. – Passage
Peg. – Pegunungan
Pen. – Peninsula, Péninsule
Phil. – Philippines
Pk. – Peak
Plat. – Plateau
Prov. – Province, Provincial
Pt. – Point
Pta. – Ponta, Punta
Pte. – Pointe
Qué. – Québec
Queens. – Queensland
R. – Rio, River
R.I. – Rhode Island
Ra. – Range
Raj. – Rajasthan
Recr. – Recreational, Récréatif
Reg. – Region
Rep. – Republic
Res. – Reserve, Reservoir
Rhld-Pfz. – Rheinland-Pfalz
S. – South, Southern, Sur
Si. Arabia – Saudi Arabia
S.C. – South Carolina
S. Dak. – South Dakota
S.I. – South Island
S. Leone – Sierra Leone
Sa. – Serra, Sierra
Sask. – Saskatchewan

Scot. – Scotland
Sd. – Sound
Sev. – Severnaya
Sib. – Siberia
Sprs. – Springs
St. – Saint
Sta. – Santa
Ste. – Sainte
Sto. – Santo
Str. – Strait, Stretto
Switz. – Switzerland
Tas. – Tasmania
Tenn. – Tennessee
Terr. – Territory, Territoire
Tex. – Texas
Tg. – Tanjung
Trin. & Tob. – Trinidad & Tobago
U.A.E. – United Arab Emirates
U.K. – United Kingdom
U.S.A. – United States of America
Ut. P. – Uttar Pradesh
Va. – Virginia
Vdkhr. – Vodokhranilishche
Vdskh. – Vodoskhovyshche
Vf. – Vîrful
Vic. – Victoria
Vol. – Volcano
Vt. – Vermont
W. – Wadi, West
W. Va. – West Virginia
Wall. & F. Is. – Wallis and Futuna Is.
Wash. – Washington
Wis. – Wisconsin
Wlkp. – Wielkopolski
Wyo. – Wyoming
Yorks. – Yorkshire

A

A 'Âli an Nîl □ *Sudan* 81 F3
A Baña *Spain* 36 C2
A Cañiza *Spain* 36 C2
A Coruña *Spain* 36 B2
A Estrada *Spain* 36 C2
A Fonsagrada *Spain* 36 B3
A Guarda *Spain* 36 D2
A Gudiña *Spain* 36 C3
A Rúa *Spain* 36 C3
Aabenraa *Denmark* 11 J3
Aabybro *Denmark* 11 G3
Aachen *Germany* 24 E2
Aalborg *Denmark* 11 G3
Aalborg Bugt *Denmark* 11 H4
Aalen *Germany* 25 G6
Aalestrup *Denmark* 11 H3
Aalsmeer *Belgium* 17 D4
Aalten *Neths.* 17 C6
Aalter *Belgium* 17 C3
Äänekoski *Finland* 8 E21
Aarau *Switz.* 25 H4
Aarberg *Switz.* 25 H3
Aare ➤ *Switz.* 25 H4
Aargau □ *Switz.* 25 H4
Aarhus = Århus *Denmark* 11 H4
Aars *Denmark* 11 H3
Aarschot *Belgium* 17 D4
Aba *China* 58 A3
Aba *Dem. Rep. of the Congo* 86 B3
Aba *Nigeria* 83 D6
Âbâ, Jazîrat *Sudan* 81 E3
Abaco I. *Bahamas* 120 A4
Abadab, J. *Sudan* 80 D4
Ābādān *Iran* 71 D6
Abade *Ethiopia* 81 F4
Ābādeh *Iran* 71 D7
Abadin *Spain* 36 B3
Abadla *Algeria* 78 B5
Abaetetuba *Brazil* 125 D9
Abagnar Qi = Xilinhot *China* 56 C9
Abah, Tanjung *Indonesia* 63 K18
Abai *Paraguay* 127 B4
Abak *Nigeria* 83 E6
Abakaliki *Nigeria* 83 D6
Abakan *Russia* 53 D10
Abala *Niger* 83 C5
Abalak *Niger* 83 B6
Abalemma *Niger* 83 B6
Abana *Turkey* 72 B6
Abancay *Peru* 124 F4
Abano Terme *Italy* 41 C8
Abarán *Spain* 39 G3
Abariringa *Kiribati* 96 H10
Abarqū *Iran* 71 D7
Abashiri *Japan* 54 B12
Abashiri-Wan *Japan* 54 C12
Abaújszántó *Hungary* 28 B6
Abava ➤ *Latvia* 30 A8
Ābay = Nîl el Azraq ➤ *Sudan* 81 E3
Abay *Kazakhstan* 52 E8
Abaya, L. *Ethiopia* 81 F4
Abaza *Russia* 52 D9
Abbadia di Fiastra △ *Italy* 41 E10
Abbadia San Salvatore *Italy* 41 F8
'Abbāsābād *Iran* 71 C8
Abbay = Nîl el Azraq ➤ *Sudan* 81 D3
Abbaye, Pt. *U.S.A.* 112 B9
Abbé, L. *Ethiopia* 81 E5
Abbeville *France* 19 B8
Abbeville *Ala., U.S.A.* 117 F12
Abbeville *La., U.S.A.* 116 G8
Abbeville *S.C., U.S.A.* 117 D13
Abbeyfeale *Ireland* 12 D2
Abbiategrasso *Italy* 40 C5
Abbot Ice Shelf *Antarctica* 5 D16
Abbotsford *Canada* 102 D4
Abbottabad *Pakistan* 68 B5
ABC Islands = Netherlands Antilles □ *W. Indies* 124 A5
Abd al Kūrī *Yemen* 75 E5
Ābdar *Iran* 71 D7
'Abdolābād *Iran* 71 C8
Abdulpur *Bangla.* 69 G13
Abéché *Chad* 79 F10
Abejar *Spain* 38 D2
Abekr *Sudan* 81 E2
Abel Tasman △ *N.Z.* 91 D4
Abengourou *Ivory C.* 82 D4
Abenójar *Spain* 37 G6
Åbenrå = Aabenraa *Denmark* 11 J3
Abensberg *Germany* 25 G7
Abeokuta *Nigeria* 83 D5
Aber *Uganda* 86 B3
Aberaeron *U.K.* 15 E3
Aberayron = Aberaeron *U.K.* 15 E3
Aberchirder *U.K.* 13 D6
Abercorn *Australia* 95 D5
Aberdare *U.K.* 15 F4
Aberdare ➤ *Kenya* 86 C4
Aberdare Ra. *Kenya* 86 C4
Aberdeen *Australia* 95 E5
Aberdeen *Canada* 103 C7

Aberdeen *S. Africa* 88 E3
Aberdeen *U.K.* 13 D6
Aberdeen *Idaho, U.S.A.* 108 E7
Aberdeen *Md., U.S.A.* 113 F15
Aberdeen *Miss., U.S.A.* 117 E10
Aberdeen *S. Dak., U.S.A.* 112 C4
Aberdeen *Wash., U.S.A.* 110 D3
Aberdeen, City of □ *U.K.* 13 D6
Aberdeenshire □ *U.K.* 13 D6
Aberdovey = Aberdyfi *U.K.* 15 E3
Aberdyfi *U.K.* 15 E3
Aberfeldy *U.K.* 13 E5
Aberfoyle *U.K.* 13 E4
Abergavenny *U.K.* 15 F4
Abergele *U.K.* 14 D4
Abernathy *U.S.A.* 116 E4
Aberystwyth *U.K.* 15 E3
Abhā *Si. Arabia* 80 D5
Abhar *Iran* 73 D13
Abhayapuri *India* 69 F14
Abia □ *Nigeria* 83 D6
Abide *Turkey* 47 C11
Abidiya *Sudan* 80 D3
Abidjan *Ivory C.* 82 D4
Abilene *Kans., U.S.A.* 112 F5
Abilene *Tex., U.S.A.* 116 E5
Abingdon *U.K.* 15 F6
Abingdon *U.S.A.* 113 G13
Abington Reef *Australia* 94 B4
Abitau ➤ *Canada* 103 B7
Abitibi ➤ *Canada* 104 C4
Abitibi, L. *Canada* 104 C4
Abiy Adi *Ethiopia* 81 E4
Abiyata-Shala △ *Ethiopia* 81 F4
Abkhaz Republic = Abkhazia □ *Georgia* 35 J5
Abkhazia □ *Georgia* 35 J5
Abminga *Australia* 95 D1
Abnûb *Egypt* 80 B3
Åbo = Turku *Finland* 32 B2
Abocho *Nigeria* 83 D6
Abohar *India* 68 D6
Aboisso *Ivory C.* 82 D4
Abomey *Benin* 83 D5
Abong-Mbang *Cameroon* 84 D2
Abonnema *Nigeria* 83 E6
Abony *Hungary* 28 C5
Aboso *Ghana* 82 D4
Abou-Deïa *Chad* 79 F9
Aboyne *U.K.* 13 D6
Abra Pampa *Argentina* 126 A2
Abraham L. *Canada* 102 C5
Abrantes *Portugal* 37 F2
Abreojos, Pta. *Mexico* 118 B2
Abri *Esh Shamâliya, Sudan* 80 C3
Abri *Janub Kordofân, Sudan* 81 E3
Abrolhos, Banco *Brazil* 125 F11
Abrud *Romania* 28 D8
Abruzzo □ *Italy* 41 F10
Absaroka Range *U.S.A.* 108 D9
Abtenau *Austria* 26 D6
Abu *India* 68 G5
Abū al Abyad *U.A.E.* 71 E7
Abū al Khaşīb *Iraq* 71 D6
Abū 'Alī *Si. Arabia* 71 E6
Abū 'Alī ➤ *Lebanon* 74 A4
Abu Ballas *Egypt* 80 C2
Abu Deleiq *Sudan* 81 D3
Abu Dhabi = Abū Z̧aby *U.A.E.* 71 E7
Abu Dis *Sudan* 80 D3
Abu Dom *Sudan* 81 D3
Abū Du'ān *Syria* 73 D8
Abu el Gaïn, W. ➤ *Egypt* 74 F2
Abu Fatma, Ras *Sudan* 80 C4
Abū Gabra *Sudan* 81 E2
Abu Ga'da, W. ➤ *Egypt* 74 F1
Abu Gelba *Sudan* 81 E3
Abu Gubeiha *Sudan* 81 E3
Abu Habl, Khawr ➤ *Sudan* 81 E3
Abū Ḩadrīyah *Si. Arabia* 71 E6
Abu Hamed *Sudan* 80 D3
Abu Haraz *An Nîl el Azraq, Sudan* 80 D3
Abu Haraz *El Gezira, Sudan* 81 E3
Abu Haraz *Esh Shamâliya, Sudan* 80 D3
Abū Higar *Sudan* 81 E3
Abū Kamāl *Syria* 73 E9
Abu Kuleiwat *Sudan* 81 E2
Abū Madd, Ra's *Si. Arabia* 70 E3
Abu Matariq *Sudan* 81 E2
Abu Mendi *Ethiopia* 81 E4
Abū Mūsā *U.A.E.* 71 E7
Abū Qaşr *Sudan* 80 D3
Abu Qir *Egypt* 80 H7
Abu Qireiya *Egypt* 80 C4
Abu Qurqas *Egypt* 80 B3
Abu Shagara, Ras *Sudan* 80 C4
Abū Shanab *Sudan* 81 E2
Abu Simbel *Egypt* 80 C3
Abū Şukhayr *Iraq* 73 G11
Abu Sultân *Egypt* 80 H8
Abu Tabari *Sudan* 80 D2
Abu Tig *Egypt* 80 B3
Abu Tiga *Sudan* 81 E3
Abu Tineitin *Sudan* 81 E3

Abû Uruq *Sudan* 81 D3
Abû Zabad *Sudan* 81 E2
Abū Z̧āby *U.A.E.* 71 E7
Abū Zeydābād *Iran* 71 C6
Abuja *Nigeria* 83 D6
Abukuma-Gawa ➤ *Japan* 54 E10
Abukuma-Sammyaku *Japan* 54 F10
Abunā *Brazil* 124 E5
Abunã ➤ *Brazil* 124 E5
Abune Yosef *Ethiopia* 81 E4
Abut Hd. *N.Z.* 91 E3
Abuye Meda *Ethiopia* 81 E4
Abwong *Sudan* 81 F3
Åby *Sweden* 11 F10
Aby, Lagune *Ivory C.* 82 D4
Abyad *Sudan* 81 E2
Acadia △ *U.S.A.* 113 C19
Açailândia *Brazil* 125 D9
Acajutla *El Salv.* 120 D2
Acámbaro *Mexico* 118 C4
Acanthus *Greece* 44 F7
Acaponeta *Mexico* 118 C3
Acapulco *Mexico* 119 D5
Acarai, Serra *Brazil* 124 C7
Acarigua *Venezuela* 124 B5
Acatlán *Mexico* 119 D5
Acayucán *Mexico* 119 D6
Accéglio *Italy* 40 D4
Accomac *U.S.A.* 113 G16
Accous *France* 20 E3
Accra *Ghana* 83 D4
Accrington *U.K.* 14 D5
Acebal *Argentina* 126 C3
Aceh □ *Indonesia* 62 D1
Acerra *Italy* 43 B7
Aceuchal *Spain* 37 G4
Achaia □ *Greece* 46 C3
Achalpur *India* 66 J10
Acharnes *Greece* 46 C5
Acheloos ➤ *Greece* 46 C3
Achenkirch *Austria* 26 D4
Achensee *Austria* 26 D4
Achentrias *Greece* 47 G7
Acher *India* 68 H5
Achern *Germany* 25 G4
Achill Hd. *Ireland* 12 C1
Achill I. *Ireland* 12 C1
Achim *Germany* 24 B5
Achinsk *Russia* 53 D10
Achladokambos *Greece* 46 D4
Acıgöl *Turkey* 47 D11
Acıpayam *Turkey* 47 D11
Acireale *Italy* 43 E8
Ackerman *U.S.A.* 117 E10
Acklins I. *Bahamas* 121 B5
Acme *Canada* 102 C6
Acme *U.S.A.* 114 C5
Aconcagua, Cerro *Argentina* 126 C2
Aconquija, Mt. *Argentina* 126 B2
Açores, Is. dos *Atl. Oc.* 78 a
Acornhoek *S. Africa* 89 C5
Acquapendente *Italy* 41 F8
Acquasanta Terme *Italy* 41 F10
Acquasparta *Italy* 41 F9
Acquaviva delle Fonti *Italy* 43 B9
Ácqui Terme *Italy* 40 D5
Acraman, L. *Australia* 95 E2
Acre = 'Akko *Israel* 74 C4
Acre □ *Brazil* 124 E4
Acre ➤ *Brazil* 124 E5
Acri *Italy* 43 C9
Actium *Greece* 46 C2
Acton *Canada* 114 C4
Ad Dammām *Si. Arabia* 71 E6
Ad Dawādimī *Si. Arabia* 70 E5
Ad Dawhah *Qatar* 71 E6
Ad Dawr *Iraq* 73 E10
Ad Dir'īyah *Si. Arabia* 70 E5
Ad Dīwānīyah *Iraq* 73 F11
Ad Dujayl *Iraq* 73 F11
Ad Duwayd *Si. Arabia* 70 D4
Ada *Ghana* 83 D5
Ada *Serbia* 28 E5
Ada *Minn., U.S.A.* 112 B5
Ada *Okla., U.S.A.* 116 D6
Adabiya *Egypt* 74 F1
Adair, C. *Canada* 101 B12
Adaja ➤ *Spain* 36 D6
Adak I. *U.S.A.* 106 a
Adamaoua □ *Cameroon* 83 D7
Adamaoua, Massif de l' *Cameroon* 83 D7
Adamawa □ *Nigeria* 83 D7
Adamawa Highlands = Adamaoua, Massif de l' *Cameroon* 83 D7
Adamello, Mte. *Italy* 40 B7
Adamello △ *Italy* 40 B7
Adami Tulu *Ethiopia* 81 F4
Adaminaby *Australia* 95 F4
Adams *Mass., U.S.A.* 115 D11
Adams *N.Y., U.S.A.* 115 C8

Adams *Wis., U.S.A.* 112 D9
Adams, Mt. *U.S.A.* 110 D5
Adam's Bridge *Sri Lanka* 66 Q11
Adams L. *Canada* 102 C5
Adam's Peak *Sri Lanka* 66 R12
Adamuz *Spain* 37 G6
Adana *Turkey* 72 D6
Adana □ *Turkey* 72 D6
Adanero *Spain* 36 E6
Adapazarı = Sakarya *Turkey* 72 B4
Adar Gwagwa, J. *Sudan* 80 C4
Adarama *Sudan* 81 D3
Adarte *Eritrea* 81 E5
Adaut *Indonesia* 63 F8
Adavale *Australia* 95 D3
Adda ➤ *Italy* 40 C6
Addis Ababa = Addis Abeba *Ethiopia* 81 F4
Addis Abeba *Ethiopia* 81 F4
Addis Alem *Ethiopia* 81 F4
Addis Zemen *Ethiopia* 81 E4
Addison *U.S.A.* 114 D7
Addo *S. Africa* 88 E4
Addo △ *S. Africa* 88 E4
Adebour *Niger* 83 C7
Ādeh *Iran* 70 B5
Adel *U.S.A.* 117 F13
Adelaide *Australia* 95 E2
Adelaide *S. Africa* 88 E4
Adelaide I. *Antarctica* 5 C17
Adelaide Pen. *Canada* 100 C10
Adelaide River *Australia* 92 B5
Adelaide Village *Bahamas* 120 A4
Adelanto *U.S.A.* 111 L9
Adele I. *Australia* 92 C3
Adélie, Terre *Antarctica* 5 C10
Adélie Land = Adélie, Terre *Antarctica* 5 C10
Adelsk *Belarus* 30 E10
Ademuz *Spain* 38 E3
Aden = Al 'Adan *Yemen* 75 E4
Aden, G. of *Ind. Oc.* 75 E4
Adendorp *S. Africa* 88 E3
Aderbissinat *Niger* 83 B6
Adh Dhayd *U.A.E.* 71 E7
Adhoi *India* 68 H4
Adi *Indonesia* 63 E8
Adi Arkai *Ethiopia* 81 E4
Adi Daro *Ethiopia* 81 E4
Adi Keyih *Eritrea* 81 E4
Adi Kwala *Eritrea* 81 E4
Adi Ugri *Eritrea* 81 E4
Adieu, C. *Australia* 93 F5
Adieu Pt. *Australia* 92 C3
Adigala *Ethiopia* 81 E5
Adige ➤ *Italy* 41 C9
Adigrat *Ethiopia* 81 E4
Adıgüzel Barajı *Turkey* 47 C11
Adilabad *India* 66 K11
Adilcevaz *Turkey* 73 C10
Adirondack △ *U.S.A.* 115 C10
Adirondack Mts. *U.S.A.* 115 C10
Adis Abeba = Addis Abeba *Ethiopia* 81 F4
Adıyaman *Turkey* 73 D8
Adıyaman □ *Turkey* 73 D8
Adjohon *Benin* 83 D5
Adjud *Romania* 29 D12
Adjumani *Uganda* 86 B3
Adjuntas *Puerto Rico* 121 d
Adlavik Is. *Canada* 105 B8
Adler *Russia* 35 J4
Admer *Algeria* 83 A6
Admiralty G. *Australia* 92 B4
Admiralty I. *U.S.A.* 102 B2
Admiralty Is. *Papua N. G.* 90 B7
Adnan Menderes, İzmir ✈ (ADB) *Turkey* 47 C9
Ado *Nigeria* 83 D5
Ado-Ekiti *Nigeria* 83 D6
Adok *Sudan* 81 F3
Adola *Ethiopia* 81 F5
Adolfo Ruiz Cortines, Presa *Mexico* 118 B3
Adonara *Indonesia* 63 F6
Adoni *India* 66 M10
Adony *Hungary* 28 C3
Adour ➤ *France* 20 E2
Adra *India* 69 H12
Adra *Spain* 37 J7
Adrano *Italy* 43 E7
Adrar *Mauritania* 78 D3
Adrar □ *Mauritania* 82 A3
Adrar des Iforas *Africa* 83 B5
Ádria *Italy* 41 C9
Adrian *Mich., U.S.A.* 113 E11
Adrian *Tex., U.S.A.* 116 D3
Adriatic Sea *Medit. S.* 6 G9
Adua *Indonesia* 63 E7
Adwa *Ethiopia* 81 E4
Adygea □ *Russia* 35 H5
Adzhar Republic = Ajaria □ *Georgia* 35 K6
Adzopé *Ivory C.* 82 D4
Ægean Sea *Medit. S.* 47 C7
Aerhtai Shan *Mongolia* 60 B4

Ærø *Denmark* 11 K4
Ærøskøbing *Denmark* 11 K4
Aetos *Greece* 46 D3
Afaahiti *Tahiti* 91 d
'Afak *Iraq* 73 F11
Afandou *Greece* 49 C10
Afar *Ethiopia* 81 E5
Afareaitu *Moorea* 91 d
Afghanistan ■ *Asia* 66 C4
Afikpo *Nigeria* 83 D6
Aflou *Algeria* 78 B6
Afragóla *Italy* 43 B7
Afram ➤ *Ghana* 83 D4
Afrera *Ethiopia* 81 E5
Africa 76 E6
'Afrīn *Syria* 72 D7
Afşin *Turkey* 72 C7
Afton *N.Y., U.S.A.* 115 D9
Afton *Wyo., U.S.A.* 108 E8
Afuá *Brazil* 125 D8
'Afula *Israel* 74 C4
Afyon *Turkey* 47 C12
Afyon □ *Turkey* 47 C12
Afyonkarahisar = Afyon *Turkey* 47 C12
Aga *Egypt* 80 H7
Agadès = Agadez *Niger* 83 B6
Agadez *Niger* 83 B6
Agadir *Morocco* 78 B4
Agaete *Canary Is.* 48 F4
Agaie *Nigeria* 83 D6
Again *Sudan* 81 F2
Agalega Is. *Mauritius* 3 E12
Ağapınar *Turkey* 47 B12
Agar *India* 68 H7
Agaro *Ethiopia* 81 F4
Agartala *India* 67 H17
Ağaş *Romania* 29 D11
Agassiz *Canada* 102 D4
Agats *Indonesia* 63 F9
Agawam *U.S.A.* 115 D12
Agbélouvé *Togo* 83 D5
Agboville *Ivory C.* 82 D4
Ağcabädi *Azerbaijan* 35 K8
Ağdam *Azerbaijan* 35 L8
Ağdaş *Azerbaijan* 35 K8
Agde *France* 20 E7
Agde, C. d' *France* 20 E7
Agdzhabedi = Ağcabädi *Azerbaijan* 35 K8
Agen *France* 20 D4
Agerbæk *Denmark* 11 J2
Agersø *Denmark* 11 J5
Ageyevo *Russia* 32 E9
Aggteleki △ *Hungary* 28 B5
Āgh Kand *Iran* 73 D13
Aghaggar *Algeria* 78 D7
Aghathonisi *Greece* 47 D8
Aghia Anna *Greece* 46 C5
Aghia Deka *Greece* 49 D6
Aghia Ekaterinis, Akra *Greece* 49 A3
Aghia Galini *Greece* 49 D6
Aghia Marina *Kasos, Greece* 47 F8
Aghia Marina *Leros, Greece* 47 D8
Aghia Paraskevi *Greece* 47 B7
Aghia Roumeli *Greece* 46 F5
Aghia Varvara *Greece* 49 D7
Aghiasos *Greece* 47 B8
Aghio Theodori *Greece* 46 D5
Aghion Oros □ *Greece* 45 F8
Aghios Andreas *Greece* 46 D4
Aghios Efstratios *Greece* 46 B6
Aghios Georgios *Greece* 46 D5
Aghios Ioannis, Akra *Greece* 49 D7
Aghios Isidoros *Greece* 49 C9
Aghios Kirikos *Greece* 47 D8
Aghios Matheos *Greece* 49 B3
Aghios Mironas *Greece* 47 F7
Aghios Nikolaos *Greece* 49 D7
Aghios Petros *Greece* 46 C2
Aghiou Orous, Kolpos *Greece* 44 F7
Aghireşu *Romania* 29 D8
Agia *Greece* 46 B4
Ağlasun *Turkey* 47 D12
Agly ➤ *France* 20 F7
Agnew *Australia* 93 E3
Agnibilékrou *Ivory C.* 82 D4
Agnita *Romania* 29 E9
Agnone *Italy* 41 G11
Agofie *Ghana* 83 D5
Agogna ➤ *Italy* 40 C5
Agogo *Sudan* 81 F3
Agon Coutainville *France* 18 C5
Ágordo *Italy* 41 B9
Agori *India* 69 G10
Agouna *Benin* 83 D5
Agout ➤ *France* 20 E5
Agra *India* 68 F7
Agrakhanskiuy Poluostrov *Russia* 35 J8
Agramunt *Spain* 38 D6
Agreda *Spain* 38 D3
Ağrı *Turkey* 73 C10
Ağrı □ *Turkey* 73 C10
Agri ➤ *Italy* 43 B9

Ağrı Dağı *Turkey* 73 C11
Ağrı Karakose = Ağrı *Turkey* 73 C10
Agria *Greece* 46 B5
Agrigento *Italy* 42 E6
Agrinio *Greece* 46 C3
Agrópoli *Italy* 43 B7
Agua Caliente *Mexico* 111 N10
Agua Caliente Springs *U.S.A.* 111 N10
Água Clara *Brazil* 125 H8
Agua Fria △ *U.S.A.* 109 J8
Agua Hechicera *Mexico* 111 N10
Agua Prieta *Mexico* 118 A3
Aguadilla *Puerto Rico* 121 d
Aguadulce *Panama* 120 E3
Aguanga *U.S.A.* 111 M10
Aguanish *Canada* 105 B7
Aguanus ➤ *Canada* 105 B7
Aguapey ➤ *Argentina* 126 B4
Aguaray Guazú ➤ *Paraguay* 126 A4
Aguarico ➤ *Ecuador* 124 D3
Aguaro-Guariquito △ *Venezuela* 121 E6
Aguas ➤ *Spain* 38 D4
Aguas Blancas *Chile* 126 A2
Aguas Calientes, Sierra de *Argentina* 126 B2
Aguascalientes *Mexico* 118 C4
Aguascalientes □ *Mexico* 118 C4
Agudo *Spain* 37 G6
Águeda *Portugal* 36 E2
Águeda ➤ *Spain* 36 D4
Aguelhok *Mali* 83 B5
Aguié *Niger* 83 C6
Aguila, Punta *Puerto Rico* 121 d
Aguilafuente *Spain* 36 D6
Aguilar *Spain* 37 H6
Aguilar de Campóo *Spain* 36 C6
Aguilares *Argentina* 126 B2
Aguilas *Spain* 39 H3
Agüimes *Canary Is.* 48 G4
Aguja, C. de la *Colombia* 122 B3
Agujereada, Pta. *Puerto Rico* 121 d
Agulaa *Ethiopia* 81 E4
Agulhas, C. *S. Africa* 88 E3
Agulo *Canary Is.* 48 F2
Agung, Gunung *Indonesia* 63 J18
Agur *Uganda* 86 B3
Agusan ➤ *Phil.* 61 G6
Ağva *Turkey* 45 E13
Agvali *Russia* 35 J8
Aha Mts. *Botswana* 88 B3
Ahaggar *Algeria* 78 D7
Ahamansu *Ghana* 83 D5
Ahar *Iran* 73 C12
Ahat *Turkey* 47 C12
Ahaus *Germany* 24 C2
Ahipara B. *N.Z.* 91 A4
Ahir Dağı *Turkey* 47 C12
Ahiri *India* 66 K12
Ahlat *Turkey* 73 C10
Ahlen *Germany* 24 D3
Ahmad Wal *Pakistan* 68 E4
Ahmadabad *India* 68 H5
Aḩmadābād *Khorāsān, Iran* 71 C9
Aḩmadābād *Khorāsān, Iran* 71 C8
Aḩmadī *Iran* 71 E8
Ahmadnagar *India* 66 K9
Ahmadpur *Pakistan* 68 E4
Ahmadpur Lamma *Pakistan* 68 E4
Ahmar, Mts. *Ethiopia* 81 F5
Ahmedabad = Ahmadabad *India* 68 H5
Ahmednagar = Ahmadnagar *India* 66 K9
Ahmetbey *Turkey* 45 E11
Ahmetler *Turkey* 47 C11
Ahmetli *Turkey* 47 C9
Ahoada *Nigeria* 83 D6
Ahome *Mexico* 118 B3
Ahoskie *U.S.A.* 117 C16
Ahr ➤ *Germany* 24 E3
Ahram *Iran* 71 D6
Ahrax Pt. *Malta* 49 D1
Ahrensbök *Germany* 24 A6
Ahrensburg *Germany* 24 B6
Āhū *Iran* 71 D6
Ahuachapán *El Salv.* 120 D2
Ahun *France* 19 F9
Åhus *Sweden* 11 J8
Ahvāz *Iran* 71 D6
Ahvenanmaa = Åland *Finland* 9 F19
Aḩwar *Yemen* 75 E4
Ahzar ➤ *Mali* 83 B5
Ai ➤ *India* 69 F14
Ai-Ais *Namibia* 88 D2
Ai-Ais and Fish River Canyon △ *Namibia* 88 C2
Aichach *Germany* 25 G7
Aichi □ *Japan* 55 G8
Aigle *Switz.* 25 J2
Aignay-le-Duc *France* 19 E11
Aigoual, Mt. *France* 20 D7
Aigre *France* 20 C4

Aigrettes, Pte. des *Réunion* **85** c
Aigua *Uruguay* **127** C5
Aigueperse *France* **19** F10
Aigues ➤ *France* **21** D8
Aigues-Mortes *France* **21** E8
Aigues-Mortes, G. d' *France* **21** E8
Aigües Tortes y Lago San
  Mauricio △ *Spain* **38** C4
Aiguilles *France* **21** D10
Aiguillon *France* **20** D4
Aigurande *France* **19** F8
Aihui = Heihe *China* **60** A7
Aija *Peru* **124** E3
Aikawa *Japan* **54** E9
Aiken *U.S.A.* **117** E14
Ailao Shan *China* **58** F3
Aileron *Australia* **94** C1
Aillant-sur-Tholon *France* **19** E10
Aillik *Canada* **105** A8
Ailsa Craig *U.K.* **13** F3
Aim *Russia* **53** D14
Aimere *Indonesia* **63** F6
Aimogasta *Argentina* **126** B2
Ain □ *France* **19** F12
Ain ➤ *France* **21** C9
Aïn Ben Tili *Mauritania* **78** C4
Ain Dalla *Egypt* **80** B2
Ain el Mafki *Egypt* **80** B2
Ain Girba *Egypt* **80** B2
Ain Murr *Sudan* **80** C2
Ain Qeiqab *Egypt* **80** B1
Aïn Sefra *Algeria* **78** B5
Aïn Sheikh Murzûk *Egypt* **80** B2
Ain Sudr *Egypt* **74** F2
Aïn Sukhna *Egypt* **80** J8
Aïn Témouchent *Algeria* **78** A5
Aïn Zeitûn *Egypt* **80** B2
Ainaži *Latvia* **30** D3
Ainos Oros *Greece* **46** C2
Ainsworth *U.S.A.* **112** D4
Aiquile *Bolivia* **124** G5
Aïr *Niger* **83** B6
Air Force I. *Canada* **101** C12
Air Hitam *Malaysia* **65** M4
Airaines *France* **19** C8
Airdrie *Canada* **102** C6
Airdrie *U.K.* **13** F5
Aire ➤ *France* **19** C11
Aire, I. de l' *Spain* **48** B11
Aire-sur-la-Lys *France* **19** B9
Aire-sur-l'Adour *France* **20** E3
Airlie Beach *Australia* **94** J6
Airvault *France* **18** F6
Aisch ➤ *Germany* **25** F6
Aisne □ *France* **19** C10
Aisne ➤ *France* **19** C9
Ait *India* **69** G8
Aitana, Sierra de *Spain* **39** G4
Aitkin *U.S.A.* **112** B7
Aitutaki *Cook Is.* **97** J12
Aiud *Romania* **29** D8
Aix-en-Provence *France* **21** E9
Aix-la-Chapelle = Aachen
  Germany **24** E2
Aix-les-Bains *France* **21** C9
Aixe-sur-Vienne *France* **20** C5
Aíyina = Egina *Greece* **46** D5
Aizawl *India* **67** H18
Aizenay *France* **18** F5
Aizkraukle *Latvia* **32** D3
Aizpute *Latvia* **30** B8
Aizuwakamatsu *Japan* **54** F9
Ajaccio *France* **21** G12
Ajaccio, G. d' *France* **21** G12
Ajai △ *Uganda* **86** B3
Ajaigarh *India* **69** G9
Ajalpan *Mexico* **119** D5
Ajanta Ra. *India* **66** J9
Ajari Rep. = Ajaria □
  Georgia **35** K6
Ajaria □ *Georgia* **35** K6
Ajax *Canada* **114** C5
Ajdābiyā *Libya* **79** B10
Ajdovščina *Slovenia* **41** C10
Ajibar *Ethiopia* **81** E4
Ajka *Hungary* **28** C2
'Ajlūn *Jordan* **74** C4
'Ajlūn □ *Jordan* **74** C4
'Ajmān *U.A.E.* **71** E7
Ajmer *India* **68** F6
Ajnala *India* **68** D6
Ajo *U.S.A.* **109** K7
Ajo, C. de *Spain* **36** B7
Ajok *Sudan* **81** F2
Ajuy *Phil.* **61** F5
Ak Dağ *Turkey* **47** E11
Ak Dağları *Muğla, Turkey* **47** E11
Ak Dağları *Sivas, Turkey* **72** C7
Akaba *Togo* **83** D5
Akabira *Japan* **54** C11
Akagera △ *Rwanda* **86** C3
Akaki Beseka *Ethiopia* **81** F4
Akala *Sudan* **81** D4
Akamas *Cyprus* **49** D11
Akanthou *Cyprus* **49** D12
Akarca *Turkey* **47** C11

Akaroa *N.Z.* **91** E4
Akasha *Sudan* **80** C3
Akashi *Japan* **55** G7
Akbarpur *Bihar, India* **69** G10
Akbarpur *Ut. P., India* **69** F10
Akçaabat *Turkey* **73** B8
Akçadağ *Turkey* **72** C7
Akçakale *Turkey* **73** D8
Akçakoca *Turkey* **72** B4
Akçaova *Turkey* **45** E13
Akçay *Turkey* **47** E11
Akçay ➤ *Turkey* **47** D10
Akdağ *Turkey* **47** C8
Akdağmadeni *Turkey* **72** C6
Akelamo *Indonesia* **63** D7
Åkers styckebruk *Sweden* **10** E11
Åkersberga *Sweden* **10** E12
Aketi *Dem. Rep. of the Congo* **84** D4
Akhalkalaki *Georgia* **35** K6
Akhaltsikhe *Georgia* **35** K6
Akhisar *Turkey* **47** C9
Akhmîm *Egypt* **80** B3
Akhnur *India* **69** C6
Akhtopol *Bulgaria* **45** D11
Akhtuba ➤ *Russia* **35** G8
Akhtubinsk *Russia* **35** F8
Akhty *Russia* **35** K8
Akhtyrka = Okhtyrka
  Ukraine **33** G8
Aki *Japan* **55** H6
Akimiski I. *Canada* **104** B3
Akimovka *Ukraine* **33** J8
Akita *Japan* **54** E10
Akita □ *Japan* **54** E10
Akjoujt *Mauritania* **82** B2
Akka *Mali* **82** B4
Akkaya Tepesi *Turkey* **47** D11
'Akko *Israel* **74** C4
Akköy *Turkey* **47** D9
Aklampa *Benin* **83** D5
Aklavik *Canada* **100** C6
Aklera *India* **68** G7
Akmenė *Lithuania* **30** B9
Akmenrags *Latvia* **30** B8
Akmonte = Almonte *Spain* **37** H4
Akō *Japan* **55** G7
Ako *Nigeria* **83** C7
Akôbô *Sudan* **81** F3
Akobo ➤ *Ethiopia* **81** F3
Akola *India* **66** J10
Akonolinga *Cameroon* **83** E7
Akor *Mali* **82** C3
Akordat *Eritrea* **81** D4
Akosombo Dam *Ghana* **83** D5
Akot *Sudan* **81** F3
Akoupé *Ivory C.* **82** D4
Akpatok I. *Canada* **101** C13
Åkrahamn *Norway* **9** G11
Akranes *Iceland* **8** D2
Akreïjit *Mauritania* **82** B3
Akritas, Akra *Greece* **46** E3
Akron *Colo., U.S.A.* **108** F12
Akron *Ohio, U.S.A.* **114** E3
Akrotiri *Cyprus* **49** E11
Akrotiri, Akra *Greece* **45** F9
Akrotiri Bay *Cyprus* **49** E12
Aksai Chin *China* **69** B8
Aksaray *Turkey* **72** C6
Aksaray □ *Turkey* **72** C5
Aksay = Aqsay *Kazakhstan* **52** D6
Akşehir *Turkey* **72** C4
Akşehir Gölü *Turkey* **72** C4
Akstafa = Ağstafa *Azerbaijan* **35** K7
Aksu *China* **60** B3
Aksu ➤ *Turkey* **72** D4
Aksum *Ethiopia* **81** E4
Aktash *Russia* **34** C11
Aktsyabrski *Belarus* **23** B15
Aktyubinsk = Aqtöbe
  Kazakhstan **52** D6
Aku *Nigeria* **83** D6
Akure *Nigeria* **83** D6
Akureyri *Iceland* **8** D4
Akuseki-Shima *Japan* **55** K4
Akusha *Russia* **35** J8
Akwa-Ibom □ *Nigeria* **83** E6
Akyab = Sittwe *Burma* **67** J18
Akyazı *Turkey* **72** B4
Al 'Adan *Yemen* **75** E4
Al Aḥsā = Hasa *Si. Arabia* **71** E6
Al Ajfar *Si. Arabia* **70** E4
Al Amādīyah *Iraq* **73** D10
Al 'Amārah *Iraq* **73** G12
Al Anbār □ *Iraq* **70** C4
Al 'Aqabah *Jordan* **74** F4
Al 'Aqabah □ *Jordan* **74** F4
Al Arak *Syria* **73** E8
Al 'Aramah *Si. Arabia* **70** E5
Al 'Arṭāwīyah *Si. Arabia* **70** E5
Al 'Aṣimah = 'Ammān □
  Jordan **74** D4
Al 'Assāfiyah *Si. Arabia* **70** D3
Al 'Ayn *Si. Arabia* **70** E3
Al 'Ayn *U.A.E.* **71** E7
Al 'Azīzīyah *Iraq* **73** F11

Al Bāb *Syria* **72** D7
Al Bad' *Si. Arabia* **70** D2
Al Bādī *Iraq* **70** C4
Al Baḥral Mayyit = Dead
  Sea *Asia* **74** D4
Al Balqā □ *Jordan* **74** C4
Al Bārūk, J. *Lebanon* **74** B4
Al Baṣrah *Iraq* **70** D5
Al Baṭḥā *Iraq* **70** D5
Al Batrūn *Lebanon* **74** A4
Al Baydā *Libya* **79** B10
Al Burayj *Syria* **74** A5
Al Faḍilī *Si. Arabia* **71** E6
Al Fallūjah *Iraq* **73** F10
Al Fāw *Iraq* **71** E6
Al Fujayrah *U.A.E.* **71** E8
Al Ghadaf, W. ➤ *Jordan* **74** D5
Al Ghammās *Iraq* **70** D5
Al Ghazālah *Si. Arabia* **70** E4
Al Ḥadīthah *Iraq* **73** E10
Al Ḥadīthah *Si. Arabia* **74** D6
Al Ḥaḍr *Iraq* **73** E10
Al Ḥājānah *Syria* **74** B5
Al Hajar al Gharbī *Oman* **71** E8
Al Ḥāmad *Si. Arabia* **70** D3
Al Ḥamdānīyah *Syria* **70** C3
Al Ḥamīdīyah *Syria* **74** A4
Al Ḥammār *Iraq* **70** D5
Al Ḥamrā' *Si. Arabia* **70** E3
Al Ḥamzah *Iraq* **70** D5
Al Ḥanākīyah *Si. Arabia* **70** E4
Al Ḥarūj al Aswad *Libya* **79** C9
Al Ḥasakah *Syria* **73** D9
Al Ḥasakah □ *Syria* **73** D9
Al Ḥayy *Iraq* **73** F12
Al Ḥijarah *Asia* **70** D4
Al Ḥillah *Iraq* **73** F11
Al Ḥillah *Si. Arabia* **75** B4
Al Hindīyah *Iraq* **73** F11
Al Hirmil *Lebanon* **74** A5
Al Hoceïma *Morocco* **78** A5
Al Ḥudaydah *Yemen* **75** E3
Al Ḥudūd ash
  Shamālīyah □ *Si. Arabia* **70** D4
Al Hufūf *Si. Arabia* **71** E6
Al Ḥumaydah *Si. Arabia* **70** D2
Al Ḥunayy *Si. Arabia* **71** E6
Al Īsāwīyah *Si. Arabia* **70** D3
Al Jafr *Jordan* **74** E5
Al Jāfūrah *Si. Arabia* **71** E7
Al Jaghbūb *Libya* **79** C10
Al Jahrah *Kuwait* **70** D5
Al Jalāmīd *Si. Arabia* **70** D3
Al Jamalīyah *Qatar* **71** E6
Al Janūb □ *Lebanon* **74** B4
Al Jawf *Libya* **79** D10
Al Jawf *Si. Arabia* **70** D3
Al Jawf □ *Si. Arabia* **70** D3
Al Jazair = Algeria ■ *Africa* **78** C6
Al Jazirah *Iraq* **73** E10
Al Jithāmīyah *Si. Arabia* **70** E4
Al Jubayl *Si. Arabia* **71** E6
Al Jubaylah *Si. Arabia* **70** E5
Al Jubb *Si. Arabia* **70** E4
Al Junaynah *Sudan* **79** F10
Al Kabā'ish *Iraq* **70** D5
Al Karak *Jordan* **74** D4
Al Karak □ *Jordan* **74** E5
Al Kāẓimīyah *Iraq* **73** F11
Al Khābūra *Oman* **71** F8
Al Khafji *Si. Arabia* **71** E6
Al Khalīl *West Bank* **74** D4
Al Khāliş *Iraq* **73** F11
Al Kharsānīyah *Si. Arabia* **71** E6
Al Khaṣab *Oman* **71** E8
Al Khawr *Qatar* **71** E6
Al Khidr *Iraq* **70** D5
Al Khiyām *Lebanon* **74** B4
Al Khobar *Si. Arabia* **71** E6
Al Khums *Libya* **79** B8
Al Kiswah *Syria* **74** B5
Al Kūfah *Iraq* **73** F11
Al Kufrah *Libya* **79** D10
Al Kuhayfiyah *Si. Arabia* **70** E4
Al Kūt *Iraq* **73** F11
Al Kuwayt *Kuwait* **70** D5
Al Labwah *Lebanon* **74** A5
Al Lādhiqīyah *Syria* **72** E6
Al Lādhiqīyah □ *Syria* **72** E6
Al Līth *Si. Arabia* **80** C5
Al Liwā' *Oman* **71** E8
Al Luḥayyah *Yemen* **75** D3
Al Madīnah *Iraq* **70** D5
Al Madīnah *Si. Arabia* **70** E3
Al Mafraq *Jordan* **74** C5
Al Mafraq □ *Jordan* **74** C5
Al Maghreb = Morocco ■
  N. Afr. **78** B4
Al Maḥmūdīyah *Iraq* **73** F11
Al Majma'ah *Si. Arabia* **70** E5
Al Makhruq, W. ➤ *Jordan* **74** D6
Al Makhūl *Si. Arabia* **70** D4
Al Manāmah *Bahrain* **71** E6
Al Maqwa *Kuwait* **70** D5

Al Marāḥ *Si. Arabia* **71** E6
Al Marj *Libya* **79** B10
Al Maṭlā *Kuwait* **70** D5
Al Mawsil *Iraq* **73** D10
Al Mayādin *Syria* **73** E9
Al Mazār *Jordan* **74** D4
Al Midhnab *Si. Arabia* **70** E5
Al Minā' *Lebanon* **74** A4
Al Miqdādīyah *Iraq* **73** E11
Al Mubarraz *Si. Arabia* **71** E6
Al Mudawwarah *Jordan* **74** F5
Al Mughayrā' *U.A.E.* **71** E7
Al Muḥarraq *Bahrain* **71** E6
Al Mukallā *Yemen* **75** E4
Al Mukhā *Yemen* **75** E3
Al Musayjid *Si. Arabia* **70** E3
Al Musayyib *Iraq* **73** F11
Al Muthanná □ *Iraq* **70** D5
Al Muwayh *Si. Arabia* **80** C4
Al Muwaylih *Si. Arabia* **70** E2
Al Owuho = Otukpa *Nigeria* **83** D6
Al Qādisīyah □ *Iraq* **70** D5
Al Qā'im *Iraq* **73** E9
Al Qālibah *Si. Arabia* **70** D3
Al Qāmishlī *Syria* **73** D9
Al Qaryatayn *Syria* **74** A6
Al Qaşīm □ *Si. Arabia* **70** E4
Al Qaṭ'ā *Syria* **73** E9
Al Qaṭīf *Si. Arabia* **71** E6
Al Qaṭrānah *Jordan* **74** D5
Al Qaṭrūn *Libya* **79** D9
Al Qayşūmah *Si. Arabia* **70** D5
Al Quds = Jerusalem
  Israel/West Bank **74** D4
Al Qunayṭirah *Syria* **74** C4
Al Qunfudhah *Si. Arabia* **80** D5
Al Qurnah *Iraq* **70** D5
Al Quşayr *Iraq* **70** D5
Al Quşayr *Syria* **74** A5
Al Qutayfah *Syria* **74** B5
Al 'Ubaylah *Si. Arabia* **75** C5
Al 'Uḍaylīyah *Si. Arabia* **71** E6
Al 'Ulā *Si. Arabia* **70** E3
Al 'Uqayr *Si. Arabia* **71** E6
Al 'Uwaynid *Si. Arabia* **70** E5
Al 'Uwayqīlah *Si. Arabia* **70** D4
Al 'Uyūn *Ḥijāz, Si. Arabia* **70** E3
Al 'Uyūn *Najd, Si. Arabia* **70** E4
Al 'Uzayr *Iraq* **70** D5
Al Wajh *Si. Arabia* **70** E3
Al Wakrah *Qatar* **71** E6
Al Waqbah *Si. Arabia* **70** D5
Al Wari'āh *Si. Arabia* **70** D5
Al Yaman = Yemen ■ *Asia* **75** E3
Ala *Italy* **40** C8
Ala Dağ *Turkey* **70** B2
Ala Dağları *Turkey* **73** C10
Alabama □ *U.S.A.* **117** E11
Alabama ➤ *U.S.A.* **117** F11
Alabaster *U.S.A.* **117** E11
Alaca *Turkey* **72** B6
Alacaatlı *Turkey* **47** B10
Alaçam *Turkey* **72** B6
Alaçam Dağları *Turkey* **47** B10
Alacant = Alicante *Spain* **39** G4
Alaçatı *Turkey* **47** C8
Alachua *U.S.A.* **117** G13
Alaejos *Spain* **36** D5
Alagna Valsésia *Italy* **40** C4
Alagoa Grande *Brazil* **125** E11
Alagoas □ *Brazil* **125** E11
Alagoinhas *Brazil* **125** F11
Alagón *Spain* **38** D3
Alagón ➤ *Spain* **36** F4
Alagir *Russia* **35** J7
Alahua *U.S.A.* **117** G13 *(?)*
Alai Range *Asia* —
Alajero *Canary Is.* **48** F2
Alajuela *Costa Rica* **120** D3
Alakamisy *Madag.* **89** C8
Alaknanda ➤ *India* **69** D8
Alaköl *Kazakhstan* **60** B3
Alakurtti *Russia* **8** C24
Alamarvdasht *Iran* **71** E7
Alamata *Ethiopia* **81** E4
Alameda *Calif., U.S.A.* **110** H4
Alameda *N. Mex., U.S.A.* **109** J10
Alaminos *Phil.* **61** C3
Alamo *U.S.A.* **111** H11
Alamogordo *U.S.A.* **109** K11
Alamos *Mexico* **118** B3
Alamosa *U.S.A.* **109** H11
Åland *Finland* **9** F19
Ålands hav *Europe* **9** G18
Alandroal *Portugal* **37** G3
Alange, Embalse d' *Spain* **37** G4
Alania = North Ossetia □
  Russia **35** J7
Alanís *Spain* **37** G5
Alanya *Turkey* **72** D5
Alaotra, Farihin' *Madag.* **89** B8
Alapayevsk *Russia* **52** D7
Alappuzha = Alleppey *India*
  66 Q10
Alar del Rey *Spain* **36** C6
Alaraz *Spain* **36** E5
Alarcón, Embalse de *Spain* **38** F2
Alarobia-Vohiposa *Madag.* **89** C8
Alaşehir *Turkey* **47** C10

Alaska □ *U.S.A.* **106** a
Alaska, G. of *Pac. Oc.* **106** a
Alaska Peninsula *U.S.A.* **106** a
Alaska Range *U.S.A.* **106** a
Alássio *Italy* **40** E5
Älät *Azerbaijan* **35** L9
Alatri *Italy* **41** G10
Alatyr *Russia* **34** C8
Alatyr ➤ *Russia* **34** C8
Alausi *Ecuador* **124** D3
Alava □ *Spain* **38** C2
Alava, C. *U.S.A.* **108** B1
Alaverdi *Armenia* **35** K7
Alavo = Alavus *Finland* **8** E20
Alavus *Finland* **8** E20
Alawoona *Australia* **95** E3
Alba *Italy* **40** D5
Alba □ *Romania* **29** D8
Alba Adriática *Italy* **41** F10
Alba de Tormes *Spain* **36** E5
Alba-Iulia *Romania* **29** D8
Albac *Romania* **28** D7
Albacete *Spain* **39** F3
Albacete □ *Spain* **39** G3
Albacutya, L. *Australia* **95** F3
Ålbæk *Denmark* **11** G4
Ålbæk Bugt *Denmark* **11** G4
Albaida *Spain* **39** G4
Albalate de las Nogueras
  Spain **38** E2
Albalate del Arzobispo *Spain* **38** D4
Alban *France* **20** E6
Albanel, L. *Canada* **104** B5
Albania ■ *Europe* **44** E4
Albano Laziale *Italy* **41** G9
Albany *Australia* **93** G2
Albany *Ga., U.S.A.* **117** F12
Albany *N.Y., U.S.A.* **115** D11
Albany *Oreg., U.S.A.* **108** D2
Albany *Tex., U.S.A.* **116** E5
Albany ➤ *Canada* **104** B3
Albardón *Argentina* **126** C2
Albarracín *Spain* **38** E3
Albarracín, Sierra de *Spain* **38** E3
Albatera *Spain* **39** G4
Albatross B. *Australia* **94** A3
Albegna ➤ *Italy* **41** F8
Albemarle *U.S.A.* **117** D14
Albemarle Sd. *U.S.A.* **117** C16
Albenga *Italy* **40** D5
Alberche ➤ *Spain* **36** F6
Alberdi *Paraguay* **126** B4
Albères, Mts. *France* **20** F6
Ålberga *Sweden* **11** F10
Alberga ➤ *Australia* **95** D2
Albersdorf *Germany* **24** A5
Albert *France* **19** C9
Albert, L. *Africa* **86** B3
Albert, L. *Australia* **95** F2
Albert Edward Ra. *Australia* **92** C4
Albert Lea *U.S.A.* **112** D7
Albert Nile ➤ *Uganda* **86** B3
Albert Town *Bahamas* **121** B5
Alberta □ *Canada* **102** C6
Alberti *Argentina* **126** D3
Albertinia *S. Africa* **88** E3
Albertirsa *Hungary* **28** C4
Alberton *Canada* **105** C7
Albertville *France* **21** C10
Albertville *U.S.A.* **117** D11
Albi *France* **20** E6
Albia *U.S.A.* **112** E7
Albina *Suriname* **125** B8
Albina, Ponta *Angola* **88** B1
Albino *Italy* **40** C6
Albion *Mich., U.S.A.* **113** D11
Albion *Nebr., U.S.A.* **112** E4
Albion *Pa., U.S.A.* **114** E4
Albocàcer *Spain* **38** E5
Alboloduy *Spain* **37** H7 *(?)*
Alboloduy → Albolote *Spain* **37** H7
Alborán, Medit. S. **37** K7
Alborea *Spain* **39** F3
Ålborg = Aalborg *Denmark* **11** G3
Ålborg Bugt = Aalborg
  Bugt *Denmark* **11** H4
Alborz, Reshteh-ye
  Kūhhā-ye *Iran* **71** C7
Albox *Spain* **39** H2
Albufeira *Portugal* **37** H2
Albula ➤ *Switz.* **25** J5
Albuñol *Spain* **37** J7
Alburquerque *Spain* **37** F4
Albuquerque *U.S.A.* **109** J10
Albuquerque, Cayos de
  Caribbean **120** D3
Alburg *U.S.A.* **115** B11
Alburno, Mte. *Italy* **43** B8
Alburquerque *Spain* **37** F4
Albury *Australia* **95** F4
Alcácer do Sal *Portugal* **37** G2
Alcáçovas *Portugal* **37** G2
Alcalá de Chivert *Spain* **38** E5
Alcalá de Guadaira *Spain* **37** H5
Alcalá de Henares *Spain* **38** E7
Alcalá de los Gazules *Spain* **37** J5
Alcalá del Júcar *Spain* **39** F3
Alcalá del Río *Spain* **37** H5

Alcalá del Valle *Spain* **37** J5
Alcalá la Real *Spain* **37** H7
Álcamo *Italy* **42** E5
Alcanadre *Spain* **38** C2
Alcanadre ➤ *Spain* **38** D4
Alcanede *Portugal* **37** F2
Alcanena *Portugal* **37** F2
Alcañar *Spain* **38** E5
Alcañices *Spain* **36** D4
Alcañiz *Spain* **38** D4
Alcântara *Brazil* **125** D10
Alcántara *Spain* **36** F4
Alcántara, Embalse de *Spain* **36** F4
Alcantarilla *Spain* **39** H3
Alcaracejos *Spain* **37** G6
Alcaraz *Spain* **39** G2
Alcaraz, Sierra de *Spain* **39** G2
Alcaudete *Spain* **37** H6
Alcázar de San Juan *Spain* **37** F7
Alchevsk *Ukraine* **33** H10
Alcira = Alzira *Spain* **39** F4
Alcobaça *Portugal* **37** F2
Alcobendas *Spain* **36** E7
Alcora *Spain* **38** E4
Alcorcón *Spain* **36** E7
Alcoutim *Portugal* **37** H3
Alcova *U.S.A.* **108** E10
Alcoy *Spain* **39** G4
Alcubierre, Sierra de *Spain* **38** D4
Alcublas *Spain* **38** F4
Alcúdia *Spain* **48** B10
Alcúdia, B. d' *Spain* **48** B10
Alcudia, Sierra de la *Spain* **37** G6
Aldabra Is. *Seychelles* **77** G8
Aldama *Mexico* **119** C5
Aldan *Russia* **53** D13
Aldan ➤ *Russia* **53** C13
Aldea, Pta. de la *Canary Is.* **48** G4
Aldeburgh *U.K.* **15** E9
Alder Pk. *U.S.A.* **110** K5
Alderney *U.K.* **15** H5
Aldershot *U.K.* **15** F7
Åled *Sweden* **11** H6
Aledo *U.S.A.* **112** E8
Alefa *Ethiopia* **81** E4
Aleg *Mauritania* **82** B2
Alegranza *Canary Is.* **48** E6
Alegranza, I. *Canary Is.* **48** E6
Alegre *Brazil* **127** A7
Alegrete *Brazil* **127** B4
Aleksandriya =
  Oleksandriya *Kirovohrad,
  Ukraine* **33** H7
Aleksandriya =
  Oleksandriya *Rivne,
  Ukraine* **23** C14
Aleksandriyskaya *Russia* **35** J8
Aleksandrov *Russia* **32** D10
Aleksandrov Gay *Russia* **34** E9
Aleksandrovac *Serbia* **44** C5
Aleksandrovac *Serbia* **44** B5
Aleksandrovka =
  Oleksandrovka *Ukraine* **33** H7
Aleksandrovo *Bulgaria* **45** C8
Aleksandrovsk-
  Sakhalinskiy *Russia* **53** D15
Aleksandrów Kujawski
  Poland **31** F5
Aleksandrów Łódzki *Poland* **31** G6
Aleksandry, Zemlya *Russia* **4** A10
Alekseyevka *Samara, Russia* **34** A10
Alekseyevka *Voronezh,
  Russia* **33** G10
Aleksin *Russia* **32** E9
Aleksinac *Serbia* **44** C5
Além Paraíba *Brazil* **127** A7
Alemania *Argentina* **126** B2
Alemania *Chile* **126** B2
Alençon *France* **18** D7
Alenquer *Brazil* **125** D8
Alenquer *Portugal* **37** F2
'Alenuihähä Channel *U.S.A.* **106** b
Alépé *Ivory C.* **82** D4
Aleppo = Ḥalab *Syria* **72** D7
Aléria *France* **21** F13
Alert *Canada* **101** A13
Alès *France* **21** D8
Aleşd *Romania* **28** C7
Alessándria *Italy* **40** D5
Ålesund *Norway* **8** E12
Alet-les-Bains *France* **20** F6
Aletschhorn *Switz.* **25** J4
Aleutian Basin *Pac. Oc.* **96** B9
Aleutian Is. *Pac. Oc.* **106** a
Aleutian Trench *Pac. Oc.* **4** D17
Alexander □ *U.S.A.* **112** B2
Alexander, Mt. *Australia* **93** E3
Alexander Arch. *U.S.A.* **100** D6
Alexander Bay *S. Africa* **88** D2
Alexander City *U.S.A.* **117** E12
Alexander I. *Antarctica* **5** C17
Alexandra *Australia* **95** F4
Alexandra *N.Z.* **91** G2
Alexandra Falls *Canada* **102** A5
Alexandria = El
  Iskandarîya *Egypt* **80** H7
Alexandria B.C., *Canada* **102** C4
Alexandria Ont., *Canada* **115** A10

Alexandria *Romania* 29 G10
Alexandria *S. Africa* 88 E4
Alexandria *U.K.* 13 F4
Alexandria *La., U.S.A.* 116 F8
Alexandria *Minn., U.S.A.* 112 C6
Alexandria *S. Dak., U.S.A.* 112 D5
Alexandria *Va., U.S.A.* 113 F15
Alexandria Bay *U.S.A.* 115 B9
Alexandrina, L. *Australia* 95 F2
Alexandroupoli *Greece* 45 F9
Alexis → *Canada* 105 B8
Alexis Creek *Canada* 102 C4
Aleysk *Russia* 52 D9
Alfabia *Spain* 48 B9
Alfambra *Spain* 38 E3
Alfândega da Fé *Portugal* 36 D4
Alfaro *Spain* 38 C3
Alfatar *Bulgaria* 45 C11
Alfaz del Pi *Spain* 39 G4
Alfeld *Germany* 24 D5
Alfenas *Brazil* 127 A6
Alföld *Hungary* 26 D5
Alfonsine *Italy* 41 D9
Alford *Aberds., U.K.* 13 D6
Alford *Lincs., U.K.* 14 D8
Alfred *Maine, U.S.A.* 115 C14
Alfred *N.Y., U.S.A.* 114 D7
Alfreton *U.K.* 14 D6
Alfta *Sweden* 10 C10
Alga *Kazakhstan* 52 E6
Algaida *Spain* 48 B9
Algar *Spain* 37 J5
Ålgård *Norway* 9 G11
Algarinejo *Spain* 37 H6
Algarve *Portugal* 37 J2
Algeciras *Spain* 37 J5
Algemesí *Spain* 39 F4
Alger *Algeria* 78 A6
Alger □ *Algeria* 39 J8
Alger ✈ (ALG) *Algeria* 39 J8
Algeria ■ *Algeria* 78 C6
Alghero *Italy* 42 B1
Ålghult *Sweden* 11 G9
Algiers = Alger *Algeria* 78 A6
Algoa B. *S. Africa* 88 E4
Algodonales *Spain* 37 J5
Algodor → *Spain* 36 F7
Algoma *U.S.A.* 112 C10
Algona *U.S.A.* 112 D6
Algonac *U.S.A.* 114 D2
Algonquin △ *Canada* 104 C4
Algorta *Uruguay* 128 C5
Alhama de Almería *Spain* 37 J8
Alhama de Aragón *Spain* 38 D3
Alhama de Granada *Spain* 37 H7
Alhama de Murcia *Spain* 39 H3
Alhambra *U.S.A.* 111 L8
Alhaurín el Grande *Spain* 37 J6
Alhucemas = Al Hoceïma
  Morocco 78 A5
'Alī al Gharbī *Iraq* 73 F12
'Alī ash Sharqī *Iraq* 73 F12
Äli Bayramlı *Azerbaijan* 35 L9
'Alī Khēl *Afghan.* 68 C3
Ali Sahîh *Djibouti* 81 E5
Alī Shāh *Iran* 70 B5
Ália *Italy* 42 E6
'Alīābād *Khorāsān, Iran* 71 C8
'Alīābād *Kordestān, Iran* 70 C5
'Alīābād *Yazd, Iran* 71 D7
Aliaga *Spain* 38 E4
Aliağa *Turkey* 47 C8
Aliakmonas → *Greece* 44 F6
Alibo *Ethiopia* 81 F4
Alibori → *Benin* 83 C5
Alibunar *Serbia* 28 E5
Alicante *Spain* 39 G4
Alicante □ *Spain* 39 G4
Alicante ✈ (ALC) *Spain* 39 G4
Alice *S. Africa* 88 E4
Alice *U.S.A.* 116 H5
Alice → *Queens., Australia* 94 C3
Alice → *Queens., Australia* 94 B3
Alice, Punta *Italy* 43 C10
Alice Arm *Canada* 102 B3
Alice Springs *Australia* 94 C1
Alicedale *S. Africa* 88 E4
Aliceville *U.S.A.* 117 E10
Alicudi *Italy* 43 D7
Aliganj *India* 69 F8
Aligarh *Raj., India* 68 G7
Aligarh *Ut. P., India* 68 F8
Alīgūdarz *Iran* 71 C6
Alijó *Portugal* 36 D3
Alimia *Greece* 49 C9
Alingsås *Sweden* 11 G6
Alipur *Pakistan* 68 E4
Alipur Duar *India* 67 F16
Aliquippa *U.S.A.* 114 F4
Alishan *Taiwan* 59 F13
Aliste → *Spain* 36 D5
Alitus = Alytus *Lithuania* 32 E3
Aliveri *Greece* 46 C6
Aliwal North *S. Africa* 88 E4
Alix *Canada* 102 C6
Aljezur *Portugal* 37 H2
Aljustrel *Portugal* 37 H2
Alkamari *Niger* 83 C7

Alkmaar *Neths.* 17 B4
All American Canal *U.S.A.* 109 K6
Allada *Benin* 83 D5
Allagash → *U.S.A.* 113 B19
Allah Dad *Pakistan* 68 G2
Allahabad *India* 69 G9
Allan *Canada* 103 C7
Allanche *France* 20 C6
Allanridge *S. Africa* 88 D4
Allanwater *Canada* 104 B1
Allaqi, Wadi → *Egypt* 80 C3
Allariz *Spain* 36 C3
Allassac *France* 20 C5
Ålleberg *Sweden* 11 F7
Allegany *U.S.A.* 114 D6
Allegheny → *U.S.A.* 114 F5
Allegheny Mts. *U.S.A.* 113 F13
Allegheny Plateau *U.S.A.* 113 E14
Allegheny Res. *U.S.A.* 114 E6
Allègre, Pte. *Guadeloupe* 120 b
Allègre, France 20 C7
Allen, Bog of *Ireland* 12 C5
Allen, L. *Ireland* 12 B3
Allendale *U.S.A.* 117 E14
Allende *Mexico* 118 B4
Allentown *U.S.A.* 115 F9
Allentsteig *Austria* 26 C8
Alleppey *India* 66 Q10
Allepuz *Spain* 38 E4
Aller → *Germany* 24 C5
Alleynes B. *Barbados* 121 g
Alliance *Nebr., U.S.A.* 112 D2
Alliance *Ohio, U.S.A.* 114 F3
Allier □ *France* 19 F9
Allier → *France* 19 F10
Alliford Bay *Canada* 102 C2
Alligator Pond *Jamaica* 120 a
Allinge *Denmark* 11 J8
Alliston = New Tecumseth
  Canada 114 B5
Alloa *U.K.* 13 E5
Allones *France* 18 D8
Allora *Australia* 95 D5
Allos *France* 21 D10
Alluitsup Paa *Greenland* 4 C5
Alma *Canada* 105 C5
Alma *Ga., U.S.A.* 117 F13
Alma *Kans., U.S.A.* 112 F5
Alma *Mich., U.S.A.* 113 D11
Alma *Nebr., U.S.A.* 112 E4
Alma *Wis., U.S.A.* 112 C8
Alma Ata = Almaty
  Kazakhstan 52 E8
Almacelles *Spain* 38 D5
Almada *Portugal* 37 G1
Almadén *Australia* 94 B3
Almadén *Spain* 37 G6
Almanor, L. *U.S.A.* 108 F3
Almansa *Spain* 39 G3
Almanza *Spain* 36 C5
Almanzor, Pico *Spain* 36 E5
Almanzora → *Spain* 39 H3
Almas, Munţii *Romania* 28 F7
Almassora *Spain* 38 E4
Almaty *Kazakhstan* 52 E8
Almazán *Spain* 38 D2
Almeirim *Brazil* 125 D8
Almeirim *Portugal* 37 F2
Almelo *Neths.* 17 B6
Almenar de Soria *Spain* 38 D2
Almenara *Spain* 38 F4
Almenara, Sierra de la *Spain* 39 H3
Almendra, Embalse de *Spain* 36 D4
Almendralejo *Spain* 37 G4
Almere-Stad *Neths.* 17 B5
Almería *Spain* 37 J8
Almería □ *Spain* 39 H2
Almería, G. de *Spain* 39 J2
Almetyevsk *Russia* 34 C11
Älmhult *Sweden* 11 H8
Almirante *Panama* 120 E3
Almiropotamos *Greece* 46 C6
Almiros *Greece* 46 B4
Almodôvar *Portugal* 37 H2
Almodóvar del Campo *Spain* 37 G6
Almodóvar del Río *Spain* 37 H5
Almond *U.S.A.* 114 D7
Almont *U.S.A.* 114 D1
Almonte *Canada* 115 A8
Almonte *Spain* 37 H4
Almora *India* 69 E8
Almoradí *Spain* 39 G4
Almorox *Spain* 36 E6
Almoustarat *Mali* 83 B5
Älmsta *Sweden* 10 E12
Almudévar *Spain* 38 C4
Almuñécar *Spain* 37 J7
Almunge *Sweden* 10 E12
Almuradiel *Spain* 37 G7
Almyrou, Ormos *Greece* 49 D6
Alness *U.K.* 13 D4
Alnmouth *U.K.* 14 B6
Alnwick *U.K.* 14 B6
Aloi *Uganda* 86 B3
Alon *Burma* 67 H19
Alonissos *Greece* 46 B5
Alonissos-Northern
  Sporades △ *Greece* 46 B6
Alor *Indonesia* 63 F6

Alor Setar *Malaysia* 65 J3
Álora *Spain* 37 J6
Alosno *Spain* 37 H3
Alot *India* 68 H6
Aloysius, Mt. *Australia* 93 E4
Alpaugh *U.S.A.* 110 K7
Alpe Apuane △ *Italy* 40 D7
Alpedrinha *Portugal* 36 E3
Alpena *U.S.A.* 113 C12
Alpes-de-Haute-
  Provence □ *France* 21 D10
Alpes-Maritimes □ *France* 21 E11
Alpha *Australia* 94 C4
Alpha Ridge *Arctic* 4 A2
Alphen aan den Rijn *Neths.* 17 B4
Alphios → *Greece* 46 D3
Alpiarça *Portugal* 37 F2
Alpine *Ariz., U.S.A.* 109 K9
Alpine *Calif., U.S.A.* 111 N10
Alpine *Tex., U.S.A.* 116 F3
Alps *Europe* 22 E5
Alpu *Turkey* 72 C4
Alqueta, Barragem do
  Portugal 37 G3
Alrø *Denmark* 11 J4
Als *Denmark* 11 K3
Alsace □ *France* 19 D14
Alsask *Canada* 103 C7
Alsasua *Spain* 38 C2
Alsek → *U.S.A.* 102 B1
Alsfeld *Germany* 24 E5
Alsta *Norway* 8 D15
Alston *U.K.* 14 C5
Alta *Norway* 8 B20
Alta, Sierra *Spain* 38 E3
Alta Gracia *Argentina* 126 C3
Alta Sierra *U.S.A.* 111 K8
Altaelva → *Norway* 8 B20
Altafjorden *Norway* 8 A20
Altai = Aerhtai Shan
  Mongolia 60 B4
Altai = Gorno-Altay □
  Russia 52 D9
Altamaha → *U.S.A.* 117 F14
Altamira *Brazil* 125 D8
Altamira *Chile* 126 B2
Altamira *Mexico* 119 C5
Altamira, Cuevas de *Spain* 36 B6
Altamont *U.S.A.* 115 D10
Altamura *Italy* 43 B9
Altanbulag *Mongolia* 60 A5
Altar *Mexico* 118 A2
Altar, Gran Desierto de
  Mexico 118 B2
Altata *Mexico* 118 C3
Altavista *U.S.A.* 113 G14
Altay *China* 60 B3
Altdorf *Switz.* 25 J4
Alte Mellum *Germany* 24 B4
Altea *Spain* 39 G4
Altenberg *Germany* 24 E9
Altenbruch *Germany* 24 B4
Altenburg *Germany* 24 E8
Altenkirchen
  *Mecklenburg-Vorpommern,
  Germany* 24 A9
Altenkirchen *Rhld-Pfz.,
  Germany* 24 E3
Altenmarkt *Austria* 26 D7
Alter do Chão *Portugal* 37 F3
Altınkaya Barajı *Turkey* 72 B6
Altınoluk *Turkey* 47 B8
Altınova *Turkey* 47 B8
Altıntaş *Turkey* 47 B12
Altınyaka *Turkey* 47 E12
Altınyayla *Turkey* 47 D11
Altiplano *Bolivia* 124 G5
Altkirch *France* 19 E14
Altmark *Germany* 24 C7
Altmühl → *Germany* 25 G7
Altmühltal △ *Germany* 25 G7
Altmunster *Austria* 26 D6
Alto Adige = Trentino-Alto
  Adige □ *Italy* 41 B8
Alto Araguaia *Brazil* 125 G8
Alto Cuchumatanes =
  Cuchumatanes, Sierra
  de los *Guatemala* 120 C1
Alto del Carmen *Chile* 126 B1
Alto del Inca *Chile* 126 A2
Alto Garda Bresciano △
  Italy 40 C7
Alto Ligonha *Mozam.* 87 F4
Alto Molocue *Mozam.* 87 F4
Alto Paraguay □ *Paraguay* 126 A4
Alto Paraná □ *Paraguay* 127 B5
Alton *Canada* 114 C4
Alton *U.K.* 15 F7
Alton *Ill., U.S.A.* 112 F8
Alton *N.H., U.S.A.* 115 C13
Altona *Canada* 103 D9
Altoona *U.S.A.* 114 F6
Altötting *Germany* 25 G8
Altstätten *Switz.* 25 H5
Altun Kupri *Iraq* 73 E11
Altun Shan *China* 60 C3
Alturas *U.S.A.* 108 F3

Altus *U.S.A.* 116 D5
Alubijid *Phil.* 61 G6
Alucra *Turkey* 73 B8
Aluk *Sudan* 81 F2
Alūksne *Latvia* 32 D4
Alunda *Sweden* 10 D12
Alunite *U.S.A.* 111 K12
Aluoro → *Ethiopia* 81 F3
Alupka *Ukraine* 33 K8
Alushta *Ukraine* 33 K8
Alusi *Indonesia* 63 F8
Alustante *Spain* 38 E3
Alva *U.S.A.* 116 G5
Alvaiázere *Portugal* 36 F2
Álvängen *Sweden* 11 G6
Alvão □ *Portugal* 36 D3
Alvarado *Mexico* 119 D5
Alvarado *U.S.A.* 116 E6
Alvaro Obregón, Presa
  Mexico 118 B3
Älvdalen *Sweden* 10 D8
Alvear *Argentina* 126 B4
Alverca *Portugal* 37 G1
Alvesta *Sweden* 11 H8
Alvin *U.S.A.* 116 G7
Alvinston *Canada* 114 D3
Alvito *Portugal* 37 G3
Älvkarleby *Sweden* 10 D11
Alvord Desert *U.S.A.* 108 E4
Älvros *Sweden* 10 B8
Älvsbyn *Sweden* 8 D19
Alwar *India* 68 F7
Alxa Zuoqi *China* 56 E3
Alyangula *Australia* 94 A2
Alyata = Älät *Azerbaijan* 35 L9
Alyth *U.K.* 13 E5
Alytus *Lithuania* 32 E3
Alzada *U.S.A.* 108 D11
Alzey *Germany* 25 F4
Alzira *Spain* 39 F4
Am Timan *Chad* 79 F10
Amadi *Dem. Rep. of the Congo* 86 B2
Amâdi *Sudan* 81 F3
Amadjuak L. *Canada* 101 C12
Amadora *Portugal* 37 G1
Amagansett *U.S.A.* 115 F12
Amager *Denmark* 11 J6
Amagunze *Nigeria* 83 D6
Amahai *Indonesia* 63 E7
Amaile *Samoa* 91 b
Amakusa-Shotō *Japan* 55 H5
Åmål *Sweden* 10 E6
Amalfi *Italy* 43 B7
Amaliada *Greece* 46 D3
Amalner *India* 66 J9
Amamapare *Indonesia* 63 E9
Amambaí *Brazil* 127 A4
Amambaí → *Brazil* 127 A5
Amambay □ *Paraguay* 127 A4
Amambay, Cordillera de
  S. Amer. 127 A4
Amami-Guntō *Japan* 55 L4
Amami-Ō-Shima *Japan* 55 K4
Aman, Pulau *Malaysia* 65 c
Amaná, L. *Brazil* 124 D6
Amanat → *India* 69 G11
Amanda Park *U.S.A.* 110 C3
Amankeldi *Kazakhstan* 52 D7
Amantea *Italy* 43 C9
Amapá *Brazil* 125 C8
Amapá □ *Brazil* 125 C8
Amara *Sudan* 81 F3
Amara □ *Ethiopia* 81 E4
Amarante *Brazil* 125 E10
Amarante *Portugal* 36 D2
Amaranth *Canada* 103 C9
Amareleja *Portugal* 37 G3
Amargosa *Brazil* 127 A6
Amargosa → *U.S.A.* 111 J10
Amargosa Desert *U.S.A.* 111 J10
Amargosa Range *U.S.A.* 111 J10
Amari *Greece* 49 D6
Amarillo *U.S.A.* 116 D4
Amarkantak *India* 69 H9
Amârna, Tell el' *Sudan* 80 B3
Amaro, Mte. *Italy* 41 F11
Amarpur *India* 69 G12
Amarti *Eritrea* 81 E5
Amarwara *India* 69 H8
Amasa *U.S.A.* 112 B10
Amasra *Turkey* 72 B5
Amassama *Nigeria* 83 D6
Amasya *Turkey* 72 B6
Amasya □ *Turkey* 72 B6
Amata *Australia* 93 E5
Amatikulu *S. Africa* 89 D5
Amatitlán *Guatemala* 120 D1
Amatrice *Italy* 41 F10
Amay *Belgium* 17 G5
Amazon = Amazonas →
  S. Amer. 125 D8
Amazonas □ *Brazil* 124 E6
Amazonas → *S. Amer.* 125 D8
Amba Ferit *Ethiopia* 81 E4
Ambah *India* 68 F8
Ambahakily *Madag.* 89 C7
Ambahita *Madag.* 89 C8
Ambala *India* 68 D7

Ambalavao *Madag.* 89 C8
Ambanja *Madag.* 89 A8
Ambararata *Madag.* 89 B8
Ambarchik *Russia* 53 C17
Ambaryeba *Madag.* 89 A8
Ambato *Ecuador* 124 D3
Ambato *Madag.* 89 A8
Ambato, Sierra de *Argentina* 126 B2
Ambato Boeny *Madag.* 89 B8
Ambatofinandrahana
  Madag. 89 C8
Ambatolampy *Madag.* 89 B8
Ambatomainty *Madag.* 89 B8
Ambatomanoina *Madag.* 89 B8
Ambatondrazaka *Madag.* 89 B8
Ambatosoratra *Madag.* 89 B8
Ambelonas *Greece* 46 B4
Ambenja *Madag.* 89 B8
Amberg *Germany* 25 F7
Ambergris Cay *Belize* 119 D7
Ambérieu-en-Bugey *France* 21 C9
Amberley *N.Z.* 91 E4
Ambert *France* 20 C7
Ambidédi *Mali* 82 C2
Ambikapur *India* 69 H10
Ambikol *Sudan* 80 D3
Ambilobé *Madag.* 89 A8
Amble *U.K.* 14 B6
Ambleside *U.K.* 14 C5
Ambo *Peru* 124 F3
Amboahangy *Madag.* 89 C8
Ambodifototra *Madag.* 89 B8
Ambodilazana *Madag.* 89 B8
Ambodiriana *Madag.* 89 B8
Ambohidratrimo *Madag.* 89 B8
Ambohidray *Madag.* 89 B8
Ambohimahamasina
  Madag. 89 C8
Ambohimahasoa *Madag.* 89 C8
Ambohimanga *Madag.* 89 C8
Ambohimitombo *Madag.* 89 C8
Ambohitra *Madag.* 89 A8
Amboise *France* 18 E8
Ambon *Indonesia* 63 E7
Ambondro *Madag.* 89 D8
Amboseli, L. *Kenya* 86 C4
Amboseli △ *Kenya* 86 C4
Ambositra *Madag.* 89 C8
Ambovombe *Madag.* 89 D8
Amboy *U.S.A.* 111 L11
Amboyna Cay *S. China Sea* 62 C4
Ambridge *U.S.A.* 114 F4
Ambriz *Angola* 84 F2
Amchitka I. *U.S.A.* 106 a
Amderma *Russia* 52 C7
Amdhi *India* 69 H9
Amdo *China* 67 C17
Ameca *Mexico* 118 C4
Ameca → *Mexico* 118 C3
Amecameca de Juárez
  Mexico 119 D5
Ameland *Neths.* 17 A5
Amélia *Italy* 41 F9
Amendolara *Italy* 43 C9
Amenia *U.S.A.* 115 E11
America-Antarctica Ridge
  S. Ocean 5 B2
American Falls *U.S.A.* 108 E7
American Falls Res. *U.S.A.* 108 E7
American Fork *U.S.A.* 108 F8
American Highland
  Antarctica 5 D6
American Samoa ☑ *Pac. Oc.* 91 b
American Samoa △
  Amer. Samoa 91 b
Americana *Brazil* 127 A6
Americus *U.S.A.* 117 E12
Amerigo Vespucci,
  Firenze ✈ (FLR) *Italy* 41 E8
Amersfoort *Neths.* 17 B5
Amersfoort *S. Africa* 89 D4
Amery Basin *S. Ocean* 5 C6
Amery Ice Shelf *Antarctica* 5 C6
Ames *Spain* 36 C2
Ames *U.S.A.* 112 D7
Amesbury *U.S.A.* 115 D14
Amet *India* 68 G5
Amfikleia *Greece* 46 C4
Amfilochia *Greece* 46 C3
Amfipoli *Greece* 44 F7
Amfissa *Greece* 46 C4
Amga *Russia* 53 C14
Amga → *Russia* 53 C14
Amgu *Russia* 54 B8
Amgun → *Russia* 53 D14

Amiens *France* 19 C9
Amindeo *Greece* 44 F5
Åminne *Sweden* 11 G7
Amino *Ethiopia* 81 G5
Aminuis *Namibia* 88 C2
Amīrābād *Iran* 70 C5
Amirante Is. *Seychelles* 50 J7
Amisk → *Canada* 103 B9
Amisk L. *Canada* 103 C8
Amistad, Presa de la *Mexico* 118 B4
Amistad △ *U.S.A.* 116 C4
Amite *U.S.A.* 117 F9
Amla *India* 68 J8
Amlapura = Karangasem
  Indonesia 63 J18
Amlia I. *U.S.A.* 106 a
Amlwch *U.K.* 14 D3
Amm Adam *Sudan* 81 D4
'Ammān *Jordan* 74 D4
'Ammān □ *Jordan* 74 D5
'Ammān ✈ (AMM) *Jordan* 74 D5
Ammanford *U.K.* 15 F4
Ammassalik = Tasiilaq
  Greenland 4 C6
Ammerån → *Sweden* 10 A10
Ammersee *Germany* 25 G7
Ammochostos =
  Famagusta *Cyprus* 49 D12
Ammon *U.S.A.* 108 E8
Amnat Charoen *Thailand* 64 E5
Amnura *Bangla.* 69 G13
Amo Jiang → *China* 58 F3
Åmol *Iran* 71 B7
Amorgos *Greece* 47 E7
Amory *U.S.A.* 117 E10
Amos *Canada* 104 C4
Åmot *Norway* 9 G13
Åmotfors *Sweden* 10 E6
Amoy = Xiamen *China* 59 E12
Ampanavoana *Madag.* 89 B9
Ampang *Malaysia* 65 L3
Ampangalana,
  Lakandranon' *Madag.* 89 C8
Ampanihy *Madag.* 89 C7
Amparafaravola *Madag.* 89 B8
Ampasinambo *Madag.* 89 C8
Ampasindava,
  Helodranon' *Madag.* 89 A8
Ampasindava, Saikanosy
  Madag. 89 A8
Ampenan *Indonesia* 63 K18
Amper *Nigeria* 83 D6
Amper → *Germany* 25 G7
Ampezzo *Italy* 41 B9
Amphoe Kathu *Thailand* 65 a
Amphoe Thalang *Thailand* 65 a
Ampitsikinana *Madag.* 89 A8
Ampombiantambo *Madag.* 89 A8
Amposta *Spain* 38 E5
Ampotaka *Madag.* 89 D7
Ampoza *Madag.* 89 C7
Amqui *Canada* 105 C6
Amravati *India* 66 J10
Amreli *India* 68 J4
Amritsar *India* 68 D6
Amroha *India* 69 E8
Amrum *Germany* 24 A4
Amsterdam *Neths.* 17 B4
Amsterdam *U.S.A.* 115 D10
Amsterdam ✈ (AMS) *Neths.* 17 B4
Amsterdam, I. = Nouvelle
  Amsterdam, Î. *Ind. Oc.* 3 F13
Amstetten *Austria* 26 C7
Amudarya → *Uzbekistan* 52 E6
Amund Ringnes I. *Canada* 101 B10
Amundsen Abyssal Plain
  S. Ocean 5 C14
Amundsen Basin *Arctic* 4 A
Amundsen Gulf *Canada* 100 B7
Amundsen Ridges *S. Ocean* 5 C14
Amundsen-Scott *Antarctica* 5 E
Amundsen Sea *Antarctica* 5 D15
Amungen *Sweden* 10 C9
Amuntai *Indonesia* 62 E5
Amur → *Russia* 53 D15
Amur, W. → *Sudan* 80 D3
Amurang *Indonesia* 63 D6
Amurrio *Spain* 38 B1
Amursk *Russia* 53 D14
Amusco *Spain* 36 C6
Amvrakikos Kolpos *Greece* 46 C2
Amvrosiyivka *Ukraine* 33 J10
Amyderya =
  Amudarya → *Uzbekistan* 52 E6
An Bien *Vietnam* 65 H5
An Hoa *Vietnam* 64 E7
An Nabatīyah at Tahta
  Lebanon 74 B4
An Nabk *Si. Arabia* 70 D3
An Nabk *Syria* 74 A5
An Nafūd *Si. Arabia* 70 D4
An Najaf *Iraq* 73 G11
An Nāşirīyah *Iraq* 70 D5
An Nhon *Vietnam* 64 F7
An Nîl □ *Sudan* 80 D3
An Nîl el Abyad □ *Sudan* 81 E3
An Nîl el Azraq □ *Sudan* 81 E3
An Nu'ayrīyah *Si. Arabia* 71 E6

An Nu'mānīyah *Iraq* **73** F11
An Thoi, Dao *Vietnam* **65** H5
An Uaimh *Ireland* **12** C5
Anabar → *Russia* **53** B12
Anaconda *U.S.A.* **108** C7
Anacortes *U.S.A.* **110** B4
Anacuao, Mt. *Phil.* **61** C4
Anadarko *U.S.A.* **116** D5
Anadia *Portugal* **36** E2
Anadolu *Turkey* **72** C5
Anadyr *Russia* **53** C18
Anadyr → *Russia* **53** C18
Anadyrskiy Zaliv *Russia* **53** C19
Anafi *Greece* **47** E7
Anaga, Pta. de *Canary Is.* **48** F3
Anagni *Italy* **41** G10
'Ānah *Iraq* **73** E10
Anaheim *U.S.A.* **111** M9
Anahim Lake *Canada* **102** C3
Anakapalle *India* **67** L13
Anakie *Australia* **94** C4
Anaklia *Georgia* **35** J5
Analalava *Madag.* **89** A8
Analavoka *Madag.* **89** C8
Analipsis *Greece* **49** A3
Anambar → *Pakistan* **68** D3
Anambas, Kepulauan *Indonesia* **62** D3
Anambas Is. = Anambas, Kepulauan *Indonesia* **62** D3
Anambra □ *Nigeria* **83** D6
Anamosa *U.S.A.* **112** D8
Anamur *Turkey* **72** D5
Anamur Burnu *Turkey* **72** D5
Anan *Japan* **55** H7
Anand *India* **68** H5
Ananes *Greece* **46** E6
Anantapur *India* **66** M10
Anantnag *India* **69** C6
Ananyiv *Ukraine* **29** C14
Anapa *Russia* **33** K9
Anápolis *Brazil* **125** G9
Anapu → *Brazil* **125** D8
Anār *Iran* **71** D7
Anārak *Iran* **71** C7
Anarisfjällen *Sweden* **10** A7
Anas → *India* **68** H5
Anatolia = Anadolu *Turkey* **72** C5
Anatsogno *Madag.* **89** C7
Añatuya *Argentina* **126** B3
Anaunethad L. *Canada* **103** A8
Anbyŏn *N. Korea* **57** E14
Ancares, Sierra de *Spain* **36** C4
Ancares △ *Spain* **36** C4
Ancaster *Canada* **114** C5
Ancenis *France* **18** E5
Anchor Bay *U.S.A.* **110** G3
Anchorage *U.S.A.* **100** C5
Anci *China* **56** E9
Ancohuma, Nevado *Bolivia* **124** G5
Ancón *Peru* **124** F3
Ancona *Italy* **41** E10
Ancud *Chile* **128** E2
Ancud, G. de *Chile* **128** E2
Ancy-le-Franc *France* **19** E11
Andacollo *Argentina* **126** D1
Andacollo *Chile* **126** C1
Andaingo *Madag.* **89** B8
Andalgalá *Argentina* **126** B2
Åndalsnes *Norway* **8** E12
Andalucía □ *Spain* **37** H6
Andalusia = Andalucía □ *Spain* **37** H6
Andalusia *U.S.A.* **117** F11
Andaman Is. *Ind. Oc.* **3** D14
Andaman Sea *Ind. Oc.* **62** B1
Andamooka *Australia* **95** E2
Andapa *Madag.* **89** A8
Andara *Namibia* **88** B3
Andelot-Blancheville *France* **19** D12
Andenes *Norway* **8** B17
Andenne *Belgium* **17** D5
Andéranboukane *Mali* **83** B5
Andermatt *Switz.* **25** J4
Andernach *Germany* **24** E3
Andernos-les-Bains *France* **20** D2
Anderslöv *Sweden* **11** J7
Anderson *Alaska, U.S.A.* **106** a
Anderson *Calif., U.S.A.* **108** F2
Anderson *Ind., U.S.A.* **113** E11
Anderson *Mo., U.S.A.* **112** G6
Anderson *S.C., U.S.A.* **117** D13
Anderson → *Canada* **100** C7
Anderstorp *Sweden* **11** G7
Andes *U.S.A.* **115** D10
Andes, Cord. de los *S. Amer.* **124** H5
Andfjorden *Norway* **8** B17
Andhra Pradesh □ *India* **66** L11
Andijon *Uzbekistan* **52** E8
Andikíthira = Antikythira *Greece* **46** F5
Andilamena *Madag.* **89** B8
Andīmeshk *Iran* **73** F13
Andímilos = Antimilos *Greece* **46** E6

Andíparos = Antiparos *Greece* **47** D7
Andípaxoi = Antipaxi *Greece* **46** B2
Andipsara *Greece* **47** C7
Andizhan = Andijon *Uzbekistan* **52** E8
Andoain *Spain* **38** B2
Andoany *Madag.* **89** A8
Andohahela △ *Madag.* **89** C8
Andong *S. Korea* **57** F15
Andongwei *China* **57** G10
Andoom *Australia* **94** A3
Andorra *Spain* **38** E4
Andorra ■ *Europe* **20** F5
Andorra La Vella *Andorra* **20** F5
Andover *U.K.* **15** F6
Andover *Maine, U.S.A.* **115** B14
Andover *Mass., U.S.A.* **115** D13
Andover *N.J., U.S.A.* **115** F10
Andover *N.Y., U.S.A.* **114** D7
Andover *Ohio, U.S.A.* **114** E4
Andøya *Norway* **8** B16
Andradina *Brazil* **125** H8
Andrahary *Madag.* **89** A8
Andramasina *Madag.* **89** B8
Andranopasy *Madag.* **89** C7
Andranovory *Madag.* **89** C7
Andratx *Spain* **48** B9
Andreanof Is. *U.S.A.* **106** a
Andreapol *Russia* **32** D7
Andrews *S.C., U.S.A.* **117** E15
Andrews *Tex., U.S.A.* **116** E3
Andreyevka *Russia* **34** D10
Ándria *Italy* **43** A9
Andriamena *Madag.* **89** B8
Andriandampy *Madag.* **89** C8
Andriba *Madag.* **89** B8
Andrijevica *Montenegro* **44** D3
Andringitra △ *Madag.* **89** C8
Andritsena *Greece* **46** D3
Androka *Madag.* **89** C7
Andros *Greece* **46** D6
Andros I. *Bahamas* **120** B4
Andros Town *Bahamas* **120** B4
Androscoggin → *U.S.A.* **115** C14
Andrychów *Poland* **31** J6
Andselv *Norway* **8** B18
Andújar *Spain* **37** G6
Andulo *Angola* **84** G3
Aneby *Sweden* **11** G8
Anegada *Br. Virgin Is.* **121** e
Anegada Passage *W. Indies* **121** C7
Aného *Togo* **83** D5
Anenni-Noi *Moldova* **29** D14
Aneto, Pico de *Spain* **38** C5
Anfu *China* **59** D10
Ang Mo Kio *Singapore* **65** d
Ang Thong *Thailand* **64** E3
Ang Thong, Ko *Thailand* **65** b
Ang Thong △ *Thailand* **65** H2
Angamos, Punta *Chile* **126** A1
Angara → *Russia* **53** D10
Angara-Débou *Benin* **83** C5
Angarab *Ethiopia* **81** E4
Angarsk *Russia* **53** D11
Angas Hills *Australia* **92** D4
Angaston *Australia* **95** E2
Ånge *Sweden* **10** B9
Ángel, Salto = Angel Falls *Venezuela* **124** B6
Ángel de la Guarda, I. *Mexico* **118** B2
Angel Falls *Venezuela* **124** B6
Angeles *Phil.* **61** D4
Ängelholm *Sweden* **11** H6
Angels Camp *U.S.A.* **110** G6
Ängelsberg *Sweden* **10** E10
Anger → *Ethiopia* **81** F4
Angereb → *Ethiopia* **81** E4
Ångermanälven → *Sweden* **10** A11
Ångermanland *Sweden* **8** E17
Angermünde *Germany* **24** B9
Angers *Canada* **115** A9
Angers *France* **18** E5
Angerville *France* **19** D9
Ängesån → *Sweden* **8** C20
Angikuni L. *Canada* **103** A9
Angkor *Cambodia* **64** F4
Anglès *Spain* **38** D7
Anglesey *U.K.* **14** D3
Anglesey, Isle of □ *U.K.* **14** D3
Anglet *France* **20** E2
Angleton *U.S.A.* **116** G7
Anglin → *France* **20** B4
Anglisidhes *Cyprus* **49** E12
Anglure *France* **19** D10
Angmagssalik = Tasiilaq *Greenland* **4** C6
Ango *Dem. Rep. of the Congo* **86** B2
Angoche *Mozam.* **87** F4
Angoche, I. *Mozam.* **87** F4
Angol *Chile* **126** D1
Angola *Ind., U.S.A.* **113** E11
Angola *N.Y., U.S.A.* **114** D5
Angola ■ *Africa* **85** G3
Angoulême *France* **20** C4
Angoumois *France* **20** C4

Angra do Heroismo *Azores* **78** a
Angra dos Reis *Brazil* **127** A7
Angrapa → *Russia* **30** D8
Angren *Uzbekistan* **52** E8
Angtassom *Cambodia* **65** G5
Anguang *China* **57** B12
Anguilla ☑ *W. Indies* **121** C7
Anguo *China* **56** E8
Angurugu *Australia* **94** A2
Angus □ *U.K.* **13** E6
Angwa → *Zimbabwe* **89** B5
Anhanduí → *Brazil* **127** A5
Anholt *Denmark* **11** H5
Anhua *China* **59** C8
Anhui □ *China* **59** B11
Anhwei = Anhui □ *China* **59** B11
Anichab *Namibia* **88** C1
Anidros *Greece* **47** E7
Anié *Togo* **83** D5
Animas → *U.S.A.* **109** H9
Anina *Romania* **28** E6
Aninoasa *Romania* **29** F9
Anivorano *Madag.* **89** B8
Anjar *India* **68** H4
Anji *China* **59** B12
Anjou *France* **18** E6
Anjouan *Comoros Is.* **85** a
Anjozorobe *Madag.* **89** B8
Anju *N. Korea* **57** E13
Anka *Nigeria* **83** C6
Ankaboa, Tanjona *Madag.* **89** C7
Ankang *China* **56** H5
Ankara *Turkey* **72** C5
Ankara → *Turkey* **72** C5
Ankarafantsika △ *Madag.* **89** B8
Ankaramena *Madag.* **89** C8
Ankaratra *Madag.* **85** H9
Ankarsrum *Sweden* **11** G10
Ankasakasa *Madag.* **89** B7
Ankavandra *Madag.* **89** B8
Ankazoabo *Madag.* **89** C7
Ankazobe *Madag.* **89** B8
Ankeny *U.S.A.* **112** E7
Ankilimalinika *Madag.* **89** C7
Ankilizato *Madag.* **89** C8
Ankisabe *Madag.* **89** B8
Ankober *Ethiopia* **81** F4
Ankoro *Dem. Rep. of the Congo* **86** D2
Ankororoka *Madag.* **89** D8
Anlong *China* **58** E5
Anlong *China* **58** E5
Anlu *China* **59** B9
Anmyeondo *S. Korea* **57** F14
Ånn *Sweden* **10** A6
Ann, C. *U.S.A.* **115** D14
Ann Arbor *U.S.A.* **113** D12
Anna *Russia* **34** E5
Anna *U.S.A.* **112** G9
Annaba *Algeria* **78** A7
Annaberg-Buchholz *Germany* **24** E9
Annalee → *Ireland* **12** B4
Annam *Vietnam* **64** E7
Annamitique, Chaîne *Asia* **64** D6
Annan *U.K.* **13** G5
Annan → *U.K.* **13** G5
Annapolis *U.S.A.* **113** F15
Annapolis Royal *Canada* **105** D6
Annapurna *Nepal* **69** E10
Annean, L. *Australia* **93** E2
Anneberg *Sweden* **11** G8
Annecy *France* **21** C10
Annecy, Lac d' *France* **21** C10
Annemasse *France* **19** F13
Annette I. *U.S.A.* **102** B2
Anning *China* **58** E4
Anniston *U.S.A.* **117** E12
Annobón *Atl. Oc.* **77** G4
Annonay *France* **21** C8
Annot *France* **21** E10
Annotto B. *Jamaica* **120** a
Annville *U.S.A.* **115** F8
Annweiler *Germany* **25** F3
Ano Poroia *Greece* **44** E7
Ano Siros *Greece* **46** D6
Anogia *Greece* **49** D6
Anorotsangana *Madag.* **89** A8
Anosibe *Madag.* **89** B8
Anou Mellene *Mali* **83** B5
Anoumaba *Ivory C.* **82** D4
Anping *Hebei, China* **56** E8
Anping *Liaoning, China* **57** D12
Anpu Gang *China* **58** G7
Anqing *China* **59** B11
Anqiu *China* **57** F10
Anren *China* **59** D9
Ansager *Denmark* **11** J2
Ansai *China* **56** F5
Ansan *S. Korea* **57** F14
Ansbach *Germany* **25** F6
Anse Boileau *Seychelles* **85** b
Anse Royale *Seychelles* **85** b
Anseba → *Eritrea* **81** D4
Ansfelden *Austria* **26** C7

Anshan *China* **57** D12
Anshun *China* **58** D5
Ansião *Portugal* **36** F2
Ansley *U.S.A.* **112** E4
Ansó *Spain* **38** C3
Ansoain *Spain* **38** C3
Anson *U.S.A.* **116** E5
Anson B. *Australia* **92** B5
Ansongo *Mali* **83** B5
Ansongo-Ménaka △ *Mali* **83** B5
Ansonia *U.S.A.* **115** E11
Anstruther *U.K.* **13** E6
Ansudu *Indonesia* **63** E9
Antabamba *Peru* **124** F4
Antakya = Hatay *Turkey* **72** D7
Antalaha *Madag.* **89** A9
Antalya *Turkey* **72** D4
Antalya □ *Turkey* **47** E12
Antalya Körfezi *Turkey* **72** D4
Antambohobe *Madag.* **89** C8
Antanambao-Manampotsy *Madag.* **89** B8
Antanambe *Madag.* **89** B8
Antananarivo *Madag.* **89** B8
Antananarivo □ *Madag.* **89** B8
Antanifotsy *Madag.* **89** B8
Antanimbaribe *Madag.* **89** C7
Antanimora *Madag.* **89** C8
Antarctic Pen. *Antarctica* **5** C18
Antarctica **5** E3
Antelope *Zimbabwe* **87** G2
Antequera *Paraguay* **126** A4
Antequera *Spain* **37** H6
Antero, Mt. *U.S.A.* **108** G10
Antevamena *Madag.* **89** C7
Anthony *Kans., U.S.A.* **112** G4
Anthony *N. Mex., U.S.A.* **109** K10
Anti Atlas *Morocco* **78** C4
Anti-Lebanon = Sharqi, Al Jabal ash *Lebanon* **74** B5
Antibes *France* **21** E11
Antibes, C. d' *France* **21** E11
Anticosti, Î. d' *Canada* **105** C7
Antifer, C. d' *France* **18** C7
Antigo *U.S.A.* **112** C9
Antigonish *Canada* **105** C7
Antigua *Canary Is.* **48** F5
Antigua *Guatemala* **120** D1
Antigua *W. Indies* **121** C7
Antigua & Barbuda ■ *W. Indies* **121** C7
Antikythira *Greece* **46** F5
Antilla *Cuba* **120** B4
Antilles = West Indies *Cent. Amer.* **121** D7
Antimilos *Greece* **46** E6
Antioch *U.S.A.* **110** G5
Antioche, Pertuis d' *France* **20** B2
Antioquia *Colombia* **124** B3
Antiparos *Greece* **47** D7
Antipaxi *Greece* **46** B2
Antipodes Is. *Pac. Oc.* **96** M9
Antirio *Greece* **46** C3
Antlers *U.S.A.* **116** D7
Antoetra *Madag.* **89** C8
Antofagasta *Chile* **126** A1
Antofagasta □ *Chile* **126** A2
Antofagasta de la Sierra *Argentina* **126** B2
Antofalla *Argentina* **126** B2
Antofalla, Salar de *Argentina* **126** B2
Anton *U.S.A.* **116** E3
Antongila, Helodrano *Madag.* **89** B8
Antonibé *Madag.* **89** B8
Antonibé, Presqu'île d' *Madag.* **89** A8
Antonina *Brazil* **127** B6
Antrain *France* **18** D5
Antrim *U.K.* **12** B5
Antrim *U.S.A.* **114** F3
Antrim □ *U.K.* **12** B5
Antrim, Mts. of *U.K.* **12** A5
Antrim Plateau *Australia* **92** C4
Antrodoco *Italy* **41** F10
Antropovo *Russia* **34** A6
Antsakabary *Madag.* **89** B8
Antsalova *Madag.* **89** B7
Antsenavolo *Madag.* **89** C8
Antsiafabositra *Madag.* **89** B8
Antsirabe *Antananarivo, Madag.* **89** B8
Antsirabe *Antsiranana, Madag.* **89** A8
Antsiranana *Madag.* **89** A8
Antsiranana □ *Madag.* **89** A8
Antsohihy *Madag.* **89** A8
Antsohimbondrona Serranana *Madag.* **89** A8
Antu *China* **57** C15
Antwerp = Antwerpen *Belgium* **17** C4
Antwerp *U.S.A.* **115** B9
Antwerpen *Belgium* **17** C4
Antwerpen □ *Belgium* **17** C4
Anupgarh *India* **68** E5

Anuppur *India* **69** H9
Anuradhapura *Sri Lanka* **66** Q12
Anveh *Iran* **71** E7
Anvers = Antwerpen *Belgium* **17** C4
Anvers I. *Antarctica* **5** C17
Anwen *China* **59** C13
Anxi *Fujian, China* **59** E12
Anxi *Gansu, China* **60** B4
Anxian *China* **58** B5
Anxiang *China* **59** C9
Anxious B. *Australia* **95** E1
Anyama *Ivory C.* **82** D4
Anyang *China* **56** F8
Anyang *S. Korea* **57** F14
Anyer *Indonesia* **63** G12
Anyuan *China* **59** E10
Anyue *China* **58** B5
Anza *U.S.A.* **111** M10
Anze *China* **56** F7
Anzhero-Sudzhensk *Russia* **52** D9
Ánzio *Italy* **42** A5
Ao Makham *Thailand* **65** a
Ao Phangnga △ *Thailand* **65** a
Aoga-Shima *Japan* **55** H9
Aoiz *Spain* **38** C3
Aoji *N. Korea* **57** C16
Aomen = Macau *China* **59** F9
Aomori *Japan* **54** D10
Aomori □ *Japan* **54** D10
Aonla *India* **69** E8
Aorai, Mt. *Tahiti* **91** d
Aoraki Mount Cook *N.Z.* **91** E3
Aoral, Phnum *Cambodia* **65** G5
Aosta *Italy* **40** C4
Aotearoa ■ = New Zealand ■ *Oceania* **91** D6
Aoudéras *Niger* **83** B6
Aoukâr *Mauritania* **82** B3
Aozou Strip *Chad* **79** D9
Apa → *S. Amer.* **126** A4
Apache *U.S.A.* **116** D5
Apache Junction *U.S.A.* **109** K8
Apalachee B. *U.S.A.* **117** G13
Apalachicola *U.S.A.* **117** G12
Apalachicola → *U.S.A.* **117** G12
Apam *Ghana* **83** D4
Apapa *Nigeria* **83** D5
Apaporis → *Colombia* **124** D5
Aparados da Serra △ *Brazil* **127** B5
Aparri *Phil.* **61** B4
Apateu *Romania* **28** D6
Apatin *Serbia* **28** E4
Apatity *Russia* **8** C25
Apatula = Finke *Australia* **94** D1
Apatzingán *Mexico* **118** D4
Apeldoorn *Neths.* **17** B5
Apen *Germany* **24** B3
Apennines = Appennini *Italy* **40** D7
Apensen *Germany* **24** B5
Apia *Samoa* **91** b
Apiacás, Serra dos *Brazil* **124** E7
Apies → *S. Africa* **89** D4
Apizaco *Mexico* **119** D5
Aplao *Peru* **124** G4
Apo, Mt. *Phil.* **63** C7
Apolakia *Greece* **49** C9
Apolakia, Ormos *Greece* **49** C9
Apolda *Germany* **24** D7
Apollonia = Marsá Susah *Libya* **79** B10
Apolo *Bolivia* **124** F5
Apolonia *Greece* **46** E6
Aporé → *Brazil* **125** G8
Apostle Is. *U.S.A.* **112** B8
Apostle Islands △ *U.S.A.* **112** B8
Apóstoles *Argentina* **127** B4
Apostolos Andreas, C. *Cyprus* **49** D13
Apostolovo *Ukraine* **33** J7
Apoteri *Guyana* **124** C7
Appalachian Mts. *U.S.A.* **113** G14
Äppelbo *Sweden* **10** D8
Appennini *Italy* **40** D7
Appennino Ligure *Italy* **40** D6
Appenzell-Ausser Rhoden □ *Switz.* **25** H5
Appenzell-Inner Rhoden □ *Switz.* **25** H5
Appiano *Italy* **41** B8
Apple Hill *Canada* **115** A10
Apple Valley *U.S.A.* **111** L9
Appleby-in-Westmorland *U.K.* **14** C5
Appledore *U.K.* **15** F3
Appleton *U.S.A.* **112** C9
Approuague → *Fr. Guiana* **125** C8
Apricena *Italy* **41** G12
Aprília *Italy* **42** A5
Apsheronsk *Russia* **35** H4
Apsley *Canada* **114** B6
Apt *France* **21** E9
Apuane, Alpi *Italy* **40** D7
Apucarana *Brazil* **127** A5
Apulia = Púglia □ *Italy* **43** A9

Apure → *Venezuela* **124** B5
Apurímac → *Peru* **124** F4
Apuseni, Munții *Romania* **28** D7
Āqā Jarī *Iran* **71** D6
Aqaba = Al 'Aqabah *Jordan* **74** F4
Aqaba, G. of *Red Sea* **70** D2
'Aqabah, Khalīj al = Aqaba, G. of *Red Sea* **70** D2
'Aqdā *Iran* **71** C7
Aqiq *Sudan* **80** D4
Aqiq, Khalīg *Sudan* **80** D4
'Aqrah *Iraq* **73** D10
Aqsay *Kazakhstan* **52** D6
Aqtaū *Kazakhstan* **52** E6
Aqtöbe *Kazakhstan* **52** D6
Aqtoghay *Kazakhstan* **52** E8
Aquidauana *Brazil* **125** H7
Aquila *Mexico* **118** D4
Aquiles Serdán *Mexico* **118** B3
Aquin *Haiti* **121** C5
Aquitaine □ *France* **20** D3
Ar Rachidiya = Er Rachidia *Morocco* **78** B5
Ar Rafid *Syria* **74** C4
Ar Raḥḥālīyah *Iraq* **73** F10
Ar Ramādī *Iraq* **73** F10
Ar Ramthā *Jordan* **74** C5
Ar Raqqah *Syria* **73** E8
Ar Raqqah □ *Syria* **73** D8
Ar Rass *Si. Arabia* **70** E4
Ar Rawshān *Si. Arabia* **80** C5
Ar Rayyān *Qatar* **71** E6
Ar Rifā'ī *Iraq* **70** D5
Ar Riyāḍ *Si. Arabia* **70** E5
Ar Ru'ays *Qatar* **71** E6
Ar Rukhaymīyah *Iraq* **70** D5
Ar Ruṣāfah *Syria* **73** E8
Ar Ruṭbah *Iraq* **73** F9
Ara *India* **69** G11
Ara Goro *Ethiopia* **81** F5
Ara Tera *Ethiopia* **81** F5
Arab *U.S.A.* **117** D11
'Arab, Bahr el → *Sudan* **81** F2
Arab, Khalīg el *Egypt* **80** A2
Arab, Shatt al → *Asia* **71** D6
'Araba, W. → *Egypt* **80** J8
'Arabābād *Iran* **71** C8
Araban *Turkey* **72** D7
Arabatskaya Strelka *Ukraine* **33** K8
Arabba *Italy* **41** B8
Arabia *Asia* **50** F6
Arabian Desert = Es Sahrâ' Esh Sharqîya *Egypt* **80** B3
Arabian Gulf = Persian Gulf *Asia* **71** E6
Arabian Sea *Ind. Oc.* **50** G8
Araç *Turkey* **72** B5
Aracaju *Brazil* **125** F11
Aracati *Brazil* **125** D11
Araçatuba *Brazil* **127** A5
Aracena *Spain* **37** H4
Aracena, Sierra de *Spain* **37** H4
Arachova *Greece* **46** C4
Aračinovo *Macedonia* **44** D5
Araçuaí *Brazil* **125** G10
Araçuaí → *Brazil* **125** G10
'Arad *Israel* **74** D4
Arad *Romania* **28** D6
Arad □ *Romania* **28** D6
Arādān *Iran* **71** C7
Aradhippou *Cyprus* **49** E12
Arafura Sea *E. Indies* **90** B6
Aragats *Armenia* **35** K7
Aragón □ *Spain* **38** D4
Aragón → *Spain* **38** C3
Aragona *Italy* **42** E6
Araguacema *Brazil* **125** E9
Araguaia → *Brazil* **125** E9
Araguaína *Brazil* **125** E9
Araguari *Brazil* **125** G9
Araguari → *Brazil* **125** C9
Arain *India* **68** F6
Arak *Algeria* **78** C6
Arāk *Iran* **71** C6
Araka *Sudan* **81** G3
Arakan Coast *Burma* **67** K19
Arakan Yoma *Burma* **67** K19
Arakli *Turkey* **73** B9
Araks = Aras, Rūd-e → *Asia* **35** K9
Aral *Kazakhstan* **52** E7
Aral Sea *Asia* **52** E7
Aral Tengizi = Aral Sea *Asia* **52** E7
Aralsk = Aral *Kazakhstan* **52** E7
Aralskoye More = Aral Sea *Asia* **52** E7
Aralsor, Ozero = Aralsor Köli *Kazakhstan* **35** F9
Aralsor Köli *Kazakhstan* **35** F9
Aramac *Australia* **94** C4
Aran I. *Ireland* **12** A3
Aran Is. *Ireland* **12** C2
Aranda de Duero *Spain* **36** D7
Arandān *Iran* **70** C5
Arandelovac *Serbia* **44** B4
Aranjuez *Spain* **36** E7
Aranos *Namibia* **88** C2
Aransas Pass *U.S.A.* **116** H6

Aranyaprathet *Thailand* **64** F4
Araouane *Mali* **82** B4
Arapahoe *U.S.A.* **112** E4
Arapey Grande → *Uruguay* **126** C4
Arapgir *Turkey* **73** C8
Arapiraca *Brazil* **125** E11
Arapis, Akra *Greece* **45** F8
Arapongas *Brazil* **127** A5
Ar'ar *Si. Arabia* **70** D4
Araranguá *Brazil* **127** B6
Araraquara *Brazil* **125** H9
Ararás, Serra das *Brazil* **127** B5
Ararat *Armenia* **73** C11
Ararat *Australia* **95** F3
Ararat, Mt. = Ağrı Dağı *Turkey* **73** C11
Araria *India* **69** F12
Araripe, Chapada do *Brazil* **125** E11
Araruama, L. de *Brazil* **127** A7
Aras, Rūd-e → *Asia* **35** K9
Aratâne *Mauritania* **82** B3
Arauca *Colombia* **124** B4
Arauca → *Venezuela* **124** B5
Arauco *Chile* **126** D1
Arawa *Ethiopia* **81** F5
Arawale △ *Kenya* **86** C5
Araxá *Brazil* **125** G9
Araya, Pen. de *Venezuela* **124** A6
Arba Gugu *Ethiopia* **81** F5
Arba Minch *Ethiopia* **81** F4
Arbat *Iraq* **73** E11
Árbatax *Italy* **42** C2
Arbi *Ethiopia* **81** F4
Arbīl *Iraq* **73** D11
Arbīl □ *Iraq* **73** D11
Arboga *Sweden* **10** E9
Arbois *France* **19** F12
Arbore *Ethiopia* **81** F4
Arboréa *Italy* **42** C1
Arborfield *Canada* **103** C8
Arborg *Canada* **103** C9
Arbre du Ténéré *Niger* **83** B7
Arbroath *U.K.* **13** E6
Arbuckle *U.S.A.* **110** F4
Arbus *Italy* **42** C1
Arc → *France* **21** C10
Arc-lès-Gray *France* **19** E12
Arcachon *France* **20** D2
Arcachon, Bassin d' *France* **20** D2
Arcade *U.S.A.* **114** D6
Arcadia *Fla., U.S.A.* **117** H14
Arcadia *La., U.S.A.* **116** E8
Arcadia *Pa., U.S.A.* **114** F6
Arcata *U.S.A.* **108** F1
Arcévia *Italy* **41** E9
Archanes *Greece* **47** F7
Archangel = Arkhangelsk *Russia* **52** C5
Archangelos *Greece* **49** C10
Archar *Bulgaria* **44** C6
Archbald *U.S.A.* **115** E9
Archena *Spain* **39** G3
Archer → *Australia* **94** A3
Archer B. *Australia* **94** A3
Archer Bend = Mungkan Kandju △ *Australia* **94** A3
Archers Post *Kenya* **86** B4
Arches △ *U.S.A.* **108** G9
Archidona *Spain* **37** H6
Archipel-de-Mingan △ *Canada* **105** B7
Archipiélago Chinijo △ *Canary Is.* **48** E6
Archipiélago Los Roques △ *Venezuela* **121** D6
Arci, Mte. *Italy* **42** C1
Arcidosso *Italy* **41** F8
Arcipelago de la Maddalena △ *Italy* **42** A2
Arcipelago Toscano △ *Italy* **40** F7
Arcis-sur-Aube *France* **19** D11
Arckaringa Cr. → *Australia* **95** D2
Arco *Italy* **40** C7
Arco *U.S.A.* **108** E7
Arcos de Jalón *Spain* **38** D2
Arcos de la Frontera *Spain* **37** J5
Arcos de Valdevez *Portugal* **36** D2
Arcot *India* **66** N11
Arcozelo *Portugal* **36** E3
Arctic Bay *Canada* **101** B11
Arctic Mid-Ocean Ridge *Arctic* **4** A
Arctic Ocean *Arctic* **4** B18
Arctic Red River = Tsiigehtchic *Canada* **100** C6
Arctowski *Antarctica* **5** C18
Arda → *Bulgaria* **45** E10
Arda → *Italy* **40** C7
Ardabīl *Iran* **73** C13
Ardabīl □ *Iran* **71** B6
Ardahan *Turkey* **73** B10
Ardahan □ *Turkey* **73** B10
Ardakān = Sepīdān *Iran* **71** D7
Ardakān *Iran* **71** C7
Ardala *Sweden* **11** F7
Ardales *Spain* **37** J6
Ardara *Ireland* **12** B3
Ardas → *Greece* **45** E10

Ardèche □ *France* **21** D8
Ardèche → *France* **21** D8
Ardee *Ireland* **12** C5
Arden *Canada* **114** B8
Arden *Denmark* **11** H3
Arden *Calif., U.S.A.* **110** G5
Arden *Nev., U.S.A.* **111** J11
Ardenne *Belgium* **17** E5
Ardennes = Ardenne *Belgium* **17** E5
Ardennes □ *France* **19** C11
Ardentes *France* **19** F8
Arderin *Ireland* **12** C4
Ardeşen *Turkey* **73** B9
Ardestān *Iran* **71** C7
Ardfert *Ireland* **12** D2
Ardglass *U.K.* **12** B6
Ardhéa = Aridea *Greece* **44** F6
Ardila → *Portugal* **37** G3
Ardino *Bulgaria* **45** E9
Ardivachar Pt. *U.K.* **13** D1
Ardlethan *Australia* **95** E4
Ardmore *Okla., U.S.A.* **116** D6
Ardmore *Pa., U.S.A.* **115** F9
Ardnamurchan, Pt. of *U.K.* **13** E2
Ardnave Pt. *U.K.* **13** F2
Ardon *Russia* **35** J7
Ardore *Italy* **43** D9
Ardres *France* **19** B8
Ardrossan *Australia* **95** E2
Ardrossan *U.K.* **13** F4
Ards Pen. *U.K.* **12** B6
Arduan *Sudan* **80** D3
Ardud *Romania* **28** C7
Åre *Sweden* **10** A7
Arecibo *Puerto Rico* **121** d
Areia Branca *Brazil* **125** E11
Arena, Pt. *U.S.A.* **110** G3
Arenal *Honduras* **120** C2
Arenas = Las Arenas *Spain* **36** B6
Arenas de San Pedro *Spain* **36** E5
Arendal *Norway* **9** G13
Arendsee *Germany* **24** C7
Arenys de Mar *Spain* **38** D7
Arenzano *Italy* **40** D5
Areópoli *Greece* **46** E4
Arequipa *Peru* **124** G4
Arero *Ethiopia* **81** G4
Arès *France* **20** D2
Arévalo *Spain* **36** D6
Arezzo *Italy* **41** E8
Arga *Turkey* **70** C7
Arga → *Spain* **38** C3
Argalasti *Greece* **46** B5
Argamasilla de Alba *Spain* **37** F7
Argamasilla de Calatrava *Spain* **37** G6
Arganda *Spain* **36** E7
Arganil *Portugal* **36** E2
Argedeb *Ethiopia* **81** F5
Argelès-Gazost *France* **20** E3
Argelès-sur-Mer *France* **20** F7
Argens → *France* **21** E10
Argenta *Canada* **102** C5
Argenta *Italy* **41** D8
Argentan *France* **18** D6
Argentário, Mte. *Italy* **41** F8
Argentat *France* **20** C5
Argentera *Italy* **40** D4
Argenteuil *France* **19** D9
Argentia *Canada* **105** C9
Argentiera, C. dell' *Italy* **42** B1
Argentina ■ *S. Amer.* **128** D3
Argentine Basin *Atl. Oc.* **128** F6
Argentino, L. *Argentina* **128** G2
Argenton-Château *France* **18** F6
Argenton-sur-Creuse *France* **19** F8
Argeş □ *Romania* **29** F9
Argeş → *Romania* **29** F11
Arghandab → *Afghan.* **68** D1
Argheile *Ethiopia* **81** F5
Argirades *Greece* **49** B3
Argiroupoli *Greece* **49** D6
Argo *Sudan* **80** D3
Argolida □ *Greece* **46** D4
Argolikos Kolpos *Greece* **46** D4
Argonne *France* **19** C12
Argos *Greece* **46** D4
Argos Orestiko *Greece* **44** F5
Argostoli *Greece* **46** C2
Arguedas *Spain* **38** C3
Arguello, Pt. *U.S.A.* **111** L6
Arguineguín *Canary Is.* **48** G4
Argun *Russia* **35** J7
Argun → *Russia* **53** D13
Argungu *Nigeria* **83** C5
Argus Pk. *U.S.A.* **111** K9
Argyle, L. *Australia* **92** C4
Argyll □ *U.K.* **13** E4
Argyll & Bute □ *U.K.* **13** E3
Arhavi *Turkey* **73** B9
Århus *Denmark* **11** H4
Ariadnoye *Russia* **54** B7
Ariamsvlei *Namibia* **88** D2
Ariana *Tunisia* **79** A8
Ariano Irpino *Italy* **43** A8
Aribinda *Burkina Faso* **83** C4

Arica *Chile* **124** G4
Arica *Colombia* **124** D4
Arico *Canary Is.* **48** F3
Arid, C. *Australia* **93** F3
Arida *Japan* **55** G7
Aride *Seychelles* **85** b
Aridea *Greece* **44** F6
Ariège □ *France* **20** F5
Ariège → *France* **20** E5
Arieş → *Romania* **29** D8
Arihā *Israel* **80** A4
Arila, Akra *Greece* **49** A3
Arilje *Serbia* **44** C4
Arima *Trin. & Tob.* **121** D7
Arinos → *Brazil* **124** F7
Ario de Rosales *Mexico* **118** D4
Ariogala *Lithuania* **30** C10
Aripo, Mt. *Trin. & Tob.* **125** K15
Aripuanã *Brazil* **124** E6
Aripuanã → *Brazil* **124** E6
Ariquemes *Brazil* **124** E6
Arisaig *U.K.* **13** E3
Arīsh, W. el → *Egypt* **80** A3
Arissa *Ethiopia* **81** E5
Aristazabal I. *Canada* **102** C3
Arivonimamo *Madag.* **89** B8
Ariza *Spain* **38** D2
Arizaro, Salar de *Argentina* **126** A2
Arizona *Argentina* **126** D2
Arizona □ *U.S.A.* **109** J8
Arizpe *Mexico* **118** A2
Ärjäng *Sweden* **10** E6
Arjeplog *Sweden* **8** C17
Arjepluovve = Arjeplog *Sweden* **8** C17
Arjona *Colombia* **124** A3
Arjona *Spain* **37** H6
Arjuna *Indonesia* **63** G15
Arka *Russia* **53** C15
Arkadak *Russia* **34** E6
Arkadelphia *U.S.A.* **116** D8
Arkadia □ *Greece* **46** D4
Arkaig, L. *U.K.* **13** E3
Arkalyk = Arqalyk *Kazakhstan* **52** D7
Arkansas □ *U.S.A.* **116** D8
Arkansas → *U.S.A.* **116** E9
Arkansas City *U.S.A.* **112** G5
Arkaroola *Australia* **95** E2
Arkhangelsk *Russia* **52** C5
Arkhangelskoye *Russia* **34** E5
Arki *Greece* **47** D8
Arki *India* **68** D7
Arkiko *Eritrea* **81** D4
Arklow *Ireland* **12** D5
Arkona, Kap *Germany* **24** A9
Arkösund *Sweden* **11** F10
Arkoudi *Greece* **46** C2
Arkport *U.S.A.* **114** D7
Arkticheskiy, Mys *Russia* **53** A10
Arkul *Russia* **34** B10
Arkville *U.S.A.* **115** D10
Årla *Sweden* **10** E10
Arlanda, Stockholm ✈ (ARN) *Sweden* **10** E11
Arlanza → *Spain* **36** C6
Arlanzón → *Spain* **36** C6
Arlbergpass *Austria* **26** D3
Arles *France* **21** E8
Arli *Burkina Faso* **83** C5
Arli △ *Burkina Faso* **83** C5
Arlington *S. Africa* **89** D4
Arlington *N.Y., U.S.A.* **115** E11
Arlington *Oreg., U.S.A.* **108** D3
Arlington *S. Dak., U.S.A.* **112** C5
Arlington *Tex., U.S.A.* **116** E6
Arlington *Va., U.S.A.* **113** F15
Arlington *Vt., U.S.A.* **115** C11
Arlington *Wash., U.S.A.* **110** B4
Arlington Heights *U.S.A.* **112** D10
Arlit *Niger* **78** E7
Arlon *Belgium* **17** E5
Arlparra *Australia* **94** C1
Arltunga *Australia* **94** C1
Armagh *U.K.* **12** B5
Armagh □ *U.K.* **12** B5
Armagnac *France* **20** E4
Armançon → *France* **19** E10
Armando Bermudez △ *Dom. Rep.* **121** C5
Armavir *Russia* **35** H5
Armenia *Colombia* **124** C3
Armenia ■ *Asia* **35** K7
Armeniş *Romania* **28** E7
Armenistis, Akra *Greece* **49** C9
Armentières *France* **19** B9
Armidale *Australia* **95** E5
Armilla *Spain* **37** H7
Armorique △ *France* **18** D3
Armour *U.S.A.* **112** D4
Armstrong *B.C., Canada* **102** C5
Armstrong *Ont., Canada* **104** B2
Armutlu *Bursa, Turkey* **45** F12
Armutlu *İzmir, Turkey* **47** C9
Arnarfjörður *Iceland* **8** D2
Arnaud → *Canada* **101** D13
Arnauti, C. *Cyprus* **49** D11
Arnay-le-Duc *France* **19** E11

Arnea *Greece* **44** F7
Arnedillo *Spain* **38** C2
Arnedo *Spain* **38** C2
Arnett *U.S.A.* **116** C5
Arnhem *Neths.* **17** C5
Arnhem, C. *Australia* **94** A2
Arnhem B. *Australia* **94** A2
Arnhem Land *Australia* **94** A1
Arnissa *Greece* **44** F5
Arno → *Italy* **40** E7
Arno Bay *Australia* **95** E2
Arnold *U.K.* **14** D6
Arnold *U.S.A.* **110** G6
Arnoldstein *Austria* **26** E6
Arnon → *France* **19** E9
Arnot *Canada* **103** B9
Arnøya *Norway* **8** A19
Arnprior *Canada* **115** A8
Arnsberg *Germany* **24** D4
Arnsberger Wald △ *Germany* **24** D4
Arnstadt *Germany* **24** E6
Aroa, Pte. *Moorea* **91** d
Aroab *Namibia* **88** D2
Aroania Oros *Greece* **46** D4
Aroche *Spain* **37** H4
Arochuku *Nigeria* **83** D6
Arolsen *Germany* **24** D5
Aron *India* **68** G6
Aron → *France* **19** F10
Arona *Canary Is.* **48** F3
Arona *Italy* **40** C5
Aroroy *Phil.* **61** E5
Aros → *Mexico* **118** B3
Arosa, Ría de *Spain* **36** C2
Arpajon *France* **19** D9
Arpajon-sur-Cère *France* **20** D6
Arpaşu de Jos *Romania* **29** E9
Arqalyk *Kazakhstan* **52** D7
Arrah = Ara *India* **69** G11
Arrah → *France* **18** D3
Arrah *Ivory C.* **82** D4
Arraiolos *Portugal* **37** G3
Arran *U.K.* **13** F3
Arras *France* **19** B9
Arrasate *Spain* **38** B2
Arrats → *France* **20** D4
Arreau *France* **20** F4
Arrecife *Canary Is.* **48** F6
Arrecifes *Argentina* **126** C3
Arrée, Mts. d' *France* **18** D3
Arresø *Denmark* **11** J6
Arriaga *Mexico* **119** D6
Arribes del Duero △ *Spain* **36** D4
Arrilalah *Australia* **94** C3
Arrino *Australia* **93** E2
Arriondas *Spain* **36** B5
Arromanches-les-Bains *France* **18** C6
Arronches *Portugal* **37** F3
Arros → *France* **20** E3
Arrow, L. *Ireland* **12** B3
Arrowtown *N.Z.* **91** F2
Ars *Iran* **70** B5
Ars-sur-Moselle *France* **19** C13
Arsenault L. *Canada* **103** B7
Arsenev *Russia* **54** B6
Arsi *Ethiopia* **81** F4
Arsiero *Italy* **41** C8
Arsin *Turkey* **73** B8
Arsk *Russia* **34** B9
Årsunda *Sweden* **10** D10
Arta *Greece* **46** B3
Artà *Spain* **48** B10
Arta □ *Greece* **46** B3
Arteaga *Mexico* **118** D4
Arteche *Phil.* **61** E6
Arteijo = Arteixo *Spain* **36** B2
Arteixo *Spain* **36** B2
Artem = Artyom *Azerbaijan* **35** K10
Artem *Russia* **54** C6
Artemovsk *Russia* **53** D10
Artemovsk *Ukraine* **33** H9
Artemovskiy *Russia* **35** G5
Artenay *France* **19** D8
Artern *Germany* **24** D7
Artesa de Segre *Spain* **38** D6
Artesia = Mosomane *Botswana* **88** C4
Artesia *U.S.A.* **109** K11
Arthington *Liberia* **82** D2
Arthur *Canada* **114** C4
Arthur → *Australia* **95** G3
Arthur Cr. → *Australia* **94** C2
Arthur Pt. *Australia* **94** C5
Arthur River *Australia* **93** F2
Arthur's Pass *N.Z.* **91** E3
Arthur's Pass △ *N.Z.* **91** E3
Arthur's Town *Bahamas* **121** B4
Artigas *Antarctica* **5** C18
Artigas *Uruguay* **126** C4
Artik *Armenia* **35** K6
Artillery L. *Canada* **103** A7
Artois *France* **19** B9
Artotina *Greece* **46** C4
Artrutx, C. de *Spain* **48** B10
Artsyz *Ukraine* **29** D14

Artvin *Turkey* **73** B9
Artvin □ *Turkey* **73** B9
Artyom *Azerbaijan* **35** K10
Aru, Kepulauan *Indonesia* **63** F8
Aru Is. = Aru, Kepulauan *Indonesia* **63** F8
Arua *Uganda* **86** B3
Aruanã *Brazil* **125** F8
Aruba ☑ *W. Indies* **121** D6
Arucas *Canary Is.* **48** F4
Arué *Tahiti* **91** d
Arun → *Nepal* **69** F12
Arun → *U.K.* **15** G7
Arunachal Pradesh □ *India* **67** F19
Arusha *Tanzania* **86** C4
Arusha □ *Tanzania* **86** C4
Arusha △ *Tanzania* **86** C4
Arusha Chini *Tanzania* **86** C4
Aruwimi → *Dem. Rep. of the Congo* **86** B1
Arvada *Colo., U.S.A.* **108** G11
Arvada *Wyo., U.S.A.* **108** D10
Arve → *France* **19** F13
Arvi *Greece* **47** F7
Arviat *Canada* **103** A10
Arvidsjaur *Sweden* **8** D18
Arvika *Sweden* **10** E6
Arvin *U.S.A.* **111** K8
Arwal *India* **69** G11
Arxan *China* **60** B6
Åryd *Sweden* **11** H8
Arys *Kazakhstan* **52** E7
Arzachena *Italy* **42** A2
Arzamas *Russia* **34** C6
Arzanah *U.A.E.* **71** E7
Arzew *Algeria* **78** A5
Arzgir *Russia* **35** H7
Arzignano *Italy* **41** C8
Arzúa *Spain* **36** C2
Aš *Czech Rep.* **26** A5
Ås *Sweden* **10** A8
As Pontes de García Rodríguez *Spain* **36** B3
Aş Şafā *Syria* **74** B6
As Saffānīyah *Si. Arabia* **71** E6
As Safīrah *Syria* **72** D7
Aş Şahm *Oman* **71** E8
As Sājir *Si. Arabia* **70** E5
As Salamīyah *Syria* **72** E7
As Salmān *Iraq* **70** D5
As Salṭ *Jordan* **74** C4
As Sal'w'a *Qatar* **71** E6
As Samāwah *Iraq* **70** D5
As Sanamayn *Syria* **74** B5
As Sohar = Ṣuḩār *Oman* **71** E8
As Sukhnah *Syria* **73** E8
As Sulaymānīyah *Iraq* **73** E11
As Sulaymānīyah □ *Iraq* **73** E11
As Sulaymī *Si. Arabia* **70** E4
As Sulayyil *Si. Arabia* **75** C4
As Summān *Si. Arabia* **70** E5
As Suwaydā' *Syria* **74** C5
As Suwaydā' □ *Syria* **74** C5
As Suwayq *Oman* **71** F8
Aş Şuwayrah *Iraq* **73** F11
Åsa *Sweden* **11** G6
Asab *Namibia* **88** D2
Asaba *Nigeria* **83** D6
Asad, Buḩayrat al *Syria* **73** D8
Asadābād *Iran* **73** E13
Asafo *Ghana* **82** D4
Asahi-Gawa → *Japan* **55** G6
Asahigawa *Japan* **54** C11
Asale, L. *Ethiopia* **81** E5
Asamankese *Ghana* **83** D4
Asan → *India* **69** F8
Asansol *India* **69** H12
Åsarna *Sweden* **10** B8
Asau *Samoa* **91** b
Asayita *Ethiopia* **81** E5
Asbe Teferi *Ethiopia* **81** F5
Asbesberge *S. Africa* **88** D3
Asbestos *Canada* **105** C5
Asbury Park *U.S.A.* **115** F10
Ascea *Italy* **43** B8
Ascensión *Mexico* **118** A3
Ascensión, B. de la *Mexico* **119** D7
Ascension I. *Atl. Oc.* **77** G2
Aschach an der Donau *Austria* **26** C7
Aschaffenburg *Germany* **25** F5
Aschendorf *Germany* **24** B3
Aschersleben *Germany* **24** D7
Asciano *Italy* **41** E8
Ascó *Spain* **38** D5
Áscoli Piceno *Italy* **41** F10
Áscoli Satriano *Italy* **43** A8
Ascope *Peru* **124** E3
Ascotán *Chile* **126** A2
Aseb *Eritrea* **81** E5
Åseda *Sweden* **11** G9
Åsele *Sweden* **10** C7
Asenovgrad *Bulgaria* **45** D8
Asfeld *France* **19** C11
Asfūn el Matā'na *Egypt* **80** B3
Aşgabat = Ashgabat *Turkmenistan* **71** B8
Aşgata *Cyprus* **49** E12

Ash Fork *U.S.A.* **109** J7
Ash Grove *U.S.A.* **112** G7
Ash Shabakah *Iraq* **70** D4
Ash Shamāl □ *Lebanon* **74** A5
Ash Shāmīyah *Iraq* **73** G11
Ash Shāriqah *U.A.E.* **71** E7
Ash Sharmah *Si. Arabia* **70** D2
Ash Sharqāt *Iraq* **73** E10
Ash Shaṭrah *Iraq* **70** D5
Ash Shawbak *Jordan* **70** D2
Ash Shinafiyah *Iraq* **70** D5
Ash Shu'bah *Si. Arabia* **70** D5
Ash Shumlūl *Si. Arabia* **70** E5
Ash Shūr'a *Iraq* **70** C4
Ash Shurayf *Si. Arabia* **70** E3
Ash Shuwayfāt *Lebanon* **74** B4
Ashanti □ *Ghana* **83** D4
Ashau *Vietnam* **64** D6
Ashbourne *U.K.* **14** D6
Ashburn *U.S.A.* **117** F13
Ashburton *N.Z.* **91** E3
Ashburton → *Australia* **92** D1
Ashcroft *Canada* **102** C4
Ashdod *Israel* **74** D3
Ashdown *U.S.A.* **116** E7
Asheboro *U.S.A.* **117** D15
Ashern *Canada* **103** C9
Asherton *U.S.A.* **116** G5
Asheville *U.S.A.* **117** D13
Ashewat *Pakistan* **68** D3
Asheweig → *Canada* **104** B2
Ashford *Australia* **95** D5
Ashford *U.K.* **15** F8
Ashgabat *Turkmenistan* **71** B8
Ashibetsu *Japan* **54** C11
Ashikaga *Japan* **55** F9
Ashington *U.K.* **14** B6
Ashizuri-Uwakai △ *Japan* **55** H6
Ashizuri-Zaki *Japan* **55** H6
Ashkarkot *Afghan.* **68** C2
Ashkhabad = Ashgabat *Turkmenistan* **71** B8
Āshkhāneh *Iran* **71** B8
Ashland *Kans., U.S.A.* **112** G4
Ashland *Ky., U.S.A.* **113** F12
Ashland *Maine, U.S.A.* **113** B19
Ashland *Mont., U.S.A.* **108** D10
Ashland *Ohio, U.S.A.* **114** F2
Ashland *Oreg., U.S.A.* **108** E2
Ashland *Pa., U.S.A.* **115** F8
Ashland *Va., U.S.A.* **113** G15
Ashland *Wis., U.S.A.* **112** B9
Ashley *N. Dak., U.S.A.* **112** B5
Ashley *Pa., U.S.A.* **115** E9
Ashmore and Cartier Is. *Ind. Oc.* **92** B3
Ashmore Reef *Australia* **92** B3
Ashmûn *Egypt* **80** H7
Ashmyany *Belarus* **23** A13
Ashokan Res. *U.S.A.* **115** E10
Ashqelon *Israel* **74** D3
Ashta *India* **68** H7
Ashtabula *U.S.A.* **114** E4
Ashton *S. Africa* **88** E3
Ashton *U.S.A.* **108** D8
Ashuanipi, L. *Canada* **105** B6
Ashuapmushuan → *Canada* **104** C5
Ashville *U.S.A.* **114** F6
'Āşī → *Asia* **72** D6
Asia **50** E9
Asia, Kepulauan *Indonesia* **63** D8
Asiago *Italy* **41** C8
Asifabad *India* **66** K11
Asinara *Italy* **42** A1
Asinara, G. dell' *Italy* **42** A1
Asino *Russia* **52** D9
Asipovichy *Belarus* **23** B15
'Asīr *Si. Arabia* **75** D3
Asir, Ras *Somali Rep.* **75** E5
Aşkale *Turkey* **73** C9
Askersund *Sweden* **11** F8
Askham *S. Africa* **88** D3
Askim *Norway* **9** G14
Askio, Oros *Greece* **44** F5
Askja *Iceland* **8** D5
Askøyna *Norway* **8** F11
Asl *Egypt* **80** B3
Aslan Burnu *Turkey* **47** C8
Aslanapa *Turkey* **47** B11
Asmara = Asmera *Eritrea* **81** D4
Asmera *Eritrea* **81** D4
Asnæs *Denmark* **11** J4
Åsnen *Sweden* **11** H8
Aso Kuju △ *Japan* **55** H5
Ásola *Italy* **40** C7
Asos *Greece* **46** C2
Asosa *Ethiopia* **81** E3
Asoteriba, Jebel *Sudan* **80** C4
Aspatria *U.K.* **14** C4
Aspe *Spain* **39** G4
Aspen *U.S.A.* **108** G10
Aspendos *Turkey* **72** D4
Aspermont *U.S.A.* **116** E4
Aspet *France* **20** E4
Aspiring, Mt. *N.Z.* **91** F2
Aspres-sur-Buëch *France* **21** D9
Asprokavos, Akra *Greece* **49** B4

Aspromonte △ *Italy* **43** D8
Aspur *India* **68** H6
Asquith *Canada* **103** C7
Assab = Aseb *Eritrea* **81** E5
Assâba □ *Mauritania* **82** B2
Assâba, Massif de l'
  Mauritania **82** B2
Assagny △ *Ivory C.* **82** D4
Assaikio *Nigeria* **83** D6
Assal, L. *Djibouti* **81** E5
Assam □ *India* **67** G18
Assamakka *Niger* **83** B6
Assateague Island △ *U.S.A.*
  113 F16
Asse *Belgium* **17** D4
Assémini *Italy* **42** C1
Assen *Neths.* **17** A6
Assens *Denmark* **11** J3
Assini *Ivory C.* **82** D4
Assiniboia *Canada* **103** D7
Assiniboine ⇢ *Canada* **103** D9
Assiniboine, Mt. *Canada* **102** C5
Assis *Brazil* **127** A5
Assisi *Italy* **41** E9
Assynt, L. *U.K.* **13** C3
Astaffort *France* **20** D4
Astakida *Greece* **47** F8
Astakos *Greece* **46** C3
Astana *Kazakhstan* **52** D8
Āstāneh *Iran* **71** B6
Astara *Azerbaijan* **73** C13
Āstārā *Iran* **73** C13
Asterousia *Greece* **49** E7
Asti *Italy* **40** D5
Astipalea *Greece* **47** E8
Astorga *Spain* **36** C4
Astoria *U.S.A.* **110** D3
Åstorp *Sweden* **11** H6
Astrakhan *Russia* **35** G9
Astrakhan □ *Russia* **35** G8
Astudillo *Spain* **36** C6
Asturias □ *Spain* **36** B5
Asturias ✈ (OVD) *Spain* **36** B4
Asunción *Paraguay* **126** B4
Asunción Nochixtlán
  Mexico **119** D5
Åsunden *Sweden* **11** F9
Asutri *Sudan* **81** D4
Aswa ⇢ *Uganda* **86** B3
Aswa-Lolim △ *Uganda* **86** B3
Aswad, Ra's al *Si. Arabia* **80** C4
Aswân *Egypt* **80** C3
Aswan Dam = Sadd el Aali
  Egypt **80** C3
Asyût *Egypt* **80** B3
Asyûti, Wadi ⇢ *Egypt* **80** B3
Aszód *Hungary* **28** C4
At Ţafīlah *Jordan* **74** E4
At Ţafīlah □ *Jordan* **74** E4
Aţ Ţā'if *Si. Arabia* **80** C5
At Ta'mīm □ *Iraq* **70** C5
Aţ Ţīrāq *Si. Arabia* **70** D5
Aţ Tubayq *Si. Arabia* **70** D3
Aţ Ţunayb *Jordan* **74** D4
Atabey *Turkey* **47** D12
Atacama □ *Chile* **126** B2
Atacama, Desierto de *Chile* **126** A2
Atacama, Salar de *Chile* **126** A2
Atakpamé *Togo* **83** D5
Atalanda *Greece* **46** C4
Atalaya *Peru* **124** F4
Atalaya de Femes *Canary Is.* **48** F6
Atami *Japan* **55** G9
Atamyrat *Turkmenistan* **52** F7
Atapupu *Indonesia* **63** F6
Atâr *Mauritania* **78** D3
Atarfe *Spain* **37** H7
Atari *Pakistan* **68** D6
Atascadero *U.S.A.* **110** K6
Atasū *Kazakhstan* **52** E8
Ataturk, İstanbul ✈ (IST)
  Turkey **45** F12
Atatürk Baraji *Turkey* **73** D8
Atauro *E. Timor* **63** F7
Ataviros *Greece* **49** C9
Atbara *Sudan* **80** D3
'Atbara, Nahr ⇢ *Sudan* **80** D3
Atbasar *Kazakhstan* **52** D7
Atça *Turkey* **47** D10
Atchafalaya B. *U.S.A.* **116** G9
Atchison *U.S.A.* **112** F6
Atebubu *Ghana* **83** D4
Ateca *Spain* **38** D3
Aterno ⇢ *Italy* **41** F10
Āteshān *Iran* **71** C7
Atesine, Alpi *Italy* **41** B8
Atessa *Italy* **41** F11
Atfih *Egypt* **80** J7
Ath *Belgium* **17** D3
Athabasca *Canada* **102** C6
Athabasca ⇢ *Canada* **103** B6
Athabasca, L. *Canada* **103** B7
Athabasca Sand Dunes △
  Canada **103** B7
Athamanon Oros *Greece* **46** B3
Athboy *Ireland* **12** C5
Athenry *Ireland* **12** C3
Athens = Athina *Greece* **46** D5

Athens *Ala., U.S.A.* **117** D11
Athens *Ga., U.S.A.* **117** E13
Athens *N.Y., U.S.A.* **115** D11
Athens *Ohio, U.S.A.* **113** F12
Athens *Pa., U.S.A.* **115** E8
Athens *Tenn., U.S.A.* **117** D12
Athens *Tex., U.S.A.* **116** E7
Atherley *Canada* **114** B5
Atherton *Australia* **94** B4
Athi River *Kenya* **86** C4
Athiéme *Benin* **83** D5
Athienou *Cyprus* **49** D12
Athina *Greece* **46** D5
Athina ✈ (ATH) *Greece* **46** D5
Athínai = Athina *Greece* **46** D5
Athlone *Ireland* **12** C4
Athna *Cyprus* **49** D12
Athol *U.S.A.* **115** D12
Atholl, Forest of *U.K.* **13** E5
Atholville *Canada* **105** C6
Athos *Greece* **45** F8
Athy *Ireland* **12** C5
Ati *Chad* **79** F9
Ati *Sudan* **81** E2
Atiak *Uganda* **86** B3
Atienza *Spain* **38** D2
Atiit *Sudan* **81** F3
Atik L. *Canada* **103** B9
Atikaki △ *Canada* **103** C9
Atikameg ⇢ *Canada* **104** B3
Atikokan *Canada* **104** C1
Atikonak L. *Canada* **105** B7
Atimaono *Tahiti* **91** d
Atimonan *Phil.* **61** E4
Atitlán △ *Cent. Amer.* **119** E6
Atiu *Cook Is.* **97** J12
Atka *Russia* **53** C16
Atka I. *U.S.A.* **106** a
Atkarsk *Russia* **34** E7
Atkinson *U.S.A.* **112** D4
Atlanta *Ga., U.S.A.* **117** E12
Atlanta *Tex., U.S.A.* **116** E7
Atlantic *U.S.A.* **112** E6
Atlantic City *U.S.A.* **113** F16
Atlantic-Indian Basin
  Antarctica **5** B4
Atlantic Ocean **2** D8
Atlas Mts. = Haut Atlas
  Morocco **78** B4
Atlin *Canada* **102** B2
Atlin, L. *Canada* **102** B2
Atlin △ *Canada* **102** B2
Atmore *U.S.A.* **117** F11
Atoka *U.S.A.* **116** D6
Atokos *Greece* **46** C2
Atolia *U.S.A.* **111** K9
Atrai ⇢ *Bangla.* **69** G13
Atrak = Atrek ⇢
  Turkmenistan **71** B8
Ātran *Sweden* **11** G6
Ātran ⇢ *Sweden* **11** H6
Atrauli *India* **68** E8
Atrek ⇢ *Turkmenistan* **71** B8
Atri *Italy* **41** F10
Atsiki *Greece* **47** B7
Atsuta *Japan* **54** C10
Attalla *U.S.A.* **117** D11
Attapu *Laos* **64** E6
Attawapiskat *Canada* **104** B3
Attawapiskat ⇢ *Canada* **104** B3
Attawapiskat L. *Canada* **104** B2
Attersee *Austria* **26** D6
Attica *Ind., U.S.A.* **112** E10
Attica *Ohio, U.S.A.* **114** E2
Attichy *France* **19** C10
Attigny *France* **19** C11
Attika = Attiki □ *Greece* **46** D5
Attikamagen L. *Canada* **105** B6
Attiki □ *Greece* **46** D5
Attleboro *U.S.A.* **115** E13
Attock *Pakistan* **68** C5
Attopeu = Attapu *Laos* **64** E6
Attu I. *U.S.A.* **106** a
Attur *India* **66** P11
Atuel ⇢ *Argentina* **126** D2
Åtvidaberg *Sweden* **11** F10
Atwater *U.S.A.* **110** H6
Atwood *Canada* **114** C3
Atwood *U.S.A.* **112** F3
Atyraū *Kazakhstan* **52** E6
Au Sable *U.S.A.* **114** B1
Au Sable ⇢ *U.S.A.* **113** C12
Au Sable Forks *U.S.A.* **115** B11
Au Sable Pt. *U.S.A.* **114** B1
Auasberg *Namibia* **88** C2
Aubagne *France* **21** E9
Aubarca, C. d' *Spain* **48** B7
Aube □ *France* **19** D11
Aube ⇢ *France* **19** D10
Aubenas *France* **21** D8
Aubenton *France* **19** C11
Auberry *U.S.A.* **110** H7
Aubigny-sur-Nère *France* **19** E9
Aubin *France* **20** D6
Aubrac, Mts. d' *France* **20** D7
Auburn *Ala., U.S.A.* **117** E12
Auburn *Calif., U.S.A.* **110** G5

Auburn *Ind., U.S.A.* **113** E11
Auburn *Maine, U.S.A.* **113** C18
Auburn *N.Y., U.S.A.* **115** D8
Auburn *Nebr., U.S.A.* **112** E6
Auburn *Pa., U.S.A.* **115** F8
Auburn *Wash., U.S.A.* **110** C4
Auburn Ra. *Australia* **95** D5
Auburndale *U.S.A.* **117** G14
Aubusson *France* **20** C6
Auce *Latvia* **30** B9
Auch *France* **20** E4
Auchi *Nigeria* **83** D6
Auchterarder *U.K.* **13** E5
Auchtermuchty *U.K.* **13** E5
Auckland *N.Z.* **91** B5
Auckland Is. *Pac. Oc.* **96** N8
Aude □ *France* **20** E6
Aude ⇢ *France* **20** E7
Auden *Canada* **104** B2
Auderville *France* **18** C5
Audierne *France* **18** D2
Audincourt *France* **19** E13
Audo Ra. *Ethiopia* **81** F5
Audubon *U.S.A.* **112** E6
Aue *Germany* **24** E8
Auerbach *Germany* **24** E8
Augathella *Australia* **95** D4
Aughnacloy *U.K.* **12** B5
Aughrim *Ireland* **12** C3
Augrabies Falls *S. Africa* **88** D3
Augrabies Falls △ *S. Africa* **88** D3
Augsburg *Germany* **25** G6
Augsburg-Westliche
  Wälder △ *Germany* **25** G6
Augusta *Australia* **93** F2
Augusta *Italy* **43** E8
Augusta *Ark., U.S.A.* **116** D9
Augusta *Ga., U.S.A.* **117** E14
Augusta *Kans., U.S.A.* **112** G5
Augusta *Maine, U.S.A.* **113** C19
Augusta *Mont., U.S.A.* **108** C7
Augustenborg *Denmark* **11** K3
Augustów *Poland* **30** E9
Augustus, Mt. *Australia* **93** D2
Augustus I. *Australia* **92** C3
Aujuittuq = Grise Fiord
  Canada **101** B11
Aukan *Eritrea* **81** D5
Aukrug △ *Germany* **24** A5
Aukštaitija △ *Lithuania* **9** J22
Aukum *U.S.A.* **110** G6
Auld, L. *Australia* **92** D3
Aulefille *Norway* **10** D5
Aulla *Italy* **40** D6
Aulnay *France* **20** B3
Aulne ⇢ *France* **18** D2
Aulnoye-Aymeries *France* **19** B10
Ault *France* **18** B8
Ault *U.S.A.* **108** F11
Aulus-les-Bains *France* **20** F5
Aumale *France* **19** C8
Aumont-Aubrac *France* **20** D7
Auna *Nigeria* **83** C5
Auning *Denmark* **11** H4
Aunis *France* **20** B3
Aunu'u *Amer. Samoa* **91** b
Auponhia *Indonesia* **63** E7
Aups *France* **21** E10
Aur, Pulau *Malaysia* **65** L5
Auraiya *India* **69** F8
Aurangabad *Bihar, India* **69** G11
Aurangabad *Maharashtra,*
  India **66** K9
Auray *France* **18** E4
Aurich *Germany* **24** B3
Aurillac *France* **20** D6
Auronzo di Cadore *Italy* **41** B9
Aurora *Canada* **114** C5
Aurora *S. Africa* **88** E2
Aurora *Colo., U.S.A.* **108** G11
Aurora *Ill., U.S.A.* **112** E9
Aurora *Mo., U.S.A.* **112** G7
Aurora *N.Y., U.S.A.* **115** D8
Aurora *Nebr., U.S.A.* **112** E5
Aurora *Ohio, U.S.A.* **114** E3
Aurukun *Australia* **94** A3
Aus *Namibia* **88** D2
Ausable ⇢ *Canada* **114** C3
Auschwitz = Oświęcim
  Poland **31** H6
Austerlitz = Slavkov u
  Brna *Czech Rep.* **27** B9
Austin *Minn., U.S.A.* **112** D7
Austin *Nev., U.S.A.* **108** G5
Austin *Pa., U.S.A.* **114** E6
Austin *Tex., U.S.A.* **116** F6
Austin, L. *Australia* **93** E2
Austin I. *Canada* **103** A10
Austra *Norway* **8** D14
Austral Is. = Tubuaï, Îs.
  French Polynesia **97** K13
Austral Seamount Chain
  Pac. Oc. **97** K13
Australia ■ *Oceania* **90** D6
Australian-Antarctic Basin
  S. Ocean **5** B4
Australian Capital
  Territory □ *Australia* **95** F4

Australind *Australia* **93** F2
Austria ■ *Europe* **26** E7
Austvågøya *Norway* **8** B16
Auterive *France* **20** E5
Authie ⇢ *France* **19** B8
Authon-du-Perche *France* **18** D7
Autlán de Navarro *Mexico* **118** D4
Autun *France* **19** F11
Auvergne □ *France* **20** C7
Auvergne, Mts. d' *France* **20** C6
Auvézère ⇢ *France* **20** C4
Auxerre *France* **19** E10
Auxi-le-Château *France* **19** B9
Auxonne *France* **19** E12
Auzances *France* **19** F9
Ava *U.S.A.* **112** G7
Avallon *France* **19** E10
Avalon *U.S.A.* **111** M8
Avalon Pen. *Canada* **105** C9
Avanos *Turkey* **70** B2
Avantas *Greece* **45** F9
Avaré *Brazil* **127** A6
Avawatz Mts. *U.S.A.* **111** K10
Avdan Dağı *Turkey* **45** F13
Aveiro *Brazil* **125** D7
Aveiro *Portugal* **36** E2
Aveiro □ *Portugal* **36** E2
Āvej *Iran* **71** C6
Avellaneda *Argentina* **126** C4
Avellino *Italy* **43** B7
Avenal *U.S.A.* **110** K6
Aversa *Italy* **43** B7
Avery *U.S.A.* **108** C6
Aves, I. de *W. Indies* **121** C7
Aves, Is. las *Venezuela* **121** D6
Avesnes-sur-Helpe *France* **19** B10
Avesnois △ *France* **19** B10
Avesta *Sweden* **10** D10
Aveyron □ *France* **20** D6
Aveyron ⇢ *France* **20** D5
Avezzano *Italy* **41** F10
Avgo *Greece* **47** F7
Aviá Terai *Argentina* **126** B3
Aviano *Italy* **41** B9
Aviemore *U.K.* **13** D5
Avigliana *Italy* **40** C4
Avigliano *Italy* **43** B8
Avignon *France* **21** E8
Ávila *Spain* **36** E6
Ávila □ *Spain* **36** E6
Ávila, Sierra de *Spain* **36** E5
Avila Beach *U.S.A.* **111** K6
Avilés *Spain* **36** B5
Avintes *Portugal* **36** D2
Avis *Portugal* **37** F3
Avis *U.S.A.* **114** E7
Avisio ⇢ *Italy* **40** B8
Aviz = Avis *Portugal* **37** F3
Avize *France* **19** D11
Avlonari *Greece* **46** C6
Avlum *Denmark* **11** H2
Avoca ⇢ *Australia* **95** F3
Avoca ⇢ *Ireland* **12** D5
Avola *Canada* **102** C5
Avola *Italy* **43** F8
Avon *U.S.A.* **114** D7
Avon ⇢ *Australia* **93** F2
Avon ⇢ *Bristol, U.K.* **15** F5
Avon ⇢ *Dorset, U.K.* **15** G6
Avon ⇢ *Warks., U.K.* **15** E5
Avon Park *U.S.A.* **117** H14
Avondale *Zimbabwe* **87** F3
Avonlea *Canada* **103** D8
Avonmore *Canada* **115** A10
Avonmouth *U.K.* **15** F5
Avramov *Bulgaria* **45** D11
Avranches *France* **18** D5
Avre ⇢ *France* **18** D8
Avrig *Romania* **29** E9
Avrillé *France* **18** E5
Avtovac *Bos.-H.* **44** C2
Awa-Shima *Japan* **54** E9
Awag el Baqar *Sudan* **81** E3
A'waj ⇢ *Syria* **74** B5
Awaji-Shima *Japan* **55** G7
'Awālī *Bahrain* **71** E6
Awantipur *India* **69** C6
Awasa *Ethiopia* **81** F4
Awasa, L. *Ethiopia* **81** F4
Awash *Ethiopia* **81** F5
Awash ⇢ *Ethiopia* **81** E5
Awash △ *Ethiopia* **81** F5
Awaso *Ghana* **82** D4
Awatere ⇢ *N.Z.* **91** D5
Awbārī *Libya* **79** C8
Awbārī, Idehan *Libya* **79** C8
Awe, L. *U.K.* **13** E3
Aweil *Sudan* **81** F2
Awgu *Nigeria* **83** D6
Awjilah *Libya* **79** C10
Awka *Nigeria* **83** D6
Ax-les-Thermes *France* **20** F5
Axat *France* **20** F6
Axe ⇢ *U.K.* **15** F5
Axel Heiberg I. *Canada* **101** B11
Axim *Ghana* **82** E4
Axintele *Romania* **29** F11

Axios ⇢ *Greece* **44** F6
Axminster *U.K.* **15** G4
Axvall *Sweden* **11** F7
Ay *France* **19** C11
Ayabaca *Peru* **124** D3
Ayabe *Japan* **55** G7
Ayacucho *Argentina* **126** D4
Ayacucho *Peru* **124** F4
Ayaguz = Ayaköz
  Kazakhstan **52** E9
Ayaköz *Kazakhstan* **52** E9
Ayamé *Ivory C.* **82** D4
Ayamonte *Spain* **37** H3
Ayan *Russia* **53** D14
Ayancık *Turkey* **72** B6
Ayas *Turkey* **72** B5
Ayaviri *Peru* **124** F4
Aydın *Turkey* **47** D9
Aydın □ *Turkey* **47** D9
Aydın Dağları *Turkey* **47** D10
Ayelu *Ethiopia* **81** E5
Ayenngré *Togo* **83** D5
Ayer *U.S.A.* **115** D13
Ayer Hitam *Malaysia* **65** c
Ayerbe *Spain* **38** C4
Ayer's Cliff *Canada* **115** A12
Ayers Rock = Uluru
  Australia **93** E5
Ayeyarwady =
  Irrawaddy ⇢ *Burma* **67** M19
'Ayn, Wādī al *Oman* **71** F7
Ayn Dār *Si. Arabia* **71** E7
Ayn Zālah *Iraq* **73** D10
Ayna *Spain* **39** G2
Ayod *Sudan* **81** F3
Ayolas *Paraguay* **126** B4
Ayom *Sudan* **81** F2
Ayon, Ostrov *Russia* **53** C17
Ayora *Spain* **39** F3
Ayorou *Niger* **83** C5
Ayr *Australia* **94** B4
Ayr *Canada* **114** C4
Ayr *U.K.* **13** F4
Ayr ⇢ *U.K.* **13** F4
Ayrancı *Turkey* **72** D5
Ayrancılar *Turkey* **47** C9
Ayre, Pt. of *I. of Man* **14** C3
Aysha *Ethiopia* **81** E5
Ayton *Australia* **94** B4
Aytos *Bulgaria* **45** D11
Ayu, Kepulauan *Indonesia* **63** D8
Ayutla *Guatemala* **120** D1
Ayutla de los Libres *Mexico* **119** D5
Ayvacık *Turkey* **72** C2
Ayvalık *Turkey* **47** B8
Az Zabadānī *Syria* **74** B5
Az Ẓāhirīyah *West Bank* **74** D3
Aẓ Ẓahran *Si. Arabia* **71** E6
Az Zarqā *Jordan* **74** C5
Az Zarqā' *U.A.E.* **71** E7
Az Zarqā □ *Jordan* **74** C5
Az Zāwiyah *Libya* **79** B8
Az Zībār *Iraq* **73** D11
Az Zilfī *Si. Arabia* **70** E5
Az Zubayr *Iraq* **70** D5
Az Zuqur *Yemen* **81** E5
Azad Kashmir □ *Pakistan* **69** C5
Azambuja *Portugal* **37** F2
Azamgarh *India* **69** F10
Azangaro *Peru* **124** F4
Azaouad *Mali* **82** B4
Azaoua *Niger* **83** B6
Azar Shahr *Iran* **73** D11
Azara *Nigeria* **83** D6
Azarān *Iran* **73** D12
Āzarbāyjān =
  Azerbaijan ■ *Asia* **35** K9
Āzarbāyjān-e Gharbī □ *Iran* **70** B5
Āzarbāyjān-e Sharqī □ *Iran* **70** B5
Azare *Nigeria* **83** C7
Azay-le-Rideau *France* **18** E7
A'zāz *Syria* **70** D7
Azbine = Aïr *Niger* **83** B6
Azerbaijan ■ *Asia* **35** K9
Azezo *Ethiopia* **81** E4
Azimganj *India* **69** G13
Aznalcóllar *Spain* **37** H4
Azogues *Ecuador* **124** D3
Azores = Açores, Is. dos
  Atl. Oc. **78** a
Azov *Russia* **35** G4
Azov, Sea of *Europe* **33** J9

Azovskoye More = Azov,
  Sea of *Europe* **33** J9
Azpeitia *Spain* **38** B2
Azraq ash Shīshān *Jordan* **74** D5
Aztec *U.S.A.* **109** H10
Azúa de Compostela
  Dom. Rep. **121** C5
Azuaga *Spain* **37** G5
Azuara *Spain* **38** D4
Azuer ⇢ *Spain* **37** F7
Azuero, Pen. de *Panama* **120** E3
Azuga *Romania* **29** E10
Azul *Argentina* **126** D4
Azusa *U.S.A.* **111** L9
Azzano Décimo *Italy* **41** C9
Azzel Matti, Sebkra *Algeria* **78** C6

B

Ba Be △ *Vietnam* **64** A5
Ba Don *Vietnam* **64** D6
Ba Dong *Vietnam* **65** H6
Ba Ngoi = Cam Lam *Vietnam* **65** G7
Ba Tri *Vietnam* **65** G6
Ba Vi △ *Vietnam* **64** B5
Ba Xian = Bazhou *China* **56** E9
Baa *Indonesia* **63** F6
Baamonde *Spain* **36** B3
Baardeere = Bardera
  Somali Rep. **75** G3
Baarle-Nassau *Belgium* **17** C4
Bab el Mandeb *Red Sea* **75** E3
Baba *Bulgaria* **44** D7
Bābā, Koh-i- *Afghan.* **66** B5
Baba Burnu *Turkey* **47** B8
Baba dag *Azerbaijan* **35** K9
Bābā Kalū *Iran* **71** D6
Babadag *Romania* **29** F13
Babadağ *Turkey* **47** D10
Babaeski *Turkey* **45** E11
Babahoyo *Ecuador* **124** D3
Babai = Sarju ⇢ *India* **69** F9
Babana *Nigeria* **83** C5
Babanusa *Sudan* **81** E2
Babar *Indonesia* **63** F7
Babar *Pakistan* **68** D3
Babarkach *Pakistan* **68** E3
Babayevo *Russia* **32** C8
Babb *U.S.A.* **108** B7
Babenhausen *Germany* **25** F4
Babi Besar, Pulau *Malaysia* **65** L4
Babia Gora *Europe* **31** J6
Babian Jiang ⇢ *China* **58** F3
Bābil □ *Iraq* **70** C5
Babile *Ethiopia* **81** F5
Babimost *Poland* **31** F2
Babinda *Australia* **94** B4
Babine *Canada* **102** B3
Babine ⇢ *Canada* **102** B3
Babine L. *Canada* **102** C3
Babiogórski △ *Poland* **31** J6
Babo *Indonesia* **63** E8
Babócsa *Hungary* **28** D2
Bābol *Iran* **71** B7
Bābol Sar *Iran* **71** B7
Baborów *Poland* **31** H5
Baboua *C.A.R.* **84** C2
Babruysk *Belarus* **23** B15
Babuhri *India* **68** F3
Babuna *Macedonia* **44** E5
Babura *Nigeria* **83** C6
Babusar Pass *Pakistan* **69** B5
Babušnica *Serbia* **44** C6
Babuyan Chan. *Phil.* **61** B4
Babylon *Iraq* **73** F11
Bač *Serbia* **28** E4
Bâc ⇢ *Moldova* **29** D14
Bac Can *Vietnam* **58** F5
Bac Giang *Vietnam* **58** F6
Bac Lieu *Vietnam* **65** H5
Bac Ninh *Vietnam* **58** F6
Bac Phan *Vietnam* **64** B5
Bac Quang *Vietnam* **58** F5
Bacabal *Brazil* **125** D10
Bacalar *Mexico* **119** D7
Bacan, Kepulauan *Indonesia* **63** E7
Bacarra *Phil.* **61** B4
Bacău *Romania* **29** D11
Bacău □ *Romania* **29** D11
Baccarat *France* **19** D13
Bacerac *Mexico* **118** A3
Băceşti *Romania* **29** D12
Bach Long Vi, Dao *Vietnam* **64** B6
Bach Ma △ *Vietnam* **64** D6
Bacharach *Germany* **25** E3
Bachhwara *India* **69** G11
Bachuma *Ethiopia* **81** F4
Bačina *Serbia* **44** C5
Back ⇢ *Canada* **100** C9
Bačka Palanka *Serbia* **28** E4
Bačka Topola *Serbia* **28** E4
Bäckebo *Sweden* **11** H10
Bäckefors *Sweden* **11** F6
Bäckhammar *Sweden* **10** E8
Bački Petrovac *Serbia* **28** E4
Backnang *Germany* **25** G5

Baco, Mt. _Phil._ **61** E4
Bacolod _Phil._ **61** F5
Bacqueville-en-Caux _France_ **18** C8
Bács-Kiskun □ _Hungary_ **28** D4
Bácsalmás _Hungary_ **28** D4
Bacuag = Placer _Phil._ **61** G6
Bacuk _Malaysia_ **65** J4
Bácum _Mexico_ **118** B2
Bād _Iran_ **71** C7
Bad → _U.S.A._ **112** C3
Bad Aussee _Austria_ **26** D6
Bad Axe _U.S.A._ **114** C2
Bad Bergzabern _Germany_ **25** F3
Bad Berleburg _Germany_ **24** D4
Bad Bevensen _Germany_ **24** B6
Bad Bramstedt _Germany_ **24** B5
Bad Brückenau _Germany_ **25** E5
Bad Doberan _Germany_ **24** A7
Bad Driburg _Germany_ **24** D5
Bad Ems _Germany_ **25** E3
Bad Frankenhausen
  Germany **24** D7
Bad Freienwalde _Germany_ **24** C10
Bad Goisern _Austria_ **26** D6
Bad Harzburg _Germany_ **24** D6
Bad Hersfeld _Germany_ **24** E5
Bad Hofgastein _Austria_ **26** D6
Bad Homburg _Germany_ **25** E4
Bad Honnef _Germany_ **24** E3
Bad Iburg _Germany_ **24** C4
Bad Ischl _Austria_ **26** D6
Bad Kissingen _Germany_ **25** E6
Bad Königshofen _Germany_ **25** E6
Bad Kreuznach _Germany_ **25** F3
Bad Krozingen _Germany_ **25** H3
Bad Laasphe _Germany_ **24** E4
Bad Langensalza _Germany_ **24** D6
Bad Lauterberg _Germany_ **24** D6
Bad Leonfelden _Austria_ **26** C7
Bad Liebenwerda _Germany_ **24** D9
Bad Mergentheim _Germany_ **25** F5
Bad Münstereifel _Germany_ **24** E2
Bad Nauheim _Germany_ **25** E4
Bad Neuenahr-Ahrweiler
  Germany **24** E3
Bad Neustadt _Germany_ **25** E6
Bad Oeynhausen _Germany_ **24** C4
Bad Oldesloe _Germany_ **24** B6
Bad Orb _Germany_ **25** E5
Bad Pyrmont _Germany_ **24** D5
Bad Reichenhall _Germany_ **25** H8
Bad Säckingen _Germany_ **25** H3
Bad St. Leonhard _Austria_ **26** E7
Bad Salzuflen _Germany_ **24** C4
Bad Salzungen _Germany_ **24** E6
Bad Schwartau _Germany_ **24** B6
Bad Segeberg _Germany_ **24** B6
Bad Tölz _Germany_ **25** H7
Bad Urach _Germany_ **25** G5
Bad Vöslau _Austria_ **27** D9
Bad Waldsee _Germany_ **25** H5
Bad Wildungen _Germany_ **24** D5
Bad Wimpfen _Germany_ **25** F5
Bad Windsheim _Germany_ **25** F6
Bad Zwischenahn _Germany_ **24** B4
Bada Barabil _India_ **69** H11
Badagara _India_ **66** P9
Badagri _Nigeria_ **83** D5
Badajós, L. _Brazil_ **124** D6
Badajoz _Spain_ **37** G4
Badajoz □ _Spain_ **37** G4
Badakhshān □ _Afghan._ **66** A7
Badalona _Spain_ **38** D7
Badalzai _Afghan._ **68** E1
Badampahar _India_ **67** H15
Badanah _Si. Arabia_ **70** D4
Badarinath _India_ **69** D8
Badas, Kepulauan _Indonesia_ **62** D3
Baddo → _Pakistan_ **66** F4
Bade _Indonesia_ **63** F9
Badeggi _Nigeria_ **83** D6
Badéguichéri _Niger_ **83** C6
Baden _Austria_ **27** C9
Baden _Switz._ **25** H4
Baden _U.S.A._ **114** F4
Baden-Baden _Germany_ **25** G4
Baden-Württemberg □
  Germany **25** G4
Badgastein _Austria_ **26** D6
Badger _Canada_ **105** C8
Badger _U.S.A._ **110** J7
Bādghīs □ _Afghan._ **66** B3
Badgingarra △ _Australia_ **93** F2
Badgom _India_ **69** B6
Badia Polésine _Italy_ **41** C8
Badiar △ _Guinea_ **82** C2
Badin _Pakistan_ **68** G3
Badinka △ _Mali_ **82** C3
Badlands _U.S.A._ **112** D2
Badlands △ _U.S.A._ **112** D2
Badogo _Mali_ **82** C3
Badoumbé _Mali_ **82** C2
Badrah _Iraq_ **73** F11
Badrinath _India_ **69** D8
Badulla _Sri Lanka_ **66** R12
Badung, Selat _Indonesia_ **63** K18
Baena _Spain_ **37** H6
Baengnyeongdo _S. Korea_ **57** F13

Baeza _Spain_ **37** H7
Bafang _Cameroon_ **83** D7
Bafatá _Guinea-Biss._ **82** C2
Baffin B. _N. Amer._ **101** B13
Baffin I. _Canada_ **101** C12
Bafia _Cameroon_ **83** E7
Bafilo _Togo_ **83** D5
Bafing → _Mali_ **82** C2
Bafing △ _Mali_ **82** C2
Bafliyūn _Syria_ **70** B3
Bafoulabé _Mali_ **82** C2
Bafoussam _Cameroon_ **83** D7
Bāfq _Iran_ **71** D7
Bafra _Turkey_ **72** B6
Bafra Burnu _Turkey_ **72** B7
Bāft _Iran_ **71** D8
Bafut _Cameroon_ **83** D7
Bafwasende
  Dem. Rep. of the Congo **86** B2
Bagam _Niger_ **83** B6
Bagamoyo _Tanzania_ **86** D4
Bagan Datoh _Malaysia_ **65** L3
Bagan Serai _Malaysia_ **65** K3
Baganga _Phil._ **61** H7
Bagani _Namibia_ **88** B3
Bagansiapiapi _Indonesia_ **62** D2
Bagasra _India_ **68** J4
Bagaud _India_ **68** H6
Bagawi _Sudan_ **81** E3
Bagbag _Sudan_ **81** D3
Bagdad _U.S.A._ **111** L11
Bagdarin _Russia_ **53** D12
Bagé _Brazil_ **127** C5
Bagenalstown = Muine
  Bheag _Ireland_ **12** D5
Baggs _U.S.A._ **108** F10
Bagh _Pakistan_ **69** C5
Baghain → _India_ **69** G9
Baghdād _Iraq_ **73** F11
Bagheria _Italy_ **42** D6
Baghlān _Afghan._ **66** A6
Baghlān □ _Afghan._ **66** B6
Bagley _U.S.A._ **112** B6
Bagnara Cálabra _Italy_ **43** D8
Bagnasco _Italy_ **40** D5
Bagnères-de-Bigorre _France_ **20** E4
Bagnères-de-Luchon _France_ **20** F4
Bagni di Lucca _Italy_ **40** D7
Bagno di Romagna _Italy_ **41** E8
Bagnoles-de-l'Orne _France_ **18** D6
Bagnols-sur-Cèze _France_ **21** D8
Bagnorégio _Italy_ **41** F9
Bago = Pegu _Burma_ **67** L20
Bagodar _India_ **69** G11
Bagrationovsk _Russia_ **30** D7
Bagrdan _Serbia_ **44** B5
Baguio _Phil._ **61** C4
Bağyurdu _Turkey_ **47** C9
Bagzane, Monts _Niger_ **83** B6
Bah _India_ **69** F8
Bahabón de Esgueva _Spain_ **36** D7
Bahadurganj _India_ **69** F12
Bahadurgarh _India_ **68** E7
Bahama, Canal Viejo de
  W. Indies **120** B4
Bahamas ■ _N. Amer._ **121** B5
Bahār _Iran_ **73** E13
Baharampur _India_ **69** G13
Baharîya, El Wâhat al _Egypt_ **80** B2
Baharu Pandan = Pandan
  Malaysia **65** d
Bahawalnagar _Pakistan_ **68** E5
Bahawalpur _Pakistan_ **68** E4
Bahçe _Turkey_ **72** D7
Bahçecik _Turkey_ **45** F13
Bäherden _Turkmenistan_ **71** B8
Baheri _India_ **69** E8
Bahgul → _India_ **69** F8
Bahi _Tanzania_ **86** D4
Bahi Swamp _Tanzania_ **86** D4
Bahía = Salvador _Brazil_ **125** F11
Bahía □ _Brazil_ **125** F10
Bahía, Is. de la _Honduras_ **120** C2
Bahía Blanca _Argentina_ **126** D3
Bahía de Caráquez _Ecuador_ **124** D2
Bahía Kino _Mexico_ **118** B2
Bahía Laura _Argentina_ **128** F3
Bahía Negra _Paraguay_ **124** H7
Bahir Dar _Ethiopia_ **81** E4
Bahmanzād _Iran_ **71** D6
Bahraich _India_ **69** F9
Bahrain ■ _Asia_ **71** E6
Bahror _India_ **68** F7
Bāhū Kalāt _Iran_ **71** E9
Bai _Mali_ **82** C4
Bai Bung, Mui = Ca Mau,
  Mui _Vietnam_ **65** H5
Bai Duc _Vietnam_ **64** C5
Bai Thuong _Vietnam_ **64** C5
Baia de Aramă _Romania_ **28** E7
Baia Mare _Romania_ **29** C8
Baia-Sprie _Romania_ **29** C8
Baião _Brazil_ **125** D9
Baïbokoum _Chad_ **79** G9
Baicheng _China_ **57** B12
Băicoi _Romania_ **29** E10

Baidoa _Somali Rep._ **75** G3
Baie-Comeau _Canada_ **105** C6
Baie-St-Paul _Canada_ **105** C5
Baie Ste-Anne _Seychelles_ **85** b
Baie-Trinité _Canada_ **105** C6
Baie Verte _Canada_ **105** C8
Baignes-Ste-Radegonde
  France **20** C3
Baigneux-les-Juifs _France_ **19** E11
Baihar _India_ **69** H9
Baihe _China_ **56** H6
Ba'ijī _Iraq_ **73** E10
Baijnath _India_ **69** E8
Baikal, L. = Baykal, Oz.
  Russia **53** D11
Baikonur = Bayqongyr
  Kazakhstan **52** E7
Baikunthpur _India_ **69** H10
Baile Atha Cliath = Dublin
  Ireland **12** C5
Băile Govora _Romania_ **29** E9
Băile Herculane _Romania_ **28** F7
Băile Olănești _Romania_ **29** E9
Băile Tușnad _Romania_ **29** D10
Bailén _Spain_ **37** G7
Băilești _Romania_ **29** F8
Baima _China_ **58** A3
Bain-de-Bretagne _France_ **18** E5
Bainbridge _Ga., U.S.A._ **117** F12
Bainbridge _N.Y., U.S.A._ **115** D9
Bainbridge Island _U.S.A._ **110** C4
Baing _Indonesia_ **63** F6
Bainiu _China_ **56** H7
Baiona _Spain_ **36** C2
Bā'ir _Jordan_ **74** E5
Bairiki = Tarawa _Kiribati_ **96** G9
Bairin Youqi _China_ **57** C10
Bairin Zuoqi _China_ **57** C10
Bairnsdale _Australia_ **95** F4
Bais _Phil._ **61** G5
Baisha _China_ **56** G7
Baissa _Nigeria_ **83** D7
Baitadi _Nepal_ **69** E9
Baixa Limia-Sierra do
  Xurés △ _Spain_ **36** D2
Baiyin _China_ **56** F3
Baiyü _China_ **58** B2
Baiyu Shan _China_ **56** F4
Baiyuda _Sudan_ **80** D3
Baj Baj _India_ **69** H13
Baja _Hungary_ **28** D3
Baja, Pta. _Mexico_ **118** B1
Baja California _Mexico_ **118** A1
Baja California □ _Mexico_ **118** B2
Baja California Sur □
  Mexico **118** B2
Bajag _India_ **69** H9
Bajamar _Canary Is._ **48** F3
Bajana _India_ **68** H4
Bajatrejo _Indonesia_ **63** J17
Bajera _Indonesia_ **63** J18
Bájgīrān _Iran_ **71** B8
Bajimba, Mt. _Australia_ **95** D5
Bajina Bašta _Serbia_ **44** C3
Bajmok _Serbia_ **28** E4
Bajo Nuevo _Caribbean_ **120** C4
Bajoga _Nigeria_ **83** C7
Bajool _Australia_ **94** C5
Bak _Hungary_ **28** D1
Bakassi Pen. _Cameroon_ **83** E6
Bakel _Senegal_ **82** C2
Baker _Calif., U.S.A._ **111** K10
Baker _Mont., U.S.A._ **108** C11
Baker, L. _Canada_ **100** C10
Baker, Mt. _U.S.A._ **108** B3
Baker City _U.S.A._ **108** D5
Baker I. _Pac. Oc._ **96** G10
Baker I. _U.S.A._ **102** B2
Baker L. _Australia_ **93** E4
Baker Lake _Canada_ **100** C10
Bakers Creek _Australia_ **94** C4
Bakers Dozen Is. _Canada_ **104** A4
Bakersfield _Calif., U.S.A._ **111** K8
Bakersfield _Vt., U.S.A._ **115** B12
Bakharden = Bäherden
  Turkmenistan **71** B8
Bakhchysaray _Ukraine_ **33** K7
Bakhmach _Ukraine_ **33** G7
Bäkhtarān = Kermānshāh
  Iran **73** E12
Bākhtaran =
  Kermānshāh □ _Iran_ **70** C5
Bakı _Azerbaijan_ **35** K9
Bakır → _Turkey_ **47** C9
Bakırdaği _Turkey_ **72** C6
Bakkafjörður _Iceland_ **8** C6
Baklan _Turkey_ **47** C11
Bako _Ethiopia_ **81** F4
Bako _Ivory C._ **82** D3
Bakony _Hungary_ **28** C2
Bakony Forest = Bakony
  Hungary **28** C2
Bakori _Nigeria_ **83** C6
Bakouma _C.A.R._ **84** C4
Baksan _Russia_ **35** J6
Bakswaho _India_ **69** G8
Baku = Bakı _Azerbaijan_ **35** K9

Bakundi _Nigeria_ **83** D7
Bakutis Coast _Antarctica_ **5** D15
Baky = Bakı _Azerbaijan_ **35** K9
Bala _Canada_ **114** A5
Bala _Senegal_ **82** C2
Bâla _Turkey_ **72** C5
Bala _U.K._ **14** E4
Bala, L. _U.K._ **14** E4
Balabac I. _Phil._ **62** C5
Balabac Str. _E. Indies_ **62** C5
Balabagh _Afghan._ **68** B4
Ba'labakk _Lebanon_ **74** B5
Balabalangan, Kepulauan
  Indonesia **62** E5
Bălăciţa _Romania_ **29** F8
Balad _Iraq_ **73** F11
Balad Rūz _Iraq_ **73** F11
Bālādeh _Fārs, Iran_ **71** D6
Bālādeh _Māzandaran, Iran_ **71** B6
Balaghat _India_ **66** J12
Balaghat Ra. _India_ **66** K10
Balaguer _Spain_ **38** D5
Balakhna _Russia_ **34** B6
Balaklava _Ukraine_ **33** K7
Balakliya _Ukraine_ **33** H9
Balakovo _Russia_ **34** D8
Balamau _India_ **69** F9
Bălan _Romania_ **29** D10
Balancán _Mexico_ **119** D6
Balanivka _Ukraine_ **29** B14
Balasinor _India_ **68** H5
Balashov _Russia_ **34** E6
Balasore = Baleshwar _India_ **67** J15
Balassagyarmat _Hungary_ **28** B4
Balât _Egypt_ **80** B2
Balaton _Hungary_ **28** D2
Balaton-Felvidéki △
  Hungary **28** D2
Balatonboglár _Hungary_ **28** D2
Balatonfüred _Hungary_ **28** D2
Balatonszentgyörgy
  Hungary **28** D2
Balayan _Phil._ **61** E4
Balazote _Spain_ **39** G2
Balbieriškis _Lithuania_ **30** D10
Balbigny _France_ **21** C8
Balbina, Reprêsa de _Brazil_ **124** D7
Balboa _Panama_ **120** E4
Balbriggan _Ireland_ **12** C5
Balcarce _Argentina_ **126** D4
Balcarres _Canada_ **103** C8
Bălcești _Romania_ **29** F8
Balchik _Bulgaria_ **45** C12
Balclutha _N.Z._ **91** G2
Balcones Escarpment
  _U.S.A._ **116** G5
Balçova _Turkey_ **47** C9
Bald Hd. _Australia_ **93** G2
Bald I. _Australia_ **93** F2
Bald Knob _U.S.A._ **116** D9
Baldock L. _Canada_ **103** B9
Baldwin _Mich., U.S.A._ **113** D11
Baldwin _Pa., U.S.A._ **114** F5
Baldwinsville _U.S.A._ **115** C8
Baldy Peak _U.S.A._ **109** K9
Bale _Croatia_ **41** C10
Bale _Oromiya, Ethiopia_ **81** F5
Bale _Oromiya, Ethiopia_ **81** F5
Bale Mts. △ _Ethiopia_ **81** F5
Baleares, Is. _Spain_ **48** B10
Balearic Is. = Baleares, Is.
  Spain **48** B10
Baleine = Whale → _Canada_ **105** A6
Baleine, Petite R. de la →
  Canada **104** A4
Băleni _Romania_ **29** E12
Balya _Turkey_ **47** B9
Baler _Phil._ **61** D4
Baler Bay _Phil._ **61** D4
Baleshare _U.K._ **13** D1
Baleshwar _India_ **67** J15
Balezino _Russia_ **34** B11
Balfate _Honduras_ **120** C2
Bali _Cameroon_ **83** D7
Bali _Greece_ **49** D6
Bali _India_ **68** G5
Bali _Indonesia_ **63** J18
Bali □ _Indonesia_ **63** J18
Bali, Selat _Indonesia_ **63** J17
Bali Sea _Indonesia_ **63** J17
Balia _S. Leone_ **82** D2
Baliapal _India_ **69** J12
Baligród _Poland_ **31** J9
Balik Pulau _Malaysia_ **65** c
Balikeşir _Turkey_ **47** B9
Balıkesir □ _Turkey_ **47** B9
Balıklıçeşme _Turkey_ **45** F11
Balikpapan _Indonesia_ **62** E5
Balimbing _Phil._ **61** J1
Balingen _Germany_ **25** G4
Balint _Romania_ **28** E6
Balintang Channel _Phil._ **61** B4
Balkan Mts. = Stara
  Planina _Bulgaria_ **44** C7
Balkanabat _Turkmenistan_ **71** B7
Balkhash = Balqash
  Kazakhstan **52** E8

Balkhash, Ozero = Balqash
  Köli _Kazakhstan_ **52** E8
Ballachulish _U.K._ **13** E3
Balladonia _Australia_ **93** F3
Ballarat _Australia_ **95** F3
Ballard, L. _Australia_ **93** E3
Ballater _U.K._ **13** D5
Ballé _Mali_ **82** B3
Ballenas, Canal de _Mexico_ **118** B2
Balleny Is. _Antarctica_ **5** C11
Balleroy _France_ **18** C6
Ballerup _Denmark_ **11** J6
Ballı _Turkey_ **45** F11
Ballia _India_ **69** G11
Ballidu _Australia_ **93** F2
Ballina _Australia_ **95** D5
Ballina _Ireland_ **12** B2
Ballinasloe _Ireland_ **12** C3
Ballinger _U.S.A._ **116** F5
Ballinrobe _Ireland_ **12** C2
Ballon _France_ **18** D7
Ballons des Vosges △
  France **19** E14
Ballsh _Albania_ **44** F3
Ballston Spa _U.S.A._ **115** D11
Ballybay _Ireland_ **12** B5
Ballyboghil _Ireland_ **12** C5
Ballybunion _Ireland_ **12** D2
Ballycanew _Ireland_ **12** D5
Ballycastle _U.K._ **12** A5
Ballyclare _U.K._ **12** B6
Ballydehob _Ireland_ **12** E2
Ballygawley _U.K._ **12** B4
Ballyhaunis _Ireland_ **12** C3
Ballyheige _Ireland_ **12** D2
Ballymena _U.K._ **12** B5
Ballymoney _U.K._ **12** A5
Ballymote _Ireland_ **12** B3
Ballynahinch _U.K._ **12** B6
Ballyquintin Pt. _U.K._ **12** B6
Ballyshannon _Ireland_ **12** B3
Balmaceda _Chile_ **128** F2
Balmaseda _Spain_ **38** B1
Balmazújváros _Hungary_ **28** C6
Balmertown _Canada_ **103** C10
Balmoral _Australia_ **95** F3
Balmorhea _U.S.A._ **116** F3
Balonne → _Australia_ **95** D4
Balotra _India_ **68** G5
Balqash _Kazakhstan_ **52** E8
Balqash Köli _Kazakhstan_ **52** E8
Balrampur _India_ **69** F10
Balranald _Australia_ **95** E3
Balş _Romania_ **29** F9
Balsas → _Brazil_ **125** E9
Balsas → _Mexico_ **118** D4
Balsas del Norte _Mexico_ **119** D5
Bålsta _Sweden_ **10** E11
Balta _Romania_ **28** F7
Balta _Ukraine_ **29** B14
Baltanás _Spain_ **36** D6
Bălți _Moldova_ **29** C12
Baltic Sea _Europe_ **9** H18
Baltim _Egypt_ **80** H7
Baltimore _Ireland_ **12** E2
Baltimore _Md., U.S.A._ **113** F15
Baltimore _Ohio, U.S.A._ **114** G2
Baltinglass _Ireland_ **12** D5
Baltit _Pakistan_ **69** A6
Baltiysk _Russia_ **30** D7
Baltrum _Germany_ **24** B3
Balurghat _India_ **69** G13
Balvi _Latvia_ **32** D4
Balya _Turkey_ **47** B9
Bam _Iran_ **71** D8
Bama _China_ **58** E6
Bama _Nigeria_ **83** C7
Bamaga _Australia_ **94** A3
Bamaji L. _Canada_ **104** B1
Bamako _Mali_ **82** C3
Bamba _Mali_ **83** B4
Bambari _C.A.R._ **84** C4
Bambaroo _Australia_ **94** B4
Bambaya _Guinea_ **82** D2
Bamberg _Germany_ **25** F6
Bamberg _U.S.A._ **117** E14
Bambesi _Ethiopia_ **81** F3
Bambey _Senegal_ **82** C1
Bambili _Dem. Rep. of the Congo_ **86** B2
Bamboi _Ghana_ **82** D4
Bamburgh _U.K._ **14** B6
Bamenda _Cameroon_ **83** D7
Bamfield _Canada_ **102** D3
Bāmīān □ _Afghan._ **66** B5
Bamiancheng _China_ **57** C13
Bamkin _Cameroon_ **83** D7
Bampūr _Iran_ **71** E9
Ban _Burkina Faso_ **82** C4
Ban Ao Tu Khun _Thailand_ **65** a
Ban Ban _Laos_ **64** C4
Ban Bang Hin _Thailand_ **65** H2
Ban Bang Khu _Thailand_ **65** a
Ban Bang Rong _Thailand_ **65** a
Ban Bo Phut _Thailand_ **65** b

Ban Chaweng _Thailand_ **65** b
Ban Chiang Klang _Thailand_ **64** C3
Ban Chik _Laos_ **64** D4
Ban Choho _Thailand_ **64** E4
Ban Dan Lan Hoi _Thailand_ **64** D3
Ban Don = Surat Thani
  Thailand **65** H2
Ban Don _Vietnam_ **64** F6
Ban Don, Ao → _Thailand_ **65** H2
Ban Dong _Thailand_ **64** C3
Ban Hong _Thailand_ **64** C2
Ban Hua Thanon _Thailand_ **65** b
Ban Kaeng _Thailand_ **64** D3
Ban Kantang _Thailand_ **65** J2
Ban Karon _Thailand_ **65** a
Ban Kata _Thailand_ **65** a
Ban Keun _Laos_ **64** C4
Ban Khai _Thailand_ **64** F3
Ban Kheun _Laos_ **64** B3
Ban Khlong Khian _Thailand_ **65** a
Ban Khlong Kua _Thailand_ **65** J3
Ban Khuan _Thailand_ **65** a
Ban Khuan Mao _Thailand_ **65** J2
Ban Ko Yai Chim _Thailand_ **65** G2
Ban Kok _Thailand_ **64** D4
Ban Laem _Thailand_ **65** F2
Ban Lamai _Thailand_ **65** b
Ban Lao Ngam _Laos_ **64** E6
Ban Le Kathe _Thailand_ **64** E2
Ban Lo Po Noi _Thailand_ **65** a
Ban Mae Chedi _Thailand_ **64** C2
Ban Mae Laeng _Thailand_ **64** B2
Ban Mae Nam _Thailand_ **65** b
Ban Mae Sariang _Thailand_ **64** C1
Ban Mê Thuột = Buon Ma
  Thuot _Vietnam_ **64** F7
Ban Mi _Thailand_ **64** E3
Ban Muong Mo _Laos_ **64** C4
Ban Na Bo _Thailand_ **65** b
Ban Na Mo _Laos_ **64** D5
Ban Na San _Thailand_ **65** H2
Ban Na Tong _Laos_ **64** B3
Ban Nam Bac _Laos_ **64** B4
Ban Nam Ma _Laos_ **64** A3
Ban Ngang _Laos_ **64** E6
Ban Nong Bok _Laos_ **64** D5
Ban Nong Boua _Laos_ **64** E6
Ban Nong Pling _Thailand_ **64** E3
Ban Pak Chan _Thailand_ **65** G2
Ban Patong _Thailand_ **65** a
Ban Phai _Thailand_ **64** D4
Ban Phak Chit _Thailand_ **65** a
Ban Pong _Thailand_ **64** E2
Ban Rawai _Thailand_ **65** a
Ban Ron Phibun _Thailand_ **65** H2
Ban Sakhu _Thailand_ **65** a
Ban Sanam Chai _Thailand_ **65** J3
Ban Sangkha _Thailand_ **64** E4
Ban Tak _Thailand_ **64** D2
Ban Tako _Thailand_ **64** E4
Ban Tha Dua _Thailand_ **64** D2
Ban Tha Li _Thailand_ **64** D3
Ban Tha Nun _Thailand_ **65** a
Ban Tha Rua _Thailand_ **65** a
Ban Tha Yu _Thailand_ **65** a
Ban Thahine _Laos_ **64** E5
Ban Thong Krut _Thailand_ **65** b
Ban Xien Kok _Laos_ **64** B3
Ban Yen Nhan _Vietnam_ **64** B6
Banaba _Kiribati_ **96** H8
Banalia _Dem. Rep. of the Congo_ **86** B2
Banam _Cambodia_ **65** G5
Banamba _Mali_ **82** C3
Banana Is. _S. Leone_ **82** D2
Bananal, I. do _Brazil_ **125** F8
Banaras = Varanasi _India_ **69** G10
Banas → _Gujarat, India_ **68** H4
Banas → _Mad. P., India_ **69** G9
Bânâs, Ras _Egypt_ **80** C4
Banaz _Turkey_ **47** C11
Banaz → _Turkey_ **47** C11
Banbridge _U.K._ **12** B5
Banbury _U.K._ **15** E6
Banchory _U.K._ **13** D6
Banco _Ethiopia_ **81** F4
Bancroft _Canada_ **114** A7
Band _Romania_ **29** D9
Band Bonī _Iran_ **71** E8
Band Qīr _Iran_ **71** D6
Banda _Mad. P., India_ **69** G8
Banda _Ut. P., India_ **69** G9
Banda, Kepulauan _Indonesia_ **63** E7
Banda Aceh _Indonesia_ **62** C1
Banda Banda, Mt. _Australia_ **95** E5
Banda Elat _Indonesia_ **63** F8
Banda Is. = Banda,
  Kepulauan _Indonesia_ **63** E7
Banda Sea _Indonesia_ **63** F8
Bandai-Asahi △ _Japan_ **54** F10
Bandai-San _Japan_ **54** F10
Bandama → _Ivory C._ **82** D3
Bandama Blanc → _Ivory C._ **82** D4
Bandama Rouge → _Ivory C._ **82** D4
Bandān _Iran_ **71** D9
Bandanaira _Indonesia_ **63** E7
Bandanwara _India_ **68** F6
Bandar = Machilipatnam
  India **67** L12

Bandar-e Abbās *Iran* **71** E8
Bandar-e Anzalī *Iran* **73** D13
Bandar-e Büsehr =
    Büshehr *Iran* **71** D6
Bandar-e Chārak *Iran* **71** E7
Bandar-e Deylam *Iran* **71** D6
Bandar-e Emām
    Khomeynī *Iran* **71** D6
Bandar-e Lengeh *Iran* **71** E7
Bandar-e Maqām *Iran* **71** E7
Bandar-e Ma'shur *Iran* **71** D6
Bandar-e Rīg *Iran* **71** D6
Bandar-e Torkeman *Iran* **71** B7
Bandar Lampung =
    Tanjungkarang
    Telukbetung *Indonesia* **62** F3
Bandar Maharani = Muar
    Malaysia **65** L4
Bandar Penggaram = Batu
    Pahat *Malaysia* **65** M4
Bandar Seri Begawan *Brunei* **62** D5
Bandar Sri Aman = Sri
    Aman *Malaysia* **62** D4
Bandawe *Malawi* **87** E3
Bande *Spain* **36** C3
Bandeira, Pico da *Brazil* **127** A7
Bandera *Argentina* **126** B3
Banderas, B. de *Mexico* **118** C3
Bandhavgarh *India* **69** H9
Bandi ➔ *India* **68** F6
Bandiagara *Mali* **82** C4
Bandikui *India* **68** F7
Bandırma *Turkey* **45** F11
Bandjarmasin =
    Banjarmasin *Indonesia* **62** E4
Bandol *France* **21** E9
Bandon *Ireland* **12** E3
Bandon ➔ *Ireland* **12** E3
Bandula *Mozam.* **87** F3
Bandundu
    Dem. Rep. of the Congo **84** E3
Bandung *Indonesia* **63** G12
Bané *Burkina Faso* **83** C4
Banes *Cuba* **121** B4
Banff *Canada* **102** C5
Banff *U.K.* **13** D6
Banff △ *Canada* **102** C5
Banfora *Burkina Faso* **82** C4
Bang Fai ➔ *Laos* **64** D5
Bang Hieng ➔ *Laos* **64** D5
Bang Krathum *Thailand* **64** D3
Bang Lamung *Thailand* **64** F3
Bang Mun Nak *Thailand* **64** D3
Bang Pa In *Thailand* **64** E3
Bang Rakam *Thailand* **64** D3
Bang Saphan *Thailand* **65** G2
Bang Thao *Thailand* **65** a
Bangadundi *India* **69** J13
Bangala Dam *Zimbabwe* **87** G3
Bangalore *India* **66** N10
Banganga ➔ *India* **68** F6
Bangangté *Cameroon* **83** D7
Bangaon *India* **69** H13
Bangassou *C.A.R.* **84** D4
Banggai *Indonesia* **63** E6
Banggai, Kepulauan
    Indonesia **63** E6
Banggai Arch. = Banggai,
    Kepulauan *Indonesia* **63** E6
Banggi, Pulau *Malaysia* **62** C5
Banghāzī *Libya* **79** B10
Bangjang *Sudan* **81** E3
Bangka *Sulawesi, Indonesia* **63** D7
Bangka *Sumatera, Indonesia* **62** E3
Bangka, Selat *Indonesia* **62** E3
Bangka-Belitung □ *Indonesia* **62** E3
Bangkalan *Indonesia* **63** G15
Bangkinang *Indonesia* **62** D2
Bangko *Indonesia* **62** E2
Bangkok *Thailand* **64** F3
Bangladesh ■ *Asia* **67** H17
Bangli *Indonesia* **63** J18
Bangolo *Ivory C.* **82** D3
Bangong Co *China* **69** B8
Bangor *Down, U.K.* **12** B6
Bangor *Gwynedd, U.K.* **14** D3
Bangor *Maine, U.S.A.* **113** C19
Bangor *Pa., U.S.A.* **115** F9
Bangued *Phil.* **61** C4
Bangui *C.A.R.* **84** D3
Bangui *Phil.* **61** B4
Banguru
    Dem. Rep. of the Congo **86** B2
Bangweulu, L. *Zambia* **87** E3
Bangweulu Swamp *Zambia* **87** E3
Banhine △ *Mozam.* **89** C5
Baní *Dom. Rep.* **121** C5
Bani ➔ *Mali* **82** C4
Bani Bangou *Niger* **83** B5
Banī Sa'd *Iraq* **73** F11
Bania *Ivory C.* **82** D4
Banihal Pass *India* **69** C6
Banissa *Kenya* **86** B4
Bāniyās *Syria* **72** E6

Banja Luka *Bos.-H.* **28** F2
Banjar *India* **68** D7
Banjar ➔ *India* **69** H9
Banjarmasin *Indonesia* **62** E4
Banjul *Gambia* **82** C1
Banka *India* **69** G12
Bankas *Mali* **82** C4
Bankeryd *Sweden* **11** G8
Banket *Zimbabwe* **87** F3
Bankilaré *Niger* **83** C5
Bankipore *India* **67** G14
Banks I., *B.C., Canada* **102** C3
Banks I., *N.W.T., Canada* **100** B7
Banks Pen. *N.Z.* **91** E4
Banks Str. *Australia* **95** G4
Bankura *India* **69** H12
Bankya *Bulgaria* **44** D7
Banmankhi *India* **69** G12
Bann ➔ *Armagh, U.K.* **12** B5
Bann ➔ *L'derry., U.K.* **12** A5
Bannalec *France* **18** E3
Bannang Sata *Thailand* **65** J3
Banning *U.S.A.* **111** M10
Banno *Ethiopia* **81** G4
Bannockburn *Canada* **114** B7
Bannockburn *U.K.* **13** E5
Bannockburn *Zimbabwe* **87** G2
Bannu *Pakistan* **66** C7
Bano *India* **69** H11
Bañolas = Banyoles *Spain* **38** C7
Banon *France* **21** D9
Baños de la Encina *Spain* **37** G7
Baños de Molgas *Spain* **36** C3
Bánovce nad Bebravou
    Slovak Rep. **27** C11
Banovići *Bos.-H.* **28** F3
Bansgaon *India* **69** F10
Banská Bystrica *Slovak Rep.* **27** C12
Banská Štiavnica
    Slovak Rep. **27** C11
Bansko *Bulgaria* **44** E7
Banskobystrický □
    Slovak Rep. **27** C12
Banswara *India* **68** H6
Bantaeng *Indonesia* **63** F5
Bantaji *Nigeria* **83** D7
Bantayan *Phil.* **61** F5
Banten □ *Indonesia* **63** G11
Bantry *Ireland* **12** E2
Bantry B. *Ireland* **12** E2
Bantul *Indonesia* **63** G14
Bantva *India* **68** J4
Banya *Bulgaria* **45** D8
Banyak, Kepulauan
    Indonesia **62** D1
Banyalbufar *Spain* **48** B9
Banyo *Cameroon* **83** D7
Banyoles *Spain* **38** C7
Banyuls-sur-Mer *France* **20** F7
Banyumas *Indonesia* **63** G13
Banyuwangi *Indonesia* **63** J17
Banzare Coast *Antarctica* **5** C9
Bao Ha *Vietnam* **64** F5
Bao Lac *Vietnam* **64** A5
Bao Loc *Vietnam* **65** G6
Bao'an = Shenzhen *China* **59** F10
Baocheng *China* **56** H4
Baode *China* **56** E6
Baodi *China* **57** E9
Baoding *China* **56** E8
Baoji *China* **56** G4
Baojing *China* **58** C7
Baokang *China* **59** B8
Baoshan *Shanghai, China* **59** B13
Baoshan *Yunnan, China* **58** E2
Baotou *China* **56** D6
Baoxing *China* **58** B4
Baoying *China* **57** H10
Baoyou = Ledong *China* **64** C7
Bap *India* **68** F5
Bapatla *India* **67** M12
Bapaume *France* **19** B9
Bāqerābād *Iran* **71** C6
Ba'qūbah *Iraq* **73** F11
Baquedano *Chile* **126** A2
Bar *Montenegro* **44** D3
Bar *Ukraine* **23** D14
Bar Bigha *India* **69** G11
Bar Harbor *U.S.A.* **113** C19
Bar-le-Duc *France* **19** D12
Bar-sur-Aube *France* **19** D11
Bar-sur-Seine *France* **19** D11
Bara *India* **69** G9
Bâra *Romania* **29** C12
Bara Banki *India* **69** F9
Barabai *Indonesia* **62** E5
Baraboo *U.S.A.* **112** D10
Baracoa *Cuba* **121** B5
Baradā ➔ *Syria* **74** B5
Baradero *Argentina* **126** C4
Baraga *U.S.A.* **112** B9
Bărăganul *Romania* **29** F12
Baragoi *Kenya* **86** B4
Barah ➔ *India* **68** F6
Barahona *Dom. Rep.* **121** C5
Barahona *Spain* **38** D2
Barail Range *India* **67** G18

Barajas, Madrid ✈ (MAD)
    Spain **36** E7
Baraka *Sudan* **81** E2
Baraka ➔ *Sudan* **80** D4
Barakaldo *Spain* **38** B2
Barakar ➔ *India* **69** G12
Barakot *India* **69** J11
Barakpur *India* **69** H13
Baralaba *Australia* **94** C4
Barameiya *Sudan* **80** D4
Baramula *India* **69** B6
Baran *India* **68** G7
Baran ➔ *Pakistan* **68** G3
Barañain *Spain* **38** C3
Baranavichy *Belarus* **23** B14
Barani *Burkina Faso* **82** C4
Baranof *U.S.A.* **102** B2
Baranof I. *U.S.A.* **100** D6
Baranów Sandomierski
    Poland **31** H8
Baranya □ *Hungary* **28** E3
Baraolt *Romania* **29** D10
Barapasi *Indonesia* **63** E9
Barasat *India* **69** H13
Barat Daya, Kepulauan
    Indonesia **63** F7
Barataria B. *U.S.A.* **117** G10
Barauda *India* **68** H6
Baraut *India* **68** E7
Barbacena *Brazil* **127** A7
Barban *Croatia* **41** C11
Barbària, C. de *Spain* **48** C7
Barbaros *Turkey* **45** F11
Barbas, C. *W. Sahara* **78** D2
Barbastro *Spain* **38** C5
Barbate *Spain* **37** J5
Barberino di Mugello *Italy* **41** E8
Barberton *S. Africa* **89** D5
Barberton *U.S.A.* **114** E3
Barbezieux-St-Hilaire *France* **20** C3
Barbosa *Colombia* **124** B4
Barbourville *U.S.A.* **113** G12
Barbuda *W. Indies* **121** C7
Bârca *Romania* **29** G8
Barcaldine *Australia* **94** C4
Barcarrota *Spain* **37** G4
Barcellona Pozzo di Gotto
    Italy **43** D8
Barcelona *Spain* **38** D7
Barcelona *Venezuela* **124** A6
Barcelona □ *Spain* **38** D7
Barcelona-Prat ✈ (BCN)
    Spain **38** D7
Barceloneta *Puerto Rico* **121** d
Barcelonette *France* **21** D10
Barcelos *Brazil* **124** D6
Barcin *Poland* **31** F4
Barclayville *Liberia* **82** E3
Barcoo ➔ *Australia* **94** D3
Barcs *Hungary* **28** E2
Barczewo *Poland* **30** E7
Bärdä *Azerbaijan* **35** K8
Bardaï *Chad* **79** D9
Bardas Blancas *Argentina* **126** D2
Bardawîl, Sabkhet el *Egypt* **74** D2
Barddhaman *India* **69** H12
Bardejov *Slovak Rep.* **27** B14
Bardera *Somali Rep.* **75** G3
Bardi *Italy* **40** D6
Bardīyah *Libya* **79** B10
Bardolino *Italy* **40** C7
Bardonécchia *Italy* **40** C3
Bardsey I. *U.K.* **14** E3
Bardstown *U.S.A.* **113** G11
Bareilly *India* **69** E8
Barela *India* **69** H9
Barentin *France* **18** C7
Barenton *France* **18** D6
Barents Sea *Arctic* **4** B9
Barentu *Eritrea* **81** D4
Barfleur *France* **18** C5
Barfleur, Pte. de *France* **18** C5
Barga *Italy* **40** D7
Bargara *Australia* **94** C5
Bargas *Spain* **36** F6
Bârgăului Bistrița *Romania* **29** C9
Barge *Italy* **40** D4
Bargnop *Sudan* **81** F2
Bargteheide *Germany* **24** B6
Barguzin *Russia* **53** D11
Barh *India* **69** G11
Barhaj *India* **69** F10
Barharwa *India* **69** G12
Barhi *India* **69** G11
Bari *India* **68** F7
Bari *Italy* **43** A9
Bari Doab *Pakistan* **68** D5
Bari Sadri *India* **68** G6
Bari Sardo *Italy* **42** C2
Barīdī, Ra's *Si. Arabia* **70** E3
Barīm *Yemen* **76** E8
Bârîs *Egypt* **80** C3

Barisal *Bangla.* **67** H17
Barisal □ *Bangla.* **67** H17
Barisan, Pegunungan
    Indonesia **62** E2
Barito ➔ *Indonesia* **62** E4
Baritú △ *Argentina* **126** A3
Barjac *France* **21** D8
Barjols *France* **21** E10
Barjūj, Wadi ➔ *Libya* **79** C8
Bark L. *Canada* **114** A7
Barka = Baraka ➔ *Sudan* **80** D4
Barkakana *India* **69** H11
Barkam *China* **58** B4
Barkan *India* **68** G7
Barker *U.S.A.* **114** C6
Barkley, L. *U.S.A.* **117** C10
Barkley Sound *Canada* **102** D3
Barkly East *S. Africa* **88** E4
Barkly Homestead *Australia* **94** B2
Barkly Tableland *Australia* **94** B2
Barkly West *S. Africa* **88** D3
Barkol, Wadi ➔ *Sudan* **80** D3
Barkol *Syria* **73** E9
Barla Dağı *Turkey* **47** C12
Bârlad *Romania* **29** D12
Bârlad ➔ *Romania* **29** E12
Barlee, L. *Australia* **93** E2
Barlee, Mt. *Australia* **93** D4
Barletta *Italy* **43** A9
Barlinek *Poland* **31** F2
Barlovento *Canary Is.* **48** F2
Barlovento *C. Verde Is.* **78** b
Barlow L. *Canada* **103** A8
Barmedman *Australia* **95** E4
Barmer *India* **68** G4
Barmera *Australia* **95** E3
Barmouth *U.K.* **14** E3
Barmstedt *Germany* **24** B5
Barna ➔ *India* **69** G10
Barnagar *India* **68** H6
Barnala *India* **68** D6
Barnard Castle *U.K.* **14** C6
Barnaul *Russia* **52** D9
Barnesville *Ga., U.S.A.* **117** E12
Barnesville *Minn., U.S.A.* **112** B5
Barnet □ *U.K.* **15** F7
Barneveld *Neths.* **17** B5
Barneville-Carteret *France* **18** C5
Barnhart *U.S.A.* **116** F4
Barnsley *U.K.* **14** D6
Barnstable *U.S.A.* **113** E18
Barnstaple *U.K.* **15** F3
Barnstaple Bay = Bideford
    Bay *U.K.* **15** F3
Barnwell *U.S.A.* **117** E14
Baro *Nigeria* **83** D6
Baro ➔ *Ethiopia* **81** F3
Baroda = Vadodara *India* **68** H5
Baroda *India* **68** G7
Baroe *S. Africa* **88** E3
Baron Ra. *Australia* **92** D4
Barong *China* **58** B2
Barotseland *Zambia* **85** H4
Barouéli *Mali* **82** C3
Barpeta *India* **67** F17
Barques, Pt. Aux *U.S.A.* **114** B2
Barquísimeto *Venezuela* **124** A5
Barr, Ras el *Egypt* **80** H7
Barr Smith Range *Australia* **93** E3
Barra *Brazil* **125** F10
Barra *U.K.* **13** E1
Barra, Sd. of *U.K.* **13** D1
Barra de Navidad *Mexico* **118** D4
Barra do Corda *Brazil* **125** E9
Barra do Piraí *Brazil* **127** A7
Barra Falsa, Pta. da *Mozam.* **89** C6
Barra Hd. *U.K.* **13** E1
Barra Mansa *Brazil* **127** A7
Barraba *Australia* **95** E5
Barrackpur = Barakpur
    India **69** H13
Barradale *Australia* **92** D1
Barrafranca *Italy* **43** E7
Barraigh = Barra *U.K.* **13** E1
Barranca *Lima, Peru* **124** F3
Barranca *Loreto, Peru* **124** D3
Barranca del Cobre △
    Mexico **118** B3
Barrancabermeja *Colombia* **124** B4
Barrancas *Venezuela* **124** B6
Barrancos *Portugal* **37** G4
Barranqueras *Argentina* **126** B4
Barranquilla *Colombia* **124** A4
Barraute *Canada* **104** C4
Barre *Mass., U.S.A.* **115** D12
Barre *Vt., U.S.A.* **115** B12
Barreal *Argentina* **126** C2
Barreiras *Brazil* **125** F10
Barreirinhas *Brazil* **125** D10
Barreiro *Portugal* **37** G1
Barrême *France* **21** E10
Barren, Nosy *Madag.* **89** B7
Barretos *Brazil* **125** H9
Barrhead *Canada* **102** C6
Barrhead *U.K.* **13** F4
Barrie *Canada* **114** B5
Barrier Ra. *Australia* **95** E3
Barrier Reef *Belize* **119** D7
Barrière *Canada* **102** C4
Barrington *U.S.A.* **115** E13

Barrington L. *Canada* **103** B8
Barrington Tops *Australia* **95** E5
Barringun *Australia* **95** D4
Barro do Garças *Brazil* **125** G8
Barron *U.S.A.* **112** C8
Barrow *U.S.A.* **106** a
Barrow ➔ *Ireland* **12** D5
Barrow Creek *Australia* **94** C1
Barrow I. *Australia* **92** D2
Barrow-in-Furness *U.K.* **14** C4
Barrow Pt. *Australia* **94** A3
Barrow Ra. *Australia* **93** E4
Barrow Str. *Canada* **4** B3
Barruecopardo *Spain* **36** D4
Barruelo de Santullán *Spain* **36** C6
Barry *U.K.* **15** F4
Barry's Bay *Canada* **114** A7
Barsalogho *Burkina Faso* **83** C4
Barsat *Pakistan* **69** A5
Barsham *Syria* **73** E9
Barsi *India* **66** K9
Barsinghausen *Germany* **24** C5
Barsoi *India* **67** G15
Barstow *U.S.A.* **111** L9
Barth *Germany* **24** A8
Barthélemy, Col *Vietnam* **64** C5
Bartica *Guyana* **124** B7
Bartin *Turkey* **72** B5
Bartle Frere *Australia* **94** B4
Bartlesville *U.S.A.* **116** C7
Bartlett *Calif., U.S.A.* **110** J8
Bartlett *Tenn., U.S.A.* **117** D10
Bartlett, L. *Canada* **102** A5
Barton *U.S.A.* **115** B12
Barton upon Humber *U.K.* **14** D7
Bartoszyce *Poland* **30** D7
Bartow *U.S.A.* **117** H14
Barú, Volcan *Panama* **120** E3
Barumba
    Dem. Rep. of the Congo **86** B1
Baruth *Germany* **24** C9
Baruunsuu *Mongolia* **56** C3
Barvinkove *Ukraine* **33** H9
Barwani *India* **68** H6
Barwice *Poland* **30** E3
Barycz ➔ *Poland* **31** G3
Barysaw *Belarus* **23** A15
Barysh *Russia* **34** D8
Barzān *Iraq* **70** B5
Bârzava *Romania* **28** D6
Bas-Rhin □ *France* **19** D14
Bašaid *Serbia* **28** E5
Bāsa'idū *Iran* **71** E7
Basal *Pakistan* **68** C5
Basankusa
    Dem. Rep. of the Congo **84** D3
Basarabeasca *Moldova* **29** D13
Basarabi *Romania* **29** F13
Basarabia = Bessarabiya
    Moldova **23** E15
Basauri *Spain* **38** B2
Basawa *Afghan.* **68** B4
Bascuñán, C. *Chile* **126** B1
Basel *Switz.* **25** H3
Basel, Euroairport ✈ (BSL)
    Europe **19** E14
Basel-Landschaft □ *Switz.* **25** H3
Basento ➔ *Italy* **43** B9
Bashäkerd, Kūhhā-ye *Iran* **71** E8
Bashaw *Canada* **102** C6
Bāshī *Iran* **71** D6
Bashkir Republic =
    Bashkortostan □ *Russia* **52** D6
Bashkortostan □ *Russia* **52** D6
Bashtanivka *Ukraine* **29** E14
Basibasy *Madag.* **89** C7
Basilan *Phil.* **61** H5
Basilan Str. *Phil.* **61** H5
Basildon *U.K.* **15** F8
Basile *Eq. Guin.* **83** E6
Basile, Pico *Eq. Guin.* **83** E6
Basilicata □ *Italy* **43** B9
Basim = Washim *India* **66** J10
Basin *U.S.A.* **108** D9
Basingstoke *U.K.* **15** F6
Baskatong, Rés. *Canada* **104** C4
Baška *Croatia* **41** D11
Başkale *Turkey* **73** D10
Baskatong, Rés. *Canada* **104** C4
Başmakçı *Turkey* **47** D12
Basoda *India* **68** H7
Basoko *Dem. Rep. of the Congo* **86** B1
Basque, Pays *France* **20** E2
Basque Provinces = País
    Vasco □ *Spain* **38** C2
Basra = Al Başrah *Iraq* **70** D5
Bass Str. *Australia* **95** F4
Bassano *Canada* **102** C6
Bassano del Grappa *Italy* **41** C8
Bassar *Togo* **83** D5
Bassas da India *Ind. Oc.* **85** J7
Basse-Normandie □ *France* **18** D6
Basse-Pointe *Martinique* **120** c
Basse Santa-Su *Gambia* **82** C2
Basse-Terre *Guadeloupe* **120** b
Basse Terre *Trin. & Tob.* **125** K15

Bassein *Burma* **67** L19
Basses, Pte. des *Guadeloupe* **120** b
Basseterre *St. Kitts & Nevis* **121** C7
Bassett *U.S.A.* **112** D4
Bassi *India* **68** D7
Bassigny *France* **19** E12
Bassikounou *Mauritania* **82** B3
Bassila *Benin* **83** D5
Bassum *Germany* **24** C4
Båstad *Sweden* **11** H3
Bastak *Iran* **71** E7
Baştām *Iran* **71** B7
Bastar *India* **67** K12
Bastelica *France* **21** F13
Basti *India* **69** F10
Bastia *France* **21** F13
Bastogne *Belgium* **17** D5
Bastrop *La., U.S.A.* **116** E9
Bastrop *Tex., U.S.A.* **116** F6
Basuo = Dongfang *China* **64** C7
Bat Yam *Israel* **74** C3
Bata *Eq. Guin.* **84** D1
Bata *Romania* **28** D7
Bataan □ *Phil.* **61** D4
Batabanó *Cuba* **120** B3
Batabanó, G. de *Cuba* **120** B3
Batac *Phil.* **61** B4
Batagai *Russia* **53** C14
Batajnica *Serbia* **44** B4
Batak *Bulgaria* **45** E8
Batala *India* **68** D6
Batalha *Portugal* **36** F2
Batama *Dem. Rep. of the Congo* **86** B2
Batamay *Russia* **53** C13
Batang *China* **58** B2
Batang *Indonesia* **63** G13
Batangafo *C.A.R.* **84** C3
Batangas *Phil.* **61** E4
Batanta *Indonesia* **63** E8
Batatais *Brazil* **127** A6
Batavia *U.S.A.* **114** D6
Bataysk *Russia* **33** J10
Batchelor *Australia* **92** B5
Batdambang *Cambodia* **64** F4
Batemans B. *Australia* **95** F5
Batemans Bay *Australia* **95** F5
Bates Ra. *Australia* **93** E3
Batesburg-Leesville *U.S.A.* **117** E14
Batesville *Ark., U.S.A.* **116** D9
Batesville *Miss., U.S.A.* **117** D10
Batesville *Tex., U.S.A.* **116** G5
Bath *Canada* **115** B8
Bath *U.K.* **15** F5
Bath *Maine, U.S.A.* **113** D19
Bath *N.Y., U.S.A.* **114** D7
Bath & North East
    Somerset □ *U.K.* **15** F5
Batheay *Cambodia* **65** G5
Bathsheba *Barbados* **121** g
Bathurst *Australia* **95** E4
Bathurst *Canada* **105** C6
Bathurst *S. Africa* **88** E4
Bathurst, C. *Canada* **100** B7
Bathurst B. *Australia* **94** A3
Bathurst Harb. *Australia* **95** G4
Bathurst I. *Australia* **92** B5
Bathurst I. *Canada* **101** B11
Bathurst Inlet *Canada* **100** C9
Bati *Ethiopia* **81** E5
Batie *Burkina Faso* **82** D4
Batiki *Fiji* **91** a
Batlow *Australia* **95** F4
Batman *Turkey* **73** D9
Baṭn al Ghūl *Jordan* **74** F4
Batna *Algeria* **78** A7
Batobato = San Isidro *Phil.* **61** H7
Batočina *Serbia* **44** B5
Batoka *Zambia* **87** F2
Baton Rouge *U.S.A.* **116** F9
Batong, Ko *Thailand* **65** J2
Bátonyterenye *Hungary* **28** C4
Batopilas *Mexico* **118** B3
Batouri *Cameroon* **84** D2
Båtsfjord *Norway* **8** A23
Battambang =
    Batdambang *Cambodia* **64** F4
Batticaloa *Sri Lanka* **66** R12
Battipáglia *Italy* **43** B7
Battle *U.K.* **15** G8
Battle ➔ *Canada* **103** C7
Battle Creek *U.S.A.* **113** D11
Battle Ground *U.S.A.* **110** E4
Battle Harbour *Canada* **105** B8
Battle Lake *U.S.A.* **112** B6
Battle Mountain *U.S.A.* **108** F5
Battlefields *Zimbabwe* **87** F2
Battleford *Canada* **103** C7
Battonya *Hungary* **28** D6
Batu *Ethiopia* **81** F4
Batu, Kepulauan *Indonesia* **62** E1
Batu Caves *Malaysia* **65** L3
Batu Ferringhi *Malaysia* **65** c
Batu Gajah *Malaysia* **65** K3
Batu Is. = Batu,
    Kepulauan *Indonesia* **62** E1
Batu Pahat *Malaysia* **65** M4
Batuata *Indonesia* **63** F6

Batugondang, Tanjung *Indonesia* **63** J17
Batukau, Gunung *Indonesia* **63** J18
Batumi *Georgia* **35** K5
Batur *Indonesia* **63** J18
Batur, Danau *Indonesia* **63** J18
Batur, Gunung *Indonesia* **63** J18
Baturaja *Indonesia* **62** E2
Baturité *Brazil* **125** D11
Baturiti *Indonesia* **63** J18
Bau *Malaysia* **62** D4
Baubau *Indonesia* **63** F6
Baucau *E. Timor* **63** F7
Bauchi *Nigeria* **83** C6
Bauchi □ *Nigeria* **83** C7
Baud *France* **18** E3
Baudette *U.S.A.* **112** A6
Bauer, C. *Australia* **95** E1
Bauhinia *Australia* **94** C4
Baukau = Baucau *E. Timor* **63** F7
Bauld, C. *Canada* **101** D14
Baume-les-Dames *France* **19** E13
Baunatal *Germany* **24** D5
Baunei *Italy* **42** B2
Baure *Nigeria* **83** C6
Bauru *Brazil* **127** A6
Bausi *India* **69** G12
Bauska *Latvia* **30** B11
Bautino *Kazakhstan* **35** H10
Bautzen *Germany* **24** D10
Bauya *S. Leone* **82** D2
Bavānāt *Iran* **71** D7
Bavaniste *Serbia* **28** F5
Bavaria = Bayern □
  Germany **25** G7
Båven *Sweden* **10** E10
Bavispe → *Mexico* **118** B3
Bawdwin *Burma* **67** H20
Bawean *Indonesia* **62** F4
Bawku *Ghana* **83** C4
Bawlake *Burma* **67** K20
Bawolung *China* **58** C3
Baxley *U.S.A.* **117** F13
Baxoi *China* **58** B1
Baxter *U.S.A.* **112** B6
Baxter Springs *U.S.A.* **112** G6
Baxter State △ *U.S.A.* **113** B19
Bay, L. de *Phil.* **61** D4
Bay City *Mich., U.S.A.* **113** D12
Bay City *Tex., U.S.A.* **116** G7
Bay Minette *U.S.A.* **117** F11
Bay Roberts *Canada* **105** C9
Bay St. Louis *U.S.A.* **117** F10
Bay Springs *U.S.A.* **117** F10
Bay View *N.Z.* **91** C6
Baya *Dem. Rep. of the Congo* **87** E2
Bayamo *Cuba* **120** B4
Bayamón *Puerto Rico* **121** d
Bayan Har Shan *China* **60** C4
Bayan Hot = Alxa Zuoqi
  China **56** E3
Bayan Lepas *Malaysia* **65** c
Bayan Obo *China* **56** D5
Bayan-Ovoo = Erdenetsogt
  Mongolia **56** C4
Bayana *India* **68** F7
Bayanaūyl *Kazakhstan* **52** D8
Bayandalay *Mongolia* **56** C2
Bayanhongor *Mongolia* **60** B5
Bayard *N. Mex., U.S.A.* **109** K9
Bayard *Nebr., U.S.A.* **112** E2
Bayawan *Phil.* **61** G5
Baybay *Phil.* **61** F6
Bayburt *Turkey* **73** B9
Bayburt □ *Turkey* **73** B8
Baydhabo =
  Somali Rep. **75** G3
Bayelsa □ *Nigeria* **83** E6
Bayerische Alpen *Germany* **25** H7
Bayerische Rhön △ *Germany* **25** E6
Bayerischer Spessart △
  Germany **25** F6
Bayerischer Wald *Germany* **25** G8
Bayern □ *Germany* **25** G7
Bayeux *France* **18** C6
Bayfield *Canada* **114** C3
Bayfield *U.S.A.* **112** B8
Bayındır *Turkey* **47** C9
Baykal, Oz. *Russia* **53** D11
Baykan *Turkey* **70** B4
Baynes Mts. *Namibia* **88** B1
Bayombong *Phil.* **61** C4
Bayon *France* **19** D13
Bayona = Baiona *Spain* **36** C2
Bayonne *France* **20** E2
Bayonne *U.S.A.* **115** F10
Bayovar *Peru* **124** E2
Bayqongyr *Kazakhstan* **52** E7
Bayram-Ali = Baýramaly
  Turkmenistan **71** B9
Baýramaly *Turkmenistan* **71** B9
Bayramiç *Turkey* **47** B8
Bayreuth *Germany* **25** F7
Bayrischzell *Germany* **25** H8
Bayrūt *Lebanon* **74** B4
Bays, L. of *Canada* **114** A5
Baysville *Canada* **114** A5
Bayt Laḥm *West Bank* **74** D4

Baytown *U.S.A.* **116** G7
Bayun *Indonesia* **63** J18
Bayzo *Niger* **83** C5
Baza *Spain* **37** H8
Bazar Dyuzi *Russia* **35** K8
Bazardüzü = Bazar Dyuzi
  Russia **35** K8
Bazarny Karabulak *Russia* **34** D8
Bazarnyy Syzgan *Russia* **34** D8
Bazaruto, I. do *Mozam.* **89** C6
Bazaruto △ *Mozam.* **89** C6
Bazas *France* **20** D3
Bazhong *China* **58** B6
Bazhou *China* **56** E9
Bazmān, Kūh-e *Iran* **71** D9
Beach *U.S.A.* **112** B2
Beach City *U.S.A.* **114** F3
Beachport *Australia* **95** F3
Beachy Hd. *U.K.* **15** G8
Beacon *Australia* **93** F2
Beacon *U.S.A.* **115** E11
Beaconsfield *Australia* **95** G4
Beagle, Canal *S. Amer.* **128** H3
Beagle Bay *Australia* **92** C3
Bealanana *Madag.* **89** A8
Beals Cr. → *U.S.A.* **116** E4
Beamsville = Lincoln
  Canada **114** C5
Bear → *Calif., U.S.A.* **110** G5
Bear → *Utah, U.S.A.* **106** B4
Béar, C. *France* **20** F7
Bear I. *Ireland* **12** E2
Bear L. *Canada* **103** B9
Bear L. *U.S.A.* **108** F8
Beardmore *Canada* **104** C2
Beardmore Glacier *Antarctica* **5** E11
Beardstown *U.S.A.* **112** E8
Bearma → *India* **69** G8
Béarn *France* **20** E3
Bearpaw Mts. → *U.S.A.* **108** B9
Bearskin Lake *Canada* **104** B1
Beas → *India* **68** D6
Beas de Segura *Spain* **37** G8
Beasain *Spain* **38** B2
Beata, C. *Dom. Rep.* **121** C5
Beata, I. *Dom. Rep.* **121** C5
Beatrice *U.S.A.* **112** E5
Beatrice *Zimbabwe* **87** F3
Beatrice, C. *Australia* **94** A2
Beatton → *Canada* **102** B4
Beatton River *Canada* **102** B4
Beatty *U.S.A.* **110** J10
Beau Bassin *Mauritius* **85** d
Beaucaire *France* **21** E8
Beauce, Plaine de la *France* **19** D8
Beauceville *Canada* **105** C5
Beaudesert *Australia* **95** D5
Beaufort *France* **21** C10
Beaufort *Malaysia* **62** C5
Beaufort *N.C., U.S.A.* **117** D16
Beaufort *S.C., U.S.A.* **117** E14
Beaufort Sea *Arctic* **98** B5
Beaufort West *S. Africa* **88** E3
Beaugency *France* **19** E8
Beauharnois *Canada* **115** A11
Beaujeu *France* **19** F11
Beaujolais *France* **19** F11
Beaulieu → *Canada* **102** A6
Beaulieu-sur-Dordogne
  France **20** D5
Beaulieu-sur-Mer *France* **21** E11
Beauly *U.K.* **13** D4
Beauly → *U.K.* **13** D4
Beaumaris *U.K.* **14** D3
Beaumont *Belgium* **17** D4
Beaumont *France* **20** D4
Beaumont *U.S.A.* **116** F7
Beaumont-de-Lomagne
  France **20** E5
Beaumont-le-Roger *France* **18** C7
Beaumont-sur-Sarthe
  France **18** D7
Beaune *France* **19** E11
Beaune-la-Rolande *France* **19** D9
Beaupré *Canada* **105** C5
Beaupréau *France* **18** E6
Beauraing *Belgium* **17** D4
Beaurepaire *France* **21** C9
Beausejour *Canada* **103** C9
Beauvais *France* **19** C9
Beauval *Canada* **103** B7
Beauvoir-sur-Mer *France* **18** F4
Beauvoir-sur-Niort *France* **20** B3
Beaver *Okla., U.S.A.* **116** C4
Beaver *Pa., U.S.A.* **114** F4
Beaver *Utah, U.S.A.* **108** G7
Beaver → *B.C., Canada* **102** B4
Beaver → *Ont., Canada* **104** A2
Beaver → *Sask., Canada* **103** B7
Beaver → *U.S.A.* **116** C5
Beaver City *U.S.A.* **112** E4
Beaver Creek *Canada* **100** C5
Beaver Dam *U.S.A.* **112** D9
Beaver Falls *U.S.A.* **114** F4
Beaver Hill L. *Canada* **103** C10
Beaver I. *U.S.A.* **113** C11
Beavercreek *U.S.A.* **113** F11
Beaverhill L. *Canada* **102** C6

Beaverlodge *Canada* **102** B5
Beaverstone → *Canada* **104** B2
Beaverton *Canada* **114** B5
Beaverton *U.S.A.* **110** E4
Beawar *India* **68** F6
Beba *Madag.* **89** B7
Bebedouro *Brazil* **127** A6
Bebera, Tanjung *Indonesia* **63** K18
Beboa *Madag.* **89** B7
Bebra *Germany* **24** E5
Becán *Mexico* **119** D7
Bécancour *Canada* **113** B17
Beccles *U.K.* **15** E9
Bečej *Serbia* **28** E5
Beceni *Romania* **29** E11
Becerreá *Spain* **36** C3
Béchar *Algeria* **78** B5
Bechyně *Czech Rep.* **26** B7
Beckley *U.S.A.* **113** G13
Beckum *Germany* **24** D4
Beclean *Romania* **29** C9
Bečva → *Czech Rep.* **27** B10
Bédar *Spain* **39** H3
Bédarieux *France* **20** E7
Beddouza, Ras *Morocco* **78** B4
Bedele *Ethiopia* **81** F4
Bederkesa *Germany* **24** B4
Bedeso *Ethiopia* **81** F5
Bedford *Canada* **115** A12
Bedford *S. Africa* **88** E4
Bedford *U.K.* **15** E7
Bedford *Ind., U.S.A.* **112** F10
Bedford *Iowa, U.S.A.* **112** E6
Bedford *Ohio, U.S.A.* **114** E3
Bedford *Pa., U.S.A.* **114** F6
Bedford *Va., U.S.A.* **113** G14
Bedford, C. *Australia* **94** B4
Bedfordshire □ *U.K.* **15** E7
Będków *Poland* **31** G6
Bednja → *Croatia* **41** B13
Bednodemyanovsk *Russia* **34** D6
Bedok *Singapore* **65** d
Bedónia *Italy* **40** D6
Bedourie *Australia* **94** C2
Bedum *Neths.* **17** A6
Będzin *Poland* **31** H6
Beebe Plain *Canada* **115** A12
Beech Creek *U.S.A.* **114** E7
Beechy *Canada* **103** C7
Beef I. *Br. Virgin Is.* **121** e
Beenleigh *Australia* **95** D5
Be'er Menuḥa *Israel* **70** D2
Be'er Sheva *Israel* **74** D3
Beersheba = Be'er Sheva
  Israel **74** D3
Beeskow *Germany* **24** C10
Beestekraal *S. Africa* **89** D4
Beeston *U.K.* **14** E6
Beetzendorf *Germany* **24** C7
Beeville *U.S.A.* **116** G6
Befale *Dem. Rep. of the Congo* **84** D4
Befandriana *Mahajanga,
  Madag.* **89** B8
Befandriana *Toliara, Madag.* **89** C7
Befasy *Madag.* **89** C7
Befotaka *Antsiranana, Madag.* **89** A8
Befotaka *Fianarantsoa,
  Madag.* **89** C8
Bega *Australia* **95** F4
Bega, Canalul *Romania* **28** E5
Bégard *France* **18** D3
Beğendik *Turkey* **45** F10
Begoro *Ghana* **83** D4
Begusarai *India* **69** G12
Behābād *Iran* **71** C8
Behala *India* **69** H13
Behara *Madag.* **89** C8
Behbehān *Iran* **71** D6
Behm Canal *U.S.A.* **102** B2
Behshahr *Iran* **71** B7
Bei Jiang → *China* **59** F9
Bei'an *China* **60** B7
Beibei *China* **58** C6
Beichuan *China* **58** B5
Beihai *China* **58** G7
Beijing *China* **56** E9
Beijing □ *China* **56** E9
Beilen *Neths.* **17** B6
Beiliu *China* **59** F8
Beilngries *Germany* **25** F7
Beilpajah *Australia* **95** E3
Beilul *Eritrea* **81** E5
Beinn na Faoghla =
  Benbecula *U.K.* **13** D1
Beipan Jiang → *China* **58** E5
Beipiao *China* **57** D11
Beira *Mozam.* **87** F3
Beirut = Bayrūt *Lebanon* **74** B4
Beiseker *Canada* **102** C6
Beit Lekhem = Bayt Laḥm
  West Bank **74** D4
Beitaolaizhao *China* **57** B13
Beitbridge *Zimbabwe* **87** G3
Beiuş *Romania* **28** D7
Beizhen = Binzhou *China* **57** F10
Beizhen *China* **57** D11
Beizhengzhen *China* **57** B12

Beja *Portugal* **37** G3
Béja *Tunisia* **79** A7
Beja □ *Portugal* **37** H3
Bejaïa *Algeria* **78** A7
Béjar *Spain* **36** E5
Bejestān *Iran* **71** C8
Bekaa Valley = Al Biqā
  Lebanon **74** A5
Bekçiler *Turkey* **47** E11
Békés *Hungary* **28** D6
Békés □ *Hungary* **28** D6
Békéscsaba *Hungary* **28** D6
Bekilli *Turkey* **47** C11
Bekily *Madag.* **89** C8
Bekisopa *Madag.* **89** C8
Bekitro *Madag.* **89** C8
Bekodoka *Madag.* **89** B8
Bekoji *Ethiopia* **81** F4
Bekok *Malaysia* **65** L4
Bekopaka *Madag.* **89** B7
Bekuli *Indonesia* **63** J17
Bekwai *Ghana* **83** D4
Bela *India* **69** G10
Bela *Pakistan* **68** F2
Bela Bela *S. Africa* **89** C4
Bela Crkva *Serbia* **28** F6
Bela Palanka *Serbia* **44** C6
Bela Vista *Brazil* **126** A4
Bela Vista *Mozam.* **89** D5
Bélâbre *France* **20** B5
Belalcázar *Spain* **37** G5
Belan → *India* **69** G9
Belanovica *Serbia* **44** B4
Belarus ■ *Europe* **23** B14
Belau = Palau ■ *Palau* **90** A6
Belavenona *Madag.* **89** C8
Belawan *Indonesia* **62** D1
Belaya *Ethiopia* **81** E4
Belaya Glina *Russia* **35** G5
Belaya Kalitva *Russia* **35** F5
Belaya Tserkov = Bila
  Tserkva *Ukraine* **23** D16
Belceşti *Romania* **29** C12
Belchatów *Poland* **31** G6
Belcher Chan. *Canada* **101** B10
Belcher Is. *Canada* **104** A3
Belchite *Spain* **38** D4
Belden *U.S.A.* **110** E5
Beled Weyne = Belet Uen
  Somali Rep. **75** G4
Belém *Brazil* **125** D9
Belén *Argentina* **126** B2
Belén *Paraguay* **126** A4
Belen *Turkey* **72** D7
Belen *U.S.A.* **109** J10
Belene *Bulgaria* **45** C9
Bélesta *France* **20** F5
Belet Uen *Somali Rep.* **75** G4
Belev *Russia* **32** F9
Belevi *Turkey* **47** C9
Belfair *U.S.A.* **110** C4
Belfast *S. Africa* **89** D5
Belfast *U.K.* **12** B6
Belfast *Maine, U.S.A.* **113** C19
Belfast *N.Y., U.S.A.* **114** D6
Belfast L. *U.K.* **12** B6
Belfield *U.S.A.* **112** B2
Belfort *France* **19** E13
Belfort, Territoire de □
  France **19** E13
Belfry *U.S.A.* **108** D9
Belgaum *India* **66** M9
Belgioioso *Italy* **40** C6
Belgium ■ *Europe* **17** D4
Belgodère *France* **21** F13
Belgorod *Russia* **33** G9
Belgorod □ *Russia* **33** G9
Belgorod-Dnestrovskiy =
  Bilhorod-Dnistrovskyy
  Ukraine **33** J6
Belgrade = Beograd *Serbia* **44** B4
Belgrade *U.S.A.* **108** D8
Belgrano *Antarctica* **5** D1
Belhaven *U.S.A.* **117** D16
Beli Drim → *Europe* **44** D4
Beli Manastir *Croatia* **28** E3
Beli Timok → *Serbia* **44** C6
Bélice → *Italy* **42** E5
Belimbing *Indonesia* **63** J18
Belinskiy *Russia* **34** D6
Belinyu *Indonesia* **62** E3
Beliton Is. = Belitung
  Indonesia **62** E3
Belitung *Indonesia* **62** E3
Beliu *Romania* **28** D6
Belize ■ *Cent. Amer.* **119** D7
Belize City *Belize* **119** D7
Beljakovci *Macedonia* **44** D5
Beljanica *Serbia* **44** B5
Belkovskiy, Ostrov *Russia* **53** B14
Bell → *Canada* **104** C4
Bell I. *Canada* **105** B8
Bell-Irving → *Canada* **102** B3
Bell Peninsula *Canada* **101** C11
Bell Ville *Argentina* **126** C3
Bella *Italy* **43** B8
Bella Bella *Canada* **102** C3
Bella Coola *Canada* **102** C3

Bella Unión *Uruguay* **126** C4
Bella Vista *Corrientes,
  Argentina* **126** B4
Bella Vista *Tucuman,
  Argentina* **126** B2
Bellac *France* **20** B5
Bellágio *Italy* **40** C6
Bellaire *U.S.A.* **114** F4
Bellária *Italy* **41** D9
Bellary *India* **66** M10
Bellata *Australia* **95** D4
Belle Fourche *U.S.A.* **112** C2
Belle Fourche → *U.S.A.* **106** B6
Belle Glade *U.S.A.* **117** H14
Belle-Île *France* **18** E3
Belle Isle *Canada* **105** B8
Belle Isle, Str. of *Canada* **105** B8
Belle Plaine *U.S.A.* **112** E7
Belle Yella *Liberia* **82** D3
Belledonne *France* **21** C10
Bellefontaine *U.S.A.* **113** E12
Bellefonte *U.S.A.* **114** F7
Bellegarde *France* **19** E9
Bellegarde-en-Marche
  France **20** C6
Bellegarde-sur-Valserine
  France **19** F12
Bellême *France* **18** D7
Belleoram *Canada* **105** C8
Belleville *Canada* **114** B7
Belleville *France* **19** F11
Belleville *Ill., U.S.A.* **112** F9
Belleville *Kans., U.S.A.* **112** F5
Belleville *N.J., U.S.A.* **115** F10
Belleville *N.Y., U.S.A.* **115** C8
Belleville-sur-Vie *France* **18** F5
Bellevue *Canada* **102** D6
Bellevue *Idaho, U.S.A.* **108** E6
Bellevue *Nebr., U.S.A.* **112** E7
Bellevue *Ohio, U.S.A.* **114** E2
Bellevue *Wash., U.S.A.* **110** C4
Belley *France* **21** C9
Bellin = Kangirsuk *Canada* **101** D13
Bellinge *Denmark* **11** J4
Bellingen *Australia* **95** E5
Bellingham *U.S.A.* **110** B4
Bellingshausen Abyssal
  Plain *S. Ocean* **5** C16
Bellingshausen Sea
  Antarctica **5** C17
Bellinzona *Switz.* **25** J5
Bello *Colombia* **124** B3
Bellows Falls *U.S.A.* **115** C12
Bellpat *Pakistan* **68** E3
Bellpuig d'Urgell *Spain* **38** D6
Belluno *Italy* **41** B9
Bellwood *U.S.A.* **114** F6
Bélmez *Spain* **37** G5
Belmont *Canada* **114** D3
Belmont *S. Africa* **88** D3
Belmont *U.S.A.* **114** D6
Belmonte *Brazil* **125** G11
Belmonte *Portugal* **36** E3
Belmonte *Spain* **39** F2
Belmopan *Belize* **119** D7
Belo Horizonte *Brazil* **125** G10
Belo-sur-Mer *Madag.* **89** C7
Belo-Tsiribihina *Madag.* **89** B7
Belogorsk = Bilohirsk
  Ukraine **33** K8
Belogorsk *Russia* **53** D13
Belogradchik *Bulgaria* **44** C6
Belogradets *Bulgaria* **45** C11
Beloha *Madag.* **89** D8
Beloit *Kans., U.S.A.* **112** F4
Beloit *Wis., U.S.A.* **112** D9
Belokorovichi *Ukraine* **23** C15
Belomorsk *Russia* **52** C4
Belonia *India* **67** H17
Belopolye = Bilopillya
  Ukraine **33** G8
Belorechensk *Russia* **35** H4
Belorussia = Belarus ■
  Europe **23** B14
Beloslav *Bulgaria* **45** C11
Belovo *Bulgaria* **45** D8
Belovo *Russia* **52** D9
Belovodsk *Ukraine* **33** H10
Belozersk *Russia* **32** B9
Belozersk *Russia* **32** B9
Belpasso *Italy* **43** E7
Belpre *U.S.A.* **113** F5
Belrain *India* **69** E9
Belt *U.S.A.* **108** C8
Beltana *Australia* **95** E2
Belterra *Brazil* **125** D8
Beltinci *Slovenia* **41** B13
Belton *U.S.A.* **116** F6
Belton L. *U.S.A.* **116** F6
Beltsy = Bălţi *Moldova* **29** C12
Belturbet *Ireland* **12** B4
Belukha *Russia* **52** E9
Beluran *Malaysia* **62** C5
Beluša *Slovak Rep.* **27** B11

Belušić *Serbia* **44** C5
Belvès *France* **20** D5
Belvidere *Ill., U.S.A.* **112** D9
Belvidere *N.J., U.S.A.* **115** F9
Belvis de la Jara *Spain* **36** F6
Belyando → *Australia* **94** C4
Belyy *Russia* **32** E7
Belyy, Ostrov *Russia* **52** B8
Belyy Yar *Russia* **52** D9
Belz *Ukraine* **31** H11
Belżec *Poland* **31** H10
Belzig *Germany* **24** C8
Belzoni *U.S.A.* **117** E10
Belżyce *Poland* **31** G9
Bemaraha, Lembalemban'
  i *Madag.* **89** B7
Bemarivo *Madag.* **89** C7
Bemarivo → *Antsiranana,
  Madag.* **89** A9
Bemarivo → *Mahajanga,
  Madag.* **89** B8
Bemavo *Madag.* **89** C8
Bembéréke *Benin* **83** C5
Bembesi *Zimbabwe* **87** G2
Bembesi → *Zimbabwe* **87** F2
Bembézar → *Spain* **37** H5
Bembibre *Spain* **36** C4
Bemetara *India* **69** J9
Bemidji *U.S.A.* **112** B6
Bemolanga *Madag.* **89** B8
Ben *Iran* **71** C6
Ben Cruachan *U.K.* **13** E3
Ben Dearg *U.K.* **13** D4
Ben En △ *Vietnam* **64** C5
Ben Gardane *Tunisia* **79** B8
Ben Hope *U.K.* **13** C4
Ben Lawers *U.K.* **13** E4
Ben Lomond *N.S.W.,
  Australia* **95** E5
Ben Lomond *Tas., Australia* **95** G4
Ben Lomond *U.K.* **13** E4
Ben Luc *Vietnam* **65** G6
Ben Macdhui *U.K.* **13** D5
Ben Mhor *U.K.* **13** D1
Ben More *Argyll & Bute, U.K.* **13** E2
Ben More *Stirling, U.K.* **13** E4
Ben More Assynt *U.K.* **13** C4
Ben Nevis *U.K.* **13** E3
Ben Quang *Vietnam* **64** D6
Ben Vorlich *U.K.* **13** E4
Ben Wyvis *U.K.* **13** D4
Bena *Nigeria* **83** C6
Benalla *Australia* **95** F4
Benalmádena *Spain* **37** J6
Benares = Varanasi *India* **69** G10
Bénat, C. *France* **21** E10
Benavente *Portugal* **37** G2
Benavente *Spain* **36** C5
Benavides *U.S.A.* **116** H5
Benavides de Órbigo *Spain* **36** C5
Benbecula *U.K.* **13** D1
Benbonyathe Hill *Australia* **95** E2
Bend *U.S.A.* **108** D3
Bender Beila *Somali Rep.* **75** F5
Bendery = Tighina *Moldova* **29** D14
Bendigo *Australia* **95** F3
Bendorf *Germany* **24** E3
Benê Beraq *Israel* **74** C3
Bénéna *Mali* **82** C4
Benenitra *Madag.* **89** C8
Benešov *Czech Rep.* **26** B7
Benevento *Italy* **43** A7
Benfeld *France* **19** D14
Benga *Mozam.* **87** F3
Bengal, Bay of *Ind. Oc.* **67** M17
Bengbis *Cameroon* **83** E7
Bengbu *China* **57** H9
Benghazi = Banghāzī *Libya* **79** B10
Bengkalis *Indonesia* **62** D2
Bengkulu *Indonesia* **62** E2
Bengkulu □ *Indonesia* **62** E2
Bengough *Canada* **103** D7
Bengtsfors *Sweden* **10** E6
Benguela *Angola* **85** G2
Benguérua, I. *Mozam.* **89** C6
Benha *Egypt* **80** H7
Beni *Dem. Rep. of the Congo* **86** B2
Beni → *Bolivia* **124** F5
Beni Mazâr *Egypt* **80** B3
Beni Mellal *Morocco* **78** B4
Beni Suef *Egypt* **80** J7
Beniah L. *Canada* **102** A6
Benicarló *Spain* **38** E5
Benicàssim *Spain* **38** E5
Benidorm *Spain* **39** G4
Benin ■ *Africa* **83** D5
Benin → *Nigeria* **83** D6
Benin, Bight of *W. Afr.* **83** E5
Benin City *Nigeria* **83** D6
Benisa *Spain* **39** G5
Benitses *Greece* **49** A3
Benjamin Aceval *Paraguay* **126** A4
Benjamin Constant *Brazil* **124** D4
Benjamín Hill *Mexico* **118** A2

Benkelman U.S.A. **112** E3
Benkovac Croatia **41** D12
Bennett Canada **102** B2
Bennett, L. Australia **92** D5
Bennetta, Ostrov Russia **53** B15
Bennettsville U.S.A. **117** D15
Bennichchâb Mauritania **82** B1
Bennington N.H., U.S.A. **115** D11
Bennington Vt., U.S.A. **115** D11
Bénodet France **18** E2
Benoni S. Africa **89** D4
Benque Viejo Belize **119** D7
Bensheim Germany **25** F4
Benson Ariz., U.S.A. **109** L8
Benson Minn., U.S.A. **112** C6
Bent Iran **71** E8
Benteng Indonesia **63** F6
Bentinck I. Australia **94** B2
Bentiu Sudan **81** F2
Bento Gonçalves Brazil **127** B5
Benton Ark., U.S.A. **116** D8
Benton Calif., U.S.A. **110** H8
Benton Ill., U.S.A. **112** F9
Benton Pa., U.S.A. **115** E8
Benton Harbor U.S.A. **112** D10
Bentong Malaysia **65** L3
Bentonville U.S.A. **116** C7
Bentu Liben Ethiopia **81** F4
Benue □ Nigeria **83** D6
Benue → Nigeria **83** D6
Benxi China **57** D12
Beo Indonesia **63** D7
Beograd Serbia **44** B4
Beograd ✈ (BEG) Serbia **44** C4
Beolgyo S. Korea **57** G14
Beoumi Ivory C. **82** D3
Bepan Jiang → China **58** E6
Beppu Japan **55** H5
Beqa Fiji **91** a
Beqaa Valley = Al Biqā
   Lebanon **74** A5
Ber Mota India **68** H3
Berach → India **68** G6
Beraketa Madag. **89** C7
Berane Montenegro **44** D3
Beravina Madag. **89** B8
Berat Albania **44** F3
Berau, Teluk Indonesia **63** E8
Beravina Madag. **89** B8
Berber Sudan **80** D3
Berbera Somali Rep. **75** E4
Berbérati C.A.R. **84** D3
Berbice → Guyana **124** B7
Berceto Italy **40** D6
Berchidda Italy **42** B2
Berchtesgaden Germany **25** H8
Berchtesgaden △ Germany **25** H8
Berck France **19** B8
Berdichev = Berdychiv
   Ukraine **23** D15
Berdsk Russia **52** D9
Berdyansk Ukraine **33** J9
Berdychiv Ukraine **23** D15
Berea U.S.A. **113** G11
Berebere Indonesia **63** D7
Bereda Somali Rep. **75** E5
Berehomet Ukraine **29** B10
Berehove Ukraine **28** B7
Bereket Turkmenistan **71** B7
Berekum Ghana **82** D4
Berenice Egypt **80** C4
Berens → Canada **103** C9
Berens I. Canada **103** C9
Berens River Canada **103** C9
Beresford U.S.A. **112** D5
Berestechko Ukraine **23** C13
Bereşti Romania **29** D12
Beretău → Romania **28** C6
Berettyó → Hungary **28** D6
Berettyóújfalu Hungary **28** C6
Berevo Mahajanga, Madag. **89** B7
Berevo Toliara, Madag. **89** B7
Bereza = Byaroza Belarus **33** F3
Berezhany Ukraine **23** D13
Berezina = Byarezina →
   Belarus **23** B16
Berezivka Ukraine **33** J6
Berezna Ukraine **33** G6
Bereznik Russia **52** C5
Berezniki Russia **52** D6
Berezovo Russia **52** C7
Berezyne Ukraine **29** D14
Berga Spain **38** C6
Berga Sweden **11** G10
Bergama Turkey **47** B9
Bérgamo Italy **40** C6
Bergara Spain **38** B2
Bergby Sweden **10** D11
Bergedorf Germany **24** B6
Bergeforsen Sweden **10** B11
Bergen
   Mecklenburg-Vorpommern,
   Germany **24** A9
Bergen Niedersachsen,
   Germany **24** C5
Bergen Neths. **17** B4
Bergen Norway **8** F11
Bergen U.S.A. **114** C7

Bergen op Zoom Neths. **17** C4
Bergerac France **20** D4
Bergheim Germany **24** E2
Bergholz U.S.A. **114** F4
Bergisch Gladbach Germany **17** D7
Bergisches Land △ Germany **24** E3
Bergkamen Germany **24** D3
Bergkvara Sweden **11** H10
Bergshamra Sweden **10** E12
Bergsjö Sweden **10** C11
Bergstrasse-Odenwald △
   Germany **25** F1
Bergues France **19** B9
Bergviken Sweden **10** C10
Bergville S. Africa **89** D4
Berhala, Selat Indonesia **62** E2
Berhampore =
   Baharampur India **69** G13
Berhampur = Brahmapur
   India **67** K14
Berheci → Romania **29** E12
Bering Sea Pac. Oc. **106** a
Bering Strait Pac. Oc. **106** a
Beringovskiy Russia **53** C18
Berisso Argentina **126** C4
Berja Spain **37** J8
Berkeley U.S.A. **110** H4
Berkner I. Antarctica **5** D18
Berkovitsa Bulgaria **44** C7
Berkshire U.S.A. **115** D8
Berkshire Downs U.K. **15** F6
Berlanga Spain **37** G5
Berlenga, I. Portugal **37** F1
Berlin Germany **24** C9
Berlin Md., U.S.A. **113** F16
Berlin N.H., U.S.A. **115** B13
Berlin N.Y., U.S.A. **115** D11
Berlin Wis., U.S.A. **112** D9
Berlin □ Germany **24** C9
Berlin L. U.S.A. **114** E4
Berlin Tegel ✈ (TXL)
   Germany **24** C9
Bermeja, Sierra Spain **37** J5
Bermejo →
   Formosa,
   Argentina **126** B4
Bermejo → San Juan,
   Argentina **126** B4
Bermejo, Paso = Uspallata,
   P. de Argentina **126** C2
Bermen, L. Canada **105** B6
Bermeo Spain **38** B2
Bermillo de Sayago Spain **36** D4
Bermuda ☑ Atl. Oc. **99** F13
Bern Switz. **25** J3
Bern □ Switz. **25** J3
Bernalda Italy **43** B9
Bernalillo U.S.A. **109** J10
Bernardo de Irigoyen
   Argentina **127** B5
Bernardo O'Higgins □
   Chile **126** C1
Bernardsville U.S.A. **115** F10
Bernasconi Argentina **126** D3
Bernau Bayern, Germany **25** H8
Bernau Brandenburg, Germany **24** C9
Bernay France **18** C7
Bernburg Germany **24** D7
Berndorf Austria **26** D9
Berne = Bern Switz. **25** J3
Berne = Bern □ Switz. **25** J3
Berner Alpen Switz. **25** J3
Berneray U.K. **13** D1
Bernier I. Australia **93** D1
Bernina, Piz Switz. **25** J5
Bernkastel-Kues Germany **25** F3
Beroroha Madag. **89** C8
Béroubouay Benin **83** C5
Beroun Czech Rep. **26** B7
Berounka → Czech Rep. **26** B7
Berovo Macedonia **44** E6
Berre, Étang de France **21** E9
Berre-l'Étang France **21** E9
Berri Australia **95** E3
Berriane Algeria **78** B6
Berrigan Australia **95** F4
Berry Australia **95** E5
Berry France **19** F8
Berry Is. Bahamas **120** A4
Berryessa, L. U.S.A. **110** G4
Berryville U.S.A. **116** C8
Bersenbrück Germany **24** C3
Berseba Namibia **88** D2
Berthold U.S.A. **112** A3
Berthoud U.S.A. **108** F11
Bertincourt France **19** B9
Bertoua Cameroon **84** D2
Bertraghboy B. Ireland **12** C2
Berwick U.S.A. **115** E8
Berwick-upon-Tweed U.K. **14** B6
Berwyn Mts. U.K. **14** E4
Beryslav Ukraine **33** J7
Berzasca Romania **28** F6
Berzence Hungary **28** D2
Besal Pakistan **69** B5
Besalampy Madag. **89** B7
Besançon France **19** E13
Besar Indonesia **62** E5
Beshenkovichi Belarus **32** E5

Beška Serbia **28** E5
Beslan Russia **35** J7
Besna Kobila Serbia **44** D6
Besnard L. Canada **103** B7
Besni Turkey **72** D7
Besor, N. → Egypt **74** D3
Bessarabiya Moldova **23** E15
Bessarabka =
   Basarabeasca Moldova **29** D13
Bessèges France **21** D8
Bessemer Ala., U.S.A. **117** E11
Bessemer Mich., U.S.A. **112** B8
Bessemer Pa., U.S.A. **114** F4
Bessin France **18** C6
Bessines-sur-Gartempe
   France **20** B5
Beswick Australia **92** B5
Bet She'an Israel **74** C4
Bet Shemesh Israel **74** D4
Betafo Madag. **89** B8
Betancuria Canary Is. **48** F5
Betanzos Spain **36** B2
Bétaré Oya Cameroon **84** C2
Betatao Madag. **89** B8
Bétera Spain **39** F4
Bétérou Benin **83** D5
Bethal S. Africa **89** D4
Bethanien Namibia **88** D2
Bethany Canada **114** B6
Bethany Mo., U.S.A. **112** E6
Bethany Okla., U.S.A. **116** D6
Bethel Alaska, U.S.A. **106** a
Bethel Conn., U.S.A. **115** E11
Bethel Maine, U.S.A. **115** B14
Bethel Vt., U.S.A. **115** C12
Bethel Park U.S.A. **114** F4
Bethlehem = Bayt Lahm
   West Bank **74** D4
Bethlehem S. Africa **89** D4
Bethlehem U.S.A. **115** F9
Bethulie S. Africa **88** E4
Béthune France **19** B9
Béthune → France **18** C8
Betioky Madag. **89** C7
Betong Malaysia **62** D4
Betong Thailand **65** K3
Betoota Australia **94** D3
Betor Ethiopia **81** E4
Betpaqdala Kazakhstan **52** E8
Betroka Madag. **89** C8
Betsiamites Canada **105** C6
Betsiamites → Canada **105** C6
Betsiboka → Madag. **89** B8
Bettendorf U.S.A. **112** E8
Bettiah India **69** F11
Bettna Sweden **11** F10
Béttola Italy **40** D6
Betul India **68** J10
Betws-y-Coed U.K. **14** D4
Betxi Spain **38** F4
Betzdorf Germany **24** E3
Beuil France **21** D10
Beulah Mich., U.S.A. **112** C10
Beulah N. Dak., U.S.A. **112** B3
Beuvron → France **18** E8
Beveren Belgium **17** C4
Beverley Australia **93** F2
Beverley U.K. **14** D7
Beverly U.S.A. **115** D14
Beverly Hills Calif., U.S.A. **111** L8
Beverly Hills Fla., U.S.A. **117** G13
Beverungen Germany **24** D5
Bevoalavo Madag. **89** D7
Bewas → India **69** H8
Bewdley U.K. **15** E5
Bex Switz. **25** J3
Bexhill U.K. **15** G8
Bey Dağları Turkey **47** E12
Beyānlu Iran **70** C5
Beyazköy Turkey **45** E11
Beyçayırı Turkey **45** F10
Beydağ Turkey **47** C10
Beyin Ghana **82** D4
Beykoz Turkey **45** E13
Beyla Guinea **82** D3
Beynat France **20** C5
Beyneu Kazakhstan **52** E6
Beyoba Turkey **47** C9
Beyoğlu Turkey **45** E12
Beypazarı Turkey **72** B4
Beyşehir Turkey **72** D4
Beyşehir Gölü Turkey **72** D4
Beytüşşebap Turkey **73** D10
Bezdan Serbia **28** E3
Bezhetsk Russia **32** D9
Béziers France **20** E7
Bezwada = Vijayawada
   India **67** L12
Bhabua India **69** G10
Bhachau India **66** H7
Bhadar → Gujarat, India **68** H5
Bhadar → Gujarat, India **68** J3
Bhadarwah India **69** C6
Bhadgaon = Bhaktapur
   Nepal **69** F11
Bhadohi India **69** G10
Bhadra India **68** E6

Bhadrakh India **67** J15
Bhadran India **68** H5
Bhag Pakistan **68** E2
Bhagalpur India **69** G12
Bhagirathi → Uttaranchal,
   India **69** D8
Bhagirathi → W. Bengal,
   India **69** H13
Bhakkar Pakistan **68** D4
Bhaktapur Nepal **69** F11
Bhakra Dam India **68** D7
Bhamo Burma **67** G20
Bhandara India **66** J11
Bhanpura India **68** G6
Bhanrer Ra. India **69** H8
Bhaptiahi India **69** F12
Bharat = India ■ Asia **66** K11
Bharatpur Chhattisgarh, India **69** H9
Bharatpur Raj., India **68** F7
Bharno India **69** H11
Bharuch India **66** J8
Bhatinda India **68** D6
Bhatpara India **69** H13
Bhattu India **68** E6
Bhaun Pakistan **68** C5
Bhaunagar = Bhavnagar
   India **66** J8
Bhavnagar India **66** J8
Bhawari India **68** G5
Bhayavadar India **68** J4
Bhera Pakistan **68** C5
Bhikangaon India **68** J6
Bhilai = Bhilainagar-Durg
   India **67** J12
Bhilainagar-Durg India **67** J12
Bhilsa = Vidisha India **68** H7
Bhilwara India **68** G6
Bhima → India **66** L10
Bhimbar Pakistan **69** C6
Bhind India **69** F8
Bhinga India **69** F9
Bhinmal India **68** G5
Bhisho S. Africa **89** E4
Bhiwandi India **66** K8
Bhiwani India **68** E7
Bhogava → India **68** H5
Bhola Bangla. **67** H17
Bholari Pakistan **68** G3
Bhopal India **68** H7
Bhubaneshwar India **67** J14
Bhuj India **68** H3
Bhumiphol Res. Thailand **64** D2
Bhusawal India **66** J9
Bhutan ■ Asia **67** F17
Biafra, B. of = Bonny,
   Bight of Africa **83** E6
Biak Indonesia **63** E9
Biała Poland **31** H4
Biała → Poland **31** H7
Biała Piska Poland **30** E9
Biała Podlaska Poland **31** F10
Biała Rawska Poland **31** G7
Białobrzegi Poland **31** G7
Białogard Poland **30** D2
Białowieski △ Poland **31** F10
Białowieża Poland **31** F10
Biały Bór Poland **30** E3
Białystok Poland **31** E10
Biancavilla Italy **43** E7
Bianco Italy **43** D9
Biankouma Ivory C. **82** D3
Biaora India **68** H7
Biaro Indonesia **63** D7
Biarritz France **20** E2
Bias Indonesia **63** J18
Biasca Switz. **25** J4
Biba Egypt **80** J7
Bibai Japan **54** C10
Bibbiena Italy **41** E8
Bibby I. Canada **103** A10
Bibel → Spain **36** C3
Biberach Germany **25** G5
Bibiani Ghana **82** D4
Bibungwa
   Dem. Rep. of the Congo **86** C2
Bicaj Albania **44** E4
Bicaz Romania **29** D11
Bicaz Ardelean Romania **29** D10
Bíccari Italy **43** A8
Bicester U.K. **15** F6
Bichena Ethiopia **81** E4
Bicheno Australia **95** G4
Bichia India **69** H9
Bichvinta Georgia **35** J5
Bickerton I. Australia **94** A2
Bicske Hungary **28** C3
Bida Nigeria **83** D6
Bidar India **66** L10
Biddeford U.S.A. **113** D18
Biddwara Ethiopia **81** F4
Bideford U.K. **15** F3
Bideford Bay U.K. **15** F3
Bidhuna India **69** F8
Bidor Malaysia **65** K3
Bidyadanga Australia **92** C3
Bie Sweden **10** E10
Bhadra India **68** E6

Bié, Planalto de Angola **85** G3
Bieber U.S.A. **108** F3
Biebrza → Poland **31** E9
Biecz Poland **31** J8
Biel Switz. **25** H3
Bielawa Poland **31** H3
Bielefeld Germany **24** C4
Bielersee Switz. **25** H3
Biella Italy **40** C5
Bielsk Podlaski Poland **31** E10
Bielsko-Biała Poland **31** J6
Bien Hoa Vietnam **65** G6
Bienne = Biel Switz. **25** H3
Bienvenida Spain **37** G4
Bienville, L. Canada **104** A5
Bierné France **18** E6
Bierun Poland **31** H6
Bierutów Poland **31** G4
Biescas Spain **38** C4
Biese → Germany **24** C7
Biesiesfontein S. Africa **88** E2
Bieszczadzki △ Poland **31** J9
Bietigheim-Bissingen
   Germany **25** G5
Bieżuń Poland **31** F6
Biferno → Italy **41** G12
Big → Canada **105** B8
Big B. Canada **105** A7
Big Bear City U.S.A. **111** L10
Big Bear Lake U.S.A. **111** L10
Big Belt Mts. U.S.A. **108** C8
Big Bend Swaziland **89** D5
Big Bend △ U.S.A. **116** G3
Big Blue → U.S.A. **112** F5
Big Creek U.S.A. **110** H7
Big Cypress △ U.S.A. **117** H14
Big Desert Australia **95** F3
Big Falls U.S.A. **112** A7
Big Fork → U.S.A. **112** A7
Big Horn Mts. = Bighorn
   Mts. U.S.A. **108** D10
Big I. Canada **102** A5
Big Lake U.S.A. **116** F4
Big Moose U.S.A. **115** C10
Big Muddy Cr. → U.S.A. **108** B11
Big Pine U.S.A. **110** H8
Big Piney U.S.A. **108** E8
Big Rapids U.S.A. **113** D11
Big Rideau L. Canada **115** B8
Big River Canada **103** C7
Big Run U.S.A. **114** F6
Big Sable Pt. U.S.A. **112** C10
Big Salmon → Canada **102** A2
Big Sand L. Canada **103** B9
Big Sandy U.S.A. **108** B8
Big Sandy → U.S.A. **113** F12
Big Sandy Cr. = Sandy
   Cr. → U.S.A. **108** F9
Big Sandy Cr. → U.S.A. **108** G12
Big Sioux → U.S.A. **112** D5
Big South Fork △ U.S.A. **117** C12
Big Spring U.S.A. **116** E4
Big Stone City U.S.A. **112** C5
Big Stone Gap U.S.A. **113** G12
Big Stone L. U.S.A. **112** C5
Big Sur U.S.A. **110** J5
Big Timber U.S.A. **108** D9
Big Trout L. Canada **104** B2
Big Trout Lake Canada **104** B2
Biga Turkey **45** F11
Biga → Turkey **45** F11
Bigadiç Turkey **47** B10
Biganos France **20** D3
Biggar Canada **103** C7
Biggar U.K. **13** F5
Bigge I. Australia **92** B4
Biggenden Australia **95** D5
Biggleswade U.K. **15** E7
Biggs U.S.A. **110** F5
Bighorn U.S.A. **108** C10
Bighorn → U.S.A. **108** C10
Bighorn Canyon △ U.S.A. **108** D10
Bighorn L. U.S.A. **108** D9
Bighorn Mts. U.S.A. **108** D10
Bignona Senegal **82** C1
Bigorre France **20** E4
Bigstone L. Canada **103** C9
Biguglia, Étang de France **21** F13
Bigwa Tanzania **86** D4
Bihać Bos.-H. **41** D12
Bihar India **69** G11
Bihar □ India **69** G12
Biharamulo Tanzania **86** C3
Biharamulo △ Tanzania **86** C3
Bihariganj India **69** G12
Biharkeresztes Hungary **28** C6
Bihor □ Romania **28** D7
Bihor, Munţii Romania **28** D7
Bijagós, Arquipélago dos
   Guinea-Biss. **82** C1
Bijaipur India **68** F7
Bijapur Chhattisgarh, India **67** K12
Bijapur Karnataka, India **66** L9
Bījār Iran **73** E12
Bijawar India **69** G8
Bijela Montenegro **44** D2
Bijeljina Bos.-H. **28** F4

Bijelo Polje Montenegro **44** C3
Bijie China **58** D5
Bijnor India **68** E8
Bikaner India **68** E5
Bikapur India **69** F10
Bikeqi China **56** D6
Bikfayyā Lebanon **74** B4
Bikin Russia **54** A7
Bikin → Russia **54** A7
Bikini Atoll Marshall Is. **96** F8
Bikita Zimbabwe **89** C5
Bikoué Cameroon **83** E7
Bila Tserkva Ukraine **23** D16
Bilanga Burkina Faso **83** C4
Bilara India **68** F5
Bilaspur Chhattisgarh, India **69** H10
Bilaspur Punjab, India **68** D7
Biläsuvar Azerbaijan **73** C13
Bilauk Taungdan Thailand **64** F2
Bilbao Spain **38** B2
Bilbao ✈ (BIO) Spain **38** B2
Bilbo = Bilbao Spain **38** B2
Bilbor Romania **29** C10
Bilce-Zolote Ukraine **29** B10
Bilciureşti Romania **29** F10
Bíldudalur Iceland **8** D2
Bílé Karpaty Europe **27** B11
Bileća Bos.-H. **44** D2
Bilecik Turkey **72** B4
Bilecik □ Turkey **72** B3
Bilećko Jezero Bos.-H. **44** D2
Bilgoraj Poland **31** H9
Bilgram India **69** F9
Bilhaur India **69** F9
Bilhorod-Dnistrovskyy
   Ukraine **33** J6
Bilibino Russia **53** C17
Bilibiza Mozam. **87** E5
Bilisht Albania **44** F5
Billdal Sweden **11** G5
Billiluna Australia **92** C4
Billings U.S.A. **108** D9
Billiton Is. = Belitung
   Indonesia **62** E3
Billsta Sweden **10** A12
Billund Denmark **11** J3
Bilma Niger **79** E8
Bilo Gora Croatia **28** E2
Biloela Australia **94** C5
Bilohirsk Ukraine **33** K8
Bilopillya Ukraine **33** G8
Biloxi U.S.A. **117** F10
Bilpa Morea Claypan
   Australia **94** D3
Biltine Chad **79** F10
Bilyarsk Russia **34** C10
Bima Indonesia **63** F5
Bimban Egypt **80** C3
Bimbila Ghana **83** D5
Bimbo C.A.R. **84** D3
Bimini Is. Bahamas **120** A4
Bin Xian Heilongjiang, China **57** B14
Bin Xian Shaanxi, China **56** G5
Bin Yauri Nigeria **83** C5
Bina-Etawah India **68** G8
Binalbagan Phil. **61** F5
Binalong Australia **95** E4
Bīnālūd, Kūh-e Iran **71** B8
Binatang = Bintangu
   Malaysia **62** D4
Binche Belgium **17** D4
Binchuan China **58** E3
Binder Chad **83** D7
Bindki India **69** F9
Bindslev Denmark **11** G4
Bindura Zimbabwe **87** F3
Binefar Spain **38** D5
Bingara Australia **95** D5
Bingen Germany **25** F3
Bingerville Ivory C. **82** D4
Bingham U.S.A. **113** C19
Binghamton U.S.A. **115** D9
Bingöl Turkey **73** C9
Bingöl □ Turkey **73** C9
Bingöl Dağları Turkey **73** C9
Bingsjö Sweden **10** C9
Binh Dinh = An Nhon
   Vietnam **64** F7
Binh Khe Vietnam **64** F7
Binh Son Vietnam **64** E7
Binhai China **57** G10
Binic France **18** D4
Binisatua Spain **48** B11
Binjai Indonesia **62** D1
Binji Nigeria **83** C5
Binnaway Australia **95** E4
Binongko Indonesia **63** F6
Binscarth Canada **103** C8
Binshangul Gumuz □
   Ethiopia **81** E4
Bint Goda Sudan **81** E3
Bintan Indonesia **62** D2
Bintangau Malaysia **62** D4
Bintulu Malaysia **62** D4
Bintuni Indonesia **63** E8
Binyang China **58** F7

Binz *Germany* **24** A9
Binzert = Bizerte *Tunisia* **79** A7
Binzhou *China* **57** F10
Bío Bío □ *Chile* **126** D1
Biograd na Moru *Croatia* **41** E12
Biogradska Gora △ *Montenegro* **44** D3
Bioko *Eq. Guin.* **83** E6
Biokovo *Croatia* **41** E14
Bipindi *Cameroon* **83** E7
Bir *India* **66** K9
Bir, Ras *Djibouti* **81** E5
Bîr Abu Hashim *Egypt* **80** C3
Bîr Abu Minqar *Egypt* **80** B2
Bîr Abu Muḩammad *Egypt* **74** F3
Bi'r ad Dabbāghāt *Jordan* **74** E4
Bîr Adal Deib *Sudan* **80** C4
Bi'r al Butayyihāt *Jordan* **74** F4
Bi'r al Mārī *Jordan* **74** E4
Bi'r al Qaṭṭār *Jordan* **74** F4
Bîr 'Asal *Egypt* **80** B3
Bîr Atrun *Sudan* **80** D2
Bîr Beïda *Egypt* **74** E3
Bîr Diqnash *Egypt* **80** A2
Bîr el 'Abd *Egypt* **74** D2
Bîr el Basur *Egypt* **80** B2
Bîr el Biarât *Egypt* **74** F3
Bîr el Duweidar *Egypt* **74** E1
Bîr el Garârât *Egypt* **74** D2
Bîr el Gellaz *Egypt* **80** A2
Bîr el Heisi *Egypt* **74** F3
Bîr el Jafir *Egypt* **74** E1
Bîr el Mâlḩi *Egypt* **74** E2
Bîr el Shaqqa *Egypt* **80** A2
Bîr el Thamâda *Egypt* **74** E2
Bîr Fuad *Egypt* **80** A2
Bîr Gebeil Ḩiṣn *Egypt* **74** E2
Bi'r Ghaḑīr *Syria* **74** A6
Bîr Haimur *Egypt* **80** C3
Bîr Ḩasana *Egypt* **74** E2
Bîr Hôoker *Egypt* **80** H7
Bîr Kanayis *Egypt* **80** C3
Bîr Kaseiba *Egypt* **74** E2
Bîr Kerawein *Egypt* **80** B2
Bîr Lahfân *Egypt* **74** E2
Bîr Madkûr *Egypt* **74** E1
Bîr Maql *Egypt* **80** C3
Bîr Mîneiga *Sudan* **80** C4
Bîr Misaha *Egypt* **80** C2
Bîr Mogreïn *Mauritania* **78** C3
Bîr Murr *Egypt* **80** C3
Bi'r Muṭribah *Kuwait* **70** D5
Bîr Nakheila *Egypt* **80** C3
Bîr Qaṭia *Egypt* **74** E1
Bîr Qaṭrani *Egypt* **80** A2
Bîr Ranga *Egypt* **80** C4
Bîr Sahara *Egypt* **80** C2
Bîr Seiyâla *Egypt* **80** B3
Bîr Shalatein *Egypt* **80** C4
Bîr Shebb *Egypt* **80** C2
Bîr Shût *Egypt* **80** C4
Bîr Terfawi *Egypt* **80** C2
Bîr Umm Qubûr *Egypt* **80** C3
Bîr Ungât *Egypt* **80** C3
Bîr Za'farâna *Egypt* **80** J8
Bîr Zeidûn *Egypt* **80** C3
Birāk *Libya* **79** C8
Biramféro *Guinea* **82** C3
Biratnagar *Nepal* **69** F12
Birawa *Dem. Rep. of the Congo* **86** C2
Birch → *Canada* **102** B6
Birch Hills *Canada* **103** C7
Birch I. *Canada* **103** C9
Birch L. *N.W.T., Canada* **102** A5
Birch L. *Ont., Canada* **104** B1
Birch Mts. *Canada* **102** B6
Birch River *Canada* **103** C8
Birchip *Australia* **95** F3
Birchiş *Romania* **28** E7
Bird *Canada* **103** B10
Bird I. = Aves, I. de *W. Indies* **121** C7
Bird I. *Antarctica* **5** B1
Birdsville *Australia* **94** D2
Birdum Cr. → *Australia* **92** C5
Birecik *Turkey* **73** D8
Birein *Israel* **74** E3
Bireuen *Indonesia* **62** C1
Biri → *Sudan* **81** F2
Birifo *Gambia* **82** C2
Birigui *Brazil* **127** A5
Bîrjand *Iran* **71** C8
Birkenfeld *Germany* **25** F3
Birkenhead *U.K.* **14** D4
Birkerod *Denmark* **11** J6
Birket Qârûn *Egypt* **80** J7
Birkfeld *Austria* **26** D8
Bîrlad = Bârlad *Romania* **29** D12
Birmingham *U.K.* **15** E6
Birmingham *U.S.A.* **117** E11
Birmingham Int. ✈ (BHX) *U.K.* **15** E6
Birmitrapur *India* **67** H14
Birni Ngaouré *Niger* **83** C5
Birni Nkonni *Niger* **83** C6
Birnin Gwari *Nigeria* **83** C6
Birnin Kebbi *Nigeria* **83** C5
Birnin Kudu *Nigeria* **83** C6

Birobidzhan *Russia* **53** E14
Birr *Ireland* **12** C4
Birrie → *Australia* **95** D4
Birsilpur *India* **68** E5
Birsk *Russia* **52** D6
Birtle *Canada* **103** C8
Birur *India* **66** N9
Biryuchiy *Ukraine* **33** J8
Biržai *Lithuania* **32** D3
Birzebbuga *Malta* **49** D3
Bisa *Indonesia* **63** E7
Bisáccia *Italy* **43** A8
Bisacquino *Italy* **42** E6
Bisalpur *India* **69** E8
Bisbee *U.S.A.* **109** L9
Biscarrosse *France* **20** D2
Biscarrosse et de Parentis, Étang de *France* **20** D2
Biscay, B. of *Atl. Oc.* **6** F5
Biscayne B. *U.S.A.* **117** J14
Biscéglie *Italy* **43** A9
Bischheim *France* **19** D14
Bischofshofen *Austria* **26** D6
Bischofswerda *Germany* **24** D10
Bischwiller *France* **19** D14
Biscoe Is. *Antarctica* **5** C17
Biscotasing *Canada* **104** C3
Biševo *Croatia* **41** F13
Bisha *Eritrea* **81** D4
Bishah, W. → *Si. Arabia* **80** C5
Bishan *China* **58** C6
Bishkek *Kyrgyzstan* **52** E8
Bishnupur *India* **69** H12
Bisho = Bhisho *S. Africa* **89** E4
Bishop *Calif., U.S.A.* **110** H8
Bishop *Tex., U.S.A.* **116** H6
Bishop Auckland *U.K.* **14** C6
Bishop's Falls *Canada* **105** C8
Bishop's Stortford *U.K.* **15** F8
Bisignano *Italy* **43** C9
Bisina, L. *Uganda* **86** B3
Biskra *Algeria* **78** B7
Biskupiec *Poland* **30** E7
Bismarck *U.S.A.* **112** B3
Bismarck Arch. *Papua N. G.* **90** B7
Bismark *Germany* **24** C7
Bismil *Turkey* **73** D9
Biso *Uganda* **86** B3
Bison *U.S.A.* **112** C2
Bīsotūn *Iran* **73** E12
Bispgården *Sweden* **10** A10
Bissagos = Bijagós, Arquipélago dos *Guinea-Biss.* **82** C1
Bissau *Guinea-Biss.* **82** C1
Bissaula *Nigeria* **83** D7
Bissikrima *Guinea* **82** C2
Bissorã *Guinea-Biss.* **82** C1
Bistcho L. *Canada* **102** B5
Bistreţ *Romania* **29** G8
Bistrica = Ilirska-Bistrica *Slovenia* **41** C11
Bistriţa *Romania* **29** C9
Bistriţa → *Romania* **29** D11
Bistriţa Năsăud □ *Romania* **29** C9
Bistriţei, Munţii *Romania* **29** C10
Biswan *India* **69** F9
Bisztynek *Poland* **30** D7
Bitam *Gabon* **84** D2
Bitburg *Germany* **25** F2
Bitche *France* **19** C14
Bitkine *Chad* **79** F9
Bitlis *Turkey* **73** C10
Bitlis □ *Turkey* **73** C10
Bitola *Macedonia* **44** E5
Bitolj = Bitola *Macedonia* **44** E5
Bitonto *Italy* **43** A9
Bitter Creek *U.S.A.* **108** F9
Bitter L. = Buheirat-Murrat-el-Kubra *Egypt* **80** H8
Bitterfeld *Germany* **24** D8
Bitterfontein *S. Africa* **88** E2
Bitterroot → *U.S.A.* **108** C6
Bitterroot Range *U.S.A.* **108** C6
Bitterwater *U.S.A.* **110** J6
Bitti *Italy* **42** B2
Bittou *Burkina Faso* **83** C4
Biu *Nigeria* **83** C7
Bivolari *Romania* **29** C12
Bivolu, Vf. *Romania* **29** C10
Biwa-Ko *Japan* **55** G8
Biwabik *U.S.A.* **112** B7
Bixad *Romania* **29** C8
Bixby *U.S.A.* **116** C6
Biyang *China* **56** H7
Biysk *Russia* **52** D9
Bizana *S. Africa* **89** E4
Bizen *Japan* **55** G7
Bizerte *Tunisia* **79** A7
Bjargtangar *Iceland* **8** D1
Bjärnum *Sweden* **11** H7
Bjästa *Sweden* **10** A12
Bjelasica *Montenegro* **44** D3
Bjelašnica *Bos.-H.* **44** C3
Bjelovar *Croatia* **41** C13
Bjerringbro *Denmark* **11** H3

Björbo *Sweden* **10** D8
Björklinge *Sweden* **10** D11
Björneborg = Pori *Finland* **32** B1
Björneborg *Sweden* **10** E8
Bjørnevatn *Norway* **8** B24
Bjørnøya *Arctic* **4** B8
Bjurås *Sweden* **10** D9
Bjuv *Sweden* **11** H6
Bla *Mali* **82** C3
Blace *Serbia* **44** C5
Blachownia *Poland* **31** H5
Black = Da → *Vietnam* **58** G5
Black → *Canada* **114** B5
Black → *Ariz., U.S.A.* **109** K8
Black → *Ark., U.S.A.* **116** D9
Black → *La., U.S.A.* **116** F9
Black → *Mich., U.S.A.* **114** D2
Black → *N.Y., U.S.A.* **115** C8
Black → *Wis., U.S.A.* **112** C9
Black Bay Pen. *Canada* **104** C2
Black Birch L. *Canada* **103** B7
Black Canyon of the Gunnison △ *U.S.A.* **108** G10
Black Diamond *Canada* **102** C6
Black Duck → *Canada* **104** A2
Black Forest = Schwarzwald *Germany* **25** G4
Black Forest *U.S.A.* **108** G11
Black Hd. *Ireland* **12** C2
Black Hills *U.S.A.* **112** D2
Black I. *Canada* **103** C9
Black L. *Canada* **103** B7
Black L. *Mich., U.S.A.* **113** C11
Black L. *N.Y., U.S.A.* **115** B9
Black Lake *Canada* **103** B7
Black Mesa *U.S.A.* **116** C3
Black Mt. = Mynydd Du *U.K.* **15** F4
Black Mts. *U.K.* **15** F4
Black Range *U.S.A.* **109** K10
Black River *Jamaica* **120** a
Black River Falls *U.S.A.* **112** C8
Black Rock *Barbados* **121** g
Black Sea *Eurasia* **6** G12
Black Tickle *Canada* **105** B8
Black Volta → *Africa* **82** D4
Black Warrior → *U.S.A.* **117** E11
Blackall *Australia* **94** C4
Blackball *N.Z.* **91** E3
Blackbull *Australia* **94** B3
Blackburn *U.K.* **14** D5
Blackburn with Darwen □ *U.K.* **14** D5
Blackdown Tableland △ *Australia* **94** C4
Blackfoot *U.S.A.* **108** E7
Blackfoot → *U.S.A.* **108** C7
Blackfoot Res. *U.S.A.* **108** E8
Blackpool *U.K.* **14** D4
Blackpool □ *U.K.* **14** D4
Blackriver *U.S.A.* **114** B1
Blacks Harbour *Canada* **105** C6
Blacksburg *U.S.A.* **113** G13
Blacksod B. *Ireland* **12** B1
Blackstairs Mt. *Ireland* **12** D5
Blackstone *U.S.A.* **113** G14
Blackstone Ra. *Australia* **93** E4
Blacktown *Australia* **95** E5
Blackwater = West Road → *Canada* **102** C4
Blackwater *Australia* **94** C4
Blackwater → *Meath, Ireland* **12** C4
Blackwater → *Waterford, Ireland* **12** D4
Blackwater → *U.K.* **12** B5
Blackwater → *U.K.* **15** F8
Blackwell *U.S.A.* **116** C6
Blackwells Corner *U.S.A.* **111** K7
Bladensburg △ *Australia* **94** C3
Blaenau Ffestiniog *U.K.* **14** E4
Blaenau Gwent □ *U.K.* **15** F4
Blagaj *Bos.-H.* **44** C1
Blagnac *France* **20** E5
Blagnac, Toulouse ✈ (TLS) *France* **20** E5
Blagodarnoye = Blagodarnyy *Russia* **35** H6
Blagodarnyy *Russia* **35** H6
Blagoevgrad *Bulgaria* **44** D7
Blagoveshchensk *Russia* **53** D13
Blahkiuh *Indonesia* **63** J18
Blain *France* **18** E5
Blain *U.S.A.* **114** F7
Blaine *Minn., U.S.A.* **112** C7
Blaine *Wash., U.S.A.* **110** B4
Blaine Lake *Canada* **103** C7
Blair *U.S.A.* **112** E5
Blair Athol *Australia* **94** C4
Blair Atholl *U.K.* **13** E5
Blairgowrie *U.K.* **13** E5
Blairsden *U.S.A.* **110** F6
Blairsville *U.S.A.* **114** F5
Blaj *Romania* **29** D8
Blakang Mati, Pulau *Singapore* **65** d
Blake Pt. *U.S.A.* **112** A9
Blakely *Ga., U.S.A.* **117** F12
Blakely *Pa., U.S.A.* **115** E9
Blâmont *France* **19** D13

Blanc, C. *Spain* **48** B9
Blanc, Mont *Europe* **21** C10
Blanca, B. *Argentina* **128** D4
Blanca, Cord. *Peru* **124** E3
Blanca Peak *U.S.A.* **109** H11
Blanche, C. *Australia* **95** E1
Blanche, L. *S. Austral., Australia* **95** D2
Blanche, L. *W. Austral., Australia* **92** D3
Blanchisseuse *Trin. & Tob.* **125** K15
Blanco *S. Africa* **88** E3
Blanco *U.S.A.* **116** F5
Blanco → *Argentina* **126** C2
Blanco, C. *Costa Rica* **120** E2
Blanco, C. *U.S.A.* **108** E1
Blanda → *Iceland* **8** D3
Blandford Forum *U.K.* **15** G5
Blanding *U.S.A.* **109** H9
Blanes *Spain* **38** D7
Blangy-sur-Bresle *France* **19** C8
Blankaholm *Sweden* **11** G10
Blankenberge *Belgium* **17** C3
Blankenburg *Germany* **24** D6
Blanquefort *France* **20** D3
Blanquilla *Venezuela* **121** D7
Blanquillo *Uruguay* **127** C4
Blansko *Czech Rep.* **27** B9
Blantyre *Malawi* **87** F4
Blarney *Ireland* **12** E3
Blasdell *U.S.A.* **114** D6
Blaszki *Poland* **31** G5
Blatná *Czech Rep.* **26** B6
Blato *Croatia* **41** F13
Blaubeuren *Germany* **25** G5
Blaustein *Germany* **25** G5
Blåvands Huk *Denmark* **11** J2
Blaydon *U.K.* **14** C6
Blaye *France* **20** C3
Blaye-les-Mines *France* **20** D6
Blayney *Australia* **95** E4
Blaze, Pt. *Australia* **92** B5
Błażowa *Poland* **31** J9
Bleckede *Germany* **24** B6
Bled *Slovenia* **41** B11
Bleiburg *Austria* **26** E7
Blejeşti *Romania* **29** F10
Blekinge *Sweden* **9** H16
Blekinge län □ *Sweden* **11** H9
Blenheim *Canada* **114** D3
Blenheim *N.Z.* **91** D4
Bléone → *France* **21** D10
Blérancourt *France* **19** C10
Bletchley *U.K.* **15** F7
Blida *Algeria* **78** A6
Blidö *Sweden* **10** E12
Blidsberg *Sweden* **11** G7
Blieskastel *Germany* **25** F3
Bligh Sound *N.Z.* **91** F1
Bligh Water *Fiji* **91** a
Blind River *Canada* **104** C3
Blinisht *Albania* **44** E3
Bliss *Idaho, U.S.A.* **108** E6
Bliss *N.Y., U.S.A.* **114** D6
Blissfield *U.S.A.* **114** F3
Blitar *Indonesia* **63** H15
Blitta *Togo* **83** D5
Block I. *U.S.A.* **115** E13
Block Island Sd. *U.S.A.* **115** E13
Bloemfontein *S. Africa* **88** D4
Bloemhof *S. Africa* **88** D4
Blois *France* **18** E8
Blomskog *Sweden* **10** E6
Blomstermåla *Sweden* **11** H10
Blönduós *Iceland* **8** D3
Blongas *Indonesia* **63** K19
Blonie *Poland* **31** F7
Bloodvein → *Canada* **103** C9
Bloody Foreland *Ireland* **12** A3
Bloomer *U.S.A.* **112** C8
Bloomfield *Canada* **114** C7
Bloomfield *Iowa, U.S.A.* **112** E7
Bloomfield *N. Mex., U.S.A.* **109** H10
Bloomfield *Nebr., U.S.A.* **112** D5
Bloomington *Ill., U.S.A.* **112** E9
Bloomington *Ind., U.S.A.* **112** F10
Bloomington *Minn., U.S.A.* **112** C7
Bloomsburg *U.S.A.* **115** F8
Bloomsbury *Australia* **94** J6
Blora *Indonesia* **63** G14
Blossburg *U.S.A.* **114** E7
Blouberg *S. Africa* **89** C4
Blountstown *U.S.A.* **117** F12
Bludenz *Austria* **26** D2
Blue Earth *U.S.A.* **112** D6
Blue Hole △ *Belize* **120** C2
Blue Lagoon △ *Zambia* **87** F2
Blue Mesa Res. *U.S.A.* **108** G10
Blue Mountain Lake *U.S.A.* **115** C10
Blue Mountain Pk. *Jamaica* **120** a
Blue Mt. *U.S.A.* **115** F8
Blue Mts. *Jamaica* **120** a
Blue Mts. *Maine, U.S.A.* **115** B14
Blue Mts. *Oreg., U.S.A.* **108** D4
Blue Mud B. *Australia* **94** A2

Blue Nile = Nîl el Azraq → *Sudan* **81** D3
Blue Nile Falls *Ethiopia* **81** E4
Blue Rapids *U.S.A.* **112** F5
Blue Ridge *U.S.A.* **113** G13
Blue River *Canada* **102** C5
Bluefield *U.S.A.* **113** G13
Bluefields *Nic.* **120** D3
Bluff *Australia* **94** C4
Bluff *N.Z.* **91** G2
Bluff *U.S.A.* **109** H9
Bluff Knoll *Australia* **93** F2
Bluff Pt. *Australia* **93** E1
Bluffton *U.S.A.* **113** E11
Blumenau *Brazil* **127** B6
Blunt *U.S.A.* **112** C4
Bly *U.S.A.* **108** E3
Blyde River Canyon △ *S. Africa* **89** C5
Blyth *Canada* **114** C3
Blyth *U.K.* **14** B6
Blythe *U.S.A.* **111** M12
Blytheville *U.S.A.* **117** D10
Bo *S. Leone* **82** D2
Bo Duc *Vietnam* **65** G6
Bo Hai *China* **57** E10
Bo Xian = Bozhou *China* **56** H8
Boa Vista *Brazil* **124** C6
Boa Vista *C. Verde Is.* **78** b
Boac *Phil.* **61** E4
Boaco *Nic.* **120** D2
Bo'ai *China* **56** G7
Boal *Spain* **36** B4
Boalsburg *U.S.A.* **114** F7
Boane *Mozam.* **89** D5
Boardman *U.S.A.* **114** E4
Bobadah *Australia* **95** E4
Bobai *China* **58** F7
Bobbili *India* **67** K13
Bóbbio *Italy* **40** D6
Bobcaygeon *Canada* **114** B6
Böblingen *Germany* **25** G5
Bobo-Dioulasso *Burkina Faso* **82** C4
Bobolice *Poland* **30** E3
Boboshevo *Bulgaria* **44** D7
Bobov Dol *Bulgaria* **44** D6
Bóbr → *Poland* **31** F2
Bobraomby, Tanjon' i *Madag.* **89** A8
Bobrinets *Ukraine* **33** H7
Bobrov *Russia* **34** E5
Bobrovitsa *Ukraine* **33** G6
Bobruysk = Babruysk *Belarus* **23** B15
Boby, Pic *Madag.* **85** J9
Boca de Drago *Venezuela* **125** K15
Boca del Río *Mexico* **119** D5
Bôca do Acre *Brazil* **124** E5
Boca Raton *U.S.A.* **117** H14
Bocanda *Ivory C.* **82** D4
Bocas del Toro *Panama* **120** E3
Boceguillas *Spain* **36** D7
Bochmanivka *Ukraine* **29** C14
Bochnia *Poland* **31** J7
Bocholt *Germany* **24** D2
Bochum *Germany* **24** D3
Bockenem *Germany* **24** C6
Bocognano *France* **21** F13
Bocoyna *Mexico* **118** B3
Bocşa *Romania* **28** E6
Boda *Central Africa* **84** D3
Boda *Västernorrland, Sweden* **10** B10
Bodafors *Sweden* **11** G8
Bodaybo *Russia* **53** D12
Boddam *U.K.* **13** B7
Boddington *Australia* **93** F2
Bode Sadu *Nigeria* **83** D5
Bodega Bay *U.S.A.* **110** G3
Boden *Sweden* **8** D19
Bodenteich *Germany* **24** C6
Bodensee *Europe* **25** H5
Bodhan *India* **66** K10
Bodinga *Nigeria* **83** C6
Bodmin *U.K.* **15** G3
Bodmin Moor *U.K.* **15** G3
Bodø *Norway* **8** C16
Bodrog → *Hungary* **28** B6
Bodrum *Turkey* **47** D9
Bódva → *Hungary* **28** B5
Boën *France* **21** C8
Boende *Dem. Rep. of the Congo* **84** E4
Boerne *U.S.A.* **116** G5
Boesmans → *S. Africa* **88** E4
Boffa *Guinea* **82** C2
Bogalusa *U.S.A.* **117** F10
Bogan → *Australia* **95** D4
Bogan Gate *Australia* **95** E4
Bogandé *Burkina Faso* **83** C4
Bogantungan *Australia* **94** C4
Bogata *U.S.A.* **116** E7
Bogatić *Serbia* **44** B3
Boğazkale *Turkey* **72** B6
Boğazlıyan *Turkey* **72** C6
Bogen *Sweden* **10** D6
Bogense *Denmark* **11** J4
Bogetići *Montenegro* **44** D2

Boggabilla *Australia* **95** D5
Boggabri *Australia* **95** E5
Boglan = Solhan *Turkey* **73** C9
Bognor Regis *U.K.* **15** G7
Bogo *Phil.* **61** F6
Bogodukhov = Bohodukhiv *Ukraine* **33** G8
Bogol Manya *Ethiopia* **81** G5
Bogong, Mt. *Australia* **95** F4
Bogor *Indonesia* **63** G12
Bogoroditsk *Russia* **32** F10
Bogorodsk *Russia* **34** B6
Bogoso *Ghana* **82** D4
Bogotá *Colombia* **124** C4
Bogotol *Russia* **52** D9
Bogou *Togo* **83** C5
Bogra *Bangla.* **67** G16
Boguchany *Russia* **53** D10
Boguchar *Russia* **34** F5
Bogué *Mauritania* **82** B2
Boguslav *Ukraine* **33** H6
Boguszów-Gorce *Poland* **31** H3
Bohain-en-Vermandois *France* **19** C10
Bohdan *Ukraine* **29** B9
Bohemian Forest = Böhmerwald *Germany* **25** F9
Bohinjska Bistrica *Slovenia* **41** B11
Böhmerwald *Germany* **25** F9
Bohmte *Germany* **24** C4
Bohodukhiv *Ukraine* **33** G8
Bohol □ *Phil.* **61** G6
Bohol Sea *Phil.* **63** C6
Bohongou *Burkina Faso* **83** C5
Böhönye *Hungary* **28** D2
Bohorodchany *Ukraine* **29** B9
Bohuslän *Sweden* **11** F5
Boi *Nigeria* **83** D6
Boi, Pta. de *Brazil* **127** A6
Boiaçu *Brazil* **124** D6
Boileau, C. *Australia* **92** C3
Boing'o *Sudan* **81** F3
Boiro *Spain* **36** C2
Boise *U.S.A.* **108** E5
Boise City *U.S.A.* **116** C3
Boissevain *Canada* **103** D8
Bóite → *Italy* **41** B9
Boitzenburg *Germany* **24** B9
Boizenburg *Germany* **24** B6
Bojador, C. *W. Sahara* **78** C3
Bojana → *Albania* **44** E3
Bojano *Italy* **43** A7
Bojanowo *Poland* **31** G3
Bojden *Denmark* **11** J4
Bojnūrd *Iran* **71** B8
Bojonegoro *Indonesia* **63** G14
Boju *Nigeria* **83** D6
Boka *Serbia* **28** E5
Boka Kotorska *Montenegro* **44** D2
Bokala *Ivory C.* **82** D4
Bokani *Nigeria* **83** D6
Bokaro *India* **69** H11
Boké *Guinea* **82** C2
Bokhara → *Australia* **95** D4
Bokkos *Nigeria* **83** D6
Boknafjorden *Norway* **9** G11
Bokoro △ *Uganda* **86** B3
Bokoro *Chad* **79** F9
Bokpyin *Burma* **65** G2
Boksitogorsk *Russia* **32** C7
Bokungu *Dem. Rep. of the Congo* **84** E4
Bol *Croatia* **41** E13
Bolama *Guinea-Biss.* **82** C1
Bolan → *Pakistan* **68** E2
Bolan Pass *Pakistan* **66** E5
Bolaños → *Mexico* **118** C4
Bolaños de Calatrava *Spain* **37** G7
Bolayır *Turkey* **45** F10
Bolbec *France* **18** C7
Boldājī *Iran* **71** D6
Boldeşti-Scăeni *Romania* **29** E11
Bole *China* **60** B3
Bole *Ethiopia* **81** F4
Bole *Ghana* **82** D4
Bolekhiv *Ukraine* **23** D12
Bolesławiec *Poland* **31** G2
Bolgatanga *Ghana* **83** C4
Bolgrad = Bolhrad *Ukraine* **29** E13
Bolhrad *Ukraine* **29** E13
Bolinao *Phil.* **61** C3
Bolintin-Vale *Romania* **29** F10
Bolívar *Argentina* **126** D3
Bolivar *Mo., U.S.A.* **112** G7
Bolivar *N.Y., U.S.A.* **114** D6
Bolivar *Tenn., U.S.A.* **117** D10
Bolivia ■ *S. Amer.* **124** G6
Bolivian Plateau = Altiplano *Bolivia* **124** G5
Boljevac *Serbia* **44** C5
Bolkhov *Russia* **32** F9
Bolków *Poland* **31** H3
Bollebygd *Sweden* **11** G6
Bollène *France* **21** D8
Bollnäs *Sweden* **10** C10
Bollon *Australia* **95** D4
Bollstabruk *Sweden* **10** B11

Bolmen Sweden 11 H7
Bolobo Dem. Rep. of the Congo 84 E3
Bologna Italy 41 D8
Bologna ✕ (BLQ) Italy 41 D8
Bologoye Russia 32 D8
Bolomba Dem. Rep. of the Congo 84 D3
Bolon, Ozero Russia 60 B8
Bolonchén Mexico 119 D7
Bolótana Italy 42 B1
Boloven, Cao Nguyen Laos 64 E6
Bolpur India 69 H12
Bolsena Italy 41 F8
Bolsena, L. di Italy 41 F8
Bolshakovo Russia 30 D8
Bolshaya Chernigovka Russia 34 D10
Bolshaya Glushitsa Russia 34 D10
Bolshaya Martynovka Russia 35 G5
Bolshaya Vradiyevka Ukraine 33 J6
Bolshevik, Ostrov Russia 53 B11
Bolshoy Anyuy → Russia 53 C17
Bolshoy Begichev, Ostrov Russia 53 B12
Bolshoy Kavkas = Caucasus Mountains Eurasia 35 J7
Bolshoy Lyakhovskiy, Ostrov Russia 53 B15
Bolshoy Tyuters, Ostrov Russia 32 C4
Bolsward Neths. 17 A5
Bolt Head U.K. 15 G4
Boltaña Spain 38 C5
Boltigen Switz. 25 J3
Bolton Canada 114 C5
Bolton U.K. 14 D5
Bolton Landing U.S.A. 115 C11
Bolu Turkey 72 B4
Bolu □ Turkey 72 B4
Bolungavík Iceland 8 C2
Boluo China 59 F10
Bolvadin Turkey 72 C4
Bolzano Italy 41 B8
Bom Jesus da Lapa Brazil 125 F10
Boma Dem. Rep. of the Congo 84 F2
Bombala Australia 95 F4
Bombarral Portugal 37 F1
Bombay = Mumbai India 66 K8
Bombedor, Pta. Venezuela 125 L15
Bomboma Dem. Rep. of the Congo 84 D3
Bombombwa Dem. Rep. of the Congo 86 B2
Bomi Hills Liberia 82 D2
Bomili Dem. Rep. of the Congo 86 B2
Bømlo Norway 9 G11
Bomokandi → Dem. Rep. of the Congo 86 B2
Bomu → C.A.R. 84 D4
Bon, C. Tunisia 76 C5
Bon Acceuil Mauritius 85 d
Bon Sar Pa Vietnam 64 F6
Bonāb Iran 73 D12
Bonaigarh India 69 J11
Bonaire Neth. Ant. 121 D6
Bonampak Mexico 119 D6
Bonang Australia 95 F4
Bonanza Nic. 120 D3
Bonaparte Arch. Australia 92 B3
Boñar Spain 36 C5
Bonar Bridge U.K. 13 D4
Bonasse Trin. & Tob. 125 K15
Bonaventure Canada 105 C6
Bonavista Canada 105 C9
Bonavista, C. Canada 105 C9
Bonavista B. Canada 105 C9
Bondeno Italy 41 D8
Bondo Dem. Rep. of the Congo 86 B1
Bondoukou Ivory C. 82 D4
Bondowoso Indonesia 63 G15
Bone, Teluk Indonesia 63 E6
Bonerate Indonesia 63 F6
Bonerate, Kepulauan Indonesia 63 F6
Bo'ness U.K. 13 E5
Bonete, Cerro Argentina 126 B2
Bong Son = Hoai Nhon Vietnam 64 E7
Bonga Ethiopia 81 F4
Bongabong Phil. 61 E4
Bongandanga Dem. Rep. of the Congo 84 D4
Bongor Chad 79 F9
Bongos, Massif des C.A.R. 84 C4
Bongouanou Ivory C. 82 D4
Bonham U.S.A. 116 E6
Boni Mali 82 B4
Boni △ Kenya 86 C5
Bonifacio France 21 G13
Bonifacio, Bouches de Medit. S. 21 G13
Bonin Is. = Ogasawara Gunto Pac. Oc. 96 E6
Bonke Ethiopia 81 F4
Bonkoukou Niger 83 C5

Bonn Germany 24 E3
Bonnat France 19 F8
Bonne Terre U.S.A. 112 G8
Bonners Ferry U.S.A. 108 B5
Bonnétable France 18 D7
Bonneval France 19 D8
Bonneval-sur-Arc France 21 C11
Bonneville France 19 F13
Bonney, L. Australia 95 F3
Bonnie Rock Australia 93 F2
Bonny Nigeria 83 E6
Bonny, Bight of Africa 83 E6
Bonny-sur-Loire France 19 E9
Bonnyrigg U.K. 13 F5
Bonnyville Canada 103 C6
Bono Italy 42 B2
Bonoi Indonesia 63 E9
Bonorva Italy 42 B1
Bonsall U.S.A. 111 M9
Bontang Indonesia 62 D5
Bontebok △ S. Africa 88 E3
Bonthe S. Leone 82 D2
Bontoc Phil. 61 C4
Bonyeri Ghana 82 D4
Bonyhád Hungary 28 D3
Bonython Ra. Australia 92 D4
Bookabie Australia 93 F5
Booker U.S.A. 116 C4
Boola Guinea 82 D3
Booligal Australia 95 E3
Boonah Australia 95 D5
Boone Iowa, U.S.A. 112 D7
Boone N.C., U.S.A. 117 G14
Booneville Ark., U.S.A. 116 D8
Booneville Miss., U.S.A. 117 D10
Boonville Calif., U.S.A. 110 F3
Boonville Ind., U.S.A. 112 F10
Boonville Mo., U.S.A. 112 F7
Boonville N.Y., U.S.A. 115 C9
Boorabbin △ Australia 93 F3
Boorindal Australia 95 E4
Boorowa Australia 95 E4
Boosaaso = Bosaso Somali Rep. 75 E4
Boothia, Gulf of Canada 101 B11
Boothia Pen. Canada 100 B10
Bootle U.K. 14 D4
Booué Gabon 84 E2
Boppard Germany 25 E3
Boquete Panama 120 E3
Boquilla, Presa de la Mexico 118 B3
Boquillas del Carmen Mexico 118 B4
Bor Czech Rep. 26 B5
Bor Russia 34 B7
Bor Serbia 44 B6
Bôr Sudan 81 F3
Bor Sweden 11 G8
Bor Turkey 72 D6
Bor Mashash Israel 74 D3
Bora Bora French Polynesia 97 J12
Borah Peak U.S.A. 108 D7
Borang Sudan 81 G3
Borås Sweden 11 G6
Borāzjān Iran 71 D6
Borba Brazil 124 D7
Borba Portugal 37 G3
Borborema, Planalto da Brazil 122 D7
Borcea Romania 29 F12
Borça Turkey 73 B9
Bord Khūn-e Now Iran 71 D6
Borda, C. Australia 95 F2
Bordeaux France 20 D3
Bordeaux ✕ (BOD) France 20 D3
Borden Australia 93 F2
Borden-Carleton Canada 105 C7
Borden I. Canada 101 B8
Borden Pen. Canada 101 B11
Border Ranges △ Australia 95 D5
Borders = Scottish Borders □ U.K. 13 F6
Bordertown Australia 95 F3
Borðeyri Iceland 8 D3
Bordighera Italy 40 E4
Bordj Fly Ste. Marie Algeria 78 C5
Bordj-in-Eker Algeria 78 D7
Bordj Omar Driss Algeria 78 C7
Bore Ethiopia 81 G4
Borehamwood U.K. 15 F7
Borek Wielkopolski Poland 31 G4
Borensberg Sweden 11 F9
Borgå = Porvoo Finland 32 B3
Borgarfjörður Iceland 8 D7
Borgarnes Iceland 8 D3
Børgefjellet Norway 8 D15
Borger Neths. 17 B6
Borger U.S.A. 116 D4
Borgholm Sweden 11 H10
Bórgia Italy 43 D9
Borgo San Dalmazzo Italy 40 D4
Borgo San Lorenzo Italy 41 E8
Borgo Val di Taro Italy 40 D6
Borgo Valsugana Italy 41 B8
Borgomanero Italy 40 C5
Borgorose Italy 41 F10
Borgosésia Italy 40 C5

Borhoyn Tal Mongolia 56 C6
Bori Nigeria 83 E6
Borikhane Laos 64 C4
Borisoglebsk Russia 34 E6
Borisovka Russia 33 G9
Borja Peru 124 D3
Borja Spain 38 D3
Borjas Blancas = Les Borges Blanques Spain 38 D5
Borjomi Georgia 35 K6
Børkop Denmark 11 J3
Borkou Chad 79 E9
Borkum Germany 24 B2
Borlänge Sweden 10 D9
Borley, C. Antarctica 5 C5
Borlu Turkey 47 C10
Bormida → Italy 40 D5
Bórmio Italy 40 B7
Borna Germany 24 D8
Borne Sulinowo Poland 30 E3
Borneo E. Indies 62 D5
Bornholm Denmark 11 J8
Bornholmsgattet Europe 11 J8
Borno □ Nigeria 83 C7
Bornos Spain 37 J5
Bornova Turkey 47 C9
Bornu Yassa Nigeria 83 C7
Boro → Sudan 81 F2
Borodino Russia 32 E8
Borodino Ukraine 29 D14
Borogontsy Russia 53 C14
Boromo Burkina Faso 82 C4
Boron U.S.A. 111 L9
Borongan Phil. 61 F6
Borotangba Mts. C.A.R. 81 F2
Borotou Ivory C. 82 D3
Borovan Bulgaria 44 C7
Borovichi Russia 32 C7
Borovsk Russia 32 E9
Borrby Sweden 11 J8
Borrego Springs U.S.A. 111 M10
Borriol Spain 38 E4
Borrisokane Ireland 12 D3
Borroloola Australia 94 B2
Borşa Cluj, Romania 29 D8
Borşa Maramureş, Romania 29 C9
Borsad India 68 H5
Borsec Romania 29 D10
Borshchiv Ukraine 29 B11
Borsod-Abaúj-Zemplén □ Hungary 28 B6
Bort-les-Orgues France 20 C6
Borth U.K. 15 E3
Börtnan Sweden 10 B7
Borūjerd Iran 73 E13
Boryeong S. Korea 57 F14
Borynya Ukraine 31 J10
Boryslav Ukraine 33 G7
Boryspil Ukraine 33 G6
Borzhomi = Borjomi Georgia 35 K6
Borzna Ukraine 33 G7
Borzya Russia 53 D12
Bosa Italy 42 B1
Bosanska Dubica Bos.-H. 41 C13
Bosanska Gradiška Bos.-H. 28 E2
Bosanska Kostajnica Bos.-H. 41 C13
Bosanska Krupa Bos.-H. 41 D13
Bosanski Brod Bos.-H. 28 E2
Bosanski Novi Bos.-H. 41 C13
Bosanski Petrovac Bos.-H. 41 D13
Bosanski Šamac Bos.-H. 28 E3
Bosansko Grahovo Bos.-H. 41 D13
Bosaso Somali Rep. 75 E4
Boscastle U.K. 15 G3
Boscobelle Barbados 121 g
Bose China 58 F6
Boseong S. Korea 57 G14
Boshan China 57 F9
Boshof S. Africa 88 D4
Boshrūyeh Iran 71 C8
Bosilegrad Serbia 44 D6
Boskovice Czech Rep. 27 B9
Bosna → Bos.-H. 28 E3
Bosna i Hercegovina = Bosnia-Herzegovina ■ Europe 28 G2
Bosnia-Herzegovina ■ Europe 28 G2
Bosnik Indonesia 63 E9
Bosobolo Dem. Rep. of the Congo 84 D3
Bosporus = İstanbul Boğazı Turkey 45 E13
Bosque Farms U.S.A. 109 J10
Bossangoa C.A.R. 84 C3
Bossé Bangou Niger 83 C5
Bossier City U.S.A. 116 E8
Bosso Niger 83 C7
Bosso, Dallol → Niger 83 C5
Bostan Pakistan 68 D2
Bostānābād Iran 73 D12
Bosten Hu China 60 B3
Boston U.K. 14 E7
Boston U.S.A. 115 D13
Boston Bar Canada 102 D4
Boston Mts. U.S.A. 116 D8

Bosumtwi, L. Ghana 83 D4
Bosut → Croatia 28 E3
Boswell Canada 102 D5
Boswell U.S.A. 114 F5
Botad India 68 H4
Botan → Turkey 73 D10
Botany B. Australia 90 E8
Botene Laos 64 C3
Botev Bulgaria 45 D8
Botevgrad Bulgaria 44 D7
Bothaville S. Africa 88 D4
Bothnia, G. of Europe 8 F19
Bothwell Australia 95 G4
Bothwell Canada 114 D3
Boticas Portugal 36 D3
Botletle → Botswana 88 C3
Botlikh Russia 35 J8
Botna → Moldova 29 D14
Botoroaga Romania 29 F10
Botoşani Romania 29 C11
Botoşani □ Romania 29 C11
Botou Burkina Faso 83 C5
Botricello Italy 43 D9
Botro Ivory C. 82 D3
Botshabelo S. Africa 85 K5
Botswana ■ Africa 88 C3
Bottineau U.S.A. 112 A3
Bottnaryd Sweden 11 G7
Bottrop Germany 17 C6
Botucatu Brazil 127 A6
Botwood Canada 105 C8
Bou Djébéha Mali 82 B4
Boû Rjeïmât Mauritania 82 B1
Bou Saâda Algeria 78 A6
Bouaflé Ivory C. 82 D3
Bouaké Ivory C. 82 D3
Bouar C.A.R. 84 C3
Bouârfa Morocco 78 B5
Boucaut B. Australia 94 A1
Bouches-du-Rhône □ France 21 E9
Boucle de Baoulé △ Mali 82 C3
Boucles de la Seine Normande ◠ France 18 C7
Bouctouche Canada 105 C7
Bougainville, C. Australia 92 B4
Bougainville I. Papua N. G. 90 B8
Bougainville Reef Australia 94 B4
Bougie = Bejaïa Algeria 78 A7
Bougouni Mali 82 C3
Bouillon Belgium 17 E5
Boukombé Benin 83 C5
Boulal Mali 82 B3
Boulazac France 20 C4
Boulder Colo., U.S.A. 108 F11
Boulder Mont., U.S.A. 108 C7
Boulder City U.S.A. 111 K12
Boulder Creek U.S.A. 110 H4
Boulder Dam = Hoover Dam U.S.A. 111 K12
Bouli Mauritania 82 B2
Boulia Australia 94 C2
Bouligny France 19 C12
Boulogne → France 18 E5
Boulogne-sur-Gesse France 20 E4
Boulogne-sur-Mer France 19 B8
Bouloire France 18 E7
Boulouli Mali 82 B3
Boulsa Burkina Faso 83 C4
Boultoum Niger 83 C7
Bouma △ Fiji 91 a
Boûmdeïd Mauritania 82 B2
Boun Neua Laos 64 B3
Boun Tai Laos 64 B3
Bouna Ivory C. 82 D4
Boundary Peak U.S.A. 110 H8
Boundiali Ivory C. 82 D3
Bountiful U.S.A. 108 F8
Bounty Is. Pac. Oc. 96 M9
Bounty Trough Pac. Oc. 96 M9
Boura Mali 82 C4
Bourbon-Lancy France 19 F10
Bourbon-l'Archambault France 19 F10
Bourbonnais France 19 F10
Bourbonne-les-Bains France 19 E12
Bourbourg France 19 B9
Bourdel L. Canada 104 A5
Bourem Mali 83 B4
Bourg France 20 C3
Bourg-Argental France 21 C8
Bourg-de-Péage France 21 C9
Bourg-en-Bresse France 19 F12
Bourg-Lastic France 20 C6
Bourg-Madame France 20 F5
Bourg-St-Andéol France 21 D8
Bourg-St-Maurice France 21 C10
Bourganeuf France 20 C5
Bourgas = Burgas Bulgaria 45 D11
Bourges France 19 E9
Bourget Canada 115 A9
Bourget, Lac du France 21 C9
Bourgneuf, B. de France 18 E4
Bourgneuf-en-Retz France 18 E5
Bourgogne France 19 F11
Bourgoin-Jallieu France 21 C9
Bourgueil France 18 E7
Bourke Australia 95 E4

Bourne U.K. 14 E7
Bournemouth U.K. 15 G6
Bournemouth □ U.K. 15 G6
Bouroum Burkina Faso 83 C4
Bouse U.S.A. 111 M13
Boussac France 19 F9
Boussé Burkina Faso 83 C4
Bousso Chad 79 F9
Boussouma Burkina Faso 83 C4
Boutilimit Mauritania 82 B2
Boutonne → France 20 C3
Bouvet I. = Bouvetøya Antarctica 2 G10
Bouvetøya Antarctica 2 G10
Bouxwiller France 19 D14
Bouza Niger 83 C6
Bouzonville France 19 C13
Bova Marina Italy 43 E8
Bovalino Marina Italy 43 D9
Bovec Slovenia 41 B10
Bovill U.S.A. 108 C5
Bovino Italy 43 A8
Bovril Argentina 126 C4
Bow → Canada 102 C6
Bow Island Canada 108 B8
Bowbells U.S.A. 112 A3
Bowdle U.S.A. 112 C4
Bowelling Australia 93 F2
Bowen Argentina 126 D2
Bowen Australia 94 b4
Bowen Mts. Australia 95 F4
Bowers Basin Pac. Oc. 4 D16
Bowers Ridge Pac. Oc. 4 D17
Bowie Ariz., U.S.A. 109 K9
Bowie Tex., U.S.A. 116 E6
Bowland, Forest of U.K. 14 D5
Bowling Green Ky., U.S.A. 112 G10
Bowling Green Ohio, U.S.A. 113 E12
Bowling Green, C. Australia 94 B4
Bowling Green Bay △ Australia 94 B4
Bowman U.S.A. 112 B2
Bowman I. Antarctica 5 C8
Bowmanville = Clarington Canada 114 C6
Bowmore U.K. 13 F2
Bowral Australia 95 E5
Bowraville Australia 95 E5
Bowron → Canada 102 C4
Bowron Lake △ Canada 102 C4
Bowser L. Canada 102 B3
Bowsman Canada 103 C8
Bowwood Zambia 87 F2
Box Cr. → Australia 95 E3
Boxholm Sweden 11 F9
Boxmeer Neths. 17 C5
Boxtel Neths. 17 C5
Boyabat Turkey 72 B6
Boyalıca Turkey 45 F13
Boyang China 59 C11
Boyany Ukraine 29 B11
Boyce U.S.A. 116 F8
Boyd L. Canada 104 B4
Boyle Canada 102 C6
Boyle Ireland 12 C3
Boyne → Ireland 12 C5
Boyne City U.S.A. 113 C11
Boynitsa Bulgaria 44 C6
Boynton Beach U.S.A. 117 H14
Boyolali Indonesia 63 G14
Boyoma, Chutes Dem. Rep. of the Congo 86 B2
Boysen Res. U.S.A. 108 E9
Boyuibe Bolivia 124 G6
Boyup Brook Australia 93 F2
Boz Burun Turkey 45 F12
Boz Dağ Turkey 47 D11
Boz Dağları Turkey 47 C10
Bozburun Turkey 47 E11
Bozcaada Turkey 72 C2
Bozdoğan Turkey 47 D10
Bozeman U.S.A. 108 D8
Bozen = Bolzano Italy 41 B8
Bozhou China 56 H8
Bozkir Turkey 72 D5
Bozkurt Turkey 47 D11
Bozouls France 20 D6
Bozoum C.A.R. 84 C3
Bozova Antalya, Turkey 47 D12
Bozova Sanlıurfa, Turkey 73 D8
Bozovici Romania 28 F7
Bozüyük Turkey 47 B12
Bra Italy 40 D4
Braås Sweden 11 G9
Brabant □ Belgium 17 D4
Brabant L. Canada 103 B8
Brač Croatia 41 E13
Bracadale, L. U.K. 13 D2
Bracciano Italy 41 F9
Bracciano, L. di Italy 41 F9
Bracebridge Canada 114 A5
Bracieux France 18 E8
Bräcke Sweden 10 B9
Brackettville U.S.A. 116 G4
Brački Kanal Croatia 41 E13

Bracknell U.K. 15 F7
Bracknell Forest □ U.K. 15 F7
Brad Romania 28 D7
Brádano → Italy 43 B9
Bradenton U.S.A. 117 H13
Bradford Canada 114 B5
Bradford U.K. 14 D6
Bradford Pa., U.S.A. 114 E6
Bradford Vt., U.S.A. 115 C12
Bradley Ark., U.S.A. 116 E8
Bradley Calif., U.S.A. 110 K6
Bradley Institute Zimbabwe 87 F3
Brady U.S.A. 116 F5
Brædstrup Denmark 11 J3
Braeside Canada 115 A8
Braga Portugal 36 D2
Braga □ Portugal 36 D2
Bragadiru Romania 29 G10
Bragado Argentina 126 D3
Bragança Brazil 125 D9
Bragança Portugal 36 D4
Bragança □ Portugal 36 D4
Bragança Paulista Brazil 127 A6
Brahestad = Raahe Finland 8 D21
Brahmanbaria Bangla. 67 H17
Brahmani → India 67 J15
Brahmapur India 67 K14
Brahmaputra → Asia 69 H13
Braich-y-pwll U.K. 14 E3
Braidwood Australia 95 F4
Brăila Romania 29 E12
Brăila □ Romania 29 E12
Brainerd U.S.A. 112 B6
Braintree U.K. 15 F8
Braintree U.S.A. 115 D14
Brak → S. Africa 88 D3
Brake Germany 24 B4
Brakel Germany 24 D5
Brakna □ Mauritania 82 B2
Bräkne-Hoby Sweden 11 H9
Brakwater Namibia 88 C2
Brålanda Sweden 11 F6
Bramberg Germany 25 E6
Bramdrupdam Denmark 11 J3
Bramming Denmark 11 J2
Brämön Sweden 10 B11
Brampton Canada 114 C5
Brampton U.K. 14 C5
Bramsche Germany 24 C3
Bramton I. Australia 94 J7
Branco → Brazil 124 D6
Brandberg Namibia 88 C1
Brandenburg = Neubrandenburg Germany 24 B9
Brandenburg Germany 24 C8
Brandenburg □ Germany 24 C9
Brandfort S. Africa 88 D4
Brando France 21 F13
Brandon Canada 103 D9
Brandon U.S.A. 115 C11
Brandon B. Ireland 12 D1
Brandon Mt. Ireland 12 D1
Brandsen Argentina 126 D4
Brandvlei S. Africa 88 E3
Brandýs nad Labem Czech Rep. 26 A7
Brănești Romania 29 F11
Branford U.S.A. 115 E12
Braniewo Poland 30 D6
Bransfield Str. Antarctica 5 C18
Brańsk Poland 31 F9
Branson U.S.A. 112 G7
Brantford Canada 114 C4
Brantôme France 20 C4
Branzi Italy 40 B6
Bras d'Or L. Canada 105 C7
Brasher Falls U.S.A. 115 B10
Brasil = Brazil ■ S. Amer. 125 F9
Brasil, Planalto Brazil 122 E6
Brasiléia Brazil 124 F5
Brasília Brazil 125 G9
Brasília Legal Brazil 125 D7
Braslaw Belarus 32 E4
Braslovče Slovenia 41 B12
Braşov Romania 29 E10
Braşov □ Romania 29 E10
Brass Nigeria 83 E6
Brass → Nigeria 83 E6
Brassac-les-Mines France 20 C7
Brasschaat Belgium 17 C4
Brassey, Banjaran Malaysia 62 D5
Brassey Ra. Australia 93 E3
Brasstown Bald U.S.A. 117 D13
Brastad Sweden 11 F5
Bratan = Morozov Bulgaria 45 D9
Brateş Romania 29 E11
Bratislava Slovak Rep. 27 C10
Bratislava M.R. Štefánik ✕ (BTS) Slovak Rep. 27 C10
Bratislavský □ Slovak Rep. 27 C10
Bratsigovo Bulgaria 45 D8
Bratsk Russia 53 D11
Brattleboro U.S.A. 115 D12
Bratunac Bos.-H. 28 F4

Braunau *Austria* **26** C6
Braunschweig *Germany* **24** C6
Braunton *U.K.* **15** F3
Brava *C. Verde Is.* **78** b
Bravicea *Moldova* **29** C13
Bráviken *Sweden* **11** F10
Bravo del Norte, Rio =
 Grande, Rio → *N. Amer.* **116** J6
Brawley *U.S.A.* **111** N11
Bray *Ireland* **12** C5
Bray, Mt. *Australia* **94** A1
Bray-sur-Seine *France* **19** D10
Brazeau → *Canada* **102** C5
Brazil *U.S.A.* **112** F10
Brazil ■ *S. Amer.* **125** F9
Brazilian Highlands =
 Brasil, Planalto *Brazil* **122** E6
Brazo Sur → *S. Amer.* **126** B4
Brazos → *U.S.A.* **116** G7
Brazzaville *Congo* **84** E3
Brčko *Bos.-H.* **28** F3
Brda → *Poland* **31** E5
Brdy *Czech Rep.* **26** B6
Breaden, L. *Australia* **93** E4
Breaksea Sd. *N.Z.* **91** F1
Bream B. *N.Z.* **91** A5
Bream Hd. *N.Z.* **91** A5
Breas *Chile* **126** B1
Breaza *Romania* **29** E10
Brebes *Indonesia* **63** G13
Brechin *Canada* **114** B5
Brechin *U.K.* **13** E6
Brecht *Belgium* **17** C4
Breckenridge *Colo., U.S.A.* **108** G10
Breckenridge *Minn., U.S.A.* **112** B5
Breckenridge *Tex., U.S.A.* **116** E5
Breckland *U.K.* **15** E8
Břeclav *Czech Rep.* **27** C9
Brecon *U.K.* **15** F4
Brecon Beacons *U.K.* **15** F4
Brecon Beacons △ *U.K.* **15** F4
Breda *Neths.* **17** C4
Bredaryd *Sweden* **11** G7
Bredasdorp *S. Africa* **88** E3
Bredebro *Denmark* **11** J2
Bredstedt *Germany* **24** A4
Bree *Belgium* **17** C5
Bregalnica → *Macedonia* **44** E6
Bregenz *Austria* **26** D2
Bregovo *Bulgaria* **44** B6
Bréhal *France* **18** D5
Bréhat, Î. de *France* **18** D4
Breiðafjörður *Iceland* **8** D2
Breil-sur-Roya *France* **21** E11
Breisach *Germany* **25** G3
Brejo *Brazil* **125** D10
Bremen *Germany* **24** B4
Bremen □ *Germany* **24** B4
Bremer Bay *Australia* **93** F2
Bremer I. *Australia* **94** A2
Bremerhaven *Germany* **24** B4
Bremerton *U.S.A.* **110** C4
Bremervörde *Germany* **24** B5
Brenes *Spain* **37** H5
Brenham *U.S.A.* **116** F6
Brenne *France* **20** B5
Brenne △ *France* **20** B5
Brennerpass *Austria* **26** D4
Breno *Italy* **40** C7
Brent *U.S.A.* **117** E11
Brenta → *Italy* **41** C9
Brentwood *U.K.* **15** F8
Brentwood *Calif., U.S.A.* **110** H5
Brentwood *N.Y., U.S.A.* **115** F11
Bréscia *Italy* **40** C7
Breskens *Neths.* **17** C3
Breslau = Wrocław *Poland* **31** G4
Bresle → *France* **18** B8
Bressanone *Italy* **41** B8
Bressay *U.K.* **13** A7
Bresse *France* **19** F12
Bressuire *France* **18** F6
Brest *Belarus* **23** B12
Brest *France* **18** D2
Brest □ *Belarus* **33** F4
Brest-Litovsk = Brest
 Belarus **23** B12
Bretagne □ *France* **18** D3
Bretçu *Romania* **29** D11
Bretenoux *France* **20** D5
Breton *Canada* **102** C6
Breton, Pertuis *France* **20** B2
Breton Sd. *U.S.A.* **117** G10
Brett, C. *N.Z.* **91** A5
Bretten *Germany* **25** F4
Breuil-Cervínia *Italy* **40** C4
Brevard *U.S.A.* **117** D13
Breves *Brazil* **125** D8
Brewarrina *Australia* **95** E4
Brewer *U.S.A.* **113** C19
Brewer, Mt. *U.S.A.* **110** J8
Brewerville *Liberia* **82** D2
Brewster *N.Y., U.S.A.* **115** E11
Brewster *Ohio, U.S.A.* **114** F3
Brewster *Wash., U.S.A.* **108** B4

Brewster, Kap =
 Kangikajik *Greenland* **4** B6
Brewton *U.S.A.* **117** F11
Breyten *S. Africa* **89** D5
Breza *Bos.-H.* **28** E3
Brežice *Slovenia* **41** C12
Březnice *Czech Rep.* **26** B6
Breznik *Bulgaria* **44** D6
Brezno *Slovak Rep.* **27** C12
Brezoi *Romania* **29** E9
Brezovica *Serbia* **44** D5
Brezovo *Bulgaria* **45** D9
Bria *C.A.R.* **84** C4
Briançon *France* **21** D10
Briare *France* **19** E9
Briático *Italy* **43** D9
Bribie I. *Australia* **95** D5
Bribri *Costa Rica* **120** E3
Briceni *Moldova* **29** B12
Bricquebec *France* **18** C5
Bridgefield *Barbados* **121** g
Bridgehampton *U.S.A.* **115** F12
Bridgend *U.K.* **15** F4
Bridgend □ *U.K.* **15** F4
Bridgeport *Calif., U.S.A.* **110** G7
Bridgeport *Conn., U.S.A.* **115** E11
Bridgeport *Nebr., U.S.A.* **112** E2
Bridgeport *Tex., U.S.A.* **116** E6
Bridger *U.S.A.* **108** D9
Bridgeton *U.S.A.* **113** F16
Bridgetown *Australia* **93** F2
Bridgetown *Barbados* **121** g
Bridgetown *Canada* **105** D6
Bridgewater *Australia* **95** G4
Bridgewater *Canada* **105** D7
Bridgewater *Mass., U.S.A.* **115** E14
Bridgewater *N.Y., U.S.A.* **115** D9
Bridgewater, C. *Australia* **95** F3
Bridgnorth *U.K.* **15** E5
Bridgton *U.S.A.* **115** B14
Bridgwater *U.K.* **15** F5
Bridgwater B. *U.K.* **15** F4
Bridlington *U.K.* **14** C7
Bridlington B. *U.K.* **14** C7
Bridport *Australia* **95** G4
Bridport *U.K.* **15** G5
Briec *France* **18** D2
Brienne-le-Château *France* **19** D11
Brienon-sur-Armançon
 France **19** E10
Brienz *Switz.* **25** J4
Brienzersee *Switz.* **25** J3
Brière △ *France* **18** E4
Brig *Switz.* **25** J3
Brigg *U.K.* **14** D7
Brigham City *U.S.A.* **108** F7
Bright *Australia* **95** F4
Brighton *Australia* **95** F2
Brighton *Canada* **114** B7
Brighton *Trin. & Tob.* **125** K15
Brighton *U.K.* **15** G7
Brighton *U.S.A.* **114** C7
Brignogan-Plage *France* **18** D2
Brignoles *France* **21** E10
Brihuega *Spain* **38** E2
Brikama *Gambia* **82** C1
Brilliant *U.S.A.* **114** F4
Brilon *Germany* **24** D4
Bríndisi *Italy* **43** B10
Brinje *Croatia* **41** D12
Brinkley *U.S.A.* **116** D9
Brinnon *U.S.A.* **110** C4
Brion, Î. *Canada* **105** C8
Brionne *France* **18** C7
Brionski *Croatia* **41** D10
Brioude *France* **20** C7
Briouze *France* **18** D6
Brisbane *Australia* **95** D5
Brisbane → *Australia* **95** D5
Brisighella *Italy* **41** D8
Bristol *U.K.* **15** F5
Bristol *Conn., U.S.A.* **115** E12
Bristol *Pa., U.S.A.* **115** F10
Bristol *R.I., U.S.A.* **115** E13
Bristol *Tenn., U.S.A.* **117** C13
Bristol, City of □ *U.K.* **15** F5
Bristol B. *U.S.A.* **106** a
Bristol Channel *U.K.* **15** F3
Bristol I. *Antarctica* **5** B1
Bristol L. *U.S.A.* **109** J6
Bristow *U.S.A.* **116** D6
Britain = Great Britain *Europe* **6** E5
British Columbia □ *Canada* **102** C3
British Indian Ocean Terr.
 = Chagos Arch. ☑ *Ind. Oc.* **50** J9
British Isles *Europe* **6** E5
British Virgin Is. ☑ *W. Indies* **121** e
Brits *S. Africa* **89** D4
Britstown *S. Africa* **88** E3
Britt *Canada* **104** C3
Brittany = Bretagne □
 France **18** D3
Britton *U.S.A.* **112** C5
Brive-la-Gaillarde *France* **20** C5
Briviesca *Spain* **36** C7
Brixen = Bressanone *Italy* **41** B8
Brixham *U.K.* **15** G4
Brnaze *Croatia* **41** E13

Brnenský □ *Czech Rep.* **27** B9
Brno *Czech Rep.* **27** B9
Broach = Bharuch *India* **66** J8
Broad → *U.S.A.* **117** D14
Broad Arrow *Australia* **93** F3
Broad B. *U.K.* **13** C2
Broad Haven *Ireland* **12** B2
Broad Law *U.K.* **13** F5
Broad Sd. *Australia* **94** C4
Broadalbin *U.S.A.* **115** C10
Broadback → *Canada* **104** B4
Broadhurst Ra. *Australia* **92** D3
Broads, The *U.K.* **14** E9
Broadus *U.S.A.* **108** D11
Broager *Denmark* **11** K3
Broby *Sweden* **11** H8
Broceni *Latvia* **30** B9
Brochet *Canada* **103** B8
Brochet, L. *Canada* **103** B8
Brock I. *Canada* **101** B8
Brocken *Germany* **24** D6
Brockport *U.S.A.* **114** C7
Brockton *U.S.A.* **115** D13
Brockville *Canada* **115** B9
Brockway *Mont., U.S.A.* **108** C11
Brockway *Pa., U.S.A.* **114** E6
Brocton *U.S.A.* **114** D5
Brod *Macedonia* **44** E5
Brodarevo *Serbia* **44** C3
Brodeur Pen. *Canada* **101** B11
Brodick *U.K.* **13** F3
Brodnica *Poland* **31** E6
Brody *Ukraine* **23** C13
Brogan *U.S.A.* **108** D5
Broglie *France* **18** C7
Brok *Poland* **31** F8
Broken Arrow *U.S.A.* **116** C7
Broken Bow *Nebr., U.S.A.* **112** E4
Broken Bow *Okla., U.S.A.* **116** D7
Broken Bow Lake *U.S.A.* **116** D7
Broken Hill *Australia* **95** E3
Broken Ridge *Ind. Oc.* **96** L1
Broken River Ra. *Australia* **94** K6
Brokind *Sweden* **11** F9
Bromley □ *U.K.* **15** F8
Bromo *Indonesia* **63** G15
Bromölla *Sweden* **11** H8
Bromsgrove *U.K.* **15** E5
Brønderslev *Denmark* **11** G3
Brong-Ahafo □ *Ghana* **82** D4
Broni *Italy* **40** C6
Bronkhorstspruit *S. Africa* **89** D4
Brønnøysund *Norway* **8** D15
Bronte *Italy* **43** E7
Brook Park *U.S.A.* **114** E4
Brookhaven *U.S.A.* **117** F9
Brookings *Oreg., U.S.A.* **108** E1
Brookings *S. Dak., U.S.A.* **112** C5
Brooklin *Canada* **114** C6
Brooklyn Park *U.S.A.* **112** C7
Brooks *Canada* **102** C6
Brooks Range *U.S.A.* **106** a
Brooksville *U.S.A.* **117** G13
Brookton *Australia* **93** F2
Brookville *U.S.A.* **114** E5
Broom, L. *U.K.* **13** D3
Broome *Australia* **92** C3
Broons *France* **18** D4
Brora *U.K.* **13** C5
Brora → *U.K.* **13** C5
Brørup *Denmark* **11** J2
Brösarp *Sweden* **11** J8
Brosna → *Ireland* **12** C4
Broșteni *Mehedinți, Romania* **28** F7
Broșteni *Suceava, Romania* **29** C10
Brothers *U.S.A.* **108** E3
Brou *France* **18** D8
Brouage *France* **20** C2
Brough *U.K.* **14** C5
Brough Hd. *U.K.* **13** B5
Broughton Island =
 Qikiqtarjuaq *Canada* **101** C13
Broumov *Czech Rep.* **27** A9
Brovary *Ukraine* **33** G6
Brovst *Denmark* **11** G3
Brown, L. *Australia* **93** F2
Brown, Pt. *Australia* **95** E1
Brown City *U.S.A.* **114** C2
Brown Willy *U.K.* **15** G3
Brownfield *U.S.A.* **116** E3
Browning *U.S.A.* **108** B7
Brownsville *Oreg., U.S.A.* **108** D2
Brownsville *Pa., U.S.A.* **114** F5
Brownsville *Tenn., U.S.A.* **117** D10
Brownsville *Tex., U.S.A.* **116** J6
Brownville *U.S.A.* **115** C9
Brownwood *U.S.A.* **116** F5
Browse I. *Australia* **92** B3
Bruas *Malaysia* **65** K3
Bruay-la-Buissière *France* **19** B9
Bruce, Mt. *Australia* **92** D2
Bruce Pen. *Canada* **114** B3
Bruce Peninsula △ *Canada* **114** A3
Bruce Rock *Australia* **93** F2
Bruche → *France* **19** D14
Bruck = Bressanone *Italy* **41** B8
Bruchsal *Germany* **25** F4
Bruck an der Leitha *Austria* **27** C9
Bruck an der Mur *Austria* **26** D8

Brue → *U.K.* **15** F5
Bruges = Brugge *Belgium* **17** C3
Brugg *Switz.* **25** H4
Brugge *Belgium* **17** C3
Bruin *U.S.A.* **114** E5
Brûk, W. el → *Egypt* **74** E2
Brûlé *Canada* **102** C5
Brûlon *France* **18** E6
Brumado *Brazil* **125** F10
Brumath *France* **19** D14
Brumunddal *Norway* **8** F14
Bruneau *U.S.A.* **108** E6
Bruneau → *U.S.A.* **108** E6
Bruneck = Brunico *Italy* **41** B8
Brunei = Bandar Seri
 Begawan *Brunei* **62** D5
Brunei ■ *Asia* **62** D5
Brunflo *Sweden* **10** A8
Brunico *Italy* **41** B8
Brunna *Sweden* **10** E11
Brunnen *Switz.* **25** J4
Brunner, L. *N.Z.* **91** E3
Brunsbüttel *Germany* **24** B5
Brunssum *Neths.* **17** D5
Brunswick =
 Braunschweig *Germany* **24** C6
Brunswick *Ga., U.S.A.* **117** F14
Brunswick *Maine, U.S.A.* **113** D19
Brunswick *Md., U.S.A.* **113** F15
Brunswick *Mo., U.S.A.* **112** F7
Brunswick *Ohio, U.S.A.* **114** E3
Brunswick, Pen. de *Chile* **128** G2
Brunswick B. *Australia* **92** C3
Brunswick Junction
 Australia **93** F2
Brunt Ice Shelf *Antarctica* **5** D2
Bruntál *Czech Rep.* **27** B10
Brus Laguna *Honduras* **120** C3
Brusartsi *Bulgaria* **44** C7
Brush *U.S.A.* **108** F12
Brushton *U.S.A.* **115** B10
Brusio *Switz.* **25** J6
Brusque *Brazil* **127** B6
Brussel *Belgium* **17** D4
Brussel ✈ (BRU) *Belgium* **17** D5
Brussels = Brussel *Belgium* **17** D4
Brussels *Canada* **114** C3
Brusy *Poland* **30** E4
Bruthen *Australia* **95** F4
Bruxelles = Brussel *Belgium* **17** D4
Bruyères *France* **19** D13
Bruz *France* **18** D5
Brwinów *Poland* **31** F7
Bryagovo *Bulgaria* **45** E9
Bryan *Ohio, U.S.A.* **113** E11
Bryan *Tex., U.S.A.* **116** F6
Bryan, Mt. *Australia* **95** E2
Bryanka *Ukraine* **33** H10
Bryansk *Bryansk, Russia* **33** F8
Bryansk *Dagestan, Russia* **35** H8
Bryansk □ *Russia* **33** F8
Bryanskoye = Bryansk
 Russia **35** H8
Bryce Canyon △ *U.S.A.* **109** H7
Bryne *Norway* **9** G11
Bryson City *U.S.A.* **117** D13
Bryukhovetskaya *Russia* **33** K10
Brza Palanka *Serbia* **44** B6
Brzeg *Poland* **31** H4
Brzeg Dolny *Poland* **31** G3
Brześć Kujawski *Poland* **31** F5
Brzesko *Poland* **31** J7
Brzeziny *Poland* **31** G6
Brzozów *Poland* **31** J9

Bsharri *Lebanon* **74** A5
Bū Baqarah *U.A.E.* **71** E8
Bu Craa *W. Sahara* **78** C3
Bū Ḥasā *U.A.E.* **71** F7
Bua *Fiji* **91** a
Bua *Sweden* **11** G6
Bua Yai *Thailand* **64** E4
Buan *S. Korea* **57** G14
Buapinang *Indonesia* **63** E6
Buba *Guinea-Biss.* **82** C2
Bubanza *Burundi* **86** C2
Bubaque *Guinea-Biss.* **82** C1
Bube *Ethiopia* **81** F4
Bubi → *Zimbabwe* **87** G3
Būbiyān *Kuwait* **71** D6
Buca *Fiji* **91** a
Buca *Turkey* **47** C9
Bucak *Turkey* **47** D12
Bucaramanga *Colombia* **124** B4
Bucas Grande I. *Phil.* **61** G6
Bucasia *Australia* **94** K7
Buccaneer Arch. *Australia* **92** C3
Buccino *Italy* **43** B8
Buccoo Reef *Trin. & Tob.* **125** J16
Bucecea *Romania* **29** C11
Bucegi △ *Romania* **29** E10
Buchach *Ukraine* **23** D13
Buchan *U.K.* **13** D7
Buchan Ness *U.K.* **13** D7
Buchanan *Canada* **103** C8
Buchanan *Liberia* **82** D2
Buchanan, L. *Queens.,*
 Australia **94** C4

Buchanan, L. *W. Austral.,*
 Australia **93** E3
Buchanan, L. *U.S.A.* **116** F5
Buchanan Cr. → *Australia* **94** B2
Buchans *Canada* **105** C8
Bucharest = București
 Romania **29** F11
Buchen *Germany* **25** F5
Bucheon *S. Korea* **57** F14
Buchholz *Germany* **24** B5
Buchloe *Germany* **25** G6
Buchon, Pt. *U.S.A.* **110** K6
Buciumi *Romania* **28** C8
Buck Hill Falls *U.S.A.* **115** E9
Buckeye Lake *U.S.A.* **114** G2
Buckhannon *U.S.A.* **113** F13
Buckhaven *U.K.* **13** E5
Buckhorn L. *Canada* **114** B6
Buckie *U.K.* **13** D6
Buckingham *Canada* **104** C4
Buckingham *U.K.* **15** F7
Buckingham B. *Australia* **94** A2
Buckinghamshire □ *U.K.* **15** F7
Buckle Hd. *Australia* **92** B4
Buckleboo *Australia* **95** E2
Buckley *U.K.* **14** D4
Buckley → *Australia* **94** C2
Bucklin *U.S.A.* **112** G4
Bucks L. *U.S.A.* **110** F5
Bucquoy *France* **19** B9
București *Romania* **29** F11
București Otopeni ✈ (OTP)
 Romania **29** F11
Bucyrus *U.S.A.* **113** E12
Budacu, Vf. *Romania* **29** C10
Budalin *Burma* **67** H19
Budaörs *Hungary* **28** C3
Budapest *Hungary* **28** C4
Budapest □ *Hungary* **28** C4
Budapest ✈ (BUD) *Hungary* **28** C4
Budaun *India* **69** E8
Budd Coast *Antarctica* **5** C8
Buddusò *Italy* **42** B2
Bude *U.K.* **15** G3
Budennovsk *Russia* **35** H7
Budești *Romania* **29** F11
Budeyi *Ukraine* **29** B14
Budge Budge = Baj Baj
 India **69** H13
Budgewoi *Australia* **95** E5
Budia *Spain* **38** E2
Budjala *Dem. Rep. of the Congo* **84** D3
Budoni *Italy* **42** B2
Búdrio *Italy* **41** D8
Budva *Montenegro* **44** D2
Budzyń *Poland* **31** F3
Buea *Cameroon* **83** E6
Buellton *U.S.A.* **111** L6
Buena Esperanza *Argentina* **126** C2
Buena Park *U.S.A.* **111** M9
Buena Vista *Colo., U.S.A.* **108** G10
Buena Vista *Va., U.S.A.* **113** G14
Buena Vista Lake Bed
 U.S.A. **111** K7
Buenaventura *Colombia* **124** C3
Buenaventura *Mexico* **118** B3
Buendía, Embalse de *Spain* **38** E2
Buenos Aires *Argentina* **126** C4
Buenos Aires *Costa Rica* **120** E3
Buenos Aires □ *Argentina* **126** D4
Buenos Aires, L. *Argentina* **128** F2
Buffalo *Mo., U.S.A.* **112** G7
Buffalo *N.Y., U.S.A.* **114** D6
Buffalo *Okla., U.S.A.* **116** C5
Buffalo *S. Dak., U.S.A.* **112** C2
Buffalo *Wyo., U.S.A.* **108** D10
Buffalo → *Canada* **102** A5
Buffalo → *S. Africa* **89** D5
Buffalo △ *U.S.A.* **116** C8
Buffalo Head Hills *Canada* **102** B5
Buffalo L. *Alta., Canada* **102** C6
Buffalo L. *N.W.T., Canada* **102** A5
Buffalo Narrows *Canada* **103** B7
Buffalo Springs △ *Kenya* **86** B4
Buffels → *S. Africa* **88** D2
Buford *U.S.A.* **117** D12
Bug = Buh → *Ukraine* **33** J6
Bug → *Poland* **31** F8
Buga *Colombia* **124** C3
Bugala I. *Uganda* **86** C3
Buganda *Uganda* **86** C3
Buganga *Uganda* **86** C3
Bugasong *Phil.* **61** F5
Bugeat *France* **20** C5
Bugel, Tanjung *Indonesia* **63** G14
Bugibba *Malta* **49** D1
Bugojno *Bos.-H.* **28** E7
Bugsuk I. *Phil.* **62** C5
Buguma *Nigeria* **83** E6
Bugun *Mongolia* **60** B5
Bugungu △ *Uganda* **86** B3
Buguruslan *Russia* **52** D6
Buh → *Ukraine* **33** J6
Buharkent *Turkey* **47** D10
Buheirat-Murrat-el-Kubra
 Egypt **80** H8

Buhera *Zimbabwe* **89** B5
Bühl *Germany* **25** G4
Buhl *U.S.A.* **108** E6
Buhuşi *Romania* **29** D11
Bui △ *Ghana* **82** D4
Builth Wells *U.K.* **15** E4
Buinsk *Russia* **34** C9
Buir Nur *Mongolia* **60** B6
Buis-les-Baronnies *France* **21** D9
Buitrago del Lozoya *Spain* **36** E7
Bujalance *Spain* **37** H6
Bujanovac *Serbia* **44** D5
Bujaraloz *Spain* **38** D4
Buje *Croatia* **41** C10
Bujumbura *Burundi* **86** C2
Bük *Hungary* **28** C1
Buk *Poland* **31** F3
Bukachacha *Russia* **53** D12
Bukama
 Dem. Rep. of the Congo **87** D2
Būkān *Iran* **73** D12
Bukavu *Dem. Rep. of the Congo* **86** C2
Bukene *Tanzania* **86** C3
Bukhara = Bukhoro
 Uzbekistan **52** F7
Bukhoro *Uzbekistan* **52** F7
Bukima *Tanzania* **86** C3
Bukit Badung *Indonesia* **63** K18
Bukit Kerajaan *Malaysia* **65** c
Bukit Mertajam *Malaysia* **65** c
Bukit Ni *Malaysia* **65** d
Bukit Panjang *Singapore* **65** d
Bukit Tengah *Malaysia* **65** c
Bukittinggi *Indonesia* **62** E2
Bükk *Hungary* **28** B5
Bükki △ *Hungary* **28** B5
Bukoba *Tanzania* **86** C3
Bukum, Pulau *Singapore* **65** d
Bukuru *Nigeria* **83** D6
Bukuya *Uganda* **86** B3
Būl, Kuh-e *Iran* **71** D7
Bula *Guinea-Biss.* **82** C1
Bula *Indonesia* **63** E8
Bülach *Switz.* **25** H4
Bulahdelah *Australia* **95** E5
Bulan *Phil.* **61** E5
Bulancak *Turkey* **73** B8
Bulandshahr *India* **68** E7
Bulanık *Turkey* **73** C10
Bûlâq *Egypt* **80** B3
Bulawayo *Zimbabwe* **87** G2
Buldan *Turkey* **47** C10
Bulgan *Russia* **34** C9
Bulgar *Russia* **34** C9
Bulgaria ■ *Europe* **45** D9
Bulgheria, Monte *Italy* **43** B8
Bulgurca *Turkey* **47** C9
Buli, Teluk *Indonesia* **63** D7
Buliluyan, C. *Phil.* **61** G2
Bulim *Singapore* **65** d
Bulki *Ethiopia* **81** F4
Bulkley → *Canada* **102** B3
Bull Shoals L. *U.S.A.* **116** C8
Bullaque → *Spain* **37** G6
Bullas *Spain* **39** G3
Bulle *Switz.* **25** J3
Bulleringa △ *Australia* **94** B3
Bullhead City *U.S.A.* **111** K12
Büllingen *Belgium* **17** D6
Bullock Creek *Australia* **94** B3
Bulloo → *Australia* **95** D3
Bulloo L. *Australia* **95** D3
Bulls *N.Z.* **91** D5
Bully-les-Mines *France* **19** B9
Bulnes *Chile* **126** D1
Bulqizë *Albania* **44** E4
Bulsar = Valsad *India* **66** J8
Bultfontein *S. Africa* **88** D4
Bulukumba *Indonesia* **63** F6
Bulun *Russia* **53** B13
Bumba *Dem. Rep. of the Congo* **84** D4
Bumbești-Jiu *Romania* **29** E8
Bumbiri I. *Tanzania* **86** C3
Bumbuna *S. Leone* **82** D2
Bumhpa Bum *Burma* **67** F20
Bumi → *Zimbabwe* **87** F2
Buna *Kenya* **86** B4
Bunaken *Indonesia* **63** D6
Bunazi *Tanzania* **86** C3
Bunbah, Khalīj *Libya* **79** B10
Bunbury *Australia* **93** F2
Bunclody *Ireland* **12** D5
Buncrana *Ireland* **12** A4
Bundaberg *Australia* **95** C5
Bünde *Germany* **24** C4
Bundey → *Australia* **94** C2
Bundi *India* **68** G6
Bundjalung △ *Australia* **95** D5
Bundoran *Ireland* **12** B3
Bundukia *Sudan* **81** F3
Bung Kan *Thailand* **64** C4
Bunga → *Nigeria* **83** C6
Bungay *U.K.* **15** E9
Bungil Cr. → *Australia* **95** D4
Bungle Bungle =
 Purnululu △ *Australia* **92** C4
Bungo-Suidō *Japan* **55** H6
Bungoma *Kenya* **86** B3

Bungotakada *Japan* 55 H5
Bungu *Tanzania* 86 D4
Bunia *Dem. Rep. of the Congo* 86 B3
Bunji *Pakistan* 69 B6
Bunkie *U.S.A.* 116 F8
Bunnell *U.S.A.* 117 G14
Buñol *Spain* 39 F4
Bunsuru *Nigeria* 83 C5
Buntok *Indonesia* 62 E4
Bununu Dass *Nigeria* 83 C6
Bununu Kasa *Nigeria* 83 D6
Bunya Mts. △ *Australia* 95 D5
Bünyan *Turkey* 72 C6
Bunyu *Indonesia* 62 D5
Bunza *Nigeria* 83 C5
Buol *Indonesia* 63 D6
Buon Brieng *Vietnam* 64 F7
Buon Ma Thuot *Vietnam* 64 F7
Buong Long *Cambodia* 64 F6
Buorkhaya, Mys *Russia* 53 B14
Buqayq *Si. Arabia* 71 E6
Buqbuq *Egypt* 80 A2
Bur Acaba *Somali Rep.* 75 G3
Bûr Fuad *Egypt* 80 H8
Bûr Safâga *Egypt* 70 E2
Bûr Sa'îd *Egypt* 80 H8
Bûr Sûdân *Sudan* 80 D4
Bûr Taufiq *Egypt* 80 J8
Bura *Kenya* 86 C4
Burakin *Australia* 93 F2
Buram *Sudan* 81 E2
Burao *Somali Rep.* 75 F4
Burâq *Syria* 74 B5
Buraydah *Si. Arabia* 70 E4
Burbank *U.S.A.* 111 L8
Burda *India* 68 G6
Burdekin → *Australia* 94 B4
Burdur *Turkey* 47 D12
Burdur □ *Turkey* 47 D12
Burdur Gölü *Turkey* 47 D12
Burdwan = Barddhaman
 India 69 H12
Bure *Gojam, Ethiopia* 81 E4
Bure *Ilubabor, Ethiopia* 81 F4
Bure → *U.K.* 14 E9
Büren *Germany* 24 D4
Bureya → *Russia* 53 E13
Burford *Canada* 114 C4
Burg *Germany* 24 C7
Burg auf Fehmarn *Germany* 24 A7
Burg el Arab *Egypt* 80 H6
Burg et Tuyur *Sudan* 80 C2
Burg Stargard *Germany* 24 B9
Burgas *Bulgaria* 45 D11
Burgas □ *Bulgaria* 45 D10
Burgaski Zaliv *Bulgaria* 45 D11
Burgdorf *Germany* 24 C6
Burgdorf *Switz.* 25 H3
Burgenland □ *Austria* 27 D9
Burgeo *Canada* 105 C8
Burgersdorp *S. Africa* 88 E4
Burges, Mt. *Australia* 93 F3
Burghausen *Germany* 25 G8
Burghead *U.K.* 13 D5
Búrgio *Italy* 42 E6
Burglengenfeld *Germany* 25 F8
Burgohondo *Spain* 36 E6
Burgos *Spain* 36 C7
Burgos □ *Spain* 36 C7
Burgstädt *Germany* 24 E8
Burgsvik *Sweden* 11 G12
Burguillos del Cerro *Spain* 37 G4
Burgundy = Bourgogne □
 France 19 F11
Burhaniye *Turkey* 47 B8
Burhanpur *India* 66 J10
Burhi Gandak → *India* 69 G12
Burhner → *India* 69 H9
Buri Pen. *Eritrea* 81 D4
Burias I. *Phil.* 61 E5
Burica, Pta. *Costa Rica* 120 E3
Burien *U.S.A.* 110 C4
Burigi, L. *Tanzania* 86 C3
Burigi □ *Tanzania* 86 C3
Burin *Canada* 105 C8
Buriram *Thailand* 64 E4
Burji *Ethiopia* 81 F4
Burkburnett *U.S.A.* 116 D5
Burke → *Australia* 94 C2
Burke Chan. *Canada* 102 C3
Burketown *Australia* 94 B2
Burkina Faso ■ *Africa* 82 C4
Burk's Falls *Canada* 104 C4
Burlada *Spain* 38 C3
Burleigh Falls *Canada* 114 B6
Burley *U.S.A.* 108 E7
Burlingame *U.S.A.* 110 H4
Burlington *Canada* 114 C5
Burlington *Colo., U.S.A.* 108 G12
Burlington *Iowa, U.S.A.* 112 E8
Burlington *Kans., U.S.A.* 112 F6
Burlington *N.C., U.S.A.* 117 C15
Burlington *N.J., U.S.A.* 115 F10
Burlington *Vt., U.S.A.* 115 B11
Burlington *Wash., U.S.A.* 110 B4
Burlington *Wis., U.S.A.* 112 D9
Burma ■ *Asia* 67 J20
Burnaby I. *Canada* 102 C2

Burnet *U.S.A.* 116 F5
Burney *U.S.A.* 108 F3
Burnham *U.S.A.* 114 F7
Burnham-on-Sea *U.K.* 15 F5
Burnie *Australia* 95 G4
Burnley *U.K.* 14 D5
Burns *U.S.A.* 108 E4
Burns Junction *U.S.A.* 108 E5
Burns Lake *Canada* 102 C3
Burnside *Canada* 100 C9
Burnside, L. *Australia* 93 E3
Burnsville *U.S.A.* 112 C7
Burnt, L. *Canada* 105 B7
Burnt River *Canada* 114 B6
Burntwood → *Canada* 103 B9
Burntwood L. *Canada* 103 B8
Burqân *Kuwait* 70 D5
Burra *Australia* 95 E2
Burra *Nigeria* 83 C6
Burray *U.K.* 13 C6
Burrel *Albania* 44 E4
Burren *Ireland* 12 C2
Burren → *Ireland* 12 C3
Burren Junction *Australia* 95 E4
Burriana *Spain* 38 F4
Burrinjuck Res. *Australia* 95 F4
Burro, Serranías del *Mexico* 118 B4
Burrow Hd. *U.K.* 13 G4
Burrum Coast △ *Australia* 95 D5
Burruyacú *Argentina* 126 B3
Burry Port *U.K.* 15 F3
Bursa *Turkey* 45 F13
Bursa □ *Turkey* 72 B3
Burseryd *Sweden* 11 G7
Burstall *Canada* 103 C7
Burton *Ohio, U.S.A.* 114 E3
Burton *S.C., U.S.A.* 117 E14
Burton, L. *Canada* 104 B4
Burton upon Trent *U.K.* 14 E6
Buru *Indonesia* 63 E7
Burullus, Bahra el *Egypt* 80 H7
Burûn, Râs *Egypt* 74 D2
Burundi ■ *Africa* 86 C3
Bururi *Burundi* 86 C2
Burutu *Nigeria* 83 D6
Burwell *U.S.A.* 112 E4
Burwick *U.K.* 13 C5
Bury *U.K.* 14 D5
Bury St. Edmunds *U.K.* 15 E8
Buryatia □ *Russia* 53 D12
Buryn *Ukraine* 33 G7
Burzenin *Poland* 31 G5
Busalla *Italy* 40 D5
Busan *S. Korea* 57 G15
Busango Swamp *Zambia* 87 E2
Buşayrah *Syria* 73 E9
Busca *Italy* 40 D4
Bushat *Albania* 44 E3
Büshehr *Iran* 71 D6
Büshehr □ *Iran* 71 D6
Bushell *Canada* 103 B7
Bushenyi *Uganda* 86 C3
Bushire = Büshehr *Iran* 71 D6
Bushtyna *Ukraine* 29 B8
Busie *Ghana* 82 C4
Businga
 Dem. Rep. of the Congo 84 D4
Busko-Zdrój *Poland* 31 H7
Busovača *Bos.-H.* 28 F2
Buşra ash Shām *Syria* 74 C5
Busselton *Australia* 93 F2
Busseri → *Sudan* 81 F2
Busseto *Italy* 40 D7
Bussière-Badil *France* 20 C4
Bussolengo *Italy* 40 C7
Bussum *Neths.* 17 B5
Buşteni *Romania* 29 E10
Busto, C. *Spain* 36 B4
Busto Arsízio *Italy* 40 C5
Busu Djanoa
 Dem. Rep. of the Congo 84 D4
Busuanga I. *Phil.* 61 E3
Büsum *Germany* 24 A4
Busungbiu *Indonesia* 63 J17
Buta *Dem. Rep. of the Congo* 86 B1
Butare *Rwanda* 86 C2
Butaritari *Kiribati* 96 G9
Bute *U.K.* 13 F3
Bute Inlet *Canada* 102 C4
Butemba *Uganda* 86 B3
Butembo
 Dem. Rep. of the Congo 86 B2
Buteni *Romania* 28 D7
Butera *Italy* 43 E7
Butere *Kenya* 86 B3
Butha Qi *China* 60 B7
Butiaba *Uganda* 86 B3
Butler *Mo., U.S.A.* 112 F6
Butler *Pa., U.S.A.* 114 F5
Buton *Indonesia* 63 F6
Butte *Mont., U.S.A.* 108 C7
Butte *Nebr., U.S.A.* 112 D4
Butte Creek → *U.S.A.* 110 F5
Butterworth = Gcuwa
 S. Africa 89 E4
Butterworth *Malaysia* 65 c
Buttevant *Ireland* 12 D3
Buttfield, Mt. *Australia* 93 D4

Button B. *Canada* 103 B10
Buttonwillow *U.S.A.* 111 K7
Butty Hd. *Australia* 93 F3
Butuan *Phil.* 61 G6
Butuku-Luba *Eq. Guin.* 83 E6
Butung = Buton *Indonesia* 63 F6
Butzbach *Germany* 25 E4
Bützow *Germany* 24 B7
Buur Hakaba = Bur Acaba
 Somali Rep. 75 G3
Buxa Duar *India* 69 F13
Buxar *India* 69 G10
Buxoro = Bukhoro
 Uzbekistan 52 F7
Buxtehude *Germany* 24 B5
Buxton *U.K.* 14 D6
Buxy *France* 19 F11
Buy *Russia* 34 A5
Buyant-Uhaa *Mongolia* 60 B6
Buynaksk *Russia* 35 J8
Buyo *Ivory C.* 82 D3
Buyo, L. de *Ivory C.* 82 D3
Büyük Menderes → *Turkey* 47 D9
Büyükçekmece *Turkey* 45 E12
Büyükkarıştıran *Turkey* 45 E11
Büyükkemikli Burnu
 Turkey 45 F10
Büyükorhan *Turkey* 47 B10
Büyükyoncalı *Turkey* 45 E11
Buzançais *France* 18 F8
Buzău *Romania* 29 E11
Buzău □ *Romania* 29 E11
Buzău → *Romania* 29 E12
Buzău, Pasul *Romania* 29 E11
Buzen *Japan* 55 H5
Buzet *Croatia* 41 C10
Buzi → *Mozam.* 87 F3
Buziaş *Romania* 28 E6
Büzmeýin *Turkmenistan* 71 B8
Buzuluk *Russia* 52 D6
Buzuluk → *Russia* 34 E6
Buzzards Bay *U.S.A.* 115 E14
Bwana Mkubwe
 Dem. Rep. of the Congo 87 E2
Bwindi △ *Uganda* 86 C2
Byala *Ruse, Bulgaria* 45 C9
Byala *Varna, Bulgaria* 45 D11
Byala Slatina *Bulgaria* 44 C7
Byarezina → *Belarus* 23 B16
Byaroza *Belarus* 23 B13
Bychawa *Poland* 31 G9
Byczyna *Poland* 31 G5
Bydgoszcz *Poland* 31 E5
Byelorussia = Belarus ■
 Europe 23 B14
Byers *U.S.A.* 108 G11
Byesville *U.S.A.* 114 G3
Byfield △ *Australia* 94 C5
Byford *Australia* 93 F2
Bykhaw *Belarus* 23 B16
Bykhov = Bykhaw *Belarus* 23 B16
Bykovo *Russia* 34 F7
Bylas *U.S.A.* 109 K8
Bylot *Canada* 103 B10
Bylot I. *Canada* 101 B12
Byrd, C. *Antarctica* 5 C17
Byrock *Australia* 95 E4
Byron, C. *Australia* 95 D5
Byron Bay *Australia* 95 D5
Byrranga, Gory *Russia* 53 B11
Byrranga Mts. =
 Byrranga, Gory *Russia* 53 B11
Byrum *Denmark* 11 G5
Byske *Sweden* 8 D19
Byskeälven → *Sweden* 8 D19
Bystrytsya *Ukraine* 29 B9
Bystrzyca → *Dolnośląskie,*
 Poland 31 G3
Bystrzyca → *Lubelskie,*
 Poland 31 G9
Bystrzyca Kłodzka *Poland* 31 H3
Bytča *Slovak Rep.* 27 B11
Bytkiv *Ukraine* 29 B9
Bytom *Poland* 31 H5
Bytom Odrzański *Poland* 31 G2
Bytów *Poland* 30 D4
Byumba *Rwanda* 86 C3
Bzenec *Czech Rep.* 27 C10
Bzura → *Poland* 31 F7

C

C.W. McConaughy, L.
 U.S.A. 112 E3
Ca → *Vietnam* 64 C5
Ca Mau *Vietnam* 65 H5
Ca Mau, Mui *Vietnam* 65 H5
Ca Na *Vietnam* 65 G7
Caacupé *Paraguay* 126 B4
Caaguazú □ *Paraguay* 127 B4
Caála *Angola* 85 G3
Caamaño Sd. *Canada* 102 C3
Caazapá *Paraguay* 126 B4
Caazapá □ *Paraguay* 127 B4
Cabadbaran *Phil.* 61 G6
Cabalian = San Juan *Phil.* 61 F6
Caballeria, C. de *Spain* 48 A11

Cabana *Spain* 36 B2
Cabanaquinta *Spain* 36 B5
Cabanatuan *Phil.* 61 D4
Cabañeros △ *Spain* 37 F6
Cabanes *Spain* 38 E5
Cabano *Canada* 105 C6
Čabar *Croatia* 41 C11
Cabazon *U.S.A.* 111 M10
Cabedelo *Brazil* 125 E12
Cabeza del Buey *Spain* 37 G5
Cabezón de la Sal *Spain* 36 B6
Cabildo *Chile* 126 C1
Cabimas *Venezuela* 124 A4
Cabinda *Angola* 84 F2
Cabinda □ *Angola* 84 F2
Cabinet Mts. *U.S.A.* 108 B6
Cabo Blanco *Argentina* 128 F3
Cabo de Gata-Níjar △ *Spain* 39 J2
Cabo Frio *Brazil* 127 A7
Cabo Pantoja *Peru* 124 D3
Cabo San Lucas *Mexico* 118 C3
Cabo Verde = Cape Verde
 Is. ■ *Atl. Oc.* 78 b
Cabonga, Réservoir *Canada* 104 C4
Cabool *U.S.A.* 112 G7
Caboolture *Australia* 95 D5
Cabora Bassa Dam =
 Cahora Bassa, Reprêsa
 de *Mozam.* 87 F3
Caborca *Mexico* 118 A2
Cabot, Mt. *U.S.A.* 115 B13
Cabot Hd. *Canada* 114 A3
Cabot Str. *Canada* 105 C8
Cabra *Spain* 37 H6
Cabra Santo del Cristo *Spain* 37 H7
Cábras *Italy* 42 C1
Cabrera *Spain* 48 B9
Cabrera, Sierra *Spain* 36 C4
Cabrera △ *Spain* 39 F7
Cabri *Canada* 103 C7
Cabriel → *Spain* 39 F3
Cabugao *Phil.* 61 C4
Cacabelos *Spain* 36 C4
Çaçador *Brazil* 127 B5
Čačak *Serbia* 44 C4
Caçapava do Sul *Brazil* 127 C5
Cáccamo *Italy* 42 E6
Cacém *Portugal* 37 G1
Cáceres *Brazil* 124 G7
Cáceres *Spain* 37 F4
Cáceres □ *Spain* 36 F5
Cache Bay *Canada* 104 C4
Cache Cr. → *U.S.A.* 110 G5
Cache Creek *Canada* 102 C4
Cacheu *Guinea-Biss.* 82 C1
Cachi *Argentina* 126 B2
Cachimbo, Serra do *Brazil* 125 E7
Cachinal de la Sierra *Chile* 126 A2
Cachoeira *Brazil* 125 F11
Cachoeira do Sul *Brazil* 127 C5
Cachoeiro de Itapemirim
 Brazil 127 A7
Cachopo *Portugal* 37 H3
Cacine *Guinea-Biss.* 82 C1
Cacoal *Brazil* 124 F6
Cacólo *Angola* 84 G3
Caconda *Angola* 85 G3
Čadca *Slovak Rep.* 27 B11
Caddo *U.S.A.* 116 D6
Cader Idris *U.K.* 15 E4
Cadereyta de Jiménez
 Mexico 118 B5
Cadí, Sierra del *Spain* 38 C6
Cadí-Moixeró △ *Spain* 38 C3
Cadibarrawirracanna, L.
 Australia 95 D2
Cadillac *France* 20 D3
Cadillac *U.S.A.* 113 C11
Cadiz *Phil.* 61 F5
Cádiz *Spain* 37 J4
Cadiz *Calif., U.S.A.* 111 L11
Cadiz *Ohio, U.S.A.* 114 F4
Cádiz □ *Spain* 37 J5
Cádiz, G. de *Spain* 37 J3
Cadiz L. *U.S.A.* 109 J6
Cadney Park *Australia* 95 D1
Cadomin *Canada* 102 C5
Cadotte Lake *Canada* 102 B5
Cadours *France* 20 E5
Cadoux *Australia* 93 F2
Caen *France* 18 C6
Caernarfon *U.K.* 14 D3
Caernarfon B. *U.K.* 14 D3
Caernarvon = Caernarfon
 U.K. 14 D3
Caerphilly *U.K.* 15 F4
Caerphilly □ *U.K.* 15 F4
Caesarea *Israel* 74 C3
Caetité *Brazil* 125 F10
Cafayate *Argentina* 126 B2
Cafu *Angola* 88 B2
Cagayan → *Phil.* 61 B4
Cagayan de Oro *Phil.* 61 G6
Cagayan Is. *Phil.* 61 G4
Cagayan Sulu I. *Phil.* 61 H3
Cagli *Italy* 41 E9
Cágliari *Italy* 42 C2
Cágliari, G. di *Italy* 42 C2

Cagnano Varano *Italy* 41 G12
Cagnes-sur-Mer *France* 21 E11
Caguán → *Colombia* 124 D4
Caguas *Puerto Rico* 121 d
Caha Mts. *Ireland* 12 E2
Cahama *Angola* 88 B1
Caher *Ireland* 12 D4
Cahersiveen *Ireland* 12 E1
Cahora Bassa, L. de *Mozam.* 87 F3
Cahora Bassa, Reprêsa de
 Mozam. 87 F3
Cahore Pt. *Ireland* 12 D5
Cahors *France* 20 D5
Cahul *Moldova* 29 E13
Cai Bau, Dao *Vietnam* 58 G6
Cai Nuoc *Vietnam* 65 H5
Caia *Mozam.* 87 F4
Caianda *Angola* 87 E1
Caibarién *Cuba* 120 B4
Caibiran *Phil.* 61 F6
Caicara *Venezuela* 124 B5
Caicó *Brazil* 125 E11
Caicos Is. *Turks & Caicos* 121 B5
Caicos Passage *W. Indies* 121 B5
Caidian *China* 59 B10
Căinari *Moldova* 29 D14
Caird Coast *Antarctica* 5 D1
Cairn Gorm *U.K.* 13 D5
Cairngorm Mts. *U.K.* 13 D5
Cairngorms △ *U.K.* 13 D5
Cairnryan *U.K.* 13 G3
Cairns *Australia* 94 B4
Cairns L. *Canada* 103 C10
Cairo = El Qâhira *Egypt* 80 H7
Cairo *Ga., U.S.A.* 117 F12
Cairo *Ill., U.S.A.* 112 G9
Cairo *N.Y., U.S.A.* 115 D10
Cairo Montenotte *Italy* 40 D5
Caithness *U.K.* 13 C5
Caithness, Ord of *U.K.* 13 C5
Caja de Muertos, I.
 Puerto Rico 121 d
Cajamarca *Peru* 124 E3
Cajarc *France* 20 D5
Cajàzeiras *Brazil* 125 E11
Čajetina *Serbia* 44 C3
Çakirgol *Turkey* 73 B8
Çakırlar *Turkey* 47 E12
Čakovec *Croatia* 41 B13
Çal *Turkey* 47 C11
Cala *Spain* 37 H4
Cala → *Spain* 37 H4
Cala → *Spain* 37 H4
Cala Cadolar, Punta de =
 Rotja, Pta. *Spain* 48 C7
Cala d'Or *Spain* 48 B10
Cala en Porter *Spain* 48 B11
Cala Figuera, C. de *Spain* 48 B9
Cala Forcat *Spain* 48 B10
Cala Major *Spain* 48 B9
Cala Mezquida = Sa
 Mesquida *Spain* 48 B11
Cala Millor *Spain* 48 B10
Cala Ratjada *Spain* 48 B10
Cala Santa Galdana *Spain* 48 B10
Calaburras, Pta. de *Spain* 37 J6
Calabanga *Phil.* 61 E5
Calabar *Nigeria* 83 E6
Calabogie *Canada* 115 A8
Calabozo *Venezuela* 124 B5
Calábria □ *Italy* 43 C9
Calábria △ *Italy* 43 C9
Calaceite *Spain* 38 D5
Calacuccia *France* 21 F13
Calafat *Romania* 28 G7
Calafate *Argentina* 128 G2
Calafell *Spain* 38 D6
Calahorra *Spain* 38 C3
Calais *France* 19 B8
Calais *U.S.A.* 113 C20
Calakmul △ *Mexico* 119 D7
Calalaste, Cord. de
 Argentina 126 B2
Calama *Brazil* 124 E6
Calama *Chile* 126 A2
Calamar *Colombia* 124 A4
Calamian Group *Phil.* 61 F3
Calamocha *Spain* 38 E3
Calamonte *Spain* 37 G4
Călan *Romania* 28 E7
Calañas *Spain* 37 H4
Calanda *Spain* 38 D4
Calang *Indonesia* 62 D1
Calangiánus *Italy* 42 B2
Calapan *Phil.* 61 E4
Călăraşi *Moldova* 29 C13
Călăraşi □ *Romania* 29 F12
Călăraşi □ *Romania* 29 F12
Calasparra *Spain* 39 G3
Calatafimi *Italy* 42 E5
Calatayud *Spain* 38 D3
Calato = Kalathos *Greece* 47 E10
Calauag *Phil.* 61 E5
Calavà, C. *Italy* 43 D7
Calavite, C. *Italy* 43 E4
Calayan *Phil.* 61 B4
Calbayog *Phil.* 61 E6

Calca *Peru* 124 F4
Calcasieu L. *U.S.A.* 116 G8
Calcutta = Kolkata *India* 69 H13
Calcutta *U.S.A.* 114 F4
Caldaro *Italy* 41 B8
Caldas da Rainha *Portugal* 37 F1
Caldas de Reis *Spain* 36 C2
Calder → *U.K.* 14 D6
Caldera *Chile* 126 B1
Caldera de Taburiente △
 Canary Is. 48 F2
Caldwell *Idaho, U.S.A.* 108 E5
Caldwell *Kans., U.S.A.* 112 G5
Caldwell *Tex., U.S.A.* 116 F6
Caledon *S. Africa* 88 E2
Caledon → *S. Africa* 88 E4
Caledon B. *Australia* 94 A2
Caledonia *Canada* 114 C5
Caledonia *U.S.A.* 114 D7
Calella *Spain* 38 D7
Calemba *Angola* 88 B2
Calen *Australia* 94 J6
Calenzana *France* 21 F12
Caletones *Chile* 126 C1
Calexico *U.S.A.* 111 N11
Calf of Man → *U.K.* 14 C3
Calgary *Canada* 102 C6
Calheta *Madeira* 48 D2
Calhoun *U.S.A.* 117 D12
Cali *Colombia* 124 C3
Calicut *India* 66 P9
Caliente *U.S.A.* 109 H6
California *Mo., U.S.A.* 112 F7
California *Pa., U.S.A.* 114 F5
California □ *U.S.A.* 110 H7
California, Baja, T.N. =
 Baja California □ *Mexico* 118 B2
California, Baja, T.S. =
 Baja California Sur □
 Mexico 118 B2
California, G. de *Mexico* 118 B2
California City *U.S.A.* 111 K9
California Hot Springs
 U.S.A. 111 K8
Calilegua △ *Argentina* 126 B3
Călimăneşti *Romania* 29 E9
Călimani, Munţii *Romania* 29 C10
Calingasta *Argentina* 126 C2
Calipatria *U.S.A.* 111 M11
Calistoga *U.S.A.* 110 G4
Calitri *Italy* 43 B8
Calitzdorp *S. Africa* 88 E3
Callabonna, L. *Australia* 95 D3
Callac *France* 18 D3
Callan *Ireland* 12 D4
Callander *U.K.* 13 E4
Callao *Peru* 124 F3
Callicoon *U.S.A.* 115 E9
Calling Lake *Canada* 102 B6
Calliope *Australia* 94 C5
Callosa de Ensarriá *Spain* 39 G4
Callosa de Segura *Spain* 39 G4
Calne *U.K.* 15 F6
Calola *Angola* 88 B2
Calolbon = San Andres *Phil.* 61 E6
Calonge *Spain* 38 D8
Caloocan *Phil.* 61 D4
Calore → *Italy* 43 A7
Caloundra *Australia* 95 D5
Calpe *Spain* 39 G5
Calpella *U.S.A.* 110 F3
Calpine *U.S.A.* 110 F6
Calstock *Canada* 104 C3
Caltabellotta *Italy* 42 E6
Caltagirone *Italy* 43 E7
Caltanissetta *Italy* 43 E7
Çaltılıbük *Turkey* 45 G12
Caluire-et-Cuire *France* 19 G11
Calulo *Angola* 84 G2
Caluso *Italy* 40 C4
Calvados □ *France* 18 C6
Calvert → *Australia* 94 B2
Calvert I. *Canada* 102 C3
Calvert Ra. *Australia* 92 D3
Calvi *France* 21 F12
Calviá *Spain* 39 F7
Calvillo *Mexico* 118 C4
Calvinia *S. Africa* 88 E2
Calvo, Mte. *Italy* 41 G12
Calwa *U.S.A.* 110 J7
Calzada Almuradiel =
 Almuradiel *Spain* 37 G7
Calzada de Calatrava *Spain* 37 G7
Cam → *U.K.* 15 E8
Cam Lam *Vietnam* 65 G7
Cam Pha *Vietnam* 58 G6
Cam Ranh *Vietnam* 65 G7
Cam Xuyen *Vietnam* 64 C6
Camabatela *Angola* 84 F3
Camacha *Madeira* 48 D3
Camacupa *Angola* 85 G3
Camagüey *Cuba* 120 B4
Camaiore *Italy* 40 E7
Camaná *Peru* 124 G4
Camanche Res. *U.S.A.* 110 G6
Camaquã *Brazil* 127 C5
Camaquã → *Brazil* 127 C5
Câmara de Lobos *Madeira* 48 D3

Camarat, C. *France* **21** E10
Camarès *France* **20** E6
Camaret-sur-Mer *France* **18** D2
Camargo *Mexico* **119** B5
Camargue *France* **21** E8
Camargue △ *France* **21** E8
Camarillo *U.S.A.* **111** L7
Camariñas *Spain* **36** B1
Camarón, C. *Honduras* **120** C2
Camarones *Argentina* **128** E3
Camas *Spain* **37** H4
Camas *U.S.A.* **110** E4
Camas Valley *U.S.A.* **108** E2
Camballin *Australia* **92** C3
Cambará *Brazil* **127** A5
Cambay = Khambhat *India* **68** H5
Cambay, G. of =
  Khambhat, G. of *India* **66** J8
Cambil *Spain* **37** H7
Cambo-les-Bains *France* **20** E2
Cambodia ■ *Asia* **64** F5
Camborne *U.K.* **15** G2
Cambrai *France* **19** B10
Cambre *Spain* **36** B2
Cambria *U.S.A.* **110** K5
Cambrian Mts. *U.K.* **15** E4
Cambridge *Canada* **114** C4
Cambridge *Jamaica* **120** a
Cambridge *N.Z.* **91** B5
Cambridge *U.K.* **15** E8
Cambridge *Mass., U.S.A.* **115** D13
Cambridge *Minn., U.S.A.* **112** C7
Cambridge *N.Y., U.S.A.* **115** C11
Cambridge *Nebr., U.S.A.* **112** E3
Cambridge *Ohio, U.S.A.* **114** F3
Cambridge Bay =
  Ikaluktutiak *Canada* **100** C9
Cambridge G. *Australia* **92** B4
Cambridge Springs *U.S.A.* **114** E4
Cambridgeshire □ *U.K.* **15** E7
Cambrils *Spain* **38** D6
Cambuci *Brazil* **127** A7
Cambundi-Catembo *Angola* **84** G3
Camden *Ala., U.S.A.* **117** F11
Camden *Ark., U.S.A.* **116** E8
Camden *Maine, U.S.A.* **113** C19
Camden *N.J., U.S.A.* **115** G9
Camden *N.Y., U.S.A.* **115** C9
Camden *S.C., U.S.A.* **117** D14
Camden Sd. *Australia* **92** C3
Camdenton *U.S.A.* **112** F7
Camelford *U.K.* **15** G3
Camena *Moldova* **29** B13
Camerino *Italy* **41** E10
Cameron *Ariz., U.S.A.* **109** J8
Cameron *La., U.S.A.* **116** G8
Cameron *Mo., U.S.A.* **112** F6
Cameron *Tex., U.S.A.* **116** F6
Cameron Highlands
  Malaysia **65** K3
Cameron Hills *Canada* **102** B5
Cameroon ■ *Africa* **79** G7
Camerota *Italy* **43** B8
Cameroun → *Cameroon* **83** E6
Cameroun, Mt. *Cameroon* **83** E6
Cametá *Brazil* **125** D9
Çamiçi Gölü *Turkey* **47** D9
Camiguin □ *Phil.* **61** G6
Camiguin I. *Phil.* **61** B4
Camiling *Phil.* **61** D4
Camilla *U.S.A.* **117** F12
Caminha *Portugal* **36** D2
Camino *U.S.A.* **110** G6
Camira Creek *Australia* **95** D5
Cammal *U.S.A.* **114** E7
Cammarata *Italy* **42** E6
Camocim *Brazil* **125** D10
Camooweal *Australia* **94** B2
Camooweal Caves △
  Australia **94** C2
Camopi *Fr. Guiana* **125** C8
Camotes Is. *Phil.* **61** F6
Camotes Sea *Phil.* **61** F6
Camp Borden *Canada* **114** B5
Camp Hill *U.S.A.* **114** F8
Camp Nelson *U.S.A.* **111** J8
Camp Pendleton *U.S.A.* **111** M9
Camp Verde *U.S.A.* **109** J8
Camp Wood *U.S.A.* **116** G4
Campagna *Italy* **43** B8
Campana *Argentina* **126** C4
Campana, I. *Chile* **128** F1
Campanário *Madeira* **48** D2
Campanario *Spain* **37** G5
Campánia □ *Italy* **43** B7
Campbell *S. Africa* **88** D3
Campbell *Calif., U.S.A.* **110** H5
Campbell *Ohio, U.S.A.* **114** E4
Campbell I. *Pac. Oc.* **96** N8
Campbell L. *Canada* **103** A7
Campbell Plateau *S. Ocean* **5** A11
Campbell River *Canada* **102** C3
Campbell Town *Australia* **95** G4
Campbellford *Canada* **114** B7
Campbellpur *Pakistan* **68** C5
Campbellsville *U.S.A.* **113** G11
Campbellton *Canada* **105** C6

Campbelltown *Australia* **95** E5
Campbeltown *U.K.* **13** F3
Campeche *Mexico* **119** D6
Campeche □ *Mexico* **119** D6
Campeche, Golfo de *Mexico* **119** D6
Campello *Spain* **39** G4
Câmpeni *Romania* **28** D8
Camperdown *Australia* **95** F3
Camperville *Canada* **103** C8
Campi Salentina *Italy* **43** B11
Campíglia Maríttima *Italy* **40** E7
Campillo de Altobuey *Spain* **39** F3
Campillos *Spain* **37** H6
Câmpina *Romania* **29** E10
Campina Grande *Brazil* **125** E11
Campinas *Brazil* **127** A6
Campli *Italy* **41** F10
Campo *Spain* **38** C5
Campo de Criptana *Spain* **37** F7
Campo de Gibraltar *Spain* **37** J5
Campo Grande *Brazil* **125** H8
Campo Maior *Brazil* **125** D10
Campo Maior *Portugal* **37** F3
Campo Mourão *Brazil* **127** A5
Campo Túres *Italy* **41** B8
Campobasso *Italy* **43** A7
Campobello di Licata *Italy* **42** E6
Campobello di Mazara *Italy* **42** E5
Campofelice di Roccella *Italy* **42** E6
Campomarino *Italy* **41** G12
Camporeale *Italy* **42** E6
Camporrobles *Spain* **38** F3
Campos *Brazil* **127** A7
Campos *Spain* **48** B10
Campos Belos *Brazil* **125** F9
Campos Novos *Brazil* **127** B5
Camprodón *Spain* **38** C7
Camptonville *U.S.A.* **110** F5
Camptown *U.S.A.* **115** E8
Câmpulung *Argeş, Romania* **29** E10
Câmpulung *Suceava,*
  Romania **29** C10
Câmpuri *Romania* **29** D11
Camrose *Canada* **102** C6
Camsell Portage *Canada* **103** B7
Çamyuva *Turkey* **47** E12
Çan *Turkey* **45** F11
Can Clavo *Spain* **48** C7
Can Creu *Spain* **48** C7
Can Gio *Vietnam* **65** G6
Can Tho *Vietnam* **65** G5
Canaan *U.S.A.* **115** D11
Canada ■ *N. Amer.* **100** D10
Canada Abyssal Plain *Arctic* **4** B18
Canada Basin *Arctic* **4** B18
Cañada de Gómez *Argentina* **126** C3
Canadian *U.S.A.* **116** D4
Canadian → *U.S.A.* **116** D7
Canadian Shield *Canada* **98** D12
Canajoharie *U.S.A.* **115** D10
Çanakkale *Turkey* **45** F10
Çanakkale □ *Turkey* **45** F10
Çanakkale Boğaz *Turkey* **45** F10
Canal Flats *Canada* **102** C5
Canalejas *Argentina* **126** D2
Canals *Argentina* **126** C3
Canals *Spain* **39** G4
Canandaigua *U.S.A.* **114** D7
Canandaigua L. *U.S.A.* **114** D7
Cananea *Mexico* **118** A2
Canarias, Is. *Atl. Oc.* **48** F4
Canarias, Is. *Atl. Oc.* **48** F4
Canaries *St. Lucia* **121** f
Canarreos, Arch. de los
  Cuba **120** B3
Canary Is. = Canarias, Is.
  Atl. Oc. **48** F4
Canaseraga *U.S.A.* **114** D7
Canatlán *Mexico* **118** C4
Canaveral, C. *U.S.A.* **117** G14
Canaveral △ *U.S.A.* **117** G14
Canavieiras *Brazil* **125** G11
Canberra *Australia* **95** F4
Canby *Calif., U.S.A.* **108** F3
Canby *Minn., U.S.A.* **112** C5
Canby *Oreg., U.S.A.* **110** E4
Cancale *France* **18** D5
Canche → *France* **19** B8
Cancún *Mexico* **119** C7
Candanchu *Spain* **38** C4
Çandarlı *Turkey* **47** C8
Çandarlı Körfezi *Turkey* **47** C8
Candas *Spain* **36** B5
Candé *France* **18** E5
Candela *Italy* **43** A8
Candelaria *Argentina* **127** B4
Candelaria *Canary Is.* **48** F3
Candelario *Spain* **36** E5
Candeleda *Spain* **36** E5
Candelo *Australia* **95** F4
Candi Dasa *Indonesia* **63** J18
Candia = Iraklio *Greece* **49** D7
Candia, Sea of = Crete, Sea
  of *Greece* **47** E7
Candle L. *Canada* **103** C7
Candlemas I. *Antarctica* **5** B1

Cando *U.S.A.* **112** A4
Candon *Phil.* **61** C4
Canea = Chania *Greece* **49** D6
Canelli *Italy* **40** D5
Canelones *Uruguay* **127** C4
Cañete *Chile* **126** D1
Cañete *Peru* **124** F3
Cañete *Spain* **38** E3
Cañete de las Torres *Spain* **37** H6
Cangas *Spain* **36** C2
Cangas de Narcea *Spain* **36** B4
Cangas de Onís *Spain* **36** B5
Cangnan *China* **59** D13
Canguaretama *Brazil* **125** E11
Canguçu *Brazil* **127** C5
Canguçu, Serra do *Brazil* **127** C5
Cangwu *China* **59** F8
Cangxi *China* **58** B5
Cangyuan *China* **58** F2
Cangzhou *China* **56** E9
Caniapiscau → *Canada* **105** A6
Caniapiscau, L. *Canada* **105** B6
Canicattì *Italy* **42** E6
Canicattini Bagni *Italy* **43** E8
Caniles *Spain* **37** H8
Canim Lake *Canada* **102** C4
Canindeyú □ *Paraguay* **127** A5
Canino *Italy* **41** F8
Canisteo *U.S.A.* **114** D7
Canisteo → *U.S.A.* **114** D7
Cañitas de Felipe Pescador
  Mexico **118** C4
Cañizal *Spain* **36** D5
Canjáyar *Spain* **37** H8
Çankırı *Turkey* **72** B5
Çankırı □ *Turkey* **72** B5
Cankuzo *Burundi* **86** C3
Canmore *Canada* **102** C5
Cann River *Australia* **95** F4
Canna *U.K.* **13** D2
Cannanore *India* **66** P9
Cannes *France* **21** E11
Canning Town = Port
  Canning *India* **69** H13
Cannington *Canada* **114** B5
Cannóbio *Italy* **40** B5
Cannock *U.K.* **15** E5
Cannonball → *U.S.A.* **112** B3
Cannondale Mt. *Australia* **94** D4
Cannonsville Res. *U.S.A.* **115** D9
Cannonvale *Australia* **94** J6
Canoas *Brazil* **127** B5
Canoe L. *Canada* **103** B7
Cañon City *U.S.A.* **108** G11
Cañon de Río Blanco △
  Mexico **119** D5
Cañón del Río Lobos △ *Spain* **36** D7
Cañón del Sumidero △
  Mexico **119** D5
Canonniers Pt. *Mauritius* **85** d
Canora *Canada* **103** C8
Canosa di Púglia *Italy* **43** A9
Canowindra *Australia* **95** E4
Canso *Canada* **105** C7
Cantabria □ *Spain* **36** B7
Cantabria, Sierra de *Spain* **38** C2
Cantabrian Mts. =
  Cantábrica, Cordillera
  Spain **36** C5
Cantábrica, Cordillera *Spain* **36** C5
Cantal □ *France* **20** C6
Cantal, Plomb du *France* **20** C6
Cantanhede *Portugal* **36** E2
Cantavieja *Spain* **38** E4
Čantavir *Serbia* **28** E4
Cantemir *Moldova* **29** D13
Canterbury *Australia* **94** D3
Canterbury *U.K.* **15** F9
Canterbury Bight *N.Z.* **91** F3
Canterbury Plains *N.Z.* **91** E3
Cantil *U.S.A.* **111** K9
Cantillana *Spain* **37** H5
Canton = Guangzhou *China* **59** F9
Canton *Ga., U.S.A.* **117** D12
Canton *Ill., U.S.A.* **112** E8
Canton *Miss., U.S.A.* **117** E9
Canton *Mo., U.S.A.* **112** E8
Canton *N.Y., U.S.A.* **115** B9
Canton *Ohio, U.S.A.* **114** F3
Canton *Pa., U.S.A.* **114** E8
Canton *S. Dak., U.S.A.* **112** D5
Canton L. *U.S.A.* **116** C5
Cantù *Italy* **40** C6
Canudos *Brazil* **124** E7
Canumã → *Brazil* **124** D7
Canutama *Brazil* **124** E6
Canutillo *U.S.A.* **116** F1
Canvey *U.K.* **15** F8
Canyon *U.S.A.* **116** D4
Canyon De Chelly △ *U.S.A.* **109** H9
Canyonlands △ *U.S.A.* **109** G9
Canyons of the Ancients △
  U.S.A. **109** H9
Canyonville *U.S.A.* **108** E2
Cao Bang *Vietnam* **58** F6
Cao He → *China* **57** D13
Cao Lanh *Vietnam* **65** G5

Cao Xian *China* **56** G8
Cáorle *Italy* **41** C9
Cap-aux-Meules *Canada* **105** C7
Cap-Chat *Canada* **105** C6
Cap-de-la-Madeleine
  Canada **104** C5
Cap-Haïtien *Haiti* **121** C5
Cap Pt. *St. Lucia* **121** f
Capac *U.S.A.* **114** C2
Capáccio *Italy* **43** B8
Capaci *Italy* **42** D6
Capanaparo → *Venezuela* **124** B5
Capanema *Brazil* **125** D9
Capão Bonito *Brazil* **127** A6
Caparo → *Venezuela* **124** B5
Cape *Australia* **94** C4
Cape Arid △ *Australia* **93** F3
Cape Barren I. *Australia* **95** G4
Cape Breton Highlands △
  Canada **105** C7
Cape Breton I. *Canada* **105** C7
Cape Charles *U.S.A.* **113** G15
Cape Coast *Ghana* **83** D4
Cape Cod △ *U.S.A.* **113** E18
Cape Coral *U.S.A.* **117** H14
Cape Dorset *Canada* **101** C12
Cape Fear → *U.S.A.* **117** E15
Cape Girardeau *U.S.A.* **112** G9
Cape Hatteras △ *U.S.A.* **117** D17
Cape Le Grand △ *Australia* **93** F3
Cape Lookout △ *U.S.A.* **117** D16
Cape May *U.S.A.* **113** F16
Cape May Point *U.S.A.* **113** F16
Cape Melville △ *Australia* **94** A3
Cape Mount → *Liberia* **82** D2
Cape Peninsula △ *S. Africa* **88** E2
Cape Range △ *Australia* **92** D1
Cape Tormentine *Canada* **105** C7
Cape Town *S. Africa* **88** E2
Cape Tribulation △ *Australia* **94** B4
Cape Verde Is. ■ *Atl. Oc.* **78** b
Cape Vincent *U.S.A.* **115** B8
Cape York Peninsula
  Australia **94** A3
Capela *Brazil* **125** F11
Capella *Australia* **94** C4
Capendu *France* **20** E6
Capestang *France* **20** E7
Capesterre-Belle-Eau
  Guadeloupe **120** b
Capesterre-de-Marie-
  Galante *Guadeloupe* **120** b
Capim → *Brazil* **125** D9
Capistrello *Italy* **41** G10
Capitan *U.S.A.* **109** K11
Capitán Arturo Prat
  Antarctica **5** C17
Capitol Reef △ *U.S.A.* **109** G8
Capitola *U.S.A.* **110** J5
Capizzi *Italy* **43** E7
Capoche → *Mozam.* **87** F3
Capodichino, Nápoli ✈
  (NAP) *Italy* **43** B7
Capoterra *Italy* **42** C1
Cappadocia *Turkey* **72** C6
Cappraia *Italy* **40** E6
Caprara, Pta. *Italy* **42** A1
Caprarola *Italy* **41** F9
Capreol *Canada* **104** C3
Caprera *Italy* **42** A2
Capri *Italy* **43** B7
Capricorn Group *Australia* **94** C5
Capricorn Ra. *Australia* **92** D2
Caprino Veronese *Italy* **40** C7
Caprivi □ = Namíbia **88** B3
Caprivi Strip *Namibia* **88** B3
Caps et Marais d'Opale △
  France **19** B9
Captain's Flat *Australia* **95** F4
Captieux *France* **20** D3
Capulin Volcano △ *U.S.A.* **116** C3
Caquetá → *Colombia* **124** D5
Caracal *Romania* **29** F9
Caracas *Venezuela* **124** A5
Caracol *Belize* **120** C2
Caracol *Mato Grosso do Sul,*
  Brazil **126** A4
Caracol *Piauí, Brazil* **125** E10
Caráglio *Italy* **40** D4
Carajás *Brazil* **125** E8
Carajás, Serra dos *Brazil* **125** E8
Carangola *Brazil* **127** A7
Caransebeş *Romania* **28** E7
Carantec *France* **18** D3
Caraquet *Canada* **105** C6
Caras *Peru* **124** E3
Caraş Severin □ *Romania* **28** E7
Carasco *Italy* **40** D6
Caratasca, L. *Honduras* **120** C3
Caratinga *Brazil* **125** G10
Caraúbas *Brazil* **125** E11
Caravaca de la Cruz *Spain* **39** G3
Caravággio *Italy* **40** C6
Caravela *Guinea-Biss.* **82** C1
Caravelas *Brazil* **125** G11
Caraveli *Peru* **124** G4

Caravelle, Presqu'île de la
  Martinique **120** c
Caràzinho *Brazil* **127** B5
Carballeda = O Carballiño
  Spain **36** C2
Carballo *Spain* **36** B2
Carberry *Canada* **103** D9
Carbó *Mexico* **118** B2
Carbonara, C. *Italy* **42** C2
Carbondale *Colo., U.S.A.* **108** G10
Carbondale *Ill., U.S.A.* **112** G9
Carbondale *Pa., U.S.A.* **115** E9
Carbonear *Canada* **105** C9
Carboneras *Spain* **39** J3
Carboneras de Guadazaón
  Spain **38** F3
Carbónia *Italy* **42** C1
Carcabuey *Spain* **37** H6
Carcagente = Carcaixent
  Spain **39** F4
Carcaixent *Spain* **39** F4
Carcajou *Canada* **102** B5
Carcar *Phil.* **61** F5
Carcarana → *Argentina* **126** C3
Carcasse, C. *Haiti* **121** C5
Carcassonne *France* **20** E6
Carcross *Canada* **102** A2
Çardak *Çanakkale, Turkey* **45** F10
Çardak *Denizli, Turkey* **47** D11
Cardamon Hills *India* **66** Q10
Cardeña *Spain* **37** G6
Cárdenas *Cuba* **120** B3
Cárdenas *San Luis Potosí,*
  Mexico **119** C5
Cárdenas *Tabasco, Mexico* **119** D6
Cardenete *Spain* **38** F3
Cardiff *U.K.* **15** F4
Cardiff □ *U.K.* **15** F4
Cardiff-by-the-Sea *U.S.A.* **111** M9
Cardigan *U.K.* **15** E3
Cardigan B. *U.K.* **15** E3
Cardinal *Canada* **115** B9
Cardona *Spain* **38** D6
Cardona *Uruguay* **126** C4
Cardoner → *Spain* **38** D6
Cardoso, Ilha do *Brazil* **127** B5
Cardston *Canada* **102** D6
Cardwell *Australia* **94** B4
Careen L. *Canada* **103** B7
Carei *Romania* **28** C7
Careme = Ciremay
  Indonesia **63** G13
Carentan *France* **18** C5
Carey *U.S.A.* **108** E7
Carey, L. *Australia* **93** E3
Carey L. *Canada* **103** A8
Careysburg *Liberia* **82** D2
Cargèse *France* **21** F12
Carhaix-Plouguer *France* **18** D3
Carhué *Argentina* **126** D3
Caria *Turkey* **47** D10
Cariacica *Brazil* **125** H10
Cariati *Italy* **43** C9
Caribbean Sea *W. Indies* **121** D5
Cariboo Mts. *Canada* **102** C4
Caribou *U.S.A.* **113** B19
Caribou → *Man., Canada* **103** B10
Caribou → *N.W.T., Canada* **102** A3
Caribou I. *Canada* **104** C2
Caribou Is. *Canada* **102** A6
Caribou L. *Man., Canada* **103** B9
Caribou L. *Ont., Canada* **104** B2
Caribou Mts. *Canada* **102** B5
Caribou River △ *Canada* **103** B9
Caríbrod = Dimitrovgrad
  Serbia **44** D7
Carichíc *Mexico* **118** B3
Carigara *Phil.* **61** F6
Carignan *France* **19** C12
Carignano *Italy* **40** D4
Carinda *Australia* **95** E4
Cariñena *Spain* **38** D3
Carinhanha *Brazil* **125** F10
Carinhanha → *Brazil* **125** F10
Carini *Italy* **42** D6
Cariño *Spain* **36** B3
Carínola *Italy* **42** A6
Carinthia = Kärnten □
  Austria **26** E6
Caripito *Venezuela* **124** A6
Carlet *Spain* **39** F4
Carleton, Mt. *Canada* **105** C6
Carleton Place *Canada* **115** A8
Carletonville *S. Africa* **88** D4
Cârlibaba *Romania* **29** C10
Carlin *U.S.A.* **108** F5
Carlingford L. *U.K.* **12** B5
Carlinville *U.S.A.* **112** F9
Carlisle *U.K.* **14** C5
Carlisle *U.S.A.* **114** F7
Carlisle B. *Barbados* **121** g
Carlisle I. *Australia* **94** J7
Carlit, Pic *France* **20** E5
Carloforte *Italy* **42** C1
Carlos Casares *Argentina* **126** D3
Carlos Tejedor *Argentina* **126** D3
Carlow *Ireland* **12** D5
Carlow □ *Ireland* **12** D5

Carlsbad *Calif., U.S.A.* **111** M9
Carlsbad *N. Mex., U.S.A.* **109** K11
Carlsbad Caverns △ *U.S.A.*
  109 K11
Carluke *U.K.* **13** F5
Carlyle *Canada* **103** D8
Carmacks *Canada* **100** C6
Carmagnola *Italy* **40** D4
Carman *Canada* **103** D9
Carmarthen *U.K.* **15** F3
Carmarthen B. *U.K.* **15** F3
Carmarthenshire □ *U.K.* **15** F3
Carmaux *France* **20** D5
Carmel *U.S.A.* **115** E11
Carmel-by-the-Sea *U.S.A.* **110** J5
Carmel Valley *U.S.A.* **110** J5
Carmelo *Uruguay* **126** C4
Carmen *Colombia* **124** B3
Carmen *Paraguay* **127** B4
Carmen → *Mexico* **118** A3
Carmen, I. *Mexico* **118** B2
Carmen de Patagones
  Argentina **128** E4
Cármenes *Spain* **36** C5
Carmensa *Argentina* **126** D2
Carmi *Canada* **102** D5
Carmi *U.S.A.* **112** F9
Carmichael *U.S.A.* **110** G5
Carmila *Australia* **94** C4
Carmona *Costa Rica* **120** E2
Carmona *Spain* **37** H5
Carn Ban *U.K.* **13** D4
Carn Eige *U.K.* **13** D3
Carnac *France* **18** E3
Carnamah *Australia* **93** E2
Carnarvon *Australia* **93** D1
Carnarvon *S. Africa* **88** E3
Carnarvon → *Australia* **94** C4
Carnarvon Ra. *Queens.,*
  Australia **94** D4
Carnarvon Ra. *W. Austral.,*
  Australia **93** E3
Carnation *U.S.A.* **110** C5
Carncastle *U.K.* **12** B6
Carndonagh *Ireland* **12** A4
Carnduff *Canada* **103** D8
Carnegie *U.S.A.* **114** F4
Carnegie, L. *Australia* **93** E3
Carnegie Ridge *Pac. Oc.* **97** H19
Carnic Alps = Karnische
  Alpen *Europe* **26** E6
Carniche Alpi = Karnische
  Alpen *Europe* **26** E6
Carnot *C.A.R.* **84** D3
Carnot, C. *Australia* **95** E2
Carnot B. *Australia* **92** C3
Carnoustie *U.K.* **13** E6
Carnsore Pt. *Ireland* **12** D5
Caro *U.S.A.* **113** D12
Carol City *U.S.A.* **117** J14
Carolina *Brazil* **125** E9
Carolina *Puerto Rico* **121** d
Carolina *S. Africa* **89** C5
Caroline I. *Kiribati* **97** H12
Caroline Is. *Micronesia* **96** G6
Caroni *Trin. & Tob.* **125** K15
Caroní → *Venezuela* **124** B6
Caronie = Nébrodi, Monti
  Italy **43** E7
Caroona *Australia* **95** E5
Carpathians *Europe* **23** D11
Carpaţii Meridionali
  Romania **29** E9
Carpentaria, G. of *Australia* **94** A2
Carpentras *France* **21** D9
Carpi *Italy* **40** D7
Cărpineni *Moldova* **29** D13
Carpinteria *U.S.A.* **111** L7
Carpio *Spain* **36** D5
Carr Boyd Ra. *Australia* **92** C4
Carra, L. *Ireland* **12** C2
Carrabelle *U.S.A.* **117** G12
Carral *Spain* **36** B2
Carranza, Presa V. *Mexico* **118** B4
Carrara *Italy* **40** D7
Carrascal *Phil.* **61** G6
Carrascosa del Campo *Spain* **38** E2
Carrauntoohill *Ireland* **12** D2
Carrick-on-Shannon *Ireland* **12** C3
Carrick-on-Suir *Ireland* **12** D4
Carrickfergus *U.K.* **12** B6
Carrickmacross *Ireland* **12** C5
Carrieton *Australia* **95** E2
Carrillo *Mexico* **118** B4
Carrington *U.S.A.* **112** B4
Carrión → *Spain* **36** D6
Carrión de los Condes *Spain* **36** C6
Carrizal Bajo *Chile* **126** B1
Carrizalillo *Chile* **126** B1
Carrizo Cr. → *U.S.A.* **109** H12
Carrizo Plain △ *U.S.A.* **110** K7
Carrizo Springs *U.S.A.* **116** G5
Carrizozo *U.S.A.* **109** K11
Carroll *U.S.A.* **112** D6
Carrollton *Ga., U.S.A.* **117** E12
Carrollton *Ill., U.S.A.* **112** F8
Carrollton *Ky., U.S.A.* **113** F11
Carrollton *Mo., U.S.A.* **112** F7

Carrollton *Ohio, U.S.A.* **114** F3
Carron → *U.K.* **13** D4
Carron, L. *U.K.* **13** D3
Carrot → *Canada* **103** C8
Carrot River *Canada* **103** C8
Carrouges *France* **18** D6
Carrù *Italy* **40** D4
Carruthers *Canada* **103** C7
Carsa Dek *Ethiopia* **81** F4
Çarşamba *Turkey* **72** B7
Carsóli *Italy* **41** F10
Carson *Calif., U.S.A.* **111** M8
Carson *N. Dak., U.S.A.* **112** B3
Carson → *U.S.A.* **110** F8
Carson City *U.S.A.* **110** F7
Carson Sink *U.S.A.* **108** G4
Cartagena *Colombia* **124** A3
Cartagena *Spain* **39** H4
Cartago *Colombia* **124** C3
Cartago *Costa Rica* **120** E3
Cártama *Spain* **37** J6
Cartaxo *Portugal* **37** F2
Cartaya *Spain* **37** H3
Cartersville *U.S.A.* **117** D12
Carterton *N.Z.* **91** D5
Carthage *Tunisia* **42** F3
Carthage *Ill., U.S.A.* **112** E8
Carthage *Mo., U.S.A.* **112** G6
Carthage *N.Y., U.S.A.* **113** D16
Carthage *Tex., U.S.A.* **116** E7
Cartier I. *Australia* **92** B3
Cartwright *Canada* **105** B8
Caruaru *Brazil* **125** E11
Carúpano *Venezuela* **124** A6
Caruthersville *U.S.A.* **112** G9
Carvin *France* **19** B9
Carvoeiro *Brazil* **124** D6
Carvoeiro, C. *Portugal* **37** F1
Cary *U.S.A.* **117** D15
Casa, Pas de la = Envalira,
  Port d' *Europe* **38** C6
Casa Branca *Portugal* **37** G2
Casa Grande *U.S.A.* **109** K8
Casablanca *Chile* **126** C1
Casablanca *Morocco* **78** B4
Casacalenda *Italy* **41** G11
Casale Monferrato *Italy* **40** C5
Casalmaggiore *Italy* **40** D7
Casalpusterlengo *Italy* **40** C6
Casamance → *Senegal* **82** C1
Casarano *Italy* **43** B11
Casares *Spain* **37** J5
Casas Ibáñez *Spain* **39** F3
Casasimarro *Spain* **39** F2
Casatejada *Spain* **36** F5
Casavieja *Spain* **36** E6
Cascada de Basaseachic △
  Mexico **118** B3
Cascade *Seychelles* **85** b
Cascade *Idaho, U.S.A.* **108** D5
Cascade *Mont., U.S.A.* **108** C8
Cascade Locks *U.S.A.* **110** E5
Cascade Ra. *U.S.A.* **110** D5
Cascade Res. *U.S.A.* **108** D5
Cascades, Pte. des *Réunion* **85** c
Cascais *Portugal* **37** G1
Cascavel *Brazil* **127** A5
Cáscina *Italy* **40** E7
Casco B. *U.S.A.* **113** D19
Caselle Torinese *Italy* **40** C4
Caserta *Italy* **43** A7
Casey *Antarctica* **5** C8
Caseyr, Raas = Asir, Ras
  Somali Rep. **75** E5
Cashel *Ireland* **12** D4
Casiguran *Phil.* **61** C5
Casilda *Argentina* **126** C3
Casimcea *Romania* **29** F13
Casino *Australia* **95** D5
Casiquiare → *Venezuela* **124** C5
Čáslav *Czech Rep.* **26** B8
Casma *Peru* **124** E3
Casmalia *U.S.A.* **111** L6
Cásola Valsénio *Italy* **41** D8
Cásoli *Italy* **41** F11
Caspe *Spain* **38** D4
Casper *U.S.A.* **108** E10
Caspian Depression *Eurasia* **35** G9
Caspian Sea *Eurasia* **52** E6
Cass Lake *U.S.A.* **112** B7
Cassà de la Selva *Spain* **38** D7
Cassadaga *U.S.A.* **114** D5
Cassano allo Iónio *Italy* **43** C9
Cassel *France* **19** B9
Casselman *Canada* **115** A9
Casselton *U.S.A.* **112** B5
Cassiar *Canada* **102** B3
Cassiar Mts. *Canada* **102** B2
Cassino *Italy* **42** A6
Cassis *France* **21** E9
Cassville *U.S.A.* **112** G7
Castagneto Carducci *Italy* **40** E7
Castaic *U.S.A.* **111** L8
Castalia *U.S.A.* **114** E2
Castanhal *Brazil* **125** D9
Cástara *Trin. & Tob.* **125** J16
Castéggio *Italy* **40** C6

Castejón de Monegros *Spain* **38** D4
Castèl di Sangro *Italy* **41** G11
Castèl San Giovanni *Italy* **40** C6
Castèl San Pietro Terme
  Italy **41** D8
Castelbuono *Italy* **43** E7
Castelfidardo *Italy* **41** E10
Castelfiorentino *Italy* **40** E7
Castelfranco Emília *Italy* **40** D8
Castelfranco Véneto *Italy* **41** C8
Casteljaloux *France* **20** D4
Castellabate *Italy* **43** B7
Castellammare, G. di *Italy* **42** D5
Castellammare del Golfo
  Italy **42** D5
Castellammare di Stábia
  Italy **43** B7
Castellamonte *Italy* **40** C4
Castellane *France* **21** E10
Castellaneta *Italy* **43** B9
Castelli *Argentina* **126** D4
Castelló de la Plana *Spain* **38** F4
Castellón de la Plana □
  Spain **38** E4
Castellote *Spain* **38** E4
Castelmáuro *Italy* **41** G11
Castelnau-de-Médoc *France* **20** C3
Castelnau-Magnoac *France* **20** E4
Castelnaudary *France* **20** E5
Castelnovo ne' Monti *Italy* **40** D7
Castelnuovo di Val di
  Cécina *Italy* **40** E7
Castelo *Brazil* **127** A7
Castelo Branco *Portugal* **36** F3
Castelo Branco □ *Portugal* **36** F3
Castelo de Paiva *Portugal* **36** D2
Castelo de Vide *Portugal* **37** F3
Castelsardo *Italy* **42** B1
Castelsarrasin *France* **20** D5
Casteltérmini *Italy* **42** E6
Castelvetrano *Italy* **42** E5
Castets *France* **20** E2
Castiglion Fiorentino *Italy* **41** E8
Castiglione del Lago *Italy* **41** E9
Castiglione della Pescáia
  Italy **40** F7
Castiglione delle Stiviere
  Italy **40** C7
Castilblanco *Spain* **37** F5
Castile *U.S.A.* **114** D6
Castilla, Playa de *Spain* **37** J4
Castilla-La Mancha □ *Spain* **37** F7
Castilla y León □ *Spain* **38** D6
Castillo de Locubín *Spain* **37** H7
Castillon-en-Couserans
  France **20** F5
Castillonès *France* **20** D4
Castillos *Uruguay* **127** C5
Castle Dale *U.S.A.* **108** G8
Castle Douglas *U.K.* **13** G5
Castle Rock *Colo., U.S.A.* **108** G11
Castle Rock *Wash., U.S.A.* **110** D4
Castlebar *Ireland* **12** C2
Castlebay *U.K.* **13** E1
Castleblaney *Ireland* **12** B5
Castlederg *U.K.* **12** B4
Castleford *U.K.* **14** D6
Castlegar *Canada* **102** D5
Castlemaine *Australia* **95** F3
Castlemaine *Ireland* **12** D2
Castlepollard *Ireland* **12** C4
Castlerea *Ireland* **12** C3
Castlereagh → *Australia* **95** E4
Castlereagh B. *Australia* **94** A2
Castleton *U.S.A.* **115** C11
Castletown *I. of Man* **14** C3
Castletown Bearhaven
  Ireland **12** E2
Castor *Canada* **102** C6
Castor → *Canada* **104** B4
Castorland *U.S.A.* **115** C9
Castres *France* **20** E6
Castricum *Neths.* **17** B4
Castries *St. Lucia* **121** f
Castril *Spain* **37** H8
Castro *Brazil* **127** A6
Castro *Chile* **128** E2
Castro Alves *Brazil* **125** F11
Castro del Río *Spain* **37** H6
Castro-Urdiales *Spain* **36** B7
Castro Valley *U.S.A.* **110** H4
Castro Verde *Portugal* **37** H2
Castrojeriz *Spain* **36** C6
Castropol *Spain* **36** B4
Castroreale *Italy* **43** D8
Castrovillari *Italy* **43** C9
Castroville *U.S.A.* **110** J5
Castuera *Spain* **37** G5
Çat *Turkey* **73** C9
Cat Ba, Dao *Vietnam* **64** B6
Cat Ba △ *Vietnam* **64** B6
Cat I. *Bahamas* **121** B4
Cat L. *Canada* **104** B1
Cat Lake *Canada* **104** B1
Cat Tien △ *Vietnam* **65** G6
Cataamas *Honduras* **120** D2

Cataguases *Brazil* **127** A7
Çatak *Turkey* **73** C10
Catalão *Brazil* **125** G9
Çatalca *Turkey* **45** E12
Catalina *Canada* **105** C9
Catalina *Chile* **126** B2
Catalina *U.S.A.* **109** K8
Catalonia = Cataluña □
  Spain **38** D6
Cataluña □ *Spain* **38** D6
Çataleyzit *Turkey* **72** B6
Catamarca *Argentina* **126** B2
Catamarca □ *Argentina* **126** B2
Catanauan *Phil.* **61** E5
Catanduanes □ *Phil.* **61** E6
Catanduva *Brazil* **127** A6
Catánia *Italy* **43** E8
Catánia, G. di *Italy* **43** E8
Catanzaro *Italy* **43** D9
Catarman *Phil.* **61** E6
Catatumbo-Bari △ *Colombia* **121** E5
Catbalogan *Phil.* **61** F6
Cateel *Phil.* **61** H7
Catembe *Mozam.* **89** D5
Caterham *U.K.* **15** F7
Cathcart *S. Africa* **88** E4
Cathedral City *U.S.A.* **111** M10
Cathlamet *U.S.A.* **110** D3
Catio *Guinea-Biss.* **82** C1
Catlettsburg *U.S.A.* **113** F12
Catoche, C. *Mexico* **119** C7
Cátria, Mte. *Italy* **41** E9
Catriló *Argentina* **126** D3
Catrimani *Brazil* **124** C6
Catrimani → *Brazil* **124** C6
Catskill *U.S.A.* **115** D11
Catskill △ *U.S.A.* **115** D10
Catskill Mts. *U.S.A.* **115** D10
Catt, Mt. *Australia* **94** A1
Cattaraugus *U.S.A.* **114** D6
Catterick *U.K.* **14** C6
Cáttolica *Italy* **41** E9
Cáttolica Eraclea *Italy* **42** E6
Catuala *Angola* **88** B2
Catuane *Mozam.* **89** D5
Catur *Mozam.* **87** E4
Cauca → *Colombia* **124** B4
Caucaia *Brazil* **125** D11
Caucasus Mountains *Eurasia* **35** J7
Caudete *Spain* **39** G3
Caudry *France* **19** B10
Caulnes *France* **18** D4
Caulónia *Italy* **43** D9
Caungula *Angola* **84** F3
Cauquenes *Chile* **126** D1
Caura → *Venezuela* **124** B6
Cauresi → *Mozam.* **87** F3
Căuşani *Moldova* **29** D14
Causapscal *Canada* **105** C6
Caussade *France* **20** D5
Causse-Méjean *France* **20** D7
Causses du Quercy △ *France* **20** D5
Cauterets *France* **20** F3
Cauvery → *India* **66** P11
Caux, Pays de *France* **18** C7
Cava de' Tirreni *Italy* **43** B7
Cávado → *Portugal* **36** D2
Cavagrande del Cassibile △
  Italy **43** F8
Cavaillon *France* **21** E9
Cavalaire-sur-Mer *France* **21** E10
Cavalese *Italy* **41** B8
Cavalier *U.S.A.* **112** A5
Cavalla = Cavally → *Africa* **82** E3
Cavallo, Î. de *France* **21** G13
Cavally → *Africa* **82** E3
Cavan *Ireland* **12** B4
Cavan □ *Ireland* **12** C4
Cavárzere *Italy* **41** C9
Çavdarhisar *Turkey* **47** B11
Çavdır *Turkey* **47** D11
Cave Creek *U.S.A.* **109** K8
Cavenagh Ra. *Australia* **93** E4
Cavendish *Australia* **95** F3
Caviana, I. *Brazil* **125** C8
Cavite *Phil.* **61** D4
Cavnic *Romania* **29** C8
Cavour *Italy* **40** D4
Cavtat *Croatia* **44** D2
Cawndilla L. *Australia* **95** E3
Cawnpore = Kanpur *India* **69** F9
Caxias *Brazil* **125** D10
Caxias do Sul *Brazil* **127** B5
Çay *Turkey* **72** C4
Cay Sal Bank *Bahamas* **120** B4
Cayambe *Ecuador* **124** C3
Çaycuma *Turkey* **72** B5
Çayeli *Turkey* **73** B9
Cayenne *Fr. Guiana* **125** B8
Cayey *Puerto Rico* **121** d
Caygören Barajı *Turkey* **47** B10
Çayıralan *Turkey* **72** C6
Caylus *France* **20** D5
Cayman Brac *Cayman Is.* **120** C4
Cayman Is. ☑ *W. Indies* **120** C3
Cayman Trough *Caribbean* **98** H11
Cayres *France* **20** D7

Cayuga *U.S.A.* **115** D8
Cayuga L. *U.S.A.* **115** D8
Cazalla de la Sierra *Spain* **37** H5
Căzăneşti *Romania* **29** F12
Cazaubon *France* **20** E3
Cazaux et de Sanguinet,
  Étang de *France* **20** D2
Cazenovia *U.S.A.* **115** D9
Cazères *France* **20** E5
Cazin *Bos.-H.* **41** D12
Čazma *Croatia* **41** C13
Cazombo *Angola* **85** G4
Cazorla *Spain* **37** H7
Cazorla, Sierra de *Spain* **37** G8
Cea → *Spain* **36** C5
Ceamurlia de Jos *Romania* **29** F13
Ceanannus Mor *Ireland* **12** C5
Ceará = Fortaleza *Brazil* **125** D11
Ceará □ *Brazil* **125** E11
Ceará Mirim *Brazil* **125** E11
Ceauru, L. *Romania* **29** F8
Cebaco, I. de *Panama* **120** E3
Cebollar *Argentina* **126** B2
Cebollera, Sierra de *Spain* **38** D2
Cebreros *Spain* **36** E6
Cebu *Phil.* **61** F5
Čečava *Bos.-H.* **28** F2
Ceccano *Italy* **42** A6
Cece *Hungary* **28** D3
Cechi *Ivory C.* **82** D4
Cecil Plains *Australia* **95** D5
Cécina *Italy* **40** E7
Cécina → *Italy* **40** E7
Ceclavín *Spain* **36** F4
Cedar → *U.S.A.* **112** E8
Cedar City *U.S.A.* **109** H7
Cedar Creek Res. *U.S.A.* **116** E6
Cedar Falls *Iowa, U.S.A.* **112** D7
Cedar Falls *Wash., U.S.A.* **110** C5
Cedar Key *U.S.A.* **117** G13
Cedar L. *Canada* **103** C9
Cedar Park *U.S.A.* **116** F6
Cedar Rapids *U.S.A.* **112** E8
Cedartown *U.S.A.* **117** D12
Cedarvale *Canada* **102** B3
Cedarville *S. Africa* **89** E4
Cedeira *Spain* **36** B2
Cedral *Mexico* **118** C4
Cedro *Brazil* **125** E11
Cedros, I. *Mexico* **118** B1
Cedros B. *Trin. & Tob.* **125** K15
Ceduna *Australia* **95** E1
Cedynia *Poland* **31** F1
Cée *Spain* **36** C1
Cefalù *Italy* **43** D7
Cega → *Spain* **36** D6
Cegléd *Hungary* **28** C4
Céglie Messápico *Italy* **43** B10
Cehegín *Spain* **39** G3
Ceheng *China* **58** E5
Cehu-Silvaniei *Romania* **29** C8
Ceica *Romania* **28** D7
Ceira → *Portugal* **36** E2
Cekik *Indonesia* **63** J17
Čelákovice *Czech Rep.* **26** A7
Celano *Italy* **41** F10
Celanova *Spain* **36** C3
Celaque △ *Honduras* **120** D2
Celaya *Mexico* **118** C4
Celebes = Sulawesi *Indonesia* **63** E6
Celebes Sea *Indonesia* **63** D6
Čelić *Bos.-H.* **28** F3
Celina *U.S.A.* **113** E11
Celinac *Bos.-H.* **28** F2
Celje *Slovenia* **41** B12
Celldömölk *Hungary* **28** C2
Celle *Germany* **24** C6
Celorico da Beira *Portugal* **36** E3
Celtic Sea *Atl. Oc.* **16** F2
Çeltikçi *Turkey* **47** D12
Çemişgezek *Turkey* **73** C8
Cenderwasih, Teluk
  Indonesia **63** E9
Cengong *China* **58** D7
Ceno → *Italy* **40** D7
Centallo *Italy* **40** D4
Centelles *Spain* **38** D7
Center *N. Dak., U.S.A.* **112** B3
Center *Tex., U.S.A.* **116** F7
Centerburg *U.S.A.* **114** F2
Centerville *Calif., U.S.A.* **110** J7
Centerville *Iowa, U.S.A.* **112** E7
Centerville *Pa., U.S.A.* **114** F5
Centerville *Tenn., U.S.A.* **117** D11
Centerville *Tex., U.S.A.* **116** F7
Cento *Italy* **41** D8
Central = Tsentralnyy □
  Russia **34** D4
Central □ *Ghana* **83** D4
Central □ *Kenya* **86** C4
Central □ *Malawi* **87** E3
Central □ *Zambia* **87** E2
Central, Cordillera *Colombia* **124** C4
Central, Cordillera
  Costa Rica **120** D3

Central, Cordillera
  Dom. Rep. **121** C5
Central, Cordillera *Phil.* **61** C4
Central, Cordillera
  Puerto Rico **121** d
Central African Rep. ■
  Africa **79** G9
Central America *America* **98** H11
Central Butte *Canada* **103** C7
Central City *Colo., U.S.A.* **108** G11
Central City *Ky., U.S.A.* **112** G10
Central City *Nebr., U.S.A.* **112** E4
Central I. *Kenya* **86** B4
Central Island △ *Kenya* **86** B4
Central Kalahari □
  Botswana **88** C3
Central Makran Range
  Pakistan **66** F4
Central Pacific Basin
  Pac. Oc. **96** G10
Central Patricia *Canada* **104** B1
Central Point *U.S.A.* **108** E2
Central Russian Uplands
  Europe **6** E13
Central Siberian Plateau
  Russia **50** B12
Central Square *U.S.A.* **115** C8
Centralia *Ill., U.S.A.* **112** F9
Centralia *Mo., U.S.A.* **112** F7
Centralia *Wash., U.S.A.* **110** D4
Centre □ *Cameroon* **83** E7
Centre de Flacq *Mauritius* **85** d
Cenxi *China* **59** F8
Ceprano *Italy* **42** A6
Ceptura *Romania* **29** E11
Cepu *Indonesia* **63** G14
Ceram = Seram *Indonesia* **63** E7
Ceram Sea = Seram Sea
  Indonesia **63** E7
Cerbère, France *France* **20** F7
Cerbicales, Îs. *France* **21** G13
Cercal *Portugal* **37** H2
Cerdaña *Spain* **38** D6
Cère → *France* **20** D5
Cerea *Italy* **41** C8
Ceredigion □ *U.K.* **15** E3
Ceres *Argentina* **126** B3
Ceres *S. Africa* **88** E2
Ceres *U.S.A.* **110** H6
Céret *France* **20** F6
Cergy *France* **19** C9
Cerignola *Italy* **43** A8
Cerigo = Kythira *Greece* **46** E5
Cérilly *France* **19** F9
Cerisiers *France* **19** D10
Cerizay *France* **18** F6
Çerkeş *Turkey* **72** B5
Çerkezköy *Turkey* **45** E12
Cerknica *Slovenia* **41** C11
Cerkovica *Bulgaria* **45** C8
Cermenovo *Serbia* **44** C4
Çermik *Turkey* **73** C8
Cerna *Romania* **29** E13
Cerna → *Romania* **29** F8
Cernavodă *Romania* **29** F13
Cernay *France* **19** E14
Cernik *Croatia* **28** E2
Cerralvo *Mexico* **118** C4
Cerralvo, I. *Mexico* **118** C3
Cerritos *Mexico* **118** C4
Cerro Chato *Uruguay* **127** C4
Cerro Cofre de Perote △
  Mexico **119** D5
Cerro Corá △ *Paraguay* **127** A4
Cerro el Copey △ *Venezuela* **121** D7
Cerro Hoya △ *Panama* **120** E3
Cerro Saroche △ *Venezuela* **121** D5
Certaldo *Italy* **40** E8
Cervaro → *Italy* **43** A8
Cervati, Monte *Italy* **43** B8
Cervantes *Australia* **93** F2
Cervera *Spain* **38** D6
Cervera de Pisuerga *Spain* **36** C6
Cervera del Río Alhama
  Spain **38** D3
Cervéteri *Italy* **41** F9
Cérvia *Italy* **41** D9
Cervignano del Friuli *Italy* **41** C10
Cervinara *Italy* **43** A7
Cervione *France* **21** F13
Cervo *Spain* **36** B3
Cesar → *Colombia* **124** A4
Cesena *Italy* **41** D9
Cesenático *Italy* **41** D9
Cēsis *Latvia* **32** D3
Česká Lípa *Czech Rep.* **26** A7
Česká Rep. = Czech Rep. ■
  Europe **26** B8
Česká Třebová *Czech Rep.* **27** B9
České Budějovice *Czech Rep.* **26** C7
České Velenice *Czech Rep.* **26** C7
Českobudějovický □
  Czech Rep. **26** B7

Českomoravská Vrchovina
  Czech Rep. **26** B8
Český Brod *Czech Rep.* **26** A7
Český Krumlov *Czech Rep.* **26** C7
Český Těšín *Czech Rep.* **27** B11
Cesma → *Croatia* **41** C13
Çeşme *Turkey* **47** C8
Cessnock *Australia* **95** E5
Cesson-Sévigné *France* **18** D5
Cestas *France* **20** D3
Cestos → *Liberia* **82** D3
Cestos Sehnkwehn △ *Liberia* **82** D3
Cetate *Romania* **28** F8
Cetin Grad *Croatia* **41** C12
Cetina → *Croatia* **41** E13
Cetinje *Montenegro* **44** D2
Cetraro *Italy* **43** C8
Ceuta *N. Afr.* **78** A4
Ceva *Italy* **40** D5
Cévennes *France* **20** D7
Cévennes △ *France* **20** D7
Ceyhan *Turkey* **72** D6
Ceyhan → *Turkey* **72** D6
Ceylânpınar *Turkey* **73** D9
Ceylon = Sri Lanka ■ *Asia* **66** R12
Cèze → *France* **21** D8
Cha-am *Thailand* **64** F2
Cha Pa *Vietnam* **64** A4
Chabanais *France* **20** C4
Chabeuil *France* **21** D9
Chablais *France* **19** F13
Chablis *France* **19** E10
Chacabuco *Argentina* **126** C3
Chachapoyas *Peru* **124** E3
Chachoengsao *Thailand* **64** F3
Chachran *Pakistan* **68** E4
Chachro *Pakistan* **68** G4
Chaco □ *Argentina* **126** B3
Chaco □ *Paraguay* **126** B4
Chaco → *U.S.A.* **109** H9
Chaco △ *Argentina* **126** B4
Chaco Austral *S. Amer.* **128** B4
Chaco Boreal *S. Amer.* **124** H6
Chaco Central *S. Amer.* **128** A4
Chaco Culture △ *U.S.A.* **109** H10
Chacon, C. *U.S.A.* **102** C2
Chad ■ *Africa* **79** F8
Chad, L. = Tchad, L. *Chad* **79** F8
Chadan *Russia* **53** D10
Chadileuvú → *Argentina* **126** D2
Chadiza *Zambia* **87** E3
Chadron *U.S.A.* **112** D2
Chadyr-Lunga =
  Ciadâr-Lunga *Moldova* **29** D13
Chae Hom *Thailand* **64** C2
Chae Son △ *Thailand* **64** C2
Chaem → *Thailand* **64** C2
Chaeryŏng *N. Korea* **57** E13
Chagai Hills = Chāh Gay
  Hills *Afghan.* **66** E3
Chagda *Russia* **53** D14
Chaghcharān *Afghan.* **66** B4
Chagny *France* **19** F11
Chagoda *Russia* **32** C8
Chagos Arch. ☑ *Ind. Oc.* **50** J9
Chagres △ *Panama* **120** E4
Chagrin Falls *U.S.A.* **114** E3
Chaguanas *Trin. & Tob.* **125** K15
Chāh Ākhvor *Iran* **71** D8
Chāh Bahar *Iran* **71** E9
Chāh-e Kavīr *Iran* **71** C8
Chāh Gay Hills *Afghan.* **66** E3
Chahār Borjak *Afghan.* **66** D3
Chahār Maḥāll va
  Bakhtīarī □ *Iran* **71** C6
Chaibasa *India* **69** H11
Chaillé-les-Marais *France* **20** B2
Chainat *Thailand* **64** E3
Chaiya *Thailand* **65** H2
Chaj Doab *Pakistan* **68** C5
Chajari *Argentina* **126** C4
Chak Amru *Pakistan* **68** C6
Chaka *Sudan* **81** G3
Chakar → *Pakistan* **68** E3
Chakari *Zimbabwe* **89** B4
Chake Chake *Tanzania* **86** D4
Chakhānsūr *Afghan.* **66** D3
Chakonipau, L. *Canada* **105** A6
Chakradharpur *India* **69** H11
Chakrata *India* **68** D7
Chakwal *Pakistan* **68** C5
Chala *Peru* **124** G4
Chalais *France* **20** C4
Chalchihuites *Mexico* **118** C4
Chalcis = Halkida *Greece* **46** C5
Châlette-sur-Loing *France* **19** D9
Chaleur B. *Canada* **105** C6
Chalfant *U.S.A.* **110** H8
Chalhuanca *Peru* **124** F4
Chaliki *Greece* **46** B4
Chalindrey *France* **19** E12
Chaling *China* **59** D9
Chalisgaon *India* **66** J9
Chalk River *Canada* **104** C4
Chalky Inlet *N.Z.* **91** G1
Challans *France* **18** F5
Challapata *Bolivia* **124** G5

Challenger Deep *Pac. Oc.* **96** F6
Challenger Fracture Zone
 Pac. Oc. **97** L17
Challis *U.S.A.* **108** D6
Chalmette *U.S.A.* **117** G10
Chalon-sur-Saône *France* **19** F11
Chalonnes-sur-Loire *France* **18** E6
Châlons-en-Champagne
 France **19** D11
Chálten, Cerro = Fitz Roy,
 Cerro *Argentina* **128** F2
Châlus *France* **20** C4
Chālūs *Iran* **71** B6
Cham *Germany* **25** F8
Cham, Cu Lao *Vietnam* **64** E7
Chama *U.S.A.* **109** H10
Chamba *India* **68** C7
Chamba *Tanzania* **87** E4
Chambal → *India* **69** F8
Chamberlain *U.S.A.* **112** D4
Chamberlain → *Australia* **92** C4
Chamberlain L. *U.S.A.* **113** B19
Chambers *U.S.A.* **109** J9
Chambersburg *U.S.A.* **113** F15
Chambéry *France* **21** C9
Chambeshi → *Zambia* **84** G6
Chambly *Canada* **115** A11
Chambord *Canada* **105** C5
Chamboulive *France* **20** C5
Chamchamal *Iraq* **73** E11
Chamela *Mexico* **118** D3
Chamical *Argentina* **126** C2
Chamkar Luong *Cambodia* **65** G4
Chamoli *India* **69** D8
Chamonix-Mont Blanc
 France **21** C10
Champa *India* **69** H10
Champagne *Canada* **102** A1
Champagne *France* **19** D11
Champagnole *France* **19** F12
Champaign *U.S.A.* **112** E9
Champassak *Laos* **64** E5
Champaubert *France* **19** D10
Champawat *India* **69** E9
Champdeniers-St-Denis
 France **20** B3
Champdoré, L. *Canada* **105** A6
Champeix *France* **20** C7
Champion *U.S.A.* **114** E4
Champlain *U.S.A.* **115** B11
Champlain, L. *U.S.A.* **115** B11
Champlitte *France* **19** E12
Champotón *Mexico* **119** D6
Champua *India* **69** H11
Chamusca *Portugal* **37** F2
Chana *Thailand* **65** J3
Chañaral *Chile* **126** B1
Chanārān *Iran* **71** B8
Chanasma *India* **68** H5
Chancery Lane *Barbados* **121** g
Chanco *Chile* **126** D1
Chand *India* **69** J8
Chandan *India* **69** G12
Chandan Chauki *India* **69** E9
Chandannagar *India* **69** H13
Chandausi *India* **69** E8
Chandeleur Is. *U.S.A.* **117** G10
Chandeleur Sd. *U.S.A.* **117** G10
Chandigarh *India* **68** D7
Chandil *India* **69** H12
Chandler *Australia* **95** D1
Chandler *Canada* **105** C7
Chandler *Ariz., U.S.A.* **109** K8
Chandler *Okla., U.S.A.* **116** D6
Chandod *India* **68** J5
Chandpur *Bangla.* **67** H17
Chandra → *India* **68** D7
Chandrapur *India* **66** K11
Chānf *Iran* **71** E9
Chang *Pakistan* **68** F3
Chang, Ko *Thailand* **65** G4
Ch'ang Chiang = Chang
 Jiang → *China* **59** B13
Chang Jiang → *China* **59** B13
Chang-won *S. Korea* **57** G15
Changa *India* **69** B13
Changanacheri *India* **66** Q10
Changane → *Mozam.* **89** C5
Changbai *China* **57** D15
Changbai Shan *China* **57** C15
Changchiak'ou =
 Zhangjiakou *China* **56** D8
Ch'angchou = Changzhou
 China **59** B12
Changchun *China* **57** C13
Changchunling *China* **57** B13
Changde *China* **59** C8
Changdo-ri *N. Korea* **57** E14
Changfeng *China* **59** A11
Changhai = Shanghai
 China **59** B13
Changhua *China* **59** B12
Changhua *Taiwan* **59** E13
Changhǔngni *N. Korea* **57** D15
Changi *Singapore* **65** d

Changi, Singapore ✈ (SIN)
 Singapore **65** M4
Changjiang *China* **64** C7
Changjin *N. Korea* **57** D14
Changjin-ho *N. Korea* **57** D14
Changle *China* **59** E12
Changli *China* **57** E10
Changling *China* **57** B12
Changlun *Malaysia* **65** J3
Changning *Hunan, China* **59** D9
Changning *Sichuan, China* **58** C5
Changning *Yunnan, China* **58** E2
Changping *China* **56** D9
Changsha *China* **59** C9
Changshan *China* **59** C12
Changshan Qundao *China* **57** E12
Changshu *China* **59** B13
Changshun *China* **58** D6
Changtai *China* **59** E11
Changting *China* **59** E11
Changwu *China* **56** G4
Changxing *China* **59** B12
Changyang *China* **59** B8
Changyi *China* **57** F10
Changyǒn *N. Korea* **57** E13
Changyuan *China* **56** G8
Changzhi *China* **56** F7
Changzhou *China* **59** B12
Chanhanga *Angola* **88** B1
Chania *Greece* **49** D6
Chania □ *Greece* **49** D6
Chanion, Kolpos *Greece* **49** D5
Chanlar = Xanlar *Azerbaijan* **35** K8
Channapatna *India* **66** N10
Channel Is. *U.K.* **15** H5
Channel Is. *U.S.A.* **111** M7
Channel Islands △ *U.S.A.* **111** L7
Channel-Port aux Basques
 Canada **105** C8
Channel Tunnel *Europe* **15** F9
Channing *U.S.A.* **116** D3
Chantada *Spain* **36** C3
Chanthaburi *Thailand* **64** F4
Chantilly *France* **19** C9
Chantonnay *France* **18** F5
Chanute *U.S.A.* **112** G6
Chanza → *Spain* **37** H3
Chao Hu *China* **59** B11
Chao Phraya → *Thailand* **64** F3
Chao Phraya Lowlands
 Thailand **64** E3
Chaocheng *China* **56** F8
Chaohu *China* **59** B11
Chaoyang *Guangdong, China* **59** F11
Chaoyang *Liaoning, China* **57** D11
Chaozhou *China* **59** F11
Chapais *Canada* **104** C5
Chapala *Mozam.* **87** F4
Chapala, L. de *Mexico* **118** C4
Chapayev *Kazakhstan* **34** E10
Chapayevsk *Russia* **34** D9
Chapecó *Brazil* **127** B5
Chapel Hill *U.S.A.* **117** D15
Chapleau *Canada* **104** C3
Chaplin *Canada* **103** C7
Chaplin L. *Canada* **103** C7
Chaplino *Ukraine* **33** H9
Chaplygin *Russia* **32** F11
Chappell *U.S.A.* **112** E2
Chapra = Chhapra *India* **69** G11
Chara *Russia* **53** D12
Charadai *Argentina* **126** B4
Charagua *Bolivia* **124** G6
Charakas *Greece* **49** D7
Charambirá, Punta
 Colombia **124** C3
Charaña *Bolivia* **124** G5
Charantsavan *Armenia* **35** K7
Charanwala *India* **68** F5
Charata *Argentina* **126** B3
Charcas *Mexico* **118** C4
Charcot I. *Antarctica* **5** C17
Chard *U.K.* **15** G5
Chardon *U.S.A.* **114** E3
Chardzhou =
 Türkmenabat
 Turkmenistan **71** B9
Charente □ *France* **20** C4
Charente → *France* **20** C2
Charente-Maritime □
 France **20** C3
Charenton-du-Cher *France* **19** F9
Chari → *Chad* **79** F8
Chārīkār *Afghan.* **66** B6
Chariton *U.S.A.* **112** E7
Chariton → *U.S.A.* **112** F7
Chärjew = Türkmenabat
 Turkmenistan **71** B9
Charkhari *India* **69** G8
Charkhi Dadri *India* **68** E7
Charleroi *Belgium* **17** D4
Charleroi *U.S.A.* **114** F5
Charles, C. *U.S.A.* **113** G16
Charles, Peak *Australia* **93** F3
Charles City *U.S.A.* **112** D7
Charles de Gaulle, Paris ✈
 (CDG) *France* **19** D9

Charles L. *Canada* **103** B6
Charles Town *U.S.A.* **113** F15
Charlesbourg *Canada* **113** B18
Charleston *Ill., U.S.A.* **112** F9
Charleston *Miss., U.S.A.* **117** D9
Charleston *Mo., U.S.A.* **112** G9
Charleston *S.C., U.S.A.* **117** E15
Charleston *W. Va., U.S.A.* **113** F13
Charleston L. *Canada* **115** B9
Charleston Peak *U.S.A.* **111** J11
Charlestown *Ireland* **12** C3
Charlestown *S. Africa* **89** D4
Charlestown *Ind., U.S.A.* **113** F11
Charlestown *N.H., U.S.A.* **115** C12
Charlestown of Aberlour
 U.K. **13** D5
Charleville = Rath Luirc
 Ireland **12** D3
Charleville *Australia* **95** D4
Charleville-Mézières *France* **19** C11
Charlevoix *U.S.A.* **113** C11
Charlieu *France* **19** F11
Charlotte *Mich., U.S.A.* **113** D11
Charlotte *N.C., U.S.A.* **117** D14
Charlotte *Vt., U.S.A.* **115** B11
Charlotte Amalie
 U.S. Virgin Is. **121** e
Charlotte Harbor *U.S.A.* **117** H13
Charlotte L. *Canada* **102** C3
Charlottenberg *Sweden* **10** E6
Charlottesville *U.S.A.* **113** F14
Charlottetown *Nfld. & L.,
 Canada* **105** B8
Charlottetown *P.E.I.,
 Canada* **105** C7
Charlotteville *Trin. & Tob.* **125** J16
Charlton *Australia* **95** F3
Charlton I. *Canada* **104** B4
Charmes *France* **19** D13
Charny *Canada* **105** C5
Charnyany *Belarus* **31** G11
Charolles *France* **19** F11
Chârost *France* **19** F9
Charre *Mozam.* **87** F4
Charroux *France* **20** B4
Charsadda *Pakistan* **68** B4
Charters Towers *Australia* **94** C4
Chartres *France* **18** D8
Chartreuse △ *France* **21** C9
Chascomús *Argentina* **126** D4
Chase *Canada* **102** C5
Chasefu *Zambia* **87** E3
Chashma Barrage *Pakistan* **68** C4
Chasseneuil-sur-
 Bonnieure *France* **20** C4
Chât *Iran* **71** B7
Chatal Balkan = Udvoy
 Balkan *Bulgaria* **45** D10
Château-Arnoux-St-
 Auban *France* **21** D10
Château-Chinon *France* **19** E10
Château-d'Olonne *France* **20** B2
Château-du-Loir *France* **18** E7
Château-Gontier *France* **18** E6
Château-la-Vallière *France* **18** E7
Château-Landon *France* **19** D9
Château-Renard *France* **19** E9
Château-Renault *France* **18** E7
Château-Salins *France* **19** D13
Château-Thierry *France* **19** C10
Châteaubourg *France* **18** D5
Châteaubriant *France* **18** E5
Châteaudun *France* **18** D8
Chateaugay *U.S.A.* **115** B10
Châteaugiron *France* **18** D5
Châteauguay, L. *Canada* **105** A5
Châteaulin *France* **18** D2
Châteaumeillant *France* **19** F9
Châteauneuf-du-Faou
 France **18** D3
Châteauneuf-sur-Charente
 France **20** C3
Châteauneuf-sur-Cher
 France **19** F9
Châteauneuf-sur-Loire
 France **19** E9
Châteaurenard *France* **21** E8
Châteauroux *France* **19** F8
Châteauvillain *France* **19** D11
Châteaux, Pte. des
 Guadeloupe **120** b
Châtelaillon-Plage *France* **20** B2
Châtelguyon *France* **20** C7
Châtellerault *France* **18** F7
Châtelus-Malvaleix *France* **19** F9
Chatham = Chatham-Kent
 Canada **114** D2
Chatham = Miramichi
 Canada **105** C6
Chatham *U.K.* **15** F8
Chatham *U.S.A.* **115** D11
Chatham Is. *Pac. Oc.* **96** M10
Chatham-Kent *Canada* **114** D2
Chatham Rise *Pac. Oc.* **96** M10
Châtillon *Italy* **40** C4
Châtillon-Coligny *France* **19** E9
Châtillon-en-Diois *France* **21** D9
Châtillon-sur-Indre *France* **18** F8

Châtillon-sur-Loire *France* **19** E9
Châtillon-sur-Seine *France* **19** E11
Chatmohar *Bangla.* **69** G13
Chatra *India* **69** G11
Chatrapur *India* **67** K14
Chats, L. des *Canada* **115** A8
Chatsu *India* **68** F6
Chatsworth *Canada* **114** B4
Chatsworth *Zimbabwe* **87** F3
Chättagâm = Chittagong
 Bangla. **67** H17
Chattahoochee *U.S.A.* **117** F12
Chattahoochee → *U.S.A.* **117** F12
Chattanooga *U.S.A.* **117** D12
Chatteris *U.K.* **15** E8
Chaturat *India* **64** E3
Chau Doc *Vietnam* **65** G5
Chaudes-Aigues *France* **20** D7
Chauffailles *France* **19** F11
Chaukan Pass *Burma* **67** F20
Chaumont *France* **19** D12
Chaumont *U.S.A.* **115** B8
Chaumont-en-Vexin *France* **19** C8
Chaumont-sur-Loire *France* **18** E8
Chaunay *France* **20** B4
Chaunskaya G. *Russia* **4** C16
Chauny *France* **19** C10
Chausey, Îs. *France* **18** D5
Chaussin *France* **19** F12
Chauvigny *France* **18** F7
Chauvin *Canada* **103** C6
Chavanges *France* **19** D11
Chaves *Brazil* **125** D9
Chaves *Portugal* **36** D3
Chawang *Thailand* **65** H2
Chazelles-sur-Lyon *France* **21** C8
Chazy *U.S.A.* **115** B11
Cheb *Czech Rep.* **26** A5
Cheboksarskoye Vdkhr.
 Russia **34** B8
Cheboksary *Russia* **34** B8
Cheboygan *U.S.A.* **113** C11
Chebsara *Russia* **32** C10
Chech, Erg *Africa* **78** D5
Chechelnyk *Ukraine* **29** B14
Chechen, Ostrov *Russia* **35** H8
Chechenia □ *Russia* **35** J7
Checheno-Ingush Republic
 = Chechenia □ *Russia* **35** J7
Chechnya = Chechenia □
 Russia **35** J7
Chęciny *Poland* **31** H7
Checotah *U.S.A.* **116** D7
Chedabucto B. *Canada* **105** C7
Cheduba I. *Burma* **67** K18
Cheepie *Australia* **95** D4
Chef-Boutonne *France* **20** B3
Chegdomyn *Russia* **53** D14
Chegga *Mauritania* **78** C4
Chegutu *Zimbabwe* **87** F3
Chehalis *U.S.A.* **110** D4
Chehalis → *U.S.A.* **110** D3
Cheile Nerei-Beusnita △
 Romania **28** F6
Cheiron, Mt. *France* **21** E10
Cheju = Jeju *S. Korea* **57** H14
Cheju-do = Jeju-do *S. Korea* **57** H14
Chekalin *Russia* **32** E9
Chekhovo *Russia* **30** D7
Chekiang = Zhejiang □
 China **59** C13
Chel = Kuru, Bahr el →
 Sudan **81** F2
Chela, Sa. da *Angola* **88** B1
Chelan *U.S.A.* **108** C3
Chelan, L. *U.S.A.* **108** B3
Cheleken = Hazar
 Turkmenistan **52** F6
Cheleken Yarymadasy
 Turkmenistan **71** B7
Chelforó *Argentina* **128** D3
Chelkar = Shalqar
 Kazakhstan **52** E6
Chella *Ethiopia* **81** F4
Chelles *France* **19** D9
Chelm *Poland* **31** G10
Chelmno *Poland* **31** E5
Chelmsford *U.K.* **15** F8
Chełmża *Poland* **31** E5
Chelsea *Australia* **95** F4
Chelsea *U.S.A.* **115** C12
Cheltenham *U.K.* **15** F5
Chelva *Spain* **38** F4
Chelyabinsk *Russia* **52** D7
Chelyuskin, C. =
 Chelyuskin, Mys *Russia* **53** B11
Chelyuskin, Mys *Russia* **53** B11
Chemainus *Canada* **110** B3
Chemba *Mozam.* **85** H6
Chembar = Belinskiy *Russia* **34** D6
Chemillé *France* **18** E6
Chemin Grenier *Mauritius* **85** d
Chemnitz *Germany* **24** E8
Chemult *U.S.A.* **108** E3
Chen, Gora *Russia* **53** C15
Chenab → *Pakistan* **68** D4
Chenango Forks *U.S.A.* **115** D9

Chencha *Ethiopia* **81** F4
Chenchiang = Zhenjiang
 China **59** A12
Cheney *U.S.A.* **108** C5
Cheng Xian *China* **56** H3
Chengbu *China* **59** D8
Chengcheng *China* **56** G5
Chengchou = Zhengzhou
 China **56** G7
Chengde *China* **57** D9
Chengdong Hu *China* **59** A11
Chengdu *China* **58** B5
Chenggong *China* **58** E4
Chenggu *China* **56** H4
Chenghai *China* **59** F11
Chengjiang *China* **58** E4
Chengkou *China* **58** B7
Chengmai *China* **64** C7
Chengxi Hu *China* **59** A11
Chengyang *China* **57** F11
Chenjiagang *China* **57** G10
Chennai *India* **66** N12
Chenôve *France* **19** E12
Chenxi *China* **59** C8
Chenzhou *China* **59** E9
Cheom Ksan *Cambodia* **64** E5
Cheonan *S. Korea* **57** F14
Cheongdo *S. Korea* **57** G15
Cheongju *S. Korea* **57** F14
Cheorwon *S. Korea* **57** E14
Chepelare *Bulgaria* **45** E8
Chepén *Peru* **124** E3
Chepes *Argentina* **126** C2
Chepo *Panama* **120** E4
Chepstow *U.K.* **15** F5
Chequamegon B. *U.S.A.* **112** B8
Cher □ *France* **19** E9
Cher → *France* **18** E7
Chéradi *Italy* **43** B10
Cherasco *Italy* **40** D4
Cheraw *U.S.A.* **117** D15
Cherbourg *France* **18** C5
Cherdakly *Russia* **34** C9
Cherdyn *Russia* **52** C6
Cheremkhovo *Russia* **53** D11
Cherepanovo *Russia* **52** D9
Cherepovets *Russia* **32** C9
Chergui, Chott ech *Algeria* **78** B6
Cherikov = Cherykaw
 Belarus **23** B16
Cherkasy *Ukraine* **33** H7
Cherkasy □ *Ukraine* **33** H6
Cherkessk *Russia* **35** H6
Cherlak *Russia* **52** D8
Chernaya *Russia* **53** B9
Chernelytsya *Ukraine* **29** B10
Cherni *Bulgaria* **44** D7
Chernigov = Chernihiv
 Ukraine **33** G6
Chernihiv *Ukraine* **33** G6
Chernihiv □ *Ukraine* **33** G7
Chernivtsi *Chernivtsi,
 Ukraine* **29** B10
Chernivtsi *Vinnyts'ka,
 Ukraine* **29** B13
Chernivtsi □ *Ukraine* **29** B10
Chernobyl = Chornobyl
 Ukraine **23** C16
Chernogorsk *Russia* **53** D10
Chernomorskoye =
 Chornomorske *Ukraine* **33** K7
Chernovtsy = Chernivtsi
 Ukraine **29** B10
Chernyakhovsk *Russia* **30** D3
Chernyanka *Russia* **33** G9
Chernysheyskiy *Russia* **53** C12
Chernyye Zemli *Russia* **35** H8
Cherokee *Iowa, U.S.A.* **112** D6
Cherokee *Okla., U.S.A.* **116** C5
Cherokee Village *U.S.A.* **116** C9
Cherokees, Grand Lake O'
 The *U.S.A.* **116** C7
Cherrapunji *India* **67** G17
Cherry Valley *U.S.A.* **115** D10
Cherskiy *Russia* **53** C17
Cherskogo Khrebet *Russia* **53** C15
Chersonisos *Greece* **49** D7
Chersonisos Akrotiri *Greece* **49** D6
Chertkovo *Russia* **33** H11
Cherven *Belarus* **23** B15
Cherven-Bryag *Bulgaria* **45** C8
Chervonoarmiyske *Ukraine* **29** E13
Chervonohrad *Ukraine* **23** C13
Cherwell → *U.K.* **15** F6
Cherykaw *Belarus* **23** B16
Chesapeake *U.S.A.* **113** G15
Chesapeake B. *U.S.A.* **113** F14
Cheshire □ *U.K.* **14** D5
Cheshskaya Guba *Russia* **52** C5
Cheshunt *U.K.* **15** F7
Chesil Beach *U.K.* **15** G5
Chesley *Canada* **114** B3
Cheste *Spain* **39** F4
Chester *U.K.* **14** D5
Chester *Calif., U.S.A.* **108** F3

Chester *Ill., U.S.A.* **112** G9
Chester *Mont., U.S.A.* **108** B8
Chester *Pa., U.S.A.* **113** F16
Chester *S.C., U.S.A.* **117** D14
Chester *Vt., U.S.A.* **115** C12
Chester *W. Va., U.S.A.* **114** F4
Chester-le-Street *U.K.* **14** C6
Chesterfield *U.K.* **14** D6
Chesterfield, Îs. *N. Cal.* **90** C8
Chesterfield Inlet *Canada* **100** C10
Chesterton Ra. *Australia* **95** D4
Chesterton Range △
 Australia **95** D4
Chestertown *U.S.A.* **115** C11
Chesterville *Canada* **115** A9
Chesuncook L. *U.S.A.* **113** C19
Chéticamp *Canada* **105** C7
Chetrosu *Moldova* **29** B12
Chetumal *Mexico* **119** D7
Chetumal, B. de *Cent. Amer.* **119** D7
Chetwynd *Canada* **102** B4
Chevanceaux *France* **20** C3
Cheviot, The *U.K.* **14** B5
Cheviot Hills *U.K.* **14** B5
Cheviot Ra. *Australia* **94** D3
Chew Bahir *Ethiopia* **81** G4
Chewelah *U.S.A.* **108** B5
Chewore △ *Zimbabwe* **87** F2
Cheyenne *Okla., U.S.A.* **116** D5
Cheyenne *Wyo., U.S.A.* **108** F11
Cheyenne → *U.S.A.* **112** C3
Cheyenne Wells *U.S.A.* **108** G12
Cheyne B. *Australia* **93** F2
Chhabra *India* **68** G7
Chhaktala *India* **68** H6
Chhapra *India* **69** G11
Chhata *India* **68** F7
Chhatarpur *Jharkhand, India* **69** G11
Chhatarpur *Mad. P., India* **69** G8
Chhattisgarh □ *India* **69** J10
Chhep *Cambodia* **64** F5
Chhindwara *Mad. P., India* **69** H8
Chhindwara *Mad. P., India* **69** H8
Chhlong *Cambodia* **65** F5
Chhota Tawa → *India* **68** H7
Chhoti Kali Sindh → *India* **68** G6
Chhuikhadan *India* **69** J9
Chhuk *Cambodia* **65** G5
Chi → *Thailand* **64** E5
Chiai *Taiwan* **59** F13
Chiali *Taiwan* **59** F13
Chiamboni *Somali Rep.* **84** E8
Chianciano Terme *Italy* **41** E8
Chiang Dao *Thailand* **64** C2
Chiang Kham *Thailand* **64** C3
Chiang Khan *Thailand* **64** D3
Chiang Khong *Thailand* **58** G3
Chiang Mai *Thailand* **64** C2
Chiang Rai *Thailand* **58** H2
Chiang Saen *Thailand* **58** G3
Chianti *Italy* **41** E8
Chiapa → *Mexico* **119** D6
Chiapa de Corzo *Mexico* **119** D6
Chiapas □ *Mexico* **119** D6
Chiapas, Sa. Madre de
 Mexico **119** D6
Chiaramonte Gulfi *Italy* **43** E7
Chiaravalle *Italy* **41** E10
Chiaravalle Centrale *Italy* **43** D9
Chiari *Italy* **40** C6
Chiatura *Georgia* **35** J6
Chiautla de Tapia *Mexico* **119** D5
Chiávari *Italy* **40** D6
Chiavenna *Italy* **40** B6
Chiba *Japan* **55** G10
Chiba □ *Japan* **55** G10
Chibabava *Mozam.* **89** C5
Chibemba *Cunene, Angola* **85** H2
Chibemba *Huila, Angola* **88** B2
Chibi *Zimbabwe* **89** C5
Chibia *Angola* **85** H2
Chibougamau *Canada* **104** C5
Chibougamau, L. *Canada* **104** C5
Chibuk *Nigeria* **83** C7
Chibuto *Mozam.* **89** C5
Chic-Chocs, Mts. *Canada* **105** C6
Chicacole = Srikakulam
 India **67** K13
Chicago *U.S.A.* **112** E10
Chicago Heights *U.S.A.* **112** E10
Chichagof I. *U.S.A.* **100** D6
Chichaoua *Morocco* **78** B4
Chichén-Itzá *Mexico* **119** C7
Chicheng *China* **56** D8
Chichester *U.K.* **15** G7
Chichester Ra. *Australia* **92** D2
Chichibu *Japan* **55** F9
Chichibu-Tama △ *Japan* **55** G9
Ch'ich'ihaerh = Qiqihar
 China **53** E13
Chicholi *India* **68** H8
Chickasaw △ *U.S.A.* **116** D6
Chickasha *U.S.A.* **116** D6
Chiclana de la Frontera
 Spain **37** J4
Chiclayo *Peru* **124** E3
Chico *U.S.A.* **110** F5

Chico → Chubut, Argentina 128 E3
Chico → Santa Cruz, Argentina 128 G3
Chicomo Mozam. 89 C5
Chicomostoc Mexico 118 C4
Chicontepec Mexico 119 C5
Chicopee U.S.A. 115 D12
Chicoutimi Canada 105 C5
Chicualacuala Mozam. 89 C5
Chidambaram India 66 P11
Chidenguele Mozam. 89 C5
Chidley, C. Canada 101 C13
Chiducuane Mozam. 89 C5
Chiede Angola 88 B2
Chiefs Pt. Canada 114 B3
Chiem Hoa Vietnam 64 A5
Chiemsee Germany 25 H8
Chiengi Zambia 87 D2
Chiengmai = Chiang Mai Thailand 64 C2
Chienti → Italy 41 E10
Chieri Italy 40 C4
Chiers → France 19 C11
Chiesa in Valmalenco Italy 40 B6
Chiese → Italy 40 C7
Chieti Italy 41 F11
Chifeng China 57 C10
Chigirin Ukraine 33 H7
Chignecto B. Canada 105 C7
Chiguana Bolivia 126 A2
Chigwell U.K. 15 F8
Chihli, G. of = Bo Hai China 57 E10
Chihuahua Mexico 118 B3
Chihuahua □ Mexico 118 B3
Chiili = Shïeli Kazakhstan 52 E7
Chik Bollapur India 66 N10
Chikmagalur India 66 N9
Chikwawa Malawi 87 F4
Chilam Chavki Pakistan 69 B6
Chilanga Zambia 87 F2
Chilapa Mexico 119 D5
Chilas Pakistan 69 B6
Chilaw Sri Lanka 66 R11
Chilcotin → Canada 102 C4
Childers Australia 95 D5
Childress U.S.A. 116 D4
Chile ■ S. Amer. 128 D2
Chile Rise Pac. Oc. 97 L18
Chilecito Argentina 126 B2
Chilete Peru 124 E3
Chilia, Brațul → Romania 29 E14
Chililabombwe Zambia 87 E2
Chilin = Jilin China 57 C14
Chiliomodi Greece 46 D4
Chilka L. India 67 K14
Chilko → Canada 102 C4
Chilko L. Canada 102 C4
Chillagoe Australia 94 B3
Chillán Chile 126 D1
Chillicothe Ill., U.S.A. 112 E9
Chillicothe Mo., U.S.A. 112 F7
Chillicothe Ohio, U.S.A. 113 F12
Chilliwack Canada 102 D4
Chilo India 68 F5
Chiloane, I. Mozam. 89 C5
Chilok → Russia 53 D11
Chiloé, I. de Chile 128 E2
Chilpancingo Mexico 119 D5
Chiltern Hills U.K. 15 F7
Chilton U.S.A. 112 C9
Chilubi Zambia 87 E2
Chilubula Zambia 87 E3
Chilung Taiwan 59 E13
Chilwa, L. Malawi 87 F4
Chimaltitán Mexico 118 C4
Chimán Panama 120 E4
Chimanimani Zimbabwe 89 B5
Chimay Belgium 17 D4
Chimayo U.S.A. 109 J11
Chimbay Uzbekistan 52 E6
Chimborazo Ecuador 124 D3
Chimbote Peru 124 E3
Chimkent = Shymkent Kazakhstan 52 E7
Chimoio Mozam. 87 F3
Chimpembe Zambia 87 D2
Chin □ Burma 67 J18
Chin Hills Burma 67 H18
Chin Ling Shan = Qinling Shandi China 56 H5
China Mexico 119 B5
China ■ Asia 60 D6
China, Great Plain of Asia 50 E13
China Lake U.S.A. 111 K9
Chinan = Jinan China 56 F9
Chinandega Nic. 120 D2
Chinati Peak U.S.A. 116 G2
Chincha Alta Peru 124 F3
Chinchaga → Canada 102 B5
Chinchilla Australia 95 D5
Chinchilla de Monte Aragón Spain 39 G3
Chinchorro, Banco Mexico 119 D7
Chinchou = Jinzhou China 57 D11
Chincoteague U.S.A. 113 G16
Chinde Mozam. 87 F4
Chindwin → Burma 67 J19

Chineni India 69 C6
Chinga Mozam. 87 F4
Chingola Zambia 87 E2
Chingole Malawi 87 E3
Chinguetti Mauritania 78 D3
Chingune Mozam. 89 C5
Chinhanguanine Mozam. 89 D5
Chinhoyi Zimbabwe 87 F3
Chini India 68 D8
Chiniot Pakistan 68 D5
Chínipas Mexico 118 B3
Chinji Pakistan 68 C5
Chinju = Jinju S. Korea 57 G15
Chinko → C.A.R. 84 D4
Chinle U.S.A. 109 H9
Chinmen Taiwan 59 E13
Chinmen Tao Taiwan 59 E12
Chinnampo = Namp'o N. Korea 57 E13
Chino Japan 55 G9
Chino U.S.A. 111 L9
Chino Valley U.S.A. 109 J7
Chinon France 18 E7
Chinook U.S.A. 108 B9
Chinook Trough Pac. Oc. 96 C10
Chinsali Zambia 87 E3
Chióggia Italy 41 C9
Chíos = Hios Greece 47 C8
Chipata Zambia 87 E3
Chiperceni Moldova 29 C13
Chipindo Angola 85 G3
Chipinge Zimbabwe 87 G3
Chipinge △ Zimbabwe 87 G3
Chipiona Spain 37 J4
Chipley U.S.A. 117 F12
Chipman Canada 105 C6
Chipoka Malawi 87 E3
Chippawa → U.S.A. 112 C7
Chippenham U.K. 15 F5
Chippewa → U.S.A. 112 C7
Chippewa Falls U.S.A. 112 C8
Chipping Norton U.K. 15 F6
Chiprovtsi Bulgaria 44 C6
Chiputneticook Lakes N. Amer. 113 C10
Chiquián Peru 124 F3
Chiquibul △ Belize 120 C2
Chiquimula Guatemala 120 D2
Chiquinquira Colombia 124 B4
Chir → Russia 35 F6
Chirala India 66 M12
Chiramba Mozam. 87 F3
Chirawa India 68 E6
Chirchiq Uzbekistan 52 E7
Chiredzi Zimbabwe 89 C5
Chiricahua △ U.S.A. 109 K9
Chiricahua Peak U.S.A. 109 L9
Chiriquí, G. de Panama 120 E3
Chiriquí, L. de Panama 120 E3
Chirisa △ Zimbabwe 87 F2
Chirivira Falls Zimbabwe 87 G3
Chirmiri India 69 H10
Chirnogi Romania 29 F11
Chirpan Bulgaria 45 D9
Chirripó Grande, Cerro Costa Rica 120 E3
Chirundu Zimbabwe 89 B4
Chisamba Zambia 87 E2
Chisapani Nepal 69 E9
Chisasibi Canada 104 B4
Ch'ishan Taiwan 59 F13
Chisholm Canada 102 C6
Chisholm U.S.A. 112 B8
Chishtian Mandi Pakistan 68 E5
Chishui China 58 C5
Chishui He → China 58 C5
Chisimaio Somali Rep. 75 H3
Chisimba Falls Zambia 87 E3
Chișinău Moldova 29 C13
Chișinău ✈ (KIV) Moldova 29 C13
Chișineu Criș Romania 28 D6
Chisone → Italy 40 D4
Chisos Mts. U.S.A. 116 G3
Chistopol Russia 34 C10
Chita Russia 53 D12
Chitipa Malawi 87 D3
Chitose Japan 54 C10
Chitral Pakistan 66 B7
Chitré Panama 120 E3
Chittagong Bangla. 67 H17
Chittagong □ Bangla. 67 G17
Chittaurgarh India 68 G6
Chittoor India 66 N11
Chitungwiza Zimbabwe 87 F3
Chiusi Italy 41 E8
Chiva Spain 39 F4
Chivasso Italy 40 C4
Chivhu Zimbabwe 87 F3
Chivilcoy Argentina 126 C4
Chiwanda Tanzania 87 E3
Chixi China 59 G9
Chizarira Zimbabwe 87 F2
Chizarira △ Zimbabwe 87 F2
Chizela Zambia 87 E2
Chkalov = Orenburg Russia 52 D6
Chkolovsk Russia 34 B6
Chloride U.S.A. 111 K12

Chlumec nad Cidlinou Czech Rep. 26 A8
Chmielnik Poland 31 H7
Cho Bo Vietnam 58 G5
Cho-do N. Korea 57 E13
Cho Phuoc Hai Vietnam 65 G6
Choa Chu Kang Singapore 65 d
Choba Kenya 86 B4
Chocianów Poland 31 G2
Chociwel Poland 30 E2
Chocolate Mts. U.S.A. 111 M11
Choctawhatchee → U.S.A. 117 F11
Chodecz Poland 31 F6
Chodov Czech Rep. 26 A5
Chodzież Poland 31 F3
Choele Choel Argentina 128 D3
Choiseul St. Lucia 121 f
Choiseul Solomon Is. 90 B8
Choix Mexico 118 B3
Chojna Poland 31 F1
Chojnice Poland 30 E4
Chojnów Poland 31 G2
Chōkai-San Japan 54 E10
Choke Canyon Res. U.S.A. 116 G5
Choke Mts. Ethiopia 81 E4
Chokurdakh Russia 53 B15
Cholame U.S.A. 110 K6
Cholet France 18 E6
Cholguan Chile 126 D1
Choluteca Honduras 120 D2
Choluteca → Honduras 120 D2
Chom Bung Thailand 64 F2
Chom Thong Thailand 64 C2
Choma Zambia 87 F2
Chomolungma = Everest, Mt. Nepal 69 E12
Chomun India 68 F6
Chomutov Czech Rep. 26 A6
Chon Buri Thailand 64 F3
Chon Thanh Vietnam 65 G6
Chone Ecuador 124 D3
Chong Kai Cambodia 64 F4
Chong Mek Thailand 64 E5
Chong Phangan Thailand 65 b
Chong Samui Thailand 65 b
Chongde China 59 B13
Ch'ŏngjin N. Korea 57 D15
Chŏngju N. Korea 57 E13
Chongli China 56 D8
Chongming China 59 B13
Chongming Dao China 59 B13
Chongqing Chongqing, China 58 C6
Chongqing Sichuan, China 58 B4
Chongqing Shi □ China 58 C6
Chongren China 59 D11
Chonguene Mozam. 89 D5
Chongyi China 59 E10
Chongzuo China 58 F6
Chonos, Arch. de los Chile 128 F2
Chop Ukraine 28 B7
Chopim → Brazil 127 B5
Chor Pakistan 68 G3
Chora Greece 46 D3
Chora Sfakion Greece 49 D6
Chorbat La India 69 B7
Chorley U.K. 14 D5
Chorna Ukraine 29 C14
Chornobyl Ukraine 23 C16
Chornomorske Ukraine 33 K7
Chorolque, Cerro Bolivia 126 A2
Choroszcz Poland 31 E9
Chorregon Australia 94 C3
Chorro el Indio △ Venezuela 121 E5
Chortkiv Ukraine 23 D13
Chorzele Poland 31 E7
Chorzów Poland 31 H5
Chos-Malal Argentina 126 D1
Ch'osan N. Korea 57 D13
Choszczno Poland 31 E2
Choteau U.S.A. 108 C7
Chotěboř Czech Rep. 26 B8
Chotila India 68 H4
Chotta Udepur India 68 H6
Chowchilla U.S.A. 110 H6
Choybalsan Mongolia 60 B6
Christchurch N.Z. 91 E4
Christchurch U.K. 15 G6
Christian I. Canada 114 B4
Christiana S. Africa 88 D4
Christiansfeld Denmark 11 J3
Christiansted U.S. Virgin Is. 121 C7
Christie B. Canada 103 A6
Christina → Canada 103 B6
Christmas Cr. → Australia 92 C4
Christmas I. = Kiritimati Kiribati 97 G12
Christmas I. Ind. Oc. 96 J2
Christopher, L. Australia 93 D4
Chrudim Czech Rep. 26 B8
Chrzanów Poland 31 H6
Chtimba Malawi 87 E3
Chū = Shū Kazakhstan 52 E8
Chu → Vietnam 64 C5
Chu Lai Vietnam 64 E7
Chuak, Ko Thailand 65 b

Ch'uanchou = Quanzhou China 59 E12
Chuankou China 56 G6
Chubbuck U.S.A. 108 E7
Chūbu □ Japan 55 F8
Chubu-Sangaku △ Japan 55 F8
Chubut → Argentina 128 E3
Chuchi L. Canada 102 B4
Chuda India 68 H4
Chudovo Russia 32 C6
Chudskoye, Ozero Russia 32 C4
Chugach Mts. U.S.A. 108 F11
Chūgoku □ Japan 55 G6
Chūgoku-Sanchi Japan 55 G6
Chuguyev = Chuhuyiv Ukraine 33 H9
Chuhuyiv Ukraine 33 H9
Chuka Kenya 86 C4
Chukchi Plateau Arctic 4 B17
Chukchi Sea Russia 53 C19
Chukotskoye Nagorye Russia 53 C18
Chula Vista U.S.A. 111 N9
Chulucanas Peru 124 E2
Chulym → Russia 52 D9
Chum Phae Thailand 64 D4
Chum Saeng Thailand 64 E3
Chumar India 69 C8
Chumbicha Argentina 126 B2
Chumerna Bulgaria 45 D9
Chumikan Russia 53 D14
Chumphon Thailand 65 G2
Chumuare Mozam. 87 E3
Chuna → Russia 53 D10
Chun'an China 59 C12
Chuncheon S. Korea 57 F14
Chunchura India 69 H13
Chunga Zambia 87 F2
Chunggang-ŭp N. Korea 57 D14
Chunghwa N. Korea 57 E13
Chungju S. Korea 57 F14
Chungking = Chongqing China 58 C6
Chungyang Shanmo Taiwan 59 F13
Chunian Pakistan 68 D6
Chunya Tanzania 87 D3
Chunyang China 57 C15
Chupara Pt. Trin. & Tob. 125 K15
Chuquibamba Peru 124 G4
Chuquicamata Chile 126 A2
Chur Switz. 25 J5
Churachandpur India 67 G18
Church Stretton U.K. 15 E5
Churchill Canada 103 B10
Churchill → Man., Canada 103 B10
Churchill → Nfld. & L., Canada 105 B7
Churchill, C. Canada 103 B10
Churchill Falls Canada 105 B7
Churchill L. Canada 103 B7
Churchill Pk. Canada 102 B3
Churki India 69 H10
Churu India 68 E6
Churún Merú = Angel Falls Venezuela 124 B6
Chushal India 69 C8
Chuska Mts. U.S.A. 109 H9
Chusovoy Russia 52 D6
Chute-aux-Outardes Canada 105 C6
Chuuk = Truk Micronesia 96 G7
Chuvash Republic = Chuvashia □ Russia 34 C8
Chuvashia □ Russia 34 C8
Chuwärtah Iraq 70 C5
Chuxiong China 58 E3
Chuy Uruguay 127 C5
Chuzhou China 59 A12
Chynadiyeve Ukraine 28 B7
Ci Xian China 56 F8
Ciacova Romania 28 E6
Ciadâr-Lunga Moldova 29 D13
Ciamis Indonesia 63 G13
Cianjur Indonesia 63 G12
Cianorte Brazil 127 A5
Cibola U.S.A. 111 M12
Cicero U.S.A. 112 E10
Cicia Fiji 91 a
Cidacos → Spain 38 C3
Cide Turkey 72 B5
Ciéagas del Cataumbo △ Venezuela 121 E5
Ciechanów Poland 31 F7
Ciechanowiec Poland 31 F9
Ciechocinek Poland 31 F5
Ciego de Ávila Cuba 120 B4
Ciénaga Colombia 124 A4
Cienfuegos Cuba 120 B3
Cíes, Is. Spain 36 C2
Cieszanów Poland 31 H10
Cieszyn Poland 31 J5
Cieza Spain 39 G3

Çifteler Turkey 72 C4
Cifuentes Spain 38 E2
Cihanbeyli Turkey 72 C5
Cihuatlán Mexico 118 D4
Cijara, Embalse de Spain 37 F6
Cijara △ Spain 37 F6
Cijulang Indonesia 63 G13
Cilacap Indonesia 63 G13
Çıldır Turkey 73 B10
Çıldır Gölü Turkey 73 B10
Cili China 59 C8
Cilibia Romania 29 E12
Cilicia Turkey 72 D5
Cilento e Vallo di Diano △ Italy 43 B8
Cili China 59 C8
Cilibia Romania 29 E12
Cilicia Turkey 72 D5
Cill Chainnigh = Kilkenny Ireland 12 D4
Cilo Dağı Turkey 73 D10
Cima U.S.A. 111 K11
Cimarron Kans., U.S.A. 112 G3
Cimarron N. Mex., U.S.A. 109 H11
Cimarron → U.S.A. 116 C6
Cimişlia Moldova 29 D13
Cimone, Mte. Italy 40 D7
Çınar Turkey 73 D9
Çınarcık Turkey 45 F13
Cinca → Spain 38 D5
Cincar Bos.-H. 28 G2
Cincinnati U.S.A. 113 F11
Cincinnatus U.S.A. 115 D9
Ciney Belgium 17 D5
Cíngoli Italy 41 E10
Cinigiano Italy 41 F8
Cinto, Mte. France 21 F12
Cintruénigo Spain 38 C3
Ciocile Romania 29 F12
Ciolăneşti din Deal Romania 29 F10
Ciorani Romania 29 F11
Čiovo Croatia 41 E13
Circeo, Mte. Italy 42 A6
Çirçir Turkey 72 C7
Circle Alaska, U.S.A. 106 a
Circle Mont., U.S.A. 108 C11
Circleville U.S.A. 113 F12
Cirebon Indonesia 63 G13
Ciremay Indonesia 63 G13
Cirencester U.K. 15 F6
Cireşu Romania 28 F7
Cirey-sur-Vezouze France 19 D13
Ciriè Italy 40 C4
Cirium Cyprus 49 E11
Cirò Italy 43 C10
Cirò Marina Italy 43 C10
Ciron → France 20 D3
Cisco U.S.A. 116 E5
Cislău Romania 29 E11
Cisna Poland 31 J9
Cisnădie Romania 29 E9
Cisterna di Latina Italy 42 A5
Cisternino Italy 43 B10
Cistierna Spain 36 C5
Citeli-Ckaro = Tsiteli-Tsqaro Georgia 35 K8
Citlaltépetl = Orizaba, Pico de Mexico 119 D5
Citrus Heights U.S.A. 110 G5
Citrusdal S. Africa 88 E2
Città del Vaticano = Vatican City ■ Europe 41 G9
Città della Pieve Italy 41 F9
Città di Castello Italy 41 E9
Città Sant' Angelo Italy 41 F11
Cittadella Italy 41 C8
Cittaducale Italy 41 F9
Cittanova Italy 43 D9
Ciuc, Munţii Romania 29 D11
Ciucaş, Vf. Romania 29 E10
Ciucea Romania 28 D7
Ciuciulea Moldova 29 C12
Ciuciuleni Moldova 29 C13
Ciudad Acuña Mexico 118 B4
Ciudad Altamirano Mexico 118 D4
Ciudad Anáhuac Mexico 118 B4
Ciudad Bolívar Venezuela 124 B6
Ciudad Camargo Mexico 118 B3
Ciudad de México Mexico 119 D5
Ciudad de Valles Mexico 119 C5
Ciudad del Carmen Mexico 119 D6
Ciudad del Este Paraguay 127 B5
Ciudad Delicias = Delicias Mexico 118 B3
Ciudad Frontera Mexico 118 B4
Ciudad Guayana Venezuela 124 B6
Ciudad Guerrero Mexico 118 B3
Ciudad Guzmán Mexico 118 D4
Ciudad Juárez Mexico 118 A3
Ciudad Lerdo Mexico 118 B4
Ciudad Madero Mexico 119 C5
Ciudad Mante Mexico 119 C5
Ciudad Obregón Mexico 118 B3
Ciudad Real Spain 37 G7
Ciudad Real □ Spain 37 G7
Ciudad Rodrigo Spain 36 E4
Ciudad Victoria Mexico 119 C5
Ciudadela Spain 48 B10
Ciulniţa Romania 29 F12

Ciumeghiu Romania 28 D6
Ciuperceni Romania 28 F8
Civa Burnu Turkey 72 B7
Cividale del Friuli Italy 41 B10
Civita Castellana Italy 41 F9
Civitanova Marche Italy 41 E10
Civitavécchia Italy 41 F8
Civray France 20 B4
Çivril Turkey 47 C11
Cixerri → Italy 42 C1
Cixi China 59 B13
Cizre Turkey 73 D10
Cizur Mayor Spain 38 C3
Clackmannanshire □ U.K. 13 E5
Clacton-on-Sea U.K. 15 F9
Clain → France 18 F7
Claire, L. Canada 102 B6
Clairton U.S.A. 114 F5
Clairvaux-les-Lacs France 19 F12
Claise → France 20 B5
Clallam Bay U.S.A. 110 B2
Clamecy France 19 E10
Clanton U.S.A. 117 E11
Clanwilliam S. Africa 88 E2
Clara Ireland 12 C4
Claraville U.S.A. 111 K8
Clare Australia 95 E2
Clare U.S.A. 113 D11
Clare □ Ireland 12 D3
Clare → Ireland 12 C2
Clare I. Ireland 12 C1
Claremont Calif., U.S.A. 111 L9
Claremont N.H., U.S.A. 115 C12
Claremont Pt. Australia 94 A3
Claremore U.S.A. 116 C6
Claremorris Ireland 12 C3
Clarence → Australia 95 D5
Clarence → N.Z. 91 E4
Clarence, I. Chile 128 G2
Clarence I. Antarctica 5 C18
Clarence Str. Australia 92 B5
Clarence Town Bahamas 121 B5
Clarendon Pa., U.S.A. 114 E5
Clarendon Tex., U.S.A. 116 D4
Clarenville-Shoal Harbour Canada 105 C9
Claresholm Canada 102 D6
Clarie Coast Antarctica 5 C9
Clarinda U.S.A. 112 E6
Clarington Canada 114 C6
Clarion Iowa, U.S.A. 112 D7
Clarion Pa., U.S.A. 114 E5
Clarion → U.S.A. 114 E5
Clarion Fracture Zone Pac. Oc. 98 H7
Clark U.S.A. 112 C5
Clark, Pt. Canada 114 B3
Clark Fork U.S.A. 108 B5
Clark Fork → U.S.A. 108 B5
Clarkdale U.S.A. 109 J7
Clarke City Canada 105 B6
Clarke I. Australia 95 G4
Clarke Ra. Australia 94 J6
Clarks Fork Yellowstone → U.S.A. 108 D9
Clark's Harbour Canada 105 D6
Clarks Hill L. = J. Strom Thurmond L. U.S.A. 117 E13
Clarks Summit U.S.A. 115 E9
Clarksburg U.S.A. 113 F13
Clarksdale U.S.A. 117 D9
Clarkston U.S.A. 108 C5
Clarksville Ark., U.S.A. 116 D8
Clarksville Tenn., U.S.A. 117 C11
Clarksville Tex., U.S.A. 116 E7
Clatskanie U.S.A. 110 D3
Claude U.S.A. 116 D4
Claveria Phil. 61 B4
Clay U.S.A. 110 G5
Clay Center U.S.A. 112 F5
Claypool U.S.A. 109 K8
Claysburg U.S.A. 114 F6
Claysville U.S.A. 114 F4
Clayton N. Mex., U.S.A. 109 H12
Clayton N.Y., U.S.A. 115 B8
Clear, C. Ireland 12 E2
Clear, L. Canada 114 A7
Clear Hills Canada 102 B5
Clear I. Ireland 12 E2
Clear L. U.S.A. 110 F4
Clear Lake Iowa, U.S.A. 112 D7
Clear Lake S. Dak., U.S.A. 112 C5
Clear Lake Res. U.S.A. 108 F3
Clearfield Pa., U.S.A. 114 E6
Clearfield Utah, U.S.A. 108 F7
Clearlake U.S.A. 110 G4
Clearwater Canada 102 C4
Clearwater U.S.A. 117 H13
Clearwater → Alta., Canada 102 C6
Clearwater → Alta., Canada 103 B6
Clearwater L. Canada 103 C9
Clearwater Lake △ Canada 103 C8
Clearwater Mts. U.S.A. 108 C6
Clearwater River △ Canada 103 B7
Cleburne U.S.A. 116 E6
Clee Hills U.K. 15 E5
Cleethorpes U.K. 14 D7

Cleeve Cloud *U.K.* **15** F6
Clelles *France* **21** D9
Clemson *U.S.A.* **117** D13
Clerke Reef *Australia* **92** C2
Clermont *Australia* **94** C4
Clermont *France* **19** C9
Clermont *U.S.A.* **117** G14
Clermont-en-Argonne
 France **19** C12
Clermont-Ferrand *France* **20** C7
Clermont-l'Hérault *France* **20** E7
Clerval *France* **19** E13
Clervaux *Lux.* **17** D6
Cles *Italy* **40** B8
Clevedon *U.K.* **15** F5
Cleveland *Miss., U.S.A.* **117** E9
Cleveland *Ohio, U.S.A.* **114** E3
Cleveland *Okla., U.S.A.* **116** C6
Cleveland *Tenn., U.S.A.* **117** D12
Cleveland *Tex., U.S.A.* **116** F7
Cleveland, C. *Australia* **94** B4
Cleveland, Mt. *U.S.A.* **108** B7
Cleveland Heights *U.S.A.* **114** E3
Clevelândia *Brazil* **127** B5
Clew B. *Ireland* **12** C2
Clewiston *U.S.A.* **117** H14
Clifden *Ireland* **12** C1
Clifden *N.Z.* **91** G1
Cliffdell *U.S.A.* **110** D5
Cliffy Hd. *Australia* **93** G2
Clifton *Australia* **95** D5
Clifton *Ariz., U.S.A.* **109** K9
Clifton *Colo., U.S.A.* **108** G9
Clifton *Tex., U.S.A.* **116** F6
Clifton Beach *Australia* **94** B4
Climax *Canada* **103** D7
Clinch → *U.S.A.* **117** D12
Clingmans Dome *U.S.A.* **117** D13
Clint *U.S.A.* **116** F1
Clinton *B.C., Canada* **102** C4
Clinton *Ont., Canada* **114** C3
Clinton *N.Z.* **91** G2
Clinton *Ark., U.S.A.* **116** D8
Clinton *Conn., U.S.A.* **115** E12
Clinton *Ill., U.S.A.* **112** E9
Clinton *Ind., U.S.A.* **112** F10
Clinton *Iowa, U.S.A.* **112** E8
Clinton *Mass., U.S.A.* **115** D13
Clinton *Miss., U.S.A.* **117** E9
Clinton *Mo., U.S.A.* **112** F7
Clinton *N.C., U.S.A.* **117** D15
Clinton *Okla., U.S.A.* **116** D5
Clinton *S.C., U.S.A.* **117** D14
Clinton *Tenn., U.S.A.* **117** C12
Clinton *Wash., U.S.A.* **110** C4
Clinton C. *Australia* **94** C5
Clinton Colden L. *Canada* **100** C9
Clintonville *U.S.A.* **112** C9
Clipperton, I. *Pac. Oc.* **97** F17
Clipperton Fracture Zone
 Pac. Oc. **97** G16
Clisham *U.K.* **13** D2
Clisson *France* **18** E5
Clitheroe *U.K.* **14** D5
Clo-oose *Canada* **110** B2
Cloates, Pt. *Australia* **92** D1
Clocolan *S. Africa* **89** D4
Clodomira *Argentina* **126** B3
Clogher Hd. *Ireland* **12** C5
Clonakilty *Ireland* **12** E3
Clonakilty B. *Ireland* **12** E3
Cloncurry *Australia* **94** C3
Cloncurry *Ireland* **12** C5
Cloncurry → *Australia* **94** B3
Clondalkin *Ireland* **12** C5
Clones *Ireland* **12** B4
Clonmel *Ireland* **12** D4
Cloppenburg *Germany* **24** C4
Cloquet *U.S.A.* **112** B7
Clorinda *Argentina* **126** B4
Cloud Bay *Canada* **104** C2
Cloud Peak *U.S.A.* **108** D10
Cloudcroft *U.S.A.* **109** K11
Cloverdale *U.S.A.* **110** G4
Clovis *Calif., U.S.A.* **110** J7
Clovis *N. Mex., U.S.A.* **109** J12
Cloyes-sur-le-Loir *France* **18** E8
Cloyne *Canada* **114** B7
Cluj □ *Romania* **29** D8
Cluj-Napoca *Romania* **29** D8
Clunes *Australia* **95** F3
Cluny *France* **19** F11
Cluses *France* **19** F13
Clusone *Italy* **40** C6
Clutha → *N.Z.* **91** G2
Clwyd → *U.K.* **14** D4
Clyde *Canada* **102** C6
Clyde *N.Z.* **91** F2
Clyde *U.S.A.* **114** C8
Clyde → *U.K.* **13** F4
Clyde, Firth of *U.K.* **13** F3
Clyde Muirshiel △ *U.K.* **13** F4
Clyde River *Canada* **101** B13
Clydebank *U.K.* **13** F4
Clymer *N.Y., U.S.A.* **114** D5
Clymer *Pa., U.S.A.* **114** D5
Ćmielów *Poland* **31** H8

Côa → *Portugal* **36** D3
Coachella *U.S.A.* **111** M10
Coachella Canal *U.S.A.* **111** N12
Coahoma *U.S.A.* **116** E4
Coahuayana → *Mexico* **118** D4
Coahuila □ *Mexico* **118** B4
Coal → *Canada* **102** B3
Coalane *Mozam.* **87** F4
Coalcomán *Mexico* **118** D4
Coaldale *Canada* **102** D6
Coalgate *U.S.A.* **116** D6
Coalinga *U.S.A.* **110** J6
Coalisland *U.K.* **12** B5
Coalville *U.K.* **14** E6
Coalville *U.S.A.* **108** F8
Coamo *Puerto Rico* **121** d
Coari *Brazil* **124** D6
Coast □ *Kenya* **86** C4
Coast Mts. *Canada* **102** C3
Coast Ranges *U.S.A.* **110** G4
Coatbridge *U.K.* **13** F4
Coatepec *Mexico* **119** D5
Coatepeque *Guatemala* **120** D1
Coatesville *U.S.A.* **113** F16
Coaticook *Canada* **115** A13
Coats I. *Canada* **101** C11
Coats Land *Antarctica* **5** D1
Cobá *Mexico* **119** C7
Cobadin *Romania* **29** F13
Cobalt *Canada* **104** C4
Cobán *Guatemala* **120** C1
Çobanlar *Turkey* **47** C12
Cobar *Australia* **95** E4
Cóbh *Ireland* **12** E3
Cobija *Bolivia* **124** F5
Cobleskill *U.S.A.* **115** D10
Coboconk *Canada* **114** B6
Cobourg *Canada* **114** C6
Cobourg △ *Australia* **92** B5
Cobourg Pen. *Australia* **92** B5
Cobram *Australia* **95** F4
Coburg *Germany* **25** E6
Coca *Spain* **36** D6
Cocanada = Kakinada
 India **67** L13
Cocentaina *Spain* **39** G4
Cochabamba *Bolivia* **124** G5
Cochem *Germany* **25** E3
Cochemane *Mozam.* **87** F3
Cochin *India* **66** Q10
Cochin China =
 Nam-Phan *Vietnam* **65** G6
Cochran *U.S.A.* **117** E13
Cochrane *Alta., Canada* **102** C6
Cochrane *Ont., Canada* **104** C3
Cochrane *Chile* **128** F2
Cochrane → *Canada* **103** B8
Cochrane, L. *Chile* **128** F2
Cochranton *U.S.A.* **114** E4
Cockburn *Australia* **95** E3
Cockburn, Canal *Chile* **128** G2
Cockburn I. *Canada* **104** C3
Cockburn Ra. *Australia* **92** C4
Cockermouth *U.K.* **14** C4
Cocklebiddy *Australia* **93** F4
Cockpit Country, The
 Jamaica **120** a
Coco → *Cent. Amer.* **120** D3
Coco, I. del *Pac. Oc.* **97** G19
Cocoa *U.S.A.* **117** G14
Cocobeach *Gabon* **84** D1
Cocora *Romania* **29** F12
Cocos B. *Trin. & Tob.* **125** K15
Cocos Is. *Ind. Oc.* **96** J1
Cocos Ridge *Pac. Oc.* **97** G19
Cod, C. *U.S.A.* **113** D18
Codajás *Brazil* **124** D6
Codigoro *Italy* **41** D9
Codlea *Romania* **29** E10
Codó *Brazil* **125** D10
Codogno *Italy* **40** C6
Codróipo *Italy* **41** C10
Codru, Munţii *Romania* **28** D7
Cody *U.S.A.* **108** D9
Coe Hill *Canada* **114** B7
Coelemu *Chile* **126** D1
Coen *Australia* **94** A3
Coesfeld *Germany* **24** D3
Coeur d'Alene *U.S.A.* **108** C5
Coeur d'Alene L. *U.S.A.* **108** C5
Coevorden *Neths.* **17** B6
Cofete *Canary Is.* **48** F5
Coffeyville *U.S.A.* **112** G6
Coffin B. *Australia* **95** E2
Coffin Bay *Australia* **95** E2
Coffin Bay △ *Australia* **95** E2
Coffin Bay Peninsula
 Australia **95** E2
Coffs Harbour *Australia* **95** E5
Cofrentes *Spain* **39** F3
Cogalnic → *Moldova* **29** E14
Cogealac *Romania* **29** F13
Coghinas → *Italy* **42** B1
Coghinas, L. del *Italy* **42** B2
Cognac *France* **20** C3

Cogne *Italy* **40** C4
Cogolin *France* **21** E10
Cogolludo *Spain* **38** E1
Cohocton *U.S.A.* **114** D7
Cohocton → *U.S.A.* **114** D7
Cohoes *U.S.A.* **115** D11
Cohuna *Australia* **95** F3
Coiba, I. de *Panama* **120** E3
Coig → *Argentina* **128** G3
Coigeach, Rubha *U.K.* **13** C3
Coihaique *Chile* **128** F2
Coimbatore *India* **66** P10
Coimbra *Brazil* **124** G7
Coimbra *Portugal* **36** E2
Coimbra □ *Portugal* **36** E2
Coín *Spain* **37** J6
Coipasa, Salar de *Bolivia* **124** G5
Cojimies *Ecuador* **124** C3
Cojocna *Romania* **29** D8
Cojutepequé *El Salv.* **120** D2
Čoka *Serbia* **28** E5
Cokeville *U.S.A.* **108** E8
Colac *Australia* **95** F3
Colatina *Brazil* **125** G10
Colbeck, C. *Antarctica* **5** D13
Colborne *Canada* **114** C7
Colby *U.S.A.* **112** F3
Colca → *Peru* **124** G4
Colchester *U.K.* **15** F8
Colchester *U.S.A.* **115** E12
Cold L. *Canada* **103** C7
Coldstream *Canada* **102** C5
Coldstream *U.K.* **13** F6
Coldwater *Canada* **114** B5
Coldwater *Kans., U.S.A.* **112** G4
Coldwater *Mich., U.S.A.* **113** E11
Colebrook *U.S.A.* **115** B13
Coleman *U.S.A.* **116** F5
Coleman → *Australia* **94** B3
Colenso *S. Africa* **89** D4
Coleraine *Australia* **95** F3
Coleraine *U.K.* **12** A5
Coleridge, L. *N.Z.* **91** E3
Colesberg *S. Africa* **88** E4
Coleville *U.S.A.* **110** G7
Colfax *Calif., U.S.A.* **110** F6
Colfax *La., U.S.A.* **116** F8
Colfax *Wash., U.S.A.* **108** C5
Colhué Huapi, L. *Argentina* **128** F3
Colibaşi *Moldova* **29** E13
Colibaşi *Romania* **29** F9
Cólico *Italy* **40** B6
Coligny *France* **19** F12
Coligny *S. Africa* **89** D4
Colima *Mexico* **118** D4
Colima □ *Mexico* **118** D4
Colima, Nevado de *Mexico* **118** D4
Colina *Chile* **126** C1
Colina do Norte *Guinea-Biss.* **82** C2
Colinas *Brazil* **125** D10
Colindres *Spain* **36** B7
Coll *U.K.* **13** E2
Collaguasi *Chile* **126** A2
Collarada, Peña *Spain* **38** C4
Collarenebri *Australia* **95** D4
Colle di Val d'Elsa *Italy* **40** E8
Collécchio *Italy* **40** D7
Colleen Bawn *Zimbabwe* **87** G2
College Park *U.S.A.* **117** E12
College Station *U.S.A.* **116** F6
Collesalvetti *Italy* **40** E7
Colli Euganei △ *Italy* **41** C8
Collie *Australia* **93** F2
Collier B. *Australia* **92** C3
Collier Ra. *Australia* **93** D2
Collier Range △ *Australia* **93** D2
Collierville *U.S.A.* **117** D10
Collina, Passo di *Italy* **40** D7
Collingwood *Canada* **114** B4
Collingwood *N.Z.* **91** D4
Collins *Canada* **104** B2
Collinsville *Australia* **94** C4
Collipulli *Chile* **126** D1
Collooney *Ireland* **12** B3
Colmar *France* **19** D14
Colmars *France* **21** D10
Colmenar *Spain* **37** J6
Colmenar de Oreja *Spain* **36** E7
Colmenar Viejo *Spain* **36** E7
Colo → *Australia* **95** E5
Cologne = Köln *Germany* **24** E2
Colom, I. d'en *Spain* **48** B11
Coloma *U.S.A.* **110** G6
Colomb-Béchar = Béchar
 Algeria **78** B5
Colombey-les-Belles *France* **19** D12
Colombey-les-Deux-Églises
 France **19** D11
Colombia ■ *S. Amer.* **124** C4
Colombian Basin *S. Amer.* **98** H12
Colombo *Sri Lanka* **66** R11
Colomiers *France* **20** E5
Colón *B. Aires, Argentina* **126** C3
Colón *Entre Ríos, Argentina* **126** C4
Colón *Cuba* **120** B3
Colón *Panama* **120** E4
Colón, Arch. de *Ecuador* **122** D1

Colònia de Sant Jordi *Spain* **48** B9
Colonia del Sacramento
 Uruguay **126** C4
Colonia Dora *Argentina* **126** B3
Colonial Beach *U.S.A.* **113** F15
Colonie *U.S.A.* **115** D11
Colonna, C. *Italy* **43** C10
Colonsay *Canada* **103** C7
Colonsay *U.K.* **13** E2
Colorado □ *U.S.A.* **108** G11
Colorado → *Argentina* **128** D4
Colorado → *N. Amer.* **109** L6
Colorado → *U.S.A.* **116** G7
Colorado City *U.S.A.* **116** E4
Colorado Plateau *U.S.A.* **109** H8
Colorado River Aqueduct
 U.S.A. **111** L12
Colorado Springs *U.S.A.* **108** G11
Colorno *Italy* **40** D7
Colotlán *Mexico* **118** C4
Colstrip *U.S.A.* **108** D10
Colton *U.S.A.* **115** B10
Columbia *Ky., U.S.A.* **113** G11
Columbia *La., U.S.A.* **116** E8
Columbia *Miss., U.S.A.* **117** F10
Columbia *Mo., U.S.A.* **112** F7
Columbia *Pa., U.S.A.* **115** F8
Columbia *S.C., U.S.A.* **117** D14
Columbia *Tenn., U.S.A.* **117** D11
Columbia → *N. Amer.* **110** D2
Columbia, C. *Canada* **101** A11
Columbia, District of □
 U.S.A. **113** F15
Columbia, Mt. *Canada* **102** C5
Columbia Basin *U.S.A.* **108** C4
Columbia Falls *U.S.A.* **108** B6
Columbia Mts. *Canada* **102** C5
Columbia Plateau *U.S.A.* **108** E5
Columbiana *U.S.A.* **114** F4
Columbretes, Is. *Spain* **38** F5
Columbus *Ga., U.S.A.* **117** E12
Columbus *Ind., U.S.A.* **113** F11
Columbus *Kans., U.S.A.* **112** G6
Columbus *Miss., U.S.A.* **117** E10
Columbus *Mont., U.S.A.* **108** D9
Columbus *N. Mex., U.S.A.* **109** L10
Columbus *Nebr., U.S.A.* **112** E5
Columbus *Ohio, U.S.A.* **113** F12
Columbus *Tex., U.S.A.* **116** G6
Colunga *Spain* **36** B5
Colusa *U.S.A.* **110** F4
Colville *U.S.A.* **108** B5
Colville → *U.S.A.* **106** a
Colville, C. *N.Z.* **91** B5
Colwood *Canada* **110** B3
Colwyn Bay *U.K.* **14** D4
Coma *Ethiopia* **81** F4
Comácchio *Italy* **41** D9
Comalcalco *Mexico* **119** D6
Comallo *Argentina* **128** E2
Comana *Romania* **29** F11
Comanche *U.S.A.* **116** F5
Comandante Ferraz
 Antarctica **5** C18
Comănești *Romania* **29** D11
Comarnic *Romania* **29** E10
Comayagua *Honduras* **120** D2
Combahee → *U.S.A.* **117** E14
Combarbalá *Chile* **126** C1
Combe Martin *U.K.* **15** F3
Combeaufontaine *France* **19** E12
Comber *Canada* **114** D2
Comber *U.K.* **12** B6
Combermere *Canada* **114** A7
Comblain-au-Pont *Belgium* **17** D5
Combourg *France* **18** D5
Combrailles *France* **19** F9
Combronde *France* **20** C7
Comeragh Mts. *Ireland* **12** D4
Comet *Australia* **94** C4
Comilla *Bangla.* **67** H17
Comino *Malta* **49** C1
Comino, C. *Italy* **42** B2
Cómiso *Italy* **43** F7
Comitán de Domínguez
 Mexico **119** D6
Commentry *France* **19** F9
Commerce *Ga., U.S.A.* **117** D13
Commerce *Tex., U.S.A.* **116** E7
Commercy *France* **19** D12
Committee B. *Canada* **101** C11
Commonwealth B. *Antarctica* **5** C10
Commoron Cr. → *Australia* **95** D5
Communism Pk. = imeni
 Ismail Samani, Pik
 Tajikistan **52** F8
Como *Italy* **40** C6
Como, Lago di *Italy* **40** B6
Comodoro Rivadavia
 Argentina **128** F3
Comoé → *Ivory C.* **82** D4
Comorâşti *Romania* **28** E6
Comorin, C. =
 Kanyakumari *India* **66** Q10
Comoros ■ *Ind. Oc.* **85** a
Comox *Canada* **102** D4
Compiègne *France* **19** C9

Comporta *Portugal* **37** G2
Compostela *Mexico* **118** C4
Comprida, I. *Brazil* **127** A6
Compton *Canada* **115** A13
Compton *U.S.A.* **111** M8
Comrat *Moldova* **29** D13
Con Cuong *Vietnam* **64** C5
Con Dao △ *Vietnam* **65** H6
Con Son *Vietnam* **65** H6
Conakry *Guinea* **82** D2
Conara *Australia* **95** G4
Conceição *Mozam.* **87** F4
Conceição da Barra *Brazil* **125** G11
Conceição do Araguaia
 Brazil **125** E9
Concepción *Argentina* **126** B2
Concepción *Bolivia* **124** G6
Concepción *Chile* **126** D1
Concepción *Mexico* **119** D6
Concepción *Paraguay* **126** A4
Concepción □ *Chile* **126** D1
Concepción → *Mexico* **118** A2
Concepción, Est. de *Chile* **128** G2
Concepción, L. *Bolivia* **124** G6
Concepción, Pta. *Mexico* **118** B2
Concepción del Oro *Mexico* **118** C4
Concepción del Uruguay
 Argentina **126** C4
Conception, Pt. *U.S.A.* **111** L6
Conception B. *Canada* **105** C9
Conception B. *Namibia* **88** C1
Conception I. *Bahamas* **121** B4
Concession *Zimbabwe* **87** F3
Conches-en-Ouche *France* **18** D7
Concho *U.S.A.* **109** J9
Concho → *U.S.A.* **116** F5
Conchos → *Chihuahua,*
 Mexico **118** B4
Conchos → *Chihuahua,*
 Mexico **118** B3
Conchos → *Tamaulipas,*
 Mexico **119** B5
Concord *Calif., U.S.A.* **110** H4
Concord *N.C., U.S.A.* **117** D14
Concord *N.H., U.S.A.* **115** C13
Concordia *Antarctica* **5** D17
Concordia *Argentina* **126** C4
Concórdia *Brazil* **124** D5
Concordia *Mexico* **118** C3
Concordia *U.S.A.* **112** F5
Concrete *U.S.A.* **108** B3
Condamine *Australia* **95** D5
Condat *France* **20** C6
Condé-sur-Noireau *France* **18** D6
Condeúba *Brazil* **125** F10
Condobolin *Australia* **95** E4
Condom *France* **20** E4
Condon *U.S.A.* **108** D3
Conegliano *Italy* **41** C9
Conejera, I. = Conills, I. des
 Spain **48** B9
Conejos *Mexico* **118** B4
Conemaugh → *U.S.A.* **114** F5
Conero △ *Italy* **41** E10
Confolens *France* **20** B4
Confuso → *Paraguay* **126** B4
Congaz *Moldova* **29** D13
Conghua *China* **59** F9
Congjiang *China* **58** E7
Congleton *U.K.* **14** D5
Congo (Brazzaville) =
 Congo ■ *Africa* **84** E3
Congo (Kinshasa) =
 Congo, Dem. Rep. of
 the ■ *Africa* **84** E4
Congo ■ *Africa* **84** E3
Congo → *Africa* **84** F2
Congo, Dem. Rep. of the ■
 Africa **84** E4
Congo Basin *Africa* **84** E4
Congonhas *Brazil* **127** A7
Congress *U.S.A.* **109** J7
Conil de la Frontera *Spain* **37** J4
Conills, I. des *Spain* **48** B9
Coniston *Canada* **104** C3
Conjeeveram =
 Kanchipuram *India* **66** N11
Conklin *Canada* **103** B6
Conklin *U.S.A.* **115** D9
Conn, L. *Ireland* **12** B2
Connacht □ *Ireland* **12** C2
Conneaut *U.S.A.* **114** E4
Connecticut □ *U.S.A.* **115** E12
Connecticut → *U.S.A.* **115** E12
Connell *U.S.A.* **108** C4
Connellsville *U.S.A.* **114** F5
Connemara *Ireland* **12** C2
Connemara △ *Ireland* **12** C2
Connerré *France* **18** D7
Connersville *U.S.A.* **113** F11
Connors Ra. *Australia* **94** C4
Conques *France* **20** D6
Conquest *Canada* **103** C7
Conrad *U.S.A.* **108** B8

Conran, C. *Australia* **95** F4
Conroe *U.S.A.* **116** F7
Consecon *Canada* **114** C7
Conselheiro Lafaiete *Brazil* **127** A7
Conselve *Italy* **41** C8
Consett *U.K.* **14** C6
Consort *Canada* **103** C6
Constance = Konstanz
 Germany **25** H5
Constance, L. = Bodensee
 Europe **25** H5
Constanţa *Romania* **29** F13
Constanţa □ *Romania* **29** F13
Constantina *Spain* **37** H5
Constantine *Algeria* **78** A7
Constantia *U.S.A.* **115** C8
Constitución *Chile* **126** D1
Constitución *Uruguay* **126** C4
Constitución de 1857 △
 Mexico **118** A1
Consuegra *Spain* **37** F7
Consul *Canada* **103** D7
Contact *U.S.A.* **108** F6
Contai *India* **69** J12
Contamana *Peru* **124** E4
Contarina *Italy* **41** C9
Contas → *Brazil* **125** F11
Contes *France* **21** E11
Contoocook *U.S.A.* **115** C13
Contra Costa *Mozam.* **89** D5
Contres *France* **18** E8
Contrexéville *France* **19** D12
Contwoyto L. *Canada* **100** C8
Conversano *Italy* **43** B10
Conway = Conwy *U.K.* **14** D4
Conway = Conwy → *U.K.* **14** D4
Conway *Australia* **94** J6
Conway *Ark., U.S.A.* **116** D8
Conway *N.H., U.S.A.* **115** C13
Conway *S.C., U.S.A.* **117** E15
Conway, C. *Australia* **94** J6
Conway, L. *Australia* **95** D2
Conwy *U.K.* **14** D4
Conwy □ *U.K.* **14** D4
Conwy → *U.K.* **14** D4
Coober Pedy *Australia* **95** D1
Cooch Behar = Koch Bihar
 India **67** F13
Cooinda *Australia* **92** B5
Cook *Australia* **93** F5
Cook *U.S.A.* **112** B7
Cook, B. *Chile* **128** H3
Cook, C. *Canada* **102** C3
Cook, Mt. = Aoraki Mount
 Cook *N.Z.* **91** E3
Cook Inlet *U.S.A.* **100** D4
Cook Is. *Pac. Oc.* **97** J12
Cook Strait *N.Z.* **91** D5
Cookeville *U.S.A.* **117** C12
Cookhouse *S. Africa* **88** E4
Cookshire *Canada* **115** A13
Cookstown *U.K.* **12** B5
Cooksville *Canada* **114** C5
Cooktown *Australia* **94** B4
Coolabah *Australia* **95** E4
Cooladdi *Australia* **95** D4
Coolah *Australia* **95** E4
Coolamon *Australia* **95** E4
Coolgardie *Australia* **93** F3
Coolidge *U.S.A.* **109** K8
Coolidge Dam *U.S.A.* **109** K8
Cooma *Australia* **95** F4
Coon Rapids *U.S.A.* **112** C7
Coonabarabran *Australia* **95** E4
Coonamble *Australia* **95** E4
Coonana *Australia* **93** F3
Coondapoor *India* **66** N9
Cooninnie, L. *Australia* **95** D2
Cooper *U.S.A.* **116** E7
Cooper Cr. → *Australia* **95** D2
Cooper Ridge *Pac. Oc.* **97** G12
Cooperstown *N. Dak., U.S.A.* **112** B4
Cooperstown *N.Y., U.S.A.* **115** D10
Coorabie *Australia* **93** F5
Coorong, The *Australia* **95** F2
Coorow *Australia* **93** E2
Cooroy *Australia* **95** D5
Coos Bay *U.S.A.* **108** E1
Coosa → *U.S.A.* **117** E11
Cootamundra *Australia* **95** E4
Cootehill *Ireland* **12** B4
Copahue Paso *Argentina* **126** D1
Copainalá *Mexico* **119** D6
Copake *U.S.A.* **115** D11
Copalnic Mănăştur *Romania* **29** C8
Copán *Honduras* **120** D2
Cope *U.S.A.* **108** G12
Cope, C. *Spain* **39** H3
Copenhagen = København
 Denmark **11** J6
Copenhagen *U.S.A.* **115** C9
Copertino *Italy* **43** B11
Copiapó *Chile* **126** B1
Copiapó → *Chile* **126** B1
Coplay *U.S.A.* **115** F9
Copp L. *Canada* **102** A6
Copparo *Italy* **41** D8

Coppename → *Suriname* **125** B7
Copper Canyon =
  Barranca del Cobre △
  Mexico **118** B3
Copper Harbor *U.S.A.* **112** B10
Copper Queen *Zimbabwe* **87** F2
Copperas Cove *U.S.A.* **116** F6
Copperbelt □ *Zambia* **87** E2
Coppermine = Kugluktuk
  Canada **100** C8
Coppermine → *Canada* **100** C8
Copperopolis *U.S.A.* **110** H6
Copşa Mică *Romania* **29** D9
Coquet → *U.K.* **14** B6
Coquille *U.S.A.* **108** E1
Coquimbo *Chile* **126** C1
Coquimbo □ *Chile* **126** C1
Corabia *Romania* **29** G9
Coracora *Peru* **124** G4
Coraki *Australia* **95** D5
Coral *U.S.A.* **114** F5
Coral Gables *U.S.A.* **117** J14
Coral Harbour *Canada* **101** C11
Coral Sea *Pac. Oc.* **90** C8
Coral Sea Basin *Pac. Oc.* **96** J7
Coral Sea Islands Terr. □
  Australia **90** C8
Coral Springs *U.S.A.* **117** H14
Coraopolis *U.S.A.* **114** F4
Corato *Italy* **43** A9
Corbeil-Essonnes *France* **19** D9
Corbett △ *India* **69** E8
Corbie *France* **19** C9
Corbigny *France* **19** E11
Corbin *U.S.A.* **113** G11
Corbones → *Spain* **37** H5
Corbu *Romania* **29** F13
Corby *U.K.* **15** E7
Corcaigh = Cork *Ireland* **12** E3
Corcoran *U.S.A.* **110** J7
Corcovado △ *Costa Rica* **120** E3
Cordele *U.S.A.* **117** F13
Cordell *U.S.A.* **116** D5
Cordenòns *Italy* **41** C10
Cordes-sur-Ciel *France* **20** D5
Córdoba *Argentina* **126** C3
Córdoba *Mexico* **119** D5
Córdoba *Spain* **37** H6
Córdoba □ *Argentina* **126** C3
Córdoba □ *Spain* **37** G6
Córdoba, Sierra de
  Argentina **126** C3
Cordon *Phil.* **61** C4
Cordova *U.S.A.* **100** C5
Corella *Spain* **38** C3
Corella → *Australia* **94** B3
Corfield *Australia* **94** C3
Corfu = Kerkyra *Greece* **49** A3
Corfu ✈ (CFU) *Greece* **46** B1
Corfu, Str. of = Kerkyras,
  Notio Steno *Greece* **49** A4
Corgo = O Corgo *Spain* **36** C3
Cori *Italy* **42** A5
Coria *Spain* **36** F4
Coria del Río *Spain* **37** H4
Corigliano Cálabro *Italy* **43** C9
Coringa Is. *Australia* **94** B4
Corinth = Korinthos *Greece* **46** D4
Corinth *Miss., U.S.A.* **117** D10
Corinth *N.Y., U.S.A.* **115** C11
Corinth, G. of =
  Korinthiakos Kolpos
  Greece **46** C4
Corinth Canal *Greece* **46** D4
Corinto *Brazil* **125** G10
Corinto *Nic.* **120** D2
Cork *Ireland* **12** E3
Cork □ *Ireland* **12** E3
Cork Harbour *Ireland* **12** E3
Corlay *France* **18** D3
Corleone *Italy* **42** E6
Corleto Perticara *Italy* **43** B9
Çorlu *Turkey* **45** E11
Cormack L. *Canada* **102** A4
Cormòns *Italy* **41** C10
Cormorant *Canada* **103** C8
Cormorant L. *Canada* **103** C8
Corn Is. = Maiz, Is. del *Nic.* **120** D3
Cornalvo △ *Spain* **37** F4
Cornélio Procópio *Brazil* **127** A5
Corner Brook *Canada* **105** C8
Corneşti *Moldova* **29** C13
Corníglio *Italy* **40** D7
Corning *Ark., U.S.A.* **117** C9
Corning *Calif., U.S.A.* **108** G2
Corning *Iowa, U.S.A.* **112** E6
Corning *N.Y., U.S.A.* **114** D7
Corno Grande *Italy* **41** F10
Cornwall *Canada* **115** A10
Cornwall *U.S.A.* **115** F8
Cornwall □ *U.K.* **15** G3
Cornwall I. *Canada* **101** B10
Cornwallis I. *Canada* **101** B10
Corny Pt. *Australia* **95** E2
Coro *Venezuela* **124** A5
Coroatá *Brazil* **125** D10

Corocoro *Bolivia* **124** G5
Coroico *Bolivia* **124** G5
Coromandel *N.Z.* **91** B5
Coromandel Coast *India* **66** N12
Corona *Calif., U.S.A.* **111** M9
Corona *N. Mex., U.S.A.* **109** J11
Coronach *Canada* **103** D7
Coronado *U.S.A.* **111** N9
Coronado, B. de *Costa Rica* **120** E3
Coronados, Is. Los *Mexico* **111** N9
Coronation *Canada* **102** C6
Coronation Gulf *Canada* **100** C9
Coronation I. *Antarctica* **5** C18
Coronation Is. *Australia* **92** B3
Coronda *Argentina* **126** C3
Coronel *Chile* **126** D1
Coronel Bogado *Paraguay* **126** B4
Coronel Dorrego *Argentina* **126** D3
Coronel Oviedo *Paraguay* **126** B4
Coronel Pringles *Argentina* **126** D3
Coronel Suárez *Argentina* **126** D3
Coronel Vidal *Argentina* **126** D4
Coropuna, Nevado *Peru* **124** G4
Corowa *Australia* **95** E4
Corozal *Belize* **119** D7
Corozal Pt. *Trin. & Tob.* **125** K15
Corps *France* **21** D9
Corpus *Argentina* **127** B4
Corpus Christi *U.S.A.* **116** H6
Corpus Christi, L. *U.S.A.* **116** G6
Corral de Almaguer *Spain* **36** F7
Corralejo *Canary Is.* **48** F6
Corraun Pen. *Ireland* **12** C2
Corréggio *Italy* **40** D7
Correntes, C. das *Mozam.* **89** C6
Corrib, L. *Ireland* **12** C2
Corrientes *Argentina* **126** B4
Corrientes □ *Argentina* **126** B4
Corrientes → *Argentina* **126** C4
Corrientes → *Peru* **124** D4
Corrientes, C. *Colombia* **124** B3
Corrientes, C. *Cuba* **120** B3
Corrientes, C. *Mexico* **118** C3
Corrigan *U.S.A.* **116** F7
Corrigin *Australia* **93** F2
Corriverton *Guyana* **124** B7
Corry *U.S.A.* **114** E5
Corse □ *France* **21** G13
Corse, C. *France* **21** E13
Corse △ *France* **21** F13
Corse-du-Sud □ *France* **21** G13
Corsica = Corse □ *France* **21** G13
Corsicana *U.S.A.* **116** E6
Corte *France* **21** F13
Corte Pinto *Portugal* **37** H3
Cortegana *Spain* **37** H4
Cortés, Mar de =
  California, G. de *Mexico* **118** B2
Cortez *U.S.A.* **109** H9
Cortina d'Ampezzo *Italy* **41** B9
Cortland *N.Y., U.S.A.* **115** D8
Cortland *Ohio, U.S.A.* **114** E4
Cortona *Italy* **41** E8
Corubal → *Guinea-Biss.* **82** C2
Coruche *Portugal* **37** G2
Çoruh → *Turkey* **35** K5
Çorum *Turkey* **72** B6
Çorum □ *Turkey* **72** B6
Corumbá *Brazil* **124** G7
Corund *Romania* **29** D10
Corunna = A Coruña *Spain* **36** B2
Corvallis *U.S.A.* **108** D2
Corvette, L. de la *Canada* **104** B5
Corvo *Azores* **78** a
Corydon *U.S.A.* **112** E7
Cosalá *Mexico* **118** C3
Cosamaloapan de Carpio
  Mexico **119** D5
Cosenza *Italy* **43** C9
Coşereni *Romania* **29** F11
Coshocton *U.S.A.* **114** F3
Cosmo Newberry *Australia* **93** E3
Cosne-Cours-sur-Loire
  France **19** E9
Coso Junction *U.S.A.* **111** J9
Coso Pk. *U.S.A.* **111** J9
Cospeito *Spain* **36** B3
Cosquín *Argentina* **126** C3
Cossato *Italy* **40** C5
Cossé-le-Vivien *France* **18** E6
Cosson → *France* **18** E8
Costa Blanca *Spain* **39** G4
Costa Brava *Spain* **38** D8
Costa del Sol *Spain* **37** J6
Costa Dorada *Spain* **38** D6
Costa Mesa *U.S.A.* **111** M9
Costa Rica ■ *Cent. Amer.* **120** E3
Costa Smeralda *Italy* **42** A2
Costeşti *Romania* **29** F9
Costigliole d'Asti *Italy* **40** D5
Cosumnes → *U.S.A.* **110** G5
Coswig *Sachsen, Germany* **24** D9
Coswig *Sachsen-Anhalt,
  Germany* **24** D8

Cotabato *Phil.* **61** H6
Cotagaita *Bolivia* **126** A2
Côte d'Azur *France* **21** E11
Côte-d'Ivoire = Ivory
  Coast ■ *Africa* **82** D4
Côte d'Or *France* **19** E11
Côte-d'Or □ *France* **19** E11
Cotentin *France* **18** C5
Côtes de Meuse *France* **19** C12
Côtes-du-Nord =
  Côtes-d'Armor □ *France* **18** D4
Cotiella *Spain* **38** C5
Cotillo *Canary Is.* **48** F5
Cotiujeni *Moldova* **29** C13
Cotonou *Benin* **83** D5
Cotopaxi *Ecuador* **124** D3
Cotronei *Italy* **43** C9
Cotswold Hills *U.K.* **15** F5
Cottage Grove *U.S.A.* **108** E2
Cottbus *Germany* **24** D10
Cottonwood *U.S.A.* **109** J7
Cotulla *U.S.A.* **116** G5
Coubre, Pte. de la *France* **20** C2
Couches *France* **19** F11
Couço *Portugal* **37** G2
Coudersport *U.S.A.* **114** E6
Couedic, C. du *Australia* **95** F2
Couëron *France* **18** E5
Couesnon → *France* **18** D5
Couhé *France* **20** B4
Coulanges-sur-Yonne
  France **19** E10
Coulee City *U.S.A.* **108** C4
Coulee Dam Nat. Recr.
  Area = Lake
  Roosevelt △ *U.S.A.* **108** B4
Coulman I. *Antarctica* **5** D11
Coulommiers *France* **19** D10
Coulon → *France* **21** E9
Coulonge → *Canada* **104** C4
Coulonges-sur-l'Autize
  France **20** B3
Coulounieix-Chamiers
  France **20** C4
Coulterville *U.S.A.* **110** H6
Council *U.S.A.* **108** D5
Council Bluffs *U.S.A.* **112** E6
Council Grove *U.S.A.* **112** F5
Coupeville *U.S.A.* **110** B4
Courantyne → *S. Amer.* **124** B7
Courcelles *Belgium* **17** D4
Courchevel *France* **21** C10
Courland *U.S.A.* **110** G5
Courtenay *Canada* **102** D4
Courtenay *France* **19** D10
Courtland *U.S.A.* **110** G5
Courtrai = Kortrijk *Belgium* **17** D3
Courtright *Canada* **114** D2
Coushatta *U.S.A.* **116** E8
Coutances *France* **18** C5
Coutras *France* **20** C3
Coutts Crossing *Australia* **95** D5
Couva *Trin. & Tob.* **125** K15
Couvin *Belgium* **17** D4
Covarrubias *Spain* **36** C7
Covasna *Romania* **29** E11
Covasna □ *Romania* **29** E10
Cove I. *Canada* **114** A3
Coventry *U.K.* **15** E6
Covilhã *Portugal* **36** E3
Covington *Ga., U.S.A.* **117** E13
Covington *Ky., U.S.A.* **113** F11
Covington *Tenn., U.S.A.* **117** D10
Covington *Va., U.S.A.* **113** G14
Cowal, L. *Australia* **95** E4
Cowan, L. *Australia* **93** F3
Cowan L. *Canada* **103** C7
Cowangie *Australia* **95** F3
Cowansville *Canada* **115** A12
Coward Springs *Australia* **95** D2
Cowcowing Lakes *Australia* **93** F2
Cowdenbeath *U.K.* **13** E5
Cowell *Australia* **95** E2
Cowes *U.K.* **15** G6
Cowichan L. *Canada* **110** B2
Cowlitz → *U.S.A.* **110** D4
Cowra *Australia* **95** E4
Cox *Spain* **39** G4
Coxilha Grande *Brazil* **127** B5
Coxim *Brazil* **125** G8
Cox's Bazar *Bangla.* **67** J17
Coyote Wells *U.S.A.* **111** N11
Coyuca de Benítez *Mexico* **119** D4
Coyuca de Catalán *Mexico* **119** D4
Cozad *U.S.A.* **112** E4
Cozes *France* **20** C3
Cozumel *Mexico* **119** C7
Cozumel, Isla *Mexico* **119** C7
Crab Hill *Barbados* **121** g

Cracow = Kraków *Poland* **31** H6
Cracow *Australia* **95** D5
Cradle Mt.-Lake St. Clair △
  Australia **95** G4
Cradock *Australia* **95** E2
Cradock *S. Africa* **88** E4
Craig *U.S.A.* **108** F10
Craigavon *U.K.* **12** B5
Craigmore *Zimbabwe* **87** G3
Craik *Canada* **103** C7
Crailsheim *Germany* **25** F6
Craiova *Romania* **29** F8
Cramsie *Australia* **94** C3
Cranberry L. *U.S.A.* **115** B10
Cranberry Portage *Canada* **103** C8
Cranbrook *Australia* **93** F2
Cranbrook *Canada* **102** D5
Crandon *U.S.A.* **112** C9
Crane *Oreg., U.S.A.* **108** E4
Crane *Tex., U.S.A.* **116** F3
Crane, The *Barbados* **121** g
Cranston *U.S.A.* **115** E13
Craon *France* **18** E6
Craonne *France* **19** C10
Craponne-sur-Arzon *France* **20** C7
Crasna *Romania* **29** D12
Crasna → *Romania* **28** C7
Crasnei, Munţii *Romania* **29** C8
Crater L. *U.S.A.* **108** E2
Crater Lake △ *U.S.A.* **108** E2
Craters of the Moon △
  U.S.A. **108** E7
Crateús *Brazil* **125** E10
Crato *Brazil* **125** E11
Crato *Portugal* **37** F3
Craven, L. *Canada* **104** B4
Crawford *U.S.A.* **112** D2
Crawfordsville *U.S.A.* **112** E10
Crawley *U.K.* **15** F7
Crazy Mts. *U.S.A.* **108** C8
Crean L. *Canada* **103** C7
Crécy-en-Ponthieu *France* **19** B8
Crediton *Canada* **114** C3
Crediton *U.K.* **15** G4
Cree → *Canada* **103** B7
Cree → *U.K.* **13** G4
Cree L. *Canada* **103** B7
Creede *U.S.A.* **109** H10
Creekside *U.S.A.* **114** F5
Creel *Mexico* **118** B3
Creemore *Canada* **114** B4
Creighton *Canada* **103** C8
Creighton *U.S.A.* **112** D5
Creil *France* **19** C9
Crema *Italy* **40** C6
Cremona *Italy* **40** C7
Crepaja *Serbia* **28** E5
Crépy *France* **19** C10
Crépy-en-Valois *France* **19** C9
Cres *Croatia* **41** D11
Crescent City *U.S.A.* **108** F1
Crescentino *Italy* **40** C5
Crespo *Argentina* **126** C3
Cresson *U.S.A.* **114** F6
Crest *France* **21** D9
Cresta, Mt. *Phil.* **61** C5
Crestline *Calif., U.S.A.* **111** L9
Crestline *Ohio, U.S.A.* **114** F2
Creston *Canada* **102** D5
Creston *Calif., U.S.A.* **110** K6
Creston *U.S.A.* **112** E6
Crestview *Calif., U.S.A.* **110** H8
Crestview *Fla., U.S.A.* **117** F11
Crêt de la Neige *France* **19** F12
Crete = Kriti *Greece* **49** D7
Crete *U.S.A.* **112** E5
Crete, Sea of *Greece* **47** F7
Créteil *France* **19** D9
Creus, C. de *Spain* **38** C8
Creuse □ *France* **19** F9
Creuse → *France* **20** B4
Creutzwald *France* **19** C13
Creuzburg *Germany* **24** D6
Crèvecœur-le-Grand *France* **19** C9
Crevillente *Spain* **39** G4
Crewe *U.K.* **14** D5
Crewkerne *U.K.* **15** G5
Crianlarich *U.K.* **13** E4
Criciúma *Brazil* **127** B6
Cricova *Moldova* **29** C13
Crieff *U.K.* **13** E5
Crikvenica *Croatia* **41** C11
Crimea □ *Ukraine* **33** K8
Crimean Pen. = Krymskyy
  Pivostriv *Ukraine* **33** K8
Crimmitschau *Germany* **24** E8
Cristuru Secuiesc *Romania* **29** D10
Crişul Alb → *Romania* **28** D6
Crişul Negru → *Romania* **28** D6
Crişul Repede → *Romania* **28** D6
Criuleni *Moldova* **29** C14
Crivitz *Germany* **24** B7
Crna → *Macedonia* **44** E5
Crna Gora =
  Montenegro ■ *Europe* **44** D3
Crna Gora *Macedonia* **44** D5

Crna Reka = Crna →
  Macedonia **44** E5
Crna Trava *Serbia* **44** D6
Crni Drim → *Macedonia* **44** E4
Crni Timok → *Serbia* **44** C6
Crnoljeva Planina *Serbia* **44** D5
Črnomelj *Slovenia* **41** C12
Croagh Patrick *Ireland* **12** C2
Croatia ■ *Europe* **41** C13
Crocker, Banjaran *Malaysia* **62** C5
Crockett *U.S.A.* **116** F7
Crocodile = Umgwenya →
  Mozam. **89** D5
Crocodile Is. *Australia* **94** A1
Crocq *France* **20** C6
Crodo *Italy* **40** B5
Crohy Hd. *Ireland* **12** B3
Croisette, C. *France* **21** E9
Croisic, Pte. du *France* **18** E4
Croix, L. La *Canada* **104** C1
Croker, C. *Australia* **92** B5
Croker, C. *Canada* **114** B4
Croker I. *Australia* **92** B5
Cromarty *U.K.* **13** D4
Cromer *U.K.* **14** E9
Cromwell *N.Z.* **91** F2
Cromwell *U.S.A.* **115** E12
Cronat *France* **19** F10
Crook *U.K.* **14** C6
Crooked → *Canada* **102** C4
Crooked → *U.S.A.* **108** D3
Crooked I. *Bahamas* **121** B5
Crooked Island Passage
  Bahamas **121** B5
Crookston *Minn., U.S.A.* **112** B5
Crookston *Nebr., U.S.A.* **112** D3
Crookwell *Australia* **95** E4
Crosby *U.K.* **14** D4
Crosby *N. Dak., U.S.A.* **112** A2
Crosby *Pa., U.S.A.* **114** E6
Crosbyton *U.S.A.* **116** E4
Crosia *Italy* **43** C9
Cross → *Nigeria* **83** D6
Cross City *U.S.A.* **117** G13
Cross Fell *U.K.* **14** C5
Cross L. *Canada* **103** C9
Cross Lake *Canada* **103** C9
Cross River □ *Nigeria* **83** D6
Cross River △ *Nigeria* **83** D6
Cross Sound *U.S.A.* **100** D6
Crossett *U.S.A.* **116** E9
Crosshaven *Ireland* **12** E3
Crossmaglen *U.K.* **12** B5
Crossmolina *Ireland* **12** B2
Crossville *U.S.A.* **117** D12
Croswell *U.S.A.* **114** C2
Croton-on-Hudson *U.S.A.* **115** E11
Crotone *Italy* **43** C10
Crow → *Canada* **102** B4
Crow Agency *U.S.A.* **108** D10
Crow Hd. *Ireland* **12** E1
Crowell *U.S.A.* **116** E5
Crowley *U.S.A.* **116** F8
Crowley, L. *U.S.A.* **110** H8
Crown Point *Ind., U.S.A.* **112** E10
Crown Point *N.Y., U.S.A.* **115** C11
Crown Pt. *Trin. & Tob.* **125** J16
Crownpoint *U.S.A.* **109** J9
Crows Landing *U.S.A.* **110** H5
Crows Nest *Australia* **95** D5
Crowsnest Pass *Canada* **102** D6
Croydon *Australia* **94** B3
Croydon □ *U.K.* **15** F7
Crozet, Is. *Ind. Oc.* **3** G12
Crozon *France* **18** D2
Crusheen *Ireland* **12** D3
Cruz, C. *Cuba* **120** C4
Cruz Alta *Brazil* **127** B5
Cruz Bay *U.S. Virgin Is.* **121** e
Cruz de Incio *Spain* **36** C3
Cruz del Eje *Argentina* **126** C3
Cruzeiro *Brazil* **127** A7
Cruzeiro do Oeste *Brazil* **127** A5
Cruzeiro do Sul *Brazil* **124** E4
Cry L. *Canada* **102** B3
Crystal Bay *U.S.A.* **110** F7
Crystal Brook *Australia* **95** E2
Crystal City *U.S.A.* **116** G5
Crystal Falls *U.S.A.* **112** B9
Crystal River *U.S.A.* **117** G13
Crystal Springs *U.S.A.* **117** F9
Csenger *Hungary* **28** C7
Csongrád *Hungary* **28** D5
Csongrád □ *Hungary* **28** D5
Csorna *Hungary* **28** C2
Csurgo *Hungary* **28** D2

Cuanza → *Angola* **84** F2
Cuarto → *Argentina* **126** C3
Cuatrociénegas *Mexico* **118** B4
Cuauhtémoc *Mexico* **118** B3
Cuba *Portugal* **37** G3
Cuba *N. Mex., U.S.A.* **109** H10
Cuba *N.Y., U.S.A.* **114** D6
Cuba ■ *W. Indies* **120** B4
Cubango → *Africa* **88** B3
Çubuk *Turkey* **72** B5
Cuc Phuong △ *Vietnam* **64** B5
Cuchumatanes, Sierra de
  los *Guatemala* **120** C1
Cuckfield *U.K.* **15** F7
Cucuí *Brazil* **124** C5
Cucurpé *Mexico* **118** A2
Cuddalore *India* **66** P11
Cuddapah *India* **66** M11
Cuddapan, L. *Australia* **94** D3
Cudillero *Spain* **36** B4
Cue *Australia* **93** E2
Cuéllar *Spain* **36** D6
Cuenca *Ecuador* **124** D3
Cuenca *Spain* **38** E2
Cuenca □ *Spain* **38** F3
Cuenca, Serranía de *Spain* **38** F3
Cuenca Alta del
  Manzanares △ *Spain* **36** E7
Cuerdo del Pozo, Embalse
  de la *Spain* **38** D2
Cuernavaca *Mexico* **119** D5
Cuero *U.S.A.* **116** G6
Cuers *France* **21** E10
Cueva de la Quebrada del
  Toro △ *Venezuela* **121** D6
Cuevas del Almanzora *Spain* **39** H3
Cuevo *Bolivia* **124** H6
Cugir *Romania* **29** E8
Cugnaux *France* **20** E5
Cuhai-Bakony → *Hungary* **28** C2
Cuiabá *Brazil* **125** G7
Cuiabá → *Brazil* **125** G7
Cuijk *Neths.* **17** C5
Cuilco *Guatemala* **120** C1
Cuillin Hills *U.K.* **13** D2
Cuillin Sd. *U.K.* **13** D2
Cuilo = Kwilu →
  Dem. Rep. of the Congo **84** E3
Cuiseaux *France* **19** F12
Cuito → *Angola* **88** B3
Cuitzeo, L. de *Mexico* **118** D4
Cujmir *Romania* **28** F7
Cukai *Malaysia* **65** K4
Culbertson *U.S.A.* **108** B11
Culcairn *Australia* **95** F4
Culebra *Puerto Rico* **121** d
Culebra, Sierra de la *Spain* **36** D4
Culfa *Azerbaijan* **73** C11
Culgoa → *Australia* **95** D4
Culgoa Flood Plain △
  Australia **95** D4
Culiacán *Mexico* **118** C3
Culiacán → *Mexico* **118** C3
Culik *Indonesia* **63** J18
Culion *Phil.* **61** F4
Cúllar *Spain* **37** H8
Cullarin Ra. *Australia* **95** E4
Cullen *U.K.* **13** D6
Cullen Pt. *Australia* **94** A3
Cullera *Spain* **39** F4
Cullman *U.S.A.* **117** D11
Culloz *France* **21** C9
Culpeper *U.S.A.* **113** F14
Culuene → *Brazil* **125** F8
Culver, Pt. *Australia* **93** F3
Culverden *N.Z.* **91** E4
Cumaná *Venezuela* **124** A6
Cumaovası *Turkey* **47** C9
Cumberland, B.C., Canada* **102** D4
Cumberland *Ont., Canada* **115** A9
Cumberland *U.S.A.* **113** F14
Cumberland → *U.S.A.* **112** G9
Cumberland, L. *U.S.A.* **113** G11
Cumberland Gap △ *U.S.A.* **113** G12
Cumberland I. *U.S.A.* **117** F14
Cumberland Is. *Australia* **94** J7
Cumberland Island △
  U.S.A. **117** F14
Cumberland L. *Canada* **103** C8
Cumberland Pen. *Canada* **101** C13
Cumberland Plateau *U.S.A.*
  117 D12
Cumberland Sd. *Canada* **101** C13
Cumbernauld *U.K.* **13** F5
Cumborah *Australia* **95** D4
Cumbres de Majalca △
  Mexico **118** B3
Cumbres de Monterrey △
  Mexico **118** B4
Cumbres Mayores *Spain* **37** G4
Cumbria □ *U.K.* **14** C5
Cumbrian Mts. *U.K.* **14** C5
Cumbum *India* **66** M11
Cuminá → *Brazil* **125** D7

Cummings Mt. *U.S.A.* **111** K8
Cummins *Australia* **95** E2
Cumnock *Australia* **95** E4
Cumnock *U.K.* **13** F4
Cumpas *Mexico* **118** B3
Cumplida, Pta. *Canary Is.* **48** F2
Çumra *Turkey* **72** D5
Cunco *Chile* **128** D2
Cuncumén *Chile* **126** C1
Cunderdin *Australia* **93** F2
Cunene → *Angola* **88** B1
Cúneo *Italy* **40** D4
Çüngüş *Turkey* **70** B3
Cunillera, I. = Sa Conillera
  Spain **48** C7
Cunlhat *France* **20** C7
Cunnamulla *Australia* **95** D4
Cuorgnè *Italy* **40** C4
Cupar *Canada* **103** C8
Cupar *U.K.* **13** E5
Cupcini *Moldova* **29** B12
Cupertino *U.S.A.* **110** H4
Cupica, G. de *Colombia* **124** B3
Čuprija *Serbia* **44** C5
Curaçao *Neth. Ant.* **121** D6
Curanilahue *Chile* **126** D1
Curaray → *Peru* **124** D4
Cure → *France* **19** E10
Curepipe *Mauritius* **85** d
Curepto *Chile* **126** D1
Curiapo *Venezuela* **124** B6
Curicó *Chile* **126** C1
Curieuse *Seychelles* **85** b
Curinga *Italy* **43** D9
Curitiba *Brazil* **127** B6
Curitibanos *Brazil* **127** B5
Currabubula *Australia* **95** E5
Currais Novos *Brazil* **125** E11
Curral Velho *C. Verde Is.* **78** b
Curralinho *Brazil* **125** D9
Currane, L. *Ireland* **12** E1
Currant *U.S.A.* **108** G6
Currawinya △ *Australia* **95** D3
Current → *U.S.A.* **116** C9
Currie *Australia* **95** F3
Currie *U.S.A.* **108** F6
Curtea de Argeş *Romania* **29** E9
Curtici *Romania* **28** D6
Curtis *U.S.A.* **112** E3
Curtis Group *Australia* **95** F4
Curtis I. *Australia* **94** C5
Curuápanema → *Brazil* **125** D7
Curuçá *Brazil* **125** D9
Curuguaty *Paraguay* **127** A4
Curup *Indonesia* **62** E2
Curuzú Cuatiá *Argentina* **126** B4
Curvelo *Brazil* **125** G10
Cusco = Cuzco *Peru* **124** F4
Cushendall *U.K.* **12** A5
Cushing *U.S.A.* **116** D6
Cushing, Mt. *Canada* **102** B3
Cusihuiriáchic *Mexico* **118** B3
Cusna, Mte. *Italy* **40** D7
Cusset *France* **19** F10
Custer *U.S.A.* **112** D3
Cut Bank *U.S.A.* **108** B7
Cutchogue *U.S.A.* **115** E12
Cuthbert *U.S.A.* **117** F12
Cutler *U.S.A.* **110** J7
Cutro *Italy* **43** C9
Cuttaburra → *Australia* **95** D3
Cuttack *India* **67** J14
Cuvier, C. *Australia* **93** D1
Cuvier I. *N.Z.* **91** B5
Cuxhaven *Germany* **24** B4
Cuyahoga Falls *U.S.A.* **114** E3
Cuyahoga Valley △ *U.S.A.* **114** E3
Cuyapo *Phil.* **61** D4
Cuyo *Phil.* **61** F4
Cuyo East Pass *Phil.* **61** F4
Cuyo West Pass *Phil.* **61** F4
Cuyuni → *Guyana* **124** B7
Cuzco *Bolivia* **124** H5
Cuzco *Peru* **124** F4
Čvrsnica *Bos.-H.* **28** G2
Cwmbran *U.K.* **15** F4
Cyangugu *Rwanda* **86** C2
Cybinka *Poland* **31** F1
Cyclades *Greece* **46** E6
Cyclades □ *Greece* **46** E6
Cygnet *Australia* **95** G4
Cynthiana *U.S.A.* **113** F11
Cypress Hills *Canada* **103** D7
Cypress Hills △ *Canada* **103** D7
Cyprus ■ *Asia* **49** E12
Cyrenaica *Libya* **79** C10
Cyrene *Libya* **79** B10
Czaplinek *Poland* **30** E3
Czar *Canada* **103** C6
Czarna → *Łódzkie, Poland* **31** G6
Czarna → *Świętokrzyskie,*
  Poland **31** H8
Czarna Białostocka *Poland* **31** E10
Czarna Woda *Poland* **30** E5
Czarne *Poland* **30** E3
Czarnków *Poland* **31** F3

Czech Rep. ■ *Europe* **26** B8
Czechowice-Dziedzice *Poland* **31** J5
Czempiń *Poland* **31** F3
Czeremcha *Poland* **31** F10
Czerniejewo *Poland* **31** F4
Czersk *Poland* **30** E4
Czerwieńsk *Poland* **31** F2
Czerwionka-Leszczyny
  Poland **31** H5
Częstochowa *Poland* **31** H6
Człopa *Poland* **31** E3
Człuchów *Poland* **30** E4
Czyżew-Osada *Poland* **31** F9

D

Da → *Vietnam* **58** G5
Da Hinggan Ling *China* **60** B7
Da Lat *Vietnam* **65** G7
Da Nang *Vietnam* **64** D7
Da Qaidam *China* **60** C4
Da Yunhe → *Hopei, China* **57** E9
Da Yunhe → *Jiangsu, China* **57** G11
Da'an *China* **57** B13
Daan Viljoen △ *Namibia* **88** C2
Dab'a, Ras el *Egypt* **80** H6
Daba Shan *China* **58** B7
Dabai *Nigeria* **83** C6
Dabakala *Ivory C.* **82** D4
Dabas *Hungary* **28** C4
Dabat *Ethiopia* **81** E4
Dabbagh, Jabal *Si. Arabia* **70** E2
Dabhoi *India* **68** H5
Dabie *Poland* **31** F5
Dabie Shan *China* **59** B10
Dabilda *Cameroon* **83** C7
Dabnou *Niger* **83** C6
Dabo = Pasirkuning
  Indonesia **62** E2
Dabola *Guinea* **82** C2
Dabou *Ivory C.* **82** D4
Daboya *Ghana* **83** D4
Dabravolya *Belarus* **31** F10
Dąbrowa Białostocka
  Poland **30** F4
Dąbrowa Górnicza *Poland* **31** H6
Dąbrowa Tarnowska *Poland* **31** H7
Dabu *China* **59** E11
Dabung *Malaysia* **65** K4
Dabus → *Ethiopia* **81** E4
Dacato → *Ethiopia* **81** F5
Dacca = Dhaka *Bangla.* **69** H14
Dacca = Dhaka □ *Bangla.* **69** G14
Dachau *Germany* **25** G7
Dachigam △ *India* **68** B6
Dachstein, Hoher *Austria* **26** D6
Dačice *Czech Rep.* **26** B8
Dadanawa *Guyana* **124** C7
Daday *Turkey* **72** B5
Dade City *U.S.A.* **117** G13
Dadhar *Pakistan* **68** E2
Dadiya *Nigeria* **83** D7
Dadnah *U.A.E.* **71** E8
Dadra & Nagar Haveli □
  India **66** J8
Dadri = Charkhi Dadri *India* **68** E7
Dadu *Pakistan* **68** F2
Dadu He → *China* **58** C4
Daegu *S. Korea* **57** G15
Daejeon *S. Korea* **57** F14
Daejeong *S. Korea* **57** H14
Daet *Phil.* **61** D5
Dafang *China* **58** D5
Dafnes *Greece* **49** D7
Dafni *Greece* **46** D4
Dağ *Turkey* **47** D12
Dagana *Senegal* **82** B1
Dagash *Sudan* **80** D3
Dagestan □ *Russia* **35** J8
Dagestanskiye Ogni *Russia* **35** J9
Daghestan Republic =
  Dagestan □ *Russia* **35** J8
Daghfeli *Sudan* **80** D3
Dağlıq Qarabağ =
  Nagorno-Karabakh □
  Azerbaijan **73** C12
Dago = Hiiumaa *Estonia* **32** C2
Dagu *China* **57** E9
Daguan *China* **58** D4
Dagupan *Phil.* **61** C4
Daguragu *Australia* **92** C5
Dahab *Egypt* **80** B3
Dahlak △ *Eritrea* **81** D5
Dahlak Kebir *Eritrea* **81** D5
Dahlenburg *Germany* **24** B6
Dahlonega *U.S.A.* **117** D13
Dahme *Germany* **24** D9
Dahod *India* **68** H6
Dahong Shan *China* **59** B9
Dahongliutan *China* **69** B8
Dahra *Libya* **79** C9
Dahra *Senegal* **82** B1
Dahshūr *Egypt* **80** J7
Dahūk *Iraq* **73** D10
Dahūk □ *Iraq* **73** D10
Dai Hao *Vietnam* **64** C6

Dai-Sen *Japan* **55** G6
Dai Shan *China* **59** B14
Dai Xian *China* **56** E7
Daicheng *China* **56** E9
Daikondi = Day Kundī □
  Afghan. **66** C5
Daimiel *Spain* **37** F7
Daingean *Ireland* **12** C4
Dainkog *China* **58** A1
Daintree *Australia* **94** B4
Daintree △ *Australia* **94** B4
Daiō-Misaki *Japan* **55** G8
Dair, J. ed *Sudan* **81** E3
Dairût *Egypt* **80** B3
Daisen-Oki △ *Japan* **55** G6
Daisetsu-Zan *Japan* **54** C11
Daisetsu-Zan △ *Japan* **54** C11
Dajarra *Australia* **94** C2
Dajiawa *China* **57** F10
Dajin Chuan → *China* **58** B3
Dak Dam *Cambodia* **64** F6
Dak Nhe *Vietnam* **64** E6
Dak Pek *Vietnam* **64** E6
Dak Song *Vietnam* **65** F6
Dak Sui *Vietnam* **64** E6
Dakar *Senegal* **82** C1
Dakar □ *Senegal* **82** C1
Dakhla *W. Sahara* **78** D2
Dakhla, El Wâhât el- *Egypt* **80** B2
Dakingari *Nigeria* **83** C5
Dakor *India* **68** H5
Dakoro *Niger* **83** C6
Dakota City *U.S.A.* **112** D5
Đakovica *Serbia* **44** D4
Đakovo *Croatia* **28** E3
Dalaba *Guinea* **82** C2
Dalachi *China* **56** F3
Dalai Nur *China* **56** C9
Dālakī *Iran* **71** D6
Dalälven → *Sweden* **10** D10
Dalaman *Turkey* **47** E10
Dalaman → *Turkey* **47** E10
Dalandzadgad *Mongolia* **56** C3
Dalap-Uliga-Darrit =
  Majuro *Marshall Is.* **96** G9
Dalarna *Sweden* **10** D8
Dalarnas län □ *Sweden* **10** C8
Dālbandīn *Pakistan* **66** E3
Dalbeattie *U.K.* **13** G5
Dalbeg *Australia* **94** C4
Dalbosjön *Sweden* **11** F6
Dalby *Australia* **95** D5
Dalby *Sweden* **11** J7
Dalby Söderskog △ *Sweden* **11** J7
Dale City *U.S.A.* **113** F15
Dale Hollow L. *U.S.A.* **117** C12
Dalga *Egypt* **80** B3
Dalgán *Iran* **71** E8
Dalhart *U.S.A.* **116** C3
Dalhousie *Canada* **105** C6
Dalhousie *India* **68** C6
Dali *Shaanxi, China* **56** G5
Dali *Yunnan, China* **58** E3
Dalian *China* **57** E11
Daliang Shan *China* **58** D4
Daling He → *China* **57** D11
Dāliyat el Karmel *Israel* **74** C4
Dalj *Croatia* **28** E3
Dalkeith *U.K.* **13** F5
Dallas *Oreg., U.S.A.* **108** D2
Dallas *Tex., U.S.A.* **116** E6
Dalles, The *U.S.A.* **108** D3
Dallol *Ethiopia* **81** E5
Dalmā *U.A.E.* **71** E7
Dalmacija *Croatia* **41** E13
Dalmas, L. *Canada* **105** B5
Dalmatia = Dalmacija
  Croatia **41** E13
Dalmau *India* **69** F9
Dalmellington *U.K.* **13** F4
Dalnegorsk *Russia* **54** B7
Dalnerechensk *Russia* **54** B6
Dalnevostochnyy □ *Russia* **53** C14
Daloa *Ivory C.* **82** D3
Dalou Shan *China* **58** C6
Dalry *U.K.* **13** F4
Dalrymple, L. *Australia* **94** C4
Dalrymple, Mt. *Australia* **94** K6
Dals Långed *Sweden* **11** F6
Dalsjöfors *Sweden* **11** G7
Dalsland *Sweden* **11** F6
Daltenganj *India* **69** H11
Dalton *Ga., U.S.A.* **117** D12
Dalton *Mass., U.S.A.* **115** D11
Dalton *Nebr., U.S.A.* **112** E2
Dalton-in-Furness *U.K.* **14** C4
Dalupiri I. *Phil.* **61** B4
Dalvík *Iceland* **8** D4
Dálvvadis = Jokkmokk
  Sweden **8** C18
Dalwallinu *Australia* **93** F2
Daly → *Australia* **92** B5
Daly City *U.S.A.* **110** H4
Daly L. *Canada* **103** B7
Daly River *Australia* **92** B5
Daly Waters *Australia* **94** B1
Dalyan *Turkey* **47** E10

Dam Doi *Vietnam* **65** H5
Dam Ha *Vietnam* **64** B6
Damachova *Belarus* **31** G10
Daman *India* **66** J8
Dāmaneh *Iran* **71** C6
Damanhûr *Egypt* **80** H7
Damant L. *Canada* **103** A7
Damanzhuang *China* **56** E9
Damar *Indonesia* **63** F7
Damara *C.A.R.* **84** D3
Damaraland *Namibia* **88** C2
Damascus = Dimashq *Syria* **74** B5
Damasi *Greece* **46** B4
Damaturu *Nigeria* **83** C7
Damāvand *Iran* **71** C7
Damāvand, Qolleh-ye *Iran* **71** C7
Damba *Angola* **84** F3
Dâmboviţa □ *Romania* **29** F10
Dâmboviţa → *Romania* **29** F11
Dâmbovnic → *Romania* **29** F10
Dame Marie *Haiti* **121** C5
Dāmghān *Iran* **71** B7
Damiel = Damietta *Egypt* **80** H7
Daming *China* **56** F8
Damīr Qābū *Syria* **70** B4
Dammam = Ad Dammām
  Si. Arabia **71** E6
Dammarie-les-Lys *France* **19** D9
Dammartin-en-Goële *France* **19** C9
Damme *Germany* **24** C4
Damoh *India* **69** H12
Damoh *India* **69** H8
Dampier *Australia* **92** D2
Dampier, Selat *Indonesia* **63** E8
Dampier Arch. *Australia* **92** D2
Damrei, Chuor Phnum
  Cambodia **65** G4
Damvillers *France* **19** C12
Damyang *S. Korea* **57** G14
Dan-Gulbi *Nigeria* **83** C6
Dana *Indonesia* **63** F6
Dana, L. *Canada* **104** B4
Dana, Mt. *U.S.A.* **110** H7
Danakil Desert *Ethiopia* **81** E5
Danané *Ivory C.* **82** D3
Danao *Phil.* **61** F6
Danau Poso *Indonesia* **63** E6
Danba *China* **58** B3
Danbury *U.S.A.* **115** E11
Danby L. *U.S.A.* **109** J6
Dand *Afghan.* **68** D1
Dande △ *Zimbabwe* **87** F3
Dandeldhura *Nepal* **69** E9
Dandeli *India* **66** M9
Dandenong *Australia* **95** F4
Dandīl *Egypt* **80** J7
Dandong *China* **57** D13
Danfeng *China* **56** H6
Dangan Liedao *China* **59** F10
Dangé-St-Romain *France* **20** B4
Dângeni *Romania* **29** C11
Danger Is. = Pukapuka
  Cook Is. **97** J11
Danger Pt. *S. Africa* **88** E2
Danginpuri *Indonesia* **63** K18
Dangla *Ethiopia* **81** E4
Dangla Shan = Tanggula
  Shan *China* **60** C4
Dangora *Nigeria* **83** C6
Dangrek, Phnom *Thailand* **64** E5
Dangriga *Belize* **119** D7
Dangshan *China* **56** G9
Dangtu *China* **59** B12
Dangyang *China* **59** B8
Dani *Burkina Faso* **83** C4
Daniel *U.S.A.* **108** E8
Daniel's Harbour *Canada* **105** B8
Danielskuil *S. Africa* **88** D3
Danielson *U.S.A.* **115** E13
Danilov *Russia* **32** C11
Danilovgrad *Montenegro* **44** D3
Danilovka *Russia* **34** E7
Daning *China* **56** F6
Danja *Nigeria* **83** C6
Danjiangkou *China* **59** A8
Danjiangkou Shuiku *China* **59** A8
Dank *Oman* **71** F8
Dankalwa *Nigeria* **83** C7
Dankama *Nigeria* **83** C6
Dankhar Gompa *India* **68** C8
Dankov *Russia* **32** F10
Danlí *Honduras* **120** D2
Danmark = Denmark ■
  Europe **11** J3
Dannemora *U.S.A.* **115** B11
Dannenberg *Germany* **24** B7
Dannevirke *N.Z.* **91** D6
Dannhauser *S. Africa* **89** D5
Dansville *U.S.A.* **114** D7
Danta *India* **68** G5
Dantan *India* **69** J12
Danube = Dunărea →
  Europe **29** E14

Danvers *U.S.A.* **115** D14
Danville *Ill., U.S.A.* **112** E10
Danville *Ky., U.S.A.* **113** G11
Danville *Pa., U.S.A.* **115** F8
Danville *Va., U.S.A.* **113** G14
Danville *Vt., U.S.A.* **115** B12
Danyang *China* **59** B12
Danzhai *China* **58** D6
Danzhou *China* **64** C7
Danzig = Gdańsk *Poland* **30** D9
Dão → *Portugal* **36** E2
Dao Xian *China* **59** E8
Daocheng *China* **58** C3
Daoukro *Ivory C.* **82** D4
Dapaong *Togo* **83** C5
Dapchi *Nigeria* **83** C7
Dapitan *Phil.* **61** G5
Daqing Shan *China* **56** D6
Daqu Shan *China* **59** B14
Dar Banda *Africa* **76** F6
Dar el Beida = Casablanca
  Morocco **78** B4
Dar es Salaam *Tanzania* **86** D4
Dar Mazār *Iran* **71** D8
Dar'ā *Syria* **74** C5
Dar'ā □ *Syria* **74** C5
Dārāb *Iran* **71** D7
Daraban *Pakistan* **68** D4
Darabani *Romania* **29** B11
Daraina *Madag.* **89** A8
Daraj *Libya* **79** B8
Dārān *Iran* **71** C6
Daraw *Egypt* **80** C3
Dārayyā *Syria* **74** B5
Darazo *Nigeria* **83** C7
Darband *Pakistan* **68** B5
Darband, Kūh-e *Iran* **71** D8
Darbhanga *India* **69** F11
Darby, C. *U.S.A.* **106** B3
D'Arcy *Canada* **102** C4
Darda *Croatia* **28** E3
Dardanelle *Ark., U.S.A.* **116** D8
Dardanelle *Calif., U.S.A.* **110** G7
Dardanelles = Çanakkale
  Boğazı *Turkey* **45** F10
Dare → *Ethiopia* **81** F5
Darende *Turkey* **72** C7
Dārestān *Iran* **71** D8
Darfo *Italy* **40** C7
Dârfûr *Sudan* **79** F10
Dargai *Pakistan* **68** B4
Dargaville *N.Z.* **91** A4
Dargol *Niger* **83** C5
Darhan *Mongolia* **60** B5
Darhan Muminggan
  Lianheqi *China* **56** D6
Dari *Sudan* **81** F3
Darıca *Turkey* **72** B3
Darién, G. del *Colombia* **124** B3
Darién △ *Panama* **120** E4
Dariganga = Ovoot *Mongolia* **56** B7
Darinskoye *Kazakhstan* **34** E10
Darjeeling = Darjiling *India* **69** F13
Darjiling *India* **69** F13
Darkan *Australia* **93** F2
Darkhana *Pakistan* **68** D5
Darkhazineh *Iran* **71** D6
Darkot Pass *Pakistan* **69** A5
Darling → *Australia* **95** E3
Darling Downs *Australia* **95** D5
Darling Ra. *Australia* **93** F2
Darlington *U.K.* **14** C6
Darlington *U.S.A.* **117** D15
Darlington □ *U.K.* **14** C6
Darlington, L. *S. Africa* **88** E4
Darlot, L. *Australia* **93** E3
Darłowo *Poland* **30** D3
Dărmăneşti *Bacău, Romania* **29** D11
Dărmăneşti *Suceava,*
  Romania **29** C11
Darmstadt *Germany* **25** F4
Darnah *Libya* **79** B10
Darnall *S. Africa* **89** D5
Darney *France* **19** D13
Darnley, C. *Antarctica* **5** C6
Darnley B. *Canada* **100** C7
Daroca *Spain* **38** D3
Darou-Mousti *Senegal* **82** B1
Darr → *Australia* **94** C3
Darra Pezu *Pakistan* **68** C4
Darrequeira *Argentina* **126** D3
Darrington *U.S.A.* **108** B3
Darsser Ort *Germany* **24** A8
Dart → *U.K.* **15** G4
Dart, C. *Antarctica* **5** D14
Dartford *U.K.* **15** F8
Dartmoor *U.K.* **15** G4
Dartmoor △ *U.K.* **15** G4
Dartmouth *Canada* **105** D7
Dartmouth *U.K.* **15** G4
Dartmouth, L. *Australia* **95** D4
Dartmouth Res. *Australia* **95** D4
Dartuch, C. = Artrutx, C.
  de *Spain* **48** B10
Daruvar *Croatia* **28** E2
Darvaza *Turkmenistan* **52** E6
Darvel, Teluk = Lahad
  Datu, Telok *Malaysia* **63** D5

Darwen *U.K.* **14** D5
Darwendale *Zimbabwe* **89** B5
Darwha *India* **66** J10
Darwin *Australia* **92** B5
Darwin *U.S.A.* **111** J9
Darya Khan *Pakistan* **68** D4
Daryoi Amu =
  Amudarya → *Uzbekistan* **52** E6
Dās *U.A.E.* **71** E7
Dashen, Ras *Ethiopia* **81** E4
Dashetai *China* **56** D5
Dashkesan = Daşkäsän
  Azerbaijan **35** K7
Dashköpri *Turkmenistan* **71** B9
Dashoguz *Turkmenistan* **52** E6
Dasht *Iran* **71** B8
Dasht → *Pakistan* **66** G2
Daska *Pakistan* **68** C6
Daşkäsän *Azerbaijan* **35** K7
Dassa *Benin* **83** D5
Dasuya *India* **68** D6
Datça *Turkey* **47** E9
Datia *India* **69** G8
Datian *China* **59** E11
Datong *Anhui, China* **59** B11
Datong *Shanxi, China* **56** D7
Dattakhel *Pakistan* **68** C3
Datteln *Germany* **24** D3
Datu, Tanjung *Indonesia* **62** D3
Datu Piang *Phil.* **61** H6
Daua = Dawa → *Africa* **81** G5
Daud Khel *Pakistan* **68** C4
Daudnagar *India* **69** G11
Daugava → *Latvia* **32** D3
Daugavpils *Latvia* **32** E4
Daulpur *India* **68** F7
Daun *Germany* **25** E2
Dauphin *Canada* **103** C8
Dauphin *U.S.A.* **112** F8
Dauphin L. *Canada* **103** C9
Dauphiné *France* **21** C9
Daura *Borno, Nigeria* **83** C7
Daura *Katsina, Nigeria* **83** C6
Dausa *India* **68** F7
Dāvāçi *Azerbaijan* **35** K9
Davangere *India* **66** M9
Davao *Phil.* **61** H6
Davao G. *Phil.* **61** H6
Dāvar Panāh = Sarāvān
  Iran **71** E9
Davenport *Calif., U.S.A.* **110** H4
Davenport *Iowa, U.S.A.* **112** E8
Davenport *Wash., U.S.A.* **108** C4
Davenport Ra. *Australia* **94** C1
Daventry *U.K.* **15** E6
David *Panama* **120** E3
David City *U.S.A.* **112** E5
David Glacier *Antarctica* **5** D21
David Gorodok = Davyd
  Haradok *Belarus* **23** B14
Davidson *Canada* **103** C7
Davis *Antarctica* **5** C6
Davis *U.S.A.* **110** G5
Davis Dam *U.S.A.* **111** K12
Davis Inlet *Canada* **105** A7
Davis Mts. *U.S.A.* **116** F3
Davis Str. *N. Amer.* **98** C14
Davis Sea *Antarctica* **5** C7
Davos *Switz.* **25** J5
Davutlar *Turkey* **47** E9
Davy L. *Canada* **103** B7
Davyd Haradok *Belarus* **23** B14
Dawa → *Africa* **81** G5
Dawaki *Bauchi, Nigeria* **83** D6
Dawaki *Kano, Nigeria* **83** C6
Dawei = Tavoy *Burma* **64** E2
Dawes Ra. *Australia* **94** C5
Dawlish *U.K.* **15** G4
Dawna Ra. *Burma* **64** D2
Dawros Hd. *Ireland* **12** B3
Dawson *Canada* **100** C6
Dawson *U.S.A.* **117** F12
Dawson, I. *Chile* **128** G2
Dawson B. *Canada* **103** C8
Dawson Creek *Canada* **102** B4
Dawson Inlet *Canada* **103** A10
Dawson Ra. *Australia* **94** C4
Dawu *Hubei, China* **59** B9
Dawu *Sichuan, China* **58** B3
Dax *France* **20** E2
Daxian *China* **58** B6
Daxin *China* **58** F6
Daxindian *China* **57** F11
Daxinggou *China* **57** C15
Daxue Shan *Sichuan, China* **58** B3
Daxue Shan *Yunnan, China* **58** F2
Day Kundī □ *Afghan.* **66** C5
Dayao *China* **58** E3
Daye *China* **59** B10
Dayet en Naharat *Mali* **82** B4
Dayi *China* **58** B4
Daylesford *Australia* **95** F3
Dayong *China* **59** C8
Dayr az Zawr *Syria* **73** E9

Dayr az Zawr □ *Syria* **73** E9
Daysland *Canada* **102** C6
Dayton *Nev., U.S.A.* **110** F7
Dayton *Ohio, U.S.A.* **113** F11
Dayton *Pa., U.S.A.* **114** F5
Dayton *Tenn., U.S.A.* **117** D12
Dayton *Wash., U.S.A.* **108** C5
Dayton *Wyo., U.S.A.* **108** D10
Daytona Beach *U.S.A.* **117** G14
Dayu *China* **59** E10
Dayville *U.S.A.* **108** D4
Dazhu *China* **58** B6
Dazkırı *Turkey* **47** D11
Dazu *China* **58** C5
De Aar *S. Africa* **88** E3
De Biesbosch △ *Neths.* **17** C4
De Funiak Springs *U.S.A.* **117** F11
De Grey ➝ *Australia* **92** D2
De Haan *Belgium* **17** C3
De Hoge Veluwe △ *Neths.* **17** B5
De Hoop ◠ *S. Africa* **88** E3
De Kennemerduinen △
  Neths. **17** B4
De Land *U.S.A.* **117** G14
De Leon *U.S.A.* **116** E5
De Panne *Belgium* **17** C2
De Pere *U.S.A.* **112** C9
De Queen *U.S.A.* **116** D7
De Quincy *U.S.A.* **116** F8
De Smet *U.S.A.* **112** C5
De Soto *U.S.A.* **112** F8
De Tour Village *U.S.A.* **113** B12
De Witt *U.S.A.* **116** D9
Dead Sea *Asia* **74** D4
Deadwood *U.S.A.* **112** C2
Deadwood L. *Canada* **102** B3
Deal *U.K.* **15** F9
Deal I. *Australia* **95** F4
Dealesville *S. Africa* **88** D4
De'an *China* **59** C10
Dean ➝ *Canada* **102** C3
Dean, Forest of *U.K.* **15** F5
Dean Chan. *Canada* **102** C3
Deán Funes *Argentina* **126** C3
Dease ➝ *Canada* **102** B3
Dease L. *Canada* **102** B2
Dease Lake *Canada* **102** B2
Death Valley *U.S.A.* **111** J10
Death Valley △ *U.S.A.* **111** J9
Death Valley Junction
  U.S.A. **111** J10
Deauville *France* **18** C7
Deba *Spain* **38** B2
Deba Habe *Nigeria* **83** C7
Debaltsevo *Ukraine* **33** H10
Debao *China* **58** F6
Debar *Macedonia* **44** E4
Debark *Ethiopia* **81** E4
Debden *Canada* **103** C7
Dębica *Poland* **31** H8
Dęblin *Poland* **31** G8
Dębno *Poland* **31** F1
Débo, L. *Mali* **82** B4
DeBolt *Canada* **102** B5
Deborah East, L. *Australia* **93** F2
Deborah West, L. *Australia* **93** F2
Debrc *Serbia* **44** B3
Debre Birhan *Ethiopia* **81** F4
Debre Markos *Ethiopia* **81** E4
Debre May *Ethiopia* **81** E4
Debre Sina *Ethiopia* **81** F4
Debre Tabor *Ethiopia* **81** E4
Debre Zebit *Ethiopia* **81** E4
Debre Zevit *Ethiopia* **81** F4
Debrecen *Hungary* **28** C6
Debrzno *Poland* **30** E4
Dečani *Serbia* **44** D4
Decatur *Ala., U.S.A.* **117** D11
Decatur *Ga., U.S.A.* **117** E12
Decatur *Ill., U.S.A.* **112** F9
Decatur *Ind., U.S.A.* **113** E11
Decatur *Tex., U.S.A.* **116** E6
Decazeville *France* **20** D6
Deccan *India* **66** L11
Deception Bay *Australia* **95** D5
Deception I. *Antarctica* **5** C17
Deception L. *Canada* **103** B8
Dechang *China* **58** D4
Dechhu *India* **68** F5
Děčín *Czech Rep.* **26** A7
Decize *France* **19** F10
Deckerville *U.S.A.* **114** C2
Decollatura *Italy* **43** C9
Decorah *U.S.A.* **112** D8
Deda *Romania* **29** D9
Dedéagach =
  Alexandroupoli *Greece* **45** F9
Deder *Ethiopia* **81** F5
Dedham *U.S.A.* **115** D13
Dédougou *Burkina Faso* **82** C4
Dedovichi *Russia* **32** D5
Dee ➝ *Aberds., U.K.* **13** D6
Dee ➝ *Dumf. & Gall., U.K.* **13** G4
Dee ➝ *Wales, U.K.* **14** D4
Deep B. *Canada* **102** A5
Deepwater *Australia* **95** D5

Deer ➝ *Canada* **103** B10
Deer L. *Canada* **103** C10
Deer Lake *Nfld. & L., Canada* **105** C8
Deer Lake *Ont., Canada* **103** C10
Deer Lodge *U.S.A.* **108** C7
Deer Park *U.S.A.* **108** C5
Deer River *U.S.A.* **112** B7
Deeragun *Australia* **94** B4
Deerdepoort *S. Africa* **88** C4
Deferiet *U.S.A.* **115** B9
Degana *India* **68** F6
Dêgê *China* **58** B2
Degebe ➝ *Portugal* **37** G3
Degeberga *Sweden* **11** J8
Dégelis *Canada* **105** C6
Degema *Nigeria* **83** E6
Degerfors *Sweden* **10** E8
Degerhamn *Sweden* **11** H10
Deggendorf *Germany* **25** G8
Degh ➝ *Pakistan* **68** D5
Değirmendere *Turkey* **45** F13
Deh Bīd *Iran* **71** D7
Deh-e Shīr *Iran* **71** D7
Dehaj *Iran* **71** D7
Dehak *Iran* **71** E9
Dehdez *Iran* **71** D6
Dehej *India* **68** J5
Dehestān *Iran* **71** D7
Dehgolān *Iran* **73** E12
Dehibat *Tunisia* **79** B8
Dehlorān *Iran* **73** F12
Dehnow-e Kūhestān *Iran* **71** E8
Dehra Dun *India* **68** D8
Dehri *India* **69** G11
Dehua *China* **59** E12
Dehui *China* **57** B13
Deim Zubeir *Sudan* **81** F2
Deinze *Belgium* **17** D3
Dej *Romania* **29** C8
Deje *Sweden* **10** E7
Dejiang *China* **58** C7
Deka ➝ *Zimbabwe* **88** B4
DeKalb *U.S.A.* **112** E9
Dekemhare *Eritrea* **81** D4
Dekese *Dem. Rep. of the Congo* **84** E4
Del Mar *U.S.A.* **111** N9
Del Norte *U.S.A.* **109** H10
Del Rio *U.S.A.* **116** G4
Delai *China* **58** A3
Delambre I. *Australia* **92** D2
Delami *Sudan* **81** E3
Delano *U.S.A.* **111** K7
Delano Peak *U.S.A.* **108** G7
Delareyville *S. Africa* **88** D4
Delaronde L. *Canada* **103** C7
Delavan *U.S.A.* **112** D9
Delaware *U.S.A.* **113** E12
Delaware □ *U.S.A.* **113** F16
Delaware ➝ *U.S.A.* **115** G9
Delaware B. *U.S.A.* **113** F16
Delaware Water Gap △
  U.S.A. **115** E10
Delay ➝ *Canada* **105** A5
Delbrück *Germany* **24** D4
Delčevo *Macedonia* **44** E6
Delegate *Australia* **95** F4
Delémont *Switz.* **25** H3
Delevan *U.S.A.* **114** D6
Delft *Neths.* **17** B4
Delfzijl *Neths.* **17** A6
Delgado, C. *Mozam.* **87** E5
Delgerhet *Mongolia* **56** B6
Delgo *Sudan* **80** C3
Delhi *Canada* **114** D4
Delhi *India* **68** E7
Delhi □ *India* **68** E7
Delhi *La., U.S.A.* **116** E9
Delhi *N.Y., U.S.A.* **115** D10
Deli Jovan *Serbia* **44** B6
Delia *Canada* **102** C6
Delice *Turkey* **72** C6
Delice ➝ *Turkey* **72** B6
Delicias *Mexico* **118** B3
Delījān *Iran* **71** C6
Déline *Canada* **100** C7
Delisle *Canada* **103** C7
Delitzsch *Germany* **24** D8
Dell City *U.S.A.* **116** F2
Dell Rapids *U.S.A.* **112** D5
Delle *France* **19** E14
Delmar *U.S.A.* **115** D11
Delmenhorst *Germany* **24** B4
Delnice *Croatia* **41** C11
Delonga, Ostrova *Russia* **53** B15
Deloraine *Australia* **95** G4
Deloraine *Canada* **103** D8
Delphi *Greece* **46** C4
Delphi *U.S.A.* **112** E10
Delphos *U.S.A.* **113** E11
Delportshoop *S. Africa* **88** D3
Delray Beach *U.S.A.* **117** H14
Delsbo *Sweden* **10** C10
Delta *Colo., U.S.A.* **108** G9
Delta *Utah, U.S.A.* **108** G7
Delta □ *Nigeria* **83** D6
Delta del Ebro ➝ *Spain* **38** E5
Delta del Po ◠ *Italy* **41** D9
Delta du Saloum △ *Senegal* **82** C1

Delta Dunărea ◠ *Romania* **29** E14
Delta Junction *U.S.A.* **100** C5
Deltona *U.S.A.* **117** G14
Delungra *Australia* **95** D5
Delvada *India* **68** J4
Delvinaki *Greece* **46** B2
Delvinë *Albania* **44** G4
Demak *Indonesia* **63** G14
Demanda, Sierra de la *Spain* **38** C2
Demavend = Damāvand,
  Qolleh-ye *Iran* **71** C7
Dembecha *Ethiopia* **81** E4
Dembi *Ethiopia* **81** F4
Dembia *Dem. Rep. of the Congo* **86** B2
Dembidolo *Ethiopia* **81** F3
Demchok *India* **69** C8
Demer ➝ *Belgium* **17** D4
Demetrias *Greece* **46** B5
Demidov *Russia* **32** E6
Deming *N. Mex., U.S.A.* **109** K10
Deming *Wash., U.S.A.* **108** B4
Demini ➝ *Brazil* **124** D6
Demirci *Turkey* **47** B10
Demirköprü Baraji *Turkey* **47** C10
Demirköy *Turkey* **45** E11
Demmin *Germany* **24** B9
Demonte *Italy* **40** D4
Demopolis *U.S.A.* **117** E11
Dempo *Indonesia* **62** E2
Demyansk *Russia* **32** D7
Den Bosch =
  's-Hertogenbosch *Neths.* **17** C5
Den Burg *Neths.* **17** A4
Den Chai *Thailand* **64** D3
Den Haag =
  's-Gravenhage *Neths.* **17** B4
Den Helder *Neths.* **17** B4
Den Oever *Neths.* **17** B5
Denain *France* **19** B10
Denair *U.S.A.* **110** H6
Denau *Uzbekistan* **52** F7
Denbigh *Canada* **114** A7
Denbigh *U.K.* **14** D4
Denbighshire □ *U.K.* **14** D4
Dendang *Indonesia* **62** E3
Dendermonde *Belgium* **17** C4
Deneba *Ethiopia* **81** E4
Denge *Nigeria* **83** C6
Dengchuan *China* **58** E3
Denge *Nigeria* **83** C6
Dengfeng *China* **56** G7
Dengi *Nigeria* **83** D6
Dengkou *China* **56** D4
Dengzhou *China* **59** A9
Denham *Australia* **93** E1
Denham, Mt. *Jamaica* **120** a
Denham Ra. *Australia* **94** C4
Denham Sd. *Australia* **93** E1
Denholm *Canada* **103** C7
Denia *Spain* **39** G5
Denial B. *Australia* **95** E1
Deniliquin *Australia* **95** F3
Denison *Iowa, U.S.A.* **112** D6
Denison *Tex., U.S.A.* **116** E6
Denison Plains *Australia* **92** C4
Denizli *Turkey* **47** D11
Denizli □ *Turkey* **47** D11
Denman Glacier *Antarctica* **5** C7
Denmark *Australia* **93** F2
Denmark ■ *Europe* **11** J3
Denmark Str. *Atl. Oc.* **98** C17
Dennery *St. Lucia* **121** f
Dennison *U.S.A.* **114** F3
Denny *U.K.* **13** E5
Denpasar *Indonesia* **63** K18
Denpasar ✈ (DPS) *Indonesia* **63** K18
Denton *Mont., U.S.A.* **108** C9
Denton *Tex., U.S.A.* **116** E6
D'Entrecasteaux, Pt.
  Australia **93** F2
D'Entrecasteaux △ *Australia* **93** F2
D'Entrecasteaux Is.
  Papua N. G. **90** B8
Denu *Ghana* **83** D5
Denver *Colo., U.S.A.* **108** G11
Denver *Pa., U.S.A.* **115** F8
Denver City *U.S.A.* **116** E3
Deoband *India* **68** E7
Deogarh *India* **68** G5
Deoghar *India* **69** G12
Deolali *India* **66** K8
Deoli = Devli *India* **68** G6
Déols *France* **19** F8
Deora *India* **68** F4
Deori *India* **69** H8
Deoria *India* **69** F10
Deosai Mts. *Pakistan* **69** B6
Deosri *India* **69** F14
Depalpur *India* **68** H6
Deping *China* **57** F9
Deposit *U.S.A.* **115** D9
Depuch I. *Australia* **92** D2
Deputatskiy *Russia* **53** C14
Dêqên *China* **58** C2
Deqing *China* **59** F8

Dera Ghazi Khan *Pakistan* **68** D4
Dera Ismail Khan *Pakistan* **68** D4
Derabugti *Pakistan* **68** E3
Derawar Fort *Pakistan* **68** E4
Derby *Australia* **92** C3
Derby *U.K.* **14** E6
Derby *Conn., U.S.A.* **115** E11
Derby *Kans., U.S.A.* **112** G5
Derby *N.Y., U.S.A.* **114** D6
Derby City □ *U.K.* **14** E6
Derby Line *U.S.A.* **115** B12
Derbyshire □ *U.K.* **14** D6
Derdap △ *Serbia* **44** B6
Derdepoort *S. Africa* **88** C4
Dereham *U.K.* **15** E8
Dereköy *Turkey* **45** E11
Dereli *Turkey* **73** B8
Derg ➝ *U.K.* **12** B4
Derg, L. *Ireland* **12** D3
Dergachi = Derhaci *Ukraine* **33** G9
Derhaci *Ukraine* **33** G9
Deridder *U.S.A.* **116** F8
Derik *Turkey* **73** D9
Derinkuyu *Turkey* **72** C6
Dermantsi *Bulgaria* **45** C8
Dermott *U.S.A.* **116** E9
Dêrong *China* **58** C2
Derry = Londonderry *U.K.* **12** B4
Derry = Londonderry □
  U.K. **12** B4
Derry *N.H., U.S.A.* **115** D13
Derry *Pa., U.S.A.* **114** F5
Derryveagh Mts. *Ireland* **12** B3
Derudub *Sudan* **80** D4
Derval *France* **18** E5
Derveni *Greece* **46** C4
Derventa *Bos.-H.* **28** F2
Derwent ➝ *Cumb., U.K.* **14** C4
Derwent ➝ *Derby, U.K.* **14** E6
Derwent ➝ *N. Yorks., U.K.* **14** D7
Derwent Water *U.K.* **14** C4
Des Moines *Iowa, U.S.A.* **112** E7
Des Moines *N. Mex., U.S.A.* **109** H12
Des Moines *Wash., U.S.A.* **110** C4
Des Moines ➝ *U.S.A.* **112** E8
Desa *Romania* **28** G8
Desaguadero ➝ *Argentina* **126** C2
Desaguadero ➝ *Bolivia* **124** G5
Desantne *Ukraine* **29** E14
Desar *Malaysia* **65** d
Descanso, Pta. *Mexico* **111** N9
Descartes *France* **20** B4
Deschaillons-sur-St-
  Laurent *Canada* **105** C5
Deschambault L. *Canada* **103** C8
Deschutes ➝ *U.S.A.* **108** D3
Dese *Ethiopia* **81** E4
Deseado ➝ *Argentina* **128** F3
Desenzano del Garda *Italy* **40** C7
Desert Center *U.S.A.* **111** M11
Desert Hot Springs *U.S.A.* **111** M10
Desfina *Greece* **46** C4
Deshnok *India* **68** F5
Desierto Central de Baja
  California ◠ *Mexico* **118** B2
Deskati *Greece* **44** G5
Desna ➝ *Ukraine* **23** C16
Desnățui ➝ *Romania* **29** G8
Desolación, I. *Chile* **128** G2
Despeñaperros, Paso *Spain* **37** G7
Despeñaperros ◠ *Spain* **37** G7
Despotiko *Greece* **46** E6
Despotovac *Serbia* **44** B5
Dessau *Germany* **24** D8
Dessye = Dese *Ethiopia* **81** E4
D'Estrees B. *Australia* **95** F2
Desuri *India* **68** G5
Desvres *France* **19** B8
Det Udom *Thailand* **64** E5
Deta *Romania* **28** E6
Dete *Zimbabwe* **88** B4
Đetinja ➝ *Serbia* **44** C4
Detmold *Germany* **24** D4
Detour, Pt. *U.S.A.* **112** C10
Detroit *U.S.A.* **114** D1
Detroit Lakes *U.S.A.* **112** B6
Detva *Slovak Rep.* **27** C12
Deua △ *Australia* **95** F4
Deurne *Neths.* **17** C5
Deutsch-
  Luxemburgischer ◠
  Germany **25** F2
Deutschland =
  Germany ■ *Europe* **24** E6
Deutschlandsberg *Austria* **26** E8
Deux-Sèvres □ *France* **18** F6
Deva *Romania* **28** E7
Devakottai *India* **66** Q11
Dévaványa *Hungary* **28** C5
Deveci Dağları *Turkey* **72** B7
Devecikonağı *Turkey* **45** G12
Devecser *Hungary* **28** C2

Develi *Turkey* **72** C6
Deventer *Neths.* **17** B6
Deveron ➝ *U.K.* **13** D6
Devesel *Romania* **28** F7
Devgadh Bariya *India* **68** H5
Devikot *India* **68** F4
Devils Den *U.S.A.* **110** K7
Devils Hole = Death
  Valley ◠ *U.S.A.* **111** J9
Devils Lake *U.S.A.* **112** A4
Devils Paw *Canada* **102** B2
Devils Postpile ◠ *U.S.A.* **110** H7
Devils Tower *U.S.A.* **108** D11
Devils Tower △ *U.S.A.* **108** D11
Devin *Bulgaria* **45** E8
Devine *U.S.A.* **116** G5
Devizes *U.K.* **15** F6
Devli *India* **68** G6
Devnya *Bulgaria* **45** C11
Devoll ➝ *Albania* **44** F4
Devon *Canada* **102** C6
Devon □ *U.K.* **15** G4
Devon I. *Canada* **101** B11
Devonport *Australia* **95** G4
Devonport *N.Z.* **91** B5
Devrek *Turkey* **72** B4
Devrekâni *Turkey* **72** B5
Devrez ➝ *Turkey* **72** B6
Dewas *India* **68** H7
Dewetsdorp *S. Africa* **88** D4
Dewey *Puerto Rico* **121** d
Dexing *China* **59** C11
Dexter *Maine, U.S.A.* **113** C19
Dexter *Mo., U.S.A.* **112** G9
Dexter *N. Mex., U.S.A.* **109** K11
Dey-Dey, L. *Australia* **93** E5
Deyang *China* **58** B5
Deyhūk *Iran* **71** C8
Deyyer *Iran* **71** E6
Dezadeash L. *Canada* **102** A1
Dezfūl *Iran* **73** F13
Dezhneva, Mys *Russia* **53** C19
Dezhou *China* **56** F9
Dhadhar ➝ *India* **69** G11
Dhahaban *Si. Arabia* **80** C4
Dhahiriya = Aẕ Ẕāhirīyah
  West Bank **74** D3
Dhahran = Aẕ Ẕahrān
  Si. Arabia **71** E6
Dhak *Pakistan* **68** C5
Dhaka *Bangla.* **69** H14
Dhaka □ *Bangla.* **69** G14
Dhali *Cyprus* **49** D12
Dhamār *Yemen* **75** E3
Dhampur *India* **69** E8
Dhamtari *India* **67** J12
Dhanbad *India* **69** H12
Dhangarhi *Nepal* **69** E9
Dhankuta *Nepal* **69** F12
Dhar *India* **68** H6
Dharampur *India* **68** H6
Dharamsala = Dharmsala
  India **68** C7
Dhariwal *India* **68** D6
Dharla ➝ *Bangla.* **69** G13
Dharmapuri *India* **66** N11
Dharmjaygarh *India* **69** H10
Dharmsala *India* **68** C7
Dharni *India* **68** J7
Dharwad *India* **66** M9
Dhasan ➝ *India* **69** G8
Dhaulagiri *Nepal* **69** E10
Dhebar, L. *India* **68** G6
Dheftera *Cyprus* **49** D12
Dhenkanal *India* **67** J14
Dherinia *Cyprus* **49** D12
Dheskáti = Deskati *Greece* **44** G5
Dhī Qār □ *Iraq* **70** D5
Dhībān *Jordan* **74** D4
Dhilwan *India* **68** D6
Dhimarkhera *India* **69** H9
Dhodhekánisos =
  Dodecanese *Greece* **47** E8
Dholka *India* **68** H5
Dhomokós = Domokos
  Greece **46** B4
Dhoraji *India* **68** J4
Dhrangadhra *India* **68** H4
Dhrol *India* **68** H4
Dhuburi *India* **67** F16
Dhule *India* **66** J9
Di-ib, W. ➝ *Sudan* **80** C4
Di Linh *Vietnam* **65** G7
Di Linh, Cao Nguyen
  Vietnam **65** G7
Dia *Greece* **49** D7
Diabakania *Guinea* **82** C2
Diablo Range *U.S.A.* **110** J5
Diafarabé *Mali* **82** C4
Diala *Mali* **82** C3
Dialakoro *Mali* **82** C3
Diallassagou *Mali* **82** C4
Diamante *Argentina* **126** C3

Diamante *Italy* **43** C8
Diamante ➝ *Argentina* **126** C2
Diamantina *Brazil* **125** G10
Diamantina ➝ *Australia* **95** D2
Diamantina △ *Australia* **94** C3
Diamantino *Brazil* **125** F7
Diamond Bar *U.S.A.* **111** L9
Diamond Harbour *India* **69** H13
Diamond Is. *Australia* **94** B5
Diamond Mts. *U.S.A.* **108** G6
Diamond Springs *U.S.A.* **110** G6
Dian Chi *China* **58** E4
Dianalund *Denmark* **11** J5
Dianbai *China* **59** G8
Diancheng *China* **59** G8
Dianjiang *China* **58** B6
Diano Marina *Italy* **40** E5
Dianra *Ivory C.* **82** D3
Diaoyu Tai = Senkaku-
  Shotō *E. China Sea* **55** M1
Diapaga *Burkina Faso* **83** C5
Diapangou *Burkina Faso* **83** C5
Diariguila *Guinea* **82** C2
Dībā *U.A.E.* **71** E8
Dibai *India* **68** E8
Dibaya *Dem. Rep. of the Congo* **84** F4
Dibaya-Lubue
  Dem. Rep. of the Congo **84** E3
Dibbeen △ *Jordan* **74** C4
Dibete *Botswana* **88** C4
Dibrugarh *India* **67** F19
Dickens *U.S.A.* **116** E4
Dickinson *U.S.A.* **112** B2
Dickson *U.S.A.* **117** C11
Dickson City *U.S.A.* **115** E9
Dicle Baraji *Turkey* **73** C9
Dicle Nehri ➝ *Turkey* **73** D9
Dicomano *Italy* **41** E8
Didesa, W. ➝ *Ethiopia* **81** E4
Didi *Sudan* **81** F3
Didiéni *Mali* **82** C3
Didimoticho *Greece* **45** E10
Didsbury *Canada* **102** C6
Didwana *India* **68** F6
Die *France* **21** D9
Diébougou *Burkina Faso* **82** C4
Diecke *Guinea* **82** D3
Diefenbaker, L. *Canada* **103** C7
Diego de Almagro *Chile* **126** B1
Diego Suarez =
  Antsiranana *Madag.* **89** A8
Diekirch *Lux.* **17** E6
Diéma *Mali* **82** C3
Diembéring *Senegal* **82** C1
Diemelsee ◠ *Germany* **24** D4
Dien Ban *Vietnam* **64** E7
Dien Bien *Vietnam* **58** G4
Dien Khanh *Vietnam* **65** F7
Diepholz *Germany* **24** C4
Dieppe *France* **18** C8
Dierks *U.S.A.* **116** D7
Diest *Belgium* **17** D5
Dietikon *Switz.* **25** H4
Dieulefit *France* **21** D9
Dieuze *France* **19** D13
Dif *Somali Rep.* **75** G3
Diffa □ *Niger* **83** B7
Differdange *Lux.* **17** E5
Dig *India* **68** F7
Digba *Dem. Rep. of the Congo* **86** B2
Digby *Canada* **105** D6
Diggi *India* **68** F6
Dighinala *Bangla.* **67** H18
Dighton *U.S.A.* **112** F3
Digna *Mali* **82** C3
Digne-les-Bains *France* **21** D10
Digoin *France* **19** F11
Digor *Turkey* **73** B10
Digos *Phil.* **61** H6
Digranes *Iceland* **8** C6
Digul ➝ *Indonesia* **63** F9
Digya △ *Ghana* **83** D5
Dihang = Brahmaputra ➝
  Asia **69** H13
Dijlah, Nahr ➝ *Asia* **70** D5
Dijon *France* **19** E12
Dikhil *Djibouti* **81** E5
Dikili *Turkey* **47** B8
Dikirnis *Egypt* **80** H7
Dikkil = Dikhil *Djibouti* **81** E5
Dikodougou *Ivory C.* **82** D3
Diksmuide *Belgium* **17** C2
Dikson *Russia* **52** B9
Dikti Oros *Greece* **49** D7
Dikwa *Nigeria* **83** C7
Dila *Ethiopia* **81** F4
Dilek Yarimadisi △ *Turkey* **47** D9
Dili *E. Timor* **63** F7
Dilijan *Armenia* **35** K7
Dilinata *Greece* **46** C2
Dilizhan = Dilijan *Armenia* **35** K7
Dilj *Croatia* **28** E3
Dillenburg *Germany* **24** E4
Dilley *U.S.A.* **116** G5
Dilli = Delhi *India* **68** E7
Dilling *Sudan* **81** E2
Dillingen *Bayern, Germany* **25** G6

Dillingen *Saarland, Germany* **25** F2
Dillingham *U.S.A.* **106** a
Dillon *Canada* **103** B7
Dillon *Mont., U.S.A.* **108** D7
Dillon *S.C., U.S.A.* **117** D15
Dillon ➤ *Canada* **103** B7
Dillsburg *U.S.A.* **114** F7
Dilly *Mali* **82** C3
Dilolo *Dem. Rep. of the Congo* **84** G4
Dilos *Greece* **47** D7
Dilove *Ukraine* **29** C9
Dimas *Mexico* **118** C3
Dimashq *Syria* **74** B5
Dimashq □ *Syria* **74** B5
Dimbaza *S. Africa* **89** E4
Dimbokro *Ivory C.* **82** D4
Dimboola *Australia* **95** F3
Dîmboviţa =
Dâmboviţa ➤ *Romania* **29** F11
Dimbulah *Australia* **94** B4
Dimitrovgrad *Bulgaria* **45** D9
Dimitrovgrad *Russia* **34** C9
Dimitrovgrad *Serbia* **44** C6
Dimitrovo = Pernik *Bulgaria* **44** D7
Dimitsana *Greece* **46** D4
Dimmitt *U.S.A.* **116** D3
Dimo *Sudan* **81** F2
Dimona *Israel* **74** D4
Dimovo *Bulgaria* **44** D6
Dinagat *Phil.* **61** F6
Dinajpur *Bangla.* **67** G16
Dinan *France* **18** D5
Dīnān Āb *Iran* **71** C8
Dinant *Belgium* **17** D4
Dinapur *India* **69** G11
Dinar *Turkey* **47** C12
Dīnār, Kūh-e *Iran* **71** D6
Dinara Planina *Croatia* **41** D13
Dinard *France* **18** D4
Dinaric Alps = Dinara
Planina *Croatia* **41** D13
Dindanko *Mali* **82** C3
Dinder, Nahr ed ➤ *Sudan* **81** E3
Dinder △ *Sudan* **81** E4
Dindigul *India* **66** P11
Dindori *India* **69** H9
Ding Xian = Dingzhou *China* **56** E8
Dinga *Pakistan* **68** G2
Dingalan *Phil.* **61** D4
Ding'an *China* **64** C8
Dingbian *China* **56** F4
Dingelstädt *Germany* **24** D6
Dingle *Ireland* **12** D1
Dingle *Sweden* **11** F5
Dingle B. *Ireland* **12** D1
Dingmans Ferry *U.S.A.* **115** E10
Dingnan *China* **59** E10
Dingo *Australia* **94** C4
Dingolfing *Germany* **25** G8
Dingtao *China* **56** G8
Dinguira *Mali* **82** C2
Dinguiraye *Guinea* **82** C2
Dingwall *U.K.* **13** D4
Dingxi *China* **56** G3
Dingxiang *China* **56** E7
Dingyuan *China* **59** A11
Dingzhou *China* **56** E8
Dinh, Mui *Vietnam* **65** G7
Dinh Lap *Vietnam* **58** G6
Dinin ➤ *Ireland* **12** D4
Dinira △ *Venezuela* **121** E6
Dinokwe *Botswana* **88** C4
Dinorwic *Canada* **103** D10
Dinosaur △ *Canada* **102** C6
Dinosaur △ *U.S.A.* **108** F9
Dinuba *U.S.A.* **110** J7
Diö *Sweden* **11** H8
Dioïla *Mali* **82** C3
Dioka *Mali* **82** C2
Diongoï *Mali* **82** C3
Dionisades *Greece* **49** D8
Diósgyör *Hungary* **28** B5
Diosig *Romania* **28** C7
Diougani *Mali* **82** C4
Diouloulou *Senegal* **82** C1
Dioura *Mali* **82** C3
Diourbel *Senegal* **82** C1
Dipalpur *Pakistan* **68** D5
Diplo *Pakistan* **68** G3
Dipolog *Phil.* **61** G5
Dipperu △ *Australia* **94** C4
Dir *Pakistan* **66** B7
Diré *Mali* **82** B4
Dire Dawa *Ethiopia* **81** F5
Dirfis Oros *Greece* **46** C5
Diriamba *Nic.* **120** D2
Dirk Hartog I. *Australia* **93** E1
Dirranbandi *Australia* **95** D4
Disa *India* **68** G5
Disa *Sudan* **81** E3
Disappointment, C. *U.S.A.* **108** C1
Disappointment, L. *Australia* **92** D3
Disaster B. *Australia* **95** F4
Discovery B. *Australia* **95** F3
Disentis Muster *Switz.* **25** J4

Disina *Nigeria* **83** C6
Disko = Qeqertarsuaq
Greenland **98** C14
Disna = Dzisna ➤ *Belarus* **32** E5
Disney Reef *Tonga* **91** c
Diss *U.K.* **15** E9
Disteghil Sar *Pakistan* **69** A6
District of Columbia □
U.S.A. **113** F15
Distrito Federal □ *Brazil* **125** G9
Distrito Federal □ *Mexico* **119** D5
Disûq *Egypt* **80** H7
Diu *India* **68** J4
Dīvāndarreh *Iran* **73** E12
Dives ➤ *France* **18** C6
Dives-sur-Mer *France* **18** C6
Divichi = Dāvāçi *Azerbaijan* **35** K9
Divide *U.S.A.* **108** D7
Dividing Ra. *Australia* **93** E2
Divinópolis *Brazil* **125** H10
Divjake *Albania* **44** F3
Divnoye *Russia* **35** H6
Divo *Ivory C.* **82** D3
Divriği *Turkey* **73** C8
Diyālā □ *Iraq* **70** C5
Diyālā ➤ *Iraq* **73** F11
Diyarbakır *Turkey* **73** D9
Diyarbakır □ *Turkey* **73** D9
Diyodar *India* **68** G4
Djakarta = Jakarta
Indonesia **63** G12
Djamba *Angola* **88** B1
Djambala *Congo* **84** E2
Djanet *Algeria* **78** D7
Djawa = Jawa *Indonesia* **62** F3
Djelfa *Algeria* **78** B6
Djema *C.A.R.* **86** A2
Djenné *Mali* **82** C4
Djerba, Î. de *Tunisia* **79** B8
Djerid, Chott *Tunisia* **78** B7
Djibo *Burkina Faso* **83** C4
Djibouti *Djibouti* **81** E5
Djibouti ■ *Africa* **81** E5
Djolu *Dem. Rep. of the Congo* **84** D4
Djougou *Benin* **83** D5
Djoum *Cameroon* **84** D2
Djourab, Erg du *Chad* **79** E9
Djugu *Dem. Rep. of the Congo* **86** B3
Djukbinj △ *Australia* **92** B5
Djúpivogur *Iceland* **8** D6
Djurås *Sweden* **10** D9
Djurö △ *Sweden* **11** F7
Djursland *Denmark* **11** H4
Dmitriya Lapteva, Proliv
Russia **53** B15
Dmitriyev Lgovskiy *Russia* **33** F8
Dmitrov *Russia* **32** D9
Dmitrovsk-Orlovskiy *Russia* **33** F8
Dnepr = Dnipro ➤ *Ukraine* **33** J7
Dneprodzerzhinsk =
Dniprodzerzhynsk
Ukraine **33** H8
Dneprodzerzhinskoye
Vdkhr. =
Dniprodzerzhynske
Vdskh. *Ukraine* **33** H8
Dnepropetrovsk =
Dnipropetrovsk *Ukraine* **33** H8
Dneprorudnoye =
Dniprorudne *Ukraine* **33** J8
Dnestr = Dnister ➤ *Europe* **23** E16
Dnieper = Dnipro ➤
Ukraine **33** J7
Dniester = Dnister ➤
Europe **23** E16
Dnipro ➤ *Ukraine* **33** J7
Dniprodzerzhynsk *Ukraine* **33** H8
Dniprodzerzhynske Vdskh.
Ukraine **33** H8
Dnipropetrovsk *Ukraine* **33** H8
Dniprorudne *Ukraine* **33** J8
Dnister ➤ *Europe* **23** E16
Dnistrovskyy Lyman
Ukraine **33** J6
Dno *Russia* **32** D5
Dnyapro = Dnipro ➤
Ukraine **33** J7
Doaktown *Canada* **105** C6
Doan Hung *Vietnam* **58** G5
Doany *Madag.* **89** A8
Doba *Chad* **79** G9
Dobandi *Pakistan* **68** D2
Dobbiaco *Italy* **41** B9
Dobbyn *Australia* **94** B3
Dobczyce *Poland* **31** J7
Dobele *Latvia* **30** B10
Dobele *Latvia* **30** B10
Döbeln *Germany* **24** D9
Doberai, Jazirah *Indonesia* **63** E8

Dobiegniew *Poland* **31** F2
Doblas *Argentina* **126** D3
Dobo *Indonesia* **63** F8
Doboj *Bos.-H.* **28** F3
Dobra *Wielkopolskie, Poland* **31** G5
Dobra *Zachodnio-Pomorskie, Poland* **30** E2
Dobra *Dâmbovita, Romania* **29** F10
Dobra *Hunedoara, Romania* **28** E7
Dobre Miasto *Poland* **30** E7
Dobreşti *Romania* **28** D7
Dobrich *Bulgaria* **45** C11
Dobrinishta *Bulgaria* **44** E7
Dobříš *Czech Rep.* **26** B7
Dobrodzień *Poland* **31** H5
Dobromyl *Ukraine* **31** J9
Dobron *Ukraine* **28** B7
Dobropole *Ukraine* **33** H9
Dobrovolsk *Russia* **30** D9
Dobruja *Europe* **29** F13
Dobrush *Belarus* **23** B16
Dobrzany *Poland* **30** E2
Dobrzyń nad Wisłą *Poland* **31** F6
Doc, Mui *Vietnam* **64** D6
Docker River =
Kaltukatjara *Australia* **93** D4
Docksta *Sweden* **10** A12
Doctor Arroyo *Mexico* **118** C4
Doda *India* **69** C6
Doda, L. *Canada* **104** C4
Dodecanese *Greece* **47** E8
Dodekanisa = Dodecanese
Greece **47** E8
Dodekanisa □ *Greece* **47** E8
Dodge City *U.S.A.* **112** G3
Dodge L. *Canada* **103** B7
Dodgeville *U.S.A.* **112** D8
Dodo *Cameroon* **83** D7
Dodo *Sudan* **81** F2
Dodola *Ethiopia* **81** F4
Dodoma *Tanzania* **86** D4
Dodoma □ *Tanzania* **86** D4
Dodoni *Greece* **46** B2
Dodori △ *Kenya* **86** C5
Dodsland *Canada* **103** C7
Dodson *U.S.A.* **108** B9
Doesburg *Neths.* **17** B6
Doetinchem *Neths.* **17** C6
Dog Creek *Canada* **102** C4
Dog L. *Man., Canada* **103** C9
Dog L. *Ont., Canada* **104** C2
Doğanşehir *Turkey* **72** C7
Dogliani *Italy* **40** D4
Dogondoutchi *Niger* **83** C5
Dogran *Pakistan* **68** D5
Doğubayazıt *Turkey* **73** C11
Doguéraoua *Niger* **83** C6
Doha = Ad Dawḩah *Qatar* **71** E6
Dohazari *Bangla.* **67** H18
Dohrighat *India* **69** F10
Doi *Indonesia* **63** D7
Doi Inthanon △ *Thailand* **64** C2
Doi Khuntan △ *Thailand* **64** C2
Doi Luang *Thailand* **64** C3
Doi Luang △ *Thailand* **64** C2
Doi Saket *Thailand* **64** C2
Doi Suthep △ *Thailand* **64** C2
Dois Irmãos, Sa. *Brazil* **125** E10
Dojransko Jezero *Macedonia* **44** E6
Dokkum *Neths.* **17** A5
Dokos *Greece* **46** D5
Dokri *Pakistan* **68** F3
Dokuchayevsk *Ukraine* **33** J9
Dol-de-Bretagne *France* **18** D5
Dolac *Serbia* **44** D4
Dolak, Pulau *Indonesia* **63** F9
Dolbeau-Mistassini *Canada* **105** C5
Dole *France* **19** E12
Doleib, Wadi ➤ *Sudan* **81** E3
Dolenji Logatec *Slovenia* **41** C11
Dolgellau *U.K.* **14** E4
Dolgelley = Dolgellau *U.K.* **14** E4
Dolhasca *Romania* **29** C11
Doliana *Greece* **46** B2
Dolianova *Italy* **42** C2
Dolinskaya = Dolynska
Ukraine **33** H7
Dolj □ *Romania* **29** F8
Dollard *Neths.* **17** A7
Dolna Banya *Bulgaria* **44** D7
Dolni Chiflik *Bulgaria* **45** D11
Dolni Dŭbnik *Bulgaria* **45** C8
Dolnośląskie □ *Poland* **31** G3
Dolný Kubín *Slovak Rep.* **27** B12
Dolo *Ethiopia* **81** G5
Dolo *Italy* **41** C9
Dolomites = Dolomiti *Italy* **41** B8
Dolomiti *Italy* **41** B8
Dolomiti Bellunesi △ *Italy* **41** B9
Dolores *Argentina* **126** D4
Dolores *Uruguay* **126** C4
Dolores *U.S.A.* **109** H9
Dolores ➤ *U.S.A.* **108** G9
Dolovo *Serbia* **28** E5
Dolphin, C. *Falk. Is.* **128** G5
Dolphin and Union Str.
Canada **100** C8

Dolsk *Poland* **31** G4
Dolyna *Ukraine* **29** B9
Dolynska *Ukraine* **33** H7
Dolynske *Ukraine* **29** C14
Dolzhanskaya *Russia* **33** J9
Dom Pedrito *Brazil* **127** C5
Doma *Nigeria* **83** D6
Doma △ *Zimbabwe* **87** F3
Domaniç *Turkey* **47** B11
Domariaganj ➤ *India* **69** F10
Domasi *Malawi* **87** F4
Domažlice *Czech Rep.* **26** B5
Dombarovskiy *Russia* **52** D6
Dombås *Norway* **8** E13
Dombasle-sur-Meurthe
France **19** D13
Dombes *France* **21** C9
Dombóvár *Hungary* **28** D3
Dombrád *Hungary* **28** B6
Dome Argus *Antarctica* **5** E12
Dome C. *Antarctica* **5** D17
Dome Fuji *Antarctica* **5** D5
Domel I. = Letsôk-aw
Kyun *Burma* **65** G2
Domérat *France* **19** F9
Domeyko *Chile* **126** B1
Domeyko, Cordillera *Chile* **126** A2
Domfront *France* **18** D6
Dominador *Chile* **126** A2
Dominica ■ *W. Indies* **121** C7
Dominica Passage *W. Indies* **121** C7
Dominican Rep. ■
W. Indies **121** C5
Dömitz *Germany* **24** B7
Domme *France* **20** D5
Domnești *Romania* **29** E9
Domodóssola *Italy* **40** B5
Domokos *Greece* **46** B4
Dompaire *France* **19** D13
Dompierre-sur-Besbre
France **19** F10
Dompim *Ghana* **82** D4
Domrémy-la-Pucelle *France*
19 D12
Domvena *Greece* **46** C4
Domville, Mt. *Australia* **95** D5
Domžale *Slovenia* **41** B11
Don ➤ *Russia* **33** J10
Don ➤ *Aberds., U.K.* **13** D6
Don ➤ *S. Yorks., U.K.* **14** D7
Don, C. *Australia* **92** B5
Don Benito *Spain* **37** G5
Don Figuerero Mts. *Jamaica* **120** a
Don Sak *Thailand* **65** b
Dona Ana = Nhamaabué
Mozam. **87** F4
Doña Mencía *Spain* **37** H6
Donaghadee *U.K.* **12** B6
Donaghmore *Ireland* **12** D4
Donald *Australia* **95** F3
Donaldsonville *U.S.A.* **116** F9
Donalsonville *U.S.A.* **117** F12
Doñana △ *Spain* **37** J4
Donau = Dunărea ➤
Europe **29** E14
Donau ➤ *Austria* **27** C10
Donau Auen △ *Austria* **27** C9
Donaueschingen *Germany* **25** H4
Donauwörth *Germany* **25** G6
Doncaster *U.K.* **14** D6
Dondo *Angola* **84** F2
Dondo *Mozam.* **87** F3
Dondo, Teluk *Indonesia* **63** D6
Dondra Head *Sri Lanka* **66** S12
Donduşeni *Moldova* **29** B12
Donegal *Ireland* **12** B3
Donegal □ *Ireland* **12** B4
Donegal B. *Ireland* **12** B3
Donets ➤ *Russia* **35** G5
Donets Basin *Ukraine* **6** F13
Donetsk *Ukraine* **33** J9
Donetsk □ *Ukraine* **33** J9
Dong Ba Thin *Vietnam* **65** F7
Dong Giam *Vietnam* **64** C5
Dong Ha *Vietnam* **64** D6
Dong Hene *Laos* **64** D5
Dong Hoi *Vietnam* **64** D6
Dong Jiang ➤ *China* **59** F10
Dong Khe *Vietnam* **64** A6
Dong Ujimqin Qi *China* **56** B9
Dong Van *Vietnam* **64** A5
Dong Xoai *Vietnam* **65** G6
Donga *Nigeria* **83** D7
Donga ➤ *Nigeria* **83** D7
Dong'an *China* **59** D8
Dongara *Australia* **93** E1
Dongbei *China* **57** D13
Dongchuan *China* **58** D4
Dongco *China* **67** C14
Dongfang *China* **64** C6
Dongfeng *China* **57** C13
Donggala *Indonesia* **63** E5
Donggan *China* **58** F5

Donggang *China* **57** E13
Dongguan *China* **59** F9
Dongguang *China* **56** F9
Donghae *S. Korea* **57** F15
Donghai Dao *China* **59** G8
Donglan *China* **58** E6
Dongliu *China* **59** B11
Dongmen *China* **58** F6
Dongnae *S. Korea* **57** G15
Dongning *China* **57** B16
Dongnyi *China* **58** C3
Dongola *Sudan* **80** D3
Dongping *China* **56** G9
Dongsha Dao *China* **59** G11
Dongshan *China* **59** F11
Dongtai *China* **57** H11
Dongting Hu *China* **59** C9
Dongtou *China* **59** D13
Dongxiang *China* **59** C11
Dongxing *China* **58** G7
Dongyang *China* **59** C13
Dongzhi *China* **59** B11
Donington, C. *Australia* **95** E2
Doniphan *U.S.A.* **112** G8
Donja Stubica *Croatia* **41** C12
Donji Dušnik *Serbia* **44** C6
Donji Miholjac *Croatia* **28** E3
Donji Milanovac *Serbia* **44** B6
Donji Vakuf *Bos.-H.* **28** F2
Dønna *Norway* **8** C15
Donna *U.S.A.* **116** H5
Donnaconna *Canada* **105** C5
Donnelly's Crossing *N.Z.* **91** A4
Donnybrook *Australia* **93** F2
Donnybrook *S. Africa* **89** D4
Donora *U.S.A.* **114** F5
Donostia = Donostia-San
Sebastián *Spain* **38** B3
Donostia-San Sebastián
Spain **38** B3
Donousa *Greece* **47** D7
Donskoy *Russia* **32** F10
Donzère *France* **21** D8
Donzy *France* **19** E10
Doon ➤ *U.K.* **13** F4
Dora, L. *Australia* **92** D3
Dora Báltea ➤ *Italy* **40** C5
Dora Ripária ➤ *Italy* **40** C4
Doran L. *Canada* **103** A7
Dorchester *U.K.* **15** G5
Dorchester, C. *Canada* **101** C12
Dordabis *Namibia* **88** C2
Dordogne □ *France* **20** D5
Dordogne ➤ *France* **20** C3
Dordrecht *Neths.* **17** C4
Dordrecht *S. Africa* **88** E4
Dore ➤ *France* **20** C7
Dore, Mts. *France* **20** C6
Doré L. *Canada* **103** C7
Dorfen *Germany* **25** G8
Dorgali *Italy* **42** B2
Dori *Burkina Faso* **83** C4
Doring ➤ *S. Africa* **88** E2
Doringbos *S. Africa* **88** E2
Dorking *U.K.* **15** F7
Dormaa-Ahenkro *Ghana* **82** D4
Dormans *France* **19** C10
Dormo, Ras *Eritrea* **81** E5
Dornbirn *Austria* **26** D2
Dornes *France* **19** F10
Dorneşti *Romania* **29** C11
Dornie *U.K.* **13** D3
Dornoch *U.K.* **13** D4
Dornoch Firth *U.K.* **13** D4
Dornogovĭ □ *Mongolia* **56** C6
Doro *Mali* **83** B4
Doro, Kavo *Greece* **46** C6
Dorog *Hungary* **28** C3
Dorogobuzh *Russia* **32** E7
Dorohoi *Romania* **29** C11
Döröö Nuur *Mongolia* **60** B4
Dorr *Iran* **71** C6
Dorre I. *Australia* **93** E1
Dorrigo *Australia* **95** E5
Dorris *U.S.A.* **108** F3
Dorset *Canada* **114** A6
Dorset *U.S.A.* **114** E4
Dorset □ *U.K.* **15** G5
Dorsten *Germany* **24** D2
Dortmund *Germany* **24** D3
Dortmund-Ems-Kanal ➤
Germany **24** D3
Dörtyol *Turkey* **72** D7
Dorum *Germany* **24** B4
Doruma
Dem. Rep. of the Congo **86** B2
Dorüneh *Iran* **71** C8
Dos Bahías, C. *Argentina* **128** E3
Dos Hermanas *Spain* **37** H5
Dos Palos *U.S.A.* **110** J6
Döşemealtı *Turkey* **47** D12
Dosso *Niger* **83** C5
Dosso □ *Niger* **83** C5

Dosso △ *Niger* **83** C5
Dothan *U.S.A.* **117** F12
Doty *U.S.A.* **110** D3
Douai *France* **19** B10
Douako *Guinea* **82** D2
Douala *Cameroon* **83** E6
Douarnenez *France* **18** D2
Doubabougou *Mali* **82** C3
Double Island Pt. *Australia* **95** D5
Double Mountain Fork ➤
U.S.A. **116** E4
Doubrava ➤ *Czech Rep.* **26** A8
Doubs □ *France* **19** E13
Doubs ➤ *France* **19** F12
Doubtful Sd. *N.Z.* **91** F1
Doubtless B. *N.Z.* **91** F4
Doudeville *France* **18** C7
Doué-la-Fontaine *France* **18** E6
Douentza *Mali* **82** C4
Douentza △ *Mali* **82** B4
Douglas *I. of Man* **14** C3
Douglas *S. Africa* **88** D3
Douglas *Ariz., U.S.A.* **109** L9
Douglas *Ga., U.S.A.* **117** F13
Douglas *Wyo., U.S.A.* **108** E11
Douglas Apsley △ *Australia* **95** G4
Douglas Chan. *Canada* **102** C3
Douglas Pt. *Canada* **114** B3
Douglasville *U.S.A.* **117** E12
Doukaton, Akra *Greece* **46** C2
Doulevant-le-Château
France **19** D11
Doullens *France* **19** B9
Doumen *China* **59** F9
Douna *Mali* **82** C4
Dounreay *U.K.* **13** C5
Dourada, Serra *Brazil* **125** F9
Dourados *Brazil* **127** A5
Dourados ➤ *Brazil* **127** A5
Dourados, Serra dos *Brazil* **127** A5
Dourdan *France* **19** D9
Douro ➤ *Europe* **36** D2
Douvaine *France* **19** F13
Douvres-la-Délivrande
France **18** C6
Douze ➤ *France* **20** E3
Dove ➤ *U.K.* **14** E6
Dove Creek *U.S.A.* **109** H9
Dover *Australia* **95** G4
Dover *U.K.* **15** F9
Dover *Del., U.S.A.* **113** F16
Dover *N.H., U.S.A.* **115** C14
Dover *N.J., U.S.A.* **115** F10
Dover *Ohio, U.S.A.* **114** F3
Dover, Pt. *Australia* **93** F4
Dover, Str. of *Europe* **15** G9
Dover-Foxcroft *U.S.A.* **113** C19
Dover Plains *U.S.A.* **115** E11
Dovey = Dyfi ➤ *U.K.* **15** E3
Dovhe *Ukraine* **29** B8
Dovrefjell *Norway* **8** E13
Dow Rūd *Iran* **71** C6
Dowa *Malawi* **87** E3
Dowagiac *U.S.A.* **112** E10
Dowerin *Australia* **93** F2
Dowgha'i *Iran* **71** B8
Dowlatābād *Iran* **71** D8
Down □ *U.K.* **12** B5
Downey *Calif., U.S.A.* **111** M8
Downey *Idaho, U.S.A.* **108** E7
Downham Market *U.K.* **15** E8
Downieville *U.S.A.* **110** F6
Downpatrick *U.K.* **12** B6
Downpatrick Hd. *Ireland* **12** B2
Downsville *U.S.A.* **115** D10
Downton, Mt. *Canada* **102** C4
Dowsārī *Iran* **71** D8
Doxato *Greece* **45** E8
Doyle *U.S.A.* **110** E6
Doylestown *U.S.A.* **115** F9
Dozois, Rés. *Canada* **104** C4
Dra Khel *Pakistan* **68** F2
Drâa, C. *Morocco* **78** C3
Drâa, Oued ➤ *Morocco* **78** C3
Drac ➤ *France* **21** C9
Dračevo *Macedonia* **44** E5
Drachten *Neths.* **17** A6
Drăgăneşti *Moldova* **29** C13
Drăgăneşti-Olt *Romania* **29** F9
Drăgăneşti-Vlaşca *Romania* **29** F10
Dragaš *Serbia* **44** D4
Drăgăşani *Romania* **29** F9
Dragichyn *Belarus* **23** B13
Dragocvet *Serbia* **44** C5
Dragon's Mouths = Boca
de Drago *Venezuela* **125** K15
Dragovishtitsa *Bulgaria* **44** D6
Draguignan *France* **21** E10
Drahove *Ukraine* **29** B8
Drain *U.S.A.* **108** E2
Drake *U.S.A.* **112** B3
Drake Passage *S. Ocean* **5** B17
Drakensberg *S. Africa* **89** D4
Drama *Greece* **45** E8
Drama □ *Greece* **45** E8
Drammen *Norway* **9** G14
Drangajökull *Iceland* **8** C2

Dranov, Ostrov *Romania* **29** F14
Dras *India* **69** B6
Drastis, Akra *Greece* **49** A3
Drau = Drava *Croatia* **28** E3
Drava *Croatia* **28** E3
Drawa *Poland* **31** F2
Drawieński △ *Poland* **31** E2
Drawno *Poland* **31** E2
Drawsko Pomorskie *Poland* **30** E2
Drayton Valley *Canada* **102** C6
Dreieich *Germany* **25** E4
Dren *Serbia* **44** C4
Drenthe □ *Neths.* **17** B6
Drepano, Akra *Greece* **49** D6
Drepanum, C. *Cyprus* **49** E11
Dresden *Canada* **114** D2
Dresden *Germany* **24** D9
Dreux *France* **18** D8
Drezdenko *Poland* **31** F2
Driffield *U.K.* **14** C7
Driftwood *U.S.A.* **114** E6
Driggs *U.S.A.* **108** E8
Drin ➔ *Albania* **44** D3
Drin i Zi ➔ *Albania* **44** E4
Drina ➔ *Bos.-H.* **44** B3
Drincea ➔ *Romania* **28** F7
Drinjača ➔ *Bos.-H.* **28** F4
Driopida *Greece* **46** D6
Drissa =
    Vyerkhnyadzvinsk
    Belarus **32** E4
Drniš *Croatia* **41** E13
Drøbak *Norway* **9** G14
Drobeta-Turnu Severin
    Romania **28** F7
Drobin *Poland* **31** F6
Drochia *Moldova* **29** B12
Drogheda *Ireland* **12** C5
Drogichin = Dragichyn
    Belarus **23** B13
Drogobych = Drohobych
    Ukraine **31** J10
Drohiczyn *Poland* **31** F9
Drohobych *Ukraine* **31** J10
Droichead Atha =
    Drogheda *Ireland* **12** C5
Droichead Nua *Ireland* **12** C5
Droitwich *U.K.* **15** E5
Drôme □ *France* **21** D9
Drôme ➔ *France* **21** D8
Dromedary, C. *Australia* **95** F5
Drömling △ *Germany* **24** C7
Dromore *U.K.* **12** B4
Dromore West *Ireland* **12** B3
Dronero *Italy* **40** D4
Dronfield *U.K.* **14** D6
Dronne ➔ *France* **20** C3
Dronning Maud Land
    Antarctica **5** D3
Dronninglund *Denmark* **11** G4
Dronten *Neths.* **17** B5
Dropt ➔ *France* **20** D3
Drosendorf *Austria* **26** C8
Droué *France* **18** D8
Druk Yul = Bhutan ■ *Asia* **67** F17
Drumbo *Canada* **114** C4
Drumcliff *Ireland* **12** B3
Drumheller *Canada* **102** C6
Drummond *U.S.A.* **108** C7
Drummond I. *U.S.A.* **113** B12
Drummond Pt. *Australia* **95** E2
Drummond Ra. *Australia* **94** C4
Drummondville *Canada* **104** C5
Drumright *U.S.A.* **116** D6
Druskininkai *Lithuania* **32** E2
Drut ➔ *Belarus* **23** B16
Druya *Belarus* **32** E4
Druzhba *Bulgaria* **45** C12
Druzhina *Russia* **53** C15
Drvar *Bos.-H.* **41** D13
Drvenik *Croatia* **41** E13
Drwęca ➔ *Poland* **31** E5
Dry Harbour Mts. *Jamaica* **120** a
Dry Tortugas *U.S.A.* **117** F13
Dryanovo *Bulgaria* **45** D9
Dryden *Canada* **103** D10
Dryden *U.S.A.* **115** D8
Drygalski I. *Antarctica* **5** C7
Drygalski Ice Tongue
    Antarctica **5** D21
Drysdale ➔ *Australia* **92** B4
Drysdale I. *Australia* **94** A2
Drysdale River △ *Australia* **92** B4
Drzewica *Poland* **31** G7
Drzewiczka ➔ *Poland* **31** G7
Dschang *Cameroon* **83** D7
Du Gué ➔ *Canada* **104** A5
Du He ➔ *China* **59** A8
Du Quoin *U.S.A.* **112** F9
Du'an *China* **58** F7
Đuđa *Si. Arabia* **70** E2
Dubai = Dubayy *U.A.E.* **71** E7
Dubăsari *Moldova* **29** C14

Dubăsari Vdkhr. *Moldova* **29** C13
Dubawnt ➔ *Canada* **103** A8
Dubawnt L. *Canada* **103** A8
Dubayy *U.A.E.* **71** E7
Dubbo *Australia* **95** E4
Dubele *Dem. Rep. of the Congo* **86** B2
Dübendorf *Switz.* **25** H4
Dubica *Croatia* **41** C13
Dublin *Ireland* **12** C5
Dublin *Ga., U.S.A.* **117** E13
Dublin *Tex., U.S.A.* **116** E5
Dublin □ *Ireland* **12** C5
Dublin ✈ (DUB) *Ireland* **12** C5
Dubna *Russia* **32** D9
Dubnica nad Váhom
    Slovak Rep. **27** C11
Dubno *Ukraine* **23** C13
Dubois *Idaho, U.S.A.* **108** D7
Dubois *Pa., U.S.A.* **114** E6
Dubossary = Dubăsari
    Moldova **29** C14
Dubossary Vdkhr. =
    Dubăsari Vdkhr. *Moldova* **29** C13
Dubove *Ukraine* **29** B8
Dubovka *Russia* **35** F7
Dubovskoye *Russia* **35** G6
Dubrajpur *India* **69** H12
Dubréka *Guinea* **82** D2
Dubrovitsa = Dubrovytsya
    Ukraine **23** C14
Dubrovnik *Croatia* **44** D2
Dubrovytsya *Ukraine* **23** C14
Dubuque *U.S.A.* **112** D8
Dubysa ➔ *Lithuania* **30** C10
Duchang *China* **59** C11
Duchesne *U.S.A.* **108** F8
Duchess *Australia* **94** C2
Ducie I. *Pac. Oc.* **97** K15
Duck ➔ *U.S.A.* **117** C11
Duck Cr. ➔ *Australia* **92** D2
Duck Lake *Canada* **103** C7
Duck Mountain △ *Canada* **103** C8
Duckwall, Mt. *U.S.A.* **110** H6
Duderstadt *Germany* **24** D6
Dudhi *India* **69** G10
Dudinka *Russia* **53** C9
Dudley *U.K.* **15** E5
Dudwa *India* **69** E9
Dudwa △ *India* **69** E9
Dueñas *Spain* **36** D6
Dufftown *U.K.* **13** D5
Dufourspitz *Switz.* **25** K3
Dugi Otok *Croatia* **41** D11
Dugo Selo *Croatia* **41** C13
Duisburg *Germany* **24** D2
Duiwelskloof =
    Modjadjiskloof *S. Africa* **89** C5
Dujiangyan *China* **58** B4
Duk Fadiat *Sudan* **81** F3
Duk Faiwil *Sudan* **81** F3
Dukat *Albania* **44** F3
Dūkdamīn *Iran* **71** C8
Dukelský Průsmyk
    Slovak Rep. **27** B14
Dukhān *Qatar* **71** E6
Dukhovshchina *Russia* **32** E7
Duki *Pakistan* **66** D6
Dukla *Poland* **31** J8
Duku *Bauchi, Nigeria* **83** C7
Duku *Sokoto, Nigeria* **83** C5
Dulag *Phil.* **61** F6
Dulce *U.S.A.* **109** H10
Dulce ➔ *Argentina* **126** C3
Dulce, G. *Costa Rica* **120** E3
Dulf *Iraq* **70** C5
Dŭlgopol *Bulgaria* **45** C11
Duliu *China* **56** E9
Dullewala *Pakistan* **68** D4
Dullstroom *S. Africa* **89** D5
Dülmen *Germany* **24** D3
Dulovo *Bulgaria* **45** C11
Dulq Maghār *Syria* **73** D8
Duluth *U.S.A.* **112** B7
Dum Dum *India* **69** H13
Dum Duma *India* **67** F19
Dūmā *Syria* **74** B5
Dumaguete *Phil.* **61** G5
Dumai *Indonesia* **62** D2
Dumaran *Phil.* **61** F3
Dumas *Ark., U.S.A.* **116** E9
Dumas *Tex., U.S.A.* **116** D4
Ḍumayr *Syria* **74** B5
Dumbarton *U.K.* **13** F4
Ďumbier *Slovak Rep.* **27** C12
Dumbleyung *Australia* **93** F2
Dumboa *Nigeria* **83** C7
Dumbrăveni *Romania* **29** D9
Dumfries *U.K.* **13** F5
Dumfries & Galloway □
    U.K. **13** F5
Dumitreşti *Romania* **29** E11
Dumka *India* **69** G12
Dumlupınar *Turkey* **47** C12
Dümmer *Germany* **24** C4
Dümmer △ *Germany* **24** C4

Dumoine ➔ *Canada* **104** C4
Dumoine, L. *Canada* **104** C4
Dumont d'Urville *Antarctica* **5** C10
Dumraon *India* **69** G11
Dumyât *Egypt* **80** H7
Dumyât, Masabb *Egypt* **80** H7
Dún Dealgan = Dundalk
    Ireland **12** B5
Dún Laoghaire *Ireland* **12** C5
Dun-le-Palestel *France* **19** F8
Dun-sur-Auron *France* **19** F9
Dun-sur-Meuse *France* **19** C12
Duna = Dunărea ➔ *Europe* **29** E14
Duna-Drava △ *Hungary* **28** D3
Duna-völgyi-főcsatorna
    Hungary **28** D3
Dunaföldvár *Hungary* **28** D3
Dunagiri *India* **69** D8
Dunaj = Dunărea ➔
    Europe **29** E14
Dunajec ➔ *Poland* **31** H7
Dunajská Streda *Slovak Rep.* **27** C10
Dunakeszi *Hungary* **28** C4
Dunapataj *Hungary* **28** D3
Dunărea ➔ *Europe* **29** E14
Dunaszekcső *Hungary* **28** D3
Dunaújváros *Hungary* **28** D3
Dunav = Dunărea ➔
    Europe **29** E14
Dunavaţu de Jos *Romania* **29** F14
Dunavtsi *Bulgaria* **44** C6
Dunay *Russia* **54** C6
Dunayivtsi *Ukraine* **29** B11
Dunback *N.Z.* **91** F3
Dunbar *U.K.* **13** E6
Dunblane *U.K.* **13** E5
Duncan *Canada* **110** B3
Duncan *Ariz., U.S.A.* **109** K9
Duncan *Okla., U.S.A.* **116** D6
Duncan, L. *Canada* **104** B4
Duncan Town *Bahamas* **120** B4
Duncannon *U.S.A.* **114** F7
Duncansby Head *U.K.* **13** C5
Duncansville *U.S.A.* **114** F6
Dundaga *Latvia* **30** A9
Dundalk *Canada* **114** B4
Dundalk *Ireland* **12** B5
Dundalk *U.S.A.* **113** F15
Dundalk Bay *Ireland* **12** C5
Dundas = Uummannaq
    Greenland **4** B4
Dundas *Canada* **114** C5
Dundas, L. *Australia* **93** F3
Dundas I. *Canada* **102** C2
Dundas Str. *Australia* **92** B5
Dundee *S. Africa* **89** D5
Dundee *U.K.* **13** E6
Dundee *U.S.A.* **114** D8
Dundee City □ *U.K.* **13** E6
Dundgovĭ □ *Mongolia* **56** B4
Dundrum *U.K.* **12** B6
Dundrum B. *U.K.* **12** B6
Dunedin *N.Z.* **91** F3
Dunedin *U.S.A.* **117** G13
Dunfanaghy *Ireland* **12** A4
Dunfermline *U.K.* **13** E5
Dungannon *Canada* **114** C3
Dungannon *U.K.* **12** B5
Dungarpur *India* **68** H5
Dungarvan *Ireland* **12** D4
Dungarvan Harbour *Ireland* **12** D4
Dungeness *U.K.* **15** G8
Dunglow *Ireland* **12** B3
Dungo, L. do *Angola* **88** B2
Dungog *Australia* **95** E5
Dungu *Dem. Rep. of the Congo* **86** B2
Dungun *Malaysia* **65** K4
Dungunâb *Sudan* **80** C4
Dungunâb, Khalīg *Sudan* **80** C4
Dunhua *China* **57** C15
Dunhuang *China* **60** B4
Dunk I. *Australia* **94** B4
Dunkassa *Benin* **83** C5
Dunkeld *Australia* **95** F4
Dunkeld *U.K.* **13** E5
Dunkerque *France* **19** A9
Dunkery Beacon *U.K.* **15** F4
Dunkirk = Dunkerque
    France **19** A9
Dunkirk *U.S.A.* **114** D5
Dunkuj *Sudan* **81** E3
Dunkwa *Central, Ghana* **82** D4
Dunkwa *Central, Ghana* **83** D4
Dúnleary = Dún
    Laoghaire *Ireland* **12** C5
Dunleer *Ireland* **12** C5
Dunmanus B. *Ireland* **12** E2
Dunmanway *Ireland* **12** E2
Dunmarra *Australia* **94** B1
Dunmore *U.S.A.* **115** E9
Dunmore East *Ireland* **12** D5
Dunmore Hd. *Ireland* **12** D1
Dunmore Town *Bahamas* **120** A4
Dunn *U.S.A.* **117** D15
Dunnellon *U.S.A.* **117** G13
Dunnet Hd. *U.K.* **13** C5

Dunning *U.S.A.* **112** E3
Dunnville *Canada* **114** D5
Dunolly *Australia* **95** F3
Dunoon *U.K.* **13** F4
Dunqul *Egypt* **80** C3
Duns *U.K.* **13** F6
Dunseith *U.S.A.* **112** A3
Dunshaughlin *Ireland* **12** C5
Dunsmuir *U.S.A.* **108** F2
Dunstable *U.K.* **15** F7
Dunstan Mts. *N.Z.* **91** F2
Dunster *Canada* **102** C5
Dunvegan *U.K.* **13** D2
Dunvegan L. *Canada* **103** A7
Duolun *China* **56** C9
Duong Dong *Vietnam* **65** G4
Dupree *U.S.A.* **112** C3
Dupuyer *U.S.A.* **108** B7
Durack ➔ *Australia* **92** C4
Durack Ra. *Australia* **92** C4
Durağan *Turkey* **72** B6
Durak *Turkey* **47** B10
Durance ➔ *France* **21** E8
Durand *U.S.A.* **112** C9
Durango *Mexico* **118** C4
Durango *U.S.A.* **109** H10
Durango □ *Mexico* **118** C4
Durankulak *Bulgaria* **45** C12
Durant *Miss., U.S.A.* **117** E10
Durant *Okla., U.S.A.* **116** E6
Duratón ➔ *Spain* **36** D6
Durazno *Uruguay* **126** C4
Durazzo = Durrës *Albania* **44** E3
Durban *France* **20** F6
Durban *S. Africa* **89** D5
Durbuy *Belgium* **17** D5
Dúrcal *Spain* **37** J7
Đurđevac *Croatia* **28** D2
Düren *Germany* **24** E2
Durg = Bhilainagar-Durg
    India **67** J12
Durgapur *India* **69** H12
Durham *Canada* **114** B4
Durham *U.K.* **14** C6
Durham *Calif., U.S.A.* **110** F5
Durham *N.C., U.S.A.* **117** D15
Durham *N.H., U.S.A.* **115** C14
Durham □ *U.K.* **14** C6
Durleşti *Moldova* **29** C13
Durma *Si. Arabia* **70** E5
Durmitor *Montenegro* **44** C2
Durmitor △ *Serbia* **44** C3
Durness *U.K.* **13** C4
Durrës *Albania* **44** E3
Durrow *Ireland* **12** D4
Dursey I. *Ireland* **12** E1
Dursley *U.K.* **15** F5
Dursunbey *Turkey* **47** B10
Durtal *France* **18** E6
Duru *Dem. Rep. of the Congo* **86** B2
Duru Gölü *Turkey* **45** E12
Durusu *Turkey* **45** E12
Durūz, Jabal ad *Jordan* **74** C5
D'Urville, Tanjung *Indonesia* **63** E9
D'Urville I. *N.Z.* **91** D4
Duryea *U.S.A.* **115** E9
Ḍūsh *Egypt* **80** C3
Dushak *Turkmenistan* **71** B9
Dushan *China* **58** E6
Dushanbe *Tajikistan* **52** F7
Dusheti *Georgia* **35** J7
Dushore *U.S.A.* **115** E8
Dusky Sd. *N.Z.* **91** F1
Dussejour, C. *Australia* **92** B4
Düsseldorf *Germany* **24** D2
Düsseldorf Rhein-Ruhr ✈
    (DUS) *Germany* **24** D2
Duszniki-Zdrój *Poland* **31** H3
Dutch Harbor *U.S.A.* **106** a
Dutlwe *Botswana* **88** C3
Dutsan Wai *Nigeria* **83** C6
Dutton *Canada* **114** D3
Dutton ➔ *Australia* **94** C3
Dutywa *S. Africa* **89** E4
Duved *Sweden* **10** A6
Düvertepe *Turkey* **47** B10
Düzce *Turkey* **72** B4
Düzce □ *Turkey* **72** B4
Dve Mogili *Bulgaria* **45** C9
Dvina, Severnaya ➔ *Russia* **6** C14
Dvinsk = Daugavpils *Latvia* **32** E4
Dvor *Croatia* **41** C13
Dvůr Králové nad Labem
    Czech Rep. **26** A8
Dwarka *India* **68** H3
Dwellingup *Australia* **93** F2
Dwight *Canada* **114** A5
Dwight *U.S.A.* **112** E9
Dyakove *Ukraine* **28** B7
Dyatkovo *Russia* **32** F8
Dyatlovo = Dzyatlava
    Belarus **23** B13

Dyce *U.K.* **13** D6
Dyer, C. *Canada* **101** C13
Dyer Bay *Canada* **114** A3
Dyer Plateau *Antarctica* **5** D17
Dyersburg *U.S.A.* **117** C10
Dyfi ➔ *U.K.* **15** E3
Dyje ➔ *Czech Rep.* **27** C9
Dymer *Ukraine* **23** C16
Dynów *Poland* **31** J9
Dysart *Australia* **94** C4
Dzaoudzi *Mayotte* **85** a
Dzerzhinsk *Russia* **34** B6
Dzhalinda *Russia* **53** D13
Dzhambul = Taraz
    Kazakhstan **52** E8
Dzhankoy *Ukraine* **33** K8
Dzhanybek = Zhänibek
    Kazakhstan **34** F8
Dzharylhach, Ostriv *Ukraine* **33** J7
Dzhezkazgan =
    Zhezqazghan *Kazakhstan* **52** E7
Dzhizak = Jizzakh *Uzbekistan* **52** E7
Dzhugdzur, Khrebet *Russia* **53** D14
Dzhulynk *Ukraine* **29** B14
Dzhuryn *Ukraine* **29** B13
Dzhvari = Jvari *Georgia* **35** J6
Działdowo *Poland* **31** E7
Działoszyce *Poland* **31** H7
Działoszyn *Poland* **31** G5
Dzibilchaltún *Mexico* **119** C7
Dzierzgoń *Poland* **30** E6
Dzierżoniów *Poland* **31** H3
Dzilam de Bravo *Mexico* **119** C7
Dzisna *Belarus* **32** E5
Dzisna ➔ *Belarus* **32** E5
Dziwnów *Poland* **30** D1
Dz◈kija □ *Lithuania* **9** J21
Dzungaria = Junggar
    Pendi *China* **60** B3
Dzungarian Basin =
    Junggar Pendi *China* **60** B3
Dzüünmod *Mongolia* **60** B5
Dzyarzhynsk *Belarus* **23** B14
Dzyatlava *Belarus* **23** B13

E

E.C. Manning △ *Canada* **102** D4
Eabamet L. *Canada* **104** B2
Eads *U.S.A.* **108** G12
Eagar *U.S.A.* **109** J9
Eagle *Alaska, U.S.A.* **100** C5
Eagle *Colo., U.S.A.* **108** G10
Eagle ➔ *Canada* **105** B8
Eagle Butte *U.S.A.* **112** C3
Eagle Grove *U.S.A.* **112** D7
Eagle L. *Canada* **103** D10
Eagle L. *Calif., U.S.A.* **108** F3
Eagle L. *Maine, U.S.A.* **113** B19
Eagle Lake *Canada* **114** A6
Eagle Lake *Maine, U.S.A.* **113** B19
Eagle Lake *Tex., U.S.A.* **116** G6
Eagle Mountain *U.S.A.* **111** M11
Eagle Nest *U.S.A.* **109** H11
Eagle Pass *U.S.A.* **116** G4
Eagle Pk. *U.S.A.* **110** G7
Eagle Pt. *Australia* **92** C3
Eagle River *Mich., U.S.A.* **112** B9
Eagle River *Wis., U.S.A.* **112** C9
Eaglehawk *Australia* **95** F3
Eagles Mere *U.S.A.* **115** E8
Ealing □ *U.K.* **15** F7
Ear Falls *Canada* **103** C10
Earle *U.S.A.* **117** D9
Earlimart *U.S.A.* **111** K7
Earn ➔ *U.K.* **13** E5
Earn, L. *U.K.* **13** E4
Earnslaw, Mt. *N.Z.* **91** F2
Earth *U.S.A.* **116** D3
Easley *U.S.A.* **117** D13
East Anglia *U.K.* **14** E9
East Angus *Canada* **105** C5
East Antarctica *Antarctica* **5** D7
East Aurora *U.S.A.* **114** D6
East Ayrshire □ *U.K.* **13** F4
East Bengal *Bangla.* **67** G17
East Beskids = Vychodné
    Beskydy *Europe* **27** B15
East Brady *U.S.A.* **114** F5
East C. = Dezhneva, Mys
    Russia **53** C19
East C. *N.Z.* **91** B7
East Caroline Basin *Pac. Oc.* **96** G6
East Chicago *U.S.A.* **112** E10
East China Sea *Asia* **60** C7
East Coulee *Canada* **102** C6
East Dereham = Dereham
    U.K. **15** E8
East Dunbartonshire □ *U.K.* **13** F4
East Falkland *Falk. Is.* **128** G5
East Grand Forks *U.S.A.* **112** B5
East Greenwich *U.S.A.* **115** E13
East Grinstead *U.K.* **15** F8
East Hartford *U.S.A.* **115** E12
East Helena *U.S.A.* **108** C8
East Indies *Asia* **50** J14

East Kilbride *U.K.* **13** F4
East Lansing *U.S.A.* **113** D11
East Liverpool *U.S.A.* **114** F4
East London *S. Africa* **89** E4
East Lothian □ *U.K.* **13** F6
East Main = Eastmain
    Canada **104** B4
East Mariana Basin *Pac. Oc.* **96** F7
East Northport *U.S.A.* **115** F11
East Orange *U.S.A.* **115** F10
East Pacific Rise *Pac. Oc.* **97** J17
East Palestine *U.S.A.* **114** F4
East Pine *Canada* **102** B4
East Point *U.S.A.* **117** E12
East Providence *U.S.A.* **115** E13
East Pt., Br. Virgin Is. **121** e
East Pt. *Canada* **105** C7
East Renfrewshire □ *U.K.* **13** F4
East Retford = Retford *U.K.* **14** D7
East Riding of Yorkshire □
    U.K. **14** D7
East Rochester *U.S.A.* **114** C7
East St. Louis *U.S.A.* **112** F8
East Schelde =
    Oosterschelde ➔ *Neths.* **17** C4
East Sea = Japan, Sea of *Asia* **54** E7
East Siberian Sea *Russia* **53** B17
East Stroudsburg *U.S.A.* **115** E9
East Sussex □ *U.K.* **15** G8
East Tasman Plateau
    Pac. Oc. **96** M7
East Tawas *U.S.A.* **113** C12
East Toorale *Australia* **95** E4
East Walker ➔ *U.S.A.* **110** G7
East Windsor *U.S.A.* **115** F10
Eastbourne *N.Z.* **91** D5
Eastbourne *U.K.* **15** G8
Eastend *Canada* **103** D7
Easter Fracture Zone
    Pac. Oc. **97** K16
Easter I. = Pascua, I. de
    Chile **97** K17
Eastern □ *Ghana* **83** D4
Eastern □ *Kenya* **86** C4
Eastern □ *S. Leone* **82** D2
Eastern Cape □ *S. Africa* **88** E4
Eastern Cr. ➔ *Australia* **94** C3
Eastern Ghats *India* **66** N11
Eastern Group = Lau
    Group *Fiji* **91** a
Eastern Group *Australia* **93** F3
Eastern Transvaal =
    Mpumalanga □ *S. Africa* **89** D5
Easterville *Canada* **103** C9
Easthampton *U.S.A.* **115** D12
Eastlake *U.S.A.* **114** E3
Eastland *U.S.A.* **116** E5
Eastleigh *U.K.* **15** G6
Eastmain *Canada* **104** B4
Eastmain ➔ *Canada* **104** B4
Eastman *Canada* **115** A12
Eastman *U.S.A.* **117** E13
Easton *Md., U.S.A.* **113** F15
Easton *Pa., U.S.A.* **115** F9
Easton *Wash., U.S.A.* **110** C5
Eastport *U.S.A.* **113** C20
Eastsound *U.S.A.* **110** B4
Eaton *U.S.A.* **108** F11
Eatonia *Canada* **103** C7
Eatonton *U.S.A.* **117** E13
Eatontown *U.S.A.* **115** F10
Eatonville *U.S.A.* **110** D4
Eau Claire *U.S.A.* **112** C8
Eau Claire, Lac à l' *Canada* **104** A5
Eauripik Rise *Pac. Oc.* **96** G5
Eauze *France* **20** E4
Eban *Nigeria* **83** D5
Ebano *Mexico* **119** C5
Ebbegebirge △ *Germany* **24** D3
Ebbw Vale *U.K.* **15** F4
Ebeltoft *Denmark* **11** H4
Ebeltoft Vig *Denmark* **11** H4
Ebensburg *U.S.A.* **114** F6
Ebensee *Austria* **26** D6
Ebetsu *Japan* **54** C10
Ebey's Landing △ *U.S.A.* **110** B4
Ebian *China* **58** C4
Ebingen *Germany* **25** G5
Éboli *Italy* **43** B8
Ebolowa *Cameroon* **83** E7
Ebonda *Dem. Rep. of the Congo* **84** D4
Ebonyi □ *Nigeria* **83** D6
Ebrach *Germany* **25** F6
Ébrié, Lagune *Ivory C.* **82** D4
Ebro ➔ *Spain* **38** E5
Ebro, Embalse del *Spain* **36** C7
Ebstorf *Germany* **24** B6
Ecatepec de Morelos *Mexico* **119** D5
Eceabat *Turkey* **45** F10
Ech Chéliff *Algeria* **78** A6
Echigo-Sammyaku *Japan* **55** F9
Echinos *Greece* **45** E9
Échirolles *France* **21** C9

Echizen-Misaki *Japan* **55** G7
Echmiadzin = Yejmiadzin
  Armenia **35** K7
Echo Bay *N.W.T., Canada* **100** C8
Echo Bay *Ont., Canada* **104** C3
Echoing ↠ *Canada* **104** B1
Echterdingen, Stuttgart ✈
  (STR) *Germany* **25** G5
Echternach *Lux.* **17** E6
Echuca *Australia* **95** F3
Ecija *Spain* **37** H5
Eckental *Germany* **25** F7
Eckernförde *Germany* **24** A5
Eclipse I. *Australia* **93** G2
Eclipse Is. *Australia* **92** B4
Eclipse Sd. *Canada* **101** B12
Écommoy *France* **18** E7
Écouché *France* **18** D6
Ecrins △ *France* **21** D10
Ecuador ■ *S. Amer.* **124** D3
Écueillé *France* **18** E8
Ed *Sweden* **11** F5
Ed Dabbura *Sudan* **80** D3
Ed Da'ein *Sudan* **81** E2
Ed Damazin *Sudan* **79** F12
Ed Dâmer *Sudan* **80** D3
Ed Dar el Beida =
  Casablanca *Morocco* **78** B4
Ed Debba *Sudan* **80** D3
Ed Déffa *Egypt* **80** A2
Ed Deim *Sudan* **81** E2
Ed Dueim *Sudan* **81** E3
Edam *Canada* **103** C7
Edam *Neths.* **17** B5
Edane *Sweden* **10** E6
Eday *U.K.* **13** B6
Edd *Eritrea* **81** E5
Eddrachillis B. *U.K.* **13** C3
Eddystone *U.K.* **15** G3
Eddystone Pt. *Australia* **95** G4
Ede *Neths.* **17** B5
Ede *Nigeria* **83** D5
Édéa *Cameroon* **83** E7
Edebäck *Sweden* **10** D7
Edehon L. *Canada* **103** A9
Edekel, Adrar *Algeria* **78** D7
Edelény *Hungary* **28** B5
Eden *Australia* **95** F4
Eden *N.C., U.S.A.* **117** C15
Eden *N.Y., U.S.A.* **114** D6
Eden *Tex., U.S.A.* **116** F5
Eden ↠ *U.K.* **14** C4
Edenburg *S. Africa* **88** D4
Edendale *S. Africa* **89** D5
Edenderry *Ireland* **12** C4
Edenton *U.S.A.* **117** C16
Edenville *S. Africa* **89** D4
Eder ↠ *Germany* **24** D5
Eder-Stausee *Germany* **24** D4
Edessa *Greece* **44** F6
Edewecht *Germany* **24** B3
Edgar *U.S.A.* **112** E5
Edgartown *U.S.A.* **115** E14
Edge Hill *U.K.* **15** E6
Edgefield *U.S.A.* **117** E14
Edgeley *U.S.A.* **112** B4
Edgemont *U.S.A.* **112** D2
Edgeøya *Svalbard* **4** B9
Édhessa = Edessa *Greece* **44** F6
Edievale *N.Z.* **91** F2
Edina *Liberia* **82** D2
Edina *U.S.A.* **112** E7
Edinboro *U.S.A.* **114** E4
Edinburg *U.S.A.* **116** H5
Edinburgh *U.K.* **13** F5
Edinburgh ✈ (EDI) *U.K.* **13** F5
Edinburgh, City of □ *U.K.* **13** F5
Edineţ *Moldova* **29** B12
Edirne *Turkey* **45** E10
Edirne □ *Turkey* **45** E10
Edison *U.S.A.* **110** B4
Edithburgh *Australia* **95** F2
Edmond *U.S.A.* **116** D6
Edmonds *U.S.A.* **110** C4
Edmonton *Australia* **94** B4
Edmonton *Canada* **102** C6
Edmund L. *Canada* **104** B1
Edmundston *Canada* **105** C6
Edna *U.S.A.* **116** G6
Edo □ *Nigeria* **83** D6
Edolo *Italy* **40** B7
Edremit *Turkey* **47** B9
Edremit Körfezi *Turkey* **47** B8
Edsbro *Sweden* **10** E12
Edsbyn *Sweden* **10** C9
Edson *Canada* **102** C5
Eduardo Castex *Argentina* **126** D3
Edward ↠ *Australia* **95** F3
Edward, L. *Africa* **86** C2
Edward VII Land *Antarctica* **5** E13
Edwards *Calif., U.S.A.* **111** L9
Edwards *N.Y., U.S.A.* **115** B9
Edwards Plateau *U.S.A.* **116** F4
Edwardsville *U.S.A.* **115** E9
Edzná *Mexico* **119** D6
Edzo *Canada* **102** A5

Eeklo *Belgium* **17** C3
Eesti = Estonia ■ *Europe* **32** C3
Eferding *Austria* **26** C7
Effigy Mounds △ *U.S.A.* **112** D8
Effingham *U.S.A.* **112** F9
Eforie *Romania* **29** F13
Efxinoupoli *Greece* **46** B4
Ega ↠ *Spain* **38** C3
Égadi, Ísole *Italy* **42** E5
Egan Range *U.S.A.* **108** G6
Eganville *Canada* **114** A7
Eger = Cheb *Czech Rep.* **26** A5
Eger *Hungary* **28** C5
Eger ↠ *Hungary* **28** C5
Egersund *Norway* **9** G12
Egg L. *Canada* **103** B7
Eggegebirge Südlicher
  Teutoburger Wald △
  Germany **24** D4
Eggenburg *Austria* **26** C8
Eggenfelden *Germany* **25** G8
Éghezée *Belgium* **17** D4
Egina *Greece* **46** D5
Eginio *Greece* **44** F6
Egio *Greece* **46** C4
Égletons *France* **20** C6
Eglinton I. *Canada* **101** B8
Egmont *Canada* **102** D4
Egmont, C. *N.Z.* **91** C4
Egmont, Mt. = Taranaki,
  Mt. *N.Z.* **91** C5
Egmont △ *N.Z.* **91** C5
Egra *India* **69** J12
Eğridir *Turkey* **72** D4
Eğridir Gölü *Turkey* **72** D4
Egtved *Denmark* **11** J3
Egume *Nigeria* **83** D6
Éguzon-Chantôme *France* **19** F8
Egvekinot *Russia* **53** C19
Egyek *Hungary* **28** C5
Egypt ■ *Africa* **80** B3
Eha Amufu *Nigeria* **83** D6
Ehime □ *Japan* **55** H6
Ehingen *Germany* **25** G5
Ehrenberg *U.S.A.* **111** M12
Ehrwald *Austria* **26** D3
Eibar *Spain* **38** B2
Eichstätt *Germany* **25** G7
Eider ↠ *Germany* **24** A4
Eidsvold *Australia* **95** D5
Eidsvoll *Norway* **9** F14
Eifel *Germany* **25** E2
Eiffel Flats *Zimbabwe* **87** F3
Eiger *Switz.* **40** B5
Eigg *U.K.* **13** E2
Eighty Mile Beach *Australia* **92** C3
Eil *Somali Rep.* **75** F4
Eil, L. *U.K.* **13** E3
Eildon, L. *Australia* **95** F4
Eilean Sar = Western
  Isles □ *U.K.* **13** D1
Eilenburg *Germany* **24** D8
Ein el Luweiqa *Sudan* **81** E3
Einasleigh *Australia* **94** B3
Einasleigh ↠ *Australia* **94** B3
Einbeck *Germany* **24** D5
Eindhoven *Neths.* **17** C5
Einsiedeln *Switz.* **25** H4
Eire = Ireland ■ *Europe* **12** C4
Eiríksjökull *Iceland* **8** D3
Eirunepé *Brazil* **124** E5
Eiseb ↠ *Namibia* **88** C2
Eisenach *Germany* **24** E6
Eisenberg *Germany* **24** E7
Eisenerz *Austria* **26** D7
Eisenhüttenstadt *Germany* **24** C10
Eisenkappel *Austria* **26** E7
Eisenstadt *Austria* **27** D9
Eisfeld *Germany* **25** E6
Eisleben *Germany* **24** D7
Eislingen *Germany* **25** G5
Eivissa *Spain* **48** C7
Eixe, Serra do *Spain* **36** C4
Ejea de los Caballeros *Spain* **38** C3
Ejeda *Madag.* **89** C7
Ejura *Ghana* **83** D4
Ejutla *Mexico* **119** D5
Ekalaka *U.S.A.* **108** D11
Ekaterinburg =
  Yekaterinburg *Russia* **52** D7
Ekenäs = Tammisaari
  Finland **32** B2
Ekenässjön *Sweden* **11** G9
Ekerö *Sweden* **10** E11
Eket *Nigeria* **83** E6
Eketahuna *N.Z.* **91** D5
Ekibastuz *Kazakhstan* **52** D8
Ekiti □ *Nigeria* **83** D6
Ekoli *Dem. Rep. of the Congo* **86** C1
Ekoln *Sweden* **10** E11
Ekshärad *Sweden* **10** D7
Eksjö *Sweden* **11** G8
Ekuma ↠ *Namibia* **88** B2
Ekwan ↠ *Canada* **104** B3
Ekwan Pt. *Canada* **104** B3
El Aaiún *W. Sahara* **78** C3
El Abanico *Chile* **126** D1

El Abbasiya *Sudan* **81** E3
El 'Agrûd *Egypt* **74** E3
El 'Aiyat *Egypt* **80** J7
El 'Alamein *Egypt* **80** A2
El 'Aqaba, W. ↠ *Egypt* **74** E2
El 'Arag *Egypt* **80** B2
El Arahal *Spain* **37** H5
El Arīḥā *West Bank* **74** D4
El 'Arîsh *Egypt* **74** D2
El 'Arîsh, W. ↠ *Egypt* **74** D2
El Asnam = Ech Chéliff
  Algeria **78** A6
El Astillero *Spain* **36** B7
El Badâri *Egypt* **80** B3
El Bahrein *Egypt* **80** B2
El Ballâs *Egypt* **80** B3
El Balyana *Egypt* **80** B3
El Baqeir *Sudan* **80** D3
El Barco de Ávila *Spain* **36** E5
El Barco de Valdeorras = O
  Barco *Spain* **36** C4
El Bauga *Sudan* **80** D3
El Bawiti *Egypt* **80** B2
El Bayadh *Algeria* **78** B6
El Bierzo *Spain* **36** C4
El Bluff *Nic.* **120** D3
El Bonillo *Spain* **39** G2
El Buheirat □ *Sudan* **81** F3
El Burgo de Osma *Spain* **38** D1
El Cajon *U.S.A.* **111** N10
El Campo *U.S.A.* **116** G6
El Capitan *U.S.A.* **110** H7
El Centro *U.S.A.* **111** N11
El Cerro *Bolivia* **124** G6
El Cerro de Andévalo *Spain* **37** H4
El Compadre *Mexico* **111** N10
El Coronil *Spain* **37** H5
El Cuy *Argentina* **128** D3
El Cuyo *Mexico* **119** C7
El Dab'a *Egypt* **80** H6
El Daheir *Egypt* **74** D3
El Deir *Egypt* **80** B3
El Dere *Somali Rep.* **75** G4
El Descanso *Mexico* **111** N10
El Desemboque *Mexico* **118** A2
El Dilingat *Egypt* **80** H7
El Diviso *Colombia* **124** C3
El Djouf *Mauritania* **78** D4
El Dorado *Mexico* **118** C3
El Dorado *Ark., U.S.A.* **116** E8
El Dorado *Kans., U.S.A.* **112** G5
El Dorado *Venezuela* **124** B6
El Dorado Springs *U.S.A.* **112** G6
El 'Ein *Sudan* **81** D2
El Ejido *Spain* **37** J8
El Escorial *Spain* **36** E6
El Espinar *Spain* **36** D6
El Faiyûm *Egypt* **80** J7
El Fâsher *Sudan* **81** E2
El Fashn *Egypt* **80** J7
El Ferrol = Ferrol *Spain* **36** B2
El Fifi *Sudan* **81** E2
El Fuerte *Mexico* **118** B3
El Ga'a *Sudan* **81** E2
El Gal *Somali Rep.* **75** E5
El Garef *Sudan* **81** E3
El Gebir *Sudan* **81** E2
El Gedida *Egypt* **80** B2
El Geneina = Al Junaynah
  Sudan **79** F10
El Geteina *Sudan* **81** E3
El Gezira □ *Sudan* **81** E3
El Gir *Sudan* **80** D2
El Gîza *Egypt* **80** J7
El Gogorrón △ *Mexico* **118** C4
El Goléa *Algeria* **78** B6
El Golfo de Santa Clara
  Mexico **118** A2
El Grau *Spain* **39** G4
El Guácharo △ *Venezuela* **121** D7
El Guache △ *Venezuela* **121** E6
El Hagiz *Sudan* **81** D4
El Hâi *Egypt* **80** J7
El Hammam *Egypt* **80** A2
El Hawata *Sudan* **81** E3
El Heiz *Egypt* **80** B2
El Hideib *Sudan* **81** E3
El Hilla *Sudan* **81** E2
El 'Idisât *Egypt* **80** B3
El Iskandarîya *Egypt* **80** H7
El Istiwa'iya *Sudan* **79** G11
El Jadida *Morocco* **78** B4
El Jardal *Honduras* **120** D2
El Jebelein *Sudan* **81** E3
El Kab *Sudan* **80** D3
El Kafr el Sharqi *Egypt* **80** H7
El Kamlin *Sudan* **81** D3
El Karaba *Sudan* **80** D3
El Kef □ *Tunisia* **79** A7
El Kere *Ethiopia* **81** F5
El Khandaq *Sudan* **80** D3
El Khârga *Egypt* **80** B3
El Khartûm *Sudan* **81** D3
El Khartûm □ *Sudan* **81** D3
El Khartûm Bahrî *Sudan* **81** D3
El Kuntilla *Egypt* **74** E3

El Laqâwa *Sudan* **81** E2
El Leh *Ethiopia* **81** G4
El Leiya *Sudan* **81** D4
El Lucero *Mexico* **118** A3
El Maestrazgo *Spain* **38** E4
El Mafâza *Sudan* **81** E3
El Maghra *Egypt* **80** A2
El Mahalla el Kubra *Egypt* **80** H7
El Mahârîq *Egypt* **80** B3
El Maïmûn *Egypt* **80** J7
El Maks el Bahari *Egypt* **80** C3
El Malpais △ *U.S.A.* **109** J10
El Manshâh *Egypt* **80** B3
El Mansûra *Egypt* **80** H7
El Manzala *Egypt* **80** H7
El Marâgha *Egypt* **80** B3
El Masid *Sudan* **81** D3
El Masnou *Spain* **38** D7
El Matarîya *Egypt* **80** H8
El Meda *Ethiopia* **81** F5
El Medano *Canary Is.* **48** F3
El Metemma *Sudan* **81** D3
El Milagro *Argentina* **126** C2
El Minyâ *Egypt* **80** B3
El Monte *U.S.A.* **111** L8
El Montseny *Spain* **38** D7
El Mreyye *Mauritania* **82** B3
El Niybo *Ethiopia* **81** G4
El Obeid *Sudan* **81** E3
El Odaiya *Sudan* **81** E2
El Oro *Mexico* **119** D4
El Oued *Algeria* **78** B7
El Palmar △ *Argentina* **126** C4
El Palmito, Presa *Mexico* **118** B3
El Paso *U.S.A.* **116** F1
El Pedernoso *Spain* **39** F2
El Pedroso *Spain* **37** H5
El Pobo de Dueñas *Spain* **38** E3
El Portal *U.S.A.* **110** H7
El Porvenir *Mexico* **118** A3
El Prat de Llobregat *Spain* **38** D7
El Progreso *Honduras* **120** C2
El Pueblito *Mexico* **118** B3
El Pueblo *Canary Is.* **48** F2
El Puente del Arzobispo
  Spain **36** F5
El Puerto de Santa María
  Spain **37** J4
El Qâhira *Egypt* **80** H7
El Qantara *Egypt* **74** E1
El Qasr *Egypt* **80** B2
El Qubâbât *Egypt* **80** J7
El Queseima *Egypt* **74** E3
El Qusîya *Egypt* **80** B3
El Râshda *Egypt* **80** B2
El Real *Panama* **124** B3
El Reno *U.S.A.* **106** C7
El Rey △ *Argentina* **126** A3
El Rîdisiya *Egypt* **80** C3
El Rio *U.S.A.* **111** L7
El Ronquillo *Spain* **37** H4
El Roque, Pta. *Canary Is.* **48** F4
El Rosarito *Mexico* **118** B2
El Rubio *Spain* **37** H5
El Saff *Egypt* **80** J7
El Salto *Mexico* **118** C3
El Salvador ■ *Cent. Amer.* **120** D2
El Sauce *Nic.* **120** D2
El Saucejo *Spain* **37** H5
El Shallal *Egypt* **80** C3
El Simbillawein *Egypt* **80** H7
El Sueco *Mexico* **118** B3
El Suweis *Egypt* **80** J8
El Tabbin *Egypt* **80** J7
El Tamarâni, W. ↠ *Egypt* **74** E3
El Thamad *Egypt* **74** F3
El Tigre *Venezuela* **124** B6
El Tîh, Gebel *Egypt* **74** F2
El Tîna *Egypt* **80** H8
El Tofo *Chile* **126** B1
El Tránsito *Chile* **126** B1
El Tûr *Egypt* **70** D2
El Turbio *Argentina* **128** G2
El Uqsur *Egypt* **80** B3
El Valle △ *Spain* **39** H3
El Vendrell *Spain* **38** D6
El Vergel *Mexico* **118** B3
El Vigía *Venezuela* **124** B4
El Viso del Alcor *Spain* **37** H5
El Wabeira *Egypt* **74** F2
El Wak *Kenya* **86** B5
El Waqf *Egypt* **80** B3
El Weguet *Ethiopia* **81** F5
El Wuz *Sudan* **81** E3
Elafonisos *Greece* **46** E4
Elafonisos *Greece* **46** E4
Élancourt *France* **19** D8
Elasa *Greece* **47** F8
Elassona *Greece* **46** B4
Elat *Israel* **74** F3
Elatia *Greece* **46** C4
Elâzığ *Turkey* **73** C8
Elâzığ □ *Turkey* **73** C8
Elba *Italy* **40** F7

Elba *U.S.A.* **117** F11
Elbasan *Albania* **44** E4
Elbe ↠ *U.S.A.* **110** D4
Elbe ↠ *Europe* **24** B4
Elbe-Seitenkanal *Germany* **24** C6
Elbert, Mt. *U.S.A.* **108** G10
Elberton *U.S.A.* **117** D13
Elbeuf *France* **18** C8
Elbidtan *Turkey* **72** C7
Elbląg *Poland* **30** D6
Elbow *Canada* **103** C7
Elbrus *Russia* **35** J5
Elbufer-Drawehn △
  Germany **24** B6
Elburz Mts. = Alborz,
  Reshteh-ye Kühhä-ye
  Iran **71** C7
Elche *Spain* **39** G4
Elche de la Sierra *Spain* **39** G2
Elcho I. *Australia* **94** A2
Elda *Spain* **39** G4
Eldama Ravine *Kenya* **86** B4
Elde ↠ *Germany* **24** B7
Eldon *Mo., U.S.A.* **112** F7
Eldon *Wash., U.S.A.* **110** C3
Eldora *U.S.A.* **112** D7
Eldorado *Argentina* **127** B5
Eldorado *Canada* **114** B7
Eldorado *Ill., U.S.A.* **112** G9
Eldorado *Tex., U.S.A.* **116** F4
Eldoret *Kenya* **86** B4
Eldred *U.S.A.* **114** E6
Elea, C. *Cyprus* **49** D13
Elefantes ↠ *Africa* **89** C5
Eleanora, Pk. *Australia* **93** F3
Elefsina *Greece* **46** C5
Eleftheroupoli *Greece* **45** F8
Elektrogorsk *Russia* **32** E10
Elektrostal *Russia* **32** E10
Elele *Nigeria* **83** D6
Elemi Triangle *Africa* **81** G4
Elena *Bulgaria* **45** D9
Elephant Butte Res. *U.S.A.* **109** K10
Elephant I. *Antarctica* **5** C18
Eleshnitsa *Bulgaria* **44** E7
Eleşkirt *Turkey* **73** C10
Eleuthera *Bahamas* **120** B4
Eleutheroupoli *Greece* **45** F8
Elgin *Canada* **115** B8
Elgin *U.K.* **13** D5
Elgin *Ill., U.S.A.* **112** D9
Elgin *N. Dak., U.S.A.* **112** B3
Elgin *Oreg., U.S.A.* **108** D5
Elgin *Tex., U.S.A.* **116** F6
Elgoibar *Spain* **38** B2
Elgon, Mt. *Africa* **86** B3
Eliase *Indonesia* **63** F8
Elikonos Oros *Greece* **46** C4
Elim *Namibia* **88** B2
Elim *S. Africa* **88** E2
Elizabeth *Australia* **95** E2
Elizabeth *U.S.A.* **115** F10
Elizabeth City *U.S.A.* **117** C16
Elizabethton *U.S.A.* **117** C13
Elizabethtown *Ky., U.S.A.* **113** G11
Elizabethtown *N.Y., U.S.A.* **115** B11
Elizabethtown *Pa., U.S.A.* **115** F8
Elizondo *Spain* **38** B3
Ełk *Poland* **30** E9
Elk ↠ *Canada* **102** C5
Elk ↠ *Poland* **30** E9
Elk ↠ *U.S.A.* **117** D11
Elk City *U.S.A.* **116** D5
Elk Creek *U.S.A.* **110** F4
Elk Grove *U.S.A.* **110** G5
Elk Island △ *Canada* **102** C6
Elk Lake *Canada* **104** C3
Elk Point *Canada* **103** C6
Elk River *Idaho, U.S.A.* **108** C5
Elk River *Minn., U.S.A.* **112** C7
Elkedra ↠ *Australia* **94** C2
Elkhart *Ind., U.S.A.* **113** E11
Elkhart *Kans., U.S.A.* **112** G3
Elkhorn *Canada* **103** D8
Elkhorn ↠ *U.S.A.* **112** E5
Elkhovo *Bulgaria* **45** D10
Elkin *U.S.A.* **117** C14
Elkins *U.S.A.* **113** F14
Elkland *U.S.A.* **114** E7
Elko *Canada* **102** D5
Elko *U.S.A.* **108** F6
Elkton *U.S.A.* **114** C1
Ellas = Greece ■ *Europe* **46** B3
Ellef Ringnes I. *Canada* **101** B9
Ellen, Mt. *U.S.A.* **115** B12
Ellenburg *U.S.A.* **115** B11
Ellendale *U.S.A.* **112** B5
Ellensburg *U.S.A.* **108** C3
Ellenville *U.S.A.* **115** E10
Ellerton *Barbados* **121** g
Ellery, Mt. *Australia* **95** F4
Ellesmere, L. *N.Z.* **91** G4
Ellesmere I. *Canada* **101** B12

Ellesmere Port *U.K.* **14** D5
Ellice Is. = Tuvalu ■
  Pac. Oc. **90** B10
Ellicottville *U.S.A.* **114** D6
Elliot *Australia* **94** B1
Elliot *S. Africa* **89** E4
Elliot Lake *Canada* **104** C3
Elliotdale = Xhora *S. Africa* **89** E4
Ellis *U.S.A.* **112** F4
Elliston *Australia* **95** E1
Ellisville *U.S.A.* **117** F10
Ellon *U.K.* **13** D6
Ellore = Eluru *India* **67** L12
Ellsworth *Kans., U.S.A.* **112** F4
Ellsworth *Maine, U.S.A.* **113** C19
Ellsworth Land *Antarctica* **5** D16
Ellsworth Mts. *Antarctica* **5** D16
Ellwangen *Germany* **25** G6
Ellwood City *U.S.A.* **114** F4
Elm *Switz.* **25** J5
Elm-Lappwald △ *Germany* **24** C7
Elma *Canada* **103** D9
Elma *U.S.A.* **110** D3
Elmadağ *Turkey* **72** C5
Elmalı *Turkey* **47** E11
Elmhurst *U.S.A.* **112** E10
Elmina *Ghana* **83** D4
Elmira *Canada* **114** C4
Elmira *U.S.A.* **114** D8
Elmira Heights *U.S.A.* **114** D8
Elmore *Australia* **95** F3
Elmshorn *Germany* **24** B5
Elmvale *Canada* **114** B5
Elne *France* **20** F6
Elora *Canada* **114** C4
Elos *Greece* **46** E4
Elounda *Greece* **49** D7
Eloy *U.S.A.* **109** K8
Éloyes *France* **19** D13
Elrose *Canada* **103** C7
Elsdorf *Germany* **24** E2
Elsie *U.S.A.* **110** E3
Elsinore = Helsingør
  Denmark **11** H6
Elster ↠ *Germany* **24** D7
Elsterwerda *Germany* **24** D9
Eltanin Fracture Zone
  System *S. Ocean* **5** B14
Eltham *N.Z.* **91** C5
Elton *Russia* **35** F8
Elton, Ozero *Russia* **35** F8
Eltville *Germany* **25** E4
Eluru *India* **67** L12
Elvas *Portugal* **37** G3
Elven *France* **18** E4
Elverum *Norway* **8** F14
Elvire ↠ *Australia* **92** C4
Elvire, Mt. *Australia* **93** E2
Elvo ↠ *Italy* **40** C5
Elwell, L. = Tiber Res.
  U.S.A. **108** B8
Elwood *Ind., U.S.A.* **113** E11
Elwood *Nebr., U.S.A.* **112** E4
Elx = Elche *Spain* **39** G4
Ely *U.K.* **15** E8
Ely *Minn., U.S.A.* **112** B8
Ely *Nev., U.S.A.* **108** G6
Elyria *U.S.A.* **114** E2
Elyros *Greece* **46** F5
Elz ↠ *Germany* **25** G3
Emådalen *Sweden* **10** C8
eMalahleni *S. Africa* **89** D4
Emämrüd *Iran* **71** B7
Emån ↠ *Sweden* **11** G10
Embarcación *Argentina* **126** A3
Embarras Portage *Canada* **103** B6
Embetsu *Japan* **54** B10
Embi *Kazakhstan* **52** E6
Embi ↠ *Kazakhstan* **52** E6
Embonas *Greece* **49** C9
Embrun *France* **21** D10
Embu *Kenya* **86** C4
Emden *Germany* **24** B3
Emecik *Turkey* **47** E9
Emerald *Australia* **94** C4
Emerson *Canada* **103** D9
Emet *Turkey* **47** B11
Emi Koussi *Chad* **79** E9
Emília-Romagna □ *Italy* **40** D8
Emilius, Mte. *Italy* **40** C4
Eminabad *Pakistan* **68** C6
Emine, Nos *Bulgaria* **45** D11
Emirdağ *Turkey* **72** C5
Emissi, Tarso *Chad* **79** D9
Emlenton *U.S.A.* **114** E5
Emlichheim *Germany* **24** C2
Emmaboda *Sweden* **11** H9
Emmaus *S. Africa* **88** D3
Emmaus *U.S.A.* **115** F9
Emme ↠ *Switz.* **25** H3
Emmeloord *Neths.* **17** B5
Emmen *Neths.* **17** B6
Emmen *Switz.* **25** H4
Emmendingen *Germany* **25** G3
Emmental *Switz.* **25** J3
Emmerich *Germany* **24** D2
Emmet *Australia* **94** C3

Emmetsburg *U.S.A.* **112** D6
Emmett *Idaho, U.S.A.* **108** E5
Emmett *Mich., U.S.A.* **114** D2
Emmonak *U.S.A.* **106** a
Emo *Canada* **103** D10
Emőd *Hungary* **28** C5
Emona *Bulgaria* **45** D11
Empalme *Mexico* **118** B2
Empangeni *S. Africa* **89** D5
Empedrado *Argentina* **126** B4
Emperor Seamount Chain
  Pac. Oc. **96** D9
Emperor Trough *Pac. Oc.* **96** C9
Empoli *Italy* **40** E7
Emporia *Kans., U.S.A.* **112** F5
Emporia *Va., U.S.A.* **113** G15
Emporium *U.S.A.* **114** E6
Empress *Canada* **103** C7
Empty Quarter = Rub' al
  Khālī *Si. Arabia* **75** D4
Ems → *Germany* **24** B3
Emsdale *Canada* **114** A5
Emsdetten *Germany* **24** C3
Emu *China* **57** C15
Emu Park *Australia* **94** C5
eMuziwezinto *S. Africa* **89** E5
'En 'Avrona *Israel* **74** F4
'En Boqeq *Israel* **71** D4
'En Gedi *Israel* **71** D4
En Nahud *Sudan* **81** E2
En Nofalab *Sudan* **81** D3
Ena *Japan* **55** G8
Enana *Namibia* **88** B2
Enånger *Sweden* **10** C11
Enard B. *U.K.* **13** C3
Enare = Inarijärvi *Finland* **8** B23
Enarotali *Indonesia* **63** E9
Encampment *U.S.A.* **108** F10
Encantadas, Serra *Brazil* **127** C5
Encarnación *Paraguay* **127** B4
Encarnación de Díaz
  Mexico **118** C4
Enchi *Ghana* **82** D4
Encinitas *U.S.A.* **111** M9
Encino *U.S.A.* **109** J11
Encounter B. *Australia* **95** F2
Encs *Hungary* **28** B6
Endako *Canada* **102** C3
Endau *Kenya* **86** C4
Ende *Indonesia* **63** F6
Endeavour Str. *Australia* **94** A3
Endelave *Denmark* **11** J4
Enderbury I. *Kiribati* **96** H10
Enderby *Canada* **102** C5
Enderby Abyssal Plain
  S. Ocean **5** C5
Enderby I. *Australia* **92** D2
Enderby Land *Antarctica* **5** C5
Enderlin *U.S.A.* **112** B5
Endicott *U.S.A.* **113** D8
Endwell *U.S.A.* **115** D8
Endyalgout I. *Australia* **92** B5
Eneabba *Australia* **93** E2
Enewetak Atoll *Marshall Is.* **96** F8
Enez *Turkey* **45** F10
Enfer, Pte. d' *Martinique* **120** c
Enfield *Canada* **105** D7
Enfield *Conn., U.S.A.* **115** E12
Enfield *N.C., U.S.A.* **117** C16
Enfield *N.H., U.S.A.* **115** C12
Engadin *Switz.* **25** J6
Engaño, C. *Dom. Rep.* **121** C6
Engaño, C. *Phil.* **63** A6
Engaru *Japan* **54** B11
Engcobo = Ngcobo *S. Africa* **89** E4
Engelberg *Switz.* **25** J4
Engels *Russia* **34** E8
Engemann L. *Canada* **103** B7
Engershatu *Eritrea* **81** D4
Enggano *Indonesia* **62** F2
England *U.S.A.* **116** D9
England □ *U.K.* **15** E5
Englee *Canada* **105** B8
Englehart *Canada* **104** C4
Englewood *U.S.A.* **108** G11
English → *Canada* **103** C10
English Bazar = Ingraj
  Bazar *India* **69** G13
English Channel *Europe* **15** G6
English Company's Is., The
  Australia **94** A2
English River *Canada* **104** C1
Engures ezers *Latvia* **30** A10
Enguri → *Georgia* **35** J5
Enid *U.S.A.* **116** C6
Enipeas → *Greece* **46** B4
Enkhuizen *Neths.* **17** B5
Enköping *Sweden* **10** E11
Enle *China* **58** F3
Enna *Italy* **43** E7
Ennadai *Canada* **103** A8
Ennadai L. *Canada* **103** A8
Enngonia *Australia* **95** D4
Ennigerloh *Germany* **24** D4
Ennis *Ireland* **12** D3
Ennis *Mont., U.S.A.* **108** D8

Ennis *Tex., U.S.A.* **116** E6
Enniscorthy *Ireland* **12** D5
Enniskillen *U.K.* **12** B4
Ennistimon *Ireland* **12** D2
Enns *Austria* **26** C7
Enns → *Austria* **26** C7
Eno *Finland* **8** E24
Enonkoski *Finland* **8** E23
Enontekiö *Finland* **8** B20
Enosburg Falls *U.S.A.* **115** B12
Enping *China* **59** F9
Enriquillo *Dom. Rep.* **121** C5
Enriquillo, L. *Dom. Rep.* **121** C5
Enschede *Neths.* **17** B6
Ensenada *Argentina* **126** C4
Ensenada *Mexico* **118** A1
Ensenada de los Muertos
  Mexico **118** C2
Enshi *China* **58** B7
Ensiola, Pta. de n' *Spain* **48** B9
Ensisheim *France* **19** E14
Enterprise *Canada* **102** A5
Enterprise *Ala., U.S.A.* **117** F12
Enterprise *Oreg., U.S.A.* **108** D5
Entorno de Doñana △ *Spain* **37** J4
Entraygues-sur-Truyère
  France **20** D6
Entre Ríos *Bolivia* **126** A3
Entre Ríos □ *Argentina* **126** C4
Entrepeñas, Embalse de
  Spain **38** E2
Entroncamento *Portugal* **37** F2
Enugu *Nigeria* **83** D6
Enugu □ *Nigeria* **83** D6
Enugu Ezike *Nigeria* **83** D6
Enumclaw *U.S.A.* **110** C4
Envalira, Port d' *Europe* **38** C6
Envermeu *France* **18** C8
Enviken *Sweden* **10** D9
Enying *Hungary* **28** D3
Enza → *Italy* **40** D7
Eólie, Ís. *Italy* **43** D7
Epanomi *Greece* **44** F6
Epe *Neths.* **17** B5
Epe *Nigeria* **83** D5
Épernay *France* **19** C10
Épernon *France* **19** D8
Ephesus *Turkey* **47** D9
Ephraim *U.S.A.* **108** G8
Ephrata *Pa., U.S.A.* **115** F8
Ephrata *Wash., U.S.A.* **108** C4
Epidavros Limira *Greece* **46** E5
Épila *Spain* **38** D3
Épinac *France* **19** F11
Épinal *France* **19** D13
Epiros □ *Greece* **46** B2
Episkopi *Cyprus* **49** E11
Episkopi *Greece* **49** D6
Episkopi Bay *Cyprus* **49** E11
Epitalio *Greece* **46** D3
Eppan = Appiano *Italy* **41** B8
Eppingen *Germany* **25** F4
Epsom *U.K.* **15** F7
Epukiro *Namibia* **88** C2
Equatoria = El Istiwa'iya
  Sudan **79** G11
Equatorial Guinea ■ *Africa* **84** D1
Er Hai *China* **58** E3
Er Rachidia *Morocco* **78** B5
Er Rahad *Sudan* **81** E3
Er Rif *Morocco* **78** A5
Er Rogel *Sudan* **80** D4
Er Roseires *Sudan* **81** E3
Er Rua'at *Sudan* **81** E3
Eraclea *Italy* **41** C9
Erāwadī Myit =
  Irrawaddy → *Burma* **67** M19
Erāwadī Myitwanya =
  Irrawaddy, Mouths of
  the *Burma* **67** M19
Erba *Italy* **40** C6
Erba *Sudan* **80** D4
Erba, J. *Sudan* **80** C4
Erbaa *Turkey* **72** B7
Erbeskopf *Germany* **25** F3
Erbil = Arbīl *Iraq* **73** D11
Erbu *Ethiopia* **81** E3
Erçek *Turkey* **70** B4
Erçiş *Turkey* **73** C10
Erciyaş Dağı *Turkey* **70** B2
Érd *Hungary* **28** C3
Erdao Jiang → *China* **57** C14
Erdek *Turkey* **45** F11
Erdemli *Turkey* **72** D6
Erdene = Ulaan-Uul
  Mongolia **56** B6
Erdenetsogt *Mongolia* **56** C4
Erding *Germany* **25** G7
Erdre → *France* **18** E5
Erebus, Mt. *Antarctica* **5** D11
Erechim *Brazil* **127** B5
Ereğli *Konya, Turkey* **72** D6
Ereğli *Zonguldak, Turkey* **72** B4
Erei, Monti *Italy* **43** E7
Erenhot *China* **56** C7
Eresma → *Spain* **36** D6
Eresos *Greece* **47** B7
Erfenisdam *S. Africa* **88** D4

Erfstadt *Germany* **24** E2
Erft → *Germany* **24** D2
Erfurt *Germany* **24** E7
Ergani *Turkey* **73** C8
Ergel *Mongolia* **56** C5
Ergene → *Turkey* **45** E10
Ergeni Vozvyshennost
  Russia **35** G7
Érgli *Latvia* **32** D3
Erhlin *Taiwan* **59** F13
Eria → *Spain* **36** C5
Eriba *Sudan* **81** D4
Eriboll, L. *U.K.* **13** C4
Érice *Italy* **42** D5
Erie *U.S.A.* **114** D4
Erie, L. *N. Amer.* **114** D4
Erie Canal *U.S.A.* **114** C7
Erieau *Canada* **114** D3
Erigavo *Somali Rep.* **75** E4
Erikoussa *Greece* **49** A3
Eriksdale *Canada* **103** C9
Erimanthos *Greece* **46** D3
Erimo-misaki *Japan* **54** D11
Erin Pt. *Trin. & Tob.* **125** K15
Erinpura *India* **68** G5
Eriskay *U.K.* **13** D1
Erithres *Greece* **46** C5
Eritrea ■ *Africa* **81** E4
Erjas → *Portugal* **36** F3
Erkelenz *Germany* **24** D2
Erkner *Germany* **24** C9
Erlangen *Germany* **25** F6
Erldunda *Australia* **94** D1
Ermelo *Neths.* **17** B5
Ermelo *S. Africa* **89** D4
Ermenek *Turkey* **72** D5
Ermil *Sudan* **81** E2
Ermioni *Greece* **46** D5
Ermones *Greece* **49** A3
Ernakulam *India* **66** Q10
Erne → *Ireland* **12** B3
Erne, Lower L. *U.K.* **12** B4
Erne, Upper L. *U.K.* **12** B4
Ernée *France* **18** D6
Ernest Giles Ra. *Australia* **93** E3
Ernstberg *Germany* **25** E2
Erode *India* **66** P10
Eromanga *Australia* **95** D3
Erongo *Namibia* **88** C2
Erquy *France* **18** D4
Erramala Hills *India* **66** M11
Errer → *Ethiopia* **81** F5
Erri-Nundra △ *Australia* **95** F4
Errigal *Ireland* **12** A3
Erris Hd. *Ireland* **12** B1
Ersekë *Albania* **44** F4
Erskine *U.S.A.* **112** B6
Erstein *France* **19** D14
Ertholmene *Denmark* **11** J9
Ertil *Russia* **34** E5
Ertis = Irtysh → *Russia* **52** C7
Eruh *Turkey* **73** D10
Eruwa *Nigeria* **83** D5
Ervy-le-Châtel *France* **19** D10
Erwin *U.S.A.* **117** C13
Eryuan *China* **58** D2
Erzgebirge *Germany* **24** E8
Erzin *Russia* **53** D10
Erzincan *Turkey* **73** C8
Erzincan □ *Turkey* **73** C8
Erzurum *Turkey* **73** C9
Erzurum □ *Turkey* **73** C9
Es Caló *Spain* **48** C8
Es Canar *Spain* **48** B8
Es Mercadal *Spain* **48** B11
Es Migjorn Gran *Spain* **48** B11
Es Safiya *Sudan* **81** D3
Es Sahrâ' Esh Sharqîya
  Egypt **80** B3
Es Sînâ' *Egypt* **74** F3
Es Sûkî *Sudan* **81** E3
Es Vedrà *Spain* **48** C7
Esambo *Dem. Rep. of the Congo* **86** C1
Esan-Misaki *Japan* **54** D10
Esashi *Hokkaidō, Japan* **54** B11
Esashi *Hokkaidō, Japan* **54** D10
Esbjerg *Denmark* **11** J2
Esbo = Espoo *Finland* **32** B3
Escalante *U.S.A.* **109** H8
Escalante → *U.S.A.* **109** H8
Escalón *Mexico* **118** B4
Escambia → *U.S.A.* **117** F11
Escanaba *U.S.A.* **112** C10
Esch-sur-Alzette *Lux.* **17** E6
Eschede *Germany* **24** C6
Eschwege *Germany* **24** D6
Eschweiler *Germany* **24** E2
Escondido *U.S.A.* **111** M9
Escravos → *Nigeria* **83** D6
Escuinapa de Hidalgo
  Mexico **118** C3
Escuintla *Guatemala* **120** D1
Eséka *Cameroon* **83** E7
Eşen → *Turkey* **47** E11
Esenguly *Turkmenistan* **52** F6
Esens *Germany* **24** B3
Eresos *Greece* **47** B7
Esenyurt *Turkey* **45** E12
Estella *Spain* **38** C2

Esera → *Spain* **38** C5
Eşfahān *Iran* **71** C6
Eşfahān □ *Iran* **71** C6
Esfarāyen *Iran* **71** B8
Esfideh *Iran* **71** C8
Esgueva → *Spain* **36** D6
Esh Sham = Dimashq *Syria* **74** B5
Esh Shamâlîya □ *Sudan* **80** D2
Esha Ness *U.K.* **13** A7
Eshan *China* **58** E4
Eshkol △ *Israel* **74** D3
Eshowe *S. Africa* **89** D5
Esiama *Ghana* **82** E4
Esigodini *Zimbabwe* **89** C4
Esil = Ishim → *Russia* **52** D8
Esino → *Italy* **41** E10
Esira *Madag.* **89** C8
Esk → *Dumf. & Gall., U.K.* **13** G5
Esk → *N. Yorks., U.K.* **14** C7
Eskān *Iran* **71** E9
Esker *Canada* **105** B6
Eskifjörður *Iceland* **8** D7
Eskilsäter *Sweden* **11** F7
Eskilstuna *Sweden* **10** E10
Eskimalatya *Turkey* **73** C8
Eskimo Point = Arviat
  Canada **103** A10
Eskişehir *Turkey* **47** B12
Eskişehir □ *Turkey* **47** B12
Esla → *Spain* **36** D4
Eslāmābād-e Gharb *Iran* **73** E12
Eslāmshahr *Iran* **71** C6
Eslöv *Sweden* **11** J7
Eşme *Turkey* **47** C10
Esmeraldas *Ecuador* **124** C3
Esnagi L. *Canada* **104** C3
Espalion *France* **20** D6
España = Spain ■ *Europe* **7** H5
Espanola *Canada* **104** C3
Espanola *U.S.A.* **109** J10
Esparreguera *Spain* **38** D6
Esparta *Costa Rica* **120** E3
Espelkamp *Germany* **24** C4
Esperance *Australia* **93** F3
Esperance B. *Australia* **93** F3
Esperance Harbour *St. Lucia* **121** f
Esperanza *Antarctica* **5** C18
Esperanza *Argentina* **126** C3
Esperanza *Phil.* **61** G6
Esperanza *Puerto Rico* **121** d
Espéraza *France* **20** F6
Espichel, C. *Portugal* **37** G1
Espigão, Serra do *Brazil* **127** B5
Espinazo, Sierra del =
  Espinhaço, Serra do
  Brazil **125** G10
Espinhaço, Serra do *Brazil* **125** G10
Espinho *Portugal* **36** D2
Espinilho, Serra do *Brazil* **127** B5
Espinosa de los Monteros
  Spain **36** B7
Espírito Santo □ *Brazil* **125** H10
Espíritu Santo *Vanuatu* **90** C9
Espíritu Santo, B. del
  Mexico **119** D7
Espíritu Santo, I. *Mexico* **118** C2
Espita *Mexico* **119** C7
Espiye *Turkey* **73** B8
Espluga de Francolí *Spain* **38** D6
Espoo *Finland* **32** B3
Espuña, Sierra de *Spain* **39** H3
Espungabera *Mozam.* **89** C5
Esquel *Argentina* **128** E2
Esquimalt *Canada* **110** B3
Esquina *Argentina* **126** C4
Essaouira *Morocco* **78** B4
Essebie *Dem. Rep. of the Congo* **86** B3
Essen *Belgium* **17** C4
Essen *Germany* **24** D3
Essendon, Mt. *Australia* **93** E3
Essequibo → *Guyana* **124** B7
Essex *Canada* **114** D2
Essex *Calif., U.S.A.* **111** L11
Essex *N.Y., U.S.A.* **115** B11
Essex □ *U.K.* **15** F8
Essex Junction *U.S.A.* **115** B11
Esslingen *Germany* **25** G5
Essonne □ *France* **19** D9
Estaca de Bares, C. de *Spain* **36** B3
Estación Camacho *Mexico* **118** C4
Estación Simón *Mexico* **118** C4
Estadilla *Spain* **38** C5
Estados, I. de los *Argentina* **128** G4
Estagel *France* **20** F6
Estância *Brazil* **125** F11
Estancia *U.S.A.* **109** J10
Estārm *Iran* **71** D8
Estarreja *Portugal* **36** E2
Estats, Pic d' *Spain* **38** C6
Estcourt *S. Africa* **89** D4
Este *Italy* **41** C8
Este △ *Dom. Rep.* **121** C6
Estelí *Nic.* **120** D2
Estella *Spain* **38** C2

Estellencs *Spain* **48** B9
Estena → *Spain* **37** F6
Estepa *Spain* **37** H6
Estepona *Spain* **37** J5
Esterhazy *Canada* **103** C8
Esternay *France* **19** D10
Esterri d'Aneu *Spain* **38** C6
Estevan *Canada* **103** D8
Estevan Group *Canada* **102** C3
Estherville *U.S.A.* **112** D6
Estissac *France* **19** D10
Eston *Canada* **103** C7
Estonia ■ *Europe* **32** C3
Estoril *Portugal* **37** G1
Estouk *Mali* **83** B5
Estreito *Brazil* **125** E9
Estrela, Serra da *Portugal* **36** E3
Estrella *Spain* **37** G7
Estremoz *Portugal* **37** G3
Estrondo, Serra do *Brazil* **125** E9
Esztergom *Hungary* **28** C3
Et Tîdra *Mauritania* **82** B1
Etah *India* **69** F8
Étain *France* **19** C12
Étampes *France* **19** D9
Etanga *Namibia* **88** B1
Étaples *France* **19** B8
Etawah *India* **69** F8
Etawney L. *Canada* **103** B9
Etchojoa *Mexico* **118** B3
Ete *Nigeria* **83** D6
eThekwini = Durban
  S. Africa **89** D5
Ethel *U.S.A.* **110** D4
Ethelbert *Canada* **103** C8
Ethiopia ■ *Africa* **75** F3
Ethiopian Highlands *Ethiopia* **75** F2
Etili *Turkey* **45** G10
Etive, L. *U.K.* **13** E3
Etna *Italy* **43** E7
Etoile *Dem. Rep. of the Congo* **87** E2
Etoliko *Greece* **46** C3
Etoloakarnania □ *Greece* **46** C3
Etosha △ *Namibia* **88** B2
Etosha Pan *Namibia* **88** B2
Etowah *U.S.A.* **117** D12
Étréchy *France* **19** D9
Etrek *Turkmenistan* **71** B7
Étrépagny *France* **19** C8
Étretat *France* **18** C7
Ettelbruck *Lux.* **17** E6
Ettlingen *Germany* **25** G4
Ettrick Water → *U.K.* **13** F6
Etuku *Dem. Rep. of the Congo* **86** C2
Etulia *Moldova* **29** E13
Etzná-Tixmucuy = Edzná
  Mexico **119** D6
Eu *France* **18** B8
Eua *Tonga* **91** c
Euboea = Evia *Greece* **46** C6
Eucla *Australia* **93** F4
Euclid *U.S.A.* **114** E3
Eucumbene, L. *Australia* **95** F4
Eudora *U.S.A.* **116** E9
Eufaula *Ala., U.S.A.* **117** F12
Eufaula *Okla., U.S.A.* **116** D7
Eufaula L. *U.S.A.* **116** D7
Eugene *U.S.A.* **108** D2
Eugowra *Australia* **95** E4
Eulo *Australia* **95** D4
Eungella △ *Australia* **94** C4
Eunice *La., U.S.A.* **116** F8
Eunice *N. Mex., U.S.A.* **109** K12
Eupen *Belgium* **17** D6
Euphrates = Furāt, Nahr
  al → *Asia* **70** D5
Eure □ *France* **18** C8
Eure → *France* **18** C8
Eure-et-Loir □ *France* **18** D8
Eureka *Canada* **101** B11
Eureka *Calif., U.S.A.* **108** F1
Eureka *Kans., U.S.A.* **112** G5
Eureka *Mont., U.S.A.* **108** B6
Eureka *Nev., U.S.A.* **108** G6
Eureka *S. Dak., U.S.A.* **112** C4
Eureka, Mt. *Australia* **93** E3
Euroa *Australia* **95** F4
Europa, Île *Ind. Oc.* **85** J8
Europa, Picos de *Spain* **36** B6
Europa, Pt. *Gib.* **37** J5
Europe ■ **6** E10
Europoort *Neths.* **17** C4
Euskirchen *Germany* **24** E2
Eustis *U.S.A.* **117** G14
Eutin *Germany* **24** A6
Eutsuk L. *Canada* **102** C3
Evale *Angola* **88** B2
Evans *U.S.A.* **108** F11
Evans, L. *Canada* **104** B4
Evans City *U.S.A.* **114** F4
Evans Head *Australia* **95** D5
Evans Mills *U.S.A.* **115** B9
Evansburg *Canada* **102** C5
Evanston *Ill., U.S.A.* **112** D10
Evanston *Wyo., U.S.A.* **108** F8
Evansville *U.S.A.* **112** G10

Évaux-les-Bains *France* **19** F9
Evaz *Iran* **71** E7
Evciler *Afyon, Turkey* **47** C11
Evciler *Çanakkale, Turkey* **47** B8
Eveleth *U.S.A.* **112** B7
Evensk *Russia* **53** C16
Everard, L. *Australia* **95** E2
Everard Ranges *Australia* **93** E5
Everest, Mt. *Nepal* **69** E12
Everett *Pa., U.S.A.* **114** F6
Everett *Wash., U.S.A.* **110** C4
Everglades, The *U.S.A.* **117** J14
Everglades □ *U.S.A.* **117** J14
Everglades City *U.S.A.* **117** J14
Evergreen *Ala., U.S.A.* **117** F11
Evergreen *Mont., U.S.A.* **108** B6
Everöd *Sweden* **11** J8
Evertsberg *Sweden* **10** C7
Evesham *U.K.* **15** E6
Evia *Greece* **46** C6
Evia □ *Greece* **46** C5
Évian-les-Bains *France* **19** F13
Evinos → *Greece* **46** C3
Évisa *France* **21** F12
Evje *Norway* **9** G12
Évora *Portugal* **37** G3
Évora □ *Portugal* **37** G3
Evowghlī *Iran* **73** C11
Évreux *France* **18** C8
Evritania □ *Greece* **46** B3
Évron *France* **18** D6
Evros □ *Greece* **45** E10
Evros → *Greece* **72** B2
Evrotas → *Greece* **46** E4
Évry *France* **19** D9
Évvoia = Evia *Greece* **46** C6
Ewe, L. *U.K.* **13** D3
Ewing *U.S.A.* **112** D4
Ewo *Congo* **84** E2
Exaltación *Bolivia* **124** F5
Excelsior Springs *U.S.A.* **112** F6
Excideuil *France* **20** C5
Exe → *U.K.* **15** G4
Exeter *Canada* **114** C3
Exeter *U.K.* **15** G4
Exeter *Calif., U.S.A.* **110** J7
Exeter *N.H., U.S.A.* **115** D14
Exmoor *U.K.* **15** F4
Exmoor △ *U.K.* **15** F4
Exmouth *Australia* **92** D1
Exmouth *U.K.* **15** G4
Exmouth G. *Australia* **92** D1
Exmouth Plateau *Ind. Oc.* **96** J3
Expedition △ *Australia* **94** D4
Expedition Ra. *Australia* **94** C4
Extremadura □ *Spain* **37** F4
Exuma Sound *Bahamas* **120** B4
Eyasi, L. *Tanzania* **86** C4
Eye Pen. *U.K.* **13** C2
Eyemouth *U.K.* **13** F6
Eygues = Aigues → *France* **21** D8
Eygurande *France* **19** G9
Eyjafjörður *Iceland* **8** C4
Eymet *France* **20** D4
Eymoutiers *France* **20** C5
Eynesil *Turkey* **73** B8
Eyre (North), L. *Australia* **95** D2
Eyre (South), L. *Australia* **95** D2
Eyre, L. *Australia* **90** D6
Eyre Mts. *N.Z.* **91** F2
Eyre Pen. *Australia* **95** E2
Eysturoy *Færoe Is.* **8** E9
Eyvānkī *Iran* **71** C6
Ez Zeidab *Sudan* **80** D3
Ezcaray *Spain* **38** C1
Ežerėlis *Lithuania* **30** D10
Ezhou *China* **59** B10
Ezine *Turkey* **47** B8

F

F.Y.R.O.M. =
  Macedonia ■ *Europe* **44** E5
Faaa *Tahiti* **91** d
Faaborg *Denmark* **11** J4
Faaone *Tahiti* **91** d
Fabala *Guinea* **82** D3
Fabens *U.S.A.* **116** F1
Fabero *Spain* **36** C4
Fabriano *Italy* **41** E9
Făcăeni *Romania* **29** F12
Fachi *Niger* **79** E8
Fada *Chad* **79** E10
Fada-n-Gourma *Burkina Faso* **83** C5
Fadd *Hungary* **28** D3
Faddeyevskiy, Ostrov
  Russia **53** B15
Faddor *Sudan* **81** F3
Fadghāmī *Syria* **73** E9
Fadlab *Sudan* **81** D3
Faenza *Italy* **41** D8
Færoe Is. = Føroyar ☑ *Atl. Oc.* **8** F9
Fafa *Mali* **83** B5
Fafe *Portugal* **36** D2
Fagam *Nigeria* **83** C7
Făgăraş *Romania* **29** E9

Făgăraş, Munţii *Romania* **29** E9
Făgelmara *Sweden* **11** H9
Fagerhult *Sweden* **11** G9
Fagersta *Sweden* **10** D9
Făget *Romania* **28** E7
Făget, Munţii *Romania* **29** C8
Fagnano, L. *Argentina* **128** G3
Fagnières *France* **19** D11
Faguibine, L. *Mali* **82** B4
Fahlīān *Iran* **71** D6
Fahraj *Kermān, Iran* **71** D8
Fahraj *Yazd, Iran* **71** D7
Fai Tsi Long *Vietnam* **58** G6
Faial *Azores* **78** a
Faial *Madeira* **48** D3
Fair Haven *U.S.A.* **113** D17
Fair Hd. *U.K.* **12** A5
Fair Isle *U.K.* **16** B6
Fair Oaks *U.S.A.* **110** G5
Fairbanks *U.S.A.* **100** C5
Fairbury *U.S.A.* **112** E5
Fairfax *U.S.A.* **115** B11
Fairfield *Ala., U.S.A.* **117** E11
Fairfield *Calif., U.S.A.* **110** G4
Fairfield *Conn., U.S.A.* **115** E11
Fairfield *Idaho, U.S.A.* **108** E6
Fairfield *Ill., U.S.A.* **112** F9
Fairfield *Iowa, U.S.A.* **112** E8
Fairfield *Tex., U.S.A.* **116** F6
Fairford *Canada* **103** C9
Fairlie *N.Z.* **91** F3
Fairmead *U.S.A.* **110** H6
Fairmont *Minn., U.S.A.* **112** D6
Fairmont *W. Va., U.S.A.* **113** F13
Fairmount *Calif., U.S.A.* **111** L8
Fairmount *N.Y., U.S.A.* **115** C8
Fairplay *U.S.A.* **108** G10
Fairport *U.S.A.* **114** C7
Fairport Harbor *U.S.A.* **114** E3
Fairview *Canada* **102** B5
Fairview *Mont., U.S.A.* **108** C11
Fairview *Okla., U.S.A.* **116** C5
Fairweather, Mt. *U.S.A.* **102** B1
Faisalabad *Pakistan* **68** D5
Faith *U.S.A.* **112** C2
Faizabad *India* **69** F10
Fajardo *Puerto Rico* **121** d
Fajr, W. → *Si. Arabia* **70** D3
Fakenham *U.K.* **14** E8
Fåker *Sweden* **10** A8
Fakfak *Indonesia* **63** E8
Fakiya *Bulgaria* **45** D11
Fakobli *Ivory C.* **82** D3
Fakse *Denmark* **11** J6
Fakse Bugt *Denmark* **11** J6
Fakse Ladeplads *Denmark* **11** J6
Faku *China* **57** C12
Falaba *S. Leone* **82** D2
Falaise *France* **18** D6
Falaise, Mui *Vietnam* **64** C5
Falakro Oros *Greece* **44** E7
Falam *Burma* **67** H18
Falces *Spain* **38** C3
Fălciu *Romania* **29** D13
Falcó, C. des *Spain* **48** C7
Falcón, Presa *Mexico* **119** B5
Falcon Lake *Canada* **103** D9
Falcon Res. *U.S.A.* **116** H5
Falconara Maríttima *Italy* **41** E10
Falcone, C. del *Italy* **42** B1
Falconer *U.S.A.* **114** D5
Faléa *Mali* **82** C2
Falefa *Samoa* **91** b
Falelatai *Samoa* **91** b
Falelima *Samoa* **91** b
Falémé → *Senegal* **82** C2
Falerum *Sweden* **11** F10
Faleshty = Făleşti *Moldova* **29** C12
Făleşti *Moldova* **29** C12
Falfurrias *U.S.A.* **116** H5
Falher *Canada* **102** B5
Faliraki *Greece* **49** C10
Falkenberg *Germany* **24** D9
Falkenberg *Sweden* **11** H6
Falkensee *Germany* **24** C9
Falkirk *U.K.* **13** F5
Falkirk □ *U.K.* **13** F5
Falkland *U.K.* **13** E5
Falkland Is. ☑ *Atl. Oc.* **128** G5
Falkland Sd. *Falk. Is.* **128** G5
Falkonera *Greece* **46** E5
Falköping *Sweden* **11** F7
Fall River *U.S.A.* **115** E13
Fallbrook *U.S.A.* **111** M9
Fallon *U.S.A.* **108** G4
Falls City *U.S.A.* **112** E6
Falls Creek *U.S.A.* **114** E6
Falmouth *Jamaica* **120** a
Falmouth *U.K.* **15** G2
Falmouth *U.S.A.* **115** E14
Falsa, Pta. *Mexico* **118** B1
False B. *S. Africa* **88** E2
Falso, C. *Honduras* **120** C3
Falster *Denmark* **11** K5
Falsterbo *Sweden* **9** J15
Fălticeni *Romania* **29** C11

Falun *Sweden* **10** D9
Famagusta *Cyprus* **49** D12
Famagusta Bay *Cyprus* **49** D13
Famalé *Niger* **78** F6
Famatina, Sierra de
  Argentina **126** B2
Family L. *Canada* **103** C9
Famoso *U.S.A.* **111** K7
Fan Xian *China* **56** G8
Fana *Mali* **82** C3
Fanad Hd. *Ireland* **12** A4
Fanari *Greece* **46** B3
Fandriana *Madag.* **89** C8
Fánes-Sénnes e Braies △
  Italy **41** B9
Fang *Thailand* **58** H2
Fang Xian *China* **59** A8
Fangaga *Sudan* **80** D4
Fangak *Sudan* **81** F3
Fangchang *China* **59** B12
Fangcheng *China* **56** H7
Fangchenggang *China* **58** G7
Fangliao *Taiwan* **59** F13
Fangshan *China* **56** E6
Fangzi *China* **57** F10
Fani i Madh → *Albania* **44** E4
Fanjakana *Madag.* **89** C8
Fanjiatun *China* **57** C13
Fannich, L. *U.K.* **13** D4
Fannūj *Iran* **71** E8
Fanø *Denmark* **11** J2
Fano *Italy* **41** E10
Fanshi *China* **56** E7
Fao = Al Fāw *Iraq* **71** D6
Faqirwali *Pakistan* **68** E5
Fâqûs *Egypt* **80** H7
Far East =
  Dalnevostochnyy □
  Russia **53** C14
Far East *Asia* **50** E14
Fara in Sabina *Italy* **41** F9
Faradje *Dem. Rep. of the Congo* **86** B2
Farafangana *Madag.* **89** C8
Farāfra, El Wâhât el- *Egypt* **80** B2
Farāh *Afghan.* **66** C3
Farāh □ *Afghan.* **66** C3
Farahalana *Madag.* **89** A9
Faraid, Gebel *Egypt* **80** C4
Farako *Ivory C.* **82** D4
Faramana *Burkina Faso* **82** C4
Faranah *Guinea* **82** C2
Farasān, Jazā'ir *Si. Arabia* **75** D3
Farasan Is. = Farasān,
  Jazā'ir *Si. Arabia* **75** D3
Faratsiho *Madag.* **89** B8
Fardes → *Spain* **37** H7
Fareham *U.K.* **15** G6
Farewell *U.S.A.* **114** D5
Farewell, C. *N.Z.* **91** D4
Farewell C. = Nunap Isua
  Greenland **98** D15
Färgelanda *Sweden* **11** F5
Farghona *Uzbekistan* **52** E8
Fargo *U.S.A.* **112** B5
Fär'iah, W. al → *West Bank* **74** C4
Faribault *U.S.A.* **112** C7
Faridabad *India* **68** E6
Faridkot *India* **68** D6
Faridpur *Bangla.* **69** H13
Faridpur *India* **69** E8
Färila *Sweden* **10** C9
Farim *Guinea-Biss.* **82** C1
Farīmān *Iran* **71** C8
Farina *Australia* **95** E2
Fariones, Pta. *Canary Is.* **48** E6
Fâriskûr *Egypt* **80** H7
Färjestaden *Sweden* **11** H10
Farkadóna *Greece* **46** B4
Farleigh *Australia* **94** K7
Farmakonisi *Greece* **47** D9
Farmerville *U.S.A.* **116** E8
Farmingdale *U.S.A.* **115** F10
Farmington *Canada* **102** B4
Farmington *Calif., U.S.A.* **110** H6
Farmington *Maine, U.S.A.* **113** C18
Farmington *Mo., U.S.A.* **112** G8
Farmington *N.H., U.S.A.* **115** C13
Farmington *N. Mex., U.S.A.* **109** H9
Farmington *Utah, U.S.A.* **108** F8
Farmington → *U.S.A.* **115** E12
Farmville *U.S.A.* **113** G14
Färnäs *Sweden* **10** D8
Farne Is. *U.K.* **14** B6
Färnebofjärden △ *Sweden* **10** D10
Faro *Brazil* **125** D7
Faro *Canada* **100** C6
Faro *Portugal* **37** H3
Fårö *Sweden* **9** H18
Faro □ *Portugal* **37** H2
Faro ✈ (FAO) *Portugal* **37** H3
Fårösund *Sweden* **9** H18
Farquhar, C. *Australia* **93** D1
Farrars Cr. → *Australia* **94** D3
Farrāshband *Iran* **71** D7
Farrell *U.S.A.* **114** E4
Farrokhī *Iran* **71** C8

Farruch, C. = Ferrutx, C.
  Spain **48** B10
Fārs □ *Iran* **71** D7
Farsala *Greece* **46** B4
Farsø *Denmark* **11** H3
Farson *U.S.A.* **108** E9
Farsund *Norway* **9** G12
Fartak, Râs *Si. Arabia* **70** D2
Fartak, Ra's *Yemen* **75** D5
Fârţăneşti *Romania* **29** E12
Fartura, Serra da *Brazil* **127** B5
Faru *Nigeria* **83** C6
Fārūj *Iran* **71** B8
Fårup *Denmark* **11** H3
Farvel, Kap = Nunap Isua
  Greenland **98** D15
Farwell *U.S.A.* **116** D3
Fasā *Iran* **71** D7
Fasano *Italy* **43** B10
Fashoda *Sudan* **81** F3
Fassa *Mali* **82** C3
Fastiv *Ukraine* **23** C15
Fastnet Rock *Ireland* **12** E2
Fastov = Fastiv *Ukraine* **23** C15
Fatagar, Tanjung *Indonesia* **63** E8
Fatehabad *Haryana, India* **68** E6
Fatehabad *Ut. P., India* **68** F8
Fatehgarh *India* **69** F8
Fatehpur *Bihar, India* **69** G11
Fatehpur *Raj., India* **68** F6
Fatehpur *Ut. P., India* **69** G9
Fatehpur *Ut. P., India* **69** F9
Fatehpur Sikri *India* **68** F6
Fatesh *Russia* **33** F8
Fathai *Sudan* **81** F3
Fathom Five △ *Canada* **114** A3
Fatick *Senegal* **82** C1
Fatick □ *Senegal* **82** C1
Fatima *Canada* **105** C7
Fátima *Portugal* **37** F2
Fatoya *Guinea* **82** C3
Fatsa *Turkey* **72** B7
Faucille, Col de la *France* **19** F13
Faulkton *U.S.A.* **112** C5
Faulquemont *France* **19** C13
Faure I. *Australia* **93** E1
Fâurei *Romania* **29** E12
Fauresmith *S. Africa* **88** D4
Fauske *Norway* **8** C16
Favara *Italy* **42** F6
Faváritx, C. de *Spain* **48** B11
Faverges *France* **21** C10
Favignana *Italy* **42** F5
Favignana, I. *Italy* **42** E5
Fawcett, Pt. *Australia* **92** B5
Fawn → *Canada* **104** A2
Fawnskin *U.S.A.* **111** L10
Faxaflói *Iceland* **8** D2
Faxälven → *Sweden* **10** A10
Faya-Largeau *Chad* **79** E9
Fayd *Si. Arabia* **70** C4
Fayence *France* **21** E10
Fayette *Ala., U.S.A.* **117** E11
Fayette *Mo., U.S.A.* **112** F7
Fayetteville *Ark., U.S.A.* **116** C7
Fayetteville *N.C., U.S.A.* **117** D15
Fayetteville *Tenn., U.S.A.* **117** D11
Fayied *Egypt* **80** H8
Fayón *Spain* **38** D5
Fazao-Malfakassa △ *Togo* **83** D5
Fazilka *India* **68** D6
Fazilpur *Pakistan* **68** E4
Fdérik *Mauritania* **78** D3
Feakle *Ireland* **12** D3
Feale → *Ireland* **12** D2
Fear, C. *U.S.A.* **117** E16
Feather → *U.S.A.* **108** G3
Feather Falls *U.S.A.* **110** F5
Featherston *N.Z.* **91** D5
Featherstone *Zimbabwe* **87** F3
Fécamp *France* **18** C7
Fedala = Mohammedia
  Morocco **78** B4
Federación *Argentina* **126** C4
Féderal *Argentina* **128** C5
Federal Capital Terr. □
  Nigeria **83** D6
Federal Way *U.S.A.* **110** C4
Fedeshkūh *Iran* **71** D7
Fehérgyarmat *Hungary* **28** C7
Fehmarn *Germany* **24** A7
Fehmarn Bælt *Europe* **11** K5
Fehmarn Belt = Fehmarn
  Bælt *Europe* **11** K5
Fei Xian *China* **57** G9
Feijó *Brazil* **124** E4
Feilding *N.Z.* **91** D5
Feira de Santana *Brazil* **125** F11
Feixi *China* **59** B11
Feixiang *China* **56** F8
Fejér □ *Hungary* **28** C3
Fejø *Denmark* **11** K5
Feke *Turkey* **72** D6
Fekete → *Hungary* **28** E3
Felanitx *Spain* **48** B10
Feldbach *Austria* **26** E8

Feldberg *Baden-W., Germany* **25** H3
Feldberg
  Mecklenburg-Vorpommern,
  Germany **24** B9
Feldkirch *Austria* **26** D2
Feldkirchen *Austria* **26** E7
Felipe Carrillo Puerto
  Mexico **119** D7
Felixburg *Zimbabwe* **89** B5
Felixstowe *U.K.* **15** F9
Felletin *France* **20** C6
Fellingsbro *Sweden* **10** E9
Felton *U.S.A.* **110** H4
Feltre *Italy* **41** B8
Femer Bælt = Fehmarn
  Bælt *Europe* **11** K5
Femø *Denmark* **11** K5
Femunden *Norway* **8** E14
Fen He → *China* **56** G6
Fene *Spain* **36** B2
Fenelon Falls *Canada* **114** B6
Fener Burnu *Turkey* **47** E9
Feneroa *Ethiopia* **81** E4
Fengari *Greece* **45** F9
Feng Xian *Jiangsu, China* **56** G9
Feng Xian *Shaanxi, China* **56** H4
Fengcheng *Jiangxi, China* **59** C10
Fengcheng *Liaoning, China* **57** D13
Fengfeng *China* **56** F8
Fenggang *China* **58** D6
Fenghua *China* **59** C13
Fenghuang *China* **58** D7
Fengkai *China* **59** F8
Fengkang *Taiwan* **59** F13
Fengle *China* **59** B9
Fenglin *Taiwan* **59** F13
Fengning *China* **56** D9
Fengqing *China* **58** E2
Fengqiu *China* **56** G8
Fengrun *China* **57** E10
Fengshan *Guangxi Zhuangzu,*
  China **58** E7
Fengshan *Guangxi Zhuangzu,*
  China **58** E6
Fengshan *Taiwan* **59** F13
Fengshun *China* **59** F11
Fengtai *Anhui, China* **59** A11
Fengtai *Beijing, China* **56** E9
Fengxian *China* **59** B13
Fengxiang *China* **56** G4
Fengxin *China* **59** C10
Fengyang *China* **57** H9
Fengyi *China* **58** E3
Fengyüan *Taiwan* **59** E13
Fengzhen *China* **56** D7
Feno, C. de *France* **21** G12
Fenoarivo *Fianarantsoa,*
  Madag. **89** C8
Fenoarivo *Fianarantsoa,*
  Madag. **89** C8
Fenoarivo Afovoany *Madag.* **89** B8
Fenoarivo Atsinanana
  Madag. **89** B8
Fens, The *U.K.* **14** E7
Fensmark *Denmark* **11** J5
Fenton *U.S.A.* **113** D12
Fenxi *China* **56** F6
Fenyang *China* **56** F6
Fenyi *China* **59** D10
Feodosiya *Ukraine* **33** K8
Ferbane *Ireland* **12** C4
Ferdows *Iran* **71** C8
Fère-Champenoise *France* **19** D10
Fère-en-Tardenois *France* **19** C10
Ferentino *Italy* **41** G10
Feres *Greece* **45** F10
Ferfer *Somali Rep.* **75** F4
Fergana = Farghona
  Uzbekistan **52** E8
Fergus *Canada* **114** C4
Fergus Falls *U.S.A.* **112** B5
Feričanci *Croatia* **28** E2
Ferihegy, Budapest ✈
  (BUD) *Hungary* **28** C4
Ferkéssédougou *Ivory C.* **82** D3
Ferlach *Austria* **26** E7
Ferland *Canada* **104** B2
Ferlo, Vallée du *Senegal* **82** B2
Ferlo-Nord △ *Senegal* **82** B2
Ferlo-Sud △ *Senegal* **82** B2
Fermanagh □ *U.K.* **12** B4
Fermo *Italy* **41** E10
Fermont *Canada* **105** B6
Fermoselle *Spain* **36** D4
Fermoy *Ireland* **12** D3
Fernán Núñez *Spain* **37** H6
Fernández *Argentina* **126** B3
Fernandina Beach *U.S.A.* **117** F14
Fernando de Noronha
  Brazil **125** D12
Fernando Póo = Bioko
  Eq. Guin. **83** E6
Ferndale *U.S.A.* **110** B4
Fernie *Canada* **102** D5
Fernlees *Australia* **94** C4
Fernley *U.S.A.* **108** G4

Ferozepore = Firozpur *India* **68** D6
Ferrandina *Italy* **43** B9
Ferrara *Italy* **41** D8
Ferrato, C. *Italy* **42** C2
Ferreira do Alentejo *Portugal* **37** G2
Ferreñafe *Peru* **124** E3
Ferrerías *Spain* **48** B11
Ferret, C. *France* **20** D2
Ferrette *France* **19** E14
Ferriday *U.S.A.* **116** F9
Ferriere *Italy* **40** D6
Ferrières *France* **19** D9
Ferro, Capo *Italy* **42** A2
Ferrol *Spain* **36** B2
Ferron *U.S.A.* **108** G8
Ferrutx, C. *Spain* **48** B10
Ferryland *Canada* **105** C9
Fertile *U.S.A.* **112** B5
Fertőszentmiklós *Hungary* **28** C1
Fertőtavi △ *Hungary* **28** C1
Fès *Morocco* **78** B5
Fessenden *U.S.A.* **112** B4
Festus *U.S.A.* **112** F8
Feté Bowé *Senegal* **82** C2
Feteşti *Romania* **29** F12
Fethiye *Turkey* **47** E11
Fethiye Körfezi *Turkey* **47** E10
Fetlar *U.K.* **13** A8
Feuilles → *Canada* **101** D12
Feurs *France* **21** C8
Fez = Fès *Morocco* **78** B5
Fezzan *Libya* **79** C8
Fiambalá *Argentina* **126** B2
Fianarantsoa *Madag.* **89** C8
Fianarantsoa □ *Madag.* **89** B8
Fiche *Ethiopia* **81** F4
Fichtelgebirge *Germany* **25** E7
Fichtelgebirge △ *Germany* **25** E8
Ficksburg *S. Africa* **89** D4
Fidenza *Italy* **40** D7
Fiditi *Nigeria* **83** D5
Fife □ *U.K.* **13** E5
Fife △ *U.K.* **13** E5
Fife Ness *U.K.* **13** E6
Fifth Cataract *Sudan* **80** D3
Figari *France* **21** G13
Figeac *France* **20** D5
Figeholm *Sweden* **11** G10
Figline Valdarno *Italy* **41** E8
Figtree *Zimbabwe* **87** G2
Figueira Castelo Rodrigo
  Portugal **36** E4
Figueira da Foz *Portugal* **36** E2
Figueiró dos Vinhos *Portugal* **36** F2
Figueres *Spain* **38** C7
Figuig *Morocco* **78** B5
Fihaonana *Madag.* **89** B8
Fiherenana *Madag.* **89** B8
Fiherenana → *Madag.* **89** C7
Fiji ■ *Pac. Oc.* **91** a
Fik *Ethiopia* **81** F5
Fika *Nigeria* **83** D7
Filabres, Sierra de los *Spain* **37** H8
Filabusi *Zimbabwe* **89** C4
Filadélfia *Italy* **43** D9
Fil'akovo *Slovak Rep.* **27** C12
Filchner Ice Shelf *Antarctica* **5** D1
Filey *U.K.* **14** C7
Filey B. *U.K.* **14** C7
Filfla *Malta* **49** D1
Filiaşi *Romania* **29** F8
Filiates *Greece* **46** B2
Filiatra *Greece* **46** D3
Filicudi *Italy* **43** D7
Filingué *Niger* **83** C5
Filiourí = Lissos → *Greece* **45** E9
Filipada *Greece* **46** B2
Filipstad *Sweden* **10** E8
Filisur *Switz.* **25** J5
Fillmore *Calif., U.S.A.* **111** L8
Fillmore *Utah, U.S.A.* **108** G7
Filotio *Greece* **47** D7
Filottrano *Italy* **41** E10
Filtu *Ethiopia* **81** F5
Fina *Mali* **82** C3
Finale Emília *Italy* **41** D8
Finale Lígure *Italy* **40** D5
Fiñana *Spain* **37** H8
Finch *Canada* **115** A9
Finch Hatton *Australia* **94** K6
Findhorn → *U.K.* **13** D5
Findlay *U.S.A.* **113** E12
Finger L. *Canada* **104** B1
Finger Lakes *U.S.A.* **115** D8
Fíngoè *Mozam.* **87** E3
Finike *Turkey* **47** E12
Finike Körfezi *Turkey* **47** E12
Finiq *Albania* **44** G4
Finistère □ *France* **18** D3
Finisterre = Fisterra *Spain* **36** C1
Finisterre, C. = Fisterra, C.
  Spain **36** C1

Finke *Australia* **94** D1
Finke Gorge △ *Australia* **92** D5
Finland ■ *Europe* **8** E22
Finland, G. of *Europe* **32** C3
Finlay → *Canada* **102** B3
Finley *Australia* **95** F4
Finley *U.S.A.* **112** B5
Finn → *Ireland* **12** B4
Finnerödja *Sweden* **11** F8
Finnigan, Mt. *Australia* **94** B4
Finniss, C. *Australia* **95** E1
Finnmark *Norway* **8** B20
Finnsnes *Norway* **8** B18
Finspång *Sweden* **11** F9
Finsteraarhorn *Switz.* **25** J4
Finsterwalde *Germany* **24** D9
Fiora → *Italy* **41** F8
Fiordland △ *N.Z.* **91** F1
Fiorenzuola d'Arda *Italy* **40** D6
Firat = Furãt, Nahr al →
  Asia **70** D5
Fire Island △ *U.S.A.* **115** F11
Firebag → *Canada* **103** B6
Firebaugh *U.S.A.* **110** J6
Firedrake L. *Canada* **103** A8
Firenze *Italy* **41** E8
Firenze Amerigo
  Vespucci ✈ (FLR) *Italy* **41** E8
Firenze Pisa ✈ (PSA) *Italy* **40** E7
Firenzuola *Italy* **41** D8
Firk, Sha'ib → *Iraq* **70** D5
Firmi *France* **20** D6
Firminy *France* **21** C8
Firozabad *India* **68** F8
Firozpur *India* **68** D6
Firozpur-Jhirka *India* **68** F7
Fīrūzābād *Iran* **71** D7
Fīrūzkūh *Iran* **71** C7
Firvale *Canada* **102** C3
Fish → *Namibia* **88** D2
Fish → *S. Africa* **88** E3
Fish River Canyon *Namibia* **88** D2
Fisher B. *Canada* **103** C9
Fishers I. *U.S.A.* **115** E13
Fishguard *U.K.* **15** E3
Fishing L. *Canada* **103** C9
Fishkill *U.S.A.* **115** E11
Fismes *France* **19** C10
Fisterra *Spain* **36** C1
Fisterra, C. *Spain* **36** C1
Fitchburg *Mass., U.S.A.* **115** D13
Fitchburg *Wis., U.S.A.* **112** D9
Fitz Roy *Argentina* **128** F3
Fitz Roy, Cerro *Argentina* **128** F2
Fitzgerald *Canada* **102** B6
Fitzgerald *U.S.A.* **117** F13
Fitzgerald River △ *Australia* **93** F3
Fitzmaurice → *Australia* **92** B5
Fitzroy → *Queens., Australia* **94** C5
Fitzroy → *W. Austral.,*
  Australia **92** C3
Fitzroy Crossing *Australia* **92** C4
Fitzwilliam I. *Canada* **114** A3
Fiuggi *Italy* **41** G10
Fiume = Rijeka *Croatia* **41** C11
Fiumicino, Roma ✈ (FCO)
  Italy **41** G9
Five Points *U.S.A.* **110** J6
Fivizzano *Italy* **40** D7
Fizi *Dem. Rep. of the Congo* **86** C2
Fjällbacka *Sweden* **11** F5
Fjärdhundra *Sweden* **10** E10
Fjellerup *Denmark* **11** H4
Fjerritslev *Denmark* **11** G3
Fjugesta *Sweden* **10** E8
Flagstaff *U.S.A.* **109** J8
Flagstaff L. *U.S.A.* **115** A14
Flaherty I. *Canada* **104** A4
Flåm *Norway* **8** F12
Flambeau → *U.S.A.* **112** C8
Flamborough Hd. *U.K.* **14** C7
Fläming *Germany* **24** C8
Flaming Gorge △ *U.S.A.* **108** F9
Flaming Gorge Res. *U.S.A.* **108** F9
Flamingo, Teluk *Indonesia* **63** F9
Flanders = Flandre *Europe* **19** B9
Flandre *Europe* **19** B9
Flandre-Occidentale =
  West-Vlaanderen □
  Belgium **17** D2
Flandre-Orientale = Oost-
  Vlaanderen □ *Belgium* **17** C3
Flandreau *U.S.A.* **112** C5
Flanigan *U.S.A.* **110** E7
Flannan Is. *U.K.* **13** C1
Flåsjön *Sweden* **8** D16
Flat → *Canada* **102** A3
Flat I. *Mauritius* **85** d
Flathead L. *U.S.A.* **108** C6
Flattery, C. *Australia* **94** A4
Flattery, C. *U.S.A.* **110** B2
Flatwoods *U.S.A.* **113** F12
Fleetwood *U.K.* **14** D4
Fleetwood *U.S.A.* **115** F9
Flekkefjord *Norway* **9** G12
Flemington *U.S.A.* **114** E7

Flen *Sweden* 10 E10
Flensburg *Germany* 24 A5
Flers *France* 18 D6
Flesherton *Canada* 114 B4
Flesko, Tanjung *Indonesia* 63 D6
Fleurance *France* 20 E4
Fleurier *Switz.* 25 J2
Fleurieu Pen. *Australia* 95 F2
Flevoland □ *Neths.* 17 B5
Flin Flon *Canada* 103 C8
Flinders → *Australia* 94 B3
Flinders B. *Australia* 93 F2
Flinders Group *Australia* 94 A3
Flinders I. *S. Austral.,
  Australia* 95 E1
Flinders I. *Tas., Australia* 95 G4
Flinders Ranges *Australia* 95 E2
Flinders Reefs *Australia* 94 B4
Flint *U.K.* 14 D4
Flint *U.S.A.* 113 D12
Flint → *U.S.A.* 117 F12
Flint I. *Kiribati* 97 J12
Flintshire □ *U.K.* 14 D4
Fliseryd *Sweden* 11 G10
Flix *Spain* 38 D5
Flixecourt *France* 19 B9
Floby *Sweden* 11 F7
Floda *Sweden* 11 G6
Flodden *U.K.* 14 B5
Flogny-la-Chapelle *France* 19 E10
Floodwood *U.S.A.* 112 B7
Flora *U.S.A.* 112 F9
Florac *France* 20 D7
Florala *U.S.A.* 117 F11
Florence = Firenze *Italy* 41 E8
Florence *Ala., U.S.A.* 117 D11
Florence *Ariz., U.S.A.* 109 K8
Florence *Colo., U.S.A.* 108 G11
Florence *Oreg., U.S.A.* 108 D1
Florence *S.C., U.S.A.* 117 D15
Florence, L. *Australia* 95 D2
Florencia *Colombia* 124 C3
Florennes *Belgium* 17 D4
Florensac *France* 20 E7
Florenville *Belgium* 17 E5
Flores *Azores* 78 a
Flores *Guatemala* 120 C2
Flores *Indonesia* 63 F6
Flores I. *Canada* 102 D3
Flores Sea *Indonesia* 63 F6
Floreşti *Moldova* 29 C13
Floresville *U.S.A.* 116 G5
Floriano *Brazil* 125 E10
Florianópolis *Brazil* 127 B6
Florida *Cuba* 120 B4
Florida *Uruguay* 127 C4
Florida □ *U.S.A.* 117 G14
Florida, Straits of *U.S.A.* 120 B4
Florida B. *U.S.A.* 120 B3
Florida Keys *U.S.A.* 117 J14
Florídia *Italy* 43 E8
Florin *U.S.A.* 110 G5
Florina *Greece* 44 F5
Florina □ *Greece* 44 F5
Florissant *U.S.A.* 112 F8
Florø *Norway* 8 F11
Flower Station *Canada* 115 A8
Flowerpot I. *Canada* 114 A3
Floydada *U.S.A.* 116 E4
Fluk *Indonesia* 63 E7
Flúmen → *Spain* 38 D4
Flumendosa → *Italy* 42 C2
Fluminimaggiore *Italy* 42 C1
Flushing = Vlissingen *Neths.* 17 C3
Fluviá → *Spain* 38 C8
Fly → *Papua N. G.* 90 B7
Flying Fish, C. *Antarctica* 5 D15
Foa *Tonga* 91 c
Foam Lake *Canada* 103 C8
Foča *Bos.-H.* 44 C2
Foça *Turkey* 47 C8
Fochabers *U.K.* 13 D5
Focşani *Romania* 29 E12
Fodécontéa *Guinea* 82 C2
Fogang *China* 59 F9
Fóggia *Italy* 43 A8
Foggo *Nigeria* 83 C6
Fogo *Canada* 105 C9
Fogo C. Verde Is. *78* b
Fogo I. *Canada* 105 C9
Fohnsdorf *Austria* 26 D7
Föhr *Germany* 24 A4
Foia *Portugal* 37 H2
Foix *France* 20 F4
Fojnica *Bos.-H.* 28 G2
Fokida □ *Greece* 46 C4
Fokino *Russia* 32 F8
Fokku *Nigeria* 83 C5
Folda *Nord-Trøndelag, Norway* 8 D14
Folda *Nordland, Norway* 8 C16
Földeák *Hungary* 28 D6
Folegandros *Greece* 46 E6
Foley *Botswana* 88 C4
Foley *U.S.A.* 117 F11
Foleyet *Canada* 104 C4
Folgefonna *Norway* 9 F12

Foligno *Italy* 41 F9
Folkestone *U.K.* 15 F9
Folkston *U.S.A.* 117 F13
Follansbee *U.S.A.* 114 F4
Follónica *Italy* 40 F7
Follónica, G. di *Italy* 40 F7
Folsom L. *U.S.A.* 110 G5
Folteşti *Romania* 29 E13
Fomboni *Comoros Is.* 85 a
Fond-du-Lac *Canada* 103 B7
Fond du Lac *U.S.A.* 112 D9
Fond-du-Lac → *Canada* 103 B7
Fonda *U.S.A.* 115 D10
Fondi *Italy* 42 A6
Fonfría *Spain* 36 D4
Fongafale *Tuvalu* 90 B10
Fonni *Italy* 42 B2
Fonsagrada = A
  Fonsagrada *Spain* 36 B3
Fonseca, G. de *Cent. Amer.* 120 D2
Font-Romeu-Odeillo-Via
  France 20 F5
Fontaine-Française *France* 19 E12
Fontainebleau *France* 19 D9
Fontana *U.S.A.* 111 L9
Fontas → *Canada* 102 B4
Fonte Boa *Brazil* 124 D5
Fontem *Cameroon* 83 D6
Fontenay-le-Comte *France* 20 B3
Fontenelle Res. *U.S.A.* 108 E8
Fontur *Iceland* 8 C6
Fonuafo'ou *Tonga* 91 c
Fonualei *Tonga* 91 c
Fonyód *Hungary* 28 D2
Foochow = Fuzhou *China* 59 D12
Foping *China* 56 H5
Forbach *France* 19 C13
Forbes *Australia* 95 E4
Forbesganj *India* 69 F12
Forcados *Nigeria* 83 D6
Forcados → *Nigeria* 83 D6
Forcalquier *France* 21 E9
Forchheim *Germany* 25 F7
Ford City *Calif., U.S.A.* 111 K7
Ford City *Pa., U.S.A.* 114 F5
Førde *Norway* 8 F11
Fords Bridge *Australia* 95 D4
Fordyce *U.S.A.* 116 E8
Forécariah *Guinea* 82 D2
Forel, Mt. *Greenland* 98 C16
Foremost *Canada* 102 D6
Forest *Canada* 114 C3
Forest *U.S.A.* 117 E10
Forest City *Iowa, U.S.A.* 112 D7
Forest City *N.C., U.S.A.* 117 D14
Forest City *Pa., U.S.A.* 115 E9
Forest Grove *U.S.A.* 110 E3
Forestburg *Canada* 102 C6
Foreste Casentinesi-Monte
  Falterona-Campigna △
  Italy 41 E8
Foresthill *U.S.A.* 110 F6
Forestier Pen. *Australia* 95 G4
Forestville *Canada* 105 C6
Forestville *Calif., U.S.A.* 110 G4
Forestville *N.Y., U.S.A.* 114 D5
Forêt d'Orient △ *France* 19 D11
Forez, Mts. du *France* 20 C7
Forfar *U.K.* 13 E6
Forillon △ *Canada* 105 C7
Forks *U.S.A.* 110 C2
Forksville *U.S.A.* 115 E8
Forlì *Italy* 41 D9
Forman *U.S.A.* 112 B6
Formby Pt. *U.K.* 14 D4
Formentera *Spain* 48 C7
Formentor, C. de *Spain* 48 B10
Former Yugoslav Republic
  of Macedonia =
  Macedonia ■ *Europe* 44 E5
Fórmia *Italy* 42 A6
Formígine *Italy* 40 D7
Formosa = Taiwan ■ *Asia* 59 F13
Formosa *Argentina* 126 B4
Formosa *Brazil* 125 G9
Formosa □ *Argentina* 126 B4
Formosa, Serra *Brazil* 125 F8
Formosa B. = Ungwana B.
  Kenya 86 C5
Fornells *Spain* 48 A11
Fornos de Algodres *Portugal* 36 E3
Fornovo di Taro *Italy* 40 D7
Føroyar ☑ *Atl. Oc.* 8 F9
Forres *U.K.* 13 D5
Forrest *Australia* 93 F4
Forrest, Mt. *Australia* 93 D4
Forrest City *U.S.A.* 117 D9
Fors *Sweden* 10 D10
Forsayth *Australia* 94 B3
Forshaga *Sweden* 10 E7
Förslöv *Sweden* 11 H6
Forsmo *Sweden* 10 A11
Forssa *Finland* 32 B2
Forst *Germany* 24 D10
Forster *Australia* 95 E5
Forsvik *Sweden* 11 F8
Forsyth *U.S.A.* 108 C10

Fort Abbas *Pakistan* 68 E5
Fort Albany *Canada* 104 B3
Fort Ann *U.S.A.* 115 C11
Fort Assiniboine *Canada* 102 C6
Fort Augustus *U.K.* 13 D4
Fort Beaufort *S. Africa* 88 E4
Fort Benton *U.S.A.* 108 C8
Fort Bragg *U.S.A.* 108 G2
Fort Bridger *U.S.A.* 108 F8
Fort Chipewyan *Canada* 103 B6
Fort Clatsop △ *U.S.A.* 110 D3
Fort Collins *U.S.A.* 108 F11
Fort-Coulonge *Canada* 104 C4
Fort Covington *U.S.A.* 115 B10
Fort Dauphin = Taolanaro
  Madag. 89 D8
Fort Davis *U.S.A.* 116 F3
Fort Defiance *U.S.A.* 109 J9
Fort Dodge *U.S.A.* 112 D6
Fort Edward *U.S.A.* 115 C11
Fort Erie *Canada* 114 D6
Fort Fairfield *U.S.A.* 113 B20
Fort Frances *Canada* 103 D10
Fort Franklin = Déline
  Canada 100 C7
Fort Garland *U.S.A.* 109 H11
Fort George = Chisasibi
  Canada 104 B4
Fort Good Hope *Canada* 100 C7
Fort Hancock *U.S.A.* 116 F2
Fort Hope *Canada* 104 B2
Fort Irwin *U.S.A.* 111 K10
Fort Kent *U.S.A.* 113 B19
Fort Klamath *U.S.A.* 108 E3
Fort Laramie *U.S.A.* 108 E11
Fort Lauderdale *U.S.A.* 117 H14
Fort Liard *Canada* 102 A4
Fort Liberté *Haiti* 121 C5
Fort Lupton *U.S.A.* 108 F11
Fort MacKay *Canada* 102 B6
Fort Macleod *Canada* 102 D6
Fort McMurray *Canada* 102 B6
Fort McPherson *Canada* 100 C6
Fort Madison *U.S.A.* 112 E9
Fort Meade *U.S.A.* 117 H14
Fort Morgan *U.S.A.* 108 F12
Fort Myers *U.S.A.* 117 H14
Fort Nelson *Canada* 102 B4
Fort Nelson → *Canada* 102 B4
Fort Norman = Tulita
  Canada 100 C7
Fort Payne *U.S.A.* 117 D12
Fort Peck *U.S.A.* 108 B10
Fort Peck Dam *U.S.A.* 108 C10
Fort Peck L. *U.S.A.* 108 C10
Fort Pierce *U.S.A.* 117 H14
Fort Pierre *U.S.A.* 112 C3
Fort Plain *U.S.A.* 115 D10
Fort Portal *Uganda* 86 B3
Fort Providence *Canada* 102 A5
Fort Qu'Appelle *Canada* 103 C8
Fort Resolution *Canada* 102 A6
Fort Rixon *Zimbabwe* 87 G2
Fort Ross *U.S.A.* 110 G3
Fort Rupert =
  Waskaganish *Canada* 104 B4
Fort St. James *Canada* 102 C4
Fort St. John *Canada* 102 B4
Fort Saskatchewan *Canada* 102 C6
Fort Scott *U.S.A.* 112 G6
Fort Severn *Canada* 104 A2
Fort Shevchenko
  Kazakhstan 35 H10
Fort Simpson *Canada* 102 A4
Fort Smith *Canada* 102 B6
Fort Smith *U.S.A.* 116 D7
Fort Stockton *U.S.A.* 116 F3
Fort Sumner *U.S.A.* 109 J11
Fort Thompson *U.S.A.* 112 C4
Fort Union △ *U.S.A.* 109 J11
Fort Valley *U.S.A.* 117 E13
Fort Vermilion *Canada* 102 B5
Fort Walton Beach *U.S.A.* 117 F11
Fort Wayne *U.S.A.* 113 E11
Fort William *U.K.* 13 E3
Fort Worth *U.S.A.* 116 E6
Fort Yates *U.S.A.* 112 B3
Fort Yukon *U.S.A.* 106 a
Fortaleza *Brazil* 125 D11
Forteau *Canada* 105 B8
Fortescue → *Australia* 92 D2
Forth → *U.K.* 13 E5
Forth, Firth of *U.K.* 13 E6
Fortore → *Italy* 41 G12
Fortrose *U.K.* 13 D4
Fortuna *Spain* 39 G3
Fortuna *Calif., U.S.A.* 108 F1
Fortuna *N. Dak., U.S.A.* 112 A2
Fortune *Canada* 105 C8
Fortune B. *Canada* 105 C8
Forūr *Iran* 71 E7
Fos-sur-Mer *France* 21 E8
Fosen *Norway* 8 E14
Foshan *China* 59 F9
Fosnavåg *Norway* 8 E11
Foso *Ghana* 83 D4

Fossano *Italy* 40 D4
Fossil *U.S.A.* 108 D3
Fossil Butte △ *U.S.A.* 108 F8
Fossombrone *Italy* 41 E9
Foster *Canada* 115 A12
Foster → *Canada* 103 B7
Fosters Ra. *Australia* 94 C1
Fostoria *U.S.A.* 113 E12
Fotadrevo *Madag.* 89 C8
Fouesnant *France* 18 E2
Fougères *France* 18 D5
Foul Pt. *Sri Lanka* 66 Q12
Foula *U.K.* 13 A6
Foulness I. *U.K.* 15 F8
Foulpointe *Madag.* 89 B8
Foumban *Cameroon* 83 D7
Foumbot *Cameroon* 83 D7
Foumbouni *Comoros Is.* 85 a
Foundiougne *Senegal* 82 C1
Fountain *U.S.A.* 108 G11
Fountain Hills *U.S.A.* 109 K8
Fountain Springs *U.S.A.* 111 K8
Fourchambault *France* 19 E10
Fouriesburg *S. Africa* 88 D4
Fourmies *France* 19 B11
Fourna *Greece* 46 B3
Fourni *Greece* 47 D8
Fours *France* 19 F10
Fourth Cataract *Sudan* 79 E12
Fouta Djallon *Guinea* 82 C2
Foux, Cap-à- *Haiti* 121 C5
Foveaux Str. *N.Z.* 91 G2
Fowey *U.K.* 15 G3
Fowler *Calif., U.S.A.* 110 J7
Fowler *Colo., U.S.A.* 108 G11
Fowler, Pt. *Australia* 93 F5
Fowlers B. *Australia* 93 F5
Fowman *Iran* 73 D13
Fox → *Canada* 103 B10
Fox Creek *Canada* 102 C5
Fox Lake *Canada* 102 B6
Fox Valley *Canada* 103 C7
Foxboro *U.S.A.* 115 D13
Foxdale *Australia* 94 J6
Foxe Basin *Canada* 101 C12
Foxe Chan. *Canada* 101 C11
Foxe Pen. *Canada* 101 C12
Foxen *Sweden* 10 E5
Foxford *Ireland* 12 C2
Foxton *N.Z.* 91 J5
Foyle, Lough *U.K.* 12 A4
Foynes *Ireland* 12 D2
Foz *Spain* 36 B3
Foz do Cunene *Angola* 88 B1
Foz do Iguaçu *Brazil* 127 B5
Frackville *U.S.A.* 115 F8
Fraga *Spain* 38 D5
Fraile Muerto *Uruguay* 127 C5
Framingham *U.S.A.* 115 D13
Frampol *Poland* 31 H9
Franca *Brazil* 125 H9
Francavilla al Mare *Italy* 41 F11
Francavilla Fontana *Italy* 43 B10
France ■ *Europe* 7 F6
Frances *Australia* 95 F3
Frances → *Canada* 102 A3
Frances L. *Canada* 102 A3
Franceville *Gabon* 84 E2
Franche-Comté □ *France* 19 F12
Francis Case, L. *U.S.A.* 112 D4
Francisco Beltrão *Brazil* 127 B5
Francisco Ignacio Madero
  Coahuila, Mexico 118 B4
Francisco Ignacio Madero
  Durango, Mexico 118 C4
Francisco Ignacio Madero,
  Presa *Mexico* 118 B3
Francistown *Botswana* 89 C4
Francofonte *Italy* 43 E7
François *Canada* 105 C8
François L. *Canada* 102 C3
François Peron △ *Australia* 93 E1
Francs Pk. *U.S.A.* 108 E9
Franeker *Neths.* 17 A5
Frank Hann △ *Australia* 93 F3
Frankado *Djibouti* 81 E5
Frankenberg *Germany* 24 D4
Frankenhöhe △ *Germany* 25 F6
Frankenwald *Germany* 25 E7
Frankenwald △ *Germany* 25 E7
Frankford *Canada* 114 B7
Frankfort *S. Africa* 89 D4
Frankfort *Ind., U.S.A.* 112 E10
Frankfort *Kans., U.S.A.* 112 F5
Frankfort *Ky., U.S.A.* 113 F11
Frankfort *N.Y., U.S.A.* 115 C9
Frankfurt *Brandenburg,
  Germany* 24 C10
Frankfurt *Hessen, Germany* 25 E4
Frankfurt ✈ (FRA) *Germany* 25 E4
Fränkische Alb *Germany* 25 F7
Fränkische Rezat →
  Germany 25 F7
Fränkische Saale →
  Germany 25 E5
Fränkische Schweiz
  Germany 25 F7

Fränkische
  Schweiz-Veldensteiner
  Forst △ *Germany* 25 F7
Frankland → *Australia* 93 G2
Franklin *Ky., U.S.A.* 112 G10
Franklin *La., U.S.A.* 116 G9
Franklin *Mass., U.S.A.* 115 D13
Franklin *N.H., U.S.A.* 115 C13
Franklin *Nebr., U.S.A.* 112 E4
Franklin *Pa., U.S.A.* 114 E5
Franklin *Va., U.S.A.* 113 G15
Franklin *W. Va., U.S.A.* 113 F14
Franklin B. *Canada* 100 C7
Franklin D. Roosevelt L.
  U.S.A. 108 B4
Franklin-Gordon Wild
  Rivers △ *Australia* 95 G4
Franklin I. *Antarctica* 5 D11
Franklin L. *U.S.A.* 108 F6
Franklin Mts. *Canada* 100 C7
Franklin Str. *Canada* 100 B10
Franklinton *U.S.A.* 117 F9
Franklinville *U.S.A.* 114 D6
Frankston *Australia* 95 F4
Fränsta *Sweden* 10 B10
Frantsa Iosifa, Zemlya
  Russia 52 A7
Franz *Canada* 104 C3
Franz Josef Land = Frantsa
  Iosifa, Zemlya *Russia* 52 A7
Franz Josef Strauss ✈
  (MUC) *Germany* 25 G7
Franzburg *Germany* 24 A8
Frascati *Italy* 41 G9
Fraser *U.S.A.* 114 D2
Fraser → *B.C., Canada* 110 A3
Fraser → *Nfld. & L., Canada* 105 A7
Fraser, Mt. *Australia* 93 E2
Fraser I. *Australia* 95 D5
Fraser Lake *Canada* 102 C4
Fraserburg *S. Africa* 88 E3
Fraserburgh *U.K.* 13 D6
Fraserdale *Canada* 104 C3
Frashër *Albania* 44 F4
Frasne *France* 19 F13
Fray Bentos *Uruguay* 126 C4
Fray Jorge △ *Chile* 126 C1
Frechilla *Spain* 36 C6
Frederick *Md., U.S.A.* 113 F15
Frederick *Okla., U.S.A.* 116 D5
Frederick *S. Dak., U.S.A.* 112 C4
Fredericksburg *Pa., U.S.A.* 115 F8
Fredericksburg *Tex., U.S.A.* 116 F5
Fredericksburg *Va., U.S.A.* 113 F15
Fredericktown *Mo., U.S.A.* 112 G8
Fredericktown *Ohio, U.S.A.* 114 F2
Frederico Westphalen
  Brazil 127 B5
Fredericton *Canada* 105 C6
Fredericton Junction
  Canada 105 C6
Frederikshåb = Paamiut
  Greenland 4 C5
Frederikshamn = Hamina
  Finland 32 B4
Frederikshavn *Denmark* 11 G4
Frederikssund *Denmark* 11 J6
Frederiksted *U.S. Virgin Is.* 121 C7
Frederiksværk *Denmark* 11 J6
Fredonia *Ariz., U.S.A.* 109 H7
Fredonia *Kans., U.S.A.* 112 G6
Fredonia *N.Y., U.S.A.* 114 D5
Fredriksberg *Sweden* 10 D8
Fredrikstad *Norway* 9 G14
Free State □ *S. Africa* 88 D4
Freehold *U.S.A.* 115 F10
Freeland *U.S.A.* 115 E9
Freels, C. *Canada* 105 C9
Freeman *Calif., U.S.A.* 111 K9
Freeman *S. Dak., U.S.A.* 112 D5
Freeport *Bahamas* 120 A4
Freeport *Ill., U.S.A.* 112 D9
Freeport *N.Y., U.S.A.* 115 F11
Freeport *Ohio, U.S.A.* 114 F3
Freeport *Pa., U.S.A.* 114 F5
Freeport *Tex., U.S.A.* 116 G7
Freetown *S. Leone* 82 D2
Frégate, L. de la *Canada* 104 B5
Fregenal de la Sierra *Spain* 37 G4
Fregene *Italy* 41 G9
Fréhel, C. *France* 18 D4
Freiberg *Germany* 24 E9
Freibourg = Fribourg *Switz.* 25 J3
Freiburg *Baden-W., Germany* 25 H3
Freiburg *Niedersachsen,
  Germany* 24 B5
Freilassing *Germany* 25 H8
Freire *Chile* 128 D2
Freirina *Chile* 126 B1
Freising *Germany* 25 G7
Freistadt *Austria* 26 C7
Freital *Germany* 24 D9

Fréjus *France* 21 E10
Fremantle *Australia* 93 F2
Fremont *Calif., U.S.A.* 110 H4
Fremont *Mich., U.S.A.* 113 D11
Fremont *Nebr., U.S.A.* 112 E5
Fremont *Ohio, U.S.A.* 113 E12
Fremont → *U.S.A.* 108 G8
French Camp *U.S.A.* 110 H5
French Cays = Plana Cays
  Bahamas 121 B5
French Creek → *U.S.A.* 114 E5
French Guiana ☑ *S. Amer.* 125 C8
French Polynesia ☑ *Pac. Oc.* 97 J13
Frenchman → *N. Amer.* 108 B10
Frenchman Cr. → *U.S.A.* 112 E3
Frenštát pod Radhoštěm
  Czech Rep. 27 B11
Fresco *Ivory C.* 82 D3
Fresco → *Brazil* 125 E8
Freshfield, C. *Antarctica* 5 C10
Fresnay-sur-Sarthe *France* 18 D7
Fresnillo *Mexico* 118 C4
Fresno *U.S.A.* 110 J7
Fresno Alhandiga *Spain* 36 E5
Fresno Res. *U.S.A.* 108 B9
Freudenstadt *Germany* 25 G4
Frévent *France* 19 B9
Frew → *Australia* 94 C2
Frewsburg *U.S.A.* 114 D5
Freycinet △ *Australia* 95 G4
Freycinet Pen. *Australia* 95 G4
Freyming-Merlebach
  France 19 C13
Freyung *Germany* 25 G9
Fria *Guinea* 82 C2
Fria, C. *Namibia* 88 B1
Friant *U.S.A.* 110 J7
Frías *Argentina* 126 B2
Fribourg *Switz.* 25 J3
Fribourg □ *Switz.* 25 J3
Fridafors *Sweden* 11 H8
Friday Harbor *U.S.A.* 110 B3
Friedberg *Bayern, Germany* 25 G6
Friedberg *Hessen, Germany* 25 E4
Friedens *U.S.A.* 114 F6
Friedland *Germany* 24 B9
Friedrichshafen *Germany* 25 H5
Friedrichskoog *Germany* 24 A4
Friedrichstadt *Germany* 24 A5
Friendship *U.S.A.* 114 D6
Friesach *Austria* 26 D7
Friesack *Germany* 24 C8
Friesland □ *Neths.* 17 A5
Friesoythe *Germany* 24 B3
Frigate *Seychelles* 85 b
Friggesund *Sweden* 10 C10
Frillesås *Sweden* 11 G6
Frinnaryd *Sweden* 11 G8
Frio → *U.S.A.* 116 G5
Frio, C. *Brazil* 122 F6
Friol *Spain* 36 B3
Friona *U.S.A.* 116 D3
Fristad *Sweden* 11 G6
Fritch *U.S.A.* 116 D4
Fritsla *Sweden* 11 G6
Fritzlar *Germany* 24 D5
Friuli-Venézia Giulia □ *Italy* 41 B9
Frobisher B. *Canada* 101 C13
Frobisher Bay = Iqaluit
  Canada 101 C13
Frobisher L. *Canada* 103 B7
Frohavet *Norway* 8 E13
Frohnleiten *Austria* 26 D8
Frolovo *Russia* 34 F6
Frombork *Poland* 30 D6
Frome *U.K.* 15 F5
Frome → *U.K.* 15 G5
Frome, L. *Australia* 95 E2
Frómista *Spain* 36 C6
Front Range *U.S.A.* 106 C5
Front Royal *U.S.A.* 113 F14
Fronteira *Portugal* 37 F3
Frontera *Canary Is.* 48 G2
Frontera *Mexico* 119 D6
Fronteras *Mexico* 118 A3
Frontignan *France* 20 E7
Frosinone *Italy* 42 A6
Frostburg *U.S.A.* 113 F14
Frostisen *Norway* 8 B17
Frouard *France* 19 D13
Frövi *Sweden* 10 E9
Frøya *Norway* 8 E13
Frumoasa *Romania* 29 D10
Frunze = Bishkek *Kyrgyzstan* 52 E8
Frunzivka *Ukraine* 29 C14
Fruška Gora *Serbia* 28 E4
Fruška Gora △ *Serbia* 44 A3
Frutal *Brazil* 125 H9
Frutigen *Switz.* 25 J3
Frýdek-Místek *Czech Rep.* 27 B11
Frýdlant *Czech Rep.* 26 A8
Fryeburg *U.S.A.* 115 B14
Fryvaldov = Jeseník
  Czech Rep. 27 A10
Fthiotida □ *Greece* 46 C4
Fu Jiang → *China* 58 C6
Fu Xian = Wafangdian
  China 57 E11

Fu Xian *China* **56** G5
Fu'an *China* **59** D12
Fubian *China* **58** B4
Fucécchio *Italy* **40** E7
Fucheng *China* **56** F9
Fuchou = Fuzhou *China* **59** D12
Fuchū *Japan* **55** G6
Fuchuan *China* **59** E8
Fuchun Jiang → *China* **59** B13
Fúcino, Piana del *Italy* **41** F10
Fuding *China* **59** D13
Fuencaliente *Canary Is.* **48** F2
Fuencaliente *Spain* **37** G6
Fuencaliente, Pta. *Canary Is.* **48** F2
Fuengirola *Spain* **37** J6
Fuenlabrada *Spain* **36** E7
Fuensalida *Spain* **36** E6
Fuente-Álamo *Spain* **39** G3
Fuente-Álamo de Murcia
  Spain **39** H3
Fuente de Cantos *Spain* **37** G4
Fuente del Maestre *Spain* **37** G4
Fuente el Fresno *Spain* **37** F7
Fuente Obejuna *Spain* **37** G5
Fuente Palmera *Spain* **37** H5
Fuentes de Andalucía *Spain* **37** H5
Fuentes de Ebro *Spain* **38** D4
Fuentes de León *Spain* **37** G4
Fuentes de Oñoro *Spain* **36** E4
Fuentesaúco *Spain* **36** D5
Fuerte → *Mexico* **118** B3
Fuerte Olimpo *Paraguay* **126** A4
Fuerteventura *Canary Is.* **48** F6
Fuerteventura ✈ (FUE)
  Canary Is. **48** F6
Fufeng *China* **56** G5
Fuga I. *Phil.* **61** B4
Fugong *China* **58** D2
Fugou *China* **56** G8
Fugu *China* **56** E6
Fuhai *China* **60** B3
Fuḥaymī *Iraq* **73** E10
Fuhlsbüttel, Hamburg ✈
  (HAM) *Germany* **24** B5
Fuji *Japan* **55** G9
Fuji-Hakone-Izu △ *Japan* **55** G9
Fuji-San *Japan* **55** G9
Fuji-Yoshida *Japan* **55** G9
Fujian □ *China* **59** E12
Fujisawa *Japan* **55** G9
Fujiyama, Mt. = Fuji-San
  Japan **55** G9
Fukagawa *Japan* **54** C11
Fukien = Fujian □ *China* **59** E12
Fukuchiyama *Japan* **55** G7
Fukue-Shima *Japan* **55** H4
Fukui *Japan* **55** F8
Fukui □ *Japan* **55** G8
Fukuoka *Japan* **55** H5
Fukuoka □ *Japan* **55** H5
Fukushima *Japan* **54** F10
Fukushima □ *Japan* **54** F10
Fukuyama *Japan* **55** G6
Fulacunda *Guinea-Biss.* **82** C1
Fulaga *Fiji* **91** a
Fulda *Germany* **24** E5
Fulda → *Germany* **24** D5
Fulford Harbour *Canada* **110** B3
Fuliang *China* **59** C11
Fullerton *Calif., U.S.A.* **111** M9
Fullerton *Nebr., U.S.A.* **112** E5
Fulongquan *China* **57** B13
Fülöpszállás *Hungary* **28** D4
Fulton *Mo., U.S.A.* **112** F8
Fulton *N.Y., U.S.A.* **115** C8
Fuluälven → *Sweden* **10** C7
Fulufjället *Sweden* **10** C6
Fumay *France* **19** C11
Fumel *France* **20** D4
Fumin *China* **58** E4
Funabashi *Japan* **55** G10
Funafuti = Fongafale
  Tuvalu **90** B10
Funäsdalen *Sweden* **10** B6
Funchal *Madeira* **48** D3
Funchal ✈ (FNC) *Madeira* **48** D3
Fundación *Colombia* **124** A4
Fundão *Portugal* **36** E3
Fundu Moldovei *Romania* **29** C10
Fundulea *Romania* **29** F11
Fundy, B. of *Canada* **105** D6
Fundy △ *Canada* **105** C6
Funhalouro *Mozam.* **89** C5
Funing *Hebei, China* **57** E10
Funing *Jiangsu, China* **57** H10
Funing *Yunnan, China* **58** F5
Funiu Shan *China* **56** H7
Funsi *Ghana* **82** C4
Funtua *Nigeria* **83** C6
Fuping *Hebei, China* **56** E8
Fuping *Shaanxi, China* **56** G5
Fuqing *China* **59** E12
Fuquan *China* **58** D6
Furano *Japan* **54** C11
Furāt, Nahr al → *Asia* **70** D5
Fürg *Iran* **71** D7

Furmanov *Russia* **34** B5
Furmanovo *Kazakhstan* **34** F9
Furnás *Spain* **48** B8
Furnas, Reprêsa de *Brazil* **127** A6
Furneaux Group *Australia* **95** G4
Furqlus *Syria* **74** A6
Fürstenau *Germany* **24** C3
Fürstenberg *Germany* **24** B9
Fürstenfeld *Austria* **26** D9
Fürstenfeldbruck *Germany* **25** G7
Fürstenwalde *Germany* **24** C10
Fürth *Germany* **25** F6
Fürth im Wald *Germany* **25** F8
Furtwangen *Germany* **25** G4
Furudal *Sweden* **10** C9
Furukawa *Japan* **54** E10
Furulund *Sweden* **11** J7
Fury and Hecla Str. *Canada*
  101 C11
Fusagasuga *Colombia* **124** C4
Fuscaldo *Italy* **43** C9
Fushan *Shandong, China* **57** F11
Fushan *Shanxi, China* **56** G6
Fushë Arrëz *Albania* **44** D4
Fushë Krujë *Albania* **44** E3
Fushun *Liaoning, China* **57** D12
Fushun *Sichuan, China* **58** C5
Fusong *China* **57** C14
Füssen *Germany* **25** H6
Fustic *Barbados* **121** g
Fusui *China* **58** F6
Futog *Serbia* **28** E4
Fuwa *Egypt* **80** H7
Fuxian Hu *China* **58** E4
Fuxin *China* **57** C11
Fuyang *Anhui, China* **56** H8
Fuyang *Zhejiang, China* **59** B12
Fuyang He → *China* **56** E9
Fuying Dao *China* **59** D13
Fuyu *China* **57** B13
Fuyuan *China* **58** E5
Füzesgyarmat *Hungary* **28** C6
Fuzhou *China* **59** D12
Fylde *U.K.* **14** D5
Fyn *Denmark* **11** J4
Fyne, L. *U.K.* **13** F3
Fynshav *Denmark* **11** K3

G

Ga *Ghana* **82** D4
Gaanda *Nigeria* **83** C7
Gabarin *Nigeria* **83** C7
Gabas → *France* **20** E3
Gabela *Angola* **84** G2
Gabès *Tunisia* **79** B8
Gabès, G. de *Tunisia* **79** B8
Gabgaba, W. → *Egypt* **80** C3
Gabin *Poland* **31** F6
Gabon ■ *Africa* **84** E2
Gaborone *Botswana* **88** C4
Gabriels *U.S.A.* **115** B10
Gäbrīk *Iran* **71** E8
Gabrovo *Bulgaria* **45** D9
Gacé *France* **18** D7
Gäch Sär *Iran* **71** B6
Gachsārān *Iran* **71** D6
Gacko *Bos.-H.* **44** C2
Gadag *India* **66** M9
Gadamai *Sudan* **81** D4
Gadap *Pakistan* **68** G2
Gadarwara *India* **69** H8
Gadebusch *Germany* **24** B7
Gadein *Sudan* **81** F2
Gadhada *India* **68** J4
Gádor, Sierra de *Spain* **37** J8
Gadra *Pakistan* **68** G4
Gadsden *U.S.A.* **117** D11
Gadwal *India* **66** L10
Gadyach = Hadyach *Ukraine* **33** G8
Găeşti *Romania* **29** F10
Gaeta *Italy* **42** A6
Gaeta, G. di *Italy* **42** A6
Gaffney *U.S.A.* **117** D14
Gafsa *Tunisia* **78** B7
Gagarawa *Nigeria* **83** C6
Gagaria *India* **68** G4
Gagarin *Russia* **32** E8
Găgăuzia □ *Moldova* **29** D13
Gaggenau *Germany* **25** G4
Gaghamni *Sudan* **81** E2
Gagino *Russia* **34** C7
Gagliano del Capo *Italy* **43** C11
Gagnef *Sweden* **10** D9
Gagnoa *Ivory C.* **82** D3
Gagnon *Canada* **105** B6
Gagnon, L. *Canada* **103** A6
Gagra *Georgia* **35** J5
Gahini *Rwanda* **86** C3
Gahmar *India* **69** G10
Gai Xian = Gaizhou *China* **57** D12
Gaidouronisi *Greece* **49** E7
Gail *U.S.A.* **116** E4
Gail → *Austria* **26** E6
Gaillac *France* **20** E5
Gaillimh = Galway *Ireland* **12** C2
Gaillon *France* **18** C8

Gaines *U.S.A.* **114** E7
Gainesville *Fla., U.S.A.* **117** G13
Gainesville *Ga., U.S.A.* **117** D13
Gainesville *Mo., U.S.A.* **113** G8
Gainesville *Tex., U.S.A.* **116** E6
Gainsborough *U.K.* **14** D7
Gairdner, L. *Australia* **95** E2
Gairloch *U.K.* **13** D3
Gairloch, L. *U.K.* **13** D3
Gaizhou *China* **57** D12
Gaj *Croatia* **28** E2
Gaj → *Pakistan* **68** F2
Gakuch *Pakistan* **69** A5
Galâla, Gebel el *Egypt* **80** J8
Galán, Cerro *Argentina* **126** B2
Galana → *Kenya* **86** C5
Galanta *Slovak Rep.* **27** C10
Galapagar *Spain* **36** E7
Galápagos = Colón, Arch.
  de *Ecuador* **122** D1
Galapagos Fracture Zone
  Pac. Oc. **97** G17
Galapagos Rise *Pac. Oc.* **97** J18
Galashiels *U.K.* **13** F6
Galatas *Greece* **46** D5
Galați *Romania* **29** E13
Galați □ *Romania* **29** E12
Galatia *Turkey* **72** C5
Galatina *Italy* **43** B11
Galátone *Italy* **43** B11
Galax *U.S.A.* **113** G13
Galaxídi *Greece* **46** C4
Galcaio *Somali Rep.* **75** F4
Galdhøpiggen *Norway* **8** F13
Galeana *Chihuahua, Mexico* **118** A3
Galeana *Nuevo León, Mexico* **118** A3
Galegu *Sudan* **81** E4
Galela *Indonesia* **63** D7
Galena *U.S.A.* **106** a
Galeota Pt. *Trin. & Tob.* **125** K16
Galera *Spain* **39** H2
Galera Pt. *Trin. & Tob.* **121** D7
Galesburg *U.S.A.* **112** E8
Galestan △ *Iran* **71** B8
Galeton *U.S.A.* **114** E7
Galga *Ethiopia* **81** F4
Gali *Georgia* **35** J5
Galicea Mare *Romania* **29** F8
Galich *Russia* **34** A6
Galiche *Bulgaria* **44** C7
Galicia □ *Spain* **36** C3
Galičica △ *Macedonia* **44** E4
Galilee = Hagalil *Israel* **74** C4
Galilee, L. *Australia* **94** C4
Galilee, Sea of = Yam
  Kinneret *Israel* **74** C4
Galim *Cameroon* **83** D7
Galina Pt. *Jamaica* **120** a
Galinoporni *Cyprus* **49** D13
Galion *U.S.A.* **114** E2
Galiuro Mts. *U.S.A.* **109** K8
Galiwinku *Australia* **94** A2
Gallabat *Sudan* **81** E4
Gallan Hd. *U.K.* **13** C1
Gallarate *Italy* **40** C5
Gallatin *U.S.A.* **117** C11
Galle *Sri Lanka* **66** R12
Gállego → *Spain* **38** D4
Gallegos → *Argentina* **128** G3
Galletti → *Ethiopia* **81** F5
Galley Hd. *Ireland* **12** E3
Galliate *Italy* **40** C5
Gallinas, Pta. *Colombia* **124** A4
Gallipoli = Gelibolu *Turkey* **45** F10
Gallípoli *Italy* **43** B10
Gallipolis *U.S.A.* **113** F12
Gällivare *Sweden* **8** C19
Gallneukirchen *Austria* **26** C7
Gällö *Sweden* **10** B9
Gallo, C. *Italy* **42** D6
Gallocanta, L. de *Spain* **38** E3
Galloo I. *U.S.A.* **115** C8
Galloway *U.K.* **13** F4
Galloway, Mull of *U.K.* **13** G4
Galloway △ *U.K.* **13** F4
Gallup *U.S.A.* **109** J9
Gallur *Spain* **38** D3
Galoya *Sri Lanka* **66** Q12
Galt *U.S.A.* **110** G5
Galten *Denmark* **11** H3
Galtür *Austria* **26** E3
Galty Mts. *Ireland* **12** D3
Galtymore *Ireland* **12** D3
Galva *U.S.A.* **112** E8
Galve de Sorbe *Spain* **38** D1
Gálvez *Argentina* **126** C3
Galway *Ireland* **12** C2
Galway □ *Ireland* **12** C2
Galway B. *Ireland* **12** C2
Gam → *Vietnam* **64** B5
Gamagōri *Japan* **55** G8
Gamari, L. *Ethiopia* **81** E5
Gamawa *Nigeria* **83** C7
Gamay *Phil.* **61** E6
Gambaga *Ghana* **83** C4

Gambat *Pakistan* **68** F3
Gambela *Ethiopia* **81** F3
Gambela △ *Ethiopia* **81** F3
Gambela Hizboch □ *Ethiopia* **81** F3
Gambhir → *India* **68** F6
Gambia ■ *W. Afr.* **82** C1
Gambia → *W. Afr.* **82** C1
Gambier *U.S.A.* **114** F2
Gambier, C. *Australia* **92** B5
Gambier, Îs.
  French Polynesia **97** K14
Gambier Is. *Australia* **95** F2
Gambo *Canada* **105** C9
Gamboli *Pakistan* **68** E3
Gamboma *Congo* **84** E3
Gamka → *S. Africa* **88** E3
Gamkab → *Namibia* **88** D2
Gamla Uppsala *Sweden* **10** E11
Gamlakarleby = Kokkola
  Finland **8** E20
Gamleby *Sweden* **11** G10
Gammon → *Canada* **103** C9
Gammon Ranges △ *Australia* **95** E2
Gamo-Gofa *Ethiopia* **81** F4
Gamou *Niger* **83** C6
Gamtoos → *S. Africa* **88** E4
Gan *France* **20** E3
Gan Goriama, Mts.
  Cameroon **83** D7
Gan Jiang → *China* **59** C11
Ganado *U.S.A.* **109** J9
Gananita *Sudan* **80** D3
Gancheng *China* **64** C7
Gand = Gent *Belgium* **17** C3
Ganda *Angola* **85** G2
Gandajika
  Dem. Rep. of the Congo **84** F4
Gandak → *India* **69** G11
Gandava *Pakistan* **68** E2
Gander *Canada* **105** C9
Gander L. *Canada* **105** C9
Ganderkesee *Germany* **24** B4
Ganderowe Falls *Zimbabwe* **87** F2
Gandesa *Spain* **38** D5
Gandhi Sagar *India* **68** G6
Gandhinagar *India* **68** H5
Gandi *Nigeria* **83** C6
Gandía *Spain* **39** G4
Gandino *Italy* **40** C6
Gando, Pta. *Canary Is.* **48** G4
Gandole *Nigeria* **83** D7
Gâneb *Mauritania* **82** B2
Ganedidalem = Gani
  Indonesia **63** E7
Ganetti *Sudan* **80** D3
Ganga → *India* **69** H14
Ganga Sagar *India* **69** J13
Gangan → *India* **69** E8
Ganganagar *India* **68** E5
Gangapur *India* **68** F7
Gangara *Niger* **83** C6
Gangaw *Burma* **67** H19
Gangdisê Shan *China* **69** D9
Ganges = Ganga → *India* **69** H14
Ganges *Canada* **102** D4
Ganges *France* **20** E7
Ganges, Mouths of the *India* **69** J14
Ganggyeong *S. Korea* **57** F14
Gânghester *Sweden* **11** G7
Ganghwa *S. Korea* **57** F14
Gangi *Italy* **43** E7
Gângiova *Romania* **29** G8
Gangneung *S. Korea* **57** F15
Gangoh *India* **68** E7
Gangotri *India* **69** D8
Gangotri △ *India* **69** D8
Gangseong *S. Korea* **57** E15
Gangtok *India* **67** F16
Gangu *China* **56** G3
Gangyao *China* **57** B14
Gani *Indonesia* **63** E7
Ganj *India* **69** F8
Ganluc *China* **58** C4
Gannat *France* **19** F10
Gannett Peak *U.S.A.* **108** E9
Ganquan *China* **56** F5
Gänserdorf *Austria* **27** C9
Ganshui *China* **58** C6
Gansu □ *China* **56** G3
Ganta *Liberia* **82** D3
Gantheaume, C. *Australia* **95** F2
Gantheaume B. *Australia* **93** E1
Gantsevichi = Hantsavichy
  Belarus **23** B14
Ganye *Nigeria* **83** D7
Ganyem = Genyem
  Indonesia **63** E10
Ganyu *China* **57** G10
Ganyushkino *Kazakhstan* **35** G9
Ganzhou *China* **59** E10
Gao *Mali* **83** B4
Gao Xian *China* **58** C5
Gao'an *China* **59** C10

Gaochun *China* **59** B12
Gaohe *China* **59** F9
Gaohebu *China* **59** B11
Gaokeng *China* **59** D9
Gaolan Dao *China* **59** G9
Gaoligong Shan *China* **58** E2
Gaomi *China* **57** F10
Gaoping *China* **56** G7
Gaotang *China* **56** F9
Gaoua *Burkina Faso* **82** C4
Gaoual *Guinea* **82** C2
Gaoxiong = Kaohsiung
  Taiwan **59** F13
Gaoyang *China* **56** E8
Gaoyou *China* **59** A12
Gaoyou Hu *China* **57** H10
Gaoyuan *China* **57** F9
Gaozhou *China* **59** G8
Gap *France* **21** D10
Gapan *Phil.* **61** D4
Gapat → *India* **69** G10
Gapuwiyak *Australia* **94** A2
Gar *China* **60** C2
Gara, L. *Ireland* **12** C3
Garabogazköl Aylagy
  Turkmenistan **52** E6
Garachico *Canary Is.* **48** F3
Garachiné *Panama* **120** E4
Garafia *Canary Is.* **48** F2
Garagum *Turkmenistan* **71** B8
Garah *Australia* **95** D4
Garajonay *Canary Is.* **48** F2
Garamba △
  Dem. Rep. of the Congo **86** B2
Garango *Burkina Faso* **83** C4
Garanhuns *Brazil* **125** E11
Garautha *India* **69** G8
Garawe *Liberia* **82** E3
Garba Tula *Kenya* **86** B4
Garberville *U.S.A.* **108** F2
Garbiyang *India* **69** D9
Garbsen *Germany* **24** C5
Gard □ *France* **21** D8
Gard → *France* **21** E8
Garda, L. di *Italy* **40** C7
Gardanne *France* **21** E9
Gårdby *Sweden* **11** H10
Garde L. *Canada* **103** A7
Gardelegen *Germany* **24** C7
Garden City *Kans., U.S.A.* **117** E14
Garden City *Tex., U.S.A.* **116** F4
Garden Grove *U.S.A.* **111** M9
Gardēz *Afghan.* **68** C3
Gardiki *Greece* **46** C3
Gardiner *Maine, U.S.A.* **113** C19
Gardiner *Mont., U.S.A.* **108** D8
Gardiners I. *U.S.A.* **115** E12
Gardner *U.S.A.* **115** D13
Gardner Canal *Canada* **102** C3
Gardnerville *U.S.A.* **110** G7
Gardno, Jezioro *Poland* **30** D4
Gardo = Qardho *Somali Rep.* **75** F4
Gardone Val Trómpia *Italy* **40** C7
Gárdony *Hungary* **28** C3
Garešnica *Croatia* **41** C13
Garéssio *Italy* **40** D5
Garey *U.S.A.* **111** L6
Garfield *U.S.A.* **108** C5
Garforth *U.K.* **14** D6
Gargaliani *Greece* **46** D3
Gargan, Mt. *France* **20** C5
Gargano △ *Italy* **41** G12
Gargantua, C. *Canada* **113** B11
Gargett *Australia* **94** K6
Gargouna *Mali* **83** B5
Gargždai *Lithuania* **30** C8
Garibaldi △ *Canada* **102** D4
Gariep, L. *S. Africa* **88** E3
Garies *S. Africa* **88** E2
Garigliano → *Italy* **42** A6
Garissa *Kenya* **86** C4
Garkida *Nigeria* **83** C7
Garko *Nigeria* **83** C6
Garland *Tex., U.S.A.* **116** E6
Garland *Utah, U.S.A.* **108** F7
Garlasco *Italy* **40** C5
Garliava *Lithuania* **30** D10
Garlin *France* **20** E3
Garm *Tajikistan* **52** F8
Garmāb *Iran* **71** C8
Garmisch-Partenkirchen
  Germany **25** H7
Garmsär *Iran* **71** C7
Garner *U.S.A.* **112** D7
Garnett *U.S.A.* **112** F6
Garo Hills *India* **69** G14
Garoe *Somali Rep.* **75** F4
Garonne → *France* **20** C3
Garonne, Canal Latéral à
  la *France* **20** D4
Garoowe = Garoe *Somali Rep.* **75** F4
Garot *India* **68** G6
Garoua = Garoua *Cameroon* **83** D7
Garoua *Cameroon* **83** D7
Garpenberg *Sweden* **10** D10
Garphyttan *Sweden* **10** E8

Garrauli *India* **69** G8
Garrel *Germany* **24** C4
Garrigues *France* **20** E7
Garrison *Mont., U.S.A.* **108** C7
Garrison *N. Dak., U.S.A.* **112** B3
Garrison Res. =
  Sakakawea, L. *U.S.A.* **112** B3
Garron Pt. *U.K.* **12** A6
Garrovillas *Spain* **37** F4
Garrucha *Spain* **39** H3
Garry → *U.K.* **13** E5
Garry, L. *Canada* **100** C9
Garrygala *Turkmenistan* **71** B8
Garsen *Kenya* **86** C5
Gärsnäs *Sweden* **11** J8
Garson L. *Canada* **103** B6
Garstang *U.K.* **14** D5
Gartempe → *France* **20** B4
Gartz *Germany* **24** B10
Garu *Ghana* **83** C4
Garu *India* **69** H11
Garub *Namibia* **88** D2
Garut *Indonesia* **63** G12
Garvão *Portugal* **37** H2
Garvie Mts. *N.Z.* **91** F2
Garwa = Garoua *Cameroon* **83** D7
Garwa *India* **69** G10
Garwolin *Poland* **31** G8
Gary *U.S.A.* **112** E10
Garz *Germany* **24** A9
Garzê *China* **58** B3
Garzón *Colombia* **124** C3
Gas-San *Japan* **54** E10
Gasan Kuli = Esenguly
  Turkmenistan **52** F6
Gascogne *France* **20** E4
Gascogne, G. de *Europe* **20** E2
Gascony = Gascogne *France* **20** E4
Gascoyne → *Australia* **93** D1
Gascoyne Junction *Australia* **93** E2
Gascueña *Spain* **38** E2
Gash, Wadi → *Ethiopia* **81** D4
Gash Setit △ *Eritrea* **81** D4
Gashagar *Nigeria* **83** C7
Gashaka *Nigeria* **83** D7
Gashaka-Gumti △ *Nigeria* **83** D7
Gasherbrum *Pakistan* **69** B7
Gashua *Nigeria* **83** C7
Gasparillo *Trin. & Tob.* **125** K15
Gaspé *Canada* **105** C7
Gaspé, C. *Canada* **105** C7
Gaspé Pen. = Gaspésie,
  Pén. de la *Canada* **105** C6
Gaspésie, Pén. de la *Canada* **105** C6
Gaspésie △ *Canada* **105** C6
Gassan *Burkina Faso* **82** C4
Gassol *Nigeria* **83** D7
Gasteiz = Vitoria-Gasteiz
  Spain **38** C2
Gastonia *U.S.A.* **117** D14
Gastouni *Greece* **46** D3
Gastouri *Greece* **46** B1
Gastre *Argentina* **128** E3
Gästrikland *Sweden* **10** D10
Gata, C. *Cyprus* **49** E12
Gata, C. de *Spain* **39** J2
Gata, Sierra de *Spain* **36** E4
Gataga → *Canada* **102** B3
Gătaia *Romania* **28** E6
Gatchina *Russia* **32** C6
Gatehouse of Fleet *U.K.* **13** G4
Gates *U.S.A.* **114** C7
Gateshead *U.K.* **14** C6
Gatesville *U.S.A.* **116** F6
Gateway △ *U.S.A.* **115** F11
Gaths *Zimbabwe* **87** G3
Gatico *Chile* **126** A1
Gâtinais *France* **19** D9
Gâtine, Hauteurs de *France* **20** B3
Gatineau *Canada* **115** A9
Gatineau → *Canada* **104** C4
Gatineau △ *Canada* **104** C4
Gattaran *Phil.* **61** B4
Gattinara *Italy* **40** C5
Gatton *Australia* **95** D5
Gatun, L. *Panama* **120** E4
Gatwick, London ✈ (LGW)
  U.K. **15** F7
Gatyana *S. Africa* **89** E4
Gau *Fiji* **91** a
Gaucín *Spain* **37** J5
Gauer L. *Canada* **103** B9
Gauhati = Guwahati *India* **67** F17
Gauja → *Latvia* **30** A11
Gaujas △ *Latvia* **9** H21
Gaula → *Norway* **8** E14
Gauri Phanta *India* **69** E9
Gaustatoppen *Norway* **9** G13
Gauteng □ *S. Africa* **89** D4
Gäv Koshī *Iran* **71** D8
Gävakān *Iran* **71** D7
Gavallai △ *Liberia* **82** D3
Gavarnie *France* **20** F3
Gavāter *Iran* **71** E9
Gävbandī *Iran* **71** E7
Gavdopoula *Greece* **49** E6
Gavdos *Greece* **49** E6

Gavi *Italy* **40** D5
Gavião *Portugal* **37** F3
Gaviota *U.S.A.* **111** L6
Gãvkhũnĩ, Bãţlãq-e *Iran* **71** C7
Gävle *Sweden* **10** D11
Gävleborgs län □ *Sweden* **10** C10
Gävlebukten *Sweden* **10** D11
Gavorrano *Italy* **40** F7
Gavray *France* **18** D5
Gavrilov Yam *Russia* **32** D10
Gavrio *Greece* **46** D6
Gawachab *Namibia* **88** D2
Gawilgarh Hills *India* **66** J10
Gawler *Australia* **95** E2
Gawler Ranges *Australia* **95** E2
Gawu *Nigeria* **83** D6
Gaxun Nur *China* **60** B5
Gaya *India* **69** G11
Gaya *Niger* **83** C5
Gaya *Nigeria* **83** C6
Gayéri *Burkina Faso* **83** C5
Gaylord *U.S.A.* **113** C11
Gayndah *Australia* **95** D5
Gaysin = Haysyn
  Ukraine **29** B14
Gayvoron = Hayvoron
  Ukraine **29** B14
Gaza *Gaza Strip* **74** D3
Gaza □ *Mozam.* **89** C5
Gaza Strip ■ *Asia* **74** D3
Gazanjyk = Bereket
  Turkmenistan **71** B7
Gazaoua *Niger* **83** C6
Gãzbor *Iran* **71** D8
Gazi *Dem. Rep. of the Congo* **86** B1
Gaziantep *Turkey* **72** D7
Gaziantep □ *Turkey* **72** D7
Gazimağosa = Famagusta
  Cyprus **49** D12
Gazipaşa *Turkey* **72** D5
Gbarnga *Liberia* **82** D3
Gbekebo *Nigeria* **83** D5
Gboko *Nigeria* **83** D6
Gbongan *Nigeria* **83** D5
Gcoverega *Botswana* **88** B3
Gcuwa *S. Africa* **89** E4
Gdańsk *Poland* **30** D5
Gdańsk ✈ (GDN) *Poland* **30** D5
Gdańska, Zatoka *Poland* **30** D6
Gdov *Russia* **32** C4
Gdynia *Poland* **30** D5
Geba → *Guinea-Biss.* **82** C1
Gebe *Indonesia* **63** D7
Gebeciler *Turkey* **47** C12
Gebeit Mine *Sudan* **80** C4
Gebel Abyad *Sudan* **80** D2
Gebel Iweibid *Egypt* **80** H8
Gebze *Turkey* **45** F13
Gecha *Ethiopia* **81** F4
Gedaref *Sudan* **81** E4
Gedaref □ *Sudan* **81** E4
Gediz *Turkey* **47** B11
Gediz → *Turkey* **47** C8
Gedo *Ethiopia* **81** F4
Gèdre *France* **20** F4
Gedser *Denmark* **11** K5
Gedung, Pulau *Malaysia* **65** c
Geegully Cr. → *Australia* **92** C3
Geel *Belgium* **17** C4
Geelong *Australia* **95** F3
Geelvink B. =
  Cenderwasih, Teluk
  Indonesia **63** E9
Geelvink Chan. *Australia* **93** E1
Geesthacht *Germany* **24** B6
Geidam *Nigeria* **83** C7
Geikie → *Canada* **103** B8
Geikie Gorge △ *Australia* **92** C4
Geili *Sudan* **81** D3
Geisingen *Germany* **25** H4
Geislingen *Germany* **25** G5
Geistown *U.S.A.* **114** F6
Geita *Tanzania* **86** C3
Gejiu *China* **58** F4
Gel → *Sudan* **81** F2
Gel, Meydān-i *Iran* **71** D7
Gel River *Sudan* **81** F2
Gela *Italy* **43** E7
Gela, G. di *Italy* **43** F7
Gelahun *Liberia* **82** D2
Gelang Patah *Malaysia* **65** d
Gelderland □ *Neths.* **17** B6
Geldern *Germany* **24** D2
Geldrop *Neths.* **17** C5
Geleen *Neths.* **17** D5
Gelehun *S. Leone* **82** D2
Gelembe *Turkey* **47** B9
Gelemso *Ethiopia* **81** F5
Gelendost *Turkey* **72** C4
Gelendzhik *Russia* **33** K10
Gelib *Somali Rep.* **75** G3
Gelibolu *Turkey* **45** F10
Gelibolu Yarımadası *Turkey* **45** F10
Gelidonya Burnu *Turkey* **72** D4
Gelnhausen *Germany* **25** E5
Gelnica *Slovak Rep.* **27** C13
Gelsenkirchen *Germany* **24** D3

Gelting *Germany* **24** A5
Gelugur *Malaysia* **65** c
Gemas *Malaysia* **65** L4
Gembloux *Belgium* **17** D4
Gembu *Nigeria* **83** D7
Gemena
  Dem. Rep. of the Congo **84** D3
Gemerek *Turkey* **72** C7
Gemla *Sweden* **11** H8
Gemlik *Turkey* **45** F13
Gemlik Körfezi *Turkey* **45** F12
Gemona del Friuli *Italy* **41** B10
Gemsa *Egypt* **80** B3
Gemsbok △ *Botswana* **88** D3
Gemünden *Germany* **25** E5
Genadi *Greece* **49** C9
Genale → *Ethiopia* **81** F4
Genç *Turkey* **73** C9
Gençay *France* **20** B4
Geneina, Gebel *Egypt* **80** B3
General Acha *Argentina* **126** D3
General Alvear *B. Aires,*
  Argentina **126** D4
General Alvear *Mendoza,*
  Argentina **126** D2
General Artigas *Paraguay* **126** B4
General Belgrano *Argentina* **126** D4
General Bernardo
  O'Higgins *Antarctica* **5** C18
General Cabrera *Argentina* **126** C3
General Cepeda *Mexico* **118** B4
General Guido *Argentina* **126** D4
General Juan Madariaga
  Argentina **126** D4
General La Madrid
  Argentina **126** D3
General MacArthur *Phil.* **61** F6
General Martin Miguel de
  Güemes *Argentina* **126** A3
General Paz *Argentina* **126** B4
General Pico *Argentina* **126** D3
General Pinedo *Argentina* **126** B3
General Pinto *Argentina* **126** C3
General Roca *Argentina* **128** D3
General Santos *Phil.* **61** H6
General Toshevo *Bulgaria* **45** C12
General Treviño *Mexico* **119** B5
General Trías *Mexico* **118** B3
General Viamonte
  Argentina **126** D3
General Villegas *Argentina* **126** D3
Genesee *Idaho, U.S.A.* **108** C5
Genesee *Pa., U.S.A.* **114** E7
Genesee → *U.S.A.* **114** C7
Geneseo *Ill., U.S.A.* **112** E8
Geneseo *N.Y., U.S.A.* **114** D7
Geneva = Genève *Switz.* **25** J2
Geneva *Ala., U.S.A.* **117** F12
Geneva *N.Y., U.S.A.* **114** D8
Geneva *Nebr., U.S.A.* **112** E5
Geneva *Ohio, U.S.A.* **114** E4
Geneva, L. = Léman, L.
  Europe **19** F13
Genève *Switz.* **25** J2
Gengenbach *Germany* **25** G4
Gengma *China* **58** F2
Genichesk = Henichesk
  Ukraine **33** J8
Genil → *Spain* **37** H5
Genisea *Greece* **45** E8
Genk *Belgium* **17** D5
Genlis *France* **19** E12
Gennargentu, Mti. del *Italy* **42** B2
Gennes *France* **18** E6
Genoa = Génova *Italy* **40** D5
Genoa *Australia* **95** F4
Genoa *N.Y., U.S.A.* **115** D8
Genoa *Nebr., U.S.A.* **112** E5
Genoa *Nev., U.S.A.* **110** F7
Génova *Italy* **40** D5
Génova ✈ (GOA) *Italy* **40** D5
Génova, G. di *Italy* **40** E6
Genriyetty, Ostrov *Russia* **53** B16
Gent *Belgium* **17** C3
Genteng *Bali, Indonesia* **63** J17
Genteng *Jawa Barat,*
  Indonesia **63** G12
Genthin *Germany* **24** C8
Genyem *Indonesia* **63** E10
Genzano di Lucánia *Italy* **43** B9
Genzano di Roma *Italy* **41** G9
Geoagiu *Romania* **29** E8
Geochang *S. Korea* **57** G14
Geographe B. *Australia* **93** F2
Geographe Chan. *Australia* **93** D1
Geokchay = Göyçay
  Azerbaijan **35** K8
Georga, Zemlya *Russia* **52** A5
George *S. Africa* **88** E3
George → *Canada* **105** A6
George, L. *N.S.W., Australia* **95** F4
George, L. *S. Austral.,*
  Australia **95** F3
George, L. *W. Austral.,*
  Australia **92** D3
George, L. *Uganda* **86** B3
George, L. *Fla., U.S.A.* **117** G14

George, L. *N.Y., U.S.A.* **115** C11
George Gill Ra. *Australia* **92** D5
George Pt. *Australia* **94** J6
George River =
  Kangiqsualujjuaq *Canada*
  101 D13
George Sound *N.Z.* **91** F1
George Town *Australia* **95** G4
George Town *Bahamas* **120** B4
George Town *Cayman Is.* **120** C3
George Town *Malaysia* **65** c
George V Land *Antarctica* **5** C10
George VI Sound *Antarctica* **5** D17
George West *U.S.A.* **116** G5
Georgetown =
  Janjanbureh *Gambia* **82** C2
Georgetown *Australia* **94** B3
Georgetown *Ont., Canada* **114** C5
Georgetown *P.E.I., Canada* **105** C7
Georgetown *Guyana* **124** B7
Georgetown *Calif., U.S.A.* **110** G6
Georgetown *Colo., U.S.A.* **108** G11
Georgetown *Ky., U.S.A.* **113** F11
Georgetown *N.Y., U.S.A.* **115** D9
Georgetown *Ohio, U.S.A.* **113** F12
Georgetown *S.C., U.S.A.* **117** E15
Georgetown *Tex., U.S.A.* **116** F6
Georgia □ *U.S.A.* **117** E13
Georgia ■ *Asia* **35** J6
Georgia, Str. of *N. Amer.* **110** A3
Georgia Basin *S. Ocean* **5** B1
Georgian B. *Canada* **114** A4
Georgian Bay Islands △
  Canada **114** B5
Georgina → *Australia* **94** C2
Georgina I. *Canada* **114** B5
Georgioupoli *Greece* **49** D6
Georgiyevsk *Russia* **35** H6
Georgsmarienhütte *Germany* **24** C4
Gera *Germany* **24** E8
Geraardsbergen *Belgium* **17** D3
Geraki *Greece* **46** D4
Geral, Serra *Brazil* **127** B6
Geral de Goiás, Serra *Brazil* **125** F9
Geraldine *U.S.A.* **108** C8
Geraldton *Australia* **93** E1
Geraldton *Canada* **104** C2
Gérardmer *France* **19** D13
Gercüş *Turkey* **73** D9
Gerede *Turkey* **72** B5
Gerês, Sierra do *Portugal* **36** D3
Gereshk *Afghan.* **66** D4
Geretsried *Germany* **25** H7
Gérgal *Spain* **39** H2
Gerik *Malaysia* **65** K3
Gering *U.S.A.* **112** E2
Gerlach *U.S.A.* **108** F4
Gerlachovský štit
  Slovak Rep. **27** B13
German Planina *Macedonia* **44** D6
Germansen Landing *Canada*
  102 B4
Germantown *U.S.A.* **117** D10
Germany ■ *Europe* **24** E6
Germencik *Turkey* **47** D9
Germering *Germany* **25** G7
Germersheim *Germany* **25** F4
Germì *Iran* **73** C13
Germiston *S. Africa* **89** D4
Gernika-Lumo *Spain* **38** B2
Gernsheim *Germany* **25** F4
Gero *Japan* **55** G8
Gerokgak *Indonesia* **63** J17
Gerolzhofen *Germany* **25** F6
Gerona = Girona *Spain* **38** D7
Geropotamos → *Greece* **49** D6
Gerrard *Canada* **102** C5
Gers □ *France* **20** E4
Gers → *France* **20** D4
Gersfeld *Germany* **24** E5
Gersthofen *Germany* **25** G6
Gertak Sanggul *Malaysia* **65** c
Gertak Sanggul, Tanjung
  Malaysia **65** c
Gerung *Indonesia* **63** K19
Gerzat *France* **20** C7
Gerze *Turkey* **72** B6
Geseke *Germany* **24** D4
Geser *Indonesia* **63** E8
Gesso → *Italy* **40** D4
Gestro, Wabi → *Ethiopia* **81** G5
Getafe *Spain* **36** F7
Getinge *Sweden* **11** H6
Gettysburg *Pa., U.S.A.* **113** F15
Gettysburg *S. Dak., U.S.A.* **112** C4
Getxo *Spain* **38** B2
Getz Ice Shelf *Antarctica* **5** D14
Gevaş *Turkey* **73** C10
Gévaudan *France* **20** D7
Gevgelija *Macedonia* **44** E6
Gévora → *Spain* **37** G4
Gex *France* **19** F13
Geyikli *Turkey* **47** B8
Geyser *U.S.A.* **108** C8
Geyserville *U.S.A.* **110** G4
Geyve *Turkey* **72** B4

Ghâbat el Arab = Wang
  Kai *Sudan* **81** F2
Ghabeish *Sudan* **81** E2
Ghadāmis *Libya* **79** B8
Ghaggar → *India* **68** E6
Ghaghara → *India* **69** G11
Ghaghat → *Bangla.* **69** G13
Ghagra *India* **69** H11
Ghagra → *India* **69** F9
Ghalla, Wadi el → *Sudan* **81** E2
Ghallamane *Mauritania* **78** D4
Ghana ■ *W. Afr.* **83** D4
Ghansor *India* **69** H9
Ghanzi *Botswana* **88** C3
Gharb Bahr el Ghazâl □
  Sudan **81** F2
Gharb el Istiwa'iya □ *Sudan* **81** G3
Gharb Kordofân □ *Sudan* **81** E2
Gharbîya, Es Sahrâ el *Egypt* **80** B2
Ghardaïa *Algeria* **78** B6
Ghârib, G. *Egypt* **80** B3
Gharig *Sudan* **81** E2
Gharyān *Libya* **79** B8
Ghat *Libya* **79** D8
Ghatal *India* **69** H12
Ghatampur *India* **69** F9
Ghats, Eastern *India* **66** N11
Ghats, Western *India* **66** N9
Ghatsila *India* **69** H12
Ghaţţī *Si. Arabia* **70** D3
Ghawdex = Gozo *Malta* **49** C1
Ghazal, Bahr el → *Chad* **79** F9
Ghazâl, Bahr el → *Sudan* **81** F3
Ghaziabad *India* **68** E7
Ghazipur *India* **69** G10
Ghaznī *Afghan.* **68** C3
Ghaznī □ *Afghan.* **66** C6
Ghedi *Italy* **40** C7
Ghelari *Romania* **28** E7
Ghent = Gent *Belgium* **17** C3
Gheorghe Gheorghiu-
  Dej = Oneşti *Romania* **29** D11
Gheorgheni *Romania* **29** D10
Gherla *Romania* **29** C8
Ghidigeni *Romania* **29** D12
Ghilarza *Italy* **42** B1
Ghimeş-Făget *Romania* **29** D11
Ghīnah, Wādī al →
  Si. Arabia **70** D3
Ghisonaccia *France* **21** F13
Ghisoni *France* **21** F13
Ghizar → *Pakistan* **69** A5
Ghot Ogrein *Egypt* **80** A2
Ghotaru *India* **68** F4
Ghotki *Pakistan* **68** E3
Ghowr □ *Afghan.* **66** C4
Ghudāf, W. al → *Iraq* **73** F10
Ghughri *India* **69** H9
Ghugus *India* **66** K11
Ghulam Mohammad
  Barrage *Pakistan* **68** G3
Ghūrīān *Afghan.* **66** B2
Gia Dinh *Vietnam* **65** G6
Gia Lai = Plei Ku *Vietnam* **64** F7
Gia Nghia *Vietnam* **65** G6
Gia Ngoc *Vietnam* **64** E7
Gia Vuc *Vietnam* **64** E7
Giali *Greece* **47** E9
Gialtra *Greece* **46** C4
Giamama *Somali Rep.* **75** G3
Gianitsa *Greece* **44** F6
Giannutri *Italy* **40** F8
Giant Forest *U.S.A.* **110** J8
Giant Mts. = Krkonoše
  Czech Rep. **26** A8
Giant Sequoia △ *U.S.A.* **110** K8
Giants Causeway *U.K.* **12** A5
Gianyar *Indonesia* **63** K18
Giaros *Greece* **46** D6
Giarabub = Al Jaghbūb
  Libya **79** C10
Giaros *Greece* **46** D6
Giarre *Italy* **43** E8
Giaveno *Italy* **40** C4
Gibara *Cuba* **120** B4
Gibb River *Australia* **92** C4
Gibbon *U.S.A.* **112** E5
Gibe → *Ethiopia* **81** F4
Gibellina Nuova *Italy* **42** E5
Gibeon *Namibia* **88** D2
Gibraleón *Spain* **37** H4
Gibraltar ☑ *Europe* **37** J5
Gibraltar, Str. of *Medit. S.* **37** K5
Gibraltar Range △ *Australia* **95** D5
Gibson Desert *Australia* **92** D4
Gibsons *Canada* **102** D4
Gibsonville *U.S.A.* **110** F6
Giddings *U.S.A.* **116** F6
Gidole *Ethiopia* **81** F4
Giebnegáisi = Kebnekaise
  Sweden **8** C18
Gien *France* **19** E9
Giengen *Germany* **25** G6
Giessen *Germany* **24** E4
Gifatin, Geziret *Egypt* **80** B3
Gifhorn *Germany* **24** C6

Gifu *Japan* **55** G8
Gifu □ *Japan* **55** G8
Gigant *Russia* **35** G5
Giganta, Sa. de la *Mexico* **118** B2
Gigen *Bulgaria* **45** C8
Gigha *U.K.* **13** F3
Gíglio *Italy* **40** F7
Gignac *France* **20** E7
Gigüela → *Spain* **37** F7
Gijón *Spain* **36** B5
Gil I. *Canada* **102** C3
Gila → *U.S.A.* **109** K6
Gila Bend *U.S.A.* **109** K7
Gila Bend Mts. *U.S.A.* **109** K7
Gila Cliff Dwellings △
  U.S.A. **109** K9
Gīlān □ *Iran* **71** B6
Gilău *Romania* **29** D8
Gilbert → *Australia* **94** B3
Gilbert Is. *Kiribati* **90** A10
Gilbert River *Australia* **94** B3
Gilbert Seamounts *Pac. Oc.* **4** D18
Gilead *U.S.A.* **113** H5
Gilf el Kebîr, Hadabat el
  Egypt **80** C2
Gilford I. *Canada* **102** C3
Gilgandra *Australia* **95** E4
Gilgil *Kenya* **86** C4
Gilgit *India* **69** B6
Gilgit → *Pakistan* **69** B6
Gili △ *Mozam.* **87** F4
Gilimanuk *Indonesia* **63** J17
Giljeva Planina *Europe* **44** C3
Gillam *Canada* **103** B10
Gilleleje *Denmark* **11** H6
Gillen, L. *Australia* **93** E3
Gilles, L. *Australia* **95** E2
Gillette *U.S.A.* **108** D11
Gilliat *Australia* **94** C3
Gillingham *U.K.* **15** F8
Gilmer *U.S.A.* **116** E7
Gilmore, L. *Australia* **93** F3
Gilo → *Ethiopia* **81** F3
Gilort → *Romania* **29** F8
Gilroy *U.S.A.* **110** H5
Gimbi *Ethiopia* **81** F4
Gimcheon *S. Korea* **57** F15
Gimhae *S. Korea* **57** G15
Gimhwa *S. Korea* **57** E14
Gimie, Mt *St. Lucia* **121** f
Gimje *S. Korea* **57** G14
Gimli *Canada* **103** C9
Gimo *Sweden* **10** D12
Gimone → *France* **20** E5
Gimont *France* **20** E4
Gin Gin *Australia* **95** D5
Ginâh *Egypt* **80** B3
Gineifa *Egypt* **80** H8
Gingin *Australia* **93** F2
Gingindlovu *S. Africa* **89** D5
Ginir *Ethiopia* **81** F5
Ginosa *Italy* **43** B9
Ginzo de Limia = Xinzo de
  Limia *Spain* **36** C3
Giofyros → *Greece* **49** D7
Giohar *Somali Rep.* **75** G4
Gióia, G. di *Italy* **43** D8
Gióia del Colle *Italy* **43** B9
Gióia Táuro *Italy* **43** D8
Gioiosa Iónica *Italy* **43** D9
Gioiosa Marea *Italy* **43** D7
Giona, Oros *Greece* **46** C4
Giovi, Passo dei *Italy* **40** D5
Giovinazzo *Italy* **43** A9
Gir △ *India* **68** J4
Gir Hills *India* **68** J4
Girab *India* **68** F4
Girâfi, W. → *Egypt* **74** F3
Giraltovce *Slovak Rep.* **27** B14
Girard *Kans., U.S.A.* **112** G6
Girard *Ohio, U.S.A.* **114** E4
Girard *Pa., U.S.A.* **114** E4
Girdle Ness *U.K.* **13** D6
Giresun *Turkey* **73** B8
Giresun □ *Turkey* **73** B8
Girga *Egypt* **80** B3
Giri → *India* **68** D7
Giridih *India* **69** G12
Girifalco *Italy* **43** D9
Girifu *Kenya* **86** B4
Giro *Nigeria* **83** C5
Giromagny *France* **19** E13
Giron = Kiruna *Sweden* **8** C19
Girona *Spain* **38** D7
Girona □ *Spain* **38** C7
Gironde □ *France* **20** D3
Gironde → *France* **20** C2
Gironella *Spain* **38** C6
Girraween △ *Australia* **95** D5
Giru *Australia* **94** B4
Girvan *U.K.* **13** F4
Gisborne *N.Z.* **91** C7
Gīsān *Iran* **71** B8
Gisenyi *Rwanda* **86** C2
Gíslaved *Sweden* **11** H7
Gisors *France* **19** C8
Gitega *Burundi* **86** C2

Githio *Greece* **46** E4
Giuba → *Somali Rep.* **75** G3
Giugliano in Campania *Italy* **43** B7
Giuliana *Italy* **41** F10
Giura *Greece* **46** B6
Giurgeni *Romania* **29** F12
Giurgiu *Romania* **29** G10
Giurgiu □ *Romania* **29** F10
Giurgiuleşti *Moldova* **29** E13
Give *Denmark* **11** J3
Givet *France* **19** B11
Givors *France* **21** C8
Giyon *Ethiopia* **81** F4
Giza = El Gîza *Egypt* **80** J7
Giza Pyramids *Egypt* **80** J7
Gizab *Afghan.* **66** C5
Gizhiga *Russia* **53** C17
Gizhiginskaya Guba *Russia* **53** C16
Gizycko *Poland* **30** D8
Gizzeria *Italy* **43** D9
Gjalicë e Lumës, Mal.
  Albania **44** D4
Gjegjan *Albania* **44** E4
Gjirokastër *Albania* **44** F4
Gjoa Haven *Canada* **100** C10
Gjøvik *Norway* **8** F14
Gjuhës, Kep i *Albania* **44** F3
Glace Bay *Canada* **105** C8
Glacier △ *Canada* **102** C5
Glacier △ *U.S.A.* **108** B7
Glacier Bay △ *U.S.A.* **102** B1
Glacier Peak △ *U.S.A.* **108** B3
Gladewater *U.S.A.* **116** E7
Gladstone *Queens., Australia* **94** C5
Gladstone *S. Austral.,*
  Australia **95** E2
Gladstone *Canada* **103** C9
Gladstone *U.S.A.* **112** C10
Gladwin *U.S.A.* **113** D11
Glafsfjorden *Sweden* **10** E6
Glagah *Indonesia* **63** J17
Glągów Małopolski *Poland* **31** H8
Glåma = Glomma →
  Norway **9** G14
Gláma *Iceland* **8** D2
Glamis *U.S.A.* **111** N11
Glamoč *Bos.-H.* **41** D13
Glamorgan, Vale of □ *U.K.* **15** F4
Glarus *Switz.* **25** H5
Glarus □ *Switz.* **25** J5
Glasco *Kans., U.S.A.* **112** F5
Glasco *N.Y., U.S.A.* **115** D11
Glasgow *U.K.* **13** F4
Glasgow *Ky., U.S.A.* **113** G11
Glasgow *Mont., U.S.A.* **108** B10
Glasgow, City of □ *U.K.* **13** F4
Glasgow Int. ✈ (GLA) *U.K.* **13** F4
Glaslyn *Canada* **103** C7
Glastonbury *U.K.* **15** F5
Glastonbury *U.S.A.* **115** E12
Glauchau *Germany* **24** E8
Glava *Sweden* **10** E6
Glavice *Croatia* **41** E13
Glazov *Russia* **34** A11
Gleichen *Canada* **102** C6
Gleisdorf *Austria* **26** D8
Gleiwitz = Gliwice *Poland* **31** H5
Glen *U.S.A.* **115** B13
Glen Affric *U.K.* **13** D4
Glen Canyon *U.S.A.* **109** H8
Glen Canyon △ *U.S.A.* **109** H8
Glen Canyon Dam *U.S.A.* **109** H8
Glen Coe *U.K.* **13** E3
Glen Cove *U.S.A.* **115** F11
Glen Garry *U.K.* **13** D3
Glen Innes *Australia* **95** D5
Glen Lyon *U.S.A.* **115** E8
Glen Mor *U.K.* **13** D4
Glen More △ *U.K.* **13** D5
Glen Moriston *U.K.* **13** D4
Glen Robertson *Canada* **115** A10
Glen Spean *U.K.* **13** E4
Glen Ullin *U.S.A.* **112** B3
Glenallen *U.S.A.* **100** C5
Glénan, Ís. de *France* **18** E3
Glenariff △ *Ireland* **12** A5
Glenbeigh *Ireland* **12** D2
Glencoe *Canada* **114** D3
Glencoe *S. Africa* **89** D5
Glencoe *U.S.A.* **112** C7
Glencolumbkille *Ireland* **12** B3
Glendale *Ariz., U.S.A.* **109** K7
Glendale *Calif., U.S.A.* **111** L8
Glendale *Zimbabwe* **87** F3
Glendive *U.S.A.* **108** C11
Glendo *U.S.A.* **108** E11
Glenelg → *Australia* **95** F3
Glenfield *U.S.A.* **115** C9
Glengad Hd. *Ireland* **12** A4
Glengarriff *Ireland* **12** E2
Glenmont *U.S.A.* **114** F2
Glenmorgan *Australia* **95** D4
Glenn *U.S.A.* **110** F4
Glennamaddy *Ireland* **12** C3
Glenns Ferry *U.S.A.* **108** E6

Glenorchy *Australia* **95** G4
Glenore *Australia* **94** B3
Glenreagh *Australia* **95** E5
Glenrock *U.S.A.* **108** E11
Glenrothes *U.K.* **13** E5
Glens Falls *U.S.A.* **115** C11
Glenside *U.S.A.* **115** F9
Glenties *Ireland* **12** B3
Glenveagh △ *Ireland* **12** A3
Glenville *U.S.A.* **113** F13
Glenwood *Canada* **105** C9
Glenwood *Ark., U.S.A.* **116** D8
Glenwood *Iowa, U.S.A.* **112** E6
Glenwood *Minn., U.S.A.* **112** C6
Glenwood *Wash., U.S.A.* **110** D5
Glenwood Springs *U.S.A.* **108** G10
Glettinganes *Iceland* **8** D7
Glifada *Greece* **46** D5
Glimåkra *Sweden* **11** H8
Glin *Ireland* **12** D2
Glina *Croatia* **41** C13
Glinojeck *Poland* **31** F7
Gliwice *Poland* **31** H5
Globe *U.S.A.* **109** K8
Glodeanu Siliştea *Romania* **29** F11
Glodeni *Moldova* **29** C12
Glödnitz *Austria* **26** E7
Gloggnitz *Austria* **26** D8
Głogów *Poland* **31** G3
Głogówek *Poland* **31** H4
Glomma → *Norway* **9** G14
Glorieuses, Îs. *Ind. Oc.* **89** A8
Glosa *Greece* **46** B5
Glossop *U.K.* **14** D6
Gloucester *Australia* **95** E5
Gloucester *U.K.* **15** F5
Gloucester *U.S.A.* **115** D14
Gloucester I. *Australia* **94** J6
Gloucester Island △ *Australia* **94** J6
Gloucester Point *U.S.A.* **113** G15
Gloucestershire □ *U.K.* **15** F5
Gloversville *U.S.A.* **115** C10
Glovertown *Canada* **105** C9
Głowno *Poland* **31** G6
Głubczyce *Poland* **31** H4
Glubokiy *Russia* **35** F5
Glubokoye = Hlybokaye
    Belarus **32** E4
Głuchołazy *Poland* **31** H4
Glücksburg *Germany* **24** A5
Glückstadt *Germany* **24** B5
Glukhov = Hlukhiv *Ukraine* **33** G7
Glusk *Belarus* **23** B15
Głuszyca *Poland* **31** H3
Glyngøre *Denmark* **11** H2
Gmünd *Kärnten, Austria* **26** E6
Gmünd *Niederösterreich,*
    Austria **26** C8
Gmunden *Austria* **26** D6
Gnarp *Sweden* **10** B11
Gnesta *Sweden* **10** E11
Gniew *Poland* **30** E5
Gniewkowo *Poland* **31** F5
Gniezno *Poland* **31** F4
Gnjilane *Serbia* **44** D5
Gnoien *Germany* **24** B8
Gnosjö *Sweden* **11** G7
Gnowangerup *Australia* **93** F2
Go Cong *Vietnam* **65** G6
Gō-no-ura *Japan* **55** H4
Goa *India* **66** M8
Goa □ *India* **66** M8
Goalen Hd. *Australia* **95** F5
Goalpara *India* **67** F17
Goaltor *India* **69** H12
Goalundo Ghat *Bangla.* **69** H13
Goaso *Ghana* **82** D4
Goat Fell *U.K.* **13** F3
Goba *Ethiopia* **81** F4
Goba *Mozam.* **89** D5
Gobabis *Namibia* **88** C2
Göbel *Turkey* **45** F12
Gobi *Asia* **56** C6
Gobō *Japan* **55** H7
Gobo *Sudan* **81** F3
Göçbeyli *Turkey* **47** B9
Goch *Germany* **24** D2
Gochas *Namibia* **88** C2
Godalming *U.K.* **15** F7
Godavari → *India* **67** L13
Godavari Pt. *India* **67** L13
Godbout *Canada* **105** C6
Godda *India* **69** G12
Godech *Bulgaria* **44** C7
Goderich *Canada* **114** C3
Goderville *France* **18** C7
Godfrey Ra. *Australia* **93** D2
Godhavn = Qeqertarsuaq
    Greenland **4** C5
Godhra *India* **68** H5
Gödöllő *Hungary* **28** C4
Godoy Cruz *Argentina* **126** C2
Gods → *Canada* **104** A1
Gods L. *Canada* **104** B1
Gods River *Canada* **103** C10
Godthåb = Nuuk *Greenland* **99** C14
Goeie Hoop, Kaap die =
    Good Hope, C. of *S. Africa* **88** E2

Goéland, L. au *Canada* **104** C4
Goélands, L. aux *Canada* **105** A7
Goeree *Neths.* **17** C3
Goes *Neths.* **17** C3
Goffstown *U.S.A.* **115** C13
Gogama *Canada* **104** C3
Gogebic, L. *U.S.A.* **112** B9
Goggetti *Ethiopia* **81** F4
Gogolin *Poland* **31** H5
Gogonou *Benin* **83** C5
Gogra = Ghaghara → *India*
    69 G11
Gogriâl *Sudan* **81** F2
Gogti *Ethiopia* **81** E5
Gohana *India* **68** E7
Goharganj *India* **68** H7
Goi → *India* **68** H6
Goiânia *Brazil* **125** G9
Goiás *Brazil* **125** G8
Goiás □ *Brazil* **125** F9
Goio-Erê *Brazil* **127** A5
Góis *Portugal* **36** E2
Gojam *Ethiopia* **81** E4
Gojeb, Wabi → *Ethiopia* **81** F4
Gojō *Japan* **55** G7
Gojra *Pakistan* **68** D5
Gökçeada *Turkey* **45** F9
Gökçedağ *Turkey* **47** B10
Gökçen *Turkey* **47** C9
Gökçeören *Turkey* **47** C10
Gökçeyazı *Turkey* **47** B9
Gökırmak → *Turkey* **72** B6
Gökova *Turkey* **47** D10
Gökova Körfezi *Turkey* **47** E9
Göksu → *Turkey* **72** D6
Göksun *Turkey* **72** C7
Gökteik *Burma* **67** H20
Göktepe *Turkey* **47** D10
Gokurt *Pakistan* **68** E2
Gokwe *Zimbabwe* **89** B4
Gola *India* **69** E9
Golakganj *India* **69** F13
Golan Heights = Hagolan
    Syria **74** C4
Gołańcz *Poland* **31** F4
Goláshkerd *Iran* **71** E8
Golaya Pristen = Hola
    Pristan *Ukraine* **33** J7
Gölbaşı *Adıyaman, Turkey* **72** D7
Gölbaşı *Ankara, Turkey* **72** C5
Golchikha *Russia* **4** B12
Golconda *U.S.A.* **108** F5
Gölcük *Kocaeli, Turkey* **45** F13
Gölcük *Niğde, Turkey* **72** C6
Gold *U.S.A.* **114** E7
Gold Beach *U.S.A.* **108** E1
Gold Coast *W. Afr.* **83** E4
Gold Hill *U.S.A.* **108** F7
Gold River *Canada* **102** D3
Gołdap *Poland* **30** D9
Goldberg *Germany* **24** B8
Golden *Canada* **102** C5
Golden B. *N.Z.* **91** D4
Golden Gate *U.S.A.* **109** H2
Golden Gate Highlands △
    S. Africa **89** D4
Golden Hinde *Canada* **102** D3
Golden Lake *Canada* **114** A7
Golden Spike △ *U.S.A.* **108** F7
Golden Vale *Ireland* **12** D3
Goldendale *U.S.A.* **108** D3
Goldfield *U.S.A.* **109** H5
Goldsand L. *Canada* **103** B8
Goldsboro *U.S.A.* **117** D16
Goldsmith *U.S.A.* **116** F3
Goldthwaite *U.S.A.* **116** F5
Goleniów *Poland* **30** E1
Golestān □ *Iran* **71** B7
Golestānak *Iran* **71** D7
Goleta *U.S.A.* **111** L7
Golfito *Costa Rica* **120** E3
Golfo Aranci *Italy* **42** B2
Golfo di Orosei e del
    Gennargentu △ *Italy* **42** B2
Gölgeli Dağları *Turkey* **47** D10
Gölhisar *Turkey* **47** D11
Goliad *U.S.A.* **116** G6
Golija *Montenegro* **44** C2
Golija *Serbia* **44** C4
Golina *Poland* **31** F5
Gölköy *Turkey* **72** B7
Göllersdorf *Austria* **26** C9
Gölmarmara *Turkey* **47** C9
Golo → *France* **21** F13
Gölova *Turkey* **47** E12
Golpāyegān *Iran* **71** C6
Gölpazarı *Turkey* **72** B4
Golra *Pakistan* **68** C5
Golspie *U.K.* **13** D5
Golub-Dobrzyń *Poland* **31** E6
Golubac *Serbia* **44** B5
Golyam Perelik *Bulgaria* **45** E8
Golyama Kamchiya →
    Bulgaria **45** C11
Goma *Dem. Rep. of the Congo* **86** C2
Gomal Pass *Pakistan* **68** D3

Gomati → *India* **69** G10
Gombari
    Dem. Rep. of the Congo **86** B2
Gombe *Nigeria* **83** C7
Gömbe *Turkey* **47** E11
Gombe □ *Nigeria* **83** C7
Gombe → *Tanzania* **86** C3
Gombi *Nigeria* **83** C7
Gomel = Homyel *Belarus* **23** B16
Gomera *Canary Is.* **48** F2
Gómez Palacio *Mexico* **118** B4
Gomfi *Greece* **46** B3
Gomīshān *Iran* **71** B7
Gommern *Germany* **24** C7
Gomogomo *Indonesia* **63** F8
Gomoh *India* **69** H12
Gomotartsi *Bulgaria* **44** B6
Gompa = Ganta *Liberia* **82** D3
Gonâbād *Iran* **71** C8
Gonaïves *Haiti* **121** C5
Gonarezhou △ *Zimbabwe* **87** G3
Gonâve, G. de la *Haiti* **121** C5
Gonâve, Île de la *Haiti* **121** C5
Gonbad-e Kāvūs *Iran* **71** B7
Gönc *Hungary* **28** B6
Gonda *India* **69** F9
Gondal *India* **68** J4
Gondia *India* **66** J12
Gondola *Mozam.* **87** F3
Gondomar *Portugal* **36** D2
Gondrecourt-le-Château
    France **19** D12
Gönen *Balıkesir, Turkey* **45** F11
Gönen *Isparta, Turkey* **47** D12
Gönen → *Turkey* **45** F11
Gong Xian *China* **58** C5
Gong'an *China* **59** B9
Gongcheng *China* **59** E8
Gongga Shan *China* **58** C3
Gongguan *China* **58** G7
Gonghe *China* **60** C5
Gongju *S. Korea* **57** F14
Gongola → *Nigeria* **83** D7
Gongolgon *Australia* **95** E4
Gongshan *China* **58** D2
Gongtan *China* **58** C7
Gongzhuling *China* **57** C13
Goni *Greece* **46** B4
Goniadz *Poland* **30** E9
Goniri *Nigeria* **83** C7
Gonjo *China* **58** B2
Gonnesa *Italy* **42** C1
Gonnosfanádiga *Italy* **42** C1
Gonzaga *Phil.* **61** B5
Gonzales *Calif., U.S.A.* **110** J5
Gonzales *Tex., U.S.A.* **116** G6
González *Mexico* **119** C5
González Chaves *Argentina* **126** D3
Good Hope, C. of *S. Africa* **88** E2
Gooderham *Canada* **114** B6
Goodhouse *S. Africa* **88** D2
Gooding *U.S.A.* **108** E6
Goodland *U.S.A.* **112** F3
Goodlands *Mauritius* **85** d
Goodlow *Canada* **102** B4
Goodooga *Australia* **95** D4
Goodsprings *U.S.A.* **111** K11
Goole *U.K.* **14** D7
Goolgowi *Australia* **95** E4
Goomalling *Australia* **93** F2
Goomeri *Australia* **95** D5
Goonda *Mozam.* **87** F3
Goondiwindi *Australia* **95** D5
Goongarrie, L. *Australia* **93** F3
Goongarrie △ *Australia* **93** F3
Goonyella *Australia* **94** C4
Goose → *Canada* **105** B7
Goose Creek *U.S.A.* **117** E14
Goose L. *U.S.A.* **108** F3
Gop *India* **68** H3
Gopalganj *India* **69** F11
Göppingen *Germany* **25** G5
Gor *Spain* **37** H8
Góra *Dolnośląskie, Poland* **31** G3
Góra *Mazowieckie, Poland* **31** F7
Góra Kalwaria *Poland* **31** G8
Gorakhpur *India* **69** F10
Goražde *Bos.-H.* **28** G3
Gorbatov *Russia* **34** B6
Gorbea, Peña *Spain* **38** B2
Gorczański △ *Poland* **31** J7
Gorda, Pta. *Canary Is.* **48** F2
Gorda, Pta. *Nic.* **120** D3
Gordan B. *Australia* **92** B5
Gördes *Turkey* **47** C10
Gordon *U.S.A.* **112** D2
Gordon → *Australia* **95** G4
Gordon L. *Alta., Canada* **103** B6
Gordon L. *N.W.T., Canada* **102** A6
Gordonvale *Australia* **94** B4

Gorey *Ireland* **12** D5
Gorg *Iran* **71** D8
Gorgān *Iran* **71** B7
Gorgol □ *Mauritania* **82** B2
Gorgona *Italy* **40** E6
Gorgona, I. *Colombia* **124** C3
Gorgora *Nigeria* **81** E4
Gorgoram *Nigeria* **83** C7
Gorham *U.S.A.* **115** B13
Gori *Georgia* **35** J7
Goriganga → *India* **69** E9
Gorinchem *Neths.* **17** C4
Goris *Armenia* **73** C12
Goritsy *Russia* **32** D9
Gorízia *Italy* **41** C10
Gorj □ *Romania* **29** E8
Gorki = Horki *Belarus* **32** E6
Gorkiy = Nizhniy
    Novgorod *Russia* **34** B7
Gorkovskoye Vdkhr. *Russia* **34** B6
Gorleston *U.K.* **15** E9
Gorlice *Poland* **31** J8
Gorlovka = Horlivka
    Ukraine **33** H10
Görlitz *Germany* **24** D10
Gorman *U.S.A.* **111** L8
Gorna Dzhumayo =
    Blagoevgrad *Bulgaria* **44** D7
Gorna Oryahovitsa
    Bulgaria **45** C9
Gornja Radgona *Slovenia* **41** B13
Gornja Tuzla *Bos.-H.* **28** F3
Gornji Grad *Slovenia* **41** B11
Gornji Milanovac *Serbia* **44** B4
Gornji Vakuf *Bos.-H.* **28** G2
Gorno Ablanovo *Bulgaria* **45** C9
Gorno-Altay □ *Russia* **52** D9
Gorno-Altaysk *Russia* **52** D9
Gornyatskiy *Russia* **35** F5
Gornyy *Saratov, Russia* **34** E9
Gornyy *Sib., Russia* **54** B6
Gorodenka = Horodenka
    Ukraine **29** B10
Gorodets *Russia* **34** B6
Gorodishche =
    Horodyshche *Ukraine* **33** H6
Gorodishche *Russia* **34** D7
Gorodnya = Horodnya
    Ukraine **33** G6
Gorodok = Haradok *Belarus* **32** E6
Gorodok = Horodok
    Ukraine **33** D12
Gorodovikovsk *Russia* **35** G5
Gorokhov = Horokhiv
    Ukraine **23** C13
Gorokhovets *Russia* **34** B6
Gorom Gorom *Burkina Faso* **83** C4
Goromonzi *Zimbabwe* **87** F3
Gorong, Kepulauan
    Indonesia **63** E8
Gorongosa → *Mozam.* **89** B5
Gorongose → *Mozam.* **89** C5
Gorongoza *Mozam.* **87** F3
Gorongoza, Sa. da *Mozam.* **87** F3
Gorontalo *Indonesia* **63** D6
Gorontalo □ *Indonesia* **63** D6
Goronyo *Nigeria* **83** C6
Górowo Ilaweckie *Poland* **30** D7
Gorron *France* **18** D6
Gort *Ireland* **12** C3
Gortis *Greece* **49** D6
Góry Bystrzyckie *Poland* **31** H3
Goryachiy Klyuch *Russia* **35** H4
Goryeong *S. Korea* **57** G15
Gorzkowice *Poland* **31** G6
Górzno *Poland* **31** E6
Gorzów Śląski *Poland* **31** G5
Gorzów Wielkopolski *Poland* **31** F2
Gosford *Australia* **95** E5
Goshen *Calif., U.S.A.* **110** J7
Goshen *Ind., U.S.A.* **113** E11
Goshen *N.Y., U.S.A.* **115** E10
Goshogawara *Japan* **54** D10
Goslar *Germany* **24** D6
Gospič *Croatia* **41** D12
Gosport *U.K.* **15** G6
Gossas *Senegal* **82** C1
Gosse → *Australia* **94** B1
Gossi *Mali* **83** B4
Gossinga *Sudan* **81** F2
Gostivar *Macedonia* **44** E4
Gostyń *Poland* **31** G4
Gostynin *Poland* **31** F6
Göta älv → *Sweden* **11** G5
Göta kanal *Sweden* **11** F9
Götaland *Sweden* **11** H8
Göteborg *Sweden* **11** G5
Götene *Sweden* **11** F7
Goteşti *Moldova* **29** D14
Gotha *Germany* **24** E6
Gothenburg = Göteborg
    Sweden **11** G5
Gothenburg *U.S.A.* **112** E3
Gothèye *Niger* **83** C5
Gotland *Sweden* **11** G12
Gotlands län □ *Sweden* **11** G12

Gotō-Rettō *Japan* **55** H4
Gotse Delchev *Bulgaria* **44** E7
Gotska Sandön *Sweden* **9** G18
Götsu *Japan* **55** G6
Gott Pk. *Canada* **102** C4
Góttero, Monte *Italy* **40** D6
Göttingen *Germany* **24** D5
Gottwald = Zmiyev *Ukraine* **33** H9
Gottwaldov = Zlín
    Czech Rep. **27** B10
Goubangzi *China* **57** D11
Gouda *Neths.* **17** B4
Goudiry *Senegal* **82** C2
Goudoumaria *Niger* **83** C7
Gouéké *Guinea* **82** D3
Gouin, Rés. *Canada* **104** C5
Gouitafla *Ivory C.* **82** D3
Goulburn *Australia* **95** E4
Goulburn Is. *Australia* **94** A1
Goulia *Ivory C.* **82** D3
Goulimine *Morocco* **78** C3
Goumbou *Mali* **82** B4
Goumenissa *Greece* **44** F6
Goundam *Mali* **82** B4
Goura *Ivory C.* **82** D3
Gourbassi *Mali* **82** C2
Gourdon *France* **20** D5
Gouré *Niger* **83** C7
Gourin *France* **18** D3
Gourits → *S. Africa* **88** E3
Gourma-Rharous *Mali* **83** B4
Gournay-en-Bray *France* **19** C8
Gournes *Greece* **49** D7
Gourock *U.K.* **13** F4
Goursi *Burkina Faso* **82** C4
Gouverneur *U.S.A.* **115** B9
Gouvia *Greece* **49** A3
Gouzon *France* **19** F9
Governador Valadares
    Brazil **125** G10
Governor's Harbour
    Bahamas **120** A4
Govindgarh *India* **69** G9
Gowan Ra. *Australia* **94** D4
Gowanda *U.S.A.* **114** D6
Gower *U.K.* **15** F3
Gowna, L. *Ireland* **12** C4
Goya *Argentina* **126** B4
Göyçay *Azerbaijan* **35** K8
Goyder Lagoon *Australia* **95** D2
Goyllarisquisga *Peru* **124** F3
Göynük *Antalya, Turkey* **47** E12
Göynük *Bolu, Turkey* **72** B4
Goz Beïda *Chad* **79** F10
Goz Regeb *Sudan* **81** D4
Gozdnica *Poland* **31** G2
Gozo *Malta* **49** C1
Graaff-Reinet *S. Africa* **88** E3
Grabo *Ivory C.* **82** D3
Grabow *Germany* **24** B7
Grabów nad Prosną *Poland* **31** G5
Gračac *Croatia* **41** D12
Gračanica *Bos.-H.* **28** F3
Graçay *France* **19** E8
Gracias a Dios, C. *Honduras* **120** D3
Graciosa *Azores* **78** a
Graciosa, I. *Canary Is.* **48** E6
Grad Sofiya □ *Bulgaria* **44** D7
Gradac *Montenegro* **44** D3
Gradačac *Bos.-H.* **28** F3
Gradeška Planina *Macedonia* **44** E6
Gradets *Bulgaria* **45** D10
Gradišče *Slovenia* **41** B12
Grădiştea de Munte *Romania* **29** E8
Grado *Italy* **41** C10
Grado *Spain* **36** B4
Grady *U.S.A.* **109** J12
Graeca, Lacul *Romania* **29** F11
Grafenau *Germany* **25** G9
Gräfenberg *Germany* **25** F7
Grafham Water *U.K.* **15** E7
Grafton *Australia* **95** D5
Grafton *N. Dak., U.S.A.* **112** A5
Grafton *W. Va., U.S.A.* **113** F13
Graham *Canada* **104** C1
Graham *U.S.A.* **116** E5
Graham, Mt. *U.S.A.* **109** K9
Graham Bell, Ostrov =
    Greem-Bell, Ostrov *Russia* **52** A7
Graham I. *Canada* **102** C2
Graham Land *Antarctica* **5** C17
Grahamstown *S. Africa* **88** E4
Grahamsville *U.S.A.* **115** E10
Grahovo *Montenegro* **44** D2
Graie, Alpi *Europe* **21** C11
Grain Coast *W. Afr.* **82** E3
Grajagan *Indonesia* **63** K17
Grajagan, Teluk *Indonesia* **63** K17
Grajaú *Brazil* **125** E9
Grajaú → *Brazil* **125** D10
Grajewo *Poland* **30** E9
Gramada *Bulgaria* **44** C6
Gramat *France* **20** D5
Grammichele *Italy* **43** E7
Grámmos, Óros *Greece* **44** F4
Grampian *U.S.A.* **114** F6

Grampian Highlands =
    Grampian Mts. *U.K.* **13** E5
Grampian Mts. *U.K.* **13** E5
Grampians, The *Australia* **95** F3
Gramsh *Albania* **44** F4
Gran Canaria *Canary Is.* **48** G4
Gran Chaco *S. Amer.* **126** B3
Gran Desierto del
    Pinacate △ *Mexico* **118** A2
Gran Paradiso *Italy* **40** C4
Gran Sasso d'Itália *Italy* **41** F10
Gran Sasso e Monti Della
    Laga △ *Italy* **41** F10
Granada *Nic.* **120** D2
Granada *Spain* **37** H7
Granada *U.S.A.* **108** G12
Granada □ *Spain* **37** H7
Granadilla de Abona
    Canary Is. **48** F3
Granard *Ireland* **12** C4
Granbury *U.S.A.* **116** E6
Granby *Canada* **115** A12
Granby *U.S.A.* **108** F11
Grand → *Canada* **114** D5
Grand → *Mo., U.S.A.* **112** F7
Grand → *S. Dak., U.S.A.* **112** C3
Grand Bahama I. *Bahamas* **120** A4
Grand Baie *Mauritius* **85** d
Grand Bank *Canada* **105** C8
Grand Bassam *Ivory C.* **82** D4
Grand Béréby *Ivory C.* **82** E3
Grand-Bourg *Guadeloupe* **120** b
Grand Canal = Da
    Yunhe → *China* **57** E9
Grand Canyon *U.S.A.* **109** H7
Grand Canyon △ *U.S.A.* **109** H7
Grand Canyon-
    Parashant △ *U.S.A.* **109** H7
Grand Cayman *Cayman Is.* **120** C3
Grand Centre *Canada* **103** C6
Grand Cess *Liberia* **82** E3
Grand Coulee *U.S.A.* **108** C4
Grand Coulee Dam *U.S.A.* **108** C4
Grand Erg de Bilma *Niger* **79** E8
Grand Falls *Canada* **105** C6
Grand Falls-Windsor
    Canada **105** C8
Grand Forks *Canada* **102** D5
Grand Forks *U.S.A.* **112** B5
Grand Gorge *U.S.A.* **115** D10
Grand Haven *U.S.A.* **112** D10
Grand I. *Mich., U.S.A.* **112** B10
Grand I. *N.Y., U.S.A.* **114** D6
Grand Island *U.S.A.* **112** E4
Grand Isle *La., U.S.A.* **117** G9
Grand Isle *Vt., U.S.A.* **115** B11
Grand Junction *U.S.A.* **108** G9
Grand L. *N.B., Canada* **105** C6
Grand L. *Nfld. & L., Canada* **105** C8
Grand L. *Nfld. & L., Canada* **105** B7
Grand L. *U.S.A.* **116** G8
Grand Lahou *Ivory C.* **82** D3
Grand Lake *U.S.A.* **108** F11
Grand-Lieu, L. de *France* **18** E5
Grand Manan I. *Canada* **105** C6
Grand Marais *Mich., U.S.A.*
    113 B11
Grand Marais *Minn., U.S.A.* **104** C1
Grand-Mère *Canada* **104** C5
Grand Popo *Benin* **83** D5
Grand Portage *U.S.A.* **112** B9
Grand Prairie *U.S.A.* **116** E6
Grand Rapids *Canada* **103** C9
Grand Rapids *Mich., U.S.A.* **113** D11
Grand Rapids *Minn., U.S.A.* **112** B7
Grand St-Bernard, Col du
    Europe **25** K3
Grand Staircase-
    Escalante △ *U.S.A.* **109** H8
Grand Teton *U.S.A.* **108** E8
Grand Teton △ *U.S.A.* **108** E8
Grand Union Canal *U.K.* **15** E7
Grandas de Salime *Spain* **36** B4
Grande → *Jujuy, Argentina* **126** A2
Grande → *Mendoza,*
    Argentina **126** D2
Grande → *Bolivia* **124** G6
Grande → *Bahia, Brazil* **125** F10
Grande → *Minas Gerais,*
    Brazil **125** H8
Grande, B. *Argentina* **128** G3
Grande, Rio → *N. Amer.* **116** N6
Grande Anse *Seychelles* **85** b
Grande Baleine, R. de la →
    Canada **104** A4
Grande Cache *Canada* **102** C5
Grande Casse, Pte. de la
    France **21** C10
Grande Comore *Comoros Is.* **85** a
Grande-Entrée *Canada* **105** C7
Grande Prairie *Canada* **102** B5
Grande-Rivière *Canada* **105** C7
Grande-Terre *Guadeloupe* **120** b
Grande-Vallée *Canada* **105** C6
Grande Vigie, Pte. de la
    Guadeloupe **120** b
Grandfalls *U.S.A.* **116** F3

Grândola *Portugal* 37 G2
Grandpré *France* 19 C11
Grands Causses △ *France* 20 D6
Grands-Jardins △ *Canada* 105 C5
Grandview *Canada* 103 C8
Grandview *U.S.A.* 108 C4
Grandvilliers *France* 19 C8
Graneros *Chile* 126 C1
Grangemouth *U.K.* 13 E5
Granger *U.S.A.* 108 F9
Grängesberg *Sweden* 10 D9
Grangeville *U.S.A.* 108 D5
Granisle *Canada* 102 C3
Granite City *U.S.A.* 112 F8
Granite Falls *U.S.A.* 112 C6
Granite L. *Canada* 105 C8
Granite Mt. *U.S.A.* 111 M10
Granite Pk. *U.S.A.* 108 D9
Granitola, C. *Italy* 42 E5
Granity *N.Z.* 91 D3
Granja *Brazil* 125 D10
Granja de Moreruela *Spain* 36 D5
Granja de Torrehermosa
    Spain 37 G5
Gränna *Sweden* 11 F8
Granollers *Spain* 38 D7
Gransee *Germany* 24 B9
Grant *U.S.A.* 112 E3
Grant, Mt. *U.S.A.* 108 G4
Grant City *U.S.A.* 112 E6
Grant I. *Australia* 92 B5
Grant Range *U.S.A.* 108 G6
Grantham *U.K.* 14 E7
Grantown-on-Spey *U.K.* 13 D5
Grants *U.S.A.* 109 J10
Grants Pass *U.S.A.* 108 E2
Grantsville *U.S.A.* 108 F7
Granville *France* 18 D5
Granville N. Dak., *U.S.A.* 112 A3
Granville N.Y., *U.S.A.* 115 C11
Granville Ohio, *U.S.A.* 114 F2
Granville L. *Canada* 103 B8
Graskop *S. Africa* 89 C5
Gräsö *Sweden* 10 D12
Grass → *Canada* 103 B9
Grass Range *U.S.A.* 108 C9
Grass River △ *Canada* 103 C8
Grass Valley Calif., *U.S.A.* 110 F6
Grass Valley Oreg., *U.S.A.* 108 D3
Grassano *Italy* 43 B9
Grasse *France* 21 E10
Grassflat *U.S.A.* 114 E6
Grasslands △ *Canada* 103 D7
Grassy *Australia* 95 G3
Gråsten *Denmark* 11 K3
Grästorp *Sweden* 11 F6
Gratkorn *Austria* 26 D8
Graubünden □ *Switz.* 25 J5
Graulhet *France* 20 E5
Graus *Spain* 38 C5
Grave, Pte. de *France* 20 C2
Gravelbourg *Canada* 103 D7
Gravelines *France* 19 A9
Gravenhurst *Canada* 114 B5
Gravesend *Australia* 95 D5
Gravesend *U.K.* 15 F8
Gravina in Púglia *Italy* 43 B9
Gravois, Pointe-à- *Haiti* 121 C5
Gravone → *France* 21 G12
Gray *France* 19 E12
Grayling *U.S.A.* 113 C11
Grays *U.K.* 15 F8
Grays Harbor *U.S.A.* 108 C1
Grays L. *U.S.A.* 108 E8
Grays River *U.S.A.* 110 D3
Grayvoron *Russia* 33 G8
Graz *Austria* 26 D8
Grdelica *Serbia* 44 D6
Greasy L. *Canada* 102 A4
Great Abaco I. = Abaco I.
    Bahamas 120 A4
Great Artesian Basin
    Australia 94 C3
Great Australian Bight
    Australia 93 F5
Great Bahama Bank
    Bahamas 120 B4
Great Barrier I. *N.Z.* 91 B5
Great Barrier Reef *Australia* 94 B4
Great Barrier Reef △
    Australia 94 B4
Great Barrington *U.S.A.* 115 D11
Great Basalt Wall △
    Australia 94 B4
Great Basin *U.S.A.* 108 G5
Great Basin △ *U.S.A.* 108 G6
Great Bear → *Canada* 100 C7
Great Bear L. *Canada* 100 C8
Great Belt = Store Bælt
    Denmark 11 J4
Great Bend Kans., *U.S.A.* 112 F4
Great Bend Pa., *U.S.A.* 115 E9
Great Blasket I. *Ireland* 12 D1
Great Britain *Europe* 6 E5
Great Camanoe *Br. Virgin Is.* 121 e

Great Codroy *Canada* 105 C8
Great Divide, The = Great
    Dividing Ra. *Australia* 94 C4
Great Divide Basin *U.S.A.* 108 E9
Great Dividing Ra. *Australia* 94 C4
Great Driffield = Driffield
    U.K. 14 C7
Great Exuma I. *Bahamas* 120 B4
Great Falls *U.S.A.* 108 C8
Great Fish = Groot-Vis →
    S. Africa 88 E4
Great Guana Cay *Bahamas* 120 B4
Great Harbour Deep *Canada* 105 B8
Great Himalayan △ *India* 68 D7
Great Inagua I. *Bahamas* 121 B5
Great Indian Desert = Thar
    Desert *India* 68 F5
Great Karoo *S. Africa* 88 E3
Great Khingan Mts. = Da
    Hinggan Ling *China* 60 B7
Great Lake *Australia* 95 G4
Great Lakes *N. Amer.* 98 E11
Great Malvern *U.K.* 15 E5
Great Miami → *U.S.A.* 113 F11
Great Ormes Head *U.K.* 14 D4
Great Ouse → *U.K.* 14 E8
Great Palm I. *Australia* 94 B4
Great Pedro Bluff *Jamaica* 120 a
Great Pee Dee → *U.S.A.* 117 E15
Great Plains *N. Amer.* 98 E9
Great Ruaha → *Tanzania* 86 D4
Great Sacandaga L. *U.S.A.* 115 C10
Great Saint Bernard Pass =
    Grand St-Bernard, Col
    du *Europe* 25 K3
Great Salt Desert = Kavīr,
    Dasht-e *Iran* 71 C7
Great Salt L. *U.S.A.* 108 F7
Great Salt Lake Desert
    U.S.A. 108 F7
Great Salt Plains L. *U.S.A.* 116 C5
Great Sand Dunes △ *U.S.A.*
    109 H11
Great Sandy △ *Australia* 95 D5
Great Sandy Desert *Australia* 92 D3
Great Sandy Desert *U.S.A.* 106 B2
Great Sangi = Sangihe,
    Pulau *Indonesia* 63 D7
Great Scarcies → *S. Leone* 82 D2
Great Sea Reef *Fiji* 91 a
Great Skellig *Ireland* 12 E1
Great Slave L. *Canada* 102 A5
Great Smoky Mts. △ *U.S.A.*
    117 D13
Great Snow Mt. *Canada* 102 B4
Great Stour = Stour → *U.K.* 15 F9
Great Victoria Desert
    Australia 93 E4
Great Wall *Antarctica* 5 C18
Great Wall *China* 56 E5
Great Whernside *U.K.* 14 C6
Great Yarmouth *U.K.* 15 E9
Great Zab = Zāb al
    Kabīr → *Iraq* 73 D10
Great Zimbabwe *Zimbabwe* 87 G3
Greater Antilles *W. Indies* 121 C5
Greater London □ *U.K.* 15 F7
Greater Manchester □ *U.K.* 14 D5
Greater St. Lucia
    Wetlands △ *S. Africa* 89 D5
Greater Sudbury =
    Sudbury *Canada* 104 C3
Greater Sunda Is. *Indonesia* 62 F4
Grebenka = Hrebenka
    Ukraine 33 G7
Grebbestad *Sweden* 11 F5
Greco, C. *Cyprus* 49 E13
Greco, Mte. *Italy* 41 G10
Gredos, Sierra de *Spain* 36 E6
Greece *U.S.A.* 114 C7
Greece ■ *Europe* 46 B3
Greeley Colo., *U.S.A.* 108 F11
Greeley Nebr., *U.S.A.* 112 E4
Greely Fd. *Canada* 101 A11
Greem-Bell, Ostrov *Russia* 52 A7
Green → *Ky., U.S.A.* 112 G10
Green → *Utah, U.S.A.* 108 G9
Green B. *U.S.A.* 112 C10
Green Bay *U.S.A.* 112 C9
Green C. *Australia* 95 F5
Green Cove Springs *U.S.A.* 117 G14
Green I. = Lü Tao *Taiwan* 59 F13
Green Lake *Canada* 103 C7
Green Mts. *U.S.A.* 115 C12
Green River *Utah, U.S.A.* 108 G8
Green River *Wyo., U.S.A.* 108 F9
Green Valley *U.S.A.* 109 L8
Greenbank *U.S.A.* 110 B4
Greenbush *Mich., U.S.A.* 114 B1
Greenbush *Minn., U.S.A.* 112 A5
Greencastle *U.S.A.* 112 F10
Greene *U.S.A.* 115 D9
Greeneville *U.S.A.* 117 C13
Greenfield *Calif., U.S.A.* 110 J5
Greenfield *Calif., U.S.A.* 111 K8
Greenfield *Ind., U.S.A.* 113 F11
Greenfield *Iowa, U.S.A.* 112 E6

Greenfield *Mass., U.S.A.* 115 D12
Greenfield *Mo., U.S.A.* 112 G7
Greenfield Park *Canada* 115 A11
Greenland ☑ *N. Amer.* 99 C15
Greenland Sea *Arctic* 4 B7
Greenock *U.K.* 13 F4
Greenore *Ireland* 12 B5
Greenore Pt. *Ireland* 12 D5
Greenough *Australia* 93 E1
Greenough → *Australia* 93 E1
Greenough Pt. *Canada* 114 B3
Greenport *U.S.A.* 115 E12
Greensboro *Ga., U.S.A.* 117 E13
Greensboro *N.C., U.S.A.* 117 C15
Greensboro *Vt., U.S.A.* 115 B12
Greensburg *Ind., U.S.A.* 113 F11
Greensburg *Kans., U.S.A.* 112 G4
Greensburg *Pa., U.S.A.* 114 F5
Greenstone Pt. *U.K.* 13 D3
Greenvale *Australia* 94 B4
Greenville *Liberia* 82 D3
Greenville *Ala., U.S.A.* 117 F11
Greenville *Calif., U.S.A.* 110 E6
Greenville *Maine, U.S.A.* 113 C19
Greenville *Mich., U.S.A.* 113 D11
Greenville *Mo., U.S.A.* 112 G8
Greenville *N.C., U.S.A.* 117 D16
Greenville *N.H., U.S.A.* 115 D13
Greenville *N.Y., U.S.A.* 115 D10
Greenville *Ohio, U.S.A.* 113 E11
Greenville *Pa., U.S.A.* 114 E4
Greenville *S.C., U.S.A.* 117 D13
Greenville *Tex., U.S.A.* 116 E6
Greenwater Lake △ *Canada* 103 C8
Greenwich *Conn., U.S.A.* 115 E11
Greenwich *N.Y., U.S.A.* 115 C11
Greenwich *Ohio, U.S.A.* 114 E2
Greenwich □ *U.K.* 15 F8
Greenwood *Canada* 102 D5
Greenwood *Ark., U.S.A.* 116 D7
Greenwood *Ind., U.S.A.* 112 F10
Greenwood *Miss., U.S.A.* 117 E9
Greenwood *S.C., U.S.A.* 117 D13
Greenwood, Mt. *Australia* 92 B5
Gregbe *Ivory C.* 82 D3
Gregory *U.S.A.* 112 D4
Gregory → *Australia* 94 B2
Gregory, L. S. Austral.,
    Australia 95 D2
Gregory, L. W. Austral.,
    Australia 92 D3
Gregory, L. W. Austral.,
    Australia 93 E2
Gregory → *Australia* 92 C5
Gregory Downs *Australia* 94 B2
Gregory Ra. *Queens.,*
    Australia 94 B3
Gregory Ra. W. Austral.,
    Australia 92 D3
Greiffenberg *Germany* 24 B9
Greifswald *Germany* 24 A9
Greifswalder Bodden
    Germany 24 A9
Grein *Austria* 26 C7
Greiz *Germany* 24 E8
Gremikha *Russia* 52 C4
Grenaa *Denmark* 11 H4
Grenada *U.S.A.* 117 E10
Grenade *France* 20 E5
Grenadier I. *U.S.A.* 115 B8
Grenada ■ *W. Indies* 121 D7
Grenadines, The *St. Vincent* 121 D7
Grenchen *Switz.* 25 H3
Grenen *Denmark* 11 G4
Grenfell *Australia* 95 E4
Grenfell *Canada* 103 C8
Grenoble *France* 21 C9
Grenville, C. *Australia* 94 A3
Grenville Chan. *Canada* 102 C3
Gréoux-les-Bains *France* 21 E9
Gresham *U.S.A.* 110 E4
Gresik *Indonesia* 63 G15
Gretna *U.S.A.* 113 F5
Gretna *U.K.* 13 F5
Gretna *U.S.A.* 117 G9
Greve Strand *Denmark* 11 J6
Greven *Germany* 24 C3
Grevena *Greece* 44 F5
Grevena □ *Greece* 44 F5
Grevenbroich *Germany* 24 D2
Grevenmacher *Lux.* 17 E6
Grevesmühlen *Germany* 24 B7
Grey → *Canada* 105 C8
Grey → *N.Z.* 91 E3
Grey, C. *Australia* 94 A2
Grey Ra. *Australia* 95 D3
Greybull *U.S.A.* 108 D9
Greymouth *N.Z.* 91 E3
Greystones *Ireland* 12 C5
Greytown *N.Z.* 91 D5
Greytown *S. Africa* 89 D5
Gribanovskiy *Russia* 34 E5
Gribbell I. *Canada* 102 C3
Gribës, Mal i *Albania* 44 F3
Gridley *U.S.A.* 110 F5
Griekwastad *S. Africa* 88 D3
Griesheim *Germany* 25 F4
Grieskirchen *Austria* 26 C6

Griffin *U.S.A.* 117 E12
Griffith *Australia* 95 E4
Griffith *Canada* 114 A7
Griffith I. *Canada* 114 B4
Grignols *France* 20 D3
Grigoriopol *Moldova* 29 C14
Grimaylov = Hrymayliv
    Ukraine 23 D14
Grimes *U.S.A.* 110 F5
Grimma *Germany* 24 D8
Grimmen *Germany* 24 A9
Grimsay *U.K.* 13 D1
Grimsby *Canada* 114 C5
Grimsby *U.K.* 14 D7
Grímsey *Iceland* 8 C5
Grimshaw *Canada* 102 B5
Grimslöv *Sweden* 11 H8
Grimstad *Norway* 9 G13
Grindelwald *Switz.* 25 J4
Grindsted *Denmark* 11 J2
Grindstone I. *Canada* 115 B8
Grindu *Romania* 29 F11
Grinnell *U.S.A.* 112 E7
Grintavec *Slovenia* 41 B11
Gris-Nez, C. *France* 19 B8
Grise Fiord *Canada* 101 B11
Grisolles *France* 20 E5
Grisons = Graubünden □
    Switz. 25 J5
Grisslehamn *Sweden* 10 D12
Grmeč Planina *Bos.-H.* 41 D13
Groais I. *Canada* 105 B8
Grobiņa *Latvia* 30 B8
Groblersdal *S. Africa* 89 D4
Grobming *Austria* 26 D6
Grocka *Serbia* 44 B4
Gródek *Poland* 31 E10
Grodno = Hrodna *Belarus* 30 E10
Grodzisk Mazowiecki *Poland* 31 F7
Grodzisk Wielkopolski
    Poland 31 F3
Grodzyanka =
    Hrodzyanka *Belarus* 23 B15
Groesbeck *U.S.A.* 116 F6
Groix *France* 18 E3
Groix, Î. de *France* 18 E3
Grójec *Poland* 31 G7
Gronau *Niedersachsen,*
    Germany 24 C5
Gronau *Nordrhein-Westfalen,*
    Germany 24 C5
Grong *Norway* 8 D15
Grönhögen *Sweden* 11 H10
Groningen *Neths.* 17 A6
Groningen □ *Neths.* 17 A6
Groom *U.S.A.* 116 D4
Groot → *S. Africa* 88 E3
Groot-Berg → *S. Africa* 88 E2
Groot-Brakrivier *S. Africa* 88 E3
Groot Karasberge *Namibia* 88 D2
Groot-Kei → *S. Africa* 89 E4
Groot-Vis → *S. Africa* 88 E4
Grootdrink *S. Africa* 88 D3
Groote Eylandt *Australia* 94 A2
Grootfontein *Namibia* 88 B2
Grootlaagte → *Africa* 88 C3
Grootvloer → *S. Africa* 88 E3
Gros C. *Canada* 102 A6
Gros Islet *St. Lucia* 121 f
Gros Morne △ *Canada* 105 C8
Gros Piton *St. Lucia* 121 f
Gros Piton Pt. *St. Lucia* 121 f
Grosne → *France* 19 F11
Grossa, Pta. *Spain* 48 B8
Grossenbrode *Germany* 24 A7
Grossenhain *Germany* 24 D9
Grosser Arber *Germany* 25 F9
Grosser Plöner See *Germany* 24 A6
Grosseto *Italy* 41 F8
Grossgerungs *Austria* 26 C7
Grossglockner *Austria* 26 D5
Groswater B. *Canada* 105 B8
Groton *Conn., U.S.A.* 115 E12
Groton *N.Y., U.S.A.* 115 D8
Groton *S. Dak., U.S.A.* 112 C4
Grottáglie *Italy* 43 B10
Grottaminarda *Italy* 43 A8
Grottammare *Italy* 41 F10
Grouard Mission *Canada* 102 B5
Grouin, Pte. du *France* 18 D5
Groundhog → *Canada* 104 C3
Grouw *Neths.* 17 A5
Grove City *U.S.A.* 114 E4
Grove Hill *U.S.A.* 117 F11
Groveland *U.S.A.* 110 H6
Grover Beach *U.S.A.* 111 K6
Groves *U.S.A.* 116 G8
Groveton *U.S.A.* 115 B13
Groznjan *Croatia* 41 C10
Groznyy *Russia* 35 J7
Grubišno Polje *Croatia* 28 E2
Grudusk *Poland* 31 E7
Grudziądz *Poland* 30 E5
Gruinard B. *U.K.* 13 D3

Gruissan *France* 20 E7
Grumo Áppula *Italy* 43 A9
Grums *Sweden* 10 E7
Grünberg *Germany* 24 E4
Gründau *Germany* 25 E5
Grünstadt *Germany* 25 F4
Gruppo di Tessa △ *Italy* 40 B8
Gruvberget *Sweden* 10 C10
Gruver *U.S.A.* 116 C4
Gruyères *Switz.* 25 J3
Gruža *Serbia* 44 C4
Gryazi *Russia* 33 F10
Gryazovets *Russia* 32 C11
Grybów *Poland* 31 J7
Grycksbo *Sweden* 10 D9
Gryfice *Poland* 30 E2
Gryfino *Poland* 31 E1
Gryfów Śląski *Poland* 31 G2
Grythyttan *Sweden* 10 E8
Gstaad *Switz.* 25 J3
Gua *India* 69 H11
Gua Musang *Malaysia* 65 K3
Guacanayabo, G. de *Cuba* 120 B4
Guachípas → *Argentina* 126 B2
Guadajoz → *Spain* 37 H6
Guadalajara *Mexico* 118 C4
Guadalajara *Spain* 38 E1
Guadalajara □ *Spain* 38 E2
Guadalcanal *Solomon Is.* 90 B9
Guadalcanal *Spain* 37 G5
Guadalén → *Spain* 37 G7
Guadales *Argentina* 126 C2
Guadalete → *Spain* 37 J4
Guadalimar → *Spain* 37 G7
Guadalmena → *Spain* 37 G8
Guadalmez → *Spain* 37 G5
Guadalope → *Spain* 38 D4
Guadalquivir → *Spain* 37 J4
Guadalupe =
    Guadeloupe ☑ *W. Indies* 120 b
Guadalupe *Mexico* 111 N10
Guadalupe *Spain* 37 F5
Guadalupe *U.S.A.* 111 L6
Guadalupe → *Mexico* 111 N10
Guadalupe → *U.S.A.* 116 G6
Guadalupe, Sierra de *Spain* 37 F5
Guadalupe Bravos *Mexico* 118 A3
Guadalupe I. *Pac. Oc.* 98 G8
Guadalupe Mts. △ *U.S.A.* 116 F2
Guadalupe Peak *U.S.A.* 116 F2
Guadalupe y Calvo *Mexico* 118 B3
Guadarrama, Sierra de *Spain* 36 E7
Guadauta *Georgia* 35 J5
Guadeloupe ☑ *W. Indies* 120 b
Guadeloupe = Guadeloupe *120 b*
Guadeloupe Passage
    W. Indies 121 C7
Guadiamar → *Spain* 37 J4
Guadiana → *Portugal* 37 H3
Guadiana Menor → *Spain* 37 H7
Guadiaro → *Spain* 37 J5
Guadiato → *Spain* 37 H5
Guadiela → *Spain* 38 E2
Guadix → *Spain* 37 H7
Guafo, Boca del *Chile* 128 E2
Guaíca *Trin. & Tob.* 125 K15
Guainía □ *Colombia* 124 C5
Guaíra *Brazil* 127 A5
Guaíra □ *Paraguay* 126 B4
Guaitecas, Is. *Chile* 128 E2
Guajará-Mirim *Brazil* 124 F5
Guajira, Pen. de la *Colombia* 124 A4
Gualán *Guatemala* 120 C2
Gualdo Tadino *Italy* 41 E9
Gualeguay *Argentina* 126 C4
Gualeguaychú *Argentina* 126 C4
Gualequay → *Argentina* 126 C4
Guam ☑ *Pac. Oc.* 96 F6
Guaminí *Argentina* 126 D3
Guamúchil *Mexico* 118 B3
Guana I. *Br. Virgin Is.* 121 e
Guanabacoa *Cuba* 120 B3
Guanacaste, Cordillera del
    Costa Rica 120 D2
Guanacaste △ *Costa Rica* 120 D2
Guanaceví *Mexico* 118 B3
Guanahani = San
    Salvador I. *Bahamas* 121 B5
Guanajay *Cuba* 120 B3
Guanajuato *Mexico* 118 C4
Guanajuato □ *Mexico* 118 C4
Guandacol *Argentina* 126 B2
Guane *Cuba* 120 B3
Guang'an *China* 58 B6
Guangchang *China* 59 D11
Guangde *China* 59 B12
Guangdong □ *China* 59 F9
Guangfeng *China* 59 C12
Guanghan *China* 58 B5
Guangling *China* 56 E8
Guangnan *China* 58 E5
Guangning *China* 59 F9
Guangrao *China* 57 F10
Guangshui *China* 59 B9
Guangshun *China* 58 D6

Guangwu *China* 56 F3
Guangxi Zhuangzu
    Zizhiqu □ *China* 58 F7
Guangyuan *China* 58 A5
Guangze *China* 59 D11
Guangzhou *China* 59 F9
Guanica *Puerto Rico* 121 d
Guanipa → *Venezuela* 124 B6
Guanling *China* 58 E5
Guannan *China* 57 G10
Guantánamo *Cuba* 121 B4
Guantánamo B. *Cuba* 121 C4
Guantao *China* 56 F8
Guanyang *China* 59 E8
Guanyun *China* 57 G10
Guápiles *Costa Rica* 120 D3
Guapo B. *Trin. & Tob.* 125 K15
Guaporé *Brazil* 127 B5
Guaporé → *Brazil* 124 F5
Guaqui *Bolivia* 124 G5
Guara, Sierra de *Spain* 38 C4
Guaramacal △ *Venezuela* 121 E5
Guarapari *Brazil* 127 A7
Guarapuava *Brazil* 127 B5
Guaratinguetá *Brazil* 127 A6
Guaratuba *Brazil* 127 B6
Guarda *Portugal* 36 E3
Guarda □ *Portugal* 36 E3
Guardafui, C. = Asir, Ras
    Somali Rep. 75 E5
Guardamar del Segura *Spain* 39 G4
Guardavalle *Italy* 43 D9
Guárdia Sanframondi *Italy* 43 A7
Guardiagrele *Italy* 41 F11
Guardo *Spain* 36 C6
Guareña *Spain* 37 G4
Guareña → *Spain* 36 D5
Guárico □ *Venezuela* 124 B5
Guarujá *Brazil* 127 A6
Guarulhos *Brazil* 127 A6
Guarus *Brazil* 127 A7
Guasave *Mexico* 118 B3
Guasdualito *Venezuela* 124 B4
Guastalla *Italy* 40 D7
Guatemala *Guatemala* 120 D1
Guatemala ■ *Cent. Amer.* 120 C1
Guatemala Basin *Pac. Oc.* 97 F18
Guatemala Trench *Pac. Oc.* 98 H10
Guatopo △ *Venezuela* 121 D6
Guatuaro Pt. *Trin. & Tob.* 125 K16
Guaviare □ *Colombia* 124 C5
Guaviare → *Colombia* 124 C5
Guaxupé *Brazil* 127 A6
Guayaguayare *Trin. & Tob.* 125 K15
Guayama *Puerto Rico* 121 d
Guayaquil *Ecuador* 124 D2
Guayaquil *Mexico* 118 B1
Guayaquil, G. de *Ecuador* 124 D2
Guaymas *Mexico* 118 B2
Guba *Dem. Rep. of the Congo* 87 E2
Guba *Ethiopia* 81 E4
Gûbâl, Madîq *Egypt* 80 B3
Gúbbio *Italy* 41 E9
Guben *Germany* 24 D10
Gubin *Poland* 31 G1
Gubio *Nigeria* 83 C7
Gubkin *Russia* 33 G9
Guča *Serbia* 44 C4
Gucheng *China* 59 A8
Gudata = Guadauta *Georgia* 35 J5
Gudbrandsdalen *Norway* 8 F14
Guddu Barrage *Pakistan* 68 E3
Gudenå → *Denmark* 11 H4
Gudermes *Russia* 35 J8
Gudhjem *Denmark* 11 J8
Gudur *India* 66 M11
Guebwiller *France* 19 E14
Guecho = Getxo *Spain* 38 B2
Guékédou *Guinea* 82 D2
Guélé Mendouka *Cameroon* 83 E7
Guelmine = Goulimine
    Morocco 78 C3
Guelph *Canada* 114 C4
Guéméné-Penfao *France* 18 E5
Guéméné-sur-Scorff *France* 18 D3
Guéné *Benin* 83 C5
Guer *France* 18 E4
Guérande *France* 18 E4
Guéret *France* 19 F8
Guérigny *France* 19 E10
Guerneville *U.S.A.* 110 G4
Guernica = Gernika-Lumo
    Spain 38 B2
Guernsey *U.K.* 15 H5
Guernsey *U.S.A.* 108 E11
Guerrero □ *Mexico* 119 D5
Guessou-Sud *Benin* 83 C5
Gueugnon *France* 19 F11
Guéyo *Ivory C.* 82 D3
Gughe *Ethiopia* 81 F4
Gügher *Iran* 71 D8
Guglionesi *Italy* 41 G11
Guhakolak, Tanjung
    Indonesia 63 G12
Gui Jiang → *China* 59 F8
Guia *Canary Is.* 48 F4
Guia de Isora *Canary Is.* 48 F3

Guia Lopes da Laguna
  Brazil **127** A4
Guiana Highlands *S. Amer.* **122** C4
Guibéroua *Ivory C.* **82** D3
Guichi *China* **59** B11
Guider *Cameroon* **83** D7
Guidiguir *Niger* **83** C6
Guidimaka ☐ *Mauritania* **82** B2
Guiding *China* **58** D6
Guidong *China* **59** D9
Guidónia-Montecélio *Italy* **41** F9
Guiers, L. de *Senegal* **82** B1
Guigang *China* **58** F7
Guiglo *Ivory C.* **82** D3
Guihulñgan *Phil.* **61** F5
Guijá *Mozam.* **89** C5
Guijuelo *Spain* **36** E5
Guildford ☐ *U.K.* **15** F7
Guilford *U.S.A.* **115** E12
Guilin *China* **59** E8
Guillaume-Delisle, L.
  Canada **104** A4
Guillaumes *France* **21** D10
Guillestre *France* **21** D10
Guilvinec *France* **18** E2
Güimar *Canary Is.* **48** F3
Guimarães *Portugal* **36** D2
Guimaras ☐ *Phil.* **61** F5
Guinda *U.S.A.* **110** G4
Guinea *Africa* **76** F4
Guinea ■ *W. Afr.* **82** C2
Guinea, Gulf of *Atl. Oc.* **83** E5
Guinea-Bissau ■ *Africa* **82** C2
Güines *Cuba* **120** B3
Guingamp *France* **18** D3
Guinguinéo *Senegal* **82** C1
Guipavas *France* **18** D2
Guiping *China* **59** F8
Guipúzcoa ☐ *Spain* **38** B2
Guir *Mali* **82** B4
Guirel *Mauritania* **82** B3
Güiria *Venezuela* **124** A6
Guiscard *France* **19** C10
Guise *France* **19** C10
Guitiriz *Spain* **36** B3
Guitri *Ivory C.* **82** D3
Guiuan *Phil.* **61** F6
Guixi *China* **59** C11
Guiyang *Guizhou, China* **58** D6
Guiyang *Hunan, China* **59** E9
Guizhou ☐ *China* **58** D6
Gujan-Mestras *France* **20** D2
Gujar Khan *Pakistan* **68** C5
Gujarat ☐ *India* **68** H4
Gujiang *China* **59** D10
Gujranwala *Pakistan* **68** C6
Gujrat *Pakistan* **68** C6
Gukovo *Russia* **35** F5
Gulbarga *India* **66** L10
Gulbene *Latvia* **32** D4
Gulf, The = Persian Gulf
  Asia **71** E6
Gulf Islands △ *U.S.A.* **117** F11
Gulfport *U.S.A.* **117** F10
Gulgong *Australia* **95** E4
Gulin *China* **58** C5
Gulistan *Pakistan* **68** D2
Gull Lake *Canada* **103** C7
Gullbrandstorp *Sweden* **11** H6
Gullspång *Sweden* **11** F8
Güllük *Turkey* **47** D9
Güllük Daği ☐ *Turkey* **47** E12
Güllük Körfezi *Turkey* **47** D9
Gulma *Nigeria* **83** C5
Gulmarg *India* **69** B6
Gülnar *Turkey* **72** D5
Gülpınar *Turkey* **47** B8
Gülşehir *Turkey* **72** C6
Gülshat *Kazakhstan* **52** C8
Gulu *Uganda* **86** B3
Gŭlŭbovo *Bulgaria* **45** D9
Gulud, J. *Sudan* **81** E2
Gulwe *Tanzania* **86** D4
Gulyaypole = Hulyaypole
  Ukraine **33** J9
Gumal → *Pakistan* **68** D4
Gumbaz *Pakistan* **68** D3
Gumel *Nigeria* **83** C6
Gumi *S. Korea* **57** F15
Gumiel de Hizán *Spain* **36** D7
Gumla *India* **69** H11
Gumlu *Australia* **94** B4
Gumma ☐ *Japan* **55** F9
Gummersbach *Germany* **24** D4
Gummi *Nigeria* **83** C6
Gümüldür *Turkey* **47** C9
Gümüşçay *Turkey* **45** F11
Gümüşhacıköy *Turkey* **72** B6
Gümüşhane *Turkey* **73** B8
Gümüşsu *Turkey* **47** C11
Gumzai *Indonesia* **63** F8
Guna *Ethiopia* **81** F4
Guna *India* **68** G7
Gunbalanya *Australia* **92** B5
Gundabooka △ *Australia* **95** E4
Gundelfingen *Germany* **25** G6

Güney *Burdur, Turkey* **47** D11
Güney *Denizli, Turkey* **47** C11
Güneydoğu Toroslar *Turkey* **73** C9
Gunisao → *Canada* **103** C9
Gunisao L. *Canada* **103** C9
Gunjyal *Pakistan* **68** C4
Günlüce *Turkey* **47** E10
Gunnarskog *Sweden* **10** E6
Gunnbjørn Fjeld *Greenland* **4** C6
Gunnebo *Sweden* **11** G10
Gunnedah *Australia* **95** E5
Gunnewin *Australia* **95** D4
Gunningbar Cr. → *Australia* **95** E4
Gunnison *Colo., U.S.A.* **108** G10
Gunnison *Utah, U.S.A.* **108** G8
Gunnison → *U.S.A.* **108** G9
Gunpowder *Australia* **94** B2
Gunsan *S. Korea* **57** G14
Guntakal *India* **66** M10
Guntersville *U.S.A.* **117** D11
Guntong *Malaysia* **65** K3
Guntur *India* **67** L12
Gunungapi *Indonesia* **63** F7
Gunungsitoli *Indonesia* **62** D1
Günz → *Germany* **25** G6
Gunza *Angola* **84** G2
Günzburg *Germany* **25** G6
Gunzenhausen *Germany* **25** F6
Guo He → *China* **57** H9
Guoyang *China* **56** H9
Gupis *Pakistan* **69** A5
Gura Humorului *Romania* **29** C10
Gura-Teghii *Romania* **29** E11
Gurag *Ethiopia* **81** F4
Gurahonţ *Romania* **28** D7
Gurdaspur *India* **68** C6
Gurdon *U.S.A.* **116** E8
Güre *Balıkesir, Turkey* **47** B8
Güre *Uşak, Turkey* **47** C11
Gurgaon *India* **68** E7
Gürgentepe *Turkey* **72** B7
Gurghiu, Munţii *Romania* **29** D10
Gurgueia → *Brazil* **125** E10
Gurha *India* **68** G4
Guri, Embalse de *Venezuela* **124** B6
Gurig △ *Australia* **92** B5
Gurin *Nigeria* **83** D7
Gurjaani *Georgia* **35** K7
Gurk → *Austria* **26** E7
Gurkha *Nepal* **69** E11
Gurley *Australia* **95** D4
Gurnet Point *U.S.A.* **115** D14
Guro *Mozam.* **87** F3
Gürpınar *İstanbul, Turkey* **45** F12
Gürpınar *Van, Turkey* **73** C10
Gürsu *Turkey* **45** F13
Gurué *Mozam.* **87** F4
Gurun *Malaysia* **65** K3
Gürün *Turkey* **72** C7
Gurupá *Brazil* **125** D8
Gurupá, I. Grande de *Brazil* **125** D8
Gurupi *Brazil* **125** F9
Gurupi → *Brazil* **125** D9
Guruwe *Zimbabwe* **89** B5
Guryev = Atyraū *Kazakhstan* **52** E6
Guryevsk *Russia* **30** D7
Gus-Khrustalnyy *Russia* **34** C5
Gusau *Nigeria* **83** C6
Gusev *Russia* **30** D9
Gushan *China* **57** E12
Gushgy = Serhetabat
  Turkmenistan **71** C9
Gushi *China* **59** A10
Gushiago *Ghana* **83** D4
Gusinje *Montenegro* **44** D3
Gusinoozersk *Russia* **53** D11
Gúspini *Italy* **42** C1
Güssing *Austria* **27** D9
Gustavsberg *Sweden* **10** E12
Gustavus *U.S.A.* **102** B1
Gustine *U.S.A.* **110** H6
Güstrow *Germany* **24** B8
Gusum *Sweden* **11** F10
Guta = Kolárovo
  Slovak Rep. **27** D10
Gütersloh *Germany* **24** D4
Gutha *Australia* **93** E2
Guthalungra *Australia* **94** B4
Guthrie *Okla., U.S.A.* **116** D6
Guthrie *Tex., U.S.A.* **116** E4
Gutian *China* **59** D12
Guttenberg *U.S.A.* **112** D8
Gutu *Zimbabwe* **89** B5
Guwahati *India* **67** F17
Guy Fawkes River △
  Australia **95** D5
Guyana ■ *S. Amer.* **124** C7
Guyane française = French
  Guiana ☑ *S. Amer.* **125** C8
Guyang *China* **56** D6
Guyenne *France* **20** D4
Guymon *U.S.A.* **116** C4
Guyra *Australia* **95** E5
Guyuan *Hebei, China* **56** D8
Guyuan *Ningxia Huizu, China* **56** G4
Güzelbahçe *Turkey* **47** C8
Güzelyurt = Morphou
  Cyprus **49** D11

Guzhang *China* **58** C7
Guzhen *China* **57** H9
Guzmán, L. de *Mexico* **118** A3
Gvardeysk *Russia* **30** D8
Gvardeyskoye *Ukraine* **33** K8
Gwa *Burma* **67** L19
Gwaai *Zimbabwe* **87** F2
Gwaii → *Zimbabwe* **87** F2
Gwaii Haanas △ *Canada* **102** C2
Gwabegar *Australia* **95** E4
Gwadabawa *Nigeria* **83** C6
Gwādar *Pakistan* **66** G3
Gwagwada *Nigeria* **83** C6
Gwalior *India* **68** F8
Gwanara *Nigeria* **83** D5
Gwanda *Zimbabwe* **87** G2
Gwandu *Nigeria* **83** C5
Gwane *Dem. Rep. of the Congo* **86** B2
Gwangju *S. Korea* **57** G14
Gwanju = Gwangju
  S. Korea **57** G14
Gwaram *Nigeria* **83** C7
Gwarzo *Nigeria* **83** C6
Gwasero *Nigeria* **83** D5
Gwda → *Poland* **31** B3
Gweebarra B. *Ireland* **12** B3
Gweedore *Ireland* **12** A3
Gweru *Zimbabwe* **87** F2
Gwi *Nigeria* **83** D6
Gwinn *U.S.A.* **112** B10
Gwio Kura *Nigeria* **83** C7
Gwoza *Nigeria* **83** C7
Gwydir → *Australia* **95** D4
Gwynedd ☐ *U.K.* **14** E3
Gyandzha = Gäncä
  Azerbaijan **35** K8
Gyaring Hu *China* **60** C4
Gydanskiy Poluostrov
  Russia **52** C8
Gympie *Australia* **95** D5
Gyomaendrőd *Hungary* **28** D5
Gyöngyös *Hungary* **28** C4
Győr *Hungary* **28** C2
Győr-Moson-Sopron ☐
  Hungary **28** C2
Gypsum Pt. *Canada* **102** A6
Gypsumville *Canada* **103** C9
Gyueshevo *Bulgaria* **44** D6
Gyula *Hungary* **28** D6
Gyumri *Armenia* **35** K6
Gyzylarbat = Serdar
  Turkmenistan **71** B8
Gyzyletrek = Etrek
  Turkmenistan **71** B7
Gzhatsk = Gagarin *Russia* **32** E8

H

Ha 'Arava → *Israel* **74** E4
Ha Coi *Vietnam* **58** G6
Ha Dong *Vietnam* **58** G5
Ha Giang *Vietnam* **58** F5
Ha Karmel △ *Israel* **74** C4
Ha Long, Vinh *Vietnam* **64** B6
Ha Tien *Vietnam* **65** G5
Ha Tinh *Vietnam* **64** C5
Ha Trung *Vietnam* **64** C5
Ha Yaek Chalong *Thailand* **65** a
Haaksbergen *Neths.* **17** B6
Ha'ano *Tonga* **91** c
Ha'apai Group *Tonga* **91** c
Haapiti *Moorea* **91** d
Haapsalu *Estonia* **32** C2
Haarlem *Neths.* **17** B4
Haast → *N.Z.* **91** E2
Haast Bluff *Australia* **92** D5
Hab → *Pakistan* **68** G3
Hab Nadi Chauki *Pakistan* **68** G2
Habahe *China* **60** B3
Habaswein *Kenya* **86** B4
Habay *Canada* **102** B5
Ḥabbānīyah *Iraq* **73** F10
Ḥabbānīyah, Hawr al *Iraq* **73** F10
Habichtswald △ *Germany* **24** D5
Habo *Sweden* **11** G8
Haboro *Japan* **54** B10
Ḥabshān *U.A.E.* **71** F7
Hachenburg *Germany* **24** E3
Hachijō-Jima *Japan* **55** H9
Hachinohe *Japan* **54** D10
Hachiōji *Japan* **55** G9
Hacıbektaş *Turkey* **72** C6
Hacılar *Turkey* **72** C6
Hackås *Sweden* **10** B8
Hackensack *U.S.A.* **115** F10
Hackettstown *U.S.A.* **115** F10
Hadali *Pakistan* **68** C5
Hadarba, Ras *Sudan* **80** C4
Hadarom ☐ *Israel* **74** E4
Ḥadd, Ra's al *Oman* **75** C6
Haddington *U.K.* **13** F6
Hadejia *Nigeria* **83** C7
Hadejia → *Nigeria* **83** C7
Ḥadera *Israel* **74** C3
Ḥadera, N. → *Israel* **74** C3

Haderslev *Denmark* **11** J3
Hadhramaut =
  Ḥaḍramawt *Yemen* **75** D4
Ḥadīboh *Yemen* **75** E5
Hadim *Turkey* **72** D5
Hadong *S. Korea* **57** G14
Ḥaḍramawt *Yemen* **75** D4
Ḥadrānīyah *Iraq* **70** C4
Hadrian's Wall *U.K.* **14** B5
Hadsten *Denmark* **11** H4
Hadsund *Denmark* **11** H4
Hadyach *Ukraine* **33** G8
Haeju *N. Korea* **57** E13
Haenam *S. Korea* **57** G14
Haenertsburg *S. Africa* **89** C4
Haerhpin = Harbin *China* **57** B14
Hafar al Bāṭin *Si. Arabia* **70** D5
Ḥafirat al 'Aydā *Si. Arabia* **70** E3
Hafik *Turkey* **72** C7
Hafizabad *Pakistan* **68** C5
Haflong *India* **67** G18
Haft Gel *Iran* **71** D6
Hagalil *Israel* **74** C4
Hagby *Sweden* **11** H10
Hagen *Germany* **24** D3
Hagenow *Germany* **24** B7
Hagerman *U.S.A.* **109** K11
Hagerman Fossil Beds △
  U.S.A. **108** E6
Hagerstown *U.S.A.* **113** F15
Hagersville *Canada* **114** D4
Hagetmau *France* **20** E3
Hagfors *Sweden* **10** D7
Hagi *Japan* **55** G5
Hagolan *Syria* **74** C4
Hagondange *France* **19** C13
Hags Hd. *Ireland* **12** D2
Hague, C. de la *France* **18** C5
Hague, The =
  's-Gravenhage *Neths.* **17** B4
Haguenau *France* **19** D14
Hai Duong *Vietnam* **58** G6
Hai'an *Guangdong, China* **59** G8
Hai'an *Jiangsu, China* **59** A13
Haicheng *Fujian, China* **59** E11
Haicheng *Liaoning, China* **57** D12
Haidar Khel *Afghan.* **68** C3
Haidarâbâd = Hyderabad
  India **66** L11
Haidargarh *India* **69** F9
Haifa = Ḥefa *Israel* **74** C4
Haifeng *China* **59** F10
Haiger *Germany* **24** E4
Haikou *China* **64** B8
Ḥā'il *Si. Arabia* **70** E4
Ḥā'il → *Si. Arabia* **70** E4
Hailar *China* **60** B6
Hailey *U.S.A.* **108** E6
Haileybury *Canada* **104** C4
Hailin *China* **57** B15
Hailing Dao *China* **59** G8
Hailuoto *Finland* **8** D21
Haimen *Guangdong, China* **59** F11
Haimen *Jiangsu, China* **59** B13
Hainan ☐ *China* **64** C7
Hainan Dao *China* **64** C7
Hainan Str. = Qiongzhou
  Haixia *China* **64** B8
Hainaut ☐ *Belgium* **17** D4
Hainburg *Austria* **27** C9
Haines *Alaska, U.S.A.* **102** B1
Haines *Oreg., U.S.A.* **108** D5
Haines City *U.S.A.* **117** G14
Haines Junction *Canada* **102** A1
Hainfeld *Austria* **26** C8
Haining *China* **59** B13
Haiphong *Vietnam* **58** G6
Haitan Dao *China* **59** E12
Haiti ■ *W. Indies* **121** C5
Haiya *Sudan* **80** D4
Haiyan *China* **59** B13
Haiyang *China* **57** F11
Haiyuan *Guangxi Zhuangzu,
  China* **58** F6
Haiyuan *Ningxia Huizu, China* **56** F3
Haizhou *China* **57** G10
Haizhou Wan *China* **57** G10
Hajdú-Bihar ☐ *Hungary* **28** C6
Hajdúböszörmény *Hungary* **28** C6
Hajdúdorog *Hungary* **28** C6
Hajdúhadház *Hungary* **28** C6
Hajdúnánás *Hungary* **28** C6
Hajdúsámson *Hungary* **28** C6
Hajdúszoboszló *Hungary* **28** C6
Haji Ibrahim *Iraq* **73** D11
Hajipur *India* **69** G11
Hajjah *Yemen* **75** D3
Ḥājjī Muḥsin *Iraq* **70** C5
Ḥājjīābād *Iran* **71** D7
Ḥājjīābād-e Zarrīn *Iran* **71** C7
Hajnówka *Poland* **31** B10
Haka *Burma* **67** H18
Hakansson, Mts.
  Dem. Rep. of the Congo **87** D2
Hakkâri *Turkey* **73** D10
Hakkâri *Turkey* **73** D10
Hakkâri Dağları *Turkey* **73** C10

Hakken-Zan *Japan* **55** G7
Hakodate *Japan* **54** D10
Hakos *Namibia* **88** C2
Håksberg *Sweden* **10** D9
Haku-San *Japan* **55** F8
Haku-San △ *Japan* **55** F8
Hakui *Japan* **55** F8
Hala *Pakistan* **66** G6
Ḥalab *Syria* **72** D7
Ḥalab ☐ *Syria* **72** D7
Halabjah *Iraq* **73** E11
Halaib *Sudan* **80** C4
Halaib Triangle *Africa* **80** C4
Halasa *Sudan* **81** E3
Hālat 'Ammār *Si. Arabia* **70** D3
Halbā *Lebanon* **74** A5
Halberstadt *Germany* **24** D7
Halcombe *N.Z.* **91** D5
Halcon *Phil.* **63** B6
Halde Fjäll = Haltiatunturi
  Finland **8** B19
Halden *Norway* **9** G14
Haldensleben *Germany* **24** C7
Haldia *India* **69** H13
Haldimand *Canada* **114** D5
Haldwani *India* **69** E8
Hale → *Australia* **94** C2
Halesowen *U.K.* **15** E5
Halesworth *U.K.* **15** E9
Haleyville *U.S.A.* **117** D11
Half Assini *Ghana* **82** D4
Half Dome *U.S.A.* **110** H7
Halfmoon Bay *N.Z.* **91** G2
Halfway → *Canada* **102** B4
Halia *India* **69** G10
Haliburton *Canada* **114** A6
Halifax *Australia* **94** B4
Halifax *Canada* **105** D7
Halifax *U.K.* **14** D6
Halifax *U.S.A.* **114** F8
Halifax B. *Australia* **94** B4
Halifax I. *Namibia* **88** D2
Halīl → *Iran* **71** E8
Halki *Greece* **47** E9
Halkida *Greece* **46** C5
Halkidikí ☐ *Greece* **44** F7
Halkirk *U.K.* **13** C5
Hall Beach = Sanirajak
  Canada **101** C11
Hall in Tirol *Austria* **26** D4
Hall Pen. *Canada* **101** C13
Hall Pt. *Australia* **92** C3
Hallabro *Sweden* **11** H9
Halland *Sweden* **9** H15
Hallands län ☐ *Sweden* **11** H6
Hallands Väderö *Sweden* **11** H6
Hallandsås *Sweden* **11** H7
Halle *Belgium* **17** D4
Halle *Nordrhein-Westfalen,
  Germany* **24** C4
Halle *Sachsen-Anhalt, Germany* **24** D7
Hällefors *Sweden* **10** E8
Hälleforsnäs *Sweden* **10** E10
Hallein *Austria* **26** D6
Hällekis *Sweden* **11** F7
Hallen *Sweden* **10** A8
Hallett *Australia* **95** E2
Hallettsville *U.S.A.* **116** G6
Hallim *S. Korea* **57** H14
Hallingdalselva → *Norway* **8** F13
Hallock *U.S.A.* **112** A5
Halls Creek *Australia* **92** C4
Halls Gap *Australia* **95** F3
Hallsberg *Sweden* **10** E9
Hallstahammar *Sweden* **10** E10
Hallstatt *Austria* **26** D6
Hallstavik *Sweden* **10** D12
Hallstead *U.S.A.* **115** E9
Halmahera *Indonesia* **63** D7
Halmeu *Romania* **28** C8
Halmstad *Sweden* **11** H6
Hals *Denmark* **11** H4
Hälsingborg = Helsingborg
  Sweden **11** H6
Hälsingland *Sweden* **10** C10
Halstead *U.K.* **15** F8
Haltern *Germany* **24** D3
Haltiatunturi *Finland* **8** B19
Halton ☐ *U.K.* **14** D5
Haltwhistle *U.K.* **14** C5
Ḥālūl *Qatar* **71** E7
Halvad *India* **68** H4
Halvån → *Iran* **71** D8
Ham *France* **19** C10
Ham Tan *Vietnam* **65** G6
Ham Yen *Vietnam* **64** A5
Hamab *Namibia* **88** D2
Hamad *Sudan* **81** D3
Hamada *Japan* **55** G6
Hamadān *Iran* **73** E13
Hamadān ☐ *Iran* **71** C6
Ḥamāh *Syria* **72** E7
Hamamatsu *Japan* **55** G8
Hamar *Norway* **8** F14

Hamâta, Gebel *Egypt* **70** E2
Hambantota *Sri Lanka* **66** R12
Hamber △ *Canada* **102** C5
Hamburg *Germany* **24** B5
Hamburg *Ark., U.S.A.* **116** E9
Hamburg *N.Y., U.S.A.* **114** D6
Hamburg *Pa., U.S.A.* **115** F9
Hamburg ☐ *Germany* **24** B5
Hamburg Fuhlsbüttel ✈
  (HAM) *Germany* **24** B5
Ḥamd, W. al → *Si. Arabia* **70** E3
Hamden *U.S.A.* **115** E12
Hamdibey *Turkey* **47** B9
Häme *Finland* **32** B2
Hämeenlinna *Finland* **32** B3
Hamélé *Ghana* **82** C4
Hamelin Pool *Australia* **93** E1
Hameln *Germany* **24** C5
Hamerkaz ☐ *Israel* **74** C3
Hamersley Ra. *Australia* **92** D2
Hamhũng *N. Korea* **57** E14
Hami *China* **60** B4
Hamili *Greece* **47** F8
Hamilton *Australia* **95** F3
Hamilton *Canada* **114** C5
Hamilton *N.Z.* **91** B5
Hamilton *U.K.* **13** F4
Hamilton *Ala., U.S.A.* **117** D11
Hamilton *Mont., U.S.A.* **108** C6
Hamilton *N.Y., U.S.A.* **115** D9
Hamilton *Ohio, U.S.A.* **113** F11
Hamilton *Tex., U.S.A.* **116** F5
Hamilton → *Queens.,
  Australia* **94** C2
Hamilton → *S. Austral.,
  Australia* **95** D2
Hamilton City *U.S.A.* **110** F4
Hamilton I. *Australia* **94** J6
Hamilton Inlet *Canada* **105** B8
Hamilton Mt. *U.S.A.* **115** C10
Hamina *Finland* **32** B4
Hamirpur *H.P., India* **68** D7
Hamirpur *Ut. P., India* **69** G9
Hamitabat *Turkey* **45** E11
Hamju *N. Korea* **57** E14
Hamlet *U.S.A.* **117** D15
Hamley Bridge *Australia* **95** E2
Hamlin = Hameln *Germany* **24** C5
Hamlin *N.Y., U.S.A.* **114** C7
Hamlin *Tex., U.S.A.* **116** E4
Hamm *Germany* **24** D3
Ḥammār, Hawr al *Iraq* **70** D5
Hammarstrand *Sweden* **10** A10
Hammelburg *Germany* **25** E5
Hammeren *Denmark* **11** J8
Hammerfest *Norway* **8** A20
Hammeren *Denmark* **11** H3
Hamminkeln *Germany* **24** D2
Hammond *Ind., U.S.A.* **112** E10
Hammond *La., U.S.A.* **117** F9
Hammond *N.Y., U.S.A.* **115** B9
Hammondsport *U.S.A.* **114** D7
Hammonton *U.S.A.* **113** F16
Hamneda *Sweden* **11** H7
Hamoyet, Jebel *Sudan* **80** D4
Hampden *N.Z.* **91** F3
Hampshire ☐ *U.K.* **15** F6
Hampshire Downs *U.K.* **15** F6
Hampton *N.B., Canada* **105** C6
Hampton *Ont., Canada* **114** C6
Hampton *Ark., U.S.A.* **116** E8
Hampton *Iowa, U.S.A.* **112** D7
Hampton *N.H., U.S.A.* **115** D14
Hampton *S.C., U.S.A.* **117** E14
Hampton *Va., U.S.A.* **113** G15
Hampton Bays *U.S.A.* **115** F12
Hampton Tableland
  Australia **93** F4
Hamra *Sweden* **10** C8
Hamrat esh Sheykh *Sudan* **81** E2
Hamur *Turkey* **73** C10
Hamyang *S. Korea* **57** G14
Han i Hotit *Albania* **44** D3
Han Jiang → *China* **59** F11
Han Shui → *China* **59** B10
Hanak *Si. Arabia* **70** E3
Hanamaki *Japan* **54** E10
Hanang *Tanzania* **86** C4
Hanau *Germany* **25** E4
Hanbogd = Ihbulag
  Mongolia **56** C4
Hançalar *Turkey* **47** C11
Hânceşti *Moldova* **29** D13
Hancheng *China* **56** G6
Hanchuan *China* **59** B9
Hancock *Mich., U.S.A.* **112** B10
Hancock *N.Y., U.S.A.* **115** E9
Handa *Japan* **55** G8
Handa I. *U.K.* **13** C3
Handan *China* **56** F8
Handeni *Tanzania* **86** D4
Handlová *Slovak Rep.* **27** C11
Handub *Sudan* **80** D4
Handwara *India* **69** B6
Hanegev *Israel* **74** E4
Hanford *U.S.A.* **110** J7
Hanford Reach △ *U.S.A.* **108** C4

Hang Chat *Thailand* **64 C2**
Hang Dong *Thailand* **64 C2**
Hangang → *S. Korea* **57 F14**
Hangayn Nuruu *Mongolia* **60 B4**
Hangchou = Hangzhou *China* **59 B13**
Hanggin Houqi *China* **56 D4**
Hanggin Qi *China* **56 E5**
Hangu *China* **57 E9**
Hangzhou *China* **59 B13**
Hangzhou Wan *China* **59 B13**
Hanhongor *Mongolia* **56 C3**
Hania = Chania *Greece* **49 D6**
Ḥanīdh *Si. Arabia* **71 E6**
Ḥanīsh *Yemen* **75 E3**
Haniska *Slovak Rep.* **27 C14**
Hanjiang *China* **59 E12**
Hankinson *U.S.A.* **112 B5**
Hankö *Finland* **32 C2**
Hankou *China* **59 B10**
Hanksville *U.S.A.* **108 G8**
Hanle *India* **69 C8**
Hanmer Springs *N.Z.* **91 E4**
Hann → *Australia* **92 C4**
Hann, Mt. *Australia* **92 C4**
Hanna *Canada* **102 C6**
Hanna *U.S.A.* **108 F10**
Hannah B. *Canada* **104 B4**
Hannibal *Mo., U.S.A.* **112 F8**
Hannibal *N.Y., U.S.A.* **115 C8**
Hannik *Sudan* **80 D3**
Hannover *Germany* **24 C5**
Hanö *Sweden* **11 H8**
Hanöbukten *Sweden* **11 J8**
Hanoi *Vietnam* **58 G5**
Hanover = Hannover *Germany* **24 C5**
Hanover *Canada* **114 B3**
Hanover *S. Africa* **88 E3**
Hanover *N.H., U.S.A.* **115 C12**
Hanover *Ohio, U.S.A.* **114 F2**
Hanover *Pa., U.S.A.* **113 F15**
Hanover, I. *Chile* **128 G2**
Hans Lollik I. *U.S. Virgin Is.* **121 e**
Hansdiha *India* **69 G12**
Hanshou *China* **59 C8**
Hansi *India* **68 E6**
Hanson, L. *Australia* **95 E2**
Hanstholm *Denmark* **11 G2**
Hantsavichy *Belarus* **23 B14**
Hanumangarh *India* **68 E6**
Hanyin *China* **58 A7**
Hanyuan *China* **58 C4**
Hanzhong *China* **56 H4**
Hanzhuang *China* **57 G9**
Haora *India* **69 H13**
Haoxue *China* **59 B9**
Haparanda *Sweden* **8 D21**
Happy *U.S.A.* **116 D4**
Happy Camp *U.S.A.* **108 F2**
Happy Valley-Goose Bay *Canada* **105 B7**
Hapsu *N. Korea* **57 D15**
Hapur *India* **68 E7**
Ḥaql *Si. Arabia* **74 F3**
Har *Indonesia* **63 F8**
Har-Ayrag *Mongolia* **56 B5**
Har Hu *China* **60 C4**
Har Us Nuur *Mongolia* **60 B4**
Har Yehuda *Israel* **74 D3**
Ḥaraḍ *Si. Arabia* **75 C4**
Haradok *Belarus* **32 E6**
Härädsbäck *Sweden* **11 H8**
Haranomachi *Japan* **54 F10**
Harare *Zimbabwe* **87 F3**
Harat *Eritrea* **81 D4**
Harazé *Chad* **79 G10**
Harbin *China* **57 B14**
Harbiye *Turkey* **72 D7**
Harbo *Sweden* **10 D11**
Harboøre *Denmark* **11 H2**
Harbor Beach *U.S.A.* **114 C2**
Harbour Breton *Canada* **105 C8**
Harburg *Germany* **24 B5**
Harburger Berge △ *Germany* **24 B5**
Harda *India* **68 H7**
Hardangerfjorden *Norway* **9 F12**
Hardangervidda *Norway* **8 F12**
Hardap △ *Namibia* **88 C2**
Hardap Dam *Namibia* **88 C2**
Hardenberg *Neths.* **17 B6**
Harderwijk *Neths.* **17 B5**
Hardey → *Australia* **92 D2**
Hardin *U.S.A.* **108 D10**
Harding *S. Africa* **89 E4**
Harding Ra. *Australia* **92 C3**
Hardisty *Canada* **102 C6**
Hardoi *India* **69 F9**
Hardwar = Haridwar *India* **68 E8**
Hardwick *U.S.A.* **115 B12**
Hardy, Pen. *Chile* **128 H3**
Hardy, Pte. *St. Lucia* **121 f**
Hare B. *Canada* **105 B8**
Hareid *Norway* **8 E12**
Haren *Germany* **24 C3**
Harer *Ethiopia* **81 F5**
Harerge *Ethiopia* **81 F5**

Hareto *Ethiopia* **81 F4**
Harfleur *France* **18 C7**
Hargeisa *Somali Rep.* **75 F3**
Harghita □ *Romania* **29 D10**
Harghita, Munţii *Romania* **29 D10**
Hargshamn *Sweden* **10 D12**
Hari → *Indonesia* **62 E2**
Haria *Canary Is.* **48 E6**
Haridwar *India* **68 E8**
Harim, Jabal al *Oman* **71 E8**
Haringhata → *Bangla.* **67 J16**
Harīr, W. al → *Syria* **74 C4**
Harīrūd → *Asia* **71 B9**
Härjedalen *Sweden* **10 B7**
Harlan *Iowa, U.S.A.* **112 E6**
Harlan *Ky., U.S.A.* **113 G12**
Hârlău *Romania* **29 C11**
Harlech *U.K.* **14 E3**
Harlem *U.S.A.* **108 B9**
Hårlev *Denmark* **11 J6**
Harlingen *Neths.* **17 A5**
Harlingen *U.S.A.* **116 H6**
Harlow *U.K.* **15 F8**
Harlowton *U.S.A.* **108 C9**
Harmancık *Turkey* **47 B11**
Harmånger *Sweden* **10 C11**
Harmil *Eritrea* **81 D5**
Harnai *Pakistan* **68 D2**
Harney Basin *U.S.A.* **108 E4**
Harney L. *U.S.A.* **108 E4**
Harney Peak *U.S.A.* **112 D2**
Härnön *Sweden* **10 B12**
Härnösand *Sweden* **10 B11**
Haro *Spain* **38 C2**
Haroldswick *U.K.* **13 A8**
Harp L. *Canada* **105 A7**
Harper *Liberia* **82 E3**
Harplinge *Sweden* **11 H6**
Harr *Mauritania* **82 B2**
Harrai *India* **69 H8**
Harrand *Pakistan* **68 E4**
Harricana → *Canada* **104 B4**
Harriman *U.S.A.* **117 D12**
Harrington Harbour *Canada* **105 B8**
Harris *U.K.* **13 D2**
Harris, L. *Australia* **95 E2**
Harris, Sd. of *U.K.* **13 D1**
Harris Pt. *Canada* **114 C2**
Harrisburg *Ill., U.S.A.* **112 G9**
Harrisburg *Nebr., U.S.A.* **112 E2**
Harrisburg *Pa., U.S.A.* **114 F8**
Harrismith *S. Africa* **89 D4**
Harrison *Ark., U.S.A.* **116 C8**
Harrison *Maine, U.S.A.* **115 B14**
Harrison *Nebr., U.S.A.* **112 D2**
Harrison, C. *Canada* **105 B8**
Harrison L. *Canada* **102 D4**
Harrisonburg *U.S.A.* **113 F14**
Harrisonville *U.S.A.* **112 F6**
Harriston *Canada* **114 C4**
Harrisville *Mich., U.S.A.* **114 B1**
Harrisville *N.Y., U.S.A.* **115 B9**
Harrisville *Pa., U.S.A.* **114 E5**
Harrodsburg *U.S.A.* **113 G11**
Harrogate *U.K.* **14 C6**
Harrow □ *U.K.* **15 F7**
Harrow *Canada* **114 D2**
Harrowsmith *Canada* **115 B8**
Harry S. Truman Res. *U.S.A.* **112 F7**
Harsefeld *Germany* **24 B5**
Harsewinkel *Germany* **24 D4**
Harsin *Iran* **73 E12**
Hârşova *Romania* **29 F12**
Harstad *Norway* **8 B17**
Harsud *India* **68 H7**
Hart *U.S.A.* **114 D2**
Hart, L. *Australia* **95 E2**
Hartbees → *S. Africa* **88 D3**
Hartberg *Austria* **26 D8**
Hartford *Conn., U.S.A.* **115 E12**
Hartford *Ky., U.S.A.* **112 G10**
Hartford *S. Dak., U.S.A.* **112 D5**
Hartford *Wis., U.S.A.* **112 D9**
Hartford City *U.S.A.* **113 E11**
Hartland *Canada* **105 C6**
Hartland Pt. *U.K.* **15 F3**
Hartlepool *U.K.* **14 C6**
Hartley Bay *Canada* **102 C3**
Hartmannberge *Namibia* **88 B1**
Hartney *Canada* **103 D8**
Hârtop *Moldova* **29 D13**
Harts → *S. Africa* **88 D3**
Hartselle *U.S.A.* **117 D11**
Hartshorne *U.S.A.* **116 D7**
Hartstown *U.S.A.* **114 E4**
Hartsville *U.S.A.* **117 D14**
Hartswater *S. Africa* **88 D3**
Hartwell *U.S.A.* **117 D13**
Harunabad *Pakistan* **68 E5**
Harvand *Iran* **71 D7**
Harvey *Australia* **93 F2**
Harvey *Ill., U.S.A.* **112 E10**

Harvey *N. Dak., U.S.A.* **112 B4**
Harwich *U.K.* **15 F9**
Haryana □ *India* **68 E7**
Haryn → *Belarus* **23 B14**
Harz *Germany* **24 D6**
Harz △ *Germany* **24 D6**
Harzgerode *Germany* **24 D7**
Hasa *Si. Arabia* **71 E6**
Hasan → *Indonesia* **62 E2**
Ḥasā, W. al → *Jordan* **74 D4**
Hasaheisa *Sudan* **81 E3**
Ḥasanābād *Iran* **71 C7**
Hasankeyf *Turkey* **73 D9**
Hasa *Turkey* **45 E10**
Hasdo → *India* **69 J10**
Haselünne *Germany* **24 C3**
Hashimoto *Japan* **55 G7**
Hashtjerd *Iran* **71 C6**
Haskell *U.S.A.* **116 E5**
Haskovo = Khaskovo *Bulgaria* **45 E9**
Hasköy *Turkey* **45 E10**
Haslach *Germany* **25 G4**
Hasle *Denmark* **11 J8**
Haslemere *U.K.* **15 F7**
Haslev *Denmark* **11 J5**
Hasparren *France* **20 E2**
Hassa *Turkey* **72 D7**
Hassberge △ *Germany* **25 E6**
Hassela *Sweden* **10 B10**
Hasselt *Belgium* **17 D5**
Hassfurt *Germany* **25 E6**
Hassi Messaoud *Algeria* **78 B7**
Hässleholm *Sweden* **11 H7**
Hassloch *Germany* **25 F4**
Hästholmen *Sweden* **11 F8**
Hastings *N.Z.* **91 C6**
Hastings *U.K.* **15 G8**
Hastings *Mich., U.S.A.* **113 D11**
Hastings *Minn., U.S.A.* **112 C7**
Hastings *Nebr., U.S.A.* **112 E4**
Hastings Ra. *Australia* **95 E5**
Hästveda *Sweden* **11 H7**
Hat *Ukraine* **28 B7**
Hat Yai *Thailand* **65 J3**
Hatanbulag = Ergel *Mongolia* **56 C5**
Hatay *Turkey* **72 D7**
Hatay □ *Turkey* **72 D7**
Hatch *U.S.A.* **109 K10**
Hatchet L. *Canada* **103 B8**
Haţeg *Romania* **28 E7**
Hateruma-Shima *Japan* **55 M1**
Hatfield P.O. *Australia* **95 E3**
Hatgal *Mongolia* **60 A5**
Hathras *India* **68 F8**
Hatia *Bangla.* **67 H17**
Ḥātibah, Ra's *Si. Arabia* **80 C4**
Hato Mayor *Dom. Rep.* **121 C6**
Hatta *India* **69 G8**
Hatta *U.A.E.* **71 E8**
Hattah *Australia* **95 E3**
Hattah Kulkyne △ *Australia* **95 E3**
Hatteras, C. *U.S.A.* **117 D17**
Hattiesburg *U.S.A.* **117 F10**
Hatvan *Hungary* **28 C4**
Hau Duc *Vietnam* **64 E7**
Haugesund *Norway* **9 G11**
Haukipudas *Finland* **8 D21**
Haultain → *Canada* **103 B7**
Hauraki G. *N.Z.* **91 B5**
Hausruck *Austria* **26 C6**
Haut Atlas *Morocco* **78 B4**
Haut-Jura △ *France* **19 F9**
Haut-Languedoc △ *France* **20 E6**
Haut-Niger △ *Guinea* **82 C2**
Haut-Rhin □ *France* **19 E14**
Haute-Corse □ *France* **21 F13**
Haute-Garonne □ *France* **20 E5**
Haute-Loire □ *France* **20 C7**
Haute-Marne □ *France* **19 D12**
Haute-Normandie □ *France* **18 C7**
Haute-Saône □ *France* **19 E13**
Haute-Savoie □ *France* **21 C10**
Haute-Vienne □ *France* **20 C5**
Hautes-Alpes □ *France* **21 D10**
Hautes Fagnes = Hohes Venn *Belgium* **17 D6**
Hautes-Pyrénées □ *France* **20 F4**
Hauteville-Lompnès *France* **21 C9**
Hautmont *France* **19 B10**
Hauts-de-Seine □ *France* **19 D9**
Hauts Plateaux *Algeria* **78 B6**
Hauzenberg *Germany* **25 G9**
Havana = La Habana *Cuba* **120 B3**
Havana *U.S.A.* **112 E8**
Havant *U.K.* **15 G7**
Havârna *Romania* **29 B11**
Havasor = Kızıl *Turkey* **70 B4**
Havasu, L. *U.S.A.* **111 L12**
Havdhem *Sweden* **11 G12**
Havel → *Germany* **24 C8**
Havelian *Pakistan* **68 B5**
Havelock *Canada* **114 B7**
Havelock *N.Z.* **91 D4**
Havelock *U.S.A.* **117 D16**
Haverfordwest *U.K.* **15 F3**
Haverhill *U.K.* **15 E8**

Haverhill *U.S.A.* **115 D13**
Haverstraw *U.S.A.* **115 E11**
Håverud *Sweden* **11 F6**
Havirga *Mongolia* **56 B7**
Havířov *Czech Rep.* **27 B11**
Havlíčkův Brod *Czech Rep.* **26 B8**
Havneby *Denmark* **11 J2**
Havran *Turkey* **47 B9**
Havre *U.S.A.* **108 B9**
Havre-Aubert *Canada* **105 C7**
Havre-St.-Pierre *Canada* **105 B7**
Havsa *Turkey* **45 E10**
Havza *Turkey* **72 B6**
Haw → *U.S.A.* **117 D15**
Hawai'i *U.S.A.* **106 b**
Hawai'i □ *U.S.A.* **106 b**
Hawaiian Is. *Pac. Oc.* **106 b**
Hawaiian Ridge *Pac. Oc.* **97 E11**
Hawarden *Canada* **103 C7**
Hawarden *U.S.A.* **112 D5**
Hawea, L. *N.Z.* **91 F2**
Hawera *N.Z.* **91 C5**
Hawick *U.K.* **13 F6**
Hawk Junction *Canada* **104 C3**
Hawke B. *N.Z.* **91 C6**
Hawker *Australia* **95 E2**
Hawke's Bay *Canada* **105 B8**
Hawkesbury *Canada* **104 C5**
Hawkesbury I. *Canada* **102 C3**
Hawkesbury Pt. *Australia* **94 A1**
Hawkinsville *U.S.A.* **117 E13**
Hawley *Minn., U.S.A.* **112 B5**
Hawley *Pa., U.S.A.* **115 E9**
Ḥawrān, W. → *Iraq* **73 F10**
Hawsh Mūssá *Lebanon* **74 B4**
Hawthorne *U.S.A.* **108 G4**
Hay *Australia* **95 E3**
Hay → *Australia* **94 C2**
Hay → *Canada* **102 A5**
Hay, C. *Australia* **92 B4**
Hay I. *Canada* **114 B4**
Hay L. *Canada* **102 B5**
Hay-on-Wye *U.K.* **15 E4**
Hay River *Canada* **102 A5**
Hay Springs *U.S.A.* **112 D3**
Haya = Tehoru *Indonesia* **63 E7**
Hayachine-San *Japan* **54 E10**
Hayange *France* **19 C13**
Hayastan = Armenia ■ *Asia* **35 K7**
Haydān, W. al → *Jordan* **74 D4**
Haydarlı *Turkey* **47 C12**
Hayden *U.S.A.* **108 F10**
Haydon *Australia* **94 B3**
Hayes *U.S.A.* **112 C3**
Hayes → *Canada* **104 A1**
Hayes Creek *Australia* **92 B5**
Hayle *U.K.* **15 G2**
Hayling I. *U.K.* **15 G7**
Hayman I. *Australia* **94 J6**
Haymana *Turkey* **72 C5**
Haymen I. *Australia* **94 J6**
Hayrabolu *Turkey* **45 E11**
Hays *Canada* **102 C6**
Hays *U.S.A.* **112 F4**
Haysyn *Ukraine* **29 B14**
Hayvoron *Ukraine* **29 B14**
Hayward *Calif., U.S.A.* **110 H4**
Hayward *Wis., U.S.A.* **112 B8**
Haywards Heath *U.K.* **15 G7**
Hazafon □ *Israel* **74 C4**
Hazar *Turkmenistan* **52 F6**
Hāzārān, Kūh-e *Iran* **71 D8**
Hazard *U.S.A.* **113 G12**
Hazaribag *India* **69 H11**
Hazaribag Road *India* **69 G11**
Hazebrouck *France* **19 B9**
Hazelton *Canada* **102 B3**
Hazelton *U.S.A.* **112 B3**
Hazen *U.S.A.* **112 B3**
Hazlehurst *Ga., U.S.A.* **117 F13**
Hazlehurst *Miss., U.S.A.* **117 F9**
Hazlet *U.S.A.* **115 F10**
Hazleton *U.S.A.* **115 F9**
Hazlett, L. *Australia* **92 D4**
Hazro *Turkey* **70 B4**
He Xian *Anhui, China* **59 B12**
He Xian *Guangxi Zhuangzu, China* **59 E8**
Head of Bight *Australia* **93 F5**
Headlands *Zimbabwe* **87 F3**
Healdsburg *U.S.A.* **110 G4**
Healdton *U.S.A.* **116 D6**
Healesville *Australia* **95 F4**
Heany Junction *Zimbabwe* **89 C4**
Heard I. *Ind. Oc.* **3 G13**
Hearne *U.S.A.* **116 F6**
Hearst *Canada* **104 C3**
Heart → *U.S.A.* **112 B3**
Heart's Content *Canada* **105 C9**
Heath, Pte. *Canada* **105 C7**
Heathrow, London ✈ (LHR) *U.K.* **15 F7**
Heavener *U.S.A.* **116 D7**
Hebbronville *U.S.A.* **116 H5**
Hebei □ *China* **56 E9**
Hebel *Australia* **95 D4**
Heber *U.S.A.* **111 N11**
Heber Springs *U.S.A.* **116 D8**
Hebgen L. *U.S.A.* **108 D8**

Hebi *China* **56 G8**
Hebrides *U.K.* **6 D4**
Hebrides, Sea of the *U.K.* **13 D2**
Hebron = Al Khalīl *West Bank* **74 D4**
Hebron *Canada* **101 D13**
Hebron *N. Dak., U.S.A.* **112 B2**
Hebron *Nebr., U.S.A.* **112 E5**
Heby *Sweden* **10 E10**
Hecate Str. *Canada* **102 C2**
Hechi *China* **58 E7**
Hechingen *Germany* **25 G4**
Hechuan *China* **58 B6**
Hecla *U.S.A.* **112 C4**
Hecla I. *Canada* **103 C9**
Hedal *Norway* **10 D3**
Hede *Sweden* **10 B7**
Hedemora *Sweden* **10 D9**
Hedesunda *Sweden* **10 D10**
Heerde *Neths.* **17 B6**
Heerenveen *Neths.* **17 B5**
Heerhugowaard *Neths.* **17 B4**
Heerlen *Neths.* **17 D5**
Ḥefa *Israel* **74 C4**
Ḥefa □ *Israel* **74 C4**
Hefei *China* **59 B11**
Hefeng *China* **59 C8**
Heganglig *Sudan* **81 E3**
Hegang *China* **60 B8**
Heiban *Sudan* **81 E3**
Heichengzhen *China* **56 F4**
Heide *Germany* **24 A5**
Heidelberg *Germany* **25 F4**
Heidelberg *S. Africa* **88 E3**
Heidenau *Germany* **24 E9**
Heidenheim *Germany* **25 G6**
Heilbad Heiligenstadt *Germany* **24 D6**
Heilbron *S. Africa* **89 D4**
Heilbronn *Germany* **25 F5**
Heiligenblut *Austria* **26 D5**
Heiligenhafen *Germany* **24 A6**
Heilongjiang □ *China* **60 B7**
Heilunkiang = Heilongjiang □ *China* **60 B7**
Heimaey *Iceland* **8 E3**
Heinola *Finland* **32 B4**
Heinsberg *Germany* **24 D2**
Heinze Kyun *Burma* **64 E1**
Heishan *China* **57 D12**
Heishui *Liaoning, China* **57 C10**
Heishui *Sichuan, China* **58 A4**
Hejaz = Ḥijāz *Si. Arabia* **70 G3**
Hejian *China* **56 E9**
Hejiang *China* **58 C5**
Hejin *China* **56 G6**
Hekimhan *Turkey* **72 C7**
Hekla *Iceland* **8 E4**
Hekou *Guangdong, China* **59 F9**
Hekou *Yunnan, China* **58 F4**
Hel *Poland* **30 D5**
Helagsfjället *Sweden* **10 B6**
Helan Shan *China* **56 E3**
Helechosa *Spain* **37 F6**
Helen Atoll *Pac. Oc.* **63 D8**
Helena *Ark., U.S.A.* **117 D9**
Helena *Mont., U.S.A.* **108 C7**
Helendale *U.S.A.* **111 L9**
Helensburgh *U.K.* **13 E4**
Helensville *N.Z.* **91 B5**
Helgeland *Norway* **8 C15**
Helgasjön *Sweden* **11 H8**
Helgoland *Germany* **24 A3**
Heligoland = Helgoland *Germany* **24 A3**
Heligoland B. = Deutsche Bucht *Germany* **24 A4**
Heliopolis = Masr el Gedida *Egypt* **80 H7**
Hell Hole Gorge △ *Australia* **94 D3**
Hella *Iceland* **8 E3**
Hellas = Greece ■ *Europe* **46 B3**
Hellertown *U.S.A.* **115 F9**
Hellespont = Çanakkale Boğazı *Turkey* **45 F10**
Hellevoetsluis *Neths.* **17 C4**
Hellín *Spain* **39 G3**
Hells Canyon △ *U.S.A.* **108 D5**
Hell's Gate △ *Kenya* **86 C4**
Helmand □ *Afghan.* **66 D4**
Helmand → *Afghan.* **66 D2**
Helme → *Germany* **24 D7**
Helmeringhausen *Namibia* **88 D2**
Helmond *Neths.* **17 C5**
Helmsdale *U.K.* **13 C5**
Helmsdale → *U.K.* **13 C5**
Helmstedt *Germany* **24 C7**
Helong *China* **57 C15**
Helper *U.S.A.* **108 G8**
Helsingborg *Sweden* **11 H6**
Helsinge *Denmark* **11 H6**

Helsingfors = Helsinki *Finland* **32 B3**
Helsingør *Denmark* **11 H6**
Helsinki *Finland* **32 B3**
Helska, Mierzeja *Poland* **30 D5**
Helston *U.K.* **15 G2**
Helvellyn *U.K.* **14 C4**
Helwân *Egypt* **80 J7**
Hemel Hempstead *U.K.* **15 F7**
Hemet *U.S.A.* **111 M10**
Hemingford *U.S.A.* **112 D2**
Hemis △ *India* **68 B7**
Hemmingford *Canada* **115 A11**
Hempstead *N.Y., U.S.A.* **115 F11**
Hempstead *Tex., U.S.A.* **116 F6**
Hemse *Sweden* **11 G12**
Hemsön *Sweden* **10 B12**
Henån *Sweden* **11 F5**
Henan □ *China* **56 H8**
Henares → *Spain* **36 E7**
Henashi-Misaki *Japan* **54 D9**
Hendaye *France* **20 E2**
Hendek *Turkey* **72 B4**
Henderson *Argentina* **126 D3**
Henderson *Ky., U.S.A.* **112 G10**
Henderson *N.C., U.S.A.* **117 C15**
Henderson *Nev., U.S.A.* **111 J12**
Henderson *Tenn., U.S.A.* **117 D10**
Henderson *Tex., U.S.A.* **116 E7**
Henderson I. *Pac. Oc.* **97 K15**
Hendersonville *N.C., U.S.A.* **117 D13**
Hendersonville *Tenn., U.S.A.* **117 C11**
Hendijān *Iran* **71 D6**
Hendorābī *Iran* **71 E7**
Heng Jiang *China* **58 C5**
Heng Xian *China* **58 F7**
Hengcheng *China* **56 E4**
Hengch'un *Taiwan* **59 F13**
Hengdaohezi *China* **57 B15**
Hengelo *Neths.* **17 B6**
Hengfeng *China* **59 C10**
Hengshan *Hunan, China* **59 D9**
Hengshan *Shaanxi, China* **56 F5**
Hengshui *China* **56 F8**
Hengyang *China* **59 D9**
Henichesk *Ukraine* **33 J8**
Hénin-Beaumont *France* **19 B9**
Henley-on-Thames *U.K.* **15 F7**
Henlopen, C. *U.S.A.* **113 F16**
Hennan *Sweden* **10 B9**
Hennebont *France* **18 E3**
Hennenman *S. Africa* **88 D4**
Hennessey *U.S.A.* **116 C6**
Hennigsdorf *Germany* **24 C9**
Henri Pittier △ *Venezuela* **121 D6**
Henrietta *U.S.A.* **116 E5**
Henrietta, Ostrov = Genriyetty, Ostrov *Russia* **53 B16**
Henrietta Maria, C. *Canada* **104 A3**
Henry *U.S.A.* **112 E9**
Henryetta *U.S.A.* **116 D7**
Henryville *Canada* **115 A11**
Hensall *Canada* **114 C3**
Henstedt-Ulzburg *Germany* **24 B6**
Hentiesbaai *Namibia* **88 C1**
Hentiyn Nuruu *Mongolia* **60 B5**
Henty *Australia* **95 F4**
Henzada *Burma* **67 L19**
Hephaestia *Greece* **47 B7**
Heping *China* **59 E10**
Heppner *U.S.A.* **108 D4**
Hepu *China* **58 G7**
Hepworth *Canada* **114 B3**
Heqing *China* **58 D3**
Hequ *China* **56 E6**
Heraðsflói *Iceland* **8 D6**
Heraðsvötn → *Iceland* **8 D4**
Heraklion = Iraklio *Greece* **49 D7**
Herald Cays *Australia* **94 B4**
Herãt *Afghan.* **66 B3**
Herãt □ *Afghan.* **66 B3**
Hérault □ *France* **20 E7**
Hérault → *France* **20 E7**
Herbault *France* **18 E8**
Herbert → *Australia* **94 B4**
Herberton *Australia* **94 B4**
Herbertsdale *S. Africa* **88 E3**
Herbignac *France* **18 E4**
Herborn *Germany* **24 E4**
Herby *Poland* **31 H5**
Herceg-Novi *Montenegro* **44 D2**
Herchmer *Canada* **103 B10**
Herðubreið *Iceland* **8 D5**
Hereford *U.K.* **15 E5**
Hereford *U.S.A.* **116 D3**
Herefordshire □ *U.K.* **15 E5**
Hereke *Turkey* **45 F13**
Herencia *Spain* **37 F7**
Herentals *Belgium* **17 C4**
Herford *Germany* **24 C4**
Héricourt *France* **19 E13**
Herington *U.S.A.* **112 F5**
Herisau *Switz.* **25 H5**

Hérisson *France* **19** F9
Herkimer *U.S.A.* **115** D10
Herlong *U.S.A.* **110** E6
Herm *U.K.* **15** H5
Hermakivka *Ukraine* **29** B11
Hermann *U.S.A.* **112** F8
Hermannsburg *Australia* **92** D5
Hermannsburg *Germany* **24** C6
Hermanus *S. Africa* **88** E2
Herment *France* **20** C6
Hermidale *Australia* **95** E4
Hermiston *U.S.A.* **108** D4
Hermite, I. *Chile* **128** H3
Hermon *U.S.A.* **115** B9
Hermon, Mt. = Shaykh, J. ash *Lebanon* **74** B4
Hermosillo *Mexico* **118** B2
Hernád → *Hungary* **28** C6
Hernandarias *Paraguay* **127** B5
Hernandez *U.S.A.* **110** J6
Hernando *Argentina* **126** C3
Hernando *U.S.A.* **117** D10
Hernani *Spain* **38** B3
Herndon *U.S.A.* **114** F8
Herne *Germany* **17** C7
Herne Bay *U.K.* **15** F9
Herning *Denmark* **11** H2
Heroica Caborca = Caborca *Mexico* **118** A2
Heroica Nogales = Nogales *Mexico* **118** A2
Heron Bay *Canada* **104** C2
Heron I. *Australia* **94** C5
Herradura, Pta. de la *Canary Is.* **48** F5
Herreid *U.S.A.* **112** C3
Herrenberg *Germany* **25** G4
Herrera *Spain* **37** H6
Herrera de Alcántara *Spain* **37** F3
Herrera de Pisuerga *Spain* **36** C6
Herrera del Duque *Spain* **37** F5
Herrestad *Sweden* **11** F5
Herrin *U.S.A.* **112** G9
Herriot *Canada* **103** B8
Herrljunga *Sweden* **11** F7
Hersbruck *Germany* **25** F7
Herschel I. *Canada* **4** C1
Hershey *U.S.A.* **115** F8
Herso *Greece* **44** E6
Herstal *Belgium* **17** D5
Hertford *U.K.* **15** F7
Hertfordshire □ *U.K.* **15** F7
's-Hertogenbosch *Neths.* **17** C5
Hertsa *Ukraine* **29** B11
Hertzogville *S. Africa* **88** D4
Hervás *Spain* **36** E5
Hervey B. *Australia* **94** C5
Herzberg *Brandenburg, Germany* **24** D9
Herzberg *Niedersachsen, Germany* **24** D6
Herzliyya *Israel* **74** C3
Herzogenburg *Austria* **26** C8
Ḩeşār *Fārs, Iran* **71** D6
Ḩeşār *Markazī, Iran* **71** C6
Hesdin *France* **19** B9
Heshan *China* **58** F7
Heshui *China* **56** G5
Heshun *China* **56** F7
Hesperia *U.S.A.* **111** L9
Hesse = Hessen □ *Germany* **24** E4
Hessen □ *Germany* **24** E4
Hessenreuther und Manteler Wald △ *Germany* **25** F8
Hestra *Sweden* **11** G7
Hetauda *Nepal* **68** F11
Hetch Hetchy Aqueduct *U.S.A.* **110** H5
Hettinger *U.S.A.* **112** B2
Hettstedt *Germany* **24** D7
Heuksando *S. Korea* **57** G13
Heunghae *S. Korea* **57** F15
Heuvelton *U.S.A.* **115** B9
Heves *Hungary* **28** C5
Heves □ *Hungary* **28** C5
Hewitt *U.S.A.* **116** F6
Hexham *U.K.* **14** C5
Hexi *Yunnan, China* **58** E4
Hexi *Zhejiang, China* **59** D12
Hexigten Qi *China* **57** C9
Ḩeydarābād *Iran* **71** D7
Heysham *U.K.* **14** C5
Heyuan *China* **59** F10
Heywood *Australia* **95** F3
Heze *China* **56** G8
Hezhang *China* **58** D5
Hi, Ko *Thailand* **65** a
Hi Vista *U.S.A.* **111** L9
Hialeah *U.S.A.* **117** J14
Hiawatha *U.S.A.* **112** F6
Hibbing *U.S.A.* **112** B7
Hibbs B. *Australia* **95** G4
Hibernia Reef *Australia* **92** B3
Hickman *U.S.A.* **112** G9
Hickory *U.S.A.* **117** D14
Hicks, Pt. *Australia* **95** F4

Hicks L. *Canada* **103** A9
Hicksville *U.S.A.* **115** F11
Hida *Romania* **29** C8
Hida-Gawa → *Japan* **55** G8
Hida-Sammyaku *Japan* **55** F8
Hidaka-Sammyaku *Japan* **54** C11
Hidalgo □ *Mexico* **119** C5
Hidalgo, Presa M. *Mexico* **118** B3
Hidalgo del Parral *Mexico* **118** B3
Hiddensee *Germany* **24** A9
Hieflau *Austria* **26** D7
Hiendelaencina *Spain* **38** D2
Hierro *Canary Is.* **48** G1
Higashiajima-San *Japan* **54** F10
Higashiōsaka *Japan* **55** G7
Higgins *U.S.A.* **116** C4
Higgins Corner *U.S.A.* **110** F5
High Bridge *U.S.A.* **115** F10
High Level *Canada* **102** B5
High Point *U.S.A.* **117** D15
High Prairie *Canada* **102** B5
High River *Canada* **102** C6
High Tatra = Tatry *Slovak Rep.* **27** B13
High Veld *Africa* **76** J6
High Wycombe *U.K.* **15** F7
Highland □ *U.K.* **13** D4
Highland Park *U.S.A.* **112** D10
Highmore *U.S.A.* **112** C4
Highrock L. *Man., Canada* **103** B9
Highrock L. *Sask., Canada* **103** B7
Higüey *Dom. Rep.* **121** C6
Hihya *Egypt* **80** H7
Hiiumaa *Estonia* **32** C2
Híjar *Spain* **38** D4
Hijo = Tagum *Phil.* **61** H6
Hikari *Japan* **55** H5
Hikmak, Ras el *Egypt* **80** A2
Hiko *U.S.A.* **110** H11
Hikone *Japan* **55** G8
Hikurangi *Gisborne, N.Z.* **91** C6
Hikurangi *Northland, N.Z.* **91** A5
Hildburghausen *Germany* **24** E6
Hildesheim *Germany* **24** C5
Hill → *Australia* **93** F2
Hill City *Idaho, U.S.A.* **108** E6
Hill City *Kans., U.S.A.* **112** F4
Hill City *Minn., U.S.A.* **112** B7
Hill City *S. Dak., U.S.A.* **112** D2
Hill Island L. *Canada* **103** A7
Hillaby, Mt. *Barbados* **121** g
Hillared *Sweden* **11** G7
Hillcrest *Barbados* **121** g
Hillcrest Center *U.S.A.* **111** K8
Hillegom *Neths.* **17** B4
Hillerød *Denmark* **11** J6
Hillerstorp *Sweden* **11** G7
Hillsboro *Kans., U.S.A.* **112** F5
Hillsboro *N. Dak., U.S.A.* **112** B5
Hillsboro *Ohio, U.S.A.* **113** F12
Hillsboro *Oreg., U.S.A.* **110** E4
Hillsboro *Tex., U.S.A.* **116** E6
Hillsborough *Grenada* **121** D7
Hillsborough *U.S.A.* **115** C13
Hillsborough Channel *Australia* **94** J7
Hillsdale *Mich., U.S.A.* **113** E11
Hillsdale *N.Y., U.S.A.* **115** D11
Hillsport *Canada* **104** C2
Hillston *Australia* **95** E4
Hilo *U.S.A.* **106** b
Hilton *U.S.A.* **114** C7
Hilton Head Island *U.S.A.* **117** E14
Hilvan *Turkey* **73** D8
Hilversum *Neths.* **17** B5
Himachal Pradesh □ *India* **68** D7
Himalaya *Asia* **69** E11
Himamaylan *Phil.* **61** F5
Himarë *Albania* **44** F3
Himatnagar *India* **68** H5
Himeji *Japan* **55** G7
Himi *Japan* **55** F8
Himmerland *Denmark* **11** H3
Ḩimş *Syria* **74** A5
Ḩimş □ *Syria* **74** A6
Hinche *Haiti* **121** C5
Hinchinbrook I. *Australia* **94** B4
Hinchinbrook Island △ *Australia* **94** B4
Hinckley *U.K.* **15** E6
Hinckley *U.S.A.* **112** B7
Hindaun *India* **68** F7
Hindmarsh, L. *Australia* **95** F3
Hindsholm *Denmark* **11** J4
Hindu Bagh *Pakistan* **68** D2
Hindu Kush *Asia* **66** B7
Hindupur *India* **66** N10
Hines Creek *Canada* **102** B5
Hinesville *U.S.A.* **117** F14
Hinganghat *India* **66** J11
Hingham *U.S.A.* **108** B8
Hingir *India* **69** J10
Hingoli *India* **66** K10
Hiniragan *Phil.* **61** F5
Hinis *Turkey* **73** C9
Hinna = Imi *Ethiopia* **81** F5

Hinna *Nigeria* **83** C7
Hinnerup *Denmark* **11** H4
Hinnøya *Norway* **8** B16
Hinojosa del Duque *Spain* **37** G5
Hinsdale *U.S.A.* **115** D12
Hinterrhein → *Switz.* **25** J5
Hinthada = Henzada *Burma* **67** L19
Hinton *Canada* **102** C5
Hinton *U.S.A.* **113** G13
Hios *Greece* **47** C8
Hios □ *Greece* **47** C8
Hirado *Japan* **55** H4
Hirakud Dam *India* **67** J13
Hiran → *India* **69** H8
Hirapur *India* **69** G8
Hirara *Japan* **55** M2
Hiratsuka *Japan* **55** G9
Hirfanlı Barajı *Turkey* **72** C5
Hiroo *Japan* **54** C11
Hirosaki *Japan* **54** D10
Hiroshima *Japan* **55** G6
Hiroshima □ *Japan* **55** G6
Hirson *France* **19** C11
Hirtshals *Denmark* **11** G3
Hisar *India* **68** E6
Hisarcık *Turkey* **47** B11
Hisaria *Bulgaria* **45** D8
Ḩīt *Iraq* **73** F10
Hita *Japan* **55** H5
Hitachi *Japan* **55** F10
Hitchin *U.K.* **15** F7
Hitiaa *Tahiti* **91** d
Hitoyoshi *Japan* **55** H5
Hitra *Norway* **8** E13
Hitzacker *Germany* **24** B7
Hiva Oa *French Polynesia* **97** H14
Hixon *Canada* **102** C4
Ḩiyyon, N. → *Israel* **74** E4
Hjalmar L. *Canada* **103** A7
Hjälmaren *Sweden* **10** E9
Hjort Trench *S. Ocean* **5** B10
Hjortkvarn *Sweden* **11** F9
Hjältevad *Sweden* **11** G9
Hjo *Sweden* **11** F8
Hjørring *Denmark* **11** G3
Hkakabo Razi *Burma* **67** E20
Hlinsko *Czech Rep.* **26** B8
Hlobane *S. Africa* **89** D5
Hlohovec *Slovak Rep.* **27** C10
Hlučín *Czech Rep.* **27** B11
Hluhluwe *S. Africa* **89** D5
Hluhluwe △ *S. Africa* **89** C5
Hlukhiv *Ukraine* **33** G7
Hlyboka *Ukraine* **29** B10
Hlybokaye *Belarus* **32** E4
Hnúšťa *Slovak Rep.* **27** C12
Ho *Ghana* **83** D5
Ho Chi Minh City = Thanh Pho Ho Chi Minh *Vietnam* **65** G6
Ho Thuong *Vietnam* **64** C5
Hoa Binh *Vietnam* **58** G5
Hoa Da *Vietnam* **65** G7
Hoa Hiep *Vietnam* **65** G5
Hoai Nhon *Vietnam* **64** E7
Hoang Lien Son *Vietnam* **58** F4
Hoanib → *Namibia* **88** B2
Hoare B. *Canada* **101** C13
Hoarusib → *Namibia* **88** B2
Hobart *Australia* **95** G4
Hobart *U.S.A.* **116** D5
Hobbs *U.S.A.* **109** K12
Hobbs Coast *Antarctica* **5** D14
Hobe Sound *U.S.A.* **117** H14
Hoboken *U.S.A.* **115** F10
Hobro *Denmark* **11** H3
Hoburgen *Sweden* **11** H12
Hocalar *Turkey* **47** C11
Hochfeld *Namibia* **88** C2
Hochharz △ *Germany* **24** D6
Hochschwab *Austria* **26** D8
Höchstadt *Germany* **25** F6
Hochtaunus △ *Germany* **25** E4
Hockenheim *Germany* **25** F4
Hodaka-Dake *Japan* **55** F8
Hodeida = Al Ḩudaydah *Yemen* **75** E3
Hodgeville *Canada* **103** C7
Hodgson *Canada* **103** C9
Hodh El Gharbi □ *Mauritania* **82** B3
Hódmezővásárhely *Hungary* **28** D5
Hodna, Chott el *Algeria* **78** A6
Hodonín *Czech Rep.* **27** C10
Hœdic, Î. de *France* **18** E4
Hoek van Holland *Neths.* **17** C4
Hoengseong *S. Korea* **57** F14
Hoeryong *N. Korea* **57** C15
Hoeyang *N. Korea* **57** E14
Hof *Germany* **25** E7
Hofgeismar *Germany* **24** D5
Hofheim *Germany* **25** E4
Hofmeyr *S. Africa* **88** E4
Höfn *Iceland* **8** D6

Hofors *Sweden* **10** D10
Hofsjökull *Iceland* **8** D4
Hōfu *Japan* **55** G5
Hogan Group *Australia* **95** F4
Höganäs *Sweden* **11** H6
Hogarth, Mt. *Australia* **94** C2
Hoge Kempen △ *Belgium* **17** C5
Hoggar = Ahaggar *Algeria* **78** D7
Högsäter *Sweden* **11** F6
Høgsby *Sweden* **11** G10
Högsjö *Sweden* **10** E9
Hogsty Reef *Bahamas* **121** B5
Hoh → *U.S.A.* **110** C2
Hohd ech Chargui □ *Mauritania* **82** B3
Hohe Acht *Germany* **25** E3
Hohe Tauern *Austria* **26** D5
Hohe Tauern △ *Austria* **26** D5
Hohenau *Austria* **27** C9
Hohenems *Austria* **26** D2
Hohenloher Ebene *Germany* **25** F5
Hohenwald *U.S.A.* **117** D11
Hohenwestedt *Germany* **24** A5
Hoher Rhön = Rhön *Germany* **24** E5
Hoher Vogelsberg △ *Germany* **24** D5
Hohhot *China* **56** D6
Hohoe *Ghana* **83** D5
Hoi An *Vietnam* **64** E7
Hoi Xuan *Vietnam* **58** G5
Hoisington *U.S.A.* **112** F4
Hōjō *Japan* **55** H6
Hok *Sweden* **11** G8
Hökensås *Sweden* **11** G8
Hökerum *Sweden* **11** G7
Hokianga Harbour *N.Z.* **91** A4
Hokitika *N.Z.* **91** E3
Hokkaidō □ *Japan* **54** C11
Hol-Hol *Djibouti* **81** E5
Hola *Kenya* **86** B4
Hola Pristan *Ukraine* **33** J7
Holakas *Greece* **49** D9
Holbæk *Denmark* **11** J5
Holbrook *Australia* **95** F4
Holbrook *U.S.A.* **109** J8
Holden *U.S.A.* **108** G7
Holdenville *U.S.A.* **116** D6
Holdrege *U.S.A.* **112** E4
Holešov *Czech Rep.* **27** B10
Holetown *Barbados* **121** g
Holguín *Cuba* **120** B4
Holíč *Slovak Rep.* **27** C10
Holice *Czech Rep.* **26** A8
Höljes *Sweden* **10** D6
Hollabrunn *Austria* **26** C9
Hollams Bird I. *Namibia* **88** C1
Holland *Mich., U.S.A.* **112** D10
Holland *N.Y., U.S.A.* **114** D6
Holley *U.S.A.* **114** C6
Hollfeld *Germany* **25** F7
Hollidaysburg *U.S.A.* **114** F6
Hollis *U.S.A.* **116** D5
Hollister *Calif., U.S.A.* **110** J5
Hollister *Idaho, U.S.A.* **108** E6
Höllviken = Höllviksnäs *Sweden* **11** J6
Höllviksnäs *Sweden* **11** J6
Holly Hill *U.S.A.* **117** G14
Holly Springs *U.S.A.* **117** D10
Hollywood *U.S.A.* **117** J14
Holman *Canada* **100** B8
Hólmavík *Iceland* **8** D3
Holmen *U.S.A.* **112** D8
Holmes Reefs *Australia* **94** B4
Holmsjö *Sweden* **11** H9
Holmsjön *Västernorrland, Sweden* **10** B10
Holmsund *Sweden* **8** E19
Holmsund *Västernorrland, Sweden* **10** B9
Holod *Romania* **28** D7
Holovne *Ukraine* **31** G11
Holozubyntsi *Ukraine* **29** B11
Holroyd → *Australia* **94** A3
Holstebro *Denmark* **11** H2
Holsteinische Schweiz △ *Germany* **24** A6
Holsworthy *U.K.* **15** G3
Holton *Canada* **105** B8
Holton *U.S.A.* **112** F6
Holtville *U.S.A.* **111** N11
Holwerd *Neths.* **17** A5
Holy I. *Anglesey, U.K.* **14** D3
Holy I. *Northumberland, U.K.* **14** B6
Holyhead *U.K.* **14** D3
Holyoke *Colo., U.S.A.* **108** F12
Holyoke *Mass., U.S.A.* **115** D12
Holyrood *Canada* **105** C9
Holzkirchen *Germany* **25** H7
Holzminden *Germany* **24** D5
Homa Bay *Kenya* **86** C3

Homand *Iran* **71** C8
Homberg *Germany* **24** D5
Homburg *Germany* **25** F3
Home B. *Canada* **101** C13
Home Hill *Australia* **94** B4
Home Reef *Tonga* **91** c
Homedale *U.S.A.* **108** E5
Homer *Alaska, U.S.A.* **100** D4
Homer *La., U.S.A.* **116** E8
Homer City *U.S.A.* **114** F5
Homert △ *Germany* **24** D4
Homestead *Australia* **94** C4
Homestead *U.S.A.* **117** J14
Homestead △ *U.S.A.* **112** E5
Homoine *Mozam.* **89** C6
Homolje Planina *Serbia* **44** B5
Homorod *Romania* **29** D10
Homs = Ḩimş *Syria* **74** A5
Homyel *Belarus* **23** B16
Homyel □ *Belarus* **33** F6
Hon Chong *Vietnam* **65** G5
Hon Hai *Vietnam* **65** H7
Hon Me *Vietnam* **64** C5
Honan = Henan □ *China* **56** H8
Honaz *Turkey* **47** D11
Honbetsu *Japan* **54** C11
Honcut *U.S.A.* **110** F5
Honda, Bahía *Cuba* **120** B3
Honda Bay *Phil.* **61** G3
Hondarribia *Spain* **38** B3
Hondeklipbaai *S. Africa* **88** E2
Hondo *Japan* **55** H5
Hondo *U.S.A.* **116** G5
Hondo, Río → *Belize* **119** D7
Honduras ■ *Cent. Amer.* **120** D2
Honduras, G. de *Caribbean* **120** C2
Hønefoss *Norway* **9** F14
Honesdale *U.S.A.* **115** E9
Honey L. *U.S.A.* **110** E6
Honfleur *France* **18** C7
Høng *Denmark* **11** J5
Hong Gai *Vietnam* **58** G6
Hong He → *China* **56** H8
Hong Hu *China* **59** C9
Hong Kong □ *China* **59** F10
Hong'an *China* **59** B10
Hongcheon *S. Korea* **57** F14
Honghai Wan *China* **59** F10
Honghe *China* **58** F4
Honghu *China* **59** C9
Hongjiang *China* **58** D7
Hongliu He → *China* **56** E5
Hongor *Mongolia* **56** B7
Hongsa *Laos* **64** C3
Hongseong *S. Korea* **57** F14
Hongshui He → *China* **58** F7
Hongtong *China* **56** F6
Honguedo, Détroit d' *Canada* **105** C7
Hongwon *N. Korea* **57** E14
Hongya *China* **58** C4
Hongyuan *China* **58** A4
Hongze Hu *China* **57** H10
Honiara *Solomon Is.* **90** B8
Honiton *U.K.* **15** G4
Honjō *Japan* **54** E10
Honkorâb, Ras *Egypt* **80** C4
Honningsvåg *Norway* **8** A21
Hönö *Sweden* **11** G5
Honolulu *U.S.A.* **106** b
Hontoria del Pinar *Spain* **38** D1
Hood, Mt. *U.S.A.* **108** D3
Hood, Pt. *Australia* **93** F2
Hood River *U.S.A.* **108** D3
Hoodsport *U.S.A.* **110** C3
Hooge *Germany* **24** A4
Hoogeveen *Neths.* **17** B6
Hoogezand-Sappemeer *Neths.* **17** A6
Hooghly = Hugli → *India* **69** J13
Hooghly-Chinsura = Chunchura *India* **69** H13
Hook Hd. *Ireland* **12** D5
Hook I. *Australia* **94** J6
Hook of Holland = Hoek van Holland *Neths.* **17** C4
Hooker *U.S.A.* **116** C4
Hooker Creek = Lajamanu *Australia* **92** C5
Hoonah *U.S.A.* **102** B1
Hooper Bay *U.S.A.* **106** a
Hoopeston *U.S.A.* **112** E10
Hoopstad *S. Africa* **88** D4
Höör *Sweden* **11** J7
Hoover *U.S.A.* **117** E11
Hoover Dam *U.S.A.* **111** K12
Hooversville *U.S.A.* **114** F6
Hop Bottom *U.S.A.* **115** E9
Hopa *Turkey* **73** B9
Hope *Canada* **102** D4
Hope *Ariz., U.S.A.* **111** M13
Hope *Ark., U.S.A.* **116** E8
Hope, L. *S. Austral., Australia* **95** D2

Hope, L. *W. Austral., Australia* **93** F3
Hope, Pt. *U.S.A.* **98** C3
Hope I. *Canada* **114** B5
Hope Town *Bahamas* **120** A4
Hope Vale *Australia* **94** B4
Hopedale *Canada* **105** A7
Hopedale *U.S.A.* **115** D13
Hopefield *S. Africa* **88** E2
Hopei = Hebei □ *China* **56** E9
Hopelchén *Mexico* **119** D7
Hopetoun *Vic., Australia* **95** F3
Hopetoun *W. Austral., Australia* **93** F3
Hopetown *S. Africa* **88** D3
Hopewell *U.S.A.* **113** G15
Hopfgarten *Austria* **26** D5
Hopkins, L. *Australia* **92** D4
Hopkinsville *U.S.A.* **112** G10
Hopland *U.S.A.* **110** G3
Hoquiam *U.S.A.* **110** D3
Hora Hoverla *Ukraine* **29** B9
Horasan *Turkey* **73** B10
Horaždovice *Czech Rep.* **26** B6
Horb *Germany* **25** G4
Hörby *Sweden* **11** J7
Horcajo de Santiago *Spain* **38** F1
Hordern Hills *Australia* **92** D5
Horezu *Romania* **29** E8
Horgen *Switz.* **25** H4
Horgoš *Serbia* **28** C4
Hořice *Czech Rep.* **26** A8
Horinchove *Ukraine* **29** B8
Horinger *China* **56** D6
Horki *Belarus* **32** E6
Horlick Mts. *Antarctica* **5** E15
Horlivka *Ukraine* **33** H10
Hormak *Iran* **71** D9
Hormoz *Iran* **71** E7
Hormoz, Jaz.-ye *Iran* **71** E8
Hormozgān □ *Iran* **71** E8
Hormuz, Küh-e *Iran* **71** E7
Hormuz, Str. of *The Gulf* **71** E8
Horn *Austria* **26** C8
Horn *Sweden* **11** G9
Horn → *Canada* **102** A5
Horn, Cape = Hornos, C. de *Chile* **128** H3
Horn Head *Ireland* **12** A3
Horn I. *Australia* **94** A3
Horn Plateau *Canada* **102** A5
Hornachuelos *Spain* **37** H5
Hornavan *Sweden* **8** C17
Hornbeck *U.S.A.* **116** F8
Hornbrook *U.S.A.* **108** F2
Hornburg *Germany* **24** C6
Horncastle *U.K.* **14** D7
Horndal *Sweden* **10** D10
Hornell *U.S.A.* **114** D7
Hornell L. *Canada* **102** A5
Hornepayne *Canada* **104** C3
Horní Planá *Czech Rep.* **26** C7
Hornings Mills *Canada* **114** B4
Hornitos *U.S.A.* **110** H6
Hornos, C. de *Chile* **128** H3
Hornoy-le-Bourg *France* **19** C8
Hornsea *U.K.* **14** D7
Hornslandet *Sweden* **10** C11
Hörnum *Germany* **24** A4
Horobetsu = Noboribetsu *Japan* **54** C10
Horodenka *Ukraine* **29** B10
Horodnya *Ukraine* **33** G6
Horodok *Khmelnytskyy, Ukraine* **23** D14
Horodok *Lviv, Ukraine* **23** D12
Horodyshche *Ukraine* **33** H6
Horokhiv *Ukraine* **23** C13
Horovice *Czech Rep.* **26** B6
Horqin Youyi Qianqi *China* **57** A12
Horqueta *Paraguay* **126** A4
Horred *Sweden* **11** G6
Horse Cr. → *U.S.A.* **108** F12
Horse I. *Canada* **103** C9
Horse Is. *Canada* **105** B8
Horsefly L. *Canada* **102** C4
Horseheads *U.S.A.* **114** D8
Horsens *Denmark* **11** J3
Horsham *Australia* **95** F3
Horsham *U.K.* **15** F7
Horšovský Týn *Czech Rep.* **26** B5
Horta *Azores* **78** a
Horten *Norway* **9** G14
Hortobágy → *Hungary* **28** C6
Hortobágyi △ *Hungary* **28** C6
Horton *U.S.A.* **112** F6
Horton → *Canada* **100** C7
Horwood L. *Canada* **104** C3
Hosaina *Ethiopia* **81** F4
Ḩoseynābād *Khuzestān, Iran* **71** C6
Ḩoseynābād *Kordestān, Iran* **73** E12
Hoshangabad *India* **68** H7
Hoshiarpur *India* **68** D6
Hospet *India* **66** M10
Hoste, I. *Chile* **128** H3
Hostens *France* **20** D3
Hot *Thailand* **64** C2
Hot Creek Range *U.S.A.* **108** G5

Hot Springs *Ark., U.S.A.* **116** D8
Hot Springs *S. Dak., U.S.A.* **112** D2
Hot Springs △ *U.S.A.* **116** D8
Hotagen *Sweden* **8** E16
Hotan *China* **60** C2
Hotazel *S. Africa* **88** D3
Hotchkiss *U.S.A.* **108** G10
Hotham, C. *Australia* **92** B5
Hoting *Sweden* **8** D17
Hotolisht *Albania* **44** E4
Hotte, Massif de la *Haiti* **121** C5
Hottentotsbaai *Namibia* **88** D1
Houat, Î. de *France* **18** E4
Houdan *France* **19** D8
Houei Sai *Laos* **58** G3
Houffalize *Belgium* **17** D5
Houghton *Mich., U.S.A.* **112** B9
Houghton *N.Y., U.S.A.* **114** D6
Houghton L. *U.S.A.* **113** C11
Houghton-le-Spring *U.K.* **14** C6
Houhora Heads *N.Z.* **91** A4
Houlton *U.S.A.* **113** B20
Houma *U.S.A.* **117** G9
Houndé *Burkina Faso* **82** C4
Hourtin *France* **20** C2
Hourtin-Carcans, Étang d'
   France **20** C2
Housatonic ➤ *U.S.A.* **115** E11
Houston *Canada* **102** C3
Houston *Mo., U.S.A.* **112** G8
Houston *Tex., U.S.A.* **116** G7
Hout = Mogwadi ➤
   S. Africa **89** C4
Houtkraal *S. Africa* **88** E3
Houtman Abrolhos *Australia* **93** E1
Hovd □ *Mongolia* **60** B4
Hove *U.K.* **15** G7
Hovedstaden □ *Denmark* **11** J6
Hoven weep △ *U.S.A.* **109** H9
Hoveyzeh *Iran* **71** D6
Hovmantorp *Sweden* **11** H9
Hövsgöl *Mongolia* **56** C5
Hövsgöl Nuur *Mongolia* **60** A5
Hovsta *Sweden* **10** E9
Howakil *Eritrea* **81** D5
Howar, Wadi ➤ *Sudan* **81** D2
Howard *Australia* **95** D5
Howard *Pa., U.S.A.* **114** F7
Howard *S. Dak., U.S.A.* **112** C5
Howe *U.S.A.* **108** E7
Howe, C. *Australia* **95** F5
Howe, West Cape *Australia* **93** G2
Howe I. *Canada* **115** B8
Howell *U.S.A.* **113** D12
Howick *Canada* **115** A11
Howick *S. Africa* **89** D5
Howick Group *Australia* **94** A4
Howitt, L. *Australia* **95** D2
Howland I. *Pac. Oc.* **96** G10
Howrah = Haora *India* **69** H13
Howth *Ireland* **12** C5
Howth Hd. *Ireland* **12** C5
Höxter *Germany* **24** D5
Hoy *U.K.* **13** C5
Hoya *Germany* **24** C5
Høyanger *Norway* **8** F12
Hoyerswerda *Germany* **24** D10
Hoylake *U.K.* **14** D4
Hoyos *Spain* **36** E4
Hpa-an = Pa-an *Burma* **67** L20
Hpunan Pass *Burma* **67** F20
Hradec Králové *Czech Rep.* **26** A8
Hrádek *Czech Rep.* **27** C9
Hranice *Czech Rep.* **27** B10
Hrazdan *Armenia* **35** K7
Hrebenka *Ukraine* **33** G7
Hrisoupoli *Greece* **45** F8
Hristiana *Greece* **47** E7
Hrodna *Belarus* **30** E10
Hrodna □ *Belarus* **32** F3
Hrodzyanka *Belarus* **23** B15
Hron ➤ *Slovak Rep.* **27** D11
Hrubieszów *Poland* **31** H10
Hrubý Jeseník *Czech Rep.* **27** A10
Hrvatska = Croatia ■
   Europe **41** C13
Hrymayliv *Ukraine* **23** D14
Hrynyava *Ukraine* **29** C9
Hsenwi *Burma* **67** H20
Hsiamen = Xiamen *China* **59** E12
Hsian = Xi'an *China* **56** G5
Hsinchu *Taiwan* **59** E13
Hsinhailien =
   Lianyungang *China* **57** G10
Hsinying *Taiwan* **59** F13
Hsopket *Burma* **58** F2
Htapodia *Greece* **47** D7
Hu Xian *China* **56** G5
Hua Hin *Thailand* **64** F2
Hua Xian *Henan, China* **56** G8
Hua Xian *Shaanxi, China* **56** G5
Hua'an *China* **59** E11
Huab ➤ *Namibia* **88** B2
Huacheng *China* **59** E10
Huachinera *Mexico* **118** A3

Huacho *Peru* **124** F3
Huade *China* **56** D7
Huadian *China* **57** C14
Huadu *China* **59** F9
Huahine, Î. *French Polynesia* **97** J12
Huai Had △ *Thailand* **64** D5
Huai He ➤ *China* **59** A10
Huai Nam Dang △ *Thailand* **64** C2
Huai Yot *Thailand* **65** J2
Huai'an *Hebei, China* **56** D8
Huai'an *Jiangsu, China* **57** H10
Huaibei *China* **56** G9
Huaibin *China* **59** A10
Huaide = Gongzhuling
   China **57** C13
Huaidezhen *China* **57** C13
Huaihua *China* **58** D7
Huaiji *China* **59** F9
Huainan *China* **59** A11
Huaining *China* **59** B11
Huairen *China* **56** E7
Huairou *China* **56** D9
Huaiyang *China* **56** H8
Huaiyin *China* **57** H10
Huaiyuan
   Guangxi Zhuangzu, China **58** E7
Huaiyuan
   Anhui, China **57** H9
Huajuapán de León *Mexico* **119** D5
Hualapai Peak *U.S.A.* **109** J7
Hualien *Taiwan* **59** E13
Huallaga ➤ *Peru* **124** E3
Huambo *Angola* **85** G3
Huan Jiang ➤ *China* **56** G5
Huan Xian *China* **56** F4
Huancabamba *Peru* **124** E3
Huancane *Peru* **124** G5
Huancavelica *Peru* **124** F3
Huancayo *Peru* **124** F3
Huanchaca *Bolivia* **124** H5
Huang Hai = Yellow Sea
   China **57** G12
Huang He ➤ *China* **57** F10
Huang Xian *China* **57** F11
Huangchuan *China* **59** A10
Huanggang *China* **59** B10
Huangguoshu *China* **58** E5
Huangling *China* **56** G5
Huanglong *China* **56** G5
Huanglongtan *China* **59** A8
Huangmei *China* **59** B10
Huangpi *China* **59** B10
Huangping *China* **58** D6
Huangshan *Anhui, China* **59** B12
Huangshan *Anhui, China* **59** C12
Huangshi *China* **59** B10
Huangsongdian *China* **57** C14
Huangyan *China* **59** C13
Huangyangsi *China* **59** D8
Huaning *China* **58** E4
Huanjiang *China* **58** E7
Huanren *China* **57** D13
Huantai *China* **57** F9
Huánuco *Peru* **124** E3
Huaping *China* **58** D3
Huaraz *Peru* **124** E3
Huarmey *Peru* **124** F3
Huarong *China* **59** C9
Huascarán, Nevado *Peru* **124** E3
Huasco *Chile* **126** B1
Huasco ➤ *Chile* **126** B1
Huasna *U.S.A.* **111** K6
Huatabampo *Mexico* **118** B3
Huauchinango *Mexico* **119** C5
Huautla de Jiménez *Mexico* **119** D5
Huaxi *China* **58** D6
Huayin *China* **56** G6
Huayuan *China* **58** C7
Huayun *China* **58** B6
Huazhou *China* **59** G8
Hubbard *Ohio, U.S.A.* **114** E4
Hubbard *Tex., U.S.A.* **116** F6
Hubbart Pt. *Canada* **103** B10
Hubei □ *China* **59** B9
Hubli *India* **66** M9
Huch'ang *N. Korea* **57** D14
Hucknall *U.K.* **14** D6
Huddersfield *U.K.* **14** D6
Hude *Germany* **24** B4
Hudi *Sudan* **80** D3
Hudiksvall *Sweden* **10** C11
Hudson *Canada* **104** B1
Hudson *Mass., U.S.A.* **115** D13
Hudson *N.Y., U.S.A.* **115** D11
Hudson *Wis., U.S.A.* **112** C7
Hudson *Wyo., U.S.A.* **108** E9
Hudson ➤ *U.S.A.* **115** F11
Hudson, C. *Antarctica* **5** C20
Hudson Bay *Nunavut,
   Canada* **101** D11
Hudson Bay *Sask., Canada* **103** C8
Hudson Falls *U.S.A.* **115** C11
Hudson Mts. *Antarctica* **5** D16
Hudson Str. *Canada* **101** C13
Hudson's Hope *Canada* **102** B4
Hue *Vietnam* **64** D6
Huebra ➤ *Spain* **36** D4
Huedin *Romania* **28** D8

Huehuetenango *Guatemala* **120** C1
Huejúcar *Mexico* **118** C4
Huélamo *Spain* **38** E3
Huelgoat *France* **18** D3
Huelma *Spain* **37** H7
Huelva *Spain* **37** H4
Huelva □ *Spain* **37** H4
Huelva ➤ *Spain* **37** H5
Huentelauquén *Chile* **126** C1
Huércal-Overa *Spain* **39** H3
Huerta, Sa. de la *Argentina* **126** C2
Huertas, C. de las *Spain* **39** G4
Huerva ➤ *Spain* **38** D4
Huesca *Spain* **38** C4
Huesca □ *Spain* **38** C5
Huéscar *Spain* **39** H2
Huetamo *Mexico* **118** D4
Huete *Spain* **38** E2
Hugh ➤ *Australia* **94** D1
Hughenden *Australia* **94** C3
Hughesville *U.S.A.* **115** E8
Hugli ➤ *India* **69** J13
Hugo *Colo., U.S.A.* **108** G12
Hugo *Okla., U.S.A.* **116** D7
Hugoton *U.S.A.* **112** G3
Hui Xian = Huixian *China* **56** G7
Hui Xian *China* **56** H4
Hui'an *China* **59** E12
Hui'anbu *China* **56** F4
Huichang *China* **59** E10
Huichapan *Mexico* **119** C5
Huichon *N. Korea* **57** D14
Huidong *Guangdong, China* **59** F10
Huidong *Sichuan, China* **58** D4
Huifa He ➤ *China* **57** C14
Huila, Nevado del *Colombia* **124** C3
Huilai *China* **59** F11
Huili *China* **58** D4
Huimin *China* **57** F9
Huinan *China* **57** C14
Huinca Renancó *Argentina* **126** C3
Huining *China* **56** G3
Huinong *China* **56** E4
Huishui *China* **58** D6
Huisne ➤ *France* **18** E7
Huiting *China* **56** G9
Huitong *China* **58** D7
Huixian *China* **56** H4
Huixtla *Mexico* **119** D6
Huize *China* **58** D4
Huizhou *China* **59** F10
Hukawng Valley *Burma* **67** F20
Hukou *China* **59** C11
Hukuntsi *Botswana* **88** C3
Ḥulayfā' *Si. Arabia* **70** E4
Hulin He ➤ *China* **57** B12
Hull = Kingston upon Hull
   U.K. **14** D7
Hull *Canada* **115** A9
Hull ➤ *U.K.* **14** D7
Hulst *Neths.* **17** C4
Hultsfred *Sweden* **11** G9
Hulun Nur *China* **60** B6
Hulyaypole *Ukraine* **33** J9
Huma, Tanjung *Malaysia* **65** c
Humacao *Puerto Rico* **121** d
Humahuaca *Argentina* **126** A2
Humaitá *Brazil* **124** E6
Humaitá *Paraguay* **126** B4
Humansdorp *S. Africa* **88** E3
Humara, J. *Sudan* **81** D3
Humbe *Angola* **88** B1
Humber ➤ *U.K.* **14** D7
Humboldt *Canada* **103** C7
Humboldt *Iowa, U.S.A.* **112** D6
Humboldt *Tenn., U.S.A.* **117** D10
Humboldt ➤ *U.S.A.* **108** G4
Humboldt Gletscher =
   Sermersuaq *Greenland* **4** B4
Hume *U.S.A.* **110** J8
Hume, L. *Australia* **95** F4
Humenné *Slovak Rep.* **27** C14
Hummelsta *Sweden* **10** E10
Humphreys, Mt. *U.S.A.* **110** H8
Humphreys Peak *U.S.A.* **109** J8
Humpolec *Czech Rep.* **26** B8
Humptulips *U.S.A.* **110** C3
Hūn *Libya* **79** C9
Hun Jiang ➤ *China* **57** D13
Húnaflói *Iceland* **8** D3
Hunan □ *China* **59** D9
Hunchun *China* **57** C16
Hundested *Denmark* **11** J5
Hundewali *Pakistan* **68** D5
Hundred Mile House
   Canada **102** C4
Hunedoara *Romania* **28** E7
Hunedoara □ *Romania* **28** E7
Hünfeld *Germany* **24** E5
Hung Yen *Vietnam* **58** G6
Hunga Ha'apai *Tonga* **91** c
Hungary ■ *Europe* **27** D12
Hungary, Plain of *Europe* **6** F10
Hungerford *Australia* **95** D3
Hŭngnam ➤ *N. Korea* **57** E14
Hungt'ou Hsü = Lan Yü
   Taiwan **59**

Huni Valley *Ghana* **82** D4
Hunjiang *China* **57** D14
Hunneberg *Sweden* **11** F6
Hunnebostrand *Sweden* **11** F5
Hunsberge *Namibia* **88** D2
Hunsrück *Germany* **25** F3
Hunstanton *U.K.* **14** E8
Hunte ➤ *Germany* **24** B4
Hunter *U.S.A.* **115** D10
Hunter I. *Australia* **95** G3
Hunter I. *Canada* **102** C3
Hunter Ra. *Australia* **95** E5
Hunters Road *Zimbabwe* **87** F2
Hunterville *N.Z.* **91** C5
Huntingburg *U.S.A.* **112** F10
Huntingdon *Canada* **104** C5
Huntingdon *U.K.* **15** E7
Huntingdon *U.S.A.* **114** F6
Huntington *Ind., U.S.A.* **113** E11
Huntington *N.Y., U.S.A.* **115** F11
Huntington *Oreg., U.S.A.* **108** D5
Huntington *Utah, U.S.A.* **108** G8
Huntington *W. Va., U.S.A.* **113** F12
Huntington Beach *U.S.A.* **111** M9
Huntly *N.Z.* **91** B5
Huntly *U.K.* **13** D6
Huntsville *Canada* **114** A5
Huntsville *Ala., U.S.A.* **117** D11
Huntsville *Tex., U.S.A.* **116** F7
Hunyani ➤ *Zimbabwe* **87** F3
Hunyuan *China* **56** E7
Hunza ➤ *India* **69** B6
Huo Xian = Huozhou *China* **56** F6
Huong Khe *Vietnam* **64** C5
Huonville *Australia* **95** G4
Huoqiu *China* **59** A11
Huoshan *Anhui, China* **59** A12
Huoshan *Anhui, China* **59** B11
Huoshao Dao = Lü Tao
   Taiwan **59** F13
Huozhou *China* **56** F6
Hupeh = Hubei □ *China* **59** B9
Ḥūr *Iran* **71** D8
Hurezani *Romania* **29** F8
Hurghada *Egypt* **80** B3
Hurley *N. Mex., U.S.A.* **109** K9
Hurley *Wis., U.S.A.* **112** B8
Huron *Calif., U.S.A.* **110** J6
Huron *Ohio, U.S.A.* **114** E2
Huron *S. Dak., U.S.A.* **112** C4
Huron, L. *U.S.A.* **114** B2
Huron East *Canada* **114** C3
Hurricane *U.S.A.* **109** H7
Hurso *Ethiopia* **81** F5
Hurungwe △ *Zimbabwe* **87** F2
Hurunui ➤ *N.Z.* **91** E4
Hurup *Denmark* **11** H2
Húsavík *Iceland* **8** C5
Huşi *Romania* **29** D13
Huskvarna *Sweden* **11** G8
Hustadvika *Norway* **8** E12
Hustontown *U.S.A.* **114** F6
Hustopeče *Czech Rep.* **27** C9
Husum *Germany* **24** A5
Husum *Sweden* **10** A13
Hutchinson *Kans., U.S.A.* **112** F5
Hutchinson *Minn., U.S.A.* **112** C6
Hutte Sauvage, L. de la
   Canada **105** A7
Hüttenberg *Austria* **26** E7
Hüttener Berge △ *Germany* **24** A5
Hutton, Mt. *Australia* **95** D4
Huwun *Ethiopia* **81** G5
Huy *Belgium* **17** D5
Huzhou *China* **59** B13
Hvalpsund *Denmark* **11** H3
Hvammstangi *Iceland* **8** D3
Hvar *Croatia* **41** E13
Hvarski Kanal *Croatia* **41** E13
Hvítá ➤ *Iceland* **8** D3
Hvizdets *Ukraine* **29** B10
Hwachon-Cheosuji
   S. Korea **57** E14
Hwang Ho = Huang He ➤
   China **57** F10
Hwange *Zimbabwe* **87** F2
Hwange △ *Zimbabwe* **88** B4
Hyannis *Mass., U.S.A.* **113** E18
Hyannis *Nebr., U.S.A.* **112** E3
Hyargas Nuur *Mongolia* **60** B4
Hybo *Sweden* **10** C10
Hydaburg *U.S.A.* **102** B2
Hyde Park *U.S.A.* **115** E11
Hyden *Australia* **93** F2
Hyder *U.S.A.* **102** B2
Hyderabad *India* **66** L11
Hyderabad *Pakistan* **68** G3
Hydra *Greece* **46** D5
Hyères *France* **21** E10
Hyères, Îs. d' *France* **21** F10
Hyesan *N. Korea* **57** D15
Hyland ➤ *Canada* **102** B3
Hyltebruk *Sweden* **11** H7

Huni Valley *Ghana* **82** D4

Hymia *India* **69** C8
Hyndman Peak *U.S.A.* **108** E6
Hyōgo □ *Japan* **55** G7
Hyrum *U.S.A.* **108** F8
Hysham *U.S.A.* **108** C10
Hythe *U.K.* **15** F9
Hyūga *Japan* **55** H5
Hyvinge = Hyvinkää *Finland* **32** B3
Hyvinkää *Finland* **32** B3

I

I-n-Gall *Niger* **83** B6
I-n-Oudad *Algeria* **83** A5
I-n-Ouzzal *Algeria* **83** A5
I-n-Tadreft *Niger* **83** B6
Iablaniţa *Romania* **28** F7
Iaco ➤ *Brazil* **124** E5
Iacobeni *Romania* **29** C10
Iakora *Madag.* **89** C8
Ialomiţa □ *Romania* **29** F12
Ialomiţa ➤ *Romania* **29** F12
Ialoveni *Moldova* **29** D13
Ialpug ➤ *Moldova* **29** E13
Ianca *Romania* **29** E12
Iara *Romania* **29** D8
Iargara *Moldova* **29** D13
Iaşi *Romania* **29** C12
Iaşi □ *Romania* **29** C12
Iasmos *Greece* **45** E9
Ib ➤ *India* **69** J10
Iba *Phil.* **61** D4
Ibadan *Nigeria* **83** D5
Ibagué *Colombia* **124** C3
Iballë *Albania* **44** D4
Ibănesti *Botoşani, Romania* **29** B11
Ibănesti *Mureş, Romania* **29** D9
Ibar ➤ *Serbia* **44** C4
Ibaraki *Japan* **55** F10
Ibaraki □ *Japan* **55** F10
Ibarra *Ecuador* **124** C3
Ibb *Yemen* **75** E3
Ibba *Sudan* **81** G2
Ibba, Bahr el ➤ *Sudan* **81** F2
Ibbenbüren *Germany* **24** C3
Ibembo *Dem. Rep. of the Congo* **86** B1
Ibenga ➤ *Congo* **84** D3
Ibera, L. *Argentina* **126** B4
Iberian Peninsula *Europe* **6** H5
Iberville *Canada* **115** A11
Iberville, Lac d' *Canada* **104** A5
Ibi *Nigeria* **83** D6
Ibi *Spain* **39** G4
Ibiá *Brazil* **125** G9
Ibiapaba, Sa. da *Brazil* **125** D10
Ibicuí ➤ *Brazil* **127** B4
Ibicuy *Argentina* **126** C4
Ibiza = Eivissa *Spain* **48** C7
Ibiza ✈ (IBZ) *Spain* **39** G6
Íblei, Monti *Italy* **43** E7
Ibo *Mozam.* **87** E5
Ibonma *Indonesia* **63** E8
Ibotirama *Brazil* **125** F10
Ibrāhīm ➤ *Lebanon* **74** A4
'Ibrī *Oman* **71** F8
Ibshawâi *Egypt* **80** J7
Ibu *Indonesia* **63** D7
Ibusuki *Japan* **55** J5
Ica *Peru* **124** F3
Içá ➤ *Brazil* **124** D5
Icacos Pt. *Trin. & Tob.* **125** K15
Içana *Brazil* **124** C5
Içana ➤ *Brazil* **124** C5
İçel *Turkey* **72** D6
İçel □ *Turkey* **72** D5
Iceland ■ *Europe* **8** D4
Iceland Basin *Atl. Oc.* **4** C7
Icelandic Plateau *Arctic* **4** C7
Ich'ang = Yichang *China* **59** B8
Ichchapuram *India* **67** K14
Icheon *S. Korea* **57** F14
Ichhawar *India* **68** H7
Ichihara *Japan* **55** G10
Ichikawa *Japan* **55** G9
Ichilo ➤ *Bolivia* **124** G6
Ichinohe *Japan* **54** D10
Ichinomiya *Japan* **55** G8
Ichinoseki *Japan* **54** E10
Ichnya *Ukraine* **33** G7
Icod *Canary Is.* **48** F3
Icy C. *U.S.A.* **98** B3
Ida Grove *U.S.A.* **112** D6
Idabel *U.S.A.* **116** E7
Idaga Hamus *Ethiopia* **81** E4
Idah *Nigeria* **83** D6
Idaho □ *U.S.A.* **108** D6
Idaho City *U.S.A.* **108** E6
Idaho Falls *U.S.A.* **108** E7
Idalia △ *Australia* **94** C3
Idanha-a-Nova *Portugal* **36** F3
Idar-Oberstein *Germany* **25** F3
Idensalmi = Iisalmi *Finland* **8** E22
Idfû *Egypt* **80** C3
Ídhra = Hydra *Greece* **46** D5
Idi *Indonesia* **62** C1
Idi, Oros = Psiloritis, Oros
   Greece **49** D6
Idiofa *Dem. Rep. of the Congo* **84** E3

Idkerberget *Sweden* **10** D9
Idku, Bahra el *Egypt* **80** H7
Idlib *Syria* **72** E7
Idlib □ *Syria* **72** E7
Idre *Sweden* **10** C6
Idria *U.S.A.* **110** J6
Idrija *Slovenia* **41** C11
Idritsa *Russia* **32** D5
Idutywa = Dutywa *S. Africa* **89** E4
Ieper *Belgium* **17** D2
Ierapetra *Greece* **49** E7
Ierissos *Greece* **44** F7
Ierissos Kolpos *Greece* **44** F7
Iernut *Romania* **29** D9
Iesi *Italy* **41** E10
Iésolo *Italy* **41** C9
Ifach, Peñón de *Spain* **39** G5
Ifakara *Tanzania* **84** F7
'Ifāl, W. al ➤ *Si. Arabia* **70** D2
Ifanadiana *Madag.* **89** C8
Ife *Nigeria* **83** D5
Iférouâne *Niger* **83** B6
Iffley *Australia* **94** B3
Ifon *Nigeria* **83** D6
Iforas, Adrar des *Africa* **83** B5
Ifould, L. *Australia* **93** F5
Igalo *Montenegro* **44** D2
Iganga *Uganda* **86** B3
Igarapava *Brazil* **125** H9
Igarka *Russia* **52** C9
Igatimi *Paraguay* **127** A4
Igbetti *Nigeria* **83** D5
Igbo-Ora *Nigeria* **83** D5
Igboho *Nigeria* **83** D5
Igbor *Nigeria* **83** D6
Iğdır *Turkey* **73** C11
Igelfors *Sweden* **11** F9
Iggesund *Sweden* **10** C11
Iglésias *Italy* **42** C1
Igloolik *Canada* **101** C11
Igluligaarjuk =
   Chesterfield Inlet *Canada* **100** C10
Iglulik = Igloolik *Canada* **101** C11
'Igma, Gebel el *Egypt* **80** B3
Ignace *Canada* **104** C1
İğneada *Turkey* **45** E11
İğneada Burnu *Turkey* **45** E12
Igoumenitsa *Greece* **46** B2
Igra *Russia* **34** B11
Iguaçu ➤ *Brazil* **127** B5
Iguaçu, Cat. del *Brazil* **127** B5
Iguaçu △ *Brazil* **127** B5
Iguaçu Falls = Iguaçu, Cat.
   del *Brazil* **127** B5
Iguala *Mexico* **119** D5
Igualada *Spain* **38** D6
Iguassu = Iguaçu ➤ *Brazil* **127** B5
Iguatu *Brazil* **125** E11
Iguazú △ *Argentina* **127** B5
Iguidi, Erg *Africa* **78** C4
Iharana *Madag.* **89** A9
Ihbulag *Mongolia* **56** C4
Iheya-Shima *Japan* **55** L3
Ihiala *Nigeria* **83** D6
Ihosy *Madag.* **89** C8
Ihotry, Farihy *Madag.* **89** C7
Ihugh *Nigeria* **83** D6
Ii *Finland* **8** D21
Ii-Shima *Japan* **55** L3
Iida *Japan* **55** G8
Iijoki ➤ *Finland* **8** D21
Iisalmi *Finland* **8** E22
Iiyama *Japan* **55** F9
Iizuka *Japan* **55** H5
Ijâfene *Mauritania* **78** D4
Ijebu-Igbo *Nigeria* **83** D5
Ijebu-Ode *Nigeria* **83** D5
IJmuiden *Neths.* **17** B4
Ijo älv = Iijoki ➤ *Finland* **8** D21
IJssel ➤ *Neths.* **17** B5
IJsselmeer *Neths.* **17** B5
Ijuí *Brazil* **127** B5
Ijuí ➤ *Brazil* **127** B4
Ikalamavony *Madag.* **89** C8
Ikale *Nigeria* **83** D6
Ikaluktutiak *Canada* **100** C9
Ikang *Nigeria* **83** E6
Ikanga *Kenya* **86** C4
Ikara *Nigeria* **83** C6
Ikare *Nigeria* **83** D6
Ikaria *Greece* **47** D8
Ikast *Denmark* **11** H3
Ikeda *Japan* **55** G6
Ikeja *Nigeria* **83** D5
Ikela *Dem. Rep. of the Congo* **84** E4
Ikerre-Ekiti *Nigeria* **83** D6
Ikhtiman *Bulgaria* **44** D7
Iki *Japan* **55** H4
Ikimba L. *Tanzania* **86** C3
Ikire *Nigeria* **83** D5
İkizdere *Turkey* **73** B9
Ikom *Nigeria* **83** D6
Ikongo *Madag.* **89** C8
Ikopa ➤ *Madag.* **89** B8
Ikorongo △ *Tanzania* **86** C3
Ikot Ekpene *Nigeria* **83** D6
Ikparjuk = Arctic Bay
   Canada **101** B11

Iksan *S. Korea* **57** G14
Ikungu *Tanzania* **86** C3
Ikuntji = Haast Bluff
 Australia **92** D5
Ikurun *Nigeria* **83** D5
Ila *Nigeria* **83** D5
Ilagan *Phil.* **61** C4
Ilaka *Madag.* **89** B8
Īlām *Iran* **73** F12
Ilam *Nepal* **69** F12
Īlām □ *Iran* **70** C5
Ilan *Taiwan* **59** E13
Ilanskiy *Russia* **53** D10
Ilaro *Nigeria* **83** D5
Ilatane *Niger* **83** B5
Iława *Poland* **30** E6
Ile ➤ *Kazakhstan* **52** E8
Île-à-la-Crosse *Canada* **103** B7
Île-à-la-Crosse, Lac *Canada* **103** B7
Île-de-France □ *France* **19** D9
Ileanda *Romania* **29** C8
Ilebo *Dem. Rep. of the Congo* **84** E4
Ilek *Russia* **52** D6
Ilero *Nigeria* **83** D5
Ilesha *Kwara, Nigeria* **83** D5
Ilesha *Oyo, Nigeria* **83** D5
Ilford *Canada* **103** B9
Ilfracombe *Australia* **94** C3
Ilfracombe *U.K.* **15** F3
Ilgaz *Turkey* **72** B5
Ilgaz Dağları *Turkey* **72** B5
Ilgın *Turkey* **72** C4
Ilha de Moçambique *Mozam.* **87** F5
Ílhavo *Portugal* **36** E2
Ilhéus *Brazil* **125** F11
Ili = Ile ➤ *Kazakhstan* **52** E8
Ilia *Romania* **28** E7
Ilía □ *Greece* **46** D2
Iliamna L. *U.S.A.* **106** a
Ilias, Profítis *Greece* **49** C9
Iliç *Turkey* **73** C8
Ilıca *Turkey* **47** B9
Ilichevsk *Azerbaijan* **73** C11
Iligan *Phil.* **61** G6
Iligan Bay *Phil.* **61** G6
Ilin I. *Phil.* **61** E4
Ilion *U.S.A.* **115** D9
Ilirska-Bistrica *Slovenia* **41** C11
Ilkeston *U.K.* **14** E6
Ilkley *U.K.* **14** D6
Illampu = Ancohuma,
 Nevado *Bolivia* **124** G5
Illana B. *Phil.* **61** H5
Illapel *Chile* **126** C1
Ille-et-Vilaine □ *France* **18** D5
Ille-sur-Têt *France* **20** F6
Illéla *Niger* **83** C6
Iller ➤ *Germany* **25** G5
Illertissen *Germany* **25** G6
Illescas *Spain* **36** E7
Illetas *Spain* **48** B9
Illichivsk *Ukraine* **33** J6
Illiers-Combray *France* **18** D8
Illimani, Nevado *Bolivia* **124** G5
Illinois □ *U.S.A.* **112** E9
Illinois ➤ *U.S.A.* **112** F8
Illizi *Algeria* **78** C7
Illkirch-Graffenstaden
 France **19** D14
Íllora *Spain* **37** H7
Ilm ➤ *Germany* **24** D7
Ilma, L. *Australia* **93** E4
Ilmajoki *Finland* **8** E20
Ilmen, Ozero *Russia* **32** C6
Ilmenau *Germany* **24** E6
Ilnytsya *Ukraine* **28** B8
Ilo *Peru* **124** G4
Ilobu *Nigeria* **83** D5
Iloilo *Phil.* **61** F5
Ilomantsi *Finland* **8** E24
Ilora *Nigeria* **83** D5
Ilorin *Nigeria* **83** D5
Ilovatka *Russia* **34** E7
Ilovlya *Russia* **35** F7
Ilovlya ➤ *Russia* **35** F7
Iłowa *Poland* **31** G2
Ilubabor *Ethiopia* **81** F4
Ilva Mică *Romania* **29** C9
Ilwaco *U.S.A.* **110** D2
Ilwaki *Indonesia* **63** F7
Ilyichevsk = Illichivsk
 Ukraine **33** J6
Iłża *Poland* **31** G8
Iłżanka ➤ *Poland* **31** G8
Imabari *Japan* **55** G6
Imaloto ➤ *Madag.* **89** C8
İmamoğlu *Turkey* **72** D6
Imandra, Ozero *Russia* **8** C25
Imanombo *Madag.* **89** C8
Imari *Japan* **55** H4
Imasa *Sudan* **80** D4
Imathia □ *Greece* **44** F6
Imatra *Finland* **32** B5
Ménas *Mali* **83** B5
imeni 26 Bakinskikh
 Komissarov = Neftçala
 Azerbaijan **73** C13

imeni 26 Bakinskikh
 Komissarov *Turkmenistan* **71** B7
imeni Ismail Samani, Pik
 Tajikistan **52** F8
Imeri, Serra *Brazil* **124** C5
Imerimandroso *Madag.* **89** B8
Imfolozi △ *S. Africa* **89** D5
Imi *Ethiopia* **81** F5
Imishly = Imişli *Azerbaijan* **35** L9
Imişli *Azerbaijan* **35** L9
Imlay *U.S.A.* **108** F4
Imlay City *U.S.A.* **114** D1
Immaseri *Sudan* **81** D2
Immenstadt *Germany* **25** H6
Immingham *U.K.* **14** D7
Immokalee *U.S.A.* **117** H14
Imo □ *Nigeria* **83** D6
Imo ➤ *Nigeria* **83** E6
Ímola *Italy* **41** D8
Imotski *Croatia* **41** E14
Imperatriz *Brazil* **125** E9
Impéria *Italy* **40** E5
Imperial *Canada* **103** C7
Imperial *Calif., U.S.A.* **111** N11
Imperial *Nebr., U.S.A.* **112** E3
Imperial Beach *U.S.A.* **111** N9
Imperial Dam *U.S.A.* **111** N12
Imperial Reservoir *U.S.A.* **111** N12
Imperial Valley *U.S.A.* **111** N11
Imperieuse Reef *Australia* **92** C2
Impfondo *Congo* **84** D3
Imphal *India* **67** G18
Imphy *France* **19** F10
Imranlı *Turkey* **73** C8
İmroz = Gökçeada *Turkey* **45** F9
İmroz *Turkey* **45** F9
Imst *Austria* **26** D3
Imuris *Mexico* **118** A2
Imuruan B. *Phil.* **63** B5
In Akhmed *Mali* **83** B5
In Aleï *Mali* **82** B4
In Delimane *Mali* **83** B5
In Guezzam *Algeria* **83** B6
In Koufi *Mali* **83** B5
In Salah *Algeria* **78** C6
In Tallak *Mali* **83** B5
In Tebezas *Mali* **83** B5
Ina *Japan* **55** G9
Inagua △ *Bahamas* **121** B5
Inangahua *N.Z.* **91** D3
Inanwatan *Indonesia* **63** E8
Iñapari *Peru* **124** F5
Inari *Finland* **8** B22
Inarijärvi *Finland* **8** B23
Inawashiro-Ko *Japan* **54** F10
Inca *Spain* **48** B9
Inca de Oro *Chile* **126** B2
Incaguasi *Chile* **126** B1
Incahuasi *Argentina* **126** B2
İnce Burun *Turkey* **72** A6
İncekum Burnu *Turkey* **72** D5
İncesu *Turkey* **70** B2
Incheon *S. Korea* **57** F14
Inchiri □ *Mauritania* **82** B2
Incio = Cruz de Incio *Spain* **36** C3
İncirliova *Turkey* **47** D9
Incline Village *U.S.A.* **108** G4
Incomáti ➤ *Mozam.* **89** D5
Incudine, Mte. *France* **21** G13
Inda Silase *Ethiopia* **81** E4
Indal *Sweden* **10** B11
Indalsälven ➤ *Sweden* **10** B11
Indaw *Burma* **67** G20
Indbir *Ethiopia* **81** F4
Independence *Calif., U.S.A.* **110** J8
Independence *Iowa, U.S.A.* **112** D8
Independence *Kans., U.S.A.* **112** G6
Independence *Ky., U.S.A.* **113** F11
Independence *Mo., U.S.A.* **112** F6
Independence Fjord *Greenland* **4** A6
Independence Mts. *U.S.A.* **108** F5
Independenţa *Romania* **29** E12
Index *U.S.A.* **110** C5
India ■ *Asia* **66** K11
Indian ➤ *U.S.A.* **117** H14
Indian Cabins *Canada* **102** B5
Indian Harbour *Canada* **105** B8
Indian Head *Canada* **103** C8
Indian Lake *U.S.A.* **115** C10
Indian Springs *U.S.A.* **111** J11
Indiana *U.S.A.* **114** F5
Indiana □ *U.S.A.* **113** F11
Indianapolis *U.S.A.* **112** F10
Indianola *Iowa, U.S.A.* **112** E7
Indianola *Miss., U.S.A.* **113** J9
Indigirka ➤ *Russia* **53** B15
Indija *Serbia* **28** E5
Indio *U.S.A.* **111** M10
Indira Gandhi Canal *India* **68** F5
Indira Sagar *India* **68** H7
Indo-China *Asia* **50** G12
Indonesia ■ *Asia* **62** F5
Indore *India* **68** H6
Indramayu *Indonesia* **63** G13
Indravati ➤ *India* **67** K12
Indre □ *France* **19** F8
Indre ➤ *France* **18** E7

Indre-et-Loire □ *France* **18** E7
Indulkana *Australia* **95** D1
Indura *Belarus* **30** E10
Indus ➤ *Pakistan* **68** G2
Indus, Mouths of the
 Pakistan **68** H3
İnebolu *Turkey* **72** B5
İnecik *Turkey* **45** F11
İnegöl *Turkey* **45** F13
Ineu *Romania* **28** D6
Infantes = Villanueva de
 los Infantes *Spain* **37** G7
Infiernillo, Presa del *Mexico* **118** D4
Infiesto *Spain* **36** B5
Ingelstad *Sweden* **11** H8
Ingenio *Canary Is.* **48** G4
Ingenio Santa Ana
 Argentina **126** B2
Ingersoll *Canada* **114** C4
Ingham *Australia* **94** B4
Ingleborough *U.K.* **14** C5
Inglewood *Queens., Australia* **95** D5
Inglewood *Vic., Australia* **95** F3
Inglewood *N.Z.* **91** C5
Inglewood *U.S.A.* **111** M8
Ingólfshöfði *Iceland* **8** E5
Ingolstadt *Germany* **25** G7
Ingomar *U.S.A.* **108** C10
Ingonish *Canada* **105** C7
Ingore *Guinea-Biss.* **82** C1
Ingraj Bazar *India* **69** G13
Ingrid Christensen Coast
 Antarctica **5** C6
Ingul = Inhul ➤ *Ukraine* **33** J7
Ingulec = Inhulec *Ukraine* **33** J7
Ingulets = Inhulets ➤
 Ukraine **33** J7
Inguri = Enguri ➤ *Georgia* **35** J5
Ingushetia □ *Russia* **35** J7
Ingwavuma *S. Africa* **89** D5
Inhaca *Mozam.* **89** D5
Inhafenga *Mozam.* **89** C5
Inhambane *Mozam.* **89** C6
Inhambane □ *Mozam.* **89** C5
Inhaminga *Mozam.* **87** F4
Inharrime *Mozam.* **89** C6
Inharrime ➤ *Mozam.* **89** C6
Inhisar *Turkey* **47** A12
Inhul ➤ *Ukraine* **33** J7
Inhulec *Ukraine* **33** J7
Inhulets ➤ *Ukraine* **33** J7
Iniesta *Spain* **39** F3
Ining = Yining *China* **52** E9
Inírida ➤ *Colombia* **124** C5
Inishbofin *Ireland* **12** C1
Inisheer *Ireland* **12** C2
Inishfree B. *Ireland* **12** A3
Inishkea North *Ireland* **12** B1
Inishkea South *Ireland* **12** B1
Inishmaan *Ireland* **12** C2
Inishmore *Ireland* **12** C2
Inishmurray I. *Ireland* **12** B3
Inishshark *Ireland* **12** C1
Inishturk *Ireland* **12** C1
Inishvickillane *Ireland* **12** D1
Injibara *Ethiopia* **81** E4
Injune *Australia* **95** D4
Inklin ➤ *N. Amer.* **102** B2
Inland Kaikoura Ra. *N.Z.* **91** D4
Inland Sea = Setonaikai
 Japan **55** G6
Inle L. *Burma* **67** J20
Inlet *U.S.A.* **115** C10
Inn ➤ *Austria* **26** C6
Innamincka *Australia* **95** D3
Inner Hebrides *U.K.* **13** E2
Inner Mongolia = Nei
 Monggol Zizhiqu □ *China* **56** D7
Inner Sound *U.K.* **13** D3
Innerkip *Canada* **114** C4
Innetalling I. *Canada* **104** A4
Innisfail *Australia* **94** B4
Innisfail *Canada* **102** C6
In'noshima *Japan* **55** G6
Innsbruck *Austria* **26** D4
Innviertel *Austria* **26** C6
Inny ➤ *Ireland* **12** C4
Inongo *Dem. Rep. of the Congo* **84** E3
İnönü *Turkey* **47** B12
Inoucdjouac = Inukjuak
 Canada **101** D12
Inousses *Greece* **47** C8
Inowrocław *Poland* **31** F5
Inscription, C. *Australia* **93** E1
Insein *Burma* **67** L20
Insjön *Sweden* **10** D9
Ińsko *Poland* **30** E2
Însurăţei *Romania* **29** F12
Inta *Russia* **52** C6
Intendente Alvear
 Argentina **126** D3
İntepe *Turkey* **47** A8
Interlaken *Switz.* **25** J3
Interlaken *U.S.A.* **115** D8
International Falls *U.S.A.* **112** A7
Intiyaco *Argentina* **126** B3

Întorsura Buzăului *Romania* **29** E11
Inukjuak *Canada* **101** D12
Inútil, B. *Chile* **128** G2
Inuvik *Canada* **100** C6
Inveraray *U.K.* **13** E3
Inverbervie *U.K.* **13** E6
Invercargill *N.Z.* **91** G2
Inverclyde □ *U.K.* **13** F4
Inverell *Australia* **95** D5
Invergordon *U.K.* **13** D4
Inverloch *Australia* **95** F4
Invermere *Canada* **102** C5
Inverness *Canada* **105** C7
Inverness *U.K.* **13** D4
Inverness *U.S.A.* **117** G13
Inverurie *U.K.* **13** D6
Investigator Group *Australia* **95** E1
Investigator Str. *Australia* **95** F2
Inya *Russia* **52** D9
Inyanga *Zimbabwe* **87** F3
Inyangani *Zimbabwe* **87** F3
Inyantue *Zimbabwe* **88** B4
Inyo Mts. *U.S.A.* **110** J9
Inyokern *U.S.A.* **111** K9
Inza *Russia* **34** D8
Inzhavino *Russia* **34** D6
Iō-Jima *Japan* **55** J5
Ioánnina *Greece* **46** B2
Ioánnina □ *Greece* **46** B2
Iola *U.S.A.* **112** G6
Ion Corvin *Romania* **29** F12
Iona *U.K.* **13** E2
Ione *U.S.A.* **110** G6
Ionia *U.S.A.* **113** D11
Ionian Is. = Iónioi Nísoi
 Greece **46** C2
Ionian Sea *Medit. S.* **6** H9
Iónioi Nísoi *Greece* **46** C2
Iónioi Nísoi □ *Greece* **46** C2
Íos *Greece* **47** E7
Iowa □ *U.S.A.* **112** D7
Iowa ➤ *U.S.A.* **112** E8
Iowa City *U.S.A.* **112** E8
Iowa Falls *U.S.A.* **112** D7
Iowa Park *U.S.A.* **116** E5
Ipala *Tanzania* **86** C3
Ipameri *Brazil* **125** G9
Ipati *Greece* **46** C4
Ipatinga *Brazil* **125** G10
Ipatovo *Russia* **35** H6
Ipel' ➤ *Europe* **27** D11
Ipiales *Colombia* **124** C3
Ipin = Yibin *China* **58** C5
Ipixuna *Brazil* **124** E4
Ipoh *Malaysia* **65** K3
Ippy *C.A.R.* **84** C4
Ípsala *Turkey* **45** F10
Ipsário, Óros *Greece* **45** F8
Ipswich *Australia* **95** D5
Ipswich *U.K.* **15** E9
Ipswich *Mass., U.S.A.* **115** D14
Ipswich *S. Dak., U.S.A.* **112** C4
Ipu *Brazil* **125** D10
Iqaluit *Canada* **101** C13
Iquique *Chile* **124** H4
Iquitos *Peru* **124** D4
Irabu-Jima *Japan* **55** M2
Iracoubo *Fr. Guiana* **125** B8
Iráklia *Cyclades, Greece* **47** E7
Iráklia *Serres, Greece* **44** E7
Iráklio *Greece* **49** D7
Iráklio □ *Greece* **49** D7
Iráklion = Iráklio *Greece* **49** D7
Irala *Paraguay* **127** B5
Iran ■ *Asia* **71** C7
Iran, Pegunungan *Malaysia* **62** D4
Iran Ra. = Iran,
 Pegunungan *Malaysia* **62** D4
Īrānshahr *Iran* **71** E9
Irapuato *Mexico* **118** C4
Iraq ■ *Asia* **73** F10
Irati *Brazil* **127** B5
Irbes saurums *Latvia* **30** A9
Irbid *Jordan* **74** C4
Irbid □ *Jordan* **74** C5
Irebu *Dem. Rep. of the Congo* **84** E3
Iregua ➤ *Spain* **38** C2
Irele *Nigeria* **83** D6
Ireland ■ *Europe* **12** C4
Irgiz, Bolshaya ➤ *Russia* **34** D9
Iri = Iksan *S. Korea* **57** G14
Irian Jaya = Papua □
 Indonesia **63** E9
Irian Jaya Barat □ *Indonesia* **63** E8
Irié *Guinea* **82** D3
Iriga *Phil.* **61** E5
Iringa *Tanzania* **86** D4
Iringa □ *Tanzania* **86** D4
Iriomote △ *Japan* **55** M1
Iriomote-Jima *Japan* **55** M1
Iriona *Honduras* **120** C2
Iriri ➤ *Brazil* **125** D8
Irish Republic ■ *Europe* **12** C4
Irish Sea *Europe* **14** D3
Irkutsk *Russia* **53** D11

Irlanğalı *Turkey* **47** D11
Irma *Canada* **103** C6
Irō-Zaki *Japan* **55** G9
Iroise, Mer d' *France* **18** D2
Iron Baron *Australia* **95** E2
Iron Gate = Portile de Fier
 Europe **28** F7
Iron Knob *Australia* **95** E2
Iron Mountain *U.S.A.* **112** C9
Iron Range △ *Australia* **94** A3
Iron River *U.S.A.* **112** B9
Irondequoit *U.S.A.* **114** C7
Ironton *Mo., U.S.A.* **112** G8
Ironton *Ohio, U.S.A.* **113** F12
Ironwood *U.S.A.* **112** B8
Ironwood Forest △ *U.S.A.* **109** K8
Iroquois *Canada* **115** B9
Iroquois Falls *Canada* **104** C3
Irosin *Phil.* **61** E6
Irpin *Ukraine* **23** C16
Irrara Cr. ➤ *Australia* **95** D4
Irrawaddy □ *Burma* **67** L19
Irrawaddy ➤ *Burma* **67** M19
Irrawaddy, Mouths of the
 Burma **67** M19
Irricana *Canada* **102** C6
Irshava *Ukraine* **28** B8
Irsina *Italy* **43** B9
Irtysh ➤ *Russia* **52** C7
Irumu *Dem. Rep. of the Congo* **86** B2
Irún *Spain* **38** B3
Irunea = Pamplona *Spain* **38** C3
Irurzun *Spain* **38** C3
Irvine *Canada* **103** D6
Irvine *U.K.* **13** F4
Irvine *Calif., U.S.A.* **111** M9
Irvine *Ky., U.S.A.* **113** G12
Irving *U.S.A.* **116** E6
Irvona *U.S.A.* **114** F6
Irwin ➤ *Australia* **93** E1
Irymple *Australia* **95** E3
Is, Jebel *Sudan* **80** C4
Isa *Nigeria* **83** C6
Isa Khel *Pakistan* **68** C4
Isaac ➤ *Australia* **94** C4
Isabel *U.S.A.* **112** C3
Isabel, I. *Mexico* **118** C3
Isabela *Phil.* **61** H5
Isabela *Puerto Rico* **121** d
Isabella, Cord. *Nic.* **120** D2
Isabella Ra. *Australia* **92** D3
Isaccea *Romania* **29** E13
Ísafjarðardjúp *Iceland* **8** C2
Ísafjörður *Iceland* **8** C2
Isagarh *India* **68** G7
Isahaya *Japan* **55** H5
Isaka *Tanzania* **86** C3
Isalnita *Romania* **29** F8
Isalo △ *Madag.* **89** C8
Isan ➤ *India* **69** F9
Isana = Içana ➤ *Brazil* **124** C5
Isangano △ *Zambia* **87** E3
Isanlu Makutu *Nigeria* **83** D6
Isar ➤ *Germany* **25** G8
Isarco ➤ *Italy* **41** B8
Isaris *Greece* **46** D3
Íscar *Spain* **36** D6
Íschehisar *Turkey* **47** C12
Íschia *Italy* **42** B6
Isdell ➤ *Australia* **92** C3
Ise *Japan* **55** G8
Ise-Shima △ *Japan* **55** G8
Ise-Wan *Japan* **55** G8
Isefjord *Denmark* **11** J5
Isel ➤ *Austria* **26** E5
Iseo *Italy* **40** C7
Iseo, L. d' *Italy* **40** C7
Iseramagazi *Tanzania* **86** C3
Isère □ *France* **21** C9
Isère ➤ *France* **21** D8
Iserlohn *Germany* **24** D3
Isérnia *Italy* **43** A7
Iseyin *Nigeria* **83** D5
Isfahan = Eşfahān *Iran* **71** C6
Ishëm *Albania* **44** E3
Ishigaki *Japan* **55** M2
Ishigaki-Shima *Japan* **55** M2
Ishikari-Gawa ➤ *Japan* **54** C10
Ishikari-Sammyaku *Japan* **54** C11
Ishikari-Wan *Japan* **54** C10
Ishikawa *Japan* **55** L3
Ishikawa □ *Japan* **55** F8
Ishim *Russia* **52** D7
Ishim ➤ *Russia* **52** D8
Ishinomaki *Japan* **54** E10
Ishioka *Japan* **55** F10
Ishkuman *Pakistan* **69** A5
Ishpeming *U.S.A.* **112** B10
Isigny-sur-Mer *France* **18** C5
Işıklar Dağı *Turkey* **45** F11
Işıklı *Turkey* **47** C11
Isil Kul *Russia* **52** D8
Ísili *Italy* **42** C2
Isiolo *Kenya* **86** B4
Isiro *Dem. Rep. of the Congo* **86** B2

Isisford *Australia* **94** C3
İskenderun *Turkey* **72** D7
İskenderun Körfezi *Turkey* **72** D6
İskilip *Turkey* **72** B6
Iskŭr ➤ *Bulgaria* **45** C8
Iskŭr, Yazovir *Bulgaria* **44** D7
Iskut ➤ *Canada* **102** B2
Isla ➤ *U.K.* **13** E5
Isla Coiba △ *Panama* **120** E3
Isla Cristina *Spain* **37** H3
Isla de Salamanca △
 Colombia **121** D5
Isla Gorge △ *Australia* **94** D4
Isla Isabel △ *Mexico* **118** C3
Isla Tiburón y San
 Esteban △ *Mexico* **118** B2
Isla Vista *U.S.A.* **111** L7
İslâhiye *Turkey* **72** D7
Islam Headworks *Pakistan* **68** E5
Islamabad *Pakistan* **68** C5
Islamgarh *Pakistan* **68** F4
Islamkot *Pakistan* **68** G4
Islampur *India* **69** G11
Island = Iceland ■ *Europe* **8** D4
Island L. *Canada* **103** C10
Island Lagoon *Australia* **95** E2
Island Pond *U.S.A.* **115** B13
Islands, B. of *Canada* **105** C8
Islands, B. of *N.Z.* **91** A5
Islay *U.K.* **13** F2
Isle ➤ *France* **20** D3
Isle aux Morts *Canada* **105** C8
Isle of Wight □ *U.K.* **15** G6
Isle Royale △ *U.S.A.* **112** B9
Isleton *U.S.A.* **110** G5
Ismail = Izmayil *Ukraine* **29** E13
Ismâ'ilîya *Egypt* **80** H8
Ismaning *Germany* **25** G7
Isna *Egypt* **80** B3
Isoanala *Madag.* **89** C8
Isogstalo *India* **69** B8
Ísola del Liri *Italy* **41** G10
Ísola della Scala *Italy* **40** C7
Ísola di Capo Rizzuto *Italy* **43** D10
Ísparta *Turkey* **47** D12
Ísparta □ *Turkey* **72** D4
Isperikh *Bulgaria* **45** C10
Íspica *Italy* **43** F7
Israel ■ *Asia* **74** D3
Isratu *Eritrea* **81** D4
Issakly *Russia* **34** C10
Issia *Ivory C.* **82** D3
Issoire *France* **20** C7
Issoudun *France* **19** F8
Issyk-Kul, Ozero =
 Ysyk-Köl *Kyrgyzstan* **52** E8
Ist *Croatia* **41** D11
Istállós-kő *Hungary* **28** B5
İstanbul *Turkey* **45** E12
İstanbul □ *Turkey* **45** E12
İstanbul ✈ (IST) *Turkey* **45** F12
İstanbul Boğazı *Turkey* **45** E13
Istiéa *Greece* **46** C5
Istok *Serbia* **44** D4
Istokpoga, L. *U.S.A.* **117** H14
Istra *Croatia* **41** C10
Istres *France* **21** E8
Istria = Istra *Croatia* **41** C10
Itá *Paraguay* **126** B4
Itaberaba *Brazil* **125** F10
Itabira *Brazil* **125** G10
Itabirito *Brazil* **125** A7
Itabuna *Brazil* **125** F11
Itacaunas ➤ *Brazil* **125** E9
Itacoatiara *Brazil* **124** D7
Itaipú, Reprêsa de *Brazil* **127** B5
Itaituba *Brazil* **125** D7
Itajaí *Brazil* **127** B6
Itajubá *Brazil* **127** A6
Itaka *Tanzania* **87** D3
Itala □ *S. Africa* **89** D5
Italy ■ *Europe* **7** G8
Itamaraju *Brazil* **125** G11
Itampolo *Madag.* **89** C7
Itandrano *Madag.* **89** C8
Itapecuru-Mirim *Brazil* **125** D10
Itaperuna *Brazil* **127** A7
Itapetininga *Brazil* **127** A6
Itapeva *Brazil* **127** A6
Itapicuru ➤ *Bahia, Brazil* **125** F11
Itapicuru ➤ *Maranhão,
 Brazil* **125** D10
Itapipoca *Brazil* **125** D11
Itapuá □ *Paraguay* **127** B4
Itaquari *Brazil* **127** A7
Itaqui *Brazil* **126** B4
Itararé *Brazil* **127** A6
Itarsi *India* **68** H7
Itati *Argentina* **126** B4
Itatiaia △ *Brazil* **127** A7
Itbayat *Phil.* **61** A4
Itchen ➤ *U.K.* **15** G6
Itea *Greece* **46** C4
Itezhi Tezhi, L. *Zambia* **87** F2
Ithaca = Itháki *Greece* **46** C2
Ithaca *U.S.A.* **115** D8
Itháki *Greece* **46** C2

Iti △ *Greece* **46** C4
Itiquira ➔ *Brazil* **125** G7
Itō *Japan* **55** G9
Itoigawa *Japan* **55** F8
Iton ➔ *France* **18** C8
Itonamas ➔ *Bolivia* **124** F6
Itri *Italy* **42** A6
Itsa *Egypt* **80** J7
Íttiri *Italy* **42** B1
Ittoqqortoormiit *Greenland* **4** B6
Itu *Brazil* **127** A6
Itu *Nigeria* **83** D6
Itu Aba I. *S. China Sea* **62** B4
Ituiutaba *Brazil* **125** G9
Ituna *Canada* **103** C8
Itunge Port *Tanzania* **87** D3
Iturbe *Argentina* **126** A2
Ituri ➔ *Dem. Rep. of the Congo* **86** B2
Iturup, Ostrov *Russia* **53** E15
Ituxi ➔ *Brazil* **124** E6
Ituyuro ➔ *Argentina* **126** A3
Itzehoe *Germany* **24** B5
Ivahona *Madag.* **89** C8
Ivaí ➔ *Brazil* **127** A5
Ivalo *Finland* **8** B22
Ivalojoki ➔ *Finland* **8** B22
Ivanava *Belarus* **23** B13
Ivančice *Czech Rep.* **27** B9
Ivane-Puste *Ukraine* **29** B11
Ivăneşti *Romania* **29** D12
Ivangorod *Russia* **32** C5
Ivanhoe *Australia* **95** E3
Ivanhoe *Calif., U.S.A.* **110** J7
Ivanhoe *Minn., U.S.A.* **112** C5
Ivanhorod *Ukraine* **29** B14
Ivanić Grad *Croatia* **41** C13
Ivanjica *Serbia* **44** C4
Ivanjska *Bos.-H.* **28** F2
Ivankoyskoye Vdkhr.
  Russia **32** D9
Ivano-Frankivsk *Ukraine* **29** B9
Ivano-Frankivsk □ *Ukraine* **29** B9
Ivanovo = Ivanava *Belarus* **23** B13
Ivanovo *Russia* **32** D11
Ivanovo □ *Russia* **34** B5
Ivanščica *Croatia* **41** B13
Ivato *Madag.* **89** C8
Ivatsevichy *Belarus* **23** B13
Ivaylovgrad *Bulgaria* **45** E10
Ivinheima ➔ *Brazil* **127** A5
Ivinhema *Brazil* **127** A5
Ivohibe *Madag.* **89** C8
Ivory Coast *W. Afr.* **82** E4
Ivory Coast ■ *Africa* **82** D4
Ivösjön *Sweden* **11** H8
Ivrea *Italy* **40** C4
Ívrindi *Turkey* **47** B9
Ivujivik *Canada* **101** C12
Ivybridge *U.K.* **15** G4
Iwaizumi *Japan* **54** E10
Iwaki *Japan* **55** F10
Iwakuni *Japan* **55** G6
Iwamizawa *Japan* **54** C10
Iwanai *Japan* **54** C10
Iwata *Japan* **55** G8
Iwate □ *Japan* **54** E10
Iwate-San *Japan* **54** E10
Iwo *Nigeria* **83** D5
Iwŏn *N. Korea* **57** D15
Iwonicz-Zdrój *Poland* **31** J8
Ixiamas *Bolivia* **124** F5
Ixopo *S. Africa* **89** E5
Ixtepec *Mexico* **119** D5
Ixtlán del Río *Mexico* **118** C4
Iyal Bakhit *Sudan* **81** E2
Iyo *Japan* **55** H6
Izabal, L. de *Guatemala* **120** C2
Izamal *Mexico* **119** C7
Izberbash *Russia* **35** J8
Izbica *Poland* **31** H10
Izbica Kujawska *Poland* **31** F5
Izbiceni *Romania* **29** G9
Izena-Shima *Japan* **55** L3
Izgrev *Bulgaria* **45** C10
Izhevsk *Russia* **52** D6
Izmayil *Ukraine* **29** E13
İzmir *Turkey* **47** C9
İzmir □ *Turkey* **47** C9
İzmir Adnan Menderes ✈
  (ADB) *Turkey* **47** C9
İzmir Körfezi *Turkey* **47** C8
İzmit = Kocaeli *Turkey* **45** F13
Iznájar *Spain* **37** H6
İznik *Turkey* **72** B3
İznik Gölü *Turkey* **45** F13
Izobil'nyy *Russia* **35** H5
Izola *Slovenia* **41** C10
Izra *Syria* **74** C5
Iztochni Rodopi *Bulgaria* **45** E9
Izu-Shotō *Japan* **55** G10
Izúcar de Matamoros
  Mexico **119** D5
Izumi-Sano *Japan* **55** G7
Izumo *Japan* **55** G6
Izyaslav *Ukraine* **23** C14
Izyum *Ukraine* **33** H9

J

J.F.K. Int. ✈ (JFK) *U.S.A.* **115** F11
J. Strom Thurmond L.
  U.S.A. **117** E13
Jaba *Ethiopia* **81** F4
Jabal at Ţā'ir *Red Sea* **81** D5
Jabalón ➔ *Spain* **37** G6
Jabalpur *India* **69** H8
Jabbūl *Syria* **70** B3
Jabiru *Australia* **92** B5
Jablah *Syria* **72** E6
Jablanac *Croatia* **41** D11
Jablanica *Bos.-H.* **28** G2
Jablonec nad Nisou
  Czech Rep. **26** A8
Jablonica *Slovak Rep.* **27** C10
Jablonowo Pomorskie
  Poland **30** E6
Jablunkov *Czech Rep.* **27** B11
Jaboatão *Brazil* **125** E11
Jaboticabal *Brazil* **127** A6
Jaca *Spain* **38** C4
Jacareí *Brazil* **127** A6
Jacarèzinho *Brazil* **127** A6
Jackman *U.S.A.* **113** C18
Jacksboro *U.S.A.* **116** E5
Jackson *Barbados* **121** g
Jackson *Ala., U.S.A.* **117** F11
Jackson *Calif., U.S.A.* **110** G6
Jackson *Ky., U.S.A.* **113** G12
Jackson *Mich., U.S.A.* **113** D11
Jackson *Minn., U.S.A.* **112** D6
Jackson *Miss., U.S.A.* **117** E9
Jackson *Mo., U.S.A.* **112** G9
Jackson *N.H., U.S.A.* **115** B13
Jackson *Ohio, U.S.A.* **113** F12
Jackson *Tenn., U.S.A.* **117** D10
Jackson *Wyo., U.S.A.* **108** E8
Jackson B. *N.Z.* **91** E2
Jackson L. *U.S.A.* **108** E8
Jackson's Arm *Canada* **105** C8
Jacksonville *Ala., U.S.A.* **117** E12
Jacksonville *Ark., U.S.A.* **116** D8
Jacksonville *Calif., U.S.A.* **110** H6
Jacksonville *Fla., U.S.A.* **117** F14
Jacksonville *Ill., U.S.A.* **112** F8
Jacksonville *N.C., U.S.A.* **117** D16
Jacksonville *Tex., U.S.A.* **116** F7
Jacksonville Beach *U.S.A.* **117** F14
Jacmel *Haiti* **121** C5
Jacob Lake *U.S.A.* **109** H7
Jacobabad *Pakistan* **68** E3
Jacobina *Brazil* **125** F10
Jacques-Cartier, Dét. de
  Canada **105** C7
Jacques-Cartier, Mt. *Canada* **105** C6
Jacques-Cartier △ *Canada* **105** C5
Jacqueville *Ivory C.* **82** D4
Jacuí ➔ *Brazil* **127** C5
Jacumba *U.S.A.* **111** N10
Jacundá ➔ *Brazil* **125** D8
Jade *Germany* **24** B4
Jade Mt. = Yü Shan *Taiwan* **59** F13
Jadebusen *Germany* **24** B4
Jadovnik *Serbia* **44** C3
Jadraque *Spain* **38** E2
Jaén *Peru* **124** E3
Jaén *Spain* **37** H7
Jaén □ *Spain* **37** H7
Jafarabad *India* **68** J4
Jaffa = Tel Aviv-Yafo *Israel* **74** C3
Jaffa, C. *Australia* **95** F2
Jaffna *Sri Lanka* **66** Q12
Jaffray *Canada* **103** D10
Jaffrey *U.S.A.* **115** D12
Jagadhri *India* **68** D7
Jagadishpur *India* **69** G11
Jagdalpur *India* **67** K13
Jagersfontein *S. Africa* **88** D4
Jaghīn ➔ *Iran* **71** E8
Jagodina *Serbia* **44** B5
Jagraon *India* **68** D6
Jagst ➔ *Germany* **25** F5
Jagtial *India* **66** K11
Jaguariaíva *Brazil* **127** A6
Jaguaribe ➔ *Brazil* **125** D11
Jagüey Grande *Cuba* **120** B3
Jahanabad *India* **69** G11
Jahazpur *India* **68** G6
Jahrom *Iran* **71** D7
Jaijon *India* **68** D7
Jailolo *Indonesia* **63** D7
Jailolo, Selat *Indonesia* **63** D7
Jaipur *India* **68** F6
Jais *India* **69** F9
Jaisalmer *India* **68** F4
Jaisinghnagar *India* **69** H8
Jaitaran *India* **68** F5
Jaithari *India* **69** H8
Jājarm *Iran* **71** B8
Jajce *Bos.-H.* **28** F2
Jakam ➔ *India* **68** H6
Jakarta *Indonesia* **63** G12
Jakhal *India* **68** E6

Jakhau *India* **68** H3
Jakobstad = Pietarsaari
  Finland **8** E20
Jaba *Ethiopia* **81** F4
Jabal at Ţā'ir *Red Sea* **81** D5
Jabalón ➔ *Spain* **37** G6
Jalālābād *Afghan.* **68** B4
Jalalabad *India* **69** F8
Jalalpur Jattan *Pakistan* **68** C6
Jalama *U.S.A.* **111** L6
Jalapa *Guatemala* **120** D2
Jalapa Enríquez = Xalapa
  Mexico **119** D5
Jalasjärvi *Finland* **8** E20
Jalaun *India* **69** F8
Jalesar *India* **68** F8
Jaleswar *Nepal* **69** F11
Jalgaon *India* **66** J9
Jalībah *Iraq* **70** D5
Jalingo *Nigeria* **83** D7
Jalisco □ *Mexico* **118** D4
Jalkot *Pakistan* **69** B5
Jallas ➔ *Spain* **36** C1
Jalna *India* **66** K9
Jalón ➔ *Spain* **38** D3
Jalor *India* **68** G5
Jalpa *Mexico* **118** C4
Jalpaiguri *India* **67** F16
Jalpan *Mexico* **119** C5
Jaluit I. *Marshall Is.* **96** G8
Jalūlā *Iraq* **73** E11
Jamaame = Giamama
  Somali Rep. **75** G3
Jamaari *Nigeria* **83** C6
Jamaica ■ *W. Indies* **120** a
Jamalpur *Bangla.* **67** G16
Jamalpur *India* **69** G12
Jamalpurganj *India* **69** H13
Jamanxim ➔ *Brazil* **125** D7
Jambewangi *Indonesia* **63** J17
Jambi *Indonesia* **62** E2
Jambi □ *Indonesia* **62** E2
Jambongan, Pulau *Malaysia* **62** C5
Jambusar *India* **68** H5
James ➔ *S. Dak., U.S.A.* **112** D5
James ➔ *Va., U.S.A.* **113** G15
James B. *Canada* **104** B3
James Ranges *Australia* **92** D5
James Ross I. *Antarctica* **5** C18
Jamesabad *Pakistan* **68** G3
Jamestown *Australia* **95** E2
Jamestown *S. Africa* **88** E4
Jamestown *N. Dak., U.S.A.* **112** B4
Jamestown *N.Y., U.S.A.* **114** D5
Jamestown *Pa., U.S.A.* **114** E4
Jamīlābād *Iran* **71** C6
Jamira ➔ *India* **69** J13
Jämjö *Sweden* **11** H9
Jamkhandi *India* **66** L9
Jammerbugten *Denmark* **11** G3
Jammu *India* **68** C6
Jammu & Kashmir □ *India* **69** B7
Jamnagar *India* **68** H4
Jamni ➔ *India* **69** G8
Jampur *Pakistan* **68** E4
Jamrud *Pakistan* **68** C4
Jämsä *Finland* **32** B3
Jamshedpur *India* **69** H12
Jamtara *India* **69** H12
Jämtland *Sweden* **8** E16
Jämtlands län □ *Sweden* **10** B7
Jan L. *Canada* **103** C8
Jan Mayen *Arctic* **4** B7
Janakkala *Finland* **32** B3
Janaúba *Brazil* **125** G10
Jand *Pakistan* **68** C5
Jandaq *Iran* **71** C7
Jandía *Canary Is.* **48** F5
Jandía, Pta. de *Canary Is.* **48** F5
Jandía △ *Canary Is.* **48** F5
Jandola *Pakistan* **68** C4
Jandowae *Australia* **95** D5
Jándula ➔ *Spain* **37** G6
Janesville *U.S.A.* **112** D9
Janga *Ghana* **83** C4
Jangamo *Mozam.* **89** C6
Janghai *India* **69** G10
Jangheung *S. Korea* **57** G14
Janikowo *Poland* **31** F5
Janină = Ioannina □ *Greece* **46** B2
Janja *Bos.-H.* **28** F4
Janjanbureh *Gambia* **82** C2
Janjevo *Serbia* **44** D5
Janjgir *India* **69** J10
Janjina *Croatia* **41** F14
Janjina *Madag.* **89** C8
Janos *Mexico* **118** A3
Jánoshalma *Hungary* **28** D4
Jánosháza *Hungary* **28** C2
Jánossomorja *Hungary* **28** C2
Janów *India* **91** H6
Janów Lubelski *Poland* **31** H9
Janów Podlaski *Poland* **31** F10
Janowiec Wielkopolski
  Poland **31** F4
Januária *Brazil* **125** G10
Janub △ *Sudan* **81** F2

Janub Dârfûr □ *Sudan* **81** E2
Janub Kordofân □ *Sudan* **81** E3
Janûb Sînî □ *Egypt* **74** F2
Janubio *Canary Is.* **48** F6
Janville *France* **19** D4
Janzé *France* **18** E5
Jaora *India* **68** H6
Japan ■ *Asia* **55** G8
Japan, Sea of *Asia* **54** E7
Japan Trench *Pac. Oc.* **96** D6
Japen = Yapen *Indonesia* **63** E9
Japla *India* **69** G11
Japurá ➔ *Brazil* **124** D5
Jaquarão *Brazil* **127** C5
Jaqué *Panama* **120** E4
Jaraicejo *Spain* **37** F5
Jaraiz de la Vera *Spain* **36** E5
Jarama ➔ *Spain* **38** E1
Jaramānah *Syria* **72** F7
Jarandilla *Spain* **36** E5
Jaranwala *Pakistan* **68** D5
Jarash *Jordan* **74** C4
Jarash □ *Jordan* **74** C4
Järbo *Sweden* **10** D10
Jardim *Brazil* **126** A4
Jardín ➔ *Spain* **39** G2
Jardine River △ *Australia* **94** A3
Jardines de la Reina, Arch.
  de los *Cuba* **120** B4
Jargalang *China* **57** C12
Jari ➔ *Brazil* **125** D8
Jarīr, W. al ➔ *Si. Arabia* **70** E4
Järlåsa *Sweden* **10** E11
Jarmen *Germany* **24** B9
Järna *Dalarna, Sweden* **10** D8
Järna *Stockholm, Sweden* **10** E11
Jarnac *France* **20** C3
Jarny *France* **19** C12
Jarocin *Poland* **31** G4
Jaroměř *Czech Rep.* **26** A8
Jarosław *Poland* **31** H9
Järpås *Sweden* **11** F6
Järpen *Sweden* **10** A7
Jarrahdale *Australia* **93** F2
Jarrahi ➔ *Iran* **71** D6
Jarres, Plaine des *Laos* **64** C4
Jarso *Ethiopia* **81** F4
Jartai *China* **56** E3
Jarud Qi *China* **57** B11
Jarvis *Canada* **114** D4
Jarvis I. *Pac. Oc.* **97** H12
Jarvorník *Czech Rep.* **27** A10
Järvsö *Sweden* **10** C10
Jarwa *India* **69** F10
Jaša Tomić *Serbia* **28** E5
Jasdan *India* **68** H4
Jashpurnagar *India* **69** H11
Jasidih *India* **69** G12
Jasień *Poland* **31** G2
Jāsimīyah *Iraq* **73** F11
Jasin *Malaysia* **65** L4
Jāsk *Iran* **71** E8
Jasło *Poland* **31** J8
Jasmund *Germany* **24** A9
Jasmund △ *Germany* **24** A9
Jaso *India* **69** G9
Jasper *Alta., Canada* **102** C5
Jasper *Ont., Canada* **115** B9
Jasper *Ala., U.S.A.* **117** E11
Jasper *Fla., U.S.A.* **117** F13
Jasper *Ind., U.S.A.* **112** F10
Jasper *Tex., U.S.A.* **116** F7
Jasper △ *Canada* **102** C5
Jasrasar *India* **68** F5
Jastarnia *Poland* **30** D5
Jastrowie *Poland* **30** E3
Jastrzębie Zdrój *Poland* **31** J5
Jász-Nagykun-Szolnok □
  Hungary **28** C5
Jászapáti *Hungary* **28** C5
Jászárokszállás *Hungary* **28** C4
Jászberény *Hungary* **28** C4
Jászkisér *Hungary* **28** C5
Jászladány *Hungary* **28** C5
Jataí *Brazil* **125** G8
Jati *Pakistan* **68** G3
Jatibarang *Indonesia* **63** G13
Jatiluwih *Indonesia* **63** J18
Jatinegara *Indonesia* **63** G12
Játiva = Xàtiva *Spain* **39** G4
Jaú *Brazil* **127** A6
Jauja *Peru* **124** F3
Jaunpur *India* **69** G10
Java = Jawa *Indonesia* **62** F3
Java Sea *Indonesia* **62** E3
Java Trench *Ind. Oc.* **62** F3
Javalambre, Sa. de *Spain* **38** E4
Jávea *Spain* **39** G5
Jawa *Indonesia* **62** F3
Jawa Barat □ *Indonesia* **63** G12
Jawa Tengah □ *Indonesia* **63** G14
Jawa Timur □ *Indonesia* **63** G15
Jawad *India* **68** G6

Jawor *Poland* **31** G3
Jaworzno *Poland* **31** H6
Jaworzyna Śląska *Poland* **31** H3
Jay Peak *U.S.A.* **115** B12
Jaya, Puncak *Indonesia* **63** E9
Jayanti *India* **67** F16
Jayapura *Indonesia* **63** E10
Jaynagar *India* **69** F12
Jayrūd *Syria* **72** F7
Jayton *U.S.A.* **116** E4
Jāz Mūrīān, Hāmūn-e *Iran* **71** E8
Jazīreh-ye Shīf *Iran* **71** D6
Jazminal *Mexico* **118** C4
Jazzîn *Lebanon* **74** B4
Jean *U.S.A.* **111** K11
Jean Marie River *Canada* **102** A4
Jean-Rabel *Haiti* **121** C5
Jeanerette *U.S.A.* **116** G9
Jeanette, Ostrov =
  Zhannetty, Ostrov *Russia* **53** B16
Jeannette *U.S.A.* **114** F5
Jebāl Bārez, Kūh-e *Iran* **71** D8
Jebba *Nigeria* **83** D5
Jebel, Bahr el ➔ *Sudan* **81** F3
Jebel Dud *Sudan* **81** E3
Jebel Qerri *Sudan* **81** D3
Jecheon *S. Korea* **57** F15
Jedburgh *U.K.* **13** F6
Jedda = Jiddah *Si. Arabia* **75** C2
Jeddore L. *Canada* **105** C8
Jedlicze *Poland* **31** J8
Jędrzejów *Poland* **31** H7
Jedwabne *Poland* **31** E9
Jeetzel ➔ *Germany* **24** B7
Jefferson *Iowa, U.S.A.* **112** D6
Jefferson *Ohio, U.S.A.* **114** E4
Jefferson *Tex., U.S.A.* **116** E7
Jefferson, Mt. *Nev., U.S.A.* **108** G5
Jefferson, Mt. *Oreg., U.S.A.* **108** D3
Jefferson City *Mo., U.S.A.* **112** F7
Jefferson City *Tenn., U.S.A.* **117** C13
Jeffersontown *U.S.A.* **113** F11
Jeffersonville *U.S.A.* **113** F11
Jeffrey City *U.S.A.* **108** E10
Jega *Nigeria* **83** C5
Jeju *S. Korea* **57** H14
Jeju-do *S. Korea* **57** H14
Jēkabpils *Latvia* **32** D3
Jekyll I. *U.S.A.* **117** F14
Jelcz-Laskowice *Poland* **31** G4
Jelenia Góra *Poland* **31** H2
Jelgava *Latvia* **30** B10
Jelgava □ *Latvia* **30** B10
Jelica *Serbia* **44** C4
Jelli *Sudan* **81** F3
Jelšava *Slovak Rep.* **27** C13
Jemaja *Indonesia* **65** L5
Jemaluang *Malaysia* **65** L4
Jember *Indonesia* **63** H15
Jena *Germany* **24** C7
Jena *U.S.A.* **116** F8
Jenbach *Austria* **26** D4
Jenīn *West Bank* **74** C4
Jenkins *U.S.A.* **113** G12
Jenner *U.S.A.* **110** G3
Jennings *U.S.A.* **116** F8
Jeong-eup *S. Korea* **57** G14
Jeonju *S. Korea* **57** G14
Jepara *Indonesia* **63** G14
Jeparit *Australia* **95** F3
Jequié *Brazil* **125** F10
Jequitinhonha *Brazil* **125** G10
Jequitinhonha ➔ *Brazil* **125** G11
Jerada *Morocco* **78** B5
Jerantut *Malaysia* **65** L4
Jerejak, Pulau *Malaysia* **65** c
Jerez, Pta. *Mexico* **119** C5
Jerez de García Salinas
  Mexico **118** C4
Jerez de la Frontera *Spain* **37** J4
Jerez de los Caballeros *Spain* **37** G4
Jericho = El Arīḥā *West Bank* **74** D4
Jericho *Australia* **94** C4
Jerichow *Germany* **24** C8
Jerid, Chott el = Djerid,
  Chott *Tunisia* **78** B7
Jerilderie *Australia* **95** F4
Jermyn *U.S.A.* **115** E9
Jerome *U.S.A.* **108** E6
Jerramungup *Australia* **93** F2
Jersey *U.K.* **15** H5
Jersey City *U.S.A.* **115** F10
Jersey Shore *U.S.A.* **114** E7
Jerseyville *U.S.A.* **112** F8
Jerusalem *Israel/West Bank* **74** D4
Jervis B. *Australia* **95** F5
Jervis Inlet *Canada* **102** C3
Jerzu *Italy* **42** C2
Jesenice *Slovenia* **41** B11
Jeseník *Czech Rep.* **27** A10
Jesenké *Slovak Rep.* **27** C13
Jesi = Iesi *Italy* **41** E10

Jessnitz *Germany* **24** D8
Jessore *Bangla.* **67** H16
Jesup *U.S.A.* **117** F14
Jesús Carranza *Mexico* **119** D5
Jesús María *Argentina* **126** C3
Jetmore *U.S.A.* **112** F4
Jetpur *India* **68** J4
Jeumont *France* **19** B11
Jevnaker *Norway* **9** F14
Jewett *U.S.A.* **114** F3
Jewett City *U.S.A.* **115** E13
Jeyhūnābād *Iran* **71** C6
Jeypore *India* **67** K13
Jeziorak, Jezioro *Poland* **30** E6
Jeziorany *Poland* **30** E7
Jeziorka ➔ *Poland* **31** F8
Jha Jha *India* **69** G12
Jhabua *India* **68** H6
Jhajjar *India* **68** E7
Jhal *Pakistan* **68** E2
Jhal Jhao *Pakistan* **66** F4
Jhalawar *India* **68** G7
Jhalida *India* **69** H11
Jhalrapatan *India* **68** G7
Jhang Maghiana *Pakistan* **68** D5
Jhansi *India* **69** G8
Jhargram *India* **69** H12
Jharia *India* **69** H12
Jharsuguda *India* **67** J14
Jhelum *Pakistan* **68** C5
Jhelum ➔ *Pakistan* **68** D5
Jhilmilli *India* **69** H10
Jhudo *Pakistan* **68** G3
Jhunjhunu *India* **68** E6
Ji-Paraná *Brazil* **124** F5
Ji Xian *Hebei, China* **56** F8
Ji Xian *Henan, China* **56** G8
Ji Xian *Shanxi, China* **56** F6
Jia Xian *Henan, China* **56** H7
Jia Xian *Shaanxi, China* **56** E6
Jiading *China* **59** B13
Jiahe *China* **59** E9
Jiaji = Qionghai *China* **64** C8
Jialing Jiang ➔ *China* **58** C6
Jiamusi *China* **60** B8
Ji'an *Jiangxi, China* **59** D10
Ji'an *Jilin, China* **57** D14
Jianchang *China* **57** D11
Jianchangying *China* **57** D10
Jianchuan *China* **58** D2
Jiande *China* **59** C12
Jiang'an *China* **58** C5
Jiangbei *China* **58** C6
Jiangcheng *China* **58** F3
Jiangchuan *China* **58** E4
Jiangdi *China* **58** D4
Jiangdu *China* **59** A12
Jiange *China* **58** A5
Jianghua *China* **59** E8
Jiangjin *China* **58** C6
Jiangkou *China* **58** D7
Jiangle *China* **59** D11
Jiangling *China* **59** B9
Jiangmen *China* **59** F9
Jiangning *China* **59** B12
Jiangshan *China* **59** C12
Jiangsu □ *China* **57** H11
Jiangxi □ *China* **59** D11
Jiangyan *China* **59** A13
Jiangyin *China* **59** B13
Jiangyong *China* **59** E8
Jiangyou *China* **58** B5
Jianhe *China* **58** D7
Jianli *China* **59** C9
Jianning *China* **59** D11
Jian'ou *China* **59** D12
Jianshi *China* **58** B7
Jianshui *China* **58** F4
Jianyang *Fujian, China* **59** D12
Jianyang *Sichuan, China* **58** B5
Jiao Xian = Jiaozhou *China* **57** F11
Jiaohe *Hebei, China* **56** E9
Jiaohe *Jilin, China* **57** C14
Jiaojiang *China* **59** C13
Jiaoling *China* **59** E11
Jiaozhou *China* **57** F11
Jiaozhou Wan *China* **57** F11
Jiaozuo *China* **56** G7
Jiashan *China* **59** B13
Jiawang *China* **57** G9
Jiaxiang *China* **56** G9
Jiaxing *China* **59** B13
Jiayi = Chiai *Taiwan* **59** F13
Jiayu *China* **59** C9
Jibiya *Nigeria* **83** C6
Jibou *Romania* **29** C8
Jibuti = Djibouti ■ *Africa* **81** E5
Jicarón, I. *Panama* **120** E3
Jičín *Czech Rep.* **26** A8
Jiddah *Si. Arabia* **75** C2
Jido *India* **67** E19
Jieshou *China* **56** H8
Jiexiu *China* **56** F6
Jieyang *China* **59** F11

Jigalong *Australia* **92** D3
Jigawa □ *Nigeria* **83** C6
Jigni *India* **69** G8
Jihlava *Czech Rep.* **26** B8
Jihlava ➤ *Czech Rep.* **27** C9
Jihlavský □ *Czech Rep.* **26** B8
Jihočeský □ *Czech Rep.* **26** B7
Jihomoravský □ *Czech Rep.* **27** B9
Jijiga *Ethiopia* **75** F3
Jikamshi *Nigeria* **83** C6
Jikau *Sudan* **81** F3
Jilib = Gelib *Somali Rep.* **75** G3
Jilin *China* **57** C14
Jilin □ *China* **57** C14
Jiloca ➤ *Spain* **38** D3
Jilong = Chilung *Taiwan* **59** E13
Jim Thorpe *U.S.A.* **115** F9
Jima *Ethiopia* **81** F4
Jimbaran, Teluk *Indonesia* **63** K18
Jimbolia *Romania* **28** E5
Jimena de la Frontera *Spain* **37** J5
Jiménez *Mexico* **118** B4
Jimo *China* **57** F11
Jin Jiang ➤ *China* **59** C10
Jin Xian = Jinzhou *Hebei, China* **56** E8
Jin Xian = Jinzhou *Liaoning, China* **57** E11
Jinan *China* **56** F9
Jinchang *China* **60** C5
Jincheng *China* **56** G7
Jinchuan *China* **58** B4
Jind *India* **68** E7
Jindabyne *Australia* **95** F4
Jindo *S. Korea* **57** G14
Jindřichův Hradec *Czech Rep.* **26** B8
Jing He ➤ *China* **56** G5
Jing Shan *China* **59** B8
Jing Xian *China* **59** B12
Jing'an *China* **59** C10
Jingbian *China* **56** F5
Jingchuan *China* **56** G4
Jingde *China* **59** B12
Jingdezhen *China* **59** C11
Jingdong *China* **58** E3
Jinggangshan *China* **59** D10
Jinggu *China* **58** F3
Jinghai *China* **56** E9
Jinghong *China* **58** G3
Jingjiang *China* **59** A13
Jingle *China* **56** E6
Jingmen *China* **59** B9
Jingning *China* **56** G3
Jingpo Hu *China* **57** C15
Jingshan *China* **59** B9
Jingtai *China* **56** F3
Jingxi *China* **58** F6
Jingxing *China* **56** E8
Jingyang *China* **56** G5
Jingyu *China* **57** C14
Jingyuan *China* **56** F3
Jingzhou *China* **58** D7
Jingziguan *China* **56** H6
Jinhua *China* **59** C12
Jining *Nei Monggol Zizhiqu, China* **56** D7
Jining *Shandong, China* **56** G9
Jinja *Uganda* **86** B3
Jinjang *Malaysia* **65** L3
Jinji *China* **56** F4
Jinjiang *Fujian, China* **59** E12
Jinjiang *Yunnan, China* **58** D3
Jinjini *Ghana* **82** D4
Jinju *S. Korea* **57** G15
Jinkou *China* **59** B10
Jinkouhe *China* **58** C4
Jinmen Dao *China* **59** E12
Jinnah Barrage *Pakistan* **68** C4
Jinning *China* **58** E4
Jinotega *Nic.* **120** D2
Jinotepe *Nic.* **120** D2
Jinping *Guizhou, China* **58** D7
Jinping *Yunnan, China* **58** F4
Jinsha *China* **58** D6
Jinsha Jiang ➤ *China* **58** C5
Jinshan *China* **59** B13
Jinshi *China* **59** C8
Jintan *China* **59** B12
Jinxi *Jiangxi, China* **59** D11
Jinxi *Liaoning, China* **57** D11
Jinxian *China* **59** C11
Jinxiang *China* **56** G9
Jinyang *China* **58** D4
Jinyun *China* **59** C13
Jinzhai *China* **59** B10
Jinzhou *Hebei, China* **56** E8
Jinzhou *Liaoning, China* **57** E11
Jinzhou *Liaoning, China* **57** D11
Jiparaná ➤ *Brazil* **124** E6
Jipijapa *Ecuador* **124** D2
Jiquilpan *Mexico* **118** D4
Jirisan *S. Korea* **57** G14
Jishan *China* **56** G6
Jishou *China* **58** C7
Jishui *China* **59** D10
Jisr ash Shughūr *Syria* **72** E7
Jitarning *Australia* **93** F2

Jitra *Malaysia* **65** J3
Jiu ➤ *Romania* **29** G8
Jiudengkou *China* **56** E4
Jiujiang *Guangdong, China* **59** F9
Jiujiang *Jiangxi, China* **59** C10
Jiuling Shan *China* **59** C10
Jiulong = Kowloon *China* **59** F10
Jiulong *China* **58** C3
Jiutai *China* **57** B13
Jiuxincheng *China* **56** E8
Jiuyuhang *China* **59** B12
Jiwani *Pakistan* **66** G2
Jixi *Anhui, China* **59** B12
Jixi *Heilongjiang, China* **57** B16
Jiyang *China* **57** F9
Jiyuan *China* **56** G7
Jīzān *Si. Arabia* **75** D3
Jize *China* **56** F8
Jizera ➤ *Czech Rep.* **26** A7
Jizl, Wādī al ➤ *Si. Arabia* **70** E3
Jizō-Zaki *Japan* **55** G6
Jizzakh *Uzbekistan* **52** E7
Joaçaba *Brazil* **127** B5
Joal Fadiout *Senegal* **82** C1
João Pessoa *Brazil* **125** E12
Joaquín V. González *Argentina* **126** B3
Jobat *India* **68** H6
Jobourg, Nez de *France* **18** C5
Jódar *Spain* **37** H7
Jodhpur *India* **68** F5
Jodiya *India* **68** H4
Joensuu *Finland* **8** E23
Jõetsu *Japan* **55** F9
Jœuf *France* **19** C12
Jofane *Mozam.* **89** C5
Jogbani *India* **69** F12
Jõgeva *Estonia* **32** C4
Jogjakarta = Yogyakarta *Indonesia* **63** G14
Johannesburg *S. Africa* **89** D4
Johannesburg *U.S.A.* **111** K9
Johansfors *Sweden* **11** H9
Johilla ➤ *India* **69** H9
John Crow Mts. *Jamaica* **120** a
John Day *U.S.A.* **108** D4
John Day ➤ *U.S.A.* **108** D3
John Day Fossil Beds △ *U.S.A.* **108** D4
John D'Or Prairie *Canada* **102** B5
John H. Kerr Res. *U.S.A.* **117** C15
John o' Groats *U.K.* **13** C5
Johnnie *U.S.A.* **111** J10
John's Ra. *Australia* **94** C1
Johnson *U.S.A.* **115** B12
Johnson City *Kans., U.S.A.* **112** G3
Johnson City *N.Y., U.S.A.* **115** D9
Johnson City *Tenn., U.S.A.* **117** C13
Johnson City *Tex., U.S.A.* **116** F5
Johnsonburg *U.S.A.* **114** E6
Johnsondale *U.S.A.* **111** K8
Johnsons Crossing *Canada* **102** A2
Johnston, L. *Australia* **93** F3
Johnston Falls = Mambilima Falls *Zambia* **87** E2
Johnston I. *Pac. Oc.* **97** F11
Johnstone Str. *Canada* **102** C3
Johnstown *Ireland* **12** D4
Johnstown *N.Y., U.S.A.* **115** C10
Johnstown *Ohio, U.S.A.* **114** F2
Johnstown *Pa., U.S.A.* **114** F6
Johor, Selat *Asia* **65** d
Johor Bahru *Malaysia* **65** d
Jõhvi *Estonia* **32** C4
Joigny *France* **19** E10
Joinville *Brazil* **127** B6
Joinville *France* **19** D12
Joinville I. *Antarctica* **5** C18
Jojutla *Mexico* **119** D5
Jokkmokk *Sweden* **8** C18
Jökulsá á Bru ➤ *Iceland* **8** D6
Jökulsá á Fjöllum ➤ *Iceland* **8** C5
Jolfā *Āzarbājān-e Sharqī, Iran* **73** C11
Jolfā *Eşfahan, Iran* **71** C6
Joliet *U.S.A.* **112** E9
Joliette *Canada* **104** C5
Jolo *Phil.* **61** J4
Jolon *U.S.A.* **110** K5
Jomalig I. *Phil.* **61** D5
Jombang *Indonesia* **63** G15
Jomda *China* **58** B2
Jonava *Lithuania* **32** E3
Jones Sound *Canada* **101** B11
Jonesboro *Ark., U.S.A.* **117** D9
Jonesboro *La., U.S.A.* **116** E8
Jong ➤ *S. Leone* **82** D2
Jonglei *Sudan* **81** F3
Jonglei □ *Sudan* **81** F3
Joniškis *Lithuania* **30** B10
Jönköping *Sweden* **11** G8
Jönköpings län □ *Sweden* **11** G8
Jonquière *Canada* **105** C5
Jonsered *Sweden* **11** G6
Jonzac *France* **20** C3
Joplin *U.S.A.* **112** G6
Jora *India* **68** F6
Jordan *Mont., U.S.A.* **108** C10

Jordan *N.Y., U.S.A.* **115** C8
Jordan ■ *Asia* **74** E5
Jordan ➤ *Asia* **74** D4
Jordan Valley *U.S.A.* **108** E5
Jordanów *Poland* **31** J6
Jorhat *India* **67** F19
Jori ➤ *Norway* **10** B3
Jörn *Sweden* **8** D19
Jorong *Indonesia* **62** E4
Jørpeland *Norway* **9** G12
Jorquera ➤ *Chile* **126** B2
Jos *Nigeria* **83** D6
Jos Plateau *Nigeria* **83** D6
Jošanička Banja *Serbia* **44** C4
José Batlle y Ordóñez *Uruguay* **127** C4
Joseni *Romania* **29** D10
Joseph, L. *Nfld. & L., Canada* **105** B6
Joseph, L. *Ont., Canada* **114** A5
Joseph Bonaparte G. *Australia* **92** B4
Joshinath *India* **69** D8
Joshinetsu-Kōgen △ *Japan* **55** F9
Joshua Tree *U.S.A.* **111** L10
Joshua Tree △ *U.S.A.* **111** M10
Josselin *France* **18** E4
Jost Van Dyke I. *Br. Virgin Is.* **121** e
Jostedalsbreen *Norway* **8** F12
Jotunheimen *Norway* **8** F13
Joubertberge *Namibia* **88** B1
Joué-lès-Tours *France* **18** E7
Jourdanton *U.S.A.* **116** G5
Joutseno *Finland* **32** B5
Jovellanos *Cuba* **120** B3
Jowhar = Giohar *Somali Rep.* **75** G4
Joyeuse *France* **21** D8
Józefów *Lubelskie, Poland* **31** H10
Józefów *Mazowieckie, Poland* **31** F8
Ju Xian *China* **57** F10
Juan Aldama *Mexico* **118** C4
Juan Bautista Alberdi *Argentina* **126** B3
Juan de Fuca, Str of. *N. Amer.* **110** B3
Juán de N. *Ind. Oc.* **89** B7
Juan Fernández, Arch. de *Pac. Oc.* **122** G2
Juan José Castelli *Argentina* **126** B3
Juan L. Lacaze *Uruguay* **126** C4
Juankoski *Finland* **8** E23
Juárez *Argentina* **126** D4
Juárez *Mexico* **111** N11
Juárez *Coahuila, Mexico* **118** B4
Juárez *Sierra de Mexico* **118** A1
Juàzeiro *Brazil* **125** E10
Juàzeiro do Norte *Brazil* **125** E11
Juba = Giuba ➤ *Somali Rep.* **75** G3
Jūbā *Sudan* **81** G3
Jubany *Antarctica* **5** C18
Jubayl *Lebanon* **74** A4
Jubbah *Si. Arabia* **70** D4
Jubbal *India* **68** D7
Jubbulpore = Jabalpur *India* **69** H8
Jübek *Germany* **24** A5
Jubga *Russia* **35** H4
Jubilee L. *Australia* **93** E4
Juby, C. *Morocco* **78** C3
Júcar = Xúquer ➤ *Spain* **39** F4
Júcaro *Cuba* **120** B4
Juchitán de Zaragoza *Mexico* **119** D5
Judea = Har Yehuda *Israel* **74** D3
Judenburg *Austria* **26** D7
Judith ➤ *U.S.A.* **108** C9
Judith, Pt. *U.S.A.* **115** E13
Judith Gap *U.S.A.* **108** C9
Juelsminde *Denmark* **11** J4
Jugoslavia = Serbia ■ *Europe* **28** F5
Juigalpa *Nic.* **120** D2
Juillac *France* **20** C5
Juist *Germany* **24** B2
Juiz de Fora *Brazil* **127** A7
Jujuy □ *Argentina* **126** A2
Julesburg *U.S.A.* **108** F12
Juli *Peru* **124** G5
Julia Cr. ➤ *Australia* **94** C3
Julia Creek *Australia* **94** C3
Juliaca *Peru* **124** G4
Julian *U.S.A.* **111** M10
Julian, L. *Canada* **104** B4
Julian Alps = Julijske Alpe *Slovenia* **41** B11
Julianatop *Suriname* **125** C7
Julianehåb = Qaqortoq *Greenland* **4** C5
Jülich *Germany* **24** E2
Julijske Alpe *Slovenia* **41** B11
Julimes *Mexico* **118** B3
Jullundur *India* **68** D6
Julu *China* **56** F8
Jumbo *Zimbabwe* **87** F3
Jumbo Pk. *U.S.A.* **111** J12
Jumentos Cays *Bahamas* **120** B4
Jumilla *Spain* **39** G3
Jumla *Nepal* **69** E10
Jumna = Yamuna ➤ *India* **69** G9

Jumunjin *S. Korea* **57** F15
Junagadh *India* **68** J4
Junction *Tex., U.S.A.* **116** F5
Junction *Utah, U.S.A.* **109** G7
Junction B. *Australia* **94** A1
Junction City *Kans., U.S.A.* **112** F5
Junction City *Oreg., U.S.A.* **108** D2
Junction Pt. *Australia* **94** A1
Jundah *Australia* **94** C3
Jundiaí *Brazil* **127** A6
Juneau *U.S.A.* **102** B2
Junee *Australia* **95** E4
Jungfrau *Switz.* **25** J3
Junggar Pendi *China* **60** B3
Jungshahi *Pakistan* **68** G2
Juniata ➤ *U.S.A.* **114** F7
Junín *Argentina* **126** C3
Junín de los Andes *Argentina* **128** D2
Jūniyah *Lebanon* **74** B4
Junlian *China* **58** C5
Juntas *Chile* **126** B2
Juntura *U.S.A.* **108** E4
Jur, Nahr el ➤ *Sudan* **81** F2
Jura = Jura, Mts. du *Europe* **19** F13
Jura = Schwäbische Alb *Germany* **25** G5
Jura *U.K.* **13** F3
Jura □ *France* **19** F12
Jura □ *Switz.* **25** H3
Jūra ➤ *Lithuania* **30** C9
Jura, Mts. du *Europe* **19** F13
Jura, Sd. of *U.K.* **13** F3
Jurbarkas *Lithuania* **30** C9
Jurien *Australia* **93** F2
Jurilovca *Romania* **29** F13
Jūrmala *Latvia* **30** B10
Jurong *China* **59** B12
Jurong *Singapore* **65** d
Juruá ➤ *Brazil* **124** D5
Juruena *Brazil* **124** F7
Juruena ➤ *Brazil* **124** E7
Juruti *Brazil* **125** D7
Jussey *France* **19** E12
Justo Daract *Argentina* **126** C2
Jutaí ➤ *Brazil* **124** D5
Jüterbog *Germany* **24** D9
Juticalpa *Honduras* **120** D2
Jutland = Jylland *Denmark* **11** H3
Juuka *Finland* **8** E23
Juuventud, I. de la *Cuba* **120** B3
Juvigny-sous-Andaine *France* **18** D6
Jūy Zar *Iran* **73** F12
Juye *China* **56** G9
Juzennecourt *France* **19** D11
Jvari *Georgia* **35** J6
Jwaneng *Botswana* **85** J4
Jyderup *Denmark* **11** J5
Jylland *Denmark* **11** H3
Jyväskylä *Finland* **32** A3

K

K2 *Pakistan* **69** B7
Ka ➤ *Nigeria* **83** C5
Kaakha = Kaka *Turkmenistan* **71** B8
Kaap Plateau *S. Africa* **88** D3
Kaapkruis *Namibia* **88** C1
Kaapstad = Cape Town *S. Africa* **88** E2
Kaba *Guinea* **82** C2
Kabaena *Indonesia* **63** F6
Kabala *S. Leone* **82** D2
Kabale *Uganda* **86** C3
Kabalo *Dem. Rep. of the Congo* **86** D2
Kabambare *Dem. Rep. of the Congo* **86** C2
Kabango *Dem. Rep. of the Congo* **87** D2
Kabanjahe *Indonesia* **62** D1
Kabankalan *Phil.* **61** G5
Kabara *Fiji* **91** a
Kabara *Mali* **82** B4
Kabardinka *Russia* **33** K10
Kabardino-Balkar Republic = Kabardino-Balkaria □ *Russia* **35** J6
Kabardino-Balkaria □ *Russia* **35** J6
Kabarega Falls = Murchison Falls *Uganda* **86** B3
Kabarnet *Kenya* **86** B4
Kabasalan *Phil.* **61** H5
Kabat *Indonesia* **63** J17
Kabba *Nigeria* **83** D6
Kabi *Niger* **83** C7
Kabin Buri *Thailand* **64** F3
Kabinakagami L. *Canada* **104** C3
Kabinda *Dem. Rep. of the Congo* **84** F4
Kabna *Sudan* **80** D3
Kabompo *Zambia* **87** E1
Kabompo ➤ *Zambia* **85** G4
Kabondo *Dem. Rep. of the Congo* **87** D2

Kabongo *Dem. Rep. of the Congo* **86** D2
Kabot *Guinea* **82** C2
Kabou *Togo* **83** D5
Kabr *Sudan* **81** E2
Kabrît, G. el *Egypt* **74** F2
Kabrousse *Senegal* **82** C1
Kabūd Gonbad *Iran* **71** B8
Kābul *Afghan.* **66** B6
Kābul □ *Afghan.* **66** B6
Kābul ➤ *Pakistan* **68** C5
Kabunga *Dem. Rep. of the Congo* **86** C2
Kaburuang *Indonesia* **63** D7
Kabushiya *Sudan* **81** D3
Kabwe *Zambia* **87** E2
Kačanik *Serbia* **44** D5
Kačerginė *Lithuania* **30** D10
Kachchh, Gulf of *India* **68** H3
Kachchh, Rann of *India* **68** H4
Kachebera *Zambia* **87** E3
Kachia *Nigeria* **83** D6
Kachikau *Botswana* **88** B3
Kachin □ *Burma* **58** D1
Kachira, L. *Uganda* **86** C3
Kachiry *Kazakhstan* **52** D8
Kachisi *Ethiopia* **81** F4
Kachnara *India* **68** H6
Kachot *Cambodia* **65** G4
Kaçkar *Turkey* **73** B9
Kadan *Czech Rep.* **26** A6
Kadan Kyun *Burma* **64** F2
Kadanai ➤ *Afghan.* **68** D1
Kadarkút *Hungary* **28** D2
Kadavu *Fiji* **91** a
Kadavu Passage *Fiji* **91** a
Kade *Ghana* **83** D4
Kadhimain = Al Kāzimīyah *Iraq* **73** F11
Kadi *India* **68** H5
Kadina *Australia* **95** E2
Kadinhanı *Turkey* **72** C5
Kadiolo *Mali* **82** C3
Kadipur *India* **69** F10
Kadirli *Turkey* **72** D7
Kadiyevka = Stakhanov *Ukraine* **33** H10
Kadodo *Sudan* **81** E2
Kadoka *U.S.A.* **112** D3
Kadom *Russia* **34** C6
Kadoma *Zimbabwe* **87** F2
Kaduna *Nigeria* **83** C6
Kaduna □ *Nigeria* **83** C6
Kaduy *Russia* **32** C9
Kaédi *Mauritania* **82** B2
Kaélé *Cameroon* **83** C7
Kaeng Khoï *Thailand* **64** E3
Kaeng Kra Chan △ *Thailand* **64** F2
Kaeng Tana △ *Thailand* **64** E5
Kaesŏng *N. Korea* **57** F14
Kāf *Si. Arabia* **70** D3
Kafan = Kapan *Armenia* **73** C12
Kafanchan *Nigeria* **83** D6
Kafareti *Nigeria* **83** C7
Kaffrine *Senegal* **82** C1
Kafin *Nigeria* **83** D6
Kafin Madaki *Nigeria* **83** C6
Kafinda *Zambia* **87** E3
Kafr el Battikh *Egypt* **80** H7
Kafr el Dauwâr *Egypt* **80** H7
Kafr el Sheikh *Egypt* **80** H7
Kafue *Zambia* **87** F2
Kafue ➤ *Zambia* **85** H5
Kafue △ *Zambia* **87** F2
Kafue Flats *Zambia* **87** F2
Kafulwe *Zambia* **87** D2
Kaga *Afghan.* **68** B4
Kaga Bandoro *C.A.R.* **84** C3
Kagan *Uzbekistan* **52** F7
Kagarko *Nigeria* **83** D6
Kagawa □ *Japan* **55** G7
Kagera □ *Tanzania* **86** C3
Kagera ➤ *Uganda* **86** C3
Kağızman *Turkey* **73** B10
Kagmar *Sudan* **81** E3
Kagoshima *Japan* **55** J5
Kagoshima □ *Japan* **55** J5
Kagul = Cahul *Moldova* **29** E13
Kahak *Iran* **71** B6
Kahama *Tanzania* **86** C3
Kahan *Pakistan* **68** E3
Kahang *Malaysia* **65** L4
Kahayan ➤ *Indonesia* **62** E4
Kahe *Tanzania* **86** C4
Kahemba *Dem. Rep. of the Congo* **84** F3
Kahnūj *Iran* **71** E8
Kahoka *U.S.A.* **112** E8
Kaho'olawe *U.S.A.* **106** b
Kahramanmaraş *Turkey* **72** D7
Kahramanmaraş □ *Turkey* **72** D7
Kâhta *Turkey* **73** D8
Kahul, Ozero *Ukraine* **29** E13
Kahului *U.S.A.* **106** b

Kahurangi △ *N.Z.* **91** D4
Kahuta *Pakistan* **68** C5
Kahuzi-Biega △ *Dem. Rep. of the Congo* **86** C2
Kai, Kepulauan *Indonesia* **63** F8
Kai Besar *Indonesia* **63** F8
Kai Is. = Kai, Kepulauan *Indonesia* **63** F8
Kai Kecil *Indonesia* **63** F8
Kai Xian *China* **58** B7
Kaiama *Nigeria* **83** D5
Kaiapoi *N.Z.* **91** E4
Kaieteur Falls *Guyana* **124** B7
Kaifeng *China* **56** G8
Kaihua *China* **59** C12
Kaikohe *N.Z.* **91** A4
Kaikoura *N.Z.* **91** E4
Kailahun *S. Leone* **82** D2
Kailas = Kangrinboqe Feng *China* **69** D9
Kaili *China* **58** D6
Kailu *China* **57** C11
Kailua *U.S.A.* **106** b
Kaimaktsalan Oros = Voras Oros *Greece* **44** F5
Kaimana *Indonesia* **63** E8
Kaimanawa Mts. *N.Z.* **91** C5
Kaimganj *India* **69** F8
Kaimur Hills *India* **69** G10
Kainab ➤ *Namibia* **88** D2
Kainji Dam *Nigeria* **83** D5
Kainji Lake △ *Nigeria* **83** C5
Kainji Res. *Nigeria* **83** C5
Kainuu *Finland* **8** D23
Kaipara Harbour *N.Z.* **91** B5
Kaiping *China* **59** F9
Kaipokok B. *Canada* **105** B8
Kaira *India* **68** H5
Kairana *India* **68** E7
Kaironi *Indonesia* **63** E8
Kairouan *Tunisia* **79** A8
Kaiserslautern *Germany* **25** F3
Kaiserstuhl *Germany* **25** G3
Kaitaia *N.Z.* **91** A4
Kaitangata *N.Z.* **91** G2
Kaithal *India* **68** E7
Kaitu ➤ *Pakistan* **68** C4
Kaiyang *China* **58** D6
Kaiyuan *Liaoning, China* **57** C13
Kaiyuan *Yunnan, China* **58** F4
Kajaani *Finland* **8** D22
Kajabbi *Australia* **94** C3
Kajana = Kajaani *Finland* **8** D22
Kajang *Malaysia* **65** L3
Kajaran *Armenia* **73** C12
Kajiado *Kenya* **86** C4
Kajo Kaji *Sudan* **81** G3
Kajuru *Nigeria* **83** C6
Kaka *Sudan* **81** E3
Kaka *Turkmenistan* **71** B8
Kakabeka Falls *Canada* **104** C2
Kakamas *S. Africa* **88** D3
Kakamega *Kenya* **86** B3
Kakanj *Bos.-H.* **28** F3
Kakanui Mts. *N.Z.* **91** F3
Kakata *Liberia* **82** D2
Kakdwip *India* **69** J13
Kake *Japan* **55** G6
Kake *U.S.A.* **102** B2
Kakegawa *Japan* **55** G9
Kakeroma-Jima *Japan* **55** K4
Kakhib *Russia* **35** J8
Kakhovka *Ukraine* **33** J7
Kakhovske Vdskh. *Ukraine* **33** J7
Kakinada *India* **67** L13
Kakisa ➤ *Canada* **102** A5
Kakisa L. *Canada* **102** A5
Kakogawa *Japan* **55** G7
Kakum △ *Ghana* **83** D4
Kakuma *Kenya* **86** B3
Kakwa ➤ *Canada* **102** C5
Kāl Gūsheh *Iran* **71** D8
Kala *Nigeria* **83** C7
Kalaallit Nunaat = Greenland ☒ *N. Amer.* **99** C15
Kalabagh *Pakistan* **68** C4
Kalabahi *Indonesia* **63** F6
Kalabana *Mali* **82** C3
Kalach *Russia* **34** E5
Kalach na Donu *Russia* **35** H3
Kaladan ➤ *Burma* **67** J18
Kaladar *Canada* **114** B7
Kalahari *Africa* **88** C3
Kalahari Gemsbok △ *S. Africa* **88** D3
Kalajoki *Finland* **8** D21
Kalakamati *Botswana* **89** C4
Kalakan *Russia* **53** D12
K'alak'unlun Shank'ou = Karakoram Pass *Asia* **69** B7
Kalam *Pakistan* **69** B5
Kalama *Dem. Rep. of the Congo* **86** C2
Kalama *U.S.A.* **110** E4
Kalamaria *Greece* **44** F6

Kalamata *Greece* **46** D4
Kalamazoo *U.S.A.* **113** D11
Kalamazoo → *U.S.A.* **112** D10
Kalambaka *Greece* **46** B3
Kalambo Falls *Tanzania* **87** D3
Kalamos *Attiki, Greece* **46** C5
Kalamos *Lefkada, Greece* **46** C2
Kalan *Turkey* **70** B3
Kalankalan *Guinea* **82** C3
Kalannie *Australia* **93** F2
Kalāntarī *Iran* **71** C7
Kalao *Indonesia* **63** F6
Kalaotoa *Indonesia* **63** F6
Kälarne *Sweden* **10** B10
Kalasin *Thailand* **64** D4
Kālat *Iran* **71** E8
Kalat *Pakistan* **66** E5
Kalāteh *Iran* **71** B7
Kalāteh-ye Ganj *Iran* **71** E8
Kalathos *Greece* **47** E10
Kalaus → *Russia* **35** H7
Kalavrita *Greece* **46** C4
Kalbā *U.A.E.* **71** E8
Kalbarri *Australia* **93** E1
Kalbarri △ *Australia* **93** E1
Kalce *Slovenia* **22** F8
Kale *Antalya, Turkey* **47** E12
Kale *Denizli, Turkey* **47** D10
Kalecik *Turkey* **72** B5
Kalegauk Kyun *Burma* **64** E1
Kalehe *Dem. Rep. of the Congo* **86** C2
Kalema *Tanzania* **86** C3
Kalemie
  Dem. Rep. of the Congo **86** D2
Kalety *Poland* **31** H5
Kalewa *Burma* **67** H19
Kalgoorlie-Boulder *Australia* **93** F3
Kali → *India* **69** F8
Kali Sindh → *India* **68** G6
Kaliakra, Nos *Bulgaria* **45** C12
Kalianda *Indonesia* **62** F3
Kalibo *Phil.* **61** F5
Kalima *Dem. Rep. of the Congo* **86** C2
Kalimantan *Indonesia* **62** E4
Kalimantan Barat □
  Indonesia **62** E4
Kalimantan Selatan □
  Indonesia **62** E5
Kalimantan Tengah □
  Indonesia **62** E4
Kalimantan Timur □
  Indonesia **62** D5
Kálimnos *Greece* **47** D8
Kalimpong *India* **69** F13
Kaliningrad *Russia* **30** D7
Kaliningrad ✈ (KGD) *Russia* **30** D7
Kalininsk *Russia* **34** E7
Kalinkavichy *Belarus* **23** B15
Kalinkovichi =
  Kalinkavichy *Belarus* **23** B15
Kalinovik *Bos.-H.* **44** C2
Kalipetrovo *Bulgaria* **45** B11
Kalirachi *Greece* **47** F8
Kaliro *Uganda* **86** B3
Kalispell *U.S.A.* **108** B6
Kalisz *Poland* **31** G5
Kalisz Pomorski *Poland* **31** E2
Kalithea *Greece* **46** D5
Kaliua *Tanzania* **86** D3
Kalivia Thorikou *Greece* **46** D5
Kalix = Kalixälven →
  Sweden **8** D20
Kalix *Sweden* **8** D20
Kalixälven → *Sweden* **8** D20
Kalka *India* **68** D7
Kalkan *Turkey* **47** E11
Kalkarindji *Australia* **92** C5
Kalkaska *U.S.A.* **113** C11
Kalkfeld *Namibia* **88** C2
Kalkfontein *Botswana* **88** C3
Kalkım *Turkey* **47** B9
Kalkrand *Namibia* **88** C2
Kållandsö *Sweden* **11** F7
Kallavesi *Finland* **8** E22
Källby *Sweden* **11** F7
Kållered *Sweden* **11** G6
Kallinge *Sweden* **11** H9
Kallimasia *Greece* **47** C8
Kallinge *Sweden* **11** H9
Kallmet *Albania* **44** E3
Kallsjön *Sweden* **8** E15
Kalmalo *Nigeria* **83** C6
Kalmar *Sweden* **11** H10
Kalmar län □ *Sweden* **11** G10
Kalmar sund *Sweden* **11** H10
Kalmyk Republic =
  Kalmykia □ *Russia* **35** G8
Kalmykia □ *Russia* **35** G8
Kalna *India* **69** H13
Kalnai *India* **69** H10
Kalo Nero *Greece* **46** D3
Kalocsa *Hungary* **28** D4
Kalofer *Bulgaria* **45** D8
Kalokhorio *Cyprus* **49** E12
Kaloko *Dem. Rep. of the Congo* **86** D2
Kalol *Gujarat, India* **68** H5
Kalol *Gujarat, India* **68** H5

Kalolimnos *Greece* **47** D9
Kalomo *Zambia* **87** F2
Kaloni *Greece* **47** B8
Kaloni, Kolpos *Greece* **47** B8
Kalpi *India* **69** F8
Kaltern = Caldaro *Italy* **41** B8
Kaltukatjara *Australia* **93** D4
Kaltungo *Nigeria* **83** D7
Kalu *Pakistan* **68** G2
Kaluga *Russia* **32** E9
Kaluga □ *Russia* **32** E8
Kalulushi *Zambia* **87** E2
Kalundborg *Denmark* **11** J5
Kalush *Ukraine* **23** D13
Kaluszyn *Poland* **31** F8
Kalutara *Sri Lanka* **66** R12
Kalvarija *Lithuania* **30** D10
Kalyan *India* **66** K8
Kalyazin *Russia* **32** D9
Kam *Albania* **44** D4
Kam → *Nigeria* **83** D7
Kama *Dem. Rep. of the Congo* **86** C2
Kama → *Russia* **6** D16
Kamachumu *Tanzania* **86** C3
Kamaishi *Japan* **54** E10
Kamalia *Pakistan* **68** D5
Kaman *India* **68** F6
Kaman *Turkey* **72** C5
Kamanjab *Namibia* **88** B2
Kamapanda *Zambia* **87** E1
Kamarān *Yemen* **75** D3
Kamativi *Zimbabwe* **88** B4
Kamba *Nigeria* **83** C5
Kambalda West *Australia* **93** F3
Kambar *Pakistan* **68** F3
Kambia *S. Leone* **82** D2
Kambolé *Togo* **83** D5
Kambolé *Zambia* **87** D3
Kambos *Cyprus* **49** D11
Kambove
  Dem. Rep. of the Congo **87** E2
Kamchatka, Poluostrov
  Russia **53** D17
Kamchatka Pen. =
  Kamchatka, Poluostrov
  Russia **53** D17
Kamchiya → *Bulgaria* **45** C11
Kame Ruins *Zimbabwe* **87** G2
Kamen *Russia* **52** D9
Kamen-Rybolov *Russia* **54** B3
Kamenica *Serbia* **44** C6
Kamenica *Serbia* **44** B3
Kamenice nad Lipou
  Czech Rep. **26** B8
Kamenjak, Rt *Croatia* **41** D10
Kamenka = Kaminka
  Ukraine **33** H4
Kamenka *Kazakhstan* **34** E10
Kamenka *Penza, Russia* **34** D6
Kamenka *Voronezh, Russia* **33** G10
Kamenka Bugskaya =
  Kamyanka-Buzka
  Ukraine **23** C13
Kamenka Dneprovskaya
  = Kamyanka-
  Dniprovska *Ukraine* **33** J8
Kamennomostskiy *Russia* **35** H5
Kameno *Bulgaria* **45** D11
Kamenolomini *Russia* **35** G5
Kamensk-Shakhtinskiy
  Russia **35** F5
Kamensk Uralskiy *Russia* **52** D7
Kamenskiy *Russia* **34** E7
Kamenskoye *Russia* **53** C17
Kamenyak *Bulgaria* **45** C10
Kamenz *Germany* **24** D10
Kameoka *Japan* **55** G7
Kamet *India* **69** D8
Kamiah *U.S.A.* **108** C5
Kamień Krajeński *Poland* **30** E4
Kamień Pomorski *Poland* **30** E1
Kamienna → *Poland* **31** G8
Kamienna Góra *Poland* **31** H3
Kamieńsk *Poland* **31** G6
Kamieskroon *S. Africa* **88** E2
Kamilukuak L. *Canada* **103** A8
Kamin-Kashyrskyy *Ukraine*
  23 C13
Kamina
  Dem. Rep. of the Congo **87** D2
Kaminak L. *Canada* **103** A10
Kaministiquia *Canada* **104** C1
Kaminka *Ukraine* **33** H7
Kaminoyama *Japan* **54** E10
Kamiros *Greece* **49** C9
Kamituga
  Dem. Rep. of the Congo **86** C2
Kamla → *India* **69** G12
Kamloops *Canada* **102** C4
Kamnik *Slovenia* **41** B11
Kamo *Armenia* **35** K7
Kamo *Japan* **54** E9
Kamoke *Pakistan* **68** C6
Kamp → *Austria* **26** C8
Kampala *Uganda* **86** B3
Kampar *Malaysia* **65** K3

Kampar → *Indonesia* **62** D2
Kampen *Neths.* **17** B5
Kampene
  Dem. Rep. of the Congo **84** E5
Kamphaeng Phet *Thailand* **64** D2
Kampinoski △ *Poland* **31** F7
Kampolombo, L. *Zambia* **87** E2
Kampong Chhnang
  Cambodia **65** F5
Kampong Pengerang
  Malaysia **65** d
Kampong Punggai *Malaysia* **65** d
Kampong Saom *Cambodia* **65** G4
Kampong Saom, Chaak
  Cambodia **65** G4
Kampong Tanjong
  Langsat *Malaysia* **65** d
Kampong Telok Ramunia
  Malaysia **65** d
Kampong To *Thailand* **65** J3
Kampot *Cambodia* **65** G5
Kampti *Burkina Faso* **82** C4
Kampuchea =
  Cambodia ■ *Asia* **64** F5
Kampung Air Putih
  Malaysia **65** K4
Kampung Jerangau
  Malaysia **65** K4
Kampung Raja *Malaysia* **65** K4
Kampungbaru = Tolitoli
  Indonesia **63** D6
Kamrau, Teluk *Indonesia* **63** E8
Kamsack *Canada* **103** C8
Kamsai *Guinea* **82** C2
Kamskoye Ustye *Russia* **34** C9
Kamuchawie L. *Canada* **103** B8
Kamuela *U.S.A.* **106** b
Kamui-Misaki *Japan* **54** C10
Kamyanets-Podilskyy
  Ukraine **29** B11
Kamyanka-Buzka *Ukraine* **23** C13
Kamyanka-Dniprovska
  Ukraine **33** J8
Kamyanyets *Belarus* **31** F10
Kamyanyuki *Belarus* **31** F10
Kāmyārān *Iran* **73** E12
Kamyshin *Russia* **34** E7
Kamyzyak *Russia* **35** G9
Kan *Sudan* **81** F3
Kanaaupscow *Canada* **101** D12
Kanaaupscow → *Canada* **104** B4
Kanab *U.S.A.* **109** H7
Kanab Cr. → *U.S.A.* **109** H7
Kanacea *Lau Group, Fiji* **91** a
Kanacea *Taveuni, Fiji* **91** a
Kanagi *Japan* **54** D10
Kanairiktok → *Canada* **105** A7
Kanalia *Greece* **46** B4
Kananga
  Dem. Rep. of the Congo **84** F4
Kanash *Russia* **34** C8
Kanaskat *U.S.A.* **110** C5
Kanastraíon, Ákra =
  Paliouri, Akra *Greece* **44** G7
Kanawha → *U.S.A.* **113** F12
Kanazawa *Japan* **55** F8
Kanchanaburi *Thailand* **64** E2
Kanchenjunga *Nepal* **69** F13
Kanchipuram *India* **66** N11
Kańczuga *Poland* **31** J9
Kandaghat *India* **68** D7
Kandahār *Afghan.* **66** D4
Kandahār □ *Afghan.* **66** D4
Kandalaksha *Russia* **8** C25
Kandangan *Indonesia* **62** E5
Kandanghaur *Indonesia* **63** G13
Kandanos *Greece* **49** D5
Kandava *Latvia* **30** A9
Kandavu = Kadavu *Fiji* **91** a
Kandavu Passage =
  Kadavu Passage *Fiji* **91** a
Kandhkot *Pakistan* **68** E3
Kandhla *India* **68** E7
Kandi *Benin* **83** C5
Kandi *India* **69** H13
Kandiaro *Pakistan* **68** F3
Kandila *Greece* **46** D4
Kandıra *Turkey* **72** B4
Kandla *India* **68** H4
Kandos *Australia* **95** E4
Kandreho *Madag.* **89** B8
Kandy *Sri Lanka* **66** R12
Kane *U.S.A.* **114** E6
Kane Basin *Greenland* **98** B12
Kanel *Senegal* **82** B2
Käne'ohe *U.S.A.* **106** b
Kanevskaya *Russia* **35** G4
Kanfanar *Croatia* **41** C10
Kang *Botswana* **88** C3
Kangaba *Mali* **82** C3
Kangal *Turkey* **72** C7
Kangān *Fārs, Iran* **71** E7
Kangān *Hormozgān, Iran* **71** E8
Kangar *Malaysia* **65** J3
Kangaré *Mali* **82** C3
Kangaroo I. *Australia* **95** F2

Kangaroo Mts. *Australia* **94** C3
Kangasala *Finland* **32** B3
Kangāvar *Iran* **73** E12
Kangding *China* **58** B3
Kangdong *N. Korea* **57** E14
Kangean, Kepulauan
  Indonesia **62** F5
Kangean Is. = Kangean,
  Kepulauan *Indonesia* **62** F5
Kangen → *Sudan* **81** F3
Kanggye *N. Korea* **57** D14
Kangikajik *Greenland* **4** B6
Kangiqliniq = Rankin Inlet
  Canada **100** C10
Kangiqsualujjuaq *Canada* **101** D13
Kangiqsujuaq *Canada* **101** C12
Kangiqtugaapik = Clyde
  River *Canada* **101** B13
Kangirsuk *Canada* **101** D13
Kangkar Chemaran *Malaysia* **65** d
Kangkar Sungai Tiram
  Malaysia **65** d
Kangkar Teberau *Malaysia* **65** d
Kangping *China* **57** C12
Kangra *India* **68** C7
Kangrinboqe Feng *China* **69** D9
Kangto *China* **67** F18
Kanha △ *India* **69** H9
Kanhar → *India* **69** G10
Kani *Ivory C.* **82** D3
Kaniama
  Dem. Rep. of the Congo **86** D1
Kaniapiskau =
  Caniapiscau → *Canada* **105** A6
Kaniapiskau, L. =
  Caniapiscau, L. *Canada* **105** B6
Kanin, Poluostrov *Russia* **6** B14
Kanin Nos, Mys *Russia* **52** C5
Kanin Pen. = Kanin,
  Poluostrov *Russia* **6** B14
Kaninë *Albania* **44** F3
Kaniva *Australia* **95** F3
Kanjiža *Serbia* **28** D5
Kanjut Sar *Pakistan* **69** A6
Kankaanpää *Finland* **32** B2
Kankakee *U.S.A.* **112** E10
Kankakee → *U.S.A.* **112** E9
Kankan *Guinea* **82** C3
Kankendy = Xankändi
  Azerbaijan **73** C12
Kanker *India* **67** J12
Kankossa *Mauritania* **82** B2
Kankroli *India* **68** G5
Kannapolis *U.S.A.* **117** D14
Kannauj *India* **69** F8
Kannod *India* **66** H10
Kano *Japan* **55** G6
Kano *Nigeria* **83** C6
Kano □ *Nigeria* **83** C6
Kan'onji *Japan* **55** G6
Kanoroba *Ivory C.* **82** D3
Kanowit *Malaysia* **62** D4
Kanoya *Japan* **55** J5
Kanpetlet *Burma* **67** J18
Kanpur *India* **69** F9
Kansas □ *U.S.A.* **112** F4
Kansas → *U.S.A.* **112** F6
Kansas City *Kans., U.S.A.* **112** F6
Kansas City *Mo., U.S.A.* **112** F6
Kansenia
  Dem. Rep. of the Congo **87** E2
Kansk *Russia* **53** D10
Kansu = Gansu □ *China* **56** G3
Kantaphor *India* **68** H7
Kantchari *Burkina Faso* **83** C5
Kantché *Niger* **83** C6
Kanté *Togo* **83** D5
Kantemirovka *Russia* **33** H10
Kantharalak *Thailand* **64** E5
Kanti *India* **68** E6
Kantō □ *Japan* **55** F9
Kantō-Sanchi *Japan* **55** G9
Kanturk *Ireland* **12** D3
Kanuma *Japan* **55** F9
Kanus *Namibia* **88** D2
Kanyakumari *India* **66** Q10
Kanye *Botswana* **88** C4
Kanzenze
  Dem. Rep. of the Congo **87** E2
Kanzi, Ras *Tanzania* **86** D4
Kao *Tonga* **91** c
Kao Phara *Thailand* **65** a
Kaohsiung *Taiwan* **59** F13
Kaokoveld *Namibia* **88** B1
Kaolack *Senegal* **82** C1
Kaolack □ *Senegal* **82** C1
Kaoshan *China* **57** B13
Kapaa *U.S.A.* **106** b
Kapadvanj *India* **68** H5
Kapaklı *Turkey* **45** E11
Kapan *Armenia* **73** C12
Kapanga
  Dem. Rep. of the Congo **84** F4
Kapchagai = Qapshaghay
  Kazakhstan **52** E8
Kapela = Velika Kapela
  Croatia **41** C12

Kapelo, Akra *Greece* **46** E5
Kapema
  Dem. Rep. of the Congo **87** E2
Kapenguria *Kenya* **86** B4
Kapfenberg *Austria* **26** D8
Kapı Dağı *Turkey* **45** F11
Kapiri Mposhi *Zambia* **87** E2
Kāpīsā □ *Afghan.* **66** B6
Kapiskau → *Canada* **104** B3
Kapit *Malaysia* **62** D4
Kapiti I. *N.Z.* **91** D5
Kaplan *U.S.A.* **116** G8
Kaplice *Czech Rep.* **26** C7
Kapoe *Thailand* **65** H2
Kapoeta *Sudan* **81** G3
Kápolnásnyék *Hungary* **28** C3
Kapos → *Hungary* **28** D3
Kaposvár *Hungary* **28** D2
Kapowsin *U.S.A.* **110** D4
Kappeln *Germany* **24** A5
Kappelshamn *Sweden* **11** G12
Kapps *Namibia* **88** C2
Kaprije *Croatia* **41** E12
Kapsabet *Kenya* **86** B4
Kapsan *N. Korea* **57** D15
Kapsukas = Marijampolė
  Lithuania **30** D10
Kapuas → *Indonesia* **62** E3
Kapuas Hulu,
  Pegunungan *Malaysia* **62** D4
Kapuas Hulu Ra. =
  Kapuas Hulu,
  Pegunungan *Malaysia* **62** D4
Kapulo *Dem. Rep. of the Congo* **87** D2
Kapunda *Australia* **95** E2
Kapuni *N.Z.* **91** C5
Kapurthala *India* **68** D6
Kapuskasing *Canada* **104** C3
Kapuskasing → *Canada* **104** C3
Kapustin Yar *Russia* **35** F7
Kaputar, Mt. *Australia* **95** E5
Kaputir *Kenya* **86** B4
Kapuvár *Hungary* **28** C2
Kara *Russia* **52** C7
Kará, W. → *Si. Arabia* **80** C5
Kara Ada *Turkey* **47** E9
Kara Bogaz Gol, Zaliv =
  Garabogazköl Aylagy
  Turkmenistan **52** E6
Kara Burun *Turkey* **47** C8
Kara Kalpak Republic =
  Qoraqalpoghistan □
  Uzbekistan **52** E6
Kara Kum = Garagum
  Turkmenistan **71** B8
Kara Sea *Russia* **52** B8
Karaadilli *Turkey* **47** C12
Karabiğa *Turkey* **45** F11
Karabük *Turkey* **72** B5
Karabük □ *Turkey* **72** B5
Karaburun *Albania* **44** F3
Karaburun *Turkey* **47** C8
Karabutak = Qarabutaq
  Kazakhstan **52** E7
Karacabey *Turkey* **45** F12
Karacakılavuz *Turkey* **45** E11
Karacaköy *Turkey* **45** E12
Karacasu *Turkey* **47** D10
Karachay-Cherkessia □
  Russia **35** J5
Karachayevsk *Russia* **35** J5
Karachev *Russia* **33** F8
Karachey-Cherkessia □
  Russia **35** J5
Karachi *Pakistan* **68** G2
Karad *India* **66** L9
Karadeniz Boğazı *Turkey* **45** F13
Karaga *Ghana* **83** D4
Karaganda = Qaraghandy
  Kazakhstan **52** E8
Karagayly = Qaraghayly
  Kazakhstan **52** E8
Karaginskiy, Ostrov *Russia* **53** D17
Karagola Road *India* **69** G12
Karagüney Dağları *Turkey* **72** B6
Karahallı *Turkey* **47** C11
Karaikal *India* **66** P11
Karaikkudi *India* **66** P11
Karaisalı *Turkey* **72** D6
Karaj *Iran* **71** C6
Karak *Malaysia* **65** L4
Karakalpakstan =
  Qoraqalpoghistan □
  Uzbekistan **52** E6
Karakaya Barajı *Turkey* **73** C8
Karakelong *Indonesia* **63** D7
Karakitang *Indonesia* **63** D7
Karakoçan *Turkey* **73** C9
Karakol *Kyrgyzstan* **52** E8
Karakoram Pass *Asia* **69** B7
Karakoram Ra. *Asia* **69** B7
Karakurt *Turkey* **73** B10
Karakuwisa *Namibia* **88** B3
Karalon *Russia* **53** D12

Karama *Jordan* **74** D4
Karaman *Balıkesir, Turkey* **47** B9
Karaman *Konya, Turkey* **72** D5
Karamanlı *Turkey* **47** D11
Karamay *China* **60** B3
Karambu *Indonesia* **62** E5
Karamea Bight *N.Z.* **91** D3
Karamnasa → *India* **69** G10
Karān *Si. Arabia* **71** E6
Karand *Iran* **73** E12
Karangana *Mali* **82** C3
Karanganyar *Indonesia* **63** G13
Karangasem *Indonesia* **63** J18
Karanjia *India* **69** J11
Karankasso *Burkina Faso* **82** C4
Karaova *Turkey* **47** D9
Karapınar *Turkey* **72** D5
Karasburg *Namibia* **88** D2
Karasino *Russia* **52** C9
Karasjok *Norway* **8** B21
Karasu *Turkey* **72** B4
Karasu → *Turkey* **47** E12
Karasuk *Russia* **52** D8
Karasuyama *Japan* **55** F10
Karataş *Adana, Turkey* **72** D6
Karataş *Manisa, Turkey* **47** C10
Karataş Burnu *Turkey* **72** D6
Karatau, Khrebet =
  Qarataū *Kazakhstan* **52** E7
Karatsu *Japan* **55** H5
Karaul *Russia* **52** B9
Karauli *India* **68** F7
Karavastasë, L. e *Albania* **44** F3
Karavia *Greece* **46** E5
Karawang *Indonesia* **63** G12
Karawanken *Europe* **26** E7
Karayazı *Turkey* **73** C10
Karazhal = Qarazhal
  Kazakhstan **52** E8
Karbalā' *Iraq* **73** F11
Karbalā' □ *Iraq* **73** F10
Kårböle *Sweden* **10** C9
Karcag *Hungary* **28** C5
Karcha → *Pakistan* **69** B7
Karchana *India* **69** G9
Karczew *Poland* **31** F8
Kardam *Bulgaria* **45** C12
Kardamaina *Greece* **47** D8
Kardamili *Greece* **46** E4
Kardeljovo = Ploče *Croatia* **41** E14
Karditsa *Greece* **46** B3
Karditsa □ *Greece* **46** B3
Kärdla *Estonia* **32** C2
Kareeberge *S. Africa* **88** E3
Kareha → *India* **69** G12
Kareima *Sudan* **80** D3
Karelia □ *Russia* **8** D25
Karelian Republic =
  Karelia □ *Russia* **8** D25
Karera *India* **68** G8
Kärevändar *Iran* **71** E9
Kargasok *Russia* **52** D9
Kargat *Russia* **52** D9
Kargi *Kenya* **86** B4
Kargı *Turkey* **72** B6
Kargil *India* **69** B7
Kargopol *Russia* **32** B10
Kargowa *Poland* **31** F2
Karguéri *Niger* **83** C7
Karhal *India* **69** F8
Karia *Greece* **46** C2
Kariān *Iran* **71** E8
Karianga *Madag.* **89** C8
Kariba *Zimbabwe* **87** F2
Kariba, L. *Zimbabwe* **87** F2
Kariba Dam *Zimbabwe* **87** F2
Kariba Gorge *Zambia* **87** F2
Karibib *Namibia* **88** C2
Karies *Greece* **45** F8
Karijini △ *Australia* **92** D2
Karikal = Karaikal *India* **66** P11
Karimata, Kepulauan
  Indonesia **62** E3
Karimata, Selat *Indonesia* **62** E3
Karimata Is. = Karimata,
  Kepulauan *Indonesia* **62** E3
Karimnagar *India* **66** K11
Karimun Kecil, Pulau
  Indonesia **65** d
Karimunjawa, Kepulauan
  Indonesia **62** F4
Karin *Somali Rep.* **75** E4
Karistos *Greece* **46** C6
Karīt *Iran* **71** C8
Kariya *Japan* **55** G8
Kariyangwe *Zimbabwe* **89** B4
Karjala *Finland* **32** A5
Karkaralinsk = Qarqaraly
  Kazakhstan **52** E8
Karkheh → *Iran* **70** D5
Karkinitska Zatoka *Ukraine* **33** K7
Karkinitskiy Zaliv =
  Karkinitska Zatoka
  Ukraine **33** K7
Karkuk = Kirkūk *Iraq* **73** E11

Karkur Tohl *Egypt* **80** C2
Karl Liebknecht *Russia* **33** G8
Karla, L. = Volvi, L. *Greece* **44** F7
Karleby = Kokkola *Finland* **8** E20
Karlholmsbruk *Sweden* **10** D11
Karlino *Poland* **30** D2
Karlivka *Ukraine* **33** H8
Karlobag *Croatia* **41** D12
Karlovac *Croatia* **41** C12
Karlovarský □ *Czech Rep.* **26** A5
Karlovasi *Greece* **47** D8
Karlovka = Karlivka
  Ukraine **33** H8
Karlovo *Bulgaria* **45** D8
Karlovy Vary *Czech Rep.* **26** A5
Karlsbad = Karlovy Vary
  Czech Rep. **26** A5
Karlsborg *Sweden* **11** F8
Karlshamn *Sweden* **11** H8
Karlskoga *Sweden* **10** E8
Karlskrona *Sweden* **11** H9
Karlsruhe *Germany* **25** F4
Karlstad *Sweden* **10** E7
Karlstad *U.S.A.* **112** A5
Karlstadt *Germany* **25** F5
Karma *Niger* **83** C5
Karmėlava *Lithuania* **30** D11
Karmi'el *Israel* **74** C4
Karnak *Egypt* **80** B3
Karnal *India* **68** E7
Karnali → *Nepal* **69** E9
Karnaphuli Res. = Kaptai
  L. *Bangla.* **67** H18
Karnaprayag *India* **69** D8
Karnataka □ *India* **66** N10
Karnes City *U.S.A.* **116** G6
Karnische Alpen *Europe* **26** E6
Karnobat *Bulgaria* **45** D10
Kärnten □ *Austria* **26** E6
Karo *Mali* **82** C4
Karoi *Zimbabwe* **87** F2
Karon, Ao *Thailand* **65** a
Karonga *Malawi* **87** D3
Karoo △ *S. Africa* **88** E3
Karoonda *Australia* **95** F2
Karor *Pakistan* **68** D4
Karora *Sudan* **80** D4
Karounga *Mali* **82** B3
Karousades *Greece* **46** B1
Karpacz *Poland* **31** H2
Karpasia *Cyprus* **49** D13
Karpathos *Greece* **47** F9
Karpathos, Stenon *Greece* **47** F9
Karpatsky △ *Ukraine* **29** B9
Karpenisi *Greece* **46** C3
Karpuz Burnu = Apostolos
  Andreas, C. *Cyprus* **49** D13
Karpuzlu *Turkey* **47** D9
Karratha *Australia* **92** D2
Kars *Turkey* **73** B10
Kars □ *Turkey* **73** B10
Karsakpay *Kazakhstan* **52** E7
Karsha *Kazakhstan* **34** F10
Karshi = Qarshi *Uzbekistan* **52** F7
Karsiyang *India* **69** F13
Karsog *India* **68** D7
Karst = Kras *Croatia* **41** C10
Kartal *Turkey* **45** F13
Kartala *Comoros Is.* **85** a
Kartaly *Russia* **52** D7
Kartapur *India* **68** D6
Karthaus *U.S.A.* **114** E6
Kartuzy *Poland* **30** D5
Karufa *Indonesia* **63** E8
Karuma △ *Uganda* **86** B3
Karumba *Australia* **94** B3
Karumo *Tanzania* **86** C3
Karumwa *Tanzania* **86** C3
Kārūn → *Iran* **71** D6
Karungu *Kenya* **86** C3
Karup *Denmark* **11** H3
Karviná *Czech Rep.* **27** B11
Karwan → *India* **68** F8
Karwar *India* **66** M9
Karwendel △ *Austria* **26** D4
Karwi *India* **69** G9
Kaş *Turkey* **47** E11
Kasaba *Turkey* **47** E11
Kasache *Malawi* **87** E3
Kasai →
  Dem. Rep. of the Congo **84** E3
Kasai-Oriental □
  Dem. Rep. of the Congo **86** D1
Kasaji *Dem. Rep. of the Congo* **87** E1
Kasama *Zambia* **87** E3
Kasan *N. Korea* **57** D14
Kasandra *Greece* **44** F7
Kasandra Kolpos *Greece* **44** F7
Kasandras, Akra *Greece* **44** G7
Kasane *Namibia* **88** B3
Kasanga *Tanzania* **87** D3
Kasanka △ *Zambia* **87** E3
Kasar, Ras *Sudan* **80** D4
Kasaragod *India* **66** N9
Kasba L. *Canada* **103** A8
Kasempa *Zambia* **87** E2

Kasenga
  Dem. Rep. of the Congo **87** E2
Kasese *Uganda* **86** B3
Kasewa *Zambia* **87** E2
Kasganj *India* **69** F8
Kashabowie *Canada* **104** C1
Kashaf *Iran* **71** C9
Kāshān *Iran* **71** C6
Kashechewan *Canada* **104** B3
Kashgar = Kashi *China* **60** C2
Kashi *China* **60** C2
Kashimbo
  Dem. Rep. of the Congo **87** E2
Kashin *Russia* **32** D9
Kashipur *India* **69** E8
Kashira *Russia* **32** E10
Kashiwazaki *Japan* **55** F9
Kashk-e Kohneh *Afghan.* **66** B3
Kashkū'īyeh *Iran* **71** D7
Kāshmar *Iran* **71** C8
Kashmir *Asia* **69** C7
Kashmor *Pakistan* **68** E3
Kashpirovka *Russia* **34** D9
Kashun Noerh = Gaxun
  Nur *China* **60** B5
Kasiari *India* **69** H12
Kasimov *Russia* **34** C5
Kasinge
  Dem. Rep. of the Congo **86** D2
Kasiruta *Indonesia* **63** E7
Kaskaskia → *U.S.A.* **112** G9
Kaskattama → *Canada* **103** B10
Kaskinen *Finland* **8** E19
Kaskö = Kaskinen *Finland* **8** E19
Kaslo *Canada* **102** D5
Kasmere L. *Canada* **103** B8
Kasongo
  Dem. Rep. of the Congo **86** C2
Kasongo Lunda
  Dem. Rep. of the Congo **84** F3
Kasos *Greece* **47** F8
Kasos, Stenon *Greece* **47** F8
Kaspi *Georgia* **35** K7
Kaspichan *Bulgaria* **45** C11
Kaspiysk *Russia* **35** J8
Kaspiyskiy *Russia* **35** H8
Kassab ed Doleib *Sudan* **81** E3
Kassaba *Egypt* **80** D3
Kassalâ *Sudan* **81** D4
Kassalâ □ *Sudan* **81** D4
Kassandrino *Greece* **44** F7
Kassel *Germany* **24** D5
Kassinger *Sudan* **80** D3
Kassiopi *Greece* **49** A3
Kasson *U.S.A.* **112** C7
Kastamonu *Turkey* **72** B5
Kastamonu □ *Turkey* **72** B5
Kastav *Croatia* **41** C11
Kasteli *Greece* **49** D5
Kastelli *Greece* **49** D7
Kastellórizon = Megisti
  Greece **47** E11
Kastelo, Akra *Greece* **47** F9
Kasterlee *Belgium* **17** C4
Kastlösa *Sweden* **11** H10
Kastoria *Greece* **44** F5
Kastoria □ *Greece* **44** F5
Kastorias, L. *Greece* **44** F5
Kastorio *Greece* **46** D4
Kastornoye *Russia* **33** G10
Kastos *Greece* **46** C2
Kastrosikia *Greece* **46** B2
Kastrup, København ✈
  (CPH) *Denmark* **11** J6
Kastsyukovichy *Belarus* **32** F7
Kasulu *Tanzania* **86** C3
Kasumi *Japan* **55** G7
Kasumkent *Russia* **35** K9
Kasungu *Malawi* **87** E3
Kasungu △ *Malawi* **87** E3
Kasur *Pakistan* **68** D6
Kata Archanes *Greece* **49** D7
Kata Tjuta *Australia* **93** E5
Kataba *Zambia* **87** F2
Katagum *Nigeria* **83** C7
Katahdin, Mt. *U.S.A.* **113** C19
Katako Kombe
  Dem. Rep. of the Congo **86** C1
Katakolo *Greece* **46** D3
Katale *Tanzania* **86** C3
Katanda *Katanga,*
  Dem. Rep. of the Congo **86** D1
Katanda *Nord-Kivu,*
  Dem. Rep. of the Congo **86** C2
Katanga □
  Dem. Rep. of the Congo **86** D2
Katangi *India* **66** J11
Katanning *Australia* **93** F2
Katastari *Greece* **46** D2
Katavi △ *Tanzania* **86** D3
Katavi Swamp *Tanzania* **86** D3
Katerini *Greece* **44** F6
Katghora *India* **69** H10
Katha *Burma* **67** G20
Katherîna, Gebel *Egypt* **70** D2
Katherine *Australia* **92** B5
Katherine Gorge *Australia* **92** B5

Kathi *India* **68** J6
Kathiawar *India* **68** H4
Kathikas *Cyprus* **49** E11
Kathmandu = Katmandu
  Nepal **69** F11
Kathua *India* **68** C6
Kati *Mali* **82** C3
Katihar *India* **69** G12
Katima Mulilo *Zambia* **88** B3
Katimbira *Malawi* **87** E3
Katingan = Mendawai →
  Indonesia **62** E4
Katiola *Ivory C.* **82** D3
Katlabukh, Ozero *Ukraine* **29** E14
Katlanovo *Macedonia* **44** E5
Katmandu *Nepal* **69** F11
Katni *India* **69** H9
Kato Achaia *Greece* **46** C3
Kato Chorio *Greece* **49** D7
Kato Korakiana *Greece* **49** A3
Káto Pyrgos *Cyprus* **49** D11
Katochi *Greece* **46** C3
Katompe
  Dem. Rep. of the Congo **86** D2
Katong *Singapore* **65** d
Katonga → *Uganda* **86** B3
Katoomba *Australia* **95** E5
Katouna *Greece* **46** C3
Katowice *Poland* **31** H6
Katrancı Dağı *Turkey* **47** D12
Katrine, L. *U.K.* **13** E4
Katrineholm *Sweden* **10** E10
Katsepe *Madag.* **89** B8
Katsina *Nigeria* **83** C6
Katsina □ *Nigeria* **83** C6
Katsina Ala *Nigeria* **83** D6
Katsina Ala → *Nigeria* **83** D6
Katsumoto *Japan* **55** H4
Katsuura *Japan* **55** G10
Katsuyama *Japan* **55** F8
Kattavia *Greece* **49** D9
Kattegat *Denmark* **11** H5
Katthammarsvik *Sweden* **11** G12
Katul, J. *Sudan* **81** E2
Katumba
  Dem. Rep. of the Congo **86** D2
Katwa *India* **69** H13
Katwijk *Neths.* **17** B4
Kąty Wrocławskie *Poland* **31** G3
Kaua'i *U.S.A.* **106** b
Kauai Channel *U.S.A.* **106** b
Kaub *Germany* **25** E3
Kaudom △ *Namibia* **88** B3
Kaufbeuren *Germany* **25** H6
Kaufman *U.S.A.* **116** E6
Kauhajoki *Finland* **8** E20
Kaukauna *U.S.A.* **112** C9
Kaukauveld *Namibia* **88** C3
Kaunakakai *U.S.A.* **106** b
Kaunas *Lithuania* **30** D10
Kaunas ✈ (KUN) *Lithuania* **30** D11
Kaunia *Bangla.* **69** G13
Kaunos *Turkey* **47** E10
Kaura Namoda *Nigeria* **83** C6
Kauru *Nigeria* **83** C6
Kautokeino *Norway* **8** B20
Kauwapur *India* **69** F10
Kavacha *Russia* **53** C17
Kavadarci *Macedonia* **44** E6
Kavajë *Albania* **44** E3
Kavak *Turkey* **72** B7
Kavak Dağı *Turkey* **47** D10
Kavaklı *Turkey* **45** E11
Kavaklıdere *Turkey* **47** D10
Kavala *Greece* **45** E8
Kavala □ *Greece* **45** E8
Kavala Kolpos *Greece* **45** F8
Kavalerovo *Russia* **54** B7
Kavali *India* **66** M12
Kavār *Iran* **71** D7
Kavarna *Bulgaria* **45** C12
Kavi *India* **68** H5
Kavimba *Botswana* **88** B3
Kavīr, Dasht-e *Iran* **71** C7
Kavīr △ *Iran* **71** C7
Kavkaz *Russia* **33** K9
Kävlinge *Sweden* **11** J7
Kavos *Greece* **49** B4
Kavousi *Greece* **47** F7
Kaw *Fr. Guiana* **125** C8
Kawa *Sudan* **81** E3
Kawagama L. *Canada* **114** A6
Kawagoe *Japan* **55** G9
Kawaguchi *Japan* **55** G9
Kawambwa *Zambia* **87** D2
Kawanoe *Japan* **55** G6
Kawardha *India* **69** J9
Kawasaki *Japan* **55** G9
Kawasi *Indonesia* **63** E7
Kawawachikamach
  Canada **105** B6
Kawerau *N.Z.* **91** C6
Kawhia *N.Z.* **91** C5
Kawhia Harbour *N.Z.* **91** C5
Kawio, Kepulauan *Indonesia* **63** D7
Kawthaung *Burma* **65** H2
Kawthoolei = Kayin □
  Burma **67** L20

Kawthule = Kayin □
  Burma **67** L20
Kaxholmen *Sweden* **11** G8
Kaya *Burkina Faso* **83** C4
Kayah □ *Burma* **67** K20
Kayan → *Indonesia* **62** D5
Kaycee *U.S.A.* **108** E10
Kayeli *Indonesia* **63** E7
Kayenta *U.S.A.* **109** H8
Kayes *Mali* **82** C2
Kayes □ *Mali* **82** C2
Kayı *Turkey* **47** B12
Kayima *S. Leone* **82** D2
Kayin □ *Burma* **67** L20
Kaymakçı *Turkey* **47** C10
Kayoa *Indonesia* **63** D7
Kayomba *Zambia* **87** E1
Kaysatskoye *Russia* **34** F8
Kayseri *Turkey* **72** C6
Kayseri □ *Turkey* **72** C7
Kaysville *U.S.A.* **108** F8
Kaz Dağı *Turkey* **47** B8
Kazachye *Russia* **53** B14
Kazakhstan ■ *Asia* **52** E8
Kazan *Russia* **34** C9
Kazan → *Canada* **103** A9
Kazan-Rettō *Pac. Oc.* **96** E6
Kazanlŭk *Bulgaria* **45** D9
Kazanskaya *Russia* **34** F5
Kazatin = Kozyatyn
  Ukraine **33** H15
Kazaure *Nigeria* **83** C6
Kazbek *Russia* **35** J7
Kāzerūn *Iran* **71** D6
Kazi Magomed =
  Qazimämmäd *Azerbaijan* **35** K9
Kazimierz Dolny *Poland* **31** G8
Kazimierza Wielka *Poland* **31** H7
Kazincbarcika *Hungary* **28** B5
Kazlų Rūda *Lithuania* **30** D10
Kaztalovka *Kazakhstan* **34** F9
Kazuma Pan △ *Zimbabwe* **87** F2
Kazuno *Japan* **54** D10
Kazym → *Russia* **52** C7
Kcynia *Poland* **31** F4
Ké-Macina *Mali* **82** C3
Kea *Greece* **46** D6
Keady *U.K.* **12** B5
Kearney *U.S.A.* **112** E4
Kearny *U.S.A.* **109** K8
Kearsarge, Mt. *U.S.A.* **115** C13
Keban *Turkey* **73** C8
Keban Baraji *Turkey* **73** C8
Kebbi □ *Nigeria* **83** C5
Kébi *Ivory C.* **82** D3
Kebnekaise *Sweden* **8** C18
Kebri Dehar *Ethiopia* **75** F3
Kebumen *Indonesia* **63** G13
Kecel *Hungary* **28** D4
Kechika → *Canada* **102** B3
Keçiborlu *Turkey* **47** D12
Kecskemét *Hungary* **28** D4
Kedada *Ethiopia* **81** F4
Kédainiai *Lithuania* **30** C11
Kedarnath *India* **69** D8
Kedgwick *Canada* **105** C6
Kediri *Indonesia* **63** G15
Kedjebi *Ghana* **83** D5
Kédougou *Senegal* **82** C2
Kedros Oros *Greece* **49** D6
Kędzierzyn-Koźle *Poland* **31** H5
Keeler *U.S.A.* **110** J9
Keeley L. *Canada* **103** B7
Keeling Is. = Cocos Is.
  Ind. Oc. **96** J1
Keelung = Chilung *Taiwan* **59** E13
Keene *Canada* **114** B6
Keene *Calif., U.S.A.* **111** K8
Keene *N.H., U.S.A.* **115** D12
Keene *N.Y., U.S.A.* **115** B11
Keep River △ *Australia* **92** C4
Keeper Hill *Ireland* **12** D3
Keerweer, C. *Australia* **94** A3
Keeseville *U.S.A.* **115** B11
Keetmanshoop *Namibia* **88** D2
Keewatin *Canada* **103** D10
Keewatin → *Canada* **103** B8
Kefa *Ethiopia* **81** F4
Kefallonia *Greece* **46** C2
Kefalonia □ *Greece* **46** C2
Kefalos *Greece* **47** E8
Kefamenanu *Indonesia* **63** F6
Kefar Sava *Israel* **74** C3
Keffi *Nigeria* **83** D6
Keffin Hausa *Nigeria* **83** C6
Keflavík *Iceland* **8** D2
Keftya *Ethiopia* **81** E4
Keg River *Canada* **102** B5
Kegaska *Canada* **105** B7
Kehancha *Kenya* **86** C3
Keheili *Sudan* **80** D3
Kehl *Germany* **25** G3
Keighley *U.K.* **14** D6
Keila *Estonia* **32** C3
Keimoes *S. Africa* **88** D3
Keita *Niger* **83** C6

Keitele *Finland* **8** E22
Keith *Australia* **95** F3
Keith *U.K.* **13** D6
Keiyasi *Fiji* **91** a
Keizer *U.S.A.* **108** D2
Kejimkujik △ *Canada* **105** D6
Kejserr Franz Joseph Fd.
  Greenland **4** B6
Kekri *India* **68** G6
Kelam *Ethiopia* **81** G4
Kelamet *Eritrea* **81** D4
Kelan *China* **56** E6
Kelang = Klang *Malaysia* **65** L3
Kelantan → *Malaysia* **65** J4
Këlcyrë *Albania* **44** F4
Kelekçi *Turkey* **47** D11
Keles *Turkey* **45** G13
Kelheim *Germany* **25** G7
Kelkit *Turkey* **73** B8
Kelkit → *Turkey* **72** B7
Kellerberrin *Australia* **93** F2
Kellett, C. *Canada* **101** B7
Kelleys I. *U.S.A.* **114** E2
Kellogg *U.S.A.* **108** C5
Kells = Ceannanus Mor
  Ireland **12** C5
Kelmė *Lithuania* **30** C9
Kelmentsi *Ukraine* **29** B11
Kélo *Chad* **79** G9
Kelokedhara *Cyprus* **49** E11
Kelowna *Canada* **102** D5
Kelsey Creek *Australia* **94** J6
Kelseyville *U.S.A.* **110** G4
Kelso *N.Z.* **91** F2
Kelso *U.K.* **13** F6
Kelso *U.S.A.* **110** D4
Keluang = Kluang *Malaysia* **65** L4
Kelvington *Canada* **103** C8
Kem *Russia* **52** C4
Kema *Indonesia* **63** D7
Kemah *Turkey* **73** C8
Kemaliye *Erzincan, Turkey* **73** C8
Kemaliye *Manisa, Turkey* **47** C10
Kemalpaşa *Turkey* **47** C9
Kemaman *Malaysia* **65** K4
Kemano *Canada* **102** C3
Kemasik *Malaysia* **65** K4
Kembolcha *Ethiopia* **81** E4
Kemer *Antalya, Turkey* **47** E12
Kemer *Burdur, Turkey* **47** D12
Kemer *Muğla, Turkey* **47** E11
Kemer Baraji *Turkey* **47** D10
Kemerovo *Russia* **52** D9
Ķemeru △ *Latvia* **30** B10
Kemi *Finland* **8** D21
Kemi älv = Kemijoki →
  Finland **8** D21
Kemi träsk = Kemijärvi
  Finland **8** C22
Kemijärvi *Finland* **8** C22
Kemijoki → *Finland* **8** D21
Kemmerer *U.S.A.* **108** F8
Kemmuna = Comino *Malta* **49** C1
Kemp, L. *U.S.A.* **116** E5
Kemp Land *Antarctica* **5** C5
Kempas *Malaysia* **65** d
Kempsey *Australia* **95** E5
Kempston *Canada* **104** C5
Kempten *Germany* **25** H6
Kempton *Australia* **95** G4
Kempt, L. *Canada* **104** C5
Kemptville *Canada* **115** B9
Ken → *India* **69** G9
Kenai *U.S.A.* **100** C4
Kendai *India* **69** H10
Kendal *Indonesia* **63** G14
Kendal *U.K.* **14** C5
Kendall *Australia* **95** E5
Kendall *U.S.A.* **117** J14
Kendall → *Australia* **94** A3
Kendallville *U.S.A.* **113** E11
Kendari *Indonesia* **63** E6
Kendawangan *Indonesia* **62** E4
Kende *Nigeria* **83** C5
Kendi, Pulau *Malaysia* **65** c
Kendrapara *India* **67** J15
Kendrew *S. Africa* **88** E3
Kene Thao *Laos* **64** D3
Kenema *S. Leone* **82** D2
Keng Kok *Laos* **64** D5
Keng Tawng *Burma* **67** J21
Keng Tung *Burma* **58** G2
Kengeja *Tanzania* **86** D4
Kenhardt *S. Africa* **88** D3
Kéniéba *Mali* **82** C2
Kenitra *Morocco* **78** B4
Kenli *China* **57** F10
Kenmare *Ireland* **12** E2
Kenmare *U.S.A.* **112** A2
Kenmare River *Ireland* **12** E2
Kennebago Lake *U.S.A.* **115** A14
Kennebec *U.S.A.* **112** D4
Kennebec → *U.S.A.* **113** D19
Kennebunk *U.S.A.* **115** C14
Kennedy *Zimbabwe* **88** B4

Kennedy Ra. *Australia* **93** D2
Kennedy Range △ *Australia* **93** D2
Kenner *U.S.A.* **117** G9
Kennet → *U.K.* **15** F7
Kenneth Ra. *Australia* **93** D2
Kennett *U.S.A.* **112** G8
Kennewick *U.S.A.* **108** C4
Kenogami → *Canada* **104** B3
Kenora *Canada* **103** D10
Kenosha *U.S.A.* **112** D10
Kensington *Canada* **105** C7
Kent *Ohio, U.S.A.* **114** E3
Kent *Tex., U.S.A.* **116** F2
Kent *Wash., U.S.A.* **110** C4
Kent □ *U.K.* **15** F8
Kent Group *Australia* **95** F4
Kent Pen. *Canada* **100** C9
Kentaū *Kazakhstan* **52** E7
Kentland *U.S.A.* **112** E10
Kenton *U.S.A.* **113** E12
Kentucky □ *U.S.A.* **113** G11
Kentucky → *U.S.A.* **113** F11
Kentucky L. *U.S.A.* **113** G2
Kentville *Canada* **105** C7
Kentwood *U.S.A.* **117** F9
Kenya ■ *Africa* **86** C4
Kenya, Mt. *Kenya* **86** C4
Keo Neua, Deo *Vietnam* **64** C5
Keokuk *U.S.A.* **112** E8
Keoladeo △ *India* **68** F7
Keonjhargarh *India* **69** J11
Kep *Cambodia* **65** G5
Kep *Vietnam* **64** B6
Kepala Batas *Malaysia* **65** c
Kepez *Turkey* **45** F10
Kepi *Indonesia* **63** F9
Kepice *Poland* **30** D3
Kępno *Poland* **31** G4
Kepsut *Turkey* **47** B10
Kerala □ *India* **66** P10
Kerama-Rettō *Japan* **55** L3
Keran *Pakistan* **69** B5
Keran → *Togo* **83** C5
Kerang *Australia* **95** F3
Keranyo *Ethiopia* **81** F4
Kerao → *Sudan* **81** E3
Keratea *Greece* **46** D5
Keraudren, C. *Australia* **92** C2
Kerava *Finland* **32** B3
Kerch *Ukraine* **33** K9
Kerchenskiy Proliv *Black Sea* **33** K9
Kerchoual *Mali* **83** B5
Kerempe Burnu *Turkey* **72** A5
Keren *Eritrea* **81** D4
Kerewan *Gambia* **82** C1
Kerguelen *Ind. Oc.* **3** G13
Keri *Greece* **46** D2
Keri Kera *Sudan* **81** E3
Kericho *Kenya* **86** C4
Kerinci *Indonesia* **62** E2
Kerki = Atamyrat
  Turkmenistan **52** F7
Kerkini, L. *Greece* **44** E7
Kerkouane *Tunisia* **42** F4
Kerkrade *Neths.* **17** D6
Kerkyra *Greece* **49** A3
Kerkyra □ *Greece* **46** B1
Kerkyra ✈ (CFU) *Greece* **46** B1
Kerkyras, Notio Steno
  Greece **49** A4
Kerma *Sudan* **80** D3
Kermadec Is. *Pac. Oc.* **90** E11
Kermadec Trench *Pac. Oc.* **96** L10
Kermān *Iran* **71** D8
Kerman *U.S.A.* **110** J6
Kermān □ *Iran* **71** D8
Kermān, Bīābān-e *Iran* **71** D8
Kermānshāh *Iran* **73** E12
Kermānshāh □ *Iran* **70** C5
Kermen *Bulgaria* **45** D10
Kermit *U.S.A.* **116** F3
Kern → *U.S.A.* **111** K7
Kernhof *Austria* **26** D8
Kernow = Cornwall □ *U.K.* **15** G3
Kernville *U.S.A.* **111** K8
Keroh *Malaysia* **65** K3
Keros *Greece* **47** E7
Kérou *Benin* **83** C5
Kérouane *Guinea* **82** D3
Kerpen *Germany* **24** E2
Kerrera *U.K.* **13** E3
Kerrobert *Canada* **103** C7
Kerrville *U.S.A.* **116** F5
Kerry □ *Ireland* **12** D2
Kerry Hd. *Ireland* **12** D2
Kersa *Ethiopia* **81** F5
Kerulen → *Asia* **60** B6
Kervo = Kerava *Finland* **32** B3
Kerzaz *Algeria* **78** C5
Kesagami → *Canada* **104** B4
Kesagami L. *Canada* **104** B3
Keşan *Turkey* **45** F10
Kesennuma *Japan* **54** E10
Keshit *Iran* **71** D8
Keşiş Dağ *Turkey* **73** C8
Keskin *Turkey* **72** C5
Kestell *S. Africa* **89** D4

Kestenga *Russia* **8** D24
Keswick *U.K.* **14** C4
Keszthely *Hungary* **28** D2
Ket → *Russia* **52** D9
Keta *Ghana* **83** D5
Keta Lagoon *Ghana* **83** D5
Ketapang *Bali, Indonesia* **63** J17
Ketapang *Kalimantan, Indonesia* **62** E4
Ketchenery *Russia* **35** G7
Ketchikan *U.S.A.* **102** B2
Ketchum *U.S.A.* **108** E6
Kete Krachi *Ghana* **83** D4
Ketef, Khalîg Umm el *Egypt* **70** F2
Keti Bandar *Pakistan* **68** G2
Kétou *Benin* **83** D5
Ketri *India* **68** E6
Kętrzyn *Poland* **30** D8
Kettering *U.K.* **15** E7
Kettering *U.S.A.* **113** F11
Kettle → *Canada* **103** B11
Kettle Falls *U.S.A.* **108** B4
Kettle Pt. *Canada* **114** C2
Kettleman City *U.S.A.* **110** J7
Kęty *Poland* **31** J6
Keuka L. *U.S.A.* **114** D7
Keuruu *Finland* **32** A3
Kevelaer *Germany* **24** D2
Kewanee *U.S.A.* **112** E9
Kewaunee *U.S.A.* **112** C10
Keweenaw B. *U.S.A.* **112** B9
Keweenaw Pen. *U.S.A.* **112** B9
Keweenaw Pt. *U.S.A.* **112** B10
Key, L. *Ireland* **12** C3
Key Largo *U.S.A.* **117** J14
Key West *U.S.A.* **120** B3
Keyala *Sudan* **81** G3
Keynsham *U.K.* **15** F5
Keyser *U.S.A.* **113** F14
Kezhma *Russia* **53** D11
Kezi *Zimbabwe* **89** C4
Kežmarok *Slovak Rep.* **27** B13
Kgalagadi Transfrontier △ *Africa* **88** D3
Khabarovsk *Russia* **53** E14
Khabr *Iran* **71** D8
Khābūr → *Syria* **73** E9
Khachmas = Xaçmaz *Azerbaijan* **35** K9
Khachrod *India* **68** H6
Khadari, W. el → *Sudan* **81** E2
Khadro *Pakistan* **68** F3
Khadyzhensk *Russia* **35** H4
Khadzhilyangar = Dahongliutan *China* **69** B8
Khaga *India* **69** G9
Khagaria *India* **69** G12
Khaipur *Pakistan* **68** E5
Khair *India* **68** F7
Khairabad *India* **69** F9
Khairagarh *India* **69** J9
Khairpur *Pakistan* **68** F3
Khairpur Nathan Shah *Pakistan* **68** F2
Khairwara *India* **68** H5
Khaisor → *Pakistan* **68** D3
Khajuri Kach *Pakistan* **68** C3
Khakassia □ *Russia* **52** D9
Khakhea *Botswana* **88** C3
Khalafābād *Iran* **71** D6
Khalilabad *India* **69** F10
Khalīlī *Iran* **71** E7
Khalkhāl *Iran* **73** D13
Khalkís = Halkida *Greece* **46** C5
Khalmer Yu *Russia* **52** C7
Khalūf *Oman* **75** C6
Kham Keut *Laos* **64** C5
Khamaria *India* **69** H9
Khambhaliya *India* **68** H3
Khambhat *India* **68** H5
Khambhat, G. of *India* **66** J8
Khamīr *Iran* **71** E7
Khamir *Yemen* **75** D3
Khamīs Mushayṭ *Si. Arabia* **75** D3
Khamsa *Egypt* **74** E1
Khan → *Namibia* **88** C2
Khān Abū Shāmat *Syria* **74** B5
Khān Azād *Iraq* **70** C5
Khān Mujiddah *Iraq* **70** C4
Khān Shaykhūn *Syria* **72** E7
Khān Yūnis *Gaza Strip* **74** D3
Khanai *Pakistan* **68** D2
Khānaqīn *Iraq* **73** E11
Khānbāghī *Iran* **71** B7
Khandwa *India* **66** J10
Khandyga *Russia* **53** C14
Khāneh *Iran* **70** B5
Khanewal *Pakistan* **68** D4
Khangah Dogran *Pakistan* **68** D5
Khanh Duong *Vietnam* **64** F7
Khaniá = Chania *Greece* **49** D6
Khaniadhana *India* **68** G8
Khanka, L. *Asia* **54** B6
Khankendy = Xankändi *Azerbaijan* **73** C12
Khanna *India* **68** D7
Khanozai *Pakistan* **68** D2

Khanpur *Pakistan* **68** E4
Khanty-Mansiysk *Russia* **52** C7
Khao Laem △ *Thailand* **64** E2
Khao Laem Res. *Thailand* **64** E2
Khao Luang △ *Thailand* **65** H2
Khao Phlu *Thailand* **65** b
Khao Pu-Khao Ya △ *Thailand* **65** J2
Khao Sam Roi Yot △ *Thailand* **65** F2
Khao Sok △ *Thailand* **65** H2
Khao Yai △ *Thailand* **64** E3
Khaoen Si Nakarin △ *Thailand* **64** E2
Khapalu *Pakistan* **69** B7
Khapcheranga *Russia* **53** E12
Khaptao △ *Nepal* **69** E9
Kharabali *Russia* **35** G8
Kharagpur *India* **69** H12
Kharan Kalat *Pakistan* **66** E4
Kharānaq *Iran* **71** C7
Kharda *India* **66** K9
Khardung La *India* **69** B7
Kharg = Khārk, Jazīreh-ye *Iran* **71** D6
Khârga, El Wâhât-el *Egypt* **80** B3
Khargon *India* **66** J9
Khari → *India* **68** G6
Kharian *Pakistan* **68** C5
Kharit, Wadi el → *Egypt* **80** C3
Khārk, Jazīreh-ye *Iran* **71** D6
Kharkiv *Ukraine* **33** H9
Kharkiv □ *Ukraine* **33** H9
Kharkov = Kharkiv *Ukraine* **33** H9
Kharmanli *Bulgaria* **45** E9
Kharovsk *Russia* **32** C11
Kharsawangarh *India* **69** H11
Kharta *Turkey* **72** B3
Khartoum = El Khartûm *Sudan* **81** D3
Khasan *Russia* **54** C5
Khasavyurt *Russia* **35** J8
Khāsh *Iran* **71** D9
Khashm el Girba *Sudan* **81** E4
Khashum *Sudan* **81** E2
Khashuri *Georgia* **35** J6
Khaskovo *Bulgaria* **45** E9
Khaskovo □ *Bulgaria* **45** E9
Khatanga *Russia* **53** B11
Khatanga → *Russia* **53** B11
Khatauli *India* **68** E7
Khatra *India* **69** H12
Khātūnābād *Iran* **71** D7
Khatyrka *Russia* **53** C18
Khavda *India* **68** H3
Khawr Fakkān *U.A.E.* **71** E8
Khaybar, Ḥarrat *Si. Arabia* **70** E4
Khāzimiyah *Iraq* **70** C4
Khazzān Jabal al Awliyā *Sudan* **81** D3
Khe Bo *Vietnam* **64** C5
Khe Long *Vietnam* **64** B5
Khe Sanh *Vietnam* **64** D6
Khed Brahma *India* **68** G5
Khekra *India* **68** E7
Khemarak Phouminville = Krong Kaoh Kong *Cambodia* **65** G4
Khemisset *Morocco* **78** B4
Khemmarat *Thailand* **64** D5
Khenāmān *Iran* **71** D8
Khenchela *Algeria* **78** A7
Khersān → *Iran* **71** D6
Khersan *Ukraine* **33** J7
Kherson □ *Ukraine* **33** J7
Kheta → *Russia* **53** B11
Khewari *Pakistan* **68** F3
Khilchipur *India* **68** G7
Khilok *Russia* **53** D12
Khimki *Russia* **32** E9
Khíos = Hios *Greece* **47** C8
Khirsadoh *India* **69** H8
Khiuma = Hiiumaa *Estonia* **32** C2
Khiva *Uzbekistan* **52** E7
Khīyāv *Iran* **70** B5
Khlebarovo *Bulgaria* **45** C10
Khlong Khlung *Thailand* **64** D2
Khmelnik *Ukraine* **23** D14
Khmelnitskiy = Khmelnytskyy *Ukraine* **23** D14
Khmelnytskyy *Ukraine* **23** D14
Khmelnytskyy □ *Ukraine* **33** H4
Khmer Rep. = Cambodia ■ *Asia* **64** F5
Khoai, Hon *Vietnam* **65** H5
Khodoriv *Ukraine* **23** D13
Khodzent = Khŭjand *Tajikistan* **52** E7
Khojak Pass *Afghan.* **68** D2
Khok Kloi *Thailand* **65** a
Khok Pho *Thailand* **65** J3
Kholm *Russia* **32** D6
Kholmsk *Russia* **53** E15
Khomas Hochland *Namibia* **88** C2
Khombole *Senegal* **82** C1
Khomeyn *Iran* **71** C6

Khomeynī Shahr *Iran* **71** C6
Khomodino *Botswana* **88** C3
Khon Kaen *Thailand* **64** D4
Khong → *Cambodia* **64** F5
Khong *India* **69** E8
Khong Sedone *Laos* **64** E5
Khonuu *Russia* **53** C15
Khoper → *Russia* **34** E6
Khor el 'Atash *Sudan* **81** E3
Khorāsān □ *Iran* **71** C8
Khorat = Nakhon Ratchasima *Thailand* **64** E4
Khorat, Cao Nguyen *Thailand* **64** E4
Khorixas *Namibia* **88** C1
Khorol *Ukraine* **33** H7
Khorramābād *Khorāsān, Iran* **71** C8
Khorramābād *Lorestān, Iran* **73** F13
Khorrāmshahr *Iran* **71** D6
Khorugh *Tajikistan* **52** F8
Khosravi *Iran* **71** D6
Khosrowābād *Khuzestān, Iran* **71** D6
Khosrowābād *Kordestān, Iran* **73** E12
Khost *Pakistan* **68** D2
Khosūyeh *Iran* **71** D7
Khotyn *Ukraine* **29** B11
Khouribga *Morocco* **78** B4
Khowst *Afghan.* **68** C3
Khowst □ *Afghan.* **66** C6
Khoyniki *Belarus* **23** C15
Khrami → *Georgia* **35** K7
Khrenovoye *Russia* **34** E5
Khrysokhou B. *Cyprus* **49** D11
Khu Khan *Thailand* **64** E5
Khuan Wa *Thailand* **65** a
Khudzhand = Khŭjand *Tajikistan* **52** E7
Khuff *Si. Arabia* **70** E5
Khūgīānī *Afghan.* **68** D2
Khŭjand *Tajikistan* **52** E7
Khujner *India* **68** H7
Khulna *Bangla.* **67** H16
Khulna □ *Bangla.* **67** H16
Khulo *Georgia* **35** K6
Khumago *Botswana* **88** C3
Khunjerab △ *Pakistan* **69** A6
Khunjerab Pass = Kinjirap Daban *Asia* **66** A9
Khūnsorkh *Iran* **71** E8
Khunti *India* **69** H11
Khūr *Iran* **71** C8
Khurai *India* **68** G8
Khurayṣ *Si. Arabia* **71** E6
Khureit *Sudan* **81** E2
Khurja *India* **68** E7
Khūrmāl *Iraq* **70** C5
Khurr, Wādī al *Iraq* **70** C4
Khûsf *Iran* **71** C8
Khushab *Pakistan* **68** C5
Khust *Ukraine* **29** B8
Khutse △ *Botswana* **88** C3
Khuzdar *Pakistan* **68** F2
Khūzestān □ *Iran* **71** D6
Khvāf *Iran* **71** C9
Khvājeh *Iran* **70** B5
Khvalynsk *Russia* **34** D9
Khvānsār *Iran* **71** D7
Khvatovka *Russia* **34** D8
Khvor *Iran* **71** C7
Khvorgū *Iran* **71** E8
Khvormūj *Iran* **71** D6
Khvoy *Iran* **73** C11
Khvoynaya *Russia* **32** C8
Khyber Pass *Afghan.* **68** B4
Khyriv *Ukraine* **31** J9
Kia *Fiji* **91** a
Kiabukwa *Dem. Rep. of the Congo* **87** D1
Kiama *Australia* **95** E5
Kiamba *Phil.* **61** H6
Kiambi *Dem. Rep. of the Congo* **86** D2
Kiambu *Kenya* **86** C4
Kiangara *Madag.* **89** B8
Kiangsi = Jiangxi □ *China* **59** D11
Kiangsu = Jiangsu □ *China* **57** H11
Kiato *Greece* **46** C4
Kibæk *Denmark* **11** H2
Kibale → *Uganda* **86** B3
Kibanga Port *Uganda* **86** B3
Kibara *Tanzania* **86** C3
Kibare, Mts. *Dem. Rep. of the Congo* **86** D2
Kibira △ *Burundi* **86** C3
Kibombo *Dem. Rep. of the Congo* **86** C2
Kibondo *Tanzania* **86** C3
Kibre Mengist *Ethiopia* **81** F4
Kibris = Cyprus ■ *Asia* **49** E12
Kibumbu *Burundi* **86** C3
Kibungo *Rwanda* **86** C3
Kibuye *Burundi* **86** C2
Kibuye *Rwanda* **86** C2
Kibwesa *Tanzania* **86** D2

Kibwezi *Kenya* **86** C4
Kicasalih *Turkey* **45** E10
Kičevo *Macedonia* **44** E4
Kichha *India* **69** E8
Kichha → *India* **69** E8
Kicking Horse Pass *Canada* **102** C5
Kidal *Mali* **83** B5
Kidal □ *Mali* **83** B5
Kidderminster *U.K.* **15** E5
Kidepo Valley △ *Uganda* **86** B3
Kidete *Tanzania* **86** D4
Kidira *Senegal* **82** C2
Kidnappers, C. *N.Z.* **91** C6
Kidsgrove *U.K.* **14** D5
Kidston *Australia* **94** B3
Kidugallo *Tanzania* **86** D4
Kiel *Germany* **24** A6
Kiel Canal = Nord-Ostsee-Kanal *Germany* **24** A5
Kielce *Poland* **31** H7
Kielder Water *U.K.* **14** B5
Kieler Bucht *Germany* **24** A6
Kiembara *Burkina Faso* **82** C4
Kien Binh *Vietnam* **65** H5
Kien Tan *Vietnam* **65** G5
Kienge *Dem. Rep. of the Congo* **87** E2
Kiessé *Niger* **83** C5
Kiev = Kyyiv *Ukraine* **23** C16
Kifaya *Guinea* **82** C2
Kiffa *Mauritania* **82** B2
Kifisos → *Greece* **46** C5
Kifissia *Greece* **46** C5
Kifrī *Iraq* **73** E11
Kigali *Rwanda* **86** C3
Kigarama *Tanzania* **86** C3
Kigelle *Sudan* **81** F3
Kigezi □ *Uganda* **86** C2
Kigoma □ *Tanzania* **86** D3
Kigoma-Ujiji *Tanzania* **86** C2
Kigomasha, Ras *Tanzania* **86** C4
Kığzı *Turkey* **70** B4
Kihnu *Estonia* **32** C2
Kii-Sanchi *Japan* **55** G8
Kii-Suidō *Japan* **55** H7
Kiira Dam *Uganda* **86** B3
Kikaiga-Shima *Japan* **55** K4
Kikinda *Serbia* **28** E5
Kikládhes = Cyclades *Greece* **46** E6
Kikwit *Dem. Rep. of the Congo* **84** E3
Kil *Sweden* **10** E7
Kilafors *Sweden* **10** C10
Kilar *India* **68** C7
Kīlauea Caldera *U.S.A.* **106** b
Kilbeggan *Ireland* **12** C4
Kilbrannan Sd. *U.K.* **13** F3
Kilchu *N. Korea* **57** D15
Kilcoy *Australia* **95** D5
Kildare *Ireland* **12** C5
Kildare □ *Ireland* **12** C5
Kildinstroy *Russia* **8** B25
Kileikli *Sudan* **81** E2
Kilfinnane *Ireland* **12** D3
Kilgarvan *Ireland* **12** E2
Kilgore *U.S.A.* **116** E7
Kilgoris *Kenya* **86** C3
Kilibo *Benin* **83** D5
Kilifi *Kenya* **86** C4
Kilimanjaro *Tanzania* **86** C4
Kilimanjaro □ *Tanzania* **86** C4
Kilimli *Turkey* **72** B4
Kilindini *Kenya* **86** C4
Kilis *Turkey* **72** D7
Kilis □ *Turkey* **72** D7
Kiliya *Ukraine* **29** E14
Kilkee *Ireland* **12** D2
Kilkeel *U.K.* **12** B5
Kilkenny *Ireland* **12** D4
Kilkenny □ *Ireland* **12** D4
Kilkieran B. *Ireland* **12** C2
Kilkis *Greece* **44** F6
Kilkis □ *Greece* **44** E6
Killala *Ireland* **12** B2
Killala B. *Ireland* **12** B2
Killaloe *Canada* **114** A7
Killaloe *Ireland* **12** D3
Killarney *Australia* **95** D5
Killarney *Canada* **103** D9
Killarney *Ireland* **12** D2
Killary Harbour *Ireland* **12** C2
Killdeer *U.S.A.* **112** B2
Killeberg *Sweden* **11** H8
Killeen *U.S.A.* **116** F6
Killin *U.K.* **13** E4
Killiney *Ireland* **12** C5
Killington Pk. *U.S.A.* **115** C12
Killíni = Kyllíni *Greece* **46** D3
Killini *Greece* **46** D4
Killorglin *Ireland* **12** D2
Killybegs *Ireland* **12** B3
Kilmarnock *U.K.* **13** F4
Kilmez *Russia* **34** C10
Kilmez → *Russia* **34** B10
Kilmore *Australia* **95** F3
Kilmore Quay *Ireland* **12** D5
Kilondo *Tanzania* **87** D3
Kilosa *Tanzania* **86** D4

Kilrush *Ireland* **12** D2
Kilwa Kisiwani *Tanzania* **87** D4
Kilwa Kivinje *Tanzania* **87** D4
Kilwa Masoko *Tanzania* **87** D4
Kilwinning *U.K.* **13** F4
Kim *U.S.A.* **109** H12
Kim → *Cameroon* **83** D7
Kimaam *Indonesia* **63** F9
Kimamba *Tanzania* **86** D4
Kimba *Australia* **95** E2
Kimball *Nebr., U.S.A.* **112** E2
Kimball *S. Dak., U.S.A.* **112** D5
Kimberley *Australia* **92** C4
Kimberley *Canada* **102** D5
Kimberley *S. Africa* **88** D3
Kimberly *U.S.A.* **108** E6
Kimch'aek *N. Korea* **57** D15
Kimhae = Gimhae *S. Korea* **57** G15
Kimi *Greece* **46** C6
Kimmirut *Canada* **101** C13
Kimolos *Greece* **46** E6
Kimovsk *Moskva, Russia* **32** E9
Kimovsk *Tula, Russia* **32** E10
Kimparana *Mali* **82** C4
Kimpese *Dem. Rep. of the Congo* **84** F2
Kimry *Russia* **32** D9
Kimstad *Sweden* **11** F9
Kinabalu, Gunung *Malaysia* **62** C5
Kinango *Kenya* **86** C4
Kinaros *Greece* **47** E8
Kinaskan L. *Canada* **102** B2
Kinbasket L. *Canada* **102** C5
Kincardine *Canada* **114** B3
Kincolith *Canada* **102** C3
Kinda *Dem. Rep. of the Congo* **87** D2
Kinde *U.S.A.* **114** C2
Kinder Scout *U.K.* **14** D6
Kindersley *Canada* **103** C7
Kindia *Guinea* **82** D2
Kindu *Dem. Rep. of the Congo* **86** C2
Kinel *Russia* **34** D10
Kineshma *Russia* **34** B6
Kinesi *Tanzania* **86** C3
King, L. *Australia* **93** F2
King, Mt. *Australia* **94** D4
King City *U.S.A.* **110** J5
King Cr. → *Australia* **94** C2
King Edward → *Australia* **92** B4
King Frederick VI Land = Kong Frederik VI Kyst *Greenland* **4** C5
King George B. *Falk. Is.* **128** G4
King George I. *Antarctica* **5** C18
King George Is. *Canada* **101** D11
King I. = Kadan Kyun *Burma* **64** F2
King I. *Australia* **95** F3
King I. *Canada* **102** C3
King Leopold Ranges *Australia* **92** C4
King of Prussia *U.S.A.* **115** F9
King Sd. *Australia* **92** C3
King Sejong *Antarctica* **5** C18
King William I. *Canada* **100** C10
King William's Town *S. Africa* **88** E4
Kingait = Cape Dorset *Canada* **101** C12
Kingaok = Bathurst Inlet *Canada* **100** C9
Kingaroy *Australia* **95** D5
Kingfisher *U.S.A.* **116** D6
Kingirbān *Iraq* **70** C5
Kingisepp = Kuressaare *Estonia* **32** C2
Kingisepp *Russia* **32** C5
Kingman *Ariz., U.S.A.* **111** K12
Kingman *Kans., U.S.A.* **112** G4
Kingoonya *Australia* **95** E2
Kingri *Pakistan* **68** D3
Kings → *U.S.A.* **110** J7
Kings Canyon △ *U.S.A.* **110** J8
King's Lynn *U.K.* **14** E8
Kings Park *U.S.A.* **115** F11
Kings Peak *U.S.A.* **108** F8
Kingsbridge *U.K.* **15** G4
Kingsburg *U.S.A.* **110** J7
Kingscote *Australia* **95** F2
Kingscourt *Ireland* **12** C5
Kingsford *U.S.A.* **112** C9
Kingsland *U.S.A.* **117** F14
Kingsport *U.S.A.* **117** C13
Kingston *Canada* **115** B8
Kingston *Jamaica* **120** a
Kingston *N.Z.* **91** F2
Kingston *N.H., U.S.A.* **115** D13
Kingston *N.Y., U.S.A.* **115** E11
Kingston *Pa., U.S.A.* **115** E9
Kingston *R.I., U.S.A.* **115** E13
Kingston Pk. *U.S.A.* **111** K11
Kingston South East *Australia* **95** F2
Kingston upon Hull *U.K.* **14** D7
Kingston upon Hull □ *U.K.* **14** D7
Kingston-upon-Thames □ *U.K.* **15** F7

Kingstown *St. Vincent* **121** D7
Kingstree *U.S.A.* **117** E15
Kingsville *Canada* **114** D2
Kingsville *U.S.A.* **116** H6
Kingussie *U.K.* **13** D4
Kingwood *U.S.A.* **116** F7
Kınık *Antalya, Turkey* **47** E11
Kınık *İzmir, Turkey* **47** B9
Kinistino *Canada* **103** C7
Kinjirap Daban *Asia* **66** A9
Kinkala *Congo* **84** E2
Kinki □ *Japan* **55** H8
Kinleith *N.Z.* **91** C5
Kinlochleven *U.K.* **13** E4
Kinmount *Canada* **114** B6
Kinna *Sweden* **11** G6
Kinnairds Hd. *U.K.* **13** D6
Kinnared *Sweden* **11** G7
Kinnarp *Sweden* **11** F7
Kinneviken *Sweden* **11** F7
Kino Nuevo *Mexico* **118** B2
Kinoje → *Canada* **104** B3
Kinomoto *Japan* **55** G8
Kinoni *Uganda* **86** C3
Kinoosao *Canada* **103** B8
Kinross *U.K.* **13** E5
Kinsale *Ireland* **12** E3
Kinsale, Old Hd. of *Ireland* **12** E3
Kinsha = Chang Jiang → *China* **59** B13
Kinshasa *Dem. Rep. of the Congo* **84** E3
Kinsley *U.S.A.* **112** G4
Kinsman *U.S.A.* **114** E4
Kinston *U.S.A.* **117** D16
Kintamani *Indonesia* **63** J18
Kintampo *Ghana* **83** D4
Kintore *U.K.* **13** D6
Kintore Ra. *Australia* **92** D4
Kintyre *U.K.* **13** F3
Kintyre, Mull of *U.K.* **13** F3
Kinushseo → *Canada* **104** A3
Kinuso *Canada* **102** B5
Kinvarra *Ireland* **12** C3
Kinyangiri *Tanzania* **86** C3
Kinyeti *Sudan* **81** G3
Kinzig → *Germany* **25** G3
Kinzua *U.S.A.* **114** E6
Kioni *Greece* **46** C2
Kiosk *Canada* **104** C4
Kiowa *Kans., U.S.A.* **112** G4
Kiowa *Okla., U.S.A.* **116** D7
Kipahigan L. *Canada* **103** B8
Kipanga *Tanzania* **86** D4
Kiparissia *Greece* **46** D3
Kiparissiakos Kolpos *Greece* **46** D3
Kipawa, L. *Canada* **104** C4
Kipembawe *Tanzania* **86** D3
Kipengere Ra. *Tanzania* **87** D3
Kipili *Tanzania* **86** D3
Kipini *Kenya* **86** C5
Kipling *Canada* **103** C8
Kippure *Ireland* **12** C5
Kipushi *Dem. Rep. of the Congo* **87** E2
Kira Panagia *Greece* **46** B6
Kirane *Mali* **82** B2
Kiranomena *Madag.* **89** B8
Kiraz *Turkey* **47** C10
Kirazlı *Turkey* **45** F10
Kirchhain *Germany* **24** E5
Kirchheim *Germany* **25** G5
Kirchheimbolanden *Germany* **25** F3
Kirchschlag *Austria* **27** D9
Kireç *Turkey* **47** B10
Kirensk *Russia* **53** D11
Kirghizia = Kyrgyzstan ■ *Asia* **52** E8
Kiribati ■ *Pac. Oc.* **90** B10
Kırıkhan *Turkey* **72** D7
Kırıkkale *Turkey* **72** C5
Kirillov *Russia* **32** C10
Kirin = Jilin *China* **57** C14
Kirinyaga = Kenya, Mt. *Kenya* **86** C4
Kirishi *Russia* **32** C7
Kirishima Yaku △ *Japan* **55** J5
Kiritimati *Kiribati* **97** G12
Kırka *Turkey* **47** B12
Kırkağaç *Turkey* **47** B9
Kirkby *U.K.* **14** D5
Kirkby-in-Ashfield *U.K.* **14** D6
Kirkby Lonsdale *U.K.* **14** C5
Kirkby Stephen *U.K.* **14** C5
Kirkcaldy *U.K.* **13** E5
Kirkcudbright *U.K.* **13** G4
Kirkee *India* **66** K8
Kirkenes *Norway* **8** B24
Kirkfield *Canada* **114** B6
Kirkintilloch *U.K.* **13** F4
Kirkjubæjarklaustur *Iceland* **8** E4
Kirkkonummi *Finland* **32** B3
Kirkland *U.S.A.* **110** C4
Kirkland Lake *Canada* **104** C3
Kırklareli *Turkey* **45** E11
Kırklareli □ *Turkey* **45** E11
Kirksville *U.S.A.* **112** E7

Kirkūk *Iraq* **73** E11
Kirkwall *U.K.* **13** C6
Kirn *Germany* **25** F3
Kirov *Kaluga, Russia* **32** E8
Kirov *Kirov, Russia* **52** D5
Kirovabad = Gäncä
  Azerbaijan **35** K8
Kirovograd = Kirovohrad
  Ukraine **33** H7
Kirovohrad *Ukraine* **33** H7
Kirovohrad □ *Ukraine* **33** H6
Kirovskiy *Astrakhan, Russia* **35** H9
Kirovskiy *Kamchatka, Russia* **53** D16
Kirovskiy *Primorsk, Russia* **54** B6
Kirriemuir *U.K.* **13** E5
Kirsanov *Russia* **34** D6
Kırşehir *Turkey* **72** C6
Kirtachi *Niger* **83** C5
Kirthar △ *Pakistan* **68** F2
Kirthar Range *Pakistan* **68** F2
Kirtland *U.S.A.* **109** H9
Kiruna *Sweden* **8** C19
Kirundu
  Dem. Rep. of the Congo **86** C2
Kirya *Russia* **34** C8
Kiryū *Japan* **55** F9
Kisa *Sweden* **11** G9
Kisaga *Tanzania* **86** C3
Kisalaya *Nic.* **120** D3
Kisalföld *Hungary* **28** C2
Kisanga
  Dem. Rep. of the Congo **86** B2
Kisangani
  Dem. Rep. of the Congo **86** B2
Kisar *Indonesia* **63** F7
Kisarawe *Tanzania* **86** D4
Kisarazu *Japan* **55** G9
Kisbér *Hungary* **28** C3
Kishanganga ➤ *Pakistan* **69** B5
Kishanganj *India* **69** F13
Kishangarh *Raj., India* **68** F6
Kishangarh *Raj., India* **68** F4
Kishi *Nigeria* **83** D5
Kishinev = Chişinău
  Moldova **29** C13
Kishiwada *Japan* **55** G7
Kishtwar *India* **68** C6
Kisielice *Poland* **30** E6
Kisigo ➤ *Tanzania* **86** D3
Kisii *Kenya* **86** C3
Kisiju *Tanzania* **86** D4
Kisir *Turkey* **73** B10
Kisizi *Uganda* **86** C2
Kiskomárom = Zalakomár
  Hungary **28** D2
Kiskörei-víztároló *Hungary* **28** C5
Kiskőrös *Hungary* **28** D4
Kiskundorozsma *Hungary* **28** D5
Kiskunfélegyháza *Hungary* **28** D4
Kiskunhalas *Hungary* **28** D4
Kiskunmajsa *Hungary* **28** D4
Kiskunsági △ *Hungary* **28** D4
Kislovodsk *Russia* **35** J6
Kismayu = Chisimaio
  Somali Rep. **75** H3
Kiso-Gawa ➤ *Japan* **55** G8
Kiso-Sammyaku *Japan* **55** G8
Kisofukushima *Japan* **55** G8
Kisoro *Uganda* **86** C2
Kissamos = Kasteli *Greece* **49** D5
Kissamos, Kolpos *Greece* **49** D5
Kissidougou *Guinea* **82** D2
Kissimmee *U.S.A.* **117** G14
Kissimmee ➤ *U.S.A.* **117** H14
Kississing L. *Canada* **103** B8
Kissónerga *Cyprus* **49** E11
Kissu, J. *Sudan* **80** C2
Kistanje *Croatia* **41** E12
Kisújszállás *Hungary* **28** C5
Kisumu *Kenya* **86** C3
Kiswani *Tanzania* **86** D4
Kiswere *Tanzania* **87** D4
Kit Carson *U.S.A.* **108** G12
Kita *Mali* **82** C3
Kitaibaraki *Japan* **55** F10
Kitakami *Japan* **54** E10
Kitakami-Gawa ➤ *Japan* **54** E10
Kitakami-Sammyaku *Japan* **54** E10
Kitakata *Japan* **54** F9
Kitakyūshū *Japan* **55** H5
Kitale *Kenya* **86** B4
Kitami *Japan* **54** C11
Kitami-Sammyaku *Japan* **54** B11
Kitangiri, L. *Tanzania* **86** C3
Kitaya *Tanzania* **87** E5
Kitchener *Canada* **114** C4
Kitee *Finland* **32** A6
Kitega = Gitega *Burundi* **86** C2
Kitengo *Dem. Rep. of the Congo* **86** D1
Kitgum *Uganda* **86** B3
Kíthira = Kythira *Greece* **46** E5
Kithnos *Greece* **46** D6
Kiti *Cyprus* **49** E12
Kiti, C. *Cyprus* **49** E12
Kitimat *Canada* **102** C3

Kitinen ➤ *Finland* **8** C22
Kitiyab *Sudan* **81** D3
Kitros *Greece* **44** F6
Kitsman *Ukraine* **29** B10
Kitsuki *Japan* **55** H5
Kittakittaooloo, L. *Australia* **95** D2
Kittanning *U.S.A.* **114** F5
Kittatinny Mt. *U.S.A.* **115** F10
Kittery *U.S.A.* **115** C14
Kittilä *Finland* **8** C21
Kitui *Kenya* **86** C4
Kitwanga *Canada* **102** B3
Kitwe *Zambia* **87** E2
Kitzbühel *Austria* **26** D5
Kitzbühler Alpen *Austria* **26** D5
Kitzingen *Germany* **25** F6
Kivarli *India* **68** G5
Kivertsi *Ukraine* **23** C13
Kividhes *Cyprus* **49** E11
Kivik *Sweden* **11** J8
Kivotos *Greece* **44** F5
Kivu, L. *Dem. Rep. of the Congo* **86** C2
Kiyev = Kyyiv *Ukraine* **23** C16
Kiyevskoye Vdkhr. =
  Kyyivske Vdskh. *Ukraine* **23** C16
Kıyıköy *Turkey* **45** E12
Kizhi, Ostrov *Russia* **32** A8
Kiziguru *Rwanda* **86** C3
Kızıl Adalar *Turkey* **45** F13
Kızıl Irmak ➤ *Turkey* **72** B6
Kizil Jilga *China* **69** B8
Kizil Yurt *Russia* **35** J8
Kızılcabölük *Turkey* **47** D11
Kızılcadağ *Turkey* **47** D11
Kızılcahamam *Turkey* **72** B5
Kızıldağ △ *Turkey* **70** B1
Kızılhisar *Turkey* **72** D3
Kızılırmak *Turkey* **72** B5
Kızılkaya *Turkey* **47** D9
Kızılören *Turkey* **47** C12
Kızıltepe *Turkey* **73** D9
Kizimkazi *Tanzania* **86** D4
Kizlyar *Russia* **35** J8
Kizyl-Arvat = Serdar
  Turkmenistan **71** B8
Kjellerup *Denmark* **11** H3
Kjölur *Iceland* **8** D4
Kladanj *Bos.-H.* **28** F3
Kladnica *Serbia* **44** C4
Kladno *Czech Rep.* **26** A7
Kladovo *Serbia* **44** B6
Klaeng *Thailand* **64** F3
Klagenfurt *Austria* **26** E7
Klaipėda *Lithuania* **30** C8
Klaipėda □ *Lithuania* **30** C8
Klaksvík *Færoe Is.* **8** E9
Klamath ➤ *U.S.A.* **108** F1
Klamath Falls *U.S.A.* **108** E3
Klamath Mts. *U.S.A.* **108** F2
Klamono *Indonesia* **63** E8
Klang *Malaysia* **65** L3
Klanjec *Croatia* **41** B12
Klappan ➤ *Canada* **102** B3
Klarälven ➤ *Sweden* **10** E7
Klässbol *Sweden* **10** E6
Klatovy *Czech Rep.* **26** B6
Klawer *S. Africa* **88** E2
Klazienaveen *Neths.* **17** B6
Klé *Mali* **82** C3
Klecko *Poland* **31** F4
Kleczew *Poland* **31** F5
Kleena Kleene *Canada* **102** C4
Klein-Karas *Namibia* **88** D2
Klekovača *Bos.-H.* **41** D13
Klembivka *Ukraine* **29** B13
Klenoec *Macedonia* **44** E4
Klenovec *Slovak Rep.* **27** C12
Klerksdorp *S. Africa* **88** D4
Kleszczele *Poland* **31** F10
Kletnya *Russia* **32** F7
Kletsk = Klyetsk *Belarus* **23** B14
Kletskiy *Russia* **35** F6
Kleve *Germany* **24** D2
Klickitat *U.S.A.* **108** D3
Klickitat ➤ *U.S.A.* **110** E5
Klidhes *Cyprus* **49** D13
Klimovichi *Belarus* **32** F6
Klin *Russia* **32** D9
Klina *Serbia* **44** D4
Klinaklini ➤ *Canada* **102** C3
Klintehamn *Sweden* **11** G12
Klintsy *Russia* **33** F7
Klip ➤ *S. Africa* **89** D4
Klipdale *S. Africa* **88** E2
Klippan *Sweden* **11** H7
Klipplaat *S. Africa* **88** E3
Klishkivtsi *Ukraine* **29** B11
Klisura *Bulgaria* **45** D8
Kljajićevo *Serbia* **28** E4
Ključ *Bos.-H.* **41** D13
Klobuck *Poland* **31** H5
Klockestrand *Sweden* **10** B11
Kłodawa *Poland* **31** F5
Kłodzko *Poland* **31** H3
Klong Wang Chao △
  Thailand **64** D2
Klos *Albania* **44** E4

Klosterneuburg *Austria* **27** C9
Klosters *Switz.* **25** J5
Klötze *Germany* **24** C7
Klouto *Togo* **83** D5
Kluane △ *Canada* **102** A1
Kluane L. *Canada* **100** C6
Kluang *Malaysia* **65** L4
Kluczbork *Poland* **31** H5
Klukwan *U.S.A.* **102** B1
Klungkung *Indonesia* **63** K18
Klyetsk *Belarus* **23** B14
Klyuchevskaya, Gora
  Russia **53** D17
Knäred *Sweden* **11** H7
Knaresborough *U.K.* **14** C6
Knee L. *Man., Canada* **104** A1
Knee L. *Sask., Canada* **103** B7
Knezha *Bulgaria* **45** C8
Knight Inlet *Canada* **102** C3
Knighton *U.K.* **15** E4
Knights Ferry *U.S.A.* **110** H6
Knights Landing *U.S.A.* **110** G5
Knin *Croatia* **41** D13
Knislinge *Sweden* **11** H8
Knittelfeld *Austria* **26** D7
Knivsta *Sweden* **10** E11
Knjaževac *Serbia* **44** C6
Knob, C. *Australia* **93** F2
Knock *Ireland* **12** C3
Knockmealdown Mts.
  Ireland **12** D4
Knokke-Heist *Belgium* **17** C3
Knossos *Greece* **49** D7
Knowlton *Canada* **115** A12
Knox *U.S.A.* **112** E10
Knox Coast *Antarctica* **5** C8
Knoxville *Iowa, U.S.A.* **112** E7
Knoxville *Pa., U.S.A.* **114** E7
Knoxville *Tenn., U.S.A.* **117** D13
Knud Rasmussen Land
  Greenland **4** A5
Knysna *S. Africa* **88** E3
Knyszyn *Poland* **30** E9
Ko Kha *Thailand* **64** C2
Ko Tarutao △ *Thailand* **65** J2
Ko Yao *Thailand* **65** a
Koartac = Quaqtaq *Canada*
  101 C13
Koba *Indonesia* **63** F8
Kobarid *Slovenia* **41** B10
Kobayashi *Japan* **55** J5
Kōbe *Japan* **55** G7
Kobelyaky *Ukraine* **33** H8
København *Denmark* **11** J6
København ✈ (CPH)
  Denmark **11** J6
Kobenni *Mauritania* **82** B3
Kōbi-Sho *Japan* **55** M1
Koblenz *Germany* **24** E3
Kobo *Ethiopia* **81** E4
Kobryn *Belarus* **23** B13
Kobuleti *Georgia* **35** K5
Kobylin *Poland* **31** G4
Kobyłka *Poland* **31** F8
Kobylkino *Russia* **34** C6
Koca ➤ *U.S.A.* **45** F11
Kocabaş *Turkey* **47** D11
Kocaeli *Turkey* **45** F13
Kocaeli □ *Turkey* **45** F13
Kočane *Serbia* **44** C5
Kočani *Macedonia* **44** E6
Koçarlı *Turkey* **47** D9
Koceljevo *Serbia* **44** B3
Kočevje *Slovenia* **41** C11
Koch Bihar *India* **67** F16
Kochas *India* **69** G10
Kocher ➤ *Germany* **25** F5
Kochi = Cochin *India* **66** Q10
Kōchi *Japan* **55** H6
Kōchi □ *Japan* **55** H6
Kochiu = Gejiu *China* **58** F4
Kock *Poland* **31** G9
Kodarma *India* **69** G11
Kode *Sweden* **11** G5
Kodiak *U.S.A.* **106** a
Kodiak I. *U.S.A.* **106** a
Kodinar *India* **68** J4
Kodok *Sudan* **81** F3
Kodori ➤ *Georgia* **35** J5
Kodyma *Ukraine* **29** B14
Koedoesberge *S. Africa* **88** E3
Koes *Namibia* **88** D2
Kofçaz *Turkey* **45** E11
Koffiefontein *S. Africa* **88** D4
Kofiau *Indonesia* **63** E8
Köflach *Austria* **26** D8
Koforidua *Ghana* **83** D4
Kōfu *Japan* **55** G9
Koga *Japan* **55** F9
Kogaluc ➤ *Canada* **105** A7
Køge *Denmark* **11** J6
Køge Bugt *Denmark* **11** J6
Kogi □ *Nigeria* **83** D6
Kogin Baba *Nigeria* **83** D7
Koh-i-Khurd *Afghan.* **68** C1
Koh-i-Maran *Pakistan* **68** E2

Kohat *Pakistan* **68** C4
Kohima *India* **67** G19
Kohkīlūyeh va Būyer
  Aḥmadī □ *Iran* **71** D6
Kohler Ra. *Antarctica* **5** D15
Kohlu *Pakistan* **68** E3
Kohtla-Järve *Estonia* **32** C4
Kohylnyk ➤ *Ukraine* **29** E14
Koi Sanjaq *Iraq* **73** D11
Koillismaa *Finland* **8** D23
Koin *N. Korea* **57** D14
Koinare *Bulgaria* **45** C8
Koindu *S. Leone* **82** D2
Kojetín *Czech Rep.* **27** B10
Kojŏ *N. Korea* **57** E14
Kojonup *Australia* **93** F2
Kojūr *Iran* **71** B6
Koka *Sudan* **80** C3
Kokand = Qŭqon *Uzbekistan* **52** E8
Kokas *Indonesia* **63** E8
Kokava *Slovak Rep.* **27** C12
Kokchetav = Kökshetaū
  Kazakhstan **52** D7
Kokemäenjoki ➤ *Finland* **32** B1
Kokhma *Russia* **34** B5
Koki *Senegal* **82** B1
Kokkola *Finland* **8** E20
Koko *Nigeria* **83** C5
Koko Kyunzu *Burma* **67** M18
Kokolopozo *Ivory C.* **82** D3
Kokomo *U.S.A.* **112** E10
Kokoro *Niger* **83** C5
Koksan *N. Korea* **57** E14
Kökshetaū *Kazakhstan* **52** D7
Koksoak ➤ *Canada* **101** D13
Kokstad *S. Africa* **89** E4
Kokubu *Japan* **55** J5
Kola *Indonesia* **63** F9
Kola *Russia* **8** B25
Kola Pen. = Kolskiy
  Poluostrov *Russia* **6** B13
Kolachi ➤ *Pakistan* **68** F2
Kolahoi *India* **69** B6
Kolahun *Liberia* **82** D2
Kolaka *Indonesia* **63** E6
Kolar *India* **66** N11
Kolar Gold Fields *India* **66** N11
Kolaras *India* **68** G6
Kolari *Finland* **8** C20
Kolárovo *Slovak Rep.* **27** D10
Kolašin *Montenegro* **44** D3
Kolayat *India* **68** F5
Kolbäck *Sweden* **10** E10
Kolbäcksån ➤ *Sweden* **10** E10
Kolbermoor *Germany* **25** H8
Kolbuszowa *Poland* **31** H8
Kolda *Senegal* **82** C2
Kolda □ *Senegal* **82** C2
Koldegi *Sudan* **81** E3
Kolding *Denmark* **11** J3
Kolepom = Dolak, Pulau
  Indonesia **63** F9
Kolguyev, Ostrov *Russia* **52** C5
Kolhapur *India* **66** L9
Kolia *Ivory C.* **82** D3
Kolín *Czech Rep.* **26** A8
Kolind *Denmark* **11** H4
Kolkas rags *Latvia* **30** A9
Kolkata *India* **69** H13
Kollam = Quilon *India* **66** Q10
Kölleda *Germany* **24** D7
Kollum *Neths.* **17** A6
Kolmanskop *Namibia* **88** D2
Köln *Germany* **24** E2
Kolno *Poland* **30** E8
Koło *Poland* **31** F5
Kołobrzeg *Poland* **30** D2
Kolochava *Ukraine* **29** B8
Kolokani *Mali* **82** C3
Koloko *Burkina Faso* **82** C3
Kololo *Ethiopia* **81** F5
Kolomna *Russia* **32** E10
Kolomyya *Ukraine* **29** B10
Kolondiéba *Mali* **82** C3
Kolonodale *Indonesia* **63** E6
Kolonowskie *Poland* **31** H5
Kolosib *India* **67** G18
Kolpashevo *Russia* **52** D9
Kolpino *Russia* **32** C6
Kolpny *Russia* **33** G9
Kolskiy Poluostrov *Russia* **6** B13
Kolskiy Zaliv *Russia* **8** B26
Kolsva *Sweden* **10** E9
Kolubara ➤ *Serbia* **44** B4
Koluszki *Poland* **31** G6
Kolwezi *Dem. Rep. of the Congo* **87** E2
Kolyma ➤ *Russia* **53** C17
Kolymskoye Nagorye
  Russia **53** C16
Kôm Hamâda *Egypt* **80** H7
Kôm Ombo *Egypt* **80** C3
Komadugu Gana ➤ *Nigeria* **83** C7
Komandorskiye Is. =
  Komandorskiye Ostrova
  Russia **53** D17
Komandorskiye Ostrova
  Russia **53** D17

Komárno *Slovak Rep.* **27** D11
Komarnyky *Ukraine* **28** B8
Komárom *Hungary* **28** C3
Komárom-Esztergom □
  Hungary **28** C3
Komatipoort *S. Africa* **89** D5
Komatou Yialou *Cyprus* **49** D13
Komatsu *Japan* **55** F8
Komatsushima *Japan* **55** H7
Kombissiri *Burkina Faso* **83** C4
Kombori *Burkina Faso* **82** C4
Komboti *Greece* **46** B3
Komen *Slovenia* **41** C10
Komenda *Ghana* **83** D4
Komi □ *Russia* **52** C6
Komiža *Croatia* **41** E13
Komló *Hungary* **28** D3
Kommunarsk = Alchevsk
  Ukraine **33** H10
Kommunizma, Pik =
  imeni Ismail Samani,
  Pik *Tajikistan* **52** F8
Komodo *Indonesia* **63** F5
Komoé ➤ *Ivory C.* **82** D4
Komono *Japan* **55** F9
Komoran, Pulau *Indonesia* **63** F9
Komoro *Japan* **55** F9
Komotini *Greece* **45** E9
Komovi *Montenegro* **44** D3
Kompasberg *S. Africa* **88** E3
Kompong Bang *Cambodia* **65** F5
Kompong Cham *Cambodia* **65** G5
Kompong Chhnang =
  Kampong Chhnang
  Cambodia **65** F5
Kompong Chikreng
  Cambodia **64** F5
Kompong Kleang *Cambodia* **64** F5
Kompong Luong *Cambodia* **65** G5
Kompong Pranak *Cambodia* **64** F5
Kompong Som =
  Kampong Saom *Cambodia* **65** G4
Kompong Som, Chhung =
  Kampong Saom, Chaak
  Cambodia **65** G4
Kompong Speu *Cambodia* **65** G5
Kompong Sralau *Cambodia* **64** E5
Kompong Thom *Cambodia* **64** F5
Kompong Trabeck *Cambodia* **64** F5
Kompong Trabeck *Cambodia* **65** G5
Kompong Trach *Cambodia* **65** G5
Kompong Tralach *Cambodia* **65** G5
Komrat = Comrat *Moldova* **29** D13
Komsberg *S. Africa* **88** E3
Komsomolets, Ostrov
  Russia **53** A10
Komsomolsk *Amur, Russia* **53** D14
Komsomolsk *Ivanovo, Russia*
  32 D11
Komsomolskiy *Russia* **34** C7
Kömür Burnu *Turkey* **47** C8
Kon Tum *Vietnam* **64** E7
Kon Tum, Plateau du
  Vietnam **64** E7
Kona *Mali* **82** C4
Konakovo *Russia* **32** D9
Konar □ *Afghan.* **66** B7
Konārī *Iran* **71** D6
Konch *India* **69** G8
Konde *Tanzania* **86** C4
Kondias *Greece* **47** B7
Kondinin *Australia* **93** F2
Kondoa *Tanzania* **86** C4
Kondopaga *Russia* **32** A8
Kondratyevo *Russia* **53** D10
Kondrovo *Russia* **32** E8
Konduga *Nigeria* **83** C7
Köneürgench *Turkmenistan* **52** E6
Konevo *Russia* **32** B6
Kong = Khong ➤ *Cambodia* **64** F5
Kong *Ivory C.* **82** D4
Kong, Koh *Cambodia* **65** G4
Kong Christian IX Land
  Greenland **4** C6
Kong Christian X Land
  Greenland **4** B6
Kong Frederik IX Land
  Greenland **4** C5
Kong Frederik VI Kyst
  Greenland **4** C5
Kong Frederik VIII Land
  Greenland **4** B6
Kong Oscar Fjord *Greenland* **4** B6
Kongeå ➤ *Denmark* **11** J2
Konglu *Burma* **67** F20
Kongola *Namibia* **88** B3
Kongolo *Kasai-Or.,
  Dem. Rep. of the Congo* **86** D1
Kongolo *Katanga,
  Dem. Rep. of the Congo* **86** D2
Kongor *Sudan* **81** F3
Kongsberg *Norway* **9** G11
Kongsvinger *Norway* **9** F15
Kongwa *Tanzania* **86** D4
Koni *Dem. Rep. of the Congo* **87** E2
Koni, Mts.
  Dem. Rep. of the Congo **87** E2

Koniakari *Mali* **82** C2
Koniecpol *Poland* **31** H6
Königs Wusterhausen
  Germany **24** C9
Königsbrunn *Germany* **25** G6
Königslutter *Germany* **24** C6
Konin *Poland* **31** F5
Konispol *Albania* **44** G4
Konitsa *Greece* **46** A2
Konjic *Bos.-H.* **28** G2
Konkiep *Namibia* **88** D2
Könnern *Germany* **24** D7
Kono *S. Leone* **82** D2
Konongo *Ghana* **83** D4
Konosha *Russia* **32** B11
Kōnosu *Japan* **55** F9
Konotop *Ukraine* **33** G7
Konsankoro *Guinea* **82** D3
Końskie *Poland* **31** G7
Konstancin-Jeziorna *Poland* **31** F8
Konstantinovka =
  Kostyantynivka *Ukraine* **33** H9
Konstantinovsk *Russia* **35** G5
Konstantynów Łódzki
  Poland **31** G6
Konstanz *Germany* **25** H5
Kont *Iran* **71** E9
Kontagora *Nigeria* **83** C6
Kontcha *Cameroon* **83** D7
Kontiolahti *Finland* **8** E23
Kontokali *Greece* **49** A3
Konya *Turkey* **72** D5
Konya □ *Turkey* **72** D5
Konya Ovası *Turkey* **72** C5
Konz *Germany* **25** F2
Konza *Kenya* **86** C4
Koocanusa, L. *Canada* **108** B6
Kookynie *Australia* **93** E3
Koolyanobbing *Australia* **93** F2
Koonibba *Australia* **95** E1
Koorawatha *Australia* **95** E4
Koorda *Australia* **93** F2
Kooskia *U.S.A.* **108** C6
Kootenay ➤ *U.S.A.* **102** D5
Kootenay △ *Canada* **102** C5
Kootenay L. *Canada* **108** B5
Kootjieskolk *S. Africa* **88** E3
Kopanovka *Russia* **35** G8
Kopaonik *Serbia* **44** C4
Kopaonik △ *Serbia* **44** C4
Kópavogur *Iceland* **8** D3
Kopayhorod *Ukraine* **29** B12
Koper *Slovenia* **41** C10
Kopervik *Norway* **9** G11
Kopet Dagh *Asia* **71** B8
Kopi *Australia* **95** E2
Köping *Sweden* **10** E10
Köpingsvik *Sweden* **11** H10
Kopište *Croatia* **41** F13
Koplik *Albania* **44** D3
Köpmanholmen *Sweden* **10** A12
Kopparberg *Sweden* **10** E9
Koppeh Dāgh = Kopet
  Dagh *Asia* **71** B8
Koppies *S. Africa* **89** D4
Koppom *Sweden* **10** E6
Koprivlen *Bulgaria* **44** E7
Koprivnica *Croatia* **41** B13
Kopřivnice *Czech Rep.* **27** B11
Koprivshtitsa *Bulgaria* **45** D8
Köprübaşı *Turkey* **47** C10
Köprülü □ *Turkey* **70** B1
Kopychyntsi *Ukraine* **23** D13
Kora △ *Kenya* **86** C4
Korab *Macedonia* **44** E4
Koral *India* **68** J5
Korarou, L. *Mali* **82** B4
Korba *India* **69** H10
Korbach *Germany* **24** D4
Korbu, G. *Malaysia* **65** K3
Korçë *Albania* **44** F4
Korčula *Croatia* **41** F13
Korčulanski Kanal *Croatia* **41** E13
Kord Kūy *Iran* **71** B7
Kord Sheykh *Iran* **71** D7
Kordestān = Kurdistan
  Asia **73** D10
Kordestān □ *Iran* **70** C5
Kordofân *Sudan* **79** F11
Koré Mayroua *Niger* **83** C5
Korem *Ethiopia* **81** E4
Korenevo *Russia* **33** G8
Korenovsk *Russia* **35** H4
Korets *Ukraine* **23** C14
Korfantów *Poland* **31** H4
Korgan *Turkey* **72** B7
Korgus *Sudan* **80** D3
Korhogo *Ivory C.* **82** D3
Koribundu *S. Leone* **82** D2
Korienzé *Mali* **82** B4
Korinthía □ *Greece* **46** D4
Korinthiakos Kolpos *Greece* **46** C4

Korinthos *Greece* 46 D4
Korioumé *Mali* 82 B4
Korissa, L. *Greece* 49 B3
Kōriyama *Japan* 54 F10
Korkuteli *Turkey* 47 D12
Kormakiti, C. *Cyprus* 49 D11
Körmend *Hungary* 28 C1
Kornat *Croatia* 41 E12
Kornat △ *Croatia* 41 E12
Korneshty = Corneşti
   Moldova 29 C13
Korneuburg *Austria* 27 C9
Kórnik *Poland* 31 F4
Koro *Fiji* 91 a
Koro *Ivory C.* 82 D3
Koro *Mali* 82 C4
Koro Sea *Fiji* 91 a
Korocha *Russia* 33 G9
Köroğlu Dağları *Turkey* 72 B5
Korogwe *Tanzania* 86 D4
Koroleve *Ukraine* 29 B8
Korolevu *Fiji* 91 a
Koronadal *Phil.* 61 H6
Koroni *Greece* 46 E3
Koronia, L. *Greece* 44 F7
Koronos *Greece* 47 D7
Koronowo *Poland* 31 E4
Koropets *Ukraine* 29 B10
Koror *Palau* 96 G5
Körös → *Hungary* 28 D5
Körös Maros △ *Hungary* 28 C5
Köröstarcsa *Hungary* 28 D6
Korosten *Ukraine* 23 C15
Korostyshev *Ukraine* 23 C15
Korotoyak *Russia* 33 G10
Korovou *Fiji* 91 a
Koroyanitu △ *Fiji* 91 a
Korraraika, Helodranon' i
   Madag. 89 B7
Korsakov *Russia* 53 E15
Korsberga *Sweden* 11 G9
Korshiv *Ukraine* 29 B10
Korshunovo *Russia* 53 D12
Korsør *Denmark* 11 J5
Korsun Shevchenkovskiy
   Ukraine 33 H6
Korsze *Poland* 30 D8
Korti *Sudan* 80 D3
Kortrijk *Belgium* 17 D3
Korwai *India* 68 G7
Koryakskoye Nagorye
   Russia 53 C18
Koryukovka *Ukraine* 33 G7
Kos *Greece* 47 E9
Kosa *Ethiopia* 81 F4
Kosaya Gora *Russia* 32 E9
Kościan *Poland* 31 F3
Kościerzyna *Poland* 30 D4
Kosciusko *U.S.A.* 117 E10
Kosciuszko, Mt. *Australia* 95 F4
Kösély → *Hungary* 28 C6
Kosha *Sudan* 80 C3
Koshava *Bulgaria* 44 B7
K'oshih = Kashi *China* 60 C2
Koshiki-Rettō *Japan* 55 J4
Kosi *India* 68 F7
Kosi → *India* 69 E8
Košice *Slovak Rep.* 27 C14
Košický □ *Slovak Rep.* 27 C14
Kosiv *Ukraine* 29 B10
Kosjerić *Serbia* 44 B3
Kōşk *Turkey* 47 D10
Koskinou *Greece* 49 C10
Koslan *Russia* 52 C5
Kosmach *Ukraine* 29 B9
Kosŏng *N. Korea* 57 E15
Kosovo □ *Serbia* 44 D4
Kosovo Polje *Serbia* 44 D5
Kosovska Kamenica *Serbia* 44 D5
Kosovska Mitrovica *Serbia* 44 D4
Kossou, L. de *Ivory C.* 82 D3
Kosta *Sweden* 11 H9
Kostajnica *Croatia* 41 C13
Kostanjevica *Slovenia* 41 C12
Kostenets *Bulgaria* 44 D7
Koster *S. Africa* 88 D4
Kôstî *Sudan* 81 E3
Kostinbrod *Bulgaria* 44 D7
Kostolac *Serbia* 44 B5
Kostopil *Ukraine* 23 C14
Kostroma *Russia* 32 D11
Kostromo □ *Russia* 34 A6
Kostromskoye Vdkhr.
   Russia 32 D11
Kostryzhivka *Ukraine* 29 B10
Kostrzyn *Lubuskie, Poland* 31 F1
Kostrzyn *Wielkopolskie, Poland* 31 F4
Kostyantynivka *Ukraine* 33 H9
Kostyukovichi =
   Kastsyukovichy *Belarus* 32 F7
Koszalin *Poland* 30 D3
Kőszeg *Hungary* 28 C1
Kot Addu *Pakistan* 68 D4
Kot Kapura *India* 68 D6
Kot Moman *Pakistan* 68 C5

Kot Sultan *Pakistan* 68 D4
Kota *India* 68 G6
Kota Barrage *India* 68 G6
Kota Belud *Malaysia* 62 C5
Kota Bharu *Malaysia* 65 J4
Kota Kinabalu *Malaysia* 62 C5
Kota Kubu Bharu *Malaysia* 65 L3
Kota Tinggi *Malaysia* 65 M4
Kotaagung *Indonesia* 62 F2
Kotabaru *Indonesia* 62 E5
Kotabumi *Indonesia* 62 E2
Kotamobagu *Indonesia* 63 D6
Kotcho L. *Canada* 102 B4
Kotdwara *India* 69 E8
Kotel *Bulgaria* 45 D10
Kotelnich *Russia* 34 A9
Kotelnikovo *Russia* 35 G6
Kotelnyy, Ostrov *Russia* 53 B14
Kothari → *India* 68 G6
Köthen *Germany* 24 D7
Kothi *Chhattisgarh, India* 69 H10
Kothi *Mad. P., India* 69 G9
Kotiro *Pakistan* 68 F2
Kotka *Finland* 32 B4
Kotlas *Russia* 52 C5
Kotlenska Planina *Bulgaria* 45 D10
Kotli *Pakistan* 68 C5
Kotma *India* 69 H9
Kotmul *Pakistan* 69 B6
Koton-Karifi *Nigeria* 83 D6
Kotonkoro *Nigeria* 83 C6
Kotor *Montenegro* 44 D2
Kotor Varoš *Bos.-H.* 28 F2
Kotoriba *Croatia* 41 B13
Kotovo *Russia* 34 E7
Kotovsk *Russia* 34 D5
Kotovsk *Ukraine* 23 E15
Kotputli *India* 68 F7
Kotri *Pakistan* 68 G3
Kotronas *Greece* 46 E4
Kötschach-Mauthen *Austria* 26 E6
Kotto → *C.A.R.* 84 D4
Kotturu *India* 66 M10
Kotu Group *Tonga* 91 c
Kotuy → *Russia* 53 B11
Kotyuzhany *Ukraine* 29 B12
Kotzebue *U.S.A.* 106 a
Kotzebue Sound *U.S.A.* 98 C3
Kouchibouguac △ *Canada* 105 C6
Koudougou *Burkina Faso* 82 C4
Koufonisi *Iraklio, Greece* 49 E8
Koufonisi *Notio Aigaio, Greece* 47 E7
Kougaberge *S. Africa* 88 E3
Kouibli *Ivory C.* 82 D3
Kouilou → *Congo* 84 E2
Koula *Greece* 45 E8
Koula Moutou *Gabon* 84 E2
Koulen = Kulen *Cambodia* 64 F5
Koulikoro *Mali* 82 C3
Koulikoro □ *Mali* 82 C3
Kouloura *Greece* 49 A3
Koumala *Australia* 94 C4
Koumankou *Mali* 82 C3
Koumbia *Burkina Faso* 82 C4
Koumbia *Guinea* 82 C2
Koumboum *Guinea* 82 C2
Koumpenntoum *Senegal* 82 C2
Koumra *Chad* 79 G9
Koun-Fao *Ivory C.* 82 D4
Koundara *Guinea* 82 C2
Koundian *Guinea* 82 C3
Koungheul *Senegal* 82 C2
Kountze *U.S.A.* 116 F7
Koupéla *Burkina Faso* 83 C4
Kourémalé *Mali* 82 C3
Kouris → *Cyprus* 49 E11
Kourou *Fr. Guiana* 125 B8
Kourouba *Mali* 82 C2
Kouroukoto *Mali* 82 C2
Kourouma *Burkina Faso* 82 C4
Kourouninkoto *Mali* 82 C3
Kouroussa *Guinea* 82 C3
Koussané *Mali* 82 C2
Koussane *Senegal* 82 C2
Kousseri *Cameroon* 79 F8
Koutiala *Mali* 82 C3
Kouto *Ivory C.* 82 D3
Kouvé *Togo* 83 D5
Kouvola *Finland* 32 B4
Kovačica *Serbia* 28 E5
Kovdor *Russia* 8 C24
Kovel *Ukraine* 23 C13
Kovin *Serbia* 28 F5
Kovrov *Russia* 34 B5
Kowal *Poland* 31 F5
Kowalewo Pomorskie
   Poland 31 E5
Kowanyama *Australia* 94 B3
Kowloon *China* 59 F10
Kowŏn *N. Korea* 57 E14
Koyampattur =
   Coimbatore *India* 66 P10
Köyceğiz *Turkey* 47 E10
Köyceğiz Gölü *Turkey* 47 E10
Koyukuk → *U.S.A.* 98 C4
Koyulhisar *Turkey* 72 B7

Koyunyeri *Turkey* 45 F10
Koza = Okinawa *Japan* 55 L3
Kozak *Turkey* 47 B9
Kozan *Turkey* 72 D6
Kozani *Greece* 44 F5
Kozani □ *Greece* 44 F5
Kozara *Bos.-H.* 41 D14
Kozara △ *Bos.-H.* 28 F2
Kozarac *Bos.-H.* 41 D13
Kozelsk *Russia* 32 E8
Kozhikode = Calicut *India* 66 P9
Koziegłowy *Poland* 31 H6
Kozienice *Poland* 31 G8
Kozje *Slovenia* 41 B12
Kozloduy *Bulgaria* 44 C7
Kozlovets *Bulgaria* 45 C9
Kozlovka *Russia* 34 C9
Kozlu *Turkey* 72 B4
Kozluk *Turkey* 73 C9
Koźmin *Poland* 31 G4
Kozmodemyansk *Russia* 34 B8
Kožuchów *Poland* 31 G2
Kozyatyn *Ukraine* 23 D15
Kpabia *Ghana* 83 D4
Kpalimé *Togo* 83 D5
Kpandae *Ghana* 83 D4
Kpessi *Togo* 83 D5
Kra, Isthmus of = Kra,
   Kho Khot *Thailand* 65 G2
Kra, Kho Khot *Thailand* 65 G2
Kra Buri *Thailand* 65 G2
Kraai → *S. Africa* 88 E4
Krabi *Thailand* 65 H2
Kracheh *Cambodia* 64 F6
Kragan *Indonesia* 63 G14
Kragerø *Norway* 9 G13
Kragujevac *Serbia* 44 B4
Krajenka *Poland* 31 E3
Krakatau = Rakata, Pulau
   Indonesia 62 F3
Krakatoa = Rakata, Pulau
   Indonesia 62 F3
Krakor *Cambodia* 64 F5
Kraków *Poland* 31 H6
Kraków ✈ (KRK) *Poland* 31 H6
Kralanh *Cambodia* 64 F4
Králíky *Czech Rep.* 27 A9
Kraljevo *Serbia* 44 C4
Kralovéhradecký □
   Czech Rep. 26 A8
Královský Chlmec
   Slovak Rep. 27 C14
Kralupy nad Vltavou
   Czech Rep. 26 A7
Kramatorsk *Ukraine* 33 H9
Kramfors *Sweden* 10 B11
Krania *Greece* 44 G5
Krania Elasonas *Greece* 46 B4
Kranidi *Greece* 46 D5
Kranj *Slovenia* 41 B11
Kranjska Gora *Slovenia* 41 B10
Krankskop *S. Africa* 89 D5
Krapina *Croatia* 41 B12
Krapina → *Croatia* 41 C12
Krapkowice *Poland* 31 H4
Kras *Croatia* 41 C11
Kraskino *Russia* 54 C5
Krāslava *Latvia* 32 E4
Kraslice *Czech Rep.* 26 A5
Krasnaya Gorbatka *Russia* 34 C5
Krasnaya Polyana *Russia* 35 J5
Krasne *Ukraine* 29 D14
Krasni Okny *Ukraine* 29 C14
Kraśnik *Poland* 31 H9
Krasnoarmeisk *Ukraine* 33 H9
Krasnoarmeysk *Russia* 34 E7
Krasnoarmeyskiy *Russia* 35 G6
Krasnobród *Poland* 31 H10
Krasnodar *Russia* 35 H4
Krasnodar □ *Russia* 35 G4
Krasnodon *Ukraine* 33 H10
Krasnogorskiy *Russia* 34 B9
Krasnograd = Krasnohrad
   Ukraine 33 H8
Krasnogvardeysk *Ukraine* 33 K8
Krasnogvardeyskoye *Russia* 35 H5
Krasnohrad *Ukraine* 33 H8
Krasnokutsk *Ukraine* 33 G8
Krasnolesnyy *Russia* 33 G10
Krasnoperekopsk *Ukraine* 33 J7
Krasnorechenskiy *Russia* 54 B7
Krasnoselkup *Russia* 52 C9
Krasnoslobodsk *Mordvinia,*
   Russia 34 C6
Krasnoslobodsk *Volgograd,*
   Russia 35 F7
Krasnoturinsk *Russia* 52 D7
Krasnoyarsk *Russia* 53 D10
Krasnoyarskoye *Russia* 30 D8
Krasnoye = Krasnyy *Russia* 32 E6
Krasnoyarskiy *Russia* 35 C10
Krasnoznamensk *Russia* 30 D9
Krasnystaw *Poland* 31 H10
Krasnyy *Russia* 32 E6

Krasnyy Kholm *Russia* 32 C9
Krasnyy Kut *Russia* 34 E8
Krasnyy Liman *Ukraine* 33 H9
Krasnyy Luch *Ukraine* 33 H10
Krasny Profintern *Russia* 32 D11
Krasnyy Yar *Astrakhan,*
   Russia 35 G9
Krasnyy Yar *Samara, Russia* 34 D10
Krasnyy Yar *Volgograd,*
   Russia 34 E7
Krasnyye Baki *Russia* 34 B7
Krasnyoskolske Vdskh.
   Ukraine 33 H9
Kraszna → *Hungary* 28 B7
Kratie = Kracheh *Cambodia* 64 F6
Kratovo *Macedonia* 44 D6
Krau *Indonesia* 63 E10
Kravanh, Chuor Phnum
   Cambodia 65 G4
Krefeld *Germany* 24 D2
Kremaston, L. *Greece* 46 C3
Kremen *Croatia* 41 D12
Kremenchuk *Ukraine* 33 H7
Kremenchuksk Vdskh.
   Ukraine 33 H7
Kremenets *Ukraine* 23 C13
Kremennaya *Ukraine* 33 H10
Kremges = Svitlovodsk
   Ukraine 33 H7
Kremmen *Germany* 24 C9
Kremmling *U.S.A.* 108 F10
Kremnica *Slovak Rep.* 27 C11
Krems *Austria* 26 C8
Kremsmünster *Austria* 26 C7
Krestena *Greece* 46 D3
Kretinga *Lithuania* 30 C8
Krettsy *Russia* 32 C7
Kreuzberg *Germany* 25 E5
Kreuztal *Germany* 24 E4
Kria Vrisi *Greece* 44 F6
Kribi *Cameroon* 83 E6
Krichem *Bulgaria* 45 D8
Krichev = Krychaw *Belarus* 23 B16
Krim *Slovenia* 41 C11
Krios, Akra *Greece* 49 D5
Krishna → *India* 67 M12
Krishnanagar *India* 69 H13
Kristdala *Sweden* 11 G10
Kristiansand *Norway* 9 G13
Kristianstad *Sweden* 11 H8
Kristiansund *Norway* 8 E12
Kristiinankaupunki *Finland* 8 E19
Kristinehamn *Sweden* 10 E8
Kristinestad =
   Kristiinankaupunki
   Finland 8 E19
Kriti *Greece* 49 D7
Kritsa *Greece* 49 D7
Kriva → *Macedonia* 44 D5
Kriva Palanka *Macedonia* 44 D6
Krivaja → *Bos.-H.* 28 F3
Krivelj *Serbia* 44 B6
Krivoy Rog = Kryvyy Rih
   Ukraine 33 J7
Križevci *Croatia* 41 B13
Krk *Croatia* 41 C11
Krka → *Slovenia* 41 C12
Krka △ *Croatia* 41 E12
Krkonoše *Czech Rep.* 26 A8
Krkonoše △ *Czech Rep.* 26 A8
Krnov *Czech Rep.* 27 A10
Krobia *Poland* 31 G3
Krokees *Greece* 46 E4
Krokek *Sweden* 11 F10
Krokodil = Umgwenya →
   Mozam. 89 D5
Krokom *Sweden* 10 A8
Krokowa *Poland* 30 D5
Krolevets *Ukraine* 33 G7
Kroměříž *Czech Rep.* 27 B10
Krompachy *Slovak Rep.* 27 C13
Kromy *Russia* 33 F8
Kronach *Germany* 25 E7
Krong Kaoh Kong *Cambodia* 65 G4
Kronobergs län □ *Sweden* 11 H8
Kronprins Olav Kyst
   Antarctica 5 C5
Kronprinsesse Märtha
   Kyst *Antarctica* 5 D2
Kronshtadt *Russia* 32 C5
Kroonstad *S. Africa* 88 D4
Kröpelin *Germany* 24 A7
Kropotkin *Russia* 35 H5
Kropp *Germany* 24 A5
Krosna *Lithuania* 30 D10
Krośniewice *Poland* 31 F6
Krosno *Poland* 31 J8
Krosno Odrzańskie *Poland* 31 F2
Krotoszyn *Poland* 31 G4
Krotovka *Russia* 34 D10
Krousonas *Greece* 49 D6
Krrabë *Albania* 44 E3
Krško *Slovenia* 41 C12
Krstača *Serbia* 44 D3
Kruger △ *S. Africa* 89 C5
Krugersdorp *S. Africa* 89 D4
Kruisfontein *S. Africa* 88 E3

Krujë *Albania* 44 E3
Krulevshchina =
   Krulyewshchyna *Belarus* 32 E4
Krulyewshchyna *Belarus* 32 E4
Krumbach *Germany* 25 G6
Krumë *Albania* 44 D4
Krumovgrad *Bulgaria* 45 E9
Krung Thep = Bangkok
   Thailand 64 F3
Krupanj *Serbia* 44 B3
Krupina *Slovak Rep.* 27 C12
Krupinica → *Slovak Rep.* 27 C11
Krupki *Belarus* 23 A15
Krychaw *Belarus* 23 B16
Krymsk *Russia* 33 K10
Krymskiy Poluostrov =
   Krymskyy Pivostriv
   Ukraine 33 K8
Krymskyy Pivostriv *Ukraine* 33 K8
Krynica *Poland* 31 J7
Krynica Morska *Poland* 30 D6
Krynki *Poland* 31 E10
Krynychne *Ukraine* 29 E13
Kryvyy Rih *Ukraine* 33 J7
Kryzhopil *Ukraine* 29 B13
Krzepice *Poland* 31 H5
Krzeszów *Poland* 31 H9
Krzna → *Poland* 31 F10
Krzywiń *Poland* 31 G3
Krzyż Wielkopolski *Poland* 31 F2
Książ Wielkopolski *Poland* 31 F4
Kstovo *Russia* 34 B7
Ku, W. el → *Sudan* 81 E2
Kuah *Malaysia* 65 J2
Kuala Belait *Malaysia* 62 D4
Kuala Berang *Malaysia* 65 K4
Kuala Dungun = Dungun
   Malaysia 65 K4
Kuala Kangsar *Malaysia* 65 K3
Kuala Kelawang *Malaysia* 65 L4
Kuala Kerai *Malaysia* 65 K4
Kuala Kerian *Malaysia* 65 c
Kuala Lipis *Malaysia* 65 K4
Kuala Lumpur *Malaysia* 65 L3
Kuala Nerang *Malaysia* 65 J3
Kuala Pilah *Malaysia* 65 L4
Kuala Rompin *Malaysia* 65 L4
Kuala Selangor *Malaysia* 65 L3
Kuala Sepetang *Malaysia* 65 K3
Kuala Terengganu *Malaysia* 65 K4
Kualajelai *Indonesia* 62 E4
Kualakapuas *Indonesia* 62 E4
Kualakurun *Indonesia* 62 E4
Kualapembuang *Indonesia* 62 E4
Kualasimpang *Indonesia* 62 D1
Kuancheng *China* 57 D10
Kuandang *Indonesia* 63 D6
Kuandian *China* 57 D13
Kuangchou = Guangzhou
   China 59 F9
Kuanshan *Taiwan* 59 F13
Kuantan *Malaysia* 65 L4
Kuba = Quba *Azerbaijan* 35 K9
Kuban → *Russia* 33 K9
Kuban Depression =
   Prikubanskaya
   Nizmennost *Russia* 35 H4
Kubenskoye, Ozero *Russia* 32 C10
Kubokawa *Japan* 55 H6
Kubrat *Bulgaria* 45 C10
Kubu *Indonesia* 63 J18
Kubutambahan *Indonesia* 63 J18
Kučevo *Serbia* 44 B5
Kucha Gompa *India* 69 B7
Kuchaman *India* 68 F6
Kuchenspitze *Austria* 26 D3
Kuchinda *India* 69 J11
Kuchino-eruba-Jima *Japan* 55 J5
Kuchino-Shima *Japan* 55 K4
Kuchinotsu *Japan* 55 H5
Kuchl *Austria* 26 D6
Kuchurhan → *Ukraine* 29 D14
Kucing = Kuching *Malaysia* 62 D4
Kuçovë *Albania* 44 F3
Küçükbahçe *Turkey* 47 C8
Küçükköy *Turkey* 47 B8
Küçükkuyu *Turkey* 47 B8
Küçükmenderes → *Turkey* 47 D9
Kud → *Pakistan* 68 F2
Kuda *India* 68 H4
Kudat *Malaysia* 62 C5
Kudirkos Naumiestis
   Lithuania 30 D9
Kudremukh *India* 66 N9
Kudus *Indonesia* 63 G14
Kudowa-Zdrój *Poland* 31 H3
Kudymkar *Russia* 52 D6
Kueiyang = Guiyang *China* 58 D6
Kufra Oasis = Al Kufrah
   Libya 79 D10

Kufstein *Austria* 26 D5
Kugaaruk = Pelly Bay
   Canada 101 C11
Kugluktuk *Canada* 100 C8
Kugong I. *Canada* 104 A4
Kūh-e Jebāl Bārez *Iran* 71 D8
Kūhak *Iran* 71 E9
Kuhan *Pakistan* 68 E2
Kūhbonān *Iran* 71 D8
Kühestak *Iran* 71 E8
Kuhin *Iran* 71 B6
Kūhīrī *Iran* 71 E9
Kuhmo *Finland* 8 D23
Kuhnsdorf *Austria* 26 E7
Kūhpāyeh *Eşfahan, Iran* 71 C7
Kūhpāyeh *Kermān, Iran* 71 D8
Kührān, Kūh-e *Iran* 71 E8
Kui Buri *Thailand* 65 F2
Kuiseb → *Namibia* 88 C1
Kuito *Angola* 85 G3
Kujang *N. Korea* 57 E14
Kujawsko-Pomorskie □
   Poland 30 E5
Kuji *Japan* 54 D10
Kujū-San *Japan* 55 H5
Kukava *Ukraine* 29 B12
Kukavica *Serbia* 44 D5
Kukawa *Nigeria* 83 C7
Kukës *Albania* 44 D4
Kukmor *Russia* 34 B10
Kukup *Malaysia* 65 d
Kukup, Pulau *Malaysia* 65 d
Kukvidze *Russia* 34 E6
Kula *Bulgaria* 44 C6
Kula *Serbia* 28 E4
Kula *Turkey* 47 C10
Kulachi *Pakistan* 68 D4
Kulai *Malaysia* 65 M4
Kulaly, Ostrov = Kulaly
   Aral *Kazakhstan* 35 H10
Kulaly Aral *Kazakhstan* 35 H10
Kulasekarappattinam *India* 66 Q11
Kulautuva *Lithuania* 30 D10
Kuldīga *Latvia* 30 B8
Kuldīga □ *Latvia* 30 B8
Kuldu *Sudan* 80 E2
Kulebaki *Russia* 34 C6
Kulen *Cambodia* 64 F5
Kulen Vakuf *Bos.-H.* 41 D13
Kulgam *India* 69 C6
Kulgera *Australia* 94 D1
Kulim *Malaysia* 65 K3
Kulin *Australia* 93 F2
Kulkayu = Hartley Bay
   Canada 102 C3
Kullen *Sweden* 11 H6
Kulmbach *Germany* 25 E7
Kŭlob *Tajikistan* 52 F7
Kulp *Turkey* 73 C9
Kulpawn → *Ghana* 83 D4
Kulsary *Kazakhstan* 52 E6
Kulti *India* 69 H12
Kulu *India* 68 D7
Kulu *Turkey* 72 C5
Kulunda *Russia* 52 D8
Kulungar *Afghan.* 68 C3
Kŭlvand *Iran* 71 D7
Kulwin *Australia* 95 F3
Kulyab = Kŭlob *Tajikistan* 52 F7
Kuma → *Russia* 35 H8
Kumafşarı *Turkey* 47 D11
Kumaganum *Nigeria* 83 C7
Kumagaya *Japan* 55 F9
Kumai *Indonesia* 62 E4
Kumalar Dağı *Turkey* 47 C12
Kumamba, Kepulauan
   Indonesia 63 E9
Kumamoto *Japan* 55 H5
Kumamoto □ *Japan* 55 H5
Kumanovo *Macedonia* 44 D5
Kumara *N.Z.* 91 E3
Kumara Roadhouse
   Australia 93 D2
Kumasi *Ghana* 82 D4
Kumba *Cameroon* 83 E6
Kumbağ *Turkey* 45 F11
Kumbakonam *India* 66 P11
Kumbarilla *Australia* 95 D5
Kumbhraj *India* 68 G7
Kumbia *Australia* 95 D5
Kumbo *Cameroon* 83 D7
Kŭmch'ŏn *N. Korea* 57 E14
Kumdok *India* 69 C8
Kume-Shima *Japan* 55 L3
Kumeny *Russia* 34 B9
Kumharsain *India* 68 D7
Kumi *Uganda* 86 B3
Kumkale *Turkey* 45 G10
Kumla *Sweden* 10 E9
Kumluca *Turkey* 47 E12
Kummerower See *Germany* 24 B8
Kumo *Nigeria* 83 C7
Kumo älv =
   Kokemäenjoki → *Finland* 32 B1
Kumon Bum *Burma* 67 F20
Kumylzhenskaya *Russia* 34 F6
Kunágota *Hungary* 28 D6

Kunashir, Ostrov *Russia* **53** E15
Kunda *Estonia* **32** C4
Kunda *India* **69** G9
Kundar → *Pakistan* **68** D3
Kundelungu △
  Dem. Rep. of the Congo **87** E2
Kundelungu Ouest △
  Dem. Rep. of the Congo **87** D2
Kundian *Pakistan* **68** C4
Kundla *India* **68** J4
Kung, Ao *Thailand* **65** a
Kunga → *Bangla.* **69** J13
Kungälv *Sweden* **11** G5
Kunghit I. *Canada* **102** C2
Kungrad = Qŭnghirot
  Uzbekistan **52** E6
Kungsängen *Sweden* **10** E11
Kungsbacka *Sweden* **11** G6
Kungshamn *Sweden* **11** F5
Kungsör *Sweden* **10** E10
Kungur *Russia* **52** D6
Kungurri *Australia* **94** K6
Kunhar → *Pakistan* **69** B5
Kunhegyes *Hungary* **28** C5
Kuningan *Indonesia* **63** G13
Kunlong *Burma* **58** F2
Kunlun Shan *Asia* **60** C3
Kunmadaras *Hungary* **28** C5
Kunming *China* **58** E4
Kunów *Poland* **31** H8
Kunshan *China* **59** B13
Kunszentmárton *Hungary* **28** D5
Kunszentmiklós *Hungary* **28** C4
Kuntaur *Senegal* **82** C2
Kununurra *Australia* **92** C4
Kunwari → *India* **69** F8
Kunya-Urgench =
  Köneürgench
  Turkmenistan **52** E6
Künzelsau *Germany* **25** F5
Kuopio *Finland* **8** E22
Kupa → *Croatia* **41** C13
Kupang *Indonesia* **63** F6
Kupreanof I. *U.S.A.* **102** B2
Kupres *Bos.-H.* **28** G2
Kupyansk *Ukraine* **33** H9
Kupyansk-Uzlovoi *Ukraine* **33** H9
Kuqa *China* **60** B3
Kür → *Azerbaijan* **73** C13
Kür Dili *Azerbaijan* **73** C13
Kura = Kür → *Azerbaijan* **73** C13
Kuranda *Australia* **94** B4
Kuranga *India* **68** H3
Kurashiki *Japan* **55** G6
Kurayn *Si. Arabia* **71** E6
Kurayoshi *Japan* **55** G6
Kürdämir *Azerbaijan* **35** K9
Kurdistan *Asia* **73** D10
Kŭrdzhali *Bulgaria* **45** E9
Kure *Japan* **55** G6
Küre *Turkey* **72** B5
Küre Dağları *Turkey* **72** B6
Kuressaare *Estonia* **32** C2
Kurgan *Russia* **52** D7
Kurganinsk *Russia* **35** H5
Kurgannaya =
  Kurganinsk *Russia* **35** H5
Kuri *India* **68** F4
Kuria Maria Is. =
  Ḩallāniyat, Jazā'ir al
  Oman **75** D6
Kuridala *Australia* **94** C3
Kurigram *Bangla.* **67** G16
Kurikka *Finland* **8** E20
Kuril Basin *Pac. Oc.* **4** E15
Kuril Is. = Kurilskiye
  Ostrova *Russia* **53** E16
Kuril-Kamchatka Trench
  Pac. Oc. **96** C7
Kurilsk *Russia* **53** E15
Kurilskiye Ostrova *Russia* **53** E16
Kurino *Japan* **55** J5
Kurinskaya Kosa = Kür
  Dili *Azerbaijan* **73** C13
Kurkur *Egypt* **80** C3
Kurlovskiy *Russia* **34** C5
Kurmuk *Sudan* **81** E3
Kurnool *India* **66** M11
Kuro-Shima *Kagoshima, Japan* **55** J4
Kuro-Shima *Okinawa, Japan* **55** M2
Kuror, J. *Sudan* **80** C3
Kurow *N.Z.* **91** F3
Kurów *Poland* **31** G9
Kurram → *Pakistan* **68** C4
Kurri Kurri *Australia* **95** E5
Kurrimine *Australia* **94** B4
Kursavka *Russia* **35** H6
Kurshskaya Kosa △ *Russia* **30** C7
Kurshskiy Zaliv *Russia* **30** C8
Kuršių Nerijos △ *Lithuania* **30** C8
Kursk *Russia* **33** G9
Kursk □ *Russia* **33** G9
Kuršumlija *Serbia* **44** C5
Kuršumlijska Banja *Serbia* **44** C5
Kurşunlu *Bursa, Turkey* **45** F13
Kurşunlu *Çankırı, Turkey* **72** B5
Kurtalan *Turkey* **73** D9

Kurtbey *Turkey* **45** E10
Kuru *Sudan* **81** F2
Kuru, Bahr el → *Sudan* **81** F2
Kurucaşile *Turkey* **72** B5
Kuruçay *Turkey* **70** B3
Kuruktag *China* **60** B3
Kuruman *S. Africa* **88** D3
Kuruman → *S. Africa* **88** D3
Kurume *Japan* **55** H5
Kurun → *Sudan* **81** F2
Kurunegala *Sri Lanka* **66** R12
Kurya *Russia* **52** C6
Kus Gölü *Turkey* **45** F11
Kuşadası *Turkey* **72** D2
Kuşadası Körfezi *Turkey* **47** D8
Kusamba *Indonesia* **63** K18
Kusatsu *Japan* **55** F9
Kusawa L. *Canada* **102** A1
Kusel *Germany* **25** F3
Kushaka *Nigeria* **83** C6
Kushalgarh *India* **68** H6
Kushchevskaya *Russia* **35** G4
Kusheriki *Nigeria* **83** C6
Kushikino *Japan* **55** J5
Kushima *Japan* **55** J5
Kushimoto *Japan* **55** H7
Kushiro *Japan* **54** C12
Kushiro-Gawa → *Japan* **54** C12
Kushiro Shitsugen □ *Japan* **54** C12
Kūshk *Iran* **71** D8
Kushka = Serhetabat
  Turkmenistan **71** C9
Kūshkī *Iran* **70** C5
Kushnytsya *Ukraine* **29** B8
Kushol *India* **69** C7
Kushtia *Bangla.* **67** H16
Kushum → *Kazakhstan* **34** F10
Kuskokwim → *U.S.A.* **98** C3
Kuskokwim B. *U.S.A.* **106** a
Kusmi *India* **69** H10
Kusŏng *N. Korea* **57** E13
Kussharo-Ko *Japan* **54** C12
Kustanay = Qostanay
  Kazakhstan **52** D7
Kut, Ko *Thailand* **65** G4
Kuta *Indonesia* **63** K18
Kütahya *Turkey* **47** B11
Kütahya □ *Turkey* **47** B11
Kutaisi *Georgia* **35** J6
Kutaraja = Banda Aceh
  Indonesia **62** J2
Kutch, Gulf of = Kachchh,
  Gulf of *India* **68** H3
Kutch, Rann of =
  Kachchh, Rann of *India* **68** H4
Kutina *Croatia* **41** C13
Kutiyana *India* **68** J4
Kutjevo *Croatia* **28** E2
Kutkashen *Azerbaijan* **35** K8
Kutná Hora *Czech Rep.* **26** B8
Kutno *Poland* **31** F6
Kutse *Botswana* **88** C3
Kuttabul *Australia* **94** b
Kutu *Dem. Rep. of the Congo* **84** E3
Kutum *Sudan* **81** E1
Kúty *Slovak Rep.* **27** C10
Kuty *Ukraine* **29** B10
Kuujjuaq *Canada* **101** D13
Kuujjuarapik *Canada* **104** A4
Kuusamo *Finland* **8** D23
Kuusankoski *Finland* **32** B4
Kuvshinovo *Russia* **32** D8
Kuwait = Al Kuwayt *Kuwait* **70** D5
Kuwait ■ *Asia* **70** D5
Kuwana *Japan* **55** G8
Kuwana → *India* **69** F10
Kuybyshev = Samara
  Russia **34** D10
Kuybyshev *Russia* **52** D8
Kuybyshevo *Ukraine* **33** J9
Kuybyshevskoye Vdkhr.
  Russia **34** C9
Kuye He → *China* **56** E6
Kūyeh *Iran* **70** B5
Kuyto, Ozero *Russia* **8** D24
Kuyucak *Turkey* **47** D10
Kuyumba *Russia* **53** C10
Kuzey Anadolu Dağları
  Turkey **72** B7
Kuzmin *Serbia* **28** E4
Kuznetsk *Russia* **34** D8
Kuzomen *Russia* **52** C4
Kvænangen *Norway* **8** A19
Kværndrup *Denmark* **11** J4
Kvaløya *Norway* **8** B18
Kvänum *Sweden* **11** F7
Kvareli = Qvareli *Georgia* **35** K7
Kvarner *Croatia* **41** D11
Kvarnerič *Croatia* **41** D11
Kvicksund *Sweden* **10** E10
Kvillsfors *Sweden* **11** G9
Kvismare kanal *Sweden* **10** E9
Kvissleby *Sweden* **10** B11
Kwabhaca *S. Africa* **89** E4
Kwajalein *Marshall Is.* **96** G8
Kwakhanai *Botswana* **88** C3
Kwakoegron *Suriname* **125** B7
Kwale *Kenya* **86** C4

Kwale *Nigeria* **83** D6
KwaMashu *S. Africa* **89** D5
Kwando → *Africa* **88** B3
Kwangchow = Guangzhou
  China **59** F9
Kwango →
  Dem. Rep. of the Congo **84** E3
Kwangsi-Chuang =
  Guangxi Zhuangzu
  Zizhiqu □ *China* **58** F7
Kwangtung =
  Guangdong □ *China* **59** F9
Kwara □ *Nigeria* **83** D6
Kwataboahegan → *Canada* **104** B3
Kwatisore *Indonesia* **63** E8
KwaZulu Natal □ *S. Africa* **89** D5
Kweichow = Guizhou □
  China **58** D6
Kwekwe *Zimbabwe* **87** F2
Kwidzyn *Poland* **30** E5
Kwiha *Ethiopia* **81** E4
Kwilu →
  Dem. Rep. of the Congo **84** E3
Kwinana *Australia* **93** F2
Kwisa → *Poland* **31** G2
Kwoka *Indonesia* **63** E8
Kwolla *Nigeria* **83** D6
Kyabra Cr. → *Australia* **95** D3
Kyabram *Australia* **95** F4
Kyaikto *Burma* **64** D1
Kyakhta *Russia* **53** D11
Kyambura △ *Uganda* **86** C3
Kyancutta *Australia* **95** E2
Kyaukpadaung *Burma* **67** J19
Kyaukpyu *Burma* **67** K18
Kyaukse *Burma* **67** J20
Kybartai *Lithuania* **30** D9
Kyburz *U.S.A.* **110** G6
Kyelang *India* **68** C7
Kyenjojo *Uganda* **86** B3
Kyle *Canada* **103** C7
Kyle Dam *Zimbabwe* **87** G3
Kyle of Lochalsh *U.K.* **13** D3
Kyll → *Germany* **25** F2
Kyllburg *Germany* **25** E2
Kyllini *Greece* **46** D3
Kymijoki → *Finland* **32** B4
Kymmene älv =
  Kymijoki → *Finland* **32** B4
Kyneton *Australia* **95** F3
Kynuna *Australia* **94** C3
Kyō-ga-Saki *Japan* **55** G7
Kyoga, L. *Uganda* **86** B3
Kyogle *Australia* **95** D5
Kyom → *Sudan* **81** F2
Kyŏngju = Gyeongju
  S. Korea **57** G15
Kyŏngsŏng *N. Korea* **57** D15
Kyonpyaw *Burma* **67** L19
Kyōto *Japan* **55** G7
Kyōto □ *Japan* **55** G7
Kyparissovouno *Cyprus* **49** D12
Kyperounda *Cyprus* **49** E11
Kypros = Cyprus ■ *Asia* **49** E12
Kyrenia *Cyprus* **49** D12
Kyrgyzstan ■ *Asia* **52** E8
Kyritz *Germany* **24** C8
Kyrkhult *Sweden* **11** H8
Kyrnasivka *Ukraine* **29** B13
Kyrnychky *Ukraine* **29** E14
Kyro älv = Kyrönjoki →
  Finland **8** E19
Kyrönjoki → *Finland* **8** E19
Kystatyam *Russia* **53** C13
Kysucké Nové Mesto
  Slovak Rep. **27** B11
Kytay, Ozero *Ukraine* **29** E14
Kythira *Greece* **46** E5
Kythréa *Cyprus* **49** D12
Kyunhla *Burma* **67** H19
Kyuquot Sound *Canada* **102** D3
Kyurdamir = Kürdämir
  Azerbaijan **35** K9
Kyūshū *Japan* **55** H5
Kyūshū □ *Japan* **55** H5
Kyushu-Palau Ridge *Pac. Oc.* **96** E5
Kyūshū-Sanchi *Japan* **55** H5
Kyustendil *Bulgaria* **44** D6
Kyusyur *Russia* **53** B13
Kyyiv *Ukraine* **23** C16
Kyyiv □ *Ukraine* **33** G6
Kyyivske Vdskh. *Ukraine* **23** C16
Kyzyl *Russia* **53** D10
Kyzyl Kum *Uzbekistan* **52** E7
Kyzyl-Kyya *Kyrgyzstan* **52** E8
Kyzyl-Orda = Qyzylorda
  Kazakhstan **52** E7

L

La Albuera *Spain* **37** G4
La Alcarria *Spain* **38** E2
La Almarcha *Spain* **38** F2
La Almunia de Doña
  Godina *Spain* **38** D3
La Amistad △ *Cent. Amer.* **120** E3

Kwale *Nigeria* **83** D6
La Asunción *Venezuela* **124** A6
La Baie *Canada* **105** C5
La Banda *Argentina* **126** B3
La Bañeza *Spain* **36** C5
La Barca *Mexico* **118** C4
La Barge *U.S.A.* **108** E8
La Bastide-Puylaurent
  France **20** D7
La Baule *France* **18** E4
La Belle *U.S.A.* **117** H14
La Biche → *Canada* **102** B4
La Biche, L. *Canada* **102** C6
La Bisbal d'Empordà *Spain* **38** D8
La Brea *Trin. & Tob.* **125** K15
La Brède *France* **20** D3
La Bresse *France* **19** D13
La Bureba *Spain* **36** C7
La Calera *Chile* **126** C1
La Campana △ *Chile* **126** C1
La Campiña *Spain* **37** H6
La Canal = Sa Canal *Spain* **48** C7
La Cañiza = A Cañiza *Spain* **36** C2
La Canourgue *France* **20** D7
La Capelle *France* **19** C10
La Carlota *Argentina* **126** C3
La Carlota *Phil.* **61** F5
La Carlota *Spain* **37** H6
La Carolina *Spain* **37** G7
La Cavalerie *France* **20** D7
La Ceiba *Honduras* **120** C2
La Chaise-Dieu *France* **20** C7
La Chapelle d'Angillon
  France **19** E9
La Chapelle-St-Luc *France* **19** D11
La Chapelle-sur-Erdre *France* **18** E5
La Charité-sur-Loire *France* **19** E9
La Chartre-sur-le-Loir *France* **18** E7
La Châtaigneraie *France* **20** B3
La Châtre *France* **19** F9
La Chaux-de-Fonds *Switz.* **25** H2
La Chorrera *Panama* **120** E4
La Ciotat *France* **21** E9
La Clayette *France* **19** F11
La Cocha *Argentina* **126** B2
La Concepción *Panama* **120** E3
La Concordia *Mexico* **119** D6
La Coruña = A Coruña *Spain* **36** B2
La Coruña □ *Spain* **36** B2
La Côte-St-André *France* **21** C9
La Courtine *France* **20** C6
La Crau *Bouches-du-Rhône,*
  France **21** E8
La Crau *Var, France* **21** E10
La Crescent *U.S.A.* **112** D8
La Crete *Canada* **102** B5
La Crosse *Kans., U.S.A.* **112** F4
La Crosse *Wis., U.S.A.* **112** D8
La Cruz *Costa Rica* **120** D2
La Cruz *Mexico* **118** C3
La Désirade *Guadeloupe* **120** b
La Digue *Seychelles* **85** b
La Esmeralda *Paraguay* **126** A3
La Esperanza *Cuba* **120** B3
La Esperanza *Honduras* **120** D2
La Estrada = A Estrada *Spain* **36** C2
La Faouët *France* **18** D3
La Fayette *U.S.A.* **117** D12
La Fé *Cuba* **120** B3
La Fère *France* **19** C10
La Ferté-Bernard *France* **18** D7
La Ferté-Gaucher *France* **19** D10
La Ferté-Macé *France* **18** D6
La Ferté-St-Aubin *France* **19** E8
La Ferté-sous-Jouarre
  France **19** D10
La Ferté-Vidame *France* **18** D7
La Flèche *France* **18** E6
La Follette *U.S.A.* **117** C12
La Fregeneda *Spain* **36** E4
La Fuente de San Esteban
  Spain **36** E4
La Gacilly *France* **18** E4
La Gineta *Spain* **39** F2
La Grand'Combe *France* **21** D8
La Grande *U.S.A.* **108** D4
La Grande → *Canada* **104** B5
La Grande Deux, Rés.
  Canada **104** B4
La Grande-Motte *France* **21** E8
La Grande Quatre, Rés.
  Canada **104** B5
La Grande Trois, Rés.
  Canada **104** B4
La Grange *Calif., U.S.A.* **110** H6
La Grange *Ga., U.S.A.* **117** E12
La Grange *Tex., U.S.A.* **116** G6
La Grave *France* **21** C10
La Guaira *Venezuela* **124** A5
La Guardia = A Guarda
  Spain **36** D2
La Gudiña = A Gudiña *Spain* **36** C3
La Guerche-de-Bretagne
  France **18** E5
La Guerche-sur-l'Aubois
  France **19** F9
La Habana *Cuba* **120** B3

La Haute Vallée de
  Chevreuse △ *France* **19** D8
La Haye-du-Puits *France* **18** C5
La Horra *Spain* **36** D7
La Independencia *Mexico* **119** D6
La Isabela *Dom. Rep.* **121** C5
La Jonquera *Spain* **38** C7
La Junta *U.S.A.* **108** H12
La Laguna *Canary Is.* **48** F3
La Libertad = Puerto
  Libertad *Mexico* **118** B2
La Libertad *Guatemala* **120** C1
La Ligua *Chile* **126** C1
La Línea de la Concepción
  Spain **37** J5
La Loche *Canada* **103** B7
La Londe-les-Maures
  France **21** E10
La Lora *Spain* **36** C7
La Loupe *France* **18** D8
La Louvière *Belgium* **17** D4
La Lune *Trin. & Tob.* **125** K15
La Machine *France* **19** F10
La Maddalena *Italy* **42** A2
La Malbaie *Canada* **105** C5
La Malinche △ *Mexico* **119** D5
La Mancha *Spain* **39** F2
La Mariña *Spain* **36** B3
La Martre, L. *Canada* **102** A5
La Mesa *Mexico* **111** N10
La Mesa *U.S.A.* **111** N9
La Mesilla *U.S.A.* **109** K10
La Misión *Mexico* **118** A1
La Mothe-Achard *France* **18** F5
La Motte-Chalançon *France* **21** D9
La Motte-du-Caire *France* **21** D10
La Motte-Servolex *France* **21** C9
La Moure *U.S.A.* **112** B4
La Muela *Spain* **38** D3
La Mure *France* **21** D9
La Negra *Chile* **126** A1
La Oliva *Canary Is.* **48** F6
La Orotava *Canary Is.* **48** F3
La Oroya *Peru* **124** F3
La Pacaudière *France* **19** F10
La Palma *Canary Is.* **48** F2
La Palma *Panama* **120** E4
La Palma del Condado *Spain* **37** H4
La Paloma *Chile* **126** C1
La Pampa □ *Argentina* **126** D2
La Paragua *Venezuela* **124** B6
La Paz *Entre Ríos, Argentina* **126** C4
La Paz *San Luis, Argentina* **126** C2
La Paz *Bolivia* **124** G5
La Paz *Honduras* **120** D2
La Paz *Mexico* **118** C2
La Paz *Phil.* **61** D4
La Paz Centro *Nic.* **120** D2
La Pedrera *Colombia* **124** D5
La Pérade *Canada* **105** C5
La Perla *Mexico* **118** B3
La Perouse Str. *Asia* **54** B11
La Pesca *Mexico* **119** C5
La Piedad *Mexico* **118** C4
La Pine *U.S.A.* **108** E3
La Plata *Argentina* **126** D4
La Pobla de Lillet *Spain* **38** C6
La Pobla de Segur *Spain* **38** C5
La Pocatière *Canada* **105** C5
La Pola de Gordón *Spain* **36** C5
La Porta *France* **21** F13
La Porte *U.S.A.* **116** G7
La Presanella *Italy* **40** B7
La Puebla = Sa Pobla *Spain* **38** F8
La Puebla de Cazalla *Spain* **37** H5
La Puebla de los Infantes
  Spain **37** H5
La Puebla de Montalbán
  Spain **36** F6
La Puebla del Río *Spain* **37** H4
La Puerta de Segura *Spain* **37** G8
La Purísima *Mexico* **118** B2
La Push *U.S.A.* **110** C2
La Quiaca *Argentina* **126** A2
La Réole *France* **20** D3
La Restinga *Canary Is.* **48** G2
La Rioja *Argentina* **126** B2
La Rioja □ *Argentina* **126** B2
La Rioja □ *Spain* **38** C2
La Robla *Spain* **36** C5
La Roche-Bernard *France* **18** E4
La Roche-Canillac *France* **20** C5
La Roche-en-Ardenne
  Belgium **17** D5
La Roche-sur-Foron *France* **19** F13
La Roche-sur-Yon *France* **18** F5
La Rochefoucauld *France* **20** C4
La Rochelle *France* **20** B2
La Roda *Spain* **39** F2
La Roda de Andalucía *Spain* **37** H6
La Romaine *Canada* **105** B7
La Romana *Dom. Rep.* **121** C6
La Ronge *Canada* **103** B7
La Rumorosa *Mexico* **111** N10
La Sabina = Sa Savina *Spain* **48** C7
La Sagra *Spain* **39** H2
La Salle *U.S.A.* **112** E9
La Sanabria *Spain* **36** C4

La Santa *Canary Is.* **48** E6
La Sarre *Canada* **104** C4
La Scie *Canada* **105** C8
La Selva *Spain* **38** D7
La Selva Beach *U.S.A.* **110** J5
La Selva del Camp *Spain* **38** D6
La Serena *Chile* **126** B1
La Serena *Spain* **37** G5
La Seu d'Urgell *Spain* **38** C6
La Seyne-sur-Mer *France* **21** E9
La Sila *Italy* **43** C9
La Solana *Spain* **37** G7
La Soufrière *St. Vincent* **121** D7
La Souterraine *France* **19** F8
La Spézia *Italy* **40** D6
La Suze-sur-Sarthe *France* **18** E7
La Tagua *Colombia* **124** C4
La Teste-de-Buch *France* **20** D2
La Tortuga *Venezuela* **121** D6
La Tour-du-Pin *France* **21** C9
La Tranche-sur-Mer *France* **18** F5
La Tremblade *France* **20** C2
La Trinité *Martinique* **120** c
La Tuque *Canada* **104** C5
La Unión *Chile* **128** E2
La Unión *El Salv.* **120** D2
La Unión *Mexico* **118** D4
La Unión *Spain* **39** H4
La Urbana *Venezuela* **124** B5
La Vache Pt. *Trin. & Tob.* **125** K15
La Vall d'Uixó *Spain* **38** F4
La Vecilla de Curveño *Spain* **36** C5
La Vega *Dom. Rep.* **121** C5
La Vela de Coro *Venezuela* **124** A5
La Veleta *Spain* **37** H7
La Venta *Mexico* **119** D6
La Vergne *U.S.A.* **117** C11
La Voulte-sur-Rhône *France* **21** D8
Laa an der Thaya *Austria* **27** C9
Laaber, Grosse → *Germany* **25** G8
Laage *Germany* **24** B8
Laas Caanood = Las Anod
  Somali Rep. **75** F4
Laatzen *Germany* **24** C5
Laba → *Russia* **35** H4
Labasa *Fiji* **91** a
Labason *Phil.* **61** G5
Labastide-Murat *France* **20** D5
Labastide-Rouairoux *France* **20** E6
Labbézenga *Mali* **83** B5
Labdah = Leptis Magna
  Libya **79** B8
Labe = Elbe → *Europe* **24** B4
Labé *Guinea* **82** C2
Laberge, L. *Canada* **102** A1
Labin *Croatia* **41** C11
Labinsk *Russia* **35** H5
Labis *Malaysia* **65** L4
Labiszyn *Poland* **31** F4
Labo *Phil.* **61** D5
Laboe *Germany* **24** A6
Laborec → *Slovak Rep.* **27** C14
Laborie *St. Lucia* **121** f
Labouheyre *France* **20** D3
Laboulaye *Argentina* **126** C3
Labrador *Canada* **105** B7
Labrador City *Canada* **105** B6
Labrador Sea *Atl. Oc.* **101** D14
Lábrea *Brazil* **124** E6
Labruguière *France* **20** E6
Labuan *Malaysia* **62** C5
Labuan, Pulau *Malaysia* **62** C5
Labuha *Indonesia* **63** E7
Labuhan *Indonesia* **63** G11
Labuhanbajo *Indonesia* **63** F6
Labuk, Telok *Malaysia* **62** C5
Labyrinth, L. *Australia* **95** E2
Labytnangi *Russia* **52** C7
Laç *Albania* **44** E3
Lac-Bouchette *Canada* **105** C5
Lac Édouard *Canada* **104** C5
Lac La Biche *Canada* **102** C6
Lac La Martre = Wha Ti
  Canada **100** C8
Lac La Ronge △ *Canada* **103** B7
Lac-Mégantic *Canada* **104** C5
Lac Thien *Vietnam* **64** F7
Lacanau *France* **20** D2
Lacanau, Étang de *France* **20** D2
Lacantún → *Mexico* **119** D6
Lacara → *Spain* **37** G4
Lacaune *France* **20** E6
Lacaune, Mts. de *France* **20** E6
Laccadive Is. =
  Lakshadweep Is. *India* **3** D13
Lacepede B. *Australia* **95** F2
Lacepede Is. *Australia* **92** C3
Lacerdónia *Mozam.* **87** F4
Lacey *U.S.A.* **110** C4
Lachania *Greece* **49** D9
Lachhmangarh *India* **68** F6
Lachi *Pakistan* **68** C4
Lachine *Canada* **104** C5
Lachlan → *Australia* **95** E3
Lachute *Canada* **104** C5
Lackagh Hills *Ireland* **12** B3
Lackawanna *U.S.A.* **114** D6

Lackawaxen *U.S.A.* **115** E10
Lacolle *Canada* **115** A11
Lacombe *Canada* **102** C6
Lacona *U.S.A.* **115** C8
Láconi *Italy* **42** C2
Laconia *U.S.A.* **115** C13
Lacq *France* **20** E3
Ladakh Ra. *India* **69** C8
Lądek-Zdrój *Poland* **31** H3
Ladik *Turkey* **72** B6
Ladismith *S. Africa* **88** E3
Ladispoli *Italy* **41** G9
Lādīz *Iran* **71** D9
Ladnun *India* **68** F6
Ladoga, L. = Ladozhskoye
  Ozero *Russia* **32** B6
Ladonas → *Greece* **46** D3
Ladozhskoye Ozero *Russia* **32** B6
Ladushkin *Russia* **30** D7
Lady Elliott I. *Australia* **94** C5
Lady Grey *S. Africa* **88** E4
Ladybrand *S. Africa* **88** D4
Ladysmith *Canada* **110** B3
Ladysmith *S. Africa* **89** D4
Ladysmith *U.S.A.* **112** C8
Ladyzhnyn *Ukraine* **29** B14
Lae *Papua N. G.* **90** B7
Laem Hin Khom *Thailand* **65** b
Laem Khat *Thailand* **65** a
Laem Nga *Thailand* **65** a
Laem Ngop *Thailand* **65** F4
Laem Phan Wa *Thailand* **65** a
Laem Pho *Thailand* **65** J3
Laem Phrom Thep *Thailand* **65** a
Laem Riang *Thailand* **65** a
Laem Sam Rong *Thailand* **65** b
Laem Son *Thailand* **65** a
Laem Yamu *Thailand* **65** a
Laerma *Greece* **49** C9
Læsø *Denmark* **11** G5
Læsø Rende *Denmark* **11** G4
Lafayette *Ind., U.S.A.* **112** E10
Lafayette *La., U.S.A.* **116** F8
Lafayette *Tenn., U.S.A.* **117** C11
Laferte → *Canada* **102** A5
Lafia *Nigeria* **83** D6
Lafiagi *Nigeria* **83** D6
Lafkos *Greece* **46** B5
Lafleche *Canada* **103** D7
Lafon *Sudan* **81** F3
Lagan *Sweden* **11** H7
Lagan → *Sweden* **11** H6
Lagan → *U.K.* **12** B5
Lagarfljót → *Iceland* **8** D6
Lagdo, Rés. de *Cameroon* **79** G8
Lage *Germany* **24** D4
Lågen → *Oppland, Norway* **8** F14
Lågen → *Vestfold, Norway* **9** G14
Lägerdorf *Germany* **24** B5
Laghouat *Algeria* **78** B6
Lagnieu *France* **21** C9
Lagny-sur-Marne *France* **19** D9
Lago *Italy* **43** C9
Lago de Sanabria y
  Entorno △ *Spain* **36** C4
Lagôa *Portugal* **37** H2
Lagoa do Peixe △ *Brazil* **127** C5
Lagoa Vermelha *Brazil* **127** B5
Lagoaça *Portugal* **36** D4
Lagodekhi *Georgia* **35** K8
Lagónegro *Italy* **43** B8
Lagonoy G. *Phil.* **61** E5
Lagos *Greece* **45** E9
Lagos *Nigeria* **83** D5
Lagos *Portugal* **37** H2
Lagos □ *Nigeria* **83** D5
Lagos de Moreno *Mexico* **118** C4
Lagrange = Bidyadanga
  Australia **92** C3
Lagrange B. *Australia* **92** C3
Laguardia *Spain* **38** C2
Laguépie *France* **20** D5
Laguna *Brazil* **127** B6
Laguna *U.S.A.* **109** J10
Laguna, Sa. de la *Mexico* **118** C3
Laguna Beach *U.S.A.* **111** M9
Laguna de Duera *Spain* **36** D6
Laguna de la Restinga △
  Venezuela **121** D6
Laguna del Laja △ *Chile* **126** D1
Laguna del Tigre △
  Guatemala **120** C1
Laguna Limpia *Argentina* **126** B4
Lagunas *Chile* **126** A2
Lagunas *Peru* **124** E3
Lagunas de Chacahua △
  Mexico **119** D5
Lagunas de Montebello △
  Mexico **119** D6
Lagunas de Ruidera △ *Spain* **39** G2
Lahad Datu *Malaysia* **63** D5
Lahad Datu, Telok *Malaysia* **63** D5
Lahan Sai *Thailand* **64** E4
Lahanam *Laos* **64** D5
Lahar *India* **69** F8
Laharpur *India* **69** F9
Lahat *Indonesia* **62** E2

Lahewa *Indonesia* **62** D1
Lāhījān *Iran* **71** B6
Lahn → *Germany* **25** E3
Lahnstein *Germany* **25** E3
Laholm *Sweden* **11** H7
Laholmsbukten *Sweden* **11** H6
Lahore *Pakistan* **68** D6
Lahr *Germany* **25** G3
Lahri *Pakistan* **68** E3
Lahti *Finland* **32** B3
Lahtis = Lahti *Finland* **32** B3
Laï *Chad* **79** G9
Lai Chau *Vietnam* **58** F4
Lai'an *China* **59** A12
Laibin *China* **58** F7
Laifeng *China* **58** C7
L'Aigle *France* **18** D7
Laignes *France* **19** E11
L'Aiguillon-sur-Mer *France* **20** B2
Laila = Layla *Si. Arabia* **75** C4
Laingsburg *S. Africa* **88** E3
Lainioälven → *Sweden* **8** C20
Lairg *U.K.* **13** C4
Laisamis *Kenya* **86** B4
Laishui *China* **56** E8
Laissac *France* **20** D6
Láives *Italy* **41** B8
Laiwu *China* **57** F9
Laixi *China* **57** F11
Laiyang *China* **57** F11
Laiyuan *China* **56** E8
Laizhou *China* **57** F10
Laizhou Wan *China* **57** F10
Laja → *Mexico* **118** C4
Lajamanu *Australia* **92** C5
Lajere *Nigeria* **83** C7
Lajes *Brazil* **127** B5
Lajkovac *Serbia* **44** B4
Lajosmizse *Hungary* **28** C4
Lak Sao *Laos* **64** C5
Lakaband *Pakistan* **68** D3
Lakamané *Mali* **82** C3
Lake *U.S.A.* **108** D8
Lake Alpine *U.S.A.* **110** G7
Lake Andes *U.S.A.* **112** D4
Lake Arthur *U.S.A.* **116** F8
Lake Bindegolly △ *Australia* **95** D3
Lake Cargelligo *Australia* **95** E4
Lake Charles *U.S.A.* **116** F8
Lake City *Colo., U.S.A.* **108** G10
Lake City *Fla., U.S.A.* **117** F13
Lake City *Mich., U.S.A.* **113** C11
Lake City *Minn., U.S.A.* **112** C7
Lake City *Pa., U.S.A.* **114** D4
Lake City *S.C., U.S.A.* **117** E15
Lake Cowichan *Canada* **102** D4
Lake District △ *U.K.* **14** C5
Lake Elsinore *U.S.A.* **111** M9
Lake Eyre △ *Australia* **95** D2
Lake Gairdner △ *Australia* **95** E2
Lake George *U.S.A.* **115** C11
Lake Grace *Australia* **93** F2
Lake Harbour = Kimmirut
  Canada **101** C13
Lake Havasu City *U.S.A.* **111** L12
Lake Hughes *U.S.A.* **111** L8
Lake Isabella *U.S.A.* **111** K8
Lake Jackson *U.S.A.* **116** G7
Lake King *Australia* **93** F2
Lake Lenore *Canada* **103** C8
Lake Louise *Canada* **102** C5
Lake Malawi △ *Malawi* **87** E3
Lake Mburo △ *Uganda* **86** C3
Lake Mead △ *U.S.A.* **111** K12
Lake Meredith △ *U.S.A.* **116** D4
Lake Mills *U.S.A.* **112** D8
Lake Nakura △ *Kenya* **86** C4
Lake Placid *U.S.A.* **115** B11
Lake Pleasant *U.S.A.* **115** C10
Lake Providence *U.S.A.* **116** E9
Lake Roosevelt △ *U.S.A.* **108** B4
Lake St. Peter *Canada* **114** A6
Lake Superior △ *Canada* **104** C3
Lake Torrens △ *Australia* **95** E2
Lake Village *U.S.A.* **116** E9
Lake Wales *U.S.A.* **117** H14
Lake Worth *U.S.A.* **117** H14
Lakeba *Fiji* **91** a
Lakeba Passage *Fiji* **91** a
Lakefield *Canada* **114** B6
Lakefield △ *Australia* **94** B3
Lakehurst *U.S.A.* **115** F10
Lakeland *Australia* **94** B3
Lakeland *U.S.A.* **117** G14
Lakemba = Lakeba *Fiji* **91** a
Lakeport *Calif., U.S.A.* **110** F4
Lakeport *Mich., U.S.A.* **114** C2
Lakes Entrance *Australia* **95** F4
Lakeside *Calif., U.S.A.* **111** N10
Lakeside *Nebr., U.S.A.* **112** D2
Lakeside *Ohio, U.S.A.* **114** E2
Lakeview *U.S.A.* **108** E3
Lakeville *U.S.A.* **112** C7
Lakewood *Colo., U.S.A.* **108** G11
Lakewood *N.J., U.S.A.* **115** F10
Lakewood *N.Y., U.S.A.* **114** D5
Lakewood *Ohio, U.S.A.* **114** E3

Lakewood *Wash., U.S.A.* **110** C4
Lakha *India* **68** F4
Lakhimpur *India* **69** F9
Lakhnadon *India* **69** H8
Lakhnau = Lucknow *India* **69** F9
Lakhonpheng *Laos* **64** E5
Lakhpat *India* **68** H3
Lakin *U.S.A.* **112** G3
Lakitusaki → *Canada* **104** B3
Lakki *Greece* **49** D5
Lakki *Pakistan* **68** C4
Lakonia □ *Greece* **46** E4
Lakonikos Kolpos *Greece* **46** E4
Lakor *Indonesia* **63** F7
Lakota *Ivory C.* **82** D3
Lakota *U.S.A.* **112** A4
Laksar *India* **68** E8
Laksefjorden *Norway* **8** A22
Lakselv *Norway* **8** A21
Lakshadweep Is. *India* **3** D13
Lakshmanpur *India* **69** J11
Lakshmikantapur *India* **69** H13
Lala Musa *Pakistan* **68** C5
Lalaghat *India* **67** G18
Lalago *Tanzania* **86** C3
Lalapanzi *Zimbabwe* **87** F3
Lalapaşa *Turkey* **45** E10
L'Albufera *Spain* **39** F4
Lalganj *India* **69** G11
Lalgola *India* **69** G13
Lālī *Iran* **71** C6
Lalin *China* **57** B14
Lalín *Spain* **36** C2
Lalín He → *China* **57** B13
Lalinde *France* **20** D4
Lalitapur *Nepal* **69** F11
Lalitpur *India* **69** G8
Lalkua *India* **69** E8
Lalsot *India* **68** F7
Lam *Vietnam* **64** B6
Lam Pao Res. *Thailand* **64** D4
Lama Kara = Kara *Togo* **83** D5
Lamaing *Burma* **64** E1
Lamar *Colo., U.S.A.* **108** G12
Lamar *Mo., U.S.A.* **112** G6
Lamas *Peru* **124** E3
Lamastre *France* **21** D8
Lambach *Austria* **26** C6
Lamballe *France* **18** D4
Lambaréné *Gabon* **84** E2
Lambasa = Labasa *Fiji* **91** a
Lambay I. *Ireland* **12** C5
Lambert's Bay *S. Africa* **88** E2
Lambesc *France* **21** E9
Lambeth *Canada* **114** D3
Lambia *Greece* **46** D3
Lambomakondro *Madag.* **89** C7
Lambro → *Italy* **40** C6
Lambton Shores *Canada* **114** C3
Lame *Nigeria* **83** C6
Lame Deer *U.S.A.* **108** D10
Lamego *Portugal* **36** D3
Lamèque *Canada* **105** C7
Lameroo *Australia* **95** F3
Lamesa *U.S.A.* **116** E4
Lamia *Greece* **46** C4
Lamington △ *Australia* **95** D5
Lamitan *Phil.* **61** H5
Lammermuir Hills *U.K.* **13** F6
Lammhult *Sweden* **11** G8
Lamoille → *U.S.A.* **115** B11
Lamon B. *Phil.* **61** D5
Lamont *Canada* **102** C6
Lamont *Calif., U.S.A.* **111** K8
Lamont *Wyo., U.S.A.* **108** E10
Lamotte-Beuvron *France* **19** E9
Lampa *Peru* **124** G4
Lampang *Thailand* **64** C2
Lampasas *U.S.A.* **116** F5
Lampazos de Naranjo
  Mexico **118** B4
Lampertheim *Germany* **25** F4
Lampeter *U.K.* **15** E3
Lampman *Canada* **103** D8
Lamprechtshausen *Austria* **26** D5
Lampung □ *Indonesia* **62** F2
Lamta *India* **69** H9
Lamu *Kenya* **86** C5
Lamy *U.S.A.* **109** J11
Lan Xian *China* **56** E6
Lan Yü *Taiwan* **59**
Läna'i *U.S.A.* **106** b
Lanak La *China* **69** B8
Lanak'o Shank'ou =
  Lanak La *China* **69** B8
Lanao, L. *Phil.* **61** H6
Lanark *Canada* **115** A8
Lanark *U.K.* **13** F5
Lanbi Kyun *Burma* **65** G2
Lancang *China* **58** F2
Lancang Jiang → *China* **58** G3
Lancashire □ *U.K.* **14** D5
Lancaster *Canada* **115** A10
Lancaster *U.K.* **14** C5

Lancaster *Calif., U.S.A.* **111** L8
Lancaster *Ky., U.S.A.* **113** G11
Lancaster *N.H., U.S.A.* **115** B13
Lancaster *N.Y., U.S.A.* **114** D6
Lancaster *Ohio, U.S.A.* **113** F12
Lancaster *Pa., U.S.A.* **115** F8
Lancaster *S.C., U.S.A.* **117** D14
Lancaster *Wis., U.S.A.* **112** D8
Lancaster Sd. *Canada* **101** B11
Lancelin *Australia* **93** F2
Lanchow = Lanzhou *China* **56** F2
Lanchyn *Ukraine* **29** B9
Lanciano *Italy* **41** F11
Lancun *China* **57** F11
Land Between the Lakes △
  U.S.A. **117** C11
Landau *Bayern, Germany* **25** G8
Landau *Rhld-Pfz., Germany* **25** F4
Landeck *Austria* **26** D3
Lander *U.S.A.* **108** E9
Lander → *Australia* **92** D5
Landerneau *France* **18** D2
Landeryd *Sweden* **11** G7
Landes *France* **20** D2
Landes □ *France* **20** E3
Landes de Gascogne △
  France **20** D3
Landete *Spain* **38** F3
Landi Kotal *Pakistan* **68** B4
Landisburg *U.S.A.* **114** F7
Landmannalaugar *Iceland* **8** E4
Landquart *Switz.* **25** J5
Landrecies *France* **19** B10
Land's End *U.K.* **15** G2
Landsberg *Germany* **25** G6
Landsborough Cr. →
  Australia **94** C3
Landsbro *Sweden* **11** G8
Landshut *Germany* **25** G8
Landskrona *Sweden* **11** J6
Landstuhl *Germany* **25** F3
Landvetter *Sweden* **11** G6
Lanesboro *U.S.A.* **115** E9
Lanester *France* **18** E3
Lanett *U.S.A.* **117** E12
Lang Qua *Vietnam* **58** A5
Lang Shan *China* **56** D4
Lang Son *Vietnam* **58** G6
Lang Suan *Thailand* **65** H2
Langå *Denmark* **11** H3
La'nga Co *China* **69** D9
Langadas *Greece* **44** F7
Langadia *Greece* **46** D4
Langan *Sweden* **10** A8
Langano, L. *Ethiopia* **81** F4
Langar *Iran* **71** C9
Langara I. *Canada* **102** C2
Lângås *Sweden* **11** H6
Langdai *China* **58** D5
Langdon *U.S.A.* **112** A4
Länge Jan = Ölands södra
  udde *Sweden* **11** H10
Langeac *France* **20** C7
Langeais *France* **18** E7
Langeb Baraka → *Sudan* **80** D4
Langeberg *S. Africa* **88** E3
Langeberge *S. Africa* **88** D3
Langeland *Denmark* **11** K4
Langelands Bælt *Denmark* **11** K4
Langen *Hessen, Germany* **25** F4
Langen *Niedersachsen,
  Germany* **24** B4
Langenburg *Canada* **103** C8
Langeneß *Germany* **24** A4
Langenlois *Austria* **26** C8
Langeoog *Germany* **24** B3
Langeskov *Denmark* **11** J4
Länghem *Sweden* **11** G7
Langhirano *Italy* **40** D7
Langholm *U.K.* **13** F5
Langjökull *Iceland* **8** D3
Langkawi, Pulau *Malaysia* **65** J2
Langklip *S. Africa* **88** D3
Langkon *Malaysia* **62** C5
Langlade *St-P. & M.* **105** C8
Langley *Canada* **110** A4
Langnau *Switz.* **25** J3
Langogne *France* **20** D7
Langon *France* **20** D3
Langøya *Norway* **8** B16
Langreo *Spain* **36** B5
Langres *France* **19** E12
Langres, Plateau de *France* **19** E12
Langsa *Indonesia* **62** D1
Långsele *Sweden* **10** A11
Långshyttan *Sweden* **10** D10
Langtang △ *Nepal* **69** E11
Langtry *U.S.A.* **116** G4
Langu *Thailand* **65** J2
Langue de Barbarie △
  Senegal **82** C1
Languedoc *France* **20** E7
Languedoc-Roussillon □
  France **20** E6
Langxi *China* **59** B12

Langxiangzhen *China* **56** E9
Langzhong *China* **58** B5
Lanigan *Canada* **103** C7
Lankao *China* **56** G8
Länkäran *Azerbaijan* **73** C13
Lanmeur *France* **18** D3
Lannemezan *France* **20** E4
Lannilis *France* **18** D2
Lannion *France* **18** D3
L'Annonciation *Canada* **104** C5
Lanouaille *France* **20** C5
Lanping *China* **58** D2
Lansdale *U.S.A.* **115** F9
Lansdowne *Australia* **95** E5
Lansdowne *Canada* **115** B8
Lansdowne *India* **69** E8
Lansdowne House *Canada* **104** B2
L'Anse *U.S.A.* **112** B9
L'Anse au Loup *Canada* **105** B8
L'Anse aux Meadows
  Canada **105** B8
L'Anse la Raye *St. Lucia* **121** f
Lansford *U.S.A.* **115** F9
Lanshan *China* **59** E9
Lansing *U.S.A.* **113** D11
Lanslebourg-Mont-Cenis
  France **21** C10
Lanta Yai, Ko *Thailand* **65** J2
Lantewa *Nigeria* **83** C7
Lantian *China* **56** G5
Lanus *Argentina* **126** C4
Lanusei *Italy* **42** C2
Lanuza *Phil.* **61** G7
Lanxi *China* **59** C12
Lanzarote *Canary Is.* **48** F6
Lanzarote ✈ (ACE) *Canary Is.* **48** F6
Lanzhou *China* **56** F2
Lanzo Torinese *Italy* **40** C4
Lao → *Italy* **43** C9
Lao Bao *Laos* **64** D6
Lao Cai *Vietnam* **58** F4
Laoag *Phil.* **61** B4
Laoang *Phil.* **61** E6
Laoha He → *China* **57** C11
Laohekou *China* **59** A8
Laois □ *Ireland* **12** D4
Laon *France* **19** C10
Laona *U.S.A.* **112** C10
Laos ■ *Asia* **64** D5
Lapa *Brazil* **127** B6
Lapai *Nigeria* **83** D6
Lapalisse *France* **19** F10
Lapeer *U.S.A.* **113** D12
Lapeyrade *France* **20** D3
Lapithos *Cyprus* **49** D12
Lapland = Lappland *Europe* **8** B21
LaPorte *Ind., U.S.A.* **112** E10
Laporte *Pa., U.S.A.* **115** E8
Lapovo *Serbia* **44** B5
Lappeenranta *Finland* **32** B5
Lappland *Europe* **8** B21
Lappo = Lapua *Finland* **8** E20
Laprida *Argentina* **126** D3
Lapseki *Turkey* **45** F10
Laptev Sea *Russia* **53** B13
Lapua *Finland* **8** E20
Lāpuş → *Romania* **29** C8
Lăpuş, Munţii *Romania* **29** C8
Lăpuşna *Moldova* **29** D13
Łapy *Poland* **31** F9
Laqiya Arba'in *Sudan* **80** C2
Laqiya Umran *Sudan* **80** D2
L'Áquila *Italy* **41** F10
Lār *Āzarbājān-e Sharqī, Iran* **70** B5
Lār *Fārs, Iran* **71** E7
Larabanga *Ghana* **82** D4
Laragne-Montéglin *France* **21** D9
Laramie *U.S.A.* **108** F11
Laramie → *U.S.A.* **108** F11
Laranjeiras do Sul *Brazil* **127** B5
Larantuka *Indonesia* **63** F6
Larat *Indonesia* **63** F8
L'Arbresle *France* **21** C8
Lärbro *Sweden* **11** G12
Larde *Mozam.* **87** F4
Larder Lake *Canada* **104** C4
Lardos, Akra = Lindos,
  Akra *Greece* **49** C10
Lardos, Ormos *Greece* **49** C10
Lare *Kenya* **86** C4
Laredo *Spain* **36** B7
Laredo *U.S.A.* **116** H5
Laredo Sd. *Canada* **102** C3
Largentière *France* **21** D8
L'Argentière-la-Bessée
  France **21** D10
Largo *U.S.A.* **117** H13
Largs *U.K.* **13** F4
Lari *Italy* **40** E7
Lariang *Indonesia* **63** E5
Larimore *U.S.A.* **112** B5
Larino *Italy* **41** G11
Larisa *Greece* **46** B4
Larissas □ *Greece* **46** B4
Larkana *Pakistan* **68** F3
Larnaca *Cyprus* **49** E12
Larnaca Bay *Cyprus* **49** E12

Larne *U.K.* **12** B6
Larned *U.S.A.* **112** F4
Laroquebrou *France* **20** D6
Larose *U.S.A.* **117** G9
Larrimah *Australia* **92** C5
Larsen Ice Shelf *Antarctica* **5** C17
Laruns *France* **20** F3
Larvik *Norway* **9** G14
Larzac, Causse du *France* **20** E7
Las Alpujarras *Spain* **39** J1
Las Animas *U.S.A.* **108** G12
Las Anod *Somali Rep.* **75** F4
Las Arenas *Spain* **36** B6
Las Batuecas △ *Spain* **36** E4
Las Brenãs *Argentina* **126** B3
Las Cabezas de San Juan
  Spain **37** J5
Las Cañadas del Teide △
  Canary Is. **48** F3
Las Cejas *Argentina* **128** B4
Las Chimeneas *Mexico* **111** N10
Las Cruces *U.S.A.* **109** K10
Las Flores *Argentina* **126** D4
Las Heras *Argentina* **126** C2
Las Lajas *Argentina* **128** D2
Las Lomitas *Argentina* **126** A3
Las Marismas *Spain* **37** H4
Las Minas *Spain* **39** G3
Las Navas de la
  Concepción *Spain* **37** H5
Las Navas del Marqués *Spain* **36** E6
Las Palmas *Argentina* **126** B4
Las Palmas *Canary Is.* **48** F4
Las Palmas → *Mexico* **111** N10
Las Palmas ✈ (LPA)
  Canary Is. **48** G4
Las Palmas de Cocalán △
  Chile **126** C1
Las Pedroñas *Spain* **39** F2
Las Piedras *Uruguay* **127** C4
Las Pipinas *Argentina* **126** D4
Las Plumas *Argentina* **128** E3
Las Rosas *Argentina* **126** C3
Las Rozas *Spain* **36** E7
Las Tablas *Panama* **120** E3
Las Termas *Argentina* **126** B3
Las Toscas *Argentina* **126** B4
Las Truchas *Mexico* **118** D4
Las Tunas *Cuba* **120** B4
Las Varillas *Argentina* **126** C3
Las Vegas N. Mex., *U.S.A.* **109** J11
Las Vegas *Nev., U.S.A.* **111** J11
Las Vegas McCarran Int. ✈
  (LAS) U.S.A. **111** J11
Lasarte *Spain* **38** B2
Lascano *Uruguay* **127** C5
Lash-e Joveyn *Afghan.* **66** D2
Lashburn *Canada* **103** C7
Lashio *Burma* **67** H20
Lashkar *India* **68** F8
Łasin *Poland* **30** E6
Lasithi *Greece* **49** D7
Lasithi □ *Greece* **49** D7
Läsjerd *Iran* **71** C7
Łask *Poland* **31** G6
Łaskarzew *Poland* **31** G8
Laško *Slovenia* **41** B12
Lassay-les-Châteaux *France* **18** D6
Lassen Pk. *U.S.A.* **108** F3
Lassen Volcanic △ *U.S.A.* **108** F3
Last Mountain L. *Canada* **103** C7
Lastchance Cr. → *U.S.A.* **110** E5
Lastoursville *Gabon* **84** E2
Lastovo *Croatia* **41** F13
Lastovski Kanal *Croatia* **41** F14
Lat Yao *Thailand* **64** E2
Latacunga *Ecuador* **124** D3
Latakia = Al Lādhiqīyah
  Syria **72** E6
Latchford *Canada* **104** C4
Late *Tonga* **91** c
Latehar *India* **69** H11
Laterza *Italy* **43** B9
Latham *Australia* **93** E2
Lathen *Germany* **24** C3
Lathi *India* **68** G4
Lathrop Wells *U.S.A.* **111** J10
Latiano *Italy* **43** B10
Latina *Italy* **42** A5
Latisana *Italy* **41** C10
Latium = Lazio □ *Italy* **41** F9
Laton *U.S.A.* **110** J7
Latorytsya → *Slovak Rep.* **27** C14
Latouche Treville, C.
  Australia **92** C3
Latrobe *Australia* **95** G4
Latrobe *U.S.A.* **114** F5
Latrónico *Italy* **43** B9
Latvia ■ *Europe* **32** D2
Lau *Nigeria* **83** D7
Lau Group *Fiji* **91** a
Lauchhammer *Germany* **24** D9
Lauda-Königshofen *Germany* **25** F5
Lauenburg *Germany* **24** B6
Lauenburgische Seen △
  Germany **24** B6
Lauf *Germany* **25** F7

Laughlin *U.S.A.* **109** J6
Laujar de Andarax *Spain* **39** H2
Laukaa *Finland* **8** E21
Launceston *Australia* **95** G4
Launceston *U.K.* **15** G3
Laune → *Ireland* **12** D2
Launglon Bok *Burma* **64** F1
Laupheim *Germany* **25** G5
Laura *Australia* **94** B3
Laureana di Borrello *Italy* **43** D9
Laurel *Miss., U.S.A.* **117** F10
Laurel *Mont., U.S.A.* **108** D9
Laurel Hill *U.S.A.* **114** F5
Laurencekirk *U.K.* **13** E6
Laurens *U.S.A.* **117** D13
Laurentian Plateau *Canada* **105** B6
Lauria *Italy* **43** B8
Laurie L. *Canada* **103** B8
Laurinburg *U.S.A.* **117** D15
Laurium *U.S.A.* **112** B9
Lausanne *Switz.* **25** J2
Laut *Indonesia* **62** D3
Laut, Pulau *Indonesia* **62** E5
Laut Kecil, Kepulauan *Indonesia* **62** E5
Lauterbach *Germany* **24** E5
Lauterecken *Germany* **25** F3
Lautoka *Fiji* **91** a
Lauzès *France* **20** D5
Lava → *Russia* **30** D8
Lava Beds △ *U.S.A.* **108** F3
Lavagh More *Ireland* **12** B3
Lavagna *Italy* **40** D6
Laval *France* **18** D6
Laval-des-Rapides *Canada* **104** C5
Lavalle *Argentina* **126** B2
Lavant Station *Canada* **115** A8
Lāvar Meydān *Iran* **71** D7
Lavara *Greece* **45** E8
Lavardac *France* **20** D4
Lavaur *France* **20** E5
Lavelanet *France* **20** F5
Lavello *Italy* **43** A8
Laverton *Australia* **93** E3
Lavis *Italy* **40** B8
Lavos *Portugal* **36** E2
Lavradio *Portugal* **37** G1
Lavras *Brazil* **127** A7
Lavre *Portugal* **37** G2
Lavrio *Greece* **46** D6
Lavris *Greece* **49** D6
Lavumisa *Swaziland* **89** D5
Lavushi Manda △ *Zambia* **87** E3
Lawaki *Fiji* **91** a
Lawas *Malaysia* **62** D5
Lawele *Indonesia* **63** F6
Lawn Hill △ *Australia* **94** B2
Lawqah *Si. Arabia* **70** D4
Lawra *Ghana* **82** C4
Lawrence *N.Z.* **91** F2
Lawrence *Ind., U.S.A.* **112** F10
Lawrence *Kans., U.S.A.* **112** F6
Lawrence *Mass., U.S.A.* **115** D13
Lawrenceburg *Ind., U.S.A.* **113** F11
Lawrenceburg *Tenn., U.S.A.* **117** D11
Lawrenceville *Ga., U.S.A.* **117** E13
Lawrenceville *Pa., U.S.A.* **114** E7
Laws *U.S.A.* **110** H8
Lawton *U.S.A.* **116** D5
Lawu *Indonesia* **63** G14
Lawz, J. al *Si. Arabia* **80** B4
Laxå *Sweden* **11** F8
Laxford, L. *U.K.* **13** C3
Laxou *France* **19** D13
Lay → *Russia* **20** B2
Layla *Si. Arabia* **75** C4
Laylān *Iraq* **70** C5
Layon → *France* **18** E6
Layton *U.S.A.* **108** F8
Laytonville *U.S.A.* **108** G2
Lazarevac *Serbia* **44** B4
Lazarevskoye *Russia* **35** J4
Lazarivo *Madag.* **89** C8
Lázaro Cárdenas *Mexico* **118** D4
Lazdijai *Lithuania* **30** D10
Lazio □ *Italy* **41** F9
Lazo *Moldova* **29** C13
Lazo *Russia* **54** C6
Le Beausset *France* **21** E9
Le Bic *Canada* **105** C6
Le Blanc *France* **20** B5
Le Bleymard *France* **20** D7
Le Bourgneuf-la-Fôret *France* **18** D6
Le Bugue *France* **20** D4
Le Cateau Cambrésis *France* **19** B10
Le Caylar *France* **20** E7
Le Chambon-Feugerolles *France* **21** C8
Le Châtelet *France* **19** F9
Le Chesne *France* **19** C11
Le Cheylard *France* **21** D8
Le Conquet *France* **18** D2
Le Creusot *France* **19** F11
Le Croisic *France* **18** E4
Le Donjon *France* **19** F10

Le Dorat *France* **20** B5
Le François *Martinique* **120** c
Le Gosier *Guadeloupe* **120** b
Le Grand-Lucé *France* **18** E7
Le Grand-Pressigny *France* **18** F7
Le Grand-Quevilly *France* **18** C8
Le Gris Gris *Mauritius* **85** d
Le Havre *France* **18** C7
Le Lamentin *Martinique* **120** c
Le Lavandou *France* **21** E10
Le Lion-d'Angers *France* **18** E6
Le Louroux-Béconnais *France* **18** E6
Le Luc *France* **21** E10
Le Lude *France* **18** E7
Le Mans *France* **18** E7
Le Marin *Martinique* **120** c
Le Mars *France* **112** D5
Le Mayet-de-Montagne *France* **19** F10
Le Mêle-sur-Sarthe *France* **18** D7
Le Monastier-sur-Gazeille *France* **20** D7
Le Monêtier-les-Bains *France* **21** D10
Le Mont-Dore *France* **20** C6
Le Mont-St-Michel *France* **18** D5
Le Moule *Guadeloupe* **120** b
Le Muy *France* **21** E10
Le Palais *France* **18** E3
Le Perthus *France* **20** F6
Le Port *Réunion* **85** c
Le Prêcheur *Martinique* **120** c
Le Puy-en-Velay *France* **20** C7
Le Robert *Martinique* **120** c
Le St-Esprit *Martinique* **120** c
Le Sueur *U.S.A.* **112** C7
Le Tampon *Réunion* **85** c
Le Teil *France* **21** D8
Le Teilleul *France* **18** D6
Le Theil *France* **18** D7
Le Thillot *France* **19** E13
Le Thuy *Vietnam* **64** D6
Le Touquet-Paris-Plage *France* **19** B8
Le Tréport *France* **18** B8
Le Val-d'Ajol *France* **19** E13
Le Verdon-sur-Mer *France* **20** C2
Le Vigan *France* **20** E7
Lea → *U.K.* **15** F8
Leach *Cambodia* **65** F4
Lead *U.S.A.* **112** C2
Leader *Canada* **103** C7
Leadville *U.S.A.* **108** G10
Leaf → *U.S.A.* **117** F10
Leaf Rapids *Canada* **103** B9
Leamington *Canada* **114** D2
Leamington *U.S.A.* **108** G7
Leamington Spa = Royal Leamington Spa *U.K.* **15** E6
Le'an *China* **59** D10
Leandro Norte Alem *Argentina* **127** B4
Leane, L. *Ireland* **12** D2
Learmonth *Australia* **92** D1
Leask *Canada* **103** C7
Leatherhead *U.K.* **15** F7
Leavenworth *Kans., U.S.A.* **112** F6
Leavenworth *Wash., U.S.A.* **108** C3
Leawood *U.S.A.* **112** F6
Łeba *Poland* **30** D4
Łeba → *Poland* **30** D4
Lebach *Germany* **25** F2
Lebak *Phil.* **61** H6
Lebane *Serbia* **44** D5
Lebam *U.S.A.* **110** D3
Lebanon *Ind., U.S.A.* **112** E10
Lebanon *Kans., U.S.A.* **112** F4
Lebanon *Ky., U.S.A.* **113** G11
Lebanon *Mo., U.S.A.* **112** G7
Lebanon *N.H., U.S.A.* **115** C12
Lebanon *Oreg., U.S.A.* **108** D2
Lebanon *Pa., U.S.A.* **115** F8
Lebanon *Tenn., U.S.A.* **117** C11
Lebanon ■ *Asia* **74** B5
Lebec *Canada* **111** L8
Lebedyan *Russia* **33** F10
Lebedyn *Ukraine* **33** G8
Lebel-sur-Quévillon *Canada* **104** C4
Lebomboberge *S. Africa* **89** C5
Lębork *Poland* **30** D4
Lebrija *Spain* **37** J4
Łebsko, Jezioro *Poland* **30** D4
Lebu *Chile* **126** D1
Leca da Palmeira *Portugal* **36** D2
Lecce *Italy* **43** B11
Lecco *Italy* **40** C6
Lecco, L. di *Italy* **40** C6
Lécera *Spain* **38** D4
Lech *Austria* **26** D3
Lech → *Germany* **25** G6
Lechang *China* **59** E9
Lechena *Greece* **46** D3
Lechtaler Alpen *Austria* **26** D3
Lecontes Mills *U.S.A.* **114** E6
Lectoure *France* **20** E4
Łęczna *Poland* **31** G9

Łęczyca *Poland* **31** F6
Ledesma *Spain* **36** D5
Ledong *China* **64** C7
Leduc *Canada* **102** C6
Lee *U.S.A.* **115** D11
Lee → *Ireland* **12** E3
Lee Vining *U.S.A.* **110** H7
Leech L. *U.S.A.* **112** B6
Leechburg *U.S.A.* **114** F5
Leeds *U.K.* **14** D6
Leeds *U.S.A.* **117** E11
Leek *Neths.* **17** A6
Leek *U.K.* **14** D5
Leeman *Australia* **93** E1
Leeper *U.S.A.* **114** E5
Leer *Germany* **24** B3
Leesburg *U.S.A.* **117** G14
Leesville *U.S.A.* **116** F8
Leeton *Australia* **95** E4
Leetonia *U.S.A.* **114** F4
Leeu Gamka *S. Africa* **88** E3
Leeuwarden *Neths.* **17** A5
Leeuwin, C. *Australia* **93** F2
Leeuwin Naturaliste △ *Australia* **93** F2
Leeward Is. *Atl. Oc.* **121** C7
Lefka *Cyprus* **49** D11
Lefkada *Greece* **46** C2
Lefkimis *Greece* **49** B4
Lefkimis, Akra *Greece* **49** B4
Lefkímmi = Lefkimis *Greece* **49** B4
Lefkoniko *Cyprus* **49** D12
Lefroy *Canada* **114** B5
Lefroy, L. *Australia* **93** F3
Łeg → *Poland* **31** H8
Leganés *Spain* **36** B7
Legazpi *Phil.* **61** E5
Lège-Cap-Ferret *France* **20** D2
Lege Hida *Ethiopia* **81** F5
Legendre I. *Australia* **92** D2
Leghorn = Livorno *Italy* **40** E7
Legionowo *Poland* **31** F7
Legnago *Italy* **41** C8
Legnano *Italy* **40** C5
Legnica *Poland* **31** G3
Legrad *Croatia* **41** B13
Leh *India* **69** B7
Lehigh Acres *U.S.A.* **117** H14
Lehighton *U.S.A.* **115** F9
Lehliu *Romania* **29** F11
Leho *Sudan* **81** F3
Lehrte *Germany* **24** C5
Lehututu *Botswana* **88** C3
Lei Shui → *China* **59** D9
Leiah *Pakistan* **68** D4
Leibnitz *Austria* **26** E8
Leibo *China* **58** C4
Leicester *U.K.* **15** E6
Leicester City □ *U.K.* **15** E6
Leicestershire □ *U.K.* **15** E6
Leichhardt → *Australia* **94** B2
Leichhardt Ra. *Australia* **94** C4
Leiden *Neths.* **17** B4
Leie → *Belgium* **17** C3
Leifers = Láives *Italy* **41** B8
Leimen *Germany* **25** F4
Leine → *Germany* **24** C5
Leinefelde *Germany* **24** D6
Leinster *Australia* **93** E3
Leinster □ *Ireland* **12** C5
Leinster, Mt. *Ireland* **12** D5
Leipalingis *Lithuania* **30** D10
Leipzig *Germany* **24** D8
Leiria *Portugal* **36** F2
Leiria □ *Portugal* **36** F2
Leirvik *Norway* **9** G11
Leishan *China* **58** D7
Leisler, Mt. *Australia* **92** D4
Leith *U.K.* **13** F5
Leith Hill *U.K.* **15** F7
Leitha → *Europe* **27** D10
Leitrim *Ireland* **12** B3
Leitrim □ *Ireland* **12** B4
Leitza *Spain* **38** B3
Leiyang *China* **59** D9
Leizhou *China* **59** G8
Leizhou Bandao *China* **58** G7
Leizhou Wan *China* **59** G8
Lek → *Neths.* **17** C4
Leka *Norway* **8** D14
Lekani *Greece* **45** E8
Lekbibaj *Albania* **44** D3
Lekeitio *Spain* **38** B2
Lekoui *Burkina Faso* **82** C4
Leksand *Sweden* **10** D9
Leland *U.S.A.* **113** C11
Lelâng *Sweden* **10** E6
Leleque *Argentina* **128** E2
Lelystad *Neths.* **17** B5
Lem *Denmark* **11** H2
Lema *Nigeria* **83** C5
Lema Shilindi *Ethiopia* **81** G5
Léman, L. *Europe* **19** F13
Lembar *Indonesia* **63** K19
Lembuak *Indonesia* **63** K19
Lemera *Dem. Rep. of the Congo* **86** C2
Lemery *Phil.* **61** E4

Lemhi Ra. *U.S.A.* **108** D7
Lemmer *Neths.* **17** B5
Lemmon *U.S.A.* **112** C2
Lemon Grove *U.S.A.* **111** N9
Lemoore *U.S.A.* **110** J7
Lempdes *France* **20** C7
Lemvig *Denmark* **11** H2
Lena → *Russia* **53** B13
Lenadoon Pt. *Ireland* **12** B2
Lenart *Slovenia* **41** B12
Lenartovce *Slovak Rep.* **27** C13
Lencloître *France* **18** F7
Lendava *Slovenia* **41** B13
Lendeh *Iran* **71** D6
Lendinara *Italy* **41** C8
Lengerich *Germany* **24** C3
Lenggong *Malaysia* **65** K3
Lenggries *Germany* **25** H7
Lengshuijiang *China* **59** D8
Lengshuitan *China* **59** D8
Lengua de Vaca, Pta. *Chile* **126** C1
Lengwe △ *Malawi* **87** F3
Lengyeltóti *Hungary* **28** D2
Lenhovda *Sweden* **11** G9
Lenina, Kanal → *Russia* **35** J7
Leningrad = St. Petersburg *Russia* **32** C7
Lenino *Ukraine* **33** K8
Leninogorsk *Kazakhstan* **52** D9
Leninsk *Russia* **35** F7
Leninsk-Kuznetskiy *Russia* **52** D9
Leninskoye *Russia* **34** A8
Lenk *Switz.* **25** J3
Lenkoran = Länkäran *Azerbaijan* **73** C13
Lenmalu *Indonesia* **63** E8
Lenne → *Germany* **24** D3
Lennestadt *Germany* **24** D4
Lennox *U.S.A.* **112** D5
Lennoxville *Canada* **115** A13
Leno *Italy* **40** C7
Lenoir *U.S.A.* **117** D14
Lenoir City *U.S.A.* **117** D12
Lenore L. *Canada* **103** C8
Lenox *U.S.A.* **115** D11
Lens *France* **19** B9
Lensahn *Germany* **24** A6
Lensk *Russia* **53** C12
Lentas *Greece* **49** E6
Lentekhi *Georgia* **35** J6
Lenti *Hungary* **28** D1
Lentini *Italy* **43** E8
Lenwood *U.S.A.* **111** L9
Lenya *Burma* **65** G2
Lenzen *Germany* **24** B7
Léo *Burkina Faso* **82** C4
Leoben *Austria* **26** D8
Leodhas = Lewis *U.K.* **13** C2
Leola *U.S.A.* **112** C4
Leominster *U.K.* **15** E5
Leominster *U.S.A.* **115** D13
Léon *France* **20** E2
León *Mexico* **118** C4
León *Nic.* **120** D2
León *Spain* **36** C5
Leon *U.S.A.* **112** E7
León □ *Spain* **36** C4
León, Montes de *Spain* **36** C4
Leonardo da Vinci, Roma ✈ (FCO) *Italy* **41** G9
Leonardtown *U.S.A.* **113** F15
Leonardville *Namibia* **88** C2
Leonberg *Germany* **25** G5
Leonding *Austria* **26** C7
Leone *Amer. Samoa* **91** b
Leonessa *Italy* **41** F9
Leonforte *Italy* **43** E7
Leongatha *Australia* **95** F4
Leonidio *Greece* **46** D4
Leonora *Australia* **93** E3
Leopoldina *Brazil* **127** A7
Leopoldsburg *Belgium* **17** C5
Leoti *U.S.A.* **112** F4
Leova *Moldova* **29** D13
Leoville *Canada* **103** C7
Lepe *Spain* **37** H3
Lepel = Lyepyel *Belarus* **32** E5
Lepenou *Greece* **46** C3
Leping *China* **59** C11
Lépo, L. do *Angola* **88** B2
Lepontine, Alpi *Italy* **40** B5
Leppävirta *Finland* **8** E22
Lepsény *Hungary* **28** D3
Leptis Magna *Libya* **79** B8
Lequeitio = Lekeitio *Spain* **38** B2
Lercara Friddi *Italy* **42** E6
Léré *Chad* **83** D7
Léré *Mali* **82** B4
Lere *Bauchi, Nigeria* **83** D6
Lere *Kaduna, Nigeria* **83** C6
Leribe *Lesotho* **89** D4
Lérici *Italy* **40** D6
Lérida = Lleida *Spain* **38** D5
Lérins, Îs. de *France* **21** E11
Lerma *Spain* **36** C7
Leros *Greece* **47** D8
Lérouville *France* **19** D12

Lerum *Sweden* **11** G6
Lerwick *U.K.* **13** A7
Leş *Romania* **28** D6
Les Abrets *France* **21** C9
Les Andelys *France* **18** C8
Les Borges Blanques *Spain* **38** D5
Les Cayes *Haiti* **121** C5
Les Coteaux *Canada* **115** A10
Les Escoumins *Canada* **105** C6
Les Essarts *France* **18** F5
Les Herbiers *France* **18** F5
Les Minquiers, Plateau des *Chan. Is.* **18** D4
Les Pieux *France* **18** C5
Les Ponts-de-Cé *France* **18** E6
Les Riceys *France* **19** E11
Les Sables-d'Olonne *France* **20** B2
Les Vans *France* **21** D8
Lesbos = Lesvos *Greece* **47** B8
L'Escala *Spain* **38** C8
Leshan *China* **58** C4
Leshwe △ *Dem. Rep. of the Congo* **87** E2
Lésina *Italy* **41** G12
Lésina, L. di *Italy* **41** G12
Lesjöfors *Sweden* **10** E8
Lesko *Poland* **31** J9
Leskov I. *Antarctica* **5** B1
Leskovac *Serbia* **44** C5
Leskovik *Albania* **44** F4
Leśna *Poland* **31** G2
Lesneven *France* **18** D2
Leśnica *Poland* **31** H5
Lešnica *Serbia* **44** B3
Lesnoye *Russia* **32** C8
Lesopilnoye *Russia* **54** A7
Lesotho ■ *Africa* **89** D4
Lesozavodsk *Russia* **54** B6
Lesparre-Médoc *France* **20** C3
Lessay *France* **18** C5
Lesse → *Belgium* **17** D4
Lesse et Lomme △ *Belgium* **17** D5
Lessebo *Sweden* **11** H9
Lesser Antilles *W. Indies* **121** D7
Lesser Slave L. *Canada* **102** B5
Lesser Sunda Is. *Indonesia* **63** F6
Lessines *Belgium* **17** D3
Lester B. Pearson Int., Toronto ✈ (YYZ) *Canada* **114** C5
Lestock *Canada* **103** C8
Lesueur I. *Australia* **92** B4
Lesueur △ *Australia* **93** F2
Lésvos = Lesbos *Greece* **47** B8
Leszno *Poland* **31** G3
Letaba *S. Africa* **89** C5
Letälven → *Sweden* **10** E8
Létavértes *Hungary* **28** C6
Letchworth *U.K.* **15** F7
Letea, Ostrov *Romania* **29** E14
Lethbridge *Canada* **102** D6
Lethem *Guyana* **124** C7
Leti, Kepulauan *Indonesia* **63** F7
Leti Is. = Leti, Kepulauan *Indonesia* **63** F7
Letiahau → *Botswana* **88** C3
Leticia *Colombia* **124** D5
Leting *China* **57** E10
Letjiesbos *S. Africa* **88** E3
Letlhakane *Botswana* **88** C4
Letlhakeng *Botswana* **88** C3
Letpadan *Burma* **67** L19
Letpan *Burma* **67** K19
Letsôk-aw Kyun *Burma* **65** G2
Letterkenny *Ireland* **12** B4
Leu *Romania* **29** F9
Leucadia *U.S.A.* **111** M9
Leucate *France* **20** F7
Leucate, Étang de *France* **20** F7
Leuchars *U.K.* **13** E6
Leuk *Switz.* **25** J3
Leuşeni *Moldova* **29** D13
Leuser, G. *Indonesia* **62** D1
Leutkirch *Germany* **25** H6
Leuven *Belgium* **17** D4
Leuze-en-Hainaut *Belgium* **17** D3
Lev Tolstoy *Russia* **32** F10
Levan *Albania* **44** F3
Levanger *Norway* **8** E14
Levant, Î. du *France* **21** E10
Lévanto *Italy* **40** D6
Lévanzo *Italy* **42** D5
Levelland *U.S.A.* **116** E3
Leven *U.K.* **13** E6
Leven, L. *U.K.* **13** E5
Leven, Toraka *Madag.* **89** A8
Leveque C. *Australia* **92** C3
Leverano *Italy* **43** B10
Leverkusen *Germany* **24** D2
Levice *Slovak Rep.* **27** C11
Lévico Terme *Italy* **41** C8
Levie *France* **21** G13
Levier *France* **19** F13
Levin *N.Z.* **91** D5
Lévis *Canada* **105** C5
Levis, L. *Canada* **102** A5
Levitha *Greece* **47** D8
Levittown *N.Y., U.S.A.* **115** F11

Levittown *Pa., U.S.A.* **115** F10
Levka *Bulgaria* **45** E10
Levka Oros *Greece* **49** D6
Levkada = Lefkada *Greece* **46** C2
Levkás = Lefkada *Greece* **46** C2
Levkôsia = Nicosia *Cyprus* **49** D12
Levoča *Slovak Rep.* **27** B13
Levroux *France* **19** F8
Levski *Bulgaria* **45** C9
Levskigrad = Karlovo *Bulgaria* **45** D9
Levuka *Fiji* **91** a
Lewes *U.K.* **15** G8
Lewes *U.S.A.* **113** F16
Lewin Brzeski *Poland* **31** H4
Lewis → *U.S.A.* **110** E4
Lewis, Butt of *U.K.* **13** C2
Lewis Ra. *Australia* **92** D4
Lewis Range *U.S.A.* **108** B7
Lewis Run *U.S.A.* **114** E6
Lewisburg *Pa., U.S.A.* **114** F8
Lewisburg *Tenn., U.S.A.* **117** D11
Lewisburg *W. Va., U.S.A.* **113** G13
Lewisporte *Canada* **105** C8
Lewiston *Idaho, U.S.A.* **108** C5
Lewiston *Maine, U.S.A.* **113** C18
Lewiston *N.Y., U.S.A.* **114** C5
Lewistown *Mont., U.S.A.* **108** C9
Lewistown *Pa., U.S.A.* **114** F7
Lexington *Ill., U.S.A.* **112** E9
Lexington *Ky., U.S.A.* **113** F11
Lexington *Mich., U.S.A.* **114** C2
Lexington *Mo., U.S.A.* **112** F7
Lexington *N.C., U.S.A.* **117** D15
Lexington *N.Y., U.S.A.* **115** D10
Lexington *Nebr., U.S.A.* **112** E4
Lexington *Ohio, U.S.A.* **114** F2
Lexington *Tenn., U.S.A.* **117** D10
Lexington *Va., U.S.A.* **113** G14
Lexington Park *U.S.A.* **113** F15
Leyburn *U.K.* **14** C6
Leye *China* **58** E6
Leyland *U.K.* **14** D5
Leyre → *France* **20** D2
Leyte □ *Phil.* **61** F6
Leyte Gulf *Phil.* **61** F6
Leżajsk *Poland* **31** H9
Lezay *France* **20** B3
Lezha *Albania* **44** E3
Lezhi *China* **58** B5
Lézignan-Corbières *France* **20** E6
Lezoux *France* **20** C7
Lgov *Russia* **33** G8
Lhasa *China* **60** D4
Lhazê *China* **60** D3
Lhokkruet *Indonesia* **62** D1
Lhokseumawe *Indonesia* **62** C1
L'Hospitalet de Llobregat *Spain* **38** D7
Li *Thailand* **64** D2
Li Jiang → *China* **59** E8
Li Shui → *China* **59** C9
Li Xian *Gansu, China* **56** G3
Li Xian *Hebei, China* **56** E8
Li Xian *Hunan, China* **59** C8
Liadi *China* **58** C7
Liancheng *China* **59** E11
Liancourt Rocks = Tok-do *Asia* **55** F5
Lianga *Phil.* **61** G7
Liangcheng *Nei Monggol Zizhiqu, China* **56** D7
Liangcheng *Shandong, China* **57** G10
Liangdang *China* **56** H4
Lianghe *China* **58** E2
Lianghekou *China* **58** C7
Liangping *China* **58** B6
Liangpran *Indonesia* **62** D4
Lianhua *China* **59** D9
Lianjiang *Fujian, China* **59** D12
Lianjiang *Guangdong, China* **59** G8
Lianping *China* **59** E10
Lianshan *China* **59** E9
Lianshanguan *China* **57** D12
Lianshui *China* **57** H10
Lianyuan *China* **59** D8
Lianyungang *China* **57** G10
Lianzhou *China* **59** E9
Liao He → *China* **57** D11
Liaocheng *China* **56** F8
Liaodong Bandao *China* **57** E12
Liaodong Wan *China* **57** D11
Liaoning □ *China* **57** D12
Liaotung, G. of = Liaodong Wan *China* **57** D11
Liaoyang *China* **57** D12
Liaoyuan *China* **57** C13
Liaozhong *China* **57** D12
Liard → *Canada* **102** A4
Liard River *Canada* **102** B3
Liari *Pakistan* **68** G2
Libau = Liepāja *Latvia* **30** H9
Libby *U.S.A.* **108** B6
Libenge *Dem. Rep. of the Congo* **84** D3
Liberal *U.S.A.* **112** G3
Liberec *Czech Rep.* **26** A8

Liberecký □ *Czech Rep.* **26** A8
Liberia *Costa Rica* **120** D2
Liberia ■ *W. Afr.* **82** D3
Liberty *Mo., U.S.A.* **112** F6
Liberty *N.Y., U.S.A.* **115** E10
Liberty *Tex., U.S.A.* **116** F7
Liberty-Newark Int. ✈
(EWR) *U.S.A.* **115** F10
Libiąż *Poland* **31** H6
Lībīya, Sahrā' *Africa* **79** C10
Libo *China* **58** E6
Libobo, Tanjung *Indonesia* **63** E7
Libode *S. Africa* **89** E4
Libohovë *Albania* **44** F4
Libourne *France* **20** D3
Libramont *Belgium* **17** E5
Librazhd *Albania* **44** E4
Libreville *Gabon* **84** D1
Libya ■ *N. Afr.* **79** C9
Libyan Desert = Lībīya,
Sahrā' *Africa* **79** C10
Libyan Plateau = Ed Déffa
Egypt **80** A2
Licantén *Chile* **126** D1
Licata *Italy* **42** E6
Lice *Turkey* **73** C9
Licheng *China* **56** F7
Lichfield *U.K.* **15** E6
Lichinga *Mozam.* **87** E4
Lichtenburg *S. Africa* **88** D4
Lichtenfels *Germany* **25** E7
Lichuan *Hubei, China* **58** B7
Lichuan *Jiangxi, China* **59** D11
Licking ➜ *U.S.A.* **113** F11
Licosa, Punta *Italy* **43** B7
Licungo ➜ *Mozam.* **87** F4
Lida *Belarus* **23** B13
Liden *Sweden* **10** B10
Lidhult *Sweden* **11** H7
Lidköping *Sweden* **11** F7
Lido *Italy* **41** C9
Lido *Niger* **83** C5
Lido di Roma = Óstia, Lido
di *Italy* **41** G9
Lidoriki *Greece* **46** C4
Lidzbark *Poland* **31** E6
Lidzbark Warmiński *Poland* **30** D7
Liebenwalde *Germany* **24** C9
Lieberose *Germany* **24** D10
Liebig, Mt. *Australia* **92** D5
Liebling *Romania* **28** E6
Liechtenstein ■ *Europe* **25** H5
Liège *Belgium* **17** D5
Liège □ *Belgium* **17** D5
Liegnitz = Legnica *Poland* **31** G3
Lieksa *Finland* **8** E24
Lienart *Dem. Rep. of the Congo* **86** B2
Lienyünchiangshih =
Lianyungang *China* **57** G10
Lienz *Austria* **26** E5
Liepāja *Latvia* **30** B8
Liepāja □ *Latvia* **30** B8
Liepājas ezers *Latvia* **30** B8
Lier *Belgium* **17** C4
Liernais *France* **19** E11
Lieşti *Romania* **29** E12
Lietuva = Lithuania ■
Europe **32** E2
Liévin *France* **19** B9
Lièvre ➜ *Canada* **104** C4
Liezen *Austria* **26** D7
Liffey ➜ *Ireland* **12** C5
Lifford *Ireland* **12** B4
Liffré *France* **18** D5
Lifudzin *Russia* **54** B7
Ligao *Phil.* **61** E5
Lightning Ridge *Australia* **95** D4
Lignano Sabbiadoro *Italy* **41** C10
Ligny-en-Barrois *France* **19** D12
Ligonha ➜ *Mozam.* **87** F4
Ligonier *U.S.A.* **114** F5
Ligourio *Greece* **46** D5
Ligueil *France* **18** E7
Liguria □ *Italy* **40** D5
Ligurian Sea *Medit. S.* **40** E5
Lihou Reefs and Cays
Australia **94** B5
Lihue *U.S.A.* **106** a
Lihué Calel △ *Argentina* **126** D2
Lijiang *China* **58** D3
Likasi *Dem. Rep. of the Congo* **87** E2
Likenäs *Sweden* **10** D7
Likhoslavl *Russia* **32** D8
Likhovskoy *Russia* **33** H11
Likoma I. *Malawi* **87** E3
Likumburu *Tanzania* **87** D4
L'Île-Bouchard *France* **18** E7
L'Île-Rousse *France* **21** F12
Liling *China* **59** D9
Lilla Edet *Sweden* **11** F6
Lille *France* **19** B10
Lille Bælt *Denmark* **11** J3
Lillebonne *France* **18** C7
Lillehammer *Norway* **8** F14
Lillesand *Norway* **9** G13
Lillhärdal *Sweden* **10** C8

Lillian Pt. *Australia* **93** E4
Lillo *Spain* **36** F7
Lillooet *Canada* **102** C4
Lillooet ➜ *Canada* **102** D4
Lilongwe *Malawi* **87** E3
Liloy *Phil.* **63** C6
Lim ➜ *Europe* **44** C3
Lim Chu Kang *Singapore* **65** d
Lima *Indonesia* **63** E7
Lima *Peru* **124** F3
Lima *Mont., U.S.A.* **108** D7
Lima *Ohio, U.S.A.* **113** E11
Lima ➜ *Portugal* **36** D2
Liman *Indonesia* **63** G14
Liman *Russia* **35** H8
Limanowa *Poland* **31** J7
Limassol *Cyprus* **49** E12
Limavady *U.K.* **12** A5
Limay ➜ *Argentina* **128** D3
Limay Mahuida *Argentina* **126** D2
Limbach-Oberfrohna
Germany **24** E8
Limbang *Brunei* **62** D5
Limbara, Mte. *Italy* **42** B2
Limbaži *Latvia* **32** D3
Limbdi *India* **68** H4
Limbe *Cameroon* **83** E6
Limburg *Germany* **25** E4
Limburg □ *Belgium* **17** C5
Limburg □ *Neths.* **17** C5
Limedsforsen *Sweden* **10** D7
Limeira *Brazil* **127** A6
Limenaria *Greece* **45** F8
Limenas Chersonisou *Greece* **47** F7
Limerick *Ireland* **12** D3
Limerick □ *Ireland* **12** D3
Limestone *U.S.A.* **114** D6
Limestone ➜ *Canada* **103** B10
Limfjorden *Denmark* **11** H3
Limia = Lima ➜ *Portugal* **36** D2
Limingen *Norway* **8** D15
Limmared *Sweden* **11** G7
Limmen Bight *Australia* **94** A2
Limmen Bight ➜ *Australia* **94** B2
Limni *Greece* **46** C5
Limnos *Greece* **47** B7
Limoges *Canada* **115** A9
Limoges *France* **20** C5
Limón *Costa Rica* **120** E3
Limon *U.S.A.* **108** G12
Limone Piemonte *Italy* **40** D4
Limousin □ *France* **20** C5
Limousin, Plateaux du
France **20** C5
Limoux *France* **20** E6
Limpopo □ *S. Africa* **89** C4
Limpopo ➜ *Africa* **89** D5
Limuru *Kenya* **86** C4
Lin Xian *China* **56** F6
Lin'an *China* **59** B12
Linapacan I. *Phil.* **61** F3
Linapacan Str. *Phil.* **61** F3
Linares *Chile* **126** D1
Linares *Mexico* **119** C5
Linares *Spain* **37** G7
Linaro, Capo *Italy* **41** F8
Línas Mte. *Italy* **42** C1
Linate, Milano ✈ (LIN) *Italy* **40** C6
Lincang *China* **58** F3
Lincheng *China* **56** F8
Linchuan *China* **59** D11
Lincoln *Argentina* **126** C3
Lincoln *Canada* **114** C5
Lincoln *N.Z.* **91** E4
Lincoln *U.K.* **14** D7
Lincoln *Calif., U.S.A.* **110** G5
Lincoln *Ill., U.S.A.* **112** E9
Lincoln *Kans., U.S.A.* **112** F4
Lincoln *Maine, U.S.A.* **113** C19
Lincoln *N.H., U.S.A.* **115** B13
Lincoln *N. Mex., U.S.A.* **109** K11
Lincoln *Nebr., U.S.A.* **112** E6
Lincoln City *U.S.A.* **108** D1
Lincoln Hav = Lincoln Sea
Arctic **98** A14
Lincolnshire □ *U.K.* **14** D7
Lincolnshire Wolds *U.K.* **14** D7
Lincolnton *U.S.A.* **117** D14
Lind *U.S.A.* **108** C4
Linda *U.S.A.* **110** F5
Lindau *Germany* **25** H5
Lindeman I. *Australia* **94** J7
Linden *Guyana* **124** B7
Linden *Ala., U.S.A.* **117** E11
Linden *Calif., U.S.A.* **110** G5
Linden *Tex., U.S.A.* **116** E7
Lindenhurst *U.S.A.* **115** F11
Lindesberg *Sweden* **10** E9
Lindesnes *Norway* **9** H12
Lindi *Tanzania* **87** D4
Lindi □ *Tanzania* **87** D4
Lindi ➜
Dem. Rep. of the Congo **86** B2
Lindö *Sweden* **11** F10
Lindome *Sweden* **11** G6

Lindos *Greece* **49** C10
Lindos, Akra *Greece* **49** C10
Lindoso *Portugal* **36** D2
Lindow *Germany* **24** C8
Lindsay *Canada* **114** B6
Lindsay *Calif., U.S.A.* **110** J7
Lindsay *Okla., U.S.A.* **116** D6
Lindsborg *U.S.A.* **112** F5
Lindsdal *Sweden* **11** H10
Line Islands *Pac. Oc.* **97** H12
Linfen *China* **56** F6
Ling Xian *Hunan, China* **59** D9
Ling Xian *Shandong, China* **56** F9
Lingao *China* **64** C7
Lingayen *Phil.* **63** A6
Lingayen G. *Phil.* **61** C4
Lingbi *China* **57** H9
Lingbo *Sweden* **10** C10
Lingchuan
Guangxi Zhuangzu, China **59** E8
Lingchuan *Shanxi, China* **56** G7
Lingen *Germany* **24** C3
Lingga *Indonesia* **62** E2
Lingga, Kepulauan *Indonesia* **62** E2
Lingga Arch. = Lingga,
Kepulauan *Indonesia* **62** E2
Linghem *Sweden* **11** F9
Lingle *U.S.A.* **108** E11
Lingqiu *China* **56** E8
Lingshan *China* **58** F7
Lingshi *China* **56** F6
Lingshou *China* **56** E8
Lingshui *China* **64** C8
Lingtai *China* **56** G4
Linguère *Senegal* **82** B1
Lingui *China* **59** E8
Lingwu *China* **56** E4
Lingyuan *China* **57** D10
Lingyun *China* **58** E6
Linhai *China* **59** C13
Linhares *Brazil* **125** G10
Linhe *China* **56** D4
Linjiang *China* **57** D14
Linköping *Sweden* **11** F9
Linkou *China* **57** B16
Linli *China* **59** C8
Linnhe, L. *U.K.* **13** E3
Linqi *China* **56** G7
Linqing *China* **56** F8
Linqu *China* **57** F10
Linru *China* **56** G7
Lins *Brazil* **127** A6
Linshui *China* **58** B6
Linstead *Jamaica* **120** a
Linta ➜ *Madag.* **89** D7
Linth ➜ *Switz.* **25** H5
Linthal *Switz.* **25** J5
Linton *Ind., U.S.A.* **112** F10
Linton *N. Dak., U.S.A.* **112** B3
Lintong *China* **56** G5
Linwood *Canada* **114** C4
Linwu *China* **59** E9
Linxi *China* **57** C10
Linxia *China* **60** C5
Linxiang *China* **59** C9
Linyanti ➜ *Africa* **88** B4
Linyi *China* **57** G10
Linz *Austria* **26** C7
Linz *Germany* **24** E3
Linzhenzhen *China* **56** F5
Linzi *China* **57** F10
Lion, G. du *France* **20** E7
Lionárisso *Cyprus* **49** D13
Lioni *Italy* **43** B8
Lions, G. of = Lion, G. du
France **20** E7
Lion's Den *Zimbabwe* **87** F3
Lion's Head *Canada* **114** B3
Liozno = Lyozna *Belarus* **32** E6
Lipa *Phil.* **61** E4
Lipali *Mozam.* **87** F4
Lipany *Slovak Rep.* **27** B13
Lípari *Italy* **43** D7
Lípari, I. *Italy* **43** D7
Lípari, Is. = Eólie, Ís. *Italy* **43** D7
Lipcani *Moldova* **29** B11
Liperi *Finland* **8** E23
Lipetsk *Russia* **33** F10
Lipetsk □ *Russia* **34** D4
Lipiany *Poland* **31** E1
Liping *China* **58** D7
Lipisi *Greece* **47** D8
Lipkany = Lipcani *Moldova* **29** B11
Lipník nad Bečvou
Czech Rep. **27** B10
Lipno *Poland* **31** F6
Lipova *Romania* **28** D6
Lipovets *Ukraine* **23** D15
Lippe ➜ *Germany* **24** D2
Lippstadt *Germany* **24** D4
Lipscomb *U.S.A.* **116** C4
Lipsk *Poland* **30** E10
Lipsko *Poland* **31** G8
Liptovský Hrádok
Slovak Rep. **27** B12

Liptovský Mikuláš
Slovak Rep. **27** B12
Liptrap, C. *Australia* **95** F4
Lipu *China* **59** E8
Lira *Uganda* **86** B3
Liri ➜ *Italy* **42** A6
Liria = Lliria *Spain* **39** F4
Lisala *Dem. Rep. of the Congo* **84** D4
Lisboa *Portugal* **37** G1
Lisboa □ *Portugal* **37** F1
Lisboa ✈ (LIS) *Portugal* **37** G1
Lisbon = Lisboa *Portugal* **37** G1
Lisbon *N. Dak., U.S.A.* **112** B5
Lisbon *N.H., U.S.A.* **115** B13
Lisbon *Ohio, U.S.A.* **114** F4
Lisbon Falls *U.S.A.* **113** D18
Lisburn *U.K.* **12** B5
Lisburne, C. *U.S.A.* **4** C17
Liscannor B. *Ireland* **12** D2
Lisdoonvarna *Ireland* **12** C2
Liscia ➜ *Italy* **42** A2
Lishe Jiang ➜ *China* **58** E3
Lishi *China* **56** F6
Lishu *China* **57** C13
Lishui *Jiangsu, China* **59** B12
Lishui *Zhejiang, China* **59** C12
Lisianski I. *U.S.A.* **96** E10
Lisichansk = Lysychansk
Ukraine **33** H10
Lisieux *France* **18** C7
Liski *Russia* **33** G10
Lismore *Australia* **95** D5
Lismore *Ireland* **12** D4
Lissos ➜ *Greece* **45** E9
Lista *Norway* **9** G12
Lister, Mt. *Antarctica* **5** D11
Liston *Australia* **95** D5
Listowel *Canada* **114** C4
Listowel *Ireland* **12** D2
Lit *Sweden* **10** A8
Lit-et-Mixe *France* **20** D2
Litang *Guangxi Zhuangzu,
China* **58** F7
Litang *Sichuan, China* **58** B3
Litang Qu ➜ *China* **58** C3
Litani ➜ *Lebanon* **74** B4
Litchfield *Calif., U.S.A.* **110** E6
Litchfield *Conn., U.S.A.* **115** E11
Litchfield *Ill., U.S.A.* **112** F9
Litchfield *Minn., U.S.A.* **112** C6
Litchfield △ *Australia* **92** B5
Liteni *Romania* **29** C11
Lithgow *Australia* **95** E5
Lithino, Akra *Greece* **49** E6
Lithuania ■ *Europe* **32** E2
Litija *Slovenia* **41** B11
Lititz *U.S.A.* **115** F8
Litochoro *Greece* **44** F6
Litoměřice *Czech Rep.* **26** A7
Litomyšl *Czech Rep.* **27** B9
Litschau *Austria* **26** C8
Little Abaco *Bahamas* **120** A4
Little Barrier I. *N.Z.* **91** B5
Little Belt Mts. *U.S.A.* **108** C8
Little Bighorn Battlefield △
U.S.A. **108** D10
Little Blue ➜ *U.S.A.* **112** F5
Little Buffalo ➜ *Canada* **102** A6
Little Cayman *Cayman Is.* **120** C3
Little Churchill ➜ *Canada* **103** B9
Little Colorado ➜ *U.S.A.* **109** H8
Little Current *Canada* **104** C3
Little Current ➜ *Canada* **104** B3
Little Falls *Minn., U.S.A.* **112** C6
Little Falls *N.Y., U.S.A.* **115** C10
Little Fork ➜ *U.S.A.* **112** A7
Little Grand Rapids *Canada* **103** C9
Little Humboldt ➜ *U.S.A.* **108** F5
Little Inagua I. *Bahamas* **121** B5
Little Karoo *S. Africa* **88** E3
Little Khingan Mts. = Xiao
Hinggan Ling *China* **60** B7
Little Lake *U.S.A.* **111** K9
Little Laut Is. = Laut Kecil,
Kepulauan *Indonesia* **62** E5
Little Mecatina = Petit-
Mécatina ➜ *Canada* **105** B8
Little Minch *U.K.* **13** D2
Little Missouri ➜ *U.S.A.* **112** B2
Little Ouse ➜ *U.K.* **15** E9
Little Rann *India* **68** H4
Little Red ➜ *U.S.A.* **116** D9
Little River *N.Z.* **91** E4
Little Rock *U.S.A.* **116** D8
Little Ruaha ➜ *Tanzania* **86** D4
Little Sable Pt. *U.S.A.* **112** D10
Little Scarcies ➜ *S. Leone* **82** D2
Little Sioux ➜ *U.S.A.* **112** E5
Little Smoky ➜ *Canada* **102** C5
Little Snake ➜ *U.S.A.* **108** F9
Little Tobago *Trin. & Tob.* **125** J16
Little Valley *U.S.A.* **114** D6
Little Wabash ➜ *U.S.A.* **112** G9

Little White ➜ *U.S.A.* **112** D3
Little Zab = Zāb aş
Şaghīr ➜ *Iraq* **73** E10
Littlefield *U.S.A.* **116** E3
Littlehampton *U.K.* **15** G7
Littleton *U.S.A.* **115** B13
Liu He ➜ *China* **57** D11
Liu Jiang ➜ *China* **58** F7
Liuba *China* **56** H4
Liucheng *China* **58** E7
Liugou *China* **57** D10
Liuhe *China* **57** C13
Liuheng Dao *China* **59** C14
Liujiang *China* **58** E7
Liukang Tenggaja =
Sabalana, Kepulauan
Indonesia **63** F5
Liuli *Tanzania* **87** E3
Liupanshui *China* **58** D5
Liuwa Plain *Zambia* **85** G4
Liuyang *China* **59** C9
Liuzhou *China* **58** E7
Liuzhuang *China* **57** H11
Livada *Romania* **28** C8
Livadero *Greece* **44** F5
Livadhia *Cyprus* **49** E12
Livadi *Greece* **46** A4
Livadia *Greece* **46** C4
Livarot *France* **18** C7
Live Oak *Calif., U.S.A.* **110** F5
Live Oak *Fla., U.S.A.* **117** F13
Lively *Canada* **113** B13
Liveras *Cyprus* **49** D11
Livermore *U.S.A.* **110** H5
Livermore, Mt. *U.S.A.* **116** F2
Livermore Falls *U.S.A.* **113** C18
Liverpool *Canada* **105** D7
Liverpool *U.K.* **14** D4
Liverpool *U.S.A.* **115** C8
Liverpool Bay *U.K.* **14** D4
Liverpool Ra. *Australia* **95** E5
Livingston *Guatemala* **120** C2
Livingston *U.K.* **13** F5
Livingston *Ala., U.S.A.* **117** E10
Livingston *Calif., U.S.A.* **110** H6
Livingston *Mont., U.S.A.* **108** D8
Livingston *S.C., U.S.A.* **117** E14
Livingston *Tenn., U.S.A.* **117** C12
Livingston *Tex., U.S.A.* **116** F7
Livingston, L. *U.S.A.* **116** F7
Livingston Manor *U.S.A.* **115** E10
Livingstone *Zambia* **87** F2
Livingstone Mts. *Tanzania* **87** D3
Livingstonia *Malawi* **87** E3
Livno *Bos.-H.* **28** G2
Livny *Russia* **33** F9
Livonia *Mich., U.S.A.* **113** D12
Livonia *N.Y., U.S.A.* **114** D7
Livorno *Italy* **40** E7
Livradois-Forez △ *France* **20** E7
Livramento *Brazil* **127** C4
Livron-sur-Drôme *France* **21** D8
Livyntsi *Ukraine* **29** B11
Liwale *Tanzania* **87** D4
Liwiec ➜ *Poland* **31** F8
Liwonde △ *Malawi* **87** E4
Lixi *China* **58** D3
Lixian *China* **58** B4
Lixouri *Greece* **46** C2
Liyang *China* **59** B12
Lizard I. *Australia* **94** A4
Lizard Pt. *U.K.* **15** H2
Lizzano *Italy* **43** B10
Ljig *Serbia* **44** B4
Ljubija *Bos.-H.* **41** D13
Ljubinje *Bos.-H.* **44** D2
Ljubišnja *Europe* **44** C3
Ljubljana *Slovenia* **41** B11
Ljubljana ✈ (LJU) *Slovenia* **41** B11
Ljubno *Slovenia* **41** B11
Ljubovija *Serbia* **44** B3
Ljugarn *Sweden* **11** G12
Ljung *Sweden* **11** G7
Ljungan ➜ *Sweden* **10** B11
Ljungaverk *Sweden* **10** B10
Ljungby *Sweden* **11** H7
Ljungbyholm *Sweden* **11** H10
Ljungdalen *Sweden* **10** B6
Ljungsbro *Sweden* **11** F9
Ljungskile *Sweden* **11** F5
Ljusdal *Sweden* **10** C10
Ljusfallshammar *Sweden* **11** F9
Ljusnan ➜ *Sweden* **10** C11
Ljusne *Sweden* **10** C11
Ljutomer *Slovenia* **41** B13
Llagostera *Spain* **38** D7
Llancanelo, Salina
Argentina **126** D2
Llandeilo *U.K.* **15** F4
Llandovery *U.K.* **15** F4
Llandrindod Wells *U.K.* **15** E4
Llandudno *U.K.* **14** D4
Llanelli *U.K.* **15** F3
Llanes *Spain* **36** B6

Llangollen *U.K.* **14** E4
Llanidloes *U.K.* **15** E4
Llano *U.S.A.* **116** F5
Llano ➜ *U.S.A.* **116** F5
Llano Estacado *U.S.A.* **116** E3
Llanos *S. Amer.* **124** C4
Llanos de Challe △ *Chile* **126** B1
Llanquihue, L. *Chile* **128** E1
Llanwrtyd Wells *U.K.* **15** E4
Llebeig, C. des *Spain* **48** B9
Lleida *Spain* **38** D5
Lleida □ *Spain* **38** C6
Llentrisca, C. *Spain* **48** C7
Llera de Canales *Mexico* **119** C5
Llerena *Spain* **37** G5
Lleyn Peninsula *U.K.* **14** E3
Llico *Chile* **126** C1
Lliria *Spain* **39** F4
Llívia *Spain* **20** F5
Llobregat ➜ *Spain* **38** D7
Llodio *Spain* **38** B2
Lloret de Mar *Spain* **38** D7
Lloyd B. *Australia* **94** A3
Lloyd L. *Canada* **103** B7
Lloydminster *Canada* **103** C7
Llucena del Cid *Spain* **38** E4
Llucmajor *Spain* **48** B9
Llullaillaco, Volcán
S. Amer. **126** A2
Llullaillaco △ *Chile* **126** A2
Lo ➜ *Vietnam* **64** B5
Loa *U.S.A.* **108** G8
Loa ➜ *Chile* **126** A1
Loaita I. *S. China Sea* **62** B4
Loange ➜
Dem. Rep. of the Congo **84** E4
Loano *Italy* **40** D5
Lobatse *Botswana* **88** D4
Löbau *Germany* **24** D10
Lobenstein *Germany* **24** E7
Lobería *Argentina* **126** D4
Löberöd *Sweden* **11** J7
Łobez *Poland* **30** E2
Lobito *Angola* **85** G2
Lobo ➜ *Ivory C.* **82** D3
Lobos *Argentina* **126** D4
Lobos, I. *Mexico* **118** B2
Lobos, I. de *Canary Is.* **48** F6
Łobżenica *Poland* **31** E4
Loc Binh *Vietnam* **64** B6
Loc Ninh *Vietnam* **65** G6
Locarno *Switz.* **25** J4
Loch Baghasdail =
Lochboisdale *U.K.* **13** D1
Loch Garman = Wexford
Ireland **12** D5
Loch Lomond and the
Trossachs △ *U.K.* **13** E4
Loch Nam Madadh =
Lochmaddy *U.K.* **13** D1
Lochaber *U.K.* **13** E3
Locharbriggs *U.K.* **13** F5
Lochboisdale *U.K.* **13** D1
Loche, L. La *Canada* **103** B7
Lochem *Neths.* **17** B6
Loches *France* **18** E7
Lochgilphead *U.K.* **13** E3
Lochinvar △ *Zambia* **87** F2
Lochinver *U.K.* **13** C3
Lochmaddy *U.K.* **13** D1
Lochnagar *Australia* **94** C4
Lochnagar *U.K.* **13** E5
Lochów *Poland* **31** F8
Lochy, L. *U.K.* **13** E4
Lock *Australia* **95** E2
Lock Haven *U.S.A.* **114** E7
Lockeford *U.S.A.* **110** G5
Lockeport *Canada* **105** D6
Lockerbie *U.K.* **13** F5
Lockhart *U.S.A.* **116** G6
Lockhart, L. *Australia* **93** F2
Lockhart River *Australia* **94** A3
Lockney *U.S.A.* **116** D4
Lockport *U.S.A.* **114** C6
Locminé *France* **18** E4
Locri *Italy* **43** D9
Locronan *France* **18** D2
Lod *Israel* **74** D3
Lodeinoye Pole *Russia* **32** B7
Lodève *France* **20** E7
Lodge Bay *Canada* **105** B8
Lodge Grass *U.S.A.* **108** D10
Lodhran *Pakistan* **68** E4
Lodi *Italy* **40** C6
Lodi *Calif., U.S.A.* **110** G5
Lodi *Ohio, U.S.A.* **114** E3
Lodja *Dem. Rep. of the Congo* **86** C1
Lodosa *Spain* **38** C2
Lödöse *Sweden* **11** F6
Lodwar *Kenya* **86** B4
Łódź *Poland* **31** G6
Łódzkie □ *Poland* **31** G6
Loei *Thailand* **64** D3
Loengo *Dem. Rep. of the Congo* **86** C2
Loeriesfontein *S. Africa* **88** E2
Lofa ➜ *Liberia* **83** D2
Lofa Mano △ *Liberia* **82** D2

Lofer Austria 26 D5
Lofoten Norway 8 B16
Lofsdalen Sweden 10 B7
Lofsen → Sweden 10 B7
Loftahammar Sweden 11 G10
Loga Niger 83 C5
Logan Iowa, U.S.A. 112 E6
Logan Ohio, U.S.A. 113 F12
Logan Utah, U.S.A. 108 F8
Logan W. Va., U.S.A. 113 G13
Logan, Mt. Canada 100 C5
Logandale U.S.A. 111 J12
Logansport Ind., U.S.A. 112 E10
Logansport La., U.S.A. 116 F8
Logirim Sudan 81 G3
Logo Sudan 81 F3
Logone → Chad 79 F9
Logroño Spain 38 C2
Logrosán Spain 37 F5
Løgstør Denmark 11 H3
Løgumkloster Denmark 11 J2
Lohals Denmark 11 J4
Lohardaga India 69 H11
Loharia India 68 H6
Loharu India 68 E6
Lohja Finland 32 B3
Löhne Germany 24 C4
Lohr Germany 25 F5
Lohri Wah → Pakistan 68 F2
Loi-kaw Burma 67 K20
Loimaa Finland 32 B2
Loir → France 18 E4
Loir-et-Cher □ France 18 E8
Loire □ France 21 C8
Loire → France 18 E4
Loire Anjou Touraine ○ France 18 E6
Loire-Atlantique □ France 18 E5
Loiret □ France 19 E9
Loitz Germany 24 B9
Loja Ecuador 124 D3
Loja Spain 37 H6
Loji = Kawasi Indonesia 63 E7
Lojo = Lohja Finland 32 B3
Lojung China 58 E7
Loka Sudan 81 G3
Lokandu
  Dem. Rep. of the Congo 86 C2
Lokeren Belgium 17 C3
Lokgwabe Botswana 88 C3
Lokhvitsa Ukraine 33 G7
Lokichar Kenya 86 B4
Lokichokio Kenya 86 B3
Lokitaung Kenya 86 B4
Løkken tekojärvi Finland 8 C22
Løkken Denmark 11 G3
Loknya Russia 32 D6
Loko Nigeria 83 D6
Lokoja Nigeria 83 D6
Lokoro →
  Dem. Rep. of the Congo 84 E3
Lokot Russia 33 F8
Lol → Sudan 81 F2
Lola Guinea 82 D3
Lola, Mt. U.S.A. 110 F6
Lolgorien Kenya 86 C3
Lolibai, Gebel Sudan 81 G3
Lolimi Sudan 81 G3
Loliondo Tanzania 86 C4
Lolland Denmark 11 K5
Lollar Germany 24 E4
Lolo U.S.A. 108 C6
Lolodorf Cameroon 83 E7
Lolo → Bulgaria 44 C7
Lom Bulgaria 44 C7
Lom → Bulgaria 44 C7
Lom Kao Thailand 64 D3
Lom Sak Thailand 64 D3
Loma U.S.A. 108 C8
Loma Linda U.S.A. 111 L9
Loma Mansa S. Leone 82 D2
Lomaloma Fiji 91 a
Lomami →
  Dem. Rep. of the Congo 86 B1
Lomas de Zamóra Argentina 126 C4
Lombadina Australia 92 C3
Lombárdia □ Italy 40 C6
Lombardy = Lombárdia □ Italy 40 C6
Lombez France 20 E4
Lomblen Indonesia 63 F6
Lombok Indonesia 62 F5
Lombok, Selat Indonesia 63 K18
Lomé Togo 83 D5
Lomela Dem. Rep. of the Congo 84 E4
Lomela →
  Dem. Rep. of the Congo 84 E4
Lomianki Poland 31 F7
Lomma Sweden 11 J7
Lommel Belgium 17 C5
Lomond Canada 102 C6
Lomond, L. U.K. 13 E4
Lomonosov Ridge Arctic 4 A
Lomphat Cambodia 64 F6
Lompobatang Indonesia 63 F5
Lompoc U.S.A. 111 L6
Łomża Poland 31 E9

Lon, Ko Thailand 65 a
Loncoche Chile 128 D2
Londa India 66 M9
Londiani Kenya 86 C4
Londinières France 18 C8
London Canada 114 D3
London U.K. 15 F7
London Ky., U.S.A. 113 G11
London Ohio, U.S.A. 113 F12
London, Greater □ U.K. 15 F7
London Gatwick ✈ (LGW) U.K. 15 F7
London Heathrow ✈ (LHR) U.K. 15 F7
London Stansted ✈ (STN) U.K. 15 F8
Londonderry U.K. 12 B4
Londonderry □ U.K. 12 B4
Londonderry, C. Australia 92 B4
Londonderry, I. Chile 128 H2
Londres Argentina 128 B3
Londrina Brazil 127 A5
Lone Pine U.S.A. 110 J8
Lonely Mine Zimbabwe 89 B4
Long B. U.S.A. 117 E15
Long Beach Calif., U.S.A. 111 M8
Long Beach N.Y., U.S.A. 115 F11
Long Beach Wash., U.S.A. 110 D2
Long Branch U.S.A. 115 F11
Long Creek U.S.A. 108 D4
Long Eaton U.K. 14 E6
Long I. Australia 94 J6
Long I. Bahamas 121 B4
Long I. Canada 104 B4
Long I. Ireland 12 E2
Long I. U.S.A. 115 F11
Long Island Sd. U.S.A. 115 E12
Long L. Canada 104 C2
Long Lake U.S.A. 115 C10
Long Point B. Canada 114 D4
Long Prairie U.S.A. 112 C6
Long Prairie → U.S.A. 112 B6
Long Pt. Canada 114 D4
Long Range Mts. Canada 105 C8
Long Reef Australia 92 B4
Long Spruce Canada 103 B10
Long Str. = Longa, Proliv Russia 4 C16
Long Thanh Vietnam 65 G6
Long Xian China 56 G4
Long Xuyen Vietnam 65 G5
Longa Greece 46 E3
Longa, Proliv Russia 4 C16
Long'an China 58 F6
Longarone Italy 41 B9
Longbenton U.K. 14 B6
Longboat Key U.S.A. 117 H13
Longchang China 58 C5
Longchi China 58 C4
Longchuan Guangdong, China 59 E10
Longchuan Yunnan, China 58 E1
Longde China 56 G4
Longeau France 19 E12
Longford Australia 95 G4
Longford Ireland 12 C4
Longford □ Ireland 12 C4
Longhai China 59 E11
Longhua China 57 D9
Longhui China 59 D8
Longido Tanzania 86 C4
Longiram Indonesia 62 E5
Longkou Jiangxi, China 59 D10
Longkou Shandong, China 57 F11
Longlac Canada 104 C2
Longli China 58 D6
Longlin China 58 E5
Longling China 58 E2
Longmeadow U.S.A. 115 D12
Longmen China 59 F10
Longming China 58 F6
Longmont U.S.A. 108 F11
Longnan China 59 E10
Longnawan Indonesia 62 D4
Longobucco Italy 43 C9
Longquan China 59 C12
Longreach Australia 94 C3
Longshan China 58 C7
Longsheng China 59 E8
Longué-Jumelles France 18 E6
Longueau France 19 C9
Longueuil Canada 115 A11
Longuyon France 19 C12
Longvic France 19 E12
Longview Tex., U.S.A. 116 E7
Longview Wash., U.S.A. 110 D4
Longwy France 19 C12
Longxi China 56 G3
Longyan China 59 E11
Longyearbyen Svalbard 4 B8
Longyou China 59 C12
Longzhou China 58 F6
Lonigo Italy 41 C8
Löningen Germany 24 C3
Lonja → Croatia 41 C13
Lonoke U.S.A. 116 D9
Lonquimay Chile 128 D2

Lons-le-Saunier France 19 F12
Lönsboda Sweden 11 H8
Looe U.K. 15 G3
Lookout, C. Canada 104 A3
Lookout, C. U.S.A. 117 D16
Loolmalasin Tanzania 86 C4
Loon → Alta., Canada 102 B5
Loon → Man., Canada 103 B8
Loon Lake Canada 103 C7
Loongana Australia 93 F4
Loop Hd. Ireland 12 D2
Lop Buri Thailand 64 E3
Lop Nor = Lop Nur China 60 B4
Lop Nur China 60 B4
Lopare Bos.-H. 28 F3
Lopatin Russia 35 J8
Lopatina, Gora Russia 53 D15
Lopaye Sudan 81 F3
Lopez Phil. 61 E5
Lopez U.S.A. 115 E8
Lopez, C. Gabon 84 E1
Lopphavet Norway 8 A19
Lora → Afghan. 66 D4
Lora, Hāmūn-i- Pakistan 66 E4
Lora Cr. → Australia 95 D2
Lora del Río Spain 37 H5
Lorain U.S.A. 114 E2
Loralai Pakistan 68 D3
Lorca Spain 39 H3
Lord Howe I. Pac. Oc. 90 E8
Lord Howe Rise Pac. Oc. 96 L8
Lordsburg U.S.A. 109 K9
Lorestān □ Iran 71 C6
Loreto Brazil 125 E9
Loreto Italy 41 E10
Loreto Mexico 118 B2
Lorgues France 21 E10
Lorhosso Burkina Faso 82 C4
Lorient France 18 E3
Lórinci Hungary 28 C4
Lormi India 69 H9
Lorn U.K. 13 E3
Lorn, Firth of U.K. 13 E3
Lorne Australia 95 F3
Loronyo Sudan 81 F3
Lorovouno Cyprus 49 D11
Lörrach Germany 25 H3
Lorraine France 19 D13
Lorraine ○ France 19 D12
Los Sweden 10 C9
Los, Îles de Guinea 82 D2
Los Alamos Calif., U.S.A. 111 L6
Los Alamos N. Mex., U.S.A. 109 J10
Los Alcornocales ○ Spain 37 J5
Los Altos U.S.A. 110 H4
Los Andes Chile 126 C1
Los Angeles Chile 126 D1
Los Angeles U.S.A. 111 M8
Los Angeles, Bahia de Mexico 118 B2
Los Angeles Aqueduct U.S.A. 111 K9
Los Angeles Int. ✈ (LAX) U.S.A. 111 M8
Los Banos U.S.A. 110 H6
Los Barrios Spain 37 J5
Los Blancos Argentina 126 A3
Los Cardones △ Argentina 126 B2
Los Chiles Costa Rica 120 D3
Los Corrales de Buelna Spain 36 B6
Los Cristianos Canary Is. 48 F3
Los Gallardos Spain 39 H3
Los Gatos U.S.A. 110 H5
Los Haïtises △ Dom. Rep. 121 C6
Los Hermanos Is. Venezuela 121 D7
Los Islotes Canary Is. 48 E6
Los Llanos de Aridane Canary Is. 48 F2
Los Loros Chile 126 B1
Los Lunas U.S.A. 109 J10
Los Mochis Mexico 118 B3
Los Monegros Spain 38 D4
Los Nietos Spain 39 H4
Los Olivos U.S.A. 111 L6
Los Palacios Cuba 120 B3
Los Palacios y Villafranca Spain 37 H5
Los Reyes de Salgado Mexico 118 D4
Los Roques Is. Venezuela 121 D6
Los Santos de Maimona Spain 37 G4
Los Teques Venezuela 124 A5
Los Testigos, Is. Venezuela 124 A6
Los Vilos Chile 126 C1
Los Yébenes Spain 37 F7
Łosice Poland 31 F9
Lošinj Croatia 41 D11
Loskop Dam S. Africa 89 D4
Løsning Denmark 11 J3
Lossiemouth U.K. 13 D5
Lossnen △ Sweden 10 B6
Lostwithiel U.K. 15 G3
Lot □ France 20 D5
Lot → France 20 D4
Lot-et-Garonne □ France 20 D4
Lota Chile 126 D1

Lotagipi Swamp Sudan 81 G3
Lotfābād Iran 71 B8
Lothair S. Africa 89 D5
Lotorp Sweden 11 F9
Lötschbergtunnel Switz. 25 J3
Lotta → Europe 8 B24
Löttorp Sweden 11 G11
Lotung Taiwan 59 E13
Lotta → Europe 8 B24
Loubomo Congo 84 E2
Loudéac France 18 D4
Loudi China 59 D8
Loudonville U.S.A. 114 F2
Loudun France 18 E7
Loue → France 19 E12
Louga Senegal 82 B1
Louga □ Senegal 82 B1
Loughborough U.K. 14 E6
Lougheed I. Canada 101 B9
Loughrea Ireland 12 C3
Loughros More B. Ireland 12 B3
Louhans France 19 F12
Louis Trichardt S. Africa 89 C4
Louis XIV, Pte. Canada 104 B4
Louisa U.S.A. 113 F12
Louisbourg Canada 105 C8
Louisburgh Ireland 12 C2
Louise I. Canada 102 C2
Louiseville Canada 104 C5
Louisiade Arch. Papua N. G. 90 C8
Louisiana U.S.A. 112 F9
Louisiana □ U.S.A. 116 F9
Louisville Ky., U.S.A. 113 F11
Louisville Miss., U.S.A. 117 E10
Louisville Ohio, U.S.A. 114 F3
Louisville Ridge Pac. Oc. 96 L10
Loulay France 20 B3
Loulé Portugal 37 H3
Louny Czech Rep. 26 A6
Loup → U.S.A. 112 E5
Loup City U.S.A. 112 E4
Loups Marins, Lacs des Canada 104 A5
Lourdes France 20 E3
Lourdes-de-Blanc-Sablon Canada 105 B8
Lourinhã Portugal 37 F1
Lousã Portugal 36 E2
Louth Australia 95 E4
Louth Ireland 12 C5
Louth □ Ireland 12 C5
Louth U.K. 14 D7
Loutra Edipsou Greece 46 C5
Loutraki Greece 46 D4
Loutropoli Thermis Greece 47 B8
Louvain = Leuven Belgium 17 D4
Louviers France 18 C8
Louwsburg S. Africa 89 D5
Lovat → Russia 32 C6
Lovćen Montenegro 44 D2
Lovćen △ Serbia 44 D2
Lovech Bulgaria 45 C8
Lovech □ Bulgaria 45 C8
Loveland U.S.A. 108 F11
Lovell U.S.A. 108 D9
Lovelock U.S.A. 108 F4
Lóvere Italy 40 C7
Loviisa Finland 32 B4
Loving U.S.A. 109 K11
Lovington U.S.A. 109 K12
Lovisa = Loviisa Finland 32 B4
Lovosice Czech Rep. 26 A7
Lovran Croatia 41 C11
Lovrin Romania 28 E5
Lövstabruk Sweden 10 D11
Lövstabukten Sweden 10 D11
Low, L. Canada 104 B4
Low Pt. Australia 93 F4
Low Tatra = Nízké Tatry Slovak Rep. 27 C12
Lowa Dem. Rep. of the Congo 86 C2
Lowa →
  Dem. Rep. of the Congo 86 C2
Lowell U.S.A. 115 D13
Lowellville U.S.A. 114 E4
Löwen = Leuven Belgium 17 D4
Lower Alkali L. U.S.A. 108 F3
Lower Arrow L. Canada 102 D5
Lower Austria = Niederösterreich □ Austria 26 C8
Lower California = Baja California Mexico 118 A1
Lower Hutt N.Z. 91 D5
Lower Lake U.S.A. 110 G4
Lower Manitou L. Canada 103 D10
Lower Post Canada 102 B3
Lower Red L. U.S.A. 112 B6
Lower Saxony = Niedersachsen □ Germany 24 C4
Lower Tunguska = Tunguska, Nizhnyaya → Russia 53 C9
Lower Zambezi △ Zambia 87 F2
Lowestoft U.K. 15 E9
Lowgar □ Afghan. 66 B6
Lowicz Poland 31 F6

Lowville U.S.A. 115 C9
Loxton Australia 95 E3
Loxton S. Africa 88 E3
Loyalton U.S.A. 110 F6
Loyalty Is. = Loyauté, Îs. N. Cal. 90 D9
Loyang = Luoyang China 56 G7
Loyauté, Îs. N. Cal. 90 D9
Loyev = Loyew Belarus 23 C16
Loyew Belarus 23 C16
Loyoro Uganda 86 B3
Lož Slovenia 41 C11
Lozère □ France 20 D7
Loznica Serbia 44 B3
Lozova Ukraine 33 H9
Lü Shan China 59 C11
Lü Tao Taiwan 59 F13
Luachimo Angola 84 F4
Luajan → India 69 G11
Lualaba →
  Dem. Rep. of the Congo 86 B2
Luampa Zambia 87 F1
Luan Chau Vietnam 58 G4
Luan He → China 57 E10
Luan Xian China 57 E10
Luancheng Guangxi Zhuangzu, China 58 F7
Luancheng Hebei, China 56 F8
Luanco Spain 36 B5
Luanda Angola 84 F2
Luang, Thale Thailand 65 J3
Luang Prabang Laos 58 H4
Luangwa Zambia 87 F3
Luangwa → Zambia 87 E3
Luangwa Valley Zambia 87 E3
Luanne China 57 D9
Luanping China 57 D9
Luanshya Zambia 87 E2
Luapula □ Zambia 87 E2
Luapula → Africa 87 D2
Luarca Spain 36 B4
Luashi Dem. Rep. of the Congo 87 E1
Luau Angola 84 G4
Lubaczów Poland 31 H10
Lubań Poland 31 G2
Lubana, Ozero = Lubānas Ezers Latvia 32 D4
Lubānas Ezers Latvia 32 D4
Lubang Phil. 61 E4
Lubang Is. Phil. 61 E4
Lubango Angola 85 G2
Lubao Dem. Rep. of the Congo 86 D2
Lubartów Poland 31 G9
Lubawa Poland 30 E6
Lübbecke Germany 24 C4
Lübben Germany 24 D9
Lübbenau Germany 24 D9
Lubbock U.S.A. 116 E4
Lübeck Germany 24 B6
Lübecker Bucht Germany 24 A6
Lubefu Dem. Rep. of the Congo 86 C1
Lubefu →
  Dem. Rep. of the Congo 86 C1
Lubelskie □ Poland 31 G9
Lubero = Luofu Dem. Rep. of the Congo 86 C2
Lubersac France 20 C5
Lubicon L. Canada 102 B5
Lubień Kujawski Poland 31 F6
Lubilash →
  Dem. Rep. of the Congo 84 F4
Lubin Poland 31 G3
Lublin Poland 31 G9
Lubliniec Poland 31 H5
Lubnān = Lebanon ■ Asia 74 B5
Lubnān, Jabal Lebanon 74 B4
Lubniewice Poland 31 F2
Lubny Ukraine 33 G7
Luboń Poland 31 F3
Lubongola
  Dem. Rep. of the Congo 86 C2
L'ubotín Slovak Rep. 27 B13
Lubraniec Poland 31 F5
Lubsko Poland 31 G1
Lübtheen Germany 24 B7
Lubuagan Phil. 61 C4
Lubudi Dem. Rep. of the Congo 84 F5
Lubudi →
  Dem. Rep. of the Congo 87 D2
Lubuklinggau Indonesia 62 E2
Lubuksikaping Indonesia 62 D2
Lubumbashi
  Dem. Rep. of the Congo 87 E2
Lubunda
  Dem. Rep. of the Congo 86 D2
Lubungu Zambia 87 E2
Lubuskie □ Poland 31 F2
Lubutu Dem. Rep. of the Congo 86 C2
Luc An Chau Vietnam 64 A5
Luc-en-Diois France 21 D9
Lucan Canada 114 C3
Lucania, Mt. Canada 100 C5
Lucas Channel Canada 114 A3
Lucban Phil. 61 D4

Lucca Italy 40 E7
Lucé France 18 D8
Luce Bay U.K. 13 G4
Lucea Jamaica 120 a
Lucedale U.S.A. 117 F10
Lucena Phil. 61 E4
Lucena Spain 37 H6
Lučenec Slovak Rep. 27 C12
Lucera Italy 43 A8
Lucerne = Luzern Switz. 25 H4
Lucerne U.S.A. 110 F4
Lucerne Valley U.S.A. 111 L10
Lucero Mexico 118 A3
Luchena → Spain 39 H3
Lucheng China 56 F7
Lucheringo → Mozam. 87 E4
Lüchow Germany 24 C7
Luchuan China 59 F8
Lucia U.S.A. 110 J5
Lucinda Australia 94 B4
Luckau Germany 24 D9
Luckenwalde Germany 24 C9
Luckhoff S. Africa 88 D3
Lucknow Canada 114 C3
Lucknow India 69 F9
Luçon France 20 B2
Lüda = Dalian China 57 E11
Luda Kamchiya → Bulgaria 45 C11
Ludbreg Croatia 41 B13
Lüdenscheid Germany 24 D3
Lüderitz Namibia 88 D2
Lüderitzbaai Namibia 88 D2
Ludhiana India 68 D6
Ludian China 58 D4
Luding Qiao China 58 C4
Lüdinghausen Germany 24 D3
Ludington U.S.A. 112 D10
Ludlow U.K. 15 E5
Ludlow Calif., U.S.A. 111 L10
Ludlow Pa., U.S.A. 114 E6
Ludlow Vt., U.S.A. 115 C12
Ludus Romania 29 D9
Ludvika Sweden 10 D9
Ludwigsburg Germany 25 G5
Ludwigsfelde Germany 24 C9
Ludwigshafen Germany 25 F4
Ludwigslust Germany 24 B7
Ludza Latvia 32 D4
Lueki Dem. Rep. of the Congo 86 C2
Luena Dem. Rep. of the Congo 87 D2
Luena Zambia 87 E3
Luena Flats Zambia 85 G4
Luenha = Ruenya → Africa 87 F3
Lüeyang China 56 H4
Lufeng Guangdong, China 59 F10
Lufeng Yunnan, China 58 E4
Lufira →
  Dem. Rep. of the Congo 87 D2
Lufkin U.S.A. 116 F7
Lufupa Dem. Rep. of the Congo 87 E1
Luga Russia 32 C5
Luga → Russia 32 C5
Lugano Switz. 25 J4
Lugano, L. di Switz. 40 C6
Lugansk = Luhansk Ukraine 33 H10
Lugard's Falls Kenya 86 C4
Lugela Mozam. 87 F4
Lugenda → Mozam. 87 E4
Lugh Ganana Somali Rep. 75 G3
Lugnaquillia Ireland 12 D5
Lugo Italy 41 D8
Lugo Spain 36 B3
Lugo □ Spain 36 C3
Lugoj Romania 28 E6
Lugovoy = Qulan Kazakhstan 52 E8
Luhansk Ukraine 33 H10
Luhansk □ Ukraine 33 H10
Luhe China 59 A12
Luhe → Germany 24 B6
Luhuo China 58 B3
Lui → Angola 84 F3
Luiana Angola 88 B3
Luiana → Angola 85 H4
Luichow Pen. = Leizhou Bandao China 58 G7
Luimneach = Limerick Ireland 12 D3
Luing U.K. 13 E3
Luino Italy 40 C5
Luís Correia Brazil 125 D10
Luitpold Coast Antarctica 5 D1
Luiza Dem. Rep. of the Congo 84 F4
Luizi Dem. Rep. of the Congo 86 D2
Luján Argentina 126 C4
Lujiang China 59 B11
Lukang Taiwan 59 E13
Lukanga Swamp Zambia 87 E2
Lukenie →
  Dem. Rep. of the Congo 84 E3
Lukhisaral India 69 G12
Lüki Bulgaria 45 E8
Lukolela
  Dem. Rep. of the Congo 86 D1
Lukosi Zimbabwe 87 F2

Lukovë *Albania* **44** G3
Lukovit *Bulgaria* **45** C8
Łuków *Poland* **31** G9
Lukoyanov *Russia* **34** C7
Lukusuzi △ *Zambia* **87** E3
Luleå *Sweden* **8** D20
Luleälven → *Sweden* **8** D20
Lüleburgaz *Turkey* **45** E11
Luliang *China* **58** E4
Luling *U.S.A.* **116** G6
Lulong *China* **57** E10
Lulonga →
   Dem. Rep. of the Congo **84** D3
Lulua →
   Dem. Rep. of the Congo **84** E4
Luma *Amer. Samoa* **91** b
Lumajang *Indonesia* **63** H15
Lumbala N'guimbo *Angola* **85** G4
Lumberton *U.S.A.* **117** D15
Lumholtz △ *Australia* **94** B4
Lumsden *Canada* **103** C8
Lumsden *N.Z.* **91** F2
Lumut *Malaysia* **65** K3
Lumut, Tanjung *Indonesia* **62** E3
Luna *India* **68** H3
Lunan *China* **58** E4
Lunavada *India* **68** H5
Lunca *Romania* **29** C10
Lunca Corbului *Romania* **29** F9
Lund *Sweden* **11** J7
Lundazi *Zambia* **87** E3
Lunderskov *Denmark* **11** J3
Lundi → *Zimbabwe* **87** G3
Lundu *Malaysia* **62** D3
Lundy *U.K.* **15** F3
Lune → *U.K.* **14** C5
Lüneburg *Germany* **24** B6
Lüneburg Heath =
   Lüneburger Heide
   Germany **24** B6
Lüneburger Heide *Germany* **24** B6
Lunel *France* **21** E8
Lünen *Germany* **24** D3
Lunenburg *Canada* **105** D7
Lunéville *France* **19** D13
Lunga → *Zambia* **87** E2
Lunga Lunga *Kenya* **86** C4
Lungi Airport *S. Leone* **82** D2
Lunglei *India* **67** H18
Luni *India* **68** G5
Luni → *India* **68** G4
Luninets = Luninyets
   Belarus **23** B14
Luning *U.S.A.* **108** G4
Lunino *Russia* **34** D7
Luninyets *Belarus* **23** B14
Lunkaransar *India* **68** E5
Lunsemfwa → *Zambia* **87** E3
Lunsemfwa Falls *Zambia* **87** E2
Luo He → *China* **56** G6
Luocheng *China* **58** E7
Luochuan *China* **56** G5
Luoci *China* **58** E4
Luodian *China* **58** E6
Luoding *China* **59** F8
Luofu *Dem. Rep. of the Congo* **86** C2
Luohe *China* **56** H8
Luojiang *China* **58** B5
Luoning *China* **56** G6
Luoshan *China* **59** A10
Luotian *China* **59** B10
Luoxiao Shan *China* **59** D10
Luoyang *China* **56** G7
Luoyuan *China* **59** D12
Luozigou *China* **57** C16
Lupeni *Romania* **29** E8
Lupilichi *Mozam.* **87** E4
Łupków *Poland* **31** J9
Luoping *China* **58** E5
Luquan *China* **58** E4
Luque *Paraguay* **126** B4
Luquillo, Sierra de
   Puerto Rico **121** d
Lúras *Italy* **42** B2
Luray *U.S.A.* **113** F14
Lure *France* **19** E13
Lurgan *U.K.* **12** B5
Lusaka *Zambia* **87** F2
Lusaka □ *Zambia* **87** F2
Lusambo
   Dem. Rep. of the Congo **86** C1
Lusangaye
   Dem. Rep. of the Congo **86** C2
Luseland *Canada* **103** C7
Lusenga Plain △ *Zambia* **87** D2
Lushan *Henan, China* **56** H7
Lushan *Sichuan, China* **58** B4
Lushi *China* **56** G6
Lushui *China* **58** E2
Lüshun *China* **57** E11
Lushnjë *Albania* **44** F3
Lushoto *Tanzania* **86** C4

Lustenau *Austria* **26** D2
Lüt, Dasht-e *Iran* **71** D8
Luta = Dalian *China* **57** E11
Lutherstadt Wittenberg
   Germany **24** D8
Luton *U.K.* **15** F7
Luton □ *U.K.* **15** F7
Łutselk'e *Canada* **103** A6
Lutsk *Ukraine* **23** C13
Lutto = Lotta → *Europe* **8** B24
Lützow Holmbukta *Antarctica* **5** C4
Lutzputs *S. Africa* **88** D3
Luuq = Lugh Ganana
   Somali Rep. **75** G3
Luverne *Ala., U.S.A.* **117** F11
Luverne *Minn., U.S.A.* **112** D5
Luvua *Dem. Rep. of the Congo* **87** D2
Luvua →
   Dem. Rep. of the Congo **86** D2
Luvuvhu → *S. Africa* **89** C5
Luwegu → *Tanzania* **87** D4
Luwuk *Indonesia* **63** E6
Luxembourg *Lux.* **17** E6
Luxembourg □ *Belgium* **17** E5
Luxembourg ■ *Europe* **17** E5
Luxembourg ✈ (LUX) *Lux.* **17** E5
Luxeuil-les-Bains *France* **19** E13
Luxi *Hunan, China* **59** C8
Luxi *Yunnan, China* **58** E4
Luxi *Yunnan, China* **58** E2
Luxor = El Uqsur *Egypt* **80** B3
Luy-de-Béarn → *France* **20** E3
Luy-de-France → *France* **20** E3
Luyi *China* **56** H8
Luz-St-Sauveur *France* **20** F4
Luzern *Switz.* **25** H4
Luzern □ *Switz.* **25** H3
Luzhai *China* **58** E7
Luzhany *Ukraine* **29** B10
Luzhi *China* **58** D5
Luzhou *China* **58** C5
Luziânia *Brazil* **125** G9
Lužnice → *Czech Rep.* **26** B7
Luzon *Phil.* **61** D4
Luzon Strait *Asia* **59** G13
Luzy *France* **19** F10
Luzzi *Italy* **43** C9
Lviv *Ukraine* **23** D13
Lviv □ *Ukraine* **33** H2
Lvov = Lviv *Ukraine* **23** D13
Lwówek *Poland* **31** F3
Lwówek Śląski *Poland* **31** G2
Lyakhavichy *Belarus* **23** B14
Lyakhovskiye, Ostrova
   Russia **53** B15
Lyaki = Läki *Azerbaijan* **35** K8
Lyal I. *Canada* **114** B3
Lyaskovets *Bulgaria* **45** C9
Lyasnaya *Belarus* **31** F10
Lybster *U.K.* **13** C5
Lycaonia *Turkey* **72** D5
Lychen *Germany* **24** B9
Lychkova *Russia* **32** D7
Lycia *Turkey* **47** E11
Lyckebyån → *Sweden* **11** H9
Lycksele *Sweden* **8** D18
Lycosura *Greece* **46** D4
Lydda = Lod *Israel* **74** D3
Lyddan I. *Antarctica* **5** D2
Lydenburg *S. Africa* **89** D5
Lydia *Turkey* **47** C10
Łydynia → *Poland* **31** F7
Lyell *N.Z.* **91** D4
Lyell I. *Canada* **102** C2
Lyepyel *Belarus* **32** E5
Lygnern *Sweden* **11** G6
Lykens *U.S.A.* **115** F8
Lyman *Ukraine* **29** E14
Lyman *U.S.A.* **108** F8
Lymanske *Ukraine* **29** D14
Lyme B. *U.K.* **15** G4
Lyme Regis *U.K.* **15** G5
Lymington *U.K.* **15** G6
Łyna → *Poland* **30** D8
Lynchburg *U.S.A.* **113** G14
Lynd → *Australia* **94** B3
Lynd Ra. *Australia* **95** D4
Lynden *Canada* **114** C4
Lynden *U.S.A.* **110** B4
Lyndhurst *Australia* **95** E2
Lyndon → *Australia* **93** D1
Lyndonville *N.Y., U.S.A.* **114** C6
Lyndonville *Vt., U.S.A.* **115** B12
Lyngen *Norway* **8** B19
Lynher Reef *Australia* **92** C3
Lynn *U.S.A.* **115** D14
Lynn Haven *U.S.A.* **117** F12
Lynn Lake *Canada* **103** B8
Lynnwood *U.S.A.* **110** C4
Lynton *U.K.* **15** F4
Lyntupy *Belarus* **32** E4
Lynx L. *Canada* **103** A7
Lyon *France* **21** C8
Lyon St-Exupery ✈ (LYS)
   France **21** C9
Lyonnais *France* **21** C8
Lyons = Lyon *France* **21** C8

Lyons *Ga., U.S.A.* **117** E13
Lyons *Kans., U.S.A.* **112** F4
Lyons *N.Y., U.S.A.* **114** C8
Lyons → *Australia* **93** E2
Lyons Falls *U.S.A.* **115** C9
Lyozna *Belarus* **32** E6
Lys = Leie → *Belgium* **17** C3
Lysá nad Labem *Czech Rep.* **26** A7
Lysekil *Sweden* **11** F5
Lyskovo *Russia* **34** B7
Lystrup *Denmark* **11** H4
Lysva *Russia* **10** C10
Lysvik *Sweden* **10** D7
Lysychansk *Ukraine* **33** H10
Lytham St. Anne's *U.K.* **14** D4
Lyttelton *N.Z.* **91** E4
Lytton *Canada* **102** C4
Lyuban *Russia* **32** C6
Lyubertsy *Russia* **32** E9
Lyubim *Russia* **32** C11
Lyubimets *Bulgaria* **45** E10
Lyuboml *Ukraine* **31** G11
Lyubotyn *Ukraine* **33** H8
Lyudinovo *Russia* **32** F8

M

M.R. Stefanik,
   Bratislava ✈ (BTS)
   Slovak Rep. **27** C10
Ma → *Vietnam* **58** H5
Ma'adaba *Jordan* **74** E4
Maamba *Zambia* **88** B4
Ma'ān *Jordan* **74** E4
Ma'ān □ *Jordan* **74** F5
Maanselkä *Finland* **8** E23
Ma'anshan *China* **59** B12
Maarianhamina =
   Mariehamn *Finland* **9** F18
Ma'arrat an Nu'mān *Syria* **72** E7
Maas → *Neths.* **17** C4
Maaseik *Belgium* **17** C5
Maasin *Phil.* **63** B6
Maastricht *Neths.* **17** D5
Maave *Mozam.* **89** C5
Mababe Depression
   Botswana **88** B3
Mabalane *Mozam.* **89** C5
Mabel L. *Canada* **102** C5
Mabenge
   Dem. Rep. of the Congo **86** B1
Maberly *Canada* **115** B8
Mabian *China* **58** C4
Mabil *Ethiopia* **81** E4
Mablethorpe *U.K.* **14** D8
Mably *France* **19** F11
Maboma
   Dem. Rep. of the Congo **86** B2
Mabonto *S. Leone* **82** D2
Mabrouk *Mali* **83** B4
Mabuasehube △ *Botswana* **88** D3
Mac Bac *Vietnam* **65** H6
Macachín *Argentina* **126** D3
Macaé *Brazil* **127** A7
Macael *Spain* **39** H2
McAlester *U.S.A.* **116** D7
McAllen *U.S.A.* **116** H5
MacAlpine L. *Canada* **100** C9
Macamic *Canada* **104** C4
Macao = Macau *China* **59** F9
Macão *Portugal* **37** F3
Macapá *Brazil* **125** C8
Macarao △ *Venezuela* **121** D6
McArthur → *Australia* **94** B2
McArthur, Port *Australia* **94** B2
Macau *Brazil* **125** E11
Macau *China* **59** F9
McBride *Canada* **102** C4
McCall *U.S.A.* **108** D5
McCamey *U.S.A.* **116** F3
McCammon *U.S.A.* **108** E7
McCarran Int., Las
   Vegas ✈ (LAS) *U.S.A.* **111** J11
McCauley I. *Canada* **102** C2
McCleary *U.S.A.* **110** C3
McClenny *U.S.A.* **117** F13
Macclesfield *U.K.* **14** D5
M'Clintock Chan. *Canada* **100** B9
McClintock Ra. *Australia* **92** C4
McCloud *U.S.A.* **108** F2
McCluer I. *Australia* **92** B5
McClure *U.S.A.* **114** F7
McClure, L. *U.S.A.* **110** H6
M'Clure Str. *Canada* **101** B8
McClusky *U.S.A.* **112** B3
McComb *U.S.A.* **117** F9
McCook *U.S.A.* **112** E3
McCreary *Canada* **103** C9
McCullough Mt. *U.S.A.* **111** K11
McCusker → *Canada* **103** B7
McDame *Canada* **102** B3
McDermitt *U.S.A.* **108** F5
McDonald *U.S.A.* **114** F4
Macdonald, L. *Australia* **92** D4
McDonald Is. *Ind. Oc.* **3** G13
MacDonnell Ranges
   Australia **92** D5

MacDowell L. *Canada* **104** B1
Macduff *U.K.* **13** D6
Maceda *Spain* **36** C3
Macedonia *U.S.A.* **114** E3
Macedonia ■ *Europe* **44** E5
Maceió *Brazil* **125** E11
Maceira *Portugal* **36** F2
Macenta *Guinea* **82** D3
Macerata *Italy* **41** E10
McFarland *U.S.A.* **111** K7
McFarlane → *Canada* **103** B7
Macfarlane, L. *Australia* **95** E2
McGehee *U.S.A.* **116** E9
McGill *U.S.A.* **108** G6
Macgillycuddy's Reeks
   Ireland **12** E2
McGraw *U.S.A.* **115** D8
McGregor *U.S.A.* **112** D8
McGregor Ra. *Australia* **95** D3
McGuire, Mt. *U.S.A.* **108** D6
Mach *Pakistan* **68** E2
Māch Kowr *Iran* **71** E9
Machado = Jiparaná →
   Brazil **124** E6
Machagai *Argentina* **126** B3
Machakos *Kenya* **86** C4
Machala *Ecuador* **124** D3
Machanga *Mozam.* **89** C6
Machattie, L. *Australia* **94** C2
Machava *Mozam.* **89** D5
Machece *Mozam.* **87** F4
Macheng *China* **59** B10
Machero *Spain* **37** F6
Machhu → *India* **68** H4
Machiara △ *Pakistan* **68** B5
Machias *Maine, U.S.A.* **113** C20
Machias *N.Y., U.S.A.* **114** D6
Machichi → *Canada* **103** B10
Machico *Madeira* **48** D3
Machilipatnam *India* **67** L12
Machiques *Venezuela* **124** A4
Machupicchu *Peru* **124** F4
Machynlleth *U.K.* **15** E4
Macia *Mozam.* **89** D5
Maciejowice *Poland* **31** G8
Măcin *Romania* **29** E13
Macina *Mali* **82** C4
McInnes L. *Canada* **103** C10
McIntosh *U.S.A.* **112** C3
McIntosh L. *Canada* **103** B8
Macintosh Ra. *Australia* **93** E4
Macintyre → *Australia* **95** D5
Macizo Galaico *Spain* **36** C3
Mackay *Australia* **94** K7
Mackay *U.S.A.* **108** E7
MacKay → *Canada* **102** B6
Mackay, L. *Australia* **92** D4
McKay Ra. *Australia* **92** D3
McKeesport *U.S.A.* **114** F5
McKellar *Canada* **114** A5
McKenna *U.S.A.* **110** D4
Mackenzie *Canada* **102** B4
McKenzie *U.S.A.* **117** C10
Mackenzie → *Australia* **94** C4
Mackenzie → *Canada* **100** C6
McKenzie → *U.S.A.* **108** D2
Mackenzie Bay *Canada* **98** C6
Mackenzie City = Linden
   Guyana **124** B7
Mackenzie King I. *Canada* **101** B8
Mackenzie Mts. *Canada* **100** C7
Mackinaw City *U.S.A.* **113** C11
McKinlay *Australia* **94** C3
McKinlay → *Australia* **94** C3
McKinley, Mt. *U.S.A.* **106** a
McKinley Sea *Arctic* **4** A7
McKinney *U.S.A.* **116** E6
Mackinnon Road *Kenya* **86** C4
McKittrick *U.S.A.* **111** K7
Macklin *Canada* **103** C7
Macksville *Australia* **95** E5
McLaughlin *U.S.A.* **112** C3
Maclean *Australia* **95** D5
McLean *U.S.A.* **116** D4
McLeansboro *U.S.A.* **112** F9
Maclear *S. Africa* **89** E4
Maclear, C. *Malawi* **87** E3
Macleay → *Australia* **95** E5
McLennan *Canada* **102** B5
McLeod → *Canada* **102** C5
McLeod, L. *Australia* **93** D1
MacLeod B. *Canada* **103** A7
MacLeod Lake *Canada* **102** C4
McLoughlin, Mt. *U.S.A.* **108** E2
McMechen *U.S.A.* **114** G4
McMinnville *Oreg., U.S.A.* **108** D2
McMinnville *Tenn., U.S.A.* **117** D12
McMurdo *Antarctica* **5** D11
McMurdo Sd. *Antarctica* **5** D11
McMurray = Fort
   McMurray *Canada* **102** B6
McMurray *U.S.A.* **110** B4

Macomb *U.S.A.* **112** E8
Macomer *Italy* **42** B1
Mâcon *France* **19** F11
Macon *Ga., U.S.A.* **117** E13
Macon *Miss., U.S.A.* **117** E10
Macon *Mo., U.S.A.* **112** F7
Macossa *Mozam.* **87** F3
Macoun L. *Canada* **103** B8
Macovane *Mozam.* **89** C6
Macquarie → *Australia* **95** E4
Macquarie Harbour
   Australia **95** G4
Macquarie Is. *Pac. Oc.* **96** N7
Macquarie Ridge *S. Ocean* **5** B10
MacRobertson Land
   Antarctica **5** D6
Macroom *Ireland* **12** E3
MacTier *Canada* **114** A5
Macubela *Mozam.* **87** F4
Macugnaga *Italy* **40** C4
Macuira △ *Colombia* **121** D5
Macuiza *Mozam.* **87** F3
Macumba → *Australia* **95** D2
Macuro *Venezuela* **125** K15
Macusani *Peru* **124** F4
Macuse *Mozam.* **87** F4
Macuspana *Mexico* **119** D6
Macusse *Angola* **88** B3
Mada → *Nigeria* **83** D6
Ma'dabā □ *Jordan* **74** D4
Madadeni *S. Africa* **89** D5
Madagali *Nigeria* **83** C7
Madagascar ■ *Africa* **89** C8
Madā'in Sālih *Si. Arabia* **70** E3
Madama *Niger* **79** D8
Madame, I. *Canada* **105** C7
Madan *Bulgaria* **45** E8
Madang *Papua N. G.* **90** B7
Madaoua *Niger* **83** C6
Madara *Nigeria* **83** C7
Madaripur *Bangla.* **67** H17
Madauk *Burma* **67** L20
Madawaska *Canada* **114** A7
Madawaska → *Canada* **114** A7
Madaya *Burma* **67** H20
Madbar *Sudan* **81** F3
Maddalena *Italy* **42** A2
Maddaloni *Italy* **43** A7
Madeira *Atl. Oc.* **48** D3
Madeira → *Brazil* **124** D7
Madeleine, Îs. de la *Canada* **105** C7
Maden *Turkey* **73** C8
Madera *Mexico* **118** B3
Madera *Calif., U.S.A.* **110** J6
Madera → *U.S.A.* **114** F6
Madha *India* **66** L9
Madhavpur *India* **68** J3
Madhepura *India* **69** F12
Madhubani *India* **69** F12
Madhupur *India* **69** G12
Madhya Pradesh □ *India* **68** J8
Madidi → *Bolivia* **124** F5
Madikeri *India* **66** N9
Madikwe ⌂ *S. Africa* **89** D5
Madill *U.S.A.* **116** D6
Madimba
   Dem. Rep. of the Congo **84** E3
Ma'din *Syria* **73** E8
Madina *Mali* **82** C3
Madinani *Ivory C.* **82** D3
Madingou *Congo* **84** E2
Madirovalo *Madag.* **89** B8
Madison *Calif., U.S.A.* **110** G5
Madison *Fla., U.S.A.* **117** F13
Madison *Ind., U.S.A.* **113** F11
Madison *Nebr., U.S.A.* **112** E5
Madison *Ohio, U.S.A.* **114** E3
Madison *S. Dak., U.S.A.* **112** C5
Madison *Wis., U.S.A.* **112** D9
Madison → *U.S.A.* **108** D8
Madison Heights *U.S.A.* **113** G14
Madisonville *Ky., U.S.A.* **112** G10
Madisonville *Tex., U.S.A.* **116** F7
Madista *Botswana* **88** C4
Madiun *Indonesia* **63** G14
Mado Gashi *Kenya* **86** B4
Madoc *Canada* **114** B7
Madol *Sudan* **81** F2
Madon → *France* **19** D13
Madona *Latvia* **32** D4
Madonie *Italy* **42** E6
Madonna di Campiglio *Italy* **40** B7
Madra Dağı *Turkey* **47** B9
Madrakah, Ra's al *Oman* **75** D6
Madras = Chennai *India* **66** N12
Madras = Tamil Nadu □
   India **66** P10
Madras *U.S.A.* **108** D3
Madre, L. *U.S.A.* **116** J6
Madre, Sierra *Phil.* **61** C5
Madre de Dios → *Bolivia* **124** F5
Madre de Dios, I. *Chile* **128** G1
Madre del Sur, Sierra
   Mexico **119** D5

Madre Occidental, Sierra
   Mexico **118** B3
Madre Oriental, Sierra
   Mexico **118** C5
Madri *India* **68** G5
Madrid *Spain* **36** E7
Madrid *U.S.A.* **115** B9
Madrid □ *Spain* **36** E7
Madrid Barajas ✈ (MAD)
   Spain **36** E7
Madridejos *Spain* **37** F7
Madrigal de las Altas
   Torres *Spain* **36** D6
Madrona, Sierra *Spain* **37** G6
Madroñera *Spain* **37** F5
Madu *Sudan* **81** E2
Madura *Australia* **93** F4
Madura *Indonesia* **63** G15
Madura, Selat *Indonesia* **63** G15
Madurai *India* **66** Q11
Madurantakam *India* **66** N11
Madzhalis *Russia* **35** J8
Mae Chan *Thailand* **64** B2
Mae Hong Son *Thailand* **64** C2
Mae Khlong → *Thailand* **64** F3
Mae Phrik *Thailand* **64** D2
Mae Ping △ *Thailand* **64** D2
Mae Ramat *Thailand* **64** D2
Mae Rim *Thailand* **64** C2
Mae Sot *Thailand* **64** D2
Mae Suai *Thailand* **58** H2
Mae Tha *Thailand* **64** C2
Mae Wong △ *Thailand* **64** E2
Mae Yom △ *Thailand* **64** C3
Maebashi *Japan* **55** F9
Maella *Spain* **38** D5
Maesteg *U.K.* **15** F4
Maestra, Sierra *Cuba* **120** B4
Maevatanana *Madag.* **89** B8
Mafeking = Mafikeng
   S. Africa **88** D4
Mafeking *Canada* **103** C8
Mafeteng *Lesotho* **88** D4
Maffra *Australia* **95** F4
Mafia I. *Tanzania* **86** D4
Mafikeng *S. Africa* **88** D4
Mafra *Brazil* **127** B6
Mafra *Portugal* **37** G1
Mafungabusi Plateau
   Zimbabwe **87** F2
Magadan *Russia* **53** D16
Magadi *Kenya* **86** C4
Magadi, L. *Kenya* **86** C4
Magaliesburg *S. Africa* **89** D4
Magallanes, Estrecho de
   Chile **128** G2
Magaluf *Spain* **39** F7
Magangué *Colombia* **124** B4
Magaria *Niger* **83** C6
Magburaka *S. Leone* **82** D2
Magdalen Is. = Madeleine,
   Îs. de la *Canada* **105** C7
Magdalena *Argentina* **126** D4
Magdalena *Bolivia* **124** F6
Magdalena *U.S.A.* **109** J10
Magdalena → *Colombia* **124** A4
Magdalena → *Mexico* **118** A2
Magdalena, B. *Mexico* **118** C2
Magdalena, I. *Mexico* **118** C2
Magdalena, Llano de
   Mexico **118** C2
Magdalena de Kino *Mexico* **118** A2
Magdeburg *Germany* **24** C7
Magdelaine Cays *Australia* **94** B5
Magdub *Sudan* **81** E2
Magee *U.S.A.* **117** F10
Magelang *Indonesia* **63** G14
Magellan's Str. =
   Magallanes, Estrecho de
   Chile **128** G2
Magenta *Italy* **40** C5
Magenta, L. *Australia* **93** F2
Mageroya *Norway* **8** A21
Maggia → *Switz.* **25** J4
Maggiorasca, Mte. *Italy* **40** D6
Maggiore, Lago *Italy* **40** B5
Maggotty *Jamaica* **120** a
Maghâgha *Egypt* **80** B3
Maghama *Mauritania* **82** B2
Magherafelt *U.K.* **12** B5
Maghreb *N. Afr.* **78** B5
Magione *Italy* **41** E9
Magistralnyy *Russia* **53** D11
Maglaj *Bos.-H.* **28** F3
Magliano in Toscana *Italy* **41** F8
Máglie *Italy* **43** B11
Magnac-Laval *France* **20** B5
Magnetic Pole (North)
   Canada **101** B9
Magnetic Pole (South)
   Antarctica **5** C9
Magnisia □ *Greece* **46** B5
Magnitogorsk *Russia* **52** D6
Magnolia *Ark., U.S.A.* **116** E8
Magnolia *Miss., U.S.A.* **117** F9
Magny-en-Vexin *France* **19** C8

Mago *Fiji* **91** a
Mago △ *Ethiopia* **81** F4
Magog *Canada* **115** A12
Magoro *Uganda* **86** B3
Magoša = Famagusta
  Cyprus **49** D12
Magoulades *Greece* **49** A3
Magoye *Zambia* **87** F2
Magpie, L. *Canada* **105** B7
Magrath *Canada* **102** D6
Magre → *Spain* **39** F4
Magrur *Sudan* **81** E3
Magrur, Wadi → *Sudan* **81** D2
Magta Lahjar *Mauritania* **82** B2
Maguan *China* **58** F5
Maguarinho, C. *Brazil* **125** D9
Magude *Mozam.* **89** D5
Magurski △ *Poland* **31** J8
Maġusa = Famagusta
  Cyprus **49** D12
Maguse L. *Canada* **103** A9
Maguse Pt. *Canada* **103** A10
Magvana *India* **68** H3
Magwe *Burma* **67** J19
Magwe *Sudan* **81** G3
Magyarország =
  Hungary ■ *Europe* **27** D12
Maha Sarakham *Thailand* **64** D4
Mahābād *Iran* **73** D11
Mahabharat Lekh *Nepal* **69** E10
Mahabo *Madag.* **89** C7
Mahadeo Hills *India* **69** H8
Mahaffey *U.S.A.* **114** F6
Mahagi *Dem. Rep. of the Congo* **86** B3
Mahajamba → *Madag.* **89** B8
Mahajamba, Helodranon' i
  Madag. **89** B8
Mahajan *India* **68** E5
Mahajanga *Madag.* **89** B8
Mahajanga □ *Madag.* **89** B8
Mahajilo → *Madag.* **89** B8
Mahakam → *Indonesia* **62** E5
Mahalapye *Botswana* **88** C4
Mahale Mts. *Tanzania* **86** D3
Mahale Mts. △ *Tanzania* **86** D2
Maḥallāt *Iran* **71** C6
Māhān *Iran* **71** D8
Mahan → *India* **69** H10
Mahanadi → *India* **67** J15
Mahananda → *India* **69** G12
Mahanoro *Madag.* **89** B8
Mahanoy City *U.S.A.* **115** F8
Maharashtra □ *India* **66** J9
Mahasham, W. → *Egypt* **74** E3
Mahasoa *Madag.* **89** C8
Mahasolo *Madag.* **89** B8
Mahattat ash Shīdīyah
  Jordan **74** F4
Mahattat 'Unayzah *Jordan* **74** E4
Mahavavy → *Madag.* **89** B8
Mahaxay *Laos* **64** D5
Mahbubnagar *India* **66** L10
Maḥḍah *Oman* **71** E7
Mahdia *Tunisia* **79** A8
Mahe *India* **69** C8
Mahé *Seychelles* **85** b
Mahé ✈ (SEZ) *Seychelles* **85** b
Mahébourg *Mauritius* **85** d
Mahendragarh *India* **68** E7
Mahendranagar *Nepal* **69** E9
Mahenge *Tanzania* **87** D4
Maheno *N.Z.* **91** F3
Mahesana *India* **68** H5
Maheshwar *India* **68** H6
Mahgawan *India* **69** F8
Mahi → *India* **68** H5
Mahia Pen. *N.Z.* **91** C6
Mahilyow *Belarus* **23** B16
Mahilyow □ *Belarus* **32** E6
Mahina *Tahiti* **91** d
Mahinerangi, L. *N.Z.* **91** F2
Mahmiya *Sudan* **81** D3
Mahmud Kot *Pakistan* **68** D4
Mahmudia *Romania* **29** E14
Mahmutbey *Turkey* **47** B12
Mahmutbey *Turkey* **45** E12
Mahnomen *U.S.A.* **112** B6
Mahoba *India* **69** G8
Mahón = Maó *Spain* **48** B11
Mahon, Menorca ✈
  (MAH) *Spain* **38** F9
Mahone Bay *Canada* **105** D7
Mahopac *U.S.A.* **115** E11
Mahuta *Nigeria* **83** C5
Mahuva *India* **68** J4
Mahya Daği *Turkey* **45** E11
Mai-Ndombe, L.
  Dem. Rep. of the Congo **84** E3
Mai-Sai *Thailand* **58** G2
Mai Thon, Ko *Thailand* **65** a
Maia *Portugal* **36** D2
Maia *Spain* **38** B3
Maiais *Spain* **38** D5
Maïche *France* **19** E13
Maicurú → *Brazil* **125** D8
Máida *Italy* **43** D9
Maidan Khula *Afghan.* **68** C3

Maidenhead *U.K.* **15** F7
Maidstone *Canada* **103** C7
Maidstone *U.K.* **15** F8
Maiduguri *Nigeria* **83** C7
Maiella △ *Italy* **41** F11
Măieruş *Romania* **29** E10
Maigatari *Nigeria* **83** C6
Maignelay Montigny *France* **19** C9
Maigo *Phil.* **61** G5
Maigudo *Ethiopia* **81** F4
Maihar *India* **69** G9
Maijdi *Bangla.* **67** H17
Maikala Ra. *India* **67** J12
Maiko △
  Dem. Rep. of the Congo **86** C2
Mailani *India* **69** E9
Maillezais *France* **20** B3
Mailsi *Pakistan* **68** E5
Main → *Germany* **25** F4
Main → *U.K.* **12** B5
Main Range △ *Australia* **95** D5
Main Ridge *Trin. & Tob.* **125** J16
Mainburg *Germany* **25** G7
Maine *France* **18** D6
Maine □ *U.S.A.* **113** C19
Maine → *Ireland* **12** D2
Maine, G. of *U.S.A.* **113** D19
Maine-et-Loire □ *France* **18** E6
Maïne-Soroa *Niger* **83** C7
Maingkwan *Burma* **67** F20
Mainit, L. *Phil.* **61** G6
Mainland *Orkney, U.K.* **13** C5
Mainland *Shet., U.K.* **13** A7
Mainoru *Australia* **94** A1
Mainpuri *India* **69** F8
Maintal *Germany* **25** E4
Maintenon *France* **19** D8
Maintirano *Madag.* **89** B7
Mainz *Germany* **25** E4
Maio *C. Verde Is.* **78** b
Maipú *Argentina* **126** D4
Maiquetía *Venezuela* **124** A5
Máira → *Italy* **40** D4
Mairabari *India* **67** F18
Maisí *Cuba* **121** B5
Maisi, Pta. de *Cuba* **121** B5
Maitland *N.S.W., Australia* **95** E5
Maitland *S. Austral., Australia* **95** E2
Maitland → *Canada* **114** C3
Maitri *Antarctica* **5** D3
Maiyema *Nigeria* **83** C5
Maiyuan *China* **59** E11
Maizuru *Japan* **55** G7
Majalengka *Indonesia* **63** G13
Majene *Indonesia* **63** E5
Majete △ *Malawi* **87** F3
Majevica *Bos.-H.* **28** F3
Maji *Ethiopia* **81** F4
Majiang *China* **58** D6
Majorca = Mallorca *Spain* **48** B10
Majuro *Marshall Is.* **96** G9
Maka *Senegal* **82** C2
Makaha *Zimbabwe* **89** B5
Makak *Cameroon* **83** E7
Makale *Indonesia* **63** E5
Makalu-Barun △ *Nepal* **69** F12
Makamba *Burundi* **86** C2
Makari *Cameroon* **83** C7
Makarikari =
  Makgadikgadi Salt Pans
  Botswana **88** C4
Makarov Basin *Arctic* **4** A
Makarovo *Russia* **53** D11
Makarska *Croatia* **41** E14
Makaryev *Russia* **34** B9
Makasar = Ujung
  Pandang *Indonesia* **63** F5
Makasar, Selat *Indonesia* **63** E5
Makasar, Str. of =
  Makasar, Selat *Indonesia* **63** E5
Makat = Maqat *Kazakhstan* **52** E6
Makedonija =
  Macedonia ■ *Europe* **44** E5
Makeni *S. Leone* **82** D2
Makeyevka = Makiyivka
  Ukraine **33** H9
Makgadikgadi △ *Botswana* **88** C3
Makgadikgadi Salt Pans
  Botswana **88** C4
Makhachkala *Russia* **35** J8
Makhado = Louis
  Trichardt *S. Africa* **89** C4
Makharadze = Ozurgeti
  Georgia **35** K5
Makhfar al Buşayyah *Iraq* **70** D5
Makhmûr *Iraq* **73** E10
Makian *Indonesia* **63** D7
Makindu *Kenya* **86** C4
Makīnsk *Kazakhstan* **52** D8
Makira = San Cristóbal
  Solomon Is. **90** C9
Makiv *Ukraine* **29** B11
Makiyivka *Ukraine* **33** H9
Makkah *Si. Arabia* **80** C3
Makkovik *Canada* **105** A8

Makó *Hungary* **28** D5
Mako *Senegal* **82** C2
Makogai *Fiji* **91** a
Makokou *Gabon* **84** D2
Makongo
  Dem. Rep. of the Congo **86** B2
Makoro *Dem. Rep. of the Congo* **86** B2
Maków Mazowiecki *Poland* **31** F8
Maków Podhalański *Poland* **31** J6
Makra *Greece* **47** E7
Makrai *India* **68** H7
Makran Coast Range
  Pakistan **66** G4
Makrana *India* **68** F6
Makrany *Belarus* **31** G11
Makri *Greece* **45** F9
Makrigialos *Greece* **49** D7
Mākū *Iran* **73** C11
Makunda *Botswana* **88** C3
Makung *Taiwan* **59** F12
Makurazaki *Japan* **55** J5
Makurdi *Nigeria* **83** D6
Makwassie *S. Africa* **88** D4
Makwiro *Zimbabwe* **89** B5
Mâl → *Mauritania* **82** B2
Mal B. *Ireland* **12** D2
Mala, Pta. *Panama* **120** E3
Mala Belozërka *Ukraine* **33** J8
Malá Fatra △ *Slovak Rep.* **27** B12
Mala Kapela *Croatia* **41** D12
Mała Panew → *Poland* **31** H4
Mala Vyska *Ukraine* **33** H6
Malabang *Phil.* **61** H6
Malabar Coast *India* **66** P9
Malabon *Phil.* **61** D4
Malabu *Nigeria* **83** D7
Malacca, Straits of *Indonesia* **65** L3
Malacky *Slovak Rep.* **27** C10
Malad City *U.S.A.* **108** E7
Maladeta *Spain* **38** C5
Maladzyechna *Belarus* **23** A14
Málaga *Spain* **37** J6
Málaga □ *Spain* **37** J6
Malagarasi *Tanzania* **86** D3
Malagarasi → *Tanzania* **86** D2
Malagasy Rep. =
  Madagascar ■ *Africa* **89** C8
Malagón *Spain* **37** F7
Malagón → *Spain* **37** H3
Malahide *Ireland* **12** C5
Malaimbandy *Madag.* **89** C8
Malaita *Solomon Is.* **90** B9
Malakâl *Sudan* **81** F3
Malakand *Pakistan* **68** B4
Malakula *Vanuatu* **90** C9
Malakwal *Pakistan* **68** C5
Malamala *Indonesia* **63** E6
Malanda *Australia* **94** B4
Malang *Indonesia* **63** G15
Malangen *Norway* **8** B18
Malanje *Angola* **84** F3
Mälaren *Sweden* **10** E11
Malargüe *Argentina* **126** D2
Malartic *Canada* **104** C4
Malaryta *Belarus* **31** G11
Malatya *Turkey* **73** C8
Malatya □ *Turkey* **72** C7
Malawi ■ *Africa* **87** E3
Malawi, L. *Africa* **87** E3
Malay Pen. *Asia* **65** J3
Malaya Belozërka = Mala
  Belozërka *Ukraine* **33** J8
Malaya Vishera *Russia* **32** C7
Malaya Viska = Mala
  Vyska *Ukraine* **33** H6
Malaybalay *Phil.* **61** G6
Malāyer *Iran* **73** E13
Malaysia ■ *Asia* **65** K4
Malazgirt *Turkey* **73** C10
Malbaza *Niger* **83** C6
Malbon *Australia* **94** C3
Malbooma *Australia* **95** E1
Malbork *Poland* **30** D7
Malcésine *Italy* **40** C7
Malchin *Germany* **24** B8
Malchow *Germany* **24** B8
Malcolm *Australia* **93** E3
Malcolm, Pt. *Australia* **93** F3
Malczyce *Poland* **31** G3
Maldah *India* **69** G13
Maldegem *Belgium* **17** C3
Malden *Mass., U.S.A.* **115** D13
Malden *Mo., U.S.A.* **112** G9
Malden I. *Kiribati* **97** H12
Maldives ■ *Ind. Oc.* **50** H9
Maldon *U.K.* **15** F8
Maldonado *Uruguay* **127** C5
Maldonado, Pta. *Mexico* **119** D5
Malè *Italy* **40** B7
Malé *Maldives* **50** H9
Malé Karpaty *Slovak Rep.* **27** C10
Maleas, Akra *Greece* **46** E5
Malebo, Pool *Africa* **84** E3
Malegaon *India* **66** J9
Malei *Mozam.* **87** F4
Malek *Sudan* **81** F3
Malek Kandī *Iran* **73** D12

Malela *Dem. Rep. of the Congo* **86** C2
Malema *Mozam.* **87** E4
Maleme *Greece* **49** D5
Malerás *Sweden* **11** H9
Malerkotla *India* **68** D6
Males *Greece* **49** D7
Malesherbes *France* **19** D9
Maleshevska Planina *Europe* **44** E7
Malesina *Greece* **46** C5
Malestroit *France* **18** E4
Malfa *Italy* **43** D7
Malgobek *Russia* **35** J7
Malgomaj *Sweden* **8** D17
Malgrat de Mar *Spain* **38** D7
Malha *Sudan* **81** D2
Malhargarh *India* **68** G6
Malheur → *U.S.A.* **108** D5
Malheur L. *U.S.A.* **108** E4
Mali *Guinea* **82** C2
Mali ■ *Africa* **82** B4
Mali → *Burma* **67** G20
Mali Kanal *Serbia* **28** E4
Mali Kyun *Burma* **64** F2
Malia *Greece* **49** D7
Malia, Kolpos *Greece* **49** D7
Malibu *U.S.A.* **111** L8
Maliku *Indonesia* **63** E6
Malili *Indonesia* **63** E6
Mālilla *Sweden* **11** G9
Malimba, Mts.
  Dem. Rep. of the Congo **86** D2
Malin Hd. *Ireland* **12** A4
Malin Pen. *Ireland* **12** A4
Malindi *Kenya* **86** C5
Malines = Mechelen *Belgium* **17** C4
Malino *Indonesia* **63** D6
Malinyi *Tanzania* **87** D4
Malipo *China* **58** F5
Maliq *Albania* **44** F4
Malita *Phil.* **63** C7
Maliwun *Burma* **65** G2
Maliya *India* **68** H4
Maljenik *Serbia* **44** C5
Malka Mari △ *Kenya* **86** B5
Malkara *Turkey* **45** F10
Malkinia Górna *Poland* **31** F9
Malko Tŭrnovo *Bulgaria* **45** E11
Mallacoota Inlet *Australia* **95** F4
Mallaig *U.K.* **13** D3
Mallaoua *Niger* **83** C6
Mallawan *India* **69** F9
Mallawi *Egypt* **80** B3
Mallemort *France* **21** E9
Málles Venosta *Italy* **40** B7
Mallicolo = Malakula
  Vanuatu **90** C9
Mallorca *Spain* **48** B10
Mallorytown *Canada* **115** B9
Mallow *Ireland* **12** D3
Malmbäck *Sweden* **11** G8
Malmberget *Sweden* **8** C19
Malmédy *Belgium* **17** D6
Malmesbury *S. Africa* **88** E2
Malmivaara =
  Malmberget *Sweden* **8** C19
Malmköping *Sweden* **10** E10
Malmö *Sweden* **11** J7
Malmslätt *Sweden* **11** F9
Malmyzh *Russia* **34** B10
Malnaş *Romania* **29** D10
Malo Konare *Bulgaria* **45** D8
Maloarkhangelsk *Russia* **33** F9
Malolo *Fiji* **91** a
Malolos *Phil.* **63** B6
Malolotja △ *Swaziland* **89** D5
Malombe L. *Malawi* **87** E4
Małomice *Poland* **31** G2
Malomir *Bulgaria* **45** D10
Malone *U.S.A.* **115** B10
Malong *China* **58** E5
Małopolskie □ *Poland* **31** J7
Malorad *Bulgaria* **44** C7
Måløy *Norway* **8** F11
Maloyaroslovets *Russia* **32** E9
Malpartida *Spain* **37** F4
Malpaso *Canary Is.* **48** G1
Malpaso, Presa =
  Netzahualcóyotl, Presa
  Mexico **119** D6
Malpelo, I. de *Colombia* **124** C2
Malpica de Bergantiños
  Spain **36** B2
Malpur *India* **68** H5
Malpura *India* **68** F6
Mals = Málles Venosta *Italy* **40** B7
Malta *Mont., U.S.A.* **108** A10
Malta ■ *Europe* **49** D8
Maltahöhe *Namibia* **88** C2
Maltepe *Turkey* **45** F13
Malton *Canada* **114** C5
Malton *U.K.* **14** C7
Maluku *Indonesia* **63** E7
Maluku □ *Indonesia* **63** E7
Maluku Sea = Molucca
  Sea *Indonesia* **63** E6
Malumfashi *Nigeria* **83** C6

Malung *Sweden* **10** D7
Malungsfors *Sweden* **10** D7
Maluwe *Ghana* **82** D4
Malvan *India* **66** L8
Malvern *U.S.A.* **116** D8
Malvern Hills *U.K.* **15** E5
Malvinas, Is. = Falkland
  Is. ☑ *Atl. Oc.* **128** G5
Malý Dunaj → *Slovak Rep.* **27** D11
Malya *Tanzania* **86** C3
Malye Derbety *Russia* **35** G7
Malyn *Ukraine* **23** C15
Malyy Lyakhovskiy,
  Ostrov *Russia* **53** B15
Mama *Russia* **53** D12
Mamadysh *Russia* **34** C10
Mamanguape *Brazil* **125** E11
Mamanuca Group *Fiji* **91** a
Mamarr Mitlā *Egypt* **74** E1
Mamasa *Indonesia* **63** E5
Mambasa
  Dem. Rep. of the Congo **86** B2
Mamberamo → *Indonesia* **63** E9
Mambilima Falls *Zambia* **87** E2
Mambirima
  Dem. Rep. of the Congo **87** E2
Mambo *Tanzania* **86** C4
Mambrui *Kenya* **86** C5
Mamburao *Phil.* **61** E4
Mameigwess L. *Canada* **104** B2
Mamers *France* **18** D7
Mamfé *Cameroon* **83** D6
Mammoth *U.S.A.* **109** K8
Mammoth Cave △ *U.S.A.* **112** G10
Mamonovo *Russia* **30** D6
Mamoré → *Bolivia* **124** F5
Mamou *Guinea* **82** C2
Mamoudzou *Mayotte* **85** a
Mampong *Ghana* **83** D4
Mampatá *Guinea-Biss.* **82** C2
Mamuju *Indonesia* **63** E5
Mamry, Jezioro *Poland* **30** D8
Mamuno *Botswana* **88** C3
Mamuras *Albania* **44** E3
Man *Ivory C.* **82** D3
Man, I. of *U.K.* **14** C3
Man-Bazar *India* **69** H12
Man Na *Burma* **67** H20
Mana → *Fr. Guiana* **125** B8
Mana Pools △ *Zimbabwe* **87** F2
Manaar, G. of = Mannar,
  G. of *Asia* **66** Q11
Manacapuru *Brazil* **124** D6
Manacor *Spain* **48** B10
Manado *Indonesia* **63** D6
Managua *Nic.* **120** D2
Managua, L. de *Nic.* **120** D2
Manakara *Madag.* **89** C8
Manali *India* **68** C7
Manama = Al Manāmah
  Bahrain **71** E6
Manambao → *Madag.* **89** B7
Manambato *Madag.* **89** A8
Manambolo → *Madag.* **89** B7
Manambolosy *Madag.* **89** B8
Mananara *Madag.* **89** B8
Mananara → *Madag.* **89** C8
Mananara △ *Madag.* **89** B8
Manang
Manangoods... *Madag.* **89** C8
Mananjary *Madag.* **89** C8
Manankoro *Mali* **82** C3
Manantenina *Madag.* **89** C8
Manaos = Manaus *Brazil* **124** D7
Manapire → *Venezuela* **124** B5
Manapouri *N.Z.* **91** F1
Manapouri, L. *N.Z.* **91** F1
Manaqil *Sudan* **81** E3
Manār, Jabal *Yemen* **75** E3
Manaravolo *Madag.* **89** C8
Manas *China* **60** B3
Manas → *India* **67** F17
Manaslu *Nepal* **69** E11
Manasquan *U.S.A.* **115** F10
Manassa *U.S.A.* **109** H11
Manatí *Puerto Rico* **121** d
Manaung *Burma* **67** K18
Manaus *Brazil* **124** D7
Manavgat *Turkey* **72** D4
Manawan L. *Canada* **103** B8
Manay *Phil.* **61** H7
Manbij *Syria* **72** D7
Mancha Real *Spain* **37** H7
Manche □ *France* **18** C5
Manchegorsk *Russia* **52** C4
Manchester *U.K.* **14** D5
Manchester *Calif., U.S.A.* **110** G3
Manchester *Conn., U.S.A.* **115** E12
Manchester *Ga., U.S.A.* **117** E12
Manchester *Iowa, U.S.A.* **112** D8
Manchester *Ky., U.S.A.* **113** G12
Manchester *N.H., U.S.A.* **115** D13
Manchester *N.Y., U.S.A.* **114** D7
Manchester *Pa., U.S.A.* **115** F8
Manchester *Tenn., U.S.A.* **117** D11
Manchester *Vt., U.S.A.* **115** C11
Manchester Int. ✈ (MAN)
  U.K. **14** D5

Manchester L. *Canada* **103** A7
Manchhar L. *Pakistan* **68** F2
Manchuria = Dongbei
  China **57** D13
Manchurian Plain *China* **50** D14
Manciano *Italy* **41** F8
Mancifa *Ethiopia* **81** F5
Mand → *India* **69** J10
Mand → *Iran* **71** D7
Manda *Ludewe, Tanzania* **87** E3
Manda *Mbeya, Tanzania* **86** D3
Manda *Mbeya, Tanzania* **87** D3
Mandabé *Madag.* **89** C7
Mandaguari *Brazil* **127** A5
Mandah = Töhöm *Mongolia* **56** B5
Mandal *Norway* **9** G12
Mandala, Puncak *Indonesia* **63** E10
Mandalay *Burma* **67** J20
Mandale = Mandalay
  Burma **67** J20
Mandalgarh *India* **68** G6
Mandalgovĭ *Mongolia* **56** B4
Mandalī *Iraq* **73** F11
Mandan *U.S.A.* **112** B3
Mandaon *Phil.* **61** E5
Mandar, Teluk *Indonesia* **63** E5
Mándas *Italy* **42** C2
Mandaue *Phil.* **61** F5
Mandelieu-la-Napoule
  France **21** E10
Mandera *Kenya* **86** B5
Manderi *Kenya* **86** B5
Mandeville *Jamaica* **120** a
Mandi *India* **68** D7
Mandi Dabwali *India* **68** E6
Mandiana *Guinea* **82** C3
Mandimba *Mozam.* **87** E4
Mandioli *Indonesia* **63** E7
Mandla *India* **69** H9
Mandø *Denmark* **11** J2
Mandorah *Australia* **92** B5
Mandoto *Madag.* **89** B8
Mandoudi *Greece* **46** C5
Mandra *Greece* **46** C5
Mandra *Pakistan* **68** C5
Mandraki *Greece* **47** E9
Mandrare → *Madag.* **89** D8
Mandritsara *Madag.* **89** B8
Mandronarivo *Madag.* **89** C8
Mandsaur *India* **68** G6
Mandurah *Australia* **93** F2
Mandúria *Italy* **43** B10
Mandvi *India* **68** H3
Mandya *India* **66** N10
Mandzai *Pakistan* **68** D2
Mané *Burkina Faso* **83** C4
Maneh *Iran* **71** B8
Manengouba, Mts. *Cameroon* **83** E6
Manera *Madag.* **89** C8
Manério *Italy* **40** C7
Maneroo Cr. → *Australia* **94** C3
Manfalûț *Egypt* **80** B3
Manfredónia *Italy* **41** G12
Manfredónia, G. di *Italy* **41** G13
Manga *Burkina Faso* **83** C4
Manga *Niger* **83** C7
Mangabeiras, Chapada das
  Brazil **125** F9
Mangaia *Cook Is.* **97** K12
Mangalia *Romania* **29** G13
Mangalore *India* **66** N9
Mangan *India* **69** F13
Mangawan *India* **69** G9
Mangaweka *N.Z.* **91** C5
Manggar *Indonesia* **62** E3
Manggawitu *Indonesia* **63** E8
Mangghystaū Tübegi
  Kazakhstan **52** E6
Manggis *Indonesia* **63** J18
Mangindrano *Madag.* **89** A8
Mangkalihat, Tanjung
  Indonesia **63** D5
Mangla *Pakistan* **68** C5
Mangla Dam *Pakistan* **69** C5
Manglaur *India* **68** E7
Mangnai *China* **60** C4
Mango *Togo* **83** C5
Mango *Tonga* **91** c
Mangoche *Malawi* **87** E4
Mangoky → *Madag.* **89** C7
Mangole *Indonesia* **63** E6
Mangombe
  Dem. Rep. of the Congo **86** C2
Mangonui *N.Z.* **91** A4
Mangoro → *Madag.* **89** B8
Mangrol *Mad. P., India* **68** J4
Mangrol *Raj., India* **68** G6
Mangualde *Portugal* **36** E3
Mangueira, L. da *Brazil* **127** C5
Mangum *U.S.A.* **116** D5
Mangyshlak, Poluostrov =
  Mangghystaū Tübegi
  Kazakhstan **52** E6
Manhattan *U.S.A.* **112** F5
Manhiça *Mozam.* **89** D5
Mania → *Madag.* **89** B8
Maniago *Italy* **41** B9
Manica *Mozam.* **89** B5

Manica □ *Mozam.* **89 B5**
Manicaland □ *Zimbabwe* **87 F3**
Manicoré *Brazil* **124 E6**
Manicouagan → *Canada* **105 C6**
Manicouagan, Rés. *Canada* **105 B6**
Maniema □
  Dem. Rep. of the Congo **86 C2**
Manīfah *Si. Arabia* **71 E6**
Manifold, C. *Australia* **94 C5**
Maniganggo *China* **58 B2**
Manigotagan *Canada* **103 C9**
Manigotagan → *Canada* **103 C9**
Manihari *India* **69 G12**
Manihiki *Cook Is.* **97 J11**
Manihiki Plateau *Pac. Oc.* **97 J11**
Manika, Plateau de la
  Dem. Rep. of the Congo **87 E2**
Manikpur *India* **69 G9**
Manila *Phil.* **61 D4**
Manila *U.S.A.* **108 F9**
Manila B. *Phil.* **61 D4**
Manilla *Australia* **95 E5**
Manimpé *Mali* **82 C3**
Maningrida *Australia* **94 A1**
Maninian *Ivory C.* **82 C3**
Manipur □ *India* **67 G19**
Manipur → *Burma* **67 H19**
Manisa *Turkey* **47 C9**
Manisa □ *Turkey* **47 C9**
Manistee *U.S.A.* **112 C10**
Manistee → *U.S.A.* **112 C10**
Manistique *U.S.A.* **112 C10**
Manitoba □ *Canada* **103 B9**
Manitoba, L. *Canada* **103 C9**
Manitou *Canada* **103 D9**
Manitou, L. *Canada* **105 C7**
Manitou Is. *U.S.A.* **113 C10**
Manitou L. *Canada* **103 C7**
Manitou Springs *U.S.A.* **108 G11**
Manitoulin I. *Canada* **104 C3**
Manitouwadge *Canada* **104 C2**
Manitowoc *U.S.A.* **112 C10**
Manizales *Colombia* **124 B3**
Manja *Madag.* **89 C7**
Manjacaze *Mozam.* **89 C5**
Manjakandriana *Madag.* **89 B8**
Manjhand *Pakistan* **68 G3**
Manjil *Iran* **71 B6**
Manjimup *Australia* **93 F2**
Manjra → *India* **66 K10**
Mankato *Kans., U.S.A.* **112 F4**
Mankato *Minn., U.S.A.* **112 C6**
Mankayane *Swaziland* **89 D5**
Mankera *Pakistan* **68 D4**
Mankim *Cameroon* **83 D7**
Mankono *Ivory C.* **82 D3**
Mankota *Canada* **103 D7**
Manlay → *Üydzin Mongolia* **56 B4**
Manlleu *Spain* **38 C7**
Manmad *India* **66 J9**
Mann Ranges *Australia* **93 E5**
Manna *Indonesia* **62 E2**
Mannahill *Australia* **95 E3**
Mannar *Sri Lanka* **66 Q11**
Mannar, G. of *Asia* **66 Q11**
Mannar I. *Sri Lanka* **66 Q11**
Mannheim *Germany* **25 F4**
Manning *Canada* **102 B5**
Manning *Oreg., U.S.A.* **110 E3**
Manning *S.C., U.S.A.* **117 E14**
Mannu → *Italy* **42 C2**
Mannu, C. *Italy* **42 B1**
Mannum *Australia* **95 E2**
Mano *S. Leone* **82 D2**
Mano → *Liberia* **82 D2**
Mano River *Liberia* **82 D2**
Manoharpur *India* **69 H11**
Manokwari *Indonesia* **63 E8**
Manolada *Greece* **46 C3**
Manombo *Madag.* **89 C7**
Manono
  Dem. Rep. of the Congo **86 D2**
Manono *Samoa* **91 b**
Manoppello *Italy* **41 F11**
Manorhamilton *Ireland* **12 B3**
Manosque *France* **21 E9**
Manotick *Canada* **115 A9**
Manouane → *Canada* **105 C5**
Manouane, L. *Canada* **105 B5**
Manp'o *N. Korea* **57 D14**
Manpojin = Manp'o
  N. Korea **57 D14**
Manpur *Chhattisgarh, India* **69 H10**
Manpur *Mad. P., India* **68 H6**
Manresa *Spain* **38 D6**
Mansa *Gujarat, India* **68 H5**
Mansa *Punjab, India* **68 E6**
Mansa *Zambia* **87 E2**
Mânsåsen *Sweden* **10 A8**
Mansehra *Pakistan* **68 B5**
Mansel I. *Canada* **101 C12**
Mansfield *Australia* **95 F4**
Mansfield *U.K.* **14 D6**
Mansfield *La., U.S.A.* **116 E8**
Mansfield *Mass., U.S.A.* **115 D13**
Mansfield *Ohio, U.S.A.* **114 F2**
Mansfield *Pa., U.S.A.* **114 E7**
Mansfield *Tex., U.S.A.* **116 E6**
Mansfield, Mt. *U.S.A.* **115 B12**
Mansilla de las Mulas *Spain* **36 C5**
Mansle *France* **20 C4**
Mansoa *Guinea-Biss.* **82 C1**
Manson Creek *Canada* **102 B4**
Manta *Ecuador* **124 D2**
Mantadia △ *Madag.* **89 B8**
Mantalingajan, Mt. *Phil.* **61 G2**
Mantare *Tanzania* **86 C3**
Manteca *U.S.A.* **110 H5**
Manteo *U.S.A.* **117 D17**
Mantes-la-Jolie *France* **19 D8**
Manthani *India* **66 K11**
Manti *U.S.A.* **108 G8**
Mantiqueira, Serra da
  Brazil **127 A7**
Manton *U.S.A.* **113 C11**
Mantorp *Sweden* **11 F9**
Mántova *Italy* **40 C7**
Mänttä *Finland* **32 A3**
Mantua = Mántova *Italy* **40 C7**
Manturovo *Russia* **34 A7**
Manu *Peru* **124 F4**
Manu → *Peru* **124 F4**
Manu'a Is. *Amer. Samoa* **91 b**
Manuel Alves → *Brazil* **125 F9**
Manui *Indonesia* **63 E6**
Manukau *N.Z.* **91 B5**
Manuripi → *Bolivia* **124 F5**
Many *U.S.A.* **116 F8**
Manyani *Kenya* **86 C4**
Manyara, L. *Tanzania* **86 C4**
Manyas *Turkey* **45 F11**
Manyava *Ukraine* **29 B9**
Manych → *Russia* **35 G5**
Manych-Gudilo, Ozero
  Russia **35 G6**
Manyonga → *Tanzania* **86 C3**
Manyoni *Tanzania* **86 D3**
Manzai *Pakistan* **68 C4**
Manzala, Bahra el *Egypt* **80 H7**
Manzanar △ *U.S.A.* **110 J7**
Manzanares *Spain* **37 F7**
Manzaneda *Spain* **36 C3**
Manzanillo *Cuba* **120 B4**
Manzanillo *Mexico* **118 D4**
Manzanillo, Pta. *Panama* **120 E4**
Manzano Mts. *U.S.A.* **109 J10**
Manzariyeh *Iran* **71 C6**
Manzhouli *China* **60 B6**
Manzini *Swaziland* **89 D5**
Manzur Vadisi △ *Turkey* **70 B3**
Mao *Chad* **79 F9**
Maó *Spain* **48 B11**
Maoke, Pegunungan
  Indonesia **63 E9**
Maolin *China* **57 C12**
Maoming *China* **59 G8**
Maopi T'ou *China* **59 G13**
Maouri, Dallol → *Niger* **83 C5**
Maoxian *China* **58 B4**
Maoxing *China* **57 B13**
Mapam Yumco *China* **69 D9**
Mapastepec *Mexico* **119 D6**
Maphrao, Ko *Thailand* **65 a**
Mapia, Kepulauan *Indonesia* **63 D8**
Mapimí *Mexico* **118 B4**
Mapimí, Bolsón de *Mexico* **118 B4**
Maping *China* **59 B9**
Mapinga *Tanzania* **86 D4**
Mapinhane *Mozam.* **89 C6**
Maple Creek *Canada* **103 D7**
Maple Valley *U.S.A.* **110 C4**
Mapleton *U.S.A.* **108 D2**
Mapuera → *Brazil* **124 D7**
Mapulanguene *Mozam.* **89 C5**
Mapungubwe △ *S. Africa* **87 G2**
Maputo *Mozam.* **89 D5**
Maputo □ *Mozam.* **89 D5**
Maputo, B. de *Mozam.* **89 D5**
Maputo △ *Mozam.* **89 D5**
Maqat *Kazakhstan* **52 E6**
Maqiaohe *China* **57 B16**
Maqnā *Si. Arabia* **70 D2**
Maquan He →
  Brahmaputra → *Asia* **69 H13**
Maqueda *Spain* **36 E6**
Maquela do Zombo *Angola* **84 F3**
Maquinchao *Argentina* **128 E3**
Maquoketa *U.S.A.* **112 D8**
Mar, Serra do *Brazil* **127 B6**
Mar Chiquita, L. *Argentina* **126 C3**
Mar del Plata *Argentina* **126 D4**
Mar Menor *Spain* **39 H4**
Mara *Tanzania* **86 C3**
Mara □ *Tanzania* **86 C3**
Maraã *Brazil* **124 D5**
Maraa *Tahiti* **91 d**
Marabá *Brazil* **125 E9**
Maracá, I. de *Brazil* **125 C8**
Maracaibo *Venezuela* **124 A4**
Maracaibo, L. de *Venezuela* **124 B4**
Maracaju *Brazil* **127 A4**
Maracas Bay Village
  Trin. & Tob. **125 K15**
Maracay *Venezuela* **124 A5**

Maracena *Spain* **37 H7**
Maradi *Niger* **83 C6**
Maradi □ *Niger* **83 C6**
Marägheh *Iran* **73 D12**
Marāh *Si. Arabia* **70 E5**
Marahoué △ *Ivory C.* **82 D3**
Marais du Cotentin et du
  Bessin △ *France* **18 C5**
Marais Poitevin, Val de
  Sèvre et Vendée △ *France* **20 B3**
Marajó, I. de *Brazil* **125 D9**
Marakele △ *S. Africa* **89 E4**
Maralal *Kenya* **86 B4**
Maralinga *Australia* **93 F5**
Maramampy → *Tanzania* **86 C3**
Maramara *S. Leone* **82 D2**
Maran *Malaysia* **65 L4**
Marana *U.S.A.* **109 K8**
Maranboy *Australia* **92 B5**
Maranchón *Spain* **38 D2**
Marand *Iran* **73 C11**
Marang *Malaysia* **65 K4**
Maranguape *Brazil* **125 D11**
Maranhão = São Luís
  Brazil **125 D10**
Maranhão □ *Brazil* **125 E9**
Marano, L. di *Italy* **41 C10**
Maranoa → *Australia* **95 D4**
Marañón → *Peru* **124 D4**
Marão *Mozam.* **89 C5**
Maraş = Kahramanmaraş
  Turkey **72 D7**
Mărăşeşti *Romania* **29 E12**
Maratea *Italy* **43 C8**
Marateca *Portugal* **37 G2**
Marathasa *Cyprus* **49 E11**
Marathokambos *Greece* **47 D8**
Marathon *Australia* **94 C3**
Marathon *Canada* **104 C2**
Marathon *N.Y., U.S.A.* **115 D8**
Marathon *Tex., U.S.A.* **116 F3**
Marathónas *Greece* **46 C5**
Marathóvouno *Cyprus* **49 D12**
Maratua *Indonesia* **63 D5**
Maraval *Trin. & Tob.* **125 K15**
Maravatío *Mexico* **118 D4**
Marawi City *Phil.* **61 H6**
Marāwih *U.A.E.* **71 E7**
Marazliyivka *Ukraine* **29 D15**
Marbella *Spain* **37 J6**
Marble Bar *Australia* **92 D2**
Marble Falls *U.S.A.* **116 F5**
Marblehead *U.S.A.* **115 D14**
Marburg *Germany* **24 E5**
Marca, Pta. Da *Angola* **85 H2**
Marcal → *Hungary* **28 C2**
Marcali *Hungary* **28 D2**
Marcaria *Italy* **40 C7**
Mărcăuţi *Moldova* **29 B12**
March *U.K.* **15 E8**
Marche *France* **20 B5**
Marche □ *Italy* **41 E10**
Marche-en-Famenne
  Belgium **17 D5**
Marchena *Spain* **37 H5**
Marches = Marche □ *Italy* **41 E10**
Marchesale □ *Italy* **43 D9**
Marciana Marina *Italy* **40 F7**
Marcianise *Italy* **43 A7**
Marcigny *France* **19 F11**
Marcillat-en-Combraille
  France **19 F9**
Marck *France* **19 B8**
Marckolsheim *France* **19 D14**
Marco Island *U.S.A.* **117 J14**
Marcos Juárez *Argentina* **126 C3**
Mărculeşti *Moldova* **29 C13**
Marcus I. = Minami-Tori-
  Shima *Pac. Oc.* **96 E7**
Marcy, Mt. *U.S.A.* **115 B11**
Mardan *Pakistan* **68 B5**
Mardarivka *Ukraine* **29 C14**
Mardin *Turkey* **73 D9**
Mårdsjö *Sweden* **10 A9**
Marécchia → *Italy* **41 D9**
Maree, L. *U.K.* **13 D3**
Mareeba *Australia* **94 B4**
Mareetsane *S. Africa* **88 D4**
Maremma *Italy* **41 F8**
Maremma □ *Italy* **40 F8**
Maréna *Kayes, Mali* **82 C2**
Maréna *Koulikouro, Mali* **82 C3**
Marengo *U.S.A.* **112 E7**
Marennes *France* **20 C2**
Marerano *Madag.* **89 C7**
Maréttimo *Italy* **42 E5**
Mareuil *France* **20 C4**
Marfa *U.S.A.* **116 F2**
Marfa Pt. *Malta* **49 D1**
Marganets = Marhanets
  Ukraine **33 J8**
Margaret → *Australia* **92 C4**
Margaret Bay *Canada* **102 C3**
Margaret L. *Canada* **102 B5**

Margaret River *Australia* **93 F2**
Margarita, I. de *Venezuela* **124 A6**
Margariti *Greece* **46 B2**
Margaritovo *Russia* **54 C7**
Margate *S. Africa* **89 E5**
Margate *U.K.* **15 F9**
Margeride, Mts. de la *France* **20 D7**
Margherita di Savóia *Italy* **43 A9**
Margherita Pk. *Uganda* **86 B3**
Marghita *Romania* **28 C7**
Margonin *Poland* **31 F4**
Margosatubig *Phil.* **61 H5**
Mārgow, Dasht-e *Afghan.* **66 D3**
Marguerite *Canada* **102 C4**
Marhanets *Ukraine* **33 J8**
Mari El □ *Russia* **34 B8**
Mari Indus *Pakistan* **68 C4**
Mari Republic = Mari El □
  Russia **34 B8**
María, Sa. de *Spain* **39 H2**
María Elena *Chile* **126 A2**
María Grande *Argentina* **126 C4**
Maria I. *N. Terr., Australia* **94 A2**
Maria I. *Tas., Australia* **95 G4**
Maria Island △ *Australia* **95 G4**
Maria van Diemen, C. *N.Z.* **91 A4**
Mariager *Denmark* **11 H3**
Mariager Fjord *Denmark* **11 H4**
Mariakani *Kenya* **86 C4**
Mariala △ *Australia* **95 D4**
Marian *Australia* **94 K6**
Marian L. *Canada* **102 A5**
Mariana Trench *Pac. Oc.* **96 F6**
Marianna *U.S.A.* **117 F12**
Mariannelund *Sweden* **11 G9**
Mariánské Lázně *Czech Rep.* **26 B5**
Marías → *U.S.A.* **108 C8**
Marías, Islas *Mexico* **118 C3**
Mariato, Punta *Panama* **120 E3**
Mariazell *Austria* **26 D8**
Maribo *Denmark* **11 K5**
Maribor *Slovenia* **41 B12**
Marico → *Africa* **88 C4**
Maricopa *Ariz., U.S.A.* **109 K7**
Maricopa *Calif., U.S.A.* **111 K7**
Marīdī *Sudan* **81 G2**
Marīdī, Wadi → *Sudan* **81 F2**
Marié → *Brazil* **124 D5**
Marie Byrd Land *Antarctica* **5 D14**
Marie-Galante *Guadeloupe* **120 b**
Mariecourt =
  Kangiqsujuaq *Canada* **101 C12**
Mariefred *Sweden* **10 E11**
Mariehamn *Finland* **9 F18**
Marieholm *Sweden* **11 J7**
Mariembourg *Belgium* **17 D4**
Marienbad = Mariánské
  Lázně *Czech Rep.* **26 B5**
Marienberg *Germany* **24 E9**
Mariental *Namibia* **88 C2**
Marienville *U.S.A.* **114 E5**
Mariestad *Sweden* **11 F7**
Marietta *Ga., U.S.A.* **117 E12**
Marietta *Ohio, U.S.A.* **113 F13**
Marieville *Canada* **115 A11**
Mariga → *Nigeria* **83 C6**
Marignane *France* **21 E9**
Marihatag *Phil.* **61 G7**
Mariinsk *Russia* **52 D9**
Mariinskiy Posad *Russia* **34 B8**
Marijampolė *Lithuania* **30 D10**
Marijampolė □ *Lithuania* **30 D10**
Marília *Brazil* **127 A6**
Marín *Spain* **36 C2**
Marina *U.S.A.* **110 J5**
Marinduque *Phil.* **63 B6**
Marine City *U.S.A.* **114 D2**
Marineo *Italy* **42 E6**
Marinette *U.S.A.* **112 C10**
Maringá *Brazil* **127 A5**
Marinha Grande *Portugal* **36 F2**
Marino *Italy* **41 G9**
Marion *Ala., U.S.A.* **117 E11**
Marion *Ill., U.S.A.* **112 G9**
Marion *Ind., U.S.A.* **113 E11**
Marion *Iowa, U.S.A.* **112 D8**
Marion *Kans., U.S.A.* **112 F5**
Marion *N.C., U.S.A.* **117 D13**
Marion *Ohio, U.S.A.* **113 E12**
Marion *S.C., U.S.A.* **117 D15**
Marion *Va., U.S.A.* **113 G13**
Marion, L. *U.S.A.* **117 E14**
Mariposa *U.S.A.* **110 H7**
Mariscal Estigarribia
  Paraguay **126 A3**
Maritime Alps =
  Maritimes, Alpes *Europe* **21 D11**
Maritimes, Alpes *Europe* **21 D11**
Maritsa = Evros → *Greece* **72 B2**
Maritsa *Greece* **49 C10**
Mariupol *Ukraine* **33 J9**
Mariusa △ *Venezuela* **121 E7**
Marīvān *Iran* **73 E12**
Marj 'Uyūn *Lebanon* **74 B4**
Marka = Merca *Somali Rep.* **75 G3**
Marka *Si. Arabia* **80 D5**
Markam *China* **58 C2**

Markaryd *Sweden* **11 H7**
Markdale *Canada* **114 B4**
Marked Tree *U.S.A.* **117 D9**
Markelsdorfer Huk *Germany* **24 A7**
Market Drayton *U.K.* **14 E5**
Market Harborough *U.K.* **15 E7**
Market Rasen *U.K.* **14 D7**
Markham *Canada* **114 C5**
Markham, Mt. *Antarctica* **5 E11**
Marki *Poland* **31 F8**
Märkische Schweiz △
  Germany **24 C10**
Markkleeberg *Germany* **24 D8**
Markleeville *U.S.A.* **110 G7**
Markopoulo *Greece* **46 D5**
Markovac *Serbia* **44 B5**
Markovo *Russia* **53 C17**
Markoye *Burkina Faso* **83 C5**
Marks *Russia* **34 E8**
Marksville *U.S.A.* **116 F8**
Markt Schwaben *Germany* **25 G7**
Marktoberdorf *Germany* **25 H6**
Marktredwitz *Germany* **25 E8**
Marl *Germany* **24 D3**
Marla *Australia* **95 D1**
Marlbank *Canada* **114 B7**
Marlboro *U.S.A.* **115 E11**
Marlborough *Australia* **94 C4**
Marlborough *U.K.* **15 F6**
Marlborough *U.S.A.* **115 D13**
Marlborough Downs *U.K.* **15 F6**
Marle *France* **19 C10**
Marlin *U.S.A.* **116 F6**
Marlow *Germany* **24 A8**
Marlow *U.K.* **15 F7**
Marlow *U.S.A.* **116 D6**
Marmagao *India* **66 M8**
Marmande *France* **20 D4**
Marmara *Turkey* **45 F11**
Marmara, Sea of =
  Marmara Denizi *Turkey* **45 F12**
Marmara Denizi *Turkey* **45 F12**
Marmara Gölü *Turkey* **47 C10**
Marmaris *Turkey* **47 E10**
Marmaris Limanı *Turkey* **47 E10**
Marmion, Mt. *Australia* **93 E2**
Marmion L. *Canada* **104 C1**
Marmolada, Mte. *Italy* **41 B8**
Marmolejo *Spain* **37 G6**
Marmora *Canada* **114 B7**
Mármora, La *Italy* **42 C2**
Marnay *France* **19 E12**
Marne *Germany* **24 B5**
Marne □ *France* **19 D11**
Marne → *France* **19 D9**
Marneuli *Georgia* **35 K7**
Maroala *Madag.* **89 B8**
Maroantsetra *Madag.* **89 B8**
Maroelaboom *Namibia* **88 B2**
Marofandilia *Madag.* **89 C7**
Marojejy △ *Madag.* **89 A8**
Marolambo *Madag.* **89 C8**
Maromandia *Madag.* **89 A8**
Maromokotro *Madag.* **89 A8**
Marondera *Zimbabwe* **87 F3**
Maroni → *Fr. Guiana* **125 B8**
Maroochydore *Australia* **95 D5**
Maroona *Australia* **95 F3**
Maros → *Hungary* **28 D5**
Marosakoa *Madag.* **89 B8**
Maroseranana *Madag.* **89 B8**
Maróstica *Italy* **41 C8**
Marotandrano *Madag.* **89 B8**
Marotaolano *Madag.* **89 A8**
Maroua *Cameroon* **83 C7**
Marovato *Madag.* **89 B8**
Marovoay *Madag.* **89 B8**
Marquard *S. Africa* **88 D4**
Marquesas Fracture Zone
  Pac. Oc. **97 H15**
Marquesas Is. =
  Marquises, Îs.
  French Polynesia **97 H14**
Marquette *U.S.A.* **112 B10**
Marquis *St. Lucia* **121 f**
Marquise *France* **19 B8**
Marquises, Îs.
  French Polynesia **97 H14**
Marra, Djebel *Sudan* **79 F10**
Marra, Gebel *Sudan* **81 F2**
Marracuene *Mozam.* **89 D5**
Marradi *Italy* **41 D8**
Marrakech *Morocco* **78 B4**
Marratxi *Spain* **38 F7**
Marrawah *Australia* **95 G3**
Marree *Australia* **95 D2**
Marrero *U.S.A.* **117 G9**
Marrimane *Mozam.* **89 C5**
Marromeu *Mozam.* **89 B6**
Marromeu △ *Mozam.* **89 B6**
Marrubane *Mozam.* **87 F4**
Marrúbiu *Italy* **42 C1**
Marrupa *Mozam.* **87 E4**

Mars Hill *U.S.A.* **113 B20**
Marsá 'Alam *Egypt* **80 B3**
Marsá Matrûh *Egypt* **80 A2**
Marsá Sha'b *Sudan* **80 C4**
Marsá Susah *Libya* **79 B10**
Marsabit *Kenya* **86 B4**
Marsabit △ *Kenya* **86 B4**
Marsala *Italy* **42 E5**
Marsalforn *Malta* **49 C1**
Mârşani *Romania* **29 F9**
Marsberg *Germany* **24 D4**
Marsciano *Italy* **41 F9**
Marsden *Australia* **95 E4**
Marseillan *France* **20 E7**
Marseille *France* **21 E9**
Marseille-Marignane ✈
  (MRS) *France* **21 E9**
Marseilles = Marseille
  France **21 E9**
Marsh I. *U.S.A.* **116 G9**
Marshall *Liberia* **82 D2**
Marshall *Ark., U.S.A.* **116 D8**
Marshall *Mich., U.S.A.* **113 D11**
Marshall *Minn., U.S.A.* **112 C6**
Marshall *Mo., U.S.A.* **112 F7**
Marshall *Tex., U.S.A.* **116 E7**
Marshall → *Australia* **94 C2**
Marshall Is. ■ *Pac. Oc.* **90 A10**
Marshalltown *U.S.A.* **112 D8**
Marshbrook *Zimbabwe* **89 B5**
Marshfield *Mo., U.S.A.* **112 G7**
Marshfield *Vt., U.S.A.* **115 B12**
Marshfield *Wis., U.S.A.* **112 C8**
Marshūn *Iran* **71 B6**
Mársico Nuovo *Italy* **43 B8**
Märsta *Sweden* **10 E11**
Marstal *Denmark* **11 K4**
Marstrand *Sweden* **11 G5**
Mart *U.S.A.* **116 F6**
Marta → *Italy* **41 F8**
Martaban *Burma* **67 L20**
Martaban, G. of *Burma* **67 L20**
Martano *Italy* **43 B11**
Martapura *Kalimantan,*
  Indonesia **62 E4**
Martapura *Sumatera,*
  Indonesia **62 E2**
Marte *Nigeria* **83 C7**
Marte R. Gómez, Presa
  Mexico **119 B5**
Martel *France* **20 D5**
Martelange *Belgium* **17 E5**
Martellago *Italy* **41 C9**
Martés, Sierra *Spain* **39 F4**
Martfû *Hungary* **28 C5**
Martha's Vineyard *U.S.A.* **115 E14**
Martigné-Ferchaud *France* **18 E5**
Martigny *Switz.* **25 J3**
Martigues *France* **21 E9**
Martin *Slovak Rep.* **27 B11**
Martin *S. Dak., U.S.A.* **112 D3**
Martin *Tenn., U.S.A.* **117 C10**
Martín → *Spain* **38 D4**
Martin L. *U.S.A.* **117 E12**
Martina Franca *Italy* **43 B10**
Martinborough *N.Z.* **91 D5**
Martinez *Calif., U.S.A.* **110 G4**
Martinez *Ga., U.S.A.* **117 E13**
Martinique ☑ *W. Indies* **120 c**
Martinique Passage
  W. Indies **121 C7**
Martino *Greece* **46 C5**
Martinópolis *Brazil* **127 A5**
Martin's Bay *Barbados* **121 g**
Martins Ferry *U.S.A.* **114 F4**
Martinsberg *Austria* **26 C8**
Martinsburg *Pa., U.S.A.* **114 F6**
Martinsburg *W. Va., U.S.A.* **113 F15**
Martinsicuro *Italy* **41 F10**
Martinsville *Ind., U.S.A.* **112 F10**
Martinsville *Va., U.S.A.* **113 G14**
Marton *N.Z.* **91 D5**
Martorell *Spain* **38 D6**
Martos *Spain* **37 H7**
Martuni *Armenia* **35 K7**
Maru *Nigeria* **83 C6**
Marudi *Malaysia* **62 D4**
Maruf *Afghan.* **66 D5**
Marugame *Japan* **55 G6**
Marunga *Angola* **88 B3**
Marungu, Mts.
  Dem. Rep. of the Congo **86 D3**
Marv Dasht *Iran* **71 D7**
Marvast *Iran* **71 D7**
Marvejols *France* **20 D7**
Marvel Loch *Australia* **93 F2**
Marwar *India* **68 G5**
Mary *Turkmenistan* **71 B9**
Maryborough = Port
  Laoise *Ireland* **12 C4**
Maryborough *Queens.,*
  Australia **95 D5**
Maryborough *Vic., Australia* **95 F3**
Maryfield *Canada* **103 D8**
Maryland □ *U.S.A.* **113 F15**
Maryland Junction *Zimbabwe* **87 F3**
Maryport *U.K.* **14 C4**

Mary's Harbour *Canada* 105 B8
Marystown *Canada* 105 C8
Marysville *Canada* 102 D5
Marysville *Calif., U.S.A.* 110 F5
Marysville *Kans., U.S.A.* 112 F5
Marysville *Mich., U.S.A.* 114 D2
Marysville *Ohio, U.S.A.* 113 E12
Marysville *Wash., U.S.A.* 110 B4
Maryville *Mo., U.S.A.* 112 E6
Maryville *Tenn., U.S.A.* 117 D13
Marzūq *Libya* 79 C8
Marzūq, Idehân *Libya* 79 D8
Masada *Israel* 74 D4
Masahunga *Tanzania* 86 C3
Masai *Malaysia* 65 d
Masai Mara △ *Kenya* 86 C4
Masai Steppe *Tanzania* 86 C4
Masaka *Uganda* 86 C3
Masalembo, Kepulauan
  Indonesia 62 F4
Masalima, Kepulauan
  Indonesia 62 F5
Masallı *Azerbaijan* 73 C13
Masamba *Indonesia* 63 E6
Masan *S. Korea* 57 G15
Masandam, Ra's *Oman* 71 E8
Masasi *Tanzania* 87 E4
Masaya *Nic.* 120 D2
Masba *Nigeria* 83 C7
Masbate *Phil.* 61 E5
Máscali *Italy* 43 E8
Mascara *Algeria* 78 A6
Mascota *Mexico* 118 C4
Masela *Indonesia* 63 F7
Maseru *Lesotho* 88 D4
Mashaba *Zimbabwe* 87 G3
Mashābih *Si. Arabia* 70 E3
Mashan *China* 58 F7
Mashar *Sudan* 81 F2
Mashatu △ *Botswana* 89 C4
Mashegu *Nigeria* 83 D6
Masherbrum *Pakistan* 69 B7
Mashhad *Iran* 71 B8
Mashi *Nigeria* 83 C6
Mashīz *Iran* 71 D8
Mashkel, Hāmūn-i- *Pakistan* 71 D9
Mashki Chāh *Pakistan* 66 E3
Mashonaland *Zimbabwe* 85 H6
Mashonaland Central □
  Zimbabwe 89 B5
Mashonaland East □
  Zimbabwe 89 B5
Mashonaland West □
  Zimbabwe 89 B4
Mashrakh *India* 69 F11
Mashtaga = Maştağa
  Azerbaijan 35 K10
Masi Manimba
  Dem. Rep. of the Congo 84 E3
Masindi *Uganda* 86 B3
Masindi Port *Uganda* 86 B3
Maşīrah *Oman* 75 C6
Maşīrah, Khalīj *Oman* 75 C6
Masisi *Dem. Rep. of the Congo* 86 C2
Masjed Soleyman *Iran* 71 D6
Mask, L. *Ireland* 12 C2
Maskin *Oman* 71 F8
Maslen Nos *Bulgaria* 45 D11
Maslinica *Croatia* 41 E13
Masnou = El Masnou *Spain* 38 D7
Masoala, Tanjon' i *Madag.* 89 B9
Masoala △ *Madag.* 89 B9
Masoarivo *Madag.* 89 B7
Masohi = Amahai *Indonesia* 63 E7
Masomeloka *Madag.* 89 C8
Mason *Nev., U.S.A.* 110 G7
Mason *Tex., U.S.A.* 116 F5
Mason City *U.S.A.* 112 D8
Maspalomas *Canary Is.* 48 G4
Maspalomas, Pta. *Canary Is.* 48 G4
Masqat *Oman* 75 C6
Masr el Gedida *Egypt* 80 H7
Massa *Italy* 40 D7
Massa Maríttima *Italy* 40 E7
Massachusetts □ *U.S.A.* 115 D13
Massachusetts B. *U.S.A.* 115 D14
Massafra *Italy* 43 B10
Massakory *Chad* 79 F9
Massanella *Spain* 48 B9
Massangena *Mozam.* 89 C5
Massango *Angola* 84 F3
Massat *France* 20 F5
Massawa = Mitsiwa *Eritrea* 81 D4
Massena *U.S.A.* 115 B10
Massénya *Chad* 79 F9
Masset *Canada* 102 C2
Masseube *France* 20 E4
Massiac *France* 20 C7
Massiah Street *Barbados* 121 g
Massif Central *France* 20 D7
Massif des Bauges △ *France* 19 G13
Massigui *Mali* 82 C3
Massillon *U.S.A.* 114 F3
Massinga *Mozam.* 89 C6
Massingir *Mozam.* 89 C5
Masson-Angers *Canada* 115 A9
Masson I. *Antarctica* 5 C7

Maştağa *Azerbaijan* 35 K10
Mastanli = Momchilgrad
  Bulgaria 45 E9
Masterton *N.Z.* 91 D5
Mastic *U.S.A.* 115 F12
Mastuj *Pakistan* 69 A5
Mastung *Pakistan* 66 E5
Mastūrah *Si. Arabia* 80 C4
Masty *Belarus* 23 B13
Masuda *Japan* 55 G5
Masvingo *Zimbabwe* 87 G3
Masvingo □ *Zimbabwe* 87 G3
Maswa △ *Tanzania* 86 C3
Maszewo *Poland* 30 E2
Mat → *Albania* 44 E1
Mata-au = Clutha → *N.Z.* 91 G2
Matabeleland North □
  Zimbabwe 87 F2
Matabeleland South □
  Zimbabwe 87 G2
Matachel → *Spain* 37 G4
Matachewan *Canada* 104 C3
Matadi *Dem. Rep. of the Congo* 84 F2
Matagalpa *Nic.* 120 D2
Matagami *Canada* 104 C4
Matagami, L. *Canada* 104 C4
Matagorda B. *U.S.A.* 116 G6
Matagorda I. *U.S.A.* 116 G6
Mataiea *Tahiti* 91 d
Matak *Indonesia* 62 D3
Matala *Greece* 49 E6
Matam *Senegal* 82 B2
Matamey *Niger* 83 C6
Matamoros *Campeche,*
  Mexico 119 D6
Matamoros *Coahuila, Mexico* 118 B4
Matamoros *Tamaulipas,*
  Mexico 119 B5
Ma'tan as Sarra *Libya* 79 D10
Matandu → *Tanzania* 87 D3
Matane *Canada* 105 C6
Matang *China* 58 F5
Matankari *Niger* 83 C5
Matanomadh *India* 68 H3
Matanzas *Cuba* 120 B3
Matapa *Botswana* 88 C3
Matapan, C. = Tenaro,
  Akra *Greece* 46 E4
Matapédia *Canada* 105 C6
Matapo △ *Zimbabwe* 87 G2
Matara *Sri Lanka* 66 S12
Mataram *Indonesia* 63 K19
Matarani *Peru* 124 G4
Mataranka *Australia* 92 B5
Matarma, Râs *Egypt* 74 E1
Mataró *Spain* 38 D7
Matarraña → *Spain* 38 D5
Mataruška Banja *Serbia* 44 C4
Matatiele *S. Africa* 89 E4
Mataura *N.Z.* 91 G2
Matavai, B. de *Tahiti* 91 d
Matehuala *Mexico* 118 C4
Mateke Hills *Zimbabwe* 87 G3
Matelot *Trin. & Tob.* 125 K15˝
Matera *Italy* 43 B9
Matese, Monti del *Italy* 43 A7
Mateur = *Italy* 43 A7
Mátészalka *Hungary* 28 C7
Matetsi *Zimbabwe* 87 F2
Matfors *Sweden* 10 B11
Matha *France* 20 C3
Matheniko △ *Uganda* 86 B3
Mathis *U.S.A.* 116 G6
Mathraki *Greece* 49 A3
Mathura *India* 68 F7
Mati *Phil.* 61 H7
Matiakoali *Burkina Faso* 83 C5
Matiali *India* 69 F13
Matías Romero *Mexico* 119 D5
Matibane *Mozam.* 87 E5
Matiri Ra. *N.Z.* 91 D4
Matjiesfontein *S. Africa* 88 E3
Matla → *India* 69 H13
Matlamanyane *Botswana* 88 B4
Matli *Pakistan* 68 G3
Matlock *U.K.* 14 D6
Matna *Sudan* 81 E4
Mato Grosso □ *Brazil* 125 F8
Mato Grosso, Planalto do
  Brazil 125 G8
Mato Grosso do Sul □
  Brazil 125 G8
Matobo = Matapo △
  Zimbabwe 87 G2
Matochkin Shar *Russia* 52 B6
Matopo Hills *Zimbabwe* 87 G2
Matopos *Zimbabwe* 87 G2
Matosinhos *Portugal* 36 D2
Matour *France* 19 F11
Matroosberg *S. Africa* 88 E2
Maţruḩ *Oman* 75 C6
Matsena *Nigeria* 83 C7
Matsesta *Russia* 35 J4
Matsu Tao *Taiwan* 59 E13
Matsue *Japan* 55 G6

Matsum, Ko *Thailand* 65 b
Matsumae *Japan* 54 D10
Matsumoto *Japan* 55 F9
Matsusaka *Japan* 55 G8
Matsuura *Japan* 55 H4
Matsuyama *Japan* 55 H6
Mattagami → *Canada* 104 B3
Mattancheri *India* 66 Q10
Mattawa *Canada* 104 C4
Matterhorn *Switz.* 25 K3
Mattersburg *Austria* 27 D9
Matthew Town *Bahamas* 121 B5
Matthews Ridge *Guyana* 124 B6
Mattice *Canada* 104 C3
Mattituck *U.S.A.* 115 F12
Mattō *Japan* 55 F8
Mattoon *U.S.A.* 112 F9
Matuba *Mozam.* 89 C5
Matucana *Peru* 124 F3
Matuku *Fiji* 91 a
Matūn = Khowst *Afghan.* 68 C3
Matura *Trin. & Tob.* 125 K15
Maturín *Venezuela* 124 B6
Matusadona △ *Zimbabwe* 87 F2
Matveyev Kurgan *Russia* 33 J10
Matxitxako, C. *Spain* 38 B2
Mau *Mad. P., India* 69 F8
Mau *Ut. P., India* 69 G10
Mau *Ut. P., India* 69 G10
Mau Escarpment *Kenya* 86 C4
Mau Ranipur *India* 69 G8
Maua *Kenya* 86 C4
Maubeuge *France* 19 B10
Maubin *Burma* 67 L19
Maubourguet *France* 20 E4
Maud, Pt. *Australia* 92 D1
Maud Rise *S. Ocean* 5 C3
Maude *Australia* 95 E3
Maudin Sun *Burma* 67 M19
Maués *Brazil* 124 D7
Mauganj *India* 69 G9
Maughold Hd. *I. of Man* 14 C3
Mauguio *France* 20 E7
Maui *U.S.A.* 106 b
Maulamyaing =
  Moulmein *Burma* 67 L20
Maule □ *Chile* 126 D1
Mauléon-Licharre *France* 20 E3
Maumee *U.S.A.* 113 E12
Maumee → *U.S.A.* 113 E12
Maumere *Indonesia* 63 F6
Maumusson, Pertuis de
  France 20 C2
Maun *Botswana* 88 C3
Mauna Kea *U.S.A.* 106 b
Mauna Loa *U.S.A.* 106 b
Maungmagan Kyunzu
  Burma 64 E1
Maungu *Kenya* 86 C4
Maupin *U.S.A.* 108 D3
Maure-de-Bretagne *France* 18 E5
Maurepas, L. *U.S.A.* 117 F9
Maures *France* 21 E10
Mauriac *France* 20 C6
Maurice, L. *Australia* 93 E5
Mauricie △ *Canada* 104 C5
Maurienne *France* 21 C10
Mauritania ■ *Africa* 78 E3
Mauritius ■ *Ind. Oc.* 85 d
Mauron *France* 18 D4
Maurs *France* 20 D6
Mauston *U.S.A.* 112 D8
Mauterndorf *Austria* 26 D6
Mauthen *Austria* 26 E6
Mauvezin *France* 20 E4
Mauzé-sur-le-Mignon
  France 20 B3
Mavli *India* 68 G5
Mavrovë *Albania* 44 F3
Mavrovo △ *Macedonia* 44 E4
Mavuradonha Mts.
  Zimbabwe 87 F3
Mawa *Dem. Rep. of the Congo* 86 B2
Mawai *India* 69 H9
Mawana *India* 68 E7
Mawand *Pakistan* 68 E3
Mawjib, W. al → *Jordan* 74 D4
Mawk Mai *Burma* 67 J20
Mawlaik *Burma* 67 H19
Mawlamyine = Moulmein
  Burma 67 L20
Mawqaq *Si. Arabia* 70 E4
Mawson Base *Antarctica* 5 C6
Mawson Coast *Antarctica* 5 C6
Max *U.S.A.* 112 B3
Maxcanú *Mexico* 119 C6
Maxesibeni *S. Africa* 89 E4
Maxhamish L. *Canada* 102 B4
Maxixe *Mozam.* 89 C6
Maxville *Canada* 115 A10
Maxwell *U.S.A.* 110 F4
Maxwelton *Australia* 94 C3
May, C. *U.S.A.* 113 F16
May Pen *Jamaica* 120 a
Maya → *Russia* 53 D14
Maya Mts. *Belize* 119 D7
Mayaguana *Bahamas* 121 B5

Mayagüez *Puerto Rico* 121 d
Mayahi *Niger* 83 C6
Mayaky *Ukraine* 29 C14
Mayals = Maials *Spain* 38 D5
Mayāmey *Iran* 71 B7
Mayang *China* 58 D7
Mayanup *Australia* 93 F2
Mayapán *Mexico* 119 C7
Mayarí *Cuba* 121 B4
Mayaro B. *Trin. & Tob.* 125 K16
Maybell *U.S.A.* 108 F9
Maybole *U.K.* 13 F4
Maychew *Ethiopia* 81 E4
Maydān *Iraq* 73 E11
Maydan *Ukraine* 29 B8
Maydena *Australia* 95 G4
Mayen *Germany* 25 E7
Mayenne *France* 18 D6
Mayenne □ *France* 18 D6
Mayenne → *France* 18 E6
Mayer *U.S.A.* 109 J7
Mayerthorpe *Canada* 102 C5
Mayfield *Ky., U.S.A.* 112 G9
Mayfield *N.Y., U.S.A.* 115 C10
Mayhill *U.S.A.* 109 K11
Maykop *Russia* 35 H5
Maymyo *Burma* 64 A1
Maynard *Mass., U.S.A.* 115 D13
Maynard *Wash., U.S.A.* 110 C4
Maynard Hills *Australia* 93 E2
Mayne → *Australia* 94 C3
Maynooth *Ireland* 12 C5
Mayo *Canada* 100 C6
Mayo □ *Ireland* 12 C2
Mayo *Ireland* 12 C2
Mayo → *Nigeria* 83 D7
Mayo Faran *Nigeria* 83 D7
Mayon Volcano *Phil.* 61 E5
Mayor I. *N.Z.* 91 B6
Mayorga *Spain* 36 C5
Mayotte ☑ *Ind. Oc.* 85 a
Mayraira Pt. *Phil.* 61 B4
Maysān □ *Iraq* 70 D5
Maysville *U.S.A.* 113 F12
Mayu *Indonesia* 63 D7
Mayya *Russia* 53 C14
Mazabuka *Zambia* 87 F2
Mazagán = El Jadida
  Morocco 78 B4
Mazagão *Brazil* 125 D8
Mazamet *France* 20 E6
Mazán *Peru* 124 D4
Māzandarān □ *Iran* 71 B7
Mazapil *Mexico* 118 C4
Mazara del Vallo *Italy* 42 E5
Mazarrón *Spain* 39 H3
Mazarrón, G. de *Spain* 39 H3
Mazaruni → *Guyana* 124 B7
Mazatán *Mexico* 118 B2
Mazatenango *Guatemala* 120 D1
Mazatlán *Mexico* 118 C3
Mažeikiai *Lithuania* 30 B9
Māzhān *Iran* 71 C8
Mazinān *Iran* 71 B8
Mazoe *Mozam.* 87 F3
Mazoe □ *Mozam.* 87 F3
Mazoe → *Mozam.* 87 F3
Mazowieckie □ *Poland* 31 F8
Mazrûb *Sudan* 81 E2
Mazu Dao *China* 59 D12
Mazurian Lakes =
  Mazurski, Pojezierze
  Poland 30 E7
Mazurski, Pojezierze *Poland* 30 E7
Mazyr *Belarus* 23 B15
Mba *Fiji* 91 a
Mbaba *Senegal* 82 C1
Mbabane *Swaziland* 89 D5
Mbagne *Mauritania* 82 B2
M'bahiakro *Ivory C.* 82 D4
Mbaïki *C.A.R.* 84 D3
Mbala *Zambia* 87 D3
Mbalabala *Zimbabwe* 89 C4
Mbale *Uganda* 86 B3
Mbalmayo *Cameroon* 83 E7
Mbam → *Cameroon* 83 E7
Mbamba Bay *Tanzania* 87 E3
Mbandaka
  Dem. Rep. of the Congo 84 D3
Mbanga *Cameroon* 83 E6
Mbanza Congo *Angola* 84 F2
Mbanza Ngungu
  Dem. Rep. of the Congo 84 F2
Mbarangandu *Tanzania* 87 D4
Mbarara *Uganda* 86 C3
Mbatto *Ivory C.* 82 D4
Mbengga = Beqa *Fiji* 91 a
Mbenkuru → *Tanzania* 87 D4
Mberengwa *Zimbabwe* 87 G2
Mberengwa, Mt. *Zimbabwe* 87 G2
Mberubu *Nigeria* 83 D6
Mbesuma *Zambia* 87 E3
Mbeya *Tanzania* 87 D3
Mbeya □ *Tanzania* 86 D3
Mbhashe → *S. Africa* 89 E4

M'bili *Sudan* 81 F2
Mbinga *Tanzania* 87 E4
Mbini = Río Muni □
  Eq. Guin. 84 D2
Mboki *C.A.R.* 81 F2
M'bonge *Cameroon* 83 E6
Mboro *Senegal* 82 B1
M'boukou, Rés. de *Cameroon* 83 D7
Mboune *Senegal* 82 C2
Mbour *Senegal* 82 C1
Mbout *Mauritania* 82 B2
Mbuji-Mayi
  Dem. Rep. of the Congo 86 D1
Mbulu *Tanzania* 86 C4
Mburucuyá *Argentina* 126 B4
Mchinja *Tanzania* 87 D4
Mchinji *Malawi* 87 E3
Mdantsane *S. Africa* 85 L5
Mead, L. *U.S.A.* 111 J12
Meade *U.S.A.* 112 G4
Meade → *U.S.A.* 106 A9
Meadow Lake *Canada* 103 C7
Meadow Lake △ *Canada* 103 C7
Meadow Valley Wash →
  U.S.A. 111 J12
Meadville *U.S.A.* 114 E4
Meaford *Canada* 114 B4
Mealhada *Portugal* 36 E2
Mealy Mts. *Canada* 105 B8
Meander River *Canada* 102 B5
Meares, C. *U.S.A.* 108 D1
Mearim → *Brazil* 125 D10
Meath □ *Ireland* 12 C5
Meath Park *Canada* 103 C7
Meaulne *France* 19 F9
Meaux *France* 19 D9
Mebechi-Gawa → *Japan* 54 D10
Mebulu, Tanjung *Indonesia* 63 K18
Mecanhelas *Mozam.* 87 F4
Mecca = Makkah *Si. Arabia* 80 C4
Mecca *U.S.A.* 111 M10
Mechanicsburg *U.S.A.* 114 F8
Mechanicville *U.S.A.* 115 D11
Mechara *Ethiopia* 81 F5
Mechelen *Belgium* 17 C4
Mecheria *Algeria* 78 B5
Mechernich *Germany* 24 E2
Mechetinskaya *Russia* 35 G5
Mecidiye *Turkey* 45 F10
Mecitözü *Turkey* 72 B6
Mecklenburg *Germany* 22 B7
Mecklenburg-
  Vorpommern □ *Germany* 24 B8
Mecklenburger Bucht
  Germany 24 A7
Meconta *Mozam.* 87 E4
Mecsek *Hungary* 28 D3
Meda *Portugal* 36 E3
Medan *Indonesia* 62 D1
Médanos de Coro △
  Venezuela 121 D6
Medanosa, Pta. *Argentina* 128 F3
Mede *Italy* 40 C5
Médéa *Algeria* 78 A6
Mededa *Bos.-H.* 28 G4
Medellín *Colombia* 124 B3
Medelpad *Sweden* 10 B10
Medemblik *Neths.* 17 B5
Mederdra *Mauritania* 82 B1
Medford *Mass., U.S.A.* 115 D13
Medford *Oreg., U.S.A.* 108 E2
Medford *Wis., U.S.A.* 112 C8
Medgidia *Romania* 29 F13
Media Agua *Argentina* 126 C2
Media Luna *Argentina* 126 C2
Medianeira *Brazil* 127 B5
Mediaş *Romania* 29 D9
Medicina *Italy* 41 D8
Medicine Bow *U.S.A.* 108 F10
Medicine Bow Mts. *U.S.A.* 108 F10
Medicine Bow Pk. *U.S.A.* 108 F10
Medicine Hat *Canada* 103 D6
Medicine Lake *U.S.A.* 108 B11
Medicine Lodge *U.S.A.* 112 G4
Medina = Al Madīnah
  Si. Arabia 70 E3
Medina *N. Dak., U.S.A.* 112 B4
Medina *N.Y., U.S.A.* 114 C6
Medina *Ohio, U.S.A.* 114 E3
Medina → *U.S.A.* 116 G5
Medina de Pomar *Spain* 36 C7
Medina de Ríoseco *Spain* 36 D5
Medina del Campo *Spain* 36 D6
Medina L. *U.S.A.* 116 G5
Medina Sidonia *Spain* 37 J5
Medinaceli *Spain* 38 D2
Medinipur *India* 69 H12
Mediterranean Sea *Europe* 6 H7
Médoc *France* 20 C3
Medulin *Croatia* 41 D10
Medveđa *Serbia* 44 D5
Medvedevo *Russia* 34 B8
Medveditsa → *Tver, Russia* 32 D9
Medveditsa → *Volgograd,*
  Russia 34 F6
Medvedok *Russia* 34 B10
Medvezhi, Ostrava *Russia* 53 B17

Medvezhyegorsk *Russia* 52 C4
Medway □ *U.K.* 15 F8
Medway → *U.K.* 15 F8
Medzev *Slovak Rep.* 27 C13
Medzilaborce *Slovak Rep.* 27 B14
Međitlija *Macedonia* 44 F5
Meekatharra *Australia* 93 E2
Meeker *U.S.A.* 108 F10
Meelpaeg L. *Canada* 105 C8
Meersburg *Germany* 25 H5
Meerut *India* 68 E7
Meeteetse *U.S.A.* 108 D9
Mega *Ethiopia* 81 G4
Megalo Horio *Greece* 47 E9
Megalonisos *Greece* 46 D6
Megalopoli *Greece* 46 D4
Meganisi *Greece* 46 C2
Megara *Greece* 46 D5
Megasini *India* 69 J12
Megdovas = Tavropos →
  Greece 46 B3
Megève *France* 21 C10
Meghalaya □ *India* 67 G17
Meghezez *Ethiopia* 81 F4
Meghna → *Bangla.* 67 H17
Mégiscane, L. *Canada* 104 C4
Megisti *Greece* 47 E11
Megra *Russia* 32 B9
Mehadia *Romania* 28 F7
Meharry, Mt. *Australia* 92 D2
Mehedeby *Sweden* 10 D11
Mehedinţi □ *Romania* 28 F7
Meheisa *Sudan* 80 D3
Mehlville *U.S.A.* 112 F8
Mehndawal *India* 69 F10
Mehr Jān *Iran* 71 C7
Mehrābād *Iran* 73 D12
Mehrān *Iran* 73 F12
Mehrgarh *Pakistan* 68 E2
Mehriz *Iran* 71 D7
Mehun-sur-Yèvre *France* 19 E9
Mei Jiang → *China* 59 E11
Mei Xian *China* 56 G4
Meicheng *China* 59 C12
Meichengzhen *China* 59 C8
Meichuan *China* 59 B10
Meighen I. *Canada* 101 B10
Meigu *China* 58 C4
Meihekou *China* 57 C13
Meiktila *Burma* 67 J19
Meinerzhagen *Germany* 24 D3
Meiningen *Germany* 24 E6
Meira, Serra de *Spain* 36 B3
Meiringen *Switz.* 25 J4
Meishan *China* 58 B4
Meissen *Germany* 24 D9
Meissner *Germany* 24 D5
Meissner-Kaufunger
  Wald △ *Germany* 24 D5
Meitan *China* 58 D6
Meizhou *China* 59 E11
Meja *India* 69 G10
Mejillones *Chile* 126 A1
Mekdela *Ethiopia* 81 E4
Mekele *Ethiopia* 81 E4
Mekerghene, Sebkra *Algeria* 78 C6
Mekhtar *Pakistan* 66 D6
Meknès *Morocco* 78 B4
Meko *Nigeria* 83 D5
Mekong → *Asia* 65 H6
Mekongga *Indonesia* 63 E6
Mekrou → *Benin* 83 C5
Mekvari = Kür →
  Azerbaijan 73 C13
Mel *Italy* 41 B9
Melagiri Hills *India* 66 N10
Melaka *Malaysia* 65 L4
Melalap *Malaysia* 62 C5
Melambes *Greece* 49 E6
Melanesia *Pac. Oc.* 96 H7
Melanesian Basin *Pac. Oc.* 96 G8
Melaya *Indonesia* 63 J17
Melbourne *Australia* 95 F4
Melbourne *U.S.A.* 117 G14
Melchor Múzquiz *Mexico* 118 B4
Melchor Ocampo *Mexico* 118 C4
Méldola *Italy* 41 D9
Meldorf *Germany* 24 A5
Melegnano *Italy* 40 C6
Melenci *Serbia* 28 E5
Melenki *Russia* 34 C5
Mélèzes → *Canada* 104 A5
Melfi *Italy* 43 B8
Melfort *Canada* 103 C8
Melfort *Zimbabwe* 87 F3
Melgaço *Portugal* 36 C2
Melgar de Fernamental
  Spain 36 C6
Melhus *Norway* 8 E14
Melide *Spain* 36 C2
Meligales *Greece* 46 D3
Melilla *N. Afr.* 78 A5
Melilli *Italy* 43 E8
Melipilla *Chile* 126 C1
Melissa, Akra *Greece* 49 D6
Melissa Oros *Greece* 47 D8
Melita *Canada* 103 D8

Mélito di Porto Salvo *Italy* **43** E8
Melitopol *Ukraine* **33** J8
Melk *Austria* **26** C8
Mellan Fryken *Sweden* **10** E7
Mellansel *Sweden* **8** E18
Melle *France* **20** B3
Melle *Germany* **24** C4
Mellen *U.S.A.* **112** B8
Mellerud *Sweden* **11** F6
Mellette *U.S.A.* **112** C4
Mellid = Melide *Spain* **36** C2
Mellieha *Malta* **49** D1
Mellit *Sudan* **81** E2
Mellrichstadt *Germany* **24** E6
Melnik *Bulgaria* **44** E7
Mělník *Czech Rep.* **26** A7
Melnytsya Podilska *Ukraine* **29** B11
Melo *Uruguay* **127** C5
Melolo *Indonesia* **63** F6
Melouprey *Cambodia* **64** F5
Melrhir, Chott *Algeria* **78** B7
Melrose *Australia* **95** E4
Melrose *U.K.* **13** F6
Melrose *Minn., U.S.A.* **112** C6
Melrose *N. Mex., U.S.A.* **109** J12
Melstone *U.S.A.* **108** C10
Melsungen *Germany* **24** D5
Melton Mowbray *U.K.* **14** E7
Melun *France* **19** D9
Melut *Sudan* **81** E3
Melville, C. *Australia* **103** C8
Melville, C. *Australia* **94** A3
Melville, L. *Canada* **105** B8
Melville B. *Australia* **94** A2
Melville I. *Australia* **92** B5
Melville I. *Canada* **101** B8
Melville Pen. *Canada* **101** C11
Melvin, Lough *Ireland* **12** B3
Mélykút *Hungary* **28** D4
Memaliaj *Albania* **44** F3
Memba *Mozam.* **87** E5
Memboro *Indonesia* **63** F5
Membrilla *Spain* **37** G2
Memel = Klaipėda *Lithuania* **30** C8
Memel *S. Africa* **89** D4
Memmingen *Germany* **25** H6
Mempawah *Indonesia* **62** D3
Memphis *Egypt* **80** J7
Memphis *Mich., U.S.A.* **114** D2
Memphis *Tenn., U.S.A.* **117** D9
Memphis *Tex., U.S.A.* **116** D4
Memphrémagog, L. *N. Amer.* **115** B12
Mena *Ukraine* **33** G7
Mena *U.S.A.* **116** D7
Mena → *Ethiopia* **81** F5
Menai Strait *U.K.* **14** D3
Ménaka *Mali* **83** B5
Menan = Chao Phraya → *Thailand* **64** F3
Menarandra → *Madag.* **89** D7
Menard *U.S.A.* **116** F5
Menard Fracture Zone *Pac. Oc.* **97** M18
Menawashei *Sudan* **81** E1
Mendaña Fracture Zone *Pac. Oc.* **97** J18
Mendawai → *Indonesia* **62** E4
Mende *France* **20** D7
Mendebo Mts. *Ethiopia* **81** F4
Mendeleyev Ridge *Arctic* **4** B17
Menden *Germany* **24** D3
Menderes *Turkey* **47** C9
Mendhar *India* **69** C6
Mendi *Ethiopia* **81** F4
Mendip Hills *U.K.* **15** F5
Mendocino *U.S.A.* **108** G2
Mendocino, C. *U.S.A.* **108** F1
Mendocino Fracture Zone *Pac. Oc.* **97** D13
Mendota *Calif., U.S.A.* **110** J6
Mendota *Ill., U.S.A.* **112** E9
Mendoyo *Indonesia* **63** J17
Mendoza *Argentina* **126** C2
Mendoza □ *Argentina* **126** C2
Mene Grande *Venezuela* **124** B4
Menemen *Turkey* **47** C9
Menen *Belgium* **17** D3
Menfi *Italy* **42** E5
Mengdingjie *China* **58** F2
Mengeš *Slovenia* **41** B11
Menggala *Indonesia* **62** E3
Menghai *China* **58** G3
Mengíbar *Spain* **37** H7
Mengjin *China* **56** G7
Mengla *China* **58** G3
Menglian *China* **58** F3
Mengshan *China* **59** E8
Mengyin *China* **57** G9
Mengzhe *China* **58** F3
Mengzi *China* **58** F4
Menihek *Canada* **105** B6
Menihek L. *Canada* **105** B6
Menin = Menen *Belgium* **17** D3
Menindee *Australia* **95** E3
Menindee L. *Australia* **95** E3

Meningie *Australia* **95** F2
Menjangan, Pulau *Indonesia* **63** J17
Menlo Park *U.S.A.* **110** H4
Menominee *U.S.A.* **112** C10
Menominee → *U.S.A.* **112** C10
Menomonie *U.S.A.* **112** C8
Menongue *Angola* **85** G3
Menorca *Spain* **48** B11
Menorca ✈ (MAH) *Spain* **38** F9
Mentakab *Malaysia* **65** L4
Mentawai, Kepulauan *Indonesia* **62** E1
Menton *France* **21** E11
Mentor *U.S.A.* **114** E3
Menzies *Australia* **93** E3
Me'ona *Israel* **74** B4
Meoqui *Mexico* **118** B3
Mepaco *Mozam.* **87** F3
Meppel *Neths.* **17** B6
Meppen *Germany* **24** C3
Mequinenza *Spain* **38** D5
Mequinenza, Embalse de *Spain* **38** D5
Mer *France* **18** E8
Merak *Indonesia* **63** F12
Meramangye, L. *Australia* **93** E5
Meran = Merano *Italy* **41** B8
Merano *Italy* **41** B8
Merate *Italy* **40** C6
Merauke *Indonesia* **63** F10
Merbein *Australia* **95** E3
Merbuk, Gunung *Indonesia* **63** J17
Merca *Somali Rep.* **75** G3
Mercantour △ *France* **21** D10
Mercato Saraceno *Italy* **41** E9
Merced *U.S.A.* **110** H6
Merced → *U.S.A.* **110** H6
Merced Pk. *U.S.A.* **110** H7
Mercedes *B. Aires, Argentina* **126** C4
Mercedes *Corrientes, Argentina* **126** B4
Mercedes *San Luis, Argentina* **126** C2
Mercedes *Uruguay* **126** C4
Merceditas *Chile* **126** B1
Mercer *N.Z.* **91** B5
Mercer *U.S.A.* **114** E4
Mercer Island *U.S.A.* **110** C4
Mercury *U.S.A.* **111** J11
Mercy, C. *Canada* **101** C13
Merdrignac *France* **18** D4
Mere *U.K.* **15** F5
Meredith, C. *Falk. Is.* **128** G4
Meredith, L. *U.S.A.* **116** D4
Merefa *Ukraine* **33** H9
Merei *Romania* **29** E11
Merga = Nukheila *Sudan* **80** D2
Mergui *Burma* **64** F2
Mergui Arch. = Myeik Kyunzu *Burma* **65** G1
Méribel-les-Allues *France* **21** C10
Meriç *Turkey* **45** F10
Meriç → *Turkey* **45** F10
Mérida *Mexico* **119** C7
Mérida *Spain* **37** G4
Mérida *Venezuela* **124** B4
Mérida, Cord. de *Venezuela* **124** B4
Meriden *U.K.* **15** E6
Meriden *U.S.A.* **115** E12
Meridian *Calif., U.S.A.* **110** F5
Meridian *Idaho, U.S.A.* **108** E5
Meridian *Miss., U.S.A.* **117** E10
Mérignac *France* **20** D3
Merinda *Australia* **94** C4
Mering *Germany* **25** G6
Meringa *Nigeria* **83** C7
Merir *Pac. Oc.* **63** D8
Merirumã *Brazil* **125** C8
Merkel *U.S.A.* **116** E4
Mermaid Reef *Australia* **92** C2
Merowe *Sudan* **80** D3
Merowe Dam *Sudan* **80** D3
Merredin *Australia* **93** F2
Merrick *U.K.* **13** F4
Merrickville *Canada* **115** B9
Merrill *Oreg., U.S.A.* **108** E3
Merrill *Wis., U.S.A.* **112** C9
Merrimack → *U.S.A.* **115** D14
Merriman *U.S.A.* **112** D3
Merritt *Canada* **102** C4
Merritt Island *U.S.A.* **117** G14
Merriwa *Australia* **95** E5
Merry I. *Canada* **104** A4
Merryville *U.S.A.* **116** F8
Mersa Fatma *Eritrea* **81** E5
Mersch *Lux.* **17** E6
Merse → *Italy* **41** E8
Mersea I. *U.K.* **15** F8
Merseburg *Germany* **24** D7
Mersey → *U.K.* **14** D4
Merseyside □ *U.K.* **14** D4
Mersin = İçel *Turkey* **72** D6
Mersing *Malaysia* **65** L4
Merta *India* **68** F6
Merta Road *India* **68** F5

Merthyr Tydfil *U.K.* **15** F4
Merthyr Tydfil □ *U.K.* **15** F4
Merti *Kenya* **86** B4
Mértola *Portugal* **37** H3
Mertzon *U.S.A.* **116** F4
Méru *France* **19** C9
Meru *Kenya* **86** B4
Meru *Tanzania* **86** C4
Meru △ *Kenya* **86** B4
Merville *France* **19** B9
Méry-sur-Seine *France* **19** D10
Merzifon *Turkey* **72** B6
Merzig *Germany* **25** F2
Mesa *U.S.A.* **109** K8
Mesa Verde △ *U.S.A.* **109** H9
Mesagne *Italy* **43** B10
Mesanagros *Greece* **49** C9
Mesaoría *Cyprus* **49** D12
Meschede *Germany* **24** D4
Mescit *Turkey* **73** B9
Mesfinto *Ethiopia* **81** E4
Mesgouez, L. *Canada* **104** B5
Meshchovsk *Russia* **32** E8
Meshed = Mashhad *Iran* **71** B8
Meshoppen *U.S.A.* **115** E8
Meshra er Req *Sudan* **81** F2
Mesilinka → *Canada* **102** B4
Meslay-du-Maine *France* **18** E6
Mesocco *Switz.* **25** J5
Mesologi *Greece* **46** C3
Mesongi *Greece* **49** B3
Mesopotamia = Al Jazirah *Iraq* **73** E10
Mesopotamia *U.S.A.* **114** E4
Mesopotamia *Greece* **46** B2
Mesoraca *Italy* **43** C9
Mésou Volímais = Volimes *Greece* **46** D2
Mesquite *U.S.A.* **109** H6
Messaad *Algeria* **78** B6
Messac *France* **18** E5
Messalo → *Mozam.* **87** E4
Méssamena *Cameroon* **83** E7
Messara, Kolpos *Greece* **49** D6
Messina = Musina *S. Africa* **89** C5
Messina *Italy* **43** D8
Messina, Str. di *Italy* **43** D8
Messini *Greece* **46** D4
Messinia □ *Greece* **46** D3
Messiniakos Kolpos *Greece* **46** E4
Messkirch *Germany* **25** H5
Messlingen *Sweden* **10** B6
Mesta → *Bulgaria* **44** E7
Mesta, Akra *Greece* **47** C7
Mestanza *Spain* **37** G6
Mestre *Italy* **41** C9
Mesudiye *Turkey* **72** B7
Meta → *S. Amer.* **124** B5
Meta Incognita Pen. *Canada* **101** C13
Metabetchouan *Canada* **105** C5
Metairie *U.S.A.* **117** G9
Metalici, Munţii *Romania* **28** D7
Metaline Falls *U.S.A.* **108** B5
Metallifere, Colline *Italy* **40** E8
Metán *Argentina* **126** B3
Metangula *Mozam.* **87** E3
Metauro → *Italy* **41** E10
Metema *Ethiopia* **81** E4
Metengobalame *Mozam.* **87** E3
Methana *Greece* **46** D5
Methoni *Greece* **46** D3
Methven *N.Z.* **91** E3
Metil *Mozam.* **87** F4
Metkovets *Bulgaria* **44** C7
Metković *Croatia* **41** E14
Metlakatla *U.S.A.* **100** D6
Metlika *Slovenia* **41** C12
Metropolis *U.S.A.* **112** G9
Metsovo *Greece* **46** B3
Metu *Ethiopia* **81** F4
Metz *France* **19** C13
Metzingen *Germany* **25** G5
Meulaboh *Indonesia* **62** D1
Meung-sur-Loire *France* **19** E8
Meureudu *Indonesia* **62** C1
Meurthe → *France* **19** D13
Meurthe-et-Moselle □ *France* **19** D13
Meuse □ *France* **19** C12
Meuse → *Europe* **17** D5
Meuselwitz *Germany* **24** D8
Mexia *U.S.A.* **116** F6
Mexiana, I. *Brazil* **125** D9
Mexicali *Mexico* **111** N11
Mexican Plateau *Mexico* **98** G9
Mexican Water *U.S.A.* **109** H9
México *Mexico* **119** D5
Mexico *Maine, U.S.A.* **115** B14
Mexico *Mo., U.S.A.* **112** F8
Mexico *N.Y., U.S.A.* **115** C8
México □ *Mexico* **119** D5
Mexico ■ *Cent. Amer.* **118** C4
México, Ciudad de *Mexico* **119** D5
Mexico, G. of *Cent. Amer.* **119** C7
Mexico B. *U.S.A.* **115** C8
Meydán-e Naftūn *Iran* **71** D6

Meydani, Ra's-e *Iran* **71** E8
Meyenburg *Germany* **24** B8
Meyers Chuck *U.S.A.* **102** B2
Meymac *France* **20** C6
Meymaneh *Afghan.* **66** B4
Meyrueis *France* **20** D7
Meyssac *France* **20** C5
Meyzieu *France* **21** C9
Mezdra *Bulgaria* **44** C7
Mèze *France* **20** E7
Mezen *Russia* **52** C9
Mezen → *Russia* **6** B14
Mézenc, Mt. *France* **21** D8
Mezeş, Munţii *Romania* **28** C8
Mezha → *Russia* **32** E6
Mezhdurechenskiy *Russia* **52** D7
Mézidon-Canon *France* **18** C6
Mézières-en-Brenne *France* **20** B5
Mézilhac *France* **21** D8
Mézin *France* **20** D4
Mezőberény *Hungary* **28** D6
Mezőfalva *Hungary* **28** D3
Mezőhegyes *Hungary* **28** D5
Mezőkövácsháza *Hungary* **28** D5
Mezőkövesd *Hungary* **28** C5
Mézos *France* **20** D2
Mezőtúr *Hungary* **28** C5
Mezquital *Mexico* **118** C4
Mezzolombardo *Italy* **40** B8
Mfolozi → *S. Africa* **89** D5
Mgeta *Tanzania* **87** D4
Mglin *Russia* **33** F7
Mhlaba Hills *Zimbabwe* **87** F3
Mhow *India* **68** H6
Miahuatlán *Mexico* **119** D5
Miajadas *Spain* **37** F5
Miami *Fla., U.S.A.* **117** J14
Miami *Okla., U.S.A.* **116** C7
Miami *Tex., U.S.A.* **116** D4
Miami Beach *U.S.A.* **117** J14
Mian Xian *China* **56** H4
Mianchi *China* **56** G6
Mīāndarreh *Iran* **71** C7
Mīāndowāb *Iran* **73** D12
Miandrivazo *Madag.* **89** B8
Mīāneh *Iran* **73** D12
Mianning *China* **58** C4
Mianwali *Pakistan* **68** C4
Mianyang *China* **58** B5
Mianzhu *China* **58** B5
Miaoli *Taiwan* **59** E13
Miarinarivo *Antananarivo, Madag.* **89** B8
Miarinarivo *Toamasina, Madag.* **89** B8
Miariravaratra *Madag.* **89** C8
Miass *Russia* **52** D7
Miastko *Poland* **30** E3
Mica *S. Africa* **89** C5
Micăsasa *Romania* **29** D9
Michalovce *Slovak Rep.* **27** C14
Michigan □ *U.S.A.* **113** C11
Michigan, L. *U.S.A.* **112** D10
Michigan City *U.S.A.* **112** E10
Michika *Nigeria* **83** C7
Michipicoten I. *Canada* **104** C2
Michoacán □ *Mexico* **118** D4
Michurin *Bulgaria* **45** D11
Michurinsk *Russia* **34** D5
Mico, Pta. *Nic.* **120** D3
Micoud *St. Lucia* **121** f
Micronesia *Pac. Oc.* **96** G7
Micronesia, Federated States of ■ *Pac. Oc.* **90** A8
Mid-Pacific Seamounts *Pac. Oc.* **96** F10
Midai *Indonesia* **62** D3
Midale *Canada* **103** D8
Middelburg *Neths.* **17** C3
Middelburg *Eastern Cape, S. Africa* **88** E4
Middelburg *Mpumalanga, S. Africa* **89** D4
Middelfart *Denmark* **11** J3
Middelpos *S. Africa* **88** E3
Middelwit *S. Africa* **88** C4
Middle Alkali L. *U.S.A.* **108** F3
Middle America Trench = Guatemala Trench *Pac. Oc.* **98** H10
Middle Bass I. *U.S.A.* **114** E2
Middle East *Asia* **50** F7
Middle Fork Feather → *U.S.A.* **110** F5
Middle I. *Australia* **93** F3
Middle Loup → *U.S.A.* **112** E4
Middle Sackville *Canada* **105** D7
Middleboro *U.S.A.* **115** E14
Middleburg *Fla., U.S.A.* **117** F14
Middleburg *Pa., U.S.A.* **114** F7
Middleburgh *U.S.A.* **115** D10
Middlebury *U.S.A.* **115** B11
Middlemount *Australia* **94** C4
Middleport *N.Y., U.S.A.* **114** C6
Middleport *Ohio, U.S.A.* **113** F12

Middlesboro *U.S.A.* **113** G12
Middlesbrough *U.K.* **14** C6
Middlesbrough □ *U.K.* **14** C6
Middlesex *Belize* **120** C2
Middlesex *N.J., U.S.A.* **115** F10
Middlesex *N.Y., U.S.A.* **114** D7
Middleton *Australia* **94** C3
Middleton *Canada* **105** D6
Middleton Cr. → *Australia* **94** C3
Middletown *U.K.* **12** B5
Middletown *Calif., U.S.A.* **110** G4
Middletown *Conn., U.S.A.* **115** E12
Middletown *N.Y., U.S.A.* **115** E10
Middletown *Ohio, U.S.A.* **113** F11
Middletown *Pa., U.S.A.* **115** F8
Midge Point *Australia* **94** J6
Midhurst *U.K.* **15** G7
Mīdī *Yemen* **81** D5
Midi, Canal du → *France* **20** E5
Midi d'Ossau, Pic du *France* **20** F3
Midi-Pyrénées □ *France* **20** E5
Midland *Australia* **93** F2
Midland *Canada* **114** B5
Midland *Calif., U.S.A.* **111** M12
Midland *Mich., U.S.A.* **113** D11
Midland *Pa., U.S.A.* **114** F4
Midland *Tex., U.S.A.* **116** F3
Midlands □ *Zimbabwe* **87** F2
Midleton *Ireland* **12** E3
Midlothian *U.S.A.* **116** E6
Midlothian □ *U.K.* **13** F5
Midongy, Tangorombohitr' i *Madag.* **89** C8
Midongy Atsimo *Madag.* **89** C8
Midou → *France* **20** E3
Midouze → *France* **20** E3
Midsayap *Phil.* **61** H6
Midtjylland □ *Denmark* **11** H2
Midu *China* **58** E3
Midway Is. *Pac. Oc.* **96** E10
Midway Wells *U.S.A.* **111** N11
Midwest *U.S.A.* **107** B9
Midwest *Wyo., U.S.A.* **108** E10
Midwest City *U.S.A.* **116** D6
Midyat *Turkey* **73** D9
Midzŏr *Bulgaria* **44** C7
Mie □ *Japan* **55** G8
Miechów *Poland* **31** H7
Miedwie, Jezioro *Poland* **31** E1
Międzybórz *Poland* **31** G4
Międzychód *Poland* **31** F2
Międzylesie *Poland* **31** H3
Międzyrzec Podlaski *Poland* **31** G9
Międzyrzecz *Poland* **31** F2
Międzyzdroje *Poland* **30** E1
Miejska Górka *Poland* **31** G3
Miélan *France* **20** E4
Mielec *Poland* **31** H8
Mienga *Angola* **88** B2
Miercurea-Ciuc *Romania* **29** D10
Miercurea Sibiului *Romania* **29** E8
Mieres *Spain* **36** B5
Mieroszów *Poland* **31** H3
Mieso *Ethiopia* **81** F5
Mieszkowice *Poland* **31** F1
Mifflintown *U.S.A.* **114** F7
Mifraz Ḥefa *Israel* **74** C4
Migennes *France* **19** E10
Migliarino *Italy* **41** D8
Migliarino-San Rossore-Massaciuccoli △ *Italy* **40** E7
Migori *Kenya* **86** C3
Miguel Alemán, Presa *Mexico* **119** D5
Migueiturra *Spain* **37** G7
Mihăileni *Romania* **29** C11
Mihăileşti *Romania* **29** F10
Mihailovca *Moldova* **29** D13
Mihalgazi *Turkey* **47** A12
Mihaliççık *Turkey* **72** C4
Mihara *Japan* **55** G6
Mikha-Tskhakaya = Senaki *Georgia* **35** J6
Mikhailovka = Mykhaylivka *Ukraine* **33** J8
Mikhaylov *Russia* **32** E10
Mikhaylovgrad = Montana *Bulgaria* **44** C7
Mikhaylovka *Russia* **34** E6
Mikhnevo *Russia* **32** E9
Mikines *Greece* **46** D4
Mikkeli *Finland* **32** B5
Mikkwa → *Canada* **102** B6
Mikniya *Sudan* **81** D3
Mikołajki *Poland* **30** E8
Míkonos = Mykonos *Greece* **47** D7
Mikri Prespa, L. *Greece* **44** F5
Mikro Derio *Greece* **45** E10
Mikstat *Poland* **31** G4
Mikulov *Czech Rep.* **27** C9
Mikumi *Tanzania* **86** D4
Mikumi △ *Tanzania* **86** D4
Milaca *U.S.A.* **112** C7
Milagro *Ecuador* **124** D3
Milagros *Phil.* **61** E5

Milan = Milano *Italy* **40** C6
Milan *Mo., U.S.A.* **112** E7
Milan *Tenn., U.S.A.* **117** D10
Milange *Mozam.* **87** F4
Milano *Italy* **40** C6
Milano Linate ✈ (LIN) *Italy* **40** C6
Milanoa *Madag.* **89** A8
Milâs *Turkey* **47** D9
Milatos *Greece* **49** D7
Milazzo *Italy* **43** D8
Milbank *U.S.A.* **112** C5
Milbanke Sd. *Canada* **102** C3
Milden *Canada* **103** C7
Mildenhall *U.K.* **15** E8
Mildmay *Canada* **114** B3
Mildura *Australia* **95** E3
Mile *China* **58** E4
Miles *Australia* **95** D5
Miles City *U.S.A.* **108** C11
Mileşti *Moldova* **29** C13
Milestone *Canada* **103** D8
Mileto *Italy* **43** D8
Miletto, Mte. *Italy* **43** A7
Miletus *Turkey* **47** D9
Milevsko *Czech Rep.* **26** B7
Milford *Calif., U.S.A.* **110** E6
Milford *Conn., U.S.A.* **115** E11
Milford *Del., U.S.A.* **113** F16
Milford *Mass., U.S.A.* **115** D13
Milford *N.H., U.S.A.* **115** D13
Milford *Pa., U.S.A.* **115** E10
Milford *Utah, U.S.A.* **108** G7
Milford Haven *U.K.* **15** F2
Milford Sd. *N.Z.* **91** F1
Milford Sound *N.Z.* **91** F1
Milḥ, Baḥr al = Razāzah, Buḥayrat ar *Iraq* **73** F10
Milicz *Poland* **31** G4
Milies *Greece* **46** B5
Milikapiti *Australia* **92** B5
Miling *Australia* **93** F2
Militello in Val di Catánia *Italy* **43** E7
Milk, Wadi el → *Sudan* **80** D3
Milk River *Canada* **102** D6
Mill I. *Antarctica* **5** C8
Mill Valley *U.S.A.* **110** H4
Millárs → *Spain* **38** F4
Millau *France* **20** D7
Millbridge *Canada* **114** B7
Millbrook *Canada* **114** B6
Millbrook *Ala., U.S.A.* **117** E11
Millbrook *N.Y., U.S.A.* **115** E11
Mille Lacs, L. des *Canada* **104** C1
Mille Lacs L. *U.S.A.* **112** B7
Milledgeville *U.S.A.* **117** E13
Millen *U.S.A.* **117** E14
Millennium I. = Caroline I. *Kiribati* **97** H12
Miller *U.S.A.* **112** C4
Millerovo *Russia* **35** F5
Millersburg *Ohio, U.S.A.* **114** F3
Millersburg *Pa., U.S.A.* **114** F8
Millerton *U.S.A.* **115** E11
Millerton L. *U.S.A.* **110** J7
Millet *St. Lucia* **121** f
Millevaches, Plateau de *France* **20** C6
Millheim *U.S.A.* **114** F7
Millicent *Australia* **95** F3
Millington *U.S.A.* **117** D10
Millinocket *U.S.A.* **113** C19
Millmerran *Australia* **95** D5
Millom *U.K.* **14** C4
Mills L. *Canada* **102** A5
Millsboro *U.S.A.* **114** G5
Millstream Chichester △ *Australia* **92** D2
Millstreet *Ireland* **12** D2
Milltown Malbay *Ireland* **12** D2
Millville *N.J., U.S.A.* **113** F16
Millville *Pa., U.S.A.* **115** E8
Millwood L. *U.S.A.* **116** E8
Milna *Croatia* **41** E13
Milne → *Australia* **94** C2
Milo *U.S.A.* **113** C19
Milon, Akra *Greece* **49** C10
Milos *Greece* **46** E6
Miłosław *Poland* **31** F4
Milot *Albania* **44** E3
Milparinka *Australia* **95** D3
Milpitas *U.S.A.* **110** H5
Miltenberg *Germany* **25** F5
Milton *N.S., Canada* **105** D7
Milton *Ont., Canada* **114** C5
Milton *N.Z.* **91** G2
Milton *Calif., U.S.A.* **110** G6
Milton *Fla., U.S.A.* **117** F11
Milton *Pa., U.S.A.* **114** F8
Milton *Vt., U.S.A.* **115** B11
Milton-Freewater *U.S.A.* **108** D4
Milton Keynes *U.K.* **15** E7
Milton Keynes □ *U.K.* **15** E7
Miluo *China* **59** C9
Milverton *Canada* **114** C4
Milwaukee *U.S.A.* **112** D10
Milwaukee Deep *Atl. Oc.* **121** C6

Milwaukie *U.S.A.* **110** E4
Mim *Ghana* **82** D4
Mimizan *France* **20** D2
Mimoň *Czech Rep.* **26** A7
Min Jiang → *Fujian, China* **59** E12
Min Jiang → *Sichuan, China* **58** C5
Min Xian *China* **56** G3
Minā' Jabal 'Alī *U.A.E.* **71** E7
Mina Pirquitas *Argentina* **126** A2
Mīnā Su'ud *Si. Arabia* **71** D6
Mīnā'al Aḥmadī *Kuwait* **71** D6
Minago → *Canada* **103** C9
Minaki *Canada* **103** D10
Minamata *Japan* **55** H5
Minami-Arapusa △ *Japan* **55** G9
Minami-Tori-Shima *Pac. Oc.* **96** E7
Minas *Uruguay* **127** C4
Minas, Sierra de las
  Guatemala **120** C2
Minas Basin *Canada* **105** C7
Minas de Riotinto *Spain* **37** H4
Minas Gerais □ *Brazil* **125** G9
Minatitlán *Mexico* **119** D6
Minbu *Burma* **67** J19
Minchinabad *Pakistan* **68** D5
Mincio → *Italy* **40** C7
Minčol *Slovak Rep.* **27** B13
Mindanao *Phil.* **61** H6
Mindanao Sea = Bohol Sea
  Phil. **63** C6
Mindanao Trench *Pac. Oc.* **61** F7
Mindel → *Germany* **25** G6
Mindelheim *Germany* **25** G6
Mindelo *C. Verde Is.* **78** b
Minden *Canada* **114** B6
Minden *Germany* **24** C4
Minden *La., U.S.A.* **116** E8
Minden *Nev., U.S.A.* **110** G7
Mindiptana *Indonesia* **63** F10
Mindoro *Phil.* **61** E4
Mindoro Str. *Phil.* **61** E4
Mine *Japan* **55** G5
Minehead *U.K.* **15** F4
Mineola *N.Y., U.S.A.* **115** F11
Mineola *Tex., U.S.A.* **116** E7
Mineral King *U.S.A.* **110** J8
Mineral Wells *U.S.A.* **116** E5
Mineralnyye Vody *Russia* **35** H6
Minersville *U.S.A.* **115** F8
Minerva *U.S.A.* **114** F3
Minervino Murge *Italy* **43** A9
Minetto *U.S.A.* **115** C8
Mingäçevir *Azerbaijan* **35** K8
Mingäçevir Su Anbarı
  Azerbaijan **35** K8
Mingan *Canada* **105** B7
Mingechaur = Mingäçevir
  Azerbaijan **35** K8
Mingechaurskoye
  Vdkhr. = Mingäçevir Su
  Anbarı *Azerbaijan* **35** K8
Mingela *Australia* **94** B4
Mingenew *Australia* **93** E2
Mingera Cr. → *Australia* **94** C2
Minggang *China* **59** A10
Mingguang *China* **59** A11
Mingin *Burma* **67** H19
Mingir *Moldova* **29** D13
Minglanilla *Spain* **39** F3
Minglun *China* **58** E7
Mingo Junction *U.S.A.* **114** F4
Mingora *Pakistan* **68** B5
Mingorria *Spain* **36** E6
Mingshan *China* **58** B4
Mingteke Daban =
  Mintaka Pass *Pakistan* **69** A6
Mingxi *China* **59** D11
Mingyuegue *China* **57** C15
Minho = Miño → *Spain* **36** D2
Minho *China* **59** E12
Minićevo *Serbia* **28** C7
Minidoka *U.S.A.* **108** E7
Minigwal, L. *Australia* **93** E3
Minilya → *Australia* **93** D1
Minilya Roadhouse *Australia* **93** D1
Minipi L. *Canada* **105** B7
Mink L. *Canada* **102** A5
Minkammen *Sudan* **81** F3
Minna *Nigeria* **83** D6
Minneapolis *Kans., U.S.A.* **112** F5
Minneapolis *Minn., U.S.A.* **112** C7
Minnedosa *Canada* **103** C9
Minnesota □ *U.S.A.* **112** B6
Minnesota → *U.S.A.* **112** C7
Minnewaukan *U.S.A.* **112** A4
Minnipa *Australia* **95** E2
Minnitaki L. *Canada* **104** C1
Mino *Japan* **55** G8
Miño *Spain* **36** B2
Miño → *Spain* **36** D2
Minoa *Greece* **47** F7
Minorca = Menorca *Spain* **48** B11
Minot *U.S.A.* **112** A3
Minqin *China* **56** D5
Minqing *China* **59** D12
Minsen *Germany* **24** B3
Minsk *Belarus* **23** B14

Minsk □ *Belarus* **32** F4
Mińsk Mazowiecki *Poland* **31** F8
Mintabie *Australia* **95** D1
Mintaka Pass *Pakistan* **69** A6
Minto *Canada* **105** C6
Minto, L. *Canada* **104** A5
Minton *Canada* **103** D8
Minturn *U.S.A.* **108** G10
Minturno *Italy* **42** A6
Minûf *Egypt* **80** H7
Minusinsk *Russia* **53** D10
Minutang *India* **67** E20
Minvoul *Gabon* **84** D2
Minya el Qamh *Egypt* **80** H7
Minya Konka = Gongga
  Shan *China* **58** C3
Mionica *Bos.-H.* **28** F3
Mionica *Serbia* **44** B4
Miquelon *Canada* **104** C4
Miquelon *St-P. & M.* **105** C8
Mira *Italy* **41** C9
Mira *Portugal* **36** E2
Mira → *Portugal* **37** H2
Mira por vos Cay *Bahamas* **121** B5
Mirabella Eclano *Italy* **43** A7
Mirabello, Kolpos *Greece* **49** D7
Mirador-Río Azul △
  Guatemala **120** C2
Miraj *India* **66** L9
Miram Shah *Pakistan* **68** C4
Miramar *Argentina* **126** D4
Miramar *Mozam.* **89** C6
Miramas *France* **21** E8
Mirambeau *France* **20** C3
Miramichi *Canada* **105** C6
Miramichi B. *Canada* **105** C7
Miramont-de-Guyenne
  France **20** D4
Miranda *Brazil* **125** H7
Miranda → *Brazil* **124** G7
Miranda de Ebro *Spain* **38** C2
Miranda do Corvo *Portugal* **36** E2
Miranda do Douro *Portugal* **36** D4
Mirande *France* **20** E4
Mirandela *Portugal* **36** D3
Mirándola *Italy* **40** D8
Mirandópolis *Brazil* **127** A5
Mirango *Malawi* **87** E3
Mirani *Australia* **94** K6
Mirano *Italy* **41** C9
Miras *Albania* **44** F4
Mirassol *Brazil* **127** A6
Mirbāṭ *Oman* **75** D5
Mirear *Egypt* **80** C4
Mirebeau *France* **18** F7
Mirebeau-sur-Bèze *France* **19** E12
Mirecourt *France* **19** D13
Mires *Greece* **49** D6
Mirgorod = Myrhorod
  Ukraine **33** H7
Miri *Malaysia* **62** D4
Miriam Vale *Australia* **94** C5
Miribel *France* **19** G11
Mirim, L. *S. Amer.* **127** C5
Mīrjāveh *Iran* **71** D9
Mirnyy *Antarctica* **5** C14
Mirnyy *Russia* **53** C12
Miroč *Serbia* **44** B6
Mirokhan *Pakistan* **68** F3
Mirond L. *Canada* **103** B8
Mirosławiec *Poland* **30** E3
Mirpur *Pakistan* **69** B6
Mirpur Batoro *Pakistan* **68** G3
Mirpur Bibiwari *Pakistan* **68** E2
Mirpur Khas *Pakistan* **68** G3
Mirpur Sakro *Pakistan* **68** G2
Mirria *Niger* **83** C6
Mirsk *Poland* **31** H2
Mirtağ *Turkey* **70** B4
Mirtoo Sea *Greece* **46** D5
Miryang *S. Korea* **57** G15
Mirzaani *Georgia* **35** K8
Mirzapur *India* **69** G10
Mirzapur-cum-
  Vindhyachal =
  Mirzapur *India* **69** G10
Misantla *Mexico* **119** D5
Misawa *Japan* **54** D10
Miscou I. *Canada* **105** C7
Mish'āb, Ra's al *Si. Arabia* **71** D6
Mishan *China* **60** B8
Mishawaka *U.S.A.* **112** E10
Mishbih, Gebel *Egypt* **80** C3
Mishima *Japan* **55** G9
Misión *Mexico* **111** N10
Misiones □ *Argentina* **127** B5
Misiones □ *Paraguay* **126** B4
Miskah *Si. Arabia* **70** E4
Miskitos, Cayos *Nic.* **120** D3
Miskolc *Hungary* **28** B5
Misoke *Dem. Rep. of the Congo* **86** C2
Misool *Indonesia* **63** E8
Miṣr = Egypt ■ *Africa* **80** B3
Mizen Hd. *Cork, Ireland* **12** E2
Mizen Hd. *Wicklow, Ireland* **12** D5
Miṣrātah *Libya* **79** B9

Missanabie *Canada* **104** C3
Missinaibi → *Canada* **104** B3
Missinaibi L. *Canada* **104** C3
Mission *Canada* **102** D4
Mission *S. Dak., U.S.A.* **112** D3
Mission *Tex., U.S.A.* **116** H5
Mission Beach *Australia* **94** B4
Mission Viejo *U.S.A.* **111** M9
Missirah *Senegal* **82** C1
Missisa L. *Canada* **104** B2
Missisicabi → *Canada* **104** B4
Mississagi → *Canada* **104** C3
Mississauga *Canada* **114** C5
Mississippi □ *U.S.A.* **117** E10
Mississippi → *U.S.A.* **117** G10
Mississippi L. *Canada* **115** A8
Mississippi River Delta
  U.S.A. **117** G10
Mississippi Sd. *U.S.A.* **117** F10
Missoula *U.S.A.* **108** C6
Missouri □ *U.S.A.* **112** F7
Missouri → *U.S.A.* **112** F8
Missouri City *U.S.A.* **116** G7
Missouri Valley *U.S.A.* **112** E6
Mist *U.S.A.* **110** E3
Mistassibi → *Canada* **105** B5
Mistassini → *Canada* **105** C5
Mistassini, L. *Canada* **104** B5
Mistastin, L. *Canada* **105** A7
Mistelbach *Austria* **27** C9
Misterbianco *Italy* **43** E8
Mistinibi, L. *Canada* **105** A7
Mistissini *Canada* **105** C5
Mistretta *Italy* **43** E7
Misty L. *Canada* **103** B8
Misurata = Miṣrātah *Libya* **79** B9
Mît Ghamr *Egypt* **80** H7
Mitatib *Sudan* **81** D4
Mitchell *Australia* **95** D4
Mitchell *Canada* **114** C4
Mitchell *Nebr., U.S.A.* **112** E2
Mitchell *Oreg., U.S.A.* **108** D3
Mitchell *S. Dak., U.S.A.* **112** D4
Mitchell → *Australia* **94** B3
Mitchell, Mt. *U.S.A.* **117** D13
Mitchell-Alice Rivers △
  Australia **94** B3
Mitchell Ra. *Australia* **94** A2
Mitchelstown *Ireland* **12** D3
Mitha Tiwana *Pakistan* **68** C5
Mithi *Pakistan* **68** G3
Mithimna *Greece* **47** B8
Mithrao *Pakistan* **68** F3
Mitilini *Greece* **47** B8
Mitilinii *Greece* **47** D8
Mitla Pass = Mamarr
  Mitlā *Egypt* **74** E1
Mito *Japan* **55** F10
Mitrofanovka *Russia* **33** H10
Mitrovica = Kosovska
  Mitrovica *Serbia* **44** D4
Mitsamiouli *Comoros Is.* **85** a
Mitsinjo *Madag.* **89** B8
Mitsiwa *Eritrea* **81** D4
Mitsiwa Channel *Eritrea* **81** D5
Mitsukaidō *Japan* **55** F9
Mittagong *Australia* **95** E5
Mittelberg *Austria* **26** D3
Mittelfranken □ *Germany* **25** F6
Mittellandkanal → *Germany* **24** C4
Mittenwalde *Germany* **24** C9
Mittersill *Austria* **26** D5
Mitterteich *Germany* **25** F8
Mittimatalik = Pond Inlet
  Canada **101** B12
Mittweida *Germany* **24** E8
Mitú *Colombia* **124** C4
Mitumba *Tanzania* **86** D3
Mitumba, Mts.
  Dem. Rep. of the Congo **86** D2
Mitwaba
  Dem. Rep. of the Congo **87** D2
Mityana *Uganda* **86** B3
Mixteco → *Mexico* **119** D5
Miyagi □ *Japan* **54** E10
Miyah, W. el → *Egypt* **80** C3
Miyah, W. el → *Syria* **70** C3
Miyake-Jima *Japan* **55** G9
Miyako *Japan* **54** E10
Miyako-Jima *Japan* **55** M2
Miyako-Rettō *Japan* **55** M2
Miyakonojō *Japan* **55** J5
Miyani *India* **68** J3
Miyanoura-Dake *Japan* **55** J5
Miyazaki *Japan* **55** J5
Miyazaki □ *Japan* **55** H5
Miyazu *Japan* **55** G7
Miyet, Bahr el = Dead Sea
  Asia **74** D4
Miyi *China* **58** D4
Miyoshi *Japan* **55** G6
Miyun *China* **56** D9
Miyun Shuiku *China* **57** D9
Mizan Teferi *Ethiopia* **81** F4
Mizdah *Libya* **79** B8

Mizhhirya *Ukraine* **29** B8
Mizhi *China* **56** F6
Mizil *Romania* **29** F11
Mizoram □ *India* **67** H18
Mizpe Ramon *Israel* **74** E3
Mizuho *Antarctica* **5** D5
Mizusawa *Japan* **54** E10
Mjällby *Sweden* **11** H8
Mjöbäck *Sweden* **11** G6
Mjölby *Sweden* **11** F9
Mjörn *Sweden* **11** G6
Mjøsa *Norway* **8** F14
Mkata *Tanzania* **86** D4
Mkhaya △ *Swaziland* **89** D5
Mkhuze △ *S. Africa* **89** D4
Mkokotoni *Tanzania* **86** D4
Mkomazi *Tanzania* **86** C4
Mkomazi → *S. Africa* **89** E5
Mkomazi △ *Tanzania* **86** C4
Mkulwe *Tanzania* **87** D3
Mkumbi, Ras *Tanzania* **86** D4
Mkushi *Zambia* **87** E2
Mkushi River *Zambia* **87** E2
Mkuze *S. Africa* **89** D5
Mladá Boleslav *Czech Rep.* **26** A7
Mladenovac *Serbia* **44** B4
Mlala Hills *Tanzania* **86** D3
Mlange = Mulanje *Malawi* **87** F4
Mlava → *Serbia* **44** B5
Mława *Poland* **31** E7
Mlawula △ *Swaziland* **89** D5
Mlinište *Bos.-H.* **41** D13
Mljet *Croatia* **41** F14
Mljet △ *Croatia* **41** F14
Mljetski Kanal *Croatia* **41** F14
Młynary *Poland* **30** D6
Mmabatho *S. Africa* **88** D4
Mmathethe *Botswana* **88** D4
Mme *Cameroon* **83** D7
Mnichovo Hradiště
  Czech Rep. **26** A7
Mo i Rana *Norway* **8** C16
Moa *Cuba* **121** B4
Moa *Indonesia* **63** F7
Moa → *S. Leone* **82** D2
Moab *U.S.A.* **108** G9
Moala *Fiji* **91** a
Moama *Australia* **95** F3
Moamba *Mozam.* **89** D5
Moapa *U.S.A.* **111** J12
Moate *Ireland* **12** C4
Moba *Dem. Rep. of the Congo* **86** D2
Mobārakābād *Iran* **71** D7
Mobaye *C.A.R.* **84** D4
Mobayi *Dem. Rep. of the Congo* **84** D4
Moberley Lake *Canada* **102** B4
Moberly *U.S.A.* **112** F7
Mobile *U.S.A.* **117** F10
Mobile B. *U.S.A.* **117** F11
Mobridge *U.S.A.* **112** C3
Moc Chau *Vietnam* **58** B5
Moc Hoa *Vietnam* **65** G5
Mocabe Kasari
  Dem. Rep. of the Congo **87** D2
Moçambique =
  Mozambique ■ *Africa* **87** F4
Moçâmedes *Mozam.* **87** F5
Mocanaqua *U.S.A.* **115** E8
Moce *Fiji* **91** a
Mochima △ *Venezuela* **121** D7
Mochos *Greece* **49** D7
Mochudi *Botswana* **88** C4
Mocimboa da Praia *Mozam.* **87** E5
Mociu *Romania* **29** D9
Mocoa *Colombia* **124** C3
Mococa *Brazil* **127** A6
Mocorito *Mexico* **118** B3
Moctezuma *Mexico* **118** B3
Moctezuma → *Mexico* **119** C5
Mocuba *Mozam.* **87** F4
Modane *France* **21** C10
Modasa *India* **68** H5
Modder → *S. Africa* **88** D3
Modderrivier *S. Africa* **88** D3
Módena *Italy* **40** D7
Modena *U.S.A.* **109** H7
Modesto *U.S.A.* **110** H6
Módica *Italy* **43** F7
Modimolle *S. Africa* **89** C4
Modjadjiskloof *S. Africa* **89** C5
Mödling *Austria* **27** C9
Modo *Sudan* **81** F3
Modra *Slovak Rep.* **27** C10
Modriča *Bos.-H.* **28** F3
Moe *Australia* **95** F4
Moebase *Mozam.* **87** F4
Moëlan-sur-Mer *France* **18** E3
Moengo *Suriname* **125** B8
Moga *India* **68** D6
Mogadishu = Muqdisho
  Somali Rep. **75** G4
Mogador = Essaouira
  Morocco **78** B4
Mogadouro *Portugal* **36** D4

Mogalakwena → *S. Africa* **89** C4
Mogami-Gawa → *Japan* **54** E10
Mogán *Canary Is.* **48** G4
Mogaung *Burma* **67** G20
Mogi das Cruzes *Brazil* **127** A6
Mogi-Guaçu → *Brazil* **127** A6
Mogi-Mirim *Brazil* **127** A6
Mogielnica *Poland* **31** G7
Mogige *Ethiopia* **81** F4
Mogilev = Mahilyow
  Belarus **23** B16
Mogilev-Podolskiy =
  Mohyliv-Podilskyy
  Ukraine **29** B12
Mogilno *Poland* **31** F4
Mogincual *Mozam.* **87** F5
Mogliano Véneto *Italy* **41** C9
Mogocha *Russia* **53** D12
Mogok *Burma* **67** H20
Mogollon Rim *U.S.A.* **109** J8
Mógoro *Italy* **42** C1
Mograt *Sudan* **80** D3
Moguer *Spain* **37** H4
Mogumber *Australia* **93** F2
Mogwadi → *S. Africa* **89** C4
Mohács *Hungary* **28** E3
Mohales Hoek *Lesotho* **88** E4
Mohall *U.S.A.* **112** A3
Moḥammadābād *Iran* **71** B8
Mohammedia *Morocco* **78** B4
Mohana → *India* **69** G11
Mohanlalganj *India* **69** F9
Mohave, L. *U.S.A.* **111** K12
Mohave Desert → *U.S.A.* **111** K11
Mohawk → *U.S.A.* **115** D11
Moheda *Sweden* **11** G8
Mohéli *Comoros Is.* **85** a
Mohenjodaro *Pakistan* **68** F3
Moher, Cliffs of *Ireland* **12** D2
Mohicanville Res. *U.S.A.* **114** F2
Möhne → *Germany* **24** D3
Mohns Ridge *Arctic* **4** B7
Mohoro *Tanzania* **86** D4
Mohyliv-Podilskyy *Ukraine* **29** B12
Moia *Sudan* **81** F2
Moidart, L. *U.K.* **13** E3
Moineşti *Romania* **29** D11
Moira → *Canada* **114** B7
Moirans *France* **21** C9
Moirans-en-Montagne
  France **19** F12
Moisaküla *Estonia* **32** C3
Moisie *Canada* **105** B6
Moisie → *Canada* **105** B6
Moissac *France* **20** D5
Moita *Portugal* **37** G2
Moixent *Spain* **39** G4
Möja *Sweden* **10** E12
Mojácar *Spain* **39** H3
Mojados *Spain* **36** D6
Mojave *U.S.A.* **111** K8
Mojave → *U.S.A.* **111** K11
Mojave Desert *U.S.A.* **111** L10
Mojiang *China* **58** F3
Mojo → *Ethiopia* **81** F5
Mojo *Bolivia* **126** A2
Mojo *Ethiopia* **81** F4
Mojokerto *Indonesia* **63** G15
Mokai *N.Z.* **91** C5
Mokambo
  Dem. Rep. of the Congo **87** E2
Mokameh *India* **69** G11
Mokau *N.Z.* **91** C5
Mokelumne → *U.S.A.* **110** G5
Mokelumne Hill *U.S.A.* **110** G6
Mokhotlong *Lesotho* **89** D4
Möklinta *Sweden* **10** D10
Mokokchung *India* **67** F19
Mokolo *Cameroon* **83** C7
Mokolo → *S. Africa* **89** C4
Mokopane *S. Africa* **89** C4
Mokra Gora *Europe* **44** D4
Mokronog *Slovenia* **41** C12
Moksha → *Russia* **34** C6
Mokshan *Russia* **34** D7
Mokwa *Nigeria* **83** D6
Mol *Belgium* **17** C5
Mola di Bari *Italy* **43** A10
Molai *Greece* **46** E4
Molale *Ethiopia* **81** E4
Molara *Italy* **42** B2
Molat *Croatia* **41** D11
Molchanovo *Russia* **52** D9
Mold *U.K.* **14** D4
Moldava nad Bodvou
  Slovak Rep. **27** C14
Moldavia = Moldova ■
  Europe **29** C13
Moldavia *Romania* **29** D12
Molde *Norway* **8** E12
Moldova ■ *Europe* **29** C13
Moldova Nouă *Romania* **28** F6
Moldoveanu, Vf. *Romania* **29** E9
Moldoviţa *Romania* **29** C10

Mole → *U.K.* **15** F7
Mole △ *Ghana* **83** D4
Mole Creek *Australia* **95** G4
Molepolole *Botswana* **88** C4
Molfetta *Italy* **43** A9
Molina de Aragón *Spain* **38** E3
Molina de Segura *Spain* **39** G3
Moline *U.S.A.* **112** E8
Molinella *Italy* **41** D8
Molinos *Argentina* **126** B2
Moliro *Dem. Rep. of the Congo* **86** D3
Moliterno *Italy* **43** B8
Molkom *Sweden* **10** E7
Mölle *Sweden* **11** H6
Molledo *Spain* **36** B6
Mollendo *Peru* **124** G4
Mollerin, L. *Australia* **93** F2
Mollerussa *Spain* **38** D5
Mollina *Spain* **37** H6
Mölln *Germany* **24** B6
Mölltorp *Sweden* **11** F8
Mölnlycke *Sweden* **11** G6
Molo *Kenya* **86** C4
Molochansk *Ukraine* **33** J8
Molochnoye, Ozero *Ukraine* **33** J8
Molodechno =
  Maladzyechna *Belarus* **23** A14
Molodezhnaya *Antarctica* **5** C9
Molodove *Ukraine* **29** D14
Moloka'i *U.S.A.* **106** b
Molokai Fracture Zone
  Pac. Oc. **97** C15
Molong *Australia* **95** E4
Molopo → *Africa* **88** D3
Molos *Greece* **46** C4
Molsheim *France* **19** D14
Molson L. *Canada* **103** C9
Molteno *S. Africa* **88** E4
Molu *Indonesia* **63** F8
Molucca Sea *Indonesia* **63** E6
Moluccas = Maluku
  Indonesia **63** E7
Moma *Dem. Rep. of the Congo* **86** C1
Moma *Mozam.* **87** F4
Mombasa *Kenya* **86** C4
Mombetsu *Japan* **54** B11
Mombuey *Spain* **36** C4
Momchilgrad *Bulgaria* **45** E9
Momi *Dem. Rep. of the Congo* **86** C2
Mompós *Colombia* **124** B4
Møn *Denmark* **11** K6
Mon □ *Burma* **67** L20
Mona, Canal de la = Mona
  Passage *W. Indies* **121** C6
Mona, Isla *Puerto Rico* **121** C6
Mona, Pta. *Costa Rica* **120** E3
Mona Passage *W. Indies* **121** C6
Monaca *U.S.A.* **114** F4
Monaco ■ *Europe* **21** E11
Monadhliath Mts. *U.K.* **13** D4
Monadnock, Mt. *U.S.A.* **115** D12
Monaghan *Ireland* **12** B5
Monaghan □ *Ireland* **12** B5
Monahans *U.S.A.* **116** F3
Monapo *Mozam.* **87** E5
Monar, L. *U.K.* **13** D3
Monarch Mt. *Canada* **102** C3
Monashee Mts. *Canada* **102** C5
Monasterevin *Ireland* **12** C4
Monastir = Bitola *Macedonia* **44** E5
Monastir *Tunisia* **79** A8
Moncada *Phil.* **61** D4
Moncalieri *Italy* **40** C4
Moncalvo *Italy* **40** C5
Moncão *Portugal* **36** C2
Moncarapacho *Portugal* **37** H3
Moncayo, Sierra del *Spain* **38** D3
Monchegorsk *Russia* **8** C25
Mönchengladbach *Germany* **24** D2
Monchique *Portugal* **37** H2
Moncks Corner *U.S.A.* **117** E14
Monclova *Mexico* **118** B4
Moncontour *France* **18** D4
Moncton *Canada* **105** C7
Mondariz *Spain* **36** C2
Mondego → *Portugal* **36** E2
Mondego, C. *Portugal* **36** E2
Mondeodo *Indonesia* **63** E6
Mondeville *France* **18** C6
Mondolfo *Italy* **41** E10
Mondoñedo *Spain* **36** B3
Mondovì *Italy* **40** D4
Mondragon *Phil.* **61** E6
Mondragone *Italy* **42** A6
Mondrain I. *Australia* **93** F3
Moneague *Jamaica* **120** a
Monemvasia *Greece* **46** E5
Moneron, Ostrov *Russia* **54** A10
Monessen *U.S.A.* **114** F5
Monesterio *Spain* **37** G4
Monestier-de-Clermont
  France **21** D9
Monett *U.S.A.* **112** G7
Moneymore *U.K.* **12** B5
Monfalcone *Italy* **41** C10
Monflanquin *France* **20** D4
Monforte *Portugal* **37** F3

Monforte de Lemos *Spain* **36** C3
Mong Cai *Vietnam* **64** B6
Mong Hsu *Burma* **58** G2
Mong Kung *Burma* **67** J20
Mong Nai *Burma* **67** J20
Mong Pawk *Burma* **67** H21
Mong Ping *Burma* **58** G2
Mong Ton *Burma* **67** J21
Mong Wa *Burma* **67** J22
Mong Yai *Burma* **67** H21
Mongalla *Sudan* **81** F3
Mongers, L. *Australia* **93** E2
Monghyr = Munger *India* **69** G12
Mongibello = Etna *Italy* **43** E7
Mongo *Chad* **79** F9
Mongo → *S. Leone* **82** D2
Mongolia ■ *Asia* **53** E10
Mongolia, Plateau of *Asia* **50** D12
Mongonu *Nigeria* **83** C7
Mongu *Zambia* **85** H4
Mônguas *Angola* **88** B2
Monifieth *U.K.* **13** E6
Monistrol-sur-Loire *France* **21** C8
Monkey Bay *Malawi* **87** E4
Monkey Mia *Australia* **93** E1
Monkey River *Belize* **119** D7
Moński *Poland* **30** E9
Monkoto
 Dem. Rep. of the Congo **84** E4
Monkton *Canada* **114** C3
Monmouth *U.K.* **15** F5
Monmouth *Ill., U.S.A.* **112** E8
Monmouth *Oreg., U.S.A.* **108** D2
Monmouthshire □ *U.K.* **15** F5
Mono L. *U.S.A.* **110** H7
Monolith *U.S.A.* **111** K8
Monolithos *Greece* **49** C9
Monongahela → *U.S.A.* **114** F5
Monópoli *Italy* **43** B10
Monor *Hungary* **28** C4
Monos I. *Trin. & Tob.* **125** K15
Monóvar *Spain* **39** G4
Monreal del Campo *Spain* **38** E3
Monreale *Italy* **42** D6
Monroe *Ga., U.S.A.* **117** E13
Monroe *La., U.S.A.* **116** E8
Monroe *Mich., U.S.A.* **113** E12
Monroe *N.C., U.S.A.* **117** D14
Monroe *N.Y., U.S.A.* **115** E10
Monroe *Utah, U.S.A.* **108** G7
Monroe *Wash., U.S.A.* **110** C5
Monroe *Wis., U.S.A.* **112** D9
Monroe City *U.S.A.* **112** F8
Monroeton *U.S.A.* **115** E8
Monroeville *Ala., U.S.A.* **117** F11
Monroeville *Pa., U.S.A.* **114** F5
Monrovia *Liberia* **82** D2
Mons *Belgium* **17** D3
Møns Klint *Denmark* **11** K6
Monsaraz *Portugal* **37** G3
Monse *Indonesia* **63** E6
Monségur *France* **20** D4
Monsélice *Italy* **41** C8
Mönsterås *Sweden* **11** G10
Mont Cenis, Col du *France* **21** C10
Mont-de-Marsan *France* **20** E3
Mont-Joli *Canada* **105** C6
Mont-Laurier *Canada* **104** C4
Mont-Louis *Canada* **105** C6
Mont Peko △ *Ivory C.* **82** D3
Mont-roig del Camp *Spain* **38** D5
Mont-St-Michel, Le *France* **18** D5
Mont Sangbe △ *Ivory C.* **82** D3
Mont-Tremblant △ *Canada* **104** C5
Montabaur *Germany* **24** E3
Montagnac *France* **20** E7
Montagnana *Italy* **41** C8
Montagne d'Ambre △
 Madag. **89** A8
Montagne de Reims △
 France **19** C11
Montagu *S. Africa* **88** E3
Montagu I. *Antarctica* **5** B1
Montague *Canada* **105** C7
Montague, I. *Mexico* **118** A2
Montague Ra. *Australia* **93** E2
Montague Sd. *Australia* **92** B4
Montaigu *France* **18** F5
Montalbán *Spain* **38** E4
Montalbano Iónico *Italy* **43** B9
Montalbo *Spain* **38** F2
Montalcino *Italy* **41** E8
Montalegre *Portugal* **36** D3
Montalto *Italy* **43** D8
Montalto di Castro *Italy* **41** F8
Montalto Uffugo *Italy* **43** C9
Montalvo *U.S.A.* **111** L7
Montamarta *Spain* **36** D5
Montana *Bulgaria* **44** C7
Montaña *Peru* **124** E4
Montana □ *Bulgaria* **44** C7
Montana □ *U.S.A.* **108** C9
Montaña Clara, I. *Canary Is.* **48** E6
Montañas de Malaga △
 Spain **37** J6
Montánchez *Spain* **37** F4
Montargil *Portugal* **37** F2

Montargis *France* **19** E9
Montauban *France* **20** D5
Montauk *U.S.A.* **115** E13
Montauk Pt. *U.S.A.* **115** E13
Montbard *France* **19** E11
Montbarrey *France* **19** E12
Montbéliard *France* **19** E13
Montblanc *Spain* **38** D6
Montbrison *France* **21** C8
Montcalm, Pic de *France* **20** F5
Montceau-les-Mines *France* **19** F11
Montcenis *France* **21** B8
Montclair *U.S.A.* **115** F10
Montcornet *France* **19** C11
Montcuq *France* **20** D5
Montdidier *France* **19** C9
Monte Albán *Mexico* **119** D5
Monte Alegre *Brazil* **125** D8
Monte Azul *Brazil* **125** G10
Monte-Carlo *Monaco* **21** E11
Monte Caseros *Argentina* **126** C4
Monte Comán *Argentina* **126** C2
Monte Crísti *Dom. Rep.* **121** C5
Monte Cucco △ *Italy* **41** E9
Monte Lindo → *Paraguay* **126** A4
Monte Patria *Chile* **126** C1
Monte Quemado *Argentina* **126** B3
Monte Redondo *Portugal* **36** F2
Monte Rio *U.S.A.* **110** G4
Monte San Giovanni
 Campano *Italy* **42** A6
Monte San Savino *Italy* **41** E8
Monte Sant' Ángelo *Italy* **41** G12
Monte Santu, C. di *Italy* **42** B2
Monte Sibillini △ *Italy* **41** F10
Monte Subasio △ *Italy* **41** E9
Monte Vista *U.S.A.* **109** H10
Monteagudo *Argentina* **127** B5
Montealegre del Castillo
 Spain **39** G3
Montebello *Canada* **104** C5
Montebello Iónico *Italy* **43** E8
Montebello Is. *Australia* **92** D2
Montebelluna *Italy* **41** C9
Montebourg *France* **18** C5
Montecastrilli *Italy* **41** F9
Montecatini Terme *Italy* **40** E7
Montecito *U.S.A.* **111** L7
Montecristo *Italy* **40** F7
Montefalco *Italy* **41** F9
Montefiascone *Italy* **41** F9
Montefrío *Spain* **37** H7
Montegiórgio *Italy* **41** E10
Montego Bay *Jamaica* **120** a
Montehermoso *Spain* **36** E4
Montejicar *Spain* **37** H7
Montélimar *France* **21** D8
Montella *Italy* **43** B8
Montellano *Spain* **37** J5
Montello *U.S.A.* **112** D9
Montemor-o-Novo *Portugal* **37** G2
Montemor-o-Velho *Portugal* **36** E2
Montemorelos *Mexico* **119** B5
Montendre *France* **20** C3
Montenegro *Brazil* **127** B5
Montenegro ■ *Europe* **44** D3
Montenero di Bisáccia *Italy* **41** G11
Montepuez *Mozam.* **87** E4
Montepuez → *Mozam.* **87** E5
Montepulciano *Italy* **41** E8
Montereale *Italy* **41** F10
Montereau-Faut-Yonne
 France **19** D9
Monterey *U.S.A.* **110** J5
Monterey B. *U.S.A.* **110** J5
Montería *Colombia* **124** B3
Monteros *Argentina* **126** B2
Monterotondo *Italy* **41** F9
Monterrey *Mexico* **118** B4
Montes Azules △ *Mexico* **119** D6
Montes Claros *Brazil* **125** G10
Montesano *U.S.A.* **110** D3
Montesano sulla
 Marcellana *Italy* **43** B8
Montesárchio *Italy* **43** A7
Montescaglioso *Italy* **43** B9
Montesilvano *Italy* **41** F11
Montesinho △ *Portugal* **36** D4
Montevarchi *Italy* **41** E8
Montevideo *Uruguay* **127** C4
Montevideo *U.S.A.* **112** C6
Montezuma *U.S.A.* **112** E7
Montezuma Castle △
 U.S.A. **109** J8
Montfaucon *France* **18** E5
Montfaucon-d'Argonne
 France **19** C12
Montfaucon-en-Velay
 France **21** C8
Montfort-le-Gesnois *France* **18** D7
Montfort-sur-Meu *France* **18** D5
Montfragüe △ *Spain* **37** F5
Montgenèvre *France* **21** D10
Montgomery *U.K.* **15** E4
Montgomery *Ala., U.S.A.* **117** E11
Montgomery *Pa., U.S.A.* **114** E8
Montgomery *W. Va., U.S.A.*
 113 F13

Montgomery City *U.S.A.* **112** F8
Montguyon *France* **20** C3
Monthermé *France* **19** C11
Monthey *Switz.* **25** J2
Monthois *France* **19** C11
Monti *Italy* **42** B2
Monti Lucrétili △ *Italy* **41** F9
Monti Picentini △ *Italy* **43** B8
Monti Simbruini △ *Italy* **41** G10
Monticelli d'Ongina *Italy* **40** C6
Monticello *Ark., U.S.A.* **116** E9
Monticello *Fla., U.S.A.* **117** F13
Monticello *Ind., U.S.A.* **112** E10
Monticello *Iowa, U.S.A.* **112** D8
Monticello *Ky., U.S.A.* **113** G11
Monticello *Minn., U.S.A.* **112** C7
Monticello *Miss., U.S.A.* **117** F9
Monticello *N.Y., U.S.A.* **115** E10
Monticello *Utah, U.S.A.* **109** H9
Montichiari *Italy* **40** C7
Montier-en-Der *France* **19** D11
Montignac *France* **20** C5
Montigny-les-Metz *France* **19** C13
Montigny-sur-Aube *France* **19** E11
Montijo *Portugal* **37** G2
Montijo *Spain* **37** G4
Montilla *Spain* **37** H6
Montivilliers *France* **18** C7
Montluçon *France* **19** F9
Montmagny *Canada* **105** C5
Montmarault *France* **19** F9
Montmartre *Canada* **103** C8
Montmédy *France* **19** C12
Montmélian *France* **21** C10
Montmirail *France* **19** D9
Montmoreau-St-Cybard
 France **20** C4
Montmorillon *France* **20** B4
Montmort-Lucy *France* **19** D10
Monto *Australia* **94** C5
Montoire-sur-le-Loir *France* **18** E7
Montongbuwoh *Indonesia* **63** K19
Montoro *France* **37** G6
Montório al Vomano *Italy* **41** F10
Montour Falls *U.S.A.* **114** D8
Montoursville *U.S.A.* **114** E8
Montpelier *Idaho, U.S.A.* **108** E8
Montpelier *Vt., U.S.A.* **115** B12
Montpellier *France* **20** E7
Montpezat-de-Quercy
 France **20** D5
Montpon-Ménestérol *France* **20** D4
Montréal *Canada* **115** A11
Montréal *Aude, France* **20** E6
Montréal *Gers, France* **20** E4
Montreal → *Canada* **104** C3
Montreal L. *Canada* **103** C7
Montreal Lake *Canada* **103** C7
Montredon-Labessonnié
 France **20** E6
Montrésor *France* **18** E8
Montret *France* **19** F12
Montreuil *Pas-de-Calais,
 France* **19** B8
Montreuil *Seine-St-Denis,
 France* **19** D9
Montreuil-Bellay *France* **18** E6
Montreux *Switz.* **25** J2
Montrevel-en-Bresse *France* **19** F12
Montrichard *France* **18** E8
Montrose *U.K.* **13** E6
Montrose *Colo., U.S.A.* **108** G10
Montrose *Pa., U.S.A.* **115** E9
Monts, Pte. des *Canada* **105** C6
Montsalvy *France* **20** D6
Montsauche-les-Settons
 France **19** E11
Montsec, Serra del *Spain* **38** C5
Montseny △ *Spain* **38** D2
Montserrat *Spain* **38** D6
Montserrat ☑ *W. Indies* **121** C7
Montuenga *Spain* **36** D6
Montuiri *Spain* **48** B9
Monywa *Burma* **67** H19
Monza *Italy* **40** C6
Monze *Zambia* **87** F2
Monze, C. *Pakistan* **68** G2
Monzón *Spain* **38** D5
Mooers *U.S.A.* **115** B11
Mooi → *S. Africa* **89** D5
Mooi River *S. Africa* **89** D4
Moonah → *Australia* **94** C2
Moonda, L. *Australia* **94** D3
Moonie *Australia* **95** D5
Moonie → *Australia* **95** D4
Moonta *Australia* **95** E2
Moora *Australia* **93** F2
Moorcroft *U.S.A.* **108** D11
Moore → *Australia* **93** F2
Moore, L. *Australia* **93** E2
Moore Park *Australia* **94** C5
Moore Res. *U.S.A.* **115** B13
Moore River *Australia* **93** F2 d
Moorea *French Polynesia* **91** d
Moorefield *U.S.A.* **113** F14
Moorfoot Hills *U.K.* **13** F5

Moorhead *U.S.A.* **112** B5
Moormerland *Germany* **24** B3
Moorpark *U.S.A.* **111** L8
Moorreesburg *S. Africa* **88** E2
Moorrinya △ *Australia* **94** C3
Moosburg *Germany* **25** G7
Moose → *Canada* **104** B3
Moose → *U.S.A.* **115** C9
Moose Creek *Canada* **115** A10
Moose Factory *Canada* **104** B3
Moose Jaw *Canada* **103** C7
Moose Jaw → *Canada* **103** C7
Moose Lake *Canada* **103** C8
Moose Lake *U.S.A.* **112** B7
Moose Mountain △ *Canada* **103** D8
Moosehead L. *U.S.A.* **113** C19
Mooselookmeguntic L.
 U.S.A. **115** B14
Moosilauke, Mt. *U.S.A.* **115** B13
Moosomin *Canada* **103** C8
Moosonee *Canada* **104** B3
Moosup *U.S.A.* **115** E13
Mopane *S. Africa* **89** C4
Mopeia Velha *Mozam.* **87** F4
Mopipi *Botswana* **88** C3
Mopoi *C.A.R.* **86** A2
Mopti *Mali* **82** C4
Mopti □ *Mali* **82** C4
Moqatta *Sudan* **81** E4
Moqor *Afghan.* **68** C2
Moquegua *Peru* **124** G4
Mór *Hungary* **28** C3
Mora *Cameroon* **83** C7
Móra *Portugal* **37** G2
Mora *Spain* **37** F7
Mora *Sweden* **10** C8
Mora *Minn., U.S.A.* **112** C7
Mora *N. Mex., U.S.A.* **109** J11
Mora de Rubielos *Spain* **38** E4
Mòra d'Ebre *Spain* **38** D5
Mòra la Nova *Spain* **38** D5
Morača → *Montenegro* **44** D3
Moradabad *India* **69** E8
Morafenobe *Madag.* **89** B7
Morąg *Poland* **30** E6
Moral de Calatrava *Spain* **37** G7
Moraleja *Spain* **36** E4
Moramanga *Madag.* **89** B8
Moran *Kans., U.S.A.* **112** G6
Moran *Wyo., U.S.A.* **108** E8
Moranbah *Australia* **94** C4
Morano Cálabro *Italy* **43** C9
Morant Bay *Jamaica* **120** a
Morant Cays *Jamaica* **120** C4
Morant Pt. *Jamaica* **120** a
Morar *India* **68** F8
Morar, L. *U.K.* **13** E3
Moratalla *Spain* **39** G3
Moratuwa *Sri Lanka* **66** R11
Morava → *Slovak Rep.* **27** C9
Moravia *U.S.A.* **115** D8
Moravian Hts. =
 Českomoravská
 Vrchovina *Czech Rep.* **26** B8
Moravica → *Serbia* **44** C4
Moravița *Romania* **28** E6
Moravská Třebová
 Czech Rep. **27** B9
Moravské Budějovice
 Czech Rep. **26** B8
Morawa *Australia* **93** E2
Morawhanna *Guyana* **124** B7
Moray □ *U.K.* **13** D5
Moray Firth *U.K.* **13** D5
Morbach *Germany* **25** F3
Morbegno *Italy* **40** B6
Morbi *India* **68** H4
Morbihan □ *France* **18** E4
Mörbylånga *Sweden* **11** H10
Morcenx *France* **20** D3
Morcone *Italy* **43** A7
Mordelles *France* **18** D5
Morden *Canada* **103** D9
Mordoğan *Turkey* **47** C8
Mordovian Republic =
 Mordvinia □ *Russia* **34** C7
Mordovo *Russia* **34** D5
Mordvinia □ *Russia* **34** C7
Mordy *Poland* **31** F9
Moreau → *U.S.A.* **112** C3
Morebeng *S. Africa* **89** C4
Morecambe *U.K.* **14** C5
Morecambe B. *U.K.* **14** C5
Moree *Australia* **95** D4
Morehead *U.S.A.* **113** F12
Morehead City *U.S.A.* **117** D16
Morel → *India* **68** F7
Morelia *Mexico* **118** D4
Morella *Australia* **94** C3
Morella *Spain* **38** E4
Morelos *Mexico* **118** B3
Morelos □ *Mexico* **119** D5
Morena, Sierra *Spain* **37** G7
Morena *India* **68** F8
Moreni *Romania* **29** F10
Moreno Valley *U.S.A.* **111** M10

Moresby I. *Canada* **102** C2
Morestel *France* **21** C9
Moreton I. *Australia* **95** D5
Moreton Island △ *Australia* **95** D5
Moreuil *France* **19** C9
Morey *Spain* **48** B10
Morez *France* **19** F13
Morgan *U.S.A.* **108** F8
Morgan City *U.S.A.* **116** G9
Morgan Hill *U.S.A.* **110** H5
Morganfield *U.S.A.* **112** G10
Morganton *U.S.A.* **117** D14
Morgantown *U.S.A.* **113** F14
Morgenzon *S. Africa* **89** D4
Morges *Switz.* **25** J2
Morghak *Iran* **71** D8
Morgongåva *Sweden* **10** E10
Morhange *France* **19** D13
Morhar → *India* **69** G11
Mori *Italy* **40** C7
Mori *Japan* **54** C10
Moriarty *U.S.A.* **109** J10
Moribaya *Guinea* **82** D3
Morice L. *Canada* **102** C3
Moriki *Nigeria* **83** C6
Morinville *Canada* **102** C6
Morioka *Japan* **54** E10
Moris *Mexico* **118** B3
Morlaàs *France* **20** E3
Morlaix *France* **18** D3
Mörlunda *Sweden* **11** G9
Mormanno *Italy* **43** C8
Mormant *France* **19** D9
Mornington *Australia* **95** F4
Mornington, I. *Chile* **128** F1
Mornington I. *Australia* **94** B2
Mornos → *Greece* **46** C3
Moro *Pakistan* **68** F2
Moro *Sudan* **81** E3
Moro → *Pakistan* **68** E2
Moro G. *Phil.* **61** H5
Morocco ■ *N. Afr.* **78** B4
Morogoro *Tanzania* **86** D4
Morogoro □ *Tanzania* **86** D4
Moroleón *Mexico* **118** C4
Morombe *Madag.* **89** C7
Moron *Argentina* **126** C4
Morón *Cuba* **120** B4
Morón de Almazán *Spain* **38** D2
Morón de la Frontera *Spain* **37** H5
Morona → *Peru* **124** D3
Morondava *Madag.* **89** C7
Morondo *Ivory C.* **82** D3
Morongo Valley *U.S.A.* **111** L10
Moroni *Comoros Is.* **85** a
Moroni *U.S.A.* **108** G8
Moronou *Ivory C.* **82** D4
Morotai *Indonesia* **63** D7
Moroto *Uganda* **86** B3
Moroto, Mt. *Uganda* **86** B3
Morozov *Bulgaria* **45** D9
Morozovsk *Russia* **35** F5
Morpeth *U.K.* **14** B6
Morphou *Cyprus* **49** D11
Morphou Bay *Cyprus* **49** D11
Morrilton *U.S.A.* **116** D8
Morrinhos *Brazil* **125** G9
Morrinsville *N.Z.* **91** B5
Morris *Canada* **103** D9
Morris *Ill., U.S.A.* **112** E9
Morris *Minn., U.S.A.* **112** C6
Morris *N.Y., U.S.A.* **115** D9
Morris *Pa., U.S.A.* **114** E7
Morris, Mt. *Australia* **93** E5
Morris Jesup, Kap *Greenland* **98** A16
Morrisburg *Canada* **115** B9
Morristown *Ariz., U.S.A.* **109** K7
Morristown *N.J., U.S.A.* **115** F10
Morristown *N.Y., U.S.A.* **115** B9
Morristown *Tenn., U.S.A.* **117** C13
Morrisville *N.Y., U.S.A.* **115** D9
Morrisville *Pa., U.S.A.* **115** F10
Morrisville *Vt., U.S.A.* **115** B12
Morro, Pta. *Chile* **126** B1
Morro Bay *U.S.A.* **110** K6
Morro del Jable *Canary Is.* **48** F5
Morro Jable, Pta. de
 Canary Is. **48** F5
Morrocoy △ *Venezuela* **121** D6
Morrosquillo, G. de
 Colombia **120** E4
Mörrum *Sweden* **11** H8
Morrumbene *Mozam.* **89** C6
Mörrumsån → *Sweden* **11** H8
Mors *Denmark* **11** H2
Morshansk *Russia* **34** D5
Mörsil *Sweden* **10** A7
Mortagne → *France* **19** D13
Mortagne-au-Perche *France* **18** D7
Mortagne-sur-Gironde
 France **20** C3
Mortagne-sur-Sèvre *France* **18** F6
Mortain *France* **18** D6
Mortara *Italy* **40** C5
Morteau *France* **19** E13
Morteros *Argentina* **126** C3
Mortlach *Canada* **103** C7

Mortlake *Australia* **95** F3
Morton *Tex., U.S.A.* **116** E3
Morton *Wash., U.S.A.* **110** D4
Moruga *Trin. & Tob.* **125** K15
Morundah *Australia* **95** E4
Moruya *Australia* **95** F5
Morvan *France* **19** E11
Morven *Australia* **95** D4
Morvern *U.K.* **13** E3
Morwell *Australia* **95** F4
Moryń *Poland* **31** F1
Morzine *France* **19** F13
Mosalsk *Russia* **32** E8
Mosbach *Germany* **25** F5
Moščenica *Croatia* **41** C11
Mosciano Sant' Ángelo
 Italy **41** F10
Moscos Is. *Burma* **64** F1
Moscow = Moskva *Russia* **32** E9
Moscow *Idaho, U.S.A.* **108** C5
Moscow *Pa., U.S.A.* **115** E9
Mosel → *Europe* **19** B14
Moselle = Mosel → *Europe* **19** B14
Moselle □ *France* **19** D13
Moses Lake *U.S.A.* **108** C4
Mosgiel *N.Z.* **91** F3
Moshaweng → *S. Africa* **88** D3
Moshchnyy, Ostrov *Russia* **9** F22
Moshi *Tanzania* **86** C4
Moshupa *Botswana* **88** C4
Mosina *Poland* **31** F3
Mosjøen *Norway* **8** D15
Moskenesøya *Norway* **8** C15
Moskenstraumen *Norway* **8** C15
Moskva *Russia* **32** E9
Moskva □ *Russia* **32** D9
Moskva → *Russia* **32** E10
Moslavačka Gora *Croatia* **41** C13
Mosomane *Botswana* **88** C4
Mosonmagyaróvár *Hungary* **28** C2
Mošorin *Serbia* **28** E5
Mospino *Ukraine* **33** J9
Mosquera *Colombia* **124** C3
Mosquero *U.S.A.* **109** J12
Mosquera *Spain* **38** E4
Mosquitia *Honduras* **120** C3
Mosquito Coast =
 Mosquitia *Honduras* **120** C3
Mosquito Creek L. *U.S.A.* **114** E4
Mosquito L. *Canada* **103** A8
Mosquitos, G. de los
 Panama **120** E3
Moss *Norway* **9** G14
Moss Vale *Australia* **95** E5
Mossaka *Congo* **84** E3
Mossbank *Canada* **103** D7
Mossburn *N.Z.* **91** F2
Mosselbaai *S. Africa* **88** E3
Mossendjo *Congo* **84** E2
Mossgiel *Australia* **95** E3
Mossman *Australia* **94** B4
Mossoró *Brazil* **125** E11
Mossuril *Mozam.* **87** E5
Most *Czech Rep.* **26** A6
Mosta *Malta* **49** D1
Mostaganem *Algeria* **78** A6
Mostar *Bos.-H.* **28** G2
Mostardas *Brazil* **127** C5
Mostiska = Mostyska
 Ukraine **31** J10
Móstoles *Spain* **36** E7
Mostyska *Ukraine* **31** J10
Mosul = Al Mawşil *Iraq* **73** D10
Mota *Ethiopia* **81** E4
Mota del Cuervo *Spain* **39** F2
Mota del Marqués *Spain* **36** D5
Motagua → *Guatemala* **120** C2
Motala *Sweden* **11** F9
Motaze *Mozam.* **89** C5
Moţca *Romania* **29** C11
Moth *India* **69** G8
Motherwell *U.K.* **13** F5
Motihari *India* **69** F11
Motilla del Palancar *Spain* **39** F3
Motnik *Slovenia* **41** B11
Motovun *Croatia* **41** C10
Motozintla de Mendoza
 Mexico **119** D6
Motril *Spain* **37** J7
Motru *Romania* **28** F7
Motru → *Romania* **29** F8
Mott *U.S.A.* **112** B2
Móttola *Italy* **43** B10
Motueka *N.Z.* **91** D4
Motueka → *N.Z.* **91** D4
Motul *Mexico* **119** C7
Mouchalagane → *Canada* **105** B6
Mouding *China* **58** E3
Moudjeria *Mauritania* **82** B2
Moudon *Switz.* **25** J2
Moudros *Greece* **47** B7
Mouila *Gabon* **84** E2
Moulamein *Australia* **95** F3
Moule à Chique, C. *St. Lucia* **121** f

Mouliana *Greece* **49** D7
Moulins *France* **19** F10
Moulmein *Burma* **67** L20
Moulouya, O. → *Morocco* **78** B5
Moultrie *U.S.A.* **117** F13
Moultrie, L. *U.S.A.* **117** E14
Mound City *Mo., U.S.A.* **112** E6
Mound City *S. Dak., U.S.A.* **112** C3
Moundou *Chad* **79** G9
Moundsville *U.S.A.* **114** G4
Moung *Cambodia* **64** F4
Mount Airy *U.S.A.* **117** C14
Mount Albert *Canada* **114** B5
Mount Aspiring △ *N.Z.* **91** F2
Mount Barker *S. Austral., Australia* **95** F2
Mount Barker *W. Austral., Australia* **93** F2
Mount Bellew Bridge *Ireland* **12** C3
Mount Brydges *Canada* **114** D3
Mount Burr *Australia* **95** F3
Mount Carmel = Ha Karmel △ *Israel* **74** C4
Mount Carmel *Ill., U.S.A.* **112** F10
Mount Carmel *Pa., U.S.A.* **115** F8
Mount Clemens *U.S.A.* **114** D2
Mount Coolon *Australia* **94** C4
Mount Darwin *Zimbabwe* **87** F3
Mount Desert I. *U.S.A.* **113** C19
Mount Dora *U.S.A.* **117** G14
Mount Edziza △ *Canada* **102** B2
Mount Elgon △ *E. Afr.* **86** B3
Mount Field △ *Australia* **95** G4
Mount Fletcher *S. Africa* **89** E4
Mount Forest *Canada* **114** C4
Mount Frankland △ *Australia* **92** F2
Mount Gambier *Australia* **95** F3
Mount Garnet *Australia* **94** B4
Mount Holly *U.S.A.* **115** G10
Mount Holly Springs *U.S.A.* **114** F7
Mount Hope *N.S.W., Australia* **95** E4
Mount Hope *S. Austral., Australia* **95** E2
Mount Isa *Australia* **94** C2
Mount Jewett *U.S.A.* **114** E6
Mount Kaputar △ *Australia* **95** E5
Mount Kenya △ *Kenya* **86** C4
Mount Kilimanjaro △ *Tanzania* **86** C4
Mount Kisco *U.S.A.* **115** E11
Mount Laguna *U.S.A.* **111** N10
Mount Larcom *Australia* **94** C5
Mount Lofty Ranges *Australia* **95** E2
Mount Magnet *Australia* **93** E2
Mount Maunganui *N.Z.* **91** B6
Mount Molloy *Australia* **94** B4
Mount Morgan *Australia* **94** C5
Mount Morris *U.S.A.* **114** D7
Mount Pearl *Canada* **105** C9
Mount Penn *U.S.A.* **115** F9
Mount Perry *Australia* **95** D5
Mount Pleasant *Iowa, U.S.A.* **112** E8
Mount Pleasant *Mich., U.S.A.* **113** D11
Mount Pleasant *Pa., U.S.A.* **114** F5
Mount Pleasant *S.C., U.S.A.* **117** E15
Mount Pleasant *Tenn., U.S.A.* **117** D11
Mount Pleasant *Tex., U.S.A.* **116** E7
Mount Pleasant *Utah, U.S.A.* **108** G8
Mount Pocono *U.S.A.* **115** E9
Mount Rainier △ *U.S.A.* **110** D5
Mount Revelstoke △ *Canada* **102** C5
Mount Robson △ *Canada* **102** C5
Mount St. Helens △ *U.S.A.* **110** D4
Mount Selinda *Zimbabwe* **89** C5
Mount Shasta *U.S.A.* **108** F2
Mount Signal *U.S.A.* **111** N11
Mount Sterling *Ill., U.S.A.* **112** F8
Mount Sterling *Ky., U.S.A.* **113** F12
Mount Surprise *Australia* **94** B3
Mount Union *U.S.A.* **114** F7
Mount Upton *U.S.A.* **115** D9
Mount Vernon *Ill., U.S.A.* **112** F9
Mount Vernon *Ind., U.S.A.* **112** G10
Mount Vernon *N.Y., U.S.A.* **115** F11
Mount Vernon *Ohio, U.S.A.* **114** F2
Mount Vernon *Wash., U.S.A.* **110** B4
Mount William △ *Australia* **95** G4
Mounta, Akra *Greece* **46** C2
Mountain Ash *U.K.* **15** F4
Mountain Center *U.S.A.* **111** M10
Mountain City *Nev., U.S.A.* **108** F6
Mountain City *Tenn., U.S.A.* **117** C14
Mountain Dale *U.S.A.* **115** E10
Mountain Grove *U.S.A.* **112** G7
Mountain Home *Ark., U.S.A.* **116** C8

Mountain Home *Idaho, U.S.A.* **108** E6
Mountain Iron *U.S.A.* **112** B7
Mountain Pass *U.S.A.* **111** K11
Mountain View *Ark., U.S.A.* **116** D8
Mountain View *Calif., U.S.A.* **110** H4
Mountain View *Hawai'i, U.S.A.* **106** b
Mountain Zebra △ *S. Africa* **88** E4
Mountainair *U.S.A.* **109** J10
Mountlake Terrace *U.S.A.* **110** C4
Mountmellick *Ireland* **12** C4
Mountrath *Ireland* **12** D4
Moura *Australia* **94** C4
Moura *Brazil* **124** D6
Moura *Portugal* **37** G3
Mourão *Portugal* **37** G3
Mourdi, Dépression du *Chad* **79** E10
Mourenx *France* **20** E3
Mouri *Ghana* **83** D4
Mourilyan *Australia* **94** B4
Mourmelon-le-Grand *France* **19** C11
Mourne → *U.K.* **12** B4
Mourne Mts. *U.K.* **12** B5
Mournies *Greece* **49** D6
Mouscron *Belgium* **17** D3
Moussoro *Chad* **79** F9
Mouthe *France* **19** F13
Moutier *Switz.* **25** H3
Moutong *Indonesia* **63** D6
Mouy *France* **19** C9
Mouzaki *Greece* **46** B3
Mouzon *France* **19** C12
Movas *Mexico* **118** B3
Moville *Ireland* **12** A4
Mowandjum *Australia* **92** C3
Moy → *Ireland* **12** B2
Moya *Comoros Is.* **85** a
Moyale *Kenya* **81** G4
Moyamba *S. Leone* **82** D2
Moyen Atlas *Morocco* **78** B4
Moyne, L. Le *Canada* **105** A6
Moyo *Indonesia* **62** F5
Moyobamba *Peru* **124** E3
Moyyero → *Russia* **53** C11
Moyynqum *Kazakhstan* **52** E8
Moyynty *Kazakhstan* **52** E8
Mozambique = Moçambique *Mozam.* **87** F5
Mozambique ■ *Africa* **87** F4
Mozambique Chan. *Africa* **89** B7
Mozdok *Russia* **35** J7
Mozdūrān *Iran* **71** B9
Mozhaysk *Russia* **32** E9
Mozhga *Russia* **34** B11
Mozhnābād *Iran* **71** C9
Mozirje *Slovenia* **41** B11
Mozyr = Mazyr *Belarus* **23** B15
Mpanda *Tanzania* **86** D3
Mpésoba *Mali* **82** C3
Mphoengs *Zimbabwe* **89** C4
Mpika *Zambia* **87** E3
Mpulungu *Zambia* **87** D3
Mpumalanga *S. Africa* **89** D5
Mpumalanga □ *S. Africa* **89** D5
Mpwapwa *Tanzania* **86** D4
Mqanduli *S. Africa* **89** E4
Mqinvartsveri = Kazbek *Russia* **35** J7
Mrągowo *Poland* **30** E8
Mramor *Serbia* **44** C5
Mrkonjić Grad *Bos.-H.* **28** E7
Mrkopalj *Croatia* **41** C11
Mrocza *Poland* **31** E4
Msaken *Tunisia* **79** A8
Msambansovu *Zimbabwe* **87** F3
M'sila *Algeria* **78** A6
Msoro *Zambia* **87** E3
Msta → *Russia* **32** C6
Mstislavl = Mstsislaw *Belarus* **23** A16
Mstsislaw *Belarus* **23** A16
Mszana Dolna *Poland* **31** J7
Mszczonów *Poland* **31** G7
Mtama *Tanzania* **87** E4
Mtamvuna = Mthamvuna → *S. Africa* **89** E5
Mthamvuna → *S. Africa* **89** E5
Mthatha *S. Africa* **89** E4
Mtilikwe → *Zimbabwe* **87** G3
Mtito Andei *Kenya* **86** C4
Mtsensk *Russia* **32** F9
Mtskheta *Georgia* **35** K7
Mtubatuba *S. Africa* **89** D5
Mtwalume *S. Africa* **89** E5
Mtwara-Mikindani *Tanzania* **87** E5
Mu Gia, Deo *Vietnam* **64** D5
Mu Ko Chang △ *Thailand* **65** G4
Mu Us Shamo *China* **56** E5
Muang Chiang Rai = Chiang Rai *Thailand* **58** H2
Muang Khong *Laos* **64** E5

Muang Lamphun *Thailand* **64** C2
Muang Mai *Thailand* **65** a
Muang Pak Beng *Laos* **58** H3
Muar *Malaysia* **65** L4
Muarabungo *Indonesia* **62** E2
Muaraenim *Indonesia* **62** E2
Muarajuloi *Indonesia* **62** E4
Muarakaman *Indonesia* **62** E5
Muaratebo *Indonesia* **62** E2
Muaratembesi *Indonesia* **62** E2
Muaratewe *Indonesia* **62** E4
Mubarakpur *India* **69** F10
Mubarraz = Al Mubarraz *Si. Arabia* **71** E6
Mubende *Uganda* **86** B3
Mubi *Nigeria* **83** C7
Mucajaí → *Brazil* **124** C6
Muchachos, Roque de los *Canary Is.* **48** F2
Müchen *Germany* **24** D7
Muchinga Mts. *Zambia* **87** E3
Muchkapskiy *Russia* **34** E6
Muchuan *China* **58** C5
Muck *U.K.* **13** E2
Muckadilla *Australia* **95** D4
Muckle Flugga *U.K.* **13** A8
Mucur *Turkey* **72** C6
Mucuri *Brazil* **125** G11
Mucusso *Angola* **88** B3
Muda *Canary Is.* **48** F6
Mudanjiang *China* **57** B15
Mudanya *Turkey* **45** F12
Muddy Cr. → *U.S.A.* **108** G8
Mudgee *Australia* **95** E4
Mudjatik → *Canada* **103** B7
Mudurnu *Turkey* **72** B4
Muecate *Mozam.* **87** E4
Mueda *Mozam.* **87** E4
Mueller Ranges *Australia* **92** C4
Muende *Mozam.* **87** E3
Muerto, Mar *Mexico* **119** D6
Mufu Shan *China* **59** C10
Mufulira *Zambia* **87** E2
Mufumbiro Range *Africa* **86** C2
Mugardos *Spain* **36** B2
Muge → *Portugal* **37** F2
Múggia *Italy* **41** C10
Mughal Sarai *India* **69** G10
Mughayrā' *Si. Arabia* **70** D3
Mugi *Japan* **55** H7
Mugia = Muxía *Spain* **36** B1
Mugila, Mts. *Dem. Rep. of the Congo* **86** D2
Muğla *Turkey* **47** D10
Muğla □ *Turkey* **47** D10
Muglad *Sudan* **81** E2
Müglizh *Bulgaria* **45** D9
Mugu *Nepal* **69** E10
Muhammad, Râs *Egypt* **70** E2
Muhammad Qol *Sudan* **80** C4
Muhammadabad *India* **69** F10
Muhesi → *Tanzania* **86** D4
Mühlacker *Germany* **25** G4
Mühldorf *Germany* **25** G8
Mühlhausen *Germany* **24** D6
Mühlig Hofmann fjell *Antarctica* **5** D3
Mühlviertel *Austria* **26** C7
Muhos *Finland* **8** D21
Muhu *Estonia* **32** C2
Muhutwe *Tanzania* **86** C3
Muine Bheag *Ireland* **12** D5
Muir, L. *Australia* **93** F2
Muir of Ord *U.K.* **13** D4
Mujnak = Muynak *Uzbekistan* **52** E6
Muka, Tanjung *Malaysia* **65** c
Mukacheve *Ukraine* **28** B7
Mukachevo = Mukacheve *Ukraine* **28** B7
Mukah *Malaysia* **62** D4
Mukandwara *India* **68** G6
Mukawwa, Geziret *Egypt* **80** C4
Mukawwar *Sudan* **80** C4
Mukdahan *Thailand* **64** D5
Mukden = Shenyang *China* **57** D12
Mukerian *India* **68** D6
Mukhavets *Belarus* **31** F10
Mukhtolovo *Russia* **34** C6
Mukinbudin *Australia* **93** F2
Mukishi *Dem. Rep. of the Congo* **87** D1
Mukomuko *Indonesia* **62** E2
Mukomwenze *Dem. Rep. of the Congo* **86** D2
Muktsar *India* **68** D6
Mukur = Moqor *Afghan.* **68** C2
Mukutawa → *Canada* **103** C9
Mukwela *Zambia* **87** F2
Mula *Spain* **39** G3
Mula → *Pakistan* **68** F2
Mulange *Dem. Rep. of the Congo* **86** D2
Mulanje *Malawi* **87** F4
Mulanje, Mt. *Malawi* **87** F4
Mulchén *Chile* **126** D1
Mulde → *Germany* **24** D8

Mule Creek Junction *U.S.A.* **108** E11
Muleba *Tanzania* **86** C3
Mulegé *Mexico* **118** B2
Muleshoe *U.S.A.* **116** D3
Muletta, Gara *Ethiopia* **81** F5
Mulgrave *Canada* **105** C7
Mulhacén *Spain* **37** H7
Mülheim *Germany* **24** D2
Mulhouse *France* **19** E14
Muli *China* **58** D3
Mulifanua *Samoa* **91** b
Muling *China* **57** B16
Muling → *China* **57** B16
Mull *U.K.* **13** E3
Mull, Sound of *U.K.* **13** E3
Mullaittivu *Sri Lanka* **66** Q12
Mullen *U.S.A.* **112** D3
Mullens *U.S.A.* **113** G13
Muller, Pegunungan *Indonesia* **62** D4
Mullet Pen. *Ireland* **12** B1
Mullewa *Australia* **93** E2
Müllheim *Germany* **25** H3
Mulligan → *Australia* **94** D2
Mullingar *Ireland* **12** C4
Mullins *U.S.A.* **117** D15
Mullsjö *Sweden* **11** G7
Mullumbimby *Australia* **95** D5
Mulobezi *Zambia* **87** F2
Mulonga Plain *Zambia* **85** H4
Mulroy B. *Ireland* **12** A4
Multai *India* **69** J11
Multan *Pakistan* **68** D4
Mulumbe, Mts. *Dem. Rep. of the Congo* **87** D2
Mulungushi Dam *Zambia* **87** E2
Mulvane *U.S.A.* **112** G5
Mulwad *Sudan* **80** D3
Mumbai *India* **66** K8
Mumbwa *Zambia* **87** F2
Mumias *Kenya* **86** C4
Mumra *Russia* **35** H8
Mun → *Thailand* **64** E5
Muna *Indonesia* **63** F6
Munabao *India* **68** G4
Munamagi *Estonia* **32** D4
Muncan *Indonesia* **63** K18
Muncar *Indonesia* **63** J17
Münchberg *Germany* **25** E7
Müncheberg *Germany* **24** C10
München *Germany* **25** G7
München Franz Josef Strauss Int. ✈ (MUC) *Germany* **25** G7
Munchen-Gladbach = Mönchengladbach *Germany* **24** D2
Munch'ŏn *N. Korea* **57** E14
Muncho Lake *Canada* **102** B3
Muncie *U.S.A.* **113** E11
Muncoonie L. West *Australia* **94** D2
Mundabbera *Australia* **95** D5
Munday *U.S.A.* **116** E5
Münden *Germany* **24** D5
Münden △ *Germany* **24** D5
Mundiwindi *Australia* **92** D3
Mundo → *Spain* **39** G2
Mundo Novo *Brazil* **125** F10
Mundra *India* **68** H3
Mundrabilla *Australia* **93** F4
Munera *Spain* **39** F2
Mungallala *Australia* **95** D4
Mungallala Cr. → *Australia* **95** D4
Mungana *Australia* **94** B3
Mungaoli *India* **68** G8
Mungari *Mozam.* **87** F3
Mungbere *Dem. Rep. of the Congo* **86** B2
Mungeli *India* **69** H9
Munger *India* **69** G12
Mungkan Kandju △ *Australia* **94** A3
Munich = München *Germany* **25** G7
Munising *U.S.A.* **112** B10
Munka-Ljungby *Sweden* **11** H6
Munkebo *Denmark* **11** J4
Munkedal *Sweden* **11** F5
Munkfors *Sweden* **10** E7
Munku-Sardyk *Russia* **53** D11
Münnerstadt *Germany* **25** E6
Muñoz Gamero, Pen. *Chile* **128** G2
Munroe L. *Canada* **103** B9
Munsan *S. Korea* **57** F14
Munster *France* **19** D14
Münster *Niedersachsen, Germany* **24** C6
Münster *Nordrhein-Westfalen, Germany* **24** D3
Munster □ *Ireland* **12** D3
Muntadgin *Australia* **93** F2
Muntele Mare, Vf. *Romania* **29** D8
Muntok *Indonesia* **62** E3
Munyama *Zambia* **87** F2
Munzur Dağları *Turkey* **73** C8
Muong Beng *Laos* **58** G3
Muong Boum *Vietnam* **58** F4

Muong Et *Laos* **64** B5
Muong Hai *Laos* **58** G3
Muong Hiem *Laos* **64** B4
Muong Houn *Laos* **58** G3
Muong Hung *Vietnam* **58** G4
Muong Kau *Laos* **64** E5
Muong Khao *Laos* **64** C4
Muong Khoua *Laos* **58** G4
Muong Liep *Laos* **64** C3
Muong May *Laos* **64** E5
Muong Ngeun *Laos* **58** G3
Muong Ngoi *Laos* **58** G4
Muong Nhie *Vietnam* **58** F4
Muong Nong *Laos* **64** D6
Muong Ou Tay *Laos* **58** F3
Muong Oua *Laos* **64** C3
Muong Peun *Laos* **58** G4
Muong Phalane *Laos* **64** D5
Muong Phieng *Laos* **64** C3
Muong Phine *Laos* **64** D6
Muong Sai *Laos* **58** G3
Muong Saiapoun *Laos* **64** C3
Muong Sen *Vietnam* **64** C5
Muong Sing *Laos* **58** G3
Muong Son *Laos* **58** G5
Muong Soui *Laos* **64** C4
Muong Va *Laos* **58** G4
Muong Xia *Vietnam* **64** B5
Muonio *Finland* **8** C20
Muonio älv = Muonionjoki → *Finland* **8** C20
Muonioälven = Muonionjoki → *Finland* **8** C20
Muonionjoki → *Finland* **8** C20
Muping *China* **57** F11
Mupoi *Sudan* **81** F2
Muqaddam, Wadi → *Sudan* **80** D3
Muqdisho *Somali Rep.* **75** G4
Mur → *Austria* **27** E9
Mûr-de-Bretagne *France* **18** D4
Muradiye *Manisa, Turkey* **47** C9
Muradiye *Van, Turkey* **73** C10
Murakami *Japan* **54** E9
Murallón, Cerro *Chile* **128** F2
Muranda *Rwanda* **86** C2
Murang'a *Kenya* **86** C4
Murashi *Russia* **52** D5
Murat *France* **20** C6
Murat → *Turkey* **73** C9
Murat Dağı *Turkey* **47** C11
Muratlı *Turkey* **45** E11
Murato *France* **21** F13
Murau *Austria* **26** D7
Murava *Belarus* **31** F11
Muravera *Italy* **42** C2
Murayama *Japan* **54** E10
Murça *Portugal* **36** D3
Murchison → *Australia* **93** E1
Murchison, Mt. *Antarctica* **5** D11
Murchison Falls *Uganda* **86** B3
Murchison Falls △ *Uganda* **86** B3
Murchison Ra. *Australia* **94** C1
Murchison Rapids *Malawi* **87** F3
Murcia *Spain* **39** G3
Murcia □ *Spain* **39** H3
Murdo *U.S.A.* **112** D3
Murdoch Pt. *Australia* **94** A3
Mürefte *Turkey* **45** F11
Mureș □ *Romania* **29** D9
Mureș → *Romania* **28** D5
Mureșul = Mureș → *Romania* **28** D5
Muret *France* **20** E5
Murewa *Zimbabwe* **89** B5
Murfreesboro *N.C., U.S.A.* **117** C16
Murfreesboro *Tenn., U.S.A.* **117** D11
Murgab = Murghob *Tajikistan* **52** F8
Murgap → *Turkmenistan* **71** B9
Murgenella *Australia* **92** B5
Murgeni *Romania* **29** D13
Murgha Kibzai *Pakistan* **68** D3
Murghob *Tajikistan* **52** F8
Murgon *Australia* **95** D5
Muri *India* **69** H11
Muria *Indonesia* **63** G14
Muriaé *Brazil* **127** A7
Murias de Paredes *Spain* **36** C4
Muriel Mine *Zimbabwe* **87** F3
Murliganj *India* **69** G12
Murmansk *Russia* **8** B25
Murmashi *Russia* **8** B25
Murnau *Germany* **25** H7
Muro *France* **21** F12
Muro *Spain* **48** B10
Muro, C. de *France* **21** G12
Muro de Alcoy *Spain* **39** G4
Muro Lucano *Italy* **43** B8
Murom *Russia* **34** C6
Muroran *Japan* **54** C10
Muros *Spain* **36** C1
Muros y de Noya, Ría de *Spain* **36** C1
Muroto *Japan* **55** H7
Muroto-Misaki *Japan* **55** H7

Murovani Kurylivtsi *Ukraine* **29** B12
Murowana Goślina *Poland* **31** F3
Murphy *U.S.A.* **108** E5
Murphys *U.S.A.* **110** G6
Murrat *Sudan* **80** D2
Murrat Wells *Sudan* **80** C3
Murray *Ky., U.S.A.* **112** G9
Murray *Utah, U.S.A.* **108** F8
Murray → *Australia* **95** F2
Murray, L. *U.S.A.* **117** D14
Murray Bridge *Australia* **95** F2
Murray Fracture Zone *Pac. Oc.* **97** D14
Murray Harbour *Canada* **105** C7
Murray River △ *Australia* **95** E3
Murraysburg *S. Africa* **88** E3
Murree *Pakistan* **68** C5
Murrieta *U.S.A.* **111** M9
Murro di Porco, Capo *Italy* **43** F8
Murrumbidgee → *Australia* **95** E3
Murrumburrah *Australia* **95** E4
Murrurundi *Australia* **95** E5
Murshid *Sudan* **80** C3
Murshidabad *India* **69** G13
Murska Sobota *Slovenia* **41** B13
Murtle L. *Canada* **102** C5
Murtoa *Australia* **95** F3
Murtosa *Portugal* **36** E2
Murungu *Tanzania* **86** C3
Mururoa *French Polynesia* **97** K14
Murwara *India* **69** H9
Murwillumbah *Australia* **95** D5
Mürz → *Austria* **26** D8
Mürzzuschlag *Austria* **26** D8
Muş *Turkey* **73** C9
Muş □ *Turkey* **73** C9
Mûsa, Gebel *Egypt* **70** D2
Musa Khel *Pakistan* **68** D3
Mûsa Qal'eh *Afghan.* **66** C4
Musafirkhana *India* **69** F9
Musala *Bulgaria* **44** D7
Musala *Indonesia* **62** D1
Musan *N. Korea* **57** C15
Musangu *Dem. Rep. of the Congo* **87** E1
Musasa *Tanzania* **86** C3
Musay'īd *Qatar* **71** E6
Muscat = Masqaț *Oman* **75** C6
Muscatine *U.S.A.* **112** E8
Muscle Shoals *U.S.A.* **117** D11
Musengedsi = Unsengedsi → *Zimbabwe* **87** F3
Musgrave Harbour *Canada* **105** C9
Musgrave Ranges *Australia* **93** E5
Mushie *Dem. Rep. of the Congo* **84** E3
Mushin *Nigeria* **83** D5
Musi → *Indonesia* **62** E2
Musina *S. Africa* **89** C5
Muskeg → *Canada* **102** A4
Muskegon *U.S.A.* **112** D10
Muskegon → *U.S.A.* **112** D10
Muskegon Heights *U.S.A.* **112** D10
Muskogee *U.S.A.* **116** D7
Muskoka, L. *Canada* **114** B5
Muskwa → *Canada* **102** B4
Muslīmiyah *Syria* **70** B3
Musmar *Sudan* **80** D4
Musofu *Zambia* **87** E2
Musoma *Tanzania* **86** C3
Musquaro, L. *Canada* **105** B7
Musquodoboit Harbour *Canada* **105** C7
Musselburgh *U.K.* **13** F5
Musselshell → *U.S.A.* **108** C10
Mussende *Angola* **84** G3
Mussidan *France* **20** C4
Mussomeli *Italy* **42** E6
Mussoorie *India* **68** D8
Mussuco *Angola* **88** B2
Mustafakemalpaşa *Turkey* **45** F12
Mustang *Nepal* **69** E10
Musters, L. *Argentina* **128** F3
Musudan *N. Korea* **57** D15
Muswellbrook *Australia* **95** E5
Muszyna *Poland* **31** J7
Mût *Egypt* **80** B2
Mut *Turkey* **72** D5
Mutanda *Mozam.* **89** C5
Mutanda *Zambia* **87** E2
Mutare *Zimbabwe* **87** F3
Mutawintji △ *Australia* **95** E3
Mutha *Kenya* **86** C4
Muting *Indonesia* **63** F10
Mutki = Mirtağ *Turkey* **70** B4
Mutoko *Zimbabwe* **89** B5
Mutomo *Kenya* **86** C4
Mutoray *Russia* **53** C11
Mutsamudu *Comoros Is.* **85** a
Mutshatsha *Dem. Rep. of the Congo* **87** E1
Mutsu *Japan* **54** D10
Mutsu-Wan *Japan* **54** D10
Muttaburra *Australia* **94** C3
Muttalip *Turkey* **47** B12
Mutton I. *Ireland* **12** D2
Mutuáli *Mozam.* **87** E4

Mutum Biyu *Nigeria* 83 D7
Muweilih *Egypt* 74 E3
Muxía *Spain* 36 B1
Muy Muy *Nic.* 120 D2
Muyinga *Burundi* 86 C3
Muynak *Uzbekistan* 52 E6
Muyunkum, Peski =
　Moyynqum *Kazakhstan* 52 E8
Muzaffarabad *Pakistan* 69 B5
Muzaffargarh *Pakistan* 68 D4
Muzaffarnagar *India* 68 E7
Muzaffarpur *India* 69 F11
Muzafirpur *Pakistan* 68 D3
Muzhi *Russia* 52 C7
Muzillac *France* 18 E4
Muzūra *Egypt* 80 J7
Mvôlô *Sudan* 81 F2
Mvuma *Zimbabwe* 87 F3
Mvurwi *Zimbabwe* 87 F3
Mwabvi △ *Malawi* 87 F3
Mwadui *Tanzania* 86 C3
Mwali = Mohéli *Comoros Is.* 85 a
Mwambo *Tanzania* 87 E5
Mwandi *Zambia* 87 F1
Mwanza
　Dem. Rep. of the Congo 86 D2
Mwanza *Tanzania* 86 C3
Mwanza *Zambia* 87 F1
Mwanza □ *Tanzania* 86 C3
Mwaya *Tanzania* 87 D3
Mweelrea *Ireland* 12 C2
Mweka *Dem. Rep. of the Congo* 84 E4
Mwene-Ditu
　Dem. Rep. of the Congo 84 F4
Mwenezi *Zimbabwe* 87 G3
Mwenezi → *Mozam.* 87 G3
Mwenga
　Dem. Rep. of the Congo 86 C2
Mweru, L. *Zambia* 87 D2
Mweru Wantipa △ *Zambia* 87 D2
Mweza Range *Zimbabwe* 87 G3
Mwilambwe
　Dem. Rep. of the Congo 86 D2
Mwimbi *Tanzania* 87 D3
Mwingi *Kenya* 86 C4
Mwinilunga *Zambia* 87 E1
My Tho *Vietnam* 65 G6
Myajlar *India* 68 F4
Myanaung *Burma* 67 K19
Myanmar = Burma ■ *Asia* 67 J20
Myaungmya *Burma* 67 L19
Mycenæ = Mikines *Greece* 46 D4
Myedna *Belarus* 31 G10
Myeik Kyunzu *Burma* 65 G1
Myerstown *U.S.A.* 115 F8
Myingyan *Burma* 67 J19
Myitkyina *Burma* 67 G20
Myjava *Slovak Rep.* 27 C10
Mykhaylivka *Ukraine* 33 J8
Mykines *Færoe Is.* 8 E9
Mykolayiv *Ukraine* 33 J7
Mykolayiv □ *Ukraine* 33 J6
Mykonos *Greece* 47 D7
Mymensingh *Bangla.* 67 G17
Mynydd Du *U.K.* 15 F4
Mýrdalsjökull *Iceland* 8 E4
Myrhorod *Ukraine* 33 H7
Myrtle Beach *U.S.A.* 117 E15
Myrtle Creek *U.S.A.* 108 E2
Myrtle Point *U.S.A.* 108 E1
Myrtou *Cyprus* 49 D12
Mysia *Turkey* 45 G11
Myślenice *Poland* 31 J6
Myślibórz *Poland* 31 F1
Mysłowice *Poland* 31 H6
Mysore = Karnataka □
　India 66 N10
Mysore *India* 66 N10
Mystic *U.S.A.* 115 E13
Myszków *Poland* 31 H6
Myszyniec *Poland* 30 E8
Mytishchi *Russia* 32 E9
Mývatn *Iceland* 8 D5
Mže → *Czech Rep.* 26 B6
Mzimba *Malawi* 87 E3
Mzimkulu → *S. Africa* 89 E5
Mzimvubu → *S. Africa* 89 E4
Mzuzu *Malawi* 87 E3

N

Na Hearadh = Harris *U.K.* 13 D2
Na Noi *Thailand* 64 C3
Na Phao *Laos* 64 D5
Na Sam *Vietnam* 58 F6
Na San *Vietnam* 64 B5
Na Thon *Thailand* 65 b
Naab → *Germany* 25 F8
Na'am *Sudan* 81 F2
Na'am → *Sudan* 81 F2
Naantali *Finland* 32 B1
Naas *Ireland* 12 C5
Nababeep *S. Africa* 88 D2
Nabadwip = Navadwip
　India 69 H13
Nabawa *Australia* 93 E1
Nabberu, L. *Australia* 93 E3

Nabburg *Germany* 25 F8
Naberezhnyye Chelny
　Russia 34 C11
Nabeul *Tunisia* 79 A8
Nabha *India* 68 D7
Nabīd *Iran* 71 D8
Nabire *Indonesia* 63 E9
Nabisar *Pakistan* 68 G3
Nabisipi → *Canada* 105 B7
Nabiswera *Uganda* 86 B3
Nāblus = Nābulus *West Bank* 74 C4
Naboomspruit *S. Africa* 89 C4
Nabou *Burkina Faso* 82 C4
Nabouwalu *Fiji* 91 a
Nabua *Phil.* 61 E5
Nābulus *West Bank* 74 C4
Nacala *Mozam.* 87 E5
Nacala-Velha *Mozam.* 87 E5
Nacaome *Honduras* 120 D2
Nacaroa *Mozam.* 87 E4
Naches *U.S.A.* 108 C3
Naches → *U.S.A.* 110 D6
Nachicapau, L. *Canada* 105 A6
Nachingwea *Tanzania* 87 E4
Nachna *India* 68 F4
Náchod *Czech Rep.* 26 A9
Nacimiento, L. *U.S.A.* 110 K6
Naco *Mexico* 118 A2
Nacogdoches *U.S.A.* 116 F7
Nácori Chico *Mexico* 118 B3
Nacozari de García *Mexico* 118 A3
Nacula *Fiji* 91 a
Nádendal = Naantali *Finland* 32 B1
Nadi *Fiji* 91 a
Nadi *Sudan* 80 D3
Nadiad *India* 68 H5
Nădlac *Romania* 28 D5
Nador *Morocco* 78 B5
Nadur *Malta* 49 C1
Nadūshan *Iran* 71 C7
Nadvirna *Ukraine* 29 B9
Nadvornaya = Nadvirna
　Ukraine 29 B9
Nadym *Russia* 52 C8
Nadym → *Russia* 52 C8
Nærbø *Norway* 9 G11
Næstved *Denmark* 11 J5
Nafada *Nigeria* 83 C7
Nafpaktos *Greece* 46 C3
Nafplio *Greece* 46 D4
Naft-e Safīd *Iran* 71 D6
Naftshahr *Iran* 73 E11
Nafud Desert = An Nafūd
　Si. Arabia 70 D4
Nag Hammâdi *Egypt* 80 B3
Naga *Phil.* 61 E5
Nagagami → *Canada* 104 B3
Nagahama *Japan* 55 G8
Nagai *Japan* 54 E10
Nagaland □ *India* 67 G19
Nagano *Japan* 55 F9
Nagano □ *Japan* 55 F9
Nagaoka *Japan* 55 F9
Nagappattinam *India* 66 P11
Nagar → *Bangla.* 69 G13
Nagar Parkar *Pakistan* 68 G4
Nagasaki *Japan* 55 H4
Nagasaki □ *Japan* 55 H4
Nagato *Japan* 55 G5
Nagaur *India* 68 F5
Nagda *India* 68 H6
Nagercoil *India* 66 Q10
Nagina *India* 69 E8
Naginimara *India* 67 F19
Nagīneh *Iran* 71 C8
Nagir *Pakistan* 69 A6
Naglarby *Sweden* 10 D9
Nagles Mts. *Ireland* 12 D3
Nagod *India* 69 G9
Nagold *Germany* 25 G4
Nagold → *Germany* 25 G4
Nagoorin *Australia* 94 C5
Nagorno-Karabakh □
　Azerbaijan 73 C12
Nagornyy *Russia* 53 D13
Nagoya *Japan* 55 G8
Nagpur *India* 66 J11
Nagua *Dom. Rep.* 121 C6
Naguabo *Puerto Rico* 121 d
Nagyatád *Hungary* 28 D2
Nagyecsed *Hungary* 28 C7
Nagykálló *Hungary* 28 C6
Nagykanizsa *Hungary* 28 D2
Nagykáta *Hungary* 28 C4
Nagykőrös *Hungary* 28 C4
Naha *Japan* 55 L3
Nahan *India* 68 D7
Nahanni △ *Canada* 102 A4
Nahanni Butte *Canada* 102 A4
Nahargarh *Mad. P., India* 68 G6
Nahargarh *Raj., India* 68 G7
Nahariyya *Israel* 74 F6
Nahāvand *Iran* 73 E13
Nahe → *Germany* 25 F3
Nahirne *Ukraine* 29 J5
Nahîya, W. → *Egypt* 80 B3
Nahuel Huapi, L. *Argentina* 128 E2
Nahuelbuta △ *Chile* 126 D1

Nai Yong *Thailand* 65 a
Naicá *Mexico* 118 B3
Naicam *Canada* 103 C8
Naikoon △ *Canada* 102 C2
Naila *Germany* 25 E7
Naimisharanya *India* 69 F9
Nain *Canada* 105 A7
Nā'īn *Iran* 71 C7
Naini Tal *India* 69 E8
Nainpur *India* 69 H9
Naintré *France* 18 F7
Nainwa *India* 68 G6
Naipu *Romania* 29 F10
Nairai *Fiji* 91 a
Nairn *U.K.* 13 D5
Nairobi *Kenya* 86 C4
Nairobi △ *Kenya* 86 C4
Naissaar *Estonia* 32 C3
Naita, Mt. *Ethiopia* 81 F4
Naitaba *Fiji* 91 a
Naivasha *Kenya* 86 C4
Naivasha, L. *Kenya* 86 C4
Najac *France* 20 D5
Najaf = An Najaf *Iraq* 73 G11
Najafābād *Iran* 71 C6
Najd *Si. Arabia* 75 B3
Nájera *Spain* 38 C2
Najerilla → *Spain* 38 C2
Najibabad *India* 68 E8
Najin *N. Korea* 57 C16
Najmah *Si. Arabia* 71 E6
Najrān *Si. Arabia* 75 D3
Naju *S. Korea* 57 G14
Nakadōri-Shima *Japan* 55 H4
Nakalagba
　Dem. Rep. of the Congo 86 B2
Nakaminato *Japan* 55 F10
Nakamura *Japan* 55 H6
Nakano *Japan* 55 F9
Nakano-Shima *Japan* 55 K4
Nakashibetsu *Japan* 54 C12
Nakfa *Eritrea* 81 D4
Nakfa △ *Eritrea* 81 D4
Nakha Yai, Ko *Thailand* 65 a
Nakhichevan = Naxçıvan
　Azerbaijan 73 C11
Nakhichevan Rep. =
　Naxçıvan □ *Azerbaijan* 73 C11
Nakhl *Egypt* 74 F2
Nakhl-e Taqī *Iran* 71 E7
Nakhodka *Russia* 54 C6
Nakhon Nayok *Thailand* 64 E3
Nakhon Pathom *Thailand* 64 F3
Nakhon Phanom *Thailand* 64 D5
Nakhon Ratchasima
　Thailand 64 E4
Nakhon Sawan *Thailand* 64 E3
Nakhon Si Thammarat
　Thailand 65 H3
Nakhon Thai *Thailand* 64 D3
Nakhtarana *India* 68 H3
Nakina *Canada* 104 B2
Nakło nad Notecią *Poland* 31 E4
Nako *Burkina Faso* 82 C4
Nakodar *India* 68 D6
Nakskov *Denmark* 11 K5
Naktong → *S. Korea* 57 G15
Nakuru *Kenya* 86 C4
Nakuru, L. *Kenya* 86 C4
Nakusp *Canada* 102 C5
Nal *Pakistan* 68 F2
Nal → *Pakistan* 68 G1
Nalázi *Mozam.* 89 C5
Nalchik *Russia* 35 J6
Nałęczów *Poland* 31 G9
Nalerigu *Ghana* 83 C4
Nalgonda *India* 66 L11
Nalhati *India* 69 G12
Naliya *India* 68 H3
Nallamalai Hills *India* 66 M11
Nallıhan *Turkey* 72 B4
Nalón → *Spain* 36 B4
Nalubaale Dam *Uganda* 86 B3
Nam Can *Vietnam* 65 H5
Nam-ch'on *N. Korea* 57 E14
Nam Co *China* 60 C4
Nam Dinh *Vietnam* 58 G6
Nam Du, Hon *Vietnam* 65 H5
Nam Nao △ *Thailand* 64 D3
Nam Ngum Res. *Laos* 64 C4
Nam-Phan *Vietnam* 65 G6
Nam Phong *Thailand* 64 D4
Nam Tha *Laos* 58 G3
Nam Tok *Thailand* 64 E2
Namacunde *Angola* 88 B2
Namacurra *Mozam.* 89 B6
Namak, Daryācheh-ye *Iran* 71 C7
Namak, Kavir-e *Iran* 71 C8
Namakzār, Daryācheh-ye
　Iran 71 C9
Namaland *Namibia* 88 C2
Namanga *Kenya* 86 C4
Namangan *Uzbekistan* 52 E8
Namapa *Mozam.* 87 E4
Namaqualand *S. Africa* 88 E2
Namasagali *Uganda* 86 B3
Namber *Indonesia* 63 E8

Nambour *Australia* 95 D5
Nambouwalu =
　Nabouwalu *Fiji* 91 a
Nambucca Heads *Australia* 95 E5
Nambung △ *Australia* 93 F2
Namche Bazar *Nepal* 69 F12
Namchonjŏm =
　Nam-ch'on *N. Korea* 57 E14
Namecunda *Mozam.* 87 E4
Namenalala *Fiji* 91 a
Nameponda *Mozam.* 87 F4
Námēšt' nad Oslavou
　Czech Rep. 27 B9
Námestovo *Slovak Rep.* 27 B12
Nametil *Mozam.* 87 F4
Namew L. *Canada* 103 C8
Namgia *India* 69 D8
Namhkam *Burma* 58 E1
Namib Desert *Namibia* 88 C2
Namib-Naukluft △ *Namibia* 88 C2
Namibe *Angola* 85 H2
Namibe □ *Angola* 88 B1
Namibia ■ *Africa* 88 C2
Namibwoestyn = Namib
　Desert *Namibia* 88 C2
Namīn *Iran* 73 C13
Namlea *Indonesia* 63 E7
Namoi → *Australia* 95 E4
Nampa *U.S.A.* 108 E5
Nampala *Mali* 82 B3
Namp'o *N. Korea* 57 E13
Nampō-Shotō *Japan* 55 J10
Nampula *Mozam.* 87 F4
Namrole *Indonesia* 63 E7
Namse Shankou *China* 59 E10
Namsen → *Norway* 8 D14
Namsos *Norway* 8 D14
Namtok Chat Trakan △
　Thailand 64 D3
Namtok Mae Surin △
　Thailand 64 C2
Namtsy *Russia* 53 C13
Namtu *Burma* 67 H20
Namtumbo *Tanzania* 87 E4
Namu *Canada* 102 C3
Namuka-i-Lau *Fiji* 91 a
Namur *Belgium* 17 D4
Namur □ *Belgium* 17 D4
Namuruputh *Kenya* 86 B4
Namutoni *Namibia* 88 B2
Namwala *Zambia* 87 F2
Namwon *S. Korea* 57 G14
Namyang *N. Korea* 57 C15
Namysłów *Poland* 31 G4
Nan *Thailand* 64 C3
Nan → *Thailand* 64 E3
Nan-ch'ang = Nanchang
　China 59 C10
Nan Ling *China* 59 E8
Nan Xian *China* 59 C9
Nana *Romania* 29 F11
Nana Kru *Liberia* 82 E3
Nanaimo *Canada* 102 D4
Nanam *N. Korea* 57 D15
Nanan *China* 59 E12
Nanango *Australia* 95 D5
Nan'ao *China* 59 F11
Nanao *Japan* 55 F8
Nanbu *China* 58 B6
Nanchang *China* 59 C10
Nancheng *China* 59 D11
Nanchong *China* 58 B6
Nanchuan *China* 58 C6
Nancy *France* 19 D13
Nanda Devi *India* 69 D8
Nanda Devi △ *India* 69 D8
Nanda Kot *India* 69 D9
Nandan *China* 58 E6
Nandan *Japan* 55 G7
Nanded *India* 66 K10
Nandewar Ra. *Australia* 95 E5
Nandi = Nadi *Fiji* 91 a
Nandigram *India* 69 H12
Nandurbar *India* 66 J9
Nandyal *India* 66 M11
Nanfeng *Guangdong, China* 59 F8
Nanfeng *Jiangxi, China* 59 D11
Nanga-Eboko *Cameroon* 83 E7
Nanga Parbat *Pakistan* 69 B6
Nangade *Mozam.* 87 E4
Nangapinoh *Indonesia* 62 E4
Nangarhār □ *Afghan.* 66 B7
Nangatayap *Indonesia* 62 E4
Nangeya Mts. *Uganda* 86 B3
Nangis *France* 19 D10
Nangong *China* 56 F8
Nanhua *China* 58 E3
Nanhuang *China* 57 F11
Nanhui *China* 59 B13
Nanjeko *Zambia* 87 F1
Nanji Shan *China* 59 D13
Nanjian *China* 58 E3
Nanjing *Fujian, China* 59 E11
Nanjing *Jiangsu, China* 59 A12
Nanjirinji *Tanzania* 87 D4

Nankana Sahib *Pakistan* 68 D5
Nankang *China* 59 E10
Nanking = Nanjing *China* 59 A12
Nankoku *Japan* 55 H6
Nanling *China* 59 B12
Nanning *China* 58 F7
Nannup *Australia* 93 F2
Nanpan Jiang → *China* 58 E6
Nanpara *India* 69 F9
Nanpi *China* 56 E9
Nanping *Fujian, China* 59 D12
Nanping *Henan, China* 59 C9
Nanri Dao *China* 59 E12
Nanripe *Mozam.* 87 E4
Nansei-Shotō =
　Ryūkyū-rettō *Japan* 55 M3
Nansen Basin *Arctic* 4 A10
Nansen Sd. *Canada* 101 A10
Nanshan I. *S. China Sea* 62 B5
Nansio *Tanzania* 86 C3
Nant *France* 20 D7
Nanterre *France* 19 D9
Nantes *France* 18 E5
Nantiat *France* 20 B5
Nant'ou *Taiwan* 59 F13
Nantua *France* 19 F12
Nantucket *U.S.A.* 113 E18
Nantucket I. *U.S.A.* 113 E18
Nantwich *U.K.* 14 D5
Nanty Glo *U.S.A.* 114 F6
Nanuku Passage *Fiji* 91 a
Nanuque *Brazil* 125 G10
Nanusa, Kepulauan
　Indonesia 63 D7
Nanutarra Roadhouse
　Australia 92 D2
Nanxi *China* 58 C5
Nanxiong *China* 59 E10
Nanyang *China* 56 H7
Nanyi Hu *China* 59 B12
Nanyuki *Kenya* 86 B4
Nanzhang *China* 59 B8
Nao, C. de la *Spain* 39 G5
Naococane, L. *Canada* 105 B5
Naoussa *Cyclades, Greece* 47 D7
Naoussa *Imathia, Greece* 44 F6
Naozhou Dao *China* 59 G8
Napa *U.S.A.* 110 G4
Napa → *U.S.A.* 110 G4
Napanee *Canada* 114 B8
Napanoch *U.S.A.* 115 E10
Nape *Laos* 64 C5
Nape Pass = Keo Neua,
　Deo *Vietnam* 64 C5
Napier *N.Z.* 91 C6
Napier Broome B. *Australia* 92 B4
Napier Pen. *Australia* 94 A2
Napierville *Canada* 115 A11
Naples = Nápoli *Italy* 43 B7
Naples *U.S.A.* 117 H14
Napo *China* 58 F5
Napo → *Peru* 124 D4
Napoleon *N. Dak., U.S.A.* 112 B4
Napoleon *Ohio, U.S.A.* 113 E11
Nápoli *Italy* 43 B7
Nápoli, G. di *Italy* 43 B7
Nápoli Capodichino ✈
　(NAP) *Italy* 43 B7
Napopo *Dem. Rep. of the Congo* 86 B2
Naqâda *Egypt* 80 B3
Naqadeh *Iran* 73 D11
Naqb, Ra's an *Jordan* 74 F4
Naqqāsh *Iran* 71 C6
Nara *Japan* 55 G7
Nara *Mali* 82 B3
Nara □ *Japan* 55 G8
Nara Canal *Pakistan* 68 G3
Nara Visa *U.S.A.* 109 J12
Naracoorte *Australia* 95 F3
Naradhan *Australia* 95 E4
Naraini *India* 69 G9
Naranjos *Mexico* 119 C5
Narasapur *India* 67 L12
Narathiwat *Thailand* 65 J3
Narayanganj *Bangla.* 67 H17
Narayanpet *India* 66 L10
Narberth *U.K.* 15 F3
Narbonne *France* 20 E7
Narcea → *Spain* 36 B4
Nardīn *Iran* 71 B7
Nardò *Italy* 43 B11
Narembeen *Australia* 93 F2
Nares Str. *Arctic* 98 A13
Naretha *Australia* 93 F3
Narew → *Poland* 31 F7
Nari → *Pakistan* 68 F2
Narin → *Afghan.* 66 A6
Narindra, Helodranon' i
　Madag. 89 A8
Narita *Japan* 55 G10
Nariva Swamp *Trin. & Tob.* 125 K15
Närke *Sweden* 10 E8
Narmada → *India* 68 J5

Narman *Turkey* 73 B9
Narnaul *India* 68 E7
Narni *Italy* 41 F9
Naro *Ghana* 82 C4
Naro Fominsk *Russia* 32 E9
Narodnaya *Russia* 6 B17
Narok *Kenya* 86 C4
Narón *Spain* 36 B2
Narooma *Australia* 95 F5
Narowal *Pakistan* 68 C6
Narrabri *Australia* 95 E4
Narran → *Australia* 95 D4
Narrandera *Australia* 95 E4
Narrogin *Australia* 93 F2
Narromine *Australia* 95 E4
Narrow Hills △ *Canada* 103 C8
Narsimhapur *India* 69 H8
Narsinghgarh *India* 68 H7
Nartes, L. e *Albania* 44 F3
Nartkala *Russia* 35 J6
Naruto *Japan* 55 G7
Narva *Estonia* 32 C5
Narva → *Russia* 32 C5
Narva Bay = Narva Laht
　Estonia 9 G22
Narva Laht *Estonia* 9 G22
Narvik *Norway* 8 B17
Narvskoye Vdkhr. *Russia* 32 C5
Narwana *India* 68 E7
Narwiański △ *Poland* 31 F9
Naryan-Mar *Russia* 52 C6
Narym *Russia* 52 D9
Naryn *Kyrgyzstan* 52 E8
Naryn Qum *Kazakhstan* 35 G9
Nasa *Norway* 8 C16
Nasau *Fiji* 91 a
Năsăud *Romania* 29 C9
Nasca = Nazca *Peru* 124 F4
Naseby *N.Z.* 91 F3
Naselle *U.S.A.* 110 D3
Naser, Buheirat en *Egypt* 80 C3
Nashua *Mont., U.S.A.* 108 B10
Nashua *N.H., U.S.A.* 115 D13
Nashville *Ark., U.S.A.* 116 E8
Nashville *Ga., U.S.A.* 117 F13
Nashville *Tenn., U.S.A.* 117 C11
Našice *Croatia* 28 E3
Nasielsk *Poland* 31 F7
Nasik *India* 66 K8
Nasipit *Phil.* 61 G6
Nasir *Sudan* 81 F3
Nasirabad *India* 68 F6
Nasirabad *Pakistan* 68 E3
Nasiriyah = An Nāşirīyah
　Iraq 70 D5
Naskaupi → *Canada* 105 B7
Naso *Italy* 43 D7
Naşrābād *Iran* 71 C6
Naşrīān-e Pā'īn *Iran* 70 C5
Nass → *Canada* 102 C3
Nassarawa *Nigeria* 83 D6
Nassarawa □ *Nigeria* 83 D6
Nassau *Bahamas* 120 A4
Nassau *U.S.A.* 115 D11
Nassau, B. *Chile* 128 H3
Nasser, L. = Naser,
　Buheirat en *Egypt* 80 C3
Nassian *Ivory C.* 82 D4
Nässjö *Sweden* 11 G8
Nastapoka → *Canada* 104 A4
Nastapoka, Is. *Canada* 104 A4
Näsum *Sweden* 11 H8
Näsviken *Sweden* 10 C10
Nata *Botswana* 88 C4
Nata → *Botswana* 88 C4
Natal *Brazil* 125 E11
Natal *Indonesia* 62 D1
Natal Drakensberg △
　S. Africa 89 D4
Natalinci *Serbia* 28 F5
Naţanz *Iran* 71 C6
Natashquan *Canada* 105 B7
Natashquan → *Canada* 105 B7
Natchez *U.S.A.* 116 F9
Natchitoches *U.S.A.* 116 F8
Natewa B. *Fiji* 91 a
Nathalia *Australia* 95 F4
Nathdwara *India* 68 G5
Nati, Pta. *Spain* 48 A10
Natimuk *Australia* 95 F3
Nation → *Canada* 102 B4
National City *U.S.A.* 111 N9
Natitingou *Benin* 83 C5
Natividad, I. *Mexico* 118 B1
Natkyizin *Burma* 64 E1
Natron, L. *Tanzania* 86 C4
Natrona Heights *U.S.A.* 114 F5
Natrûn, W. el → *Egypt* 80 H7
Nättraby *Sweden* 11 H9
Natukanaoka Pan *Namibia* 88 B2
Natuna Besar, Kepulauan
　Indonesia 62 D3
Natuna Is. = Natuna
　Besar, Kepulauan
　Indonesia 62 D3
Natuna Selatan,
　Kepulauan *Indonesia* 62 D3

Natural Bridge *U.S.A.* **115** B9
Natural Bridges △ *U.S.A.* **109** H9
Naturaliste, C. *Tas., Australia* **95** G4
Naturaliste, C. *W. Austral., Australia* **90** E4
Naturaliste Plateau *Ind. Oc.* **96** L3
Nau Qala *Afghan.* **68** B3
Naucelle *France* **20** D6
Nauders *Austria* **26** E3
Nauen *Germany* **24** C8
Naugatuck *U.S.A.* **115** E11
Naujaat = Repulse Bay *Canada* **101** C11
Naujoji Akmenė *Lithuania* **30** B9
Naumburg *Germany* **24** D7
Nauru ■ *Pac. Oc.* **90** B9
Naushahra = Nowshera *Pakistan* **66** C8
Naushahro *Pakistan* **68** F3
Naushon I. *U.S.A.* **115** E14
Nausori *Fiji* **91** a
Nauta *Peru* **124** D4
Nautanwa *India* **69** F10
Naute △ *Namibia* **88** D2
Nautla *Mexico* **119** C5
Nava *Mexico* **118** B4
Nava *Spain* **36** B5
Nava del Rey *Spain* **36** D5
Navadwip *India* **69** H13
Navahermosa *Spain* **37** F6
Navahrudak *Belarus* **23** B13
Navajo Res. *U.S.A.* **109** H10
Navalcarnero *Spain* **36** E6
Navalmoral de la Mata *Spain* **36** F5
Navalvillar de Pela *Spain* **37** F5
Navan = An Uaimh *Ireland* **12** C5
Navapolatsk *Belarus* **32** E5
Navarin, Mys *Russia* **4** C16
Navarino, I. *Chile* **128** H3
Navarra □ *Spain* **38** C3
Navarre *U.S.A.* **114** F3
Navarro → *U.S.A.* **110** F3
Navas de San Juan *Spain* **37** G7
Navasota *U.S.A.* **116** F6
Navassa I. *W. Indies* **121** C5
Nävekvarn *Sweden* **11** F10
Naver → *U.K.* **13** C4
Navia *Spain* **36** B4
Navia → *Spain* **36** B4
Navia de Suarna *Spain* **36** C3
Navibandar *India* **68** J3
Navidad *Chile* **126** C1
Naviraí *Brazil* **127** A5
Naviti *Fiji* **91** a
Navlakhi *India* **68** H4
Navlya *Russia* **33** F8
Năvodari *Romania* **29** F13
Navoi = Nawoiy *Uzbekistan* **52** E7
Navojoa *Mexico* **118** B3
Navolato *Mexico* **118** C3
Navrongo *Ghana* **83** C4
Navsari *India* **66** J8
Navua *Fiji* **91** a
Nawa Kot *Pakistan* **68** E4
Nawab Khan *Pakistan* **68** D3
Nawabganj *Ut. P., India* **69** F9
Nawabganj *Ut. P., India* **69** E8
Nawabshah *Pakistan* **68** F3
Nawada *India* **69** G11
Nawakot *Nepal* **69** F11
Nawalgarh *India* **68** F6
Nawanshahr *India* **69** C6
Nawar, Dasht-i- *Afghan.* **68** C3
Nawi *Sudan* **80** D3
Nawoiy *Uzbekistan* **52** E7
Naxçıvan *Azerbaijan* **73** C11
Naxçıvan □ *Azerbaijan* **73** C11
Naxos *Greece* **47** D7
Nay *France* **20** E3
Nay, Mui *Vietnam* **62** B3
Nāy Band *Büshehr, Iran* **71** E7
Nāy Band *Khorāsān, Iran* **71** C8
Nayakhan *Russia* **53** C16
Nayarit □ *Mexico* **118** C4
Nayau *Fiji* **91** a
Nayé *Senegal* **82** C2
Nayong *China* **58** D5
Nayoro *Japan* **54** B11
Nayyāl, W. → *Si. Arabia* **70** D3
Nazaré *Brazil* **125** F11
Nazaré *Portugal* **37** F1
Nazareth = Naẕerat *Israel* **74** C4
Nazareth *U.S.A.* **115** F9
Nazas *Mexico* **118** B4
Nazas → *Mexico* **118** B4
Nazca *Peru* **124** F4
Nazca Ridge *Pac. Oc.* **97** K19
Naze *Japan* **55** K4
Naze, The *U.K.* **15** F9
Naẕerat *Israel* **74** C4
Nāzik *Iran* **73** C11
Nazilli *Turkey* **47** D10
Nazko *Canada* **102** C4
Nazko → *Canada* **102** C4
Nazret *Ethiopia* **81** F4
Nchanga *Zambia* **87** E2
Ncheu *Malawi* **87** E3

Ndala *Tanzania* **86** C3
Ndalatando *Angola* **84** F2
Ndareda *Tanzania* **86** C4
Ndélé *C.A.R.* **84** C4
Ndali *Benin* **83** D5
Ndikinimeki *Cameroon* **83** E7
N'Dioum *Senegal* **82** B2
Ndjamena *Chad* **79** F8
Ndola *Zambia* **87** E2
Ndomo → *S. Africa* **89** D5
Ndoto Mts. *Kenya* **86** B4
Nduguti *Tanzania* **86** C3
Nea Alikarnassos *Greece* **47** F7
Nea Anchialos *Greece* **46** B4
Nea Epidavros *Greece* **46** D5
Nea Ionia *Greece* **46** B4
Nea Kalikratia *Greece* **44** F7
Nea Makri *Greece* **46** C5
Nea Moudania *Greece* **44** F7
Nea Visa *Greece* **45** E10
Nea Zichni *Greece* **44** E7
Neagh, Lough *U.K.* **12** B5
Neah Bay *U.S.A.* **110** B2
Neale, L. *Australia* **92** D5
Neales → *Australia* **95** D2
Neamţ □ *Romania* **29** C11
Neapoli *Kozani, Greece* **44** F5
Neapoli *Kriti, Greece* **49** D7
Neapoli *Lakonia, Greece* **46** E5
Near Is. *U.S.A.* **106** a
Neath *U.K.* **15** F4
Neath Port Talbot □ *U.K.* **15** F4
Nebbou *Burkina Faso* **83** C4
Nebine Cr. → *Australia* **95** D4
Nebitdag = Balkanabat *Turkmenistan* **71** B7
Nebo *Australia* **94** C4
Nebolchy *Russia* **32** C7
Nebraska □ *U.S.A.* **112** E4
Nebraska City *U.S.A.* **112** E6
Nébrodi, Monti *Italy* **43** E7
Necedah *U.S.A.* **112** C8
Nechako → *Canada* **102** C4
Neches → *U.S.A.* **116** G8
Nechisar △ *Ethiopia* **81** F4
Neckar → *Germany* **25** F4
Neckartal-Odenwald △ *Germany* **25** F5
Necochea *Argentina* **126** D4
Neda *Spain* **36** B2
Neda → *Greece* **46** D3
Nedelino *Bulgaria* **45** E9
Nedelišće *Croatia* **41** B13
Nederland = Netherlands ■ *Europe* **17** C5
Nedoboyivtsi *Ukraine* **29** B11
Needles *Canada* **102** D5
Needles *U.S.A.* **111** L12
Needles, The *U.K.* **15** G6
Ñeembucú □ *Paraguay* **126** B4
Neemuch = Nimach *India* **68** G6
Neenah *U.S.A.* **112** C9
Neepawa *Canada* **103** C9
Neftçala *Azerbaijan* **73** C13
Neftegorsk *Russia* **35** H4
Neftekumsk *Russia* **35** H7
Nefyn *U.K.* **14** E3
Négala *Mali* **82** C3
Negapatam = Nagappattinam *India* **66** P11
Negara *Indonesia* **63** J17
Negaunee *U.S.A.* **112** B10
Negele *Ethiopia* **81** F4
Negev Desert = Hanegev *Israel* **74** E4
Negoiul, Vf. *Romania* **29** E9
Negombo *Sri Lanka* **66** R11
Negotin *Serbia* **44** B6
Negotino *Macedonia* **44** E6
Negra, Peña *Spain* **36** C4
Negra, Pta. *Mauritania* **78** D2
Negra, Pta. *Peru* **124** D2
Negrais, C. = Maudin Sun *Burma* **67** M19
Negreşti *Romania* **29** D12
Negreşti-Oaş *Romania* **29** C8
Negril *Jamaica* **120** a
Negro → *Argentina* **128** E4
Negro → *Brazil* **124** D7
Negro → *Uruguay* **126** C4
Negros *Phil.* **61** G5
Negru Vodă *Romania* **29** G13
Neguac *Canada* **105** C6
Nehalem → *U.S.A.* **110** E3
Nehavand *Iran* **71** C6
Nehbandān *Iran* **71** D9
Nehoiu *Romania* **29** E11
Nei Monggol Zizhiqu □ *China* **56** D7
Neiafu *Tonga* **91** c
Neigh *Romania* **94** K6
Netherdale *Australia* **94** K6
Netherlands ■ *Europe* **17** C5
Netherlands Antilles ☒ *W. Indies* **124** A5

Neilton *U.S.A.* **108** C2
Neiqiu *China* **56** F8
Neiva *Colombia* **124** C3
Neixiang *China* **56** H6
Nejanilini L. *Canada* **103** B9
Nejd = Najd *Si. Arabia* **75** B3
Nejo *Ethiopia* **81** F4
Nekā *Iran* **71** B7
Nekemte *Ethiopia* **81** F4
Nêkheb *Egypt* **80** B3
Neksø *Denmark* **11** J9
Nelas *Portugal* **36** E3
Nelia *Australia* **94** C3
Nelidovo *Russia* **32** D7
Neligh *U.S.A.* **112** D4
Nelkan *Russia* **53** D14
Nellore *India* **66** M11
Nelson *Canada* **102** D5
Nelson *N.Z.* **91** D4
Nelson *U.K.* **14** D5
Nelson *Ariz., U.S.A.* **109** J7
Nelson *Nev., U.S.A.* **111** K12
Nelson → *Canada* **103** C9
Nelson, C. *Australia* **95** F3
Nelson, Estrecho *Chile* **128** G2
Nelson Forks *Canada* **102** B4
Nelson House *Canada* **103** B9
Nelson L. *Canada* **103** B8
Nelson Lakes △ *N.Z.* **91** D4
Nelspoort *S. Africa* **88** E3
Nelspruit *S. Africa* **89** D5
Néma *Mauritania* **82** B3
Neman → *Lithuania* **30** C8
Neman *Russia* **30** D9
Nemea *Greece* **46** D4
Nemeiben L. *Canada* **103** B7
Nemërçkë, Mal *Albania* **44** F4
Nemira, Vf. *Romania* **29** D11
Nemiscau *Canada* **104** B4
Nemiscau, L. *Canada* **104** B4
Nemours *France* **19** D9
Nemšová *Slovak Rep.* **27** C11
Nemuro *Japan* **54** C12
Nemuro-Kaikyō *Japan* **54** C12
Nemyriv *Ukraine* **31** H10
Nen Jiang → *China* **57** B13
Nenagh *Ireland* **12** D3
Nenasi *Malaysia* **65** L4
Nene → *U.K.* **15** E8
Nenita *Greece* **47** C8
Nenjiang *China* **60** B7
Neno *Malawi* **87** F3
Neo Chori *Greece* **46** C3
Neochori *Greece* **46** B2
Neodesha *U.S.A.* **112** G7
Neon Petritsi *Greece* **44** E7
Neora Valley △ *India* **69** F13
Neosho *U.S.A.* **112** G6
Neosho → *U.S.A.* **116** C7
Nepal ■ *Asia* **69** F11
Nepalganj *Nepal* **69** E9
Nepalganj Road *Nepal* **69** E9
Nephi *U.S.A.* **108** G8
Nephin *Ireland* **12** B2
Nephin Beg Range *Ireland* **12** C2
Nepi *Italy* **41** F9
Nepomuk *Czech Rep.* **26** B6
Neptune *U.S.A.* **115** F10
Nera → *Italy* **41** F9
Nera → *Romania* **28** F6
Nérac *France* **20** D4
Nerang *Australia* **95** D5
Nerastro, Sarīr *Libya* **79** D10
Neratovice *Czech Rep.* **26** A7
Nerchinsk *Russia* **53** D12
Nereju *Romania* **29** E11
Nerekhta *Russia* **32** B7
Neresnytsya *Ukraine* **29** B8
Néret, L. *Canada* **105** B5
Neretvanski Kanal *Croatia* **41** E14
Neringa *Lithuania* **30** C8
Neris → *Lithuania* **32** E3
Nerja *Spain* **37** J7
Nerl → *Russia* **32** D11
Nerpio *Spain* **39** G2
Nerva *Spain* **37** H4
Nervi *Italy* **40** D6
Neryungri *Russia* **53** D13
Nescopeck *U.S.A.* **115** E8
Nesebŭr *Bulgaria* **45** D11
Ness, L. *U.K.* **13** D4
Ness City *U.S.A.* **112** F4
Nesterov *Russia* **30** D9
Nesterov *Ukraine* **23** C12
Nestorio *Greece* **44** F5
Nestos → *Greece* **45** E8
Nesvady *Slovak Rep.* **27** D11
Nesvizh = Nyasvizh *Belarus* **23** B14
Netanya *Israel* **74** C3
Netarhat *India* **69** H11
Nete → *Belgium* **17** C4

Neto → *Italy* **43** C10
Netrang *India* **68** J5
Nettancourt *France* **19** D11
Nettetal *Germany* **24** D2
Nettilling L. *Canada* **101** C12
Nettuno *Italy* **42** A5
Netzahualcóyotl, Presa *Mexico* **119** D6
Neu-Isenburg *Germany* **25** E4
Neu-Ulm *Germany* **25** G6
Neubrandenburg *Germany* **24** B9
Neubukow *Germany* **24** A7
Neuburg *Germany* **25** G7
Neuchâtel *Switz.* **25** J2
Neuchâtel □ *Switz.* **25** J2
Neuchâtel, Lac de *Switz.* **25** J2
Neudau *Austria* **26** D9
Neuenhagen *Germany* **24** C9
Neuenhaus *Germany* **24** C2
Neuf-Brisach *France* **19** D14
Neufahrn *Bayern, Germany* **25** G8
Neufahrn *Bayern, Germany* **25** G7
Neufchâteau *Belgium* **17** E5
Neufchâteau *France* **19** D12
Neufchâtel-en-Bray *France* **18** C8
Neufchâtel-sur-Aisne *France* **19** C11
Neuhaus *Germany* **24** B6
Neuillé-Pont-Pierre *France* **18** E7
Neuilly-St-Front *France* **19** C10
Neukalen *Germany* **24** B8
Neumarkt *Germany* **25** F7
Neumayer *Antarctica* **5** D17
Neumünster *Germany* **24** A5
Neung-sur-Beuvron *France* **19** E8
Neunkirchen *Austria* **26** D9
Neunkirchen *Germany* **25** F3
Neuquén *Argentina* **128** D3
Neuquén □ *Argentina* **126** D2
Neuruppin *Germany* **24** C8
Neusäss *Germany* **25** G6
Neuse → *U.S.A.* **117** D16
Neusiedl *Austria* **27** D9
Neusiedler See *Austria* **27** D9
Neusiedler See-Seewinkel △ *Austria* **27** D9
Neuss *Germany* **24** D2
Neussargues-Moissac *France* **20** C7
Neustadt *Bayern, Germany* **25** F8
Neustadt *Bayern, Germany* **25** G7
Neustadt *Bayern, Germany* **25** F6
Neustadt *Bayern, Germany* **25** E7
Neustadt *Brandenburg, Germany* **24** C8
Neustadt *Hessen, Germany* **24** E5
Neustadt *Niedersachsen, Germany* **24** C5
Neustadt *Rhld-Pfz., Germany* **25** F4
Neustadt *Sachsen, Germany* **24** D10
Neustadt *Schleswig-Holstein, Germany* **24** A6
Neustadt *Thüringen, Germany* **24** E7
Neustrelitz *Germany* **24** B9
Neuvic *France* **20** C6
Neuville-sur-Saône *France* **21** C8
Neuvy-le-Roi *France* **18** E7
Neuvy-St-Sépulchre *France* **19** F8
Neuvy-sur-Barangeon *France* **19** E9
Neuwerk *Germany* **24** B4
Neuwied *Germany* **24** E3
Neva → *Russia* **32** C6
Nevada *Iowa, U.S.A.* **112** D7
Nevada *Mo., U.S.A.* **112** G6
Nevada □ *U.S.A.* **108** G5
Nevada City *U.S.A.* **110** F4
Nevado, Cerro *Argentina* **126** D2
Nevado de Colima = Volcán de Colima △ *Mexico* **118** D4
Nevado de Tres Cruces △ *Chile* **126** B2
Nevel *Russia* **32** D5
Nevers *France* **19** F10
Nevertire *Australia* **95** E4
Nevesinje *Bos.-H.* **44** C2
Neville *Canada* **103** D7
Nevinnomyssk *Russia* **35** H6
Nevis *St. Kitts & Nevis* **121** C7
Nevrokop = Gotse Delchev *Bulgaria* **44** E7
Nevşehir *Turkey* **72** C6
Nevşehir □ *Turkey* **72** C6
Nevskoye *Russia* **30** D9
New → *U.S.A.* **113** F13
New Aiyansh *Canada* **102** B3
New Albany *Ind., U.S.A.* **113** F11
New Albany *Miss., U.S.A.* **117** D10
New Albany *Pa., U.S.A.* **115** E8
New Amsterdam *Guyana* **124** B7
New Angledool *Australia* **95** D4
New Baltimore *U.S.A.* **114** D2
New Bedford *U.S.A.* **115** E14
New Berlin *N.Y., U.S.A.* **115** D9
New Berlin *Pa., U.S.A.* **114** F8
New Bern *U.S.A.* **117** D16
New Bethlehem *U.S.A.* **114** F5

New Bight *Bahamas* **121** B4
New Bloomfield *U.S.A.* **114** F7
New Boston *U.S.A.* **116** F7
New Braunfels *U.S.A.* **116** G5
New Brighton *N.Z.* **91** E4
New Brighton *U.S.A.* **114** F4
New Britain *Papua N. G.* **90** B8
New Britain *U.S.A.* **115** E12
New Brunswick *U.S.A.* **115** F10
New Brunswick □ *Canada* **105** C6
New Bussa *Nigeria* **83** D5
New Caledonia ☑ *Pac. Oc.* **90** D9
New Caledonia Trough *Pac. Oc.* **96** L8
New Castile = Castilla-La Mancha □ *Spain* **37** F7
New Castle *Ind., U.S.A.* **113** F11
New Castle *Pa., U.S.A.* **114** F4
New City *U.S.A.* **115** E11
New Concord *U.S.A.* **114** G3
New Cumberland *U.S.A.* **114** F4
New Cuyama *U.S.A.* **111** L7
New Delhi *India* **68** E7
New Denver *Canada* **102** D5
New Don Pedro Res. *U.S.A.* **110** H6
New England *U.S.A.* **107** B12
New England *N. Dak., U.S.A.* **112** B2
New England Ra. *Australia* **95** E5
New Forest △ *U.K.* **15** G6
New Galloway *U.K.* **13** F4
New Glasgow *Canada* **105** C7
New Guinea *Oceania* **90** B6
New Hamburg *Canada* **114** C4
New Hampshire □ *U.S.A.* **115** C13
New Hampton *U.S.A.* **112** D7
New Hanover *S. Africa* **89** D5
New Hartford *U.S.A.* **115** C9
New Haven *Conn., U.S.A.* **115** E12
New Haven *Mich., U.S.A.* **114** D2
New Hazelton *Canada* **102** B3
New Hebrides = Vanuatu ■ *Pac. Oc.* **90** C9
New Holland *U.S.A.* **115** F8
New Iberia *U.S.A.* **116** G9
New Ireland *Papua N. G.* **90** B8
New Jersey □ *U.S.A.* **113** F16
New Kensington *U.S.A.* **114** F5
New Lexington *U.S.A.* **113** F12
New Liskeard *Canada* **104** C4
New London *Conn., U.S.A.* **115** E12
New London *Ohio, U.S.A.* **114** E2
New London *Wis., U.S.A.* **112** C9
New Madrid *U.S.A.* **112** G9
New Martinsville *U.S.A.* **113** F13
New Meadows *U.S.A.* **108** D5
New Melones L. *U.S.A.* **110** H6
New Mexico □ *U.S.A.* **109** J11
New Milford *Conn., U.S.A.* **115** E11
New Milford *Pa., U.S.A.* **115** E9
New Norcia *Australia* **93** F2
New Norfolk *Australia* **95** G4
New Orleans *U.S.A.* **117** G9
New Philadelphia *U.S.A.* **114** F3
New Plymouth *N.Z.* **91** C5
New Plymouth *U.S.A.* **108** E5
New Port Richey *U.S.A.* **117** G13
New Providence *Bahamas* **120** A4
New Quay *U.K.* **15** E3
New Radnor *U.K.* **15** E4
New Richmond *Canada* **105** C6
New Richmond *U.S.A.* **112** C7
New River Gorge △ *U.S.A.* **113** G13
New Roads *U.S.A.* **116** F9
New Rochelle *U.S.A.* **115** F11
New Rockford *U.S.A.* **112** B4
New Romney *U.K.* **15** G8
New Ross *Ireland* **12** D5
New Salem *U.S.A.* **112** B3
New Scone = Scone *U.K.* **13** E5
New Siberian I. = Novaya Sibir, Ostrov *Russia* **53** B16
New Siberian Is. = Novosibirskiye Ostrova *Russia* **53** B15
New Smyrna Beach *U.S.A.* **117** G14
New South Wales □ *Australia* **95** E4
New Tecumseth *Canada* **114** B5
New Town *U.S.A.* **112** B2
New Tredegar *U.K.* **15** F4
New Ulm *U.S.A.* **112** C6
New Waterford *Canada* **105** C7
New-Wes-Valley *Canada* **105** C9
New Westminster *Canada* **110** A4
New York *U.S.A.* **115** F11
New York □ *U.S.A.* **115** D9
New York J.F. Kennedy Int. ✈ (JFK) *U.S.A.* **115** F11
New Zealand ■ *Oceania* **91** D6
Newaj → *India* **68** G7
Newala *Tanzania* **87** E4
Newark *Del., U.S.A.* **113** F16
Newark *N.J., U.S.A.* **115** F10
Newark *N.Y., U.S.A.* **114** C7
Newark *Ohio, U.S.A.* **114** F2
Newark Liberty Int. ✈ (EWR) *U.S.A.* **115** F10

Newark-on-Trent *U.K.* **14** D7
Newark Valley *U.S.A.* **115** D8
Newberg *U.S.A.* **108** D2
Newberry *Mich., U.S.A.* **113** B11
Newberry *S.C., U.S.A.* **117** D14
Newberry Springs *U.S.A.* **111** L10
Newboro L. *Canada* **115** B8
Newbridge = Droichead Nua *Ireland* **12** C5
Newburgh *Canada* **114** B8
Newburgh *U.S.A.* **115** E10
Newbury *U.K.* **15** F6
Newbury *U.S.A.* **115** B12
Newbury *Vt., U.S.A.* **115** B12
Newburyport *U.S.A.* **115** D14
Newcastle *Australia* **95** E5
Newcastle *N.B., Canada* **105** C6
Newcastle *Ont., Canada* **104** D4
Newcastle *S. Africa* **89** D4
Newcastle *U.K.* **12** B6
Newcastle *Calif., U.S.A.* **110** G5
Newcastle *Wyo., U.S.A.* **108** L11
Newcastle Emlyn *U.K.* **15** E3
Newcastle Ra. *Australia* **92** C5
Newcastle-under-Lyme *U.K.* **14** D5
Newcastle-upon-Tyne *U.K.* **14** C6
Newcastle Waters *Australia* **94** B1
Newcastle West *Ireland* **12** D2
Newcomb *U.S.A.* **115** C10
Newcomerstown *U.S.A.* **114** F3
Newell *Australia* **94** B4
Newell *U.S.A.* **112** C2
Newfane *U.S.A.* **114** C6
Newfield *U.S.A.* **115** D8
Newfound L. *U.S.A.* **115** C13
Newfoundland *Canada* **105** C8
Newfoundland *U.S.A.* **115** E9
Newfoundland & Labrador □ *Canada* **105** B8
Newhaven *U.K.* **15** G8
Newkirk *U.S.A.* **116** C6
Newlyn *U.K.* **15** G2
Newman *Australia* **92** D2
Newman *U.S.A.* **110** H5
Newmarket *Canada* **114** B5
Newmarket *Ireland* **12** D2
Newmarket *U.K.* **15** E8
Newmarket *U.S.A.* **115** C14
Newnan *U.S.A.* **117** E12
Newport *Ireland* **12** C2
Newport *I. of W., U.K.* **15** G6
Newport *Newport, U.K.* **15** F5
Newport *Ark., U.S.A.* **116** D9
Newport *Ky., U.S.A.* **113** F11
Newport *N.H., U.S.A.* **115** C12
Newport *N.Y., U.S.A.* **115** C9
Newport *Oreg., U.S.A.* **108** D1
Newport *Pa., U.S.A.* **114** F7
Newport *R.I., U.S.A.* **115** E13
Newport *Tenn., U.S.A.* **117** D13
Newport *Vt., U.S.A.* **115** B12
Newport *Wash., U.S.A.* **108** B5
Newport □ *U.K.* **15** F4
Newport Beach *U.S.A.* **111** M9
Newport News *U.S.A.* **113** G15
Newport Pagnell *U.K.* **15** E7
Newquay *U.K.* **15** G2
Newry *U.K.* **12** B5
Newton *Ill., U.S.A.* **112** F9
Newton *Iowa, U.S.A.* **112** E7
Newton *Kans., U.S.A.* **112** F5
Newton *Miss., U.S.A.* **117** E10
Newton *N.C., U.S.A.* **117** D14
Newton *N.J., U.S.A.* **115** E10
Newton *Tex., U.S.A.* **116** F8
Newton Abbot *U.K.* **15** G4
Newton Aycliffe *U.K.* **14** C6
Newton Falls *U.S.A.* **114** E4
Newton Stewart *U.K.* **13** G4
Newtonmore *U.K.* **13** D4
Newtown *U.K.* **15** E4
Newtownabbey *U.K.* **12** B6
Newtownards *U.K.* **12** B6
Newtownbarry = Bunclody *Ireland* **12** D5
Newtownstewart *U.K.* **12** B4
Newville *U.S.A.* **114** F7
Nexon *France* **20** C5
Neya *Russia* **34** A6
Neyrīz *Iran* **71** D7
Neyshābūr *Iran* **71** B8
Nezhin = Nizhyn *Ukraine* **33** G6
Nezperce *U.S.A.* **108** C5
Nezvysko *Ukraine* **29** B10
Ngabang *Indonesia* **62** D3
Ngabordamlu, Tanjung *Indonesia* **63** F8
N'Gage *Angola* **84** F3
Ngala *Nigeria* **83** C7
Ngambé *Centre, Cameroon* **83** D7
Ngambé *Littoral, Cameroon* **83** E7
Ngami Depression *Botswana* **88** C3
Ngamo *Zimbabwe* **87** F2
Ngangala *Sudan* **81** G3
Nganglong Kangri *China* **69** C9

Ngao *Thailand* **64** C2
Ngaoundéré *Cameroon* **84** C2
Ngapara *N.Z.* **91** F3
Ngara *Tanzania* **86** C3
Ngawi *Indonesia* **63** G14
Ngcobo *S. Africa* **89** E4
Nghia Lo *Vietnam* **58** G5
Ngoboli *Sudan* **81** G3
Ngoma *Malawi* **87** E3
Ngomahura *Zimbabwe* **87** G3
Ngomba *Tanzania* **87** D3
Ngomeni, Ras *Kenya* **86** C5
Ngong *Kenya* **86** C4
Ngop *Sudan* **81** F3
Ngoring Hu *China* **60** C4
Ngorkou *Mali* **82** B4
Ngorongoro *Tanzania* **86** C4
Ngorongoro ◠ *Tanzania* **86** C4
Ngozi *Burundi* **86** C2
Ngudu *Tanzania* **86** C3
Nguigmi *Niger* **79** F8
Nguila *Cameroon* **83** E7
Nguiu *Australia* **92** B5
Ngukurr *Australia* **94** A1
Ngunga *Tanzania* **86** C3
Nguru *Nigeria* **83** C7
Nguru Mts. *Tanzania* **86** D4
Ngusi *Malawi* **87** E3
Nguyen Binh *Vietnam* **58** F5
Nha Trang *Vietnam* **65** F7
Nhacoongo *Mozam.* **89** C6
Nhamaabué *Mozam.* **87** F4
Nhamundá → *Brazil* **125** D7
Nhill *Australia* **95** F3
Nho Quan *Vietnam* **58** G5
Nhulunbuy *Australia* **94** A2
Nia-nia *Dem. Rep. of the Congo* **86** B2
Niafounké *Mali* **82** B4
Niagara Falls *Canada* **114** C5
Niagara Falls *U.S.A.* **114** C6
Niagara-on-the-Lake
 Canada **114** C5
Niah *Malaysia* **62** D4
Niamey *Niger* **83** C5
Niandan-Koro *Guinea* **82** C3
Nianforando *Guinea* **82** D2
Niangara
 Dem. Rep. of the Congo **86** B2
Niangbo *Ivory C.* **82** D3
Niangoloko *Burkina Faso* **82** C4
Niantic *U.S.A.* **115** E12
Niaro *Sudan* **81** E3
Nias *Indonesia* **62** D1
Niassa □ *Mozam.* **87** E4
Niassa ◠ *Mozam.* **87** E4
Nibāk *Si. Arabia* **71** E7
Nibe *Denmark* **11** H3
Nicaragua ■ *Cent. Amer.* **120** D2
Nicaragua, L. de *Nic.* **120** D2
Nicastro *Italy* **43** D9
Nice *France* **21** E11
Nice-Côte-d'Azur ✈ (NCE)
 France **21** E11
Niceville *U.S.A.* **117** F11
Nichicun, L. *Canada* **105** B5
Nichinan *Japan* **55** J5
Nicholás, Canal *W. Indies* **120** B3
Nicholasville *U.S.A.* **113** G11
Nichols *U.S.A.* **115** D8
Nicholson *Australia* **92** C4
Nicholson *U.S.A.* **115** E10
Nicholson → *Australia* **94** B2
Nicholson L. *Canada* **103** A8
Nicholson Ra. *Australia* **93** E2
Nicholville *U.S.A.* **115** B10
Nicobar Is. *Ind. Oc.* **3** D14
Nicola *Canada* **102** C4
Nicolls Town *Bahamas* **120** A4
Nicosia *Cyprus* **49** D12
Nicosia *Italy* **43** E7
Nicótera *Italy* **43** D8
Nicoya *Costa Rica* **120** D2
Nicoya, G. de *Costa Rica* **120** E3
Nicoya, Pen. de *Costa Rica* **120** E2
Nida *Lithuania* **30** C8
Nidd → *U.K.* **14** D6
Nidda *Germany* **25** E5
Nidda → *Germany* **25** E4
Nidwalden □ *Switz.* **25** J4
Nidzica *Poland* **31** E7
Niebüll *Germany* **24** A4
Nied → *Germany* **19** C13
Niederaula *Germany* **24** E5
Niederbayern □ *Germany* **25** G8
Niederbronn-les-Bains
 France **19** D14
Niedere Tauern *Austria* **26** D7
Niederlausitz *Germany* **24** D9
Niederösterreich □ *Austria* **26** C8
Niedersachsen □ *Germany* **24** C4
Niedersächsisches
 Wattenmeer ◠ *Germany* **24** B3
Niekerkshoop *S. Africa* **88** D3
Niellé *Ivory C.* **82** C3
Niemba *Dem. Rep. of the Congo* **86** D2
Niemen = Nemunas →
 Lithuania **30** C8

Niemodlin *Poland* **31** H4
Nienburg *Germany* **24** C5
Niepołomice *Poland* **31** H7
Niers → *Germany* **24** D1
Niesky *Germany* **24** D10
Nieszawa *Poland* **31** F5
Nieu Bethesda *S. Africa* **88** E3
Nieuw Amsterdam
 Suriname **125** B7
Nieuw Nickerie *Suriname* **125** B7
Nieuwoudtville *S. Africa* **88** E2
Nieuwpoort *Belgium* **17** C2
Nieves, Pico de las *Canary Is.* **48** G4
Nièvre □ *France* **19** E10
Niga *Mali* **82** C3
Niğde *Turkey* **72** D6
Niğde □ *Turkey* **72** D6
Nigel *S. Africa* **89** D4
Niger □ *Nigeria* **83** D6
Niger ■ *W. Afr.* **83** D6
Niger → *W. Afr.* **83** D6
Niger Delta *Africa* **83** E6
Nigeria ■ *W. Afr.* **83** D6
Nighasin *India* **69** E9
Nightcaps *N.Z.* **91** F2
Nigríta *Greece* **44** F7
Niğde *Turkey* **72** D6
Niğde □ *Turkey* **72** D6
Nigel *S. Africa* **89** D4
Nihon = Japan ■ *Asia* **55** G8
Nii-Jima *Japan* **55** G9
Niigata *Japan* **54** F9
Niigata □ *Japan* **55** F9
Niihama *Japan* **55** H6
Ni'ihau *U.S.A.* **106** b
Niimi *Japan* **55** G6
Niitsu *Japan* **54** F9
Níjar *Spain* **39** J2
Nijil *Jordan* **74** E4
Nijkerk *Neths.* **17** B5
Nijmegen *Neths.* **17** C5
Nijverdal *Neths.* **17** B6
Nīk Pey *Iran* **73** D13
Nike *Nigeria* **83** D6
Nikel *Russia* **8** B24
Nikiniki *Indonesia* **63** F6
Nikísiani *Greece* **45** F8
Nikíti *Greece* **45** F8
Nikki *Benin* **83** D5
Nikkō *Japan* **55** F9
Nikkō ◠ *Japan* **55** F9
Nikolayev = Mykolayiv
 Ukraine **33** J7
Nikolayevsk *Russia* **34** E7
Nikolayevsk-na-Amur
 Russia **53** D15
Nikolsk *Russia* **34** D8
Nikolskoye *Russia* **53** D17
Nikopol *Bulgaria* **45** C8
Nikopol *Ukraine* **33** J8
Nikópolis *Greece* **46** B2
Niksar *Turkey* **72** B7
Nīkshahr *Iran* **71** E9
Nikšić *Montenegro* **44** D2
Nîl, Nahr en → *Africa* **80** H7
Nîl el Abyad → *Sudan* **81** D3
Nîl el Azraq → *Sudan* **81** D3
Nila *Indonesia* **63** F7
Niland *U.S.A.* **111** M11
Nile = Nîl, Nahr en →
 Africa **80** H7
Nile Delta *Egypt* **80** H7
Niles *Mich., U.S.A.* **112** E10
Niles *Ohio, U.S.A.* **114** E4
Nilüfer → *Turkey* **45** F12
Nim Ka Thana *India* **68** F6
Nimach *India* **68** G6
Nimba, Mt. *Guinea* **82** D3
Nimbahera *India* **68** G6
Nîmes *France* **21** E8
Nimfaíon, Ákra = Pines,
 Akra *Greece* **45** F8
Nimmitabel *Australia* **95** F4
Nimule *Sudan* **81** G3
Nimule ◠ *Sudan* **81** G3
Nin *Croatia* **41** D12
Nīnawā *Iraq* **73** D10
Nīnawā □ *Iraq* **70** B4
Nindigully *Australia* **95** D4
Nineveh = Nīnawā *Iraq* **73** D10
Ning Xian *China* **56** G4
Ningaloo ◠ *Australia* **92** D1
Ning'an *China* **57** B15
Ningbo *China* **59** C13
Ningcheng *China* **57** D10
Ningde *China* **59** D12
Ningdu *China* **59** D10
Ninggang *China* **59** D9
Ningguo *China* **59** B12
Ninghai *China* **59** C13
Ninghua *China* **59** D11
Ningi *Nigeria* **83** C6
Ningjin *China* **56** F8
Ningjing Shan *China* **58** C2
Ningling *China* **56** G8
Ningming *China* **58** F6
Ningnan *China* **58** D4
Ningpo = Ningbo *China* **59** C13
Ningqiang *China* **56** H4
Ningshan *China* **56** H5

Ningsia Hui A.R. =
 Ningxia Huizu
 Zizhiqu □ *China* **56** F4
Ningwu *China* **56** E7
Ningxia Huizu Zizhiqu □
 China **56** F4
Ningxiang *China* **59** C9
Ningyang *China* **56** G9
Ningyuan *China* **59** E8
Ninh Binh *Vietnam* **58** G5
Ninh Giang *Vietnam* **64** B6
Ninh Hoa *Vietnam* **64** F7
Ninh Ma *Vietnam* **64** F7
Nini-Suhien ◠ *Ghana* **82** D4
Ninove *Belgium* **17** D4
Nioaque *Brazil* **127** A4
Niobrara *U.S.A.* **112** D5
Niobrara → *U.S.A.* **112** D4
Niokolo-Koba ◠ *Senegal* **82** C2
Niono *Mali* **82** C3
Nionsamoridougou *Guinea* **82** D3
Nioro du Rip *Senegal* **82** C1
Nioro du Sahel *Mali* **82** B3
Niort *France* **20** B3
Nipawin *Canada* **103** C8
Nipf jället *Sweden* **10** C6
Nipigon *Canada* **104** C2
Nipigon, L. *Canada* **104** C2
Nipishish L. *Canada* **105** B7
Nipissing, L. *Canada* **104** C4
Nipomo *U.S.A.* **111** K6
Nippon = Japan ■ *Asia* **55** G8
Nipton *U.S.A.* **111** K11
Niquelândia *Brazil* **125** F9
Nīr *Iran* **73** C12
Nirasaki *Japan* **55** G9
Nirmal *India* **66** K11
Nirmali *India* **69** F12
Niš *Serbia* **44** C5
Nisa *Portugal* **37** F3
Nišāb *Si. Arabia* **70** D5
Nişāb *Yemen* **75** E4
Nišava → *Serbia* **44** C5
Niscemi *Italy* **43** E7
Nishinomiya *Japan* **55** G7
Nishino'omote *Japan* **55** J5
Nishiwaki *Japan* **55** G7
Niška Banja *Serbia* **44** C6
Niskibi → *Canada* **104** A2
Nisko *Poland* **31** H9
Nisporeni *Moldova* **29** C13
Nisqually → *U.S.A.* **110** C4
Nissaki *Greece* **49** A3
Nissan → *Sweden* **11** H6
Nissíros *Greece* **47** E9
Nissum Bredning *Denmark* **11** H2
Nissum Fjord *Denmark* **11** H2
Nitchequon *Canada* **105** B5
Niterói *Brazil* **127** A7
Nith → *Canada* **114** C4
Nith → *U.K.* **13** F5
Nitmiluk ◠ *Australia* **92** B5
Nitra *Slovak Rep.* **27** C11
Nitra → *Slovak Rep.* **27** D11
Nitriansky □ *Slovak Rep.* **27** C11
Nittenau *Germany* **25** F8
Niue *Pac. Oc.* **97** J11
Niulan Jiang → *China* **58** D4
Niut *Indonesia* **62** D4
Niutou Shan *China* **59** C13
Niuzhuang *China* **57** D12
Nivala *Finland* **8** E21
Nivelles *Belgium* **17** D4
Nivernais *France* **19** E10
Niverville *Canada* **103** D9
Niwas *India* **69** H9
Nixa *U.S.A.* **112** G7
Nixon *U.S.A.* **116** G6
Nizamabad *India* **66** K11
Nizamghat *India* **67** E19
Nizip *Turkey* **72** D7
Nízké Tatry *Slovak Rep.* **27** C12
Nízké Tatry ◠ *Slovak Rep.* **27** C12
Nízký Jeseník *Czech Rep.* **27** B10
Nizwá *Oman* **75** C6
Nizza Monferrato *Italy* **40** D5
Njakwa *Malawi* **87** E3
Njanji *Zambia* **87** E3
Njazidja = Grande Comore
 Comoros Is. **85** a
Njegoš *Montenegro* **44** D2

Njinjo *Tanzania* **87** D4
Njombe *Tanzania* **87** D3
Njombe → *Tanzania* **86** D4
Njurundabommen *Sweden* **10** B11
Nkambe *Cameroon* **83** D7
Nkana *Zambia* **87** E2
Nkandla *S. Africa* **89** D5
Nkawkaw *Ghana* **83** D4
Nkayi *Zimbabwe* **87** F2
Nkhotakota *Malawi* **87** E3
Nkhotakota □ *Malawi* **87** E3
Nkongsamba *Cameroon* **83** E6
Nkurenkuru *Namibia* **88** B2
Nkwanta *Ghana* **82** D4
Nmai → *Burma* **58** F2
Noakhali = Maijdi *Bangla.* **67** H17
Nobel *Canada* **114** A4
Nobeoka *Japan* **55** H5
Noblejas *Spain* **36** F7
Noblesville *U.S.A.* **112** E10
Noboribetsu *Japan* **54** C10
Noccundra *Australia* **95** D3
Noce → *Italy* **40** B7
Nocera Inferiore *Italy* **43** B7
Nocera Umbra *Italy* **41** E9
Noci *Italy* **43** B10
Nocona *U.S.A.* **116** E6
Nocrich *Romania* **29** E9
Noda *Japan* **55** G9
Nogales *Mexico* **118** A2
Nogales *U.S.A.* **109** L8
Nogaro *France* **20** E3
Nogat → *Poland* **30** E5
Nōgata *Japan* **55** H5
Nogent *France* **19** D12
Nogent-le-Rotrou *France* **18** D7
Nogent-sur-Seine *France* **19** D10
Noggerup *Australia* **93** F2
Noginsk *Moskva, Russia* **32** E10
Noginsk *Tunguska, Russia* **53** C10
Nogoa → *Australia* **94** C4
Nogoyá *Argentina* **126** C4
Nógrád □ *Hungary* **28** C4
Noguera Pallaresa → *Spain* **38** D5
Noguera Ribagorzana →
 Spain **38** D5
Nohar *India* **68** E6
Nohfelden *Germany* **25** F3
Nohta *India* **69** H8
Noia *Spain* **36** C2
Noire, Montagne *France* **20** E6
Noires, Mts. *France* **18** D3
Noirétable *France* **20** C7
Noirmoutier, Î. de *France* **18** F4
Noirmoutier-en-l'Île *France* **18** F4
Nojane *Botswana* **88** C3
Nojima-Zaki *Japan* **55** G9
Nok Kundi *Pakistan* **66** E3
Nok Ta Phao, Ko *Thailand* **65** b
Nokaneng *Botswana* **88** B3
Nokia *Finland* **32** B2
Nokomis *Canada* **103** C8
Nokomis L. *Canada* **103** B8
Nola *C.A.R.* **84** D3
Nola *Italy* **43** B7
Nolay *France* **19** F11
Noli, C. di *Italy* **40** D5
Nolinsk *Russia* **34** B9
Noma Omuramba →
 Namibia **88** B3
Nombre de Dios *Panama* **120** E4
Nome *U.S.A.* **106** a
Nomo-Zaki *Japan* **55** H4
Nomuka *Tonga* **91** c
Nomuka Group *Tonga* **91** c
Nonacho L. *Canada* **103** A7
Nonancourt *France* **18** D8
Nonda *Australia* **94** C3
None *Italy* **40** D4
Nong Chang *Thailand* **64** E2
Nong Het *Laos* **64** C4
Nong Khai *Thailand* **64** D4
Nong'an *China* **57** B13
Ngongoma *S. Africa* **89** D5
Nongsa *Indonesia* **65** d
Nonoava *Mexico* **118** B3
Nonsan *S. Korea* **57** F14
Nonthaburi *Thailand* **64** F3
Nontron *France* **20** C4
Nonza *France* **21** F13
Noonamah *Australia* **92** B5
Noondie, L. *Australia* **93** E2
Noord Brabant □ *Neths.* **17** C5
Noord Holland □ *Neths.* **17** B4
Noordbeveland *Neths.* **17** C3
Noordoostpolder *Neths.* **17** B5
Noordwijk *Neths.* **17** B4
Noosa Heads *Australia* **95** D5
Nootka I. *Canada* **102** D3
Nopiming ◠ *Canada* **103** C9
Nora *Eritrea* **81** D5
Nora *Sweden* **10** E9
Nóra → *Italy* **40** C6
Noralee *Canada* **102** C3
Noranda =
 Rouyn-Noranda *Canada* **104** C4
Norberg *Sweden* **10** D9
Nórcia *Italy* **41** F10

Norco *U.S.A.* **111** M9
Nord □ *Cameroon* **83** D7
Nord □ *France* **19** B10
Nord-Kivu □
 Dem. Rep. of the Congo **86** C2
Nord-Ostsee-Kanal *Germany* **24** A5
Nord-Ouest □ *Cameroon* **83** D7
Nord-Pas-de-Calais □ *France* **19** B9
Nordaustlandet *Svalbard* **4** B9
Nordborg *Denmark* **11** J3
Nordby *Denmark* **11** J2
Norddeich *Germany* **24** B3
Nordegg *Canada* **102** C5
Norden *Germany* **24** B3
Nordenham *Germany* **24** B4
Norderney *Germany* **24** B3
Norderstedt *Germany* **24** B6
Nordfjord *Norway* **8** F11
Nordfriesische Inseln
 Germany **24** A4
Nordhausen *Germany* **24** D6
Nordhorn *Germany* **24** C3
Norðoyar *Færoe Is.* **8** E9
Nördingen-Nol *Sweden* **11** G6
Nordingrå *Sweden* **10** B12
Nordjylland □ *Denmark* **11** G3
Nordkapp *Norway* **8** A21
Nordkapp *Svalbard* **4** A9
Nordkinnhalvøya *Norway* **8** A22
Nördlicher Teutoburger
 Wald-Wiehengebirge ◠
 Germany **24** C4
Nördlingen *Germany* **25** G6
Nordrhein-Westfalen □
 Germany **24** D3
Nordstrand *Germany* **24** A4
Nordvik *Russia* **53** B12
Nore → *Ireland* **12** D4
Norfolk *Canada* **114** D4
Norfolk *Nebr., U.S.A.* **112** D5
Norfolk *Va., U.S.A.* **113** G15
Norfolk □ *U.K.* **15** E8
Norfolk Broads ◠ *U.K.* **15** E9
Norfolk I. *Pac. Oc.* **90** D9
Norfolk Ridge *Pac. Oc.* **96** K8
Norfork L. *U.S.A.* **116** C8
Norge = Norway ■ *Europe* **8** E14
Norilsk *Russia* **53** C9
Norma, Mt. *Australia* **94** C3
Normal *U.S.A.* **112** E9
Norman *U.S.A.* **116** D6
Norman → *Australia* **94** B3
Norman Wells *Canada* **100** C7
Normanby → *Australia* **94** A3
Normandie-Maine □ *France* **18** D6
Normandin *Canada* **104** C5
Normanhurst, Mt. *Australia* **93** E3
Normanton *Australia* **94** B3
Normétal *Canada* **104** C4
Norquay *Canada* **103** C8
Norquinco *Argentina* **128** E2
Norra Dellen *Sweden* **10** C10
Norra Kvill ◠ *Sweden* **11** G9
Norra Ulvön *Sweden* **10** A12
Norrahammar *Sweden* **11** G8
Norrbottens län □ *Sweden* **8** C19
Nørre Åby *Denmark* **11** J3
Nørre Alslev *Denmark* **11** K5
Nørresundby *Denmark* **11** G3
Norrhult-Klavreström
 Sweden **11** G9
Norris Point *Canada* **105** C8
Norristown *U.S.A.* **115** F9
Norrköping *Sweden* **11** F10
Norrland *Sweden* **8** E16
Norrsundet *Sweden* **10** D11
Norrtälje *Sweden* **10** E12
Norseman *Australia* **93** F3
Norsk *Russia* **53** D14
Norte, Pta. del *Canary Is.* **48** G2
Norte, Serra do *Brazil* **124** F7
North, C. *Canada* **105** C7
North Adams *U.S.A.* **115** D11
North America **98** F10
North Arm *Canada* **102** A5
North Augusta *U.S.A.* **117** E14
North Australian Basin
 Ind. Oc. **96** J3
North Ayrshire □ *U.K.* **13** F4
North Bass I. *U.S.A.* **114** E2
North Battleford *Canada* **103** C7
North Bay *Canada* **104** C4
North Belcher Is. *Canada* **104** A4
North Bend *Oreg., U.S.A.* **108** E1
North Bend *Pa., U.S.A.* **114** E7
North Bend *Wash., U.S.A.* **110** C5
North Bennington *U.S.A.* **115** D11
North Berwick *U.K.* **13** E6
North Berwick *U.S.A.* **115** C14
North, C. *Canada* **105** C7
North, C. *N.Z.* **91** A4
North Canadian → *U.S.A.* **116** D7
North Canton *U.S.A.* **114** F3
North Cape = Nordkapp
 Norway **8** A21
North Caribou L. *Canada* **104** B1
North Carolina □ *U.S.A.* **117** D15

North Cascades △ *U.S.A.* **108** B3
North Channel *Canada* **104** C3
North Channel *U.K.* **13** F3
North Charleston *U.S.A.* **117** E15
North Chicago *U.S.A.* **112** D10
North Creek *U.S.A.* **115** C11
North Dakota □ *U.S.A.* **112** B3
North Downs *U.K.* **15** F8
North East *U.S.A.* **114** D5
North East Frontier
 Agency = Arunachal
 Pradesh □ *India* **67** F19
North East Lincolnshire □
 U.K. **14** D7
North Eastern □ *Kenya* **86** B5
North Esk → *U.K.* **13** E6
North European Plain
 Europe **6** E10
North Foreland *U.K.* **15** F9
North Fork *U.S.A.* **110** H7
North Fork American →
 U.S.A. **110** G5
North Fork Feather →
 U.S.A. **110** F5
North Fork Grand →
 U.S.A. **112** C3
North Fork Red → *U.S.A.* **116** D5
North Frisian Is. =
 Nordfriesische Inseln
 Germany **24** A4
North Gower *Canada* **115** A9
North Hd. *Australia* **93** F1
North Henik L. *Canada* **103** A9
North Highlands *U.S.A.* **110** G5
North Horr *Kenya* **86** B4
North I. *Kenya* **86** B4
North I. *N.Z.* **91** C5
North I. *Seychelles* **85** b
North Kingsville *U.S.A.* **114** E4
North Kitui ◠ *Kenya* **86** C4
North Knife → *Canada* **103** B10
North Koel → *India* **69** G10
North Korea ■ *Asia* **57** E14
North Lakhimpur *India* **67** F19
North Lanarkshire □ *U.K.* **13** F5
North Las Vegas *U.S.A.* **111** J11
North Lincolnshire □ *U.K.* **14** D7
North Little Rock *U.S.A.* **116** D8
North Loup → *U.S.A.* **112** E4
North Luangwa △ *Zambia* **87** E3
North Magnetic Pole
 Canada **101** B9
North Mankato *U.S.A.* **112** C6
North Minch *U.K.* **13** C3
North Moose L. *Canada* **103** C8
North Myrtle Beach *U.S.A.* **117** E15
North Nahanni → *Canada* **102** A4
North Olmsted *U.S.A.* **114** E3
North Ossetia □ *Russia* **35** J7
North Pagai, I. = Pagai
 Utara, Pulau *Indonesia* **62** E2
North Palisade *U.S.A.* **110** H8
North Platte *U.S.A.* **112** E3
North Platte → *U.S.A.* **112** E3
North Pole *Arctic* **4** A
North Portal *Canada* **103** D8
North Powder *U.S.A.* **108** D5
North Pt. *Barbados* **121** g
North Pt. *Trin. & Tob.* **125** J16
North Pt. *U.S.A.* **114** A1
North Rhine Westphalia =
 Nordrhein-Westfalen □
 Germany **24** D3
North River *Canada* **105** B8
North Ronaldsay *U.K.* **13** B6
North Saskatchewan →
 Canada **103** C7
North Sea *Europe* **6** D6
North Seal → *Canada* **103** B9
North Somerset □ *U.K.* **15** F5
North Sydney *Canada* **105** C7
North Syracuse *U.S.A.* **115** C8
North Taranaki Bight *N.Z.* **91** C5
North Thompson →
 Canada **102** C4
North Tonawanda *U.S.A.* **114** C6
North Troy *U.S.A.* **115** B12
North Twin I. *Canada* **104** B4
North Tyne → *U.K.* **14** B5
North Uist *U.K.* **13** D1
North Vancouver *Canada* **110** A3
North Vernon *U.S.A.* **113** F11
North Wabasca L. *Canada* **102** B6
North Walsham *U.K.* **14** E9
North West = Severo-
 Zapadnyy □ *Russia* **52** C4
North-West □ *S. Africa* **88** D4
North West C. *Australia* **92** D1
North West Frontier □
 Pakistan **68** C4
North West Highlands *U.K.* **13** D4
North West River *Canada* **105** B7
North Western □ *Zambia* **87** E2
North Wildwood *U.S.A.* **113** F16
North York Moors *U.K.* **14** C7
North York Moors △ *U.K.* **14** C7
North Yorkshire □ *U.K.* **14** C6

Northallerton *U.K.* **14** C6
Northam *Australia* **93** F2
Northam *S. Africa* **88** C4
Northampton *Australia* **93** E1
Northampton *U.K.* **15** E7
Northampton *Mass., U.S.A.* **115** D12
Northampton *Pa., U.S.A.* **115** F9
Northamptonshire □ *U.K.* **15** E7
Northbridge *U.S.A.* **115** D13
Northcliffe *Australia* **93** F2
Northeast Pacific Basin *Pac. Oc.* **97** D13
Northeast Providence Chan. *W. Indies* **120** A4
Northeim *Germany* **24** D6
Northern = Limpopo □ *S. Africa* **89** C4
Northern □ *Ghana* **83** D4
Northern □ *Malawi* **87** E3
Northern □ *S. Leone* **82** D2
Northern □ *Zambia* **87** E3
Northern Areas □ *Pakistan* **69** A5
Northern Cape □ *S. Africa* **88** D3
Northern Circars *India* **67** L13
Northern Indian L. *Canada* **103** B9
Northern Ireland □ *U.K.* **12** B5
Northern Lau Group *Fiji* **91** a
Northern Light L. *Canada* **104** C1
Northern Marianas ☒ *Pac. Oc.* **96** F6
Northern Province □ *S. Africa* **89** C4
Northern Range *Trin. & Tob.* **125** K15
Northern Sporades = Vóreioi Sporádhes *Greece* **46** B5
Northern Territory □ *Australia* **92** D5
Northfield *Minn., U.S.A.* **112** C7
Northfield *Vt., U.S.A.* **115** B12
Northland □ *N.Z.* **91** A4
Northome *U.S.A.* **112** B6
Northport *Ala., U.S.A.* **117** E11
Northport *Wash., U.S.A.* **108** B5
Northumberland □ *U.K.* **14** B6
Northumberland, C. *Australia* **95** F3
Northumberland Is. *Australia* **94** C4
Northumberland Str. *Canada* **105** C7
Northville *U.S.A.* **115** C10
Northwest Pacific Basin *Pac. Oc.* **96** D8
Northwest Providence Channel *W. Indies* **120** A4
Northwest Territories □ *Canada* **100** C8
Northwich *U.K.* **14** D5
Northwood *Iowa, U.S.A.* **112** D7
Northwood *N. Dak., U.S.A.* **112** B5
Norton *U.S.A.* **112** F4
Norton *Zimbabwe* **87** F3
Norton Sd. *U.S.A.* **106** a
Nortorf *Germany* **24** A5
Norwalk *Calif., U.S.A.* **111** M8
Norwalk *Conn., U.S.A.* **115** E11
Norwalk *Iowa, U.S.A.* **112** C7
Norwalk *Ohio, U.S.A.* **114** E2
Norway *Maine, U.S.A.* **113** C18
Norway *Mich., U.S.A.* **112** C10
Norway ■ *Europe* **8** E14
Norway House *Canada* **103** C9
Norwegian B. *Canada* **101** B11
Norwegian Basin *Atl. Oc.* **4** C7
Norwegian Sea *Atl. Oc.* **6** B6
Norwich *Canada* **114** D4
Norwich *U.K.* **15** E9
Norwich *Conn., U.S.A.* **115** E12
Norwich *N.Y., U.S.A.* **115** D9
Norwood *Canada* **114** B7
Norwood *U.S.A.* **115** B10
Nosappu-Misaki *Japan* **54** C12
Noshiro *Japan* **54** D10
Nosivka *Ukraine* **33** G6
Nosovka = Nosivka *Ukraine* **33** G6
Noşratābād *Iran* **71** D8
Noss Hd. *U.K.* **13** C5
Nossebro *Sweden* **11** F6
Nossob → *S. Africa* **88** D3
Nossombougou *Mali* **82** C3
Nosy Barren *Madag.* **89** H8
Nosy Bé *Madag.* **85** G9
Nosy Boraha *Madag.* **89** B8
Nosy Lava *Madag.* **89** A8
Nosy Varika *Madag.* **89** C8
Noteć → *Poland* **31** F2
Notikewin → *Canada* **102** B5
Notio Aigaio = Notíos Aiyaíon □ **47** E7
Notíos Aiyaíon □ **47** E7
Notíos Evvoïkos Kólpos *Greece* **46** C5
Noto *Italy* **43** F8
Noto, G. di *Italy* **43** F8
Notodden *Norway* **9** G13
Notre Dame B. *Canada* **105** C8

Notre-Dame-de-Koartac = Quaqtaq *Canada* **101** C13
Notre-Dame-des-Bois *Canada* **115** A13
Notre-Dame-d'Ivugivic = Ivujivik *Canada* **101** C12
Notre-Dame-du-Nord *Canada* **104** C4
Notsé *Togo* **83** D5
Nottawasaga B. *Canada* **114** B4
Nottaway → *Canada* **104** B4
Nottingham *U.K.* **14** E6
Nottingham, City of □ *U.K.* **14** E6
Nottingham I. *Canada* **101** C12
Nottinghamshire □ *U.K.* **14** D6
Nottoway → *U.S.A.* **113** G15
Notwane → *Botswana* **88** C4
Nouâdhibou *Mauritania* **78** D2
Nouâdhibou, Râs *Mauritania* **78** D2
Nouakchott *Mauritania* **82** B1
Nouâmghâr *Mauritania* **82** B1
Nouméa *N. Cal.* **90** D9
Nouna *Burkina Faso* **82** C4
Noupoort *S. Africa* **88** E3
Nouveau Comptoir = Wemindji *Canada* **104** B4
Nouvelle Amsterdam, Î. *Ind. Oc.* **3** F13
Nouvelle-Calédonie = New Caledonia ☒ *Pac. Oc.* **90** D9
Nouzonville *France* **19** C11
Nová Baňa *Slovak Rep.* **27** C11
Nová Bystřice *Czech Rep.* **26** B8
Nova Casa Nova *Brazil* **125** E10
Nova Esperança *Brazil* **127** A5
Nova Friburgo *Brazil* **127** A7
Nova Gaia = Cambundi-Catembo *Angola* **84** G3
Nova Gorica *Slovenia* **41** C10
Nova Gradiška *Croatia* **28** E2
Nova Iguaçu *Brazil* **127** A7
Nova Iorque *Brazil* **125** E10
Nova Kakhovka *Ukraine* **33** J7
Nova Lamego *Guinea-Biss.* **82** C2
Nova Lima *Brazil* **127** A7
Nova Lusitânia *Mozam.* **87** F3
Nova Mambone *Mozam.* **89** C6
Nova Odesa *Ukraine* **33** J6
Nová Paka *Czech Rep.* **26** A8
Nova Pavova *Serbia* **28** F5
Nova Scotia □ *Canada* **105** C7
Nova Siri *Italy* **43** B9
Nova Sofala *Mozam.* **89** C5
Nova Ushytsya *Ukraine* **29** B12
Nova Varoš *Serbia* **44** C3
Nova Venécia *Brazil* **125** G10
Nova Zagora *Bulgaria* **45** D10
Novaci *Macedonia* **44** E5
Novaci *Romania* **29** E8
Novafeltria *Italy* **41** E9
Novannenskiy = Novoannenskiy *Russia* **34** E6
Novar *Canada* **114** A5
Novara *Italy* **40** C5
Novato *U.S.A.* **110** G4
Novaya Kakhovka = Nova Kakhovka *Ukraine* **33** J7
Novaya Kazanka = Zhangaqala *Kazakhstan* **35** F9
Novaya Ladoga *Russia* **32** B7
Novaya Lyalya *Russia* **52** D7
Novaya Sibir, Ostrov *Russia* **53** B16
Novaya Zemlya *Russia* **52** B6
Nové Mesto *Slovak Rep.* **27** C10
Nové Město na Moravě *Czech Rep.* **26** B9
Nové Město nad Metují *Czech Rep.* **27** A9
Nové Zámky *Slovak Rep.* **27** C11
Novelda *Spain* **39** G4
Novellara *Italy* **40** D7
Noventa Vicentina *Italy* **41** C8
Novgorod *Russia* **32** C6
Novgorod □ *Russia* **32** C7
Novgorod-Severskiy = Novhorod-Siverskyy *Ukraine* **33** G7
Novhorod-Siverskyy *Ukraine* **33** G7
Novi Bečej *Serbia* **28** E5
Novi Iskar *Bulgaria* **44** D7
Novi Kneževac *Serbia* **28** D5
Novi Lígure *Italy* **40** D5
Novi Pazar *Bulgaria* **45** C11
Novi Pazar *Serbia* **44** C4
Novi Sad *Serbia* **28** E4
Novi Slankamen *Serbia* **28** E5
Novi Travnik *Bos.-H.* **28** F2
Novi Vinodolski *Croatia* **41** C11
Novigrad *Istra, Croatia* **41** C10
Novigrad *Zadar, Croatia* **41** D12
Novigradsko More *Croatia* **41** D12
Novo Hamburgo *Brazil* **127** B5
Novo Ivanivka *Ukraine* **29** E14
Novo Mesto *Slovenia* **41** C12
Novo Miloševo *Serbia* **28** E5
Novo Remanso *Brazil* **125** E10
Novoaleksandrovsk *Russia* **35** H5
Novoaleksandrovskaya = Novoaleksandrovsk *Russia* **35** H5

Novoaltaysk *Russia* **52** D9
Novoannenskiy *Russia* **34** E6
Novoazovsk *Ukraine* **33** J10
Novocheboksarsk *Russia* **34** B8
Novocherkassk *Russia* **35** G5
Novodevichye *Russia* **34** D9
Novogrudok = Navahrudak *Belarus* **23** B13
Novohrad-Volynskyy *Ukraine* **23** C14
Novokachalinsk *Russia* **54** B5
Novokhopersk *Russia* **34** E5
Novokuybyshevsk *Russia* **34** D9
Novokuznetsk *Russia* **52** D9
Novolazarevskaya *Antarctica* **5** D3
Novomirgorod *Ukraine* **33** H6
Novomoskovsk *Russia* **32** E10
Novomoskovsk *Ukraine* **33** H8
Novopolotsk = Navapolatsk *Belarus* **32** E5
Novorossiysk *Russia* **33** K9
Novorybnoye *Russia* **53** B11
Novorzhev *Russia* **32** D5
Novosej *Albania* **44** E4
Novoselytsya *Ukraine* **29** B11
Novoshakhtinsk *Russia* **33** J10
Novosibirsk *Russia* **52** D9
Novosibirskiye Ostrova *Russia* **53** B15
Novosil *Russia* **33** F9
Novosokolniki *Russia* **32** D6
Novotitarovskaya *Russia* **35** H4
Novotroitsk *Russia* **52** D6
Novoukrayinka *Ukraine* **33** H6
Novouljanovsk *Russia* **34** C9
Novouzensk *Russia* **34** E9
Novovolynsk *Ukraine* **31** H11
Novovoronezhskiy *Russia* **33** G10
Novoyavoriske *Ukraine* **31** J10
Novozybkov *Russia* **33** F6
Novska *Croatia* **41** C14
Novvy Urengoy *Russia* **52** C8
Nový Bor *Czech Rep.* **26** A7
Nový Bug = Novyy Buh *Ukraine* **33** J7
Nový Bydžov *Czech Rep.* **26** A8
Novy Dvor *Belarus* **31** F11
Novy Dwór Mazowiecki *Poland* **31** F7
Nový Jičín *Czech Rep.* **27** B11
Novyy Afon *Georgia* **35** J5
Novyy Buh *Ukraine* **33** J7
Novyy Oskol *Russia* **33** G9
Novyy Port *Russia* **52** C8
Now Shahr *Iran* **71** B6
Nowa Deba *Poland* **31** H8
Nowa Ruda *Poland* **31** H3
Nowa Sarzyna *Poland* **31** H9
Nowa Sól *Poland* **31** G2
Nowata *U.S.A.* **116** C7
Nowbarān *Iran* **71** C6
Nowe *Poland* **30** E5
Nowe Miasteczko *Poland* **31** G2
Nowe Miasto *Poland* **31** G7
Nowe Miasto Lubawskie *Poland* **30** E6
Nowe Skalmierzyce *Poland* **31** G4
Nowe Warpno *Poland* **30** E1
Nowghāb *Iran* **71** C8
Nowgong *Assam, India* **67** F18
Nowgong *Mad. P., India* **69** G8
Nowogard *Poland* **30** E2
Nowogród *Poland* **31** E8
Nowogród Bobrzanski *Poland* **31** G2
Nowogrodziec *Poland* **31** G2
Nowra *Australia* **95** E5
Nowshera *Pakistan* **66** C8
Nowy Dwór Gdański *Poland* **30** D6
Nowy Sącz *Poland* **31** J7
Nowy Staw *Poland* **30** D6
Nowy Targ *Poland* **31** J7
Nowy Tomyśl *Poland* **31** F3
Nowy Wiśnicz *Poland* **31** J7
Noxen *U.S.A.* **115** E8
Noyabr'sk *Russia* **52** C8
Noyant *France* **18** E7
Noyers *France* **19** E10
Noyon *France* **19** C10
Noyon *Mongolia* **56** C2
Nozay *France* **18** E5
Nqutu *S. Africa* **89** D5
Nsanje *Malawi* **87** F4
Nsawam *Ghana* **83** D4
Nsomba *Zambia* **87** E2
Nsukka *Nigeria* **83** D6
Ntui *Cameroon* **83** E7
Nu Jiang → *China* **58** E2
Nu Shan *China* **58** E2
Nuba Mts. = Nubah, Jibalan *Sudan* **81** E3
Nubah, Jibalan *Sudan* **81** E3
Nubia *Africa* **76** D7
Nubian Desert = Nûbîya, Es Sahrâ en *Sudan* **80** D3
Nûbîya, Es Sahrâ en *Sudan* **80** C3
Nubledo *Spain* **36** B5

Nuboai *Indonesia* **63** E9
Nubra → *India* **69** B7
Nucet *Romania* **28** D7
Nueces → *U.S.A.* **116** H6
Nueltin L. *Canada* **103** A9
Nueva Carteya *Spain* **37** H6
Nueva Ciudad Guerrero *Mexico* **119** B5
Nueva Gerona *Cuba* **120** B3
Nueva Palmira *Uruguay* **126** C4
Nueva Rosita *Mexico* **118** B4
Nueva San Salvador *El Salv.* **120** D2
Nueva Tabarca *Spain* **39** G4
Nuéve de Julio *Argentina* **126** D3
Nuevitas *Cuba* **120** B4
Nuevo, G. *Argentina* **128** E4
Nuevo Casas Grandes *Mexico* **118** A3
Nuevo Laredo *Mexico* **119** B5
Nuevo León □ *Mexico* **118** C5
Nuevo Rocafuerte *Ecuador* **124** D3
Nugget Pt. *N.Z.* **91** G2
Nugrus, Gebel *Egypt* **80** C3
Nuhaka *N.Z.* **91** C6
Nuhuda *Iraq* **73** F10
Nukey Bluff *Australia* **95** E2
Nukhayb *Iraq* **73** F10
Nukheila *Sudan* **80** D2
Nuku Hiva *French Polynesia* **97** H13
Nuku'alofa *Tonga* **91** c
Nukus *Uzbekistan* **52** E6
Nules *Spain* **38** F4
Nullagine *Australia* **92** D3
Nullagine → *Australia* **92** D3
Nullarbor *Australia* **93** F5
Nullarbor △ *Australia* **93** F2
Nullarbor Plain *Australia* **93** F4
Numalla, L. *Australia* **95** D3
Numan *Nigeria* **83** D7
Numata *Japan* **55** F9
Numatinna → *Sudan* **81** F2
Numaykoos Lake △ *Canada* **103** B9
Numazu *Japan* **55** G9
Numbulwar *Australia* **94** A2
Numfoor *Indonesia* **63** E8
Numurkah *Australia* **95** F4
Nunaksaluk I. *Canada* **105** A7
Nunap Isua *Greenland* **98** D15
Nunavut □ *Canada* **101** C11
Nunda *U.S.A.* **114** D7
Nuneaton *U.K.* **15** E6
Nungarin *Australia* **93** F2
Nungo *Mozam.* **87** E4
Nungwe *Tanzania* **86** C3
Nunivak I. *U.S.A.* **106** a
Nunkun *India* **69** C7
Núoro *Italy* **42** B2
Nūrābād *Iran* **71** E8
Nure → *Italy* **40** C6
Nuremberg = Nürnberg *Germany* **25** F7
Nuri *Mexico* **118** B3
Nuri *Sudan* **80** D3
Nuriootpa *Australia* **95** E2
Nuristān □ *Afghan.* **66** B7
Nurlat *Russia* **34** C10
Nurmes *Finland* **8** E23
Nürnberg *Germany* **25** F7
Nurpur *Pakistan* **68** D4
Nurra, La *Italy* **42** B1
Nurran, L. = Terewah, L. *Australia* **95** D4
Nurrari Lakes *Australia* **93** E5
Nurri *Italy* **42** C2
Nürtingen *Germany* **25** G5
Nurzec → *Poland* **31** F9
Nus *Italy* **40** C4
Nusa Barung *Indonesia* **63** H15
Nusa Dua *Indonesia* **63** K18
Nusa Kambangan *Indonesia* **63** G13
Nusa Tenggara Barat □ *Indonesia* **62** F5
Nusa Tenggara Timur □ *Indonesia* **63** F6
Nusaybin *Turkey* **73** D9
Nushki *Pakistan* **68** E2
Nuuk *Greenland* **99** C14
Nuupere, Pte. *Moorea* **91** d
Nuwakot *Nepal* **69** E10
Nuwayb'ī, W. an → *Si. Arabia* **74** F3
Nuweiba' *Egypt* **70** D2
Nuwerus *S. Africa* **88** E2
Nuweveldberge *S. Africa* **88** E3
Nuyts, Pt. *Australia* **93** G2
Nuyts Arch. *Australia* **95** E1
Nxai Pan △ *Botswana* **88** B3
Nxau-Nxau *Botswana* **88** B3
Nyaake *Liberia* **82** E3
Nyabing *Australia* **93** F2
Nyack *U.S.A.* **115** E11
Nyagan *Russia* **52** C7
Nyahanga *Tanzania* **86** C3
Nyahua *Tanzania* **86** D3
Nyahururu *Kenya* **86** B4
Nyaingêntanglha Shan *China* **60** D4

Nyakanazi *Tanzania* **86** C3
Nyakrom *Ghana* **83** D4
Nyamandhlovu *Zimbabwe* **87** F2
Nyambiti *Tanzania* **86** C3
Nyamlell *Sudan* **81** F2
Nyamwaga *Tanzania* **86** C3
Nyandekwa *Tanzania* **86** C3
Nyanding → *Sudan* **81** F3
Nyandoma *Russia* **32** B11
Nyanga △ *Zimbabwe* **87** F3
Nyangana *Namibia* **88** B3
Nyanguge *Tanzania* **86** C3
Nyankpala *Ghana* **83** D4
Nyanza *Rwanda* **86** C2
Nyanza □ *Kenya* **86** C3
Nyanza-Lac *Burundi* **86** C2
Nyaponges *Sudan* **81** F3
Nyasa, L. = Malawi, L. *Africa* **87** E3
Nyasvizh *Belarus* **23** B14
Nyazura *Zimbabwe* **87** F3
Nyazwidzi → *Zimbabwe* **87** G3
Nyborg *Denmark* **11** J4
Nybro *Sweden* **11** H9
Nyda *Russia* **52** C8
Nyeri *Kenya* **86** C4
Nyerol *Sudan* **81** F3
Nyhammar *Sweden* **10** D8
Nyika △ *Malawi* **87** E3
Nyinahin *Ghana* **82** D4
Nyíradony *Hungary* **28** C6
Nyírbátor *Hungary* **28** C7
Nyíregyháza *Hungary* **28** C6
Nyiru, Mt. *Kenya* **86** B4
Nykarleby = Uusikaarlepyy *Finland* **8** E20
Nykøbing *Nordjylland, Denmark* **11** H2
Nykøbing *Sjælland, Denmark* **11** K5
Nykøbing *Sjælland, Denmark* **11** J5
Nyköping *Sweden* **11** F11
Nykroppa *Sweden* **10** E8
Nykvarn *Sweden* **10** E11
Nyland *Sweden* **10** A11
Nylstroom = Modimolle *S. Africa* **89** C4
Nymagee *Australia* **95** E4
Nymboida → *Australia* **95** D5
Nymburk *Czech Rep.* **26** A8
Nynäshamn *Sweden* **11** F11
Nyngan *Australia* **95** E4
Nyoma Rap *India* **69** C8
Nyoman = Nemunas → *Lithuania* **30** C8
Nyon *Switz.* **25** J2
Nyons *France* **21** D9
Nyou *Burkina Faso* **83** C4
Nysa *Poland* **31** H4
Nysa → *Europe* **24** C10
Nysa Kłodzka → *Poland* **31** H4
Nysäter *Sweden* **10** E6
Nyssa *U.S.A.* **108** E5
Nystad = Uusikaupunki *Finland* **32** B1
Nysted *Denmark* **11** K5
Nyunzu *Dem. Rep. of the Congo* **86** D2
Nyurba *Russia* **53** C12
Nyzhankovychi *Ukraine* **31** J9
Nyzhnohirskyy *Ukraine* **33** K8
Nyzhny Vorota *Ukraine* **28** B8
Nzébéla *Guinea* **82** D3
Nzega *Tanzania* **86** C3
Nzérékoré *Guinea* **82** D3
Nzeto *Angola* **84** F2
Nzilo, Chutes de *Dem. Rep. of the Congo* **87** E2
N'zo → *Ivory C.* **82** D3
N'zo → *Ivory C.* **82** D3
Nzubuka *Tanzania* **86** C3
Nzwani = Anjouan *Comoros Is.* **85** a

O

O Barco *Spain* **36** C4
O Carballiño *Spain* **36** C2
O Corgo *Spain* **36** C3
O Le Pupū Pu'e △ *Samoa* **91** b
O Pino *Spain* **36** C2
O Porriño *Spain* **36** C2
Ō-Shima *Hokkaidō, Japan* **54** D10
Ō-Shima *Shizuoka, Japan* **55** G9
Oa, Mull of *U.K.* **13** F2
Oacoma *U.S.A.* **112** D4
Oahe, L. *U.S.A.* **112** C3
Oahe Dam *U.S.A.* **112** C3
O'ahu *U.S.A.* **106** b
Oak Harbor *U.S.A.* **110** B4
Oak Hill *U.S.A.* **113** G13
Oak Island *U.S.A.* **112** B8
Oak Ridge *U.S.A.* **117** C12
Oak View *U.S.A.* **111** L7

Oakan-Dake *Japan* **54** C12
Oakdale *Calif., U.S.A.* **110** H6
Oakdale *La., U.S.A.* **116** F8
Oakes *U.S.A.* **112** B4
Oakesdale *U.S.A.* **108** C5
Oakey *Australia* **95** D5
Oakfield *U.S.A.* **114** C6
Oakham *U.K.* **15** E7
Oakhurst *U.S.A.* **110** H7
Oakland *U.S.A.* **110** H4
Oakley *Idaho, U.S.A.* **108** E7
Oakley *Kans., U.S.A.* **112** F3
Oakover → *Australia* **92** D3
Oakridge *U.S.A.* **108** E2
Oakville *Canada* **114** C5
Oakville *U.S.A.* **110** D3
Oamaru *N.Z.* **91** F3
Oancea *Romania* **29** E12
Oasi Faunistica di Vendicari △ *Italy* **43** F8
Oasis *Calif., U.S.A.* **110** H9
Oasis *Calif., U.S.A.* **111** M10
Oates Land *Antarctica* **5** C11
Oatlands *Australia* **95** G4
Oatman *U.S.A.* **111** K12
Oaxaca *Mexico* **119** D5
Oaxaca □ *Mexico* **119** D5
Ob → *Russia* **52** C7
Oba *Canada* **104** C3
Obala *Cameroon* **83** E7
Obama *Japan* **55** G7
Oban *Nigeria* **83** D6
Oban *U.K.* **13** E3
Obbia *Somali Rep.* **75** F4
Obera *Argentina* **127** B4
Oberammergau *Germany* **25** H6
Oberasbach *Germany* **25** F6
Oberbayern □ *Germany* **25** G7
Oberdrauburg *Austria* **26** E5
Obere Donau △ *Germany* **25** G5
Oberer Bayerischer Wald △ *Germany* **25** F8
Oberfranken □ *Germany* **25** E7
Oberhausen *Germany* **24** D2
Oberkirch *Germany* **25** G4
Oberlausitz *Germany* **24** D10
Oberlin *Kans., U.S.A.* **112** F3
Oberlin *La., U.S.A.* **116** F8
Oberlin *Ohio, U.S.A.* **114** E2
Obernai *France* **19** D14
Oberndorf *Germany* **25** G4
Oberon *Australia* **95** E4
Oberösterreich □ *Austria* **26** C7
Oberpfalz □ *Germany* **25** F8
Oberpfälzer Wald *Germany* **25** F8
Oberpfälzer Wald △ *Germany* **25** F8
Oberstdorf *Germany* **25** H6
Obertyn *Ukraine* **29** B10
Oberursel *Germany* **25** E4
Oberwart *Austria* **27** D9
Obi, Kepulauan *Indonesia* **63** E7
Obiaruku *Nigeria* **83** D6
Óbidos *Brazil* **125** D7
Óbidos *Portugal* **37** F1
Obihiro *Japan* **54** C11
Obilatu *Indonesia* **63** E7
Obilnoye *Russia* **35** G7
Obing *Germany* **25** G8
Objat *France* **20** C5
Obluchye *Russia* **53** E14
Obninsk *Russia* **32** E9
Obo *C.A.R.* **86** A2
Oboa, Mt. *Uganda* **86** B3
Obock *Djibouti* **81** E5
Obodivka *Ukraine* **29** B14
Oborniki *Poland* **31** F3
Oborniki Śląskie *Poland* **31** G3
Oboyan *Russia* **33** G9
Obozerskaya = Obozerskiy *Russia* **52** C5
Obozerskiy *Russia* **52** C5
Obrenovac *Serbia* **44** B4
Obrovac *Croatia* **41** D12
Obruk *Turkey* **72** C5
Obshchi Syrt *Russia* **6** E16
Obskaya Guba *Russia* **52** C8
Obuasi *Ghana* **83** D4
Obubra *Nigeria* **83** D6
Obudu *Nigeria* **83** D6
Obwalden □ *Switz.* **25** J4
Obzor *Bulgaria* **45** D11
Ocala *U.S.A.* **117** G13
Ocampo *Chihuahua, Mexico* **118** B3
Ocampo *Tamaulipas, Mexico* **119** C5
Ocaña *Spain* **36** F7
Occidental, Cordillera *Colombia* **124** C3
Occidental, Grand Erg *Algeria* **78** B6
Ocean City *Md., U.S.A.* **113** F16
Ocean City *N.J., U.S.A.* **113** F16
Ocean City *Wash., U.S.A.* **110** C2
Ocean Falls *Canada* **102** C3
Ocean I. = Banaba *Kiribati* **96** H8

Ocean Park *U.S.A.* 110 D2
Oceano *U.S.A.* 111 K6
Oceanport *U.S.A.* 115 F10
Oceanside *U.S.A.* 111 M9
Ochagavía *Spain* 38 C3
Ochakiv *Ukraine* 33 J6
Ochamchira *Georgia* 35 J5
Ochi, Oros *Greece* 46 C6
Ochil Hills *U.K.* 13 E5
Ocho Rios *Jamaica* 120 a
Ochsenfurt *Germany* 25 F6
Ochsenhausen *Germany* 25 G5
Ocilla *U.S.A.* 117 F13
Ockelbo *Sweden* 10 D10
Ocmulgee → *U.S.A.* 117 F13
Ocna Mureş *Romania* 29 D8
Ocna Sibiului *Romania* 29 E9
Ocnele Mari *Romania* 29 E9
Ocniţa *Moldova* 29 B12
Oconee → *U.S.A.* 117 F13
Oconomowoc *U.S.A.* 112 D9
Oconto *U.S.A.* 112 C10
Oconto Falls *U.S.A.* 112 C9
Ocosingo *Mexico* 119 D6
Ocotal *Nic.* 120 D2
Ocotlán *Jalisco, Mexico* 118 C4
Ocotlán *Oaxaca, Mexico* 119 D5
Ocreza → *Portugal* 37 F3
Ócsa *Hungary* 28 C4
Octeville *France* 18 C5
Oda *Ghana* 83 D4
Ōda *Japan* 55 G6
Oda, J. *Sudan* 80 C4
Ódáðahraun *Iceland* 8 D5
Ōdaejin *N. Korea* 57 D15
Öðåkra *Sweden* 11 H6
Odate *Japan* 54 D10
Odawara *Japan* 55 G9
Odda *Norway* 9 F12
Odder *Denmark* 11 J4
Odei → *Canada* 103 B9
Odemira *Portugal* 37 H2
Ödemiş *Turkey* 47 C9
Odendaalsrus *S. Africa* 88 D4
Odensbacken *Sweden* 10 E9
Odense *Denmark* 11 J4
Odenwald = Neckartal-
  Odenwald △ *Germany* 25 F5
Odenwald *Germany* 25 F5
Oder → *Europe* 24 B10
Oder-Havel Kanal *Germany* 24 C10
Oderzo *Italy* 41 C9
Odesa *Ukraine* 33 J6
Odesa □ *Ukraine* 33 J5
Ödeshög *Sweden* 11 F8
Odessa = Odesa *Ukraine* 33 J6
Odessa *Canada* 115 B8
Odessa *Tex., U.S.A.* 116 F3
Odessa *Wash., U.S.A.* 108 C4
Odiakwe *Botswana* 88 C4
Odiel → *Spain* 37 H4
Odienné *Ivory C.* 82 D3
Odintsovo *Russia* 32 E9
Odiongan *Phil.* 61 E4
Odolanów *Poland* 31 G4
O'Donnell *U.S.A.* 116 E4
Odorheiu Secuiesc *Romania* 29 D10
Odoyevo *Russia* 32 F9
Odra = Oder → *Europe* 24 B10
Odra → *Spain* 36 C6
Odžaci *Serbia* 28 E4
Odžak *Bos.-H.* 28 E3
Odzi *Zimbabwe* 89 B5
Odzi → *Zimbabwe* 89 B5
Oebisfelde *Germany* 24 C6
Oeiras *Brazil* 125 E10
Oeiras *Portugal* 37 G1
Oelrichs *U.S.A.* 112 D2
Oelsnitz *Germany* 25 E8
Oelwein *U.S.A.* 112 D8
Oeno I. *Pac. Oc.* 97 K14
Oenpelli = Gunbalanya
  Australia 92 B5
Oetz *Austria* 26 D3
Of *Turkey* 73 B9
Ofanto → *Italy* 43 A9
Offa *Nigeria* 83 D5
Offaly □ *Ireland* 12 C4
Offenbach *Germany* 25 E4
Offenburg *Germany* 25 G3
Officer Cr. → *Australia* 93 E5
Offida *Italy* 41 F10
Ofidousa *Greece* 47 E8
Ofolanga *Tonga* 91 c
Ofotfjorden *Norway* 8 B17
Ofu *Amer. Samoa* 91 b
Ōfunato *Japan* 54 E10
Oga *Japan* 54 E9
Oga-Hantō *Japan* 54 E9
Ogaden *Ethiopia* 75 F3
Ōgaki *Japan* 55 G8
Ogallala *U.S.A.* 112 E3
Ogasawara Gunto *Pac. Oc.* 96 E6
Ogbomosho *Nigeria* 83 D5
Ogden *U.S.A.* 108 F8
Ogdensburg *U.S.A.* 115 B9

Ogea Driki *Fiji* 91 a
Ogea Levu *Fiji* 91 a
Ogeechee → *U.S.A.* 117 F14
Ogilby *U.S.A.* 111 N12
Oglio → *Italy* 40 C7
Óglio Nord △ *Italy* 40 C6
Óglio Sud △ *Italy* 40 C7
Ogmore *Australia* 94 C4
Ognon → *France* 19 E12
Ogoja *Nigeria* 83 D6
Ogoki *Canada* 104 B2
Ogoki → *Canada* 104 B2
Ogoki L. *Canada* 104 B2
Ogoki Res. *Canada* 104 B2
Ogooué → *Gabon* 84 E1
Ogosta → *Bulgaria* 44 C7
Ogowe = Ogooué → *Gabon* 84 E1
Ogr = Sharafa *Sudan* 81 E2
Ograźden *Macedonia* 44 E6
Ogre *Latvia* 32 D3
Ogrein *Sudan* 80 D3
Ogulin *Croatia* 41 C12
Ogun □ *Nigeria* 83 D5
Ogurchinskiy, Ostrov
  Turkmenistan 71 B7
Oguta *Nigeria* 83 D6
Ogwashi-Uku *Nigeria* 83 D6
Ogwe *Nigeria* 83 E6
Ohai *N.Z.* 91 F2
Ohakune *N.Z.* 91 C5
Ohata *Japan* 54 D10
Ohau, L. *N.Z.* 91 F2
Ohio □ *U.S.A.* 114 F2
Ohio → *U.S.A.* 112 G9
Ohře → *Czech Rep.* 26 A7
Ohre → *Germany* 24 C7
Ohrid *Macedonia* 44 E4
Ohridsko Jezero *Macedonia* 44 E4
Ohrigstad *S. Africa* 89 C5
Öhringen *Germany* 25 F5
Oi Qu → *China* 58 C2
Oiapoque *Brazil* 125
Oikou *China* 57 E9
Oil City *U.S.A.* 114 E5
Oil Springs *Canada* 114 D2
Oildale *U.S.A.* 111 K7
Oinousa = Inousses *Greece* 47 C8
Oise □ *France* 19 C9
Oise → *France* 19 C9
Oiseaux du Djoudj △ *Senegal* 82 B1
Oistins *Barbados* 121 g
Oistins B. *Barbados* 121 g
Ōita *Japan* 55 H5
Ōita □ *Japan* 55 H5
Oiticica *Brazil* 125 E10
Ojai *U.S.A.* 111 L7
Ojcowski △ *Poland* 31 H6
Ojinaga *Mexico* 118 B4
Ojiya *Japan* 55 F9
Ojo Caliente *Mexico* 118 C4
Ojos del Salado, Cerro
  Argentina 126 B2
Oka → *Russia* 34 B7
Okaba *Indonesia* 63 F9
Okahandja *Namibia* 88 C2
Okanagan L. *Canada* 102 D5
Okandja *Gabon* 84 E2
Okanogan *U.S.A.* 108 B4
Okanogan → *U.S.A.* 108 B4
Okanogan Range *N. Amer.* 102 D5
Okány *Hungary* 28 D6
Okapi △
  Dem. Rep. of the Congo 86 B2
Okaputa *Namibia* 88 C2
Okara *Pakistan* 68 D5
Okaukuejo *Namibia* 88 B2
Okavango Delta *Botswana* 88 B3
Okavango Swamp =
  Okavango Delta *Botswana* 88 B3
Okaya *Japan* 55 F9
Okayama *Japan* 55 G6
Okayama □ *Japan* 55 G6
Okazaki *Japan* 55 G8
Oke-Iho *Nigeria* 83 D5
Okeechobee *U.S.A.* 117 H14
Okeechobee, L. *U.S.A.* 117 H14
Okefenokee △ *U.S.A.* 117 F13
Okefenokee Swamp *U.S.A.*
  117 F13
Okehampton *U.K.* 15 G4
Okene *Nigeria* 83 D6
Oker → *Germany* 24 C6
Okęcie, Warszawa ✕
  (WAW) *Poland* 31 F7
Okha *India* 68 H3
Okha *Russia* 53 D15
Okhotsk *Russia* 53 D15
Okhotsk, Sea of *Asia* 53 D15
Okhotskiy Perevoz *Russia* 53 C14
Okhtyrka *Ukraine* 33 G8
Oki-Shotō *Japan* 55 F6
Okiep *S. Africa* 88 D2
Okigwi *Nigeria* 83 D6
Okija *Nigeria* 83 D6
Okinawa *Japan* 55 L4
Okinawa □ *Japan* 55 L4
Okinawa-Guntō *Japan* 55 L4

Okinawa-Jima *Japan* 55 L4
Okino-erabu-Shima *Japan* 55 L4
Okitipupa *Nigeria* 83 D5
Oklahoma □ *U.S.A.* 116 D6
Oklahoma City *U.S.A.* 116 D6
Okmulgee *U.S.A.* 116 D7
Oknitsa = Ocniţa *Moldova* 29 B12
Oko, W. → *Sudan* 80 C4
Okolo *Uganda* 86 B3
Okolona *U.S.A.* 117 E10
Okombahe *Namibia* 88 C2
Okonek *Poland* 30 B3
Okotoks *Canada* 102 C6
Okrika *Nigeria* 83 E6
Oksibil *Indonesia* 63 E10
Oksikyy =
  Aktsyabrski *Belarus* 23 B15
Oktyabrsk *Kazakhstan* 52 E6
Oktyabrsk *Russia* 34 D9
Oktyabrskiy *Russia* 35 G5
Oktyabrskoy Revolyutsii,
  Ostrov *Russia* 53 B10
Oktyabrskoye =
  Zhovtneve *Ukraine* 33 J7
Okulovka *Russia* 32 C7
Okuru *N.Z.* 91 E2
Okushiri-Tō *Japan* 54 C9
Okuta *Nigeria* 83 D5
Okwa → *Botswana* 88 C3
Ola *U.S.A.* 116 D8
Ólafsfjörður *Iceland* 8 C4
Ólafsvík *Iceland* 8 D2
Olaine *Latvia* 30 B10
Olancha *U.S.A.* 111 J8
Olancha Pk. *U.S.A.* 111 J8
Olanchito *Honduras* 120 C2
Öland *Sweden* 11 H10
Ölands norra udde *Sweden* 11 G11
Ölands södra udde *Sweden* 11 H10
Olargues *France* 20 E6
Olary *Australia* 95 E3
Olascoaga *Argentina* 126 D3
Olathe *U.S.A.* 112 F6
Olavarría *Argentina* 126 D3
Oława *Poland* 31 H4
Olbernhau *Germany* 24 E9
Ólbia *Italy* 42 B2
Ólbia, G. di *Italy* 42 B2
Olching *Germany* 25 G7
Olcott *U.S.A.* 114 C6
Old Bahama Chan. =
  Bahama, Canal Viejo de
  W. Indies 120 B4
Old Baldy Pk. = San
  Antonio, Mt. *U.S.A.* 111 L9
Old Bridge *U.S.A.* 115 F10
Old Castile = Castilla y
  Leon □ *Spain* 36 D6
Old Crow *Canada* 100 C6
Old Dale *U.S.A.* 111 L11
Old Forge *N.Y., U.S.A.* 115 C10
Old Forge *Pa., U.S.A.* 115 E9
Old Perlican *Canada* 105 C9
Old Shinyanga *Tanzania* 86 C3
Old Speck Mt. *U.S.A.* 115 B14
Old Town *U.S.A.* 113 C19
Old Washington *U.S.A.* 114 F3
Old Wives L. *Canada* 103 C7
Oldbury *U.K.* 15 F5
Oldcastle *Ireland* 12 C4
Oldeani *Tanzania* 86 C4
Oldenburg *Niedersachsen,
  Germany* 24 B4
Oldenburg
  Schleswig-Holstein, Germany 24 A6
Oldenzaal *Neths.* 17 B6
Oldham *U.K.* 14 D5
Oldman → *Canada* 102 D6
Oldmeldrum *U.K.* 13 D6
Olds *Canada* 102 C6
Olduvai Gorge *Tanzania* 86 C4
Oldziyt *Mongolia* 56 B5
Olean *U.S.A.* 114 D6
Olecko *Poland* 30 D9
Oléggio *Italy* 40 C5
Oleiros *Portugal* 36 F3
Oleiros *Spain* 36 B2
Olekma → *Russia* 53 C13
Olekminsk *Russia* 53 C13
Oleksandriya *Kirovohrad,
  Ukraine* 33 H7
Oleksandriya *Rivne, Ukraine* 23 C14
Oleksandrivka *Ukraine* 33 H7
Olema *U.S.A.* 110 G4
Olenegorsk *Russia* 8 B25
Olenek *Russia* 53 C12
Olenek → *Russia* 53 B13
Olenino *Russia* 32 D7
Oléron, Î. d' *France* 20 C2
Olesk *Ukraine* 31 G11
Oleśnica *Poland* 31 G4
Olesno *Poland* 31 H5
Olevsk *Ukraine* 23 C14
Olga *Russia* 53 E14
Olga, L. *Canada* 104 C4

Olgas, The = Kata Tjuta
  Australia 93 E5
Ølgod *Denmark* 11 J2
Olhão *Portugal* 37 H3
Olhopil *Ukraine* 29 B14
Olhovatka *Russia* 30 D9
Olib *Croatia* 41 D11
Oliena *Italy* 42 B2
Oliete *Spain* 38 D4
Olifants = Elefantes →
  Africa 89 C5
Olifants → *Namibia* 88 C2
Olifantshoek *S. Africa* 88 D3
Ólimbos *Greece* 47 F9
Ólimbos, Óros = Olymbos
  Oros *Greece* 44 F6
Olímpia *Brazil* 127 A6
Olimpos-Beydaglari △
  Turkey 47 E12
Olinda *Brazil* 125 E12
Olite *Spain* 38 C3
Oliva *Argentina* 126 C3
Oliva *Spain* 39 G4
Oliva, Punta del *Spain* 36 B5
Oliva de la Frontera *Spain* 37 G4
Olivares *Spain* 38 F2
Olive Branch *U.S.A.* 117 D10
Olivehurst *U.S.A.* 110 F5
Oliveira de Azeméis *Portugal* 36 E2
Oliveira do Douro *Portugal* 36 D2
Olivenza *Spain* 37 G3
Oliver *Canada* 102 D5
Oliver L. *Canada* 103 B8
Olivet *France* 19 E8
Olkhovka *Russia* 34 F7
Olkusz *Poland* 31 H6
Ollagüe *Chile* 126 A2
Olmedo *Spain* 36 D6
Olmeto *France* 21 G12
Olney *Ill., U.S.A.* 112 F9
Olney *Tex., U.S.A.* 116 E5
Olofström *Sweden* 11 H8
Oloitokitok *Kenya* 86 C4
Oloma *Cameroon* 83 E7
Olomane → *Canada* 105 B7
Olomouc *Czech Rep.* 27 B10
Olomoucký □ *Czech Rep.* 27 B10
Olonets *Russia* 32 B8
Olongapo *Phil.* 61 D4
Olonne-sur-Mer *France* 20 B2
Oloron, Gave d' → *France* 20 E3
Oloron-Ste-Marie *France* 20 E3
Olosega *Amer. Samoa* 91 b
Olosenga = Swains I.
  Amer. Samoa 97 J11
Olot *Spain* 38 C7
Olovo *Bos.-H.* 28 F3
Olovyannaya *Russia* 53 D12
Oloy → *Russia* 53 C16
Olsberg *Germany* 24 D4
Olshammar *Sweden* 11 F8
Olshanka *Ukraine* 33 H6
Olshany *Ukraine* 33 G8
Olsztyn *Poland* 30 E7
Olsztynek *Poland* 30 E7
Olt □ *Romania* 29 F9
Olt → *Romania* 29 G9
Olten *Switz.* 25 H3
Olteniţa *Romania* 29 F11
Olton *U.S.A.* 116 D3
Oltu *Turkey* 73 B9
Oluan Pi *Taiwan* 59 G13
Olula del Rio *Spain* 39 H2
Olur *Turkey* 73 B10
Olutanga *Phil.* 61 H5
Olvega *Spain* 38 D2
Olvera *Spain* 37 J5
Olymbos *Cyprus* 49 D12
Olymbos Oros *Greece* 44 F6
Olympia *Greece* 46 D3
Olympia *U.S.A.* 110 D4
Olympic △ *U.S.A.* 110 C3
Olympic Dam *Australia* 95 E2
Olympic Mts. *U.S.A.* 110 C3
Olympus *Cyprus* 49 E11
Olympus, Mt. = Olymbos
  Oros *Greece* 44 F6
Olympus, Mt. = Uludağ
  Turkey 45 F13
Olympus, Mt. *U.S.A.* 110 C3
Olyphant *U.S.A.* 115 E9
Om → *Russia* 52 D8
Om Hajer *Eritrea* 81 E4
Om Koi *Thailand* 64 D2
Ōma *Japan* 54 D10
Ōmachi *Japan* 55 F8
Omae-Zaki *Japan* 55 G9
Ōmagari *Japan* 54 E10
Omagh *U.K.* 12 B4
Omagh □ *U.K.* 12 B4
Omaha *U.S.A.* 112 E6
Omak *U.S.A.* 108 B4
Omalos *Greece* 49 D5
Oman ■ *Asia* 75 C6
Oman, G. of *Asia* 71 E8
Omaruru *Namibia* 88 C2
Omaruru → *Namibia* 88 C1

Omate *Peru* 124 G4
Ombai, Selat *Indonesia* 63 F6
Omboué *Gabon* 84 E1
Ombrone → *Italy* 40 F8
Omdurmân *Sudan* 81 D3
Omegna *Italy* 40 C5
Omemee *Canada* 114 B6
Omeonga
  Dem. Rep. of the Congo 86 C1
Ometepe, I. de *Nic.* 120 D2
Ometepec *Mexico* 119 D5
Ominato *Japan* 54 D10
Omineca → *Canada* 102 B4
Omineca Mts. *Canada* 102 B3
Omiš *Croatia* 41 E13
Omišalj *Croatia* 41 C11
Ōmiya = Saitama *Japan* 55 G9
Omme Å → *Denmark* 11 J2
Ommen *Neths.* 17 B6
Ömnögovi □ *Mongolia* 56 C3
Omo → *Ethiopia* 81 F4
Omo ○ *Ethiopia* 81 F4
Omo Valley *Ethiopia* 81 F4
Omodeo, L. *Italy* 42 B1
Omodhos *Cyprus* 49 E11
Omoko *Nigeria* 83 D6
Omolon → *Russia* 53 C16
Omono-Gawa → *Japan* 54 E10
Omsk *Russia* 52 D8
Omsukchan *Russia* 53 C16
Ōmu *Japan* 54 B11
Omul, Vf. *Romania* 29 E10
Omulew → *Poland* 31 E8
Ōmura *Japan* 55 H4
Omuramba Omatako →
  Namibia 88 B2
Omuramba Ovambo →
  Namibia 88 B2
Omurtag *Bulgaria* 45 C10
Ōmuta *Japan* 55 H5
Oña *Spain* 36 C7
Onaga *U.S.A.* 112 F5
Onalaska *U.S.A.* 112 D8
Onancock *U.S.A.* 113 G16
Onang *Indonesia* 63 E5
Onangue, L. *Gabon* 84 E2
Onaping L. *Canada* 104 C3
Onavas *Mexico* 118 B3
Onawa *U.S.A.* 112 D5
Oncócua *Angola* 88 B1
Onda *Spain* 38 F4
Ondangwa *Namibia* 88 B2
Ondarroa *Spain* 38 B2
Ondava → *Slovak Rep.* 27 C14
Ondjiva *Angola* 88 B2
Ondo *Nigeria* 83 D5
Ondo □ *Nigeria* 83 D6
Öndörshil *Mongolia* 56 B5
Öndörhaan *Mongolia* 56 B6
One Tree *Australia* 95 E3
Oneata *Fiji* 91 a
Onega *Russia* 52 C4
Onega → *Russia* 6 C13
Onega, L. = Onezhskoye
  Ozero *Russia* 32 B8
Oneida *U.S.A.* 115 C9
Oneida L. *U.S.A.* 115 C9
O'Neill *U.S.A.* 112 D5
Onekotan, Ostrov *Russia* 53 E16
Onema *Dem. Rep. of the Congo* 86 C1
Oneonta *U.S.A.* 115 D10
Oneşti *Romania* 29 D11
Onezhskoye Ozero *Russia* 32 B8
Ongarue *N.Z.* 91 C5
Ongers → *S. Africa* 88 E3
Ongerup *Australia* 93 F2
Ongjin *N. Korea* 57 F13
Ongkharak *Thailand* 64 E3
Ongniud Qi *China* 57 C10
Ongoka
  Dem. Rep. of the Congo 86 C2
Ongole *India* 66 M12
Ongon = Havirga *Mongolia* 56 B7
Oni *Georgia* 35 J6
Onida *U.S.A.* 112 C3
Onilahy → *Madag.* 89 C7
Onitsha *Nigeria* 83 D6
Ono *Fiji* 91 a
Onoda *Japan* 55 G5
Ons, I. de *Spain* 36 C2
Onsala *Sweden* 11 G6
Onslow *Australia* 92 D2
Onslow B. *U.S.A.* 117 D16
Ontake-San *Japan* 55 G8
Ontario *Calif., U.S.A.* 111 L9
Ontario *Oreg., U.S.A.* 108 D5
Ontario □ *Canada* 104 B2
Ontario, L. *N. Amer.* 114 C7
Ontinyent *Spain* 39 G4
Ontonagon *U.S.A.* 112 B9
Ontur *Spain* 39 G3
Onyx *U.S.A.* 111 K8
Oodnadatta *Australia* 95 D2
Ooldea *Australia* 93 F5

Oombulgurri *Australia* 92 C4
Oorindi *Australia* 94 C3
Oost-Vlaanderen □ *Belgium* 17 C3
Oostende *Belgium* 17 C2
Oosterhout *Neths.* 17 C4
Oosterschelde → *Neths.* 17 C4
Oosterwolde *Neths.* 17 B6
Ootacamund =
  Udagamandalam *India* 66 P10
Ootsa L. *Canada* 102 C3
Op Luang △ *Thailand* 64 C2
Opaka *Bulgaria* 45 C10
Opala *Dem. Rep. of the Congo* 86 C1
Opalenica *Poland* 31 F3
Opan *Bulgaria* 45 D9
Opanake *Sri Lanka* 66 R12
Opasatika *Canada* 104 C3
Opasquia △ *Canada* 104 B1
Opatija *Croatia* 41 C11
Opatów *Poland* 31 H8
Opava *Czech Rep.* 27 B10
Opelika *U.S.A.* 117 E12
Opelousas *U.S.A.* 116 F8
Opémisca, L. *Canada* 104 C5
Opheim *U.S.A.* 108 B10
Ophthalmia Ra. *Australia* 92 D2
Opi *Nigeria* 83 D6
Opinaca → *Canada* 104 B4
Opinaca, Rés. *Canada* 104 B4
Opinnagau → *Canada* 104 B3
Opiscotéo, L. *Canada* 105 B6
Opobo *Nigeria* 83 E6
Opochka *Russia* 32 D5
Opoczno *Poland* 31 G7
Opol *Phil.* 61 G6
Opole *Poland* 31 H4
Opole Lubelskie *Poland* 31 G8
Opolskie □ *Poland* 31 H5
Oponono L. *Namibia* 88 B2
Oporto = Porto *Portugal* 36 D2
Opotiki *N.Z.* 91 C6
Opp *U.S.A.* 117 F11
Oppdal *Norway* 8 E13
Óppido Mamertina *Italy* 43 D8
Opportunity *U.S.A.* 108 C5
Oprişor *Romania* 28 F8
Oprtalj *Croatia* 41 C10
Opua *N.Z.* 91 A5
Opunake *N.Z.* 91 C4
Opuzen *Croatia* 41 E14
Ora *Cyprus* 49 E12
Oracle *U.S.A.* 109 K8
Oradea *Romania* 28 C6
Öræfajökull *Iceland* 8 D5
Orahovac *Serbia* 44 D4
Orahovica *Croatia* 28 E2
Orai *India* 69 G8
Oraison *France* 21 E9
Oral = Zhayyq →
  Kazakhstan 6 F16
Oral *Kazakhstan* 34 E10
Oran *Algeria* 78 A5
Orange *Australia* 95 E4
Orange *France* 21 D8
Orange *Calif., U.S.A.* 111 M9
Orange *Mass., U.S.A.* 115 D12
Orange *Tex., U.S.A.* 116 F8
Orange *Va., U.S.A.* 113 F14
Orange → *S. Africa* 88 D2
Orange, C. *Brazil* 125 C8
Orange Cove *U.S.A.* 110 J7
Orange Free State = Free
  State □ *S. Africa* 88 D4
Orange Grove *U.S.A.* 116 H6
Orange Walk *Belize* 119 D7
Orangeburg *U.S.A.* 117 E14
Orangeville *Canada* 114 C4
Orango *Guinea-Biss.* 82 C1
Orani *Phil.* 61 D4
Oranienburg *Germany* 24 C9
Oranje = Orange →
  S. Africa 88 D2
Oranjemund *Namibia* 88 D2
Oranjerivier *S. Africa* 88 D3
Oranjestad *Aruba* 121 D5
Orapa *Botswana* 85 J5
Orarak *Sudan* 81 F3
Oras *Phil.* 61 E6
Orašje *Bos.-H.* 28 E3
Orăştie *Romania* 29 E8
Orava → *Slovak Rep.* 27 B12
Orava, Vodna nádrž
  Slovak Rep. 27 B12
Oraviţa *Romania* 28 E6
Orb → *France* 20 E7
Orba → *Italy* 40 D5
Ørbæk *Denmark* 11 J4
Orbe *Switz.* 25 J2
Orbec *France* 18 C7
Orbetello *Italy* 41 F8
Órbigo → *Spain* 36 C5
Orbisonia *U.S.A.* 114 F7
Orbost *Australia* 95 F4
Örbyhus *Sweden* 10 D11
Orcadas *Antarctica* 5 C18
Orcas I. *U.S.A.* 110 B4

Orce *Spain* 39 H2
Orce ➤ *Spain* 39 H2
Orchard City *U.S.A.* 108 G10
Orchard Homes *U.S.A.* 108 C6
Orchid I. = Lan Yü *Taiwan* 59
Orchies *France* 19 B10
Orchila, I. *Venezuela* 121 D6
Orchilla, Pta. *Canary Is.* 48 G1
Órcia ➤ *Italy* 41 F8
Orco ➤ *Italy* 40 C4
Orcutt *U.S.A.* 111 L6
Ord *U.S.A.* 112 E4
Ord ➤ *Australia* 92 C4
Ord, Mt. *Australia* 92 C4
Ord Mts. *U.S.A.* 111 L10
Ordenes = Ordes *Spain* 36 B2
Orderville *U.S.A.* 109 H7
Ordes *Spain* 36 B2
Ordesa y Monte Perido △ *Spain* 38 C4
Ording = St-Peter-Ording *Germany* 24 A4
Ordos = Mu Us Shamo *China* 56 E5
Ordu *Turkey* 72 B7
Ordu □ *Turkey* 72 B7
Ordubad *Azerbaijan* 73 C12
Orduña *Álava, Spain* 38 C2
Orduña *Granada, Spain* 37 H7
Ordway *U.S.A.* 108 G12
Ordzhonikidze *Ukraine* 33 J8
Ore *Dem. Rep. of the Congo* 86 B2
Ore Mts. = Erzgebirge *Germany* 24 E8
Orebić *Croatia* 41 F14
Örebro *Sweden* 10 E9
Örebro län □ *Sweden* 10 E8
Orecchiella △ *Italy* 40 D7
Oregon *U.S.A.* 112 D9
Oregon □ *U.S.A.* 108 E3
Oregon City *U.S.A.* 110 E4
Oregon Dunes △ *U.S.A.* 108 E1
Öregrund *Sweden* 10 D12
Öregrundsgrepen *Sweden* 10 D12
Orekhov = Orikhiv *Ukraine* 33 J8
Orekhovo-Zuyevo *Russia* 32 E10
Orel *Russia* 33 F9
Orel □ *Russia* 33 F9
Orel ➤ *Ukraine* 33 H8
Orellana *Spain* 37 F5
Orellana, Canal de *Spain* 37 F5
Orellana, Embalse de *Spain* 37 F5
Orem *U.S.A.* 108 F8
Ören *Turkey* 47 D9
Orenburg *Russia* 52 D6
Örencik *Turkey* 47 B11
Orense = Ourense *Spain* 36 C3
Orense □ *Spain* 36 C3
Orepuki *N.Z.* 91 G1
Orestes Pereyra *Mexico* 118 B3
Orestiada *Greece* 45 E10
Øresund *Europe* 11 J6
Orfanos Kolpos *Greece* 44 F7
Orford Ness *U.K.* 15 E9
Organ Pipe Cactus △ *U.S.A.* 109 K7
Organos, Pta. de los *Canary Is.* 48 F2
Organyà *Spain* 38 C6
Orgaz *Spain* 37 F7
Orgeyev = Orhei *Moldova* 29 C13
Orhaneli *Turkey* 45 G12
Orhaneli ➤ *Turkey* 45 G12
Orhangazi *Turkey* 45 F13
Orhei *Moldova* 29 C13
Orhon Gol ➤ *Mongolia* 60 A5
Ória *Italy* 43 B10
Oriental, Cordillera *Colombia* 124 B4
Oriental, Grand Erg *Algeria* 78 B7
Orientale □ *Dem. Rep. of the Congo* 86 B2
Oriente *Argentina* 126 D3
Orihuela *Spain* 39 G4
Orihuela del Tremedal *Spain* 38 E3
Orikhiv *Ukraine* 33 J8
Orikum *Albania* 44 F3
Orillia *Canada* 114 B5
Orinoco ➤ *Venezuela* 124 B6
Orion *Canada* 103 D6
Oriskany *U.S.A.* 115 C9
Orissa □ *India* 67 K14
Orissaare *Estonia* 32 C2
Oristano *Italy* 42 C1
Oristano, G. di *Italy* 42 C1
Orizaba *Mexico* 119 D5
Orizaba, Pico de *Mexico* 119 D5
Orizare *Bulgaria* 45 D11
Orjen *Bos.-H.* 44 D2
Orjiva *Spain* 37 J7
Orkanger *Norway* 8 E13
Örkelljunga *Sweden* 11 H7
Örken *Sweden* 11 G9
Örkény *Hungary* 28 C4
Orkla ➤ *Norway* 8 E13
Orkney *S. Africa* 88 D4
Orkney □ *U.K.* 13 B5
Orkney Is. *U.K.* 13 B6

Orland *U.S.A.* 110 F4
Orlando *U.S.A.* 117 G14
Orlando, C. d' *Italy* 43 D7
Orléanais *France* 19 E9
Orléans *France* 19 E8
Orleans *U.S.A.* 115 B12
Orléans, Î. d' *Canada* 105 C5
Orlice ➤ *Czech Rep.* 26 A8
Orlivka *Ukraine* 29 E13
Orlov *Slovak Rep.* 27 B13
Orlov Gay *Russia* 34 E9
Orlová *Czech Rep.* 27 B11
Orlovat *Serbia* 28 E5
Orly, Paris ✈ (ORY) *France* 19 D9
Ormara *Pakistan* 66 G4
Ormea *Italy* 40 D4
Ormília *Greece* 44 F7
Ormoc *Phil.* 61 F6
Ormond *N.Z.* 91 C6
Ormond Beach *U.S.A.* 117 G14
Ormož *Slovenia* 41 B13
Ormskirk *U.K.* 14 D5
Ormstown *Canada* 115 A11
Ornans *France* 19 E13
Orne □ *France* 18 D7
Orne ➤ *France* 18 C6
Orneta *Poland* 30 D7
Ornö *Sweden* 10 E12
Örnsköldsvik *Sweden* 10 A12
Oro *N. Korea* 57 D14
Oro ➤ *Mexico* 118 B3
Oro Grande *U.S.A.* 111 L9
Oro Valley *U.S.A.* 109 K8
Orobie, Alpi *Italy* 40 B6
Orobie Bergamasche △ *Italy* 40 C6
Orobie Valtellinesi △ *Italy* 40 B6
Orocué *Colombia* 124 C4
Orodara *Burkina Faso* 82 C4
Orodo *Nigeria* 83 D6
Orofino *U.S.A.* 108 C5
Orohena, Mt. *Tahiti* 91 d
Orol Dengizi = Aral Sea *Asia* 52 E7
Oromíya □ *Ethiopia* 81 F5
Oromocto *Canada* 105 C6
Oron *Nigeria* 83 E6
Orono *Canada* 114 C6
Orono *U.S.A.* 113 C19
Oronsay ➤ *U.K.* 13 E2
Oropesa *Spain* 36 F5
Oroquieta *Phil.* 61 G5
Orosei *Italy* 42 B2
Orosei, G. di *Italy* 42 B2
Orosháza *Hungary* 28 D5
Oroszlány *Hungary* 28 C3
Orotukan *Russia* 53 C16
Oroville *Calif., U.S.A.* 110 F5
Oroville *Wash., U.S.A.* 108 B4
Oroville, L. *U.S.A.* 110 F5
Orrefors *Sweden* 11 H9
Orroroo *Australia* 95 E2
Orrviken *Sweden* 10 A8
Orrville *U.S.A.* 114 F3
Orsa *Sweden* 10 C8
Orsara di Púglia *Italy* 43 A8
Orsasjön *Sweden* 10 C8
Orsha *Belarus* 32 E6
Örsjö *Sweden* 11 H9
Orsk *Russia* 52 D6
Orşova *Romania* 28 F7
Ørsted *Denmark* 11 H4
Örsundsbro *Sweden* 10 E11
Orta, L. d' *Italy* 40 C5
Orta Nova *Italy* 43 A8
Ortaca *Turkey* 47 E10
Ortakent *Turkey* 47 D9
Ortaklar *Turkey* 47 D9
Ortaköy *Çorum, Turkey* 72 B6
Ortaköy *Niğde, Turkey* 72 C6
Orte *Italy* 41 F9
Ortegal, C. *Spain* 36 B3
Orthez *France* 20 E3
Ortigueira *Spain* 36 B3
Orting *U.S.A.* 110 C4
Ortisei *Italy* 41 B8
Ortles *Italy* 40 B7
Ortón ➤ *Bolivia* 124 F5
Ortona *Italy* 41 F11
Ortonville *U.S.A.* 112 C5
Orūmīyeh *Iran* 73 D11
Orūmīyeh, Daryācheh-ye *Iran* 73 D11
Orune *Italy* 42 B2
Oruro *Bolivia* 124 G5
Orust *Sweden* 11 F5
Oruzgān □ *Afghan.* 66 C5
Orvault *France* 18 E5
Orvieto *Italy* 41 F9
Orwell *N.Y., U.S.A.* 115 C9
Orwell *Ohio, U.S.A.* 114 E4
Orwell ➤ *U.K.* 15 F9
Orwigsburg *U.S.A.* 115 F8
Oryakhovo *Bulgaria* 44 C7
Orynyn *Ukraine* 29 B11
Orzinuovi *Italy* 40 C6
Orzyc ➤ *Poland* 31 F8
Orzysz *Poland* 30 E8
Osa ➤ *Poland* 30 E5

Osa, Pen. de *Costa Rica* 120 E3
Osage *U.S.A.* 112 D7
Osage ➤ *U.S.A.* 112 F8
Osage City *U.S.A.* 112 F6
Ōsaka *Japan* 55 G7
Osan *S. Korea* 57 F14
Osawatomie *U.S.A.* 112 F6
Osborne *U.S.A.* 112 F4
Osceola *Ark., U.S.A.* 117 D10
Osceola *Iowa, U.S.A.* 112 E7
Oschatz *Germany* 24 D9
Oschersleben *Germany* 24 C7
Óschiri *Italy* 42 B2
Oscoda *U.S.A.* 114 B1
Osečina *Serbia* 44 B3
Ösel = Saaremaa *Estonia* 32 C2
Osery *Russia* 32 E10
Osgoode *Canada* 115 A9
Osh *Kyrgyzstan* 52 E8
Oshakati *Namibia* 85 H3
Oshawa *Canada* 114 C6
Oshigambo *Namibia* 88 B2
Oshkosh *Nebr., U.S.A.* 112 E2
Oshkosh *Wis., U.S.A.* 112 C9
Oshmyany = Ashmyany *Belarus* 23 A13
Oshnovīyeh *Iran* 70 B5
Oshogbo *Nigeria* 83 D5
Oshtorīnān *Iran* 73 E13
Oshwe *Dem. Rep. of the Congo* 84 E3
Osi *Nigeria* 83 D6
Osieczna *Poland* 31 G3
Ósilo *Italy* 42 B1
Ósimo *Italy* 41 E10
Osintorf *Belarus* 32 E6
Osipovichi = Asipovichy *Belarus* 23 B15
Osiyan *India* 68 F5
Osizweni *S. Africa* 89 D5
Oskaloosa *U.S.A.* 112 E7
Oskarshamn *Sweden* 11 G10
Oskarström *Sweden* 11 H6
Oskélanéo *Canada* 104 C4
Öskemen *Kazakhstan* 52 E9
Oskol ➤ *Ukraine* 33 H9
Oslo *Norway* 9 G14
Oslob *Phil.* 61 G5
Oslofjorden *Norway* 9 G14
Osmanabad *India* 66 K10
Osmancık *Turkey* 72 B6
Osmaniye *Turkey* 72 D7
Osmanlı *Turkey* 45 E10
Ösmo *Sweden* 10 F11
Osnabrück *Germany* 24 C4
Ośno Lubuskie *Poland* 31 F1
Osoblaha *Czech Rep.* 27 A10
Osogovska Planina *Macedonia* 44 D6
Osório *Brazil* 127 B5
Osorno *Chile* 128 E2
Osorno *Spain* 36 C6
Osorno, Vol. *Chile* 128 D2
Osoyoos *Canada* 102 D5
Osøyro *Norway* 8 F11
Ospika ➤ *Canada* 102 B4
Osprey Reef *Australia* 94 A4
Oss *Neths.* 17 C5
Ossa, Mt. *Australia* 95 G4
Ossa, Oros *Greece* 46 B4
Ossabaw I. *U.S.A.* 117 F14
Ossi *Italy* 42 B1
Ossining *U.S.A.* 115 E11
Ossipee *U.S.A.* 115 C13
Ossokmanuan L. *Canada* 105 B7
Ossora *Russia* 53 D17
Ostashkov *Russia* 32 D7
Östavall *Sweden* 10 B9
Ostend = Oostende *Belgium* 17 C2
Oster *Ukraine* 23 C16
Österbotten = Pohjanmaa *Finland* 8 E20
Osterburg *Germany* 24 C7
Osterburg *U.S.A.* 114 F6
Osterburken *Germany* 25 F5
Österbybruk *Sweden* 11 D11
Österbymo *Sweden* 11 G9
Österdalälven *Sweden* 10 C7
Østerdalen *Norway* 10 C14
Österfärnebo *Sweden* 10 D10
Österforse *Sweden* 10 A11
Osterholz-Scharmbeck *Germany* 24 B4
Østerild *Denmark* 11 G2
Östermyra = Seinäjoki *Finland* 8 E20
Osterode *Germany* 24 D6
Österreich = Austria ■ *Europe* 26 E7
Östersund *Sweden* 10 A8

Östervåla *Sweden* 10 D11
Ostfriesische Inseln *Germany* 24 B3
Ostfriesland *Germany* 24 B3
Östhammar *Sweden* 10 D12
Óstia, Lido di *Italy* 41 G9
Ostíglia *Italy* 41 C8
Östmark *Sweden* 10 D6
Ostrava *Czech Rep.* 27 B11
Ostróda *Poland* 30 E6
Ostrogozhsk *Russia* 33 G10
Ostroh *Ukraine* 23 C14
Ostrołęka *Poland* 31 E8
Ostrov *Bulgaria* 45 C8
Ostrov *Czech Rep.* 26 A5
Ostrov *Romania* 29 F12
Ostrov *Russia* 32 D5
Ostrów Lubelski *Poland* 31 G9
Ostrów Mazowiecka *Poland* 31 F8
Ostrów Wielkopolski *Poland* 31 G4
Ostrowiec-Świętokrzyski *Poland* 31 H8
Ostrożac *Bos.-H.* 28 G2
Ostrzeszów *Poland* 31 G4
Ostseebad Kühlungsborn *Germany* 24 A7
Osttirol □ *Austria* 26 E5
Ostuni *Italy* 43 B10
Osum ➤ *Albania* 44 F4
Osŭm ➤ *Bulgaria* 45 C8
Ōsumi-Kaikyō *Japan* 55 J5
Ōsumi-Shotō *Japan* 55 J5
Osun □ *Nigeria* 83 D5
Osuna *Spain* 37 H5
Oswegatchie ➤ *U.S.A.* 115 B9
Oswego *U.S.A.* 115 C8
Oswego ➤ *U.S.A.* 115 C8
Oswestry *U.K.* 14 E4
Oświęcim *Poland* 31 H6
Otaci *Moldova* 29 B12
Otago □ *N.Z.* 91 F2
Otago Harbour *N.Z.* 91 F3
Otaheite B. *Trin. & Tob.* 125 K15
Ōtake *Japan* 55 G6
Otaki *N.Z.* 91 D5
Otaru *Japan* 54 C10
Otaru-Wan = Ishikari-Wan *Japan* 54 C10
Otava ➤ *Czech Rep.* 26 B7
Otavalo *Ecuador* 124 C3
Otavi *Namibia* 88 B2
Otchinjau *Angola* 88 B1
Otelec *Romania* 28 E5
Otelnuk, L. *Canada* 105 A6
Otelu Roşu *Romania* 28 E7
Otero de Rey = Outeiro de Rei *Spain* 36 B3
Othello *U.S.A.* 108 C4
Othoni *Greece* 46 B1
Othris, Oros *Greece* 46 B4
Oti ➤ *Togo* 83 C5
Otjiwarongo *Namibia* 88 C2
Otmuchów *Poland* 31 H4
Oto Tolu Group *Tonga* 91 c
Otočac *Croatia* 41 D12
Otoineppu *Japan* 54 B11
Otok *Croatia* 41 E13
Otopeni, Bucureşti ✈ (OTP) *Romania* 29 F11
Otorohanga *N.Z.* 91 C5
Otoskwin ➤ *Canada* 104 B2
Otra ➤ *Norway* 9 G13
Otradnyy *Russia* 34 D10
Otranto *Italy* 43 B11
Otranto, C. d' *Italy* 43 B11
Otranto, Str. of *Italy* 43 B11
Otrokovice *Czech Rep.* 27 B10
Otse *S. Africa* 88 D4
Ōtsu *Japan* 55 G7
Ōtsuki *Japan* 55 G9
Ottawa = Outaouais ➤ *Canada* 104 C5
Ottawa *Canada* 115 A9
Ottawa *Ill., U.S.A.* 112 E9
Ottawa *Kans., U.S.A.* 112 F6
Ottawa Is. *Canada* 101 D11
Ottélé *Cameroon* 83 E7
Ottensheim *Austria* 26 C7
Otter Cr. ➤ *U.S.A.* 115 B11
Otter L. *Canada* 103 B8
Otterup *Denmark* 11 J4
Otterville *Canada* 114 D4
Ottery St. Mary *U.K.* 15 G4
Otto Beit Bridge *Zimbabwe* 87 F2
Ottosdal *S. Africa* 88 D4
Ottumwa *U.S.A.* 112 E7
Otu *Nigeria* 83 D5
Oturkpo *Nigeria* 83 D6
Otway, B. *Chile* 128 G2
Otway, C. *Australia* 95 F3
Otwock *Poland* 31 F8
Otyniya *Ukraine* 29 B9
Ovid *U.S.A.* 115 D8
Ovidiopol *Ukraine* 33 J16
Ovidiu *Romania* 29 F13
Ötztaler Ache ➤ *Austria* 26 D3
Ötztaler Alpen *Austria* 26 E3

Ou ➤ *Laos* 64 B4
Ou Neua *Laos* 58 F3
Ou-Sammyaku *Japan* 54 E10
Ouachita *U.S.A.* 116 D8
Ouachita, L. *U.S.A.* 116 D8
Ouachita Mts. *U.S.A.* 116 D7
Ouagadougou *Burkina Faso* 83 C4
Ouahigouya *Burkina Faso* 82 C4
Ouahran = Oran *Algeria* 78 A5
Ouallâta *Mauritania* 82 B3
Ouallam *Niger* 83 C5
Ouallene *Algeria* 78 D6
Ouargaye *Burkina Faso* 83 C5
Ouargla *Algeria* 78 B7
Ouarkoye *Burkina Faso* 82 C4
Ouarra ➤ *C.A.R.* 84 C4
Ouarzazate *Morocco* 78 B4
Ouassouas *Mali* 83 B5
Ouatagouna *Mali* 83 B5
Oubangi ➤ *Dem. Rep. of the Congo* 84 E3
Ouche ➤ *France* 19 E12
Ouddorp *Neths.* 17 C3
Oude Rijn ➤ *Neths.* 17 C4
Oudeïka *Mali* 83 B4
Oudenaarde *Belgium* 17 D3
Oudon ➤ *France* 18 E6
Oudtshoorn *S. Africa* 88 E3
Ouellé *Ivory C.* 82 D4
Ouémé ➤ *Benin* 83 D5
Ouessa *Burkina Faso* 82 C4
Ouessant, Î. d' *France* 18 D1
Ouesso *Congo* 84 D3
Ouest □ *Cameroon* 83 D7
Ouest, Pte. de l' *Canada* 105 C7
Ouezzane *Morocco* 78 B4
Ougarou *Burkina Faso* 83 C5
Oughter, L. *Ireland* 12 B4
Oughterard *Ireland* 12 C2
Ouidah *Benin* 83 D5
Ouidi *Niger* 83 C7
Ouistreham *France* 18 C6
Oujda *Morocco* 78 B5
Oujeft *Mauritania* 82 A2
Oulainen *Finland* 8 D21
Ould Yenjé *Mauritania* 82 B2
Oulins *France* 21 C8
Oulu *Finland* 8 D21
Oulujärvi *Finland* 8 D22
Oulujoki ➤ *Finland* 8 D21
Oulx *Italy* 40 C3
Oum Chalouba *Chad* 79 E10
Oum Hadjer *Chad* 79 F9
Oumé *Ivory C.* 82 D3
Ounasjoki ➤ *Finland* 8 C21
Ounguati *Namibia* 88 C2
Ounianga Sérir *Chad* 79 E10
Our ➤ *Lux.* 17 E6
Oura, Akra *Greece* 47 C8
Ouranoupoli *Greece* 44 F7
Ourârene *Niger* 83 B6
Ouray *U.S.A.* 109 G10
Ourcq ➤ *France* 19 C10
Ourense *Spain* 36 C3
Ouricuri *Brazil* 125 E10
Ourinhos *Brazil* 127 A6
Ourique *Portugal* 37 H2
Ouro Fino *Brazil* 127 A6
Ouro Prêto *Brazil* 127 A7
Ouro Sogui *Senegal* 82 B2
Ouro-Ndia *Mali* 82 B4
Oursi *Burkina Faso* 83 C4
Ourthe ➤ *Belgium* 17 D5
Ouse ➤ *E. Sussex, U.K.* 15 G8
Ouse ➤ *N. Yorks., U.K.* 14 D7
Oust *France* 20 F5
Oust ➤ *France* 18 E4
Outamba-Kilimi △ *S. Leone* 82 D2
Outaouais ➤ *Canada* 104 C5
Outardes ➤ *Canada* 105 C6
Outer Hebrides *U.K.* 13 D1
Outes = Serra de Outes *Spain* 36 C2
Outjo *Namibia* 88 C2
Outlook *Canada* 103 C7
Outokumpu *Finland* 8 E23
Outreau *France* 19 B8
Ouvèze ➤ *France* 21 E8
Ouyen *Australia* 95 F3
Ouzouer-le-Marché *France* 19 E8
Ovada *Italy* 40 D5
Ovalau *Fiji* 91 a
Ovalle *Chile* 126 C1
Ovamboland = Ovambo *Namibia* 88 B2
Ovar *Portugal* 36 E2
Overath *Germany* 24 E3
Overflakkee *Neths.* 17 C4
Overijssel □ *Neths.* 17 B6
Overland Park *U.S.A.* 112 F6
Overton *U.S.A.* 111 J12
Övertorneå *Sweden* 8 C20
Överum *Sweden* 11 F10

Oviksfjällen *Sweden* 10 A7
Oviši *Latvia* 30 A8
Ovoot *Mongolia* 56 B7
Övör Hangay □ *Mongolia* 56 B2
Ovoro *Nigeria* 83 D6
Øvre Årdal *Norway* 8 F12
Øvre Fryken *Sweden* 10 E7
Ovruch *Ukraine* 23 C15
Owaka *N.Z.* 91 G2
Owambo = Ovamboland *Namibia* 88 B2
Owasco L. *U.S.A.* 115 D8
Owase *Japan* 55 G8
Owatonna *U.S.A.* 112 C7
Owbeh *Afghan.* 66 B3
Owego *U.S.A.* 115 D8
Owen Falls Dam = Nalubaale Dam *Uganda* 86 B3
Owen Sound *Canada* 114 B4
Owen Stanley Ra. *Papua N. G.* 90 B7
Oweniny ➤ *Ireland* 12 B2
Owens ➤ *U.S.A.* 110 J9
Owens L. *U.S.A.* 111 J9
Owensboro *U.S.A.* 112 G10
Owerri *Nigeria* 83 D6
Owl ➤ *Canada* 103 B10
Owo *Nigeria* 83 D6
Owosso *U.S.A.* 113 D11
Owyhee *U.S.A.* 108 F5
Owyhee ➤ *U.S.A.* 108 E5
Owyhee, L. *U.S.A.* 108 E5
Ox Mts. = Slieve Gamph *Ireland* 12 B3
Öxarfjörður *Iceland* 8 C5
Oxbow *Canada* 103 D8
Oxelösund *Sweden* 11 F11
Oxford *N.Z.* 91 E4
Oxford *U.K.* 15 F6
Oxford *Mass., U.S.A.* 115 D13
Oxford *Miss., U.S.A.* 117 D10
Oxford *N.C., U.S.A.* 117 C15
Oxford *N.Y., U.S.A.* 115 D9
Oxford *Ohio, U.S.A.* 113 F11
Oxford, L. *Canada* 103 C9
Oxfordshire □ *U.K.* 15 F6
Oxia *Greece* 46 C3
Oxie *Sweden* 11 J7
Oxilithos *Greece* 46 C6
Oxnard *U.S.A.* 111 L7
Oxsjövålen *Sweden* 10 B7
Oxus = Amudarya ➤ *Uzbekistan* 52 E6
Oya *Malaysia* 62 D4
Oyama *Japan* 55 F9
Oyambre △ *Spain* 36 B6
Oyem *Gabon* 84 D2
Oyen *Canada* 103 C6
Oykel ➤ *U.K.* 13 D4
Oymyakon *Russia* 53 C15
Oyo *Nigeria* 83 D5
Oyo □ *Nigeria* 83 D5
Oyonnax *France* 19 F12
Oyster Bay *U.S.A.* 115 F11
Ōyūbari *Japan* 54 C11
Özalp *Turkey* 73 C10
Ozamiz *Phil.* 61 G5
Ozark *Ala., U.S.A.* 117 F12
Ozark *Ark., U.S.A.* 116 D8
Ozark *Mo., U.S.A.* 112 G7
Ozark Plateau *U.S.A.* 112 G8
Ozarks, L. of the *U.S.A.* 112 F7
Ożarów *Poland* 31 H8
Ózd *Hungary* 28 B5
Ozernoye *Russia* 34 E10
Ozero Svityaz *Ukraine* 31 G10
Ozersk *Russia* 30 D8
Ozette, L. *U.S.A.* 110 B2
Ozieri *Italy* 42 B2
Ozimek *Poland* 31 H5
Ozinki *Russia* 34 E9
Ozona *U.S.A.* 116 F4
Ozorków *Poland* 31 G6
Ozren *Bos.-H.* 28 G3
Ozuluama *Mexico* 119 C5
Ozun *Romania* 29 E11
Ozurgeti *Georgia* 35 K5

P

Pa *Burkina Faso* 82 C4
Pa-an *Burma* 67 L20
Pa Mong Dam *Thailand* 64 D4
Pa Sak ➤ *Thailand* 64 E3
Paamiut *Greenland* 4 C5
Paar ➤ *Germany* 25 G7
Paarl *S. Africa* 88 E2
Pab Hills *Pakistan* 68 F2
Pabbay *U.K.* 13 D1
Pabianice *Poland* 31 G6
Pabna *Bangla.* 67 G16
Pabo *Uganda* 86 B3
Pacaja ➤ *Brazil* 125 D8
Pacaraima, Sa. *S. Amer.* 124 C6
Pacasmayo *Peru* 124 E3
Paceco *Italy* 42 E5
Pachhar *India* 68 G7

Pachia *Greece* 47 E7
Pachino *Italy* 43 F8
Pachitea → *Peru* 124 E4
Pachmarhi *India* 69 H8
Pachnes *Greece* 49 D6
Pachpadra *India* 68 G5
Pachuca *Mexico* 119 C5
Pacific Antarctic Ridge
  Pac. Oc. 5 B13
Pacific Grove *U.S.A.* 110 J5
Pacific Ocean 97 G14
Pacific Rim △ *Canada* 110 B2
Pacifica *U.S.A.* 110 H4
Pacitan *Indonesia* 63 H14
Packwood *U.S.A.* 110 D5
Pacov *Czech Rep.* 26 B8
Pacy-sur-Eure *France* 18 C8
Padaido, Kepulauan
  Indonesia 63 E9
Padang *Indonesia* 62 E2
Padang Endau *Malaysia* 65 L4
Padangpanjang *Indonesia* 62 E2
Padangsidempuan *Indonesia* 62 D1
Padborg *Denmark* 11 K3
Paddle Prairie *Canada* 102 B5
Paddockwood *Canada* 103 C7
Paderborn *Germany* 24 D4
Padeş, Vf. *Romania* 28 E7
Padina *Romania* 29 F12
Padma *India* 69 G11
Pádova *Italy* 41 C8
Padra *India* 68 H5
Padrauna *India* 69 F10
Padre I. *U.S.A.* 116 H6
Padre Island △ *U.S.A.* 116 H6
Padrón *Spain* 36 C2
Padstow *U.K.* 15 G3
Padua = Pádova *Italy* 41 C8
Paducah *Ky., U.S.A.* 112 G9
Paducah *Tex., U.S.A.* 116 D4
Padul *Spain* 37 H7
Paea *Tahiti* 91 d
Paeroa *N.Z.* 91 B5
Paesana *Italy* 40 D4
Pafúri *Mozam.* 89 C5
Pag *Croatia* 41 D12
Paga *Ghana* 83 C4
Pagadian *Phil.* 61 H5
Pagai Selatan, Pulau
  Indonesia 62 E2
Pagai Utara, Pulau *Indonesia* 62 E2
Pagalu = Annobón *Atl. Oc.* 77 G4
Pagara *India* 69 G9
Pagastikos Kolpos *Greece* 46 B5
Pagatan *Indonesia* 62 E5
Page *U.S.A.* 109 H8
Pagégiai *Lithuania* 30 C8
Pago Pago *Amer. Samoa* 91 b
Pagosa Springs *U.S.A.* 109 H10
Pagwa River *Canada* 104 B2
Pähala *U.S.A.* 106 b
Pahang → *Malaysia* 65 L4
Pahiatua *N.Z.* 91 D5
Pahokee *U.S.A.* 117 H14
Pahrump *U.S.A.* 111 J11
Pahute Mesa *U.S.A.* 110 H10
Pai *Thailand* 64 C2
Paicines *U.S.A.* 110 J5
Paide *Estonia* 32 C3
Paignton *U.K.* 15 G4
Paiho *Taiwan* 59 F13
Päijänne *Finland* 32 B3
Pailani *India* 69 G8
Pailin *Cambodia* 64 F4
Paimpol *France* 18 D3
Painan *Indonesia* 62 E2
Painesville *U.S.A.* 114 E3
Paint Hills = Wemindji
  Canada 104 B4
Paint L. *Canada* 103 B9
Painted Desert *U.S.A.* 109 H8
Paintsville *U.S.A.* 113 G12
País Vasco □ *Spain* 38 C2
Paisley *Canada* 114 B3
Paisley *U.K.* 13 F4
Paisley *U.S.A.* 108 E3
Paita *Peru* 124 E2
Paiva → *Portugal* 36 D2
Paizhou *China* 59 B9
Pajares *Spain* 36 B5
Pajares, Puerto de *Spain* 36 C5
Pajęczno *Poland* 31 G5
Pak Lay *Laos* 64 C3
Pak Phanang *Thailand* 65 H3
Pak Sane *Laos* 64 C4
Pak Song *Laos* 64 E6
Pak Suong *Laos* 58 H4
Pakaur *India* 69 G12
Pakch'ǒn *N. Korea* 57 E13
Pakenham *Canada* 115 A8
Pakistan ■ *Asia* 68 E4
Pakkading *Laos* 64 C4
Paklenica △ *Croatia* 41 D12
Pakokku *Burma* 67 J19
Pakość *Poland* 31 F5
Pakowki L. *Canada* 103 D6

Pakpattan *Pakistan* 68 D5
Pakrac *Croatia* 28 E2
Pakruojis *Lithuania* 30 C10
Paks *Hungary* 28 D3
Paktīā □ *Afghan.* 66 C6
Paktīkā □ *Afghan.* 66 C6
Pakwach *Uganda* 86 B3
Pakxe *Laos* 64 E5
Pal Lahara *India* 69 J11
Pala *Chad* 79 G9
Pala *Dem. Rep. of the Congo* 86 D2
Pala *U.S.A.* 111 M9
Palabek *Uganda* 86 B3
Palacios *U.S.A.* 116 G6
Palafrugell *Spain* 38 D8
Palagiano *Italy* 43 B10
Palagonía *Italy* 43 E7
Palagruža *Croatia* 41 F13
Palaiseau *France* 19 D9
Palam *India* 66 K10
Palamás *Greece* 46 B4
Palamòs *Spain* 38 D8
Palampur *India* 68 C7
Palamut *Turkey* 47 C9
Palana *Australia* 95 F4
Palana *Russia* 53 D16
Palanan *Phil.* 61 C5
Palanan Pt. *Phil.* 61 C5
Palandri *Pakistan* 69 C5
Palanga *Lithuania* 30 C8
Palangkaraya *Indonesia* 62 E4
Palani *India* 66 P10
Palani Hills *India* 66 P10
Palanpur *India* 68 G5
Palapye *Botswana* 88 C4
Palas *Pakistan* 69 B5
Palas de Rei *Spain* 36 C3
Palashi *India* 69 H13
Palasponga *India* 69 J11
Palatka *Russia* 53 C16
Palatka *U.S.A.* 117 G14
Palau *Italy* 42 A2
Palau ■ *Palau* 90 A6
Palauk *Burma* 64 F2
Palawan *Phil.* 61 G3
Palayankottai *India* 66 Q10
Palazzo, Pte. *France* 21 F12
Palazzo San Gervásio *Italy* 43 B8
Palazzolo Acréide *Italy* 43 E7
Paldiski *Estonia* 32 C3
Pale *Bos.-H.* 28 G3
Palekastro *Greece* 49 D8
Paleleh *Indonesia* 63 D6
Palembang *Indonesia* 62 E2
Palencia *Spain* 36 C6
Palencia □ *Spain* 36 C6
Palenque *Mexico* 119 D6
Paleochora *Greece* 49 D5
Paleokastritsa *Greece* 49 A3
Paleometokho *Cyprus* 49 D12
Palermo *Italy* 42 D6
Palermo *U.S.A.* 108 G3
Palermo ✕ (PMO) *Italy* 42 D6
Paleros *Greece* 46 C2
Palestina *Chile* 128 A3
Palestine *Asia* 74 D4
Palestine *U.S.A.* 116 F7
Palestrina *Italy* 41 G9
Paletwa *Burma* 67 J18
Palghat *India* 66 P10
Palgrave, Mt. *Australia* 92 D2
Pali *India* 68 G5
Palikir *Micronesia* 96 G7
Palinuro *Italy* 43 B8
Palinuro, C. *Italy* 43 B8
Paliouri, Akra *Greece* 44 G7
Palisades Res. *U.S.A.* 108 E8
Palitana *India* 68 J4
Palizada *Mexico* 119 D6
Palk Bay *Asia* 66 Q11
Palk Strait *Asia* 66 Q11
Palkānah *Iraq* 70 C5
Palkot *India* 69 H11
Pallanza = Verbánia *Italy* 40 C5
Pallarenda *Australia* 94 B4
Pallasovka *Russia* 34 E8
Pallës, Bishti i *Albania* 44 E3
Pallinup → *Australia* 93 F2
Pallisa *Uganda* 86 B3
Pallu *India* 68 E6
Palm Bay *U.S.A.* 117 G14
Palm Beach *U.S.A.* 117 H14
Palm Coast *U.S.A.* 117 G14
Palm Desert *U.S.A.* 111 M10
Palm Is. *Australia* 94 B4
Palm Springs *U.S.A.* 111 M10
Palma *Mozam.* 87 E5
Palma, B. de *Spain* 48 B9
Palma de Mallorca *Spain* 48 B9
Palma de Mallorca ✕
  (PMI) *Spain* 39 F7
Palma del Río *Spain* 37 H5
Palma di Montechiaro *Italy* 42 F6
Palma Soriano *Cuba* 120 B4
Palmares *Brazil* 125 E11
Palmarola *Italy* 42 B5
Palmas *Brazil* 127 B5

Palmas, C. *Liberia* 82 E3
Pálmas, G. di *Italy* 42 D1
Palmdale *U.S.A.* 111 L8
Palmeira das Missões *Brazil* 127 B5
Palmeira dos Índios *Brazil* 125 E11
Palmela *Portugal* 37 G2
Palmer *Antarctica* 5 C17
Palmer *U.S.A.* 100 C5
Palmer → *Australia* 94 B3
Palmer Arch. *Antarctica* 5 C17
Palmer Lake *U.S.A.* 108 G11
Palmer Land *Antarctica* 5 D18
Palmerston *Australia* 92 B5
Palmerston *Canada* 114 C4
Palmerston *N.Z.* 91 F3
Palmerston North *N.Z.* 91 D5
Palmerton *U.S.A.* 115 F9
Palmetto *U.S.A.* 117 H13
Palmi *Italy* 43 D8
Palmira = Tudmur *Syria* 73 E8
Palmira *Colombia* 124 C3
Palmyra = Tudmur *Syria* 73 E8
Palmyra *Mo., U.S.A.* 112 F8
Palmyra *N.J., U.S.A.* 115 F9
Palmyra *N.Y., U.S.A.* 114 C7
Palmyra *Pa., U.S.A.* 115 F8
Palmyra Is. *Pac. Oc.* 97 G11
Palo Alto *U.S.A.* 110 H4
Palo Seco *Trin. & Tob.* 125 K15
Palo Verde *U.S.A.* 111 M12
Palo Verde △ *Costa Rica* 120 D2
Paloich *Sudan* 81 E3
Palomar Mt. *U.S.A.* 111 M10
Palompon *Phil.* 61 F6
Palopo *Indonesia* 63 E6
Palos, C. de *Spain* 39 H4
Palos de la Frontera *Spain* 37 H4
Palos Verdes, Pt. *U.S.A.* 111 M8
Palos Verdes Estates *U.S.A.* 111 M8
Pålsboda *Sweden* 10 E9
Palu *Indonesia* 63 E5
Palu *Turkey* 73 C9
Paluke *Liberia* 82 D3
Paluzza *Italy* 41 B10
Palwal *India* 68 E7
Pama *Burkina Faso* 83 C5
Pama △ *Burkina Faso* 83 C5
Pamanukan *Indonesia* 63 G12
Pamekasan *Indonesia* 63 G15
Pamenang *Indonesia* 63 J19
Pamiers *France* 20 E5
Pamir *Tajikistan* 52 F8
Pamlico → *U.S.A.* 117 D16
Pamlico Sd. *U.S.A.* 117 D17
Pampa *U.S.A.* 116 D4
Pampa de las Salinas
  Argentina 126 C2
Pampanua *Indonesia* 63 E6
Pampas *Argentina* 126 D3
Pampas *Peru* 124 F4
Pamphylia *Turkey* 72 D4
Pamplona *Colombia* 124 B4
Pamplona *Spain* 38 C3
Pampoenpoort *S. Africa* 88 E3
Pamukçu *Turkey* 47 B9
Pamukkale *Turkey* 47 D11
Pan de Azúcar △ *Chile* 126 B1
Pan Xian *China* 58 E5
Pana *U.S.A.* 112 F9
Panabo *Phil.* 61 H6
Panaca *U.S.A.* 109 H6
Panagyurishte *Bulgaria* 45 D8
Panaitan *Indonesia* 63 G11
Panaji *India* 66 M8
Panamá *Panama* 120 E4
Panama ■ *Cent. Amer.* 120 E4
Panamá, G. de *Panama* 120 E4
Panama, Isthmus of
  Cent. Amer. 98 H12
Panama Basin *Pac. Oc.* 97 G19
Panama Canal *Panama* 120 E4
Panama City *U.S.A.* 117 F12
Panamint Range *U.S.A.* 111 J9
Panamint Springs *U.S.A.* 111 J9
Panão *Peru* 124 E3
Panaon I. *Phil.* 61 F6
Panare *Thailand* 65 J3
Panarea *Italy* 43 D8
Panaro → *Italy* 41 D8
Panay *Phil.* 61 F5
Panay G. *Phil.* 63 B6
Pančevo *Serbia* 28 B5
Panch'iao *Taiwan* 59 E13
Panciu *Romania* 29 E12
Pancorbo, Desfiladero *Spain* 36 C7
Pâncota *Romania* 28 D6
Panda *Mozam.* 89 C5
Pandan *Malaysia* 65 d
Pandan *Antique, Phil.* 61 F5
Pandan, Catanduanes, *Phil.* 61 D6
Pandan, Selat *Singapore* 65 d
Pandan Tampoi = Tampoi
  Malaysia 65 d
Pandegelang *Indonesia* 63 G12
Pandhana *India* 68 J7
Pandharpur *India* 66 L9
Pando *Uruguay* 127 C4

Pando, L. = Hope, L.
  Australia 95 D2
Pandokratoras *Greece* 49 A3
Pandora *Costa Rica* 120 E3
Pandrup *Denmark* 11 G3
Panevéggio-Pale di San
  Martino △ *Italy* 41 B8
Panevèžys *Lithuania* 32 E3
Panfilovo *Russia* 34 E6
Pang-Long *Burma* 67 H21
Pang Sida △ *Thailand* 64 E4
Pang-Yang *Burma* 67 H21
Panga *Dem. Rep. of the Congo* 86 B2
Pangaíon Óros *Greece* 45 E8
Pangalanes, Canal des =
  Ampangalana,
  Lakandranon' *Madag.* 89 C8
Pangani *Tanzania* 86 D4
Pangani → *Tanzania* 86 D4
Pangfou = Bengbu *China* 57 H9
Pangil *Dem. Rep. of the Congo* 86 C2
Pangkah, Tanjung
  Indonesia 63 G15
Pangkajene *Indonesia* 63 E5
Pangkalanbrandan
  Indonesia 62 D1
Pangkalanbuun *Indonesia* 62 E4
Pangkalpinang *Indonesia* 62 E3
Pangnirtung *Canada* 101 C13
Pangong Tso *India* 68 B8
Panguitch *U.S.A.* 109 H7
Pangutaran Group *Phil.* 61 H4
Panhandle *U.S.A.* 116 D4
Pani Mines *India* 68 H5
Pania-Mutombo
  Dem. Rep. of the Congo 86 D1
Panikota I. *India* 68 J4
Panipat *India* 68 E7
Panjal Range = Pir Panjal
  Range *India* 68 C7
Panjang, Hon *Vietnam* 65 H4
Panjgur *Pakistan* 66 F4
Panjim = Panaji *India* 66 M8
Panjin *China* 57 D12
Panjnad → *Pakistan* 68 E4
Panjnad Barrage *Pakistan* 68 E4
Panjwai *Afghan.* 68 D1
Pankshin *Nigeria* 83 D6
Panmunjŏm *N. Korea* 57 F14
Panna *India* 69 G9
Panna △ *India* 69 G8
Panna Hills *India* 69 G9
Pannawonica *Australia* 92 D2
Pannga, Tanjung *Indonesia* 63 K19
Pannirtuuq =
  Pangnirtung *Canada* 101 C13
Pano Akil *Pakistan* 68 F3
Pano Lefkara *Cyprus* 49 E12
Pano Panayia *Cyprus* 49 E11
Panorama *Brazil* 127 A5
Panormos *Greece* 49 D6
Pansemal *India* 68 J6
Panshan = Panjin *China* 57 D12
Panshi *China* 57 C14
Pantanal *Brazil* 124 H7
Pantanos de Centla △
  Mexico 119 D6
Pantar *Indonesia* 63 F6
Pante Macassar *E. Timor* 63 F6
Pante Makasar = Pante
  Macassar *E. Timor* 63 F6
Pantelleria *Italy* 42 F4
Pantón *Spain* 36 C3
Pánuco *Mexico* 119 C5
Panyam *Nigeria* 83 D6
Panyu *China* 59 F9
Panzhihua *China* 58 D3
Páola *Italy* 43 C9
Paola *Malta* 49 D2
Paola *U.S.A.* 112 F6
Paonia *U.S.A.* 108 G10
Paopao *Moorea* 91 d
Paoting = Baoding *China* 56 E8
Paot'ou = Baotou *China* 56 D6
Paoua *C.A.R.* 84 C3
Pápa *Hungary* 28 C2
Papa Stour *U.K.* 13 A7
Papa Westray *U.K.* 13 B6
Papagayo → *Mexico* 119 D5
Papagayo, G. de *Costa Rica* 120 D2
Papakura *N.Z.* 91 B5
Papantla *Mexico* 119 C5
Papar *Malaysia* 62 C5
Papara *Tahiti* 91 d
Paparoa *N.Z.* 91 E3
Papas, Akra *Greece* 46 C3
Papeete *Tahiti* 91 d
Papenburg *Germany* 24 B3
Papenoo *Tahiti* 91 d
Papenoo → *Tahiti* 91 d
Papetoai *Moorea* 91 d
Paphlagonia *Turkey* 72 B5
Paphos *Cyprus* 49 E11
Papikio Oros *Greece* 45 E9
Paposo *Chile* 126 B1
Papoutsa *Cyprus* 49 E12
Papua □ *Indonesia* 63 E9

Papua, G. of *Papua N. G.* 90 B7
Papua New Guinea ■
  Oceania 90 B7
Papudo *Chile* 126 C1
Papuk *Croatia* 28 E2
Papun *Burma* 67 K20
Papunya *Australia* 92 D5
Pará = Belém *Brazil* 125 D9
Pará □ *Brazil* 125 D8
Paraburdoo *Australia* 92 D2
Paracale *Phil.* 61 D5
Paracatu *Brazil* 125 G9
Paracel Is. = S. China Sea 62 A4
Parachilna *Australia* 95 E2
Parachinar *Pakistan* 68 C4
Paraćin *Serbia* 44 C5
Paradas *Spain* 37 H5
Paradela *Spain* 36 C3
Paradip *India* 67 J15
Paradise *Calif., U.S.A.* 110 F5
Paradise *Nev., U.S.A.* 111 J11
Paradise → *Canada* 105 B8
Paradise Hill *Canada* 103 C7
Paradise River *Canada* 105 B8
Paradise Valley *U.S.A.* 108 F5
Paradisi *Greece* 49 C10
Parado *Indonesia* 63 F5
Paragould *U.S.A.* 117 C9
Paragua → *Venezuela* 124 B6
Paraguaçu → *Brazil* 125 F11
Paraguaçu Paulista *Brazil* 127 A5
Paraguaná, Pen. de
  Venezuela 124 A5
Paraguarí *Paraguay* 126 B4
Paraguarí □ *Paraguay* 126 B4
Paraguay ■ *S. Amer.* 126 A4
Paraguay → *Paraguay* 126 B4
Paraíba = João Pessoa
  Brazil 125 E12
Paraíba □ *Brazil* 125 E11
Paraíba do Sul → *Brazil* 127 A7
Parainen *Finland* 32 B2
Paraíso *Mexico* 119 D6
Parak *Iran* 71 E7
Parakhino Paddubye *Russia* 32 C7
Parakou *Benin* 83 D5
Paralimni *Cyprus* 49 D12
Paralio Astros *Greece* 46 D4
Paramaribo *Suriname* 125 B7
Páramos del Batallón y La
  Negra △ *Venezuela* 121 E5
Paramushir, Ostrov *Russia* 53 D16
Paran → *Israel* 74 E4
Paraná *Argentina* 126 C3
Paraná *Brazil* 125 F9
Paraná □ *Brazil* 127 A5
Paraná → *Argentina* 126 C4
Paranaguá *Brazil* 127 B6
Paranaíba *Brazil* 125 G8
Paranaíba → *Brazil* 125 H8
Paranapanema → *Brazil* 127 A5
Paranapiacaba, Serra do
  Brazil 127 A6
Paranas *Phil.* 61 F6
Paranavaí *Brazil* 127 A5
Parang *Maguindanao, Phil.* 63 C6
Parang *Sulu, Phil.* 61 J4
Parângul Mare, Vf. *Romania* 29 E8
Paraparaumu *N.Z.* 91 D5
Paraspori, Akra *Greece* 47 F9
Paray-le-Monial *France* 19 F11
Parbati → *Mad. P., India* 68 G7
Parbati → *Raj., India* 68 F7
Parbhani *India* 66 K10
Parchim *Germany* 24 B7
Parczew *Poland* 31 G9
Pardes Hanna-Karkur *Israel* 74 C3
Pardilla *Spain* 36 D7
Pardo → *Bahia, Brazil* 125 G11
Pardo → *Mato Grosso, Brazil* 127 A5
Pardoo Roadhouse *Australia* 92 D2
Pardubice *Czech Rep.* 26 A8
Pardubický □ *Czech Rep.* 26 B8
Pare *Indonesia* 63 G15
Pare Mts. *Tanzania* 86 C4
Parecis, Serra dos *Brazil* 124 F7
Paredes de Nava *Spain* 36 C6
Paren *Russia* 53 C17
Parent *Canada* 104 C5
Parent, L. *Canada* 104 C4
Parentis-en-Born *France* 20 D2
Parepare *Indonesia* 63 E5
Parfino *Russia* 32 D6
Parfuri → *Venezuela* 125 K14
Pargas = Parainen *Finland* 32 B2
Pargo, Pta. do *Madeira* 48 D2
Paria → *U.S.A.* 109 H8
Paria, G. de *Venezuela* 125 K14
Pariaguán *Venezuela* 124 B6
Paricutín, Cerro *Mexico* 118 D4
Parigi *Indonesia* 63 E6
Parika *Guyana* 124 B7
Parikia *Greece* 47 D7
Parikkala *Finland* 32 B5
Parima, Serra *Brazil* 124 C6
Parinari *Peru* 124 D4

Pariñas, Pta. *S. Amer.* 122 D2
Parincea *Romania* 29 D12
Pariparti Kyun *Burma* 67 M18
Parintins *Brazil* 125 D7
Paris *Canada* 114 C4
Paris *France* 19 D9
Paris *Idaho, U.S.A.* 108 E8
Paris *Ky., U.S.A.* 113 F11
Paris *Tenn., U.S.A.* 117 C10
Paris *Tex., U.S.A.* 116 E7
Paris, Ville de □ *France* 19 D9
Paris Charles de Gaulle ✕
  (CDG) *France* 19 D9
Paris Orly ✕ (ORY) *France* 19 D9
Parish *U.S.A.* 115 C8
Parishville *U.S.A.* 115 B10
Park *U.S.A.* 110 B4
Park City *U.S.A.* 112 G5
Park Falls *U.S.A.* 112 C8
Park Head *Canada* 114 B3
Park Hills *U.S.A.* 112 G8
Park Range *U.S.A.* 108 F10
Park Rapids *U.S.A.* 112 B6
Park River *U.S.A.* 112 A5
Park Rynie *S. Africa* 89 E5
Parkå Bandar *Iran* 71 E8
Parkano *Finland* 32 A2
Parker *Ariz., U.S.A.* 111 L12
Parker *Pa., U.S.A.* 114 E5
Parker Dam *U.S.A.* 111 L12
Parkersburg *U.S.A.* 113 F13
Parkes *Australia* 95 E4
Parkfield *U.S.A.* 110 K6
Parkhill *Canada* 114 C3
Parkland *U.S.A.* 110 C4
Parkston *U.S.A.* 112 D5
Parksville *Canada* 102 D4
Parkway *U.S.A.* 110 G5
Parla *Spain* 36 E7
Pârlița *Moldova* 29 C12
Parma *Italy* 40 D7
Parma *Idaho, U.S.A.* 108 E5
Parma *Ohio, U.S.A.* 114 E3
Parma → *Italy* 40 D7
Parnaguá *Brazil* 125 F10
Parnaíba *Brazil* 125 D10
Parnaíba → *Brazil* 125 D10
Parnassos *Greece* 46 C4
Parnitha *Greece* 46 C5
Parnitha △ *Greece* 46 C5
Parnonas Oros *Greece* 46 D4
Pärnu *Estonia* 32 C3
Paro Dzong *Bhutan* 69 F13
Paroo → *Australia* 95 E3
Paroo-Darling △ *Australia* 95 E3
Paros *Greece* 47 D7
Parowan *U.S.A.* 109 H7
Parpaillon *France* 21 D10
Parral *Chile* 126 D1
Parras *Mexico* 118 B4
Parrett → *U.K.* 15 F4
Parris I. *U.S.A.* 117 E14
Parrsboro *Canada* 105 C7
Parry I. *Canada* 114 A4
Parry Is. *Canada* 101 B9
Parry Sound *Canada* 114 A5
Parsaloi *Kenya* 86 B4
Parsberg *Germany* 25 F7
Parsęta → *Poland* 30 D2
Parsnip → *Canada* 102 B4
Parsons *U.S.A.* 112 G6
Parsons Ra. *Australia* 94 A2
Partanna *Italy* 42 E5
Partenio △ *Italy* 43 B7
Parthenay *France* 18 F6
Partinico *Italy* 42 D6
Partizansk *Russia* 54 C6
Partizánske *Slovak Rep.* 27 C11
Partridge I. *Canada* 104 A2
Partry Mts. *Ireland* 12 C2
Paru → *Brazil* 125 D8
Parvān □ *Afghan.* 66 B6
Parvatipuram *India* 67 K13
Parvatsar *India* 68 F6
Påryd *Sweden* 11 H9
Parys *S. Africa* 88 D4
Pas, Pta. des *Spain* 48 C7
Pas, The *Canada* 103 C8
Pas-de-Calais □ *France* 19 B9
Pasada *Spain* 36 B5
Pasaje → *Argentina* 126 B3
Pasalimani *Turkey* 45 F11
Pasar *Indonesia* 63 J17
Pasay *Phil.* 61 D4
Pascagoula *U.S.A.* 117 F10
Pascagoula → *U.S.A.* 117 F10
Paşcani *Romania* 29 C11
Pasco *U.S.A.* 108 C4
Pasco, Cerro de *Peru* 124 F3
Pasco I. *Australia* 92 D2
Pascoag *U.S.A.* 115 E13
Pascua, I. de *Chile* 97 K17
Pasewalk *Germany* 24 B9
Pasfield L. *Canada* 103 B7

Pasha → *Russia* **32** B7
Pasinler *Turkey* **73** C9
Pasir Mas *Malaysia* **65** J4
Pasir Panjang *Singapore* **65** d
Pasir Putih *Malaysia* **65** K4
Pasirian *Indonesia* **63** H15
Pasirkuning *Indonesia* **62** E2
Påskallavik *Sweden* **11** G10
Paskūh *Iran* **71** E9
Pasłęk *Poland* **30** D6
Pasłęka → *Poland* **30** D6
Pasley, C. *Australia* **93** F3
Pašman *Croatia* **41** E12
Pasni *Pakistan* **66** G3
Paso Cantinela *Mexico* **111** N11
Paso de Indios *Argentina* **128** E3
Paso de los Libres *Argentina* **126** B4
Paso de los Toros *Uruguay* **126** C4
Paso Robles *U.S.A.* **110** K6
Paspébiac *Canada* **105** C6
Pasrur *Pakistan* **68** C6
Passage East *Ireland* **12** D5
Passage West *Ireland* **12** E3
Passaic *U.S.A.* **115** F10
Passau *Germany* **25** G9
Passero, C. *Italy* **43** F8
Passo Fundo *Brazil* **127** B5
Passos *Brazil* **125** H9
Passow *Germany* **24** B10
Passy *France* **21** C10
Pastavy *Belarus* **32** E4
Pastaza → *Peru* **124** D3
Pasto *Colombia* **124** C3
Pastrana *Spain* **38** E2
Pasuruan *Indonesia* **63** G15
Pasym *Poland* **30** E7
Pásztó *Hungary* **28** C4
Patagonia *Argentina* **128** F3
Patagonia *Argentina* **109** L8
Patambar *Iran* **71** D9
Patan = Lalitapur *Nepal* **69** F11
Patan *India* **68** H5
Patani *Indonesia* **63** D7
Pătârlagele *Romania* **29** E11
Pataudi *India* **68** E7
Patchewollock *Australia* **95** F3
Patchogue *U.S.A.* **115** F11
Pate *Kenya* **86** C5
Patea *N.Z.* **91** C5
Pategi *Nigeria* **83** D6
Patensie *S. Africa* **88** E3
Paterna *Spain* **39** F4
Paternion *Austria* **26** E6
Paternò *Italy* **43** E7
Pateros *U.S.A.* **108** B4
Paterson *U.S.A.* **115** F10
Paterson Ra. *Australia* **92** D3
Pathankot *India* **68** C6
Pathein = Bassein *Burma* **67** L19
Pathfinder Res. *U.S.A.* **108** E10
Pathiu *Thailand* **65** G2
Pathum Thani *Thailand* **64** E3
Pati *Indonesia* **63** G14
Patía → *Colombia* **124** C3
Patiala *Punjab, India* **68** D7
Patiala *Ut. P., India* **69** F8
Patine Kouka *Senegal* **82** C2
Patitiri *Greece* **46** B5
Patkai Bum *India* **67** F19
Patmos *Greece* **47** D8
Patna *India* **69** G11
Patnos *Turkey* **73** C10
Pato Branco *Brazil* **127** B5
Patonga *Uganda* **86** B3
Patos *Albania* **44** F3
Patos *Brazil* **125** E11
Patos, L. dos *Brazil* **127** C5
Patos, Río de los →
   Argentina **126** C2
Patos de Minas *Brazil* **125** G9
Patquía *Argentina* **126** C2
Patra *Greece* **46** C3
Patraikos Kolpos *Greece* **46** C3
Patras = Patra *Greece* **46** C3
Patriot Hills *Antarctica* **5** E16
Patrocínio *Brazil* **125** G9
Pattada *Italy* **42** B2
Pattani *Thailand* **65** J3
Pattaya *Thailand* **64** F3
Patten *U.S.A.* **113** B19
Patterson *Calif., U.S.A.* **110** H5
Patterson *La., U.S.A.* **116** G9
Patterson, Mt. *U.S.A.* **110** G7
Patti *Punjab, India* **68** D6
Patti *Ut. P., India* **69** G10
Patti *Italy* **43** D7
Pattoki *Pakistan* **68** D5
Patton *U.S.A.* **114** F6
Patuakhali *Bangla.* **67** H17
Patuanak *Canada* **103** B7
Patuca → *Honduras* **120** C3
Patuca, Punta *Honduras* **120** C3
Patuca → *Honduras* **120** D2
Pătulele *Romania* **28** F7
Patvinsuo △ *Finland* **8** E24
Pátzcuaro *Mexico* **118** D4

Pau *France* **20** E3
Pau, Gave de → *France* **20** E2
Pauillac *France* **20** C3
Pauk *Burma* **67** J19
Paul I. *Canada* **105** A7
Paul Smiths *U.S.A.* **115** B10
Paulatuk *Canada* **100** C7
Paulhan *France* **20** E7
Paulistana *Brazil* **125** E10
Paulo Afonso *Brazil* **125** E11
Paulpietersburg *S. Africa* **89** D5
Pauls Valley *U.S.A.* **116** D6
Pauma Valley *U.S.A.* **111** M10
Pauri *India* **69** D8
Pāveh *Iran* **73** E12
Pavelets *Russia* **32** F10
Pavia *Italy* **40** C6
Pavilion *U.S.A.* **114** D6
Pavilly *France* **18** C7
Pāvilosta *Latvia* **30** B8
Pavlikeni *Bulgaria* **45** C9
Pavlodar *Kazakhstan* **52** D8
Pavlograd = Pavlohrad
   Ukraine **33** H8
Pavlohrad *Ukraine* **33** H8
Pavlovo *Russia* **34** C6
Pavlovsk *Russia* **34** E5
Pavlovskaya *Russia* **35** G4
Pavlovskiy-Posad *Russia* **32** E10
Pavullo nel Frignano *Italy* **40** D7
Pawai, Pulau *Singapore* **65** d
Pawayan *India* **69** E9
Pawhuska *U.S.A.* **116** C6
Pawling *U.S.A.* **115** E11
Pawnee *U.S.A.* **116** C6
Pawnee City *U.S.A.* **112** E5
Pawtucket *U.S.A.* **115** E13
Paxi *Greece* **46** B2
Paximadia *Greece* **49** E6
Paxton *U.S.A.* **112** E9
Payakumbuh *Indonesia* **62** E2
Payerne *Switz.* **25** J2
Payette *U.S.A.* **108** D5
Payne Bay = Kangirsuk
   Canada **101** D13
Paynes Find *Australia* **93** E2
Paynesville *Liberia* **82** D2
Paynesville *U.S.A.* **112** C6
Pays de la Loire □ *France* **18** E6
Paysandú *Uruguay* **126** C4
Payson *Ariz., U.S.A.* **109** J8
Payson *Utah, U.S.A.* **108** F8
Paz → *Guatemala* **120** D1
Paz, B. de la *Mexico* **118** C2
Pāzanān *Iran* **71** D6
Pazar *Turkey* **73** B9
Pazarcık *Turkey* **72** D7
Pazardzhik *Bulgaria* **45** D8
Pazarköy *Turkey* **47** B9
Pazarlar *Turkey* **47** C11
Pazaryeri *Turkey* **47** B11
Pazaryolu *Turkey* **73** B9
Pazin *Croatia* **41** C10
Pčinja → *Macedonia* **44** E5
Pe Ell *U.S.A.* **110** D3
Peabody *U.S.A.* **115** D14
Peace → *Canada* **102** B6
Peace Point *Canada* **102** B6
Peace River *Canada* **102** B5
Peach Springs *U.S.A.* **109** J7
Peachland *Canada* **102** D5
Peachtree City *U.S.A.* **117** E12
Peak, The = Kinder Scout
   U.K. **14** D6
Peak Charles △ *Australia* **93** F3
Peak District △ *U.K.* **14** D6
Peak Hill *N.S.W., Australia* **95** E4
Peak Hill *W. Austral.,
   Australia* **93** E2
Peak Ra. *Australia* **94** C4
Peake Cr. → *Australia* **95** D2
Peal de Becerro *Spain* **37** H7
Peale, Mt. *U.S.A.* **108** G9
Pearblossom *U.S.A.* **111** L9
Pearl → *U.S.A.* **117** F10
Pearl City *U.S.A.* **106** b
Pearl Harbor *U.S.A.* **106** b
Pearl River = Zhu Jiang →
   China **59** F9
Pearl River *U.S.A.* **115** E10
Pearsall *U.S.A.* **116** G5
Pearson Int. Toronto ✈
   (YYZ) *Canada* **114** C5
Peary Land *Greenland* **4** A6
Pease → *U.S.A.* **116** D5
Peawanuck *Canada* **101** D11
Pebane *Mozam.* **87** F4
Pebas *Peru* **124** D4
Pebble Beach *U.S.A.* **110** J5
Peč *Serbia* **44** D4
Péccioli *Italy* **40** E7
Pechea *Romania* **29** E12
Pechenga *Russia* **8** B24
Pechenizhyn *Ukraine* **29** B9
Pechiguera, Pta. *Canary Is.* **48** F6

Pechnezhskoye Vdkhr.
   Ukraine **33** G9
Pechora *Russia* **52** C6
Pechora → *Russia* **6** B16
Pechorskaya Guba *Russia* **52** C6
Pechory *Russia* **32** D4
Pecica *Romania* **28** D6
Pecka *Serbia* **44** B3
Pécora, C. *Italy* **42** C1
Pecos *N. Mex., U.S.A.* **109** J11
Pecos *Tex., U.S.A.* **116** F3
Pecos → *U.S.A.* **116** G4
Pécs *Hungary* **28** D3
Pedder, L. *Australia* **95** G4
Pedernales *Dom. Rep.* **121** C5
Pedirka *Australia* **95** D2
Pedieos → *Cyprus* **49** D12
Pedra Azul *Brazil* **125** G10
Pedra Lume *C. Verde Is.* **78** b
Pedreguer *Spain* **39** G5
Pedreiras *Brazil* **125** D10
Pedro Afonso *Brazil* **125** E9
Pedro Cays *Jamaica* **120** C4
Pedro de Valdivia *Chile* **126** A2
Pedro Juan Caballero
   Paraguay **127** A4
Pedro Muñoz *Spain* **37** F8
Pedrógão Grande *Portugal* **36** F2
Pee Dee = Great Pee
   Dee → *U.S.A.* **117** E15
Peebinga *Australia* **95** E3
Peebles *U.K.* **13** F5
Peekskill *U.S.A.* **115** E11
Peel *I. of Man* **14** C3
Peel → *Australia* **95** E5
Peel → *Canada* **100** C6
Peel Sd. *Canada* **100** B10
Peene → *Germany* **24** A9
Peera Peera Poolanna L.
   Australia **95** D2
Peerless Lake *Canada* **102** B6
Peers *Canada* **102** C5
Pegasus Bay *N.Z.* **91** E4
Peggau *Austria* **26** D8
Pegnitz *Germany* **25** F7
Pegnitz → *Germany* **25** F6
Pego *Spain* **39** G4
Pegu *Burma* **67** L20
Pegu Yoma *Burma* **67** K20
Pehčevo *Macedonia* **44** E6
Pehlivanköy *Turkey* **45** E10
Pehuajó *Argentina* **126** D3
Pei Xian = Pizhou *China* **56** G9
Peikang *Taiwan* **59** F13
Peine *Chile* **126** A2
Peine *Germany* **24** C6
Peip'ing = Beijing *China* **56** E9
Peipus, L. = Chudskoye,
   Ozero *Russia* **32** C4
Peissenberg *Germany* **25** H7
Peitz *Germany* **24** D10
Peixe *Brazil* **125** F9
Peixe → *Brazil* **125** H8
Pek → *Serbia* **44** B5
Pekalongan *Indonesia* **63** G13
Pekan *Malaysia* **65** L4
Pekan Nenas *Malaysia* **65** d
Pekanbaru *Indonesia* **62** D2
Pekin *U.S.A.* **112** E9
Peking = Beijing *China* **56** E9
Pekutatan *Indonesia* **63** J17
Pela *Greece* **44** F6
Péla *Guinea* **82** D3
Pelabuhan Klang *Malaysia* **65** L3
Pelabuhan Ratu, Teluk
   Indonesia **63** G12
Pelabuhanratu *Indonesia* **63** G12
Pélagos = Kira Panagia
   Greece **46** B6
Pelaihari *Indonesia* **62** E4
Pelat, Mt. *France* **21** D10
Pelée, Mt. *Martinique* **120** c
Pelee, Pt. *Canada* **104** D3
Pelee I. *Canada* **114** E2
Pelekech *Kenya* **86** B4
Peleng *Indonesia* **63** E6
Pelentong *Malaysia* **65** d
Pélézi *Ivory C.* **82** D3
Pelhřimov *Czech Rep.* **26** B8
Pelican *U.S.A.* **102** B1
Pelican L. *Canada* **103** C8
Pelican Narrows *Canada* **103** B8
Pelister △ *Macedonia* **44** F5
Pelješac *Croatia* **41** F14
Pelkosenniemi *Finland* **8** C22
Pella *S. Africa* **88** D2
Pella *U.S.A.* **112** E7
Pella □ *Greece* **44** F6
Pello *Finland* **8** C20
Pellworm *Germany* **24** A4
Pelly → *Canada* **102** A1
Pelly Bay *Canada* **101** C11
Peloponnese □ *Greece* **46** D4
Peloritani, Monti *Italy* **43** D8

Pelorus Sd. *N.Z.* **91** D4
Pelotas *Brazil* **127** C5
Pelotas → *Brazil* **127** B5
Pelovo *Bulgaria* **45** C8
Pelplin *Poland* **30** E5
Pelvoux, Massif du *France* **21** D10
Pemalang *Indonesia* **63** G13
Pemanggil, Pulau *Malaysia* **65** L5
Pematangsiantar *Indonesia* **62** D1
Pemba *Mozam.* **87** E5
Pemba *Zambia* **87** F2
Pemba Channel *Tanzania* **86** D4
Pemba I. *Tanzania* **86** D4
Pemberton *Australia* **93** F2
Pemberton *Canada* **102** C4
Pembina → *Canada* **102** C6
Pembroke *Canada* **104** C4
Pembroke *U.K.* **15** F3
Pembroke □ *U.K.* **15** F3
Pembrokeshire Coast △
   U.K. **15** F2
Pen-y-Ghent *U.K.* **14** C5
Peña, Sierra de la *Spain* **38** C4
Peña de Francia, Sierra de
   la *Spain* **36** E4
Peñafiel *Portugal* **36** D2
Peñafiel *Spain* **36** D6
Peñaflor *Spain* **37** H5
Peñalara *Spain* **36** E4
Penamacôr *Portugal* **36** E3
Penang = Pinang *Malaysia* **65** c
Penápolis *Brazil* **127** A6
Peñaranda de Bracamonte
   Spain **36** E4
Peñarroya *Spain* **38** E4
Peñarroya-Pueblonuevo
   Spain **37** G5
Penarth *U.K.* **15** F4
Peñas, C. de *Spain* **36** B5
Peñas, G. de *Chile* **128** F2
Peñas de San Pedro *Spain* **39** G3
Peñas del Chache *Canary Is.* **48** E6
Peñausende *Spain* **36** D5
Pench △ *India* **69** J8
Pench'i = Benxi *China* **57** D12
Pend Oreille → *U.S.A.* **108** B5
Pend Oreille, L. *U.S.A.* **108** B5
Pendalofos *Greece* **44** F5
Pendembu *Eastern, S. Leone* **82** D2
Pendembu *Northern, S. Leone* **82** D2
Pender B. *Australia* **92** C3
Pendik *Turkey* **45** F13
Pendjari → *Benin* **83** C5
Pendjari △ *Benin* **83** C5
Pendleton *U.S.A.* **108** D4
Pendra *India* **69** H9
Peneda-Gerês △ *Portugal* **36** D2
Penedo *Brazil* **125** F11
Penelokan *Indonesia* **63** J18
Penetanguishene *Canada* **114** B5
Penfield *U.S.A.* **114** E6
Pengalengan *Indonesia* **63** G12
Penge *Kasai-Or.,
   Dem. Rep. of the Congo* **86** D1
Penge *Sud-Kivu,
   Dem. Rep. of the Congo* **86** C2
P'enghu Ch'üntou *Taiwan* **59** F12
Penglai *China* **57** F11
Pengshan *China* **58** B4
Pengshui *China* **58** C7
Penguin *Australia* **95** G4
Pengxi *China* **58** B5
Pengze *China* **59** C11
Penhalonga *Zimbabwe* **87** F3
Peniche *Portugal* **37** F1
Penicuik *U.K.* **13** F5
Penida, Nusa *Indonesia* **63** K18
Peninnes, Alpes =
   Pennine, Alpi *Alps* **25** J3
Peninsular Malaysia □
   Malaysia **65** L4
Peñíscola *Spain* **38** E5
Penitente, Serra do *Brazil* **125** E9
Penkridge *U.K.* **14** E5
Penmark *France* **18** E2
Penmarch, Pte. de *France* **18** E2
Penn Hills *U.S.A.* **114** F5
Penn Yan *U.S.A.* **114** D7
Penna, Punta della *Italy* **41** F11
Pennant *Canada* **103** C7
Penne *Italy* **41** F11
Penner → *India* **66** M12
Pennine, Alpi *Alps* **25** J3
Pennines *U.K.* **14** C5
Pennington *U.S.A.* **110** F5
Pennino, Mte. *Italy* **41** F9
Pennsburg *U.S.A.* **115** F9
Pennsylvania □ *U.S.A.* **113** E15
Penny Ice Cap *Canada* **102** C4
Penny Str. *Canada* **101** B8
Peno *Russia* **32** D7
Penobscot → *U.S.A.* **113** C19
Penobscot B. *U.S.A.* **113** C19
Penola *Australia* **95** F3
Penong *Australia* **93** F5

Penonomé *Panama* **120** E3
Penrhyn *Cook Is.* **97** H12
Penrith *Australia* **95** E5
Penrith *U.K.* **14** C5
Penryn *U.K.* **15** G2
Pensacola *U.S.A.* **117** F11
Pensacola Mts. *Antarctica* **5** E1
Pense *Canada* **103** C8
Penshurst *Australia* **95** F3
Penticton *Canada* **102** D5
Pentland *Australia* **94** C4
Pentland Firth *U.K.* **13** C5
Pentland Hills *U.K.* **13** F5
Pentland Hills △ *U.K.* **13** F5
Penza *Russia* **34** D7
Penza □ *Russia* **34** D7
Penzance *U.K.* **15** G2
Penzberg *Germany* **25** H7
Penzhino *Russia* **53** C17
Penzhinskaya Guba *Russia* **53** C17
Penzhou *China* **58** B4
Penzlin *Germany* **24** B9
Peoria *Ariz., U.S.A.* **109** K7
Peoria *Ill., U.S.A.* **112** E9
Pepacton Res. *U.S.A.* **115** D10
Pepani → *S. Africa* **88** D3
Pepel *S. Leone* **82** D2
Peqin *Albania* **44** E3
Pera Hd. *Australia* **94** A3
Perabumulih *Indonesia* **62** E2
Perachora *Greece* **46** C4
Perak □ *Malaysia* **65** K3
Perales de Alfambra *Spain* **38** E4
Perales del Puerto *Spain* **36** E4
Perama *Kerkyra, Greece* **49** A3
Perama *Kriti, Greece* **49** D6
Perancak *Indonesia* **63** J17
Peräpohjola *Finland* **8** C22
Perast *Montenegro* **44** D2
Percé *Canada* **105** C7
Perche *France* **18** D8
Perche, Collines du *France* **18** D7
Percival Lakes *Australia* **92** D4
Percy *France* **18** D5
Percy Is. *Australia* **94** C5
Perdido, Mte. *Spain* **38** C5
Perdu, Mt. = Perdido, Mte.
   Spain **38** C5
Perechyn *Ukraine* **28** B7
Perehinske *Ukraine* **29** B9
Pereira *Colombia* **124** C3
Perelazovskiy *Russia* **35** F6
Perenjori *Australia* **93** E2
Peresecina *Moldova* **29** C13
Pereslavi-Zalesskiy *Russia* **32** D10
Pereyaslav-Khmelnytskyy
   Ukraine **33** G6
Pereyma *Ukraine* **29** B14
Pérez, I. *Mexico* **119** C7
Perg *Austria* **26** C7
Pergamino *Argentina* **126** C3
Pergau → *Malaysia* **65** K3
Pérgine Valsugana *Italy* **41** B8
Pérgola *Italy* **41** E9
Perham *U.S.A.* **112** B6
Perhentian, Kepulauan
   Malaysia **65** K4
Peri → *Turkey* **73** C8
Periam *Romania* **28** D5
Péribonka → *Canada* **105** C5
Péribonka, L. *Canada* **105** B5
Perico *Argentina* **126** A2
Pericos *Mexico* **118** B3
Périers *France* **18** C5
Périgord *France* **20** D4
Périgord-Limousin △ *France* **20** C4
Périgueux *France* **20** C4
Perijá, Sierra de *Colombia* **124** B4
Perijá △ *Venezuela* **121** E5
Peristera *Greece* **46** B5
Peristerona → *Cyprus* **49** D12
Perito Moreno *Argentina* **128** F2
Perivol = Dragovishtitsa
   Bulgaria **44** D6
Perkasie *U.S.A.* **115** F9
Perković *Croatia* **41** E13
Perlas, Arch. de las *Panama* **104** E4
Perlas, Punta de *Nic.* **120** D3
Perleberg *Germany* **24** B7
Perlez *Serbia* **28** E5
Perm *Russia* **52** D6
Përmet *Albania* **44** F4
Pernambuco = Recife
   Brazil **125** E12
Pernambuco □ *Brazil* **125** E11
Pernatty Lagoon *Australia* **95** E2
Pernik *Bulgaria* **44** D7
Peron Is. *Australia* **92** B5
Peron Pen. *Australia* **93** E1
Péronne *France* **19** C9
Perosa Argentina *Italy* **40** D4
Perow *Canada* **102** C3
Perpignan *France* **20** F6
Perris *U.S.A.* **111** M9
Perros-Guirec *France* **18** D3

Perry *Fla., U.S.A.* **117** F13
Perry *Ga., U.S.A.* **117** E13
Perry *Iowa, U.S.A.* **112** E6
Perry *Okla., U.S.A.* **116** C6
Perryton *U.S.A.* **116** C4
Perryville *U.S.A.* **112** G9
Persan *France* **19** C9
Persberg *Sweden* **10** E8
Persembe *Turkey* **72** B7
Persepolis *Iran* **71** D7
Pershotravensk *Ukraine* **23** C14
Persia = Iran ■ *Asia* **71** C7
Persian Gulf *Asia* **71** E6
Perstorp *Sweden* **11** H7
Perth *Australia* **93** F2
Perth *Canada* **115** B8
Perth *U.K.* **13** E5
Perth & Kinross □ *U.K.* **13** E5
Perth Amboy *U.S.A.* **115** F10
Perth-Andover *Canada* **105** C6
Perth Basin *Ind. Oc.* **96** L2
Pertuis *France* **21** E9
Pertusato, C. *France* **21** G13
Peru *Ind., U.S.A.* **112** E10
Peru *N.Y., U.S.A.* **115** B11
Peru ■ *S. Amer.* **124** D4
Peru Basin *Pac. Oc.* **97** J18
Peru-Chile Trench *Pac. Oc.* **124** G3
Perúgia *Italy* **41** E9
Perušić *Croatia* **41** D12
Pervomaysk *Russia* **34** C6
Pervomaysk *Ukraine* **33** H6
Pervouralsk *Russia* **52** D6
Pésaro *Italy* **41** E9
Pescadores = P'enghu
   Ch'üntou *Taiwan* **59** F12
Pescara *Italy* **41** F11
Pescara → *Italy* **41** F11
Peschanokopskoye *Russia* **35** G5
Péscia *Italy* **40** E7
Pescina *Italy* **41** F10
Peshawar *Pakistan* **68** B4
Peshkopi *Albania* **44** E4
Peshtera *Bulgaria* **45** D8
Peshtigo *U.S.A.* **112** C10
Peski *Russia* **34** E6
Pêso da Régua *Portugal* **36** D3
Pesqueira *Brazil* **125** E11
Pessac *France* **20** D3
Pest □ *Hungary* **28** C4
Pestovo *Russia* **32** C8
Pestravka *Russia* **34** D9
Petah Tiqwa *Israel* **74** C3
Petalidi *Greece* **46** E4
Petaling Jaya *Malaysia* **65** L3
Petaloudes *Greece* **49** C10
Petaluma *U.S.A.* **110** G4
Pétange *Lux.* **17** E5
Petaro *Pakistan* **68** G3
Petas *Greece* **46** B3
Petatlán *Mexico* **118** D4
Petauke *Zambia* **87** E3
Petawawa *Canada* **104** C4
Petén Itzá, L. *Guatemala* **120** C2
Peter I. *Br. Virgin Is.* **121** e
Peter I. Øy *Antarctica* **5** C16
Peter Pond L. *Canada* **103** B7
Peterbell *Canada* **104** C3
Peterborough *Australia* **95** E2
Peterborough *Canada* **114** B6
Peterborough *U.K.* **15** E7
Peterborough *U.S.A.* **115** D13
Peterborough □ *U.K.* **15** E7
Peterculter *U.K.* **13** D6
Peterhead *U.K.* **13** D7
Peterlee *U.K.* **14** C6
Petermann Ranges *Australia* **93** E5
Petersburg *Alaska, U.S.A.* **100** D6
Petersburg *Pa., U.S.A.* **114** F6
Petersburg *Va., U.S.A.* **113** G15
Petersburg *W. Va., U.S.A.* **113** F14
Petersfield *U.K.* **15** F7
Petershagen *Germany* **24** C4
Petília Policastro *Italy* **43** C9
Petit Goâve *Haiti* **121** C5
Petit Jardin *Canada* **105** C8
Petit Lac Manicouagan
   Canada **105** B6
Petit-Mécatina → *Canada* **105** B8
Petit-Mécatina, Î. du
   Canada **105** B8
Petit Piton *St. Lucia* **121** f
Petit-Saguenay *Canada* **105** C5
Petit Saint Bernard, Col du
   Italy **21** C10
Petitcodiac *Canada* **105** C6
Petite Terre, Îles de la
   Guadeloupe **120** b
Petitot → *Canada* **102** A4
Petitsikapau L. *Canada* **105** B6
Petlad *India* **68** H5
Peto *Mexico* **119** C7
Petone *N.Z.* **91** D5
Petorca *Chile* **126** C1
Petoskey *U.S.A.* **113** C11

Petra *Jordan* **74** E4
Petra *Spain* **48** B10
Petra, Ostrova *Russia* **4** B13
Petra Velikogo, Zaliv *Russia* **54** C6
Petrel = Petrer *Spain* **39** G4
Petrella, Monte *Italy* **42** A6
Petrer *Spain* **39** G4
Petreto-Bicchisano *France* **21** G12
Petrich *Bulgaria* **44** E7
Petrified Forest △ *U.S.A.* **109** J9
Petrijanec *Croatia* **41** B13
Petrikov = Pyetrikaw
   Belarus **23** B15
Petrila *Romania* **29** E8
Petrinja *Croatia* **41** C13
Petrodvorets *Russia* **32** C5
Petrolândia *Brazil* **125** E11
Petrolia *Canada* **114** D2
Petrolina *Brazil* **125** E10
Petropavl *Kazakhstan* **52** D7
Petropavlovsk = Petropavl
   Kazakhstan **52** D7
Petropavlovsk-
   Kamchatskiy *Russia* **53** D16
Petropavlovskiy =
   Akhtubinsk *Russia* **35** F8
Petrópolis *Brazil* **127** A7
Petroşani *Romania* **29** E8
Petrova Gora *Croatia* **41** C12
Petrovac *Montenegro* **44** D2
Petrovac *Serbia* **44** B5
Petrovaradin *Serbia* **28** E4
Petrovsk *Russia* **34** D7
Petrovsk-Zabaykalskiy
   Russia **53** D11
Petrovskaya *Russia* **33** K9
Petrozavodsk *Russia* **32** B8
Petrus Steyn *S. Africa* **89** D4
Petrusburg *S. Africa* **88** D4
Petzeck *Austria* **26** E5
Peumo *Chile* **126** C1
Peureulak *Indonesia* **62** D1
Pevek *Russia* **53** C18
Peveragno *Italy* **40** D4
Peyrehorade *France* **20** E2
Peyruis *France* **21** D9
Pézenas *France* **20** E7
Pezinok *Slovak Rep.* **27** C10
Pfaffenhofen *Germany* **25** G7
Pfälzerwald △ *Germany* **25** F5
Pfarrkirchen *Germany* **25** G8
Pfeffenhausen *Germany* **25** G7
Pforzheim *Germany* **25** G4
Pfullendorf *Germany* **25** H5
Pfungstadt *Germany* **25** F4
Pha Taem △ *Thailand* **64** E5
Phaestos *Greece* **49** D6
Phagwara *India* **68** D6
Phala *Botswana* **88** C4
Phalera = Phulera *India* **68** F6
Phalodi *India* **68** F5
Phalsbourg *France* **19** D14
Phaluai, Ko *Thailand* **65** b
Phan *Thailand* **64** C2
Phan Rang *Vietnam* **65** G7
Phan Ri = Hoa Da *Vietnam* **65** G7
Phan Thiet *Vietnam* **65** G7
Phanae *Greece* **47** C7
Phanat Nikhom *Thailand* **64** F3
Phangan, Ko *Thailand* **65** H3
Phangnga *Thailand* **65** H2
Phangnga, Ao *Thailand* **65** a
Phanom Sarakham *Thailand* **64** F3
Phaphund *India* **69** F8
Pharenda *India* **69** F10
Pharr *U.S.A.* **116** H5
Phatthalung *Thailand* **65** J3
Phayao *Thailand* **64** C2
Phelps *U.S.A.* **114** D7
Phelps L. *Canada* **103** B8
Phenix City *U.S.A.* **117** E12
Phet Buri *Thailand* **64** F2
Phetchabun *Thailand* **64** D3
Phetchabun, Thiu Khao
   Thailand **64** E3
Phetchaburi = Phet Buri
   Thailand **64** F2
Phi Phi, Ko *Thailand* **65** J2
Phiafay *Laos* **64** E6
Phibun Mangsahan *Thailand* **64** E5
Phichai *Thailand* **64** D3
Phichit *Thailand* **64** D3
Philadelphia *Miss., U.S.A.* **117** E10
Philadelphia *N.Y., U.S.A.* **115** B9
Philadelphia *Pa., U.S.A.* **115** G9
Philip *U.S.A.* **112** C3
Philipi *Greece* **45** E8
Philippeville *Belgium* **17** D4
Philippi *U.S.A.* **113** F13
Philippi L. *Australia* **94** C2
Philippine Basin *Pac. Oc.* **96** F5
Philippine Sea *Pac. Oc.* **96** F4
Philippine Trench =
   Mindanao Trench *Pac. Oc.* **61** F7
Philippines ■ *Asia* **61** F5
Philippolis *S. Africa* **88** E4
Philippopolis = Plovdiv
   Bulgaria **45** D8

Philipsburg *Canada* **115** A11
Philipsburg *Mont., U.S.A.* **108** C7
Philipsburg *Pa., U.S.A.* **114** F6
Philipstown = Daingean
   Ireland **12** C4
Philipstown *S. Africa* **88** E3
Phillip I. *Australia* **95** F4
Phillips *U.S.A.* **112** C8
Phillipsburg *Kans., U.S.A.* **112** F4
Phillipsburg *N.J., U.S.A.* **115** F9
Philmont *U.S.A.* **115** D11
Philomath *U.S.A.* **108** D2
Phimai *Thailand* **64** E4
Phitsanulok *Thailand* **64** D3
Phnom Dangrek *Thailand* **64** E5
Phnom Penh *Cambodia* **65** G5
Phnum Penh = Phnom
   Penh *Cambodia* **65** G5
Phoenicia *U.S.A.* **115** D10
Phoenix *Mauritius* **85** d
Phoenix *Ariz., U.S.A.* **109** K7
Phoenix *N.Y., U.S.A.* **115** C8
Phoenix Is. *Kiribati* **96** H10
Phoenixville *U.S.A.* **115** F9
Phon *Thailand* **64** E4
Phon Tiou *Laos* **64** D5
Phong → *Thailand* **64** D4
Phong Saly *Laos* **58** G4
Phong Tho *Vietnam* **64** A4
Phonhong *Laos* **64** C4
Phonum *Thailand* **65** H2
Phra Nakhon Si
   Ayutthaya *Thailand* **64** E3
Phra Thong, Ko *Thailand* **65** H2
Phrae *Thailand* **64** C3
Phrom Phiram *Thailand* **64** D3
Phrygia *Turkey* **72** C4
Phu Bia *Laos* **64** C4
Phu Chong-Na Yoi △
   Thailand **64** E6
Phu Dien *Vietnam* **64** C5
Phu Hin Rang Kla △
   Thailand **64** D3
Phu Kradung △ *Thailand* **64** D3
Phu Loi *Laos* **64** B4
Phu Luang △ *Thailand* **64** D3
Phu Ly *Vietnam* **58** G5
Phu Phan △ *Thailand* **64** D4
Phu Quoc, Dao *Vietnam* **65** G4
Phu Tho *Vietnam* **58** G5
Phuc Yen *Vietnam* **58** G5
Phuket *Thailand* **65** a
Phuket, Ko *Thailand* **65** a
Phul *India* **68** D6
Phulad *India* **68** G5
Phulchari *Bangla.* **69** G13
Phulera *India* **68** F6
Phulpur *India* **69** G10
Phun Phin *Thailand* **65** H2
Phulera *India* **68** F6
Piacenza *Italy* **40** C6
Piai, Tanjung *Malaysia* **65** d
Pian Cr. → *Australia* **95** E4
Pian-Upe △ *Uganda* **86** B3
Piana *France* **21** F12
Pianella *Italy* **41** F11
Pianosa *Puglia, Italy* **41** F12
Pianosa *Toscana, Italy* **40** F7
Piapot *Canada* **103** D7
Pias *Portugal* **37** G3
Piaseczno *Poland* **31** F8
Piaski *Poland* **31** G9
Piastów *Poland* **31** F7
Piatra *Romania* **29** G10
Piatra Craiului △ *Romania* **29** E10
Piatra Neamţ *Romania* **29** D11
Piatra Olt *Romania* **29** F9
Piauí □ *Brazil* **125** E10
Piauí → *Brazil* **125** E10
Piave → *Italy* **41** C9
Piazza Ármerina *Italy* **43** E7
Pibor → *Sudan* **81** F3
Pibor Post *Sudan* **81** F3
Picardie □ *France* **19** C10
Picardie, Plaine de *France* **19** C9
Picardy = Picardie □
   France **19** C10
Picayune *U.S.A.* **117** F10
Picerno *Italy* **43** B8
Pichhor *India* **69** G8
Pichilemu *Chile* **126** C1
Pichor *India* **69** G8
Pickerel L. *Canada* **104** C1
Pickering *U.K.* **14** C7
Pickering, Vale of *U.K.* **14** C7
Pickle Lake *Canada* **104** B1
Pickwick L. *U.S.A.* **117** D10
Pico *Azores* **78** a
Pico Bonito △ *Honduras* **120** C2
Pico Truncado *Argentina* **128** F3
Picos *Brazil* **125** E10
Picos de Europa △ *Spain* **36** B6
Picton *Australia* **95** E5
Picton *Canada* **114** B7
Picton *N.Z.* **91** D5
Pictou *Canada* **105** C7

Picture Butte *Canada* **102** D6
Pictured Rocks △ *U.S.A.* **112** B10
Picún Leufú *Argentina* **128** D3
Pidbuzh *Ukraine* **31** J10
Pidurutalagala *Sri Lanka* **66** R12
Piechowice *Poland* **31** H2
Piedimonte Matese *Italy* **43** A7
Piedmont = Piemonte □
   Italy **40** D5
Piedmont *Ala., U.S.A.* **117** E12
Piedmont *S.C., U.S.A.* **107** D10
Piedra → *Spain* **38** D3
Piedrabuena *Spain* **37** G6
Piedrahita *Spain* **36** E5
Piedralaves *Spain* **36** E6
Piedras Blancas *Spain* **36** B5
Piedras Negras *Mexico* **118** B4
Piekary Śląskie *Poland* **31** H5
Pieksämäki *Finland* **32** A4
Pielinen *Finland* **8** E23
Piemonte □ *Italy* **40** D5
Pienaarsrivier *S. Africa* **89** D4
Pieniężno *Poland* **30** D7
Pieninský △ *Europe* **27** B13
Pieńsk *Poland* **31** G2
Piercefield *U.S.A.* **115** B10
Pierceland *Canada* **103** C7
Pieria □ *Greece* **44** F6
Pierpont *U.S.A.* **114** E4
Pierre *U.S.A.* **112** C3
Pierre-Buffière *France* **20** C5
Pierre-de-Bresse *France* **19** F12
Pierrefontaine-les-Varans
   France **19** E13
Pierrefort *France* **20** D6
Pierrelatte *France* **21** D8
Pierreville *Trin. & Tob.* **125** K16
Pieštany *Slovak Rep.* **27** C10
Piešting *Austria* **27** C9
Pieszyce *Poland* **31** H3
Piet Retief *S. Africa* **89** D5
Pietarsaari *Finland* **8** E20
Pietermaritzburg *S. Africa* **89** D5
Pietersburg = Polokwane
   S. Africa **89** C4
Pietragalla *Italy* **43** B8
Pietrasanta *Italy* **40** E7
Pietroşiţa *Romania* **29** E10
Pietrosul, Vf. *Maramureş,*
   Romania **29** C9
Pietrosul, Vf. *Suceava,*
   Romania **29** C10
Pieve di Cadore *Italy* **41** B9
Pieve di Teco *Italy* **40** D4
Pievepélago *Italy* **40** D7
Pigaditsa *Greece* **44** G5
Pigeon L. *Canada* **114** B6
Piges *Greece* **46** B3
Piggott *U.S.A.* **117** C9
Pigna *Italy* **40** E4
Pigüe *Argentina* **126** D3
Pihani *India* **69** F9
Pihlajavesi *Finland* **32** B5
Pijijiapan *Mexico* **119** D6
Pikalevo *Russia* **32** C8
Pikangikum *Canada* **103** C10
Pikes Peak *U.S.A.* **108** G11
Piketberg *S. Africa* **88** E2
Pikeville *U.S.A.* **113** G12
Pikou *China* **57** E12
Pikwitonei *Canada* **103** B9
Piła *Poland* **31** E3
Pila *Spain* **39** G3
Pilanesberg △ *S. Africa* **88** D4
Pilani *India* **68** E6
Pilar *Paraguay* **126** B4
Pilar de la Horadada *Spain* **39** H4
Pilat △ *France* **21** C8
Pilawa *Poland* **31** G8
Pilaya → *Bolivia* **124** H6
Pilbara *Australia* **92** D2
Pilcomayo → *Paraguay* **126** B4
Pilea *Greece* **44** F6
Pilgrim's Rest *S. Africa* **89** C5
Pilgrimstad *Sweden* **10** B9
Pili *Greece* **47** E9
Pilibhit *India* **69** E8
Pilica → *Poland* **31** G8
Pilio, Oros *Greece* **46** B5
Pilipinas = Philippines ■
   Asia **61** F5
Pilis *Hungary* **28** C4
Pilisvörösvár *Hungary* **28** C3
Pilkhawa *India* **68** E7
Pilliga *Australia* **95** E4
Pilos *Greece* **46** E3
Pilot Mound *Canada* **103** D9
Pilot Point *U.S.A.* **116** E6
Pilot Rock *U.S.A.* **108** D4
Pilštanj *Slovenia* **41** B12
Piltene *Latvia* **30** A8
Pilzno *Poland* **31** J8
Pima *U.S.A.* **109** K9
Pimba *Australia* **95** E2
Pimenta Bueno *Brazil* **124** F6
Pimentel *Peru* **124** E3
Pin Valley △ *India* **68** D7

Pina de Ebro *Spain* **38** D4
Pinamalayan *Phil.* **61** E4
Pinang *Malaysia* **65** c
Pinar, C. des *Spain* **38** B10
Pinar del Río *Cuba* **120** B3
Pınarbaşı *Çanakkale, Turkey* **47** B8
Pınarbaşı *Kayseri, Turkey* **72** C7
Pınarhisar *Turkey* **45** E11
Pinatubo, Mt. *Phil.* **61** D3
Pinawa *Canada* **103** C9
Pincehely *Hungary* **28** D3
Pinchang *China* **58** B6
Pincher Creek *Canada* **102** D6
Pinchi L. *Canada* **102** C4
Pinckneyville *U.S.A.* **112** F9
Píndar *Australia* **93** E2
Pindi Gheb *Pakistan* **68** C5
Pindiga *Nigeria* **83** D7
Pindos △ *Greece* **46** B3
Pindos Oros *Greece* **46** B3
Pindus Mts. = Pindos Oros
   Greece **46** B3
Pine → *B.C., Canada* **102** B4
Pine → *Sask., Canada* **103** B7
Pine, C. *Canada* **105** C9
Pine Bluff *U.S.A.* **116** D8
Pine Bluffs *U.S.A.* **108** F11
Pine City *U.S.A.* **112** C7
Pine Cr. → *U.S.A.* **114** E7
Pine Creek *Australia* **92** B5
Pine Falls *Canada* **103** C9
Pine Flat L. *U.S.A.* **110** J7
Pine Grove *U.S.A.* **115** F8
Pine Hill *Australia* **94** C4
Pine Pass *Canada* **102** B4
Pine Point *Canada* **102** A6
Pine Ridge *U.S.A.* **112** D2
Pine River *Canada* **103** C8
Pine River *U.S.A.* **112** B6
Pine Valley *U.S.A.* **111** N10
Pinecrest *U.S.A.* **110** G6
Pinedale *Calif., U.S.A.* **110** J7
Pinedale *Wyo., U.S.A.* **108** E9
Pinega → *Russia* **52** C5
Pinehouse L. *Canada* **103** B7
Pineimuta → *Canada* **104** B1
Pinerolo *Italy* **40** D4
Pines, Akra *Greece* **45** F8
Pineto *Italy* **41** F11
Pinetop-Lakeside *U.S.A.* **109** J9
Pinetown *S. Africa* **89** D5
Pineville *U.S.A.* **116** F8
Piney *France* **19** D11
Ping → *Thailand* **64** E3
Pingaring *Australia* **93** F2
Pingba *China* **58** D6
Pingbian *China* **58** F4
Pingchuan *China* **58** D3
Pingding *China* **56** F7
Pingdingshan *China* **56** H7
Pingdong *Taiwan* **59** F13
Pingdu *China* **57** F10
Pingelly *Australia* **93** F2
Pingguo *China* **58** F6
Pinghe *China* **59** E11
Pinghu *China* **59** B13
Pingjiang *China* **59** C9
Pingle *China* **59** E8
Pingli *China* **58** A7
Pingliang *China* **56** G4
Pinglu *China* **56** E9
Pingluo *China* **56** E4
Pingnan *Fujian, China* **59** D12
Pingnan *Guangxi Zhuangzu,*
   China **59** F8
Pingquan *China* **57** D10
Pingrup *Australia* **93** F2
Pingshan *China* **58** C5
Pingtan *China* **59** E12
Pingtang *China* **58** E6
P'ingtung *Taiwan* **59** F13
Pingwu *China* **56** H3
Pingxiang
   Guangxi Zhuangzu, China **58** F6
Pingxiang *Jiangxi, China* **59** D9
Pingyao *China* **56** F7
Pingyi *China* **57** G9
Pingyin *China* **56** F9
Pingyuan *Guangdong, China* **59** E10
Pingyuan *Shandong, China* **56** F9
Pingyuanjie *China* **58** F4
Pinhal *Brazil* **127** A6
Pinhal Novo *Portugal* **37** G2
Pinheiro *Brazil* **125** D9
Pinheiro Machado *Brazil* **127** C5
Pinhel *Portugal* **36** E3
Pini *Indonesia* **62** D1
Pinios → *Ilia, Greece* **46** D3
Pinios → *Trikala, Greece* **46** B4
Pinjarra *Australia* **93** F2
Pink Mountain *Canada* **102** B4
Pinkafeld *Austria* **27** D9
Pinnacles △ *U.S.A.* **110** J5
Pinnaroo *Australia* **95** F3
Pinneberg *Germany* **24** B5

Pinon Hills *U.S.A.* **111** L9
Pinos *Mexico* **118** C4
Pinos, Mt. *U.S.A.* **111** L7
Pinos Pt. *U.S.A.* **109** H3
Pinos Puente *Spain* **37** H7
Pinrang *Indonesia* **63** E5
Pins, Pte. aux *Canada* **114** D3
Pinsk *Belarus* **23** B14
Pintados *Chile* **124** H5
Pinyang *China* **59** D13
Pinyug *Russia* **52** C5
Pioche *U.S.A.* **109** H6
Piombino *Italy* **40** F7
Piombino, Canale di *Italy* **40** F7
Pioner, Ostrov *Russia* **53** B10
Pionerskiy *Russia* **30** D7
Pionki *Poland* **31** G8
Piopiotaki = Milford Sd. *N.Z.* **91** F1
Piorini, L. *Brazil* **124** D6
Piotrków Trybunalski
   Poland **31** G6
Piove di Sacco *Italy* **41** C9
Pip *Iran* **71** E9
Pipar *India* **68** F5
Pipar Road *India* **68** F5
Piparia *Mad. P., India* **68** H8
Piparia *Mad. P., India* **68** J7
Piperi *Greece* **46** B6
Pipestone *U.S.A.* **112** D5
Pipestone → *Canada* **104** B2
Pipestone Cr. → *Canada* **103** D8
Piplan *Pakistan* **68** C4
Piploda *India* **68** H6
Pipmuacan, Rés. *Canada* **105** C5
Pippingarra *Australia* **92** D2
Pipriac *France* **18** E5
Piqua *U.S.A.* **113** E11
Piquiri → *Brazil* **127** A5
Pir Panjal Range *India* **68** C7
Pīr Sohrāb *Iran* **71** E9
Pira *Benin* **83** D5
Piracicaba *Brazil* **127** A6
Piracuruca *Brazil* **125** D10
Pirae *Tahiti* **91** d
Piræus = Pireas *Greece* **46** D5
Piraiévs = Pireas *Greece* **46** D5
Pirajuí *Brazil* **127** A6
Piram I. *India* **68** J5
Pirané *Argentina* **126** B4
Pirano = Piran *Slovenia* **41** C10
Pirapora *Brazil* **125** G10
Pirawa *India* **68** G7
Pirdop *Bulgaria* **45** D8
Pireas *Greece* **46** D5
Pirgi *Greece* **47** C7
Pirgos *Ilia, Greece* **46** D3
Pirgos *Kriti, Greece* **47** F7
Pirgovo *Bulgaria* **45** C9
Piri → *Russia* **52** D6
Piribebuy *Paraguay* **126** B4
Pirimapun *Indonesia* **63** F9
Pirin △ *Bulgaria* **44** E7
Pirin Planina *Bulgaria* **44** E7
Pírineos = Pyrénées *Europe* **20** F4
Piripiri *Brazil* **125** D10
Pirlangimpi *Australia* **92** B5
Pirmasens *Germany* **25** F3
Pirna *Germany* **24** E9
Pirot *Serbia* **44** C6
Piru *Indonesia* **63** E7
Piru *U.S.A.* **111** L8
Piryatin = Pyryatyn *Ukraine* **33** G7
Pisa *Italy* **40** E7
Pisa → *Poland* **31** E8
Pisa, Firenze ✈ (PSA) *Italy* **40** E7
Pisagne *Italy* **40** C7
Pisagua *Chile* **124** G4
Pisarovina *Croatia* **41** C12
Pisco *Peru* **124** F3
Piscu *Romania* **29** E12
Pishan *China* **60** C2
Pishcha *Ukraine* **31** G10
Pishchanka *Ukraine* **29** B13
Pīshīn *Iran* **71** E9
Pishin *Pakistan* **68** D2
Pishin Lora → *Pakistan* **68** E1
Pisidia *Turkey* **72** D4
Pising *Indonesia* **63** F6
Pismo Beach *U.S.A.* **111** K6
Piso, L. *Liberia* **82** D2
Pissila *Burkina Faso* **83** C4
Pissis, Cerro *Argentina* **126** B2
Pissos *France* **20** D3
Pissouri *Cyprus* **49** E11
Pisticci *Italy* **43** B9
Pistóia *Italy* **40** E7
Pistol B. *Canada* **103** A10
Pisuerga → *Spain* **36** D6
Pisz *Poland* **30** E8
Pita *Guinea* **82** C2
Pitarpunga L. *Australia* **95** E3
Pitcairn I. *Pac. Oc.* **97** K14
Pitch L. *Trin. & Tob.* **125** K15
Piteå *Sweden* **8** D19
Piteälven → *Sweden* **8** D19

Piterka *Russia* **34** E8
Piteşti *Romania* **29** F9
Pithapuram *India* **67** L13
Pithara *Australia* **93** F2
Pithio *Greece* **45** E10
Pithiviers *France* **19** D9
Pithoragarh *India* **69** E9
Pithoro *Pakistan* **68** G3
Pitigliano *Italy* **41** F8
Pitkyaranta *Russia* **32** B6
Pitlochry *U.K.* **13** E5
Pitsilia *Cyprus* **49** E12
Pitt I. *Canada* **102** C3
Pittsburg *Calif., U.S.A.* **110** G5
Pittsburg *Kans., U.S.A.* **112** G6
Pittsburg *Tex., U.S.A.* **116** E7
Pittsburgh *U.S.A.* **114** F5
Pittsfield *Ill., U.S.A.* **112** F8
Pittsfield *Maine, U.S.A.* **113** C19
Pittsfield *Mass., U.S.A.* **115** D11
Pittsfield *N.H., U.S.A.* **115** C13
Pittston *U.S.A.* **115** E9
Pittsworth *Australia* **95** D5
Pituri → *Australia* **94** C2
Piura *Peru* **124** E2
Piva → *Montenegro* **44** C2
Piwniczna *Poland* **31** J7
Pixley *U.S.A.* **110** K7
Pizarra *Spain* **37** J6
Pizhou *China* **56** G9
Pizzo *Italy* **43** D9
Placentia *Canada* **105** C9
Placentia B. *Canada* **105** C9
Placer *Masbate, Phil.* **61** F5
Placer *Surigao N., Phil.* **61** G6
Placerville *U.S.A.* **110** G6
Placetas *Cuba* **120** B4
Plačkovica *Macedonia* **44** E6
Plainfield *N.J., U.S.A.* **115** F10
Plainfield *Ohio, U.S.A.* **114** F3
Plainfield *Vt., U.S.A.* **115** C12
Plains *Mont., U.S.A.* **108** C6
Plains *Tex., U.S.A.* **116** E3
Plainview *Nebr., U.S.A.* **112** D5
Plainview *Tex., U.S.A.* **116** D4
Plainwell *U.S.A.* **113** D11
Plaisance *France* **20** E4
Plaistow *U.S.A.* **115** D13
Plaka *Greece* **47** B7
Plaka, Akra *Greece* **49** D8
Plakenska Planina
   Macedonia **44** E5
Planá *Czech Rep.* **26** B5
Plana Cays *Bahamas* **121** B5
Planada *U.S.A.* **110** H6
Plancoët *France* **18** D4
Plandište *Serbia* **28** E6
Plano *U.S.A.* **116** E6
Plant City *U.S.A.* **117** G13
Plaquemine *U.S.A.* **116** F9
Plasencia *Spain* **36** E4
Plaški *Croatia* **41** C12
Plaster City *U.S.A.* **111** N11
Plaster Rock *Canada* **105** C6
Plastun *Russia* **54** B8
Plasy *Czech Rep.* **26** B6
Plata, Río de la → *S. Amer.* **126** C4
Plátani → *Italy* **42** E6
Platanos *Greece* **49** D5
Plateau □ *Nigeria* **83** D6
Platte *U.S.A.* **112** D4
Platte → *Mo., U.S.A.* **112** F6
Platte → *Nebr., U.S.A.* **112** E6
Platteville *U.S.A.* **112** D8
Plattling *Germany* **25** G8
Plattsburgh *U.S.A.* **115** B11
Plattsmouth *U.S.A.* **112** E6
Plau *Germany* **24** B8
Plauen *Germany* **24** E8
Plauer See *Germany* **24** B8
Plav *Montenegro* **44** D3
Plavinas *Latvia* **32** D3
Plavnica *Montenegro* **44** D3
Plavno *Croatia* **41** D13
Plavsk *Russia* **32** F9
Playa Blanca *Canary Is.* **48** F6
Playa Blanca Sur *Canary Is.* **48** F6
Playa de las Americas
   Canary Is. **48** F3
Playa de Mogán *Canary Is.* **48** G4
Playa del Carmen *Mexico* **119** C7
Playa del Inglés *Canary Is.* **48** G4
Playa Esmeralda *Canary Is.* **48** F5
Playgreen L. *Canada* **103** C9
Pleasant Bay *Canada* **105** C7
Pleasant Hill *U.S.A.* **110** H4
Pleasant Mount *U.S.A.* **115** E9
Pleasanton *Calif., U.S.A.* **110** H5
Pleasanton *Tex., U.S.A.* **116** G5
Pleasantville *N.J., U.S.A.* **113** F16
Pleasantville *Pa., U.S.A.* **114** E5
Pléaux *France* **20** C6
Plei Ku *Vietnam* **64** F7
Plélan-le-Grand *France* **18** D4
Pléneuf-Val-André *France* **18** D4
Pleniţa *Romania* **29** F8
Plenty → *Australia* **94** C2

Plenty, B. of *N.Z.* **91** B6
Plentywood *U.S.A.* **108** B11
Plérin *France* **18** D4
Plessisville *Canada* **105** C5
Plestin-les-Grèves *France* **18** D3
Pleszew *Poland* **31** G4
Pleternica *Croatia* **28** E2
Plétipi, L. *Canada* **105** B5
Pleven *Bulgaria* **45** C8
Plevlja *Montenegro* **44** C3
Plevna *Canada* **114** B8
Plitvička Jezera △ *Croatia* **41** D12
Plješevica *Croatia* **41** D12
Ploaghe *Italy* **42** B1
Ploče *Croatia* **41** E14
Płock *Poland* **31** F6
Plöckenpass *Italy* **41** B9
Plöckenstein *Germany* **25** G9
Ploemeur *France* **18** E3
Ploërmel *France* **18** E4
Ploieşti *Romania* **29** F11
Plomari *Greece* **47** C8
Plombières-les-Bains *France* **19** E13
Plomin *Croatia* **41** C11
Plön *Germany* **24** A6
Plonge, Lac la *Canada* **103** B7
Płońsk *Poland* **31** F7
Plopeni *Romania* **29** E10
Plopişului, Munţii *Romania* **28** C7
Płoty *Poland* **30** E2
Plouaret *France* **18** D3
Plouay *France* **18** E3
Ploučnice → *Czech Rep.* **26** A7
Ploudalmézeau *France* **18** D2
Plouescat *France* **18** D2
Plougasnou *France* **18** D3
Plougastel-Daoulas *France* **18** D2
Plouguerneau *France* **18** D2
Plouha *France* **18** D3
Plouhinec *France* **18** E2
Plovdiv *Bulgaria* **45** D8
Plovdiv □ *Bulgaria* **45** D8
Plum *U.S.A.* **114** F5
Plum I. *U.S.A.* **115** E12
Plumas *U.S.A.* **110** F6
Plummer *U.S.A.* **108** C5
Plumtree *Zimbabwe* **87** G2
Plungė *Lithuania* **30** C8
Pluvigner *France* **18** E3
Plužine *Montenegro* **44** C2
Plymouth *Trin. & Tob.* **125** J16
Plymouth *U.K.* **15** G3
Plymouth *Calif., U.S.A.* **110** G6
Plymouth *Ind., U.S.A.* **112** E10
Plymouth *Mass., U.S.A.* **115** E14
Plymouth *N.C., U.S.A.* **117** D16
Plymouth *N.H., U.S.A.* **115** C13
Plymouth *Pa., U.S.A.* **115** E9
Plymouth *Wis., U.S.A.* **112** D10
Plympton-Wyoming *Canada* **114** D2
Plynlimon = Pumlumon Fawr *U.K.* **15** E4
Plyusa *Russia* **32** C5
Plyusa → *Russia* **32** C5
Plzeň *Czech Rep.* **26** B6
Plzeňský □ *Czech Rep.* **26** B6
Pniewy *Poland* **31** F3
Pô *Burkina Faso* **83** C4
Po → *Italy* **41** D9
Po, Foci del *Italy* **41** D9
Pô △ *Burkina Faso* **83** C4
Po Hai = Bo Hai *China* **57** E10
Pobé *Benin* **83** D5
Pobé *Burkina Faso* **83** C4
Pobeda *Russia* **53** C15
Pobedy, Pik *Kyrgyzstan* **52** E8
Pobla de Segur *Spain* **38** C5
Pobladura del Valle *Spain* **36** C5
Pocahontas *U.S.A.* **112** D6
Pocatello *U.S.A.* **108** E7
Počátky *Czech Rep.* **26** B8
Pochep *Russia* **33** F7
Pochinki *Russia* **34** C7
Pochinok *Russia* **32** E7
Pöchlarn *Austria* **26** C8
Pocking *Germany* **25** G9
Pocomoke City *U.S.A.* **113** F16
Poços de Caldas *Brazil* **127** A6
Podbořany *Czech Rep.* **26** A6
Poddębice *Poland* **31** G5
Poděbrady *Czech Rep.* **26** A8
Podensac *France* **20** D3
Podenzano *Italy* **40** D6
Podgorač *Croatia* **28** E3
Podgorica *Montenegro* **44** D3
Podgorie *Albania* **44** F4
Podilska Vysochyna *Ukraine* **29** B13
Podkarpackie □ *Poland* **31** H9
Podkova *Bulgaria* **45** E9
Podlapača *Croatia* **41** D12
Podlaskie □ *Poland* **31** E10
Podoleni *Romania* **29** D11
Podolínec *Slovak Rep.* **27** B13

Podolsk *Russia* **32** E9
Podor *Senegal* **82** B1
Podporozhye *Russia* **32** B8
Podu Iloaiei *Romania* **29** C12
Podu Turcului *Romania* **29** D12
Podujevo *Serbia* **44** D5
Podyjí □ *Czech Rep.* **26** C8
Poel *Germany* **24** B6
Pofadder *S. Africa* **88** D2
Poggiardo *Italy* **43** B11
Poggibonsi *Italy* **40** E8
Póggio Mirteto *Italy* **41** F9
Pogoanele *Romania* **29** F12
Pogorzela *Poland* **31** G4
Pogradec *Albania* **44** F4
Pogranichnyy *Russia* **54** B5
Poh *Indonesia* **63** E6
Pohang *S. Korea* **57** F15
Pohjanmaa *Finland* **8** E20
Pohnpei *Micronesia* **96** G7
Pohorelá *Slovak Rep.* **27** C13
Pohořelice *Czech Rep.* **27** C9
Pohorje *Slovenia* **41** B12
Pohri *India* **68** G6
Poiana Mare *Romania* **28** G8
Poiana Ruscăi, Munţii *Romania* **28** E7
Poiana Stampei *Romania* **29** C10
Poinsett, C. *Antarctica* **5** C8
Point Arena *U.S.A.* **110** G3
Point Baker *U.S.A.* **102** B2
Point Edward *Canada* **114** D3
Point Fortin *Trin. & Tob.* **125** K15
Point Hope *U.S.A.* **106** a
Point L. *Canada* **100** C8
Point Lisas Industrial Estate *Trin. & Tob.* **125** K15
Point Pedro *Sri Lanka* **66** Q12
Point Pelee △ *Canada* **114** E2
Point Pleasant *N.J., U.S.A.* **115** F10
Point Pleasant *W. Va., U.S.A.* **113** F12
Point Reyes △ *U.S.A.* **110** G2
Pointe-à-Pitre *Guadeloupe* **120** b
Pointe-au-Pic = La Malbaie *Canada* **105** C5
Pointe-Claire *Canada* **115** A11
Pointe-Gatineau *Canada* **115** A9
Pointe-Noire *Congo* **84** E2
Pointe-Noire *Guadeloupe* **120** b
Poio *Spain* **36** C2
Poirino *Italy* **40** D4
Poisonbush Ra. *Australia* **92** D3
Poissonnier Pt. *Australia* **92** C2
Poitiers *France* **18** F7
Poitou *France* **20** B3
Poitou-Charentes □ *France* **20** B4
Poix-de-Picardie *France* **19** C8
Poix-Terron *France* **19** C11
Pojoaque *U.S.A.* **109** J10
Pokaran *India* **68** F4
Pokataroo *Australia* **95** D4
Pokhara *Nepal* **69** E10
Pokhvistnevo *Russia* **34** D11
Poko *Dem. Rep. of the Congo* **86** B2
Poko *Sudan* **81** F3
Pokrov *Russia* **32** E10
Pokrovsk *Russia* **53** C13
Pokrovskoye *Russia* **33** J10
Pola = Pula *Croatia* **41** D10
Pola *Russia* **32** D7
Pola de Allande *Spain* **36** B4
Pola de Lena *Spain* **36** B5
Pola de Siero *Spain* **36** B5
Pola de Somiedo *Spain* **36** B5
Polacca *U.S.A.* **109** J8
Polan *Iran* **71** E9
Pol'ana *Slovak Rep.* **27** C12
Poland ■ *Europe* **31** G3
Polanica-Zdrój *Poland* **31** H3
Połaniec *Poland* **31** H8
Polanów *Poland* **30** D3
Polar Bear △ *Canada* **104** A2
Polatlı *Turkey* **72** C5
Polatsk *Belarus* **32** E5
Polcura *Chile* **126** D1
Połczyn-Zdrój *Poland* **30** E3
Poleski △ *Poland* **31** G10
Polessk *Russia* **30** D8
Polesye = Pripet Marshes *Europe* **23** B15
Polgar *Hungary* **28** C6
Poli *Cameroon* **83** C7
Policastro, G. di *Italy* **43** C8
Police *Poland* **30** E1
Police, Pte. *Seychelles* **85** b
Polichnitos *Greece* **47** B8
Polička *Czech Rep.* **27** B9
Policoro *Italy* **43** B9
Poliegos *Greece* **46** E6
Polignano a Mare *Italy* **43** A9
Poligny *France* **19** F12
Polillo Is. *Phil.* **61** D5
Polillo Strait *Phil.* **61** D4
Polis *Cyprus* **49** D11
Polístena *Italy* **43** D9

Polk *U.S.A.* **114** E5
Polkowice *Poland* **31** G3
Polla *Italy* **43** B8
Pollachi *India* **66** P10
Pollença *Spain* **48** B10
Pollença, B. de *Spain* **48** B10
Póllica *Italy* **43** B8
Pollino, Mte. *Italy* **43** C9
Pollino △ *Italy* **43** C9
Polna *Russia* **32** C5
Polnovat *Russia* **52** C7
Pology *Ukraine* **33** J9
Polokwane *S. Africa* **89** C4
Polokwane → *S. Africa* **89** C5
Polonne *Ukraine* **23** C14
Polonnoye = Polonne *Ukraine* **23** C14
Polski Trŭmbesh *Bulgaria* **45** C9
Polsko Kosovo *Bulgaria* **45** C9
Poltár *Slovak Rep.* **27** C12
Poltava *Ukraine* **33** H8
Poltava □ *Ukraine* **33** G7
Pôltsamaa *Estonia* **32** C3
Polunochnoye *Russia* **52** C7
Polya *Estonia* **32** C4
Polyana *Ukraine* **28** B7
Polyarny *Russia* **8** B25
Polyarnyye Zori *Russia* **8** C25
Polynesia *Pac. Oc.* **97** F11
Polynésie française = French Polynesia ☑ *Pac. Oc.* **97** J13
Pomarance *Italy* **40** E7
Pombal *Portugal* **36** F2
Pombia *Greece* **49** E6
Pomene *Mozam.* **89** C6
Pomézia *Italy* **42** A5
Pomichna *Ukraine* **33** H6
Pomona *Australia* **95** D5
Pomona *U.S.A.* **111** L9
Pomorie *Bulgaria* **45** D11
Pomorskie □ *Poland* **30** D5
Pomorskie, Pojezierze *Poland* **30** E3
Pomos *Cyprus* **49** D11
Pomos, C. *Cyprus* **49** D11
Pompano Beach *U.S.A.* **117** H14
Pompei *Italy* **43** B7
Pompey *France* **19** D13
Pompeys Pillar *U.S.A.* **108** D10
Pompeys Pillar △ *U.S.A.* **108** D10
Pompton Lakes *U.S.A.* **115** F10
Ponape = Pohnpei *Micronesia* **96** G7
Ponask L. *Canada* **104** B1
Ponca *U.S.A.* **112** D5
Ponca City *U.S.A.* **116** C6
Ponce *Puerto Rico* **121** d
Ponchatoula *U.S.A.* **117** F9
Poncheville, L. *Canada* **104** B4
Pond *U.S.A.* **111** K7
Pond Inlet *Canada* **101** B12
Pondicherry = Puducherry *India* **66** P11
Ponds, I. of *Canada* **105** B8
Ponferrada *Spain* **36** C4
Pongo, Wadi → *Sudan* **81** F2
Poniatowa *Poland* **31** G9
Poniec *Poland* **31** G3
Ponikva *Slovenia* **41** B12
Ponnani *India* **66** P9
Ponoka *Canada* **102** C6
Ponorogo *Indonesia* **63** G14
Pons = Ponts *Spain* **38** D6
Pons *France* **20** C3
Ponsul → *Portugal* **36** F3
Pont-à-Mousson *France* **19** D13
Pont-Audemer *France* **18** C7
Pont-Aven *France* **18** E3
Pont Canavese *Italy* **40** C4
Pont-d'Ain *France* **19** F12
Pont-de-Roide *France* **19** E13
Pont-de-Salars *France* **20** D6
Pont-de-Vaux *France* **19** F11
Pont-de-Veyle *France* **19** F11
Pont-du-Château *France* **19** G10
Pont-l'Abbé *France* **18** E2
Pont-l'Évêque *France* **18** C7
Pont-St-Esprit *France* **21** D8
Pont-St-Martin *Italy* **40** C4
Pont-Ste-Maxence *France* **19** C9
Pont-sur-Yonne *France* **19** D10
Ponta Delgada *Azores* **78** a
Ponta do Sol *Madeira* **48** D2
Ponta Grossa *Brazil* **127** B5
Ponta Pora *Brazil* **127** A4
Pontacq *France* **20** E3
Pontailler-sur-Saône *France* **19** E12
Pontarlier *France* **19** F13
Pontassieve *Italy* **41** E8
Pontaumur *France* **20** C6
Pontcharra *France* **21** C10
Pontchartrain, L. *U.S.A.* **117** F9
Pontchâteau *France* **18** E4
Ponte da Barca *Portugal* **36** D2

Ponte de Sor *Portugal* **37** F2
Ponte dell'Ólio *Italy* **40** D6
Ponte di Legno *Italy* **40** B7
Ponte do Lima *Portugal* **36** D2
Ponte do Pungué *Mozam.* **87** F3
Ponte Nova *Brazil* **127** A7
Ponte-Leccia *France* **21** F13
Ponte nelle Alpi *Italy* **41** B9
Ponteareas *Spain* **36** C2
Pontebba *Italy* **41** B10
Ponteceso *Spain* **36** B2
Pontecorvo *Italy* **42** A6
Pontedeume *Spain* **36** B2
Ponteix *Canada* **103** D7
Pontevedra *Spain* **36** C2
Pontevedra □ *Spain* **36** C2
Pontevedra, R. de → *Spain* **36** C2
Pontevico *Italy* **40** C7
Pontiac *Ill., U.S.A.* **112** E9
Pontiac *Mich., U.S.A.* **113** D12
Pontian Kechil *Malaysia* **65** d
Pontianak *Indonesia* **62** E3
Pontine Is. = Ponziane, Ísole *Italy* **42** B5
Pontine Mts. = Kuzey Anadolu Dağları *Turkey* **72** B7
Pontínia *Italy* **42** A6
Pontivy *France* **18** D4
Pontoise *France* **19** C9
Ponton → *Canada* **102** B5
Pontorson *France* **18** D5
Pontrémoli *Italy* **40** D6
Pontrieux *France* **18** D3
Ponts *Spain* **38** D6
Pontypool *Canada* **114** B6
Pontypool *U.K.* **15** F4
Ponza *Italy* **42** B5
Ponziane, Ísole *Italy* **42** B5
Poochera *Australia* **95** E1
Poole *U.K.* **15** G6
Poole □ *U.K.* **15** G6
Poona = Pune *India* **66** K8
Pooncarie *Australia* **95** E3
Poopelloe L. *Australia* **95** E3
Poopó, L. de *Bolivia* **124** G5
Popayán *Colombia* **124** C3
Poperinge *Belgium* **17** D2
Popilta L. *Australia* **95** E3
Popina *Bulgaria* **45** B10
Popio L. *Australia* **95** E3
Poplar *U.S.A.* **108** B11
Poplar → *Canada* **103** C9
Poplar Bluff *U.S.A.* **112** G8
Poplarville *U.S.A.* **117** F10
Popocatépetl, Volcán *Mexico* **119** D5
Popokabaka *Dem. Rep. of the Congo* **84** F3
Pópoli *Italy* **41** F10
Popovača *Croatia* **41** C13
Popovo *Bulgaria* **45** C10
Poppberg *Germany* **25** F7
Poppi *Italy* **41** E8
Poprad *Slovak Rep.* **27** B13
Poprad → *Slovak Rep.* **27** B13
Porali → *Pakistan* **68** G2
Porbandar *India* **68** J3
Porcher I. *Canada* **102** C2
Porcuna *Spain* **37** H6
Porcupine → *Canada* **103** B8
Porcupine → *U.S.A.* **106** a
Porcupine Gorge △ *Australia* **94** C3
Pordenone *Italy* **41** C9
Pordim *Bulgaria* **45** C8
Poreč *Croatia* **41** C10
Poretskoye *Russia* **34** C8
Pori *Finland* **32** B1
Pori *Greece* **46** F5
Porkhov *Russia* **32** D5
Porlamar *Venezuela* **124** A6
Porlezza *Italy* **40** B6
Porma → *Spain* **36** C5
Pornic *France* **18** E4
Poronaysk *Russia* **53** E15
Poros *Greece* **46** D5
Poroshiri-Dake *Japan* **54** C11
Poroszló *Hungary* **28** C5
Poroto Mts. *Tanzania* **87** D3
Porpoise B. *Antarctica* **5** C9
Porquerolles, Î. de *France* **21** F10
Porrentruy *Switz.* **25** H3
Porreres *Spain* **48** B10
Porsangerfjorden *Norway* **8** A21
Porsgrunn *Norway* **9** G13
Port Alberni *Canada* **102** D4
Port Alfred *S. Africa* **88** E4
Port Alice *Canada* **102** C3
Port Allegany *U.S.A.* **114** E6
Port Allen *U.S.A.* **116** F9
Port Alma *Australia* **94** C5
Port Angeles *U.S.A.* **110** B3
Port Antonio *Jamaica* **120** a
Port Aransas *U.S.A.* **116** H6
Port Arthur *Australia* **95** G4
Port Arthur *U.S.A.* **116** H6
Port au Choix *Canada* **105** B8

Port au Port B. *Canada* **105** C8
Port-au-Prince *Haiti* **121** C5
Port Augusta *Australia* **95** E2
Port Austin *U.S.A.* **114** B2
Port Bell *Uganda* **86** B3
Port Bergé Vaovao *Madag.* **89** B8
Port Blandford *Canada* **105** C9
Port-Bouët *Ivory C.* **82** D4
Port Bradshaw *Australia* **94** A2
Port Broughton *Australia* **95** E2
Port Burwell *Canada* **114** D4
Port Canning *India* **69** H13
Port-Cartier *Canada* **105** B6
Port Chalmers *N.Z.* **91** F3
Port Charlotte *U.S.A.* **117** H13
Port Chester *U.S.A.* **115** F11
Port Clements *Canada* **102** C2
Port Clinton *U.S.A.* **113** E12
Port Colborne *Canada* **114** D5
Port Coquitlam *Canada* **110** A4
Port Credit *Canada* **114** C5
Port Curtis *Australia* **94** C5
Port d'Alcúdia *Spain* **48** B10
Port Dalhousie *Canada* **114** C5
Port d'Andratx *Spain* **48** B9
Port Darwin *Australia* **92** B5
Port Darwin *Falk. Is.* **128** G5
Port Davey *Australia* **95** G4
Port-de-Bouc *France* **21** E8
Port-de-Paix *Haiti* **121** C5
Port de Pollença *Spain* **48** B10
Port de Sóller *Spain* **48** B9
Port Dickson *Malaysia* **65** L3
Port Douglas *Australia* **94** B4
Port Dover *Canada* **114** D4
Port Edward *Canada* **102** C2
Port Elgin *Canada* **114** B3
Port Elizabeth *S. Africa* **88** E4
Port Ellen *U.K.* **13** F2
Port-en-Bessin-Huppain *France* **18** C6
Port Erin *I. of Man* **14** C3
Port Essington *Australia* **92** B5
Port Ewen *U.S.A.* **115** E11
Port Fairy *Australia* **95** F3
Port Fouâd = Bûr Fuad *Egypt* **80** H8
Port Gamble *U.S.A.* **110** C4
Port-Gentil *Gabon* **84** E1
Port Germein *Australia* **95** E2
Port Gibson *U.S.A.* **116** F9
Port Glasgow *U.K.* **13** F4
Port Harcourt *Nigeria* **83** E6
Port Hardy *Canada* **102** C3
Port Harrison = Inukjuak *Canada* **101** D12
Port Hawkesbury *Canada* **105** C7
Port Hedland *Australia* **92** D2
Port Henry *U.S.A.* **115** B11
Port Hood *Canada* **105** C7
Port Hope *Canada* **114** C6
Port Hope *U.S.A.* **114** C2
Port Hope Simpson *Canada* **105** B8
Port Hueneme *U.S.A.* **111** L7
Port Huron *U.S.A.* **114** D2
Port Iliç *Azerbaijan* **73** C13
Port Jefferson *U.S.A.* **115** F11
Port Jervis *U.S.A.* **115** E10
Port-Joinville *France* **18** F4
Port Katon *Russia* **33** J10
Port Kelang = Pelabuhan Klang *Malaysia* **65** L3
Port Kenny *Australia* **95** E1
Port-la-Nouvelle *France* **20** E7
Port Laoise *Ireland* **12** C4
Port Lavaca *U.S.A.* **116** G6
Port Leyden *U.S.A.* **115** C9
Port Lincoln *Australia* **95** E2
Port Loko *S. Leone* **82** D2
Port Louis *France* **18** E3
Port-Louis *Guadeloupe* **120** b
Port Louis *Mauritius* **85** d
Port MacDonnell *Australia* **95** F3
Port McNeill *Canada* **102** C3
Port Macquarie *Australia* **95** E5
Port Maria *Jamaica* **120** a
Port Matilda *U.S.A.* **114** F6
Port Mellon *Canada* **102** D4
Port-Menier *Canada* **105** C7
Port Moody *Canada* **110** A4
Port Morant *Jamaica* **120** a
Port Moresby *Papua N. G.* **90** B7
Port Musgrave *Australia* **94** A3
Port-Navalo *France* **18** E4
Port Neches *U.S.A.* **116** G8
Port Nolloth *S. Africa* **88** D2
Port Nouveau-Québec = Kangiqsualujjuaq *Canada* **101** D12
Port of Spain *Trin. & Tob.* **121** D7
Port Orange *U.S.A.* **117** G14
Port Orchard *U.S.A.* **110** C4
Port Orford *U.S.A.* **108** E1
Port Pegasus *N.Z.* **91** G1

Port Perry *Canada* **114** B6
Port Phillip B. *Australia* **95** F3
Port Pirie *Australia* **95** E2
Port Renfrew *Canada* **110** B2
Port Roper *Australia* **94** A2
Port Rowan *Canada* **114** D4
Port Safaga = Bûr Safâga *Egypt* **70** G4
Port Said = Bûr Sa'îd *Egypt* **80** H8
Port St. Joe *U.S.A.* **117** G12
Port St. Johns = Umzimvubu *S. Africa* **89** E4
Port-St-Louis-du-Rhône *France* **21** E8
Port St. Lucie *U.S.A.* **117** H14
Port-Ste-Marie *France* **20** D4
Port Sanilac *U.S.A.* **114** C2
Port Severn *Canada* **114** B5
Port Shepstone *S. Africa* **89** E5
Port Simpson *Canada* **102** C2
Port Stanley = Stanley *Falk. Is.* **128** G5
Port Stanley *Canada* **114** D3
Port Sudan = Bûr Sûdân *Sudan* **80** D4
Port Sulphur *U.S.A.* **117** G10
Port-sur-Saône *France* **19** E13
Port Talbot *U.K.* **15** F4
Port Taufiq = Bûr Taufiq *Egypt* **80** J8
Port Townsend *U.S.A.* **110** B4
Port-Vendres *France* **20** F7
Port Vila *Vanuatu* **90** C7
Port Vladimir *Russia* **8** B25
Port Wakefield *Australia* **95** E2
Port Washington *U.S.A.* **112** D2
Porta Orientalis *Romania* **23** F12
Portacloy *Ireland* **12** B2
Portadown *U.K.* **12** B5
Portaferry *U.K.* **12** B6
Portage *Pa., U.S.A.* **114** F6
Portage *Wis., U.S.A.* **112** D9
Portage la Prairie *Canada* **103** D9
Portageville *U.S.A.* **112** G9
Portalegre *Portugal* **37** F3
Portalegre □ *Portugal* **37** F3
Portales *U.S.A.* **109** J12
Portarlington *Ireland* **12** C4
Portbou *Spain* **38** C8
Portel *Portugal* **37** G3
Portela, Lisboa ✈ (LIS) *Portugal* **37** G1
Porter L. *N.W.T., Canada* **103** A7
Porter L. *Sask., Canada* **103** B7
Porterville *S. Africa* **88** E2
Porterville *U.S.A.* **110** J8
Portes-lès-Valence *France* **21** D8
Porthcawl *U.K.* **15** F4
Porthill *U.S.A.* **108** B5
Porthmadog *U.K.* **14** E3
Portile de Fier *Europe* **28** F7
Portimão *Portugal* **37** H2
Portishead *U.K.* **15** F5
Portiţei, Gura *Romania* **29** F14
Portknockie *U.K.* **13** D6
Portland *N.S.W., Australia* **95** E5
Portland *Vic., Australia* **95** F3
Portland *Canada* **115** B8
Portland *Conn., U.S.A.* **115** E12
Portland *Maine, U.S.A.* **113** D18
Portland *Mich., U.S.A.* **113** D11
Portland *Oreg., U.S.A.* **110** E4
Portland *Pa., U.S.A.* **115** F9
Portland *Tex., U.S.A.* **116** H6
Portland, I. of *U.K.* **15** G5
Portland B. *Australia* **95** F3
Portland Bight *Jamaica* **120** a
Portland Bill *U.K.* **15** G5
Portland Canal *U.S.A.* **102** B2
Portland Int. ✈ (PDX) *U.S.A.* **110** E4
Portland Pt. *Jamaica* **120** a
Portmadoc = Porthmadog *U.K.* **14** E3
Portmore *Jamaica* **120** a
Porto *France* **21** F12
Porto *Portugal* **36** D2
Porto □ *Portugal* **36** D2
Porto, G. de *France* **21** F12
Pôrto Alegre *Brazil* **127** C5
Porto Azzurro *Italy* **40** F7
Porto Cristo *Spain* **48** B10
Pôrto de Móz *Brazil* **125** D8
Porto Empédocle *Italy* **42** E6
Pôrto Esperança *Brazil* **124** G7
Porto Franco *Brazil* **125** E9
Porto Inglês *C. Verde Is.* **78** b
Pôrto Mendes *Brazil* **127** A5
Porto Moniz *Madeira* **48** D2
Pôrto Murtinho *Brazil* **124** H7
Pôrto Nacional *Brazil* **125** F9
Porto-Novo *Benin* **83** D5
Porto Petro *Spain* **48** B10
Porto San Giórgio *Italy* **41** E10
Porto Sant' Elpídio *Italy* **41** E10
Porto Santo, I. de *Madeira* **78** B2
Porto Santo Stéfano *Italy* **40** F8

Pôrto São José *Brazil* **127** A5
Pôrto Seguro *Brazil* **125** G11
Porto Tolle *Italy* **41** D9
Porto Tórres *Italy* **42** B1
Pôrto União *Brazil* **127** B5
Porto-Vecchio *France* **21** G13
Pôrto Velho *Brazil* **124** E6
Portobelo *Panama* **120** E4
Portoferráio *Italy* **40** F7
Portogruaro *Italy* **41** C9
Portola *U.S.A.* **110** F6
Portomaggiore *Italy* **41** D8
Portoscuso *Italy* **42** C1
Portovénere *Italy* **40** D6
Portoviejo *Ecuador* **124** D2
Portpatrick *U.K.* **13** G3
Portree *U.K.* **13** D2
Portrush *U.K.* **12** A5
Portsmouth *Dominica* **121** C7
Portsmouth *U.K.* **15** G6
Portsmouth *N.H., U.S.A.* **115** C14
Portsmouth *Ohio, U.S.A.* **113** F12
Portsmouth *R.I., U.S.A.* **115** E13
Portsmouth *Va., U.S.A.* **113** G15
Portsmouth □ *U.K.* **15** G6
Portsoy *U.K.* **13** D6
Portstewart *U.K.* **12** A5
Porttipahdan tekojärvi
 Finland **8** B22
Portugal ■ *Europe* **36** F3
Portugalete *Spain* **38** B1
Portumna *Ireland* **12** C3
Portville *U.S.A.* **114** D6
Porvenir *Chile* **128** G2
Porvoo *Finland* **32** B3
Porzuna *Spain* **37** F6
Posada *Italy* **42** B2
Posada → *Italy* **42** B2
Posadas *Argentina* **127** B4
Posadas *Spain* **37** H5
Poschiavo *Switz.* **25** J6
Posets *Spain* **38** C5
Posht-e Badam *Iran* **71** C7
Posidium *Greece* **47** F9
Poso *Indonesia* **63** E6
Posse *Brazil* **125** F9
Possession I. *Antarctica* **5** D11
Pössneck *Germany* **24** E7
Possum Kingdom L. *U.S.A.* **116** E5
Post *U.S.A.* **116** E4
Post Falls *U.S.A.* **108** C5
Postavy = Pastavy *Belarus* **32** E4
Poste-de-la-Baleine =
 Kuujjuarapik *Canada* **104** A4
Postmasburg *S. Africa* **88** D3
Postojna *Slovenia* **41** C11
Poston *U.S.A.* **111** M12
Postville *Canada* **105** B8
Potamós *Antikythira, Greece* **46** F5
Potamós *Kythira, Greece* **46** E4
Potchefstroom *S. Africa* **88** D4
Potcoava *Romania* **29** F9
Poteau *U.S.A.* **116** D7
Poteet *U.S.A.* **116** G5
Potenza *Italy* **43** B8
Potenza → *Italy* **41** E10
Potenza Picena *Italy* **41** E10
Poteriteri, L. *N.Z.* **91** G1
Potgietersrus = Mokopane
 S. Africa **89** C4
Poti *Georgia* **35** J5
Potiskum *Nigeria* **83** C7
Potlogi *Romania* **29** F10
Potomac → *U.S.A.* **113** F14
Potosí *Bolivia* **124** G5
Potosí Mt. *U.S.A.* **111** K11
Pototan *Phil.* **61** F5
Potrerillos *Chile* **126** B2
Potsdam *Germany* **24** C9
Potsdam *U.S.A.* **115** B10
Pottenstein *Germany* **25** F7
Pottersville *U.S.A.* **115** C11
Pottstown *U.S.A.* **115** F9
Pottsville *U.S.A.* **115** F8
Pottuvil *Sri Lanka* **66** R12
P'otzu *Taiwan* **59** F13
Pouance *France* **18** E5
Pouce Coupé *Canada* **102** B4
Poughkeepsie *U.S.A.* **115** E11
Pouilly-sur-Loire *France* **19** E9
Poulaphouca Res. *Ireland* **12** C5
Poulsbo *U.S.A.* **110** C4
Poultney *U.S.A.* **115** C11
Poulton-le-Fylde *U.K.* **14** D5
Pouso Alegre *Brazil* **127** A6
Pout *Senegal* **82** C1
Pouthisat *Cambodia* **64** F4
Pouzauges *France* **18** F6
Pova de Santa Iria *Portugal* **37** G1
Považská Bystrica
 Slovak Rep. **27** B11
Poverty B. *N.Z.* **91** C7
Povlen *Serbia* **44** B3
Póvoa de Lanhosa *Portugal* **36** D2
Póvoa de Varzim *Portugal* **36** D2
Povorino *Russia* **34** E6

Povungnituk = Puvirnituq
 Canada **101** C12
Powassan *Canada* **104** C4
Poway *U.S.A.* **111** N9
Powder → *U.S.A.* **108** C11
Powder River *U.S.A.* **108** E10
Powell *U.S.A.* **108** D9
Powell, L. *U.S.A.* **109** H8
Powell River *Canada* **102** D4
Powers *U.S.A.* **112** C10
Powys □ *U.K.* **15** E4
Poyang Hu *China* **59** C11
Poyarkovo *Russia* **53** E13
Poysdorf *Austria* **27** C9
Poza de la Sal *Spain* **36** C7
Poza Rica *Mexico* **119** C5
Pozanti *Turkey* **72** D6
Požarevac *Serbia* **44** B5
Požega *Croatia* **28** E2
Požega *Serbia* **44** C4
Poznań *Poland* **31** F3
Poznań ✈ (POZ) *Poland* **31** F3
Pozo *U.S.A.* **111** K6
Pozo Alcón *Spain* **37** H8
Pozo Almonte *Chile* **124** H5
Pozo Colorado *Paraguay* **126** A4
Pozoblanco *Spain* **37** G6
Pozzallo *Italy* **43** F7
Pozzomaggiore *Italy* **42** B1
Pozzuoli *Italy* **43** B7
Pra → *Ghana* **83** D4
Prabuty *Poland* **30** E6
Prača *Bos.-H.* **28** C3
Prachatice *Czech Rep.* **26** B6
Prachin Buri *Thailand* **64** F3
Prachuap Khiri Khan
 Thailand **65** G2
Pradelles *France* **20** D7
Prades *France* **20** F6
Prado *Brazil* **125** G11
Prado del Rey *Spain* **37** J5
Præstø *Denmark* **11** J6
Pragersko *Slovenia* **41** B12
Prague = Praha *Czech Rep.* **26** A7
Praha *Czech Rep.* **26** A7
Praha ✈ (PRG) *Czech Rep.* **26** A7
Prahecq *France* **20** B3
Prahova □ *Romania* **29** E10
Prahova → *Romania* **29** F10
Prahovo *Serbia* **44** B6
Praia *C. Verde Is.* **78** b
Praia a Mare *Italy* **43** C8
Praid *Romania* **29** D10
Prainha *Amazonas, Brazil* **124** E6
Prainha *Pará, Brazil* **125** D8
Prairie *Australia* **94** C3
Prairie City *U.S.A.* **108** D4
Prairie Dog Town Fork
 Red → *U.S.A.* **116** D5
Prairie du Chien *U.S.A.* **112** D8
Prairies, L. of the *Canada* **103** C8
Pramanda *Greece* **46** B3
Prampram *Ghana* **83** D5
Pran Buri *Thailand* **64** F2
Prang *Ghana* **83** D4
Prapat *Indonesia* **62** D1
Praslin *Seychelles* **85** b
Praso, Akra *Greece* **49** D9
Prästmon *Sweden* **10** A11
Praszka *Poland* **31** G5
Prata *Brazil* **125** G9
Pratabpur *India* **69** H10
Pratapgarh *Raj., India* **68** G6
Pratapgarh *Ut. P., India* **69** G9
Pratas Is. = Dongsha Dao
 China **59** F5
Prato *Italy* **40** E8
Prátola Peligna *Italy* **41** F10
Prats-de-Mollo-la-Preste
 France **20** F6
Pratt *U.S.A.* **112** G4
Prattville *U.S.A.* **117** E11
Pravdinsk *Kaliningrad, Russia* **30** D8
Pravdinsk *Nizhniy Novgorod,
 Russia* **34** B6
Pravets *Bulgaria* **44** D7
Pravia *Spain* **36** B4
Praya *Indonesia* **62** F5
Pré-en-Pail *France* **18** D6
Precipice △ *Australia* **95** D5
Predáppio *Italy* **41** D8
Predazzo *Italy* **41** B8
Predeal *Romania* **29** E10
Predejane *Serbia* **44** D6
Preeceville *Canada* **103** C8
Preetz *Germany* **24** A6
Pregolya → *Russia* **30** D7
Pregrada *Croatia* **41** B12
Preiļi *Latvia* **32** D4
Preko *Croatia* **41** D12
Prelog *Croatia* **41** B13
Prémery *France* **19** E10
Premià de Mar *Spain* **38** D7
Premont *U.S.A.* **116** H5
Premuda *Croatia* **41** D11

Prentice *U.S.A.* **112** C8
Prenzlau *Germany* **24** B9
Preobrazheniye *Russia* **54** C6
Preparis North Channel
 Ind. Oc. **67** M18
Preparis South Channel
 Ind. Oc. **67** M18
Přerov *Czech Rep.* **27** B10
Prescott *Canada* **115** B9
Prescott *Ariz., U.S.A.* **109** J7
Prescott *Ark., U.S.A.* **116** E8
Prescott Valley *U.S.A.* **109** J7
Preservation Inlet *N.Z.* **91** G1
Preševo *Serbia* **44** D5
Presho *U.S.A.* **112** D3
Presicce *Italy* **43** C11
Presidencia de la Plaza
 Argentina **126** B4
Presidencia Roque Saenz
 Peña *Argentina* **126** B3
Presidente Epitácio *Brazil* **125** H8
Presidente Hayes □
 Paraguay **126** A4
Presidente Prudente *Brazil* **127** A5
Presidio *Mexico* **118** B4
Presidio *U.S.A.* **116** G2
Preslav *Bulgaria* **45** C10
Preslavska Planina
 Bulgaria **45** C10
Prešov *Slovak Rep.* **27** B14
Prešovský □ *Slovak Rep.* **27** B13
Prespa *Bulgaria* **45** E8
Prespa, L. = Prespansko
 Jezero *Macedonia* **44** F5
Prespa △ *Greece* **44** F5
Prespansko Jezero *Macedonia* **44** F5
Presque I. *U.S.A.* **114** D4
Presque Isle *U.S.A.* **113** B19
Prestatyn *U.K.* **14** D4
Prestea *Ghana* **82** D4
Presteigne *U.K.* **15** E5
Přeštice *Czech Rep.* **26** B6
Preston *Canada* **114** D4
Preston *U.K.* **14** D5
Preston *Idaho, U.S.A.* **108** E8
Preston *Minn., U.S.A.* **112** D7
Preston, C. *Australia* **92** D2
Prestonsburg *U.S.A.* **113** G12
Prestranda *Norway* **10** E3
Prestwick *U.K.* **13** F4
Pretoria *S. Africa* **89** D4
Preuilly-sur-Claise *France* **18** F7
Preveza *Greece* **46** C2
Preveza □ *Greece* **46** B2
Prey Veng *Cambodia* **65** G5
Priazovskoye *Ukraine* **33** J8
Pribilof Is. *U.S.A.* **106** a
Priboj *Serbia* **44** C3
Příbram *Czech Rep.* **26** B7
Price *U.S.A.* **108** G8
Price I. *Canada* **102** C3
Prichard *U.S.A.* **117** F10
Priego *Spain* **38** E2
Priego de Córdoba *Spain* **37** H6
Priekule *Latvia* **30** B8
Priekule *Lithuania* **30** C8
Prien *Germany* **25** H8
Prienai *Lithuania* **30** D10
Prieska *S. Africa* **88** D3
Priest L. *U.S.A.* **108** B5
Priest River *U.S.A.* **108** B5
Priest Valley *U.S.A.* **110** J6
Prievidza *Slovak Rep.* **27** C11
Prignitz *Germany* **24** B7
Prijedor *Bos.-H.* **41** D13
Prijepolje *Serbia* **44** C3
Prikaspiyskaya
 Nizmennost = Caspian
 Depression *Eurasia* **35** G9
Prikro *Ivory C.* **82** D4
Prikubanskaya
 Nizmennost *Russia* **35** H4
Prilep *Macedonia* **44** E5
Priluki = Pryluky *Ukraine* **33** G7
Prime Seal I. *Australia* **95** G4
Primo Tapia *Mexico* **111** N10
Primorsk *Kaliningrad, Russia* **30** D6
Primorsk *St. Petersburg,
 Russia* **32** B5
Primorsko *Bulgaria* **45** D11
Primorsko-Akhtarsk
 Russia **33** J10
Primorskoye *Ukraine* **33** J9
Primrose L. *Canada* **103** C7
Prince Albert *Canada* **103** C7
Prince Albert *S. Africa* **88** E3
Prince Albert △ *Canada* **103** C7
Prince Albert Mts. *Antarctica* **5** D11
Prince Albert Pen. *Canada* **100** B8
Prince Albert Sd. *Canada* **100** B8
Prince Alfred, C. *Canada* **101** B7
Prince Charles I. *Canada* **101** C12
Prince Charles Mts. *Antarctica* **5** D6
Prince Edward Fracture
 Zone *Ind. Oc.* **5** A4
Prince Edward I. □ *Canada* **105** C7
Prince Edward Is. *Ind. Oc.* **3** G11

Prince Edward Pt. *Canada* **114** C8
Prince George *Canada* **102** C4
Prince Gustaf Adolf Sea
 Canada **101** B9
Prince of Wales, C. *U.S.A.* **98** C3
Prince of Wales I. *Australia* **94** A3
Prince of Wales I. *Canada* **100** B10
Prince of Wales I. *U.S.A.* **100** D6
Prince Patrick I. *Canada* **101** B8
Prince Regent Inlet *Canada* **101** B11
Prince Rupert *Canada* **102** C2
Princes Town *Trin. & Tob.* **125** K15
Princess Charlotte B.
 Australia **94** A3
Princess Elizabeth Trough
 S. Ocean **5** C7
Princess May Ranges
 Australia **92** C4
Princess Royal I. *Canada* **102** C3
Princeton *Canada* **102** D4
Princeton *Calif., U.S.A.* **110** F4
Princeton *Ill., U.S.A.* **112** E9
Princeton *Ind., U.S.A.* **112** F10
Princeton *Ky., U.S.A.* **112** G10
Princeton *Mo., U.S.A.* **112** E7
Princeton *N.J., U.S.A.* **115** F10
Princeton *W. Va., U.S.A.* **113** G13
Príncipe *São Tomé & Príncipe* **76** F4
Príncipe da Beira *Brazil* **124** F6
Prineville *U.S.A.* **108** D3
Prins Harald Kyst *Antarctica* **5** D4
Prinsesse Astrid Kyst
 Antarctica **5** D3
Prinsesse Ragnhild Kyst
 Antarctica **5** D4
Prinzapolca *Nic.* **120** D3
Prior, C. *Spain* **36** B2
Priozersk *Russia* **32** B6
Pripet = Prypyat → *Europe* **23** C16
Pripet Marshes *Europe* **23** B15
Pripyat Marshes = Pripet
 Marshes *Europe* **23** B15
Pripyats = Prypyat →
 Europe **23** C16
Prislop, Pasul *Romania* **29** C9
Pristen *Russia* **33** G9
Priština *Serbia* **44** D5
Pritzwalk *Germany* **24** B8
Privas *France* **21** D8
Priverno *Italy* **42** A6
Privolzhsk *Russia* **34** B5
Privolzhskaya
 Vozvyshennost *Russia* **34** E7
Privolzhskiy *Russia* **34** E8
Privolzhskiy □ *Russia* **34** B10
Privolzhye *Russia* **34** D9
Priyutnoye *Russia* **35** G6
Prizren *Serbia* **44** D4
Prizzi *Italy* **42** E6
Prnjavor *Bos.-H.* **28** F2
Probolinggo *Indonesia* **63** G15
Prochowice *Poland* **31** G3
Proctor *U.S.A.* **115** C11
Proddatur *India* **66** M11
Prodhromos *Cyprus* **49** E11
Proença-a-Nova *Portugal* **36** F3
Profondeville *Belgium* **17** D4
Progreso *Coahuila, Mexico* **118** B4
Progreso *Yucatán, Mexico* **119** C7
Progress *Antarctica* **5** C6
Prokhladnyy *Russia* **35** J7
Prokletije *Albania* **44** D3
Prokopyevsk *Russia* **52** D9
Prokuplje *Serbia* **44** C5
Proletarsk *Russia* **35** G5
Proletarskaya = Proletarsk
 Russia **35** G5
Prome *Burma* **67** K19
Prophet → *Canada* **102** B4
Prophet River *Canada* **102** B4
Propriá *Brazil* **125** F11
Propriano *France* **21** G12
Proserpine *Australia* **94** J6
Prosna → *Poland* **31** F4
Prospect *U.S.A.* **115** C9
Prosser *U.S.A.* **108** C4
Prostějov *Czech Rep.* **27** B10
Prostki *Poland* **30** E9
Proston *Australia* **95** D5
Proszowice *Poland* **31** H7
Proti *Greece* **46** D3
Provadiya *Bulgaria* **45** C11
Provence *France* **21** E9
Provence-Alpes-Côte
 d'Azur □ *France* **21** D10
Providence *Ky., U.S.A.* **112** G10
Providence *R.I., U.S.A.* **115** E13
Providence Bay *Canada* **104** C3
Providence Mts. *U.S.A.* **111** K11
Providencia, I. de *Colombia* **120** D3
Provideniya *Russia* **53** C19
Provincetown *U.S.A.* **113** D18
Provins *France* **19** D10
Provo *U.S.A.* **108** F8
Provost *Canada* **103** C6

Prudhoe Bay *U.S.A.* **106** a
Prudhoe I. *Australia* **94** C4
Prud'homme *Canada* **103** C7
Prudnik *Poland* **31** H4
Prüm *Germany* **25** E2
Prundu *Romania* **29** F11
Pruszcz Gdański *Poland* **30** D5
Pruszków *Poland* **31** F7
Prut → *Romania* **29** E13
Pruzhany *Belarus* **23** B13
Prydz B. *Antarctica* **5** C6
Pryluky *Ukraine* **33** G7
Pryor *U.S.A.* **116** C7
Prypyat → *Europe* **23** C16
Przasnysz *Poland* **31** E7
Przedbórz *Poland* **31** G6
Przedecz *Poland* **31** F5
Przemków *Poland* **31** G2
Przemyśl *Poland* **31** J9
Przeworsk *Poland* **31** H9
Przewóz *Poland* **31** G1
Przhevalsk = Karakol
 Kyrgyzstan **52** E8
Przysucha *Poland* **31** G7
Psachna *Greece* **46** C5
Psara *Greece* **47** C7
Psathoura *Greece* **46** B6
Psel → *Ukraine* **33** H7
Pserimos *Greece* **47** E9
Psira *Greece* **49** D7
Pskov *Russia* **32** D5
Pskov □ *Russia* **32** D5
Pskovskoye, Ozero *Russia* **32** D5
Psunj *Croatia* **28** E2
Pteleos *Greece* **46** B4
Ptich = Ptsich → *Belarus* **23** B15
Ptichia = Vido *Greece* **49** A3
Ptolemaida *Greece* **44** F5
Ptsich → *Belarus* **23** B15
Ptuj *Slovenia* **41** B12
Ptujska Gora *Slovenia* **41** B12
Pu Xian *China* **56** F6
Pua *Thailand* **64** C3
Puán *Argentina* **126** D3
Pu'an *China* **58** E5
Pu'apu'a *Samoa* **91** b
Pubei *China* **58** F7
Pucallpa *Peru* **124** E4
Pucheng *China* **59** D12
Pucheni *Romania* **29** E10
Puchheim *Germany* **25** G7
Puch'on = Bucheon
 S. Korea **57** F14
Púchov *Slovak Rep.* **27** B11
Puciosa *Romania* **29** E10
Pučišća *Croatia* **41** E13
Puck *Poland* **30** D5
Pucka, Zatoka *Poland* **30** D5
Pudasjärvi *Finland* **8** D22
Puding *China* **58** D5
Pudozh *Russia* **32** B9
Puducherry *India* **66** P11
Pudukkottai *India* **66** P11
Puebla *Mexico* **119** D5
Puebla □ *Mexico* **119** D5
Puebla de Alcocer *Spain* **37** G5
Puebla de Don Fadrique
 Spain **39** H2
Puebla de Don Rodrigo *Spain* **37** F6
Puebla de Guzmán *Spain* **37** H3
Puebla de la Calzada *Spain* **37** G4
Puebla de Sanabria *Spain* **36** C4
Puebla de Trives = Pobra
 de Trives *Spain* **36** C3
Pueblo *U.S.A.* **108** G11
Pueblo Hundido *Chile* **126** B1
Puelches *Argentina* **126** D2
Puelén *Argentina* **126** D2
Puente Alto *Chile* **126** C1
Puente-Genil *Spain* **37** H6
Puente la Reina *Spain* **38** C3
Puenteareas = Ponteareas
 Spain **36** C2
Puentedeume =
 Pontedeume *Spain* **36** B2
Puentes de Garcia
 Rodriguez = As Pontes
 de García Rodríguez *Spain* **36** B3
Pu'er *China* **58** F3
Puerca, Pta. *Puerto Rico* **121** d
Puerco → *U.S.A.* **109** J10
Puerto Aisén *Chile* **128** F2
Puerto Ángel *Mexico* **119** D5
Puerto Arista *Mexico* **119** D6
Puerto Armuelles *Panama* **120** E3
Puerto Ayacucho *Venezuela* **124** B5
Puerto Barrios *Guatemala* **120** C2
Puerto Bermejo *Argentina* **126** B4
Puerto Bermúdez *Peru* **124** F4
Puerto Bolívar *Ecuador* **124** D3
Puerto Cabello *Venezuela* **124** A5
Puerto Cabezas *Nic.* **120** D3
Puerto Cabo Gracias á Dios
 Nic. **120** D3

Puerto Carreño *Colombia* **124** B5
Puerto Castilla *Honduras* **120** C2
Puerto Chicama *Peru* **124** E3
Puerto Coig *Argentina* **128** G3
Puerto Cortés *Costa Rica* **120** E3
Puerto Cortés *Honduras* **120** C2
Puerto Cumarebo *Venezuela* **124** A5
Puerto de Alcudia = Port
 d'Alcúdia *Spain* **48** B10
Puerto de Cabrera *Spain* **48** B9
Puerto de Gran Tarajal
 Canary Is. **48** F5
Puerto de la Cruz *Canary Is.* **48** F3
Puerto de los Angeles △
 Mexico **118** C3
Puerto de Mazarrón *Spain* **39** H3
Puerto de Pozo Negro
 Canary Is. **48** F6
Puerto de Sóller = Port de
 Sóller *Spain* **48** B9
Puerto de Somosierra *Spain* **36** D7
Puerto del Carmen *Canary Is.* **48** F6
Puerto del Rosario *Canary Is.* **48** F6
Puerto Deseado *Argentina* **128** F3
Puerto Escondido *Mexico* **119** D5
Puerto Heath *Bolivia* **124** F5
Puerto Inírida *Colombia* **124** C5
Puerto Juárez *Mexico* **119** C7
Puerto La Cruz *Venezuela* **124** A6
Puerto Leguízamo *Colombia* **124** D4
Puerto Libertad *Mexico* **118** B2
Puerto Limón *Colombia* **124** C4
Puerto Lobos *Argentina* **128** E3
Puerto Lumbreras *Spain* **39** H3
Puerto Madryn *Argentina* **128** E3
Puerto Maldonado *Peru* **124** F5
Puerto Manatí *Cuba* **120** B4
Puerto Montt *Chile* **128** E2
Puerto Morazán *Nic.* **120** D2
Puerto Morelos *Mexico* **119** C7
Puerto Natales *Chile* **128** G2
Puerto Padre *Cuba* **120** B4
Puerto Páez *Venezuela* **124** B5
Puerto Peñasco *Mexico* **118** A2
Puerto Pinasco *Paraguay* **126** A4
Puerto Plata *Dom. Rep.* **121** C5
Puerto Pollensa = Port de
 Pollença *Spain* **48** B10
Puerto Princesa *Phil.* **61** G3
Puerto Quepos *Costa Rica* **120** E3
Puerto Real *Spain* **37** J4
Puerto Rico *Canary Is.* **48** G4
Puerto Rico ☑ *W. Indies* **121** d
Puerto Rico Trench *Atl. Oc.* **121** C6
Puerto San Julián *Argentina* **128** F3
Puerto Sastre *Paraguay* **126** A4
Puerto Serrano *Spain* **37** J5
Puerto Suárez *Bolivia* **124** G7
Puerto Vallarta *Mexico* **118** C3
Puerto Varas *Chile* **128** E2
Puerto Wilches *Colombia* **124** B4
Puertollano *Spain* **37** G6
Pueu *Tahiti* **91** d
Pueyrredón, L. *Argentina* **128** F2
Púez Odle △ *Italy* **41** B8
Puffin I. *Ireland* **12** E1
Pugachev *Russia* **34** D9
Pugal *India* **68** E5
Puge *China* **58** D4
Pugu *Tanzania* **86** D3
Puget Sound *U.S.A.* **108** C2
Puget-Théniers *France* **21** E10
Pugödong *N. Korea* **57** C16
Púglia □ *Italy* **43** A9
Pugu *Tanzania* **86** D3
Pūgünzi *Iran* **71** E8
Pui *Romania* **28** E8
Puieşti *Romania* **29** D12
Puig Major *Spain* **48** B9
Puigcerdà *Spain* **38** C6
Puigmal *Spain* **38** C7
Puigpunyent *Spain* **48** B9
Puijiang *China* **58** B4
Puisaye, Collines de la
 France **19** E10
Puiseaux *France* **19** D9
Pujehun *S. Leone* **82** D2
Pujiang *China* **59** C12
Pujon-ho *N. Korea* **57** D14
Pukaki, L. *N.Z.* **91** F3
Pukapuka *Cook Is.* **97** J11
Pukaskwa △ *Canada* **104** C3
Pukatawagan *Canada* **103** B8
Pukchin *N. Korea* **57** D13
Pukch'ŏng *N. Korea* **57** D15
Pukë *Albania* **44** D3
Pukekohe *N.Z.* **91** B5
Pukhrayan *India* **69** F8
Pukou *China* **59** A12
Pula *Croatia* **41** D10
Pula *Italy* **42** C1
Pulacayo *Bolivia* **124** H5
Pulai *Malaysia* **65** d
Pulandian *China* **57** E11
Pulaski *N.Y., U.S.A.* **115** C8
Pulaski *Tenn., U.S.A.* **117** D11

Pulaski *Va., U.S.A.* **113** G13
Pulau → *Indonesia* **63** F9
Puławy *Poland* **31** G8
Pulga *U.S.A.* **110** F5
Pulicat L. *India* **66** N12
Pullman *U.S.A.* **108** C5
Pulog, Mt. *Phil.* **61** C4
Pültusk *Poland* **31** F8
Pülümür *Turkey* **73** C8
Pumlumon Fawr *U.K.* **15** E4
Puná, I. *Ecuador* **124** D2
Punaauia *Tahiti* **91** d
Punakaiki *N.Z.* **91** E3
Punakha Dzong *Bhutan* **67** F16
Punasar *India* **68** F5
Punata *Bolivia* **124** G5
Punch *India* **69** C6
Punch → *Pakistan* **68** C5
Punda Maria *S. Africa* **89** C5
Pune *India* **66** K8
P'ungsan *N. Korea* **57** D15
Pungue, Ponte de *Mozam.* **87** F3
Puning *China* **59** F11
Punjab □ *India* **68** D7
Punjab □ *Pakistan* **68** E6
Puno *Peru* **124** G4
Punpun → *India* **69** G11
Punta, Cerro de *Puerto Rico* **121** d
Punta Alta *Argentina* **128** D4
Punta Arenas *Chile* **128** G2
Punta de Díaz *Chile* **126** B1
Punta del Hidalgo *Canary Is.* **48** F3
Punta Gorda *Belize* **119** D7
Punta Gorda *U.S.A.* **117** H13
Punta Prieta *Mexico* **118** B2
Punta Prima *Spain* **48** B11
Punta Umbria *Spain* **37** H4
Puntarenas *Costa Rica* **120** E3
Punto Fijo *Venezuela* **124** A4
Punxsatawney *U.S.A.* **114** F6
Pupuan *Indonesia* **63** J18
Puqi *China* **59** C9
Puquio *Peru* **124** F4
Pur → *Russia* **52** C8
Puracé, Vol. *Colombia* **124** C3
Puračić *Bos.-H.* **28** F3
Puralia = Puruliya *India* **69** H12
Puranpur *India* **69** E9
Purbeck, Isle of *U.K.* **15** G5
Purcell *U.S.A.* **116** D6
Purcell Mts. *Canada* **102** D5
Puri *India* **67** K14
Purmerend *Neths.* **17** B4
Purnia *India* **69** G12
Purnululu △ *Australia* **92** C4
Pursat = Pouthisat *Cambodia* **64** F4
Purukcahu *Indonesia* **62** E4
Puruliya *India* **69** H12
Purus → *Brazil* **124** D6
Puruvesi *Finland* **32** B5
Purvis *U.S.A.* **117** F10
Pŭrvomay *Bulgaria* **45** D9
Purwa *India* **69** F9
Purwakarta *Indonesia* **63** G12
Purwodadi *Indonesia* **63** G14
Purwokerto *Indonesia* **63** G13
Puryŏng *N. Korea* **57** C15
Pusa *India* **69** G11
Pusan = Busan *S. Korea* **57** G15
Pushkin *Russia* **32** C6
Pushkino *Moskva, Russia* **32** D9
Pushkino *Saratov, Russia* **34** E8
Püspökladány *Hungary* **28** C6
Pustoshka *Russia* **32** D5
Puszczykowo *Poland* **31** F3
Putahow L. *Canada* **103** B8
Putao *Burma* **67** F20
Putararu *N.Z.* **91** C5
Putbus *Germany* **24** A9
Putian *China* **59** E12
Putignano *Italy* **43** B10
Puting, Tanjung *Indonesia* **62** E4
Putlitz *Germany* **24** B8
Putna *Romania* **29** C10
Putna → *Romania* **29** E12
Putnam *U.S.A.* **115** E13
Putnok *Hungary* **28** B5
Putorana, Gory *Russia* **53** C10
Putrajaya *Malaysia* **65** L3
Puttalam *Sri Lanka* **66** Q11
Puttgarden *Germany* **24** A7
Püttlingen *Germany* **25** F2
Putumayo → *S. Amer.* **124** D5
Putuo *China* **59** C14
Putussibau *Indonesia* **62** D4
Putyla *Ukraine* **29** B10
Puvirnituq *Canada* **101** C12
Puy-de-Dôme *France* **20** C6
Puy-de-Dôme □ *France* **20** C7
Puy-l'Évêque *France* **20** D5
Puyallup *U.S.A.* **110** C4
Puyang *China* **56** G8
Puylaurens *France* **20** E6
Pŭzeh Rīg *Iran* **71** E8
Puzhaykove *Ukraine* **29** B14
Pwani □ *Tanzania* **86** D4

Pweto *Dem. Rep. of the Congo* **87** D2
Pwllheli *U.K.* **14** E3
Pya-ozero *Russia* **8** C24
Pyana → *Russia* **34** C8
Pyapon *Burma* **67** L19
Pyasina → *Russia* **53** B9
Pyatigorsk *Russia* **35** H6
Pyatykhatky *Ukraine* **33** H7
Pydna *Greece* **44** F6
Pyè = Prome *Burma* **67** K19
Pyeongtaek *S. Korea* **57** F14
Pyetrikaw *Belarus* **23** B15
Pyhäjoki *Finland* **8** D21
Pyinmana *Burma* **67** K20
Pyla, C. *Cyprus* **49** E12
Pymatuning Res. *U.S.A.* **114** E4
Pyŏktong *N. Korea* **57** D13
Pyŏnggang *N. Korea* **57** E14
P'yŏngsong *N. Korea* **57** E13
P'yŏngyang *N. Korea* **57** E13
Pyote *U.S.A.* **116** F3
Pyramid L. *U.S.A.* **108** F4
Pyramid Pk. *U.S.A.* **111** J10
Pyramids *Egypt* **80** J7
Pyrénées *Europe* **20** F4
Pyrénées △ *France* **20** F3
Pyrénées-Atlantiques □ *France* **20** E3
Pyrénées-Orientales □ *France* **20** F6
Pyryatyn *Ukraine* **33** G7
Pyrzyce *Poland* **31** E1
Pyskowice *Poland* **31** H5
Pytalovo *Russia* **32** D4
Pyu *Burma* **67** K20
Pyzdry *Poland* **31** F4

Q

Qaanaaq *Greenland* **4** B4
Qabirri → *Azerbaijan* **35** K8
Qachasnek *S. Africa* **89** E4
Qa'el Jafr *Jordan* **74** E5
Qa'emābād *Iran* **71** D9
Qā'emshahr *Iran* **71** B7
Qagan Nur *China* **56** C8
Qahremānshahr = Kermānshāh *Iran* **73** E12
Qaidam Pendi *China* **60** C4
Qajarīyeh *Iran* **73** E12
Qala, Ras il *Malta* **49** C1
Qala-i-Jadid = Spīn Būldak *Afghan.* **68** D2
Qala Point = Qala, Ras il *Malta* **49** C1
Qala Viala *Pakistan* **68** D2
Qala Yangi *Afghan.* **68** B2
Qal'at al Akhḍar *Si. Arabia* **70** E3
Qal'at Dīzah *Iraq* **73** D11
Qal'at Ṣāliḥ *Iraq* **70** D5
Qal'at Sukkar *Iraq* **73** G12
Qalyûb *Egypt* **80** H7
Qamani'tuaq = Baker Lake *Canada* **100** C10
Qamdo *China* **58** B1
Qamea *Fiji* **91** a
Qamruddin Karez *Pakistan* **68** D3
Qandahār = Kandahār *Afghan.* **66** D4
Qandahār = Kandahār □ *Afghan.* **66** D4
Qapān *Iran* **71** B7
Qapshaghay *Kazakhstan* **52** E8
Qaqortoq *Greenland* **4** C5
Qâra *Egypt* **80** B2
Qara Qash → *China* **69** B8
Qarabutaq *Kazakhstan* **52** E7
Qaraçala *Azerbaijan* **35** L9
Qaraghandy *Kazakhstan* **52** E8
Qaraghayly *Kazakhstan* **52** E8
Qārah *Si. Arabia* **70** D4
Qarataū *Kazakhstan* **52** E7
Qarataū *Zhambyl, Kazakhstan* **52** E8
Qarazhal *Kazakhstan* **52** E8
Qardho = Gardo *Somali Rep.* **75** F4
Qardud *Sudan* **81** E2
Qareh → *Iran* **73** C12
Qareh Tekān *Iran* **71** B6
Qarnein *U.A.E.* **71** E7
Qarqan He → *China* **60** C3
Qarqaraly *Kazakhstan* **52** E8
Qarrasa *Sudan* **81** E3
Qarshi *Uzbekistan* **52** F7
Qartabā *Lebanon* **74** A4
Qaryat al Gharab *Iraq* **70** D5
Qaryat al 'Ulyā *Si. Arabia* **70** E5
Qasr 'Amra *Jordan* **70** D3
Qaşr-e Qand *Iran* **71** E9
Qaşr-e Shīrīn *Iran* **70** C5
Qasr Farâfra *Egypt* **80** B2
Qatanā *Syria* **74** B5
Qatar ■ *Asia* **71** E6
Qatlīsh *Iran* **71** B8
Qattâra *Egypt* **80** A2
Qattâra, Munkhafed el *Egypt* **80** B2

Qattâra Depression = Qattâra, Munkhafed el *Egypt* **80** B2
Qausiuittuq = Resolute *Canada* **101** B10
Qawām al Ḥamzah = Al Ḥamzah *Iraq* **70** D5
Qāyen *Iran* **71** C8
Qazaqstan = Kazakhstan ■ *Asia* **52** E8
Qazimämmäd *Azerbaijan* **35** K9
Qazvīn *Iran* **71** B6
Qazvīn □ *Iran* **71** B6
Qeissan *Sudan* **81** E3
Qena *Egypt* **80** B3
Qena, W. → *Egypt* **80** B3
Qeqertarsuaq *Greenland* **4** C5
Qeqertarsuaq *Greenland* **98** C14
Qeshlāq *Iran* **73** E12
Qeshm *Iran* **71** E8
Qeys *Iran* **71** E7
Qezel Owzen → *Iran* **71** B6
Qezi'ot *Israel* **74** E3
Qi Xian *China* **56** G8
Qian Gorlos *China* **57** B13
Qian Xian *China* **56** G5
Qiancheng *China* **58** D7
Qianjiang *Guangxi Zhuangzu, China* **58** F7
Qianjiang *Hubei, China* **59** B9
Qianjiang *Sichuan, China* **58** C7
Qianshan *China* **59** B11
Qianwei *China* **58** C4
Qianxi *China* **58** D6
Qianyang *Hunan, China* **59** D8
Qianyang *Shaanxi, China* **56** G4
Qianyang *Zhejiang, China* **59** B12
Qiaojia *China* **58** D4
Qichun *China* **59** B10
Qidong *Hunan, China* **59** D9
Qidong *Jiangsu, China* **59** B13
Qijiang *China* **58** C6
Qikiqtarjuaq *Canada* **101** C13
Qila Saifullāh *Pakistan* **68** D3
Qilian Shan *China* **60** C4
Qimen *China* **59** C11
Qin He → *China* **56** G7
Qin Jiang → *Guangxi Zhuangzu, China* **58** F7
Qin Jiang → *Jiangxi, China* **59** D10
Qin Ling = Qinling Shandi *China* **56** H5
Qin'an *China* **56** G3
Qing Xian *China* **56** E9
Qingcheng *China* **57** F9
Qingfeng *China* **56** G8
Qinghai □ *China* **60** C4
Qinghai Hu *China* **60** C5
Qinghecheng *China* **57** D13
Qinghemen *China* **57** D11
Qingjian *China* **56** F6
Qingjiang = Huaiyin *China* **57** H10
Qingliu *China* **59** D11
Qinglong *China* **58** E5
Qingping *China* **58** D5
Qingpu *China* **59** B13
Qingshui *China* **56** G4
Qingshuihe *China* **56** E6
Qingtian *China* **59** C13
Qingtongxia Shuiku *China* **56** F3
Qingxi *China* **58** D7
Qingxu *China* **56** F7
Qingyang *Anhui, China* **59** B11
Qingyang *Gansu, China* **56** F4
Qingyi Jiang → *China* **58** C4
Qingyuan *Guangdong, China* **59** F9
Qingyuan *Liaoning, China* **57** C13
Qingyuan *Zhejiang, China* **59** D12
Qingyun *China* **57** F9
Qingzhen *China* **58** D6
Qinhuangdao *China* **57** E10
Qinling Shandi *China* **56** H5
Qinshui *China* **56** G7
Qinyang = Jiyuan *China* **56** G7
Qinyuan *China* **56** F7
Qinzhou *China* **58** G7
Qionghai *China* **64** C8
Qionglai *China* **58** B4
Qionglai Shan *China* **58** B4
Qiongzhou Haixia *China* **64** B8
Qiqihar *China* **53** E13
Qiraîya, W. → *Egypt* **74** E3
Qiryat Ata *Israel* **74** C4
Qiryat Gat *Israel* **74** D3
Qiryat Mal'akhi *Israel* **74** D3
Qiryat Shemona *Israel* **74** B4
Qiryat Yam *Israel* **74** C4
Qishan *China* **56** G4
Qitai *China* **60** B3
Qiubei *China* **58** E5
Qixia *China* **57** F11
Qiyang *China* **59** D8
Qizlaġac Körfäzi *Azerbaijan* **73** C13
Qojūr *Iran* **70** B5
Qom *Iran* **71** C6
Qom □ *Iran* **71** C6

Qomolangma Feng = Everest, Mt. *Nepal* **69** E12
Qomsheh *Iran* **71** D6
Qoqon = Qŭqon *Uzbekistan* **52** E8
Qoraqalpoghistan □ *Uzbekistan* **52** E6
Qorveh *Iran* **73** E12
Qostanay *Kazakhstan* **52** D7
Qoṭūr *Iran* **73** C11
Qu Jiang → *China* **58** B6
Qu Xian *China* **58** B6
Quabbin Res. *U.S.A.* **115** D12
Quairading *Australia* **93** F2
Quakenbrück *Germany* **24** C3
Quakertown *U.S.A.* **115** F9
Qualicum Beach *Canada* **102** D4
Quambatook *Australia* **95** F3
Quambone *Australia* **95** E4
Quamby *Australia* **94** C3
Quan Long = Ca Mau *Vietnam* **65** H5
Quanah *U.S.A.* **116** D5
Quang Ngai *Vietnam* **64** E7
Quang Tri *Vietnam* **64** D6
Quang Yen *Vietnam* **58** G6
Quannan *China* **59** E10
Quanzhou *Fujian, China* **59** E12
Quanzhou *Guangxi Zhuangzu, China* **59** E8
Qu'Appelle → *Canada* **103** C8
Quaqtaq *Canada* **101** C13
Quaraí *Brazil* **126** C4
Quarré-les-Tombes *France* **19** E11
Quarteira *Portugal* **37** H2
Quartu Sant'Élena *Italy* **42** C2
Quartzsite *U.S.A.* **111** M12
Quatre Bornes *Mauritius* **85** d
Quatsino Sd. *Canada* **102** C3
Quba *Azerbaijan* **35** K9
Qŭchān *Iran* **71** B8
Queanbeyan *Australia* **95** F4
Québec *Canada* **105** C5
Québec □ *Canada* **105** C6
Quebrada del Condorito △ *Argentina* **126** C3
Quedlinburg *Germany* **24** D7
Queen Alexandra Ra. *Antarctica* **5** E11
Queen Charlotte City *Canada* **102** C2
Queen Charlotte Is. *Canada* **102** C2
Queen Charlotte Sd. *Canada* **102** C3
Queen Charlotte Strait *Canada* **102** C3
Queen Elizabeth △ *Uganda* **86** C3
Queen Elizabeth △ *U.K.* **13** E4
Queen Elizabeth Is. *Canada* **101** B10
Queen Mary Land *Antarctica* **5** D7
Queen Maud G. *Canada* **100** C9
Queen Maud Land = Dronning Maud Land *Antarctica* **5** D3
Queen Maud Mts. *Antarctica* **5** E13
Queens Channel *Australia* **92** C4
Queenscliff *Australia* **95** F3
Queensland □ *Australia* **94** C3
Queenstown *Australia* **95** G4
Queenstown *N.Z.* **91** F2
Queenstown *Singapore* **65** d
Queenstown *S. Africa* **88** E4
Queets *U.S.A.* **110** C2
Queguay Grande → *Uruguay* **126** C4
Queimadas *Brazil* **125** F11
Quelimane *Mozam.* **87** F4
Quellón *Chile* **128** E2
Quelpart = Jeju-do *S. Korea* **57** H14
Queluz *Portugal* **37** G1
Quemado *N. Mex., U.S.A.* **109** J9
Quemado *Tex., U.S.A.* **116** G4
Quemoy = Chinmen *Taiwan* **59** E13
Quemú-Quemú *Argentina* **126** D3
Quequén *Argentina* **126** D4
Querétaro *Mexico* **118** C4
Querétaro □ *Mexico* **118** C5
Querfurt *Germany* **24** D7
Quérigut *France* **20** F6
Querqueville *France* **18** C5
Quesada *Spain* **37** H7
Queshan *China* **56** H8
Quesnel *Canada* **102** C4
Quesnel → *Canada* **102** C4
Quesnel L. *Canada* **102** C4
Questa *U.S.A.* **109** H11
Questembert *France* **18** E4
Quetico △ *Canada* **104** C1
Quetta *Pakistan* **68** D2
Queyras △ *France* **21** D10
Quezaltenango = Guatemala **120** D1
Quezon City *Phil.* **61** D4
Qufār *Si. Arabia* **70** E4
Qui Nhon *Vietnam* **64** F7
Quibala *Angola* **84** G2
Quibaxe *Angola* **84** F2
Quibdo *Colombia* **124** B3

Quiberon *France* **18** E3
Quiberon, Presqu'île de *France* **18** E3
Quickborn *Germany* **24** B5
Quiet L. *Canada* **102** A2
Quiindy *Paraguay* **126** B4
Quilá *Mexico* **118** C3
Quilán, C. *Chile* **128** E2
Quilcene *U.S.A.* **110** C4
Quilimarí *Chile* **126** C1
Quilino *Argentina* **126** C3
Quill Lakes *Canada* **103** C8
Quillabamba *Peru* **124** F4
Quillagua *Chile* **126** A2
Quillaicillo *Chile* **126** C1
Quillan *France* **20** F6
Quillota *Chile* **126** C1
Quilon *India* **66** Q10
Quilpie *Australia* **95** D3
Quilpué *Chile* **126** C1
Quilua *Mozam.* **87** F4
Quimilí *Argentina* **126** B3
Quimper *France* **18** E2
Quimperlé *France* **18** E3
Quinault → *U.S.A.* **110** C2
Quincy *Calif., U.S.A.* **110** F6
Quincy *Fla., U.S.A.* **117** F12
Quincy *Ill., U.S.A.* **112** F8
Quincy *Mass., U.S.A.* **115** D14
Quincy *Wash., U.S.A.* **108** C4
Quines *Argentina* **126** C2
Quinga *Mozam.* **87** F5
Quingey *France* **19** E12
Quintana de la Serena *Spain* **37** G5
Quintana Roo □ *Mexico* **119** D7
Quintanar de la Orden *Spain* **37** F7
Quintanar de la Sierra *Spain* **38** D2
Quintanar del Rey *Spain* **39** F3
Quintero *Chile* **126** C1
Quintin *France* **18** D4
Quinto *Spain* **38** D4
Quípar → *Spain* **39** G3
Quirihue *Chile* **126** D1
Quirindi *Australia* **95** E5
Quirinópolis *Brazil* **125** G8
Quiroga *Spain* **36** C3
Quissac *France* **21** E8
Quissanga *Mozam.* **87** E5
Quissico *Mozam.* **89** C5
Quitilipi *Argentina* **126** B3
Quitman *U.S.A.* **117** F13
Quito *Ecuador* **124** D3
Quixadá *Brazil* **125** D11
Quixaxe *Mozam.* **87** F5
Qujing *China* **58** E5
Qulan *Kazakhstan* **52** E8
Qul'ân, Jazâ'ir *Egypt* **70** E2
Qul'ân, Jazâ'ir *Egypt* **70** E2
Quneitra *Syria* **74** B4
Qŭnghirot *Uzbekistan* **52** E6
Qu'nyido *China* **58** B2
Quoin I. *Australia* **92** B4
Quoin Pt. *S. Africa* **88** E2
Quorn *Australia* **95** E2
Qŭqon *Uzbekistan* **52** E8
Qurein *Sudan* **81** E3
Qurnat as Sawdā' *Lebanon* **74** A5
Qûs *Egypt* **80** B3
Qusar *Azerbaijan* **35** K9
Quşaybā' *Si. Arabia* **70** E4
Qusaybah *Iraq* **73** E9
Quseir *Egypt* **70** E2
Qūshchī *Iran* **73** D11
Quthing *Lesotho* **89** E4
Qūṭīābād *Iran* **73** E13
Quwo *China* **56** G6
Quyang *China* **56** E8
Quynh Nhai *Vietnam* **64** B4
Quyon *Canada* **115** A8
Quzhou *China* **59** C12
Quzi *China* **56** F4
Qvareli *Georgia* **35** K7
Qyzylorda *Kazakhstan* **52** E7

R

Ra, Ko *Thailand* **65** H2
Raab *Austria* **26** C6
Raahe *Finland* **8** D21
Raalte *Neths.* **17** B6
Raasay *U.K.* **13** D2
Raasay, Sd. of *U.K.* **13** D2
Rab *Croatia* **41** D11
Raba *Indonesia* **63** F5
Rába → *Hungary* **28** C2
Raba → *Poland* **31** J7
Rabaçal → *Portugal* **36** D3
Rabah *Nigeria* **83** C6
Rabai *Kenya* **86** C4
Rabak *Sudan* **81** E3
Rabastens *France* **20** E5
Rabastens-de-Bigorre *France* **20** E4
Rabat = Victoria *Malta* **49** C1
Rabat *Malta* **49** D1
Rabat *Morocco* **78** B4

Rabaul *Papua N. G.* **90** B8
Rabi *Fiji* **91** a
Rābigh *Si. Arabia* **75** C2
Rabka *Poland* **31** J6
Râbniţa *Moldova* **29** C14
Rābor *Iran* **71** D8
Rača *Serbia* **44** B4
Răcăciuni *Romania* **29** D11
Răcăşdia *Romania* **28** F6
Racconigi *Italy* **40** D4
Race, C. *Canada* **105** C9
Rach Gia *Vietnam* **65** G5
Rachid *Mauritania* **82** B2
Raciąż *Poland* **31** F7
Racibórz *Poland* **31** H5
Racichy *Belarus* **31** F10
Racine *U.S.A.* **112** D10
Radama, Nosy *Madag.* **89** A8
Radama, Saikanosy *Madag.* **89** A8
Radan *Serbia* **44** D5
Rădăuţi *Romania* **29** C10
Rădăuţi-Prut *Romania* **29** B11
Radbuza → *Czech Rep.* **26** B6
Radcliff *U.S.A.* **113** G11
Radeberg *Germany* **24** D9
Radebeul *Germany* **24** D9
Radeče *Slovenia* **41** B12
Radekhiv *Ukraine* **23** C13
Radekhov = Radekhiv *Ukraine* **23** C13
Radenthein *Austria* **26** E6
Radew → *Poland* **30** D2
Radford *U.S.A.* **113** G13
Radhanpur *India* **68** H4
Radhwa, Jabal *Si. Arabia* **70** E3
Radika → *Macedonia* **44** E4
Radisson *Qué., Canada* **104** B4
Radisson *Sask., Canada* **103** C7
Radium Hot Springs *Canada* **102** C5
Radlje ob Dravi *Slovenia* **41** B12
Radnevo *Bulgaria* **45** D9
Radnice *Czech Rep.* **26** B6
Radnor Forest *U.K.* **15** E4
Radolfzell *Germany* **25** H4
Radom *Poland* **31** G8
Radomir *Bulgaria* **44** D6
Radomka → *Poland* **31** G8
Radomsko *Poland* **31** G6
Radomyshl *Ukraine* **23** C15
Radomyśl Wielki *Poland* **31** H8
Radoszyce *Poland* **31** G7
Radoviš *Macedonia* **44** E6
Radovljica *Slovenia* **41** B11
Radstadt *Austria* **26** D6
Radstock, C. *Australia* **95** E1
Răducăneni *Romania* **29** D12
Raduša *Macedonia* **44** D5
Radvanichy *Belarus* **31** F11
Radviliškis *Lithuania* **30** C10
Radville *Canada* **103** D8
Raḍwá, J. *Si. Arabia* **80** C4
Radymno *Poland* **31** J9
Radzanów *Poland* **31** F7
Radziejów *Poland* **31** F5
Radzyń Chełmiński *Poland* **30** E5
Radzyń Podlaski *Poland* **31** G9
Rae *Canada* **102** A5
Rae Bareli *India* **69** F9
Rae Isthmus *Canada* **101** C11
Raeren *Belgium* **17** D6
Raeside, L. *Australia* **93** E3
Raetihi *N.Z.* **91** C5
Rafaela *Argentina* **126** C3
Rafah *Gaza Strip* **74** D3
Rafai *C.A.R.* **86** B1
Raffadali *Italy* **42** E6
Raffili *Sudan* **81** F2
Rafḥā *Si. Arabia* **70** D4
Rafsanjān *Iran* **71** D8
Raft Pt. *Australia* **92** C3
Râgâ *Sudan* **81** F2
Raga → *Sudan* **81** F2
Ragachow *Belarus* **23** B16
Ragag *Sudan* **81** E1
Ragama *Sri Lanka* **66** R11
Ragged, Mt. *Australia* **93** F3
Ragged Pt. *Barbados* **121** g
Raghunathpalli *India* **69** H11
Raghunathpur *India* **69** H12
Raglan *N.Z.* **91** B5
Ragusa *Italy* **43** F7
Raha *Indonesia* **63** E6
Rahad, Nahr ed → *Sudan* **81** E3
Rahaeng = Tak *Thailand* **64** D2
Rahatgarh *India* **69** H8
Rahden *Germany* **24** C4
Raheita *Eritrea* **81** E5
Rahimyar Khan *Pakistan* **68** E4
Rāhjerd *Iran* **71** C6
Rahole △ *Kenya* **86** B4
Rahon *India* **68** D7
Raiatéa, Î. *French Polynesia* **97** J12
Raichur *India* **66** L10
Raiganj *India* **69** G13
Raigarh *India* **67** J13
Raijua *Indonesia* **63** F6

Raikot *India* **68** D6
Railton *Australia* **95** G4
Rainbow Bridge △ *U.S.A.* **109** H8
Rainbow Lake *Canada* **102** B5
Rainier *U.S.A.* **110** D4
Rainier, Mt. *U.S.A.* **110** D5
Rainy L. *Canada* **103** D10
Rainy River *Canada* **103** D10
Raippaluoto *Finland* **8** E19
Raipur *India* **67** J12
Ra'is *Si. Arabia* **80** C4
Raisen *India* **68** H8
Raisio *Finland* **32** B2
Raj Nandgaon *India* **67** J12
Raj Nilgiri *India* **69** J12
Raja, Ujung *Indonesia* **62** D1
Raja Ampat, Kepulauan *Indonesia* **63** E8
Rajahmundry *India* **67** L12
Rajaji △ *India* **68** D8
Rajang → *Malaysia* **62** D4
Rajanpur *Pakistan* **68** E4
Rajapalaiyam *India* **66** Q10
Rajasthan □ *India* **68** F5
Rajasthan Canal = Indira Gandhi Canal *India* **68** F5
Rajauri *India* **69** C6
Rajgarh *Mad. P., India* **68** G7
Rajgarh *Raj., India* **68** F7
Rajgarh *Raj., India* **68** E6
Rajgir *India* **69** G11
Rajgród *Poland* **30** E9
Rajkot *India* **68** H4
Rajmahal Hills *India* **69** G12
Rajpipla *India* **66** J8
Rajpur *India* **68** H6
Rajpura *India* **68** D7
Rajshahi *Bangla.* **67** G16
Rajshahi □ *Bangla.* **69** G13
Rajula *India* **68** J4
Rakaia *N.Z.* **91** E4
Rakaia → *N.Z.* **91** E4
Rakan, Ra's *Qatar* **71** E6
Rakaposhi *Pakistan* **69** A6
Rakata, Pulau *Indonesia* **62** F3
Rakhiv *Ukraine* **29** B9
Rakhni *Pakistan* **68** D3
Rakhni → *Pakistan* **68** D3
Rakhny-Lisovi *Ukraine* **29** B13
Rakiraki *Fiji* **91** a
Rakitnoye *Russia* **54** B7
Rakitovo *Bulgaria* **45** E8
Rakiura △ *N.Z.* **91** G1
Rakoniewice *Poland* **31** F3
Rakops *Botswana* **88** C3
Rakovica *Croatia* **41** D12
Rakovník *Czech Rep.* **26** A6
Rakovski *Bulgaria* **45** D8
Rakvere *Estonia* **32** C4
Raleigh *U.S.A.* **117** D15
Ralik Chain *Pac. Oc.* **96** G8
Ralja *Serbia* **44** B4
Ralls *U.S.A.* **116** E4
Ralston *U.S.A.* **114** E8
Ram → *Canada* **102** A4
Rām Allāh *West Bank* **74** D4
Rama *Nic.* **120** D3
Ramacca *Italy* **43** E7
Ramakona *India* **69** J8
Ramales de la Victoria *Spain* **36** B7
Rāmallāh = Rām Allāh *West Bank* **74** D4
Raman *Thailand* **65** J3
Ramanathapuram *India* **66** Q11
Ramanetaka, B. de *Madag.* **89** A8
Ramanujganj *India* **69** H10
Ramat Gan *Israel* **74** C3
Ramatlhabama *S. Africa* **88** D4
Ramban *India* **69** C6
Rambervillers *France* **19** D13
Rambi = Rabi *Fiji* **91** a
Rambipuji *Indonesia* **63** H15
Rambouillet *France* **19** D8
Rame Hd. *Australia* **95** F4
Ramechhap *Nepal* **69** F12
Ramenskoye *Russia* **32** E10
Ramganga → *India* **69** F8
Ramgarh *Jharkhand, India* **69** H11
Ramgarh *Raj., India* **68** F6
Ramgarh *Raj., India* **68** F4
Rāmhormoz *Iran* **71** D6
Ramīān *Iran* **71** B7
Ramingining *Australia* **94** A2
Ramla *Israel* **74** D3
Ramlu *Eritrea* **81** E5
Ramm = Rum *Jordan* **74** F4
Ramm, Jabal *Jordan* **74** F4
Râmna → *Romania* **29** E12
Ramnad = Ramanathapuram *India* **66** Q11
Ramnagar *Jammu & Kashmir, India* **69** C6
Ramnagar *Uttaranchal, India* **69** E8
Ramnäs *Sweden* **10** E10
Ramnous *Greece* **46** C6

Ramon *Russia* **33** G10
Ramona *U.S.A.* **111** M10
Ramonville-St-Agne *France* **20** E5
Ramore *Canada* **104** C3
Ramos → *Nigeria* **83** D6
Ramotswa *Botswana* **88** C4
Rampur *H.P., India* **68** D7
Rampur *Mad. P., India* **68** H5
Rampur *Ut. P., India* **69** E8
Rampur Hat *India* **69** G12
Rampura *India* **68** G6
Ramrama Tola *India* **69** J8
Ramree I. *Burma* **67** K19
Rāmsar *Iran* **71** B6
Ramsey *I. of Man* **14** C3
Ramsey *U.S.A.* **115** E10
Ramsey L. *Canada* **104** C3
Ramsgate *U.K.* **15** F9
Ramsjö *Sweden* **10** B9
Ramstein *Germany* **25** F3
Ramtek *India* **66** J11
Ramu *Kenya* **86** B5
Ramvik *Sweden* **10** B11
Rana Pratap Sagar Dam *India* **68** G6
Ranaghat *India* **69** H13
Ranahu *Pakistan* **68** G3
Ranau *Malaysia* **62** C5
Rancagua *Chile* **126** C1
Rance → *France* **18** D5
Rancheria → *Canada* **102** A3
Ranchester *U.S.A.* **108** D10
Ranchi *India* **69** H11
Rancho Cordova *U.S.A.* **110** G5
Rancho Cucamonga *U.S.A.* **111** L9
Randalstown *U.K.* **12** B5
Randan *France* **19** F10
Randazzo *Italy* **43** E7
Randers *Denmark* **11** H4
Randers Fjord *Denmark* **11** H4
Randfontein *S. Africa* **89** D4
Randle *U.S.A.* **110** D5
Randolph *Mass., U.S.A.* **115** D13
Randolph *N.Y., U.S.A.* **114** D6
Randolph *Utah, U.S.A.* **108** F8
Randolph *Vt., U.S.A.* **115** C12
Randsburg *U.S.A.* **111** K9
Råneälven → *Sweden* **8** D20
Rangae *Thailand* **65** J3
Rangaunu B. *N.Z.* **91** A4
Range, The *Zimbabwe* **87** F3
Rangeley *U.S.A.* **115** B14
Rangeley L. *U.S.A.* **115** B14
Rangely *U.S.A.* **108** F9
Ranger *U.S.A.* **116** E5
Rangia *India* **67** F17
Rangiora *N.Z.* **91** E4
Rangitaiki → *N.Z.* **91** B6
Rangitata → *N.Z.* **91** E3
Rangitoto ke to tonga = D'Urville I. *N.Z.* **91** D4
Rangkasbitung *Indonesia* **63** G12
Rangon → *Burma* **67** L20
Rangoon *Burma* **67** L20
Rangpur *Bangla.* **67** G16
Rangsit *Thailand* **64** F3
Ranibennur *India* **66** M9
Raniganj *Ut. P., India* **69** F9
Raniganj *W. Bengal, India* **67** H15
Ranikhet *India* **69** E8
Raniwara *India* **68** G5
Ranka *India* **69** H10
Ranken → *Australia* **94** C2
Rankin *U.S.A.* **116** F4
Rankin Inlet *Canada* **100** C10
Rankins Springs *Australia* **95** E4
Rankweil *Austria* **26** D2
Rannoch, L. *U.K.* **13** E4
Rannoch Moor *U.K.* **13** E4
Ranobe, Helodranon' i *Madag.* **89** C7
Ranohira *Madag.* **89** C8
Ranomafana *Toamasina, Madag.* **89** C8
Ranomafana *Toliara, Madag.* **89** C8
Ranomafana △ *Madag.* **89** C8
Ranomena *Madag.* **89** C8
Ranong *Thailand* **65** H2
Ranotsara Nord *Madag.* **89** C8
Rānsa *Iran* **71** C6
Ransiki *Indonesia* **63** E8
Rantabe *Madag.* **89** B8
Rantauprapat *Indonesia* **62** D1
Rantemario *Indonesia* **63** E5
Ranthambore △ *India* **68** F7
Rantoul *U.S.A.* **112** E9
Ranum *Denmark* **11** H3
Ranyah, W. → *Si. Arabia* **80** C5
Raon l'Étape *France* **19** D13
Raoping *China* **59** F11
Raoyang *China* **56** E8
Rap, Ko *Thailand* **65** b
Rapa *French Polynesia* **97** K13
Rapa Nui = Pascua, I. de *Chile* **97** K17
Rapallo *Italy* **40** D6

Rapar *India* **68** H4
Rāpch *Iran* **71** E8
Raper, C. *Canada* **101** C13
Rapid City *U.S.A.* **112** C2
Rapid River *U.S.A.* **112** C10
Rapla *Estonia* **32** C3
Rapti → *India* **69** F11
Rapu Rapu I. *Phil.* **61** E6
Rara △ *Nepal* **69** E10
Rarotonga *Cook Is.* **97** K12
Ra's al 'Ayn *Syria* **73** D9
Ra's al Khaymah *U.A.E.* **71** E7
Râs el Mâ *Mali* **82** B4
Râs Ghârib *Egypt* **80** B3
Râs Mallap *Egypt* **80** B3
Râs Muhammad △ *Egypt* **80** B3
Rasca, Pta. de la *Canary Is.* **48** G3
Rashad *Sudan* **81** E3
Rashîd *Egypt* **80** H7
Rashîd, Masabb *Egypt* **80** H7
Rashmi *India* **68** G6
Rasht *Iran* **73** D13
Rasi Salai *Thailand* **64** E5
Raska *Serbia* **44** C4
Râsnov *Romania* **29** E11
Rason L. *Australia* **93** E3
Raşova *Romania* **29** F12
Rasovo *Bulgaria* **44** C7
Rasra *India* **69** G10
Rasskazovo *Russia* **34** D5
Rast *Romania* **29** G8
Rastatt *Germany* **25** G4
Rastede *Germany* **24** B4
Rǎstolița *Romania* **29** D9
Rasul *Pakistan* **68** C5
Rat → *Canada* **103** D9
Rat Buri *Thailand* **64** F2
Rat Islands *U.S.A.* **106** a
Rat L. *Canada* **103** B9
Ratak Chain *Pac. Oc.* **96** G8
Rätan *Sweden* **10** B8
Ratangarh *India* **68** E6
Raţāwī *Iraq* **70** D5
Rath *India* **69** G8
Rath Luirc *Ireland* **12** D3
Rathangan *Ireland* **12** C4
Rathdrum *Ireland* **12** D5
Rathenow *Germany* **24** C8
Rathkeale *Ireland* **12** D3
Rathlin I. *U.K.* **12** A5
Rathmelton *Ireland* **12** A4
Ratibor = Racibórz *Poland* **31** H5
Rätikon *Austria* **26** D2
Ratingen *Germany* **24** D2
Ratlam *India* **68** H6
Ratnagiri *India* **66** L8
Ratodero *Pakistan* **68** F3
Raton *U.S.A.* **109** H11
Rattaphum *Thailand* **65** J3
Ratten *Austria* **26** D8
Rattray Hd. *U.K.* **13** D7
Rättvik *Sweden* **10** D9
Ratz, Mt. *Canada* **102** B2
Ratzeburg *Germany* **24** B6
Raub *Malaysia* **65** L3
Rauch *Argentina* **126** D4
Raudales *Mexico* **119** D6
Raufarhöfn *Iceland* **8** C6
Raufoss *Norway* **8** F14
Raukumara Ra. *N.Z.* **91** C6
Rauma *Finland* **32** B1
Raumo = Rauma *Finland* **32** B1
Raung, Gunung *Indonesia* **63** J17
Raurkela *India* **69** H11
Rausu-Dake *Japan* **54** B12
Rāut → *Moldova* **29** C14
Rava-Ruska *Ukraine* **31** H10
Rava Russkaya = Rava-Ruska *Ukraine* **31** H10
Ravalli *U.S.A.* **108** C6
Ravānsar *Iran* **73** E12
Ravanusa *Italy* **42** E6
Rāvar *Iran* **71** D8
Ravena *U.S.A.* **115** D11
Ravenna *Italy* **41** D9
Ravenna *Nebr., U.S.A.* **112** E4
Ravenna *Ohio, U.S.A.* **114** E3
Ravensburg *Germany* **25** H5
Ravenshoe *Australia* **94** B4
Ravensthorpe *Australia* **93** F3
Ravenswood *Australia* **94** C4
Ravenswood *U.S.A.* **113** F13
Ravna Gora *Croatia* **41** C11
Ravna Reka *Serbia* **44** B5
Ravne na Koroškem *Slovenia* **41** B11
Rawa Mazowiecka *Poland* **31** G7
Rawalpindi *Pakistan* **68** C5
Rawang *Malaysia* **65** L3
Rawene *N.Z.* **91** A4

Rawicz *Poland* **31** G3
Rawka → *Poland* **31** F7
Rawlinna *Australia* **93** F4
Rawlins *U.S.A.* **108** F10
Rawlinson Ra. *Australia* **93** D4
Rawson *Argentina* **128** E3
Raxaul *Trin. & Tob.* **125** K16
Ray *U.S.A.* **112** A2
Ray, C. *Canada* **105** C8
Raya Ring, Ko *Thailand* **65** a
Rayadurg *India* **66** M10
Rayagada *India* **67** K13
Rāyen *Iran* **71** D8
Rayleigh *U.K.* **15** F8
Raymond *Canada* **102** D6
Raymond *Calif., U.S.A.* **110** H7
Raymond *N.H., U.S.A.* **115** C13
Raymond *Wash., U.S.A.* **110** D3
Raymondville *U.S.A.* **116** H6
Raymore *Canada* **103** C8
Rayón *Mexico* **118** B2
Rayong *Thailand* **64** F3
Rayville *U.S.A.* **116** E9
Raz, Pte. du *France* **18** D2
Razan *Iran* **73** E13
Ražana *Serbia* **44** B3
Ražanj *Serbia* **44** C5
Razāzah, Buḩayrat ar *Iraq* **73** F10
Razāzah, L. = Razāzah, Buḩayrat ar *Iraq* **73** F10
Razdelna *Bulgaria* **45** C11
Razdel'naya = Rozdilna *Ukraine* **29** D15
Razdolnoye *Russia* **54** C5
Razdolnoye *Ukraine* **33** K7
Razeh *Iran* **71** C6
Razgrad *Bulgaria* **45** C10
Razim, Lacul *Romania* **29** F14
Razlog *Bulgaria* **44** E7
Razmak *Pakistan* **68** C3
Ré, Î. de *France* **20** B2
Reading *U.K.* **15** F7
Reading *U.S.A.* **115** F9
Reading □ *U.K.* **15** F7
Realicó *Argentina* **126** D3
Réalmont *France* **20** E6
Ream *Cambodia* **65** G4
Reay Forest *U.K.* **13** C4
Rebais *France* **19** D10
Rebi *Indonesia* **63** F8
Rebiana *Libya* **79** D10
Rebiana, Sahrâ' *Libya* **79** D10
Reboly *Russia* **8** E24
Rebun-Tō *Japan* **54** B10
Recanati *Italy* **41** E10
Recaş *Romania* **28** E6
Recco *Italy* **40** D6
Recherche, Arch. of the *Australia* **93** F3
Rechna Doab *Pakistan* **68** D5
Rechytsa *Belarus* **23** B16
Recife *Brazil* **125** E12
Recife *Seychelles* **85** b
Recklinghausen *Germany* **17** C7
Reconquista *Argentina* **126** B4
Recreo *Argentina* **126** B2
Recz *Poland* **31** E2
Red → *U.S.A.* **116** F9
Red Bank *U.S.A.* **115** F10
Red Bay *Canada* **105** B8
Red Bluff *U.S.A.* **108** F2
Red Bluff Res. *U.S.A.* **109** L12
Red Cliffs *Australia* **95** E3
Red Cloud *U.S.A.* **112** E4
Red Creek *U.S.A.* **115** C8
Red Deer *Canada* **102** C6
Red Deer → *Alta., Canada* **103** C7
Red Deer → *Man., Canada* **103** C8
Red Deer L. *Canada* **103** C8
Red Hook *U.S.A.* **115** E11
Red Indian L. *Canada* **105** C8
Red L. *Canada* **103** C10
Red Lake *Canada* **103** C10
Red Lake Falls *U.S.A.* **112** B5
Red Lake Road *Canada* **103** C10
Red Lodge *U.S.A.* **108** D9
Red Mountain *U.S.A.* **111** K9
Red Oak *U.S.A.* **112** E7
Red River of the North → *N. Amer.* **112** A5
Red Rock *Canada* **104** C2
Red Rock, L. *U.S.A.* **112** E7
Red Rocks Pt. *Australia* **93** F4
Red Sea *Asia* **75** C2
Red Slate Mt. *U.S.A.* **110** H8
Red Sucker L. *Canada* **104** B1
Red Tower Pass = Turnu Roşu, P. *Romania* **29** E9
Red Wing *U.S.A.* **112** C7
Reda *Poland* **30** D5
Redang *Malaysia* **65** K4
Redange *Lux.* **17** E5
Redcar *U.K.* **14** C6
Redcar & Cleveland □ *U.K.* **14** C7
Redcliff *Canada* **108** A8
Redcliffe *Australia* **95** D5

Reddersburg *S. Africa* **88** D4
Redding *U.S.A.* **108** F2
Redditch *U.K.* **15** E6
Redfield *U.S.A.* **112** C4
Redford *U.S.A.* **115** B11
Redhead *Trin. & Tob.* **125** K16
Redkino *Russia* **32** D9
Redlands *U.S.A.* **111** M9
Redmond *Oreg., U.S.A.* **108** D3
Redmond *Wash., U.S.A.* **110** C4
Redon *France* **18** E4
Redonda *Antigua & B.* **121** C7
Redondela *Spain* **36** C2
Redondo *Portugal* **37** G3
Redondo Beach *U.S.A.* **111** M8
Redruth *U.K.* **15** G2
Redvers *Canada* **103** D8
Redwater *Canada* **102** C6
Redwood *U.S.A.* **115** B9
Redwood △ *U.S.A.* **108** F1
Redwood City *U.S.A.* **110** H4
Redwood Falls *U.S.A.* **112** C6
Ree, L. *Ireland* **12** C3
Reed City *U.S.A.* **113** D11
Reed L. *Canada* **103** C8
Reedley *U.S.A.* **110** J7
Reedsburg *U.S.A.* **112** D8
Reedsport *U.S.A.* **108** E1
Reedsville *U.S.A.* **114** F7
Reefton *N.Z.* **91** E3
Rees *Germany* **24** D2
Reese → *U.S.A.* **108** F5
Refahiye *Turkey* **73** C8
Reftele *Sweden* **11** G7
Refugio *U.S.A.* **116** G6
Rega → *Poland* **30** D2
Regalbuto *Italy* **43** E7
Regen *Germany* **25** G9
Regen → *Germany* **25** F8
Regensburg *Germany* **25** F8
Regenstauf *Germany* **25** F8
Reggâne = Zaouiet Reggâne *Algeria* **78** C6
Reggello *Italy* **41** E8
Réggio di Calábria *Italy* **43** D8
Réggio nell'Emília *Italy* **40** D7
Reghin *Romania* **29** D9
Regina *Canada* **103** C8
Regina Beach *Canada* **103** C8
Registro *Brazil* **127** A6
Reguengos de Monsaraz *Portugal* **37** G3
Rehar → *India* **69** H10
Rehli *India* **69** H8
Rehoboth *Namibia* **88** C2
Rehovot *Israel* **74** D3
Reichenbach *Germany* **24** E8
Reid *Australia* **93** F4
Reidsville *U.S.A.* **117** C15
Reigate *U.K.* **15** F7
Reillo *Spain* **38** F3
Reims *France* **19** C11
Reina Adelaida, Arch. *Chile* **128** G2
Reina Sofia, Tenerife ✈ (TFS) *Canary Is.* **48** F3
Reinbek *Germany* **24** B6
Reindeer → *Canada* **103** B8
Reindeer I. *Canada* **103** C9
Reindeer L. *Canada* **103** B8
Reinga, C. *N.Z.* **91** A4
Reinosa *Spain* **36** B6
Reitz *S. Africa* **89** D4
Reivilo *S. Africa* **88** D3
Rejaf *Sudan* **81** G3
Rejmyre *Sweden* **11** F9
Rejowiec Fabryczny *Poland* **31** G10
Reka → *Slovenia* **41** C11
Rekovac *Serbia* **44** C5
Reliance *Canada* **103** A7
Rémalard *France* **18** D7
Remarkable, Mt. *Australia* **95** E2
Rembang *Indonesia* **63** G14
Remedios *Panama* **120** E3
Remeshk *Iran* **71** E8
Remetea *Romania* **29** D10
Remich *Lux.* **17** E6
Remiremont *France* **19** D13
Remo *Ethiopia* **81** F5
Remontnoye *Russia* **35** G6
Remoulins *France* **21** E8
Remscheid *Germany* **17** C7
Ren Xian *China* **56** F8
Rendang *Indonesia* **63** J18
Rende *Italy* **43** C9
Rendina *Greece* **46** B3
Rendsburg *Germany* **24** A5
Renfrew *Canada* **114** A8
Renfrewshire □ *U.K.* **13** F4
Rengat *Indonesia* **62** E2
Rengo *Chile* **126** C1
Renhua *China* **59** E9
Renhuai *China* **58** D6
Reni *Ukraine* **29** E13
Renk *Sudan* **81** E3
Renmark *Australia* **95** E3
Rennell Sd. *Canada* **102** C2

Renner Springs *Australia* **94** B1
Rennes *France* **18** D5
Rennick Glacier *Antarctica* **5** D21
Rennie L. *Canada* **103** A7
Reno *U.S.A.* **110** F7
Reno → *Italy* **41** D9
Renovo *U.S.A.* **114** E7
Renqiu *China* **56** E9
Rens *Denmark* **11** K3
Renshou *China* **58** C5
Rensselaer *Ind., U.S.A.* **112** E10
Rensselaer *N.Y., U.S.A.* **115** D11
Rentería *Spain* **38** B3
Renton *U.S.A.* **110** C4
Réo *Burkina Faso* **82** C4
Reocín *Spain* **36** B6
Reotipur *India* **69** G10
Répcelak *Hungary* **28** C2
Republic *Mo., U.S.A.* **112** G7
Republic *Wash., U.S.A.* **108** B4
Republican → *U.S.A.* **112** F5
Repulse B. *Australia* **94** J6
Repulse Bay *Canada* **101** C11
Requena *Peru* **124** E4
Requena *Spain* **39** F3
Réquista *France* **20** D6
Reşadiye = Datça *Turkey* **47** E9
Reşadiye *Turkey* **72** B7
Reşadiye Yarımadası *Turkey* **47** E9
Resavica *Serbia* **44** B5
Resen *Macedonia* **44** E5
Reserve *U.S.A.* **109** K9
Resht = Rasht *Iran* **73** D13
Resistencia *Argentina* **126** B4
Reşiţa *Romania* **28** E6
Resko *Poland* **30** E2
Reso = Raisio *Finland* **32** B2
Resolute *Canada* **101** B10
Resolution I. *Canada* **101** C13
Resolution I. *N.Z.* **91** F1
Ressano Garcia *Mozam.* **89** D5
Reston *Canada* **103** D8
Reszel *Poland* **30** D8
Retalhuleu *Guatemala* **120** D1
Retenue, L. de *Dem. Rep. of the Congo* **87** E2
Retezat, Munţii *Romania* **28** E8
Retezat △ *Romania* **28** E7
Retford *U.K.* **14** D7
Rethel *France* **19** C11
Rethem *Germany* **24** C5
Rethimno *Greece* **49** D6
Rethimno □ *Greece* **49** D6
Reti *Pakistan* **68** E3
Retiche, Alpi *Switz.* **25** J6
Retiers *France* **18** E5
Retortillo *Spain* **36** E4
Retournac *France* **21** C8
Rétság *Hungary* **28** C4
Réunion ☑ *Ind. Oc.* **85** c
Reus *Spain* **38** D6
Reuterstadt Stavenhagen *Germany* **24** B8
Reutlingen *Germany* **25** G5
Reutte *Austria* **26** D3
Reval = Tallinn *Estonia* **32** C3
Revel *France* **20** E6
Revelganj *India* **69** G11
Revelstoke *Canada* **102** C5
Reventazón *Peru* **124** E2
Revigny-sur-Ornain *France* **19** D11
Revillagigedo, Is. de *Pac. Oc.* **118** D2
Revin *France* **19** C11
Revúca *Slovak Rep.* **27** C13
Revuè → *Mozam.* **87** F3
Rewa *India* **69** G9
Rewari *India* **68** E7
Rexburg *U.S.A.* **108** E8
Rey *Iran* **71** C6
Rey, I. del *Panama* **120** E4
Rey, I. del *Mexico* **118** B4
Rey Malabo *Eq. Guin.* **83** D6
Reyðarfjörður *Iceland* **8** D6
Reyes, Pt. *U.S.A.* **110** H3
Reyhanlı *Turkey* **72** D7
Reykjahlið *Iceland* **8** D5
Reykjanes *Iceland* **8** E2
Reykjavík *Iceland* **8** D3
Reynolds Ra. *Australia* **92** D5
Reynoldsville *U.S.A.* **114** E6
Reynosa *Mexico* **119** B5
Rēzekne *Latvia* **32** D4
Rezovo *Bulgaria* **45** D12
Rezina *Moldova* **29** C13
Rezvān *Iran* **71** E8
Rgotina *Serbia* **44** B6
Rhayader *U.K.* **15** E4
Rheda-Wiedenbrück *Germany* **24** D4
Rhede *Germany* **24** D2
Rhein → *Europe* **17** C6
Rhein-Main-Donau-Kanal *Germany* **25** F7
Rhein-Ruhr, Düsseldorf ✈ (DUS) *Germany* **24** C6
Rhein-Taunus △ *Germany* **25** E4

Rhein-Westerwald △ Germany **24** E3
Rheinbach Germany **24** E2
Rheine Germany **24** C3
Rheinfelden Germany **25** H3
Rheinhessen-Pfalz □ Germany **25** F3
Rheinland-Pfalz □ Germany **25** E2
Rheinsberg Germany **24** B8
Rhin = Rhein → Europe **17** C6
Rhine = Rhein → Europe **17** C6
Rhinebeck U.S.A. **115** E11
Rhineland-Palatinate = Rheinland-Pfalz □ Germany **25** E2
Rhinelander U.S.A. **112** C9
Rhinns Pt. U.K. **13** F2
Rhino Camp Uganda **86** B3
Rhir, Cap Morocco **78** B4
Rho Italy **40** C6
Rhode Island □ U.S.A. **115** E13
Rhodes Greece **49** C10
Rhodes ✈ (RHO) Greece **47** E10
Rhodope Mts. = Rhodopi Planina Bulgaria **45** E8
Rhodopi Planina Bulgaria **45** E8
Rhön Germany **24** E5
Rhondda U.K. **15** F4
Rhondda Cynon Taff □ U.K. **15** F4
Rhône □ France **21** C8
Rhône → France **21** E8
Rhône-Alpes □ France **21** C9
Rhum U.K. **13** E2
Rhyl U.K. **14** D4
Ri-Aba Eq. Guin. **83** E6
Ria Formosa △ Portugal **37** H3
Riachão Brazil **125** E9
Riangnom Sudan **81** F3
Riaño Spain **36** C6
Rians France **21** E9
Riansáres → Spain **37** F7
Riasi India **69** C6
Riau □ Indonesia **62** E2
Riau, Kepulauan Indonesia **62** D2
Riau Arch. = Riau, Kepulauan Indonesia **62** D2
Riaza Spain **36** D7
Riaza → Spain **36** D7
Riba de Saelices Spain **38** E2
Riba-Roja de Turia Spain **39** F4
Ribadavia Spain **36** C2
Ribadeo Spain **36** B3
Ribadesella Spain **36** B5
Ribado Nigeria **83** D7
Ribao Cameroon **83** D7
Ribas = Ribes de Freser Spain **38** C7
Ribas do Rio Pardo Brazil **125** H8
Ribauè Mozam. **87** E4
Ribble → U.K. **14** D5
Ribe Denmark **11** J2
Ribeauvillé France **19** D14
Ribécourt-Dreslincourt France **19** C9
Ribeira = Santa Uxía Spain **36** C2
Ribeira Brava Madeira **78** D2
Ribeira Grande C. Verde Is. **78** b
Ribeirão Prêto Brazil **127** A6
Ribemont France **19** C10
Ribera Italy **42** E6
Ribérac France **20** C4
Riberalta Bolivia **124** F5
Ribes de Freser Spain **38** C7
Ribnica Slovenia **41** C11
Ribnitz-Damgarten Germany **24** A8
Ričany Czech Rep. **26** B7
Riccarton N.Z. **91** E4
Ríccia Italy **43** A7
Riccione Italy **41** E9
Rice U.S.A. **111** L12
Rice L. Canada **114** B6
Rice Lake U.S.A. **112** C8
Rich, C. Canada **114** B4
Richard Toll Senegal **82** B1
Richards Bay S. Africa **89** D5
Richardson → Canada **103** B6
Richardson Lakes U.S.A. **113** C18
Richardson Springs U.S.A. **110** F5
Riche, C. Australia **93** F2
Richelieu France **18** E7
Richey U.S.A. **108** C11
Richfield U.S.A. **108** G7
Richfield Springs U.S.A. **115** D10
Richford U.S.A. **115** B12
Richibucto Canada **105** C7
Richland Ga., U.S.A. **117** E12
Richland Wash., U.S.A. **108** C4
Richland Center U.S.A. **112** D8
Richlands U.S.A. **113** G13
Richmond Australia **94** C3
Richmond N.Z. **91** D4
Richmond U.K. **14** C6
Richmond Calif., U.S.A. **110** H4
Richmond Ind., U.S.A. **113** F11
Richmond Ky., U.S.A. **113** G11
Richmond Mich., U.S.A. **114** D2
Richmond Mo., U.S.A. **112** F7

Richmond Tex., U.S.A. **116** G7
Richmond Utah, U.S.A. **108** F8
Richmond Va., U.S.A. **113** G15
Richmond Vt., U.S.A. **115** B12
Richmond Hill Canada **114** C5
Richmond Ra. Australia **95** D5
Richtersveld △ S. Africa **88** D2
Richwood U.S.A. **113** F13
Ricla Spain **38** D3
Ridder = Leninogorsk Kazakhstan **52** D9
Riddlesburg U.S.A. **114** F6
Ridgecrest U.S.A. **111** K9
Ridgefield Conn., U.S.A. **115** E11
Ridgefield Wash., U.S.A. **110** E4
Ridgeland Miss., U.S.A. **117** E9
Ridgeland S.C., U.S.A. **117** E14
Ridgetown Canada **114** D3
Ridgewood U.S.A. **115** F10
Ridgway U.S.A. **114** E6
Riding Mountain △ Canada **103** C9
Ridley, Mt. Australia **93** F3
Riebeek-Oos S. Africa **88** E4
Ried Austria **26** C6
Riedlingen Germany **25** G5
Riedstadt Germany **25** F4
Rienza → Italy **41** B8
Riesa Germany **24** D9
Riesi Italy **43** E7
Rietavas Lithuania **30** C8
Rietbron S. Africa **88** E3
Rietfontein Namibia **88** C3
Rieti Italy **41** F9
Rieupeyroux France **20** D6
Riez France **21** E10
Rif = Er Rif Morocco **78** A5
Riffe L. U.S.A. **110** D4
Rifle U.S.A. **108** G10
Rift Valley Africa **76** G7
Rift Valley → Kenya **86** B4
Rīga Latvia **30** B11
Rīga ✈ (RIX) Latvia **30** B10
Riga, G. of Latvia **30** A10
Rigacikun Nigeria **83** C6
Rīgān Iran **71** D8
Rīgas Jūras Līcis = Riga, G. of Latvia **30** A10
Rigaud Canada **115** A10
Rigby U.S.A. **108** E8
Rigestān Afghan. **66** D4
Riggins U.S.A. **108** D5
Rignac France **20** D6
Rigolet Canada **105** B8
Rihand Dam India **69** G10
Riihimäki Finland **32** B3
Riiser-Larsen-halvøya Antarctica **5** C4
Rijau Nigeria **83** C6
Rijeka Croatia **41** C11
Rijeka Crnojevića Montenegro **44** D3
Rijssen Neths. **17** B6
Rika → Ukraine **29** B8
Rike Ethiopia **81** E4
Rikuchū-Kaigan △ Japan **54** E11
Rikuzentakada Japan **54** E10
Rila Bulgaria **44** D7
Rila Planina Bulgaria **44** D7
Riley U.S.A. **108** E4
Rima → Nigeria **83** C6
Rimah, Wadi ar → Si. Arabia **70** E4
Rimau, Pulau Malaysia **65** c
Rimavská Sobota Slovak Rep. **27** C13
Rimbey Canada **102** C6
Rimbo Sweden **10** E12
Rimersburg U.S.A. **114** E5
Rimforsa Sweden **11** F9
Rimi Nigeria **83** C6
Rímini Italy **41** D9
Rimouski Canada **105** C6
Rimrock U.S.A. **110** D5
Rinca Indonesia **63** F5
Rincón de la Victoria Spain **37** J6
Rincón de Romos Mexico **118** C4
Rinconada Argentina **126** A2
Rind → India **69** G9
Ringarum Sweden **11** F10
Ringas India **68** F6
Ringe Denmark **11** J4
Ringgold Is. Fiji **91** a
Ringim Nigeria **83** C6
Ringkøbing Denmark **11** H2
Ringkøbing Fjord Denmark **11** H2
Ringsjön Sweden **11** J7
Ringsted Denmark **11** J5
Ringvassøya Norway **8** B18
Ringwood U.S.A. **115** E10
Rinia Greece **47** D7
Rinjani Indonesia **62** F5
Rinteln Germany **24** C5
Río, Punta del Spain **39** J2
Río Branco Brazil **124** E5
Río Branco Uruguay **127** C5
Río Bravo Mexico **119** B5
Río Bravo △ N. Amer. **118** B4

Río Bravo del Norte → Mexico **119** B5
Rio Brilhante Brazil **127** A5
Río Claro Brazil **127** A6
Río Claro Trin. & Tob. **121** D7
Río Colorado Argentina **128** D4
Río Cuarto Argentina **126** C3
Rio das Pedras Mozam. **89** C6
Rio de Janeiro Brazil **127** A7
Rio de Janeiro □ Brazil **127** A7
Rio do Sul Brazil **127** B6
Río Dulce △ Guatemala **120** C2
Río Gallegos Argentina **128** G3
Río Grande Argentina **128** G3
Rio Grande Brazil **127** C5
Río Grande Mexico **118** C4
Río Grande Nic. **120** D3
Rio Grande Puerto Rico **121** d
Río Grande → N. Amer. **116** H5
Rio Grande City U.S.A. **116** H5
Río Grande de Santiago → Mexico **118** C3
Rio Grande do Norte □ Brazil **125** E11
Rio Grande do Sul □ Brazil **127** C5
Río Hato Panama **120** E3
Río Lagartos Mexico **119** C7
Río Largo Brazil **125** E11
Rio Maior Portugal **37** F2
Rio Marina Italy **40** F7
Río Mulatos Bolivia **124** G5
Río Muni □ Eq. Guin. **84** D2
Rio Negro Brazil **127** B6
Rio Pardo Brazil **127** C5
Río Pilcomayo △ Argentina **126** B4
Río Platano △ Honduras **120** C3
Rio Rancho U.S.A. **109** J10
Río Segundo Argentina **126** C3
Río Tercero Argentina **126** C3
Rio Tinto Portugal **36** D2
Río Verde Brazil **125** G8
Río Verde Mexico **119** C5
Rio Vista U.S.A. **110** G5
Ríobamba Ecuador **124** D3
Ríohacha Colombia **124** A4
Riom France **20** C7
Riom-ès-Montagnes France **20** C6
Rion-des-Landes France **20** E3
Rionero in Vúlture Italy **43** B8
Rioni → Georgia **35** J5
Ríos Spain **36** D3
Ríosucio Colombia **124** B3
Riou L. Canada **103** B7
Rioz France **19** E13
Ripatransone Italy **41** F10
Ripley Canada **114** B3
Ripley Calif., U.S.A. **111** M12
Ripley N.Y., U.S.A. **114** D5
Ripley Tenn., U.S.A. **117** D10
Ripley W. Va., U.S.A. **113** F13
Ripoll Spain **38** C7
Ripon U.K. **14** C6
Ripon Calif., U.S.A. **110** H5
Ripon Wis., U.S.A. **112** D9
Riposto Italy **43** E8
Risan Montenegro **44** D2
Riscle France **20** E3
Rishā', W. ar → Si. Arabia **70** E5
Rishiri-Rebun-Sarobetsu △ Japan **54** B10
Rishiri-Tō Japan **54** B10
Rishon le Ẕiyyon Israel **74** D3
Risle → France **18** C7
Risnjak △ Croatia **41** C11
Rison U.S.A. **116** E8
Risør Norway **9** G13
Rita Blanca Cr. → U.S.A. **116** D3
Riti Nigeria **83** D6
Ritter, Mt. U.S.A. **110** H7
Rittman U.S.A. **114** F3
Ritzville U.S.A. **108** C4
Riva del Garda Italy **40** C7
Riva Lígure Italy **40** E4
Rivadavia B. Aires, Argentina **126** D3
Rivadavia Mendoza, Argentina **126** C2
Rivadavia Salta, Argentina **126** A3
Rivadavia Chile **126** B1
Rivarolo Canavese Italy **40** C4
Rivas Nic. **120** D2
Rive-de-Gier France **21** C8
River Cess Liberia **82** D3
River Jordan Canada **110** B2
Rivera Argentina **126** D3
Rivera Uruguay **127** C4
Riverbank U.S.A. **110** H6
Riverdale U.S.A. **110** J7
Riverhead U.S.A. **115** F12
Riverhurst Canada **103** C7
Rivers Canada **103** C8
Rivers □ Nigeria **83** E6
Rivers Inlet Canada **102** C3
Riversdale S. Africa **88** E3
Riverside U.S.A. **111** M9
Riverton Australia **95** E2
Riverton Canada **103** C9

Riverton N.Z. **91** G2
Riverton U.S.A. **108** E9
Rives France **21** C9
Rivesaltes France **20** F6
Riviera U.S.A. **111** K12
Riviera di Levante Italy **40** D6
Riviera di Ponente Italy **40** D5
Rivière-au-Renard Canada **105** C7
Rivière-du-Loup Canada **105** C6
Rivière-Pentecôte Canada **105** C6
Rivière-Pilote Martinique **120** c
Rivière St-Paul Canada **105** B8
Rivière-Salée Martinique **120** c
Rivne Odesa, Ukraine **29** D14
Rivne Rivne, Ukraine **23** C14
Rivne □ Ukraine **33** G4
Rívoli Italy **40** C4
Rivoli B. Australia **95** F3
Rixheim France **19** E14
Riyadh = Ar Riyāḍ Si. Arabia **70** E5
Riyadh al Khabrā' Si. Arabia **70** E4
Riza Greece **44** F7
Rize Turkey **73** B9
Rize □ Turkey **73** B9
Rizhao China **57** G10
Rizokarpaso Cyprus **49** D13
Rizzuto, C. Italy **43** D10
Rjukan Norway **9** G13
Ro Greece **47** E11
Roa Spain **36** D7
Road Town Br. Virgin Is. **121** e
Roan Plateau U.S.A. **108** G9
Roanne France **19** F11
Roanoke Ala., U.S.A. **117** E12
Roanoke Va., U.S.A. **113** G14
Roanoke → U.S.A. **117** D16
Roanoke I. U.S.A. **117** D17
Roanoke Rapids U.S.A. **117** C16
Roatán Honduras **120** C2
Robāt Sang Iran **71** C8
Robāṭkarīm Iran **71** C6
Robāṭkarīm □ Iran **71** B6
Robbins I. Australia **95** G4
Róbbio Italy **40** C5
Robe → Australia **92** D2
Robe Australia **95** F2
Röbel Germany **24** B8
Robert Lee U.S.A. **116** F4
Robertsdale U.S.A. **114** F6
Robertsganj India **69** G10
Robertson S. Africa **88** E2
Robertson I. Antarctica **5** C18
Robertson Ra. Australia **92** D3
Robertsport Liberia **82** D2
Robertstown Australia **95** E2
Roberval Canada **105** C5
Robeson Chan. N. Amer. **4** A4
Robesonia U.S.A. **115** F8
Robi Ethiopia **81** F4
Robinson U.S.A. **112** F10
Robinson → Australia **94** B2
Robinson Ra. Australia **93** E2
Robinvale Australia **95** E3
Robledo Spain **39** G2
Roblin Canada **103** C8
Roboré Bolivia **124** G7
Robson, Mt. Canada **102** C5
Robstown U.S.A. **116** H6
Roca, C. de Portugal **37** G1
Roca Partida, I. Mexico **118** D2
Rocas, I. Brazil **125** D12
Rocca Imperiale Italy **41** D8
Roccadáspide Italy **43** B8
Roccastrada Italy **41** F8
Roccella Iónica Italy **43** D9
Rocciamelone, Monte = Roche Melon Italy **21** C11
Rocha Uruguay **127** C5
Rochdale U.K. **14** D5
Roche Melon Italy **21** C11
Rochechouart France **20** C4
Rochefort Belgium **17** D5
Rochefort France **20** C3
Rochefort-en-Terre France **18** E4
Rochelle U.S.A. **112** E9
Rocher River Canada **102** A6
Rocheservière France **18** F5
Rochester U.K. **15** F8
Rochester Ind., U.S.A. **112** E10
Rochester Minn., U.S.A. **112** C7
Rochester N.H., U.S.A. **115** C14
Rochester N.Y., U.S.A. **114** C7
Rociu Romania **29** F10
Rock → Canada **102** A3
Rock, The Australia **95** F4
Rock Creek U.S.A. **114** E4
Rock Falls U.S.A. **112** E9
Rock Hill U.S.A. **117** D14
Rock Island U.S.A. **112** E8
Rock Port U.S.A. **112** E6
Rock Rapids U.S.A. **112** D5
Rock Sound Bahamas **120** B4
Rock Springs Mont., U.S.A. **108** C10
Rock Springs Wyo., U.S.A. **108** F9
Rock Valley U.S.A. **112** D5
Rockall Atl. Oc. **6** D3

Rockdale Tex., U.S.A. **116** F6
Rockdale Wash., U.S.A. **110** C5
Rockeby = Mungkan Kandju △ Australia **94** A3
Rockefeller Plateau Antarctica **5** E14
Rockford U.S.A. **112** D9
Rockglen Canada **103** D7
Rockhampton Australia **94** C5
Rockingham Australia **93** F2
Rockingham N.C., U.S.A. **117** D15
Rockingham Vt., U.S.A. **115** C12
Rockingham B. Australia **94** B4
Rocklake U.S.A. **112** A4
Rockland Canada **115** A9
Rockland Idaho, U.S.A. **108** E7
Rockland Maine, U.S.A. **113** C19
Rockland Mich., U.S.A. **112** B9
Rocklin U.S.A. **110** G5
Rockly B. Trin. & Tob. **125** J16
Rockmart U.S.A. **117** D12
Rockport Mass., U.S.A. **115** D14
Rockport Tex., U.S.A. **116** G6
Rocksprings U.S.A. **116** F4
Rockville Conn., U.S.A. **115** E12
Rockville Md., U.S.A. **113** F15
Rockwall U.S.A. **116** E6
Rockwell City U.S.A. **112** D6
Rockwood Canada **114** C4
Rockwood Maine, U.S.A. **113** C19
Rockwood Tenn., U.S.A. **117** D12
Rocky Ford U.S.A. **108** G12
Rocky Gully Australia **93** F2
Rocky Harbour Canada **105** C8
Rocky Island L. Canada **104** C3
Rocky Lane Canada **102** B5
Rocky Mount U.S.A. **117** D16
Rocky Mountain △ U.S.A. **108** F11
Rocky Mountain House Canada **102** C6
Rocky Mts. N. Amer. **108** B6
Rocky Point Namibia **88** B2
Rocroi France **19** C11
Rod Pakistan **66** E3
Roda Greece **49** A3
Rödby Denmark **11** K5
Rødbyhavn Denmark **11** K5
Roddickton Canada **105** B8
Rødding Denmark **11** J3
Rödeby Sweden **11** H9
Rødekro Denmark **11** J3
Rodenkirchen Germany **24** B4
Rodez France **20** D6
Rodhos = Rhodes Greece **49** C10
Rodi Gargánico Italy **41** G12
Rodia Greece **49** D7
Rodna Romania **29** C9
Rodnei, Munţii Romania **29** C9
Rodney Canada **114** D3
Rodney, C. N.Z. **91** B5
Rodniki Russia **34** B5
Rodolivos Greece **44** F7
Rodonit, Kepi i Albania **44** E3
Rodopi □ Greece **45** E9
Rodopos Greece **49** D5
Rodriguez Ind. Oc. **3** E13
Roe → U.K. **12** A5
Roebling U.S.A. **115** F10
Roebourne Australia **92** D2
Roebuck B. Australia **92** C3
Roermond Neths. **17** C6
Roes Welcome Sd. Canada **101** C11
Roeselare Belgium **17** D3
Rogachev = Ragachow Belarus **23** B16
Rogačica Serbia **44** B3
Rogagua, L. Bolivia **124** F5
Rogaška Slatina Slovenia **41** B12
Rogatec Slovenia **41** B12
Rogatica Bos.-H. **28** G4
Rogatyn Ukraine **23** D13
Rogers U.S.A. **116** C7
Rogers City U.S.A. **113** C12
Rogersville Canada **105** C6
Rogersville U.S.A. **117** C13
Roggan → Canada **104** B4
Roggan L. Canada **104** B4
Roggeveen Basin Pac. Oc. **97** L18
Roggeveldberge S. Africa **88** E3
Roggiano Gravina Italy **43** C9
Rogliano France **21** F13
Rogliano Italy **43** C9
Rogoaguado, L. Bolivia **124** F5
Rogojampi Indonesia **63** J17
Rogoźno Poland **31** F3
Rogue → U.S.A. **108** E1
Rohan France **18** D4
Rohnert Park U.S.A. **110** G4
Rohri Pakistan **68** F3
Rohri Canal Pakistan **68** F3
Rohtak India **68** E7
Roi Et Thailand **64** D4
Roja Latvia **30** A9
Rojas Argentina **126** C3
Rojo, C. Mexico **119** C5
Rokan → Indonesia **62** D2
Rokel → S. Leone **82** D2

Rokiškis Lithuania **32** E3
Rokitno Russia **33** G8
Rokycany Czech Rep. **26** B6
Rolândia Brazil **127** A5
Rolla Mo., U.S.A. **112** G8
Rolla N. Dak., U.S.A. **112** A4
Rolleston Australia **94** C4
Rollingstone Australia **94** B4
Rom Sudan **81** F3
Roma Australia **95** D4
Roma Italy **41** G9
Roma Sweden **11** G12
Roma Fiumicino ✈ (FCO) Italy **41** G9
Roma-Los Saenz U.S.A. **116** H5
Romain, C. U.S.A. **117** E15
Romaine → Canada **105** B7
Roman Bulgaria **44** C7
Roman Romania **29** D11
Roman-Kosh, Gora Ukraine **33** K8
Romanche → France **21** C9
Romang Indonesia **63** F7
Români Egypt **74** E1
Romania ■ Europe **29** D10
Romanija Bos.-H. **28** G3
Romano, Cayo Cuba **120** B4
Romans-sur-Isère France **21** C9
Romanshorn Switz. **25** H5
Rombari Sudan **81** E3
Romblon Phil. **61** E5
Rome = Roma Italy **41** G9
Rome Ga., U.S.A. **117** D12
Rome N.Y., U.S.A. **115** C9
Rome Pa., U.S.A. **115** E8
Rometta Italy **43** D8
Romilly-sur-Seine France **19** D10
Romney U.S.A. **113** F14
Romney Marsh U.K. **15** F8
Romny Ukraine **33** G7
Rømø Denmark **11** J2
Romodan Ukraine **33** G7
Romodanovo Russia **34** C7
Romont Switz. **25** J2
Romorantin-Lanthenay France **19** E8
Romsdalen Norway **8** E12
Romsey U.K. **15** G6
Ron Vietnam **64** D6
Rona U.K. **13** D3
Ronan U.S.A. **108** C6
Roncador, Cayos Colombia **120** D3
Roncador, Serra do Brazil **125** F8
Ronciglione Italy **41** F9
Ronco → Italy **41** D9
Ronda Spain **37** J5
Ronda, Serranía de Spain **37** J5
Rondane Norway **8** F13
Rondônia □ Brazil **124** F6
Rondonópolis Brazil **125** G8
Rong, Koh Cambodia **65** G4
Rong Jiang → China **58** E7
Rong Xian Guangxi Zhuangzu, China **59** F8
Rong Xian Sichuan, China **58** C5
Rong'an China **58** E7
Rongchang China **58** C5
Ronge, L. la Canada **103** B7
Rongjiang China **58** E7
Rongshui China **58** E7
Rønne Denmark **11** J8
Ronne Ice Shelf Antarctica **5** D18
Ronneby Sweden **11** H9
Rønnebyån → Sweden **11** H9
Rönneshytta Sweden **11** F9
Ronsard, C. Australia **93** D1
Ronse Belgium **17** D3
Roodepoort S. Africa **89** D4
Roof Butte U.S.A. **109** H9
Rooiboklaagte → Namibia **88** C3
Rooniu, Mt. Tahiti **91** d
Roorkee India **68** E7
Roosendaal Neths. **17** C4
Roosevelt U.S.A. **108** F9
Roosevelt → Brazil **124** E6
Roosevelt, Mt. Canada **102** B3
Roosevelt I. Antarctica **5** D12
Ropczyce Poland **31** H8
Roper → Australia **94** A2
Roper Bar Australia **94** A1
Roque Pérez Argentina **126** D4
Roquefort France **20** D3
Roquemaure France **21** D8
Roquetas de Mar Spain **39** J2
Roquetes Spain **38** E5
Roquevaire France **21** E9
Roraima □ Brazil **124** C6
Roraima, Mt. Venezuela **124** B6
Røros Norway **8** E14
Rorschach Switz. **25** H5
Rosa Zambia **87** D3
Rosa, Monte Europe **40** C4
Rosal de la Frontera Spain **37** H3
Rosalia U.S.A. **108** C5
Rosamond U.S.A. **111** L8
Rosans France **21** D9
Rosario Argentina **126** C3
Rosário Brazil **125** D10

Rosario *Baja Calif., Mexico* **118** B1
Rosario *Sinaloa, Mexico* **118** C3
Rosario *Paraguay* **126** A4
Rosario de la Frontera
　Argentina **126** B3
Rosario de Lerma *Argentina* **126** A2
Rosario del Tala *Argentina* **126** C4
Rosário do Sul *Brazil* **127** C5
Rosarito *Mexico* **111** N9
Rosarno *Italy* **43** D8
Rosas = Roses *Spain* **38** C8
Roscoe *U.S.A.* **115** E10
Roscoff *France* **18** D3
Roscommon *Ireland* **12** C3
Roscommon □ *Ireland* **12** C3
Roscrea *Ireland* **12** D4
Rose → *Australia* **94** A2
Rose, L. *Bahamas* **121** B5
Rose Belle *Mauritius* **85** d
Rose Blanche-Harbour Le
　Cou *Canada* **105** C8
Rose Hill *Mauritius* **85** d
Rose Pt. *Canada* **102** C2
Rose Valley *Canada* **103** C8
Roseau *Dominica* **121** C7
Roseau → *U.S.A.* **112** A6
Rosebery *Australia* **95** G4
Rosebud *S. Dak., U.S.A.* **112** D3
Rosebud *Tex., U.S.A.* **116** F6
Roseburg *U.S.A.* **108** E2
Rosehearty *U.K.* **13** D6
Roseires Res. *Sudan* **79** F12
Roseland *U.S.A.* **110** G4
Rosemary *Canada* **102** C6
Rosenberg *U.S.A.* **116** G7
Rosendaël *France* **19** A9
Rosenheim *Germany* **25** H8
Roses *Spain* **38** C8
Roses, G. de *Spain* **38** C8
Roseto degli Abruzzi *Italy* **41** F11
Rosetown *Canada* **103** C7
Rosetta = Rashîd *Egypt* **80** H7
Roseville *Calif., U.S.A.* **110** G5
Roseville *Mich., U.S.A.* **114** D2
Rosewood *Australia* **95** D5
Roshkhvâr *Iran* **71** C8
Rosières-en-Santerre *France* **19** C9
Rosignano Maríttimo *Italy* **40** E7
Rosignol *Guyana* **124** B7
Roşiori de Vede *Romania* **29** F10
Rositsa *Bulgaria* **45** C11
Rositsa → *Bulgaria* **45** C9
Roskilde *Denmark* **11** J6
Roskovec *Albania* **44** F3
Roslavl *Russia* **32** F7
Rosmaninhal *Portugal* **36** F3
Rosmead *S. Africa* **88** E4
Røsnæs *Denmark* **11** J4
Rosolini *Italy* **43** F7
Rosporden *France* **18** E3
Ross *Australia* **95** G4
Ross *N.Z.* **91** E3
Ross Béthio *Mauritania* **82** B1
Ross Dependency *Antarctica* **5** D12
Ross I. *Antarctica* **5** D11
Ross Ice Shelf *Antarctica* **5** E12
Ross L. *U.S.A.* **108** B3
Ross-on-Wye *U.K.* **15** F5
Ross River *Australia* **94** C1
Ross River *Canada* **102** A2
Ross Sea *Antarctica* **5** D11
Rossall Pt. *U.K.* **14** D4
Rossan Pt. *Ireland* **12** B3
Rossano *Italy* **43** C9
Rossburn *Canada* **103** C8
Rosseau *Canada* **114** A5
Rosseau, L. *Canada* **114** A5
Rosses, The *Ireland* **12** A3
Rossignol, L. *Canada* **104** B5
Rossignol, L. *Canada* **105** D6
Rossiya = Russia ■ *Eurasia* **53** C11
Rossland *Canada* **102** D5
Rosslare *Ireland* **12** D5
Rosslare Harbour *Ireland* **12** D5
Rosslau *Germany* **24** D8
Rosso *Mauritania* **82** B1
Rosso, C. *France* **21** F12
Rossosh *Russia* **33** G10
Røssvatnet *Norway* **8** D16
Røst *Norway* **8** C15
Rosthern *Canada* **103** C7
Rostock *Germany* **24** A8
Rostov *Don, Russia* **33** J10
Rostov *Sverdlovsk, Russia* **32** D10
Rostov □ *Russia* **35** F5
Rostrenen *France* **18** D3
Roswell *Ga., U.S.A.* **117** D12
Roswell *N. Mex., U.S.A.* **109** K11
Rota *Spain* **37** J4
Rotan *U.S.A.* **116** E4
Rotenburg *Hessen, Germany* **24** E5
Rotenburg *Niedersachsen,
　Germany* **24** B5
Roth *Germany* **25** F7
Rothaargebirge *Germany* **24** D4
Rothaargebirge △ *Germany* **24** D4
Rothenburg ob der Tauber
　Germany **25** F6

Rother → *U.K.* **15** G8
Rothera *Antarctica* **5** C17
Rotherham *U.K.* **14** D6
Rothes *U.K.* **13** D5
Rothesay *Canada* **105** C6
Rothesay *U.K.* **13** F3
Roti *Indonesia* **63** F6
Rotja, Pta. *Spain* **39** G6
Roto *Australia* **95** E4
Rotondo, Mte. *France* **21** F13
Rotoroa, L. *N.Z.* **91** D4
Rotorua *N.Z.* **91** C6
Rotorua, L. *N.Z.* **91** C6
Rott → *Germany* **25** G9
Rottenburg *Germany* **25** G4
Rottenmann *Austria* **26** D7
Rotterdam *Neths.* **17** C4
Rotterdam *U.S.A.* **115** D10
Rottne *Sweden* **11** G8
Rottnest I. *Australia* **93** F2
Rottumeroog *Neths.* **17** A6
Rottweil *Germany* **25** G4
Rotuma *Fiji* **90** C10
Roubaix *France* **19** B10
Roudnice nad Labem
　Czech Rep. **26** A7
Rouen *France* **18** C8
Rouergue *France* **20** D5
Rouillac *France* **20** C3
Rouleau *Canada* **103** C8
Round I. *Mauritius* **85** d
Round Mountain *U.S.A.* **108** G5
Round Mt. *Australia* **95** E5
Round Rock *U.S.A.* **116** F6
Roundup *U.S.A.* **108** C9
Rousay *U.K.* **13** B5
Rouses Point *U.S.A.* **115** B11
Rouseville *U.S.A.* **114** E5
Rousse = Ruse *Bulgaria* **45** C9
Roussenski Lom △ *Bulgaria* **45** C10
Roussillon *Isère, France* **21** C8
Roussillon *Pyrénées-Or.,
　France* **20** F6
Rouxville *S. Africa* **88** E4
Rouyn-Noranda *Canada* **104** C4
Rovaniemi *Finland* **8** C21
Rovato *Italy* **40** C7
Rovenki *Ukraine* **33** H10
Rovereto *Italy* **40** C8
Rovigo *Italy* **41** C8
Rovinj *Croatia* **41** C10
Rovno = Rivne *Ukraine* **23** C14
Rovnoye *Russia* **34** E8
Rovuma = Ruvuma →
　Tanzania **87** E5
Row'ān *Iran* **71** C6
Rowena *Australia* **95** D4
Rowley Shoals *Australia* **92** C2
Roxa *Guinea-Biss.* **82** C1
Roxas *Capiz, Phil.* **61** F5
Roxas *Isabela, Phil.* **61** C4
Roxas *Mind. Or., Phil.* **61** E4
Roxboro *U.S.A.* **117** C15
Roxborough *Trin. & Tob.* **125** J16
Roxburgh *N.Z.* **91** F2
Roxbury *U.S.A.* **114** F7
Roxby Downs *Australia* **95** E2
Roxen *Sweden* **11** F9
Roy *Mont., U.S.A.* **108** C9
Roy *N. Mex., U.S.A.* **109** J11
Roy *Utah, U.S.A.* **108** F7
Royal Bardia △ *Nepal* **69** E9
Royal Canal *Ireland* **12** C4
Royal Chitawan △ *Nepal* **69** F11
Royal Leamington Spa *U.K.* **15** E6
Royal Natal △ *S. Africa* **89** D4
Royal Tunbridge Wells *U.K.* **15** F8
Royale, Isle *U.S.A.* **112** B9
Royan *France* **20** C2
Roye *France* **19** C9
Royston *U.K.* **15** E7
Rožaj *Montenegro* **44** D4
Różan *Poland* **31** F8
Rozay-en-Brie *France* **19** D9
Rozdilna *Ukraine* **33** J6
Rozhnyativ *Ukraine* **29** B9
Rozhyshche *Ukraine* **23** C13
Rožmitál pod Třemšínem
　Czech Rep. **26** B6
Rožňava *Slovak Rep.* **27** C13
Rozogi *Poland* **30** E8
Rozoy-sur-Serre *France* **19** C11
Roztoczański △ *Poland* **31** H10
Rozzano *Italy* **40** C6
Rrëshen *Albania* **44** E3
Rrogozhinë *Albania* **44** E3
Rtanj *Serbia* **44** C5
Rtishchevo *Russia* **34** D6
Rúa = A Rúa *Spain* **36** C3
Ruacaná *Namibia* **88** B1
Ruaha △ *Tanzania* **86** D3
Ruahine Ra. *N.Z.* **91** C6
Ruapehu *N.Z.* **91** C5
Ruapuke I. *N.Z.* **91** G2
Ruâq, W. → *Egypt* **74** F2
Rub' al Khālī *Si. Arabia* **75** D4
Rubeho Mts. *Tanzania* **86** D4

Rubezhnoye = Rubizhne
　Ukraine **33** H10
Rubh a' Mhail *U.K.* **13** F2
Rubha Hunish *U.K.* **13** D2
Rubha Robhanais = Lewis,
　Butt of *U.K.* **13** C2
Rubi *Spain* **38** D7
Rubicon → *U.S.A.* **110** G5
Rubicone → *Italy* **41** D9
Rubik *Albania* **44** E3
Rubino *Ivory C.* **82** D4
Rubio *Venezuela* **124** B4
Rubizhne *Ukraine* **33** H10
Rubondo △ *Tanzania* **86** C3
Ruby L. *U.S.A.* **108** F6
Ruby Mts. *U.S.A.* **108** F6
Rubyvale *Australia* **94** C4
Rucheng *China* **59** E9
Ruciane-Nida *Poland* **30** E8
Rūd Sar *Iran* **71** B6
Ruda *Sweden* **11** G10
Ruda Śląska *Poland* **31** H5
Rudall *Australia* **95** E2
Rudall → *Australia* **92** D3
Rudall River △ *Australia* **92** D3
Rüdersdorf *Germany* **24** C9
Rudewa *Tanzania* **87** E3
Rudkøbing *Denmark* **11** K4
Rudky *Ukraine* **31** J10
Rudna *Poland* **31** G3
Rudnik *Bulgaria* **45** D11
Rudnik *Poland* **31** H9
Rudnik *Serbia* **44** B4
Rudnya *Russia* **32** E6
Rudnyy *Kazakhstan* **52** D7
Rudo *Bos.-H.* **28** G4
Rudolfa, Ostrov *Russia* **52** A6
Rudolstadt *Germany* **24** E7
Rudong *China* **59** A13
Rudozem *Bulgaria* **45** E8
Rudyard *U.S.A.* **113** B11
Rue *France* **19** B8
Ruenya → *Africa* **87** F3
Rufa'a *Sudan* **81** E3
Rufiji → *Tanzania* **86** D4
Rufino *Argentina* **126** C3
Rufisque *Senegal* **82** C1
Rufunsa *Zambia* **87** F2
Rugao *China* **59** A13
Rugby *U.K.* **15** E6
Rugby *U.S.A.* **112** A4
Rügen *Germany* **24** A9
Rügen △ *Germany* **24** A9
Rugles *France* **18** D7
Ruhengeri *Rwanda* **86** C2
Ruhla *Germany* **24** E6
Ruhland *Germany* **24** D9
Ruhnu *Estonia* **30** A10
Ruhr → *Germany* **24** D2
Ruhuhu → *Tanzania* **87** E3
Rui'an *China* **59** D13
Ruichang *China* **59** C10
Ruidoso *U.S.A.* **109** K11
Ruijin *China* **59** D10
Ruili *China* **58** E1
Ruivo, Pico *Madeira* **48** D3
Ruj *Bulgaria* **44** D6
Rujen *Macedonia* **44** D6
Rujm Tal'at al Jamā'ah
　Jordan **74** E4
Ruk *Pakistan* **68** F3
Rukhla *Pakistan* **68** C4
Ruki →
　Dem. Rep. of the Congo **84** E3
Rukwa □ *Tanzania* **86** D3
Rukwa, L. *Tanzania* **86** D3
Rulhieres, C. *Australia* **92** B4
Rum = Rhum *U.K.* **13** E2
Rum *Jordan* **74** F4
Rum Cay *Bahamas* **121** B5
Rum Jungle *Australia* **92** B5
Ruma *Serbia* **28** E4
Ruma △ *Kenya* **86** C3
Rumāḥ *Si. Arabia* **70** E5
Rumania = Romania ■
　Europe **29** D10
Rumaylah *Iraq* **70** D5
Rumbêk *Sudan* **81** F2
Rumburk *Czech Rep.* **26** A7
Rumford *U.S.A.* **115** B14
Rumia *Poland* **30** D5
Rumilly *France* **21** C9
Rumoi *Japan* **54** C10
Rumonge *Burundi* **86** C2
Rumson *U.S.A.* **115** F11
Rumuruti *Kenya* **86** B4
Runan *China* **56** H8
Runanga *N.Z.* **91** E3
Runaway, C. *N.Z.* **91** B6
Runaway Bay *Jamaica* **120** a
Runcorn *U.K.* **14** D5
Rundu *Namibia* **88** B2
Rungwa *Tanzania* **86** D3
Rungwa → *Tanzania* **86** D3

Rungwa △ *Tanzania* **86** D3
Rungwe *Tanzania* **87** D3
Rungwe, Mt. *Tanzania* **84** F6
Runka *Nigeria* **83** C6
Runn *Sweden* **10** D9
Runton Ra. *Australia* **92** D3
Ruokolahti *Finland* **32** B5
Ruoqiang *China* **60** C3
Rupa *India* **67** F18
Rupar *India* **68** D7
Rupat *Indonesia* **62** D2
Rupea *Romania* **29** D10
Rupen → *India* **68** H4
Rupert *U.S.A.* **108** E7
Rupert → *Canada* **104** B4
Rupert B. *Canada* **104** B4
Rupert House =
　Waskaganish *Canada* **104** B4
Rupsa *India* **69** J12
Rur → *Germany* **24** D1
Rurrenabaque *Bolivia* **124** F5
Rus → *Spain* **39** F2
Rusambo *Zimbabwe* **87** F3
Rusape *Zimbabwe* **87** F3
Ruschuk = Ruse *Bulgaria* **45** C9
Ruse *Bulgaria* **45** C9
Ruse □ *Bulgaria* **45** C10
Ruşeţu *Romania* **29** F12
Rush *Ireland* **12** C5
Rushan *China* **57** F11
Rushden *U.K.* **15** E7
Rushmore, Mt. *U.S.A.* **112** D2
Rushville *Ill., U.S.A.* **112** E8
Rushville *Ind., U.S.A.* **113** F11
Rushville *Nebr., U.S.A.* **112** D2
Russas *Brazil* **125** D11
Russell *Canada* **103** C8
Russell *Kans., U.S.A.* **112** F4
Russell *N.Y., U.S.A.* **115** B9
Russell *Pa., U.S.A.* **114** E5
Russell Cave △ *U.S.A.* **117** D12
Russell L. *Man., Canada* **103** B8
Russell L. *N.W.T., Canada* **102** A5
Russellkonda *India* **67** K14
Russellville *Ala., U.S.A.* **117** D11
Russellville *Ark., U.S.A.* **116** D8
Russellville *Ky., U.S.A.* **112** G10
Rüsselsheim *Germany* **25** F4
Russi *Italy* **41** D9
Russia ■ *Eurasia* **53** C11
Russian → *U.S.A.* **110** G3
Russkoye Ustie *Russia* **4** B15
Rust *Austria* **27** D9
Rustam *Pakistan* **68** B5
Rustam Shahr *Pakistan* **68** F2
Rustavi *Georgia* **35** K7
Rustenburg *S. Africa* **88** D4
Ruston *U.S.A.* **116** E8
Rutana *Burundi* **86** C3
Rute *Spain* **37** H6
Ruteng *Indonesia* **63** F6
Rutherford *U.S.A.* **110** G4
Ruth *U.S.A.* **114** C2
Rutland *U.S.A.* **115** C12
Rutland □ *U.K.* **15** E7
Rutland Water *U.K.* **15** E7
Rutledge → *Canada* **103** A6
Rutledge L. *Canada* **103** A6
Rutqa, W. → *Syria* **73** E9
Rutshuru
　Dem. Rep. of the Congo **86** C2
Ruvo di Púglia *Italy* **43** A9
Ruvu *Tanzania* **86** D4
Ruvu → *Tanzania* **86** D4
Ruvuba △ *Burundi* **86** C2
Ruvuma □ *Tanzania* **87** E4
Ruvuma → *Tanzania* **87** E5
Ruwais *U.A.E.* **71** E7
Ruwenzori *Africa* **86** B2
Ruwenzori △ *Uganda* **86** B2
Ruya → *Zimbabwe* **89** B5
Ruyigi *Burundi* **86** C3
Ruyuan *China* **59** E9
Ruzayevka *Russia* **34** C7
Ružomberok *Slovak Rep.* **27** B12
Ruzyně, Praha ✈ (PRG)
　Czech Rep. **26** A7
Rwanda ■ *Africa* **86** C3
Ryakhovo *Bulgaria* **45** C10
Ryan, L. *U.K.* **13** G3
Ryazan *Russia* **32** E10
Ryazan □ *Russia* **34** C4
Ryazhsk *Russia* **32** F11
Rybachiy *Russia* **30** C7
Rybachiy Poluostrov *Russia* **8** B25
Rybinsk *Russia* **32** C10
Rybinskoye Vdkhr. *Russia* **32** C10
Rybnik *Poland* **31** H5
Rybnitsa = Râbniţa
　Moldova **29** C14
Rybnoye *Russia* **32** E10
Rycroft *Canada* **102** B5
Ryd *Sweden* **11** H8

Rydaholm *Sweden* **11** H8
Ryde *U.K.* **15** G6
Ryderwood *U.S.A.* **110** D3
Rydzyna *Poland* **31** G3
Rye *U.K.* **15** G8
Rye → *U.K.* **14** C7
Rye Bay *U.K.* **15** G8
Rye Patch Res. *U.S.A.* **108** F4
Ryegate *U.S.A.* **108** C9
Ryki *Poland* **31** G8
Ryley *Canada* **102** C6
Rylsk *Russia* **33** G8
Rylstone *Australia* **95** E4
Rymanów *Poland* **31** J8
Ryn *Poland* **30** E8
Ryn Peski = Naryn Qum
　Kazakhstan **35** G9
Ryōtsu *Japan* **54** E9
Rypin *Poland* **31** E6
Ryssby *Sweden* **11** H8
Rysy *Europe* **27** B13
Ryūgasaki *Japan* **55** G10
Ryukyu Is. =
　Ryūkyū-rettō *Japan* **55** M3
Ryūkyū-rettō *Japan* **55** M3
Rzepin *Poland* **31** F1
Rzeszów *Poland* **31** H8
Rzhev *Russia* **32** D8

S

Sa *Thailand* **64** C3
Sa Canal *Spain* **48** C7
Sa Conillera *Spain* **48** C7
Sa Dec *Vietnam* **65** G5
Sa Dragonera *Spain* **48** B9
Sa Mesquida *Spain* **48** B11
Sa Pobla *Spain* **38** F8
Sa Savina *Spain* **48** C7
Sa'ādatābād *Fārs, Iran* **71** D7
Sa'ādatābād *Hormozgān, Iran* **71** D7
Sa'ādatābād *Kermān, Iran* **71** D7
Saale → *Germany* **24** D7
Saaler Bodden *Germany* **24** A8
Saalfeld *Germany* **24** E7
Saalfelden *Austria* **26** D5
Saane → *Switz.* **25** H3
Saanich *Canada* **110** B3
Saar → *Europe* **17** E6
Saar-Hunsrück △ *Germany* **25** F2
Saarbrücken *Germany* **25** F2
Saarburg *Germany* **25** F2
Saaremaa *Estonia* **32** C2
Saarijärvi *Finland* **8** E21
Saariselkä *Finland* **8** B23
Saarland □ *Germany* **25** F2
Saarlouis *Germany* **25** F2
Sab 'Ābar *Syria* **72** F7
Saba *W. Indies* **121** C7
Šabac *Serbia* **44** B3
Sabadell *Spain* **38** D7
Sabah □ *Malaysia* **62** C5
Sabak Bernam *Malaysia* **65** L3
Sabalān, Kūhhā-ye *Iran* **73** C12
Sabalana, Kepulauan
　Indonesia **63** F5
Sábana de la Mar *Dom. Rep.* **121** C6
Sábanalarga *Colombia* **124** A4
Sabang *Indonesia* **62** C1
Săbăoani *Romania* **29** C11
Sabará *Brazil* **125** G10
Sabarmati → *India* **68** H5
Sabattis *U.S.A.* **115** B10
Sabáudia *Italy* **42** A6
Saberania *Indonesia* **63** E9
Sabhā *Libya* **79** C8
Sabi → *India* **68** E7
Sabidana, J. *Sudan* **80** D4
Sabie *S. Africa* **89** D5
Sabinal *Mexico* **118** A3
Sabinal *U.S.A.* **116** G5
Sabiñánigo *Spain* **38** C4
Sabinar, Punta del *Spain* **39** J2
Sabinas *Mexico* **118** B4
Sabinas → *Mexico* **118** B4
Sabinas Hidalgo *Mexico* **118** B4
Sabine → *U.S.A.* **116** G8
Sabine L. *U.S.A.* **116** G8
Sabine Pass *U.S.A.* **116** G8
Sabinov *Slovak Rep.* **27** B14
Sabinsville *U.S.A.* **114** E7
Sabirabad *Azerbaijan* **35** K9
Sablayan *Phil.* **61** E4
Sable *U.S.A.* **105** A6
Sable, C. *Canada* **105** D6
Sable, C. *U.S.A.* **120** A3
Sable I. *Canada* **105** D8
Sablé-sur-Sarthe *France* **18** E6
Sabonkafi *Niger* **83** C6
Sabor → *Portugal* **36** D3
Sabou *Burkina Faso* **82** C4
Sabres *France* **20** D3
Sabrina Coast *Antarctica* **5** C9
Sabugal *Portugal* **36** E3
Sabulubbek *Indonesia* **62** E1
Sabuncu *Turkey* **47** B12
Sabzevār *Iran* **71** B8

Sabzvārān *Iran* **71** D8
Sac City *U.S.A.* **112** D6
Sacedón *Spain* **38** E2
Săcele *Romania* **29** E10
Sacheon *S. Korea* **57** G15
Sachigo → *Canada* **104** A2
Sachigo, L. *Canada* **104** B1
Sachimbo *Angola* **84** F4
Sachkhere *Georgia* **35** K6
Sachsen □ *Germany* **24** E9
Sachsen-Anhalt □ *Germany* **24** D7
Sächsische Schweiz △
　Germany **24** E10
Sacile *Italy* **41** C9
Sackets Harbor *U.S.A.* **115** C8
Sackville *Canada* **105** C7
Saco *Maine, U.S.A.* **115** C14
Saco *Mont., U.S.A.* **108** B10
Sacramento *U.S.A.* **110** G5
Sacramento → *U.S.A.* **110** G5
Sacramento Mts. *U.S.A.* **109** K11
Sacramento Valley *U.S.A.* **110** G5
Sacratif, C. *Spain* **37** J7
Săcueni *Romania* **28** C7
Sada *Spain* **36** B2
Sada-Misaki *Japan* **55** H6
Sádaba *Spain* **38** C3
Sadabad *India* **68** F8
Sadani *Tanzania* **86** D4
Sadao *Thailand* **65** J3
Sadd el Aali *Egypt* **80** C3
Saddle Mt. *U.S.A.* **110** E3
Sade *Nigeria* **83** C7
Sadimi *Dem. Rep. of the Congo* **87** D1
Sadiola *Mali* **82** C2
Sa'dīyah, Hawr as *Iraq* **73** F12
Sado *Japan* **54** F9
Sado → *Portugal* **37** G2
Sadon *Russia* **35** J6
Sadovoye *Russia* **35** G7
Sadra *India* **68** H5
Sadri *India* **68** G5
Sæby *Denmark* **11** G4
Saegertown *U.S.A.* **114** E4
Saelices *Spain* **38** F2
Safaalan *Turkey* **45** E12
Safaga *Egypt* **80** B3
Şafājah *Si. Arabia* **70** E3
Šafárikovo = Tornal'a
　Slovak Rep. **27** C13
Safata B. *Samoa* **91** b
Säffle *Sweden* **10** E6
Safford *U.S.A.* **109** K9
Saffron Walden *U.K.* **15** E8
Safi *Morocco* **78** B4
Şafiābād *Iran* **71** B8
Safid Dasht *Iran* **71** C6
Safid Kūh *Afghan.* **66** B3
Safid Rūd → *Iran* **71** B6
Safipur *India* **69** F9
Şāfītā *Syria* **72** E7
Safonovo *Russia* **32** E7
Safranbolu *Turkey* **72** B5
Saft Rashîn *Egypt* **80** J7
Safune *Samoa* **91** b
Şafwān *Iraq* **70** D5
Sag Harbor *U.S.A.* **115** F12
Saga *Japan* **55** H5
Saga □ *Japan* **55** H5
Sagae *Japan* **54** E10
Sagaing *Burma* **67** J19
Sagala *Mali* **82** C3
Sagamore *U.S.A.* **114** F5
Saganaga L. *Canada* **112** A8
Sagar *Karnataka, India* **66** M9
Sagar *Mad. P., India* **69** H8
Sagara, L. *Tanzania* **86** D3
Sagarmatha = Everest, Mt.
　Nepal **69** E12
Sagarmatha △ *Nepal* **69** F12
Sagay *Phil.* **61** F5
Saginaw *U.S.A.* **113** D12
Saginaw B. *U.S.A.* **113** D12
Sagleipie *Liberia* **82** D3
Saglouc = Salluit *Canada* **101** C12
Sagone *France* **21** F12
Sagone, G. de *France* **21** F12
Sagres *Portugal* **37** J2
Sagua la Grande *Cuba* **120** B3
Saguache *U.S.A.* **108** G10
Saguaro △ *U.S.A.* **109** K8
Saguenay → *Canada* **105** C5
Sagunt *Spain* **38** F4
Sagunto = Sagunt *Spain* **38** F4
Sagwara *India* **68** H6
Sahaba *Sudan* **80** D3
Sahagún *Spain* **36** C5
Saḥam al Jawlān *Syria* **74** C4
Sahamandrevo *Madag.* **89** C8
Sahand, Kūh-e *Iran* **73** D12
Sahara *Africa* **78** D6
Saharan Atlas = Saharien,
　Atlas *Algeria* **78** B6
Saharanpur *India* **68** E7
Saharien, Atlas *Algeria* **78** B6
Saharsa *India* **69** G12
Sahasinaka *Madag.* **89** C8

Sahaswan *India* **69** E8
Saheira, W. el ⇥ *Egypt* **74** E2
Sahel *Africa* **78** E5
Sahel, Canal du *Mali* **82** C3
Sahibganj *India* **69** G12
Sāḥilīyat *Iraq* **73** F10
Sahiwal *Pakistan* **68** D5
Şaḥneh *Iran* **73** E12
Sahrawi = Western
  Sahara ■ *Africa* **78** D3
Sahuaripa *Mexico* **118** B3
Sahuarita *U.S.A.* **109** L8
Sahuayo de Díaz *Mexico* **118** C4
Šahy *Slovak Rep.* **27** C11
Sai ⇥ *India* **69** G10
Sai Buri *Thailand* **65** J3
Sa'id Bundâs *Sudan* **79** G10
Sa'īdābād = Sīrjān *Iran* **71** D7
Sa'īdābād *Iran* **71** B7
Sa'īdīyeh *Iran* **71** B6
Saidpur *Bangla.* **67** G16
Saidpur *India* **69** G10
Saidu Sharif *Pakistan* **69** B5
Saignes *France* **20** C6
Saigō *Japan* **55** F6
Saigon = Thanh Pho Ho
  Chi Minh *Vietnam* **65** G6
Saijō *Japan* **55** H6
Saikai △ *Japan* **55** H4
Saikanosy Masoala *Madag.* **89** B9
Saikhoa Ghat *India* **67** F19
Saiki *Japan* **55** H5
Sailana *India* **68** H6
Saillans *France* **21** D9
Sailolof *Indonesia* **63** E8
Saimaa *Finland* **32** B5
Saimbeyli *Turkey* **72** D7
Saimen = Saimaa *Finland* **32** B5
Şa'in Dezh *Iran* **73** D12
St. Abb's Head *U.K.* **13** F6
St-Affrique *France* **20** E6
St-Agrève *France* **21** C8
St-Aignan *France* **18** E8
St. Alban's *Canada* **105** C8
St. Albans *U.K.* **15** F7
St. Albans *Vt., U.S.A.* **115** B11
St. Albans *W. Va., U.S.A.* **113** F13
St. Alban's Head *U.K.* **15** G5
St. Albert *Canada* **102** C6
St-Amand-en-Puisaye
  France **19** E10
St-Amand-les-Eaux *France* **19** B10
St-Amand-Montrond *France* **19** F9
St-Amarin *France* **19** E14
St-Amour *France* **19** F12
St-André *Réunion* **85** c
St-André-de-Cubzac *France* **20** D3
St-André-les-Alpes *France* **21** E10
St. Andrew's *Canada* **105** C8
St. Andrews *U.K.* **13** E6
St-Anicet *Canada* **115** A10
St. Annes *Canada* **103** D9
St. Anns B. *Canada* **105** C7
St. Ann's Bay *Jamaica* **120** a
St. Anthony *Canada* **105** B8
St. Anthony *U.S.A.* **108** E8
St-Antoine *Canada* **105** C7
St-Antonin-Noble-Val
  France **20** D5
St. Arnaud *Australia* **95** F3
St-Astier *France* **20** C4
St-Aubin-du-Cormier *France* **18** D5
St-Augustin *Canada* **105** B8
St-Augustin ⇥ *Canada* **105** B8
St. Augustine *U.S.A.* **117** G14
St-Aulaye *France* **20** C4
St. Austell *U.K.* **15** G3
St-Avold *France* **19** C13
St. Barbe *Canada* **105** B8
St-Barthélemy *W. Indies* **121** C7
St-Béat *France* **20** E4
St. Bees Hd. *U.K.* **14** C4
St. Bees I. *Australia* **94** J7
St-Benoît *Réunion* **85** c
St-Benoît-du-Sault *France* **20** B5
St-Bonnet-en-Champsaur
  France **21** D10
St-Brevin-les-Pins *France* **18** E4
St-Brice-en-Coglès *France* **18** D5
St. Bride's *Canada* **105** C9
St. Brides B. *U.K.* **15** F2
St-Brieuc *France* **18** D4
St-Calais *France* **18** E7
St-Cast-le-Guildo *France* **18** D4
St. Catharines *Canada* **114** C5
St. Catherines I. *U.S.A.* **117** F14
St. Catherine's Pt. *U.K.* **15** G6
St-Céré *France* **20** D5
St-Cergue *Switz.* **25** J2
St-Cernin *France* **20** C6
St-Chamond *France* **21** C8
St. Charles *Ill., U.S.A.* **112** E9
St. Charles *Md., U.S.A.* **113** F15
St. Charles *Mo., U.S.A.* **112** F8
St. Charles *Va., U.S.A.* **113** G12
St-Chély-d'Apcher *France* **20** D7
St-Chinian *France* **20** E6

St. Christopher-Nevis = St.
  Kitts & Nevis ■ *W. Indies* **121** C7
St-Ciers-sur-Gironde *France* **20** C3
St. Clair *Mich., U.S.A.* **114** D2
St. Clair *Pa., U.S.A.* **115** F8
St. Clair ⇥ *U.S.A.* **114** D2
St. Clair, L. *N. Amer.* **114** D2
St. Clairsville *U.S.A.* **114** F4
St-Claud *France* **20** C4
St. Claude *Canada* **103** D9
St-Claude *France* **19** F12
St. Clears *U.K.* **15** F3
St-Clet *Canada* **115** A10
St. Cloud *Fla., U.S.A.* **117** G14
St. Cloud *Minn., U.S.A.* **112** C6
St. Cricq, C. *Australia* **93** E1
St. Croix *U.S. Virgin Is.* **121** C7
St-Croix △ *France* **112** C7
St. Croix ⇥ *U.S.A.* **112** C7
St. Croix Falls *U.S.A.* **112** C7
St-Cyprien *France* **20** F7
St-Cyr-sur-Mer *France* **21** E9
St. David's *Canada* **105** C8
St. David's *U.K.* **15** F2
St. David's Head *U.K.* **15** F2
St-Denis *France* **19** D9
St-Denis *Réunion* **85** c
St-Denis ✈ (RUN) *Réunion* **85** c
St-Dié *France* **19** D13
St-Dizier *France* **19** D11
St-Égrève *France* **21** C9
St. Elias, Mt. *U.S.A.* **100** C5
St. Elias Mts. *N. Amer.* **102** A1
St-Éloy-les-Mines *France* **19** F9
St-Émilion *France* **20** D3
St-Étienne *France* **21** C8
St-Étienne-de-Tinée *France* **21** D10
St-Étienne-du-Rouvray
  France **18** C8
St. Eugène *Canada* **115** A10
St. Eustatius *W. Indies* **121** C7
St-Exupery, Lyon ✈ (LYS)
  France **21** C9
St-Fargeau *France* **19** E10
St-Félicien *Canada* **104** C5
St-Florent *France* **21** F13
St-Florent, G. de *France* **21** F13
St-Florent-sur-Cher *France* **19** F9
St-Florentin *France* **19** E10
St-Flour *France* **20** C7
St. Francis *U.S.A.* **112** F3
St. Francis ⇥ *U.S.A.* **117** D9
St. Francis, C. *S. Africa* **88** E3
St. Francisville *U.S.A.* **116** F9
St-François, L. *Canada* **115** A10
St-Fulgent *France* **18** F5
St-Gabriel *Canada* **104** C5
St. Gallen = Sankt Gallen
  Switz. **25** H5
St-Galmier *France* **19** G11
St-Gaudens *France* **20** E4
St-Gaultier *France* **20** B5
St-Gengoux-le-National
  France **19** F11
St-Geniez-d'Olt *France* **20** D6
St. George *Australia* **95** D4
St. George *Canada* **105** C6
St. George *S.C., U.S.A.* **117** E14
St. George *Utah, U.S.A.* **109** H7
St. George, C. *Canada* **105** C8
St. George, C. *U.S.A.* **117** G12
St. George Ra. *Australia* **92** C4
St. George's *Canada* **105** C8
St. Georges *Canada* **105** C5
St. George's *Grenada* **121** D7
St. George's B. *Canada* **105** C8
St. Georges Basin *N.S.W.,*
  Australia **95** F5
St. Georges Basin
  W. Austral., Australia **92** C4
St. George's Channel *Europe* **12** E6
St. Georges Hd. *Australia* **95** F5
St-Georges-lès-
  Baillargeaux *France* **20** B4
St-Germain-de-Calberte
  France **20** D7
St-Germain-en-Laye *France* **19** D9
St-Germain-Lembron *France* **20** C7
St-Gervais-d'Auvergne
  France **19** F9
St-Gervais-les-Bains *France* **21** C10
St-Gildas, Pte. de *France* **18** E4
St-Gilles *France* **21** E8
St-Girons *Ariège, France* **20** F5
St-Girons *Landes, France* **20** E2
St. Gotthard P. = San
  Gottardo, P. del *Switz.* **25** J4
St. Helena *Atl. Oc.* **76** H3
St. Helena *U.S.A.* **108** G2
St. Helena, Mt. *U.S.A.* **110** G4
St. Helena B. *S. Africa* **88** E2
St. Helens *Australia* **95** G4
St. Helens *U.K.* **14** D5
St. Helens *U.S.A.* **110** E4
St. Helens, Mt. *U.S.A.* **110** D4
St. Helier *U.K.* **15** H5
St-Herblain *France* **18** E5
St-Hilaire-du-Harcouët
  France **18** D5

St-Hippolyte *France* **19** E13
St-Hippolyte-du-Fort *France* **20** E7
St-Honoré-les-Bains *France* **19** F10
St-Hubert *Belgium* **17** D5
St-Hyacinthe *Canada* **104** C5
St. Ignace *Mich., U.S.A.* **113** C11
St. Ignace I. *Canada* **104** C2
St. Ignatius *U.S.A.* **108** C6
St-Imier *Switz.* **25** H2
St. Ives *Cambs., U.K.* **15** E7
St. Ives *Corn., U.K.* **15** G2
St-James *France* **18** D5
St. James *U.S.A.* **112** D6
St-Jean ⇥ *Canada* **105** B7
St-Jean, L. *Canada* **105** C5
St-Jean-d'Angély *France* **20** C3
St-Jean-de-Braye *France* **19** E8
St-Jean-de-Luz *France* **20** E2
St-Jean-de-Maurienne
  France **21** C10
St-Jean-de-Monts *France* **18** F4
St-Jean-du-Gard *France* **20** D7
St-Jean-en-Royans *France* **21** C9
St-Jean-Pied-de-Port *France* **20** E2
St-Jean-Port-Joli *Canada* **105** C5
St-Jean-sur-Richelieu
  Canada **115** A11
St-Jérôme *Canada* **104** C5
St. John *Canada* **105** C6
St. John *U.S.A.* **112** F4
St. John ⇥ *Liberia* **82** D2
St. John ⇥ *N. Amer.* **113** C20
St. John, C. *Canada* **105** C8
St. John I. *U.S. Virgin Is.* **121** e
St. John's *Antigua & B.* **121** C7
St. John's *Canada* **105** C9
St. Johns *Ariz., U.S.A.* **109** J9
St. Johns *Mich., U.S.A.* **113** D11
St. Johns ⇥ *U.S.A.* **117** F14
St. John's Pt. *Ireland* **12** B3
St. Johnsbury *U.S.A.* **115** B12
St. Johnsville *U.S.A.* **115** C10
St-Joseph *Martinique* **120** c
St-Joseph *Réunion* **85** c
St. Joseph *La., U.S.A.* **116** F9
St. Joseph *Mo., U.S.A.* **112** F6
St. Joseph ⇥ *U.S.A.* **112** D10
St. Joseph, I. *Canada* **104** C3
St. Joseph, L. *Canada* **104** B1
St-Jovite *Canada* **104** C5
St-Juéry *France* **20** E6
St-Julien-Chapteuil *France* **21** C8
St-Julien-de-Vouvantes
  France **18** E5
St-Julien-en-Genevois
  France **19** F13
St-Junien *France* **20** C4
St-Just-en-Chaussée *France* **19** C9
St-Just-en-Chevalet *France* **20** C7
St. Kilda *U.K.* **16** C2
St. Kitts & Nevis ■
  W. Indies **121** C7
St. Laurent *Canada* **103** C9
St-Laurent-de-la-Salanque
  France **20** F6
St-Laurent-du-Pont *France* **21** C9
St-Laurent-en-Grandvaux
  France **19** F12
St-Laurent-Médoc *France* **20** C3
St. Lawrence *Australia* **94** C4
St. Lawrence *Canada* **105** C8
St. Lawrence ⇥ *Canada* **105** C6
St. Lawrence, Gulf of
  Canada **105** C7
St. Lawrence I. *U.S.A.* **106** a
St. Lawrence Islands △
  Canada **115** B9
St. Leonard *Canada* **105** C6
St-Leu *Réunion* **85** c
St-Lewis ⇥ *Canada* **105** B8
St-Lô *France* **18** C5
St-Louis *France* **19** E14
St-Louis *Guadeloupe* **120** b
St-Louis *Réunion* **85** c
St. Louis *Senegal* **82** B1
St. Louis *U.S.A.* **112** F9
St. Louis □ *Senegal* **82** B2
St. Louis ⇥ *U.S.A.* **112** B7
St-Loup-sur-Semouse
  France **19** E13
St. Lucia ■ *W. Indies* **121** f
St. Lucia, L. *S. Africa* **89** D5
St. Lucia Channel *W. Indies* **121** D7
St. Maarten ☑ *W. Indies* **121** C7
St. Magnus B. *U.K.* **13** A7
St-Maixent-l'École *France* **20** B3
St-Malo *France* **18** D4
St-Malo, G. de *France* **18** D4
St-Mandrier-sur-Mer *France* **21** E9
St-Marc *Haiti* **121** C5
St-Marcellin *France* **21** C9
St-Marcouf, Îs. *France* **18** C5
St. Maries *U.S.A.* **108** C5
St-Martin ☑ *W. Indies* **121** C7
St-Martin, C. *Martinique* **120** c
St. Martin, L. *Canada* **103** C9

St-Martin-de-Crau *France* **21** E8
St-Martin-de-Ré *France* **20** B2
St-Martin-d'Hères *France* **21** C9
St-Martin-Vésubie *France* **21** D11
St. Martins *Barbados* **121** g
St-Martory *France* **20** E4
St. Mary Pk. *Australia* **95** E2
St. Marys *Australia* **95** G4
St. Marys *Canada* **114** C3
St. Mary's *Corn., U.K.* **15** H1
St. Mary's *Orkney, U.K.* **13** C6
St. Marys *Ga., U.S.A.* **117** F14
St. Marys *Pa., U.S.A.* **114** E6
St. Mary's, C. *Canada* **105** C9
St. Mary's B. *Canada* **105** C9
St. Marys Bay *Canada* **105** D6
St-Mathieu, Pte. *France* **18** D2
St. Matthew I. *U.S.A.* **106** a
St-Maurice ⇥ *Canada* **104** C5
St. Mawes *U.K.* **15** G2
St-Maximin-la-Ste-Baume
  France **21** E9
St-Médard-en-Jalles *France* **20** D3
St-Méen-le-Grand *France* **18** D4
St-Mihiel *France* **19** D12
St-Nazaire *France* **18** E4
St. Neots *U.K.* **15** E7
St-Nicolas-de-Port *France* **19** D13
St-Niklaas *Belgium* **17** C4
St-Omer *France* **19** B9
St-Palais-sur-Mer *France* **20** C2
St-Pamphile *Canada* **105** C6
St-Pardoux-la-Rivière
  France **20** C4
St-Pascal *Canada* **105** C5
St. Paul *Canada* **102** C6
St-Paul *France* **21** D10
St-Paul *Réunion* **85** c
St. Paul *Minn., U.S.A.* **112** C7
St. Paul *Nebr., U.S.A.* **112** E4
St-Paul ⇥ *Canada* **105** B6
St. Paul ⇥ *Liberia* **82** D2
St. Paul, I. *Ind. Oc.* **3** F13
St-Paul-de-Fenouillet *France* **20** F6
St. Paul I. *Canada* **105** C7
St-Paul-lès-Dax *France* **20** E2
St-Péray *France* **21** D8
St. Peter *U.S.A.* **112** C7
St-Peter-Ording *Germany* **24** A4
St. Peter Port *U.K.* **15** H5
St. Peters *N.S., Canada* **105** C7
St. Peters *P.E.I., Canada* **105** C7
St. Petersburg =
  Sankt-Peterburg *Russia* **32** C6
St. Petersburg *U.S.A.* **117** H13
St-Philbert-de-Grand-Lieu
  France **18** E5
St-Phillippe *Réunion* **85** c
St-Pie *Canada* **115** A12
St-Pierre *Martinique* **120** c
St-Pierre *Réunion* **85** c
St-Pierre *St-P. & M.* **105** C8
St-Pierre, L. *Canada* **104** C5
St-Pierre-d'Oléron *France* **20** C2
St-Pierre-en-Port *France* **18** C7
St-Pierre-et-Miquelon ☑
  N. Amer. **105** C8
St-Pierre-le-Moûtier *France* **19** F10
St-Pierre-sur-Dives *France* **18** C6
St-Pol-de-Léon *France* **18** D3
St-Pol-sur-Mer *France* **19** A9
St-Pol-sur-Ternoise *France* **19** B9
St-Pons *France* **20** E6
St-Pourçain-sur-Sioule
  France **19** F10
St-Priest *France* **21** C8
St-Quay-Portrieux *France* **18** D4
St-Quentin *Canada* **105** C6
St-Quentin *France* **19** C10
St-Rambert-d'Albon *France* **21** C8
St-Raphaël *France* **21** E10
St. Regis *U.S.A.* **108** C6
St-Renan *France* **18** D2
St-Saëns *France* **18** C8
St-Savin *France* **20** B4
St-Savinien *France* **20** C3
St. Sebastien, Tanjon' i
  Madag. **89** A8
St-Seine-l'Abbaye *France* **19** E11
St-Sernin-sur-Rance *France* **20** E6
St-Sever *France* **20** E3
St-Siméon *Canada* **105** C5
St. Simons I. *U.S.A.* **117** F14
St. Simons Island *U.S.A.* **117** F14
St. Stephen *Canada* **105** C6
St-Sulpice *France* **20** E5
St-Sulpice-Laurière *France* **20** B5
St-Sulpice-les-Feuilles *France* **20** B5
St-Syprien = St-Cyprien
  France **20** F7
St-Thégonnec *France* **18** D3
St. Thomas *Canada* **114** D3
St. Thomas I. *U.S. Virgin Is.* **121** e
St-Tite *Canada* **104** C5
St-Tropez *France* **21** E10
St-Troud = St. Truiden
  Belgium **17** D5

St. Truiden *Belgium* **17** D5
St-Vaast-la-Hougue *France* **18** C5
St-Valery-en-Caux *France* **18** C7
St-Valéry-sur-Somme *France* **19** B8
St-Vallier *France* **19** F11
St-Vallier-de-Thiey *France* **21** E10
St-Varent *France* **18** F6
St-Vaury *France* **20** B5
St. Vincent = São Vicente
  C. Verde Is. **78** b
St. Vincent *Italy* **40** C4
St. Vincent, G. *Australia* **95** F2
St. Vincent & the
  Grenadines ■ *W. Indies* **121** D7
St-Vincent-de-Tyrosse
  France **20** E2
St. Vincent Passage
  W. Indies **121** D7
St-Vith *Belgium* **17** D6
St-Vivien-de-Médoc *France* **20** C2
St. Walburg *Canada* **103** C7
St-Yrieix-la-Perche *France* **20** C5
Ste-Adresse *France* **18** C7
Ste-Agathe-des-Monts
  Canada **104** C5
Ste-Anne *Guadeloupe* **120** b
Ste-Anne *Seychelles* **85** b
Ste-Anne, L. *Canada* **105** B6
Ste-Anne-des-Monts-
  Tourelle *Canada* **105** C6
Ste-Croix *Switz.* **25** J2
Ste-Énimie *France* **20** D7
Ste-Foy-la-Grande *France* **20** D4
Ste. Genevieve *U.S.A.* **112** G8
Ste-Hermine *France* **20** B2
Ste-Livrade-sur-Lot *France* **20** D4
Ste-Marguerite ⇥ *Canada* **105** B6
Ste-Marie *Canada* **105** C5
Ste-Marie *Martinique* **120** c
Ste-Marie *Réunion* **85** c
Ste-Marie, Île = Nosy
  Boraha *Madag.* **89** B8
Ste-Marie-aux-Mines
  France **19** D14
Ste-Maure-de-Touraine
  France **18** E7
Ste-Maxime *France* **21** E10
Ste-Menehould *France* **19** C11
Ste-Mère-Église *France* **18** C5
Ste-Rose *Guadeloupe* **120** b
Ste-Rose *Réunion* **85** c
Ste. Rose du Lac *Canada* **103** C9
Ste-Savine *France* **19** D11
Ste-Sigolène *France* **21** C8
Saintes *France* **20** C3
Saintes, Îs. des *Guadeloupe* **120** b
Stes-Maries-de-la-Mer
  France **21** E8
Saintfield *U.K.* **12** B6
Saintonge *France* **20** C3
Saipan *N. Marianas* **96** F6
Sairang *India* **67** H18
Sairecábur, Cerro *Bolivia* **126** A2
Saitama *Japan* **55** G9
Saitama □ *Japan* **55** F9
Saiteli = Kadınhanı *Turkey* **72** C5
Saiți *Moldova* **29** D14
Saiyid *Pakistan* **68** D3
Saiyid *Pakistan* **68** F3
Sajama *Bolivia* **124** G5
Sajan *Serbia* **28** E5
Sajó ⇥ *Hungary* **28** C6
Sajószentpéter *Hungary* **28** B5
Sajum *India* **69** C8
Sak ⇥ *S. Africa* **88** E3
Saka *Kenya* **86** B4
Sakaba *Nigeria* **83** C6
Sakai *Japan* **55** G7
Sakaide *Japan* **55** G6
Sakaiminato *Japan* **55** G6
Sakākah *Si. Arabia* **70** D4
Sakakawea, L. *U.S.A.* **112** B3
Sakami ⇥ *Canada* **104** B4
Sakami, L. *Canada* **104** B4
Sâkâne, 'Erg i-n *Mali* **83** A4
Sakania
  Dem. Rep. of the Congo **87** E2
Sakaraha *Madag.* **89** C7
Sakartvelo = Georgia ■ *Asia* **35** J6
Sakarya *Turkey* **72** B4
Sakarya □ *Turkey* **72** B4
Sakarya ⇥ *Turkey* **72** B4
Sakashima-Guntō *Japan* **55** M2
Sakassou *Ivory C.* **82** D3
Sakata *Japan* **54** E9
Sakchu *N. Korea* **57** D13
Sakeny ⇥ *Madag.* **89** C8
Sakété *Benin* **83** D5
Sakha □ *Russia* **53** C14
Sakhalin *Russia* **53** D15
Sakhalinskiy Zaliv *Russia* **53** D15
Şaki *Azerbaijan* **35** K8
Šakiai *Lithuania* **30** D10
Sakon Nakhon *Thailand* **64** D5
Sakrand *Pakistan* **68** F3
Sakri *India* **69** F12
Sakrivier *S. Africa* **88** E3

Sakskøbing *Denmark* **11** K5
Sakuma *Japan* **55** G8
Sakurai *Japan* **55** G7
Saky *Ukraine* **33** K7
Sal △ *C. Verde Is.* **78** b
Sal ⇥ *Russia* **35** G5
Sal Rei *C. Verde Is.* **78** b
Sala *Eritrea* **81** D4
Sala ⇥ *Eritrea* **81** D4
Sala *Sweden* **10** E10
Sala *Slovak Rep.* **27** C10
Sala ⇥ *Eritrea* **81** D4
Sala Consilina *Italy* **43** B8
Sala-y-Gómez *Pac. Oc.* **97** K17
Sala y Gómez Ridge *Pac. Oc.* **97** K17
Salaberry-de-Valleyfield
  Canada **115** A10
Salacgrīva *Latvia* **30** A11
Salada, L. *Mexico* **109** K6
Saladas *Argentina* **126** B4
Saladillo *Argentina* **126** D4
Salado ⇥ *B. Aires, Argentina*
  126 D4
Salado ⇥ *La Pampa,*
  Argentina **128** D3
Salado ⇥ *Santa Fe,*
  Argentina **126** C3
Salado ⇥ *Mexico* **116** H5
Salaga *Ghana* **83** D4
Şālah *Syria* **74** C4
Ṣalāḥ ad Dīn □ *Iraq* **70** C4
Sălaj □ *Romania* **28** C8
Salakos *Greece* **49** C9
Salala *Liberia* **82** D2
Salala *Sudan* **80** C4
Salālah *Oman* **75** D5
Salamanca *Chile* **126** C1
Salamanca *Spain* **36** E5
Salamanca *U.S.A.* **114** D6
Salamanca □ *Spain* **36** E5
Salāmatābād *Iran* **70** C5
Salamina *Greece* **46** D5
Salamis *Cyprus* **49** D12
Salar de Atacama *Chile* **126** A2
Salar de Uyuni *Bolivia* **124** H5
Sălard *Romania* **28** C7
Salas *Spain* **36** B4
Salas de los Infantes *Spain* **36** C7
Salatiga *Indonesia* **63** G14
Salaverry *Peru* **124** E3
Salawati *Indonesia* **63** E8
Salaya *India* **68** H3
Salayar *Indonesia* **63** F6
Salazar ⇥ *Spain* **38** C3
Salbris *France* **19** E9
Salcia *Romania* **29** G9
Sălciua *Romania* **29** D8
Salcombe *U.K.* **15** G4
Saldaña *Spain* **36** C6
Saldanha *S. Africa* **88** E2
Saldanha B. *S. Africa* **88** E2
Saldus *Latvia* **30** B9
Saldus □ *Latvia* **30** B9
Sale *Australia* **95** F4
Sale *Italy* **40** D5
Salé *Morocco* **78** B4
Sale *U.K.* **14** D5
Salekhard *Russia* **52** C7
Salelologa *Samoa* **91** b
Salem *India* **66** P11
Salem *Ill., U.S.A.* **112** F9
Salem *Ind., U.S.A.* **112** F10
Salem *Mass., U.S.A.* **115** D14
Salem *Mo., U.S.A.* **112** G8
Salem *N.H., U.S.A.* **115** D13
Salem *N.J., U.S.A.* **113** F16
Salem *N.Y., U.S.A.* **115** C11
Salem *Ohio, U.S.A.* **114** F4
Salem *Oreg., U.S.A.* **108** D2
Salem *S. Dak., U.S.A.* **112** D5
Salem *Va., U.S.A.* **113** G13
Salemi *Italy* **42** E5
Sälen *Sweden* **10** C7
Salernes *France* **21** E10
Salerno *Italy* **43** B7
Salerno, G. di *Italy* **43** B7
Salford *U.K.* **14** D5
Salgir ⇥ *Ukraine* **33** K8
Salgótarján *Hungary* **28** B4
Salgueiro *Brazil* **125** E11
Salibabu *Indonesia* **63** D7
Salibea = Salybia
  Trin. & Tob. **125** K15
Salida *U.S.A.* **108** G10
Salies-de-Béarn *France* **20** E3
Salihli *Turkey* **72** C3
Salihorsk *Belarus* **23** B14
Salima *Malawi* **85** G6
Salina *Italy* **43** D7
Salina *Kans., U.S.A.* **112** F5
Salina *Utah, U.S.A.* **108** G8
Salina Cruz *Mexico* **119** D5
Salina di Margherita di
  Savoia ⇥ *Italy* **43** A9
Salinas *Brazil* **125** G10
Salinas *Chile* **126** A2
Salinas *Ecuador* **124** D2

Salinas *U.S.A.* **110** J5
Salinas → *Guatemala* **119** D6
Salinas → *U.S.A.* **110** J5
Salinas, B. de *Nic.* **120** D2
Salinas, Pampa de las
  Argentina **126** C2
Salinas Ambargasta
  Argentina **126** B3
Salinas de Hidalgo *Mexico* **118** C4
Salinas Grandes *Argentina* **126** C3
Salinas Pueblo Missions △
  U.S.A. **109** J10
Salinas Valley *U.S.A.* **110** J5
Saline → *Ark., U.S.A.* **116** E8
Saline → *Kans., U.S.A.* **112** F5
Saline di Trapani e
  Paceco □ *Italy* **42** E5
Salines, C. de ses *Spain* **48** B10
Salinópolis *Brazil* **125** D9
Salins-les-Bains *France* **19** F12
Salir *Portugal* **37** H2
Salisbury *Australia* **95** E2
Salisbury *U.K.* **15** F6
Salisbury *Md., U.S.A.* **113** F16
Salisbury *N.C., U.S.A.* **117** D14
Salisbury I. *Canada* **101** C12
Salisbury Plain *U.K.* **15** F6
Săliște *Romania* **29** E8
Salka *Nigeria* **83** C5
Şalkhad *Syria* **74** C5
Salkove *Ukraine* **29** B14
Salla *Finland* **8** C23
Sallanches *France* **21** C10
Sallent *Spain* **38** D6
Salles *France* **20** D3
Salles-Curan *France* **20** D6
Salling *Denmark* **11** H2
Salliq = Coral Harbour
  Canada **101** C11
Sallisaw *U.S.A.* **116** D7
Sallom *Sudan* **80** D4
Salluit *Canada* **101** C12
Salmās *Iran* **73** C11
Salmerón *Spain* **38** E2
Salmo *Canada* **102** D5
Salmon *U.S.A.* **108** D7
Salmon → *Canada* **102** C4
Salmon → *U.S.A.* **108** D5
Salmon Arm *Canada* **102** C5
Salmon Gums *Australia* **93** F3
Salmon River Mts. *U.S.A.* **108** D6
Salo *Finland* **32** B2
Salò *Italy* **40** C7
Salobreña *Spain* **37** J7
Salome *U.S.A.* **111** M13
Salon *India* **69** F9
Salon-de-Provence *France* **21** E9
Salonica = Thessaloniki
  Greece **44** F6
Salonta *Romania* **28** D6
Salor → *Spain* **37** F3
Salou *Spain* **38** D6
Salou, C. de *Spain* **38** D6
Saloum → *Senegal* **82** C1
Salpausselkä *Finland* **32** B4
Salsacate *Argentina* **126** C2
Salses *France* **20** F6
Salsk *Russia* **35** G5
Salso → *Italy* **42** E6
Salsomaggiore Terme *Italy* **40** D6
Salt *Spain* **38** D7
Salt → *Canada* **102** B6
Salt → *U.S.A.* **109** K7
Salt Fork Red → *U.S.A.* **116** D5
Salt L. *Australia* **95** E3
Salt Lake City *U.S.A.* **108** F8
Salt Range *Pakistan* **68** C5
Salta *Argentina* **126** A2
Salta □ *Argentina* **126** A2
Saltara *Italy* **41** E9
Saltash *U.K.* **15** G3
Saltburn by the Sea *U.K.* **14** C7
Saltcoats *U.K.* **13** F4
Saltee Is. *Ireland* **12** D5
Saltfjellet *Norway* **8** C16
Saltfjorden *Norway* **8** C16
Saltholm *Denmark* **11** J6
Saltillo *Mexico* **118** B4
Salto *Argentina* **126** C3
Salto *Uruguay* **126** C4
Salto del Guaíra *Paraguay* **127** A5
Salton City *U.S.A.* **111** M11
Salton Sea *U.S.A.* **111** M11
Saltpond *Ghana* **83** D4
Saltsburg *U.S.A.* **114** F5
Saltsjöbaden *Sweden* **10** E12
Saluda → *U.S.A.* **117** D14
Salûm *Egypt* **80** A2
Salûm, Khâlig el *Egypt* **80** A2
Salur *India* **67** K13
Saluzzo *Italy* **40** D4
Salvador *Brazil* **125** F11
Salvador *Canada* **103** C7
Salvador, El □ *Cent. Amer.* **120** D2
Salvador, L. *U.S.A.* **117** G9
Salvaterra de Magos
  Portugal **37** F2

Sálvora, I. de *Spain* **36** C2
Salween → *Burma* **67** L20
Salyan *Azerbaijan* **73** C13
Salybia *Trin. & Tob.* **125** K15
Salza → *Austria* **26** D7
Salzach → *Austria* **26** C5
Salzburg *Austria* **26** D6
Salzburg □ *Austria* **26** D6
Salzgitter *Germany* **24** C6
Salzkotten *Germany* **24** D4
Salzwedel *Germany* **24** C7
Sam *India* **68** F4
Sam Neua *Laos* **58** G5
Sam Ngao *Thailand* **64** D2
Sam Rayburn Res. *U.S.A.* **116** F7
Sam Son *Vietnam* **64** C5
Sam Teu *Laos* **64** C5
Sama de Langreo =
  Langreo *Spain* **36** B5
Samagaltay *Russia* **53** D10
Samales Group *Phil.* **61** J5
Samâlût *Egypt* **80** B3
Samana *India* **68** D7
Samana Cay *Bahamas* **121** B5
Samandağ *Turkey* **72** D6
Samandıra *Turkey* **45** F13
Samanga *Tanzania* **87** D4
Samangān □ *Afghan.* **66** B5
Samangwa
  Dem. Rep. of the Congo **86** C1
Samani *Japan* **54** C11
Samanli Dağları *Turkey* **45** F13
Samar *Phil.* **61** F6
Samara *Russia* **34** D10
Samara → *Russia* **34** D10
Samara → *Ukraine* **33** H8
Samaria = Shōmrōn
  West Bank **74** C4
Samaria *Greece* **49** D5
Samaria △ *Greece* **46** F5
Samarinda *Indonesia* **62** E5
Samarkand = Samarqand
  Uzbekistan **52** F7
Samarqand *Uzbekistan* **52** F7
Sāmarrā' *Iraq* **73** E10
Samastipur *India* **69** G11
Şamaxı *Azerbaijan* **35** K9
Samba *Dem. Rep. of the Congo* **86** C2
Samba *India* **69** C6
Sambalpur *India* **67** J14
Sambar, Tanjung *Indonesia* **62** E4
Sambas *Indonesia* **62** D3
Sambava *Madag.* **89** A9
Sambhal *India* **69** E8
Sambhar *India* **68** F6
Sambhar L. *India* **68** F6
Sambiase *Italy* **43** D9
Sambir *Ukraine* **31** J10
Sambor *Cambodia* **64** F6
Samborombón, B. *Argentina* **126** D4
Sambuca di Sicília *Italy* **42** E6
Samburu △ *Kenya* **86** B4
Samcheok *S. Korea* **57** F15
Same *Tanzania* **86** C4
Samer *France* **19** B8
Samfya *Zambia* **87** E2
Sami *Greece* **46** C2
Şämkir *Azerbaijan* **35** K8
Şamlı *Turkey* **47** B9
Samnah *Si. Arabia* **70** E3
Samo Alto *Chile* **126** C1
Samobor *Croatia* **41** C12
Samoëns *France* **19** F13
Şamorīn *Slovak Rep.* **27** C10
Samorogouan *Burkina Faso* **82** C4
Samos *Greece* **47** D8
Samoš *Serbia* **28** E5
Samos *Spain* **36** C3
Samos □ *Greece* **47** D8
Samothráki = Mathraki
  Greece **49** A3
Samothraki *Greece* **45** F9
Samoylovka *Russia* **34** E6
Sampa *Ghana* **82** D4
Sampacho *Argentina* **126** C3
Sampalan *Indonesia* **63** K18
Sampang *Indonesia* **63** G15
Samper de Calanda *Spain* **38** D4
Sampéyre *Italy* **40** D4
Sampit *Indonesia* **62** E4
Sampit, Teluk *Indonesia* **62** E4
Samrong *Cambodia* **64** E4
Samrong *Thailand* **64** E3
Samsø *Denmark* **11** J4
Samsø Bælt *Denmark* **11** J4
Samsun *Turkey* **72** B7
Samsun □ *Turkey* **72** B7
Samtredia *Georgia* **35** J6
Samui, Ko *Thailand* **65** b
Samur → *Russia* **35** K9
Samurskiy Khrebet *Russia* **35** K8
Samusole
  Dem. Rep. of the Congo **87** E1
Samut Prakan *Thailand* **64** F3

Samut Songkhram *Thailand* **64** F3
Samwari *Pakistan* **68** E2
San *Mali* **82** C4
San → *Cambodia* **64** F5
San → *Poland* **31** H8
San Adrián *Spain* **38** C3
San Adrián, C. de *Spain* **36** B2
San Agustin, C. *Phil.* **61** H7
San Agustín de Valle Fértil
  Argentina **126** C2
San Ambrosio *Pac. Oc.* **122** F3
San Andreas *U.S.A.* **110** G6
San Andres *Phil.* **61** E6
San Andrés, I. de *Caribbean* **120** D3
San Andrés del Rabanedo
  Spain **36** C5
San Andres Mts. *U.S.A.* **109** K10
San Andrés Tuxtla *Mexico* **119** D5
San Angelo *U.S.A.* **116** F4
San Anselmo *U.S.A.* **110** H4
San Antonio *Belize* **119** D7
San Antonio *Chile* **126** C1
San Antonio *Phil.* **61** D4
San Antonio *N. Mex., U.S.A.*
  109 K10
San Antonio *Tex., U.S.A.* **116** G5
San Antonio → *U.S.A.* **116** G6
San Antonio, C. *Argentina* **126** D4
San Antonio, C. de *Cuba* **120** B3
San Antonio, C. de *Spain* **39** G5
San Antonio, Mt. *U.S.A.* **111** L9
San Antonio de los Baños
  Cuba **120** B3
San Antonio de los Cobres
  Argentina **126** A2
San Antonio Oeste
  Argentina **128** E4
San Arcángelo *Italy* **43** B9
San Ardo *U.S.A.* **110** J6
San Augustín *Canary Is.* **48** G4
San Augustine *U.S.A.* **116** F7
San Bartolomé *Canary Is.* **48** F6
San Bartolomé de Tirajana
  Canary Is. **48** G4
San Bartolomeo in Galdo
  Italy **43** A8
San Benedetto del Tronto
  Italy **41** F10
San Benedetto Po *Italy* **40** C7
San Benedicto, I. *Mexico* **118** D2
San Benito *U.S.A.* **116** H6
San Benito → *U.S.A.* **110** J5
San Benito Mt. *U.S.A.* **110** J6
San Bernardino *U.S.A.* **111** L9
San Bernardino Mts. *U.S.A.*
  111 L10
San Bernardino Str. *Phil.* **61** E6
San Bernardo *Chile* **126** C1
San Bernardo, I. de
  Colombia **124** B3
San Blas *Mexico* **118** B3
San Blas, Arch. de *Panama* **120** E4
San Blas, C. *U.S.A.* **117** G12
San Bonifacio *Italy* **41** C8
San Borja *Bolivia* **124** F5
San Buenaventura =
  Ventura *U.S.A.* **111** L7
San Buenaventura *Mexico* **118** B4
San Carlos = Sant Carles
  Spain **48** B8
San Carlos *Argentina* **126** C2
San Carlos *Chile* **126** D1
San Carlos *Baja Calif. S.,
  Mexico* **118** C2
San Carlos *Coahuila, Mexico* **118** B4
San Carlos *Nic.* **120** D3
San Carlos *Neg. Occ., Phil.* **61** F5
San Carlos *Pangasinan, Phil.* **61** D4
San Carlos *Uruguay* **127** C5
San Carlos *U.S.A.* **109** K8
San Carlos *Venezuela* **124** B5
San Carlos de Bariloche
  Argentina **128** E2
San Carlos de Bolívar
  Argentina **128** D4
San Carlos de la Rápita =
  Sant Carles de la Ràpita
  Spain **38** E5
San Carlos del Zulia
  Venezuela **124** B4
San Carlos L. *U.S.A.* **109** K8
San Cataldo *Italy* **42** E6
San Celoni = Sant Celoni
  Spain **38** D7
San Clemente *Chile* **126** D1
San Clemente *Spain* **39** F2
San Clemente *U.S.A.* **111** M9
San Clemente I. *U.S.A.* **111** N8
San Cristóbal = Es Migjorn
  Gran *Spain* **48** B11
San Cristóbal *Argentina* **126** C3
San Cristóbal *Dom. Rep.* **121** C5
San Cristóbal *Solomon Is.* **90** C9
San Cristóbal *Venezuela* **124** B4
San Cristóbal de las Casas
  Mexico **119** D6
San Damiano d'Asti *Italy* **40** D5

San Daniele del Friuli *Italy* **41** B10
San Diego *Calif., U.S.A.* **111** N9
San Diego *Tex., U.S.A.* **116** H5
San Diego, C. *Argentina* **128** G3
San Diego de la Unión
  Mexico **118** C4
San Diego Int. ✈ (SAN)
  U.S.A. **111** N9
San Dimitri, Ras *Malta* **49** C1
San Dimitri Point = San
  Dimitri, Ras *Malta* **49** C1
San Donà di Piave *Italy* **41** C9
San Estanislao *Paraguay* **126** A4
San Esteban de Gormaz
  Spain **38** D1
San Felice Circeo *Italy* **42** A6
San Felice sul Panaro *Italy* **41** D8
San Felipe *Chile* **126** C1
San Felipe *Mexico* **118** A2
San Felipe *Venezuela* **124** A5
San Felipe → *U.S.A.* **111** M11
San Félix *Chile* **126** B1
San Félix *Pac. Oc.* **122** F2
San Fernando = Sant
  Ferran *Spain* **48** C7
San Fernando *Chile* **126** C1
San Fernando *Mexico* **119** C5
San Fernando *La Union, Phil.* **61** C4
San Fernando *Pampanga,
  Phil.* **61** D4
San Fernando *Spain* **37** J4
San Fernando *Trin. & Tob.* **121** D7
San Fernando *U.S.A.* **111** L8
San Fernando de Apure
  Venezuela **124** B5
San Fernando de Atabapo
  Venezuela **124** C5
San Fernando di Púglia *Italy* **43** A9
San Francisco *Argentina* **126** C3
San Francisco *U.S.A.* **110** H4
San Francisco → *U.S.A.* **109** K9
San Francisco, C. de
  Colombia **122** C3
San Francisco, Paso de
  S. Amer. **126** B2
San Francisco de Macorís
  Dom. Rep. **121** C5
San Francisco del Monte
  de Oro *Argentina* **126** C2
San Francisco del Oro
  Mexico **118** B3
San Francisco Int. ✈ (SFO)
  U.S.A. **110** H4
San Francisco Javier =
  Sant Francesc de
  Formentera *Spain* **48** C7
San Fratello *Italy* **43** D7
San Gabriel *Ecuador* **124** C3
San Gabriel Chilac *Mexico* **119** D5
San Gabriel Mts. *U.S.A.* **111** L9
San Gavino Monreale *Italy* **42** C1
San German *Puerto Rico* **121** d
San Gimignano *Italy* **40** E8
San Giórgio di Nogaro *Italy* **41** C10
San Giórgio Iónico *Italy* **43** B10
San Giovanni Bianco *Italy* **40** C6
San Giovanni in Fiore *Italy* **43** C9
San Giovanni in Persiceto
  Italy **41** D8
San Giovanni Rotondo
  Italy **41** G12
San Giovanni Valdarno *Italy* **41** E8
San Giuliano Terme *Italy* **40** E7
San Gorgonio Mt. *U.S.A.* **111** L10
San Gottardo, P. del *Switz.* **25** J4
San Gregorio *Uruguay* **127** C4
San Gregorio *U.S.A.* **110** H4
San Guiseppe Jato *Italy* **42** E6
San Ignacio *Belize* **119** D7
San Ignacio *Bolivia* **124** G6
San Ignacio *Mexico* **118** B2
San Ignacio *Paraguay* **126** B4
San Ignacio, L. *Mexico* **118** B2
San Ildefonso, C. *Phil.* **61** D5
San Isidro *Argentina* **126** C4
San Isidro *Phil.* **61** H7
San Jacinto *U.S.A.* **111** M10
San Jaime = Sant Jaume
  Spain **48** B11
San Javier *Misiones,
  Argentina* **127** B4
San Javier *Santa Fe,
  Argentina* **126** C4
San Javier *Bolivia* **124** G6
San Javier *Chile* **126** D1
San Jerónimo Taviche
  Mexico **119** D5
San Joaquin *U.S.A.* **110** J6
San Joaquin → *U.S.A.* **110** G5
San Joaquin Valley *U.S.A.* **110** J6
San Jon *U.S.A.* **109** J12
San Jordi = Sant Jordi *Spain* **48** B9
San Jorge *Argentina* **126** C3
San Jorge, B. *Mexico* **118** A2
San Jorge, G. *Argentina* **128** F3
San Martín → *Bolivia* **124** F6
San José = San Josep *Spain* **48** C7

San José *Costa Rica* **120** E3
San José *Guatemala* **120** D1
San Jose *Mind. Occ., Phil.* **61** E4
San Jose *Nueva Ecija, Phil.* **61** D4
San Jose *U.S.A.* **110** H5
San Jose → *U.S.A.* **109** J10
San José, I. *Mexico* **118** C2
San José de Buenavista *Phil.* **63** B6
San José de Chiquitos
  Bolivia **124** G6
San José de Feliciano
  Argentina **126** C4
San José de Jáchal *Argentina* **126** C2
San José de Mayo *Uruguay* **126** C4
San José del Cabo *Mexico* **118** C3
San José del Guaviare
  Colombia **124** C4
San Josep *Spain* **48** C7
San Juan *Argentina* **126** C2
San Juan *Phil.* **61** E6
San Juan *Puerto Rico* **121** d
San Juan *Trin. & Tob.* **125** K15
San Juan □ *Argentina* **126** C2
San Juan → *Argentina* **126** C2
San Juan → *Nic.* **120** D3
San Juan → *U.S.A.* **109** H8
San Juan Bautista = Sant
  Joan de Labritja *Spain* **48** B8
San Juan Bautista *Paraguay* **126** B4
San Juan Bautista *U.S.A.* **110** J5
San Juan Capistrano *U.S.A.*
  111 M9
San Juan Cr. → *U.S.A.* **110** J5
San Juan de Alicante *Spain* **39** G4
San Juan de Guadalupe
  Mexico **118** C4
San Juan de la Costa *Mexico*
  118 C2
San Juan de los Lagos
  Mexico **118** C4
San Juan de los Morros
  Venezuela **124** B5
San Juan del Norte *Nic.* **120** D3
San Juan del Norte, B. de
  Nic. **120** D3
San Juan del Río *Mexico* **119** C5
San Juan del Sur *Nic.* **120** D2
San Juan I. *U.S.A.* **110** B3
San Juan Island △ *U.S.A.* **110** B4
San Juan Mts. *U.S.A.* **109** H10
San Just, Sierra de *Spain* **38** E4
San Justo *Argentina* **126** C3
San Kamphaeng *Thailand* **64** C2
San Lázaro, C. *Mexico* **118** C2
San Leandro *U.S.A.* **110** H4
San Leonardo de Yagüe
  Spain **38** D1
San Lorenzo = Sant
  Llorenç des Cardassar
  Spain **48** B10
San Lorenzo *Argentina* **126** C3
San Lorenzo *Ecuador* **124** C3
San Lorenzo *Paraguay* **126** B4
San Lorenzo → *Mexico* **118** C3
San Lorenzo, I. *Mexico* **118** B2
San Lorenzo, Mte. *Argentina* **128** F2
San Lorenzo de la Parrilla
  Spain **38** F2
San Lorenzo de Morunys =
  Sant Llorenç de
  Morunys *Spain* **38** C6
San Lucas = Cabo San
  Lucas *Mexico* **118** C3
San Lucas *Bolivia* **124** H5
San Lucas *Mexico* **118** B2
San Lucas *U.S.A.* **110** J5
San Lucas, C. *Mexico* **118** C3
San Lúcido *Italy* **43** C9
San Luis *Argentina* **126** C2
San Luis *Cuba* **120** B3
San Luis *Guatemala* **120** C2
San Luis *Ariz., U.S.A.* **109** K6
San Luis *Colo., U.S.A.* **109** H11
San Luis □ *Argentina* **126** C2
San Luis, I. *Mexico* **118** B2
San Luis, Sierra de
  Argentina **126** C2
San Luis de la Paz *Mexico* **118** C4
San Luis Obispo *U.S.A.* **111** K6
San Luis Potosí *Mexico* **118** C4
San Luis Potosí □ *Mexico* **118** C4
San Luis Res. *U.S.A.* **110** H5
San Luis Río Colorado
  Mexico **118** A2
San Manuel *U.S.A.* **109** K8
San Marco, C. *Italy* **42** C1
San Marco Argentano *Italy* **43** C9
San Marco in Lámis *Italy* **41** G12
San Marcos *Guatemala* **120** D1
San Marcos *Calif., U.S.A.* **111** M9
San Marcos *Tex., U.S.A.* **116** G6
San Marcos, I. *Mexico* **118** B2
San Marino *San Marino* **41** E9
San Marino ■ *Europe* **41** E9
San Martín *Antarctica* **5** C17
San Martín *Argentina* **128** G3
San Martín → *Bolivia* **124** F6

San Martín, L. *Argentina* **128** F2
San Martín de la Vega *Spain* **36** E7
San Martín de los Andes
  Argentina **128** E2
San Martín de
  Valdeiglesias *Spain* **36** E6
San Mateo = Sant Mateu
  Baleares, Spain **48** B7
San Mateo = Sant Mateu
  Valencia, Spain **38** E5
San Mateo *Phil.* **61** C4
San Mateo *U.S.A.* **110** H4
San Matías *Bolivia* **124** G7
San Matías, G. *Argentina* **128** E4
San Miguel = Sant Miguel
  Spain **48** B7
San Miguel *El Salv.* **120** D2
San Miguel *Panama* **120** E4
San Miguel *U.S.A.* **110** K6
San Miguel → *Bolivia* **124** F6
San Miguel de Tucumán
  Argentina **126** B2
San Miguel del Monte
  Argentina **126** D4
San Miguel I. *U.S.A.* **111** L6
San Miniato *Italy* **40** E7
San Nicolás *Canary Is.* **48** G4
San Nicolas *Phil.* **61** B4
San Nicolás de los Arroyos
  Argentina **126** C3
San Nicolas I. *U.S.A.* **111** M7
San Onofre *U.S.A.* **111** M9
San Pablo *Bolivia* **126** A2
San Pablo *Phil.* **61** D4
San Pablo *U.S.A.* **110** H4
San Páolo di Civitate *Italy* **41** G12
San Pedro *B. Aires, Argentina*
  126 C4
San Pedro *Misiones,
  Argentina* **127** B5
San Pedro *Chile* **126** C1
San Pedro *Ivory C.* **82** E3
San Pedro *Mexico* **118** C2
San Pedro □ *Paraguay* **126** A4
San Pedro → *Chihuahua,
  Mexico* **118** B3
San Pedro → *Nayarit,
  Mexico* **118** C3
San Pedro → *U.S.A.* **109** K8
San Pedro, Pta. *Chile* **126** B1
San Pedro, Sierra de *Spain* **37** F4
San Pedro Channel *U.S.A.* **111** M8
San Pedro de Atacama
  Chile **126** A2
San Pedro de Jujuy
  Argentina **126** A3
San Pedro de las Colonias
  Mexico **118** B4
San Pedro de Macorís
  Dom. Rep. **121** C6
San Pedro del Norte *Nic.* **120** D3
San Pedro del Paraná
  Paraguay **126** B4
San Pedro del Pinatar *Spain* **39** H4
San Pedro Mártir, Sierra
  Mexico **118** A1
San Pedro Mártir △ *Mexico* **118** A1
San Pedro Ocampo =
  Melchor Ocampo *Mexico* **118** C4
San Pedro Pochutla *Mexico* **119** D5
San Pedro Sula *Honduras* **120** C2
San Pedro Tututepec
  Mexico **119** D5
San Pietro *Italy* **42** C1
San Pietro Vernótico *Italy* **43** B11
San Rafael *Argentina* **126** C2
San Rafael *Calif., U.S.A.* **110** H4
San Rafael *N. Mex., U.S.A.* **109** J10
San Rafael Mt. *U.S.A.* **111** L7
San Rafael Mts. *U.S.A.* **111** L7
San Ramón de la Nueva
  Orán *Argentina* **126** A3
San Remo *Italy* **40** E4
San Roque *Argentina* **126** B4
San Roque *Spain* **37** J5
San Rosendo *Chile* **126** D1
San Saba *U.S.A.* **116** F5
San Salvador *El Salv.* **120** D2
San Salvador *Spain* **48** B10
San Salvador de Jujuy
  Argentina **126** A3
San Salvador I. *Bahamas* **121** B5
San Salvo *Italy* **41** F11
San Sebastián = Donostia-
  San Sebastián *Spain* **38** B3
San Sebastián *Argentina* **128** G3
San Sebastián *Puerto Rico* **121** d
San Sebastián de la
  Gomera *Canary Is.* **48** F2
San Serra = Son Serra
  Spain **48** B10
San Serverino Marche *Italy* **41** E10
San Severo *Italy* **41** G12
San Simeon *U.S.A.* **110** K5
San Simon *U.S.A.* **109** K9
San Stéfano di Cadore *Italy* **41** B9
San Stino di Livenza *Italy* **41** C9

San Telmo = Sant Elm *Spain* **48** B9
San Telmo *Mexico* **118** A1
San Tiburcio *Mexico* **118** C4
San Valentín, Mte. *Chile* **128** F2
San Vicente de Alcántara
  Spain **37** F3
San Vicente de la Barquera
  Spain **36** B6
San Vincente del Raspeig
  Spain **39** G4
San Vincenzo *Italy* **40** E7
San Vito *Costa Rica* **120** E3
San Vito *Italy* **42** C2
San Vito, C. *Italy* **42** D5
San Vito al Tagliamento
  Italy **41** C9
San Vito Chietino *Italy* **41** F11
San Vito dei Normanni
  Italy **43** B10
Sana' *Yemen* **75** D3
Sana → *Bos.-H.* **41** C13
Sanaba *Burkina Faso* **82** C4
Sanae IV *Antarctica* **5** D2
Şanāfir *Si. Arabia* **80** D4
Sanaga → *Cameroon* **83** E6
Sanaloa, Presa *Mexico* **118** C3
Sanana *Indonesia* **63** E7
Sanand *India* **68** H5
Sanandaj *Iran* **73** E12
Sanandita *Bolivia* **126** A3
Sanary-sur-Mer *France* **21** E9
Sanawad *India* **68** H7
Sancellas = Sencelles *Spain* **48** B9
Sancergues *France* **19** E9
Sancerre *France* **19** E9
Sancerrois, Collines du
  France **19** E9
Sancha He → *China* **58** D6
Sanchahe *China* **57** B14
Sánchez *Dom. Rep.* **121** C6
Sanchor *India* **68** G4
Sancoins *France* **19** F9
Sancti Spíritus *Cuba* **120** B4
Sancy, Puy de *France* **20** C6
Sand = Polokwane →
  S. Africa **89** C5
Sand Hills *U.S.A.* **112** D3
Sand Lakes △ *Canada* **103** B9
Sand Springs *U.S.A.* **116** C6
Sanda *Japan* **55** G7
Sandakan *Malaysia* **62** C5
Sandan = Sambor *Cambodia* **64** F6
Sandanski *Bulgaria* **44** E7
Sandaré *Mali* **82** C2
Sandared *Sweden* **11** G6
Sandarne *Sweden* **10** C11
Sanday *Japan* **55** G7
Sanday *U.K.* **13** B6
Sande *Norway* **10** E4
Sandefjord *Norway* **9** G14
Sanders *U.S.A.* **109** J9
Sanderson *U.S.A.* **116** F3
Sandersville *U.S.A.* **117** E13
Sandfire Roadhouse
  Australia **92** C3
Sandfly L. *Canada* **103** B7
Sandfontein *Namibia* **88** C2
Sandhammaren *Sweden* **11** J8
Sandheads, The *India* **69** J13
Sandía *Peru* **124** F5
Sandıklı *Turkey* **47** C12
Sandila *India* **69** F9
Sandnes *Norway* **9** G11
Sandnessjøen *Norway* **8** C15
Sandoa *Dem. Rep. of the Congo* **84** F4
Sandomierz *Poland* **31** H8
Sândominic *Romania* **29** D10
Sandover → *Australia* **94** C2
Sandoway = Thandwe
  Burma **67** K19
Sandoy *Færoe Is.* **8** F9
Sandpoint *U.S.A.* **108** B5
Sandray *U.K.* **13** E1
Sandringham *U.K.* **14** E8
Sandstone *Australia* **93** E2
Sandu *China* **58** E6
Sandusky *Mich., U.S.A.* **114** C2
Sandusky *Ohio, U.S.A.* **114** E2
Sandveld *Namibia* **88** C3
Sandvig *Denmark* **11** J8
Sandviken *Sweden* **10** D10
Sandwich, C. *Australia* **94** B4
Sandwich B. *Canada* **105** B8
Sandwich B. *Namibia* **88** C1
Sandy *Oreg., U.S.A.* **110** E4
Sandy *Pa., U.S.A.* **114** E6
Sandy Bay *Canada* **103** B8
Sandy Bight *Australia* **93** F3
Sandy C. *Queens., Australia* **94** C5
Sandy C. *Tas., Australia* **95** G3
Sandy Cay *Bahamas* **121** B4
Sandy Cr. → *U.S.A.* **108** F9
Sandy L. *Canada* **104** B1
Sandy Lake *Canada* **104** B1
Sandy Utah, U.S.A. **108** F8
Sandy Valley *U.S.A.* **111** K11
Sånfjällets △ *Sweden* **10** B7
Sanford *Fla., U.S.A.* **117** G14

Sanford *Maine, U.S.A.* **115** C14
Sanford *N.C., U.S.A.* **117** D15
Sanford → *Australia* **93** E2
Sanford, Mt. *U.S.A.* **100** C5
Sang-i-Masha *Afghan.* **68** C2
Sanga *Mozam.* **87** E4
Sanga → *Congo* **84** E3
Sangamner *India* **66** K9
Sanganeb Atoll △ *Sudan* **80** D4
Sangar *Afghan.* **68** C1
Sangar *Russia* **53** C13
Sangar Sarai *Afghan.* **68** B4
Sangaredi *Guinea* **82** C2
Sangarh → *Pakistan* **68** D4
Sangasso *Mali* **82** C3
Sangatte *France* **19** B8
Sangay *Ecuador* **124** D3
Sange *Dem. Rep. of the Congo* **86** D2
Sangeang *Indonesia* **63** F5
Sângeorz-Băi *Romania* **29** C9
Sanger *U.S.A.* **110** J7
Sângera *Moldova* **29** D13
Sangerhausen *Germany* **24** D7
Sanggan He → *China* **56** E9
Sanggau *Indonesia* **62** D4
Sanghar *Pakistan* **68** F3
Sangihe, Kepulauan
  Indonesia **63** D7
Sangihe, Pulau *Indonesia* **63** D7
Sangju *S. Korea* **57** F15
Sangkapura *Indonesia* **62** F4
Sangkhla *Thailand* **64** E2
Sangkulirang *Indonesia* **62** D5
Sangla *Pakistan* **68** D5
Sangli *India* **66** L9
Sangmélima *Cameroon* **83** E7
Sangod *India* **68** G7
Sangre de Cristo Mts.
  U.S.A. **109** H11
Sangre Grande *Trin. & Tob.* **125** K15
Sangro → *Italy* **41** F11
Sangrur *India* **68** D6
Sangudo *Canada* **102** C6
Sangue → *Brazil* **124** F7
Sangüesa *Spain* **38** C3
Sanguinaires, Îs. *France* **21** G12
Sangzhi *China* **59** C8
Sanhala *Ivory C.* **82** C3
Sanibel *U.S.A.* **117** H13
Sanikiluaq *Canada* **104** A4
Sanin-Kaigan △ *Japan* **55** G7
Sanirajak *Canada* **101** C11
Sanjawi *Pakistan* **68** D3
Sanje *Uganda* **86** C3
Sanjiang *China* **58** E7
Sanjo *Japan* **54** F9
Sankh → *India* **69** H11
Sankt Andrä *Austria* **26** E7
Sankt Anton *Austria* **25** H6
Sankt Augustin *Germany* **24** E3
Sankt Blasien *Germany* **25** H4
Sankt Gallen *Switz.* **25** H5
Sankt Gallen □ *Switz.* **25** H5
Sankt Goar *Germany* **25** E3
Sankt Ingbert *Germany* **25** F3
Sankt Johann im Pongau
  Austria **26** D6
Sankt Johann in Tirol
  Austria **26** D5
Sankt Michel = Mikkeli
  Finland **32** B4
Sankt Moritz *Switz.* **25** J5
Sankt-Peterburg *Russia* **32** C6
Sankt Pölten *Austria* **26** C8
Sankt Ulrich = Ortisei *Italy* **41** B8
Sankt Valentin *Austria* **26** C7
Sankt Veit an der Glan
  Austria **26** E7
Sankt Wendel *Germany* **25** F3
Sankt Wolfgang *Austria* **26** D6
Sankuru →
  Dem. Rep. of the Congo **84** E4
Sanliurfa *Turkey* **73** D8
Sanliurfa □ *Turkey* **73** D8
Sanlúcar de Barrameda
  Spain **37** J4
Sanluri *Italy* **42** C1
Sânmartin *Romania* **29** D10
Sanmen *China* **59** C13
Sanmenxia *China* **56** G6
Sanming *China* **59** D11
Sannaspos *S. Africa* **88** D4
Sannicandro Gargánico
  Italy **41** G12
Sânnicolau Mare *Romania* **28** D5
Sannieshof *S. Africa* **88** D4
Sannīn, J. *Lebanon* **74** B4
Sanniquellie *Liberia* **82** D3
Sannûr, W. → *Egypt* **80** B3
Sanok *Poland* **31** J9
Sanquhar *U.K.* **13** F5
Sans Souci *Trin. & Tob.* **125** K16
Sansanding *Mali* **82** C3
Sansepolcro *Italy* **41** E9
Sansha *China* **59** D13
Sanshui *China* **59** F9
Sanski Most *Bos.-H.* **41** D13

Sansui *China* **58** D7
Sant Antoni de Portmany
  Spain **48** C7
Sant Boi de Llobregat *Spain* **38** D7
Sant Carles *Spain* **48** B8
Sant Carles de la Ràpita
  Spain **38** E5
Sant Celoni *Spain* **38** D7
Sant Elm *Spain* **48** B9
Sant Feliu de Guíxols *Spain* **38** D8
Sant Feliu de Llobregat
  Spain **38** D7
Sant Ferran *Spain* **48** C7
Sant Francesc de
  Formentera *Spain* **48** C7
Sant Jaume *Spain* **48** B11
Sant Joan de Labritja *Spain* **48** B8
Sant Jordi *Ibiza, Spain* **48** C7
Sant Jordi *Mallorca, Spain* **48** B9
Sant Jordi, G. de *Spain* **38** E6
Sant Llorenç de Morunys
  Spain **38** C6
Sant Llorenç del Munt y
  l'Obac △ *Spain* **38** D3
Sant Llorenç des Cardassar
  Spain **48** B10
Sant Mateu *Baleares, Spain* **48** B7
Sant Mateu *Valencia, Spain* **38** E5
Sant Miquel *Spain* **48** B7
Sant' Ágata Militello *Italy* **43** D7
Santa Agnès *Spain* **48** B7
Santa Ana *Bolivia* **124** F5
Santa Ana *El Salv.* **120** D2
Santa Ana *Mexico* **118** A2
Santa Ana *U.S.A.* **111** M9
Sant' Ángelo Lodigiano *Italy* **40** C6
Sant' Antíoco *Italy* **42** C1
Santa Bárbara *Chile* **126** D1
Santa Bárbara *Honduras* **120** D2
Santa Bárbara *Mexico* **118** B3
Santa Bárbara *Spain* **38** E5
Santa Barbara *U.S.A.* **111** L7
Santa Bárbara, Mt. *Spain* **39** H2
Santa Barbara Channel
  U.S.A. **111** L7
Santa Barbara I. *U.S.A.* **111** M7
Santa Catalina, Gulf of
  U.S.A. **111** N9
Santa Catalina, I. *Mexico* **118** B2
Santa Catalina I. *U.S.A.* **111** M8
Santa Catarina □ *Brazil* **127** B6
Santa Catarina, I. de *Brazil* **127** B6
Santa Caterina di Pittinuri
  Italy **42** B1
Santa Caterina Villarmosa
  Italy **43** E7
Santa Cecília *Brazil* **127** B5
Santa Clara *Cuba* **120** B4
Santa Clara *Calif., U.S.A.* **110** H5
Santa Clara *Utah, U.S.A.* **109** H7
Santa Clara de Olimar
  Uruguay **127** C5
Santa Clara Valley *U.S.A.* **110** J5
Santa Clarita *U.S.A.* **111** L8
Santa Clotilde *Peru* **124** D4
Santa Coloma de Farners
  Spain **38** D7
Santa Coloma de
  Gramenet *Spain* **38** D7
Santa Comba *Spain* **36** B2
Santa Croce Camerina *Italy* **43** F7
Santa Croce di Magliano
  Italy **41** G11
Santa Cruz *Argentina* **128** G3
Santa Cruz *Bolivia* **124** G6
Santa Cruz *Chile* **126** C1
Santa Cruz *Costa Rica* **120** D2
Santa Cruz *Madeira* **48** D3
Santa Cruz *Phil.* **61** D4
Santa Cruz *U.S.A.* **110** J4
Santa Cruz → *Argentina* **128** G3
Santa Cruz de la Palma
  Canary Is. **48** F2
Santa Cruz de la Palma ✈
  (SPC) *Canary Is.* **48** F2
Santa Cruz de Mudela *Spain* **37** G7
Santa Cruz de Tenerife
  Canary Is. **48** F3
Santa Cruz del Norte *Cuba* **120** B3
Santa Cruz del Retamar
  Spain **36** E6
Santa Cruz del Sur *Cuba* **120** B4
Santa Cruz do Rio Pardo
  Brazil **127** A6
Santa Cruz do Sul *Brazil* **127** B5
Santa Cruz I. *U.S.A.* **111** M7
Santa Cruz Is. *Solomon Is.* **90** C9
Santa Cruz Mts. *Jamaica* **120** a
Santa Domingo, Cay
  Bahamas **120** B4
Sant' Egídio alla Vibrata
  Italy **41** F10
Santa Elena *Argentina* **126** C4
Santa Elena, C. *Costa Rica* **120** D2
Sant' Eufémia, G. di *Italy* **43** D9
Santa Eulària des Riu *Spain* **48** C8
Santa Fé *Argentina* **126** C3

Santa Fé *Spain* **37** H7
Santa Fe *U.S.A.* **109** J11
Santa Fé □ *Argentina* **126** C3
Santa Fé do Sul *Brazil* **125** H8
Santa Filomena *Brazil* **125** E9
Santa Fiora *Italy* **41** F8
Santa Gertrudis *Spain* **48** C7
Santa Giustina *Italy* **41** B9
Santa Inês *Brazil* **125** F11
Santa Inés *Brazil* **37** G5
Santa Inés, I. *Chile* **128** G2
Santa Isabel *Argentina* **126** D2
Santa Isabel do Morro
  Brazil **125** F8
Santa Lucía *Corrientes,
  Argentina* **126** B4
Santa Lucía *San Juan,
  Argentina* **126** C2
Santa Lucía *Spain* **39** H4
Santa Lucía *Uruguay* **126** C4
Santa Lucia Range *U.S.A.* **110** K5
Santa Luzia *C. Verde Is.* **78** b
Santa Margalida *Spain* **48** B10
Santa Margarita *Argentina* **126** D3
Santa Margarita *U.S.A.* **110** K6
Santa Margarita → *U.S.A.* **111** M9
Santa Margarita, I. *Mexico* **118** C2
Santa Margherita *Italy* **42** D1
Santa Margherita Ligure
  Italy **40** D6
Santa María *Argentina* **126** B2
Santa Maria *Azores* **78** a
Santa Maria *Brazil* **127** B5
Santa Maria *C. Verde Is.* **78** b
Santa Maria *Phil.* **61** C4
Santa Maria *U.S.A.* **111** L6
Santa María → *Mexico* **118** A3
Santa María, B. de *Mexico* **118** C3
Santa María, C. de *Portugal* **37** J3
Santa Maria Cápua Vétere
  Italy **43** A7
Santa Maria da Feira
  Portugal **36** E2
Santa Maria da Vitória
  Brazil **125** F10
Santa María del Camí *Spain* **48** B9
Santa Maria di Léuca, C.
  Italy **43** C11
Santa María la Real de
  Nieva *Spain* **36** D6
Santa Marinella *Italy* **41** F8
Santa Marta *Colombia* **124** A4
Santa Marta, Sierra
  Nevada de *Colombia* **124** A4
Santa Marta de Tormes
  Spain **36** E5
Santa Marta Grande, C.
  Brazil **127** B6
Santa Marta Ortigueira,
  Ría de *Spain* **36** B3
Santa Maura = Lefkada
  Greece **46** C2
Santa Monica *U.S.A.* **111** M8
Santa Monica Mts. △
  U.S.A. **111** L8
Santa Olalla *Huelva, Spain* **37** H4
Santa Olalla *Toledo, Spain* **36** E6
Santa Paula *U.S.A.* **111** L7
Santa Pola *Spain* **39** G4
Santa Ponça *Spain* **48** B9
Santa Rosa *La Pampa,
  Argentina* **126** D3
Santa Rosa *San Luis,
  Argentina* **126** C2
Santa Rosa *Brazil* **127** B5
Santa Rosa *Calif., U.S.A.* **110** G4
Santa Rosa *N. Mex., U.S.A.* **109** J11
Santa Rosa and San
  Jacinto Mts. △ *U.S.A.* **111** M10
Santa Rosa de Copán
  Honduras **120** D2
Santa Rosa de Río Primero
  Argentina **126** C3
Santa Rosa del Sara *Bolivia* **124** G6
Santa Rosa I. *Calif., U.S.A.* **111** M6
Santa Rosa I. *Fla., U.S.A.* **117** F11
Santa Rosa Range *U.S.A.* **108** F5
Santa Rosalía *Mexico* **118** B2
Santa Sylvina *Argentina* **126** B3
Santa Tecla = Nueva San
  Salvador *El Salv.* **120** D2
Santa Teresa *Argentina* **126** C3
Santa Teresa *Australia* **94** C1
Santa Teresa *Mexico* **119** B5
Santa Teresa △ *Uruguay* **127** C5
Santa Teresa di Riva *Italy* **43** E8
Santa Teresa Gallura *Italy* **42** A2
Santa Uxía *Spain* **36** C2
Santa Vitória do Palmar
  Brazil **127** C5
Santa Ynez → *U.S.A.* **111** L6
Santa Ynez Mts. *U.S.A.* **111** L6
Santa Ysabel *U.S.A.* **111** M10
Santadi *Italy* **42** C1
Santaella *Spain* **37** H6
Santai *China* **58** B5
Santa Fé *Argentina* **126** C3
Santana *Madeira* **48** D3

Sântana *Romania* **28** D6
Santana, Coxilha de *Brazil* **127** C4
Santana do Livramento
  Brazil **127** C4
Santander *Spain* **36** B7
Santander Jiménez *Mexico* **119** C5
Santanilla, Is. *Honduras* **120** C3
Santanyí *Spain* **48** B10
Santaquin *U.S.A.* **108** G8
Santarcángelo di
  Romagna *Italy* **41** D9
Santarém *Brazil* **125** D8
Santarém *Portugal* **37** F2
Santarém □ *Portugal* **37** F2
Santaren Channel *W. Indies* **120** B4
Santee *U.S.A.* **111** N10
Santee → *U.S.A.* **117** E15
Sant'Éramo in Colle *Italy* **43** B9
Santerno → *Italy* **41** D8
Santhià *Italy* **40** C5
Santi-Quaranta = Sarandë
  Albania **44** G3
Santiago = Río Grande de
  Santiago → *Mexico* **118** C3
Santiago = São Tiago
  C. Verde Is. **78** b
Santiago *Brazil* **127** B5
Santiago *Canary Is.* **48** F2
Santiago *Chile* **126** C1
Santiago *Panama* **120** E3
Santiago *Phil.* **61** C4
Santiago □ *Chile* **126** C1
Santiago → *Peru* **124** D3
Santiago, Punta de *Eq. Guin.* **83** E6
Santiago de Compostela
  Spain **36** C2
Santiago de Cuba *Cuba* **120** C4
Santiago de los Caballeros
  Dom. Rep. **121** C5
Santiago del Estero
  Argentina **126** B3
Santiago del Estero □
  Argentina **126** B3
Santiago do Cacém *Portugal* **37** G2
Santiago Ixcuintla *Mexico* **118** C3
Santiago Jamiltepec *Mexico* **119** D5
Santiago Papasquiaro
  Mexico **118** C3
Santiago Pinotepa
  Nacional *Mexico* **119** D5
Santiaguillo, L. de *Mexico* **118** C4
Santiguila *Mali* **82** C3
Santillana *Spain* **36** B6
Santisteban del Puerto *Spain* **37** G7
Santo Amaro *Brazil* **125** F11
Santo Anastácio *Brazil* **127** A5
Santo André *Brazil* **127** A6
Santo Ângelo *Brazil* **127** B5
Santo Antão *C. Verde Is.* **78** b
Santo António do Içá *Brazil* **124** D5
Santo Antônio do Leverger
  Brazil **125** G7
Santo Domingo *Dom. Rep.* **121** C6
Santo Domingo *Baja Calif.,
  Mexico* **118** A1
Santo Domingo
  Baja Calif. S., Mexico **118** B2
Santo Domingo *Nic.* **120** D3
Santo Domingo de la
  Calzada *Spain* **38** C2
Santo Domingo de los
  Colorados *Ecuador* **124** D3
Santo Domingo Pueblo
  U.S.A. **109** J10
Santo Stéfano di Camastro
  Italy **43** D7
Santo Tirso *Portugal* **36** D2
Santo Tomás *Mexico* **118** A1
Santo Tomás *Peru* **124** F4
Santo Tomé *Argentina* **127** B4
Santo Tomé de Guayana =
  Ciudad Guayana
  Venezuela **124** B6
Santomera *Spain* **39** G3
Santoña *Spain* **36** B7
Santorini *Greece* **47** E7
Santos *Brazil* **127** A6
Santos, Sierra de los *Spain* **37** G5
Santos Dumont *Brazil* **127** A7
Sanur *Indonesia* **63** K18
Sanwer *India* **68** H6
Sanxenxo *Spain* **36** C2
Sanya *China* **64** D7
Sanyuan *China* **56** G5
São Bartolomeu de
  Messines *Portugal* **37** H2
São Bernardo do Campo
  Brazil **127** A6
São Borja *Brazil* **127** B4
São Brás de Alportel *Portugal* **37** H3
São Carlos *Brazil* **127** A6
São Cristóvão *Brazil* **125** F11
São Domingos *Brazil* **125** F9
São Domingos *Guinea-Biss.* **82** C1
São Filipe *C. Verde Is.* **78** b
São Francisco *Brazil* **125** G10

São Francisco → *Brazil* **125** F11
São Francisco do Sul *Brazil* **127** B6
São Gabriel *Brazil* **127** C5
São Gonçalo *Brazil* **127** A7
Sao Hill *Tanzania* **87** D4
São João *Guinea-Biss.* **82** C1
São João da Boa Vista
  Brazil **127** A6
São João da Madeira
  Portugal **36** E2
São João da Pesqueira
  Portugal **36** D3
São João del Rei *Brazil* **127** A7
São João do Araguaia
  Brazil **125** E9
São João do Piauí *Brazil* **125** E10
São Joaquim *Brazil* **127** B6
São Joaquim △ *Brazil* **127** B6
São Jorge *Azores* **78** a
São Jorge, Pta. de *Madeira* **48** D3
São José *Brazil* **127** B5
São José do Norte *Brazil* **127** C5
São José do Rio Prêto *Brazil* **127** A6
São José dos Campos *Brazil* **127** A6
São Leopoldo *Brazil* **127** B5
São Lourenço *Brazil* **127** A6
São Lourenço → *Brazil* **125** G7
São Lourenço, Pta. de
  Madeira **48** D3
São Lourenço do Sul *Brazil* **127** C5
São Luís *Brazil* **125** D10
São Luís Gonzaga *Brazil* **127** B5
São Marcos → *Brazil* **125** G9
São Marcos, B. de *Brazil* **125** D10
São Martinho da Cortiça
  Portugal **36** E2
São Mateus *Brazil* **125** G11
São Mateus do Sul *Brazil* **127** B6
São Miguel *Azores* **78** a
São Miguel do Oeste *Brazil* **127** B5
São Nicolau *C. Verde Is.* **78** b
São Paulo *Brazil* **127** A6
São Paulo □ *Brazil* **127** A6
São Paulo de Olivença
  Brazil **124** D5
São Pedro do Sul *Portugal* **36** E2
São Roque *Madeira* **48** D3
São Roque, C. de *Brazil* **125** E12
São Sebastião, I. de *Brazil* **127** A6
São Sebastião do Paraíso
  Brazil **127** A6
São Teotónio *Portugal* **37** H2
São Tiago *C. Verde Is.* **78** b
São Tomé, C. de *São Tomé & Príncipe* **76** F4
São Tomé, C. de *Brazil* **127** A7
São Tomé & Príncipe ■
  Africa **77** F4
São Vicente *Brazil* **127** A6
São Vicente *C. Verde Is.* **78** b
São Vicente *Madeira* **48** D2
São Vicente, C. de *Portugal* **37** H1
Saona, I. *Dom. Rep.* **121** C6
Saône → *France* **19** G11
Saône-et-Loire □ *France* **19** F11
Saonek *Indonesia* **63** E8
Sapam, Ao *Thailand* **65** a
Sapanca *Turkey* **72** B4
Saparua *Indonesia* **63** E7
Sapele *Nigeria* **83** D6
Sapelo I. *U.S.A.* **117** F14
Sapes *Greece* **45** E9
Şaphane *Turkey* **47** B11
Sapi △ *Zimbabwe* **87** F2
Sapienza *Greece* **46** E3
Sapo △ *Liberia* **82** D3
Sapone *Burkina Faso* **83** C4
Saposoa *Peru* **124** E3
Sapotskiña *Belarus* **30** E10
Sapouy *Burkina Faso* **83** C4
Sapozhok *Russia* **34** D5
Sapphire *Australia* **94** C4
Sappho *U.S.A.* **110** B2
Sapporo *Japan* **54** C10
Sapri *Italy* **43** B8
Sapulpa *U.S.A.* **116** D6
Saqqez *Iran* **73** D12
Sar Dasht
  Āzarbāyjān-e Gharbī, Iran **73** D11
Sar Dasht *Khuzestān, Iran* **71** C6
Sar-e Pol □ *Afghan.* **66** B4
Sar Gachîneh = Yāsūj *Iran* **71** D6
Sar Planina *Macedonia* **44** E4
Sara *Burkina Faso* **82** C4
Sara *Phil.* **61** F5
Šara △ *Serbia* **44** D5
Sara Buri = Saraburi
  Thailand **64** E3
Sarāb *Iran* **73** D12
Sarabadi *Iraq* **70** C5
Saraburi *Thailand* **64** E3
Saradiya *India* **68** J4
Saraféré *Mali* **82** B4
Saragossa = Zaragoza *Spain* **38** D4
Saraguro *Ecuador* **124** D3
Sarahs *Turkmenistan* **71** B9
Sarai Naurang *Pakistan* **68** C4
Saraikela *India* **69** H11

Saraiu Romania 29 F13
Sarajevo Bos.-H. 28 G3
Sarakhs = Sarahs
   Turkmenistan 71 B9
Saran, Gunung Indonesia 62 E4
Saranac Lake U.S.A. 115 B10
Saranac Lakes U.S.A. 115 B10
Saranda Tanzania 86 D3
Sarandë Albania 44 G3
Sarandí del Yi Uruguay 127 C4
Sarandí Grande Uruguay 126 C4
Sarangani B. Phil. 61 J6
Sarangani Is. Phil. 61 J6
Sarangarh India 67 J13
Saransk Russia 34 C7
Sarapul Russia 52 D6
Sarasota U.S.A. 117 H13
Sarata Ukraine 29 D14
Sarata → Ukraine 29 E14
Saratoga Calif., U.S.A. 110 H4
Saratoga Wyo., U.S.A. 108 F10
Saratoga △ U.S.A. 115 D11
Saratoga Springs U.S.A. 115 C11
Saratok Malaysia 62 D4
Saratov Russia 34 E7
Saratov △ Russia 34 E8
Sarāvān Iran 71 E9
Saravane Laos 64 E6
Sarawak □ Malaysia 62 D4
Saray Tekirdağ, Turkey 45 E11
Saray Van, Turkey 73 C11
Saraya Senegal 82 C2
Saraycık Turkey 47 B11
Sarayköy Turkey 47 D10
Saraylar Turkey 45 F11
Sarayönü Turkey 72 C5
Sarbāz Iran 71 E9
Sarbīsheh Iran 71 C8
Sárbogárd Hungary 28 D3
Sarca → Italy 40 C7
Sarcelles France 19 D9
Sarda → India 69 F9
Sardarshahr India 68 E6
Sardegna □ Italy 42 B1
Sardhana India 68 E7
Sardina, Pta. Canary Is. 48 F4
Sardinia = Sardegna □ Italy 42 B1
Sardis Turkey 47 C10
Sārdūīyeh = Dar Mazār Iran 71 D8
Saren Indonesia 63 J18
S'Arenal Spain 48 B9
Sarentino Italy 41 B8
Sarera, G. of Indonesia 90 B6
Saréyamou Mali 82 B4
Sargasso Sea Atl. Oc. 98 G13
Sargodha Pakistan 68 C5
Sarh Chad 79 G9
Sarhala Ivory C. 82 D3
Sārī Iran 71 B7
Sari d'Orcino France 21 F12
Saria Greece 47 F9
Saria India 69 J10
Sariab Pakistan 68 D2
Saribeyler Turkey 47 B9
Sarıgöl Turkey 72 C3
Sarıkamış Turkey 73 B10
Sarıkaya Turkey 72 C6
Sarikei Malaysia 62 D4
Sarıköy Turkey 45 F11
Sarila India 69 G8
Sarina Australia 94 C4
Sariñena Spain 38 D4
Sarita U.S.A. 116 H6
Sariwŏn N. Korea 57 E13
Sarıyar Barajı Turkey 72 B4
Sarıyer Turkey 45 E13
Sarju → India 69 F9
Sark U.K. 15 H5
Sarkad Hungary 28 D6
Sarkari Tala India 68 F4
Şarkışla Turkey 72 C7
Şarköy Turkey 45 F11
Sarlat-la-Canéda France 20 D5
Sărmaşag Romania 28 C7
Sărmaşu Romania 29 D9
Sarmi Indonesia 63 E9
Sarmiento Argentina 128 F3
Sarmizegetusa Romania 28 E7
Särna Sweden 10 C7
Sarnano Italy 41 E10
Sarnen Switz. 25 J4
Sarnia Canada 114 D2
Sarno Italy 43 B7
Sarnthein = Sarentino Italy 41 B8
Särö Sweden 11 G5
Sarolangun Indonesia 62 E2
Saronikos Kolpos Greece 46 D5
Saronno Italy 40 C6
Saros Körfezi Turkey 45 F10
Sárospatak Hungary 28 B6
Sarpsborg Norway 9 G14
Sarqan Kazakhstan 52 E8
Sarracín Spain 36 C7
Sarralbe France 19 D14
Sarre = Saar → Europe 17 E6
Sarre Italy 40 C4
Sarre France 19 D14
Sarre-Union France 19 D14

Sarrebourg France 19 D14
Sarreguemines France 19 C14
Sarria Spain 36 C3
Sarrión Spain 38 E4
Sarro Mali 82 C3
Sarstedt Germany 24 C5
Sartène France 21 G12
Sarthe □ France 18 D7
Sarthe → France 18 E6
Sartilly France 18 D5
Saruhanlı Turkey 47 C9
Sáruna → Pakistan 68 F2
Sárvár Hungary 28 C1
Sarvestān Iran 71 D7
Sarvar India 68 F6
Särvfjället Sweden 10 B7
Sárviz → Hungary 28 D3
Sary-Tash Kyrgyzstan 52 F8
Sarych, Mys Ukraine 33 K7
Saryshaghan Kazakhstan 52 E8
Sarzana Italy 40 D6
Sarzeau France 18 E4
Sasan Gir India 68 J4
Sasaram India 69 G11
Sasebo Japan 55 H4
Saser India 69 B7
Saskatchewan □ Canada 103 C7
Saskatchewan → Canada 103 C8
Saskatoon Canada 103 C7
Saskylakh Russia 53 B12
Saslaya △ Nic. 120 D2
Sasolburg S. Africa 89 D4
Sasovo Russia 34 C5
Sassandra Ivory C. 82 E3
Sassandra → Ivory C. 82 E3
Sássari Italy 42 B1
Sassnitz Germany 24 A9
Sasso Marconi Italy 41 D8
Sassocorvaro Italy 41 E9
Sassoferrato Italy 41 E9
Sasstown Liberia 82 E3
Sassuolo Italy 40 D7
Sástago Spain 38 D4
Sasyk, Ozero Ukraine 29 E14
Sata-Misaki Japan 55 J5
Satadougou Mali 82 C2
Satakunda = Satakunta
   Finland 32 B2
Satakunta Finland 32 B2
Satama-Soukoura Ivory C. 82 D4
Satara India 66 L8
Satara S. Africa 89 C5
Satbarwa India 69 H11
Sätenäs Sweden 11 F6
Säter Sweden 10 D9
Satevó Mexico 118 B3
Satilla → U.S.A. 117 F14
Satmala Hills
   Andhra Pradesh, India 66 K11
Satmala Hills Maharashtra,
   India 66 J9
Satna India 69 G9
Šator Bos.-H. 41 D13
Sátoraljaújhely Hungary 28 B6
Satpura △ India 68 H8
Satpura Ra. India 66 J10
Satrup Germany 24 A5
Satsuna-Shotō Japan 55 K5
Sattahip Thailand 64 F3
Satu Mare Romania 28 C7
Satu Mare □ Romania 28 C8
Satui Indonesia 62 E5
Satun Thailand 65 J3
Satupa'itea Samoa 91 b
Saturnina → Brazil 124 F7
Sauce Argentina 126 C4
Sauceda Mexico 118 B4
Saucillo Mexico 118 B3
Sauda Norway 9 G12
Sauðárkrókur Iceland 8 D4
Saudi Arabia ■ Asia 70 B3
Sauerland Germany 22 C4
Saugeen → Canada 114 B3
Saugerties U.S.A. 115 D11
Saugues France 20 D7
Saugus U.S.A. 111 L8
Saujon France 20 C3
Sauk Centre U.S.A. 112 C6
Sauk Rapids U.S.A. 112 C6
Saulgau Germany 25 G5
Saulieu France 19 E11
Sault France 21 D9
Sault Ste. Marie Canada 104 C3
Sault Ste. Marie U.S.A. 113 B11
Saumlaki Indonesia 63 F8
Saumur France 18 E6
Saunders, C. N.Z. 91 F3
Saunders I. Antarctica 5 B1
Saunders Pt. Australia 93 E4
Sauri Nigeria 83 C6
Saurimo Angola 84 F4
Sausalito U.S.A. 110 H4
Sauveterre-de-Béarn France 20 E3
Sauzé-Vaussais France 20 B4
Savá Honduras 120 C2
Sava Italy 43 B10

Sava → Serbia 28 F5
Savage U.S.A. 108 C11
Savage I. = Niue Pac. Oc. 97 J11
Savage River Australia 95 G4
Savai'i Samoa 91 b
Savalou Benin 83 D5
Savane Mozam. 87 F4
Savanna U.S.A. 112 D8
Savanna-la-Mar Jamaica 120 a
Savannah Ga., U.S.A. 117 E14
Savannah Mo., U.S.A. 112 F6
Savannah Tenn., U.S.A. 117 D10
Savannah → U.S.A. 117 E14
Savannakhet Laos 64 D5
Savant L. Canada 104 B1
Savant Lake Canada 104 B1
Săvârşin Romania 28 D7
Savaştepe Turkey 47 B9
Savé Benin 83 D5
Save → France 20 E5
Save → Mozam. 89 C5
Sāveh Iran 71 C6
Savelugu Ghana 83 D4
Săveni Romania 29 C11
Saverdun France 20 E5
Saverne France 19 D14
Savigliano Italy 40 D4
Savigny-sur-Braye France 18 E7
Sávio → Italy 41 D9
Savnik Montenegro 44 D3
Savoie □ France 21 C10
Savona Italy 40 D5
Savona U.S.A. 114 D7
Savonlinna Finland 32 B5
Savoy = Savoie □ France 21 C10
Şavşat Turkey 73 B10
Sävsjö Sweden 11 G8
Savur Turkey 70 B4
Savusavu Fiji 91 a
Savusavu B. Fiji 91 a
Sawahlunto Indonesia 62 E2
Sawai Indonesia 63 E7
Sawai Madhopur India 68 G7
Sawaleke Fiji 91 a
Sawang Daen Din Thailand 64 D4
Sawankhalok Thailand 64 D2
Sawara Japan 55 G10
Sawatch Range U.S.A. 108 G10
Sawel Mt. U.K. 12 B4
Sawi Thailand 65 G2
Sawla Ghana 82 D4
Sawmills Zimbabwe 87 F2
Sawtooth △ U.S.A. 108 D6
Sawtooth Range U.S.A. 108 D6
Sawu Indonesia 63 F6
Sawu Sea Indonesia 63 F6
Saxby → Australia 94 B3
Saxmundham U.K. 15 E9
Saxony = Sachsen □
   Germany 24 E9
Saxony, Lower =
   Niedersachsen □ Germany 24 C4
Saxton U.S.A. 114 F6
Say Mali 82 C4
Say Niger 83 C5
Saya Nigeria 83 D5
Sayabec Canada 105 C6
Sayaboury Laos 64 C3
Sayán Peru 124 F3
Sayan, Vostochnyy Russia 53 D10
Sayan, Zapadnyy Russia 53 D10
Saydā Lebanon 74 B4
Sayhandulaan = Oldziyt
   Mongolia 56 B5
Sayhūt Yemen 75 D5
Saykhin Kazakhstan 35 F8
Saylac = Zeila Somali Rep. 75 E3
Saynshand =
   Buyant-Uhaa Mongolia 60 B6
Sayre Okla., U.S.A. 116 D5
Sayre Pa., U.S.A. 115 E8
Sayreville U.S.A. 115 F10
Sayula Mexico 118 D4
Sayward Canada 102 C3
Sazanit Albania 44 F3
Sázava → Czech Rep. 26 B7
Sazin Pakistan 69 B5
Sazlika → Bulgaria 45 E9
Scaër France 18 D3
Scafell Pike U.K. 14 C4
Scalea Italy 43 C8
Scalloway U.K. 13 A7
Scalpay U.K. 13 D3
Scandia Canada 102 C6
Scandiano Italy 40 D7
Scandicci Italy 41 E8
Scandinavia Europe 8 E15
Scansano Italy 41 F8
Scapa Flow U.K. 13 C5
Scappoose U.S.A. 110 E4
Scarámia, Capo Italy 43 F7
Scarba U.K. 13 E3
Scarborough Trin. & Tob. 121 D7
Scarborough U.K. 14 C7

Scariff I. Ireland 12 E1
Scarp U.K. 13 C1
Scarpe-Escaut △ France 19 B10
Scebeli, Wabi → Somali Rep. 75 G3
Šćedro Croatia 41 E13
Schaal See Germany 24 B6
Schaalsee △ Germany 24 B6
Schaffhausen Switz. 25 H4
Schagen Neths. 17 B4
Schaghticoke U.S.A. 115 D11
Scharding Austria 26 C6
Scharhörn Germany 24 B4
Scheessel Germany 24 B5
Schefferville =
   Kawawachikamach
   Canada 105 B6
Scheibbs Austria 26 C8
Schelde → Belgium 17 C4
Schell Creek Ra. U.S.A. 108 G6
Schellsburg U.S.A. 114 F6
Schenectady U.S.A. 115 D11
Schenevus U.S.A. 115 D10
Scherfede Germany 24 D5
Schesslitz Germany 25 F7
Schiedam Neths. 17 C4
Schiermonnikoog Neths. 17 A6
Schiltigheim France 19 D14
Schinousa Greece 47 E7
Schio Italy 41 C8
Schiphol, Amsterdam ✈
   (AMS) Neths. 17 B4
Schladming Austria 26 D6
Schlanders = Silandro Italy 40 B7
Schlei → Germany 24 A5
Schleiden Germany 24 E2
Schleswig Germany 24 A5
Schleswig-Holstein □
   Germany 24 A5
Schlüchtern Germany 25 E5
Schmalkalden Germany 24 E6
Schmölln Germany 24 E8
Schneeberg Austria 26 D8
Schneeberg Germany 24 E8
Schneverdingen Germany 24 B5
Schœlcher Martinique 120 c
Schoharie U.S.A. 115 D10
Schoharie Cr. → U.S.A. 115 D10
Scholls U.S.A. 110 E4
Schönberg
   Mecklenburg-Vorpommern,
   Germany 24 B6
Schönberg
   Schleswig-Holstein, Germany 24 A6
Schönbuch △ Germany 25 G5
Schönebeck Germany 24 C7
Schongau Germany 25 H6
Schöningen Germany 24 C6
Schopfheim Germany 25 H3
Schorndorf Germany 25 G5
Schortens Germany 24 B3
Schouten I. Australia 95 G4
Schouten Is. = Supiori
   Indonesia 63 E9
Schouwen Neths. 17 C3
Schramberg Germany 25 G4
Schrankogel Austria 26 D4
Schreiber Canada 104 C2
Schrems Austria 26 C8
Schrobenhausen Germany 25 G7
Schroffenstein Namibia 88 D2
Schroon Lake U.S.A. 115 C11
Schruns Austria 26 D2
Schuler Canada 103 C6
Schumacher Canada 104 C3
Schurz U.S.A. 108 G4
Schuyler U.S.A. 112 E5
Schuylerville U.S.A. 115 C11
Schuylkill → U.S.A. 115 G9
Schuylkill Haven U.S.A. 115 F8
Schwabach Germany 25 F7
Schwaben □ Germany 25 G6
Schwäbisch-Fränkischer
   Wald △ Germany 25 G5
Schwäbisch Gmünd
   Germany 25 G5
Schwäbisch Hall Germany 25 F5
Schwäbische Alb Germany 25 G5
Schwabmünchen Germany 25 G6
Schwalmstadt Germany 24 E5
Schwandorf Germany 25 F8
Schwaner, Pegunungan
   Indonesia 62 E4
Schwanewede Germany 24 B4
Schwarmstedt Germany 24 C5
Schwarze Elster → Germany 24 D8
Schwarzenberg Germany 24 E8
Schwarzrand Namibia 88 D2
Schwarzwald Germany 25 G4
Schwaz Austria 26 D4
Schwechat Austria 27 C9
Schwechat, Wien ✈ (VIE)
   Austria 27 C9
Schwedt Germany 24 B10
Schweinfurt Germany 25 E6
Schweiz = Switzerland ■
   Europe 25 J4

Schweizer-Reneke S. Africa 88 D4
Schwenningen =
   Villingen-
   Schwenningen Germany 25 G4
Schwerin Germany 24 B7
Schweriner See Germany 24 B7
Schwetzingen Germany 25 F4
Schwyz Switz. 25 H4
Schwyz □ Switz. 25 H4
Sciacca Italy 42 E6
Scicli Italy 43 F7
Sciliar △ Italy 41 B8
Scilla Italy 43 D8
Scilly, Isles of U.K. 15 H1
Ścinawa Poland 31 G3
Scione Greece 44 G7
Scioto → U.S.A. 113 F12
Scituate U.S.A. 115 D14
Scobey U.S.A. 108 B11
Scone Australia 95 E5
Scone U.K. 13 E5
Scordia Italy 43 E7
Scoresbysund =
   Ittoqqortoormiit Greenland 4 B6
Scornicesti Romania 29 F9
Scotia Calif., U.S.A. 108 F1
Scotia N.Y., U.S.A. 115 D11
Scotia Sea Antarctica 5 B18
Scotland Canada 114 C4
Scotland □ U.K. 13 E5
Scott Antarctica 5 D11
Scott, C. Australia 92 B4
Scott City U.S.A. 112 F3
Scott Glacier Antarctica 5 C8
Scott I. Antarctica 5 C11
Scott Is. Canada 102 C3
Scott L. Canada 103 B7
Scott Reef Australia 92 B3
Scottburgh S. Africa 89 E5
Scottdale U.S.A. 114 F5
Scottish Borders □ U.K. 13 F6
Scotts Valley U.S.A. 110 H4
Scottsbluff U.S.A. 112 E2
Scottsboro U.S.A. 117 D11
Scottsburg U.S.A. 113 F11
Scottsdale Australia 95 G4
Scottsdale U.S.A. 109 K8
Scottsville Ky., U.S.A. 112 G10
Scottsville N.Y., U.S.A. 114 C7
Scottville U.S.A. 112 D10
Scranton U.S.A. 115 E9
Scugog, L. Canada 114 B6
Scunthorpe U.K. 14 D7
Scuol Schuls Switz. 25 J6
Scutari = Shkodër Albania 44 D3
Scutari = Üsküdar Turkey 45 F13
Sea Is. U.S.A. 117 F14
Seabrook, L. Australia 93 F2
Seaford U.K. 15 G8
Seaford U.S.A. 113 F16
Seaforth Australia 94 J6
Seaforth Canada 114 C3
Seaforth, L. U.K. 13 D2
Seagraves U.S.A. 116 E3
Seaham U.K. 14 C6
Seal → Canada 103 B10
Seal L. Canada 105 B7
Sealy U.S.A. 116 G6
Searchlight U.S.A. 111 K12
Searcy U.S.A. 116 D9
Searles L. U.S.A. 111 K9
Seascale U.K. 14 C4
Seaside Calif., U.S.A. 110 J5
Seaside Oreg., U.S.A. 110 E3
Seaspray Australia 95 F4
Seattle U.S.A. 110 C4
Seattle-Tacoma Int. ✈
   (SEA) U.S.A. 110 C4
Seaview Ra. Australia 94 B4
Sebago L. U.S.A. 115 C14
Sebago Lake U.S.A. 115 C14
Sebastián Vizcaíno, B.
   Mexico 118 B2
Sebastopol = Sevastopol
   Ukraine 33 K7
Sebastopol U.S.A. 110 G4
Sebba Burkina Faso 83 C5
Sebderat Eritrea 81 D4
Sébékoro Mali 82 C3
Seben Turkey 72 B4
Şebeş Romania 29 E8
Sebeşului, Munţii Romania 29 E8
Sebewaing U.S.A. 113 D12
Sebha = Sabhā Libya 79 C8
Sébi Mali 82 B4
Şebinkarahisar Turkey 73 B8
Şebiş Romania 28 D7
Sebnitz Germany 24 E10
Sebring Fla., U.S.A. 117 H14
Sebring Ohio, U.S.A. 114 F3
Sebringville Canada 114 C3
Sebta = Ceuta N. Afr. 78 A4
Sebuku Indonesia 62 E5
Sebuku, Teluk Malaysia 62 D5
Sečanj Serbia 28 E5

Secchia → Italy 40 C8
Sechelt Canada 102 D4
Sechura, Desierto de Peru 124 E2
Seclin France 19 B10
Secondigny France 18 F6
Sečovce Slovak Rep. 27 C14
Secretary I. N.Z. 91 F1
Secunderabad India 66 L11
Security U.S.A. 108 G11
Sedalia U.S.A. 112 F7
Sedan France 19 C11
Sedan U.S.A. 112 G5
Sedano Spain 36 C7
Sedbergh U.K. 14 C5
Seddon N.Z. 91 D5
Seddonville N.Z. 91 D4
Sedé Boqér Israel 74 E3
Sedeh Fārs, Iran 71 D7
Sedeh Khorāsān, Iran 71 C8
Séderon France 21 D9
Sederot Israel 74 D3
Sédhiou Senegal 82 C1
Sedico Italy 41 B9
Sedley Canada 103 C8
Sedona U.S.A. 109 J8
Sedova, Pik Russia 52 B6
Sedro-Woolley U.S.A. 110 B4
Šeduva Lithuania 30 C10
Sędziszów Poland 31 H7
Sędziszów Małopolski Poland 31 H8
Seebad Ahlbeck Germany 24 B10
Seefeld in Tirol Austria 26 D4
Seehausen Germany 24 C7
Seeheim Namibia 88 D2
Seeheim-Jugenheim
   Germany 25 F4
Seeis Namibia 88 C2
Seekoei → S. Africa 88 E4
Seeley's Bay Canada 115 B8
Seelow Germany 24 C10
Sées France 18 D7
Seesen Germany 24 D6
Seevetal Germany 24 B6
Seewinkel = Neusiedler
   See-Seewinkel △ Austria 27 D9
Sefadu S. Leone 82 D2
Seferihisar Turkey 47 C8
Séfeto Mali 82 C3
Sefwi Bekwai Ghana 82 D4
Segamat Malaysia 65 L4
Şegarcea Romania 29 F8
Ségbana Benin 83 C5
Segbwema S. Leone 82 D2
Segesta Italy 42 E5
Seget Indonesia 63 E8
Segonzac France 20 C3
Segorbe Spain 38 F4
Ségou Mali 82 C3
Ségou □ Mali 82 C3
Segovia = Coco →
   Cent. Amer. 120 D3
Segovia Spain 36 E6
Segovia □ Spain 36 E6
Segré France 18 E6
Segre → Spain 38 D5
Séguéla Ivory C. 82 D3
Séguénéga Burkina Faso 83 C4
Seguin U.S.A. 116 G6
Segundo → Argentina 126 C3
Segura → Spain 39 G4
Segura, Sierra de Spain 39 G2
Seh Konj, Küh-e Iran 71 D8
Seh Qal'eh Iran 71 C9
Sehitwa Botswana 88 C3
Sehlabathebe △ Lesotho 89 D4
Sehore India 68 H7
Sehwan Pakistan 68 F2
Şeica Mare Romania 29 D9
Seikan Tunnel Japan 54 D10
Seil U.K. 13 E3
Seiland Norway 8 A20
Seilhac France 20 C5
Seiling U.S.A. 116 C5
Seille → Moselle, France 19 C13
Seille → Saône-et-Loire,
   France 19 F11
Sein, Î. de France 18 D2
Seinäjoki Finland 8 E20
Seine → France 18 C7
Seine, B. de la France 18 C6
Seine-et-Marne □ France 19 D10
Seine-Maritime □ France 18 C7
Seine-St-Denis □ France 19 D9
Seini Russia 32 D5
Seirijai Lithuania 30 D10
Seistan = Sīstān Asia 71 D9
Seistan, Daryācheh-ye =
   Sīstān, Daryācheh-ye
   Iran 71 D9
Sejerø Denmark 11 J5
Sejerø Bugt Denmark 11 J5
Sejny Poland 30 D10
Seka Ethiopia 81 F4
Sekayu Indonesia 62 E2
Seke Tanzania 86 C3
Sekenke Tanzania 86 C3

Seki *Turkey* **47** E11
Sekondi-Takoradi *Ghana* **82** E4
Sekota *Ethiopia* **81** E4
Seksna *Russia* **32** C10
Sekudai *Malaysia* **65** d
Sekuma *Botswana* **88** C3
Selah *U.S.A.* **108** C3
Selama *Malaysia* **65** K3
Selárgius *Italy* **42** C2
Selaru *Indonesia* **63** F8
Selatan, Selat *Malaysia* **65** c
Selb *Germany* **25** E8
Selby *U.K.* **14** D6
Selby *U.S.A.* **112** C3
Selca *Croatia* **41** E13
Selçuk *Turkey* **47** D9
Selden *U.S.A.* **112** F3
Sele → *Italy* **43** B7
Selebi-Pikwe *Botswana* **89** C4
Selemdzha → *Russia* **53** D13
Selendi *Manisa, Turkey* **47** C10
Selendi *Manisa, Turkey* **47** C9
Selenga = Selenge
  Mörön → *Asia* **60** A5
Selenge Mörön → *Asia* **60** A5
Selenicë *Albania* **44** F3
Selenter See *Germany* **24** A6
Sélestat *France* **19** D14
Seletan, Tanjung *Indonesia* **62** E4
Selevac *Serbia* **44** B4
Sélibabi *Mauritania* **82** B2
Seliger, Ozero *Russia* **32** D7
Seligman *U.S.A.* **109** J7
Şelîmă *Turkey* **73** B10
Selîma, El Wâhât el *Sudan* **80** C2
Selimiye *Turkey* **47** D9
Selinda Spillway →
  Botswana **88** B3
Selinsgrove *U.S.A.* **114** F8
Selizharovo *Russia* **32** D7
Selkirk *Canada* **103** C9
Selkirk *U.K.* **13** F6
Selkirk I. = Horse I. *Canada* **103** C9
Selkirk Mts. *Canada* **100** D8
Sellafield *U.K.* **14** C4
Sellama *Sudan* **81** E2
Sellia *Greece* **49** D6
Sellières *France* **19** F12
Sells *U.S.A.* **109** L8
Sellye *Hungary* **28** E2
Selma *Ala., U.S.A.* **117** E11
Selma *Calif., U.S.A.* **110** J7
Selma *N.C., U.S.A.* **117** D15
Selmer *U.S.A.* **117** D10
Selongey *France* **19** E12
Selous ○ *Tanzania* **87** D4
Selowandoma Falls
  Zimbabwe **87** G3
Selpele *Indonesia* **63** E8
Selsey Bill *U.K.* **15** G7
Seltso *Russia* **32** F8
Seltz *France* **19** D15
Selu *Indonesia* **63** F8
Sélune → *France* **18** D5
Selva = La Selva del Camp
  Spain **38** D6
Selva *Argentina* **126** B3
Selva Lancandona =
  Montes Azules ○ *Mexico* **119** D6
Selvas *Brazil* **124** E5
Selwyn L. *Canada* **103** B8
Selwyn Mts. *Canada* **100** C6
Selwyn Ra. *Australia* **94** C3
Selyatyn *Ukraine* **29** C10
Seman → *Albania* **44** F3
Semarang *Indonesia* **63** G14
Sembabule *Uganda* **86** C3
Sembawang *Singapore* **65** d
Sembung *Indonesia* **63** J18
Şemdinli *Turkey* **73** D11
Sémé *Senegal* **82** B2
Semeih *Sudan* **81** E3
Semenanjung
  Blambangan *Indonesia* **63** K17
Semenov *Russia* **34** B7
Semenovka *Chernihiv,*
  Ukraine **33** F7
Semenovka *Kremenchuk,*
  Ukraine **33** H7
Semeru *Indonesia* **63** H15
Semey *Kazakhstan* **52** D8
Semikarakorskiy *Russia* **35** G5
Semiluki *Russia* **33** G10
Seminoe Res. *U.S.A.* **108** G10
Seminole *Okla., U.S.A.* **116** D6
Seminole *Tex., U.S.A.* **116** E3
Seminole Draw → *U.S.A.* **116** E3
Semipalatinsk = Semey
  Kazakhstan **52** D9
Semirara Is. *Phil.* **61** F4
Semitau *Indonesia* **62** D4
Semiyarka *Kazakhstan* **52** D8
Semiyarskoye =
  Semiyarka *Kazakhstan* **52** D8
Semmering P. *Austria* **26** D8
Semnān *Iran* **71** C7
Semnān □ *Iran* **71** C7

Semporna *Malaysia* **63** D5
Semuda *Indonesia* **62** E4
Semur-en-Auxois *France* **19** E11
Sen → *Cambodia* **64** F5
Senā *Iran* **71** D6
Sena *Mozam.* **87** F4
Sena Madureira *Brazil* **124** E5
Senador Pompeu *Brazil* **125** E11
Senaki *Georgia* **35** J6
Senanga *Zambia* **85** H4
Senatobia *U.S.A.* **117** D10
Sencelles *Spain* **48** B9
Sendafa *Ethiopia* **81** F4
Sendai *Kagoshima, Japan* **55** J5
Sendai *Miyagi, Japan* **54** E10
Sendai-Wan *Japan* **54** E10
Senden *Bayern, Germany* **25** G6
Senden *Nordrhein-Westfalen,*
  Germany **24** D3
Sendhwa *India* **68** J6
Sene → *Ghana* **83** D4
Senec *Slovak Rep.* **27** C10
Seneca *U.S.A.* **117** D13
Seneca Falls *U.S.A.* **115** D8
Seneca L. *U.S.A.* **114** D8
Senecaville L. *U.S.A.* **114** G3
Senegal ■ *W. Afr.* **82** C2
Sénégal → *W. Afr.* **82** C2
Senegambia *Africa* **76** E2
Senekal *S. Africa* **89** D4
Senftenberg *Germany* **24** D10
Senga Hill *Zambia* **87** D3
Senge Khambab =
  Indus → *Pakistan* **68** G2
Sengiley *Russia* **34** D9
Sengua → *Zimbabwe* **87** F2
Senhor-do-Bonfim *Brazil* **125** F10
Senica *Slovak Rep.* **27** C10
Senigállia *Italy* **41** E10
Senio → *Italy* **41** D9
Senirkent *Turkey* **47** C12
Senise *Italy* **43** B9
Senj *Croatia* **41** D11
Senja *Norway* **8** B17
Senkaku-Shotō *E. China Sea* **55** M1
Senkuang *Indonesia* **65** d
Senlis *France* **19** C10
Senmonorom *Cambodia* **64** F6
Sennâr *Sudan* **81** E3
Sennâr □ *Sudan* **81** E3
Senneterre *Canada* **104** C4
Senno *Belarus* **32** E5
Sénnori *Italy* **42** B1
Seno *Laos* **64** D5
Senonches *France* **18** D8
Senorbì *Italy* **42** C2
Senožeče *Slovenia* **41** C11
Sens *France* **19** D10
Senta *Serbia* **28** E5
Sentani *Indonesia* **63** E10
Sentery = Lubao
  Dem. Rep. of the Congo **86** D2
Sentinel *U.S.A.* **109** K7
Šentjur *Slovenia* **41** B12
Sentosa *Singapore* **65** d
Senya Beraku *Ghana* **83** D4
Seo de Urgel = La Seu
  d'Urgell *Spain* **38** C6
Seogwipo *S. Korea* **57** H14
Seohara *India* **69** E8
Seonath → *India* **69** J10
Seondha *India* **69** F8
Seongnam *S. Korea* **57** F14
Seoni *India* **69** H8
Seoni Malwa *India* **68** H8
Seonsan *S. Korea* **57** F15
Seosan *S. Korea* **57** F14
Seoul *S. Korea* **57** F14
Sepīdān *Iran* **71** D7
Sep'o *N. Korea* **57** E14
Sępólno Krajeńskie *Poland* **30** E4
Sepone *Laos* **64** D6
Sępopol *Poland* **30** D8
Sept-Îles *Canada* **105** B6
Septemvri *Bulgaria* **45** D8
Sepúlveda *Spain* **36** D7
Sequeros *Spain* **36** E4
Sequim *U.S.A.* **110** B3
Sequoia △ *U.S.A.* **110** J8
Serafimovich *Russia* **34** F6
Seraing *Belgium* **17** D5
Serakhis → *Cyprus* **49** D11
Seram *Indonesia* **63** E7
Seram Sea *Indonesia* **63** E7
Seranantsara *Madag.* **89** B8
Serang *Indonesia* **63** G12
Serangoon *Singapore* **65** d
Serasan *Indonesia* **62** D3
Seravezza *Italy* **40** E7
Şerbettar *Turkey* **45** E10
Serbia □ *Serbia* **44** C5
Serbia ■ *Europe* **44** C4
Şercaia *Romania* **29** E10
Serdar *Turkmenistan* **71** B8
Serdo *Ethiopia* **81** E5
Serdobsk *Russia* **34** D7

Sered' *Slovak Rep.* **27** C10
Seredka *Russia* **32** C5
Seredkye *Ukraine* **28** B7
Seremban *Malaysia* **65** L3
Serengeti △ *Tanzania* **86** C4
Serengeti Plain *Tanzania* **86** C4
Serenje *Zambia* **87** E3
Seret → *Ukraine* **29** B10
Sereth = Siret → *Romania* **29** E12
Sergach *Russia* **34** C7
Sergen *Turkey* **45** E11
Sergino *Russia* **52** C7
Sergipe □ *Brazil* **125** F11
Sergiyev Posad *Russia* **32** D10
Serhetabat *Turkmenistan* **71** C9
Seria *Brunei* **62** D4
Serian *Malaysia* **62** D4
Seriate *Italy* **40** C6
Seribu, Kepulauan *Indonesia* **62** F3
Sericho *Kenya* **86** B4
Sérifontaine *France* **19** C8
Serifos *Greece* **46** D6
Sérignan *France* **20** E7
Sérigny → *Canada* **105** A6
Serik *Turkey* **72** D4
Seringapatam Reef *Australia* **92** B3
Serinhisar *Turkey* **47** D11
Seririt *Indonesia* **63** J17
Sermaize-les-Bains *France* **19** D11
Sermata *Indonesia* **63** F7
Sermersuaq *Greenland* **4** B4
Sérmide *Italy* **41** D8
Sernovodsk *Russia* **34** D10
Sernur *Russia* **34** B9
Serón *Spain* **39** H2
Seròs *Spain* **38** D5
Serov *Russia* **52** D7
Serowe *Botswana* **88** C4
Serpa *Portugal* **37** H3
Serpeddì, Punta *Italy* **42** C2
Serpentara *Italy* **42** C2
Serpentine Lakes *Australia* **93** E4
Serpent's Mouth = Sierpe,
  Bocas de la *Venezuela* **125** L15
Serpis → *Spain* **39** G4
Serpneve *Ukraine* **29** D14
Serpukhov *Russia* **32** E9
Serra da Estrela → *Portugal* **36** E3
Serra de Outes *Spain* **36** C2
Serra do Navio *Brazil* **125** C8
Serra San Bruno *Italy* **43** D9
Serradilla *Spain* **36** F4
Serramanna *Italy* **42** C1
Serra d'Aire e
  Candeeiros △ *Portugal* **37** F2
Serravalle Scrívia *Italy* **40** D5
Serre → *France* **21** D9
Serres *France* **21** D9
Serres *Greece* **44** E7
Serres □ *Greece* **44** E7
Serrezuela *Argentina* **126** C2
Serrinha *Brazil* **125** F11
Sersale *Italy* **43** C9
Sertã *Portugal* **36** F2
Sertanópolis *Brazil* **127** A5
Sêrtar *China* **58** A3
Serua *Indonesia* **63** F8
Serui *Indonesia* **63** E9
Serule *Botswana* **88** C4
Servia *Greece* **44** F6
Serzedelo *Portugal* **36** D2
Ses Salines *Spain* **48** B10
Sese Is. *Uganda* **86** C3
Sesepe *Indonesia* **63** E7
Sesfontein *Namibia* **88** B1
Sesheke *Zambia* **88** B3
Sésia → *Italy* **40** C5
Sesimbra *Portugal* **37** G1
Sessa Aurunca *Italy* **42** A6
S'Espalmador *Spain* **48** C7
S'Espardell *Spain* **48** C7
S'Estanyol *Spain* **48** B9
Sestao *Spain* **38** B2
Sesto Calende *Italy* **40** C5
Sesto San Giovanni *Italy* **40** C6
Sestri Levante *Italy* **40** D6
Sestriere *Italy* **40** D3
Sestroretsk *Russia* **32** B6
Sestrunj *Croatia* **41** D11
Sestu *Italy* **42** C2
Setana *Japan* **54** C9
Sète *France* **20** E7
Sete Lagôas *Brazil* **125** G10
Sétif *Algeria* **78** A7
Seto *Japan* **55** G8
Setonaikai *Japan* **55** G6
Setonaikai △ *Japan* **55** G6
Settat *Morocco* **78** B4
Séttimo Torinese *Italy* **40** C4
Setting L. *Canada* **103** C9
Settle *U.K.* **14** C5
Settlement, The *Br. Virgin Is.* **121** e

Settlers *S. Africa* **89** C4
Setúbal *Portugal* **37** G2
Setúbal □ *Portugal* **37** G2
Setúbal, B. de *Portugal* **37** G2
Seugne → *France* **20** C3
Seul, Lac *Canada* **104** B1
Seurre *France* **19** F12
Sevan *Armenia* **35** K7
Sevan, Ozero = Sevana
  Lich *Armenia* **35** K7
Sevana Lich *Armenia* **35** K7
Sevastopol *Ukraine* **33** K7
Seven Sisters *Canada* **102** C3
Sever → *Spain* **37** F3
Sévérac-le-Château *France* **20** D7
Severn → *Canada* **104** A2
Severn → *U.K.* **15** F5
Severn L. *Canada* **104** B1
Severnaya Zemlya *Russia* **53** B11
Severo-Kurilsk *Russia* **53** D16
Severo-Yeniseyskiy *Russia* **53** C10
Severo-Zapadnyy □ *Russia* **52** C4
Severočeský □ *Czech Rep.* **26** A7
Severodonetsk =
  Syeverodonetsk *Ukraine* **33** H10
Severodvinsk *Russia* **52** C4
Severomoravský □
  Czech Rep. **27** B10
Severomorsk *Russia* **8** B25
Severouralsk *Russia* **52** C7
Sevier → *U.S.A.* **108** G7
Sevier Desert *U.S.A.* **108** G7
Sevier L. *U.S.A.* **108** G7
Sevilla *Spain* **37** H5
Sevilla □ *Spain* **37** H5
Seville = Sevilla *Spain* **37** H5
Sevlievo *Bulgaria* **45** C9
Sevnica *Slovenia* **41** B12
Sèvre-Nantaise → *France* **18** E5
Sèvre-Niortaise → *France* **20** B3
Sevsk *Russia* **33** F8
Sewa → *S. Leone* **82** D2
Sewani *India* **68** E6
Seward *Alaska, U.S.A.* **100** C5
Seward *Nebr., U.S.A.* **112** E5
Seward *Pa., U.S.A.* **114** F5
Seward Peninsula *U.S.A.* **106** a
Sewell *Chile* **126** C1
Sewer *Indonesia* **63** F8
Sewickley *U.S.A.* **114** F4
Sexsmith *Canada* **102** B5
Seychelles ■ *Ind. Oc.* **85** b
Seyðisfjörður *Iceland* **8** D7
Seydişehir *Turkey* **72** D4
Seydvān *Iran* **73** C11
Seyhan → *Turkey* **72** D6
Seyhan Baraji *Turkey* **72** D6
Seyitgazi *Turkey* **47** B12
Seyitömer *Turkey* **47** B11
Seym → *Ukraine* **33** G7
Seymen *Turkey* **45** E11
Seymour *Australia* **95** F4
Seymour *S. Africa* **89** E4
Seymour *Conn., U.S.A.* **115** E11
Seymour *Ind., U.S.A.* **113** F11
Seymour *Tex., U.S.A.* **116** E5
Seyne *France* **21** D10
Seyssel *France* **21** C9
Sežana *Slovenia* **41** C10
Sézanne *France* **19** D10
Sezze *Italy* **42** A6
Sfântu Gheorghe *Covasna,*
  Romania **29** E10
Sfântu Gheorghe *Tulcea,*
  Romania **29** F14
Sfântu Gheorghe,
  Brațul → *Romania* **29** F14
Sfax *Tunisia* **79** B8
Sha Xi → *China* **59** D12
Sha Xian *China* **59** D11
Shaanxi □ *China* **56** G5
Shaba = Katanga □
  Dem. Rep. of the Congo **86** D2
Shaba ○ *Kenya* **86** B4
Shaballe = Scebeli,
  Wabi → *Somali Rep.* **75** G3
Shabla *Bulgaria* **45** C12
Shabogamo L. *Canada* **105** B6
Shabunda
  Dem. Rep. of the Congo **86** C2
Shache *China* **60** C2
Shackleton Fracture Zone
  S. Ocean **5** B18
Shackleton Ice Shelf
  Antarctica **5** C8
Shackleton Inlet *Antarctica* **5** E11
Shādegān *Iran* **71** D6
Shadi *China* **59** D10
Shadi *India* **69** C7
Shadrinsk *Russia* **52** D7
Shadyside *U.S.A.* **114** G4
Shaffa *Nigeria* **83** C7
Shafter *U.S.A.* **111** K7
Shaftesbury *U.K.* **15** F5
Shagamu *Nigeria* **83** D5
Shagram *Pakistan* **69** A5
Shah Alizai *Pakistan* **68** E2
Shah Bunder *Pakistan* **68** G2

Shahabad *Punjab, India* **68** D7
Shahabad *Raj., India* **68** G7
Shahabad *Ut. P., India* **69** F8
Shahadpur *Pakistan* **68** G3
Shahbā *Syria* **74** C5
Shahdād *Iran* **71** D8
Shahdād, Namakzār-e *Iran* **71** D8
Shahdadkot *Pakistan* **68** F2
Shahdol *India* **69** H9
Shahe *China* **56** F8
Shahganj *India* **69** F10
Shahgarh *India* **68** F3
Shahjahanpur *India* **69** F8
Shahpur *India* **68** H7
Shahpur *Baluchistan, Pakistan* **68** E3
Shahpur *Punjab, Pakistan* **68** C5
Shahpur Chakar *Pakistan* **68** F3
Shahpura *Mad. P., India* **69** H9
Shahpura *Raj., India* **68** G6
Shahr-e Bābak *Iran* **71** D7
Shahr-e Kord *Iran* **71** C6
Shāhrakht *Iran* **71** C9
Shahrig *Pakistan* **68** D2
Shahukou *China* **56** D7
Shaikhabad *Afghan.* **68** B3
Shajapur *India* **68** H7
Shakargarh *Pakistan* **68** C6
Shakawe *Botswana* **88** B3
Shaker Heights *U.S.A.* **114** E3
Shakhty *Russia* **35** G5
Shakhunya *Russia* **34** B8
Shaki *Nigeria* **83** D5
Shāksam Valley *Asia* **69** A7
Shala, L. *Ethiopia* **81** F4
Shali *Russia* **35** J7
Shallow Lake *Canada* **114** B3
Shalqar *Kazakhstan* **52** E6
Shalskiy *Russia* **32** B9
Shaluli Shan *China* **58** B2
Shām *Iran* **71** E8
Shām, Bādiyat ash *Asia* **70** C3
Shamāl Bahr el Ghazal □
  Sudan **81** F3
Shamāl Dārfūr □ *Sudan* **81** E2
Shamāl Kordofān □ *Sudan* **81** E3
Shamāl Sīnî □ *Egypt* **74** E2
Shamattawa *U.S.A.* **104** A1
Shamattawa → *Canada* **104** A2
Shambe *Sudan* **81** F3
Shambu *Ethiopia* **81** F4
Shamil *Iran* **71** E8
Shamkhor = Şämkir
  Azerbaijan **35** K8
Shāmkūh *Iran* **71** C8
Shamli *India* **68** E7
Shammar, Jabal *Si. Arabia* **70** E4
Shamo = Gobi *Asia* **56** C6
Shamo, L. *Ethiopia* **81** F4
Shamokin *U.S.A.* **115** F8
Shamrock *U.S.A.* **116** D4
Shamva *Zimbabwe* **87** F3
Shan □ *Burma* **67** J21
Shan Xian *China* **56** G9
Shanan → *Ethiopia* **81** F5
Shanchengzhen *China* **57** C13
Shāndak *Iran* **71** D9
Shandon *U.S.A.* **110** K6
Shandong □ *China* **57** G10
Shandong Bandao *China* **57** F11
Shang Xian = Shangzhou
  China **56** H5
Shanga *Nigeria* **78** F6
Shangalowe
  Dem. Rep. of the Congo **87** E2
Shangani *Zimbabwe* **89** B4
Shangani → *Zimbabwe* **87** F2
Shangbancheng *China* **57** D10
Shangcheng *China* **59** B10
Shangchuan Dao *China* **59** G9
Shangdu *China* **56** D7
Shanggao *China* **59** C10
Shanghai *China* **59** B13
Shanghai Shi □ *China* **59** B13
Shanghang *China* **59** E11
Shanghe *China* **57** F9
Shanglin *China* **58** F7
Shangnan *China* **56** H6
Shangqiu *China* **56** G8
Shangrao *China* **59** C11
Shangshui *China* **56** C6
Shangsi *China* **58** F6
Shangyou *China* **59** E10
Shangyu *China* **59** B13
Shangzhi *China* **57** B14
Shangzhou *China* **56** H5
Shanhetun *China* **57** B14
Shani *Nigeria* **83** C7
Shanklin *U.K.* **15** G6
Shannon *N.Z.* **91** D5
Shannon → *Ireland* **12** D2
Shannon ✕ (SNN) *Ireland* **12** D3
Shannon, Mouth of the
  Ireland **12** D2
Shannon △ *Australia* **93** F2
Shannonbridge *Ireland* **12** C3

Shansi = Shanxi □ *China* **56** F7
Shantar, Ostrov Bolshoy
  Russia **53** D14
Shantipur *India* **69** H13
Shantou *China* **59** F11
Shantung = Shandong □
  China **57** G10
Shanwei *China* **59** F10
Shanxi □ *China* **56** F7
Shanyang *China* **56** H5
Shanyin *China* **56** E7
Shaodong *China* **59** D8
Shaoguan *China* **59** E9
Shaoshan *China* **59** D9
Shaowu *China* **59** D11
Shaoxing *China* **59** C13
Shaoyang *Hunan, China* **59** D8
Shaoyang *Hunan, China* **59** D8
Shap *U.K.* **14** C5
Shapinsay *U.K.* **13** B6
Shaqq el Gi'eifer → *Sudan* **81** D2
Shaqra' *Si. Arabia* **70** E5
Shaqrā' *Yemen* **75** E4
Sharafa *Sudan* **81** E2
Sharafkhāneh *Iran* **73** C11
Sharashova *Belarus* **31** F11
Sharbot Lake *Canada* **115** B8
Shari *Japan* **54** C12
Sharjah = Ash Shāriqah
  U.A.E. **71** E7
Shark B. *Australia* **93** E1
Shark Bay △ *Australia* **93** E1
Sharon *Mass., U.S.A.* **115** D13
Sharon *Pa., U.S.A.* **114** E4
Sharon Springs *Kans.,*
  U.S.A. **112** F3
Sharon Springs *N.Y., U.S.A.*
  115 D10
Sharp Pt. *Australia* **94** A3
Sharpe L. *Canada* **104** B1
Sharpsville *U.S.A.* **114** E4
Sharq el Istiwa'iya □ *Sudan* **81** G3
Sharqi, Al Jabal ash *Lebanon* **74** B5
Sharya *Russia* **34** A7
Shasha *Ethiopia* **81** F4
Shashemene *Ethiopia* **81** F4
Shashi *Botswana* **89** C4
Shashi *China* **59** B9
Shashi → *Africa* **87** G2
Shasta, Mt. *U.S.A.* **108** F2
Shasta L. *U.S.A.* **108** F2
Shatawi *Sudan* **81** F3
Shatsk *Russia* **34** C5
Shatsk *Ukraine* **31** G10
Shatskiy Rise *Pac. Oc.* **96** D7
Shatskyi △ *Ukraine* **31** G10
Shatt al Arab *Asia* **71** D6
Shatura *Russia* **32** E10
Shaumyani = Shulaveri
  Georgia **35** K7
Shaunavon *Canada* **103** D7
Shaver L. *U.S.A.* **110** H7
Shaw → *Australia* **92** D2
Shaw I. *Australia* **94** J7
Shawanaga *Canada* **114** A4
Shawangunk Mts. *U.S.A.* **115** E10
Shawano *U.S.A.* **112** C9
Shawinigan *Canada* **104** C5
Shawmari, J. ash *Jordan* **74** E5
Shawnee *U.S.A.* **116** D6
Shay Gap *Australia* **92** D3
Shayang *China* **59** B9
Shaybārā *Si. Arabia* **70** E3
Shayib el Banat, Gebel *Egypt* **80** B3
Shaykh, J. ash *Lebanon* **74** B4
Shaykh Miskīn *Syria* **74** C5
Shaykh Sa'īd *Iraq* **73** F12
Shchekino *Russia* **32** E9
Shchigry *Russia* **33** G9
Shchors *Ukraine* **33** G6
Shchūchīnsk *Kazakhstan* **52** D8
She Xian *Anhui, China* **59** C12
She Xian *Hebei, China* **56** F7
Shebekino *Russia* **33** G9
Shebele = Scebeli, Wabi →
  Somali Rep. **75** G3
Sheboygan *U.S.A.* **112** D10
Shebshi Mts. *Nigeria* **83** D7
Shediac *Canada* **105** C7
Sheelin, L. *Ireland* **12** C4
Sheep Haven *Ireland* **12** A4
Sheep Range *U.S.A.* **111** J11
Sheerness *U.K.* **15** F8
Sheet Harbour *Canada* **105** D7
Sheffield *U.K.* **14** D6
Sheffield *Ala., U.S.A.* **117** D11
Sheffield *Mass., U.S.A.* **115** D11
Sheffield *Pa., U.S.A.* **114** E5
Shehojele *Ethiopia* **81** E4
Shehong *China* **58** B5
Sheikh Idris *Sudan* **81** E3
Sheikh Zayed Canal *Egypt* **80** C3
Sheikhpura *India* **69** G11
Shek Hasan *Ethiopia* **81** E4
Shekhupura *Pakistan* **68** D5

Sheki = Şaki *Azerbaijan* **35** K8
Shelburne *N.S., Canada* **105** D6
Shelburne *Ont., Canada* **114** B4
Shelburne *U.S.A.* **115** B11
Shelburne B. *Australia* **94** A3
Shelby *Mich., U.S.A.* **112** D10
Shelby *Mont., U.S.A.* **108** B8
Shelby *N.C., U.S.A.* **117** D14
Shelby *Ohio, U.S.A.* **114** F2
Shelbyville *Ill., U.S.A.* **112** F9
Shelbyville *Ind., U.S.A.* **113** F11
Shelbyville *Ky., U.S.A.* **113** F11
Shelbyville *Tenn., U.S.A.* **117** D11
Sheldon *U.S.A.* **112** D6
Sheldrake *Canada* **105** B7
Shelengo, Khawr ~ *Sudan* **81** E2
Shelikhova, Zaliv *Russia* **53** D16
Shell Lakes *Australia* **93** E4
Shellbrook *Canada* **103** C7
Shellharbour *Australia* **95** E5
Shelon ~ *Russia* **32** C6
Shelter I. *U.S.A.* **115** E12
Shelton *Conn., U.S.A.* **115** E11
Shelton *Wash., U.S.A.* **110** C3
Shemakha = Şamaxi
   Azerbaijan **35** K9
Shêmri *Albania* **44** D4
Shemsi *Sudan* **80** D2
Shen Xian *China* **56** F8
Shenandoah *Iowa, U.S.A.* **112** E6
Shenandoah *Pa., U.S.A.* **115** F8
Shenandoah *Va., U.S.A.* **113** F14
Shenandoah ~ *U.S.A.* **113** F15
Shenandoah △ *U.S.A.* **113** F14
Shenchi *China* **56** E7
Shendam *Nigeria* **83** D6
Shendî *Sudan* **80** D3
Shenge *S. Leone* **82** D2
Shengfang *China* **56** E9
Shëngjergj *Albania* **44** E4
Shëngjin *Albania* **44** E3
Shengzhou *China* **59** C13
Shenmu *China* **56** E6
Shennongjia *China* **59** B8
Shenqiu *China* **56** H8
Shensi = Shaanxi □ *China* **56** G5
Shenyang *China* **57** D12
Shenzhen *China* **59** F10
Sheo *India* **68** F4
Sheopur Kalan *India* **68** G7
Shepetivka *Ukraine* **23** C14
Shepetovka = Shepetivka
   Ukraine **23** C14
Shepparton *Australia* **95** F4
Sheppey, I. of *U.K.* **15** F8
Shepton Mallet *U.K.* **15** F5
Sheqi *China* **56** H7
Sher Qila *Pakistan* **69** A6
Sherab *Sudan* **81** E1
Sherborne *U.K.* **15** G5
Sherbro ~ *S. Leone* **82** D2
Sherbro I. *S. Leone* **82** D2
Sherbrooke *N.S., Canada* **105** C7
Sherbrooke *Qué., Canada* **115** A13
Sherburne *U.S.A.* **115** D9
Shereik *Sudan* **80** D3
Shergarh *India* **68** F5
Sherghati *India* **69** G11
Sheridan *Ark., U.S.A.* **116** D8
Sheridan *Wyo., U.S.A.* **108** D10
Sheringham *U.K.* **14** E9
Sherkin I. *Ireland* **12** E2
Sherkot *India* **69** E8
Sherman *U.S.A.* **116** E6
Sherpur *India* **69** G10
Sherridon *Canada* **103** B8
Sherwood Forest *U.K.* **14** D6
Sherwood Park *Canada* **102** C6
Sheslay ~ *Canada* **102** B2
Shethanei L. *Canada* **103** B9
Shetland □ *U.K.* **13** A7
Shetland Is. *U.K.* **13** A7
Shetrunji ~ *India* **68** J5
Shevchenkovo *Ukraine* **29** E14
Shewa *Ethiopia* **81** F4
Shewa Gimira *Ethiopia* **81** F4
Shey-Phoksundo △ *Nepal* **69** E10
Sheyenne ~ *U.S.A.* **112** B5
Shibām *Yemen* **75** D4
Shibata *Japan* **54** E9
Shibecha *Japan* **54** C12
Shibetsu *Japan* **54** B11
Shibīn el Kôm *Egypt* **80** H7
Shibīn el Qanâtir *Egypt* **80** H7
Shibing *China* **58** D7
Shibogama L. *Canada* **104** B2
Shibushi *Japan* **55** J5
Shicheng *China* **59** D11
Shickshinny *U.S.A.* **115** E8
Shickshock Mts. =
   Chic-Chocs, Mts. *Canada* **105** C6
Shidao *China* **57** F12
Shidian *China* **58** E2
Shido *Japan* **55** G7
Shiel, L. *U.K.* **13** E3

Shield, C. *Australia* **94** A2
Shīeli *Kazakhstan* **52** E7
Shifang *China* **58** B5
Shiga □ *Japan* **55** G8
Shigu *China* **58** D2
Shiguaigou *China* **56** D6
Shihchiachuangi =
   Shijiazhuang *China* **56** E8
Shihezi *China* **60** B3
Shijak *Albania* **44** E3
Shijiazhuang *China* **56** E8
Shijiu Hu *China* **59** B12
Shikarpur *India* **69** F8
Shikarpur *Pakistan* **68** F3
Shikohabad *India* **69** F8
Shikoku □ *Japan* **55** H6
Shikoku-Sanchi *Japan* **55** H6
Shikotsu-Ko *Japan* **54** C10
Shikotsu-Tōya △ *Japan* **54** C10
Shiliguri *India* **67** F16
Shiliu = Changjiang *China* **64** C7
Shilka *Russia* **53** D12
Shilka ~ *Russia* **53** D13
Shillelagh *Ireland* **12** D5
Shillington *U.S.A.* **115** F9
Shillong *India* **67** G17
Shilo *West Bank* **74** C4
Shilong *China* **59** F9
Shilou *China* **56** F6
Shilovo *Russia* **34** C5
Shimabara *Japan* **55** H5
Shimada *Japan* **55** G9
Shimane □ *Japan* **55** G6
Shimanovsk *Russia* **53** D13
Shimba Hills △ *Kenya* **86** C4
Shimen *China* **59** C8
Shimenjie *China* **59** C11
Shimian *China* **58** C4
Shimizu *Japan* **55** G9
Shimla *India* **68** D7
Shimodate *Japan* **55** F9
Shimoga *India* **66** N9
Shimoni *Kenya* **86** C4
Shimonoseki *Japan* **55** H5
Shimpuru Rapids *Namibia* **88** B2
Shimsk *Russia* **32** C6
Shin, L. *U.K.* **13** C4
Shinan *China* **58** F7
Shinano-Gawa ~ *Japan* **55** F9
Shināş *Oman* **71** E8
Shīndand *Afghan.* **66** C3
Shinglehouse *U.S.A.* **114** E6
Shingū *Japan* **55** H7
Shingwidzi ~ *S. Africa* **89** C5
Shinjō *Japan* **54** E10
Shinkafe *Nigeria* **83** C6
Shinkolobwe
   Dem. Rep. of the Congo **84** G5
Shinshār *Syria* **74** A5
Shinyanga *Tanzania* **86** C3
Shinyanga □ *Tanzania* **86** C3
Shio-no-Misaki *Japan* **55** H7
Shiogama *Japan* **54** E10
Shiojiri *Japan* **55** F8
Shipchenski Prokhod
   Bulgaria **45** D9
Shiping *China* **58** F4
Shippagan *Canada* **105** C7
Shippensburg *U.S.A.* **114** F7
Shippenville *U.S.A.* **114** E5
Shiprock *U.S.A.* **109** H9
Shiqian *China* **58** D7
Shiqma, N. ~ *Israel* **74** D3
Shiquan *China* **56** H5
Shiquan He = Indus ~
   Pakistan **68** G2
Shīr Kūh *Iran* **71** D7
Shiragami-Misaki *Japan* **54** D10
Shirakawa *Fukushima, Japan* **55** F10
Shirakawa *Gifu, Japan* **55** F8
Shirane-San *Gumma, Japan* **55** F9
Shirane-San *Yamanashi,
   Japan* **55** G9
Shiraoi *Japan* **54** C10
Shīrāz *Iran* **71** D7
Shirbīn *Egypt* **80** H7
Shire ~ *Africa* **87** F4
Shiretoko-Misaki *Japan* **54** B12
Shirinab ~ *Pakistan* **68** D2
Shiriya-Zaki *Japan* **54** D10
Shiroishi *Japan* **54** F10
Shirshov Ridge *Pac. Oc.* **96** B8
Shīrvān *Iran* **71** B8
Shirwa, L. = Chilwa, L.
   Malawi **87** F4
Shishi *China* **59** E12
Shishou *China* **59** C9
Shitai *China* **59** B11
Shivpuri *India* **68** G7
Shixian *China* **57** C15
Shixing *China* **59** E10
Shiyan *China* **59** A8
Shiyata *Egypt* **80** B2
Shizhu *China* **58** C7
Shizong *China* **58** E5
Shizuishan *China* **56** E4
Shizuoka *Japan* **55** G9

Shizuoka □ *Japan* **55** G9
Shkhara *Georgia* **73** A10
Shklov = Shklow *Belarus* **23** A16
Shklow *Belarus* **23** A16
Shkodër *Albania* **44** D3
Shkumbini ~ *Albania* **44** E3
Shmidta, Ostrov *Russia* **53** A10
Shō-Gawa ~ *Japan* **55** F8
Shoal L. *Canada* **103** D9
Shoal Lake *Canada* **103** C8
Shōdo-Shima *Japan* **55** G7
Sholapur = Solapur *India* **66** L9
Shōmrōn *West Bank* **74** C4
Shoreham by Sea *U.K.* **15** G7
Shori ~ *Pakistan* **68** E3
Shorkot Road *Pakistan* **68** D5
Shoshone *Calif., U.S.A.* **111** K10
Shoshone *Idaho, U.S.A.* **108** E6
Shoshone L. *U.S.A.* **108** D8
Shoshone Mts. *U.S.A.* **108** G5
Shoshong *Botswana* **88** C4
Shoshoni *U.S.A.* **108** E9
Shostka *Ukraine* **33** G7
Shou Xian *China* **59** A11
Shouchang *China* **59** C12
Shouguang *China* **57** F10
Shouning *China* **59** D12
Shouyang *China* **56** F7
Show Low *U.S.A.* **109** J8
Shpola *Ukraine* **33** H6
Shpykiv *Ukraine* **29** B13
Shqipëria = Albania ■
   Europe **44** E4
Shreveport *U.S.A.* **116** E8
Shrewsbury *U.K.* **15** E5
Shri Mohangarh *India* **68** F4
Shrirampur *India* **69** H13
Shropshire □ *U.K.* **15** E5
Shū *Kazakhstan* **52** E8
Shuangbai *China* **58** E3
Shuangcheng *China* **57** B14
Shuangfeng *China* **59** D9
Shuanggou *China* **57** G9
Shuangjiang *China* **58** F2
Shuangliao *China* **57** C12
Shuangshanzi *China* **57** D10
Shuangyang *China* **57** C13
Shuangyashan *China* **60** B8
Shubrâ el Kheima *Egypt* **80** H7
Shubrâ Khit *Egypt* **80** H7
Shucheng *China* **59** B11
Shugozero *Russia* **32** C8
Shuguri Falls *Tanzania* **87** D4
Shuiji *China* **59** D12
Shuiye *China* **56** F8
Shujalpur *India* **68** H7
Shukpa Kunzang *India* **69** B8
Shulan *China* **57** B14
Shulaveri *Georgia* **35** K7
Shule *China* **60** C2
Shumagin Is. *U.S.A.* **106** a
Shumen *Bulgaria* **45** C10
Shumerlya *Russia* **34** C8
Shumikha *Russia* **52** D7
Shunchang *China* **59** D11
Shunde *China* **59** F9
Shungay *Kazakhstan* **35** F8
Shuo Xian = Shuozhou
   China **56** E7
Shuozhou *China* **56** E7
Shūr ~ *Fārs, Iran* **71** D7
Shūr ~ *Kermān, Iran* **71** D8
Shūr ~ *Yazd, Iran* **71** D7
Shūr Āb *Iran* **71** C6
Shūr Gaz *Iran* **71** D8
Shūrāb *Iran* **71** C8
Shūrjestān *Iran* **71** D7
Shurugwi *Zimbabwe* **87** F3
Shūsf *Iran* **71** D9
Shūsh *Iran* **73** F13
Shūshtar *Iran* **71** D6
Shuswap L. *Canada* **102** C5
Shuya *Russia* **34** B5
Shuyang *China* **57** G10
Shūzū *Iran* **71** D7
Shwebo *Burma* **67** H19
Shwegu *Burma* **67** G20
Shweli ~ *Burma* **67** H20
Shymkent *Kazakhstan* **52** E7
Shyok *India* **69** B8
Shyok ~ *Pakistan* **69** B6
Shyroke *Odesa, Ukraine* **29** E15
Shyroke *Ternopil, Ukraine* **28** B8
Si Chon *Thailand* **65** H2
Si Kiang = Xi Jiang ~ *China* **59** F9
Si Lanna △ *Thailand* **64** C2
Si-ngan = Xi'an *China* **56** G5
Si Prachan *Thailand* **64** E3
Si Racha *Thailand* **64** F3
Si Xian *China* **57** H9
Siachen Glacier *Asia* **69** B7
Siahaf ~ *Pakistan* **68** E3
Siahan Range *Pakistan* **66** F4
Siaksriindrapura *Indonesia* **62** D2
Sialkot *Pakistan* **68** C6
Siam = Thailand ■ *Asia* **64** E4
Sian = Xi'an *China* **56** G5

Sian Ka'an △ *Mexico* **119** D7
Sianów *Poland* **30** D3
Siantan *Indonesia* **62** D3
Siāreh *Iran* **71** D9
Siargao I. *Phil.* **61** G7
Siari *Pakistan* **69** B7
Siasi *Phil.* **53** C6
Siasi I. *Phil.* **61** J4
Siatista *Greece* **44** F5
Siau *Indonesia* **63** D7
Siazan = Siyäzän *Azerbaijan* **35** K9
Sibâi, Gebel el *Egypt* **70** E2
Sibang *Indonesia* **63** K18
Sibayi, L. *S. Africa* **89** D5
Sibdu *Sudan* **81** E2
Sibenik *Croatia* **41** E12
Siberia = Sibirskiy □ *Russia* **53** D10
Siberia *Russia* **4** D13
Siberut *Indonesia* **62** E1
Sibi *Pakistan* **68** E2
Sibil = Oksibil *Indonesia* **63** E10
Sibiloi △ *Kenya* **86** B4
Sibirskiy □ *Russia* **53** D10
Sibirtsevo *Russia* **54** B5
Sibiti *Congo* **84** E2
Sibiu *Romania* **29** E9
Sibiu □ *Romania* **29** E9
Sibley *U.S.A.* **112** D6
Sibolga *Indonesia* **62** D1
Sibsagar *India* **67** F19
Sibu *Malaysia* **62** D4
Sibuco *Phil.* **61** H5
Sibuguey B. *Phil.* **61** H5
Sibut *C.A.R.* **84** C3
Sibutu *Phil.* **63** D5
Sibutu Group *Phil.* **61** J3
Sibutu Passage *E. Indies* **63** D5
Sibuyan I. *Phil.* **61** E5
Sibuyan Sea *Phil.* **61** E5
Sic *Romania* **29** D8
Sicamous *Canada* **102** C5
Siccus ~ *Australia* **95** E2
Sichuan □ *China* **58** B5
Sichuan Pendi *China* **58** B5
Sicilia *Italy* **43** E7
Sicily = Sicilia *Italy* **43** E7
Sicily, Str. of *Medit. S.* **42** E4
Sicuani *Peru* **124** F4
Šid *Serbia* **28** E4
Sidamo *Ethiopia* **81** G4
Sidaouet *Niger* **83** B6
Sidari *Greece* **49** A3
Siddhapur *India* **68** H5
Siddipet *India* **66** K11
Sidensjö *Sweden* **10** A12
Sidéradougou *Burkina Faso* **82** C4
Siderno *Italy* **43** E9
Sideros, Akra *Greece* **49** D8
Sidhauli *India* **69** F9
Sidhi *India* **69** G9
Sîdi Abd el Rahmân *Egypt* **80** A2
Sîdi Barrâni *Egypt* **80** A2
Sidi-bel-Abbès *Algeria* **78** A5
Sîdi Haneish *Egypt* **80** A2
Sidi Ifni *Morocco* **78** C3
Sîdi Omar *Egypt* **80** A1
Sidirokastro *Greece* **44** E7
Sidlaw Hills *U.K.* **13** E5
Sidley, Mt. *Antarctica* **5** D14
Sidmouth *U.K.* **15** G4
Sidmouth, C. *Australia* **94** A3
Sidney *Canada* **110** B3
Sidney *Mont., U.S.A.* **108** C11
Sidney *N.Y., U.S.A.* **115** D9
Sidney *Nebr., U.S.A.* **112** E2
Sidney *Ohio, U.S.A.* **113** E11
Sidney Lanier, L. *U.S.A.* **117** D12
Sido *Mali* **82** C3
Sidoarjo *Indonesia* **63** G15
Sidon = Saydā *Lebanon* **74** B4
Sidra, G. of = Surt, Khalīj
   Libya **79** B9
Siedlce *Poland* **31** F9
Sieg ~ *Germany* **24** E3
Siegburg *Germany* **24** E3
Siegen *Germany* **24** E4
Siem Pang *Cambodia* **64** E6
Siem Reap = Siemreab
   Cambodia **64** F4
Siemiatycze *Poland* **31** F9
Siemreab *Cambodia* **64** F4
Siena *Italy* **41** E8
Sieniawa *Poland* **31** H9
Sieradz *Poland* **31** G5
Sieraków *Poland* **31** F3
Sierck-les-Bains *France* **19** C13
Sierning *Austria* **26** C7
Sierpc *Poland* **31** F6
Sierpe, Bocas de la
   Venezuela **125** L15
Sierra Blanca *U.S.A.* **116** F2
Sierra Blanca Peak *U.S.A.* **109** K11
Sierra City *U.S.A.* **110** F6
Sierra Colorada *Argentina* **128** E3
Sierra de Aracena y Picas
   de Aroche △ *Spain* **37** H4

Sierra de Bahoruco △
   Dom. Rep. **121** C5
Sierra de Baza △ *Spain* **39** H2
Sierra de Castril △ *Spain* **39** H2
Sierra de Espuña △ *Spain* **39** H3
Sierra de Grazalema △ *Spain* **37** J5
Sierra de Gredos △ *Spain* **36** E5
Sierra de Hornachuelos △
   Spain **37** H5
Sierra de Huétor △ *Spain* **37** H7
Sierra de La Culata △
   Venezuela **121** E5
Sierra de Lancandón △
   Guatemala **120** C1
Sierra de las Nieves △ *Spain* **37** J6
Sierra de las Quijadas △
   Argentina **126** C2
Sierra de María-Los
   Vélez △ *Spain* **39** H2
Sierra de San Luis △
   Venezuela **121** D6
Sierra de San Pedro Mártir,
   Parque Nacional △
   Mexico **118** A1
Sierra de São Mamede △
   Portugal **37** F3
Sierra de Yeguas *Spain* **37** H6
Sierra Gorda *Chile* **126** A2
Sierra Leone ■ *W. Afr.* **82** D2
Sierra Madre *Mexico* **119** D6
Sierra Madre Occidental
   Mexico **118** B3
Sierra Madre Oriental
   Mexico **118** C5
Sierra Mágina △ *Spain* **37** H7
Sierra Mojada *Mexico* **118** B4
Sierra Nevada *Spain* **37** H7
Sierra Nevada *U.S.A.* **110** H8
Sierra Nevada △ *Spain* **37** H7
Sierra Nevada △ *Venezuela* **121** E5
Sierra Nevada de Santa
   Marta △ *Colombia* **121** D5
Sierra Norte de Seville △
   Spain **37** H5
Sierra Subbéticas △ *Spain* **37** H6
Sierra Vista *U.S.A.* **109** L8
Sierras de Cardeña y
   Montoro △ *Spain* **37** G6
Sierras de Cazorla, Segura
   y las Villas △ *Spain* **39** J2
Sierraville *U.S.A.* **110** F6
Sierre *Switz.* **25** J3
Sifani *Ethiopia* **81** E5
Sifié *Ivory C.* **82** D3
Sifnos *Greece* **46** E6
Sifton *Canada* **103** C8
Sifton Pass *Canada* **102** B3
Sig *Algeria* **78** A5
Sigatoka *Fiji* **91** a
Sigean *France* **20** E6
Sighetu-Marmaţiei *Romania* **29** C8
Sighişoara *Romania* **29** D9
Sigli *Indonesia* **62** C1
Siglufjörður *Iceland* **8** C4
Sigmaringen *Germany* **25** G5
Signa *Italy* **40** E8
Signakhi = Tsnori *Georgia* **35** K7
Signal de Botrang *Belgium* **17** D6
Signal Pk. *U.S.A.* **111** M12
Signy *L. Antarctica* **5** C18
Signy-l'Abbaye *France* **19** C11
Sigsig *Ecuador* **124** D3
Sigüenza *Spain* **38** D2
Siguiri *Guinea* **82** C3
Sigulda *Latvia* **32** D3
Sihora *India* **69** H9
Sihui *China* **59** F9
Siikajoki ~ *Finland* **8** D21
Siilinjärvi *Finland* **8** E22
Siirt *Turkey* **73** D9
Siirt □ *Turkey* **73** D9
Sijarira Ra. = Chizarira
   Zimbabwe **87** F2
Sika *India* **68** H3
Sikanni Chief ~ *Canada* **102** B4
Sikao *Thailand* **65** J2
Sikar *India* **68** F6
Sikasso *Mali* **82** C3
Sikasso □ *Mali* **82** C3
Sikeston *U.S.A.* **112** G9
Sikhote Alin, Khrebet *Russia* **54** B8
Sikhote Alin Ra. = Sikhote
   Alin, Khrebet *Russia* **54** B8
Sikia *Greece* **44** F7
Sikinos *Greece* **46** E6
Sikkim □ *India* **67** F16
Siklós *Hungary* **28** E3
Sil ~ *Spain* **36** C3
Silacayoapan *Mexico* **119** D5
Šilalė *Lithuania* **30** C9
Silandro *Italy* **40** B7
Silawad *India* **68** J6
Silay *Phil.* **61** F5
Silba *Croatia* **41** D11
Silchar *India* **67** G18
Silcox *Canada* **103** B10
Siler City *U.S.A.* **117** D15

Silesia = Śląsk *Poland* **22** C9
Silgarhi Doti *Nepal* **69** E9
Silghat *India* **67** F18
Silhouette *Seychelles* **85** b
Sili *Burkina Faso* **82** C4
Silifke *Turkey* **72** D5
Siliguri = Shiliguri *India* **67** F16
Siling Co *China* **60** C3
Silistea Nouă *Romania* **29** F10
Silistra *Bulgaria* **45** B11
Silivri *Turkey* **45** E12
Siljan *Sweden* **10** D8
Siljansnäs *Sweden* **10** D8
Silkeborg *Denmark* **11** H3
Silkwood *Australia* **94** B4
Silla *Spain* **39** F4
Sillajhuay, Cordillera *Chile* **124** G5
Sillamäe *Estonia* **32** C4
Sillé-le-Guillaume *France* **18** D6
Silleda *Spain* **36** C2
Silloth *U.K.* **14** C4
Silo *Greece* **45** E9
Siloam Springs *U.S.A.* **116** C7
Silopi *Turkey* **73** D10
Silsbee *U.S.A.* **116** F7
Siluko *Nigeria* **83** D6
Silvan *Turkey* **73** C9
Silvani *India* **69** H8
Silver City *U.S.A.* **109** K9
Silver Cr. ~ *U.S.A.* **108** E4
Silver Creek *U.S.A.* **114** D5
Silver L. *U.S.A.* **110** G6
Silver Lake *Calif., U.S.A.* **111** K10
Silver Lake *Oreg., U.S.A.* **108** E3
Silverdalen *Sweden* **11** G9
Silvermine Mts. *Ireland* **12** D3
Silverton *Colo., U.S.A.* **109** H10
Silverton *Tex., U.S.A.* **116** D4
Silves *Portugal* **37** H2
Silvi Marina *Italy* **41** F11
Silvies ~ *U.S.A.* **108** E4
Silvrettahorn *Switz.* **40** B7
Silwa Bahari *Egypt* **80** C3
Silz *Austria* **26** D3
Simaltala *India* **69** G12
Simanggang = Sri Aman
   Malaysia **62** D4
Simao *China* **58** F3
Simard, L. *Canada* **104** C4
Sīmareh ~ *Iran* **73** F12
Simav *Turkey* **47** B10
Simav ~ *Turkey* **45** F12
Simav Dağları *Turkey* **47** B10
Simba *Tanzania* **86** C3
Simbach *Germany* **25** G9
Simbirsk *Russia* **34** C9
Simbo *Tanzania* **86** C2
Simcoe *Canada* **104** D3
Simcoe, L. *Canada* **114** B5
Simdega *India* **69** H11
Simeonovgrad *Bulgaria* **45** D9
Simeria *Romania* **28** E8
Simeto ~ *Italy* **43** E8
Simeulue *Indonesia* **62** D1
Simferopol *Ukraine* **33** K8
Simi *Greece* **47** E9
Simi Valley *U.S.A.* **111** L8
Simien Mts. △ *Ethiopia* **81** E4
Simikot *Nepal* **69** E9
Simitli *Bulgaria* **44** E7
Simla = Shimla *India* **68** D7
Simlångsdalen *Sweden* **11** H7
Şimleu-Silvaniei *Romania* **28** C7
Simlipal △ *India* **69** J12
Simmern *Germany* **25** F3
Simmie *Canada* **103** D7
Simmler *U.S.A.* **111** K7
Simnas *Lithuania* **30** D10
Simo älv = Simojoki ~
   Finland **8** D21
Simojoki ~ *Finland* **8** D21
Simojovel *Mexico* **119** D6
Simonette ~ *Canada* **102** B5
Simonstown *S. Africa* **88** E2
Simontornya *Hungary* **28** D3
Simpang Empat *Malaysia* **65** c
Simplon Pass *Switz.* **25** J4
Simplontunnel *Switz.* **25** J4
Simpson Desert *Australia* **94** D2
Simpson Desert △ *Australia* **94** C2
Simpson Pen. *Canada* **101** C11
Simrishamn *Sweden* **11** J8
Simushir, Ostrov *Russia* **53** E16
Sin Cowe I. *S. China Sea* **62** C4
Sinabang *Indonesia* **62** D1
Sinadogo *Somali Rep.* **75** F4
Sinai = Es Sînâ' *Egypt* **74** F3
Sinai, Mt. = Mûsa, Gebel
   Egypt **70** D2
Sinaia *Romania* **29** E10
Sinaloa □ *Mexico* **118** C3
Sinaloa de Leyva *Mexico* **118** B3
Sinalunga *Italy* **41** E8
Sinan *China* **58** D7
Sînandrei *Romania* **28** E6

Sinarades *Greece* 49 A3
Sincan *Turkey* 72 B5
Sincanlı *Turkey* 47 C12
Sincelejo *Colombia* 124 B3
Sinch'ang *N. Korea* 57 D15
Sinch'ŏn *N. Korea* 57 E13
Sinclair *U.S.A.* 108 F10
Sinclair Mills *Canada* 102 C4
Sinclair's B. *U.K.* 13 C5
Sinclairville *U.S.A.* 114 D5
Sincorá, Serra do *Brazil* 125 F10
Sind = Sindh □ *Pakistan* 68 G3
Sind *Pakistan* 68 G3
Sind → *Jammu & Kashmir, India* 69 B6
Sind → *Mad. P., India* 69 F8
Sind Sagar Doab *Pakistan* 68 D4
Sindal *Denmark* 11 G4
Sindangan *Phil.* 61 G5
Sindangbarang *Indonesia* 63 G12
Sinde *Zambia* 87 F2
Sindelfingen *Germany* 25 G4
Sindh □ *Pakistan* 68 G3
Sındırgı *Turkey* 47 B10
Sindou *Burkina Faso* 82 C3
Sindri *India* 69 H12
Sine → *Senegal* 82 C1
Sinegorskiy *Russia* 35 G5
Sinekli *Turkey* 45 E12
Sinelnikovo = Synelnykove *Ukraine* 33 H8
Sinendé *Benin* 83 C5
Sines *Portugal* 37 H2
Sines, C. de *Portugal* 37 H2
Sineu *Spain* 48 B10
Sinfra *Ivory C.* 82 D3
Sing Buri *Thailand* 64 E3
Singa *Sudan* 81 E3
Singalila △ *India* 69 F13
Singapore ■ *Asia* 65 d
Singapore, Straits of *Asia* 65 d
Singapore Changi ✈ (SIN) *Singapore* 65 M4
Singaraja *Indonesia* 63 J18
Singatoka = Sigatoka *Fiji* 91 a
Singen *Germany* 25 H4
Singida *Tanzania* 86 C3
Singida □ *Tanzania* 86 D3
Singkaling Hkamti *Burma* 67 G19
Singkang *Indonesia* 63 E6
Singkawang *Indonesia* 62 D3
Singkep *Indonesia* 62 E2
Singleton *Australia* 95 E5
Singleton, Mt. *N. Terr., Australia* 92 D5
Singleton, Mt. *W. Austral., Australia* 93 E2
Singö *Sweden* 10 D12
Singoli *India* 68 G6
Singora = Songkhla *Thailand* 65 J3
Sinhung *N. Korea* 57 D14
Siniscóla *Italy* 42 B2
Sinj *Croatia* 41 E13
Sinjai *Indonesia* 63 F6
Sinjajevina *Montenegro* 44 D3
Sinjār *Iraq* 73 D9
Sinkat *Sudan* 80 D4
Sinkiang = Xinjiang Uygur Zizhiqu □ *China* 60 B3
Sinmak *N. Korea* 57 E14
Sinmi-do *N. Korea* 57 E13
Sínnai *Italy* 42 C2
Sinnamary *Fr. Guiana* 125 B8
Sinni → *Italy* 43 B9
Sinnuris *Egypt* 80 J7
Sinoie, Lacul *Romania* 29 F13
Sinop *Turkey* 72 A6
Sinop □ *Turkey* 72 B6
Sinor *India* 68 J5
Sinp'o *N. Korea* 57 E15
Sinsheim *Germany* 25 F4
Sinsk *Russia* 53 C13
Sintang *Indonesia* 62 D4
Sinton *U.S.A.* 116 G6
Sintra *Portugal* 37 G1
Sintra-Cascais △ *Portugal* 37 G1
Sinŭiju *N. Korea* 57 D13
Sinyukha → *Ukraine* 33 H6
Sinzig *Germany* 24 E3
Sio → *Hungary* 28 D3
Siocon *Phil.* 61 H5
Siófok *Hungary* 28 D3
Sion *Switz.* 25 J3
Sion Mills *U.K.* 12 B4
Sioux Center *U.S.A.* 112 D5
Sioux City *U.S.A.* 112 D5
Sioux Falls *U.S.A.* 112 D5
Sioux Lookout *Canada* 104 B1
Sioux Narrows *Canada* 103 D10
Sipadan *Malaysia* 63 D5
Sipalay *Phil.* 61 G5
Sipan *Croatia* 44 D1
Siparia *Trin. & Tob.* 125 K15
Sipil Dağı △ *Turkey* 47 C9
Siping *China* 57 C13
Sipiwesk L. *Canada* 103 B9
Siple *Antarctica* 5 D7

Šipovo *Bos.-H.* 28 F2
Sipra → *India* 68 H6
Sipura *Indonesia* 62 E1
Siquia → *Nic.* 120 D3
Siquijor *Phil.* 61 G5
Siquirres *Costa Rica* 120 D3
Şīr Abu Nu'ayr *U.A.E.* 71 E7
Şīr Banī Yās *U.A.E.* 71 E7
Sir Edward Pellew Group *Australia* 94 B2
Sir Graham Moore Is. *Australia* 92 B4
Sir James MacBrien, Mt. *Canada* 100 C7
Sira → *Norway* 9 G12
Siracusa *Italy* 43 E8
Sirajganj *Bangla.* 69 G13
Sirakoro *Mali* 82 C3
Şiran *Turkey* 73 B8
Sirasso *Ivory C.* 82 D3
Sirathu *India* 69 G9
Sīrdān *Iran* 73 D13
Sire *Ethiopia* 81 F4
Siren *U.S.A.* 112 C7
Sirente-Velino △ *Italy* 41 F10
Sirer *Spain* 48 C7
Siret *Romania* 29 C11
Siret → *Romania* 29 E12
Sirghāyā *Syria* 74 B5
Şiria *Romania* 28 D6
Sirinath △ *Thailand* 65 a
Sirino, Mte. *Italy* 43 B8
Sīrjān *Iran* 71 D7
Sirmaur *India* 69 G9
Sirna *Greece* 47 E8
Şırnak *Turkey* 73 D10
Sirohi *India* 68 G5
Sironj *India* 68 G7
Síros = Syros *Greece* 46 D6
Sirretta Pk. *U.S.A.* 111 K8
Sīrrī *Iran* 71 E7
Sirsa *India* 68 E6
Sirsa → *India* 69 F8
Siruela *Spain* 37 G5
Sisak *Croatia* 41 C13
Sisaket *Thailand* 64 E5
Sisante *Spain* 39 F2
Sisargas, Is. *Spain* 36 B2
Sishen *S. Africa* 88 D3
Sishui *Henan, China* 56 G7
Sishui *Shandong, China* 57 G9
Sisipuk L. *Canada* 103 B8
Sisophon *Cambodia* 64 F4
Sisseton *U.S.A.* 112 C5
Sissonne *France* 19 C10
Sīstān *Asia* 71 D9
Sīstān, Daryācheh-ye *Iran* 71 D9
Sīstān va Balūchestān □ *Iran* 71 E9
Sisteron *France* 21 D9
Sisters *U.S.A.* 108 D3
Sisters, The *Seychelles* 85 b
Siswa Bazar *India* 69 F10
Sitakili *Mali* 82 C2
Sitamarhi *India* 69 F11
Sitampiky *Madag.* 89 B8
Sitapur *India* 69 F9
Siteki *Swaziland* 89 D5
Sitges *Spain* 38 D6
Sithonia *Greece* 44 F7
Sitia *Greece* 49 D8
Sitito-Ozima Ridge *Pac. Oc.* 96 E6
Sitka *U.S.A.* 100 B1
Sitoti *Botswana* 88 C3
Sitra *Egypt* 80 B2
Sittang Myit → *Burma* 67 L20
Sittard *Neths.* 17 C5
Sittensen *Germany* 24 B5
Sittingbourne *U.K.* 15 F8
Sittona *Eritrea* 81 E4
Sittoung = Sittang Myit → *Burma* 67 L20
Sittwe *Burma* 67 J18
Situbondo *Indonesia* 63 G16
Si'umu *Samoa* 91 b
Siuna *Nic.* 120 D3
Siuri *India* 69 H12
Siutghiol, Lacul *Romania* 29 F13
Sīvand *Iran* 71 D7
Sivas *Turkey* 72 C7
Sivas □ *Turkey* 72 C7
Sivaslı *Turkey* 47 C11
Siverek *Turkey* 73 D8
Sivrihisar *Turkey* 72 C4
Sîwa *Egypt* 80 B2
Sîwa, El Wâhât es *Egypt* 80 B2
Siwa Oasis = Sîwa, El Wâhât es *Egypt* 80 B2
Siwalik Range *Nepal* 69 F10
Siwan *India* 69 F11
Siwana *India* 68 G5
Six Cross Roads *Barbados* 121 g
Sixmilebridge *Ireland* 12 D3
Sixth Cataract *Sudan* 81 D3
Siyāl, Jazā'ir → *Egypt* 80 C4
Siyäzän *Azerbaijan* 35 K9
Siziwang Qi *China* 56 D6

Sjælland *Denmark* 11 J5
Sjælland □ *Denmark* 11 J5
Sjællands Odde *Denmark* 11 J5
Sjenica *Serbia* 44 C3
Sjöbo *Sweden* 11 J7
Sjötofta *Sweden* 11 G7
Sjötorp *Sweden* 11 F8
Sjumen = Shumen *Bulgaria* 45 C10
Sjuntorp *Sweden* 11 F6
Skadarsko Jezero *Europe* 44 D3
Skadovsk *Ukraine* 33 J7
Skælskor *Denmark* 11 J5
Skærbæk *Denmark* 11 J2
Skaftafell *Iceland* 8 D5
Skaftafell △ *Iceland* 8 D5
Skagafjörður *Iceland* 8 D4
Skagastølstindane *Norway* 8 F12
Skagaströnd *Iceland* 8 D3
Skagen *Denmark* 11 G4
Skagern *Sweden* 10 E8
Skagerrak *Denmark* 11 G2
Skagit → *U.S.A.* 110 B4
Skagway *U.S.A.* 100 B1
Skala-Podilska *Ukraine* 29 B11
Skala Podolskaya = Skala-Podilska *Ukraine* 29 B11
Skalat *Ukraine* 23 D13
Skalbmierz *Poland* 31 H7
Skälderviken *Sweden* 11 H6
Skalica *Slovak Rep.* 27 C10
Skallingen *Denmark* 11 J2
Skalni Dol = Kamenyak *Bulgaria* 45 C10
Skanderborg *Denmark* 11 H3
Skåne *Sweden* 11 J7
Skåne län □ *Sweden* 11 H7
Skaneateles *U.S.A.* 115 D8
Skaneateles L. *U.S.A.* 115 D8
Skänninge *Sweden* 11 F9
Skanör med Falsterbo *Sweden* 11 J6
Skantzoura *Greece* 46 B6
Skara *Sweden* 11 F7
Skärblacka *Sweden* 11 F9
Skardu *Pakistan* 69 B6
Skåre *Sweden* 10 E7
Skärhamn *Sweden* 11 G5
Skarszewy *Poland* 30 D5
Skaryszew *Poland* 31 G8
Skarżysko-Kamienna *Poland* 31 G7
Skattkärr *Sweden* 10 E7
Skattungbyn *Sweden* 10 C8
Skawina *Poland* 31 J6
Skebobruk *Sweden* 10 E12
Skegness *U.K.* 14 D8
Skeldon = Corriverton *Guyana* 124 B7
Skeleton Coast *Namibia* 85 J2
Skeleton Coast △ *Namibia* 88 C1
Skellefteå *Sweden* 8 D19
Skellefteälven → *Sweden* 8 D19
Skelleftehamn *Sweden* 8 D19
Skender Vakuf *Bos.-H.* 28 F2
Skerries, The *U.K.* 14 D3
Skerries, Sd. of *U.K.* 13 D3
Skhidnytsya *Ukraine* 31 J10
Skhíza *Greece* 46 E3
Ski *Norway* 9 G14
Skiathos *Greece* 46 B5
Skibbereen *Ireland* 12 E2
Skiddaw *U.K.* 14 C4
Skidegate *Canada* 102 C2
Skidra *Greece* 44 F6
Skien *Norway* 9 G13
Skierniewice *Poland* 31 G7
Skikda *Algeria* 78 A7
Skillingaryd *Sweden* 11 G8
Skillinge *Sweden* 11 J8
Skilloura *Cyprus* 49 D12
Skinari, Akra *Greece* 46 D2
Skinnskatteberg *Sweden* 10 E9
Skipton *U.K.* 14 D5
Skiring, C. *Senegal* 82 C1
Skirmish Pt. *Australia* 94 A1
Skiropoula *Greece* 46 C6
Skíros *Greece* 46 C6
Skivarp *Sweden* 11 J7
Skive *Denmark* 11 H3
Skjálfandafljót → *Iceland* 8 D5
Skjálfandi *Iceland* 8 C5
Skjern *Denmark* 11 J2
Skoczów *Poland* 31 J5
Škofja Loka *Slovenia* 41 B11
Skoghall *Sweden* 10 E7
Skogstorp *Sweden* 10 E10
Skoki *Poland* 31 F4
Skole *Ukraine* 23 D12
Skopelos *Greece* 46 B5
Skopi *Greece* 49 D8
Skopin *Russia* 32 F10
Skopje *Macedonia* 44 D5
Skopje ✈ (SKP) *Macedonia* 44 E5
Skórcz *Poland* 30 E5
Skørping *Denmark* 11 H3
Skövde *Sweden* 11 F7

Skovorodino *Russia* 53 D13
Skowhegan *U.S.A.* 113 C19
Skradin *Croatia* 41 E12
Skrea *Sweden* 11 H6
Skrunda *Latvia* 30 B9
Skrwa → *Poland* 31 F6
Skukuskogen △ *Sweden* 10 A12
Skull *Ireland* 12 E2
Skultorp *Sweden* 11 F7
Skultuna *Sweden* 10 E10
Skunk → *U.S.A.* 112 E8
Skuodas *Lithuania* 30 B8
Skurup *Sweden* 11 J7
Skutskär *Sweden* 10 D11
Skvyra *Ukraine* 23 D15
Skwierzyna *Poland* 31 F2
Skye *U.K.* 13 D2
Skykomish *U.S.A.* 108 C3
Skyros = Skiros *Greece* 46 C6
Skyttorp *Sweden* 10 D11
Slade Pt. *Australia* 94 K7
Slættaratindur *Færoe Is.* 8 E9
Slagelse *Denmark* 11 J5
Slamet *Indonesia* 63 G13
Slane *Ireland* 12 C5
Slaney → *Ireland* 12 D5
Slangberge *S. Africa* 88 E3
Slănic *Romania* 29 E10
Slano *Croatia* 44 D1
Slantsy *Russia* 32 C5
Slaný *Czech Rep.* 26 A7
Slane *Ireland* 12 C5
Slangberge *S. Africa* 88 E3
Slate Is. *Canada* 104 C2
Slatina *Croatia* 28 E2
Slatina *Romania* 29 F9
Slatina Timiş *Romania* 28 E7
Slatington *U.S.A.* 115 F9
Slaton *U.S.A.* 116 E4
Slave → *Canada* 102 A6
Slave Coast *W. Afr.* 83 D5
Slave Lake *Canada* 102 B6
Slave Pt. *Canada* 102 A5
Slavgorod *Russia* 52 D8
Slavinja *Serbia* 44 C6
Slavkov u Brna *Czech Rep.* 27 B9
Slavkovský Les △ *Czech Rep.* 26 A5
Slavonija *Europe* 28 E2
Slavonski Brod *Croatia* 28 E3
Slavsk *Russia* 30 C8
Slavska *Ukraine* 29 B8
Slavskoye *Russia* 30 D7
Slavuta *Ukraine* 23 C14
Slavyanka *Russia* 54 C5
Slavyanovo *Bulgaria* 45 C8
Slavyansk = Slovyansk *Ukraine* 33 H9
Slavyansk-na-Kubani *Russia* 33 K10
Sława *Poland* 31 G3
Slawharad *Belarus* 23 B16
Sławno *Poland* 30 D3
Slawobrze *Poland* 30 E2
Sleaford *U.K.* 14 D7
Sleaford B. *Australia* 95 E2
Sleat, Sd. of *U.K.* 13 D3
Sleeper Is. *Canada* 101 D11
Sleeping Bear Dunes △ *U.S.A.* 112 C10
Sleepy Eye *U.S.A.* 112 C6
Slemon L. *Canada* 102 A5
Šlesin *Poland* 31 F5
Slide Mt. *U.S.A.* 115 E10
Slidell *U.S.A.* 117 F10
Sliema *Malta* 49 D2
Slieve Aughty *Ireland* 12 C3
Slieve Bloom *Ireland* 12 C4
Slieve Donard *U.K.* 12 B6
Slieve Gamph *Ireland* 12 B3
Slieve Gullion *U.K.* 12 B5
Slieve League *Ireland* 12 B3
Slieve Mish *Ireland* 12 D2
Slievenamon *Ireland* 12 D4
Sligeach = Sligo *Ireland* 12 B3
Sligo *Ireland* 12 B3
Sligo *U.S.A.* 114 E5
Sligo □ *Ireland* 12 B3
Sligo B. *Ireland* 12 B3
Slippery Rock *U.S.A.* 114 E4
Slite *Sweden* 11 G12
Slīteres △ *Latvia* 30 A9
Sliven *Bulgaria* 45 D10
Slivnitsa *Bulgaria* 44 D7
Slobidka *Ukraine* 29 C14
Slobozia *Moldova* 29 D14
Slobozia *Argeş, Romania* 29 F10
Slobozia *Ialomiţa, Romania* 29 F12
Slocan *Canada* 102 D5
Slomniki *Poland* 31 H7
Slonim *Belarus* 23 B13
Slough *U.K.* 15 F7
Slough □ *U.K.* 15 F7
Sloughhouse *U.S.A.* 110 G5

Slovak Rep. ■ *Europe* 27 C13
Slovakia = Slovak Rep. ■ *Europe* 27 C13
Slovakian Ore Mts. = Slovenské Rudohorie *Slovak Rep.* 27 C12
Slovenia ■ *Europe* 41 C11
Slovenija = Slovenia ■ *Europe* 41 C11
Slovenj Gradec *Slovenia* 41 B12
Slovenska = Slovak Rep. ■ *Europe* 27 C13
Slovenska Bistrica *Slovenia* 41 B12
Slovenské Konjice *Slovenia* 41 B12
Slovenské Rudohorie *Slovak Rep.* 27 C12
Slovenský Raj △ *Slovak Rep.* 27 C13
Slovyansk *Ukraine* 33 H9
Słubice *Poland* 31 F1
Sluch → *Ukraine* 23 C14
Sluis *Neths.* 17 C3
Slůnchev Bryag *Bulgaria* 45 D11
Slunj *Croatia* 41 C12
Słupca *Poland* 31 F4
Słupia → *Poland* 30 D3
Słupsk *Poland* 30 D4
Slurry *S. Africa* 88 D4
Slutsk *Belarus* 23 B14
Slyne Hd. *Ireland* 12 C1
Slyudyanka *Russia* 53 D11
Småland *Sweden* 11 G9
Smålandsfarvandet *Denmark* 11 J5
Smålandsstenar *Sweden* 11 G7
Smalltree L. *Canada* 103 A8
Smallwood Res. *Canada* 105 B7
Smarhon *Belarus* 23 A14
Smarje *Slovenia* 41 B12
Smartt Syndicate Dam *S. Africa* 88 E3
Smartville *U.S.A.* 110 F5
Smeaton *Canada* 103 C8
Smedby *Sweden* 11 H10
Smederevo *Serbia* 44 B4
Smederevska Palanka *Serbia* 44 B4
Smedjebacken *Sweden* 10 D9
Smela = Smila *Ukraine* 33 H6
Smerwick Harbour *Ireland* 12 D1
Smethport *U.S.A.* 114 E6
Smidovich *Russia* 53 E14
Šmigiel *Poland* 31 F3
Smila *Ukraine* 33 H6
Smilyan *Bulgaria* 45 E8
Smith *Canada* 102 B6
Smith Center *U.S.A.* 112 F4
Smith River △ *U.S.A.* 108 F2
Smithburne → *Australia* 94 B3
Smithers *Canada* 102 C3
Smithfield *S. Africa* 89 E4
Smithfield *N.C., U.S.A.* 117 D15
Smithfield *Utah, U.S.A.* 108 F8
Smithton *Australia* 95 G4
Smithville *Canada* 114 C5
Smithville *U.S.A.* 116 F6
Smoky → *Canada* 102 B5
Smoky Bay *Australia* 95 E1
Smoky Hill → *U.S.A.* 112 F5
Smoky Hills *U.S.A.* 112 F4
Smoky Lake *Canada* 102 C6
Smøla *Norway* 8 E13
Smolensk *Russia* 32 E7
Smolensk □ *Russia* 32 E7
Smolikas, Oros *Greece* 44 F4
Smolník *Slovak Rep.* 27 C13
Smolyan *Bulgaria* 45 E8
Smooth Rock Falls *Canada* 104 C3
Smoothstone L. *Canada* 103 C7
Smorgon = Smarhon *Belarus* 23 A14
Smotrych *Ukraine* 29 B11
Smotrych → 29 B11
Smulţi *Romania* 29 E12
Smyadovo *Bulgaria* 45 C11
Smygehamn *Sweden* 11 J7
Smyrna = İzmir *Turkey* 47 C9
Smyrna *U.S.A.* 113 F16
Snæfell *Iceland* 8 D6
Snaefell *I. of Man* 14 C3
Snæfellsjökull *Iceland* 8 D2
Snake → *U.S.A.* 108 C4
Snake I. *Australia* 95 F4
Snake Range *U.S.A.* 108 G6
Snake River Plain *U.S.A.* 108 E7
Snasahögarna *Sweden* 10 A6
Snåsavatnet *Norway* 8 D15
Snedsted *Denmark* 11 H2
Sneek *Neths.* 17 A5
Sneem *Ireland* 12 E2
Sneeuberge *S. Africa* 88 E3
Snejbjerg *Denmark* 11 H2
Snelling *U.S.A.* 110 H6
Snezhnoye *Ukraine* 33 J10
Snežnik *Slovenia* 41 C11
Snøhetta *Norway* 8 E13
Sněžka *Europe* 30 A8
Snizort, L. *U.K.* 13 D2

Śnieżka *Europe* 26 A8
Snigirevka = Snihurivka *Ukraine* 33 J7
Snihurivka *Ukraine* 33 J7
Snina *Slovak Rep.* 27 C15
Snizort, L. *U.K.* 13 D2
Snohetta *Norway* 8 E13
Snohomish *U.S.A.* 110 C4
Snoqualmie Pass *U.S.A.* 110 C5
Snoul *Cambodia* 65 F6
Snow Hill *U.S.A.* 113 F16
Snow Lake *Canada* 103 C8
Snow Mt. *Calif., U.S.A.* 110 F4
Snow Mt. *Maine, U.S.A.* 115 A14
Snow Shoe *U.S.A.* 114 E7
Snowbird L. *Canada* 103 A8
Snowdon *U.K.* 14 D3
Snowdonia △ *U.K.* 14 D4
Snowdrift = Łutselk'e *Canada* 103 A6
Snowdrift → *Canada* 103 A6
Snowflake *U.S.A.* 109 J8
Snowshoe Pk. *U.S.A.* 108 B6
Snowtown *Australia* 95 E2
Snowville *U.S.A.* 108 F7
Snowy → *Australia* 95 F4
Snowy Mt. *U.S.A.* 115 C10
Snowy Mts. *Australia* 95 F4
Snug Corner *Bahamas* 121 B5
Snyatyn *Ukraine* 29 B10
Snyder *Okla., U.S.A.* 116 D5
Snyder *Tex., U.S.A.* 116 E4
Soahanina *Madag.* 89 B7
Soalala *Madag.* 89 B8
Soaloka *Madag.* 89 B8
Soamanonga *Madag.* 89 C7
Soanierana-Ivongo *Madag.* 89 B8
Soanindraniny *Madag.* 89 B8
Şoarş *Romania* 29 E9
Soavina *Madag.* 89 C8
Soavinandriana *Madag.* 89 B8
Sob → *Ukraine* 29 B14
Soba *Nigeria* 83 C6
Sobat, Nahr → *Sudan* 81 F3
Soběslav *Czech Rep.* 26 B7
Sobhapur *India* 68 H8
Sobinka *Russia* 32 E11
Sobótka *Poland* 31 H3
Sobra *Croatia* 41 F14
Sobradinho, Reprêsa de *Brazil* 125 E10
Sobral *Brazil* 125 D10
Sobrance *Slovak Rep.* 27 C15
Sobreira Formosa *Portugal* 36 F3
Soc Giang *Vietnam* 58 F6
Soc Trang *Vietnam* 65 H5
Soča → *Europe* 26 E6
Socastee *U.S.A.* 117 E15
Sochaczew *Poland* 31 F7
Soch'e = Shache *China* 60 C2
Sochi *Russia* 35 J4
Sochos *Greece* 44 F7
Société, Îs. de la *French Polynesia* 97 J12
Society Is. = Société, Îs. de la *French Polynesia* 97 J12
Socompa, Portezuelo de *Chile* 126 A2
Socorro *N. Mex., U.S.A.* 109 J10
Socorro *Tex., U.S.A.* 116 F1
Socorro, I. *Mexico* 118 D2
Socotra *Yemen* 75 E5
Socovos *Spain* 39 G3
Socuéllamos *Spain* 39 F2
Soda L. *U.S.A.* 109 J5
Soda Plains *India* 69 B8
Soda Springs *U.S.A.* 108 E8
Sodankylä *Finland* 8 C22
Soddy-Daisy *U.S.A.* 117 D12
Söderala *Sweden* 10 C10
Söderåsen △ *Sweden* 11 H7
Söderbärke *Sweden* 10 D9
Söderfors *Sweden* 10 D11
Söderhamn *Sweden* 10 C11
Söderköping *Sweden* 11 F10
Södermanland *Sweden* 9 G17
Södermanlands län □ *Sweden* 10 E10
Södertälje *Sweden* 10 E11
Sodiri *Sudan* 81 E2
Sodo *Ethiopia* 81 F4
Södra Dellen *Sweden* 10 C10
Södra Finnskoga *Sweden* 10 D6
Södra Sandby *Sweden* 11 J7
Södra Ulvön *Sweden* 10 B12
Södra Vi *Sweden* 11 G9
Sodražica *Slovenia* 41 C11
Sodus *U.S.A.* 114 C7
Sodwana Bay △ *S. Africa* 89 D5
Soekmekaar = Morebeng *S. Africa* 89 C4
Soest *Germany* 24 D4
Soest *Neths.* 17 B5
Sofades *Greece* 46 B4
Sofala □ *Mozam.* 89 B5
Sofara *Mali* 82 C4

Sofia = Sofiya *Bulgaria* **44 D7**
Sofia ➤ *Madag.* **89 B8**
Sofievka *Ukraine* **33 H7**
Sofiko *Greece* **46 D5**
Sofiya *Bulgaria* **44 D7**
Sofiya □ *Bulgaria* **44 D7**
Sofiya ✈ (SOF) *Bulgaria* **44 D7**
Sofrana *Greece* **47 E8**
Sōfu-Gan *Japan* **55 K10**
Sogakofe *Ghana* **83 D5**
Sogamoso *Colombia* **124 B4**
Sogār *Iran* **71 E8**
Sögel *Germany* **24 C3**
Sogndalsfjøra *Norway* **8 F12**
Søgne *Norway* **9 G12**
Sognefjorden *Norway* **8 F11**
Söğüt *Bilecik, Turkey* **47 A12**
Söğüt *Burdur, Turkey* **47 D11**
Söğüt Dağı *Turkey* **47 D11**
Söğütköy *Turkey* **47 E10**
Soh *Iran* **71 C6**
Sohâg *Egypt* **80 B3**
Sohagpur *India* **68 H8**
Soignies *Belgium* **17 D4**
Soin *Burkina Faso* **82 C4**
Soira *Eritrea* **81 E4**
Soissons *France* **19 C10**
Sōja *Japan* **55 G6**
Sojat *India* **68 G5**
Sok ➤ *Russia* **34 D10**
Sokal *Ukraine* **23 C13**
Sokcho *S. Korea* **57 E15**
Söke *Turkey* **47 D9**
Sokelo *Dem. Rep. of the Congo* **87 D1**
Sokhumi *Georgia* **35 J5**
Soko Banja *Serbia* **44 C5**
Sokol *Russia* **32 C11**
Sokolac *Bos.-H.* **28 G3**
Sokółka *Poland* **30 E10**
Sokolo *Ségou, Mali* **82 C3**
Sokolo *Sikasso, Mali* **82 C3**
Sokolov *Czech Rep.* **26 A5**
Sokolów Małopolski *Poland* **31 H9**
Sokołów Podlaski *Poland* **31 F9**
Sokoły *Poland* **31 F9**
Sokoto *Nigeria* **83 C6**
Sokoto □ *Nigeria* **83 C6**
Sokoto ➤ *Nigeria* **83 C5**
Sokyrnytsya *Ukraine* **29 B8**
Sokyryany *Ukraine* **29 B13**
Sol Iletsk *Russia* **52 D6**
Sola ➤ *Poland* **31 H6**
Solai *Kenya* **86 B4**
Solan *India* **68 D7**
Solana Beach *U.S.A.* **111 N9**
Solander I. *N.Z.* **91 G1**
Solano *Phil.* **61 C4**
Solapur *India* **66 L9**
Solca *Romania* **29 C10**
Solda Gölü *Turkey* **47 D11**
Soldăneşti *Moldova* **29 C13**
Soldeu *Andorra* **38 C6**
Soldotna *U.S.A.* **100 C4**
Soléa *Cyprus* **49 D12**
Solec Kujawski *Poland* **31 E5**
Soledad *Colombia* **124 A4**
Soledad *U.S.A.* **110 J5**
Soledad *Venezuela* **124 B6**
Solent, The *U.K.* **15 G6**
Solenzara *France* **21 G13**
Solesmes *France* **19 B10**
Solfonntaggen *Norway* **9 F12**
Solhan *Turkey* **73 C9**
Soligorsk = Salihorsk
  Belarus **23 B14**
Solihull *U.K.* **15 E6**
Solikamsk *Russia* **52 D6**
Solila *Madag.* **89 C8**
Solimões = Amazonas ➤
  S. Amer. **125 D8**
Solin *Croatia* **41 E13**
Solingen *Germany* **24 D3**
Söll *Austria* **25 H8**
Sollebrunn *Sweden* **11 F6**
Solleftea *Sweden* **10 A11**
Sóller *Spain* **48 B9**
Sollentuna *Sweden* **10 E11**
Sollerön *Sweden* **10 D8**
Solling *Germany* **24 D5**
Solling-Vogler △ *Germany* **24 D5**
Solnechnogorsk *Russia* **32 D9**
Solo ➤ *Indonesia* **63 G15**
Solofra *Italy* **43 B7**
Sologne *France* **19 E8**
Solok *Indonesia* **62 E2**
Sololá *Guatemala* **120 D1**
Sololo *Kenya* **86 B4**
Solomon, N. Fork ➤ *U.S.A.* **112 F4**
Solomon, S. Fork ➤ *U.S.A.* **112 F4**
Solomon Is. ■ *Pac. Oc.* **90 B8**
Solomon Rise *Pac. Oc.* **96 G7**
Solon *China* **60 B7**
Solon Springs *U.S.A.* **112 B8**
Solor *Indonesia* **63 F6**
Solotcha *Russia* **32 E10**
Solothurn *Switz.* **25 H3**

Solothurn □ *Switz.* **25 H3**
Solotvyn *Ukraine* **29 B9**
Solsona *Spain* **38 C6**
Solt *Hungary* **28 D4**
Šolta *Croatia* **41 E13**
Soltānābād *Khorāsān, Iran* **71 C8**
Soltānābād *Khorāsān, Iran* **71 B8**
Soltau *Germany* **24 C5**
Soltsy *Russia* **32 C6**
Solunska Glava *Macedonia* **44 E5**
Solvang *U.S.A.* **111 L6**
Solvay *U.S.A.* **115 C8**
Sölvesborg *Sweden* **11 H8**
Solway Firth *U.K.* **14 C4**
Solwezi *Zambia* **87 E2**
Sōma *Japan* **54 F10**
Soma *Turkey* **47 B9**
Somabhula *Zimbabwe* **89 B4**
Somali Pen. *Africa* **75 F4**
Somali Rep. ■ *Africa* **75 F4**
Somalia = Somali Rep. ■
  Africa **75 F4**
Somaliland □ *Somali Rep.* **75 F4**
Sombernon *France* **19 E11**
Sombor *Serbia* **28 E4**
Sombra *Canada* **114 D2**
Sombrerete *Mexico* **118 C4**
Sombrero *Anguilla* **121 C7**
Şomcuta Mare *Romania* **29 C8**
Somdari *India* **68 G5**
Someido △ *Spain* **36 B4**
Somers *U.S.A.* **108 B6**
Somerset *Ky., U.S.A.* **113 G11**
Somerset *Mass., U.S.A.* **115 E13**
Somerset *Pa., U.S.A.* **114 F5**
Somerset □ *U.K.* **15 F5**
Somerset I. *Canada* **100 B10**
Somerset East *S. Africa* **88 E4**
Somerset West *S. Africa* **88 E2**
Somersworth *U.S.A.* **115 C14**
Somerton *U.S.A.* **109 K6**
Somerville *U.S.A.* **115 F10**
Someş ➤ *Romania* **28 C7**
Someşul Mare ➤ *Romania* **29 C8**
Somme □ *France* **19 C9**
Somme ➤ *France* **19 B8**
Somme, B. de la *France* **18 B8**
Sommen *Jönköping, Sweden* **11 F8**
Sommen *Östergötland, Sweden* **11 F9**
Sommepy-Tahure *France* **19 C11**
Sömmerda *Germany* **24 D7**
Sommesous *France* **19 D11**
Sommières *France* **21 E8**
Somnath *India* **68 J4**
Somogy □ *Hungary* **28 D2**
Somogyszob *Hungary* **28 D2**
Somosomo *Fiji* **91 a**
Somosomo Str. *Fiji* **91 a**
Somoto *Nic.* **120 D2**
Sompolno *Poland* **31 F5**
Somport, Puerto de *Spain* **38 C4**
Son ➤ *India* **69 G11**
Son Ha *Vietnam* **64 E7**
Son Hoa *Vietnam* **64 F7**
Son La *Vietnam* **58 G4**
Son Serra *Spain* **48 B10**
Son Servera *Spain* **38 F8**
Son Tay *Vietnam* **58 G5**
Soná *Panama* **120 E3**
Sonamarg *India* **69 B6**
Sonamukhi *India* **69 H12**
Sonar ➤ *India* **69 G8**
Sönch'ön *N. Korea* **57 E13**
Sondags ➤ *S. Africa* **88 E4**
Söndalo *India* **40 B7**
Sondar *India* **69 C6**
Sønder Felding *Denmark* **11 J2**
Sønder Omme *Denmark* **11 J2**
Sønderborg *Denmark* **11 K3**
Sondershausen *Germany* **24 D6**
Sóndrio *Italy* **40 B6**
Sone *Mozam.* **87 F3**
Sonepur *India* **67 J13**
Song *Nigeria* **83 D7**
Song Cau *Vietnam* **64 F7**
Song Hong ➤ *Vietnam* **58 F5**
Song Xian *China* **56 G7**
Songan *Indonesia* **63 J18**
Songea *Tanzania* **87 E4**
Songeons *France* **19 C8**
Songhua Hu *China* **57 C14**
Songhua Jiang ➤ *China* **60 B8**
Songimvelo △ *S. Africa* **89 D5**
Songjiang *China* **59 B13**
Sŏngjin = Kimch'aek
  N. Korea **57 D15**
Songkan *China* **58 C6**
Songkhla *Thailand* **65 J3**
Songming *China* **58 E4**
Songnim *N. Korea* **57 E13**
Songo *Mozam.* **85 H6**
Songo *Sudan* **79 G10**
Songpan *China* **58 A4**
Songtao *China* **58 C7**
Songwe *Dem. Rep. of the Congo* **86 C2**
Songwe ➤ *Africa* **87 D3**

Songxi *China* **59 D12**
Songzi *China* **59 B8**
Sonhat *India* **69 H10**
Sonid Youqi *China* **56 C7**
Sonipat *India* **68 E7**
Sonkach *India* **68 H7**
Sonkovo *Russia* **32 D9**
Sonmiani *Pakistan* **68 G2**
Sonmiani B. *Pakistan* **68 G2**
Sonnino *Italy* **42 A6**
Sono ➤ *Brazil* **125 E9**
Sonoma *U.S.A.* **110 G4**
Sonora *Calif., U.S.A.* **110 H6**
Sonora *Tex., U.S.A.* **116 F4**
Sonora □ *Mexico* **118 B2**
Sonora ➤ *Mexico* **118 B2**
Sonoran Desert *U.S.A.* **111 L12**
Sonoyta *Mexico* **118 A2**
Sonqor *Iran* **73 E12**
Sonseca *Spain* **37 F7**
Sonsonate *El Salv.* **120 D2**
Sonstorp *Sweden* **11 F9**
Sonthofen *Germany* **25 H6**
Soochow = Suzhou *China* **59 B13**
Sop Hao *Laos* **58 G5**
Sop Prap *Thailand* **64 D2**
Sopelana *Spain* **38 B2**
Sopi *Indonesia* **63 D7**
Sopot *Bulgaria* **45 D8**
Sopot *Poland* **30 D5**
Sopot *Serbia* **44 B4**
Sopotnica *Macedonia* **44 E5**
Sopron *Hungary* **28 C1**
Sopur *India* **69 B6**
Sør-Rondane *Antarctica* **5 D4**
Sorah *Pakistan* **68 F3**
Söråker *Sweden* **10 B11**
Sorano *Italy* **41 F8**
Soraon *India* **69 G9**
Sorbas *Spain* **39 H2**
Sörbygden *Sweden* **10 B10**
Sore *France* **20 D3**
Sorel-Tracy *Canada* **104 C5**
Soresina *Italy* **40 C6**
Sörforsa *Sweden* **10 C10**
Sórgono *Italy* **42 B1**
Sorgues *France* **21 D8**
Sorgun *Turkey* **72 C6**
Soria *Spain* **38 D2**
Soria □ *Spain* **38 D2**
Soriano *Uruguay* **126 C4**
Soriano nel Cimino *Italy* **41 F9**
Sorkh, Kuh-e *Iran* **71 C8**
Sorø *Denmark* **11 J5**
Soro *Guinea* **82 C3**
Soroca *Moldova* **29 B13**
Sorocaba *Brazil* **127 A6**
Soroki = Soroca *Moldova* **29 B13**
Sorong *Indonesia* **63 E8**
Soroni *Greece* **49 C10**
Soroti *Uganda* **86 B3**
Sørøya *Norway* **8 A20**
Sørøysundet *Norway* **8 A20**
Sorraia ➤ *Portugal* **37 G2**
Sorrell *Australia* **95 G4**
Sorrento *Italy* **43 B7**
Sorsele *Sweden* **8 D17**
Sörsjön *Sweden* **10 C7**
Sorso *Italy* **42 B1**
Sorsogon *Phil.* **61 E6**
Sortavala *Russia* **32 B6**
Sortino *Italy* **43 E8**
Sortland *Norway* **8 B16**
Sorvizhi *Russia* **34 B9**
Sos del Rey Católico *Spain* **38 C3**
Soscumica, L. *Canada* **104 B4**
Sósdala *Sweden* **11 H7**
Sosna ➤ *Russia* **33 F10**
Sosnovka *Kirov, Russia* **34 B10**
Sosnovka *Tambov, Russia* **34 D5**
Sosnovyy Bor *Russia* **32 C5**
Sosnowiec *Poland* **31 H6**
Sospel *France* **21 E11**
Sossus Vlei *Namibia* **88 C2**
Šoštanj *Slovenia* **41 B12**
Sŏsura *N. Korea* **57 C16**
Sot ➤ *India* **69 F8**
Sotik *Kenya* **86 C4**
Sotkamo *Finland* **8 D23**
Soto del Barco *Spain* **36 B4**
Soto la Marina *Mexico* **119 C5**
Soto la Marina ➤ *Mexico* **119 C5**
Soto y Amío *Spain* **36 C5**
Sotrondio *Spain* **36 B5**
Sotuta *Mexico* **119 C7**
Souanké *Congo* **84 D2**
Soubré *Ivory C.* **82 D3**
Souda *Greece* **49 D6**
Soudas, Ormos *Greece* **49 D6**
Souderton *U.S.A.* **115 F9**
Soufli *Greece* **45 E10**

Soufrière *Guadeloupe* **120 b**
Soufrière *St. Lucia* **121 f**
Soufrière Bay *Dominica* **121 f**
Souillac *France* **20 D5**
Souilly *France* **19 C12**
Soukhouma *Laos* **64 E5**
Sŏul = Seoul *S. Korea* **57 F14**
Soulac-sur-Mer *France* **20 C2**
Soultz-sous-Forêts *France* **19 D14**
Sound, The = Øresund
  Europe **11 J6**
Sound, The *U.K.* **15 G3**
Sounio, Akra *Greece* **46 D6**
Sources, Mt. aux *Lesotho* **89 D4**
Soure *Brazil* **125 D9**
Soure *Portugal* **36 E2**
Souris *Man., Canada* **103 D8**
Souris *P.E.I., Canada* **105 C7**
Souris ➤ *N. Amer.* **112 A4**
Sourou ➤ *Africa* **82 C4**
Sourpi *Greece* **46 B4**
Sousa *Brazil* **125 E11**
Sousel *Portugal* **37 G3**
Sousse *Tunisia* **79 A8**
Soustons *France* **20 E2**
Sout ➤ *S. Africa* **88 E2**
South Africa ■ *Africa* **88 E3**
South America *122 E5*
South Aulatsivik I. *Canada* **105 A7**
South Australia □ *Australia* **95 E2**
South Australian Basin
  Ind. Oc. **96 L4**
South Ayrshire □ *U.K.* **13 F4**
South Baldy Pk. *U.S.A.* **109 J10**
South Bass I. *U.S.A.* **114 E2**
South Bend *Ind., U.S.A.* **112 E10**
South Bend *Wash., U.S.A.* **110 D3**
South Boston *U.S.A.* **113 G14**
South Branch *Canada* **105 C8**
South Brook *Canada* **105 C8**
South Bruny I. *Australia* **95 G4**
South C. *Australia* **90 F7**
South Carolina □ *U.S.A.* **117 E14**
South Charleston *U.S.A.* **113 F13**
South China Sea *Asia* **62 C4**
South Cumberland Is. △
  Australia **94 J7**
South Dakota □ *U.S.A.* **112 C4**
South Deerfield *U.S.A.* **115 D12**
South Downs *U.K.* **15 G7**
South East C. *Australia* **95 G4**
South East Is. *Australia* **93 F3**
South Esk ➤ *U.K.* **13 E6**
South Fiji Basin *Pac. Oc.* **96 K9**
South Foreland *U.K.* **15 F9**
South Fork American ➤
  U.S.A. **110 G5**
South Fork Feather ➤
  U.S.A. **110 F5**
South Fork Grand ➤
  U.S.A. **112 C2**
South Fork Milk ➤ *U.S.A.*
  108 B10
South Fork Republican ➤
  U.S.A. **112 E3**
South Georgia *Antarctica* **128 G9**
South Gloucestershire □
  U.K. **15 F5**
South Hadley *U.S.A.* **115 D12**
South Haven *U.S.A.* **112 D10**
South Henik L. *Canada* **103 A9**
South Horr *Kenya* **86 B4**
South I. *Kenya* **86 B4**
South I. *N.Z.* **91 F3**
South Indian Lake *Canada* **103 B9**
South Invercargill *N.Z.* **91 G2**
South Island □ *N.Z.* **91 F3**
South Kitui △ *Kenya* **86 C4**
South Knife ➤ *Canada* **103 B10**
South Koel ➤ *India* **69 H11**
South Korea ■ *Asia* **57 G15**
South Lake Tahoe *U.S.A.* **110 G6**
South Lanarkshire □ *U.K.* **13 F5**
South Loup ➤ *U.S.A.* **112 E4**
South Luangwa △ *Zambia* **87 E3**
South Magnetic Pole
  Antarctica **5 C9**
South Milwaukee *U.S.A.* **112 D10**
South Molton *U.K.* **15 F4**
South Moose L. *Canada* **103 C8**
South Nahanni ➤ *Canada* **102 A4**
South Nation ➤ *Canada* **115 A9**
South Natuna Is. =
  Natuna Selatan,
  Kepulauan *Indonesia* **62 D3**
South Negril Pt. *Jamaica* **120 a**
South Orkney Is. *Antarctica* **5 C18**
South Ossetia □ *Georgia* **35 J7**
South Pagai = Pagai
  Selatan, Pulau *Indonesia* **62 E2**
South Paris *U.S.A.* **115 B14**
South Pittsburg *U.S.A.* **117 D12**
South Platte ➤ *U.S.A.* **112 E3**
South Pole *Antarctica* **5 E**
South Porcupine *Canada* **104 C3**
South Portland *U.S.A.* **113 D18**

South Pt. *Barbados* **121 g**
South Pt. *U.S.A.* **114 B1**
South River *Canada* **104 C4**
South River *U.S.A.* **115 F10**
South Ronaldsay *U.K.* **13 C6**
South Sandwich Is. *Antarctica* **5 B1**
South Sandwich Trench
  Atl. Oc. **5 B1**
South Saskatchewan ➤
  Canada **103 C7**
South Seal ➤ *Canada* **103 B9**
South Shetland Is. *Antarctica* **5 C18**
South Shields *U.K.* **14 C6**
South Sioux City *U.S.A.* **112 D5**
South Sister *U.S.A.* **108 D3**
South Taranaki Bight *N.Z.* **91 C5**
South Tasman Rise *S. Ocean* **5 A10**
South Thompson ➤
  Canada **102 C4**
South Twin I. *Canada* **104 B4**
South Tyne ➤ *U.K.* **14 C5**
South Uist *U.K.* **13 D1**
South Valley *U.S.A.* **109 J10**
South Wellesley Is. *Australia* **94 B2**
South West C. *Australia* **95 G4**
South West C. *N.Z.* **91 G1**
South Williamsport *U.S.A.* **114 E8**
South Yorkshire □ *U.K.* **14 D6**
Southampton *Canada* **114 B3**
Southampton *U.K.* **15 G6**
Southampton *U.S.A.* **115 F12**
Southampton □ *U.K.* **15 G6**
Southampton I. *Canada* **101 C11**
Southaven *U.S.A.* **117 D9**
Southbank *Canada* **102 C3**
Southbridge *N.Z.* **91 E4**
Southbridge *U.S.A.* **115 D12**
Southend *Canada* **103 B8**
Southend-on-Sea *U.K.* **15 F8**
Southend-on-Sea □ *U.K.* **15 F8**
Southern = Janub □ *Sudan* **81 F2**
Southern = Yedebub
  Biheroch Bihereseboch
  na Hizboch □ *Ethiopia* **81 F4**
Southern = Yuzhnyy □
  Russia **35 H5**
Southern □ *Malawi* **87 F4**
Southern □ *S. Leone* **82 D2**
Southern □ *Zambia* **87 F2**
Southern Alps *N.Z.* **91 E3**
Southern Cross *Australia* **93 F2**
Southern Indian L. *Canada* **103 B9**
Southern Lau Group *Fiji* **91 a**
Southern Ocean *Antarctica* **5 C6**
Southern Pines *U.S.A.* **117 D15**
Southern Uplands *U.K.* **13 F5**
Southington *U.S.A.* **115 E12**
Southland □ *N.Z.* **91 F1**
Southold *U.S.A.* **115 E13**
Southport *Australia* **95 D5**
Southport *U.K.* **14 D4**
Southport *U.S.A.* **114 D8**
Southwest ➤ *Australia* **95 G4**
Southwest Pacific Basin
  Pac. Oc. **5 A12**
Southwold *U.K.* **15 E9**
Southwood △ *Australia* **95 D5**
Soutpansberg *S. Africa* **89 C4**
Souvigny *France* **19 F10**
Sovata *Romania* **29 D10**
Soverato *Italy* **43 D9**
Sovetsk *Kaliningrad, Russia* **30 C8**
Sovetsk *Kirov, Russia* **34 B9**
Sovicille *Italy* **41 E8**
Sovetskiy *S. Africa* **89 D4**
Soweto *S. Africa* **89 D4**
Sōya-Kaikyō = La Perouse
  Str. *Asia* **54 B11**
Sōya-Misaki *Japan* **54 B10**
Soyaux *France* **20 C4**
Soyo *Angola* **84 F2**
Sozh ➤ *Belarus* **23 B16**
Sozopol *Bulgaria* **45 D11**
Spa *Belgium* **17 D5**
Spain ■ *Europe* **7 H5**
Spalding *Australia* **95 E2**
Spalding *U.K.* **14 E7**
Spanaway *U.S.A.* **110 C4**
Spangler *U.S.A.* **114 F6**
Spanish *Canada* **104 C3**
Spanish Fork *U.S.A.* **108 F8**
Spanish Town *Br. Virgin Is.* **121 e**
Spanish Town *Jamaica* **120 a**
Sparks *U.S.A.* **110 F7**
Sparreholm *Sweden* **10 E10**
Sparta = Sparti *Greece* **46 D4**
Sparta *Mich., U.S.A.* **113 D11**
Sparta *N.J., U.S.A.* **115 E10**
Sparta *Wis., U.S.A.* **112 D8**
Spartanburg *U.S.A.* **117 D14**
Spartansburg *U.S.A.* **114 E5**
Sparti *Greece* **46 D4**
Spartivento, C. *Calabria, Italy* **43 E9**
Spartivento, C. *Sard., Italy* **42 D1**
Sparwood *Canada* **102 D6**
Spas-Demensk *Russia* **32 E7**
Spas-Klepiki *Russia* **32 E11**
Spassk Dalniy *Russia* **54 B6**

Spassk-Ryazanskiy *Russia* **32 E11**
Spatha, Akra *Greece* **49 D5**
Spatsizi ➤ *Canada* **102 B3**
Spatsizi Plateau
  Wilderness △ *Canada* **102 B3**
Spean ➤ *U.K.* **13 E4**
Spearfish *U.S.A.* **112 C2**
Spearman *U.S.A.* **116 C4**
Speculator *U.S.A.* **115 C10**
Speia *Moldova* **29 D14**
Speightstown *Barbados* **121 g**
Speke Gulf *Tanzania* **86 C3**
Spello *Italy* **41 F9**
Spence Bay = Taloyoak
  Canada **100 C10**
Spencer *Idaho, U.S.A.* **108 D7**
Spencer *Iowa, U.S.A.* **112 D6**
Spencer *N.Y., U.S.A.* **115 D8**
Spencer *Nebr., U.S.A.* **112 D5**
Spencer, C. *Australia* **95 F2**
Spencer B. *Namibia* **88 D1**
Spencer G. *Australia* **95 E2**
Spencerville *Canada* **115 B9**
Spences Bridge *Canada* **102 C4**
Spennymoor *U.K.* **14 C6**
Spenser Mts. *N.Z.* **91 E4**
Spentrup *Denmark* **11 H4**
Sperchios ➤ *Greece* **46 C4**
Sperrin Mts. *U.K.* **12 B5**
Spessart *Germany* **25 F5**
Spetses *Greece* **46 D5**
Spey ➤ *U.K.* **13 D5**
Speyer *Germany* **25 F4**
Spezand *Pakistan* **68 E2**
Spezzano Albanese *Italy* **43 C9**
Spiddle *Ireland* **12 C2**
Spiekeroog *Germany* **24 B3**
Spiez *Switz.* **25 J3**
Spili *Greece* **49 D6**
Spilimbergo *Italy* **41 B9**
Spīn Būldak *Afghan.* **68 D2**
Spinalónga *Greece* **49 D7**
Spinazzola *Italy* **43 B9**
Spineni *Romania* **29 F9**
Spirit Lake *U.S.A.* **110 D4**
Spirit River *Canada* **102 B5**
Spiritwood *Canada* **103 C7**
Spišská Nová Ves
  Slovak Rep. **27 C13**
Spišské Podhradie
  Slovak Rep. **27 B13**
Spital *Austria* **26 D7**
Spithead *U.K.* **15 G6**
Spittal an der Drau *Austria* **26 E6**
Spitzbergen = Svalbard *Arctic* **4 B8**
Spjelkavik *Norway* **8 E12**
Split *Croatia* **41 E13**
Split ✈ (SPU) *Croatia* **41 E13**
Split L. *Canada* **103 B9**
Split Lake *Canada* **103 B9**
Splitski Kanal *Croatia* **41 E13**
Splügenpass *Switz.* **25 J5**
Spofford *U.S.A.* **116 G4**
Spokane *U.S.A.* **108 C5**
Spoleto *Italy* **41 F9**
Spooner *U.S.A.* **112 C8**
Sporyy Navolok, Mys *Russia* **52 B7**
Sprague *U.S.A.* **108 C5**
Spratly I. *S. China Sea* **62 C4**
Spratly Is. *S. China Sea* **62 C4**
Spray *U.S.A.* **108 D4**
Spreča ➤ *Bos.-H.* **28 F3**
Spree ➤ *Germany* **24 C9**
Spreewald *Germany* **24 D9**
Spremberg *Germany* **24 D10**
Sprengisandur *Iceland* **8 D4**
Spring City *U.S.A.* **115 F9**
Spring Creek *U.S.A.* **108 F6**
Spring Garden *U.S.A.* **110 F6**
Spring Hall *Barbados* **121 g**
Spring Hill *U.S.A.* **117 G13**
Spring Mts. *U.S.A.* **111 J11**
Spring Valley *Calif., U.S.A.* **111 N10**
Spring Valley *Nev., U.S.A.* **111 J11**
Springbok *S. Africa* **88 D2**
Springboro *U.S.A.* **114 E4**
Springdale *Canada* **105 C8**
Springdale *U.S.A.* **116 C7**
Springe *Germany* **24 C5**
Springer *U.S.A.* **109 H11**
Springerville *U.S.A.* **109 J9**
Springfield *Canada* **114 D4**
Springfield *N.Z.* **91 E3**
Springfield *Colo., U.S.A.* **109 H12**
Springfield *Ill., U.S.A.* **112 F9**
Springfield *Mass., U.S.A.* **115 D12**
Springfield *Mo., U.S.A.* **112 G8**
Springfield *Ohio, U.S.A.* **113 F12**
Springfield *Oreg., U.S.A.* **108 D2**
Springfield *Tenn., U.S.A.* **117 C11**
Springfield *Vt., U.S.A.* **115 C12**
Springfontein *S. Africa* **88 E4**
Springhill *Canada* **105 C7**
Springhill *U.S.A.* **116 E8**
Springhouse *Canada* **102 C4**
Springs *S. Africa* **89 D4**
Springsure *Australia* **94 C4**

Springvale *U.S.A.* **115** C14
Springville *Calif., U.S.A.* **110** J8
Springville *N.Y., U.S.A.* **114** D6
Springville *Utah, U.S.A.* **108** F8
Springwater *U.S.A.* **114** D7
Spruce-Creek *U.S.A.* **114** F6
Spruce Knob-Seneca
　Rocks △ *U.S.A.* **113** F14
Spruce Mt. *U.S.A.* **115** B12
Spur *U.S.A.* **116** E4
Spurn Hd. *U.K.* **14** D8
Spuž *Montenegro* **44** D3
Spuzzum *Canada* **102** D4
Squam L. *U.S.A.* **115** C13
Squamish *Canada* **102** D4
Square Islands *Canada* **105** B8
Squillace, G. di *Italy* **43** D9
Squinzano *Italy* **43** B11
Squires, Mt. *Australia* **93** E4
Srbac *Bos.-H.* **28** E2
Srbica *Serbia* **44** D4
Srbija = Serbia ■ *Europe* **44** C4
Srbobran *Serbia* **28** E4
Sre Ambel *Cambodia* **65** G4
Sre Khtum *Cambodia* **65** F6
Sre Umbell = Sre Ambel
　Cambodia **65** G4
Srebrenica *Bos.-H.* **28** F4
Sredinny Ra. = Sredinnyy
　Khrebet *Russia* **53** D17
Sredinnyy Khrebet *Russia* **53** D17
Središče *Slovenia* **41** B13
Sredna Gora *Bulgaria* **45** D8
Srednekolymsk *Russia* **53** C16
Sredni Rodopi *Bulgaria* **45** E8
Srednogorie *Bulgaria* **45** D8
Śrem *Poland* **31** F4
Sremska Mitrovica *Serbia* **28** F4
Sremski Karlovci *Serbia* **28** E4
Srepok → *Cambodia* **64** F6
Sretensk *Russia* **53** D12
Sri Aman *Malaysia* **62** D4
Sri Lanka ■ *Asia* **66** R12
Srikakulam *India* **67** K13
Srinagar *India* **69** B6
Srinagarind Res. *Thailand* **64** E2
Środa Śląska *Poland* **31** G3
Środa Wielkopolski *Poland* **31** F4
Srono *Indonesia* **63** J17
Srpska Crnja *Serbia* **28** E5
Srpski Itebej *Serbia* **28** E5
Staaten → *Australia* **94** B3
Staaten River △ *Australia* **94** B3
Staberhuk *Germany* **24** A7
Stade *Germany* **24** B5
Stadskanaal *Neths.* **17** A6
Stadtallendorf *Germany* **24** E5
Stadthagen *Germany* **24** C5
Stadtlohn *Germany* **24** D2
Stadtroda *Germany* **24** E7
Staffa *U.K.* **13** E2
Staffanstorp *Sweden* **11** J7
Stafford *U.K.* **14** E5
Stafford *U.S.A.* **112** G4
Stafford Springs *U.S.A.* **115** E12
Staffordshire □ *U.K.* **14** E5
Stagnone *Italy* **42** E5
Stagnone di Marsala △ *Italy* **42** E5
Staines *U.K.* **15** F7
Stainz *Austria* **26** E8
Stakhanov *Ukraine* **33** H10
Stalać *Serbia* **44** C5
Stalida *Greece* **49** D7
Stallarholmen *Sweden* **10** E11
Ställdalen *Sweden* **10** E8
Stalowa Wola *Poland* **31** H9
Stalybridge *U.K.* **14** D5
Stamford *Australia* **94** C3
Stamford *U.K.* **15** E7
Stamford *Conn., U.S.A.* **115** E11
Stamford *N.Y., U.S.A.* **115** D10
Stamford *Tex., U.S.A.* **116** E5
Stampriet *Namibia* **88** C2
Stamps *U.S.A.* **116** E8
Stančevo = Kalipetrovo
　Bulgaria **45** B11
Standerton *S. Africa* **89** D4
Standish *U.S.A.* **113** D12
Stanford *S. Africa* **88** E2
Stanford *U.S.A.* **108** C8
Stånga *Sweden* **11** G12
Stanger *S. Africa* **89** D5
Stängselåsen =
　Salpausselkä *Finland* **32** B4
Stanišić *Serbia* **28** E4
Stanislaus → *U.S.A.* **110** H5
Stanisławów *Poland* **31** F8
Stanley *Australia* **95** G4
Stanley *Falk. Is.* **128** G5
Stanley *U.K.* **14** C6
Stanley *Idaho, U.S.A.* **108** D6
Stanley *N. Dak., U.S.A.* **112** A2
Stanley *N.Y., U.S.A.* **114** D7
Stanley Mission *Canada* **103** B8
Stanovoy Khrebet *Russia* **53** D14
Stanovoy Ra. = Stanovoy
　Khrebet *Russia* **53** D14

Stansmore Ra. *Australia* **92** D4
Stansted, London ✈ (STN)
　U.K. **15** F8
Stanthorpe *Australia* **95** D5
Stanton *U.S.A.* **116** E4
Stanwood *U.S.A.* **110** B4
Staples *U.S.A.* **112** B6
Stapleton *U.S.A.* **112** E3
Staporków *Poland* **31** G7
Star City *Canada* **103** C8
Star Lake *U.S.A.* **115** B9
Stará L'ubovňa *Slovak Rep.* **27** B13
Stara Moravica *Serbia* **28** E4
Stara Pazova *Serbia* **28** F5
Stara Planina *Bulgaria* **44** C7
Stara Sil *Ukraine* **31** J9
Stará Turá *Slovak Rep.* **27** C10
Stara Ushytsya *Ukraine* **29** B12
Stara Zagora *Bulgaria* **45** D9
Starachowice *Poland* **31** G8
Staraya Russa *Russia* **32** D6
Starbuck I. *Kiribati* **97** H12
Starचहiojd *Romania* **29** E11
Starcke △ *Australia* **94** A4
Stargard Szczeciński *Poland* **30** E2
Stari Bar *Montenegro* **44** D3
Stari Trg *Slovenia* **41** C12
Staritsa *Russia* **32** D8
Starke *U.S.A.* **117** G13
Starkville *U.S.A.* **117** E10
Starnberg *Germany* **25** H7
Starnberger See *Germany* **25** H7
Starobilsk *Ukraine* **33** H10
Starodub *Russia* **33** F7
Starogard Gdański *Poland* **30** E5
Starokonstantinov =
　Starokonstyantyniv
　Ukraine **23** D14
Starokonstyantyniv
　Ukraine **23** D14
Starokozache *Ukraine* **29** D14
Starominskaya *Russia* **33** J10
Staroshcherbinovskaya
　Russia **33** J10
Start Pt. *U.K.* **15** G4
Stary Sącz *Poland* **31** J7
Staryy Biryuzyak *Russia* **35** H8
Staryy Chartoriysk *Ukraine* **23** C13
Staryy Krym *Ukraine* **33** K8
Staryy Oskol *Russia* **33** G9
Staryy Sambir *Ukraine* **31** J9
Stassfurt *Germany* **24** D7
Staszów *Poland* **31** H8
State College *U.S.A.* **114** F7
Stateline *U.S.A.* **110** G7
Staten = Estados, I. de
　Los *Argentina* **128** G4
Staten I. *U.S.A.* **115** F10
Statesboro *U.S.A.* **117** E14
Statesville *U.S.A.* **117** D14
Statia = St. Eustatius
　W. Indies **121** C7
Stauffer *U.S.A.* **111** L7
Staunton *Ill., U.S.A.* **112** F9
Staunton *Va., U.S.A.* **113** F14
Stavanger *Norway* **9** G11
Staveley *N.Z.* **91** E3
Stavelot *Belgium* **17** D5
Stavern *Norway* **9** G14
Stavoren *Neths.* **17** B5
Stavropol *Russia* **35** H6
Stavropol □ *Russia* **35** G6
Stavros *Cyprus* **49** D11
Stavros *Kriti, Greece* **49** D6
Stavros *Thessaloniki, Greece* **44** F7
Stavros, Akra *Greece* **49** D6
Stavroupoli *Greece* **45** E8
Stawell *Australia* **95** F3
Stawell → *Australia* **94** C3
Stawiski *Poland* **30** E9
Stawiszyn *Poland* **31** G5
Stayner *Canada* **114** B4
Stayton *U.S.A.* **108** D2
Steamboat Springs *U.S.A.* **108** F10
Steblevë *Albania* **44** E4
Steele *U.S.A.* **112** B4
Steelton *U.S.A.* **114** F8
Steen River *Canada* **102** B5
Steens Mt. *U.S.A.* **108** E4
Steenwijk *Neths.* **17** B6
Steep Pt. *Australia* **93** E1
Steep Rock *Canada* **103** C9
Ştefan Vodă *Moldova* **29** D14
Ştefăneşti *Romania* **29** C12
Stefanie △ *Ethiopia* **81** G4
Stefanie L. = Chew Bahir
　Ethiopia **81** G4
Stefansson Bay *Antarctica* **5** C5
Stege *Denmark* **11** K6
Ştei *Romania* **28** D7
Steiermark □ *Austria* **26** D8
Steigerwald *Germany* **25** F6
Steigerwald △ *Germany* **25** F6
Steilacoom *U.S.A.* **110** C4
Steilrandberge *Namibia* **88** B1
Steinbach *Canada* **103** D9
Steinfurt *Germany* **24** C3

Steinhausen *Namibia* **88** C2
Steinheim *Germany* **24** D5
Steinhuder Meer *Germany* **24** C4
Steinhuder Meer △ *Germany* **24** C5
Steinkjer *Norway* **8** D14
Steinkopf *S. Africa* **88** D2
Steinwald △ *Germany* **25** F8
Stellarton *Canada* **105** C7
Stellenbosch *S. Africa* **88** E2
Stelvio, Paso dello *Italy* **40** B7
Stenay *France* **19** C12
Stendal *Germany* **24** C7
Stende *Latvia* **30** A9
Stenhamra *Sweden* **10** E11
Stenshuvud △ *Sweden* **11** J8
Stenstorp *Sweden* **11** F7
Stenungsund *Sweden* **11** F5
Steornabhaigh =
　Stornoway *U.K.* **13** C2
Stepanakert = Xankändi
　Azerbaijan **73** C12
Stepanavan *Armenia* **35** K7
Stephens Creek *Australia* **95** E3
Stephens I. *Canada* **102** C2
Stephens L. *Canada* **103** B9
Stephenville *Canada* **105** C8
Stephenville *U.S.A.* **116** E5
Stepnica *Poland* **30** E1
Steppe *Asia* **50** C7
Sterea Ellas □ *Greece* **46** C4
Sterkstroom *S. Africa* **88** E4
Sterling *Colo., U.S.A.* **108** F12
Sterling *Ill., U.S.A.* **112** E9
Sterling *Kans., U.S.A.* **112** F4
Sterling City *U.S.A.* **116** F4
Sterling Heights *U.S.A.* **113** D12
Sterling Run *U.S.A.* **114** E6
Sterlitamak *Russia* **52** D6
Sternberg *Germany* **24** B7
Šternberk *Czech Rep.* **27** B10
Sternes *Greece* **49** D6
Sterzing = Vipiteno *Italy* **41** B8
Stettin = Szczecin *Poland* **30** E1
Stettiner Haff *Germany* **24** B10
Stettler *Canada* **102** C6
Steubenville *U.S.A.* **114** F4
Stevenage *U.K.* **15** F7
Stevens Point *U.S.A.* **112** C9
Stevenson *U.S.A.* **110** E5
Stevenson → *Australia* **95** D2
Stevenson L. *Canada* **103** C9
Stevensville *U.S.A.* **108** C6
Stevns Klint *Denmark* **11** J6
Stewart *Canada* **102** B3
Stewart *U.S.A.* **110** F7
Stewart → *Canada* **100** C6
Stewart, C. *Australia* **94** A1
Stewart, I. *Chile* **128** G2
Stewart I. *N.Z.* **91** G1
Stewarts Point *U.S.A.* **110** G3
Stewartville *U.S.A.* **112** D7
Stewiacke *Canada* **105** C7
Steynsburg *S. Africa* **88** E4
Steyr *Austria* **26** C7
Steyr → *Austria* **26** C7
Steytlerville *S. Africa* **88** E3
Stia *Italy* **41** E8
Stigler *U.S.A.* **116** D7
Stigliano *Italy* **43** B9
Stigtomta *Sweden* **11** F10
Stikine → *Canada* **102** B2
Stilfontein *S. Africa* **88** D4
Stilida *Greece* **46** C4
Stillwater *N.Z.* **91** E3
Stillwater *N.Y., U.S.A.* **115** D11
Stillwater *Okla., U.S.A.* **116** C6
Stillwater Range *U.S.A.* **108** G4
Stillwater Res. *U.S.A.* **115** C9
Stilo, Pta. *Italy* **43** D9
Stilwell *U.S.A.* **116** D7
Stînga Nistrului = *Moldova* **29** C14
Stirling *Canada* **114** B7
Stirling *U.K.* **13** E5
Stirling □ *U.K.* **13** E4
Stirling Ra. *Australia* **93** F2
Stirling Range △ *Australia* **93** F2
Stittsville *Canada* **115** A9
Stjernøya *Norway* **8** A20
Stjørdalshalsen *Norway* **8** E14
Stockach *Germany* **25** H5
Stockaryd *Sweden* **11** G8
Stockerau *Austria* **27** C9
Stockholm *Sweden* **10** E12
Stockholm Arlanda ✈
　(ARN) *Sweden* **10** E11
Stockholms län □ *Sweden* **10** E12
Stockport *U.K.* **14** D5
Stocksbridge *U.K.* **14** D6
Stockton *Calif., U.S.A.* **110** H5
Stockton *Kans., U.S.A.* **112** F4
Stockton *Mo., U.S.A.* **112** G8
Stockton-on-Tees *U.K.* **14** C7
Stockton-on-Tees □ *U.K.* **14** C6
Stockton Plateau *U.S.A.* **116** F3
Stoczek Łukowski *Poland* **31** G8

Stöde *Sweden* **10** B10
Stoeng Treng *Cambodia* **64** F5
Stoer, Pt. of *U.K.* **13** C3
Stogovo *Macedonia* **44** E4
Stoholm *Denmark* **11** H3
Stoke-on-Trent *U.K.* **14** D5
Stoke-on-Trent □ *U.K.* **14** D5
Stokes △ *Australia* **93** F3
Stokes Pt. *Australia* **95** G3
Stokes Ra. *Australia* **92** C5
Stokksnes *Iceland* **8** D6
Stokmarknes *Norway* **8** B16
Stolac *Bos.-H.* **44** C1
Stolberg *Germany* **24** E2
Stolbovoy, Ostrov *Russia* **53** B14
Stolbtsy = Stowbtsy *Belarus* **23** B14
Stolin *Belarus* **23** C14
Stöllet *Sweden* **10** D7
Stolnici *Romania* **29** F9
Stomio *Greece* **49** D5
Ston *Croatia* **41** F14
Stone *U.K.* **14** E5
Stoneboro *U.S.A.* **114** E4
Stonehaven *U.K.* **13** E6
Stonehenge *Australia* **94** C3
Stonehenge *U.K.* **15** F6
Stonewall *Canada* **103** C9
Stony L. *Man., Canada* **103** B9
Stony L. *Ont., Canada* **114** B6
Stony Point *U.S.A.* **115** E11
Stony Pt. *U.S.A.* **115** C8
Stony Rapids *Canada* **103** B7
Stony Tunguska =
　Tunguska,
　Podkamennaya →
　Russia **53** C10
Stonyford *U.S.A.* **110** F4
Stopnica *Poland* **31** H7
Storå *Sweden* **10** E9
Storå → *Denmark* **11** H2
Stora Gla *Sweden* **10** E6
Stora Le *Sweden* **10** E5
Stora Lulevatten *Sweden* **8** C18
Storavan *Sweden* **8** D18
Stord *Norway* **9** G11
Store Bælt *Denmark* **11** J4
Store Heddinge *Denmark* **11** J6
Store Mosse △ *Sweden* **11** G7
Storebro *Sweden* **11** G9
Storfors *Sweden* **10** E8
Storlien *Sweden* **10** A6
Storm B. *Australia* **95** G4
Storm Lake *U.S.A.* **112** D7
Stormberge *S. Africa* **88** E4
Stormsrivier *S. Africa* **88** E3
Stornoway *U.K.* **13** C2
Storo *Italy* **40** C7
Storozhinets =
　Storozhynets *Ukraine* **29** B10
Storozhynets *Ukraine* **29** B10
Storrs *U.S.A.* **115** E12
Storsjön *Gävleborg, Sweden* **10** D10
Storsjön *Jämtland, Sweden* **10** B7
Storsjön *Jämtland, Sweden* **10** A8
Storuman *Sweden* **8** D17
Storuman, L. *Sweden* **8** D17
Storvätteshågna *Sweden* **10** B6
Storvik *Sweden* **10** D10
Storvreta *Sweden* **10** E11
Stouffville *Canada* **114** C5
Stoughton *Canada* **103** D8
Stour → *Dorset, U.K.* **15** G6
Stour → *Kent, U.K.* **15** F9
Stour → *Suffolk, U.K.* **15** F9
Stourbridge *U.K.* **15** E5
Stout L. *Canada* **103** C10
Stove Pipe Wells Village
　U.S.A. **111** J9
Støvring *Denmark* **11** H3
Stow *U.S.A.* **114** E3
Stowbtsy *Belarus* **23** B14
Stowmarket *U.K.* **15** E9
Strabane *U.K.* **12** B4
Stracin *Macedonia* **44** D6
Stradella *Italy* **40** C6
Strahan *Australia* **95** G4
Strajitsa *Bulgaria* **45** D9
Strakonice *Czech Rep.* **26** B6
Straldzha *Bulgaria* **45** D10
Stralsund *Germany* **24** A9
Strand *S. Africa* **88** E2
Stranda *Møre og Romsdal,*
　Norway **8** E12
Stranda *Nord-Trøndelag,*
　Norway **8** E14
Strandby *Denmark* **11** G4
Strangford L. *U.K.* **12** B6
Strängnäs *Sweden* **10** E11
Stranorlar *Ireland* **12** B4
Stranraer *U.K.* **13** G3
Strasbourg *Canada* **103** C8
Strasbourg *France* **19** D14
Strasburg *Germany* **24** B9
Strășeni *Moldova* **29** C13
Stråssa *Sweden* **10** E9
Stratford *Canada* **114** C4
Stratford *N.Z.* **91** C5

Stratford *Calif., U.S.A.* **110** J7
Stratford *Conn., U.S.A.* **115** E11
Stratford *Tex., U.S.A.* **116** C3
Stratford-upon-Avon *U.K.* **15** E6
Strath Spey *U.K.* **13** D5
Strathalbyn *Australia* **95** F2
Strathaven *U.K.* **13** F4
Strathcona △ *Canada* **102** D3
Strathmore *Canada* **102** C6
Strathmore *U.K.* **13** E5
Strathmore *U.S.A.* **110** J7
Strathnaver *Canada* **102** C4
Strathpeffer *U.K.* **13** D4
Strathroy *Canada* **114** D3
Strathy Pt. *U.K.* **13** C4
Strattanville *U.S.A.* **114** E5
Stratton *U.S.A.* **115** A14
Stratton Mt. *U.S.A.* **115** C12
Straubing *Germany* **25** G8
Straumnes *Iceland* **8** C2
Strausberg *Germany* **24** C9
Strawberry → *U.S.A.* **108** F8
Straž △ *Australia* **93** F3
Strážnice *Czech Rep.* **27** C10
Středočeský □ *Czech Rep.* **26** B7
Streetsboro *U.S.A.* **114** E3
Streetsville *Canada* **114** C5
Strehaia *Romania* **29** F8
Strelcha *Bulgaria* **45** D8
Strelka *Russia* **53** D10
Streng → *Cambodia* **64** F4
Stresa *Italy* **40** C5
Streymoy *Færoe Is.* **8** E9
Strezhevoy *Russia* **52** C8
Stříbro *Czech Rep.* **26** A6
Strimonas → *Greece* **44** F7
Strofades *Greece* **46** D3
Strokestown *Ireland* **12** C3
Stroma *U.K.* **13** C5
Stromberg-Heuchelberg △
　Germany **25** F4
Strómboli *Italy* **43** D8
Stromeferry *U.K.* **13** D3
Stromness *U.K.* **13** C5
Strömsbruk *Sweden* **10** C11
Stromsburg *U.S.A.* **112** E5
Strömsnäsbruk *Sweden* **11** H7
Strömstad *Sweden* **11** F5
Strömsund *Sweden* **8** E16
Strongili *Greece* **47** E11
Strongoli *Italy* **43** C10
Strongsville *U.S.A.* **114** E3
Stronie Śląskie *Poland* **31** H3
Stronsay *U.K.* **13** B6
Stropkov *Slovak Rep.* **27** B14
Stroud *U.K.* **15** F5
Stroud Road *Australia* **95** E5
Stroudsburg *U.S.A.* **115** F9
Stroumbi *Cyprus* **49** E11
Struer *Denmark* **11** H2
Struga *Macedonia* **44** E4
Strugi Krasnyye *Russia* **32** C5
Struma → *Europe* **44** E7
Strumok *Ukraine* **29** E14
Struthers *Canada* **104** C2
Struthers *U.S.A.* **114** E4
Stryama *Bulgaria* **45** D8
Stryker *U.S.A.* **108** B6
Stryków *Poland* **31** G6
Stryy *Ukraine* **23** D12
Strzegom *Poland* **31** H3
Strzelce Krajeńskie *Poland* **31** F2
Strzelce Opolskie *Poland* **31** H5
Strzelecki Cr. → *Australia* **95** D2
Strzelecki Desert *Australia* **95** D3
Strzelin *Poland* **31** H4
Strzelno *Poland* **31** F5
Strzybnica *Poland* **31** H5
Strzyżów *Poland* **31** J8
Stuart *Fla., U.S.A.* **117** H14
Stuart *Nebr., U.S.A.* **112** D4
Stuart → *Canada* **102** C4
Stuart Bluff Ra. *Australia* **92** D5
Stuart L. *Canada* **102** C4
Stuart Ra. *Australia* **95** D1
Stubbekøbing *Denmark* **11** K6
Stuben *Austria* **26** D3
Studen Kladenets, Yazovir
　Bulgaria **45** E9
Studenka *Czech Rep.* **27** B11
Stugun *Sweden* **10** A9
Stuhr *Germany* **24** B4
Stull L. *Canada* **104** B1
Stung Treng = Stoeng
　Treng *Cambodia* **64** F5
Stupart → *Canada* **104** A1
Stupava *Slovak Rep.* **27** C10
Stupino *Russia* **32** E10
Sturgeon B. *U.S.A.* **112** C10
Sturgeon Bay *U.S.A.* **112** C10
Sturgeon Falls *Canada* **104** C4
Sturgeon L. *Alta., Canada* **102** B5
Sturgeon L. *Ont., Canada* **104** C1

Sturgeon L. *Ont., Canada* **114** B6
Sturgis *Canada* **103** C8
Sturgis *Mich., U.S.A.* **113** E11
Sturgis *S. Dak., U.S.A.* **112** C2
Sturkö *Sweden* **11** H9
Štúrovo *Slovak Rep.* **27** D11
Sturt △ *Australia* **95** D1
Sturt Cr. → *Australia* **92** C4
Sturt Stony Desert *Australia* **95** D3
Stutterheim *S. Africa* **88** E4
Stuttgart *Germany* **25** G5
Stuttgart *U.S.A.* **116** D9
Stuttgart Echterdingen ✈
　(STR) *Germany* **25** G5
Stuyvesant *U.S.A.* **115** D11
Stykkishólmur *Iceland* **8** D2
Styria = Steiermark □
　Austria **26** D8
Styrsö *Sweden* **11** G5
Su Xian = Suzhou *China* **56** H9
Suakin *Sudan* **80** D4
Suan *N. Korea* **57** E14
Suar *India* **69** E8
Subang *Indonesia* **63** G12
Subansiri → *India* **67** F18
Subarnarekha → *India* **69** H12
Subayhah *Si. Arabia* **70** D3
Subcetate *Romania* **28** E8
Subi *Indonesia* **62** D3
Subiaco *Italy* **41** G10
Subotica *Serbia* **28** D4
Suca *Ethiopia* **81** F4
Suceava *Romania* **29** C11
Suceava □ *Romania* **29** C11
Suceava → *Romania* **29** C11
Sucha-Beskidzka *Poland* **31** J6
Suchan = Partizansk *Russia* **54** C6
Suchań *Poland* **31** E2
Suchedniów *Poland* **31** G7
Suchil *Mexico* **118** C4
Suchitoto *El Salv.* **120** D2
Suchou = Suzhou *China* **59** B13
Süchow = Xuzhou *China* **57** G9
Suchowola *Poland* **30** E10
Suck → *Ireland* **12** C3
Sucre *Bolivia* **124** G5
Sućuraj *Croatia* **41** E14
Sucuriú → *Brazil* **125** H8
Sud □ *Cameroon* **83** E7
Sud, Pte. du *Canada* **105** C7
Sud-Kivu □
　Dem. Rep. of the Congo **86** C2
Sud-Ouest □ *Cameroon* **83** D6
Sud-Ouest, Pte. *Canada* **105** C7
Sud Ouest, Pte. *Mauritius* **85** d
Suda → *Russia* **32** C9
Sudak *Ukraine* **33** K8
Sudan *U.S.A.* **116** D3
Sudan ■ *Africa* **81** E3
Sudbury *Canada* **104** C3
Sudbury *U.K.* **15** E8
Sûdd *Sudan* **81** F3
Sudeifel = Deutsch-
　Luxemburgischer △
　Germany **25** F2
Süderbrarup *Germany* **24** A5
Süderlügum *Germany* **24** A4
Süderoogsand *Germany* **24** A4
Sudeten Mts. = Sudety
　Europe **27** A9
Sudety *Europe* **27** A9
Südheide △ *Germany* **24** C6
Suðuroy *Færoe Is.* **8** F9
Sudi *Tanzania* **87** E4
Sudirman, Pegunungan
　Indonesia **63** E9
Sudiți *Romania* **29** F12
Sudogda *Russia* **34** C5
Sudong, Pulau *Singapore* **65** d
Sudova Vyshnya *Ukraine* **31** J10
Sudr *Egypt* **80** B3
Sudzha *Russia* **33** G8
Sue → *Sudan* **81** F2
Sueca *Spain* **39** F4
Sŭedinenie *Bulgaria* **45** D8
Suemez I. *U.S.A.* **102** B2
Suez = El Suweis *Egypt* **80** J8
Suez, G. of = Suweis,
　Khalîg el *Egypt* **80** J8
Suez Canal = Suweis,
　Qanâ es *Egypt* **80** H8
Suffield *Canada* **102** C6
Suffolk *U.S.A.* **113** G15
Suffolk □ *U.K.* **15** E9
Şugag *Romania* **29** E8
Sugar Grove *U.S.A.* **114** E5
Sugarive → *India* **69** F12
Suğla Gölü *Turkey* **72** D5
Suhaia, Lacul *Romania* **29** G10
Şuḩār *Oman* **71** E8
Sühbaatar □ *Mongolia* **56** B8
Suhl *Germany* **24** E6
Şuhut *Turkey* **47** C12
Sui *Pakistan* **68** E3
Sui Xian *China* **56** G8
Šuica *Bos.-H.* **28** G2

Suichang *China* **59** C12
Suichuan *China* **59** D10
Suide *China* **56** F6
Suifenhe *China* **57** B16
Suihua *China* **60** B7
Suijiang *China* **58** C4
Suining *Hunan, China* **59** D8
Suining *Jiangsu, China* **57** H9
Suining *Sichuan, China* **58** B5
Suiping *China* **56** H7
Suippes *France* **19** C11
Suir → *Ireland* **12** D4
Suisse = Switzerland ■
  Europe **25** J4
Suisun City *U.S.A.* **110** G4
Suixi *China* **59** G8
Suiyang *Guizhou, China* **58** D6
Suiyang *Heilongjiang, China* **57** B16
Suizhong *China* **57** D11
Suizhou *China* **59** B9
Sujangarh *India* **68** F6
Sukabumi *Indonesia* **63** G12
Sukadana *Indonesia* **62** E4
Sukagawa *Japan* **55** F10
Sukaraja *Indonesia* **62** E4
Sukawati *Indonesia* **63** K18
Sukch'ŏn *N. Korea* **57** E13
Sukhindol *Bulgaria* **45** C9
Sukhinichi *Russia* **32** E8
Sukhona → *Russia* **52** D4
Sukhothai *Thailand* **64** D2
Sukhumi = Sokhumi *Georgia* **35** J5
Sukkur *Pakistan* **68** F3
Sukkur Barrage *Pakistan* **68** F3
Sukovo *Serbia* **44** C6
Sukri → *India* **68** G4
Sukumo *Japan* **55** H6
Sukunka → *Canada* **102** B4
Sula → *Ukraine* **33** H7
Sula, Kepulauan *Indonesia* **63** E7
Sulaco → *Honduras* **120** C2
Sulaiman Range *Pakistan* **68** D3
Sulak → *Russia* **35** J8
Sūlār *Iran* **71** D6
Sulawesi *Indonesia* **63** E6
Sulawesi Barat □ *Indonesia* **63** E5
Sulawesi Sea = Celebes Sea
  Indonesia **63** D6
Sulawesi Selatan □ *Indonesia* **63** E6
Sulawesi Tengah □ *Indonesia* **63** E6
Sulawesi Tenggara □
  Indonesia **63** E6
Sulawesi Utara □ *Indonesia* **63** D6
Sulechów *Poland* **31** F2
Sulęcin *Poland* **31** F2
Sulejów *Poland* **31** G6
Sulejówek *Poland* **31** F8
Süleymanlı *Turkey* **47** C9
Sulima *S. Leone* **82** D2
Sulina *Romania* **29** E14
Sulina, Brațul → *Romania* **29** E14
Sulingen *Germany* **24** C4
Suliţa *Romania* **29** C11
Sulitjelma *Norway* **8** C17
Sułkowice *Poland* **31** J6
Sullana *Peru* **124** D2
Süller *Turkey* **47** C11
Sullivan *Ill., U.S.A.* **112** F9
Sullivan *Ind., U.S.A.* **112** F10
Sullivan *Mo., U.S.A.* **112** F8
Sullivan Bay *Canada* **102** C3
Sullivan I. = Lanbi Kyun
  Burma **65** G2
Sullom Voe *U.K.* **13** A7
Sully-sur-Loire *France* **19** E9
Sulmierzyce *Poland* **31** G4
Sulmona *Italy* **41** F10
Süloğlu *Turkey* **45** E10
Sulphur *La., U.S.A.* **116** F8
Sulphur *Okla., U.S.A.* **116** D6
Sulphur Pt. *Canada* **102** A6
Sulphur Springs *U.S.A.* **116** E7
Sultan *Canada* **104** C3
Sultan *U.S.A.* **110** C5
Sultan Dağları *Turkey* **72** C4
Sultan Hamud *Kenya* **86** C4
Sultanhisar *Turkey* **47** D10
Sultaniça *Turkey* **45** F10
Sultaniye *Turkey* **45** F12
Sultanpur *Mad. P., India* **68** H8
Sultanpur *Punjab, India* **68** D6
Sultanpur *Ut. P., India* **69** F10
Sulu Arch. *Phil.* **61** J4
Sulu Sea *E. Indies* **61** H4
Sülüklü *Turkey* **72** C5
Sululta *Ethiopia* **81** F4
Suluova *Turkey* **72** B6
Suluq *Libya* **79** B10
Sulzbach *Germany* **25** F3
Sulzbach-Rosenberg
  Germany **25** F7
Sulzberger Ice Shelf
  Antarctica **5** E13
Sumalata *Indonesia* **63** D6
Sumampa *Argentina* **126** B3
Sumatera *Indonesia* **62** D2
Sumatera Barat □ *Indonesia* **62** E2

Sumatera Utara □ *Indonesia* **62** D1
Sumatra = Sumatera
  Indonesia **62** D2
Sumava △ *Czech Rep.* **26** C6
Sumba *Indonesia* **63** F5
Sumba, Selat *Indonesia* **63** F5
Sumbawa *Indonesia* **62** F5
Sumbawa Besar *Indonesia* **62** F5
Sumbawanga □ *Tanzania* **84** F6
Sumbe *Angola* **84** G2
Sumbu △ *Zambia* **87** D3
Sumburgh Hd. *U.K.* **13** B7
Sumdeo *India* **69** D8
Sumdo *China* **69** B8
Sumedang *Indonesia* **63** G12
Sümeg *Hungary* **28** D2
Sumeih *Sudan* **81** F2
Sumenep *Indonesia* **63** G15
Sumgait = Sumqayıt
  Azerbaijan **35** K9
Summer L. *U.S.A.* **108** E3
Summerland *Canada* **102** D5
Summerside *Canada* **105** C7
Summersville *U.S.A.* **113** F13
Summerville *Ga., U.S.A.* **117** D12
Summerville *S.C., U.S.A.* **117** E14
Summit Lake *Canada* **102** C4
Summit Peak *U.S.A.* **109** H10
Sumner *Iowa, U.S.A.* **112** D7
Sumner *Wash., U.S.A.* **110** C4
Sumoto *Japan* **55** G7
Šumperk *Czech Rep.* **27** B9
Sumqayıt *Azerbaijan* **35** K9
Sumter *U.S.A.* **117** E14
Sumy *Ukraine* **33** G8
Sumy □ *Ukraine* **33** G7
Sun City *S. Africa* **88** D4
Sun City *Ariz., U.S.A.* **109** K7
Sun City *Calif., U.S.A.* **111** M9
Sun City Center *U.S.A.* **117** H13
Sun Lakes *U.S.A.* **109** K8
Sun Valley *U.S.A.* **108** E6
Sunagawa *Japan* **54** C10
Sunan *N. Korea* **57** E13
Sunart, L. *U.K.* **13** E3
Sunburst *U.S.A.* **108** B8
Sunbury *Australia* **95** F3
Sunbury *U.S.A.* **115** F8
Sunchales *Argentina* **126** C3
Suncheon *S. Korea* **57** G14
Suncho Corral *Argentina* **126** B3
Sunch'ŏn *N. Korea* **57** E13
Suncook *U.S.A.* **115** C13
Sunda, Selat *Indonesia* **62** F3
Sunda Is. *Indonesia* **96** H2
Sunda Str. = Sunda, Selat
  Indonesia **62** F3
Sunda Trench = Java
  Trench *Ind. Oc.* **62** F3
Sundance *Canada* **103** B10
Sundance *U.S.A.* **108** D2
Sundar Nagar *India* **68** D7
Sundarbans *Asia* **67** J16
Sundarbans △ *India* **69** J13
Sundargarh *India* **67** H14
Sundays = Sondags →
  S. Africa **88** E4
Sunderland *Canada* **114** B5
Sunderland *U.K.* **14** C6
Sundown △ *Australia* **95** D5
Sundre *Canada* **102** C6
Sunds *Denmark* **11** H3
Sundsvall *Sweden* **10** B11
Sundsvallsbukten *Sweden* **10** B11
Sung Hei *Vietnam* **65** G6
Sungai Acheh *Malaysia* **65** c
Sungai Kolok *Thailand* **65** J3
Sungai Lembing *Malaysia* **65** L4
Sungai Petani *Malaysia* **65** K3
Sungaigerong *Indonesia* **62** E2
Sungailiat *Indonesia* **62** E3
Sungaipenuh *Indonesia* **62** E2
Sungari = Songhua
  Jiang → *China* **60** B8
Sunghua Chiang =
  Songhua Jiang → *China* **60** B8
Sungikai *Sudan* **81** E2
Sungurlu *Turkey* **72** B6
Sunja *Croatia* **41** C13
Sunland Park *U.S.A.* **109** L10
Sunnansjö *Sweden* **10** D8
Sunne *Sweden* **10** E7
Sunnemo *Sweden* **10** E7
Sunnyside *U.S.A.* **108** C4
Sunnyvale *U.S.A.* **110** H4
Sunrise Manor *U.S.A.* **111** J11
Suntar *Russia* **53** C12
Sunyani *Ghana* **82** D4
Suomenselkä *Finland* **8** E21
Suomi = Finland ■ *Europe* **8** E22
Suomussalmi *Finland* **8** D23
Suoyarvi *Russia* **32** A7
Supai *U.S.A.* **109** H7
Supaul *India* **69** F12
Superior *Ariz., U.S.A.* **109** K8

Superior *Mont., U.S.A.* **108** C6
Superior *Nebr., U.S.A.* **112** E4
Superior *Wis., U.S.A.* **112** B7
Superior, L. *N. Amer.* **104** C2
Supetar *Croatia* **41** E13
Suphan Buri *Thailand* **64** E3
Suphan Dağı *Turkey* **73** C10
Supiori *Indonesia* **63** E9
Supraśl *Poland* **31** E10
Supraśl → *Poland* **31** E9
Supung Shuiku *China* **57** D13
Sūq Suwayq *Si. Arabia* **70** E3
Suqian *China* **57** H10
Suqutra = Socotra *Yemen* **75** E5
Sūr *Lebanon* **74** B4
Şūr *Oman* **75** C6
Sur, Pt. *U.S.A.* **110** J5
Sura → *Russia* **34** C8
Surab *Pakistan* **68** E2
Surabaja = Surabaya
  Indonesia **63** G15
Surabaya *Indonesia* **63** G15
Surahammar *Sweden* **10** E10
Suraia *Romania* **29** E12
Surakarta *Indonesia* **63** G14
Surakhany *Azerbaijan* **35** K10
Šurany *Slovak Rep.* **27** C11
Surat *Australia* **95** D4
Surat *India* **66** J8
Surat Thani *Thailand* **65** H2
Suratgarh *India* **68** E5
Suraż *Poland* **31** F9
Surazh *Belarus* **32** E6
Surazh *Russia* **33** F7
Surduc *Romania* **29** C8
Surduc Pasul *Romania* **29** E8
Surdulica *Serbia* **44** D6
Surendranagar *India* **68** H4
Surf *U.S.A.* **111** L6
Surfers Paradise *Australia* **95** D5
Surgères *France* **20** B3
Surgut *Russia* **52** C8
Sùria *Spain* **38** D6
Suriapet *India* **66** L11
Surigao *Phil.* **61** G6
Surigao Strait *Phil.* **61** F6
Surin *Thailand* **64** E4
Surin Nua, Ko *Thailand* **65** H1
Surinam = Suriname ■
  S. Amer. **125** C7
Suriname ■ *S. Amer.* **125** C7
Suriname → *Suriname* **125** B7
Sūrmaq *Iran* **71** D7
Sürmene *Turkey* **73** B9
Surovikino *Russia* **35** F6
Surrey *Canada* **110** A4
Surrey □ *U.K.* **15** F7
Sursand *India* **69** F11
Sursar → *India* **69** F12
Sursee *Switz.* **25** H4
Sursk *Russia* **34** D7
Surskoye *Russia* **34** C8
Surt *Libya* **79** B9
Surt, Khalīj *Libya* **79** B9
Surtanahu *Pakistan* **68** F4
Surte *Sweden* **11** G6
Surtsey *Iceland* **8** E3
Sürüç *Turkey* **73** D8
Suruga-Wan *Japan* **55** G9
Susa *Italy* **40** C4
Süsä → *Denmark* **11** J5
Sušac *Croatia* **41** F13
Susak *Croatia* **41** D11
Susaki *Japan* **55** H6
Süsangerd *Iran* **73** D13
Susanville *U.S.A.* **108** F3
Susch *Switz.* **25** J6
Suşehri *Turkey* **73** B8
Sušice *Czech Rep.* **26** B6
Susleni *Moldova* **29** C13
Susner *India* **68** H7
Susong *China* **59** B11
Susquehanna *U.S.A.* **115** E9
Susquehanna → *U.S.A.* **115** G8
Susques *Argentina* **126** A2
Sussex *Canada* **105** C6
Sussex *U.S.A.* **115** E10
Sussex, E. □ *U.K.* **15** G8
Sussex, W. □ *U.K.* **15** G7
Sustut → *Canada* **102** B3
Susuman *Russia* **53** C15
Susunu *Indonesia* **63** E8
Susurluk *Turkey* **47** B10
Susuz *Turkey* **73** B10
Susz *Poland* **30** E6
Sütçüler *Turkey* **72** D4
Şuţeşti *Romania* **29** E12
Sutherland *S. Africa* **88** E3
Sutherland *U.K.* **13** C4
Sutherland *U.S.A.* **112** E3
Sutherland Falls *N.Z.* **91** F1
Sutherlin *U.S.A.* **108** E2
Suthri *India* **68** H3
Sutjeska △ *Bos.-H.* **28** G3
Sutlej → *Pakistan* **68** E4
Sutter *U.S.A.* **110** F5
Sutter Buttes *U.S.A.* **110** F5

Sutter Creek *U.S.A.* **110** G6
Sutton *Canada* **115** A12
Sutton *Nebr., U.S.A.* **112** E5
Sutton *W. Va., U.S.A.* **113** F13
Sutton → *Canada* **104** A3
Sutton Coldfield *U.K.* **15** E6
Sutton in Ashfield *U.K.* **14** D6
Sutton L. *Canada* **104** B3
Suttor → *Australia* **94** C4
Suttsu *Japan* **54** C10
Suva *Fiji* **91** a
Suva Gora *Macedonia* **44** E5
Suva Planina *Serbia* **44** C6
Suva Reka *Serbia* **44** D4
Suvorov *Russia* **32** E9
Suvorov Is. = Suwarrow
  Is. *Cook Is.* **97** J11
Suvorove *Ukraine* **29** E13
Suvorovo *Bulgaria* **45** C11
Suwałki *Poland* **30** D9
Suwana *Indonesia* **63** K18
Suwannaphum *Thailand* **64** E4
Suwannee → *U.S.A.* **117** G13
Suwanose-Jima *Japan* **55** K4
Suwarrow Is. *Cook Is.* **97** J11
Suwayq aş Şuqban *Iraq* **70** D5
Suweis, Khalîg el *Egypt* **80** J8
Suweis, Qanâ es *Egypt* **80** H8
Suwon *S. Korea* **57** F14
Suzdal *Russia* **32** D11
Suzhou *Anhui, China* **56** H9
Suzhou *Jiangsu, China* **59** B13
Suzu *Japan* **55** F8
Suzu-Misaki *Japan* **55** F8
Suzuka *Japan* **55** G8
Suzzara *Italy* **40** D7
Svalbard *Arctic* **4** B8
Svalbard Radio =
  Longyearbyen *Svalbard* **4** B8
Svalöv *Sweden* **11** J7
Svalyava *Ukraine* **28** B7
Svaneke *Denmark* **11** J9
Svängsta *Sweden* **11** H8
Svanskog *Sweden* **10** E6
Svappavaara *Sweden* **8** C19
Svärdsjö *Sweden* **10** D9
Svartå *Sweden* **10** E8
Svartisen *Norway* **8** C15
Svartvik *Sweden* **10** B11
Svatove *Ukraine* **33** H10
Svatovo = Svatove *Ukraine* **33** H10
Svay Chek *Cambodia* **64** F4
Svay Rieng *Cambodia* **65** G5
Svealand □ *Sweden* **10** D9
Svedala *Sweden* **11** J7
Sveg *Sweden* **10** B8
Svendborg *Denmark* **11** J4
Svenljunga *Sweden* **11** G7
Svenstavik *Sweden* **10** B8
Svenstrup *Denmark* **11** H3
Sverdlovsk *Ukraine* **33** H10
Sverdrup Chan. *Canada* **101** B10
Sverdrup Is. *Canada* **101** B10
Sverige = Sweden ■ *Europe* **9** H16
Svetac *Croatia* **41** E12
Sveti Nikola, Prokhod
  Europe **44** C6
Sveti Nikole *Macedonia* **44** E5
Sveti Rok *Croatia* **41** D12
Svetlaya *Russia* **54** A9
Svetlogorsk =
  Svyetlahorsk *Belarus* **23** B15
Svetlogorsk *Russia* **30** D7
Svetlograd *Russia* **35** H6
Svetlovodsk = Svitlovodsk
  Ukraine **33** H7
Svetlyy *Russia* **30** D7
Svidník *Slovak Rep.* **27** B14
Svilaja Planina *Croatia* **41** E13
Svilajnac *Serbia* **44** B5
Svilengrad *Bulgaria* **45** E10
Svir → *Russia* **32** B7
Sviritsa *Russia* **32** B7
Svishtov *Bulgaria* **45** C9
Svislach *Belarus* **31** E11
Svitava → *Czech Rep.* **27** B9
Svitavy *Czech Rep.* **27** B9
Svitlovodsk *Ukraine* **33** H7
Svizzera = Switzerland ■
  Europe **25** J4
Svobodnyy *Russia* **53** D13
Svoge *Bulgaria* **44** D7
Svolvær *Norway* **8** B16
Svratka → *Czech Rep.* **27** B9
Svrljig *Serbia* **44** C6
Svyetlahorsk *Belarus* **23** B15
Swabian Alps =
  Schwäbische Alb *Germany* **25** G5
Swaffham *U.K.* **15** E8
Swains I. *Amer. Samoa* **97** J11
Swainsboro *U.S.A.* **117** E13
Swakop → *Namibia* **88** C2
Swakopmund *Namibia* **88** C1
Swale → *U.K.* **14** C6
Swan → *Australia* **93** F2
Swan → *Canada* **103** C8
Swan Hill *Australia* **95** F3

Swan Hills *Canada* **102** C5
Swan Is. = Santanilla, Is.
  Honduras **120** C3
Swan L. *Canada* **103** C8
Swan Ra. *U.S.A.* **108** C7
Swan River *Canada* **103** C8
Swanage *U.K.* **15** G6
Swansea *Australia* **95** G4
Swansea *Canada* **114** C5
Swansea *U.K.* **15** F3
Swansea □ *U.K.* **15** F3
Swar → *Pakistan* **69** B5
Swartberge *S. Africa* **88** E3
Swartmodder *S. Africa* **88** D3
Swartnossob → *Namibia* **88** C2
Swartruggens *S. Africa* **88** D4
Swarzędz *Poland* **31** F4
Swastika *Canada* **104** C3
Swatow = Shantou *China* **59** F11
Swaziland ■ *Africa* **89** D5
Sweden ■ *Europe* **9** H16
Swedru *Ghana* **83** D4
Sweet Grass *U.S.A.* **108** B8
Sweet Home *U.S.A.* **108** D2
Sweetwater *Nev., U.S.A.* **110** G7
Sweetwater *Tenn., U.S.A.* **117** D12
Sweetwater *Tex., U.S.A.* **116** E4
Sweetwater → *U.S.A.* **108** E10
Swellendam *S. Africa* **88** E3
Swider → *Poland* **31** F8
Świdnica *Poland* **31** H3
Świdnik *Poland* **31** G9
Świdwin *Poland* **30** E2
Świebodzin *Poland* **31** H3
Świebodzin *Poland* **31** F2
Świecie *Poland* **30** E5
Swierzawa *Poland* **31** G2
Świętokrzyski △ *Poland* **31** H7
Świętokrzyskie □ *Poland* **31** H7
Świętokrzyskie, Góry *Poland* **31** H7
Swift Current *Canada* **103** C7
Swiftcurrent → *Canada* **103** C7
Swilly, L. *Ireland* **12** A4
Swindon *U.S.A.* **115** E9
Swindon □ *U.K.* **15** F6
Swinemünde =
  Świnoujście *Poland* **30** E1
Swinford *Ireland* **12** C3
Świnoujście *Poland* **30** E1
Switzerland ■ *Europe* **25** J4
Swords *Ireland* **12** C5
Swoyerville *U.S.A.* **115** E9
Syasstroy *Russia* **32** B7
Sychevka *Russia* **32** E8
Syców *Poland* **31** G4
Syddanmark □ *Denmark* **11** J2
Sydenham → *Canada* **114** D2
Sydney *Australia* **95** E5
Sydney *Canada* **105** C7
Sydney L. *Canada* **103** C10
Sydney Mines *Canada* **105** C7
Sydprøven = Alluitsup Paa
  Greenland **4** C5
Sydra, G. of = Surt, Khalīj
  Libya **79** B9
Syeverodonetsk *Ukraine* **33** H10
Syke *Germany* **24** C4
Sykesville *U.S.A.* **114** E6
Syktyvkar *Russia* **52** C6
Sylacauga *U.S.A.* **117** E11
Sylarna *Sweden* **8** E15
Sylhet *Bangla.* **67** G17
Sylhet □ *Bangla.* **67** G17
Sylt *Germany* **24** A4
Sylvan Beach *U.S.A.* **115** C9
Sylvan Lake *Canada* **102** C6
Sylvania *Ga., U.S.A.* **117** E14
Sylvania *Ohio, U.S.A.* **113** E12
Sylvester *U.S.A.* **117** F13
Sym *Russia* **52** C9
Synelnykove *Ukraine* **33** H8
Synevyr △ *Ukraine* **29** B8
Synevyrska Polyana *Ukraine* **29** B8
Synnot Ra. *Australia* **92** C4
Synyak *Ukraine* **28** B7
Syowa *Antarctica* **5** C5
Syracuse *Kans., U.S.A.* **112** G3
Syracuse *N.Y., U.S.A.* **115** C9
Syracuse *Nebr., U.S.A.* **112** E5
Syrdarya → *Kazakhstan* **52** E7
Syria ■ *Asia* **73** C5
Syrian Desert = Shām,
  Bādiyat ash *Asia* **70** C3
Syros *Greece* **46** D6
Sysslebäck *Sweden* **10** D6
Syzran *Russia* **34** D9
Szabolcs-Szatmár-Bereg □
  Hungary **28** B6
Szadek *Poland* **31** G5
Szamocin *Poland* **31** E4
Szamos → *Hungary* **28** B5
Szamotuły *Poland* **31** F3
Száraz → *Hungary* **28** D6
Szarvas *Hungary* **28** D5
Százhalombatta *Hungary* **28** C3
Szczawnica *Poland* **31** J7
Szczebrzeszyn *Poland* **31** H9

Szczecin *Poland* **30** E1
Szczecinek *Poland* **30** E3
Szczeciński, Zalew =
  Stettiner Haff *Germany* **24** B10
Szczekociny *Poland* **31** H6
Szczucin *Poland* **31** H8
Szczuczyn *Poland* **30** E9
Szczyrk *Poland* **31** J6
Szczytna *Poland* **31** H3
Szczytno *Poland* **30** E7
Szechuan Basin = Sichuan
  Pendi *China* **58** B5
Szechwan = Sichuan □
  China **58** B5
Szécsény *Hungary* **28** B4
Szeged *Hungary* **28** D5
Szeghalom *Hungary* **28** C6
Székesfehérvár *Hungary* **28** C3
Szekszárd *Hungary* **28** D3
Szendrő *Hungary* **28** B5
Szentendre *Hungary* **28** C4
Szentes *Hungary* **28** D5
Szentgotthárd *Hungary* **28** D1
Szentlőrinc *Hungary* **28** D3
Szerencs *Hungary* **28** B6
Szigetszentmiklós *Hungary* **28** C4
Szigetvár *Hungary* **28** D2
Szikszó *Hungary* **28** B5
Szklarska Poręba *Poland* **31** H2
Szlichtyngowa *Poland* **31** G3
Szob *Hungary* **28** C3
Szolnok *Hungary* **28** C5
Szombathely *Hungary* **28** C1
Szprotawa *Poland* **31** G2
Sztum *Poland* **30** E6
Sztutowo *Poland* **30** D6
Szubin *Poland* **31** E4
Szydłowiec *Poland* **31** G7
Szypliszki *Poland* **30** D10

T

Ta Khli Khok *Thailand* **64** E3
Ta Lai *Vietnam* **65** G6
Tab *Hungary* **28** D3
Tabacal *Argentina* **126** A3
Tabaco *Phil.* **61** E5
Tabagné *Ivory C.* **82** D4
Ṭābah *Si. Arabia* **70** E4
Tabanan *Indonesia* **63** K18
Tabankort *Niger* **83** B5
Ṭabas *Khorāsān, Iran* **71** C9
Ṭabas *Yazd, Iran* **71** C9
Tabasará, Serranía de
  Panama **120** E3
Tabasco □ *Mexico* **119** D6
Tabāsīn *Iran* **71** D8
Tabatinga, Serra da *Brazil* **125** F10
Taber *Canada* **102** D6
Taberg *Sweden* **11** G8
Taberg *U.S.A.* **115** C9
Tabla *Niger* **83** C5
Tablas *Phil.* **61** E5
Tablas de Daimiel △ *Spain* **37** F7
Tablas Strait *Phil.* **61** E5
Table, Pte. de la *Réunion* **85** c
Table B. *Canada* **105** B8
Table B. *S. Africa* **88** E2
Table Mt. *S. Africa* **88** E2
Table Rock L. *U.S.A.* **112** G7
Tabletop, Mt. *Australia* **94** C4
Tábor *Czech Rep.* **26** B7
Tabora *Tanzania* **86** D3
Tabora □ *Tanzania* **86** D3
Tabou *Ivory C.* **82** E3
Tabrīz *Iran* **73** C12
Tabuaeran *Kiribati* **97** G12
Tabuenca *Spain* **38** D3
Tabūk *Si. Arabia* **70** D3
Tabūk □ *Si. Arabia* **70** D3
Taburno-Camposauro △
  Italy **43** A7
Täby *Sweden* **10** E12
Tacámbaro de Codallos
  Mexico **118** D4
Tacheng *China* **60** B3
Tach'i *Taiwan* **59** E13
Tachia *Taiwan* **59** E13
Tach'ing Shan = Daqing
  Shan *China* **56** D6
Tachov *Czech Rep.* **26** B5
Tácina → *Italy* **43** D9
Tacloban *Phil.* **61** F6
Tacna *Peru* **124** G4
Tacoma *U.S.A.* **110** C4
Tacuarembó *Uruguay* **127** C4
Tademaït, Plateau du *Algeria* **78** C6
Tadio, L. *Ivory C.* **82** D3
Tadjoura *Djibouti* **81** E5
Tadjoura, Golfe de *Djibouti* **81** E5
Tadmor *N.Z.* **91** D4
Tadoule L. *Canada* **103** B9
Tadoussac *Canada* **105** C6
Tadrés △ *Niger* **83** B6
Tadzhikistan =
  Tajikistan ■ *Asia* **52** F8

Taegu = Daegu *S. Korea* **57** G15
Taegwan *N. Korea* **57** D13
Taejŏn = Daejeon *S. Korea* **57** F14
Taen, Ko *Thailand* **65** b
Tafalla *Spain* **38** C3
Tafar *Sudan* **81** F2
Tafelbaai = Table B. *S. Africa* **88** E2
Tafermaar *Indonesia* **63** F8
Tafí Viejo *Argentina* **126** B2
Tafíhān *Iran* **71** D7
Tafiré *Ivory C.* **82** D3
Tafo *Ghana* **83** D4
Tafresh *Iran* **71** C6
Taft *Iran* **71** D7
Taft *Phil.* **61** F6
Taft *U.S.A.* **111** K7
Taftan *Pakistan* **66** E2
Taftān, Kūh-e *Iran* **71** D9
Taga *Samoa* **91** b
Taga Dzong *Bhutan* **67** F16
Taganrog *Russia* **33** J10
Taganrogskiy Zaliv *Russia* **33** J10
Tagânt □ *Mauritania* **82** B3
Tagatay *Phil.* **61** D4
Tagbilaran *Phil.* **61** G5
Tággia *Italy* **40** E4
Tagish *Canada* **102** A2
Tagish L. *Canada* **102** A2
Tagliacozzo *Italy* **41** F10
Tagliamento → *Italy* **41** C10
Táglio di Po *Italy* **41** D9
Tago *Phil.* **61** G7
Tagomago *Spain* **48** B8
Tagourâret *Mauritania* **82** B3
Taguatinga *Brazil* **125** F10
Tagudin *Phil.* **61** C4
Tagum *Phil.* **61** H6
Tagus = Tejo → *Europe* **37** F2
Tahakopa *N.Z.* **91** G2
Tahan, Gunung *Malaysia* **65** K4
Tahat *Algeria* **78** D7
Tāherī *Iran* **71** E7
Tahiti *French Polynesia* **91** d
Tahiti, I. *Tahiti* **91** d
Tahlequah *U.S.A.* **116** D7
Tahoe, L. *U.S.A.* **110** G6
Tahoe City *U.S.A.* **110** F6
Tahoka *U.S.A.* **116** E4
Taholah *U.S.A.* **110** C2
Tahoua *Niger* **83** C6
Tahrūd *Iran* **71** D8
Tahsis *Canada* **102** D3
Tahta *Egypt* **80** B3
Tahtaköprü *Turkey* **45** G13
Tahtalı Dağları *Turkey* **72** C7
Tahulandang *Indonesia* **63** D7
Tahuna *Indonesia* **63** D7
Taï *Ivory C.* **82** D3
Taï △ *Ivory C.* **82** D3
Tai Hu *China* **59** B13
Tai Rom Yen △ *Thailand* **65** H2
Tai Shan *China* **57** F9
Tai'an *China* **57** F9
Taiarapu, Presqu'île de *Tahiti* **91** d
Taibei = T'aipei *Taiwan* **59** E13
Taibique *Canary Is.* **48** G2
Taibus Qi *China* **56** D8
Taicang *China* **59** B13
T'aichung *Taiwan* **59** E13
Taieri → *N.Z.* **91** G3
Taigu *China* **56** F7
Taihang Shan *China* **56** G7
Taihape *N.Z.* **91** C5
Taihe *Anhui, China* **56** H8
Taihe *Jiangxi, China* **59** D10
Taihu *China* **59** B11
Taijiang *China* **58** D7
Taikang *China* **56** G8
Tailem Bend *Australia* **95** F2
Tailfingen *Germany* **25** G5
T'ailuko *Taiwan* **59** E13
Taimyr Peninsula =
  Taymyr, Poluostrov
  Russia **53** B11
Tain *U.K.* **13** D4
T'ainan *Taiwan* **59** F13
Taining *China* **59** D11
T'aipei *Taiwan* **59** E13
Taiping *China* **59** B12
Taiping *Malaysia* **65** K3
Taipingzhen *China* **56** H6
Tairbeart = Tarbert *U.K.* **13** D2
Taishan *China* **59** F9
Taishun *China* **59** D12
Taita Hills *Kenya* **86** C4
Taitao, Pen. de *Chile* **128** F2
T'aitung *Taiwan* **59** F13
Taivalkoski *Finland* **8** D23
Taiwan ■ *Asia* **59** F13
Taiwan Strait *Asia* **59** E12
Taixing *China* **59** A13
Taiyara *Sudan* **81** E3
Taiyiba *Israel* **74** C4
Taiyuan *China* **56** F7
Taizhong = T'aichung
  Taiwan **59** E13
Taizhou *China* **59** A12

Taizhou Liedao *China* **59** C13
Ta'izz *Yemen* **75** E3
Tājābād *Iran* **71** D7
Tajikistan ■ *Asia* **52** F8
Tajima *Japan* **55** F9
Tajo = Tejo → *Europe* **37** F2
Tajrīsh *Iran* **71** C6
Tak *Thailand* **64** D2
Takāb *Iran* **73** D12
Takachiho *Japan* **55** H5
Takachu *Botswana* **88** C3
Takada *Japan* **55** F9
Takahagi *Japan* **55** F10
Takaka *N.Z.* **91** D4
Takamaka *Seychelles* **85** b
Takamatsu *Japan* **55** G7
Takaoka *Japan* **55** F8
Takapuna *N.Z.* **91** B5
Takasaki *Japan* **55** F9
Takatsuki *Japan* **55** G7
Takaungu *Kenya* **86** C4
Takayama *Japan* **55** F8
Take-Shima *Japan* **55** J5
Takefu *Japan* **55** G8
Takengon *Indonesia* **62** D1
Takeo *Japan* **55** H5
Tåkern *Sweden* **11** F8
Takeshima = Tok-do *Asia* **55** F5
Tākestān *Iran* **71** C6
Taketa *Japan* **55** H5
Takev *Cambodia* **65** G5
Takh *India* **69** C7
Takht-Sulaiman *Pakistan* **68** D3
Takikawa *Japan* **54** C10
Takla L. *Canada* **102** B3
Takla Landing *Canada* **102** B3
Takla Makan *China* **60** C3
Taklamakan Shamo =
  Takla Makan *China* **60** C3
Taku → *Canada* **102** B2
Takua Thung *Thailand* **65** a
Takum *Nigeria* **83** D6
Tal Halāl *Iran* **71** D7
Tala *Uruguay* **127** C4
Talachyn *Belarus* **32** E5
Talacogan *Phil.* **61** G6
Talagang *Pakistan* **68** C5
Talagante *Chile* **126** C1
Talak *Niger* **83** B6
Talamanca, Cordillera de
  Cent. Amer. **120** E3
Talant *France* **19** E11
Talara *Peru* **124** D2
Talas *Kyrgyzstan* **52** E8
Talas *Turkey* **72** C6
Talâta *Egypt* **74** E1
Talata Mafara *Nigeria* **83** C6
Talaud, Kepulauan *Indonesia* **63** D7
Talaud Is. = Talaud,
  Kepulauan *Indonesia* **63** D7
Talavera de la Reina *Spain* **36** F6
Talavera la Real *Spain* **37** G4
Talayan *Phil.* **61** H6
Talayuela *Spain* **36** F5
Talbandh *India* **69** H12
Talbert, Sillon de *France* **18** D3
Talbot, C. *Australia* **92** B4
Talbragar → *Australia* **95** E4
Talca *Chile* **126** D1
Talcahuano *Chile* **126** D1
Talcher *India* **67** J14
Talcho *Niger* **83** C5
Taldy Kurgan =
  Taldyqorghan *Kazakhstan* **52** E8
Taldyqorghan *Kazakhstan* **52** E8
Tālesh *Iran* **73** D13
Tālesh, Kūhhā-ye *Iran* **73** D13
Talguharai *Sudan* **80** D4
Tali Post *Sudan* **81** F3
Taliabu *Indonesia* **63** E6
Talibon *Phil.* **63** B6
Talibong, Ko *Thailand* **65** J2
Talihina *U.S.A.* **116** D7
Talisayan *Phil.* **61** G6
Taliwang *Indonesia* **62** F5
Tall 'Afar *Iraq* **73** D10
Tall Kalakh *Syria* **74** A5
Talla *Egypt* **80** B3
Talladega *U.S.A.* **117** E11
Tallahassee *U.S.A.* **117** F12
Tallangatta *Australia* **95** F4
Tallard *France* **21** D10
Tállberg *Sweden* **10** D9
Tallering Pk. *Australia* **93** E2
Talli *Pakistan* **68** E3
Tallinn *Estonia* **32** C3
Tallmadge *U.S.A.* **114** E3
Tallulah *U.S.A.* **116** E9
Talmont-St-Hilaire *France* **20** B2
Talne *Ukraine* **33** H6
Talodi *Sudan* **81** E3
Talovaya *Russia* **34** E5
Taloyoak *Canada* **100** C10
Talpa de Allende *Mexico* **118** C4
Talparo *Trin. & Tob.* **125** K15

Talsi *Latvia* **30** A9
Talsi □ *Latvia* **30** A9
Taltal *Chile* **126** B1
Taltson → *Canada* **102** A6
Talwood *Australia* **95** D4
Talyawalka Cr. → *Australia* **95** E3
Tam Ky *Vietnam* **64** E7
Tam Quan *Vietnam* **64** E7
Tama *U.S.A.* **112** E7
Tama △ *Ethiopia* **81** F4
Tamale *Ghana* **83** D4
Taman *Russia* **33** K9
Taman Negara △ *Malaysia* **65** K4
Tamani *Mali* **82** C3
Tamano *Japan* **55** G6
Tamanrasset *Algeria* **78** D7
Tamaqua *U.S.A.* **115** F9
Tamar → *U.K.* **15** G3
Tamarin *Mauritius* **85** d
Tamarinda *Spain* **48** B10
Tamarite de Litera *Spain* **38** D5
Tamashima *Japan* **55** G6
Tamási *Hungary* **28** D3
Tamaské *Niger* **83** C6
Tamatave = Toamasina
  Madag. **89** B8
Tamaulipas □ *Mexico* **119** C5
Tamaulipas, Sierra de
  Mexico **119** C5
Tamazula *Mexico* **118** C3
Tamazunchale *Mexico* **119** C5
Tamba-Dabatou *Guinea* **82** C2
Tambach *Kenya* **86** B4
Tambacounda *Senegal* **82** C2
Tambacounda □ *Senegal* **82** C2
Tambelan, Kepulauan
  Indonesia **62** D3
Tambellup *Australia* **93** F2
Tambo *Australia* **94** C4
Tambo de Mora *Peru* **124** F3
Tambohorano *Madag.* **89** B7
Tambora *Indonesia* **62** F5
Tambov *Russia* **34** D5
Tambov □ *Russia* **34** D5
Tambre → *Spain* **36** C2
Tambuku *Indonesia* **63** G15
Tamburâ *Sudan* **81** F2
Tâmchekket *Mauritania* **82** B2
Tâmega → *Portugal* **36** D2
Tamenglong *India* **67** G18
Tamgué, Massif du *Guinea* **82** C2
Tamiahua, L. de *Mexico* **119** C5
Tamil Nadu □ *India* **66** P10
Tamis → *Serbia* **28** F5
Tamluk *India* **69** H12
Tammerfors = Tampere
  Finland **32** B2
Tammisaari *Finland* **32** B2
Tämnaren *Sweden* **10** D11
Tamo Abu, Banjaran
  Malaysia **62** D5
Tampa *U.S.A.* **117** H13
Tampa, Tanjung *Indonesia* **63** K19
Tampa B. *U.S.A.* **117** H13
Tampere *Finland* **32** B2
Tampico *Mexico* **119** C5
Tampin *Malaysia* **65** L4
Tampoi *Malaysia* **65** d
Tamsweg *Austria* **26** D6
Tamu *Burma* **67** G19
Tamuja → *Spain* **37** F4
Tamworth *Australia* **95** E5
Tamworth *Canada* **114** B8
Tamworth *U.K.* **15** E6
Tan An *Vietnam* **65** G6
Tan Chau *Vietnam* **65** G5
Tan-Tan *Morocco* **78** C3
Tana → *Kenya* **86** C5
Tana → *Norway* **8** A23
Tana, L. *Ethiopia* **81** E4
Tana River Primate △ *Kenya* **86** C5
Tanabe *Japan* **55** H7
Tanafjorden *Norway* **8** A23
Tanahbala *Indonesia* **62** E1
Tanahgrogot *Indonesia* **62** E5
Tanahjampea *Indonesia* **63** F6
Tanahmasa *Indonesia* **62** E1
Tanahmerah *Indonesia* **63** F10
Tanakpur *India* **69** E9
Tanakura *Japan* **55** F10
Tanami Desert *Australia* **92** C4
Tanami Mine *Australia* **92** C4
Tananarive =
  Antananarivo *Madag.* **89** B8
Tánaro → *Italy* **40** D5
Tancheng *China* **57** G10
Tanch'ŏn *N. Korea* **57** D15
Tanda *Ut. P., India* **69** F10
Tanda *Ut. P., India* **69** E8
Tanda *Ivory C.* **82** D4
Tandag *Phil.* **61** G7
Tandaia *Tanzania* **87** D3
Tândărei *Romania* **29** F12
Tandaué *Angola* **88** B2
Tandil *Argentina* **126** D4
Tandil, Sa. del *Argentina* **126** D4
Tandlianwala *Pakistan* **68** D5

Tando Adam *Pakistan* **68** G3
Tando Allahyar *Pakistan* **68** G3
Tando Bago *Pakistan* **68** G3
Tando Mohommed Khan
  Pakistan **68** G3
Tandou L. *Australia* **95** E3
Tandoureh △ *Iran* **70** B8
Tandragee *U.K.* **12** B5
Tandsjöborg *Sweden* **10** C8
Tane-ga-Shima *Japan* **55** J5
Taneatua *N.Z.* **91** C6
Tanen Tong Dan = Dawna
  Ra. *Burma* **64** D2
Tanew → *Poland* **31** H9
Tanezrouft *Algeria* **78** D6
Tang, Koh *Cambodia* **65** G4
Tang, Ra's-e *Iran* **71** E8
Tang Krasang *Cambodia* **64** F5
Tanga *Tanzania* **86** D4
Tanga □ *Tanzania* **86** D4
Tanganyika, L. *Africa* **86** D3
Tangaza *Nigeria* **83** C5
Tanger *Morocco* **78** A4
Tangerang *Indonesia* **63** G12
Tangerhütte *Germany* **24** C7
Tangermünde *Germany* **24** C7
Tanggu *China* **57** E9
Tanggula Shan *China* **60** C4
Tanghe *China* **56** H7
Tanghla Range =
  Tanggula Shan *China* **60** C4
Tangier = Tanger *Morocco* **78** A4
Tangorin *Australia* **94** C3
Tangorombohitr'i Makay
  Madag. **89** C8
Tangshan *China* **57** E10
Tangtou *China* **57** G10
Tanguiéta *Benin* **83** C5
Tangxi *China* **59** C12
Tangyan He → *China* **58** C7
Tanimbar, Kepulauan
  Indonesia **63** F8
Tanimbar Is. = Tanimbar,
  Kepulauan *Indonesia* **63** F8
Taninthari = Tenasserim
  Burma **65** F2
Tanjay *Phil.* **61** G5
Tanjong Malim *Malaysia* **65** L3
Tanjong Pelepas *Malaysia* **65** d
Tanjore = Thanjavur *India* **66** P11
Tanjung *Indonesia* **62** E5
Tanjung *Phil.* **62** E5
Tanjung Tokong *Malaysia* **65** c
Tanjungbalai *Indonesia* **62** D1
Tanjungbatu *Indonesia* **62** D5
Tanjungkarang
  Telukbetung *Indonesia* **62** F3
Tanjungpandan *Indonesia* **62** E3
Tanjungpinang *Indonesia* **62** D2
Tanjungredeb *Indonesia* **62** D5
Tanjungselor *Indonesia* **62** D5
Tank *Pakistan* **68** C4
Tankhala *India* **68** J5
Tankwa-Karoo △ *S. Africa* **88** E2
Tännäs *Sweden* **10** B6
Tannersville *U.S.A.* **115** E9
Tannis Bugt *Denmark* **11** G4
Tannu Ola *Asia* **53** D10
Tannum Sands *Australia* **94** C5
Tano → *Ghana* **82** D4
Tanon Str. *Phil.* **61** F5
Tanout *Niger* **83** C6
Tanshui *Taiwan* **59** E13
Tansilla *Burkina Faso* **82** C4
Tanta *Egypt* **80** H7
Tantoyuca *Mexico* **119** C5
Tantung = Dandong *China* **57** D13
Tanumshede *Sweden* **11** F5
Tanunda *Australia* **95** E2
Tanus *France* **20** D6
Tanzania ■ *Africa* **86** D3
Tanzilla → *Canada* **102** B2
Tao, Ko *Thailand* **65** G2
Tao'an = Taonan *China* **57** B12
Tao'er He → *China* **57** B13
Taohua Dao *China* **59** C14
Taolanaro *Madag.* **89** D8
Taole *China* **56** E4
Taonan *China* **57** B12
Taormina *Italy* **43** E8
Taos *U.S.A.* **109** H11
Taoudenni *Mali* **78** D5
Taoyuan *China* **59** C8
T'aoyüan *Taiwan* **59** E13
Tapa *Estonia* **32** C3
Tapa Shan = Daba Shan
  China **58** B7
Tapachula *Mexico* **119** E6
Tapah *Malaysia* **65** K3
Tapajós → *Brazil* **125** D8
Tapaktuan *Indonesia* **62** D1
Tapanahoni → *Suriname* **125** C8
Tapanui *N.Z.* **91** F2
Tapauá → *Brazil* **124** E6
Tapes *Brazil* **127** C5
Tapeta *Liberia* **82** D3
Taphan Hin *Thailand* **64** D3

Tapia de Casariego *Spain* **36** B4
Tapirapecó, Serra *Venezuela* **124** C6
Tapo-Capara △ *Venezuela* **121** E5
Tapolca *Hungary* **28** D2
Tapti → *India* **66** J8
Tapuae-o-Uenuku *N.Z.* **91** E4
Tapul Group *Phil.* **61** J4
Tapurucuará *Brazil* **124** D5
Taquara *Brazil* **127** B5
Taquari → *Brazil* **124** G7
Tara *Australia* **95** D5
Tara *Canada* **114** B3
Tara *Russia* **52** D8
Tara *Zambia* **87** F2
Tara → *Montenegro* **44** C2
Tara △ *Serbia* **44** C3
Taraba □ *Nigeria* **83** D7
Taraba → *Nigeria* **83** D7
Tarābulus *Lebanon* **74** A4
Tarābulus *Libya* **79** B8
Taracliai = Taraclia, *Moldova* **29** E13
Taraclia *Tighina, Moldova* **29** D14
Taradehi *India* **69** H8
Tarajalejo *Canary Is.* **48** F5
Tarakan *Indonesia* **62** D5
Tarakit, Mt. *Kenya* **86** B4
Tarama-Jima *Japan* **55** M2
Taran, Mys *Russia* **30** D6
Taranagar *India* **68** E6
Taranaki □ *N.Z.* **91** C5
Taranaki, Mt. *N.Z.* **91** C5
Tarancón *Spain* **38** E1
Tarangire △ *Tanzania* **86** C4
Taransay *U.K.* **13** D1
Táranto *Italy* **43** B10
Táranto, G. di *Italy* **43** B10
Tarapacá *Colombia* **124** D5
Tarapacá □ *Chile* **126** A2
Tarapoto *Peru* **124** E3
Tarare *France* **21** C8
Tararua Ra. *N.Z.* **91** D5
Tarascon *France* **21** E8
Tarascon-sur-Ariège *France* **20** F5
Tarashcha *Ukraine* **23** D16
Tarauacá *Brazil* **124** E4
Tarauacá → *Brazil* **124** E5
Taravao *Tahiti* **91** d
Taravao, Isthme de *Tahiti* **91** d
Taravo → *France* **21** G12
Tarawa *Kiribati* **96** G9
Tarawera *N.Z.* **91** C6
Tarawera, L. *N.Z.* **91** C6
Taraz *Kazakhstan* **52** E8
Tarazona *Spain* **38** D3
Tarazona de la Mancha
  Spain **39** F3
Tarbagatay, Khrebet
  Kazakhstan **52** E9
Tarbat Ness *U.K.* **13** D5
Tarbela Dam *Pakistan* **68** B5
Tarbert *Ireland* **12** D2
Tarbert *Argyll & Bute, U.K.* **13** F3
Tarbert *W. Isles, U.K.* **13** D2
Tarbes *France* **20** E4
Tarboro *U.S.A.* **117** H7
Tărcău, Munţii *Romania* **29** D11
Tarcento *Italy* **41** B10
Tarcoola *Australia* **95** E1
Tarcoon *Australia* **95** E4
Tardets-Sorholus *France* **20** E3
Tardoire → *France* **20** C4
Taree *Australia* **95** E5
Tarfa, W. el → *Egypt* **80** B3
Tarfaya *Morocco* **78** C3
Târgoviște *Romania* **29** F10
Târgu Bujor *Romania* **29** E12
Târgu Cărbuneşti *Romania* **29** F8
Târgu Frumos *Romania* **29** C12
Târgu Jiu *Romania* **29** E8
Târgu Lăpuş *Romania* **29** C8
Târgu Mureş *Romania* **29** D9
Târgu Neamţ *Romania* **29** C11
Târgu Ocna *Romania* **29** D11
Târgu Secuiesc *Romania* **29** E11
Târguşor *Romania* **29** F13
Tărhăus, Vf. *Romania* **29** D11
Țarif *U.A.E.* **71** E7
Tarifa *Spain* **37** J5
Tarija *Bolivia* **126** A3
Tarija □ *Bolivia* **126** A3
Tariku → *Indonesia* **63** E9
Tarim Basin = Tarim Pendi
  China **60** C3
Tarim He → *China* **60** C3
Tarim Pendi *China* **60** C3
Taritatu → *Indonesia* **63** E9
Tarka → *S. Africa* **88** E4
Tarka La *Bhutan* **69** F13
Tarkastad *S. Africa* **88** E4
Tarkhankut, Mys *Ukraine* **33** K7
Tarko Sale *Russia* **52** C8
Tarkwa *Ghana* **82** D4
Tarlac *Phil.* **61** D4
Tarm *Denmark* **11** J2
Tarma *Peru* **124** F3
Tarn □ *France* **20** E6

Tarn → *France* **20** D5
Tarn-et-Garonne □ *France* **20** D5
Tarna → *Hungary* **28** C4
Târnava Mare → *Romania* **29** D8
Târnava Mică → *Romania* **29** D8
Târnăveni *Romania* **29** D9
Tarnica *Poland* **31** J9
Tarnobrzeg *Poland* **31** H8
Tarnogród *Poland* **31** H9
Tarnos *France* **20** E2
Tarnów *Poland* **31** H8
Tarnowskie Góry *Poland* **31** H5
Tärnsjö *Sweden* **10** D10
Táro → *Italy* **40** C7
Ţărom *Iran* **71** D7
Taroom *Australia* **95** D4
Taroudannt *Morocco* **78** B4
Tarp *Germany* **24** A5
Tarpon Springs *U.S.A.* **117** G13
Tarquínia *Italy* **41** F8
Tarrafal *C. Verde Is.* **78** b
Tarragona *Spain* **38** D6
Tarragona □ *Spain* **38** D6
Tarraleah *Australia* **95** G4
Tarrasa = Terrassa *Spain* **38** D7
Tàrrega *Spain* **38** D6
Tarrytown *U.S.A.* **115** E11
Tårs *Denmark* **11** G4
Tarshiha = Me'ona *Israel* **74** B4
Tarsus *Turkey* **72** D6
Tartagal *Argentina* **126** A3
Tärtär *Azerbaijan* **35** K8
Tärtär → *Azerbaijan* **35** K8
Tartas *France* **20** E3
Tartu *Estonia* **32** C4
Ţarţūs *Syria* **72** E6
Ţarţūs □ *Syria* **72** E7
Tarumizu *Japan* **55** J5
Tarussa *Russia* **32** E9
Tarutao = Ko Tarutao △
  Thailand **65** J2
Tarutao, Ko *Thailand* **65** J2
Tarutung *Indonesia* **62** D1
Tarutyne *Ukraine* **29** D14
Tarvísio *Italy* **41** B10
Taseko → *Canada* **102** C4
Tash-Kömür *Kyrgyzstan* **52** E8
Tash-Kumyr =
  Tash-Kömür *Kyrgyzstan* **52** E8
Tashauz = Dashoguz
  Turkmenistan **52** E6
Tashi Chho Dzong =
  Thimphu *Bhutan* **67** F16
Ţashk, Daryācheh-ye *Iran* **71** D7
Tashkent = Toshkent
  Uzbekistan **52** E7
Tashtagol *Russia* **52** D9
Tasiilaq *Greenland* **4** C6
Tasik Kenyir *Malaysia* **65** K4
Tasikmalaya *Indonesia* **63** G13
Tåsinge *Denmark* **11** J4
Tåsjön *Sweden* **8** D16
Taskan *Russia* **53** C16
Tasker *Niger* **83** C7
Taşköprü *Turkey* **72** B6
Tasman B. *N.Z.* **91** D4
Tasman Basin *Pac. Oc.* **96** M7
Tasman Mts. *N.Z.* **91** D4
Tasman Pen. *Australia* **95** G4
Tasman Sea *Pac. Oc.* **90** E9
Tasmania □ *Australia* **95** G4
Tasmanian Wilderness
  World Heritage Area △
  Australia **95** G4
Tăşnad *Romania* **28** C7
Tassili n'Ajjer *Algeria* **78** C7
Tassili-Oua-n-Ahaggar
  Algeria **78** D7
Tassili Tin-Rerhoh *Algeria* **83** A5
Tata *Hungary* **28** C3
Tata *Morocco* **78** C4
Tatabánya *Hungary* **28** C3
Tataouine *Tunisia* **79** B8
Tatarbunary *Ukraine* **29** E14
Tatarsk *Russia* **52** D8
Tatarstan □ *Russia* **34** C10
Tatatua, Pte. *Tahiti* **91** d
Tateyama *Japan* **55** G9
Tathlina L. *Canada* **102** A5
Tathra *Australia* **95** F4
Tatinnai L. *Canada* **103** A9
Tatla Lake *Canada* **102** C4
Tatlısu *Turkey* **45** F11
Tatnam, C. *Canada* **103** B10
Tatra = Tatry *Slovak Rep.* **27** B13
Tatranský △ *Slovak Rep.* **27** B13
Tatry *Slovak Rep.* **27** B13
Tatshenshini → *Canada* **102** B1
Tatsuno *Japan* **55** G7
Tatta *Pakistan* **68** G2
Tatuí *Brazil* **127** A6

Tatum U.S.A. 109 K12
Tat'ung = Datong China 56 D7
Tatvan Turkey 73 C10
Ta'ū Amer. Samoa 91 b
Taubaté Brazil 127 A6
Tauberbischofsheim Germany 25 F5
Taucha Germany 24 D8
Tauern Austria 22 E7
Tauern-tunnel Austria 26 D6
Taufikia Sudan 81 F3
Taulé France 18 D3
Taumarunui N.Z. 91 C5
Taumaturgo Brazil 124 E4
Taung S. Africa 88 D3
Taungdwingyi Burma 67 J19
Taunggyi Burma 67 J20
Taungup Burma 67 K19
Taunsa Pakistan 68 D4
Taunsa Barrage Pakistan 68 D4
Taunton U.K. 15 F4
Taunton U.S.A. 115 E13
Taunus Germany 25 E4
Taupo N.Z. 91 C6
Taupo, L. N.Z. 91 C5
Tauragė Lithuania 30 C9
Tauragė □ Lithuania 30 C9
Tauranga N.Z. 91 B6
Tauranga Harb. N.Z. 91 B6
Taureau, Rés. Canada 104 C5
Taurianova Italy 43 D9
Taurus Mts. = Toros
   Dağları Turkey 72 D5
Tauste Spain 38 D3
Tautira Tahiti 91 d
Tauz = Tovuz Azerbaijan 35 K7
Tavas Turkey 47 D11
Tavastehus =
   Hämeenlinna Finland 32 B3
Tavda Russia 52 D7
Tavda → Russia 52 D7
Tavernes de la Valldigna
   Spain 39 F4
Taveta Kenya 86 C4
Taveuni Fiji 91 a
Taviano Italy 43 C11
Tavignano → France 21 F13
Tavira Portugal 37 H3
Tavistock Canada 114 C4
Tavistock U.K. 15 G3
Tavolara Italy 42 B2
Távora → Portugal 36 D3
Tavoy Burma 64 E2
Tavropos → Greece 46 B3
Tavşanlı Turkey 47 B11
Tavua Fiji 91 a
Tavuki Fiji 91 a
Taw → U.K. 15 F3
Tawa → India 68 H8
Tawas City U.S.A. 113 C12
Tawau Malaysia 62 D5
Taweisha Sudan 81 E2
Tawi-Tawi Phil. 63 C6
Tawu Taiwan 59 F13
Taxco Mexico 119 D5
Taxila Pakistan 68 C5
Tay → U.K. 13 E5
Tay, Firth of U.K. 13 E5
Tay, L. Australia 93 F3
Tay, L. U.K. 13 E4
Tay △ U.K. 13 E5
Tay Ninh Vietnam 65 G6
Tayabamba Peru 124 E3
Tayabas Bay Phil. 61 E4
Taygetos Oros Greece 46 D4
Taylakova Russia 52 D8
Taylakovy = Taylakova
   Russia 52 D8
Taylor Canada 102 B4
Taylor Nebr., U.S.A. 112 E4
Taylor Pa., U.S.A. 115 E9
Taylor Tex., U.S.A. 116 F6
Taylor, Mt. U.S.A. 109 J10
Taylorville U.S.A. 112 F9
Taymā Si. Arabia 70 E3
Taymyr, Oz. Russia 53 B11
Taymyr, Poluostrov Russia 53 B11
Tayport U.K. 13 E6
Tayrona △ Colombia 121 D5
Tayshet Russia 53 D10
Taytay Phil. 61 F3
Tāyyebād Iran 71 C9
Tāyyebād □ Iran 71 C9
Taz → Russia 52 C8
Taza Morocco 78 B5
Tāza Khurmātū Iraq 73 E11
Tazawa-Ko Japan 54 E10
Tazin → Canada 103 B7
Tazin L. Canada 103 B7
Tazovskiy Russia 52 C8
Tbilisi Georgia 35 K7
Tchad = Chad ■ Africa 79 F8
Tchad, L. Chad 79 F8
Tchaourou Benin 83 D5
Tch'eng-tou = Chengdu
   China 58 B5
Tchentlo L. Canada 102 B4

Tchetti Benin 83 D5
Tchibanga Gabon 84 E2
Tchien Liberia 82 D3
Chin Tabaraden Niger 83 B6
Tch'ong-k'ing =
   Chongqing China 58 C6
Tczew Poland 30 D5
Te Anau, L. N.Z. 91 F1
Te Aroha N.Z. 91 B5
Te Awamutu N.Z. 91 C5
Te Ika a Maui = North I.
   N.Z. 91 C5
Te Kuiti N.Z. 91 C5
Te-n-Dghâmcha, Sebkhet
   Mauritania 82 B1
Te Puke N.Z. 91 B6
Te Waewae B. N.Z. 91 G1
Te Wai Pounamu = South
   I. N.Z. 91 F3
Teaca Romania 29 D9
Teague U.S.A. 116 F6
Teahupoo Tahiti 91 d
Teano Italy 43 A7
Teapa Mexico 119 D6
Teba Spain 37 J6
Tebakang Malaysia 62 D4
Teberda Russia 35 J5
Teberu Malaysia 65 d
Tébessa Algeria 78 A7
Tebicuary → Paraguay 126 B4
Tebingtinggi Riau, Indonesia 62 E2
Tebingtinggi
   Sumatera Utara, Indonesia 62 D1
Tebulos Georgia 35 J7
Tecate Mexico 111 N10
Tecer Dağları Turkey 72 C7
Tech → France 20 F7
Techiman Ghana 82 D4
Techirghiol Romania 29 F13
Tecka Argentina 128 E2
Tecomán Mexico 118 D4
Tecopa U.S.A. 111 K10
Tecoripa Mexico 118 B3
Tecuala Mexico 118 C3
Tecuci Romania 29 E12
Tecumseh Canada 114 D2
Tecumseh Mich., U.S.A. 113 D12
Tecumseh Okla., U.S.A. 116 D6
Tedzhen = Tejen
   Turkmenistan 52 F7
Tees → U.K. 14 C6
Tees B. U.K. 14 C6
Teeswater Canada 114 C3
Tefé Brazil 124 D6
Tefenni Turkey 47 D11
Tegal Indonesia 63 G13
Tegallalang Indonesia 63 J18
Tegalsari Indonesia 63 J17
Tegel, Berlin ✈ (TXL)
   Germany 24 C9
Tegernsee Germany 25 H7
Teggiano Italy 43 B8
Tegid, L. = Bala, L. U.K. 14 E4
Tegina Nigeria 83 C6
Tegucigalpa Honduras 120 D2
Teguidda i-n-Tessoum Niger 83 B6
Tehachapi U.S.A. 111 K8
Tehachapi Mts. U.S.A. 111 L8
Tehamiyam Sudan 80 D4
Tehilla Sudan 80 D4
Téhini Ivory C. 82 D4
Tehoru Indonesia 63 E7
Tehrān Iran 71 C6
Tehrān □ Iran 71 C6
Tehri India 69 D8
Tehuacán Mexico 119 D5
Tehuantepec Mexico 119 D5
Tehuantepec, G. de Mexico 119 D5
Tehuantepec, Istmo de
   Mexico 119 D6
Teide, Pico de Canary Is. 48 F3
Teifi → U.K. 15 E3
Teigebyen Norway 10 D5
Teign → U.K. 15 G4
Teignmouth U.K. 15 G4
Teius Romania 29 D8
Teixeira Pinto Guinea-Biss. 82 C1
Tejakula Indonesia 63 J18
Tejam India 69 E9
Tejen Turkmenistan 52 F7
Tejen → Turkmenistan 71 B9
Tejo → Europe 37 F2
Tejon Pass U.S.A. 111 L8
Tekamah U.S.A. 112 E5
Tekapo, L. N.Z. 91 E3
Tekax Mexico 119 C7
Teke Turkey 45 E13
Tekeli Kazakhstan 52 E8
Tekeze → Ethiopia 81 E4
Tekija Serbia 44 B6
Tekirdağ Turkey 45 F11
Tekirdağ □ Turkey 45 E11
Tekirova Turkey 47 E12
Tekkali India 67 K14
Tekke Turkey 72 B7
Tekman Turkey 73 C9

Tekoa U.S.A. 108 C5
Tekong Besar, Pulau
   Singapore 65 d
Tel Aviv ✈ (TLV) Israel 74 C3
Tel Aviv-Yafo Israel 74 C3
Tel Lakhish Israel 74 D3
Tel Megiddo Israel 74 C4
Tela Honduras 120 C2
Telanaipura = Jambi
   Indonesia 62 E2
Telavi Georgia 35 K7
Telč Czech Rep. 26 B8
Telciu Romania 29 C9
Telde Canary Is. 48 G4
Telegraph Creek Canada 102 B2
Telekhany =
   Tsyelyakhany Belarus 23 B13
Telemark Norway 9 G12
Telén Argentina 126 D2
Teleneşti Moldova 29 C13
Teleng Iran 71 E9
Teleño Spain 36 C4
Telescope Pk. U.S.A. 111 J9
Teletaye Mali 83 B5
Telfer Mine Australia 92 C3
Telford U.K. 15 E5
Telford and Wrekin □ U.K. 14 E5
Telfs Austria 26 D4
Télimélé Guinea 82 C2
Teljo, J. Sudan 81 E2
Telkwa Canada 102 C3
Tell City U.S.A. 112 G10
Tellicherry India 66 P9
Telluride U.S.A. 109 H10
Teloloapán Mexico 119 D5
Telpos Iz Russia 6 C17
Telsen Argentina 128 E3
Telšiai Lithuania 30 C9
Telšiai □ Lithuania 30 C9
Teltow Germany 24 C9
Teluk Anson = Teluk
   Intan Malaysia 65 K3
Teluk Bahang Malaysia 65 c
Teluk Betung =
   Tanjungkarang
   Telukbetung Indonesia 62 F3
Teluk Intan Malaysia 65 K3
Teluk Kumbar Malaysia 65 c
Telukbutun Indonesia 62 D3
Telukdalem Indonesia 62 D1
Tema Ghana 83 D5
Temagami, L. Canada 104 C3
Temax Mexico 119 C7
Temba S. Africa 89 D4
Tembagapura Indonesia 63 E9
Tembe Dem. Rep. of the Congo 86 D2
Tembe △ S. Africa 89 D5
Tembleque Spain 36 F7
Temblor Range U.S.A. 111 K7
Teme → U.K. 15 E5
Temecula U.S.A. 111 M9
Temerloh Malaysia 62 D2
Teminabuan Indonesia 63 E8
Temir Kazakhstan 52 E6
Temirtau Kazakhstan 52 D8
Temirtau Russia 52 D9
Témiscamie → Canada 105 B5
Témiscaming Canada 104 C4
Témiscamingue, L. Canada 104 C4
Temnikov Russia 34 C6
Temo → Italy 42 B1
Temosachic Mexico 118 B3
Tempe U.S.A. 109 K8
Témpio Pausánia Italy 42 B2
Tempiute U.S.A. 110 H11
Temple U.S.A. 116 F6
Temple B. Australia 94 A3
Templemore Ireland 12 D4
Templeton U.S.A. 110 K6
Templeton → Australia 94 C2
Templin Germany 24 B9
Tempoal de Sánchez Mexico
   119 C5
Temryuk Russia 33 K9
Temska → Serbia 44 C6
Temuco Chile 128 D2
Temuka N.Z. 91 F3
Tenabo Mexico 119 C6
Tenaha U.S.A. 116 F7
Tenakee Springs U.S.A. 102 B1
Tenali India 67 L12
Tenancingo de Degollado
   Mexico 119 D5
Tenango del Valle Mexico 119 D5
Tenaro, Akra Greece 46 E4
Tenasserim Burma 65 F2
Tenasserim □ Burma 64 F2
Tenby U.K. 15 F3
Tenda, Colle di France 21 D11
Tendaho Ethiopia 81 E5
Tende France 21 D11
Tendelti Sudan 81 E3
Tendrovskaya Kosa Ukraine 33 J6

Tendukhera India 69 H8
Teneguía, Volcanes de
   Canary Is. 48 F2
Teneida Egypt 80 B2
Tenenkou Mali 82 C4
Ténéré Niger 83 B7
Tenerife Canary Is. 48 F3
Tenerife, Pico Canary Is. 48 G1
Tenerife Norte ✈ (TFN)
   Canary Is. 48 F3
Tenerife Sur ✈ (TFS)
   Canary Is. 48 F3
Teng Xian
   Guangxi Zhuangzu, China 59 F8
Teng Xian Shandong, China 57 G9
Tengah, Kepulauan
   Indonesia 62 F5
Tengchong China 58 E2
Tengchowfu = Penglai
   China 57 F11
Tenggarong Indonesia 62 E5
Tenggol, Pulau Malaysia 65 K4
Tengiz Köli Kazakhstan 52 D7
Tenhult Sweden 11 G8
Teniente Enciso △ Paraguay 126 A3
Teniente Rodolfo Marsh
   Antarctica 5 C18
Tenino U.S.A. 110 D4
Tenkasi India 66 Q10
Tenke Katanga,
   Dem. Rep. of the Congo 87 E2
Tenke Katanga,
   Dem. Rep. of the Congo 87 E2
Tenkodogo Burkina Faso 83 C4
Tenna → Italy 41 E10
Tennant Creek Australia 94 B1
Tennessee □ U.S.A. 117 D11
Tennessee → U.S.A. 117 C10
Teno, Pta. de Canary Is. 48 F3
Tenom Malaysia 62 C5
Tenosique Mexico 119 D6
Tenryū-Gawa → Japan 55 G8
Tenterden U.K. 15 F8
Tenterfield Australia 95 D5
Teo Spain 36 C2
Teófilo Otoni Brazil 125 G10
Tepa Indonesia 63 F7
Tepalcatepec → Mexico 118 D4
Tepecik Bursa, Turkey 45 F12
Tepecik Kütahya, Turkey 47 B11
Tepehuanes Mexico 118 B3
Tepelenë Albania 44 F4
Tepetongo Mexico 118 C4
Tepic Mexico 118 C4
Teplá Czech Rep. 26 A6
Teplice Czech Rep. 26 A6
Teplyk Ukraine 29 B14
Tepoca, C. Mexico 118 A2
Tequila Mexico 118 C4
Ter → Spain 38 C8
Ter Apel Neths. 17 B7
Téra Niger 83 C5
Tera → Spain 36 D5
Teraina Kiribati 97 G12
Terakeka Sudan 81 F3
Téramo Italy 41 F10
Terang Australia 95 F3
Terang, Teluk Indonesia 63 K19
Terazit, Massif de Niger 83 A6
Tercan Turkey 73 C9
Terceira Azores 78 a
Tercero → Argentina 126 C3
Terebovlya Ukraine 23 D13
Teregova Romania 28 E7
Tereida Sudan 81 E3
Terek → Russia 35 J8
Terepaima △ Venezuela 121 E6
Tereshka → Russia 34 E8
Teresina Brazil 125 E10
Terespol Poland 31 F10
Teresva Ukraine 29 B8
Terewah, L. Australia 95 D4
Terges → Portugal 37 H3
Tergnier France 19 C10
Teridgerie Cr. → Australia 95 E4
Terlizzi Italy 43 A9
Terme Turkey 72 B7
Termez = Termiz Uzbekistan 52 F7
Términi Imerese Italy 42 E6
Términos, L. de Mexico 119 D6
Termiz Uzbekistan 52 F7
Térmoli Italy 41 F12
Ternate Indonesia 63 D7
Terneuzen Neths. 17 C3
Terney Russia 54 B8
Terni Italy 41 F9
Ternivka Ukraine 29 B14
Ternopil Ukraine 23 D13
Ternopol = Ternopil
   Ukraine 23 D13
Terowie Australia 95 E2
Terpni Greece 44 F7
Terra Bella U.S.A. 111 K7
Terra Nova △ Canada 105 C9
Terrace Canada 102 C3

Terrace Bay Canada 104 C2
Terracina Italy 42 A6
Terralba Italy 42 C1
Terrasini Italy 42 A5
Terrassa Spain 38 D7
Terrasson-la-Villedieu
   France 20 C5
Terre Haute U.S.A. 112 F10
Terrebonne B. U.S.A. 117 G9
Terrell U.S.A. 116 E6
Terrenceville Canada 105 C9
Terry U.S.A. 108 C11
Terryville U.S.A. 115 E11
Terschelling Neths. 17 A5
Tersko-Kumskiy Kanal
   Russia 35 H7
Tertenía Italy 42 C2
Terter = Tärtär → Azerbaijan 35 K8
Teruel Spain 38 E3
Teruel □ Spain 38 E4
Tervel Bulgaria 45 C11
Tervola Finland 8 C21
Teryaweynya L. Australia 95 E3
Tešanj Bos.-H. 28 F3
Teseney Eritrea 81 D4
Tesha → Russia 34 C6
Teshio Japan 54 B10
Teshio-Gawa → Japan 54 B10
Tešica Serbia 44 C5
Tesiyn Gol → Mongolia 60 A4
Teslić Bos.-H. 28 F2
Teslin Canada 102 A2
Teslin → Canada 102 A2
Teslin L. Canada 102 A2
Tessalit Mali 83 A5
Tessaoua Niger 83 C6
Tessin Germany 24 A8
Tessit Mali 83 B5
Test → U.K. 15 G6
Testa del Gargano Italy 41 G13
Testigos, Is. Los Venezuela 121 D7
Tetas, Pta. Chile 126 A1
Tete Mozam. 87 F3
Tete □ Mozam. 87 F3
Tetachuck L. Canada 102 C3
Teterev → Ukraine 23 C16
Teterow Germany 24 B8
Teteven Bulgaria 45 D8
Tethul → Canada 102 A6
Tetiyev Ukraine 23 D15
Teton → U.S.A. 108 C8
Tétouan Morocco 78 A4
Tetovo Macedonia 44 D4
Tetufera, Mt. Tahiti 91 d
Tetyushi Russia 34 C9
Teuco → Argentina 126 B3
Teulada Italy 42 D1
Teulon Canada 103 C9
Teun Indonesia 63 F7
Teuri-Tō Japan 54 B10
Teutoburger Wald Germany 24 C4
Tevere → Italy 41 G9
Tevere → Italy 41 G9
Teverya Israel 74 C4
Teviot → U.K. 13 F6
Tewantin Australia 95 D5
Tewkesbury U.K. 15 F5
Texada I. Canada 102 D4
Texarkana Ark., U.S.A. 116 E7
Texarkana Tex., U.S.A. 116 E7
Texas Australia 95 D5
Texas □ U.S.A. 116 F5
Texas City U.S.A. 116 G7
Texel Neths. 17 A4
Texline U.S.A. 116 C3
Texoma, L. U.S.A. 116 E6
Teyateyaneng Lesotho 85 K5
Teykovo Russia 32 D11
Teziutlán Mexico 119 D5
Tezpur India 67 F18
Tezzeron L. Canada 102 C4
Tha-anne → Canada 103 A10
Tha Deua Laos 64 D4
Tha Deua Laos 64 C4
Tha Pla Thailand 64 D3
Tha Rua Thailand 64 E3
Tha Sala Thailand 65 H2
Tha Song Yang Thailand 64 D1
Thaba Putsoa Lesotho 89 D4
Thabana Ntlenyana Lesotho 89 D4
Thabazimbi S. Africa 89 C4
Thādiq Si. Arabia 70 E5
Thai Binh Vietnam 58 G6
Thai Muang Thailand 65 H2
Thai Nguyen Vietnam 58 G5
Thailand ■ Asia 64 E4
Thailand, G. of Asia 65 G3
Thakhek Laos 64 D5
Thal Pakistan 68 C4
Thal Desert Pakistan 68 D4
Thala La = Hkakabo Razi
   Burma 67 E20
Thalabarivat Cambodia 64 F5

Thallon Australia 95 D4
Thalu, Ko Thailand 65 b
Thalwil Switz. 25 H4
Thames N.Z. 91 B5
Thames → Canada 114 D2
Thames → U.K. 15 F8
Thames → U.S.A. 115 E12
Thames Estuary U.K. 15 F8
Thamesford Canada 114 C4
Thamesville Canada 114 D3
Than India 68 H4
Than Uyen Vietnam 64 B4
Thana Gazi India 68 F7
Thandla India 68 H6
Thandwe Burma 67 K19
Thane India 66 K8
Thanesar India 68 D7
Thangool Australia 94 C5
Thanh Hoa Vietnam 64 C5
Thanh Hung Vietnam 65 H5
Thanh Pho Ho Chi Minh
   Vietnam 65 G6
Thanh Thuy Vietnam 64 A5
Thanjavur India 66 P11
Thann France 19 E14
Thano Bula Khan Pakistan 68 G2
Thaolintoa L. Canada 103 A9
Thaon-les-Vosges France 19 D13
Thap Lan △ Thailand 64 E4
Thap Sakae Thailand 65 G2
Thap Than Thailand 64 E2
Thar Desert India 68 F5
Tharad India 68 G4
Thargomindah Australia 95 D3
Tharp Fracture Zone
   S. Ocean 5 B14
Tharrawaddy Burma 67 L19
Tharthār, Buḩayrat ath
   Iraq 73 E10
Tharthar, L. = Tharthār,
   Buḩayrat ath Iraq 73 E10
Tharthār, W. ath → Iraq 73 E10
Thasopoula Greece 45 F8
Thasos Greece 45 F8
That Khe Vietnam 58 F6
Thatcher Ariz., U.S.A. 109 K9
Thatcher Colo., U.S.A. 109 H11
Thaton Burma 67 L20
Thau, Bassin de France 20 E7
Thaungdut Burma 67 G19
Thayer U.S.A. 112 G8
Thayetmyo Burma 67 K19
Thazi Burma 67 J20
The Broads U.K. 14 E9
The Everglades U.S.A. 117 J14
The Gulf = Persian Gulf Asia 71 E6
The Hague =
   's-Gravenhage Neths. 17 B4
The Pas Canada 103 C8
The Wash U.K. 14 E8
The Weald U.K. 15 F8
Thebes = Thiva Greece 46 C5
Thebes Egypt 80 B3
Thedford Canada 114 C3
Thedford U.S.A. 112 E3
Theebine Australia 95 D5
Thekulthili L. Canada 103 A7
Thelon → Canada 103 A8
Thénezay France 18 F5
Thenon France 20 C5
Theodore Australia 94 C5
Theodore Canada 103 C8
Theodore U.S.A. 117 F10
Theodore Roosevelt △
   U.S.A. 112 B3
Theodore Roosevelt L.
   U.S.A. 109 K8
Thepha Thailand 65 J3
Thérain → France 19 C9
Theresa U.S.A. 115 B9
Thermopolis U.S.A. 108 E9
Thermopylae Greece 46 C4
Thesprotia □ Greece 46 B2
Thessalon Canada 104 C3
Thessaloniki Greece 44 F6
Thessaloniki □ Greece 44 F7
Thessaloniki ✈ (SKG) Greece 44 F7
Thessaloniki, Gulf of =
   Thessaloniki Kolpos
   Greece 44 F6
Thessaloniki Kolpos Greece 44 F6
Thessaly □ Greece 46 B4
Thetford U.K. 15 E8
Thetford Mines Canada 105 C5
Theun → Laos 64 C5
Theunissen S. Africa 88 D4
Thevenard Australia 95 E1
Thiamis → Greece 46 B2
Thiberville France 18 C7
Thicket Portage Canada 103 B9
Thief River Falls U.S.A. 112 A5
Thiel Mts. Antarctica 5 E16
Thiene Italy 41 C8
Thiérache France 19 C10
Thiers France 20 C7
Thiès Senegal 82 C1
Thiès □ Senegal 82 C1

Thiesi Italy 42 B1
Thiet Sudan 81 F2
Thika Kenya 86 C4
Thille-Boubacar Senegal 82 B1
Thimphu Bhutan 67 F16
Thina → S. Africa 89 E4
Þingvallavatn Iceland 8 D3
Thionville France 19 C13
Thira = Santorini Greece 47 E7
Thirasia Greece 47 E7
Third Cataract Sudan 80 D3
Thirsk U.K. 14 C6
Thiruvananthapuram = Trivandrum India 66 Q10
Thisted Denmark 11 H2
Thistle I. Australia 95 F2
Thithia = Cicia Fiji 91 a
Thiva Greece 46 C5
Thiviers France 20 C4
Thizy France 19 F11
Þjórsá → Iceland 8 E3
Thlewiaza → Canada 103 A10
Thmar Puok Cambodia 64 F4
Tho Vinh Vietnam 64 C5
Thoa → Canada 103 A7
Thoen Thailand 64 D2
Thoeng Thailand 64 C3
Thohoyandou S. Africa 85 J6
Tholdi Pakistan 69 B7
Thomas U.S.A. 116 D5
Thomas, L. Australia 95 D2
Thomaston U.S.A. 117 E12
Thomasville Ala., U.S.A. 117 F11
Thomasville Ga., U.S.A. 117 F13
Thomasville N.C., U.S.A. 117 D14
Thompson Canada 103 B9
Thompson U.S.A. 115 E9
Thompson → Canada 102 C4
Thompson → U.S.A. 112 F7
Thompson Falls U.S.A. 108 C6
Thompson Pk. U.S.A. 108 F2
Thompson Springs U.S.A. 108 G9
Thompsontown U.S.A. 114 F7
Thomson U.S.A. 117 E13
Thomson → Australia 94 C3
Thônes France 21 C10
Thong Yang Thailand 65 b
Thonon-les-Bains France 19 F13
Thorez Ukraine 33 H10
Þórisvatn Iceland 8 D4
Thornaby on Tees U.K. 14 C6
Thornbury Canada 114 B4
Thorne U.K. 14 D7
Thornhill Canada 102 C3
Thornton U.S.A. 108 G11
Thorold Canada 114 C5
Þórshöfn Iceland 8 C6
Thouarcé France 18 E6
Thouars France 18 F6
Thouet → France 18 E6
Thouin, C. Australia 92 D2
Thousand Oaks U.S.A. 111 L8
Thrace Turkey 45 F10
Thrace, Sea of Greece 45 F8
Three Forks U.S.A. 108 D8
Three Gorges Dam China 59 B8
Three Hills Canada 102 C6
Three Hummock I. Australia 95 G3
Three Pagodas Pass Asia 64 E2
Three Points, C. Ghana 82 E4
Three Rivers Calif., U.S.A. 110 J8
Three Rivers Tex., U.S.A. 116 L5
Three Springs Australia 93 E2
Throssell, L. Australia 93 E3
Throssell Ra. Australia 92 D3
Thrushton △ Australia 95 D4
Thua → Kenya 86 C4
Thuan Hoa Vietnam 65 H5
Thubun Lakes Canada 103 A6
Thueyts France 21 D8
Thuin Belgium 17 D4
Thuir France 20 F6
Thule = Qaanaaq Greenland 4 B4
Thule Air Base = Uummannaq Greenland 4 B4
Thun Switz. 25 J3
Thunder B. U.S.A. 114 B1
Thunder Bay Canada 104 C2
Thunersee Switz. 25 J3
Thung Salaeng Luang △ Thailand 64 D3
Thung Song Thailand 65 H2
Thunkar Bhutan 67 F17
Thuong Tra Vietnam 64 D6
Thur → Switz. 25 H5
Thurgau □ Switz. 25 H5
Thüringen □ Germany 24 D6
Thüringer Wald Germany 24 E6
Thurles Ireland 12 D4
Thurn P. Austria 26 D5
Thurrock □ U.K. 15 F8
Thursday I. Australia 94 A3
Thurso Canada 104 C4
Thurso U.K. 13 C5
Thurso → U.K. 13 C5
Thurston I. Antarctica 5 D16
Thury-Harcourt France 18 D6

Thutade L. Canada 102 B3
Thy Denmark 11 H2
Thyborøn Denmark 11 H2
Thyolo Malawi 87 F4
Ti-n-Amzi → Niger 83 B5
Ti-n-Barraouene, O. → Africa 83 B5
Ti-n-Zaouatene Algeria 83 B5
Ti-Tree Australia 94 C1
Tiadiaye Senegal 82 C1
Tian Shan Asia 60 B3
Tianchang China 59 A12
Tiandeng China 58 F6
Tiandong China 58 F6
Tian'e China 58 E6
Tianhe China 58 E6
Tianjin China 57 E9
Tiankoura Burkina Faso 82 C4
Tianlin China 58 E6
Tianmen China 59 B9
Tianquan China 58 B4
Tianshifu China 57 D13
Tianshui China 56 G3
Tiantai China 59 C13
Tianyang China 58 F6
Tianyar Indonesia 63 J18
Tianzhen China 56 D8
Tianzhu China 58 D6
Tianzhuangtai China 57 D12
Tiarei Tahiti 91 d
Tiaret Algeria 78 A6
Tiassalé Ivory C. 82 D4
Tibagi Brazil 127 A5
Tibagi → Brazil 127 A5
Tībastī, Sarīr Libya 79 D9
Tibati Cameroon 83 D7
Tibe Ethiopia 81 F4
Tiber = Tevere → Italy 41 G9
Tiber Res. U.S.A. 108 B8
Tiberias = Teverya Israel 74 C4
Tiberias, L. = Yam Kinneret Israel 74 C4
Tibesti Chad 79 D9
Tibet = Xizang Zizhiqu □ China 60 C3
Tibet, Plateau of Asia 50 E10
Tibiao Phil. 61 F5
Tibiri Niger 83 C6
Þibleş, Vf. Romania 29 C9
Þibleşului, Munţii Romania 29 C9
Tibnī Syria 73 E8
Tibro Sweden 11 F8
Tiburón, I. Mexico 118 B2
Ticao I. Phil. 61 E5
Tîchît Mauritania 82 B3
Ticho Ethiopia 81 F4
Ticino □ Switz. 25 J4
Ticino → Switz. 25 J4
Ticleni Romania 29 F8
Ticul Mexico 119 C7
Tidaholm Sweden 11 F7
Tidan Sweden 11 F8
Tiddim Burma 67 H18
Tidioute U.S.A. 114 E5
Tidjikja Mauritania 82 B2
Tidore Indonesia 63 D7
Tiébissou Ivory C. 82 D3
Tiefa China 57 C12
Tiel Neths. 17 C5
Tiel Senegal 82 C1
Tieling China 57 C12
Tielt Belgium 17 C3
Tien Shan = Tian Shan Asia 60 B3
Tien-tsin = Tianjin China 57 E9
Tien Yen Vietnam 64 B6
Tienching = Tianjin China 57 E9
Tienen Belgium 17 D4
Tiénigbé Ivory C. 82 D3
Tientsin = Tianjin China 57 E9
Tieri Australia 94 C4
Tierp Sweden 10 D11
Tierra Amarilla Chile 126 B1
Tierra Amarilla U.S.A. 109 H10
Tierra Colorada Mexico 119 D5
Tierra de Barros Spain 37 G4
Tierra de Campos Spain 36 C6
Tierra del Fuego, I. Gr. de Argentina 128 J3
Tiétar → Spain 36 F4
Tieté → Brazil 127 A5
Tiffin U.S.A. 113 E12
Tifton U.S.A. 117 F13
Tifu Indonesia 63 E7
Tighina Moldova 29 D14
Tigil Russia 53 D16
Tignish Canada 105 C7
Tigray □ Ethiopia 81 E4
Tigre → Peru 124 D3
Tigre → Venezuela 124 B6
Tigris = Dijlah, Nahr → Asia 70 D5
Tigveni Romania 29 E9
Tigyaing Burma 67 H20
Tîh, Gebel el Egypt 80 B3
Tijara India 68 F7

Tijuana Mexico 111 N9
Tikal Guatemala 120 C2
Tikal △ Guatemala 120 C2
Tikamgarh India 69 G8
Tikaré Burkina Faso 83 C4
Tikhoretsk Russia 35 H5
Tikhvin Russia 32 C7
Tikiraqjuaq = Whale Cove Canada 103 A10
Tiko Cameroon 83 E6
Tikrīt Iraq 73 E10
Tiksi Russia 53 B13
Tilamuta Indonesia 63 D6
Tilburg Neths. 17 C5
Tilbury Canada 114 D2
Tilbury U.K. 15 F8
Tilcara Argentina 126 A2
Tilden U.S.A. 112 D5
Tilemsen Niger 83 B5
Tilemsi, Vallée du Mali 83 B5
Tilhar India 69 F8
Tilichiki Russia 53 C17
Tilissos Greece 49 D7
Till → U.K. 14 B5
Tillabéri Niger 83 C5
Tillamook U.S.A. 108 D2
Tillberga Sweden 10 E10
Tillia Niger 83 B5
Tillsonburg Canada 114 D4
Tillyeria Cyprus 49 D11
Tilpa Australia 95 E3
Tilt → U.K. 13 E5
Tilton U.S.A. 115 C13
Tiltonsville U.S.A. 114 F4
Tim Denmark 11 H2
Timanfaya △ Canary Is. 48 F6
Timaru N.Z. 91 F3
Timashevo Russia 34 D10
Timashevsk Russia 35 H4
Timau Kenya 86 B4
Timbaki Greece 49 D6
Timbedgha Mauritania 82 B3
Timber Creek Australia 92 C5
Timber Lake U.S.A. 112 C3
Timber Mt. U.S.A. 110 H10
Timbo Guinea 82 C2
Timbo Liberia 82 D3
Timbuktu = Tombouctou Mali 82 B4
Timeiaouine Algeria 83 A5
Timétrine, Mts. Mali 83 B4
Timfi Oros Greece 46 B2
Timfristos, Oros Greece 46 C3
Timi Cyprus 49 E11
Tîmia Niger 83 B6
Timimoun Algeria 78 C6
Timiris, Râs Mauritania 82 B1
Timiş = Tamis → Serbia 28 F5
Timiş □ Romania 28 E6
Timiskaming, L. = Témiscamingue, L. Canada 104 C4
Timişoara Romania 28 E6
Timmersdala Sweden 11 F7
Timmins Canada 104 C3
Timok → Serbia 44 B6
Timoleague Ireland 12 E3
Timor Asia 63 F7
Timor Leste = East Timor ■ Asia 63 F7
Timor Sea Ind. Oc. 92 B4
Timrå Sweden 10 B11
Tin Can Bay Australia 95 D5
Tin Ethisane Mali 83 B4
Tin Gornai Mali 83 B4
Tin Mt. U.S.A. 110 J9
Tina = Thina → S. Africa 89 E4
Tina, Khalîg el Egypt 74 D1
Tinaca Pt. Phil. 61 J6
Tinajo Canary Is. 48 E6
Tinca Romania 28 D6
Tindal Australia 92 B5
Tindouf Algeria 78 C4
Tinée → France 21 E11
Tineo Spain 36 B4
Tinfunque △ Paraguay 126 A3
Ting Jiang → China 59 E11
Tinggi, Pulau Malaysia 65 L5
Tinglev Denmark 11 K3
Tingo Maria Peru 124 E3
Tingrela Ivory C. 82 C3
Tingsryd Sweden 11 H9
Tingstäde Sweden 11 G12
Tinian N. Marianas 96 F6
Tinnevelly = Tirunelveli India 66 Q10
Tinogasta Argentina 126 B2
Tinos Greece 47 D7
Tiñoso, C. Spain 39 H3
Tinpahar India 69 G12
Tintina Argentina 126 B3
Tintinara Australia 95 F3
Tintioulé Guinea 82 C3
Tinto → Spain 37 H4

Tioga N. Dak., U.S.A. 112 A2
Tioga Pa., U.S.A. 114 E7
Tioman, Pulau Malaysia 65 L5
Tione di Trento Italy 40 B7
Tionesta U.S.A. 114 E5
Tior Sudan 81 F3
Tipperary Ireland 12 D3
Tipperary □ Ireland 12 D4
Tipton Calif., U.S.A. 110 J7
Tipton Iowa, U.S.A. 112 E8
Tipton Mt. U.S.A. 111 K12
Tiptonville U.S.A. 117 C10
Tīrān Iran 71 C6
Tīrān Si. Arabia 80 B3
Tiranë Albania 44 E3
Tiranë ✈ (TIA) Albania 44 E3
Tirano Italy 40 B7
Tirari Desert Australia 95 D2
Tiraspol Moldova 29 D14
Tirdout Mali 83 B4
Tire Turkey 47 C9
Tirebolu Turkey 73 B8
Tiree U.K. 13 E2
Tiree, Passage of U.K. 13 E2
Tîrgovişte = Târgovişte Romania 29 F10
Tîrgu Jiu = Târgu Jiu Romania 29 F8
Tîrgu Mureş = Târgu Mureş Romania 29 D9
Tirich Mir Pakistan 66 A7
Tiriolo Italy 43 D9
Tiriro Guinea 82 C3
Tiritiri o te Moana = Southern Alps N.Z. 91 E3
Tirnavos Greece 46 B4
Tirodi India 66 J11
Tirol □ Austria 26 D3
Tirso → Italy 42 C1
Tirstrup Denmark 11 H4
Tiruchchirappalli India 66 P11
Tirunelveli India 66 Q10
Tirupati India 66 N11
Tiruppur India 66 P10
Tiruvannamalai India 66 N11
Tisa → Serbia 28 E5
Tisdale Canada 103 C8
Tishomingo U.S.A. 116 D6
Tisjön Sweden 10 D7
Tisnaren Sweden 11 F9
Tišnov Czech Rep. 27 B9
Tisovec Slovak Rep. 27 C12
Tisza = Tisa → Serbia 28 E5
Tiszaföldvár Hungary 28 D5
Tiszafüred Hungary 28 C5
Tiszalök Hungary 28 B6
Tiszavasvári Hungary 28 C6
Tit-Ary Russia 53 B13
Titaguas Spain 38 F3
Titao Burkina Faso 83 C4
Titel Serbia 28 E5
Tithwal Pakistan 69 B5
Titicaca, L. S. Amer. 124 G5
Titiwa Nigeria 83 C7
Tito Italy 43 B8
Titova Korenica Croatia 41 D12
Titu Romania 29 F10
Titule Dem. Rep. of the Congo 86 B2
Titusville Fla., U.S.A. 117 G14
Titusville Pa., U.S.A. 114 E5
Tivaouane Senegal 82 C1
Tivat Montenegro 44 D2
Tivedens △ Sweden 11 F8
Tiverton U.K. 15 G4
Tivoli Italy 41 G9
Tiyo Eritrea 81 E5
Tizi-Ouzou Algeria 78 A6
Tizimín Mexico 119 C7
Tiznit Morocco 78 C4
Tjæreborg Denmark 11 J2
Tjällmo Sweden 11 F9
Tjeggelvas Sweden 8 C17
Tjiegelvas = Tjeggelvas Sweden 8 C17
Tjirebon = Cirebon Indonesia 63 G13
Tjluring Indonesia 63 J17
Tjörn Sweden 11 K3
Tkibuli = Tqibuli Georgia 35 J6
Tkvarcheli = Tqvarcheli Georgia 35 J5
Tlacotalpan Mexico 119 D5
Tlahualilo de Zaragoza Mexico 118 B4
Tlaquepaque Mexico 118 C4
Tlaxcala Mexico 119 D5
Tlaxcala □ Mexico 119 D5
Tlaxiaco Mexico 119 D5
Tlemcen Algeria 78 B5
Tlumach Ukraine 29 B10
Tłuszcz Poland 31 F8
Tlyarata Russia 35 J8
To Bong Vietnam 64 F7
Toa Payoh Singapore 65 d

Toad → Canada 102 B4
Toad River Canada 102 B3
Toamasina Madag. 89 B8
Toamasina □ Madag. 89 B8
Toay Argentina 126 D3
Toba China 58 B1
Toba Japan 55 G8
Toba, Danau Indonesia 62 D1
Toba Kakar Pakistan 68 D3
Toba Tek Singh Pakistan 68 D5
Tobago Trin. & Tob. 121 D7
Tobarra Spain 39 G3
Tobelo Indonesia 63 D7
Tobermory Canada 114 A3
Tobermory U.K. 13 E2
Tobi Pac. Oc. 63 D8
Tobi-Shima Japan 54 D9
Tobin, L. Australia 92 D4
Tobin, L. Canada 103 C8
Toblach = Dobbiaco Italy 41 B9
Toboali Indonesia 62 E3
Tobol → Russia 52 D7
Toboli Indonesia 63 E6
Tobolsk Russia 52 D7
Tobor Senegal 82 C1
Tobruk = Tubruq Libya 79 B10
Tobyhanna U.S.A. 115 E9
Tobyl = Tobol → Russia 52 D7
Tocantinópolis Brazil 125 E9
Tocantins □ Brazil 125 F9
Tocantins → Brazil 125 D9
Toccoa U.S.A. 117 D13
Toce → Italy 40 C5
Tochi → Pakistan 68 C4
Tochigi Japan 55 F9
Tochigi □ Japan 55 F9
Tocina Spain 37 H5
Töcksfors Sweden 10 E5
Toco Trin. & Tob. 125 K16
Toconao Chile 126 A2
Tocopilla Chile 126 A1
Tocumwal Australia 95 F4
Tocuyo → Venezuela 124 A5
Todd → Australia 94 C2
Todeli Indonesia 63 E6
Todenyang Kenya 86 B4
Todgarh India 68 G5
Todi Italy 41 F9
Todos os Santos, B. de Brazil 125 F11
Todos Santos Mexico 118 C2
Todtnau Germany 25 H3
Toe Hd. U.K. 13 D1
Toecé Burkina Faso 83 C4
Tofield Canada 102 C6
Tofino Canada 102 D3
Töfsingdalens △ Sweden 10 B6
Tofua Tonga 91 c
Tōgane Japan 55 G10
Togba Mauritania 82 B2
Togian, Kepulauan Indonesia 63 E6
Togliatti Russia 34 D9
Togo ■ W. Afr. 83 D5
Togtoh China 56 D6
Tohiea, Mt. Moorea 91 d
Tohma → Turkey 72 C8
Tōhoku □ Japan 54 E10
Töhöm Mongolia 56 B5
Toinya Sudan 81 F2
Toiyabe Range U.S.A. 108 G5
Tojikiston = Tajikistan ■ Asia 52 F8
Tojo Indonesia 63 E6
Tōjō Japan 55 G6
Tok U.S.A. 100 C5
Tok-do Asia 55 F5
Tokachi-Dake Japan 54 C11
Tokachi-Gawa → Japan 54 C11
Tokaj Hungary 28 B6
Tokala Indonesia 63 E6
Tōkamachi Japan 55 F9
Tokanui N.Z. 91 G2
Tokar Sudan 80 D4
Tokara-Rettō Japan 55 K4
Tokarahi N.Z. 91 F3
Tokashiki-Shima Japan 55 L3
Tokat Turkey 72 B7
Tokat □ Turkey 72 B7
Tokeland U.S.A. 110 D3
Tokelau Is. ■ Pac. Oc. 96 H10
Tokmak Kyrgyzstan 52 E8
Tokmak Ukraine 33 J8
Toko Ra. Australia 94 C2
Tokoro-Gawa → Japan 54 B12
Toku Tonga 91 c
Tokuno-Shima Japan 55 L4
Tokushima Japan 55 G7
Tokushima □ Japan 55 H7
Tokuyama Japan 55 G5
Tōkyō Japan 55 G9
Tolaga Bay N.Z. 91 E6
Tolbukhin = Dobrich Bulgaria 45 C11
Toledo Brazil 127 A5
Toledo Spain 36 F6
Toledo Ohio, U.S.A. 113 E12

Toledo Oreg., U.S.A. 108 D2
Toledo Wash., U.S.A. 108 C2
Toledo, Montes de Spain 37 F6
Toledo Bend Res. U.S.A. 116 F8
Tolentino Italy 41 E10
Tolfa Italy 41 F8
Tolga Australia 94 B4
Toliara Madag. 89 C7
Toliara □ Madag. 89 C8
Tolima Colombia 124 C3
Tolitoli Indonesia 63 D6
Tolkmicko Poland 30 D6
Tollarp Sweden 11 J7
Tollensee Germany 24 B9
Tollhouse U.S.A. 110 H7
Tolmachevo Russia 32 C5
Tolmezzo Italy 41 B10
Tolmin Slovenia 41 B10
Tolna Hungary 28 D3
Tolna □ Hungary 28 D3
Tolo, Teluk Indonesia 63 E6
Tolochin = Talachyn Belarus 32 E5
Tolosa Spain 38 B2
Tolox Spain 37 J6
Toluca Mexico 119 D5
Tom Burke S. Africa 89 C4
Tom Price Australia 92 D2
Toma Burkina Faso 82 C4
Tomah U.S.A. 112 D8
Tomahawk U.S.A. 112 C9
Tomai Moldova 29 D13
Tomakomai Japan 54 C10
Tomales U.S.A. 110 G4
Tomales B. U.S.A. 110 G3
Tomanivi Fiji 91 a
Tomar Portugal 37 F2
Tomaros, Oros Greece 46 B2
Tomarza Turkey 72 C6
Tomashevka Belarus 31 G10
Tomashpil Ukraine 29 B13
Tomaszów Lubelski Poland 31 H10
Tomaszów Mazowiecki Poland 31 G7
Tomatlán Mexico 118 D3
Tombadonkéa Guinea 82 C2
Tombe Sudan 81 F3
Tombador, Serra do Brazil 124 F7
Tombe Angola 88 B1
Tomé Chile 126 D1
Tomelilla Sweden 11 J7
Tomelloso Spain 37 F7
Tomini Indonesia 63 D6
Tomini, Teluk Indonesia 63 E6
Tominian Mali 82 C4
Tomiño Spain 36 D2
Tomintoul U.K. 13 D5
Tomislavgrad Bos.-H. 28 G2
Tomkinson Ranges Australia 93 E4
Tommot Russia 53 D13
Tomnop Ta Suos Cambodia 65 G5
Tomo → Colombia 124 B5
Toms Place U.S.A. 110 H8
Toms River U.S.A. 115 G10
Tomsk Russia 52 D9
Tomtabacken Sweden 11 G8
Tona Spain 38 D7
Tonalá Chiapas, Mexico 119 D6
Tonalá Jalisco, Mexico 118 C4
Tonale, Passo del Italy 40 B7
Tonantins Brazil 124 D5
Tonasket U.S.A. 108 B4
Tonawanda U.S.A. 114 D6
Tonb Iran 71 E7
Tonbridge U.K. 15 F8
Tondano Indonesia 63 D6
Tondela Portugal 36 E2
Tønder Denmark 11 K2
Tondi Kiwindi Niger 83 C5
Tondibi Mali 83 B4
Tondoro Namibia 88 B2
Tone → Australia 93 F2
Tone-Gawa → Japan 55 F9
Tonekābon Iran 71 B6
Tong Xian China 56 E9
Tong-Yeong S. Korea 57 G15
Tônga Sudan 81 F3
Tonga ■ Pac. Oc. 91 c
Tonga Trench Pac. Oc. 96 J10
Tongaat S. Africa 89 D5
Tong'an China 59 E12
Tongareva = Penrhyn Cook Is. 97 H12
Tongariro △ N.Z. 91 C5
Tongatapu Tonga 91 c
Tongatapu Group Tonga 91 c
Tongbai China 59 A9
Tongcheng Anhui, China 59 B11
Tongcheng Hubei, China 59 C9
Tongchuan China 56 G5
Tongdao China 58 D7
Tongeren Belgium 17 D5
Tonggu China 59 C10
Tongguan China 56 G6

Tonghai China 58 E4
Tonghua China 57 D13
Tongjiang China 58 B6
Tongjosŏn Man N. Korea 57 E15
Tongking, G. of = Tonkin, G. of Asia 64 C7
Tongliang China 58 C6
Tongliao China 57 C12
Tongling China 59 B11
Tonglu China 59 C12
Tongnan = Anyue China 58 B5
Tongobory Madag. 89 C7
Tongoy Chile 126 C1
Tongren China 58 D7
Tongres = Tongeren Belgium 17 D5
Tongsa Dzong Bhutan 67 F17
Tongshi China 64 C7
Tongue U.K. 13 C4
Tongue → U.S.A. 108 C11
Tongwei China 56 G3
Tongxiang China 59 B13
Tongxin China 56 F3
Tongyang N. Korea 57 E14
Tongyu China 57 B12
Tongzi China 58 C6
Tonj Sudan 81 F2
Tonj → Sudan 81 F2
Tonk India 68 F6
Tonkawa U.S.A. 116 C6
Tonkin = Bac Phan Vietnam 64 B5
Tonkin, G. of Asia 64 C7
Tonle Sap Cambodia 65 F5
Tonnay-Charente France 20 C3
Tonneins France 20 D4
Tonnerre France 19 E10
Tönning Germany 24 A4
Tono Japan 54 E10
Tonopah U.S.A. 109 G5
Tonosí Panama 120 E3
Tons → Haryana, India 68 D7
Tons → Ut. P., India 69 F10
Tønsberg Norway 9 G14
Tonto △ U.S.A. 109 K8
Tonumea Tonga 91 c
Tonya Turkey 73 B8
Toobanna Australia 94 B4
Toodyay Australia 93 F2
Tooele U.S.A. 108 F7
Toompine Australia 95 D3
Toora Australia 95 F4
Toora-Khem Russia 53 D10
Toowoomba Australia 95 D5
Top-ozero Russia 8 D25
Top Springs Australia 92 C5
Topalu Romania 29 F13
Topaz U.S.A. 110 G7
Topeka U.S.A. 112 F6
Topl'a → Slovak Rep. 27 C14
Topley Canada 102 C3
Toplica → Serbia 44 C5
Toplița Romania 29 D10
Topocalma, Pta. Chile 126 C1
Topock U.S.A. 111 L12
Topola Serbia 44 B4
Topolčani Macedonia 44 E5
Topoľčany Slovak Rep. 27 C11
Topolnitsa → Bulgaria 45 D8
Topolobampo Mexico 118 B3
Topoloveni Romania 29 F10
Topolovgrad Bulgaria 45 D10
Topolvățu Mare Romania 28 E6
Toppenish U.S.A. 108 C3
Topraisar Romania 29 F13
Topusko Croatia 41 C12
Torà Spain 38 D6
Tora Kit Sudan 81 E3
Toraka Vestale Madag. 89 B7
Torata Peru 124 G4
Torbalı Turkey 47 C9
Torbat-e Heydārīyeh Iran 71 C8
Torbat-e Jām Iran 71 C9
Torbay Canada 105 C9
Torbay □ U.K. 15 G4
Torbjörntorp Sweden 11 F7
Tordesillas Spain 36 D6
Töreboda Sweden 11 F8
Torekov Sweden 11 H6
Torellò Spain 38 C7
Toreno Spain 36 C4
Torfaen □ U.K. 15 F4
Torgau Germany 24 D8
Torgelow Germany 24 B10
Torhamn Sweden 11 H9
Torhout Belgium 17 C3
Torhovytsya Ukraine 29 B10
Tori Ethiopia 81 F3
Tori-Shima Japan 55 J10
Torigni-sur-Vire France 18 C6
Torija Spain 38 E1
Torino Italy 40 C4
Torit Sudan 81 G3
Torkamān Iran 73 D12
Torkovichi Russia 32 C6
Tormac Romania 28 E6
Tormes → Spain 36 D4
Tornado Mt. Canada 102 D6
Tornal'a Slovak Rep. 27 C13
Torneå = Tornio Finland 8 D21
Torneälven → Europe 8 D21
Torneträsk Sweden 8 B18
Tornio Finland 8 D21
Tornionjoki = Torneälven → Europe 8 D21
Tornquist Argentina 126 D3
Toro Baleares, Spain 48 B11
Toro Zamora, Spain 36 D5
Torö Sweden 11 F11
Toro, Cerro del Chile 126 B2
Toro ⌂ Uganda 86 C3
Toro Pk. U.S.A. 111 M10
Törökszentmiklós Hungary 28 C5
Toronto Canada 114 C5
Toronto U.S.A. 114 F4
Toronto Lester B. Pearson Int. ✕ (YYZ) Canada 114 C5
Toropets Russia 32 D6
Tororo Uganda 86 B3
Toros Dağları Turkey 72 D5
Torpa India 69 H11
Torquay U.K. 15 G4
Torquemada Spain 36 C6
Torrance U.S.A. 111 M8
Torrão Portugal 37 G2
Torre Annunziata Italy 43 B7
Torre de Moncorvo Portugal 36 D3
Torre del Campo Spain 37 H7
Torre del Greco Italy 43 B7
Torre del Mar Spain 37 J6
Torre-Pacheco Spain 39 H4
Torre Péllice Italy 40 D4
Torreblanca Spain 38 E5
Torrecampo Spain 37 G6
Torrecilla en Cameros Spain 38 C2
Torredembarra Spain 38 D6
Torredonjimeno Spain 37 H7
Torrejón de Ardoz Spain 36 E7
Torrejoncillo Spain 36 F4
Torrelaguna Spain 36 E7
Torrelavega Spain 36 B6
Torremaggiore Italy 41 G12
Torremolinos Spain 37 J6
Torrens, L. Australia 95 E2
Torrens Cr. → Australia 94 C4
Torrens Creek Australia 94 C4
Torrent Spain 39 F4
Torrenueva Spain 37 G7
Torreón Mexico 118 B4
Torreperogil Spain 37 G7
Torres Brazil 127 B5
Torres Mexico 118 B2
Torres Novas Portugal 37 F2
Torres Strait Australia 90 B7
Torres Vedras Portugal 37 F1
Torrevieja Spain 39 H4
Torrey U.S.A. 108 G8
Torridge → U.K. 15 G3
Torridon, L. U.K. 13 D3
Torrijos Spain 36 F6
Tørring Denmark 11 J3
Torrington Conn., U.S.A. 115 E11
Torrington Wyo., U.S.A. 108 E11
Torroella de Montgrì Spain 38 C8
Torrox Spain 37 J7
Torsås Sweden 11 H9
Torsby Sweden 10 D6
Torshälla Sweden 10 E10
Tórshavn Færoe Is. 8 E9
Torslanda Sweden 11 G5
Torsö Sweden 11 F7
Tortola Br. Virgin Is. 121 e
Tórtoles de Esgueva Spain 36 D6
Tortolì Italy 42 C2
Tortona Italy 40 D5
Tortorici Italy 43 D7
Tortosa Spain 38 E5
Tortosa, C. Spain 38 E5
Tortosendo Portugal 36 E3
Tortue, Î. de la Haiti 121 B5
Tortuguero △ Costa Rica 120 D3
Tortum Turkey 73 B9
Ţorūd Iran 71 C7
Torul Turkey 73 B8
Toruń Poland 31 E5
Torun Ukraine 29 B8
Tory I. Ireland 12 A3
Torysa → Slovak Rep. 27 C14
Torzhok Russia 32 D8
Torzym Poland 31 F2
Tosa Japan 55 H6
Tosa-Shimizu Japan 55 H6
Tosa-Wan Japan 55 H6
Toscana □ Italy 40 E8
Toscano, Arcipelago Italy 40 F7
Toshka Egypt 80 C3
Toshka Lakes Egypt 80 C3
Toshkent Uzbekistan 52 E7
Tosno Russia 32 C6
Tossa de Mar Spain 38 D7
Tösse Sweden 11 F6
Tostado Argentina 126 B3
Tostedt Germany 24 B5
Tostón, Pta. de Canary Is. 48 F5
Tosu Japan 55 H5
Tosya Turkey 72 B6
Toszek Poland 31 H5
Totana Spain 39 H3
Totebo Sweden 11 G10
Toteng Botswana 88 C3
Tôtes France 18 C8
Tótkomlós Hungary 28 D5
Totma Russia 52 D5
Totnes U.K. 15 G4
Totness Suriname 125 B7
Toto Nigeria 83 D6
Totonicapán Guatemala 120 D1
Totoya, I. Fiji 91 a
Totten Glacier Antarctica 5 C8
Tottenham Australia 95 E4
Tottenham Canada 114 B5
Tottori Japan 55 G7
Tottori □ Japan 55 G7
Touaret Niger 83 A6
Touba Ivory C. 82 D3
Touba Senegal 82 C1
Toubkal, Djebel Morocco 78 B4
Toucy France 19 E10
Tougan Burkina Faso 82 C4
Touggourt Algeria 78 B7
Tougouri Burkina Faso 83 C4
Tougué Guinea 82 C2
Toukoto Mali 82 C3
Toul France 19 D12
Toulepleu Ivory C. 82 D3
Touliu Taiwan 59 F13
Toulon France 21 E9
Toulouse France 20 E5
Toulouse Blagnac ✕ (TLS) France 20 E5
Toummo Niger 79 D8
Toumodi Ivory C. 82 D3
Tounan Taiwan 59 F13
Toungo Nigeria 83 D7
Toungoo Burma 67 K20
Touques → France 18 C7
Touraine France 18 E7
Tourcoing France 19 B10
Touriñán, C. Spain 36 B1
Tournai Belgium 17 D3
Tournan-en-Brie France 19 D9
Tournay France 20 E4
Tournon-St-Martin France 18 F7
Tournon-sur-Rhône France 21 C8
Tournus France 19 F11
Tours France 18 E7
Toussoro, Mt. C.A.R. 84 C4
Touws → S. Africa 88 E3
Touwsrivier S. Africa 88 E3
Tovarkovskiy Russia 32 F10
Tovste Ukraine 29 B10
Tovuz Azerbaijan 35 K7
Towada Japan 54 D10
Towada-Hachimantai △ Japan 54 D10
Towada-Ko Japan 54 D10
Towanda U.S.A. 115 E8
Tower U.S.A. 112 B7
Towerhill Cr. → Australia 94 C3
Towner U.S.A. 112 A3
Townsend U.S.A. 108 C8
Townshend I. Australia 94 C5
Townsville Australia 94 B4
Towraghondī Afghan. 66 B3
Towson U.S.A. 113 F15
Towuti, Danau Indonesia 63 E6
Toya-Ko Japan 54 C10
Toyama Japan 55 F8
Toyama □ Japan 55 F8
Toyama-Wan Japan 55 F8
Toyapakeh Indonesia 63 K18
Toyohashi Japan 55 G8
Toyokawa Japan 55 G8
Toyonaka Japan 55 G7
Toyooka Japan 55 G7
Toyota Japan 55 G8
Tozeur Tunisia 78 B7
Tozkhurmato Iraq 73 E11
Tqibuli Georgia 35 J6
Tqvarcheli Georgia 35 J5
Trá Li = Tralee Ireland 12 D2
Tra On Vietnam 65 H5
Trabancos → Spain 36 D5
Traben-Trarbach Germany 25 F3
Trabzon Turkey 73 B8
Trabzon □ Turkey 73 B8
Tracadie-Sheila Canada 105 C7
Tracy Calif., U.S.A. 110 H5
Tracy Minn., U.S.A. 112 C6
Tradate Italy 40 C5
Trade Town Liberia 82 D3
Trafalgar, C. Spain 37 J4
Tragonhsi Greece 47 D7
Traian Brăila, Romania 29 E12
Traian Tulcea, Romania 29 E13
Trail Canada 102 D5
Trainor L. Canada 102 A4
Trakai △ Lithuania 9 J21
Trákhonas Cyprus 49 D12
Tralee Ireland 12 D2
Tralee B. Ireland 12 D2
Tramore Ireland 12 D4
Tramore B. Ireland 12 D4
Tran Ninh, Cao Nguyen Laos 64 C4
Tranås Sweden 11 F8
Tranbjerg Denmark 11 H4
Trancas Argentina 126 B2
Trancoso Portugal 36 E3
Tranebjerg Denmark 11 J4
Tranemo Sweden 11 G7
Trang Thailand 65 J2
Trangahy Madag. 89 B7
Trangan Indonesia 63 F8
Trangie Australia 95 E4
Trångsviken Sweden 10 A7
Trani Italy 43 A9
Tranoroa Madag. 89 C8
Tranqueras Uruguay 127 C4
Transantarctic Mts. Antarctica 5 E12
Transcarpathia = Zakarpattya □ Ukraine 29 B8
Transilvania Romania 29 D9
Transilvanian Alps = Carpaţii Meridionali Romania 29 E9
Transnistria = Stînga Nistrului □ Moldova 29 C14
Transtrand Sweden 10 C7
Transtrandsfjällen Sweden 10 C6
Transylvania = Transilvania Romania 29 D9
Trápani Italy 42 D5
Trapper Pk. U.S.A. 108 D6
Traralgon Australia 95 F4
Trarza □ Mauritania 82 B2
Trasacco Italy 41 G10
Trăscău, Munţii Romania 29 D8
Trasimeno, L. Italy 41 E9
Träslövsläge Sweden 11 G6
Trasvase Tajo-Segura, Canal de Spain 38 E2
Trat Thailand 65 F4
Tratani → Pakistan 68 E3
Traun Austria 26 C7
Traunreut Germany 25 H8
Traunsee Austria 26 D6
Traunstein Germany 25 H8
Travellers L. Australia 95 E3
Travemünde Germany 24 B6
Travers, Mt. N.Z. 91 E4
Traverse City U.S.A. 113 C11
Travis, L. U.S.A. 116 F6
Travnik Bos.-H. 28 F2
Trawbreaga B. Ireland 12 A4
Trbovlje Slovenia 41 B12
Trébbia → Italy 40 C6
Trebel → Germany 24 B9
Trébeurden France 18 D3
Trebević △ Bos.-H. 28 G3
Třebíč Czech Rep. 26 B8
Trebinje Bos.-H. 44 D2
Trebisacce Italy 43 C9
Trebišnjica → Bos.-H. 44 D2
Trebišov Slovak Rep. 27 C14
Trebižat → Bos.-H. 41 E14
Trebnje Slovenia 41 C12
Třeboň Czech Rep. 26 B7
Trebonne Australia 94 B4
Třeboňsko ⌂ Czech Rep. 26 B7
Trebujena Spain 37 J4
Trecate Italy 40 C5
Tregaron U.K. 15 E4
Tregnago Italy 41 C8
Tregrosse Is. Australia 94 B5
Tréguier France 18 D3
Trégunc France 18 E3
Treherne Canada 103 D9
Tréia Italy 41 E10
Treignac France 20 C5
Treinta y Tres Uruguay 127 C5
Treis-karden Germany 25 E3
Treklyano Bulgaria 44 D6
Trelawney Zimbabwe 89 B5
Trélazé France 18 E6
Trelew Argentina 128 E3
Trélissac France 20 C4
Trelleborg Sweden 11 J7
Tremadog Bay U.K. 14 E3
Trémiti Italy 41 F12
Tremonton U.S.A. 108 F7
Tremp Spain 38 C5
Trenche → Canada 104 C5
Trenčiansky □ Slovak Rep. 27 C11
Trenčín Slovak Rep. 27 C11
Trenggalek Indonesia 63 H14
Trenque Lauquen Argentina 126 D3
Trent → Canada 114 B7
Trent → U.K. 14 D7
Trentino-Alto Adige □ Italy 41 B8
Trento Italy 40 B8
Trenton = Quinte West Canada 114 B7
Trenton Mo., U.S.A. 112 E7
Trenton N.J., U.S.A. 115 F10
Trenton Nebr., U.S.A. 112 E3
Trepassey Canada 105 C9
Trepuzzi Italy 43 B11
Tres Arroyos Argentina 126 D3
Três Corações Brazil 127 A6
Três Lagoas Brazil 125 H8
Tres Lomas Argentina 126 D3
Tres Montes, C. Chile 128 F1
Tres Pinos U.S.A. 110 J5
Três Pontas Brazil 127 A6
Tres Puentes Chile 126 B1
Tres Puntas, C. Argentina 128 F3
Três Rios Brazil 127 A7
Tres Valles Mexico 119 D5
Tresco U.K. 15 H1
Treska → Macedonia 44 E5
Treskavica Bos.-H. 28 G3
Trespaderne Spain 36 C7
Tresticklan △ Sweden 11 F5
Trets France 21 E9
Treuchtlingen Germany 25 G6
Treuenbrietzen Germany 24 C8
Trevi Italy 41 F9
Treviglio Italy 40 C6
Trevinca, Peña Spain 36 C4
Treviso Italy 41 C9
Trévoux France 21 C8
Trgovište Serbia 44 D6
Triabunna Australia 95 G4
Trianda Greece 49 C10
Triangle Zimbabwe 89 C5
Triaucourt-en-Argonne France 19 D12
Tribal Areas □ Pakistan 68 C4
Tribsees Germany 24 A8
Tribulation, C. Australia 94 B4
Tribune U.S.A. 112 F3
Tricárico Italy 43 B9
Tricase Italy 43 C11
Trichinopoly = Tiruchchirappalli India 66 P11
Trichonida, L. Greece 46 C3
Trichur India 66 P10
Trida Australia 95 E4
Trier Germany 25 F2
Trieste Italy 41 C10
Trieste, G. di Italy 41 C10
Trieux → France 18 D3
Triggiano Italy 43 A9
Triglav Slovenia 41 B10
Triglavski △ Slovenia 41 B10
Trigno → Italy 41 F11
Trigueros Spain 37 H4
Trikala Greece 46 B3
Trikala □ Greece 46 B3
Trikeri Greece 46 B5
Trikomo Cyprus 49 D12
Trikora, Puncak Indonesia 63 E9
Trilj Croatia 41 E13
Trillo Spain 38 E2
Trim Ireland 12 C5
Trimmu Dam Pakistan 68 D5
Trincomalee Sri Lanka 66 Q12
Trindade Brazil 125 G9
Trindade, I. Atl. Oc. 2 F8
Třinec Czech Rep. 27 B11
Trinidad Bolivia 124 F6
Trinidad Cuba 120 B4
Trinidad Trin. & Tob. 121 D7
Trinidad Uruguay 126 C4
Trinidad U.S.A. 109 H11
Trinidad → Mexico 119 D5
Trinidad & Tobago ■ W. Indies 121 D7
Trinitápoli Italy 43 A9
Trinity Canada 105 C9
Trinity U.S.A. 116 F7
Trinity → Calif., U.S.A. 108 F2
Trinity → Tex., U.S.A. 116 G7
Trinity B. Canada 105 C9
Trinity Hills Trin. & Tob. 125 K15
Trinity Is. U.S.A. 106 a
Trinity Range U.S.A. 108 F4
Trinkitat Sudan 80 D4
Trino Italy 40 C5
Trinway U.S.A. 114 F2
Triolet Mauritius 85 d
Trionto, C. Italy 43 C9
Triora Italy 40 D4
Tripoli = Tarābulus Lebanon 74 A4
Tripoli = Tarābulus Libya 79 B8
Tripoli Greece 46 D4
Tripolitania N. Afr. 79 B8
Tripura □ India 67 H18
Tripylos Cyprus 49 E11
Trischen Germany 24 A4
Tristan da Cunha Atl. Oc. 77 K2
Trisul India 69 D8
Trivandrum India 66 Q10
Trivento Italy 41 G11
Trizin Greece 46 D5
Trnava Slovak Rep. 27 C10
Trnavský □ Slovak Rep. 27 C10
Troarn France 18 C6
Trochu Canada 102 C6
Trodely I. Canada 104 B4
Trogir Croatia 41 E13
Troglav Croatia 41 E13
Tróia Italy 43 A8
Troilus, L. Canada 104 B5
Troina Italy 43 E7
Trois-Pistoles Canada 105 C6
Trois-Rivières Canada 104 C5
Trois-Rivières Guadeloupe 120 b
Troisdorf Germany 24 E3
Troitsk Russia 52 D7
Troitsko Pechorsk Russia 52 C6
Troitskoye Russia 35 G7
Trölladyngja Iceland 8 D5
Trollhättan Sweden 11 F6
Trollheimen Norway 8 E13
Trombetas → Brazil 125 D7
Tromsø Norway 8 B18
Trona U.S.A. 111 K9
Tronador, Mte. Argentina 128 E2
Trøndelag Norway 8 D14
Trondheim Norway 8 E14
Trondheimsfjorden Norway 8 E14
Trönninge Sweden 11 H6
Tronto → Italy 41 F10
Troodos Cyprus 49 E11
Troon U.K. 13 F4
Tropea Italy 43 D8
Tropic U.S.A. 109 H7
Tropojë Albania 44 D4
Trosa Sweden 11 F11
Trostan U.K. 12 A5
Trostberg Germany 25 G8
Trostyanets Sumy, Ukraine 33 G8
Trostyanets Vinnyts'ka, Ukraine 29 B14
Trou Gras Pt. St. Lucia 121 f
Trout → Canada 102 A5
Trout L. N.W.T., Canada 102 A4
Trout L. Ont., Canada 103 C10
Trout Lake Canada 102 B6
Trout Lake U.S.A. 110 E5
Trout River Canada 105 C8
Trout Run U.S.A. 114 E7
Trouville-sur-Mer France 18 C7
Trowbridge U.K. 15 F5
Troy Turkey 47 B8
Troy Ala., U.S.A. 117 F12
Troy Kans., U.S.A. 112 F6
Troy Mo., U.S.A. 112 F8
Troy Mont., U.S.A. 108 B6
Troy N.Y., U.S.A. 115 D11
Troy Ohio, U.S.A. 113 E11
Troy Pa., U.S.A. 115 E8
Troyan Bulgaria 45 D8
Troyes France 19 D11
Trpanj Croatia 41 E14
Trstenik Serbia 44 C5
Trubchevsk Russia 33 F7
Truchas Pk. U.S.A. 109 J11
Trucial States = United Arab Emirates ■ Asia 71 F7
Truckee U.S.A. 110 F6
Trudfront Russia 35 H8
Trudovoye Russia 54 C6
Trujillo Honduras 120 C2
Trujillo Peru 124 E3
Trujillo Spain 37 F5
Trujillo U.S.A. 109 J11
Trujillo Venezuela 124 B4
Truk Micronesia 96 G7
Trumann U.S.A. 117 D9
Trumansburg U.S.A. 115 D8
Trumbull, Mt. U.S.A. 109 H7
Trŭn Bulgaria 44 D6
Trun France 18 D7
Trundle Australia 95 E4
Trung-Phan = Annam Vietnam 64 E7
Truro Canada 105 C7
Truro U.K. 15 G2
Truskavets Ukraine 23 D12
Trŭstenik Bulgaria 45 C8
Trustrup Denmark 11 H4
Trutch Canada 102 B4
Truth or Consequences U.S.A. 109 K10
Trutnov Czech Rep. 26 A8
Truxton U.S.A. 115 D8
Truyère → France 20 D6
Tryavna Bulgaria 45 D9
Tryonville U.S.A. 114 E5
Trzcianka Poland 31 E3
Trzciel Poland 31 F2
Trzcińsko Zdrój Poland 31 F1
Trzebiatów Poland 30 D2
Trzebiez Poland 30 E1
Trzebnica Poland 31 G4
Trzemeszno Poland 31 F4
Tržič Slovenia 41 B11
Tsagan Aman Russia 35 G8
Tsamandas Greece 46 B2
Tsandi Namibia 88 B1
Tsaratanana Madag. 89 B8
Tsaratanana, Mt. de = Maromokotro Madag. 89 A8
Tsaratanana ⌂ Madag. 89 A8
Tsarevo Bulgaria 45 D9
Tsaritsani Greece 46 B4
Tsau Botswana 88 C3
Tsavo Kenya 86 C4
Tsavo East △ Kenya 86 C4

Tsavo West △ *Kenya* **86** C4
Tsebrykove *Ukraine* **33** J6
Tsentralnyy □ *Russia* **34** D4
Tses *Namibia* **88** D3
Tsetserleg *Mongolia* **60** B5
Tsévié *Togo* **83** D5
Tshabong *Botswana* **88** D3
Tshane *Botswana* **88** C3
Tshela *Dem. Rep. of the Congo* **84** E2
Tshesebe *Botswana* **89** C4
Tshibeke
   Dem. Rep. of the Congo **86** C2
Tshibinda
   Dem. Rep. of the Congo **86** C2
Tshikapa
   Dem. Rep. of the Congo **84** F4
Tshilenge
   Dem. Rep. of the Congo **86** D1
Tshinsenda
   Dem. Rep. of the Congo **87** E2
Tshofa *Dem. Rep. of the Congo* **86** D2
Tshwane = Pretoria *S. Africa* **89** D4
Tshwane *Botswana* **88** C3
Tsigara *Botswana* **88** C4
Tsihombe *Madag.* **89** D8
Tsiigehtchic *Canada* **100** C6
Ts'il-os △ *Canada* **102** C4
Tsimlyansk *Russia* **35** G6
Tsimlyansk Res. =
   Tsimlyanskoye Vdkhr.
   Russia **35** F6
Tsimlyanskoye Vdkhr.
   Russia **35** F6
Tsinan = Jinan *China* **56** F9
Tsineng *S. Africa* **88** D3
Tsinghai = Qinghai □ *China* **60** C4
Tsingtao = Qingdao *China* **57** F11
Tsingy de Bemaraha △
   Madag. **89** B8
Tsingy de Namoroka △
   Madag. **89** B8
Tsinjoarivo *Madag.* **89** B8
Tsinjomitondraka *Madag.* **89** B8
Tsirigo = Kythira *Greece* **46** F5
Tsiroanomandidy *Madag.* **89** B8
Tsiteli-Tsqaro *Georgia* **35** K8
Tsitondroina *Madag.* **89** C8
Tsitsikamma △ *S. Africa* **88** E3
Tsivilsk *Russia* **34** C8
Tsivory *Madag.* **89** C8
Tskhinvali *Georgia* **35** J7
Tsna → *Russia* **34** C6
Tsnori *Georgia* **35** K7
Tso Moriri, L. *India* **69** C8
Tsobis *Namibia* **88** B2
Tsodilo Hill *Botswana* **88** B3
Tsogttsetsiy = Baruunsuu
   Mongolia **56** C3
Tsolo *S. Africa* **89** E4
Tsomo *S. Africa* **89** E4
Tsu *Japan* **55** G8
Tsu L. *Canada* **102** A6
Tsuchiura *Japan* **55** F10
Tsuen Wan *China* **59** F10
Tsugaru-Kaikyō *Japan* **54** D10
Tsumeb *Namibia* **88** B2
Tsumis *Namibia* **88** C2
Tsuruga *Japan* **55** G8
Tsurugi-San *Japan* **55** H7
Tsuruoka *Japan* **54** E9
Tsushima *Gifu, Japan* **55** G8
Tsushima *Nagasaki, Japan* **55** G4
Tsuyama *Japan* **55** G7
Tsvetkovo *Ukraine* **33** H6
Tsyelyakhany *Belarus* **23** B13
Tua → *Portugal* **36** D3
Tual *Indonesia* **63** F8
Tualatin *U.S.A.* **110** E4
Tuam *Ireland* **12** C3
Tuamotu, Ís.
   French Polynesia **97** J13
Tuamotu Arch. =
   Tuamotu, Ís.
   French Polynesia **97** J13
Tuamotu Ridge *Pac. Oc.* **97** K14
Tuanfeng *China* **59** B10
Tuanxi *China* **58** D6
Tuao *Phil.* **61** C4
Tuapse *Russia* **35** H4
Tuapere *N.Z.* **91** G1
Tuas *Singapore* **65** d
Tuatapere *N.Z.* **91** G1
Tuba City *U.S.A.* **109** H8
Tuban *Indonesia* **63** G15
Tubani *Botswana* **88** C3
Tubarão *Brazil* **127** B6
Tūbās *West Bank* **74** C4
Tubas → *Namibia* **88** C2
Tübingen *Germany* **25** G5
Tubou *Fiji* **91** a
Tubruq *Libya* **79** B10
Tubuaï, Ís. *French Polynesia* **97** K13
Tuc Trung *Vietnam* **65** G6
Tucacas *Venezuela* **124** A5
T'uch'ang *Taiwan* **59** E13
Tuchodi → *Canada* **102** B3
Tuchola *Poland* **30** E4
Tuchów *Poland* **31** J8

Tuckanarra *Australia* **93** E2
Tucson *U.S.A.* **109** K8
Tucumán □ *Argentina* **126** B2
Tucumcari *U.S.A.* **109** J12
Tucupita *Venezuela* **124** B6
Tucuruí *Brazil* **125** D9
Tucuruí, Reprêsa de *Brazil* **125** D9
Tuczno *Poland* **31** E3
Tudela *Spain* **38** C3
Tudmur *Syria* **73** E8
Tudor, L. *Canada* **105** A6
Tudora *Romania* **29** C11
Tuella → *Portugal* **36** D3
Tugela → *S. Africa* **89** D5
Tuguegarao *Phil.* **61** C4
Tugur *Russia* **53** D14
Tui *Spain* **36** C2
Tuineje *Canary Is.* **48** F5
Tukangbesi, Kepulauan
   Indonesia **63** F6
Tukarak I. *Canada* **104** A4
Tukayyid *Iraq* **70** D5
Tukhlya *Ukraine* **29** B8
Tukkae, Ao *Thailand* **65** a
Tukobo *Ghana* **82** D4
Tuktoyaktuk *Canada* **100** C6
Tukums *Latvia* **30** B10
Tukums □ *Latvia* **30** B10
Tukuyu *Tanzania* **87** D3
Tula *Hidalgo, Mexico* **119** C5
Tula *Tamaulipas, Mexico* **119** C5
Tula *Nigeria* **83** D7
Tula *Russia* **32** E9
Tula □ *Russia* **32** F9
Tulancingo *Mexico* **119** C5
Tulare *Serbia* **44** D5
Tulare *U.S.A.* **110** J7
Tulare Lake Bed *U.S.A.* **110** K7
Tularosa *U.S.A.* **109** K10
Tulbagh *S. Africa* **88** E2
Tulcán *Ecuador* **124** C3
Tulcea *Romania* **29** E14
Tulcea □ *Romania* **29** E13
Tulchyn *Ukraine* **29** B13
Tüledi Araldary *Kazakhstan* **35** H10
Tüleh *Iran* **71** C7
Tulemalu L. *Canada* **103** A9
Tulgheş *Romania* **29** D10
Tuli *Zimbabwe* **87** G2
Tulia *U.S.A.* **116** D4
Tuliszków *Poland* **31** F5
Tulita *Canada* **100** C7
Tullahoma *U.S.A.* **117** D11
Tullamore *Australia* **95** E4
Tullamore *Ireland* **12** C4
Tulle *France* **20** C5
Tulln *Austria* **26** C9
Tullow *Ireland* **12** D5
Tullus *Sudan* **81** E1
Tully *Australia* **94** B4
Tully → *U.S.A.* **115** D8
Tulnici *Romania* **29** E11
Tulovo *Bulgaria* **45** D9
Tulsa *U.S.A.* **116** C7
Tulsequah *Canada* **102** B2
Tulu Milki *Ethiopia* **81** F4
Tulu Welel *Ethiopia* **81** F3
Tulua *Colombia* **124** C3
Tuluceşti *Romania* **29** E13
Tulun *Russia* **53** D11
Tulungagung *Indonesia* **63** H14
Tuma → *Russia* **32** E11
Tuma → *Nic.* **120** D3
Tumacacori △ *U.S.A.* **109** L8
Tumaco *Colombia* **124** C3
Tumatumari *Guyana* **124** B7
Tumba *Sweden* **10** E11
Tumba, L.
   Dem. Rep. of the Congo **84** E3
Tumbarumba *Australia* **95** F4
Tumbaya *Argentina* **126** A2
Tumbes *Peru* **124** D2
Tumbler Ridge *Canada* **102** B4
Tumbur *Sudan* **81** G3
Tumbwe
   Dem. Rep. of the Congo **87** E2
Tumby Bay *Australia* **95** E2
Tumd Youqi *China* **56** D6
Tumen *China* **57** C15
Tumen Jiang → *China* **57** C16
Tumeremo *Venezuela* **124** B6
Tumkur *India* **66** N10
Tump *Pakistan* **66** F3
Tumpat *Malaysia* **65** J4
Tumu *Ghana* **82** C4
Tumucumaque, Serra
   Brazil **125** C8
Tumut *Australia* **95** F4
Tumwater *U.S.A.* **110** C4
Tuna *India* **68** H4
Tunadal *Sweden* **10** B11
Tunapuna *Trin. & Tob.* **125** K15
Tunas de Zaza *Cuba* **120** B4
Tunbridge Wells = Royal
   Tunbridge Wells *U.K.* **15** F8

Tunçbilek *Turkey* **47** B11
Tunceli *Turkey* **73** C8
Tunceli □ *Turkey* **73** C8
Tuncurry *Australia* **95** E5
Tundla *India* **68** F8
Tundubai *Sudan* **80** D2
Tunduru *Tanzania* **87** E4
Tundzha → *Bulgaria* **45** E10
Tungabhadra → *India* **66** M11
Tungaru *Sudan* **81** E3
Tungla *Nic.* **120** D3
Tungsha Tao = Dongsha
   Dao *China* **59** G11
Tungshih *Taiwan* **59** E13
Tungsten *Canada* **102** A3
Tunguska, Nizhnyaya →
   Russia **53** C9
Tunguska,
   Podkamennaya →
   Russia **53** C10
Tunica *U.S.A.* **117** D9
Tunis *Tunisia* **78** A7
Tunis ✈ (TUN) *Tunisia* **42** F3
Tunisia ■ *Africa* **79** A7
Tunja *Colombia* **124** B4
Tunkhannock *U.S.A.* **115** E9
Tunliu *China* **56** F7
Tunnel Creek △ *Australia* **92** C4
Tunnsjøen *Norway* **8** D15
Tunø *Denmark* **11** J4
Tunungayualok I. *Canada* **105** A7
Tunuyán *Argentina* **126** C2
Tunuyán → *Argentina* **126** C2
Tuo Jiang → *China* **58** C5
Tuolumne *U.S.A.* **110** H6
Tuolumne → *U.S.A.* **110** H5
Tūp Āghāj *Iran* **73** D12
Tupã *Brazil* **127** A5
Tupelo *U.S.A.* **117** D10
Tupik *Russia* **32** E7
Tupinambaranas *Brazil* **124** D7
Tupiza *Bolivia* **126** A2
Tupižnica *Serbia* **44** C6
Tupman *U.S.A.* **111** K7
Tupper *Canada* **102** B4
Tupper Lake *U.S.A.* **115** B10
Tupungato, Cerro *S. Amer.* **126** C2
Tuquan *China* **57** B11
Túquerres *Colombia* **124** C3
Tura *Russia* **53** C11
Turabah *Hā'il, Si. Arabia* **70** D4
Turabah *Makkah, Si. Arabia* **80** C5
Tūrān *Iran* **71** C8
Turan *Russia* **53** D10
Turayf *Si. Arabia* **70** D3
Turbacz *Poland* **31** J7
Turbe *Bos.-H.* **28** F2
Turčianske Teplice
   Slovak Rep. **27** C11
Turcoaia *Romania* **29** E13
Turda *Romania* **29** D8
Turek *Poland* **31** F5
Turén *Venezuela* **124** B5
Turfan = Turpan *China* **60** B3
Turgeon → *Canada* **104** C4
Türgovishte *Bulgaria* **45** C10
Turgut *Turkey* **47** D10
Turgutlu *Turkey* **47** C9
Turhal *Turkey* **72** B7
Turia → *Spain* **39** F4
Turiaçu *Brazil* **125** D9
Turiaçu → *Brazil* **125** D9
Turiec → *Slovak Rep.* **27** C11
Turin = Torino *Italy* **40** C4
Turka *Ukraine* **31** J10
Turkana, L. *Africa* **86** B4
Türkeli *Turkey* **45** F11
Turkestan = Türkistan
   Kazakhstan **52** E7
Túrkeve *Hungary* **28** C5
Turkey ■ *Eurasia* **72** C7
Turkey Creek = Warmun
   Australia **92** C4
Turki *Russia* **34** D6
Türkistan *Kazakhstan* **52** E7
Türkmenabat *Turkmenistan* **71** B9
Türkmenbashi *Turkmenistan* **71** A7
Turkmenistan ■ *Asia* **52** F6
Türkmenli *Turkey* **47** B8
Türkoğlu *Turkey* **72** D7
Turks & Caicos Is. ☑
   W. Indies **121** B5
Turks Island Passage
   W. Indies **121** B5
Turku *Finland* **32** B2
Turkwel → *Kenya* **86** B4
Turlock *U.S.A.* **110** H6
Turnagain → *Canada* **102** B3
Turnagain, C. *N.Z.* **91** D6
Turneffe Is. *Belize* **119** D7
Turner *U.S.A.* **108** B9
Turner Pt. *Australia* **94** A1
Turner Valley *Canada* **102** C6
Turners Falls *U.S.A.* **115** D12

Turnhout *Belgium* **17** C4
Türnitz *Austria* **26** D8
Turnor L. *Canada* **103** B7
Turnov *Czech Rep.* **26** A8
Turnu Măgurele *Romania* **29** G9
Turnu Roşu, P. *Romania* **29** E9
Tŭrnovo = Veliko Tŭrnovo
   Bulgaria **45** C9
Turobin *Poland* **31** H9
Turpan *China* **60** B3
Turrës, Kala e *Albania* **44** E3
Turriff *U.K.* **13** D6
Tursāq *Iraq* **73** F11
Tursi *Italy* **43** B9
Turtle Head I. *Australia* **94** A3
Turtle Is. *S. Leone* **82** D2
Turtle L. *Canada* **103** C7
Turtle Lake *U.S.A.* **112** B3
Turtleford *Canada* **103** C7
Turuépano △ *Venezuela* **121** D7
Turukhansk *Russia* **53** C9
Turzovka *Slovak Rep.* **27** B11
Tuscaloosa *U.S.A.* **117** E11
Tuscánia *Italy* **41** F8
Tuscany = Toscana □ *Italy* **40** E8
Tuscarawas → *U.S.A.* **114** F3
Tuscarora Mt. *U.S.A.* **114** F7
Tuscola *Ill., U.S.A.* **114** F1
Tuscola *Tex., U.S.A.* **116** E5
Tuscumbia *U.S.A.* **117** D11
Tuskegee *U.S.A.* **117** E12
Tuszyn *Poland* **31** G6
Tutak *Turkey* **73** C10
Tutayev *Russia* **32** D10
Tuticorin *India* **66** Q11
Tutin *Serbia* **44** D4
Tutóia *Brazil* **125** D10
Tutong *Brunei* **62** D4
Tutrakan *Bulgaria* **45** B10
Tuttle Creek L. *U.S.A.* **112** F5
Tuttlingen *Germany* **25** H4
Tutuala *E. Timor* **63** F7
Tutuila *Amer. Samoa* **91** b
Tutume *Botswana* **85** J5
Tutun *Egypt* **80** J7
Tuva □ *Russia* **53** D10
Tuvalu ■ *Pac. Oc.* **90** B10
Tuvuca *Fiji* **91** a
Tuxer Alpen *Austria* **26** D4
Tuxpan *Mexico* **119** C5
Tuxtla Gutiérrez *Mexico* **119** D6
Tuy = Tui *Spain* **36** C2
Tuy An *Vietnam* **64** F7
Tuy Duc *Vietnam* **65** F6
Tuy Hoa *Vietnam* **64** F7
Tuy Phong *Vietnam* **65** G7
Tuya L. *Canada* **102** B2
Tuyen Hoa *Vietnam* **64** D6
Tuyen Quang *Vietnam* **58** G5
Tüysarkān *Iran* **73** E13
Tuz Gölü *Turkey* **72** C5
Ṭūz Khurmātū =
   Tozkhurmato *Iraq* **73** E11
Tuzi *Montenegro* **44** D3
Tuzigoot △ *U.S.A.* **109** J7
Tuzla *Bos.-H.* **28** F3
Tuzlov → *Russia* **33** J10
Tuzluca *Turkey* **73** B10
Tuzly *Ukraine* **29** E15
Tvååker *Sweden* **11** G6
Tvardiţa *Moldova* **29** D13
Tver *Russia* **32** D8
Tver □ *Russia* **32** D8
Tvrdošin *Slovak Rep.* **27** B12
Tvrdošovce *Slovak Rep.* **27** C11
Tvŭrditsa *Bulgaria* **45** D9
Twain *U.S.A.* **110** E5
Twain Harte *U.S.A.* **110** G6
Twardogóra *Poland* **31** G4
Tweed *Canada* **114** B7
Tweed → *U.K.* **13** F6
Tweed Heads *Australia* **95** D5
Tweedsmuir △ *Canada* **102** C3
Twentynine Palms *U.S.A.* **111** L10
Twillingate *Canada* **105** C9
Twin Bridges *U.S.A.* **108** D7
Twin Falls *Canada* **105** B7
Twin Falls *U.S.A.* **108** E6
Twin Valley *U.S.A.* **112** B5
Twinsburg *U.S.A.* **114** E3
Twistringen *Germany* **24** C4
Twitchell Res. *U.S.A.* **111** L6
Two Harbors *U.S.A.* **112** B8
Two Hills *Canada* **102** C6
Two Rivers *U.S.A.* **112** C10
Two Rocks *Australia* **93** F2
Twofold B. *Australia* **95** F4
Tyachiv *Ukraine* **23** D12
Tychy *Poland* **31** H5
Tyczyn *Poland* **31** J9
Tykocin *Poland* **31** E9
Tyler *Minn., U.S.A.* **112** C6
Tyler *Tex., U.S.A.* **116** E7
Tyligul → *Ukraine* **33** J6
Tymanivka *Ukraine* **29** B13
Týn nad Vltavou *Czech Rep.* **26** B7

Tynda *Russia* **53** D13
Tyndall *U.S.A.* **112** D5
Tyne → *U.K.* **14** C6
Tyne & Wear □ *U.K.* **14** B6
Tynemouth *U.K.* **14** B6
Tyre = Sūr *Lebanon* **74** B4
Tyresta △ *Sweden* **10** E12
Tyrifjorden *Norway* **9** F14
Tyringe *Sweden* **11** H7
Tyrnyauz *Russia* **35** J5
Tyrol = Tirol □ *Austria* **26** D3
Tyrone *U.S.A.* **114** F6
Tyrone □ *U.K.* **12** B4
Tyrrell → *Australia* **95** F3
Tyrrell, L. *Australia* **95** F3
Tyrrell L. *Canada* **103** A7
Tyrrhenian Sea *Medit. S.* **6** G8
Tysfjorden *Norway* **8** B17
Tysmenytsya *Ukraine* **29** B9
Tystberga *Sweden* **11** F11
Tytuvėnai *Lithuania* **30** C10
Tyub Karagan, Mys =
   Tüpqarghan Muyis
   Kazakhstan **35** H10
Tyuleni, Ostrova = Tüledi
   Araldary *Kazakhstan* **35** H10
Tyuleniy *Russia* **35** H8
Tyuleniy, Mys *Azerbaijan* **35** K10
Tyumen *Russia* **52** D7
Tywi → *U.K.* **15** F3
Tywyn *U.K.* **15** E3

U

U Taphao *Thailand* **64** F3
U.S.A. = United States of
   America ■ *N. Amer.* **106** C7
U.S. Virgin Is. ☑ *W. Indies* **121** e
Uanle Uen *Somali Rep.* **75** G3
Uatumã → *Brazil* **124** D7
Uaupés *Brazil* **124** D5
Uaupés → *Brazil* **124** C5
Uaxactún *Guatemala* **120** C2
Ub *Serbia* **44** B4
Ubá *Brazil* **127** A7
Uba *Nigeria* **83** C7
Ubaitaba *Brazil* **125** F11
Ubangi = Oubangi →
   Dem. Rep. of the Congo **84** E3
Ubauro *Pakistan* **68** E3
Ubaye → *France* **21** D10
Ubayyiḍ, W. al → *Iraq* **73** F10
Ube *Japan* **55** H5
Úbeda *Spain* **37** G7
Uberaba *Brazil* **125** G9
Uberlândia *Brazil* **125** G9
Überlingen *Germany* **25** H5
Ubiaja *Nigeria* **83** D6
Ubin, Pulau *Singapore* **65** d
Ubolratna Res. *Thailand* **64** D4
Ubombo *S. Africa* **89** D5
Ubon Ratchathani *Thailand* **64** E5
Ubondo *Dem. Rep. of the Congo* **86** C2
Ubort → *Belarus* **23** B15
Ubrique *Spain* **37** J5
Ubud *Indonesia* **63** J18
Ubundu
   Dem. Rep. of the Congo **86** C2
Ucayali → *Peru* **124** D4
Uchab *Namibia* **88** B2
Uchiura-Wan *Japan* **54** C10
Uchquduq *Uzbekistan* **52** E7
Uchte *Germany* **24** C4
Uchur → *Russia* **53** D14
Uckermark *Germany* **24** B9
Ucluelet *Canada* **102** D3
Uda → *Russia* **53** D14
Udagamandalam *India* **66** P10
Udainagar *India* **68** H7
Udaipur *India* **68** G5
Udaipur Garhi *Nepal* **69** F12
Udala *India* **69** J12
Udbina *Croatia* **41** D12
Uddeholm *Sweden* **10** D7
Uddevalla *Sweden* **11** F5
Uddjaure *Sweden* **8** D17
Uden *Neths.* **17** C5
Udgir *India* **66** K10
Udhampur *India* **69** C6
Udi *Nigeria* **83** D6
Údine *Italy* **41** B10
Udintsev Fracture Zone
   S. Ocean **5** B13
Udmurtia □ *Russia* **52** D6
Udon Thani *Thailand* **64** D4
Udu Pt. *Fiji* **91** a
Udupi *India* **66** N9
Udvoy Balkan *Bulgaria* **45** D10
Udzungwa △ *Tanzania* **86** D4
Udzungwa Range *Tanzania* **87** D4

Ueckermünde *Germany* **24** B10
Ueda *Japan* **55** F9
Uedineniya, Os. *Russia* **4** B12
Uele → *Dem. Rep. of the Congo* **84** D4
Uelen *Russia* **53** C19
Uelzen *Germany* **24** C6
Uetersen *Germany* **24** B5
Uetze *Germany* **24** C6
Ufa *Russia* **52** D6
Uffenheim *Germany* **25** F6
Ugab → *Namibia* **88** C1
Ugalla → *Tanzania* **86** D3
Ugalla River △ *Tanzania* **86** D3
Uganda ■ *Africa* **86** B3
Ugento *Italy* **43** C11
Ugep *Nigeria* **83** D6
Ughelli *Nigeria* **83** D6
Ugie *S. Africa* **89** E4
Ugíjar *Spain* **37** J7
Ugine *France* **21** C10
Uglegorsk *Russia* **53** E15
Uglich *Russia* **32** D10
Ugljan *Croatia* **41** D12
Ugljane *Croatia* **41** E13
Ugra → *Russia* **32** E9
Uğurchin *Bulgaria* **45** C8
Uh → *Slovak Rep.* **27** C15
Uherské Hradiště *Czech Rep.* **27** B10
Uherský Brod *Czech Rep.* **27** B10
Úhlava → *Czech Rep.* **26** B6
Uhniv *Ukraine* **31** H10
Uhrichsville *U.S.A.* **114** F3
Uibhist a Deas = South
   Uist *U.K.* **13** D1
Uibhist a Tuath = North
   Uist *U.K.* **13** D1
Uig *U.K.* **13** D2
Uíge *Angola* **84** F2
Uiha *Tonga* **91** c
Uijeongbu *S. Korea* **57** F14
Ŭiju *N. Korea* **57** D13
Uinta Mts. *U.S.A.* **108** F8
Uis *Namibia* **88** C1
Uiseong *S. Korea* **57** F15
Uitenhage *S. Africa* **88** E4
Uithuizen *Neths.* **17** A6
Ujazd *Poland* **31** H5
Újfehértó *Hungary* **28** C6
Ujh → *India* **68** C6
Ujhani *India* **69** F8
Uji-guntō *Japan* **55** J4
Ujjain *India* **68** H6
Ujście *Poland* **31** E3
Újszász *Hungary* **28** C5
Ujung Pandang *Indonesia* **63** F6
Uka *Russia* **53** D17
Ukara I. *Tanzania* **86** C3
Uke-Shima *Japan* **55** K4
Ukerewe I. *Tanzania* **86** C3
Ukholovo *Russia* **34** D5
Ukhrul *India* **67** G19
Ukhta *Russia* **52** C6
Ukiah *U.S.A.* **110** F3
Ukmergė *Lithuania* **32** E3
Ukraine ■ *Europe* **33** H7
Ukwi *Botswana* **88** C3
Ulaan-Uul *Mongolia* **56** B6
Ulaanbaatar *Mongolia* **53** E11
Ulaangom *Mongolia* **60** A4
Ulaanjirem *Mongolia* **56** B3
Ulamba *Dem. Rep. of the Congo* **87** D1
Ulan Bator = Ulaanbaatar
   Mongolia **53** E11
Ulan Erge *Russia* **35** G7
Ulan Khol *Russia* **35** H8
Ulan Ude *Russia* **53** D11
Ulanów *Poland* **31** H9
Ulaş *Sivas, Turkey* **72** C7
Ulaş *Tekirdağ, Turkey* **45** E11
Ulaya *Morogoro, Tanzania* **86** D4
Ulaya *Tabora, Tanzania* **86** C3
Ulcinj *Montenegro* **44** E3
Ulco *S. Africa* **88** D3
Ule älv = Oulujoki →
   Finland **8** D21
Ule träsk = Oulujärvi
   Finland **8** D22
Uleåborg = Oulu *Finland* **8** D21
Ulefoss *Norway* **9** G13
Ulëz *Albania* **44** E4
Ulfborg *Denmark* **11** H2
Ulhasnagar *India* **66** K8
Uliastay *Mongolia* **60** B4
Uljin *S. Korea* **57** F15
Uljma *Serbia* **28** E6
Ulla → *Spain* **36** C2
Ulladulla *Australia* **95** F5
Ullapool *U.K.* **13** D3
Ullared *Sweden* **11** G6
Ulldecona *Spain* **38** E5
Ulleungdo *S. Korea* **55** F5
Ullswater *U.K.* **14** C5
Ulm *Germany* **25** G5
Ulmarra *Australia* **95** D5
Ulmeni *Buzău, Romania* **29** E11
Ulmeni *Maramureş, Romania* **29** C8

Ulonguè *Mozam.* **87** E3
Ulricehamn *Sweden* **11** G7
Ulrika *Sweden* **11** F9
Ulsan *S. Korea* **57** G15
Ulsta *U.K.* **13** A7
Ulster □ *U.K.* **12** B5
Ulstrem *Bulgaria* **45** D10
Ulubat Gölü *Turkey* **45** F12
Ulubey *Turkey* **47** C11
Uluborlu *Turkey* **47** C12
Uluçinar *Turkey* **72** D6
Uludağ *Turkey* **45** F13
Uludağ △ *Turkey* **45** F13
Uludere *Turkey* **73** D10
Uluguru Mts. *Tanzania* **86** D4
Ulukışla *Turkey* **72** D6
Ulungur He → *China* **60** B3
Uluru *Australia* **93** E5
Uluru-Kata Tjuta △
  Australia **93** E5
Ulutau *Kazakhstan* **52** E7
Uluwatu *Indonesia* **63** K18
Ulva *U.K.* **13** E2
Ulverston *U.K.* **14** C4
Ulverstone *Australia* **95** G4
Ulya *Russia* **53** D15
Ulyanovo *Russia* **30** D9
Ulyanovsk = Simbirsk
  Russia **34** C9
Ulyanovsk □ *Russia* **34** C9
Ulyasutay = Uliastay
  Mongolia **60** B4
Ulysses *U.S.A.* **112** G3
Umag *Croatia* **41** C10
Umala *Bolivia* **124** G5
'Umān = Oman ■ *Asia* **75** C6
Uman *Ukraine* **23** D16
Umaria *India* **69** H9
Umarkot *Pakistan* **68** G3
Umarpada *India* **68** J5
Umatilla *U.S.A.* **108** D4
Umbagog L. *U.S.A.* **115** B13
Umbakumba *Australia* **94** A2
Umbértide *Italy* **41** E9
Umbrella Mts. *N.Z.* **91** F2
Umbria □ *Italy* **41** F9
Umeå *Sweden* **8** E19
Umeälven → *Sweden* **8** E19
Umera *Indonesia* **63** E7
Umfuli → *Zimbabwe* **87** F2
Umfurudzi △ *Zimbabwe* **87** F3
Umgusa *Zimbabwe* **87** F2
Umgwenya → *Mozam.* **89** D5
Umim Urūmah *Si. Arabia* **80** B4
Umiujaq *Canada* **104** A4
Umka *Serbia* **44** B4
Umkomaas *S. Africa* **89** E5
Umlazi *S. Africa* **85** L6
Umm ad Daraj, J. *Jordan* **74** C4
Umm al Qaywayn *U.A.E.* **71** E7
Umm al Qittayn *Jordan* **74** C5
Umm Arda *Sudan* **81** D3
Umm Bāb *Qatar* **71** E6
Umm Badr *Sudan* **81** E2
Umm Baiyud *Sudan* **80** D3
Umm Bel *Sudan* **81** E2
Umm Birkah *Si. Arabia* **80** B4
Umm Boim *Sudan* **81** E2
Umm Dam *Sudan* **81** E3
Umm Debi *Sudan* **81** E3
Umm Dubban *Sudan* **81** D3
Umm Durman =
  Omdurmân *Sudan* **81** D3
Umm el Fahm *Israel* **74** C4
Umm Gafala *Sudan* **81** E2
Umm Gimala *Sudan* **81** E2
Umm Inderaba *Sudan* **80** D3
Umm Keddada *Sudan* **81** E2
Umm Koweika *Sudan* **81** E3
Umm Lajj *Si. Arabia* **70** E3
Umm Merwa *Sudan* **80** D3
Umm Qantur *Sudan* **81** E3
Umm Qasr *Iraq* **70** D5
Umm Qurein *Sudan* **81** F2
Umm Ruwaba *Sudan* **81** E3
Umm Saiyala *Sudan* **81** E3
Umm Shanqa *Sudan* **81** E2
Umm Shutur *Sudan* **81** F3
Umm Sidr *Sudan* **81** E2
Umm Zehetir *Egypt* **80** J8
Umnak I. *U.S.A.* **106** a
Umniati → *Zimbabwe* **87** F2
Umpqua → *U.S.A.* **108** E1
Umreth *India* **68** H5
Umtata = Mthatha *S. Africa* **89** E4
Umuahia *Nigeria* **83** D6
Umuarama *Brazil* **127** A5
Umurbey *Turkey* **45** F10
Umvukwe Ra. *Zimbabwe* **87** F3
Umzimvubu *S. Africa* **89** E4
Umzingwane → *Zimbabwe* **87** G2
Umzinto = eMuziwezinto
  S. Africa **89** E5
Una *India* **68** J4
Una → *Bos.-H.* **41** D13
Unac → *Bos.-H.* **41** D13
Unadilla *U.S.A.* **115** D9

Unalakleet *U.S.A.* **106** a
Unalaska *U.S.A.* **106** a
Unalaska I. *U.S.A.* **106** a
'Unayzah *Si. Arabia* **70** E4
'Unayzah, J. *Asia* **73** F8
Uncastillo *Spain* **38** C3
Uncía *Bolivia* **124** G5
Uncompahgre Peak *U.S.A.*
  108 G10
Uncompahgre Plateau
  U.S.A. **108** G9
Undara Volcanic △ *Australia* **94** B3
Unden *Sweden* **11** F8
Underbool *Australia* **95** F3
Undersaker *Sweden* **10** A7
Unecha *Russia* **33** F7
Ungarie *Australia* **95** E4
Ungarra *Australia* **95** E2
Ungava, Pén. d' *Canada* **101** D12
Ungava B. *Canada* **101** D13
Ungeny = Ungheni *Moldova* **29** C12
Unggi *N. Korea* **57** C16
Ungheni *Moldova* **29** C12
Ungla da Vitória *Brazil* **127** B5
Uničov *Czech Rep.* **27** B10
Uniejów *Poland* **31** G5
Unije *Croatia* **41** D11
Unimak I. *U.S.A.* **106** a
Union *Miss., U.S.A.* **117** E10
Union *Mo., U.S.A.* **112** F8
Union *S.C., U.S.A.* **117** D14
Union City *Calif., U.S.A.* **110** H4
Union City *N.J., U.S.A.* **115** F10
Union City *Pa., U.S.A.* **114** E5
Union City *Tenn., U.S.A.* **117** C10
Union Gap *U.S.A.* **108** C3
Union Springs *U.S.A.* **117** E12
Uniondale *S. Africa* **88** E3
Uniontown *U.S.A.* **113** F14
Unionville *U.S.A.* **112** E7
Unirea *Romania* **29** F12
United Arab Emirates ■ *Asia* **71** F7
United Kingdom ■ *Europe* **16** E6
United States of America ■
  N. Amer. **106** C7
Unity *Canada* **103** C7
Universales, Mtes. *Spain* **38** E3
University Park *U.S.A.* **109** K10
University Place *U.S.A.* **110** C4
Unjha *India* **68** H5
Unna *Germany* **24** D3
Unnao *India* **69** F9
Uno, Ilha *Guinea-Biss.* **82** C1
Unsengedsi → *Zimbabwe* **87** F3
Unst *U.K.* **13** A8
Unstrut → *Germany* **24** D7
Unterfranken □ *Germany* **25** F5
Unterschleissheim *Germany* **25** G7
Unuk → *Canada* **102** B2
Ünye *Turkey* **72** B7
Unzen-Amakusa △ *Japan* **55** H5
Unzha *Russia* **34** A7
Unzha → *Russia* **34** B6
Uozu *Japan* **55** F8
Upata *Venezuela* **124** B6
Upemba, L.
  Dem. Rep. of the Congo **87** D2
Upemba △
  Dem. Rep. of the Congo **87** D2
Upernavik *Greenland* **4** B5
Upington *S. Africa* **88** D3
Upleta *India* **68** J4
'Upolu *Samoa* **91** b
Upper □ *Ghana* **83** C4
Upper Alkali L. *U.S.A.* **108** F3
Upper Arrow L. *Canada* **102** C5
Upper Darby *U.S.A.* **113** F16
Upper Foster L. *Canada* **103** B7
Upper Hutt *N.Z.* **91** D5
Upper Klamath L. *U.S.A.* **108** E3
Upper Lake *U.S.A.* **110** F4
Upper Manzanilla
  Trin. & Tob. **125** K15
Upper Missouri Breaks △
  U.S.A. **108** C9
Upper Musquodoboit
  Canada **105** C7
Upper Red L. *U.S.A.* **112** A6
Upper Sandusky *U.S.A.* **113** E12
Upper Volta = Burkina
  Faso ■ *Africa* **82** C4
Upphärad *Sweden* **11** F6
Uppland *Sweden* **10** D12
Upplands-Väsby *Sweden* **10** E11
Uppsala *Sweden* **10** E11
Uppsala □ *Sweden* **10** D11
Upshi *India* **69** C7
Upstart, C. *Australia* **94** B4
Upton *U.S.A.* **112** D2
Uqsuqtuuq = Gjoa Haven
  Canada **100** C10
Ur *Iraq* **70** D5
Urad Qianqi *China* **56** D5

Urakawa *Japan* **54** C11
Ural = Uralskiy □ *Russia* **52** C7
Ural = Zhayyq → *Kazakhstan* **6** F16
Ural *Australia* **95** E4
Ural Mts. = Uralskie Gory
  Eurasia **6** C17
Uralla *Australia* **95** E5
Uralsk = Oral *Kazakhstan* **34** E10
Uralskie Gory *Eurasia* **6** C17
Uralskiy □ *Russia* **52** C7
Urambo *Tanzania* **86** D3
Urandangi *Australia* **94** C2
Uranium City *Canada* **103** B7
Uraricoera → *Brazil* **124** C6
Urasoe *Japan* **55** L3
Urawa = Saitama *Japan* **55** G9
Uray *Russia* **52** C7
'Uray'irah *Si. Arabia* **71** E6
Urbana *Ill., U.S.A.* **112** E9
Urbana *Ohio, U.S.A.* **113** E12
Urbandale *U.S.A.* **112** E7
Urbánia *Italy* **41** E9
Urbel → *Spain* **36** C7
Urbino *Italy* **41** E9
Urbión, Picos de *Spain* **38** C2
Urcos *Peru* **124** F4
Urdinarrain *Argentina* **126** C4
Urdos *France* **20** E3
Ure → *U.K.* **14** C6
Uren *Russia* **34** B7
Ures *Mexico* **118** B2
Urewera △ *N.Z.* **91** C6
Urfa = Sanliurfa *Turkey* **73** D8
Urganch *Uzbekistan* **52** E7
Urgench = Urganch
  Uzbekistan **52** E7
Ürgüp *Turkey* **70** B2
Uri *India* **69** B6
Uri □ *Switz.* **25** J4
Uribe *Colombia* **124** A4
Uribia *Colombia* **124** A4
Uricani *Romania* **28** E8
Uriondo *Bolivia* **126** A3
Urique *Mexico* **118** B3
Urique → *Mexico* **118** B3
Urk *Neths.* **17** B5
Urkiola △ *Spain* **38** B3
Urla *Turkey* **47** C8
Urlati *Romania* **29** F11
Urmia = Orūmīyeh *Iran* **73** D11
Uroševac *Serbia* **44** D5
Uroyan, Montanas de
  Puerto Rico **121** d
Urshult *Sweden* **11** H8
Uruaçu *Brazil* **125** F9
Uruapan *Mexico* **118** D4
Urubamba → *Peru* **124** F4
Uruçara *Brazil* **124** D7
Uruçui *Brazil* **125** E10
Uruguai → *Brazil* **127** B5
Uruguaiana *Brazil* **126** B4
Uruguay ■ *S. Amer.* **126** C4
Uruguay → *S. Amer.* **126** C4
Urumchi = Ürümqi *China* **52** E9
Ürümqi *China* **52** E9
Urup → *Russia* **35** H11
Urup, Ostrov *Russia* **53** E16
Uryupinsk *Russia* **34** E5
Ürzhar *Kazakhstan* **52** E9
Urzhum *Russia* **34** B9
Urziceni *Romania* **29** F11
Usa → *Russia* **52** C6
Uşak *Turkey* **47** C11
Uşak □ *Turkey* **47** C11
Usakos *Namibia* **88** C2
Ušće *Serbia* **44** C4
Usedom *Germany* **24** B10
Usedom △ *Germany* **24** B10
Useless Loop *Australia* **93** E1
'Usfān *Si. Arabia* **80** C4
Ushakova, Ostrov *Russia* **4** A12
Ushakovo *Russia* **30** D7
Ushant = Ouessant, Î. d'
  France **18** D1
Ushashi *Tanzania* **86** C3
Ushat *Sudan* **81** F2
'Ushayrah *Si. Arabia* **80** C5
Ushibuka *Japan* **55** H5
Üshtöbe *Kazakhstan* **52** E8
Ushuaia *Argentina* **128** G3
Ushumun *Russia* **53** D13
Ushytsya → *Ukraine* **29** B12
Usk *Canada* **102** C3
Usk → *U.K.* **15** F5
Uska *India* **69** F10
Üsküdar *Turkey* **45** F13
Uslar *Germany* **24** D5
Usman *Russia* **33** F10
Usoke *Tanzania* **86** D3
Usolye-Sibirskoye *Russia* **53** D11
Usoro *Nigeria* **83** D6
Uspallata, P. de *Argentina* **126** C2
Ussel *France* **20** C6
Ussuri → *Asia* **54** A7
Ussuriysk *Russia* **54** C5
Ussurka *Russia* **54** B6
Ust-Bolsheretsk *Russia* **53** D16
Ust-Buzulukskaya *Russia* **34** E6

Ust-Chaun *Russia* **53** C18
Ust-Chorna *Ukraine* **29** B8
Ust-Donetskiy *Russia* **35** G5
Ust-Ilimsk *Russia* **53** D11
Ust-Ishim *Russia* **52** D8
Ust-Kamchatsk *Russia* **53** D17
Ust-Kamenogorsk =
  Öskemen *Kazakhstan* **52** E9
Ust-Khayryuzovo *Russia* **53** D16
Ust-Kut *Russia* **53** D11
Ust-Kuyga *Russia* **53** B14
Ust-Labinsk *Russia* **35** H4
Ust-Luga *Russia* **32** C5
Ust-Maya *Russia* **53** C14
Ust-Mil *Russia* **53** D14
Ust-Nera *Russia* **53** C15
Ust-Nyukzha *Russia* **53** D13
Ust-Olenek *Russia* **53** B12
Ust-Omchug *Russia* **53** C15
Ust-Port *Russia* **52** C9
Ust-Tsilma *Russia* **52** C6
Ust-Urt = Ustyurt Plateau
  Asia **52** E6
Ustaritz *France* **20** E2
Ustecký □ *Czech Rep.* **26** A7
Uster *Switz.* **25** H4
Ústí nad Labem *Czech Rep.* **26** A7
Ústí nad Orlicí *Czech Rep.* **27** B9
Ústica *Italy* **42** D6
Ustka *Poland* **30** D3
Ustroń *Poland* **31** J5
Ustyuov = Izhevsk *Russia* **52** D6
Ustyurt Plateau *Asia* **52** E6
Ustyuzhna *Russia* **32** C9
Usu *China* **60** B3
Usuki *Japan* **55** H5
Usulután *El Salv.* **120** D2
Usumacinta → *Mexico* **119** D6
Usumbura = Bujumbura
  Burundi **86** C2
Usure *Tanzania* **86** C3
Usutuo → *Mozam.* **89** D5
Uta *Indonesia* **63** E9
Utah □ *U.S.A.* **108** G8
Utah L. *U.S.A.* **108** F8
Utansjö *Sweden* **10** B11
Utara, Selat *Malaysia* **65** c
Utarni *India* **68** F4
Utatlan *Guatemala* **120** C1
Ute Creek → *U.S.A.* **109** J12
Utebo *Spain* **38** D4
Utena *Lithuania* **32** E3
Utete *Tanzania* **86** D4
Utiariti *Brazil* **124** F7
Utica *N.Y., U.S.A.* **115** C9
Utica *Ohio, U.S.A.* **114** F2
Utiel *Spain* **39** F3
Utikuma L. *Canada* **102** B5
Utö *Sweden* **10** F12
Utopia *Australia* **94** C1
Utraula *India* **69** F10
Utrecht *Neths.* **17** B5
Utrecht *S. Africa* **89** D5
Utrecht □ *Neths.* **17** B5
Utrera *Spain* **37** H5
Utsjoki → *Finland* **8** B22
Utsunomiya *Japan* **55** F9
Uttar Pradesh □ *India* **69** F9
Uttaradit *Thailand* **64** D3
Uttaranchal □ *India* **69** D8
Uttoxeter *U.K.* **14** E6
Utuado *Puerto Rico* **121** d
Uummannaq *Greenland* **4** B4
Uummannaq *Greenland* **4** B5
Uummannarsuaq =
  Nunap Isua *Greenland* **98** D15
Uusikaarlepyy *Finland* **8** E20
Uusikaupunki *Finland* **32** B1
Uva *Russia* **34** B11
Uvac → *Serbia* **44** C3
Uvalde *U.S.A.* **116** G5
Uvarovo *Russia* **34** E6
Uvat *Russia* **52** D7
Uvinza *Tanzania* **86** D3
Uvira *Dem. Rep. of the Congo* **86** C2
Uvs Nuur *Mongolia* **60** A4
'Uwairidh, Harrat al
  Si. Arabia **70** E3
Uwajima *Japan* **55** H6
Uwanda → *Tanzania* **86** D3
Uweinat, Jebel *Sudan* **80** C1
Uxbridge *Canada* **114** B5
Uxin Qi *China* **56** E5
Uxmal *Mexico* **119** C7
Üydzin *Mongolia* **56** B4
Uyo *Nigeria* **83** D6
Üyüklü Tepe *Turkey* **47** D9
Uyûn Mûsa *Egypt* **74** F1
Uyuni *Bolivia* **124** H5
Uzbekistan ■ *Asia* **52** E7
Uzboy → *Turkmenistan* **71** B7
Uzen, Bolshoi = Uzen,
  Mal → *Kazakhstan* **35** F9

Uzen, Mal → *Kazakhstan* **35** F9
Uzerche *France* **20** C5
Uzès *France* **21** D8
Uzh → *Ukraine* **23** C16
Uzhgorod = Uzhhorod
  Ukraine **28** B7
Uzhhorod *Ukraine* **28** B7
Uzhok *Ukraine* **28** B7
Užice *Serbia* **44** C3
Uzlovaya *Russia* **32** F10
Üzümlü *Turkey* **47** E11
Uzunköprü *Turkey* **45** E10
Uzunkuyu *Turkey* **47** C8

V

Vaal → *S. Africa* **88** D3
Vaal Dam *S. Africa* **89** D4
Vaalbos △ *S. Africa* **88** D3
Vaalwater *S. Africa* **89** C4
Vaasa *Finland* **8** E19
Vabre *France* **20** E6
Vác *Hungary* **28** C4
Vacaria *Brazil* **127** B5
Vacata *Fiji* **91** a
Vacaville *U.S.A.* **110** G5
Vaccarès, Étang de *France* **21** E8
Vach → *Russia* **52** C8
Vache, Î. à *Haiti* **121** C5
Väckelsång *Sweden* **11** H8
Vacoas *Mauritius* **85** d
Väddö *Sweden* **10** D12
Väderstad *Sweden* **11** F8
Vadnagar *India* **68** H5
Vado Lígure *Italy* **40** D5
Vadodara *India* **68** H5
Vadsø *Norway* **8** A23
Vadstena *Sweden* **11** F8
Vaduz *Liech.* **25** H5
Værøy *Norway* **8** C15
Vágar *Færoe Is.* **8** E9
Vaggeryd *Sweden* **11** G8
Vaghia *Greece* **46** C5
Vagia, Akra *Greece* **49** C10
Vagney *France* **19** D13
Vagnhärad *Sweden* **11** F11
Vagos *Portugal* **36** E2
Vågsfjorden *Norway* **8** B17
Váh → *Slovak Rep.* **27** D11
Vahsel B. *Antarctica* **5** D1
Váhtjer = Gällivare *Sweden* **8** C19
Vaï *Greece* **49** D8
Vaigach *Russia* **52** B6
Vaiges *France* **18** D6
Vaihingen *Germany* **25** G4
Vaihiria, L. *Tahiti* **91** d
Vail *U.S.A.* **106** C5
Vailly-sur-Aisne *France* **19** C10
Vairao *Tahiti* **91** d
Vaisali → *India* **69** F8
Vaison-la-Romaine *France* **21** D9
Vaitogi *Amer. Samoa* **91** b
Vakarel *Bulgaria* **44** D7
Vakfıkebir *Turkey* **73** B8
Vakh → *Russia* **52** C8
Vakhtan *Russia* **34** B8
Vál *Hungary* **28** C3
Val-de-Marne □ *France* **19** D9
Val-d'Isère *France* **21** C10
Val-d'Oise □ *France* **19** C9
Val-d'Or *Canada* **104** C4
Val Grande △ *Italy* **40** B5
Val Marie *Canada* **103** D7
Val Thorens *France* **21** C10
Valaam *Russia* **32** B6
Valadares *Portugal* **36** D2
Valahia *Romania* **29** F9
Valais □ *Switz.* **25** J3
Valais, Alpes du *Switz.* **25** J3
Valandovo *Macedonia* **44** E6
Valašské Meziříčí *Czech Rep.* **27** B10
Valaxa *Greece* **49** C6
Vålberg *Sweden* **10** E7
Valbo *Sweden* **10** D10
Valbondione *Italy* **40** B7
Valcani *Romania* **28** D5
Vâlcea → *Romania* **29** F9
Valcheta *Argentina* **128** E3
Valdagno *Italy* **41** C8
Valdahon *France* **19** E13
Valdai Hills = Valdayskaya
  Vozvyshennost *Russia* **32** D7
Valday *Russia* **32** D7
Valdayskaya
  Vozvyshennost *Russia* **32** D7
Valdeazogues → *Spain* **37** G6
Valdecañas, Embalse de
  Spain **36** F5
Valdemarsvik *Sweden* **11** F10
Valdemoro *Spain* **36** E7
Valdepeñas *Spain* **37** G7
Valderaduey → *Spain* **36** D5
Valderrobres *Spain* **38** E5
Valdés, Pen. *Argentina* **128** E4
Valdez *U.S.A.* **100** C5
Valdivia *Chile* **128** D2

Valdivia Abyssal Plain
  S. Ocean **5** C6
Valdobbiádene *Italy* **41** C8
Valdosta *U.S.A.* **117** F13
Valdoviño *Spain* **36** B2
Valdres *Norway* **8** F13
Vale *Georgia* **35** K6
Vale *U.S.A.* **108** E5
Vale of Glamorgan □ *U.K.* **15** F4
Valea lui Mihai *Romania* **28** C7
Valea Mărului *Romania* **29** E12
Valemount *Canada* **102** C5
Valença *Brazil* **125** F11
Valença *Portugal* **36** C2
Valença do Piauí *Brazil* **125** E10
Valençay *France* **19** E8
Valence *France* **21** D8
Valence d'Agen *France* **20** D4
Valencia *Spain* **39** F4
Valencia *Trin. & Tob.* **125** K15
Valencia *U.S.A.* **109** J10
Valencia *Venezuela* **124** A5
Valencia □ *Spain* **39** F4
Valencia ✈ (VLC) *Spain* **39** F4
Valencia, G. de *Spain* **39** F5
Valencia de Alcántara *Spain* **37** F3
Valencia de Don Juan *Spain* **36** C5
Valencia I. *Ireland* **12** E1
Valenciennes *France* **19** B10
Văleni *Romania* **29** F9
Vălenii de Munte *Romania* **29** E11
Valensole *France* **21** E9
Valentigney *France* **19** E13
Valentim, Sa. do *Brazil* **125** E10
Valentin *Russia* **54** C7
Valentine *Nebr., U.S.A.* **112** D3
Valentine *Tex., U.S.A.* **116** F2
Valenza *Italy* **40** C5
Valera *Venezuela* **124** B4
Valga *Estonia* **32** D4
Valguarnera Caropepe *Italy* **43** E7
Valier *U.S.A.* **108** B7
Valinco, G. de *France* **21** G12
Valjevo *Serbia* **44** B3
Valka *Latvia* **32** D3
Valkeakoski *Finland* **32** B2
Valkenswaard *Neths.* **17** C5
Vall de Uxó = La Vall
  d'Uixó *Spain* **38** F4
Valla *Sweden* **11** F10
Valladolid *Mexico* **119** C7
Valladolid *Spain* **36** D6
Valladolid □ *Spain* **36** D6
Vallata *Italy* **43** A8
Valldemossa *Spain* **48** B9
Valle d'Aosta □ *Italy* **40** C4
Valle de Arán *Spain* **38** C5
Valle de la Pascua *Venezuela* **124** B5
Valle de las Palmas *Mexico* **111** N10
Valle de Santiago *Mexico* **118** C4
Valle de Zaragoza *Mexico* **118** B3
Valle del Ticino △ *Italy* **40** C6
Valle Fértil, Sierra del
  Argentina **126** C2
Valle Gran Rey *Canary Is.* **48** F2
Valle Hermoso *Mexico* **119** B5
Valle Nacional *Mexico* **119** D5
Valledupar *Colombia* **124** A4
Vallehermoso *Canary Is.* **48** F2
Vallejo *U.S.A.* **110** G4
Vallenar *Chile* **126** B1
Vallentuna *Sweden* **10** E12
Valleraugue *France* **20** D7
Vallet *France* **18** E5
Valletta *Malta* **49** D2
Valley Center *U.S.A.* **111** M9
Valley City *U.S.A.* **112** B5
Valley Falls *Oreg., U.S.A.* **108** E3
Valley Falls *R.I., U.S.A.* **115** E13
Valley of Flowers △ *India* **69** D8
Valley of the Kings *Egypt* **80** B3
Valley Springs *U.S.A.* **110** G6
Valley View *U.S.A.* **115** F8
Valley Wells *U.S.A.* **111** K11
Valleyview *Canada* **102** B5
Valli di Comácchio *Italy* **41** D9
Vallimanca, Arroyo
  Argentina **126** D4
Vallo della Lucánia *Italy* **43** B8
Vallon-Pont-d'Arc *France* **21** D8
Vallorbe *Switz.* **25** J2
Valls *Spain* **38** D6
Valmaseda = Balmaseda
  Spain **38** B1
Valmiera *Latvia* **32** D3
Valnera *Spain* **36** B7
Valognes *France* **18** C5
Valona = Vlorë *Albania* **44** F3
Valongo *Portugal* **36** D2
Valozhyn *Belarus* **23** A14
Valpaços *Portugal* **36** D3
Valparaíso *Chile* **126** C1
Valparaíso *Mexico* **118** C4
Valparaiso *U.S.A.* **112** E10
Valparaíso □ *Chile* **126** C1
Valréas *France* **21** D9

Vals *Switz.* 25 J5
Vals → *S. Africa* 88 D4
Vals, Tanjung *Indonesia* 63 F9
Vals-les-Bains *France* 21 D8
Valsad *India* 66 J8
Valtellina *Italy* 40 B6
Valuyki *Russia* 33 G10
Valverde *Canary Is.* 48 G2
Valverde del Camino *Spain* 37 H4
Valverde del Fresno *Spain* 36 E4
Vama *Romania* 29 C10
Vamdrup *Denmark* 11 J3
Våmhus *Sweden* 10 C8
Vammala *Finland* 32 B2
Vamos *Greece* 49 D6
Van *Turkey* 73 C10
Van □ *Turkey* 73 C10
Van, L. = Van Gölü *Turkey* 73 C10
Van Alstyne *U.S.A.* 116 E6
Van Blommestein Meer *Suriname* 125 C7
Van Buren *Canada* 105 C6
Van Buren *Ark., U.S.A.* 116 D7
Van Buren *Maine, U.S.A.* 113 B20
Van Buren *Mo., U.S.A.* 112 G8
Van Canh *Vietnam* 64 F7
Van Diemen, C. *N. Terr., Australia* 92 B5
Van Diemen, C. *Queens., Australia* 94 B2
Van Diemen G. *Australia* 92 B5
Van Gölü *Turkey* 73 C10
Van Horn *U.S.A.* 116 F2
Van Ninh *Vietnam* 64 F7
Van Rees, Pegunungan *Indonesia* 63 E9
Van Wert *U.S.A.* 113 E11
Van Yen *Vietnam* 58 G5
Vanadzor *Armenia* 35 K7
Vanavara *Russia* 53 C11
Vancouver *Canada* 110 A3
Vancouver *U.S.A.* 110 E4
Vancouver, C. *Australia* 93 G2
Vancouver I. *Canada* 110 B2
Vancouver Int. ✕ (YVR) *Canada* 110 A3
Vanda = Vantaa *Finland* 32 B3
Vandalia *Ill., U.S.A.* 112 F9
Vandalia *Mo., U.S.A.* 112 F8
Vandenberg Village *U.S.A.* 111 L6
Vanderbijlpark *S. Africa* 89 D4
Vandergrift *U.S.A.* 114 F5
Vanderhoof *Canada* 102 C4
Vanderkloof Dam *S. Africa* 88 E3
Vanderlin I. *Australia* 94 B2
Vänern *Sweden* 11 F7
Vänersborg *Sweden* 11 F6
Vang Vieng *Laos* 64 C4
Vanga *Kenya* 86 C4
Vangaindrano *Madag.* 89 C8
Vanguard *Canada* 103 D7
Vanino *Russia* 53 E15
Vânju Mare *Romania* 28 F7
Vännäs *Sweden* 8 E18
Vannes *France* 18 E4
Vannøya *Norway* 8 A18
Vanoise, Massif de la *France* 21 C10
Vanrhynsdorp *S. Africa* 88 E2
Vansbro *Sweden* 10 D8
Vansittart B. *Australia* 92 B4
Vantaa *Finland* 32 B3
Vanua Balavu *Fiji* 91 a
Vanua Levu *Fiji* 91 a
Vanua Vatu *Fiji* 91 a
Vanuatu ■ *Pac. Oc.* 90 C9
Vanwyksvlei *S. Africa* 88 E3
Vanzylsrus *S. Africa* 88 D3
Vapnyarka *Ukraine* 29 B13
Var □ *France* 21 E10
Var → *France* 21 E11
Vara *Sweden* 11 F6
Varades *France* 18 E5
Varáita → *Italy* 40 D4
Varallo *Italy* 40 C5
Varāmīn *Iran* 71 C6
Varāmīn □ *Iran* 71 B6
Varanasi *India* 69 G10
Varangerfjorden *Norway* 8 A23
Varangerhalvøya *Norway* 8 A23
Varano, Lago di *Italy* 41 G12
Varaždin *Croatia* 41 B13
Varazze *Italy* 40 D5
Varberg *Sweden* 11 G6
Vardak □ *Afghan.* 66 B6
Vardar = Axios → *Greece* 44 F6
Varde *Denmark* 11 J2
Varde Å → *Denmark* 11 J2
Vardø *Norway* 8 A24
Varel *Germany* 24 B4
Varella, Mui *Vietnam* 64 F7
Varėna *Lithuania* 32 E3
Varennes-sur-Allier *France* 19 F10
Varennes-Vauzelles *France* 19 E10
Vareš *Bos.-H.* 28 F3
Varese *Italy* 40 C5
Vârfurile *Romania* 28 D7
Vårgårda *Sweden* 11 F6
Varginha *Brazil* 127 A6
Vargön *Sweden* 11 F6
Varillas *Chile* 126 A1
Varkaus *Finland* 32 A4
Värmdölandet *Sweden* 10 E12
Värmeln *Sweden* 10 E6
Värmlands län □ *Sweden* 10 E6
Värmlandsbro *Sweden* 10 E7
Varna *Bulgaria* 45 C11
Varna □ *Bulgaria* 45 C11
Värnamo *Sweden* 11 G8
Varnsdorf *Czech Rep.* 26 A7
Várpalota *Hungary* 28 C3
Vars *Canada* 115 A9
Vars *France* 21 D10
Varto *Turkey* 73 C9
Varvarin *Serbia* 44 C5
Varysburg *U.S.A.* 114 D6
Varzaneh *Iran* 71 C7
Varzi *Italy* 40 D6
Varzo *Italy* 40 B5
Varzy *France* 19 E10
Vas □ *Hungary* 28 C1
Vasa = Vaasa *Finland* 8 E19
Vasa Barris → *Brazil* 125 F11
Vásárosnamény *Hungary* 28 B7
Vascão → *Portugal* 37 H3
Vaşcău *Romania* 28 D7
Vascongadas = País Vasco □ *Spain* 38 C2
Vashkivtsi *Ukraine* 29 B10
Vasht = Khāsh *Iran* 71 D9
Vasilevichi *Belarus* 23 B15
Vasiliki *Greece* 46 C2
Vasiliko *Greece* 46 C5
Vasilkov = Vasylkiv *Ukraine* 23 C16
Vaslui *Romania* 29 D12
Vaslui □ *Romania* 29 D12
Väsman *Sweden* 10 D9
Vassar *Canada* 103 D9
Vassar *U.S.A.* 113 D12
Västerås *Sweden* 10 E10
Västerbotten *Sweden* 8 D19
Västerdalälven → *Sweden* 10 D8
Västergötland *Sweden* 11 F7
Västerhaninge *Sweden* 10 E12
Västervik *Sweden* 11 G10
Västmanland *Sweden* 9 G17
Västmanlands län □ *Sweden* 10 E10
Vasto *Italy* 41 F11
Västra Götalands Län □ *Sweden* 11 F6
Vasvár *Hungary* 28 C1
Vasylivka *Ukraine* 29 E13
Vasylkiv *Ukraine* 23 C16
Vatan *France* 19 E8
Vatersay *U.K.* 13 E1
Vathia *Greece* 46 E4
Vatican City ■ *Europe* 41 G9
Vaticano, C. *Italy* 43 D8
Vatili *Cyprus* 49 D12
Vatin *Serbia* 28 E6
Vatiu = Atiu *Cook Is.* 97 J12
Vatnajökull *Iceland* 8 D5
Vatolakkos *Greece* 49 D5
Vatoloha *Madag.* 89 B8
Vatomandry *Madag.* 89 B8
Vatra-Dornei *Romania* 29 C10
Vatrak → *India* 68 H5
Vättern *Sweden* 11 F8
Vatu Vara *Fiji* 91 a
Vatulele *Fiji* 91 a
Vaucluse □ *France* 21 E9
Vaucouleurs *France* 19 D12
Vaud □ *Switz.* 25 J2
Vaudreuil-Dorion *Canada* 115 A10
Vaughn *Mont., U.S.A.* 108 C8
Vaughn *N. Mex., U.S.A.* 109 J11
Vaujours L. *Canada* 104 A5
Vaupés = Uaupés → *Brazil* 124 C5
Vaupes □ *Colombia* 124 C4
Vauvert *France* 21 E8
Vauxhall *Canada* 102 C6
Vav *India* 68 G4
Vavatenina *Madag.* 89 B8
Vava'u *Tonga* 91 c
Vava'u Group *Tonga* 91 c
Vavoua *Ivory C.* 82 D3
Vawkavysk *Belarus* 23 B13
Vaxholm *Sweden* 10 E12
Växjö *Sweden* 11 H8
Våxtorp *Sweden* 11 H7
Vaygach, Ostrov *Russia* 52 C7
Veaikevárri = Svappavaara *Sweden* 8 C19
Vechelde *Germany* 24 C6
Vechta *Germany* 24 C4
Vechte → *Neths.* 17 B6
Vecsés *Hungary* 28 C4
Veddige *Sweden* 11 G6
Vedea → *Romania* 29 G10
Vedia *Argentina* 126 C3
Vedrette di Ries-Aurina ⌂ *Italy* 41 B9
Vedum *Sweden* 11 F7
Veendam *Neths.* 17 A6
Veenendaal *Neths.* 17 B5
Vefsna → *Norway* 8 D15
Vega *Norway* 8 D14
Vega *U.S.A.* 116 D3
Vega Baja *Puerto Rico* 121 d
Vegadeo *Spain* 36 B3
Vegoritida, L. *Greece* 44 F5
Vegreville *Canada* 102 C6
Veinge *Sweden* 11 H7
Veisiejai *Lithuania* 30 D10
Vejbystrand *Sweden* 11 H6
Vejen *Denmark* 11 J3
Vejer de la Frontera *Spain* 37 J5
Vejle *Denmark* 11 J3
Vejle Fjord *Denmark* 11 J3
Vela Luka *Croatia* 41 F13
Velas, C. *Costa Rica* 120 D2
Velasco, Sierra de *Argentina* 126 B2
Velay, Mts. du *France* 20 D7
Velbert *Germany* 24 D3
Velddrif *S. Africa* 88 E2
Velebit ⌂ *Croatia* 41 D12
Velebit Planina *Croatia* 41 D12
Velebitski Kanal *Croatia* 41 D11
Veleka → *Bulgaria* 45 D11
Velencei-tó *Hungary* 28 C3
Velenje *Slovenia* 41 B12
Veles *Macedonia* 44 E5
Velestino *Greece* 46 B4
Vélez-Málaga *Spain* 37 J6
Vélez Rubio *Spain* 39 H2
Velhas → *Brazil* 125 G10
Velika *Croatia* 28 E2
Velika Gorica *Croatia* 41 C13
Velika Kapela *Croatia* 41 C12
Velika Kladuša *Bos.-H.* 41 C12
Velika Kruša *Serbia* 44 D4
Velika Morava → *Serbia* 44 B5
Velika Plana *Serbia* 44 B5
Velikaya → *Russia* 32 D5
Velikaya Kema *Russia* 54 B8
Velikaya Lepetikha *Ukraine* 33 J7
Veliké Kapušany *Slovak Rep.* 27 C15
Velike Lašče *Slovenia* 41 C11
Veliki Jastrebac *Serbia* 44 C5
Veliki Kanal *Serbia* 28 E4
Veliki Popović *Serbia* 44 B5
Velikiye Luki *Russia* 32 D6
Veliko Gradište *Serbia* 44 B5
Veliko Tŭrnovo *Bulgaria* 45 C9
Velikonda Range *India* 66 M11
Vélingara *Kolda, Senegal* 82 C2
Vélingara *Louga, Senegal* 82 B2
Velingrad *Bulgaria* 44 D7
Velino, Mte. *Italy* 41 F10
Velizh *Russia* 32 E6
Velké Karlovice *Czech Rep.* 27 B11
Velké Meziříčí *Czech Rep.* 26 B9
Vel'ký Javorník *Slovak Rep.* 27 B11
Vel'ký Krtíš *Slovak Rep.* 27 C12
Vel'ký Meder *Slovak Rep.* 27 D10
Vel'ký Tribeč *Slovak Rep.* 27 C11
Velletri *Italy* 42 A5
Vellinge *Sweden* 11 J6
Vellmar *Germany* 24 D5
Vellore *India* 66 N11
Velopoula *Greece* 46 E5
Velsk *Russia* 32 B11
Velten *Germany* 24 C9
Veluwezoom △ *Neths.* 17 B6
Velva *U.S.A.* 112 A3
Velvendos *Greece* 44 F6
Velyka Mykhaylivka *Ukraine* 29 C14
Velyki Luchky *Ukraine* 28 B7
Velykyy Bereznyy *Ukraine* 28 B7
Velykyy Bychkiv *Ukraine* 29 C9
Vemb *Denmark* 11 H2
Vemdalen *Sweden* 10 B7
Ven *Sweden* 11 J6
Venaco *France* 21 F13
Venado *Mexico* 118 C4
Venado Tuerto *Argentina* 126 C3
Venafro *Italy* 43 A7
Venarey-les-Laumes *France* 19 E11
Venaría *Italy* 40 C4
Venčane *Serbia* 44 B4
Vence *France* 21 E11
Vendas Novas *Portugal* 37 G2
Vendée □ *France* 18 F5
Vendée → *France* 18 F5
Vendéen, Bocage *France* 20 B2
Vendeuvre-sur-Barse *France* 19 D11
Vendôme *France* 18 E8
Vendrell = El Vendrell *Spain* 38 D6
Vendsyssel *Denmark* 11 G4
Vendychany *Ukraine* 29 B12
Venelles *France* 21 E9
Véneta, L. *Italy* 41 C9
Véneto □ *Italy* 41 C9
Venev *Russia* 32 E10
Venézia *Italy* 41 C9
Venézia, G. di *Italy* 41 C10
Venezuela ■ *S. Amer.* 124 B5
Venezuela, G. de *Venezuela* 124 A4
Vengurla *India* 66 M8
Venice = Venézia *Italy* 41 C9
Venice *U.S.A.* 117 H13
Vénissieux *France* 21 C8
Venjansjön *Sweden* 10 D8
Venkatapuram *India* 67 K12
Venlo *Neths.* 17 C6
Vennesla *Norway* 9 G12
Venosa *Italy* 43 B8
Venray *Neths.* 17 C6
Venta *Lithuania* 30 B9
Venta → *Latvia* 30 A8
Venta de Baños *Spain* 36 D6
Venta de Cardeña = Cardeña *Spain* 37 G6
Ventana, Punta de la *Mexico* 118 C3
Ventana, Sa. de la *Argentina* 126 D3
Ventersburg *S. Africa* 88 D4
Venterstad *S. Africa* 88 E4
Ventimíglia *Italy* 40 E4
Ventnor *U.K.* 15 G6
Ventotène *Italy* 42 B6
Ventoux, Mt. *France* 21 D9
Ventspils *Latvia* 30 A8
Ventspils □ *Latvia* 30 A8
Ventuarí → *Venezuela* 124 C5
Ventucopa *U.S.A.* 111 L7
Ventura *U.S.A.* 111 L7
Vénus, Pte. *Tahiti* 91 d
Venus B. *Australia* 95 F4
Venustiano Carranza *Mexico* 118 A1
Vera *Argentina* 126 B3
Vera *Spain* 39 H3
Veracruz *Mexico* 119 D5
Veracruz □ *Mexico* 119 D5
Veraval *India* 68 J4
Verbánia *Italy* 40 C5
Verbicaro *Italy* 43 C8
Verbier *Switz.* 25 J3
Vercelli *Italy* 40 C5
Verchovchevo *Ukraine* 33 H8
Vercors ⌂ *France* 21 D9
Verdalsøra *Norway* 8 E14
Verde → *Argentina* 128 E3
Verde → *Goiás, Brazil* 125 G8
Verde → *Mato Grosso do Sul, Brazil* 125 H8
Verde → *Chihuahua, Mexico* 118 B3
Verde → *Oaxaca, Mexico* 119 D5
Verde → *Veracruz, Mexico* 118 C4
Verde → *Paraguay* 126 A4
Verde → *U.S.A.* 106 D4
Verde, Cay *Bahamas* 120 B4
Verde Island Pass *Phil.* 61 E4
Verden *Germany* 24 C5
Verdi *U.S.A.* 110 F7
Verdikoussa *Greece* 46 B3
Verdon → *France* 21 E9
Verdon ⌂ *France* 21 E10
Verdun *France* 19 C12
Verdun-sur-le-Doubs *France* 19 F12
Vereeniging *S. Africa* 89 D4
Verga, C. *Guinea* 82 C2
Vergara *Uruguay* 127 C5
Vergato *Italy* 40 D8
Vergemont Cr. → *Australia* 94 C3
Vergennes *U.S.A.* 115 B11
Vergt *France* 20 C4
Veria *Greece* 44 F6
Verín *Spain* 36 D3
Verkhnedvinsk = Vyerkhnyadzvinsk *Belarus* 32 E4
Verkhnetulomskoye Vdkhr. *Russia* 8 B24
Verkhnevilyuysk *Russia* 53 C13
Verkhniy Baskunchak *Russia* 35 F8
Verkhovye *Russia* 33 F9
Verkhovyna *Ukraine* 29 B9
Verkhoyansk *Russia* 53 C14
Verkhoyansk Ra. = Verkhoyanskiy Khrebet *Russia* 53 C13
Verkhoyanskiy Khrebet *Russia* 53 C13
Vermenton *France* 19 E10
Vermilion *Canada* 103 C6
Vermilion *U.S.A.* 114 E2
Vermilion → *Canada* 103 C6
Vermilion → *U.S.A.* 116 G9
Vermilion Bay *Canada* 103 D10
Vermilion L. *U.S.A.* 112 B7
Vermillion *U.S.A.* 112 D5
Vermillion → *Canada* 104 C5
Vermont □ *U.S.A.* 115 C12
Vermosh *Albania* 44 D3
Vernadsky *Antarctica* 5 C17
Vernal *U.S.A.* 108 F9
Vernalis *U.S.A.* 110 H5
Vernazza *Italy* 40 D6
Verner *Canada* 104 C3
Verneuil-sur-Avre *France* 18 D7
Verneukpan *S. Africa* 88 E3
Vernier *Switz.* 25 J2
Vérnio *Italy* 40 D8
Vernon *Canada* 102 C5
Vernon *France* 18 C8
Vernon *U.S.A.* 116 D5
Vernonia *U.S.A.* 110 E3
Vero Beach *U.S.A.* 117 H14
Véroia = Veria *Greece* 44 F6
Véroli *Italy* 41 G10
Verona *Canada* 115 B8
Verona *Italy* 40 C7
Verrès *Italy* 40 C4
Versailles *France* 19 D9
Versmold *Germany* 24 C4
Vert, C. *Senegal* 82 C1
Vertou *France* 18 E5
Vertus *France* 19 D11
Verulam *S. Africa* 89 D5
Verviers *Belgium* 17 D5
Vervins *France* 19 C10
Veržej *Slovenia* 41 B13
Verzy *France* 19 C11
Vescovato *France* 21 F13
Veselí nad Lužnicí *Czech Rep.* 26 B7
Veselie *Bulgaria* 45 D11
Veselovskoye Vdkhr. *Russia* 35 G5
Veshenskaya *Russia* 34 F5
Vesle → *France* 19 C10
Vesoul *France* 19 E13
Vessigebro *Sweden* 11 H6
Vesterålen *Norway* 8 B16
Vestfjorden *Norway* 8 C16
Vestmannaeyjar *Iceland* 8 E3
Vestspitsbergen *Svalbard* 4 B8
Vestvågøya *Norway* 8 B15
Vesuvio *Italy* 43 B7
Vesuvius, Mt. = Vesuvio *Italy* 43 B7
Vesyegonsk *Russia* 32 C9
Veszprém *Hungary* 28 C2
Veszprém □ *Hungary* 28 C2
Vésztő *Hungary* 28 D6
Vetlanda *Sweden* 11 G9
Vetluga *Russia* 34 B7
Vetlugu → *Russia* 34 B8
Vetluzhskiy *Kostroma, Russia* 34 A7
Vetluzhskiy *Nizhniy Novgorod, Russia* 34 B7
Vetovo *Bulgaria* 45 C10
Vetralla *Italy* 41 F9
Vetren *Bulgaria* 45 D8
Vettore, Mte. *Italy* 41 F10
Veurne *Belgium* 17 C2
Veveno → *Sudan* 81 F3
Vevey *Switz.* 25 J2
Vevi *Greece* 44 F5
Veynes *France* 21 D9
Veys *Iran* 71 D6
Vézelay *France* 19 E10
Vézelise *France* 19 D13
Vézère → *France* 20 D4
Vezhen *Bulgaria* 45 D8
Vezirköprü *Turkey* 72 B6
Vezzani *France* 21 F13
Vi Thanh *Vietnam* 65 H5
Viacha *Bolivia* 124 G5
Viadana *Italy* 40 D7
Viamão *Brazil* 127 C5
Viana *Brazil* 125 D10
Viana *Spain* 38 C2
Viana do Alentejo *Portugal* 37 G3
Viana do Bolo *Spain* 36 C3
Viana do Castelo *Portugal* 36 D2
Viana do Castelo □ *Portugal* 36 D2
Vianden *Lux.* 17 E6
Viangchan = Vientiane *Laos* 64 D4
Vianópolis *Brazil* 125 G9
Vianos *Greece* 49 D7
Viar → *Spain* 37 H5
Viaréggio *Italy* 40 E7
Viaur → *France* 20 D5
Vibble *Sweden* 11 G12
Vibo Valéntia *Italy* 43 D9
Viborg *Denmark* 11 H3
Vibraye *France* 18 D7
Vic *Spain* 38 D7
Vic, Étang de *France* 20 E7
Vic-en-Bigorre *France* 20 E4
Vic-Fezensac *France* 20 E4
Vic-le-Comte *France* 19 G10
Vic-sur-Cère *France* 20 D6
Vícar *Spain* 39 J2
Vicenza *Italy* 41 C8
Vich = Vic *Spain* 38 D7
Vichada → *Colombia* 124 C5
Vichuga *Russia* 34 B5
Vichy *France* 19 F10
Vicksburg *U.S.A.* 111 M13
Vico *France* 21 F12
Vico, L. di *Italy* 41 F9
Vico del Gargano *Italy* 41 G12
Vicovu de Sus *Romania* 29 C10
Victor *India* 68 J4
Victor *U.S.A.* 114 D7
Victor Harbor *Australia* 95 F2
Victoria *Argentina* 126 C3
Victoria *Canada* 110 B3
Victoria *Chile* 128 D2
Victoria *Guinea* 82 C2
Victoria *Malta* 49 C1
Victoria *Phil.* 61 D4
Victoria *Romania* 29 E9
Victoria *Seychelles* 85 b
Victoria *Kans., U.S.A.* 112 F4
Victoria *Tex., U.S.A.* 116 G6
Victoria □ *Australia* 95 F3
Victoria → *Australia* 92 C4
Victoria, Grand L. *Canada* 104 C4
Victoria, L. *Africa* 86 C3
Victoria, L. *Australia* 95 E3
Victoria, Mt. *Burma* 67 J18
Victoria Beach *Canada* 103 C9
Victoria de Durango = Durango *Mexico* 118 C4
Victoria de las Tunas = Las Tunas *Cuba* 120 B4
Victoria Falls *Zimbabwe* 87 F2
Victoria Harbour *Canada* 114 B5
Victoria I. *Canada* 100 B8
Victoria L. *Canada* 105 C8
Victoria Ld. *Antarctica* 5 D11
Victoria Nile → *Uganda* 86 B3
Victoria Pk. *Belize* 119 D7
Victoria River *Australia* 92 C5
Victoria Str. *Canada* 100 C9
Victoria West *S. Africa* 88 E3
Victorias *Phil.* 61 F5
Victoriaville *Canada* 105 C5
Victorica *Argentina* 126 D2
Victorville *U.S.A.* 111 L9
Vicuña *Chile* 126 C1
Vicuña Mackenna *Argentina* 126 C3
Vidal *U.S.A.* 111 L12
Vidal Junction *U.S.A.* 111 L12
Vidalia *U.S.A.* 117 E13
Vidamlya *Belarus* 31 F10
Vidauban *France* 21 E10
Videbæk *Denmark* 11 H2
Videle *Romania* 29 F10
Vidigueira *Portugal* 37 G3
Vidin *Bulgaria* 44 C6
Vidio, C. *Spain* 36 B4
Vidisha *India* 68 H7
Vido *Greece* 49 A3
Vidra *Romania* 29 E11
Viduša *Bos.-H.* 44 D2
Vidzy *Belarus* 32 E4
Viechtach *Germany* 25 F8
Viedma *Argentina* 128 E4
Viedma, L. *Argentina* 128 F2
Vieira do Minho *Portugal* 36 D2
Vielha *Spain* 38 C5
Viella = Vielha *Spain* 38 C5
Vielsalm *Belgium* 17 D5
Vienenburg *Germany* 24 D6
Vieng Pou Kha *Laos* 58 G3
Vienna = Wien *Austria* 27 C9
Vienna *Ill., U.S.A.* 112 G9
Vienna *Mo., U.S.A.* 112 F8
Vienne *France* 21 C8
Vienne □ *France* 20 B4
Vienne → *France* 18 E7
Vientiane *Laos* 64 D4
Vientos, Paso de los *Caribbean* 121 C5
Vieques *Puerto Rico* 121 d
Vierge Pt. *St. Lucia* 121 f
Viernheim *Germany* 25 F4
Viersen *Germany* 24 D2
Vierwaldstättersee *Switz.* 25 J4
Vierzon *France* 19 E9
Vieste *Italy* 41 G13
Vietnam ■ *Asia* 64 C6
Vieux-Boucau-les-Bains *France* 20 E2
Vieux Fort *St. Lucia* 121 f
Vif *France* 21 C9
Vigan *Phil.* 61 C4
Vigévano *Italy* 40 C5
Vigia *Brazil* 125 D9
Viglas, Akra *Greece* 49 D9
Vignemalle *France* 20 F3
Vigneulles-lès-Hattonchâtel *France* 19 D12
Vignola *Italy* 40 D8
Vigo *Spain* 36 C2
Vigo, Ría de *Spain* 36 C2
Vigsø Bugt *Denmark* 11 G2
Vihiers *France* 18 E6
Vihowa *Pakistan* 68 D4
Vihowa → *Pakistan* 68 D4
Vijayawada *India* 67 L12
Vijosë → *Albania* 44 F3
Vík *Iceland* 8 E4
Vika *Sweden* 10 D8
Vikarbyn *Sweden* 10 D9
Vikeke = Viqueque *E. Timor* 63 F7
Viken *Skåne, Sweden* 11 H6
Viken *Västra Götaland, Sweden* 11 F8
Viking *Canada* 102 C6
Vikmanshyttan *Sweden* 10 D9

Vikna *Norway* **8** D14
Vikos-Aoos △ *Greece* **46** B2
Vila da Maganja *Mozam.* **87** F4
Vila da Ribeira Brava
  C. Verde Is. **78** b
Vila de Rei *Portugal* **36** F2
Vila do Bispo *Portugal* **37** H2
Vila do Conde *Portugal* **36** D2
Vila Franca de Xira *Portugal* **37** G2
Vila Gamito *Mozam.* **87** E3
Vila Gomes da Costa *Mozam.* **89** C5
Vila Machado *Mozam.* **87** F3
Vila Mouzinho *Mozam.* **87** E3
Vila Nova de Famalicão
  Portugal **36** D2
Vila Nova de Fos Côa
  Portugal **36** D3
Vila Nova de Gaia *Portugal* **36** D2
Vila Nova de Ourém *Portugal* **36** F2
Vila Pouca de Aguiar
  Portugal **36** D3
Vila Real *Portugal* **36** D3
Vila Real □ *Portugal* **36** D3
Vila-real de los Infantes
  Spain **38** F4
Vila Real de Santo António
  Portugal **37** H3
Vila Vasco da Gama *Mozam.* **87** E3
Vila Velha *Brazil* **127** A7
Vila Viçosa *Portugal* **37** G3
Vilafranca del Maestrat
  Spain **38** E4
Vilafranca del Penedès *Spain* **38** D6
Vilagarcía de Arousa *Spain* **36** C2
Vilaine → *France* **18** E4
Vilanandro, Tanjona *Madag.* **89** B7
Vilanculos *Mozam.* **89** C6
Vilanova de Castelló *Spain* **39** F4
Vilanova i la Geltrú *Spain* **38** D6
Vilar Formoso *Portugal* **36** E4
Vilaseca *Spain* **38** D6
Vilaseca-Salou = Vilaseca
  Spain **38** D6
Vilbjerg *Denmark* **11** H2
Vilcheka, Zemlya *Russia* **4** A11
Vilches *Spain* **37** G7
Vileyka *Belarus* **23** A14
Vilhelmina *Sweden* **8** D17
Vilhena *Brazil* **124** F6
Viliya = Neris → *Lithuania* **32** E3
Viljandi *Estonia* **32** C3
Vilkaviškis *Lithuania* **30** D10
Vilkija *Lithuania* **30** C10
Vilkitskogo, Proliv *Russia* **53** B11
Vilkovo = Vylkove *Ukraine* **29** E14
Villa Abecia *Bolivia* **126** A2
Villa Ana *Argentina* **126** B4
Villa Ángela *Argentina* **126** B3
Villa Bella *Bolivia* **124** F5
Villa Cañás *Argentina* **126** C3
Villa Colón *Argentina* **126** C3
Villa Constitución *Argentina* **126** C3
Villa de Arriaga *Mexico* **118** C4
Villa de María *Argentina* **126** B3
Villa de Méndez *Mexico* **119** B5
Villa del Rio *Spain* **37** H6
Villa Dolores *Argentina* **126** C2
Villa Frontera *Mexico* **118** B4
Villa Guillermina *Argentina* **126** B4
Villa Hayes *Paraguay* **126** B4
Villa Hidalgo *Mexico* **119** C5
Villa Iris *Argentina* **126** D3
Villa María *Argentina* **126** C3
Villa Mazán *Argentina* **126** B2
Villa Minozzo *Italy* **40** D7
Villa Montes *Bolivia* **126** A3
Villa Ocampo *Argentina* **126** B4
Villa Ocampo *Mexico* **118** B3
Villa Ojo de Agua *Argentina* **126** B3
Villa San Giovanni *Italy* **43** D8
Villa San José *Argentina* **126** C4
Villa San Martín *Argentina* **126** B3
Villa Santina *Italy* **41** B9
Villa Unión *Mexico* **118** C3
Villablino *Spain* **36** C4
Villacarlos *Spain* **48** B11
Villacarriedo *Spain* **36** B7
Villacarrillo *Spain* **37** G7
Villacastín *Spain* **36** E6
Villach *Austria* **26** E6
Villacidro *Italy* **42** C1
Villada *Spain* **36** C6
Villadiego *Spain* **36** C6
Villadóssola *Italy* **40** B5
Villafeliche *Spain* **38** D3
Villafranca *Spain* **38** C3
Villafranca de los Barros
  Spain **37** G4
Villafranca de los
  Caballeros *Baleares, Spain* **48** B10
Villafranca de los
  Caballeros *Toledo, Spain* **37** F7
Villafranca del Cid =
  Vilafranca del Maestrat
  Spain **38** E4
Villafranca del Panadés =
  Vilafranca del Penedès
  Spain **38** D6

Villafranca di Verona *Italy* **40** C7
Villafranca Tirrena *Italy* **43** D8
Villagrán *Mexico* **119** C5
Villaguay *Argentina* **126** C4
Villaharta *Spain* **37** G6
Villahermosa *Mexico* **119** D6
Villahermosa *Spain* **39** G2
Villaines-la-Juhel *France* **18** D6
Villajoyosa *Spain* **39** G4
Villalba *Spain* **36** B3
Villalba de Guardo *Spain* **36** C6
Villalón de Campos *Spain* **36** C5
Villalpando *Spain* **36** D5
Villaluenga *Spain* **36** E7
Villamanán *Spain* **36** C5
Villamartín *Spain* **37** J5
Villamayor de Santiago
  Spain **38** F2
Villamblard *France* **20** C4
Villanova Monteleone *Italy* **42** B1
Villanueva *U.S.A.* **109** J11
Villanueva de Castellón =
  Vilanova de Castelló *Spain* **39** F4
Villanueva de Córdoba *Spain* **37** G6
Villanueva de la Fuente
  Spain **39** G2
Villanueva de la Serena
  Spain **37** G5
Villanueva de la Sierra *Spain* **36** E4
Villanueva de los
  Castillejos *Spain* **37** H3
Villanueva de los Infantes
  Spain **37** G7
Villanueva del Arzobispo
  Spain **39** G2
Villanueva del Fresno *Spain* **37** G3
Villanueva y Geltrú =
  Vilanova i la Geltrú *Spain* **38** D6
Villaputzu *Italy* **42** C2
Villaquilambre *Spain* **36** C5
Villar del Arzobispo *Spain* **38** F4
Villar del Rey *Spain* **37** F4
Villard-de-Lans *France* **21** C9
Villarcayo *Spain* **36** C6
Villarramiel *Spain* **36** C6
Villarreal = Vila-real de los
  Infantes *Spain* **38** F4
Villarrica *Chile* **128** D2
Villarrica *Paraguay* **126** B4
Villarrobledo *Spain* **39** F2
Villarroya de la Sierra *Spain* **38** D3
Villarrubia de los Ojos *Spain* **37** F7
Villars-les-Dombes *France* **19** F12
Villasayas *Spain* **38** D2
Villaseca de los Gamitos =
  Villaseco de los Gamitos
  Spain **36** D4
Villaseco de los Gamitos
  Spain **36** D4
Villasimíus *Italy* **42** C2
Villastar *Spain* **38** E3
Villatobas *Spain* **36** F7
Villavicencio *Argentina* **126** C2
Villavicencio *Colombia* **124** C4
Villaviciosa *Spain* **36** B5
Villazón *Bolivia* **126** A2
Ville-Marie *Canada* **104** C4
Ville Platte *U.S.A.* **116** F8
Villedieu-les-Poêles *France* **18** D5
Villefort *France* **20** D7
Villefranche-de-Lauragais
  France **20** E5
Villefranche-de-Rouergue
  France **20** D6
Villefranche-du-Périgord
  France **20** D5
Villefranche-sur-Saône
  France **21** C8
Villel *Spain* **38** E3
Villemur-sur-Tarn *France* **20** E5
Villena *Spain* **39** G4
Villenauxe-la-Grande
  France **19** D10
Villenave-d'Ornon *France* **20** D3
Villeneuve-d'Ascq *France* **19** B10
Villeneuve-l'Archevêque
  France **19** D10
Villeneuve-lès-Avignon
  France **21** E8
Villeneuve-sur-Allier
  France **19** F10
Villeneuve-sur-Lot *France* **20** D4
Villeneuve-sur-Yonne
  France **19** D10
Villeréal *France* **20** D4
Villers-Bocage *France* **18** C6
Villers-Cotterêts *France* **19** C10
Villers-sur-Mer *France* **18** C6
Villersexel *France* **19** E13
Villerupt *France* **19** C12
Villers *S. Africa* **89** D4
Villingen-Schwenningen
  Germany **25** G4
Villmanstrand =
  Lappeenranta *Finland* **32** B5
Vilna *Canada* **102** C6
Vilnius *Lithuania* **32** E3

Vils *Austria* **26** D3
Vils → *Bayern, Germany* **25** G9
Vils → *Bayern, Germany* **25** F7
Vilsbiburg *Germany* **25** G8
Vilshofen *Germany* **25** G9
Vilusi *Montenegro* **44** D2
Vilvoorde *Belgium* **17** D4
Vilyuy → *Russia* **53** C13
Vilyuysk *Russia* **53** C13
Vimianzo *Spain* **36** B1
Vimioso *Portugal* **36** D4
Vimmerby *Sweden* **11** G9
Vimoutiers *France* **18** D7
Vimperk *Czech Rep.* **26** B6
Viña del Mar *Chile* **126** C1
Vinarós *Spain* **38** E5
Vincennes *U.S.A.* **112** F10
Vincent *U.S.A.* **111** L8
Vinchina *Argentina* **126** B2
Vindelälven → *Sweden* **8** E18
Vindeln *Sweden* **8** D18
Vinderup *Denmark* **11** H2
Vindhya Ra. *India* **68** H7
Vineland *U.S.A.* **113** F16
Vineuil *France* **18** E8
Vinga *Romania* **28** D6
Vingåker *Sweden* **10** E9
Vinh *Vietnam* **64** C5
Vinh Linh *Vietnam* **64** D6
Vinh Long *Vietnam* **65** G5
Vinh Yen *Vietnam* **58** G5
Vinhais *Portugal* **36** D3
Vinica *Croatia* **41** B13
Vinica *Macedonia* **44** E6
Vinica *Slovenia* **41** C12
Vinita *U.S.A.* **116** C7
Vinkovci *Croatia* **28** E3
Vinnitsa = Vinnytsya
  Ukraine **23** D15
Vinnytsya *Ukraine* **23** D15
Vinnytsya □ *Ukraine* **33** H5
Vinslöv *Sweden* **11** H7
Vinson Massif *Antarctica* **5** D16
Vintjärn *Sweden* **10** D10
Vinton *Calif., U.S.A.* **110** F6
Vinton *Iowa, U.S.A.* **112** D7
Vinton *La., U.S.A.* **116** F8
Viöl *Germany* **24** A5
Viotia □ *Greece* **46** C5
Vipava *Slovenia* **41** C10
Vipiteno *Italy* **41** B8
Viqueque *E. Timor* **63** F7
Vir *Croatia* **41** D12
Virac *Phil.* **61** E6
Virachey *Cambodia* **64** F6
Virachey △ *Cambodia* **64** E6
Virago Sd. *Canada* **102** C2
Viramgam *India* **68** H5
Virananşehir *Turkey* **73** D8
Virawah *Pakistan* **68** G4
Virbalis *Lithuania* **30** D9
Virden *Canada* **103** D8
Vire *France* **18** D6
Vire → *France* **18** C5
Vírgenes, C. *Argentina* **128** G3
Virgin → *U.S.A.* **109** H6
Virgin Gorda *Br. Virgin Is.* **121** e
Virgin Is. (British) ☑
  W. Indies **121** e
Virgin Is. (U.S.) ☑ *W. Indies* **121** e
Virgin Islands □
  U.S. Virgin Is. **121** C7
Virginia *S. Africa* **88** D4
Virginia *U.S.A.* **112** B7
Virginia □ *U.S.A.* **113** G14
Virginia Beach *U.S.A.* **113** F16
Virginia City *Mont., U.S.A.* **108** D8
Virginia City *Nev., U.S.A.* **110** F7
Virginia Falls *Canada* **102** A3
Virginiatown *Canada* **104** C4
Virje *Croatia* **41** B13
Viroqua *U.S.A.* **112** D8
Virovitica *Croatia* **28** E2
Virpazar *Montenegro* **44** D3
Virpur *India* **68** J4
Virserum *Sweden* **11** G9
Virton *Belgium* **17** E5
Virudunagar *India* **66** Q10
Virunga △
  Dem. Rep. of the Congo **86** B2
Vis *Croatia* **41** E13
Visalia *U.S.A.* **110** J7
Visayan Sea *Phil.* **61** F5
Visby *Sweden* **11** G12
Viscount Melville Sd.
  Canada **101** B9
Visé *Belgium* **17** D5
Višegrad *Bos.-H.* **28** G4
Viseu *Brazil* **125** D9
Viseu *Portugal* **36** E3
Viseu □ *Portugal* **36** E3
Vişeu de Sus *Romania* **29** C9
Vishakhapatnam *India* **67** L13
Vişina *Romania* **29** G9
Vişineşti *Moldova* **29** D13
Visingsö *Sweden* **11** F8

Viskafors *Sweden* **11** G6
Viskan → *Sweden* **11** G6
Viški Kanal *Croatia* **41** E13
Vislanda *Sweden* **11** H8
Visnagar *India* **68** H5
Višnja Gora *Slovenia* **41** C11
Viso, Mte. *Italy* **40** D4
Viso del Marqués *Spain* **37** G7
Visoko *Bos.-H.* **28** G3
Visokoi I. *Antarctica* **5** B1
Visp *Switz.* **25** J3
Vissefjärda *Sweden* **11** H9
Visselhövede *Germany* **24** C5
Vissenbjerg *Denmark* **11** J4
Vista *U.S.A.* **111** M9
Vistonida, L. *Greece* **45** E9
Vistonikos, Ormos =
  Vistonida, L. *Greece* **45** E9
Vistula = Wisła → *Poland* **30** D5
Vit → *Bulgaria* **45** C8
Vitanje *Slovenia* **41** B12
Vitebsk = Vitsyebsk *Belarus* **32** E6
Viterbo *Italy* **41** F9
Vitez *Bos.-H.* **28** F2
Viti Levu *Fiji* **91** a
Vitigudino *Spain* **36** D4
Vitim *Russia* **53** D12
Vitim → *Russia* **53** D12
Vitina *Bos.-H.* **41** E14
Vitina *Greece* **46** D4
Vítkov *Czech Rep.* **27** B10
Vitória *Brazil* **125** H10
Vitória da Conquista *Brazil*
  125 F10
Vitória de São Antão *Brazil*
  125 E11
Vitoria-Gasteiz *Spain* **38** C2
Vitosha △ *Bulgaria* **44** D7
Vitré *France* **18** D5
Vitry-le-François *France* **19** D11
Vitry-sur-Seine *France* **19** D9
Vitsand *Sweden* **10** D7
Vitsi, Oros *Greece* **44** F5
Vitsyebsk *Belarus* **32** E6
Vitsyebsk □ *Belarus* **32** E5
Vittaryd *Sweden* **11** H7
Vitteaux *France* **19** E11
Vittel *France* **19** D12
Vittória *Italy* **43** F7
Vittório Véneto *Italy* **41** C9
Vittsjö *Sweden* **11** H7
Viveiro *Spain* **36** B3
Vivian *U.S.A.* **116** E8
Viviers *France* **21** D8
Vivonne *France* **20** B4
Viwa *Fiji* **91** a
Vizcaíno, Desierto de
  Mexico **118** B2
Vizcaíno, Sierra *Mexico* **118** B2
Vizcaya □ *Spain* **38** B2
Vize *Turkey* **45** E11
Vizianagaram *India* **67** K13
Vizille *France* **21** C9
Viziñada *Croatia* **41** C10
Viziru *Romania* **29** E12
Vizzini *Italy* **43** E7
Vlaardingen *Neths.* **17** C4
Vlachiotis *Greece* **46** E4
Vlădeasa, Vf. *Romania* **28** D7
Vladičin Han *Serbia* **44** D6
Vladikavkaz *Russia* **35** J7
Vladimir *Russia* **32** D11
Vladimir □ *Russia* **34** B5
Vladimir Volynskiy =
  Volodymyr-Volynskyy
  Ukraine **23** C13
Vladimirci *Serbia* **44** B3
Vladimirovac *Serbia* **28** E5
Vladimirovka *Russia* **35** F8
Vladimirovo *Bulgaria* **44** C7
Vladimorvka *Kazakhstan* **34** E10
Vladislavovka *Ukraine* **33** K8
Vladivostok *Russia* **54** C5
Vlăhiţa *Romania* **29** D10
Vlasenica *Bos.-H.* **28** F3
Vlašić *Bos.-H.* **28** F2
Vlašim *Czech Rep.* **26** B7
Vlasinsko Jezero *Serbia* **44** D6
Vlasotince *Serbia* **44** D6
Vlieland *Neths.* **17** A4
Vlissingen *Neths.* **17** C3
Vlorë *Albania* **44** F3
Vlorës, Gjiri i *Albania* **44** F3
Vltava → *Czech Rep.* **26** A7
Vo Dat *Vietnam* **65** G6
Vobarno *Italy* **40** C7
Voćin *Croatia* **41** E13
Vöcklabruck *Austria* **26** C6
Vodice *Croatia* **41** E12
Vodňany *Czech Rep.* **26** B7
Vodnjan *Croatia* **41** D10
Voe *U.K.* **13** A7
Vogel Pk. *Nigeria* **83** D7
Vogelkop = Doberai,
  Jazirah *Indonesia* **63** E8
Vogelsberg *Germany* **24** E5
Voghera *Italy* **40** D6

Vohibinany *Madag.* **89** B8
Vohilava *Madag.* **89** C8
Vohimarina = Iharana
  Madag. **89** A9
Vohimena, Tanjon' i *Madag.* **89** D8
Vohipeno *Madag.* **89** C8
Voi *Kenya* **86** C4
Void-Vacon *France* **19** D12
Voineşti *Iaşi, Romania* **29** C12
Voineşti *Prahova, Romania* **29** E10
Voiron *France* **21** C9
Voisey B. *Canada* **105** A7
Voitsberg *Austria* **26** D8
Vojens *Denmark* **11** J3
Vojmsjön *Sweden* **8** D17
Vojnić *Croatia* **41** C12
Vojnik *Italy* **41** B12
Vojvodina □ *Serbia* **28** E5
Vokhtoga *Russia* **32** C11
Volary *Czech Rep.* **26** C6
Volborg *U.S.A.* **108** D11
Volcán de Colima = *Mexico* **118** D4
Volcano Is. = Kazan-Rettō
  Pac. Oc. **96** E6
Volcans △ *Rwanda* **86** C2
Volcans d'Auvergne △
  France **20** C6
Volchansk = Vovchansk
  Ukraine **33** H8
Volda *Norway* **8** E12
Volga → *Russia* **35** G9
Volga = Privolzhskiy □
  Russia **34** B10
Volga *Russia* **32** C10
Volga → *Russia* **35** G9
Volga Hts. =
  Privolzhskaya
  Vozvyshennost *Russia* **34** E7
Volgo-Baltiyskiy Kanal
  Russia **32** B9
Volgo-Donskoy Kanal
  Russia **35** F7
Volgodonsk *Russia* **35** G6
Volgograd *Russia* **34** F7
Volgograd □ *Russia* **34** F7
Volgogradskoye Vdkhr.
  Russia **34** B8
Volgorechensk *Russia* **34** B5
Volimes *Greece* **46** D2
Volintiri *Moldova* **29** D14
Volissos *Greece* **47** C7
Volkach *Germany* **25** F6
Völkermarkt *Austria* **26** E7
Volkhov *Russia* **32** C7
Volkhov → *Russia* **32** B7
Völklingen *Germany* **25** F2
Volkovysk = Vawkavysk
  Belarus **23** B13
Volksrust *S. Africa* **89** D4
Volnansk *Ukraine* **33** H8
Volnovakha *Ukraine* **33** J9
Volochanka *Russia* **53** B10
Volodarsk *Russia* **34** B6
Volodymyr-Volynskyy
  Ukraine **23** C13
Vologda *Russia* **32** C10
Vologda □ *Russia* **32** B10
Volokolamsk *Russia* **32** D8
Volokonovka *Russia* **33** G9
Volos *Greece* **46** B4
Volosovo *Russia* **32** C5
Volovets *Ukraine* **29** B8
Volovo *Russia* **32** F10
Volozhin = Valozhyn
  Belarus **23** A14
Volsk *Russia* **34** D8
Volta □ *Ghana* **83** D5
Volta → *Ghana* **83** D5
Volta, L. *Ghana* **83** D5
Volta Blanche = White
  Volta → *Ghana* **83** D4
Volta Redonda *Brazil* **127** A7
Voltaire, C. *Australia* **92** B4
Volterra *Italy* **40** E7
Voltri *Italy* **40** D5
Volturno → *Italy* **42** A6
Volvi, L. *Greece* **44** F7
Volyn □ *Ukraine* **33** G3
Volyně *Czech Rep.* **26** B6
Volzhsk *Russia* **34** C9
Volzhskiy *Russia* **35** F7
Vomo *Fiji* **91** a
Vondrozo *Madag.* **89** C8
Vonitsa *Greece* **46** C2
Vopnafjörður *Iceland* **8** D6
Vorarlberg □ *Austria* **26** D2
Voras Oros *Greece* **44** F5
Vorbasse *Denmark* **11** J3
Vorchdorf *Austria* **26** C6
Vorderrhein → *Switz.* **25** J5
Vordingborg *Denmark* **11** J5
Vorë *Albania* **44** E3
Voreio Aigaio □ *Greece* **47** C7
Voreppe *France* **21** C9
Vori *Greece* **46** F6
Vorios Evoikos Kolpos
  Greece **46** C5

Vorkuta *Russia* **52** C7
Vormsi *Estonia* **32** C2
Vorona → *Russia* **34** E6
Voronezh *Russia* **33** G10
Voronezh *Ukraine* **33** G7
Voronezh □ *Russia* **34** E4
Voronezh → *Russia* **33** G10
Vorontsovo-
  Aleksandrovskoye =
  Zelenokumsk *Russia* **35** H6
Vorpommersche
  Boddenlandschaft △
  Germany **24** A9
Vorskla → *Ukraine* **33** H8
Võrts Järv *Estonia* **32** C4
Võru *Estonia* **32** D4
Vosges *France* **19** D14
Vosges □ *France* **19** D13
Vosges du Nord △ *France* **19** D14
Voskopojë *Albania* **44** F4
Voskresensk *Russia* **32** E10
Voskresenskoye *Russia* **34** B7
Voss *Norway* **8** F12
Vostok *Antarctica* **5** D8
Vostok I. *Kiribati* **97** J12
Votice *Czech Rep.* **26** B7
Votsuri-Shima *Japan* **55** M1
Vouga → *Portugal* **36** E2
Vouillé *France* **18** F7
Vouxa, Akra *Greece* **49** D5
Vouzela *Portugal* **36** E2
Vouziers *France* **19** C11
Vovchansk *Ukraine* **33** G9
Vowchyn *Belarus* **31** F10
Voyageurs △ *U.S.A.* **112** A7
Voynitsa *Russia* **8** D24
Vozhe, Ozero *Russia* **32** B10
Vozhega *Russia* **32** B11
Voznesensk *Ukraine* **33** J6
Voznesenye *Russia* **32** B8
Vrå *Denmark* **11** G3
Vráble *Slovak Rep.* **27** C11
Vračevšnica *Serbia* **44** B4
Vrachneika *Greece* **46** C3
Vrancea □ *Romania* **29** E11
Vrancei, Munţii *Romania* **29** E11
Vrangelya, Ostrov *Russia* **53** B19
Vranica *Bos.-H.* **28** G2
Vranje *Serbia* **44** D5
Vranjska Banja *Serbia* **44** D6
Vranov nad Topľ'ou
  Slovak Rep. **27** C14
Vransko *Slovenia* **41** B11
Vransko Jezero *Croatia* **41** E12
Vrapčište *Macedonia* **44** E4
Vratsa *Bulgaria* **44** C7
Vrbas *Serbia* **28** E4
Vrbas → *Bos.-H.* **28** E2
Vrbnik *Croatia* **41** C11
Vrbovec *Croatia* **41** C13
Vrbovsko *Croatia* **41** C12
Vrchlabí *Czech Rep.* **26** A8
Vrede *S. Africa* **89** D4
Vredefort *S. Africa* **88** D4
Vreden *Germany* **24** C2
Vredenburg *S. Africa* **88** E2
Vredendal *S. Africa* **88** E2
Vretstorp *Sweden* **10** E8
Vrgorac *Croatia* **41** E14
Vrhnika *Slovenia* **41** C11
Vriddi *Ivory C.* **82** D4
Vrigstad *Sweden* **11** G8
Vrisses *Greece* **49** D6
Vrnograč *Bos.-H.* **41** C12
Vrondados *Greece* **47** C8
Vrpolje *Croatia* **28** E3
Vršac *Serbia* **28** E6
Vrsacki Kanal *Serbia* **28** E5
Vrútky *Slovak Rep.* **27** B11
Vryburg *S. Africa* **88** D3
Vryheid *S. Africa* **89** D5
Vsetín *Czech Rep.* **27** B11
Vu Liet *Vietnam* **64** C5
Vůcha → *Bulgaria* **45** D10
Vučitrn *Serbia* **44** D4
Vukovar *Croatia* **28** E3
Vulcan *Canada* **102** C6
Vulcan *Romania* **29** E8
Vulcăneşti *Moldova* **29** E13
Vulcano *Italy* **43** E7
Vůlchedruma *Bulgaria* **44** C7
Vulkaneshty = Vulcăneşti
  Moldova **29** E13
Vunduzi → *Mozam.* **87** F3
Vung Tau *Vietnam* **65** G6
Vunidawa *Fiji* **91** a
Vunisea *Fiji* **91** a
Vůrbitsa *Bulgaria* **45** D10
Vurshets *Bulgaria* **44** C7
Vutcani *Romania* **29** D12
Vuya *Sudan* **81** F2
Vuzlove *Ukraine* **28** B7
Vwaza △ *Malawi* **87** E3
Vyartsilya *Russia* **32** A6
Vyatka = Kirov *Russia* **52** D5
Vyatka → *Russia* **34** C10

Vyatskiye Polyany *Russia* **34** B10
Vyazemskiy *Russia* **53** E14
Vyazma *Russia* **32** E8
Vyazniki *Russia* **34** B6
Vyborg *Russia* **32** B5
Vychegda ⇥ *Russia* **52** C5
Vychodné Beskydy *Europe* **27** B15
Vyerkhnyadzvinsk *Belarus* **32** E4
Vyhoda *Ukraine* **29** B8
Vyksa *Russia* **34** C6
Vylkove *Ukraine* **29** E14
Vylok *Ukraine* **28** B7
Vynohradiv *Ukraine* **28** B8
Vyrnwy, L. *U.K.* **14** E4
Vyshkiv *Ukraine* **29** B8
Vyshkove *Ukraine* **29** B8
Vyshniy Volochek *Russia* **32** D8
Vyshzha = imeni 26
  Bakinskikh Komissarov
  Turkmenistan **71** B7
Vyškov *Czech Rep.* **27** B9
Vysokaye *Belarus* **31** F10
Vysoké Mýto *Czech Rep.* **27** B9
Vysokovsk *Russia* **32** D9
Vyšší Brod *Czech Rep.* **26** C7
Vytegra *Russia* **32** B9
Vyzhnytsya *Ukraine* **29** B10
Vyzhnytsya △ *Ukraine* **29** B10

W

W du Benin △ *Benin* **83** C5
W du Burkina Faso △
  Burkina Faso **83** C4
W du Niger △ *Niger* **83** C5
W.A.C. Bennett Dam
  Canada **102** B4
Wa *Ghana* **82** C4
Waal ⇥ *Neths.* **17** C5
Waalwijk *Neths.* **17** C5
Waat *Sudan* **81** F3
Wabakimi △ *Canada* **104** B2
Wabana *Canada* **105** C9
Wabasca ⇥ *Canada* **102** B5
Wabasca-Desmarais
  Canada **102** B6
Wabash *U.S.A.* **113** E11
Wabash ⇥ *U.S.A.* **112** G9
Wabi ⇥ *Ethiopia* **81** F5
Wabigoon L. *Canada* **103** D10
Wabowden *Canada* **103** C9
Wabu Hu *China* **59** A11
Wabuk Pt. *Canada* **104** A2
Wabush *Canada* **105** B6
Wąchock *Poland* **31** G8
Wächtersbach *Germany* **25** E5
Waco *U.S.A.* **116** F6
Waconichi, L. *Canada* **104** B5
Wad Ban Naqa *Sudan* **81** D3
Wad Banda *Sudan* **81** E2
Wad el Haddad *Sudan* **81** E3
Wad en Nau *Sudan* **81** E3
Wad Hamid *Sudan* **81** D3
Wad Medani *Sudan* **81** E3
Wad Thana *Pakistan* **68** F2
Wadai *Africa* **76** E5
Wadayama *Japan* **55** G7
Waddeneilanden *Neths.* **17** A5
Waddenzee *Neths.* **17** A5
Waddi, Chappal *Nigeria* **83** D7
Waddington *U.S.A.* **115** B9
Waddington, Mt. *Canada* **102** C3
Waddy Pt. *Australia* **95** C5
Wadebridge *U.K.* **15** G3
Wadena *Canada* **103** C8
Wadena *U.S.A.* **112** B6
Wädenswil *Switz.* **25** H4
Wadern *Germany* **25** F2
Wadeye *Australia* **92** B4
Wadhams *Canada* **102** C3
Wādī as Sīr *Jordan* **74** D4
Wâdi Gemâl *Egypt* **80** C4
Wadi Halfa *Sudan* **80** C3
Wadi Rum △ *Jordan* **74** F4
Wadian *China* **59** A9
Wadlew *Poland* **31** G6
Wadowice *Poland* **31** J6
Wadsworth *Nev., U.S.A.* **108** G4
Wadsworth *Ohio, U.S.A.* **114** E3
Waegwan *S. Korea* **57** G15
Wafangdian *China* **57** E11
Wafrah *Si. Arabia* **70** D5
Wageningen *Neths.* **17** C5
Wager B. *Canada* **101** C11
Wagga Wagga *Australia* **95** F4
Waghete *Indonesia* **63** E9
Wagin *Australia* **93** F2
Wagner *U.S.A.* **112** D4
Wagon Mound *U.S.A.* **109** H11
Wagoner *U.S.A.* **116** D7
Wągrowiec *Poland* **31** F4
Wah *Pakistan* **68** C5
Wahai *Indonesia* **63** E7
Wahiawā *U.S.A.* **106** b
Wāḩid *Egypt* **74** E1
Wahnai *Afghan.* **68** C1

Wahni *Ethiopia* **81** E4
Wahoo *U.S.A.* **112** E5
Wahpeton *U.S.A.* **112** B5
Waiau ⇥ *N.Z.* **91** E4
Waibeem *Indonesia* **63** E8
Waiblingen *Germany* **25** G5
Waidhofen an der Thaya
  Austria **26** C8
Waidhofen an der Ybbs
  Austria **26** D7
Waigeo *Indonesia* **63** E8
Waihi *N.Z.* **91** B5
Waihou ⇥ *N.Z.* **91** B5
Waika *Dem. Rep. of the Congo* **86** C2
Waikabubak *Indonesia* **63** F5
Waikaremoana, L. *N.Z.* **91** C6
Waikari *N.Z.* **91** E4
Waikato ⇥ *N.Z.* **91** B5
Waikerie *Australia* **95** E3
Waikokopu *N.Z.* **91** C6
Waikouaiti *N.Z.* **91** F3
Wailuku *U.S.A.* **106** b
Waimakariri ⇥ *N.Z.* **91** E4
Waimate *N.Z.* **91** F3
Wainganga ⇥ *India* **66** K11
Waingapu *Indonesia* **63** F6
Waini ⇥ *Guyana* **124** B7
Wainwright *Canada* **103** C6
Waiouru *N.Z.* **91** C6
Waipara *N.Z.* **91** E4
Waipawa *N.Z.* **91** C6
Waipiro *N.Z.* **91** C7
Waipoua Forest *N.Z.* **91** A4
Waipu *N.Z.* **91** A5
Waipukurau *N.Z.* **91** D6
Wairakei *N.Z.* **91** C6
Wairarapa, L. *N.Z.* **91** D5
Wairoa ⇥ *N.Z.* **91** C6
Waitaki ⇥ *N.Z.* **91** F3
Waitangi *N.Z.* **91** A5
Waitara *N.Z.* **91** C5
Waitomo Caves *N.Z.* **91** C5
Waitsburg *U.S.A.* **108** C4
Waiuku *N.Z.* **91** B5
Wajima *Japan* **55** F8
Wajir *Kenya* **86** B5
Waka *Ethiopia* **81** F4
Wakasa *Japan* **55** G7
Wakasa-Wan *Japan* **55** G7
Wakatipu, L. *N.Z.* **91** F2
Wakaw *Canada* **103** C7
Wakaya *Fiji* **91** a
Wakayama *Japan* **55** G7
Wakayama □ *Japan* **55** H7
Wake Forest *U.S.A.* **117** D15
Wake I. *Pac. Oc.* **96** F8
WaKeeney *U.S.A.* **112** C4
Wakefield *Jamaica* **120** a
Wakefield *N.Z.* **91** D4
Wakefield *U.K.* **14** D6
Wakefield *Mass., U.S.A.* **115** D13
Wakefield *Mich., U.S.A.* **112** B9
Wakkanai *Japan* **54** B10
Wakkerstroom *S. Africa* **89** D5
Wakool *Australia* **95** F3
Wakool ⇥ *Australia* **95** F3
Wakre *Indonesia* **63** E8
Wakuach, L. *Canada* **105** A6
Walamba *Zambia* **87** E2
Wałbrzych *Poland* **31** H3
Walcha *Australia* **95** E5
Walcheren *Neths.* **17** C3
Walcott *U.S.A.* **108** F10
Wałcz *Poland* **31** E3
Waldbröl *Germany* **24** E3
Waldburg Ra. *Australia* **93** D2
Waldeck *Germany* **24** D5
Walden *Colo., U.S.A.* **108** F10
Walden *N.Y., U.S.A.* **115** E10
Waldkirch *Germany* **25** G3
Waldkirchen *Germany* **25** G9
Waldkraiburg *Germany* **25** G8
Waldport *U.S.A.* **108** D1
Waldron *U.S.A.* **116** D7
Waldviertel *Austria* **26** C8
Walebing *Australia* **93** F2
Walembele *Ghana* **82** C4
Walensee *Switz.* **25** H5
Wales □ *U.K.* **15** E3
Walewale *Ghana* **83** C4
Walgett *Australia* **95** E4
Walgreen Coast *Antarctica* **5** D15
Walker *U.S.A.* **112** B6
Walker, L. *Canada* **105** B6
Walker L. *Canada* **103** C9
Walker L. *U.S.A.* **108** G4
Walkerston *Australia* **94** K7
Walkerton *Canada* **114** B3
Wall *U.S.A.* **112** C2
Walla Walla *U.S.A.* **108** C4
Wallace *Idaho, U.S.A.* **108** C6
Wallace *N.C., U.S.A.* **117** D16
Wallaceburg *Canada* **114** D2
Wallachia = Valahia
  Romania **29** F9
Wallal *Australia* **95** D4

Wallam Cr. ⇥ *Australia* **95** D4
Wallambin, L. *Australia* **93** F2
Wallangarra *Australia* **95** D5
Wallaroo *Australia* **95** E2
Walldürn *Germany* **25** F5
Wallenhorst *Germany* **24** C4
Wallenpaupack, L. *U.S.A.* **115** E9
Wallingford *U.S.A.* **115** E12
Wallis & Futuna, Is.
  Pac. Oc. **90** C11
Wallowa *U.S.A.* **108** D5
Wallowa Mts. *U.S.A.* **108** D5
Walls *U.K.* **13** A7
Walls of Jerusalem △
  Australia **95** G4
Wallula *U.S.A.* **108** C4
Wallumbilla *Australia* **95** D4
Walmsley L. *Canada* **103** A7
Walney, I. of *U.K.* **14** C4
Walnut Canyon △ *U.S.A.* **109** J8
Walnut Creek *U.S.A.* **110** H4
Walpole *Australia* **93** F2
Walpole *U.S.A.* **115** D13
Walpole-Nornalup △
  Australia **93** G2
Wals *Austria* **26** D5
Walsall *U.K.* **15** E6
Walsenburg *U.S.A.* **109** H11
Walsh *U.S.A.* **109** H11
Walsh ⇥ *Australia* **94** B3
Walsrode *Germany* **24** C5
Walter F. George Res.
  U.S.A. **117** F12
Walterboro *U.S.A.* **117** E14
Walters *U.S.A.* **116** D5
Waltershausen *Germany* **24** E6
Waltham *U.S.A.* **115** D13
Waltman *U.S.A.* **108** E10
Walton *U.S.A.* **115** D9
Walton-on-the-Naze *U.K.* **15** F9
Walvis Bay *Namibia* **88** C1
Walvisbaai = Walvis Bay
  Namibia **88** C1
Wamba *Dem. Rep. of the Congo* **86** B2
Wamba *Kenya* **86** B4
Wamba *Nigeria* **83** D6
Wamego *U.S.A.* **112** F5
Wamena *Indonesia* **63** E9
Wamsutter *U.S.A.* **108** F10
Wamulan *Indonesia* **63** E7
Wan Xian *China* **58** B5
Wana *Pakistan* **68** C3
Wanaaring *Australia* **95** D3
Wanaka *N.Z.* **91** F2
Wanaka, L. *N.Z.* **91** F2
Wan'an *China* **59** D10
Wanapitei L. *Canada* **104** C3
Wandel Sea = McKinley
  Sea *Arctic* **4** A7
Wandérama *Ivory C.* **82** D4
Wanderer *Zimbabwe* **87** F3
Wandhari *Pakistan* **68** F2
Wanding *China* **58** E2
Wandoan *Australia* **95** D4
Wang ⇥ *Thailand* **64** D2
Wang Kai *Sudan* **81** F2
Wang Noi *Thailand* **64** E3
Wang Saphung *Thailand* **64** D3
Wang Thong *Thailand* **64** D3
Wanga *Dem. Rep. of the Congo* **86** B2
Wangal *Indonesia* **63** F8
Wanganella *Australia* **95** F3
Wanganui *N.Z.* **91** C5
Wangaratta *Australia* **95** F4
Wangary *Australia* **95** E2
Wangcang *China* **58** A6
Wangcheng *China* **59** C9
Wangdu *China* **56** E8
Wangen *Germany* **25** H5
Wangerooge *Germany* **24** B3
Wangiwangi *Indonesia* **63** F6
Wangjiang *China* **59** B11
Wangmo *China* **58** E6
Wangolodougou *Ivory C.* **82** D3
Wangqing *China* **57** C15
Wankaner *India* **68** H4
Wanlaweyne = Uanle Uen
  Somali Rep. **75** G3
Wanless *Canada* **103** C8
Wanneroo *Australia* **93** F2
Wannian *China* **59** C11
Wanning *China* **64** C8
Wannoo Billabong
  Roadhouse *Australia* **93** E2
Wanon Niwat *Thailand* **64** D4
Wanquan *China* **56** D8
Wanrong *China* **56** G6
Wanshan *China* **58** D7
Wanshengchang *China* **58** C6
Wantage *U.K.* **15** F6
Wanxian *China* **58** B7
Wanyuan *China* **58** A7
Wanzai *China* **59** C10
Wapakoneta *U.S.A.* **113** E11
Wapato *U.S.A.* **108** C3
Wapawekka L. *Canada* **103** C8

Wapikopa L. *Canada* **104** B2
Wapiti ⇥ *Canada* **102** B5
Wappingers Falls *U.S.A.* **115** E11
Wapsipinicon ⇥ *U.S.A.* **112** E8
Wapusk △ *Canada* **103** B10
Warab □ *Sudan* **81** F2
Warangal *India* **66** L11
Waraseoni *India* **69** J9
Waratah *Australia* **95** G4
Waratah B. *Australia* **95** F4
Warburg *Germany* **24** D5
Warburton *Vic., Australia* **95** F4
Warburton *W. Austral.,*
  Australia **93** E4
Warburton ⇥ *Australia* **95** D2
Warburton Ra. *Australia* **93** E4
Ward *N.Z.* **91** D5
Ward ⇥ *Australia* **95** D4
Ward Mt. *U.S.A.* **110** H8
Warden *S. Africa* **89** D4
Wardha *India* **66** J11
Wardha ⇥ *India* **66** K11
Ware *Canada* **102** B3
Ware *U.S.A.* **115** D12
Waregem *Belgium* **17** D3
Wareham *U.S.A.* **115** E14
Waremme *Belgium* **17** D5
Waren *Germany* **24** B8
Warendorf *Germany* **24** D4
Warialda *Australia* **95** D5
Wariap *Indonesia* **63** E8
Warin Chamrap *Thailand* **64** E5
Warka *Poland* **31** G8
Warkopi *Indonesia* **63** E8
Warm Springs *U.S.A.* **109** G5
Warman *Canada* **103** C7
Warmbad = Bela Bela
  S. Africa **89** C4
Warmbad *Namibia* **88** D2
Warmiński-Mazurskie □
  Poland **30** D8
Warminster *U.K.* **15** F5
Warminster *U.S.A.* **115** F9
Warmun *Australia* **92** C4
Warnemünde *Germany* **24** A8
Warner Mts. *U.S.A.* **108** F3
Warner Robins *U.S.A.* **117** E13
Warnow ⇥ *Germany* **24** A8
Waroona *Australia* **93** F2
Warracknabeal *Australia* **95** F3
Warragul *Australia* **95** F4
Warrego ⇥ *Australia* **95** E4
Warrego Ra. *Australia* **94** C4
Warren *Australia* **95** E4
Warren *Ark., U.S.A.* **116** E8
Warren *Mich., U.S.A.* **113** D12
Warren *Minn., U.S.A.* **112** A5
Warren *Ohio, U.S.A.* **114** E4
Warren *Pa., U.S.A.* **114** E5
Warrenpoint *U.K.* **12** B5
Warrensburg *Mo., U.S.A.* **112** F7
Warrensburg *N.Y., U.S.A.* **115** C11
Warrenton *S. Africa* **88** D3
Warrenton *U.S.A.* **110** D3
Warri *Nigeria* **83** D6
Warrina *Australia* **95** D2
Warrington *U.K.* **14** D5
Warrington *U.S.A.* **117** F11
Warrington □ *U.K.* **14** D5
Warrnambool *Australia* **95** F3
Warroad *U.S.A.* **112** A6
Warruwi *Australia* **94** A1
Warsa *Indonesia* **63** E9
Warsak Dam *Pakistan* **68** B4
Warsaw = Warszawa *Poland* **31** F8
Warsaw *Ind., U.S.A.* **113** E11
Warsaw *N.Y., U.S.A.* **114** D6
Warsaw *Ohio, U.S.A.* **114** F3
Warstein *Germany* **24** D4
Warszawa *Poland* **31** F8
Warszawa × (WAW) *Poland* **31** F7
Warta *Poland* **31** G5
Warta ⇥ *Poland* **31** F1
Warthe = Warta *Poland* **31** F1
Waru *Indonesia* **63** E8
Warwick *Australia* **95** D5
Warwick *U.K.* **15** E6
Warwick *N.Y., U.S.A.* **115** E10
Warwick *R.I., U.S.A.* **115** E13
Warwickshire □ *U.K.* **15** E6
Wasaga Beach *Canada* **114** B4
Wasagaming *Canada* **103** C9
Wasatch Ra. *U.S.A.* **108** F8
Wasbank *S. Africa* **89** D5
Wasco *Calif., U.S.A.* **111** K7
Wasco *Oreg., U.S.A.* **108** D3
Waseca *U.S.A.* **112** C7
Wasekamio L. *Canada* **103** B7
Wash, The *U.K.* **15** E8
Washago *Canada* **114** B5
Washburn *N. Dak., U.S.A.* **112** B3
Washburn *Wis., U.S.A.* **112** B8
Washim *India* **66** J10
Washington *U.K.* **14** C6
Washington *D.C., U.S.A.* **113** F15

Washington *Ga., U.S.A.* **117** E13
Washington *Ind., U.S.A.* **112** F10
Washington *Iowa, U.S.A.* **112** E8
Washington *Mo., U.S.A.* **112** F8
Washington *N.C., U.S.A.* **117** D16
Washington *N.J., U.S.A.* **115** F10
Washington *Pa., U.S.A.* **114** F4
Washington *Utah, U.S.A.* **109** H7
Washington □ *U.S.A.* **108** C3
Washington, Mt. *U.S.A.* **115** B13
Washington Court House
  U.S.A. **113** F12
Washington I. *U.S.A.* **112** C10
Washougal *U.S.A.* **110** E4
Washpool △ *Australia* **95** D5
Wasian *Indonesia* **63** E8
Wasilków *Poland* **31** E10
Wasilla *U.S.A.* **100** C5
Wasior *Indonesia* **63** E8
Wāsiṭ □ *Iraq* **73** F11
Waskaganish *Canada* **104** B4
Waskaiowana L. *Canada* **103** B9
Waskesiu Lake *Canada* **103** C7
Wasserburg *Germany* **25** G8
Wasserkuppe *Germany* **24** E5
Wassy *France* **19** D11
Waswanipi *Canada* **104** C4
Waswanipi, L. *Canada* **104** C4
Watampone *Indonesia* **63** E6
Watamu *Kenya* **86** C5
Watarrka △ *Australia* **92** D5
Water Park Pt. *Australia* **94** C5
Water Valley *U.S.A.* **117** D10
Waterberg Plateau △
  Namibia **88** C2
Waterberge *S. Africa* **89** C4
Waterbury *Conn., U.S.A.* **115** E11
Waterbury *Vt., U.S.A.* **115** B12
Waterbury L. *Canada* **103** B8
Waterdown *Canada* **114** C5
Waterford *Canada* **114** D4
Waterford *Ireland* **12** D4
Waterford *Calif., U.S.A.* **110** H6
Waterford *Mass., U.S.A.* **114** E5
Waterford □ *Ireland* **12** D4
Waterford Harbour *Ireland* **12** D5
Waterhen L. *Canada* **103** C9
Waterloo *Belgium* **17** D4
Waterloo *Ont., Canada* **114** C4
Waterloo *Qué., Canada* **115** A12
Waterloo *S. Leone* **82** D2
Waterloo *Ill., U.S.A.* **112** F8
Waterloo *Iowa, U.S.A.* **112** D7
Waterloo *N.Y., U.S.A.* **114** D8
Watermeet *U.S.A.* **112** B9
Waterton Lakes △ *Canada* **102** D6
Watertown *Conn., U.S.A.* **115** E11
Watertown *N.Y., U.S.A.* **115** C9
Watertown *S. Dak., U.S.A.* **112** C5
Watertown *Wis., U.S.A.* **112** D9
Waterval-Boven *S. Africa* **89** D5
Waterville *Canada* **115** A13
Waterville *Maine, U.S.A.* **113** C19
Waterville *N.Y., U.S.A.* **115** D9
Waterville *Pa., U.S.A.* **114** E7
Waterville *Wash., U.S.A.* **108** C3
Watervliet *U.S.A.* **115** D11
Wates *Indonesia* **63** G14
Watford *Canada* **114** D3
Watford *U.K.* **15** F7
Watford City *U.S.A.* **112** B2
Wathaman ⇥ *Canada* **103** B8
Wathaman L. *Canada* **103** B8
Watheroo *Australia* **93** F2
Watheroo △ *Australia* **93** F2
Wating *China* **56** G4
Watkins Glen *U.S.A.* **114** D8
Watling I. = San Salvador
  I. *Bahamas* **121** B5
Watonga *U.S.A.* **116** D5
Watrous *Canada* **103** C7
Watrous *U.S.A.* **109** J11
Watsa *Dem. Rep. of the Congo* **86** B2
Watseka *U.S.A.* **112** E10
Watson *Canada* **103** C8
Watson Lake *Canada* **102** A3
Watsontown *U.S.A.* **114** E8
Watsonville *U.S.A.* **110** J5
Wattiwarriganna Cr. ⇥
  Australia **95** D2
Wattwil *Switz.* **25** H5
Watuata = Batuata *Indonesia* **63** F6
Watubela, Kepulauan
  Indonesia **63** E8
Watubela Is. = Watubela,
  Kepulauan *Indonesia* **63** E8
Wau = Wâw *Sudan* **81** F2
Waubamik *Canada* **114** A4
Waubay *U.S.A.* **112** C5
Wauchope *N.S.W., Australia* **95** E5
Wauchope *N. Terr., Australia* **94** C1
Wauchula *U.S.A.* **117** H14
Waukarlycarly, L. *Australia* **92** D3
Waukegan *U.S.A.* **112** D10
Waukesha *U.S.A.* **112** D9
Waukon *U.S.A.* **112** D8
Waupaca *U.S.A.* **112** C9

Waupun *U.S.A.* **112** D9
Waurika *U.S.A.* **116** D6
Wausau *U.S.A.* **112** C9
Wautoma *U.S.A.* **112** C9
Wauwatosa *U.S.A.* **112** D9
Waveney ⇥ *U.K.* **15** E9
Waverley *N.Z.* **91** C5
Waverly *Iowa, U.S.A.* **112** D7
Waverly *N.Y., U.S.A.* **115** E8
Wavre *Belgium* **17** D4
Wâw *Sudan* **81** F2
Wâw al Kabīr *Libya* **79** C9
Wawa *Canada* **104** C3
Wawa *Nigeria* **83** D5
Wawa *Sudan* **80** C3
Wawanesa *Canada* **103** D9
Wawona *U.S.A.* **110** H7
Waxahachie *U.S.A.* **116** E6
Way, L. *Australia* **93** E3
Waya *Fiji* **91** a
Waycross *U.S.A.* **117** F13
Wayi *Sudan* **81** F3
Wayland *U.S.A.* **114** D7
Wayne *Nebr., U.S.A.* **112** D5
Wayne *W. Va., U.S.A.* **113** F12
Waynesboro *Ga., U.S.A.* **117** E13
Waynesboro *Miss., U.S.A.* **117** F10
Waynesboro *Pa., U.S.A.* **113** F15
Waynesboro *Va., U.S.A.* **113** F14
Waynesburg *U.S.A.* **113** F13
Waynesville *U.S.A.* **117** D13
Waynoka *U.S.A.* **116** D5
Wazirabad *Pakistan* **68** C6
Wda ⇥ *Poland* **30** E5
We *Indonesia* **62** C1
Weald, The *U.K.* **15** F8
Wear ⇥ *U.K.* **14** C6
Weatherford *Okla., U.S.A.* **116** D5
Weatherford *Tex., U.S.A.* **116** E6
Weaverville *U.S.A.* **108** F2
Webb City *U.S.A.* **112** G6
Webequie *Canada* **104** B2
Webo = Nyaake *Liberia* **82** E3
Webster *Mass., U.S.A.* **115** D13
Webster *N.Y., U.S.A.* **114** C7
Webster *S. Dak., U.S.A.* **112** C5
Webster *Wis., U.S.A.* **112** D7
Webster Springs *U.S.A.* **113** F13
Weda *Indonesia* **63** D7
Weda, Teluk *Indonesia* **63** D7
Weddell Abyssal Plain
  S. Ocean **5** C2
Weddell I. *Falk. Is.* **128** G4
Weddell Sea *Antarctica* **5** D1
Wedderburn *Australia* **95** F3
Wedel *Germany* **24** B5
Wedemark *Germany* **24** C5
Wedgeport *Canada* **105** D6
Wedza *Zimbabwe* **87** F3
Wee Waa *Australia* **95** E4
Weed *U.S.A.* **108** F2
Weed Heights *U.S.A.* **110** G7
Weedsport *U.S.A.* **115** C8
Weedville *U.S.A.* **114** E6
Weenen *S. Africa* **89** D5
Weener *Germany* **24** B3
Weert *Neths.* **17** C5
Węgierska-Górka *Poland* **31** J6
Węgliniec *Poland* **31** G2
Węgorzewo *Poland* **30** D8
Węgorzyno *Poland* **30** E2
Węgrów *Poland* **31** F9
Wehda □ *Sudan* **81** F3
Wei He ⇥ *Hebei, China* **56** F8
Wei He ⇥ *Shaanxi, China* **56** G6
Weichang *China* **57** D9
Weichuan *China* **56** G7
Weida *Germany* **24** E8
Weiden *Germany* **25** F8
Weifang *China* **57** F10
Weihai *China* **57** F12
Weil *Germany* **25** H3
Weilburg *Germany* **24** E4
Weilheim *Germany* **25** H7
Weimar *Germany* **24** E7
Weinan *China* **56** G5
Weingarten *Germany* **25** F4
Weinheim *Germany* **25** F4
Weining *China* **58** D5
Weipa *Australia* **94** A3
Weir ⇥ *Australia* **95** D4
Weir ⇥ *Canada* **103** B10
Weir River *Canada* **103** B10
Weirton *U.S.A.* **114** F4
Weiser *U.S.A.* **108** D5
Weishan *Shandong, China* **57** G9
Weishan *Yunnan, China* **58** E3
Weissenburg *Germany* **25** F6
Weissenfels *Germany* **24** D7
Weisswasser *Germany* **24** D10
Weitra *Austria* **26** C7
Weixi *China* **58** D2
Weixin *China* **58** D5
Weiyuan *China* **58** D5
Weiz *Austria* **26** D8
Weizhou Dao *China* **58** G7
Wejherowo *Poland* **30** D5

Wekusko L. *Canada* **103** C9
Welch *U.S.A.* **113** G13
Weldya *Ethiopia* **81** E4
Welega *Ethiopia* **81** F3
Welford △ *Australia* **94** D3
Welkite *Ethiopia* **81** F4
Welkom *S. Africa* **88** D4
Welland *Canada* **114** D5
Welland ➤ *U.K.* **15** E7
Wellesley Is. *Australia* **94** B2
Wellingborough *U.K.* **15** E7
Wellington *Australia* **95** E4
Wellington *Canada* **114** C7
Wellington *N.Z.* **91** D5
Wellington *S. Africa* **88** E2
Wellington *Somst., U.K.* **15** G4
Wellington *Telford & Wrekin,*
 U.K. **15** E5
Wellington *Colo., U.S.A.* **108** F11
Wellington *Kans., U.S.A.* **112** G5
Wellington *Nev., U.S.A.* **110** G7
Wellington *Ohio, U.S.A.* **112** E2
Wellington *Tex., U.S.A.* **116** D4
Wellington, I. *Chile* **128** F2
Wellington, L. *Australia* **95** F4
Wellington Chan. *Canada* **101** B10
Wells *U.K.* **15** F5
Wells *Maine, U.S.A.* **115** C14
Wells *N.Y., U.S.A.* **115** C10
Wells *Nev., U.S.A.* **108** F6
Wells, L. *Australia* **93** E3
Wells, Mt. *Australia* **92** C4
Wells Gray △ *Canada* **102** C4
Wells-next-the-Sea *U.K.* **14** E8
Wells River *U.S.A.* **115** B12
Wellsboro *U.S.A.* **114** E7
Wellsburg *U.S.A.* **114** F4
Wellsville *N.Y., U.S.A.* **114** D7
Wellsville *Ohio, U.S.A.* **114** F4
Wellsville *Utah, U.S.A.* **108** F8
Wellton *U.S.A.* **109** K6
Welmel, Wabi ➤ *Ethiopia* **81** F5
Welo *Ethiopia* **81** E4
Wels *Austria* **26** C7
Welshpool *U.K.* **15** E4
Wem *U.K.* **14** E5
Wembere ➤ *Tanzania* **86** C3
Wemindji *Canada* **104** B4
Wen Xian *China* **56** G7
Wenatchee *U.S.A.* **108** C3
Wenchang *China* **64** C8
Wencheng *China* **59** D13
Wenchi *Ghana* **82** D4
Wenchow = Wenzhou
 China **59** D13
Wenchuan *China* **58** B4
Wenden *U.S.A.* **111** M13
Wendeng *China* **57** F12
Wendesi *Indonesia* **63** E8
Wendo *Ethiopia* **81** F4
Wendover *U.S.A.* **108** F6
Weng'an *China* **58** D6
Wengcheng *China* **59** E9
Wengen *Switz.* **19** F14
Wengyuan *China* **59** E10
Wenling *China* **59** C13
Wenlock ➤ *Australia* **94** A3
Wenshan *China* **58** F5
Wenshang *China* **56** G9
Wenshui *China* **56** F7
Wensleydale *U.K.* **14** C6
Wensu *China* **60** B3
Wensum ➤ *U.K.* **14** E8
Wentworth *Australia* **95** E3
Wentzel L. *Canada* **102** B6
Wenut *Indonesia* **63** E8
Wenxi *China* **56** G6
Wenxian *China* **56** H3
Wenzhou *China* **59** D13
Weott *U.S.A.* **108** F2
Wepener *S. Africa* **88** D4
Werda *Botswana* **88** D3
Werdau *Germany* **24** E8
Werder *Germany* **24** C8
Werdohl *Germany* **24** D3
Wereilu *Ethiopia* **81** E4
Weri *Indonesia* **63** E8
Werneck *Germany* **25** F6
Wernigerode *Germany* **24** D6
Werra ➤ *Germany* **24** D5
Werrimull *Australia* **95** E3
Werris Creek *Australia* **95** E5
Wertach ➤ *Germany* **25** G6
Wertheim *Germany* **25** F5
Wertingen *Germany* **25** G6
Wesel *Germany* **24** D2
Weser ➤ *Germany* **24** B4
Weser-Ems □ *Germany* **24** C3
Weserbergland *Germany* **24** C5
Weserbergland
 Schaumburg Hameln △
 Germany **24** C5
Wesiri *Indonesia* **63** F7
Weslaco *U.S.A.* **116** H6
Weslemkoon L. *Canada* **114** A7

Wesleyville *U.S.A.* **114** D4
Wessel, C. *Australia* **94** A2
Wessel Is. *Australia* **94** A2
Wesselburen *Germany* **24** A4
Wessington Springs *U.S.A.* **112** C4
West *U.S.A.* **116** F6
West Allis *U.S.A.* **112** D9
West ➤ *U.S.A.* **115** D12
West Antarctica *Antarctica* **5** D15
West Baines ➤ *Australia* **92** C4
West Bank ■ *Asia* **74** C4
West Bend *U.S.A.* **112** D9
West Bengal □ *India* **69** H13
West Berkshire □ *U.K.* **15** F6
West Beskids = Západné
 Beskydy *Europe* **27** B12
West Branch *U.S.A.* **113** C11
West Branch
 Susquehanna ➤ *U.S.A.* **115** F8
West Bromwich *U.K.* **15** E6
West Burra *U.K.* **13** A7
West Canada Cr. ➤ *U.S.A.*
 115 C10
West Caroline Basin *Pac. Oc.* **96** G5
West Chazy *U.S.A.* **115** B11
West Chester *U.S.A.* **115** G9
West Coast △ *Namibia* **88** C1
West Coast △ *S. Africa* **88** E2
West Columbia *U.S.A.* **116** G7
West Covina *U.S.A.* **111** L9
West Des Moines *U.S.A.* **112** E7
West Dunbartonshire □
 U.K. **13** F4
West End *Bahamas* **120** A4
West Falkland *Falk. Is.* **128** G4
West Fargo *U.S.A.* **112** B5
West Farmington *U.S.A.* **114** E4
West Fiji Basin *Pac. Oc.* **96** J9
West Fjord = Vestfjorden
 Norway **8** C16
West Fork Trinity ➤
 U.S.A. **116** E6
West Frankfort *U.S.A.* **112** G9
West Grand L. *U.S.A.* **113** C20
West Hartford *U.S.A.* **115** E12
West Haven *U.S.A.* **115** E12
West Hazleton *U.S.A.* **115** F9
West Helena *U.S.A.* **117** D9
West Hurley *U.S.A.* **115** E10
West Ice Shelf *Antarctica* **5** C7
West Indies *Cent. Amer.* **121** D7
West Jordan *U.S.A.* **108** F8
West Linn *U.S.A.* **110** E4
West Lorne *Canada* **114** D3
West Lothian □ *U.K.* **13** F5
West Lunga ➤ *Zambia* **87** E1
West MacDonnell △
 Australia **92** D5
West Mariana Basin *Pac. Oc.* **96** F5
West Memphis *U.S.A.* **117** D9
West Midlands □ *U.K.* **15** E6
West Mifflin *U.S.A.* **114** F5
West Milford *U.S.A.* **115** E10
West Milton *U.S.A.* **114** E8
West Monroe *U.S.A.* **116** E8
West Newton *U.S.A.* **114** F5
West Nicholson *Zimbabwe* **87** G2
West Odessa *U.S.A.* **116** F3
West Palm Beach *U.S.A.* **117** H14
West Plains *U.S.A.* **112** G8
West Point *Miss., U.S.A.* **117** E10
West Point *N.Y., U.S.A.* **115** E11
West Point *Nebr., U.S.A.* **112** E5
West Point *Va., U.S.A.* **113** G15
West Point L. *U.S.A.* **117** E12
West Pt. = Ouest, Pte. de l'
 Canada **105** C7
West Pt. *Australia* **95** F2
West Road ➤ *Canada* **102** C4
West Rutland *U.S.A.* **115** C11
West Schelde =
 Westerschelde ➤ *Neths.* **17** C3
West Seneca *U.S.A.* **114** D6
West Siberian Plain *Russia* **50** B9
West Sussex □ *U.K.* **15** G7
West-Terschelling *Neths.* **17** A5
West Valley City *U.S.A.* **108** F8
West Virginia □ *U.S.A.* **113** F13
West-Vlaanderen □ *Belgium* **17** D2
West Walker ➤ *U.S.A.* **110** G7
West Wyalong *Australia* **95** E4
West Yellowstone *U.S.A.* **108** D8
West Yorkshire □ *U.K.* **14** D6
Westall, Pt. *Australia* **95** E1
Westbrook *U.S.A.* **113** D18
Westbury *Australia* **95** G4
Westby *U.S.A.* **108** B11
Westend *U.S.A.* **111** K9
Westerland *Germany* **24** A4
Westerly *U.S.A.* **115** E13
Western □ *Ghana* **82** D4
Western □ *Kenya* **86** B3
Western □ *S. Leone* **82** D2
Western □ *Zambia* **87** F1
Western Australia □
 Australia **93** E2
Western Cape □ *S. Africa* **88** E3

Western Dvina =
 Daugava ➤ *Latvia* **32** D3
Western Ghats *India* **66** N9
Western Isles □ *U.K.* **13** D1
Western Sahara ■ *Africa* **78** D3
Western Samoa =
 Samoa ■ *Pac. Oc.* **91** b
Western Sierra Madre =
 Madre Occidental,
 Sierra *Mexico* **118** B3
Westernport *U.S.A.* **113** F14
Westerschelde ➤ *Neths.* **17** C3
Westerstede *Germany* **24** B3
Westerwald *Germany* **24** E3
Westfield *Mass., U.S.A.* **115** D12
Westfield *N.Y., U.S.A.* **114** D5
Westfield *Pa., U.S.A.* **114** E7
Westhill *U.K.* **13** D6
Westhope *U.S.A.* **112** A3
Westland △ *N.Z.* **91** E2
Westland Bight *N.Z.* **91** E3
Westlock *Canada* **102** C6
Westmar *Australia* **95** D4
Westmeath □ *Ireland* **12** C4
Westminster *Calif., U.S.A.* **111** M8
Westminster *Colo., U.S.A.* **108** G11
Westminster *Md., U.S.A.* **113** F15
Westmont *U.S.A.* **114** F6
Westmoreland *Barbados* **121** g
Westmorland *U.S.A.* **111** M11
Weston *Oreg., U.S.A.* **108** D4
Weston *W. Va., U.S.A.* **113** F13
Weston I. *Canada* **104** B4
Weston-super-Mare *U.K.* **15** F5
Westover *U.S.A.* **114** F6
Westport *Canada* **115** B8
Westport *Ireland* **12** C2
Westport *N.Z.* **91** D3
Westport *N.Y., U.S.A.* **115** B11
Westport *Oreg., U.S.A.* **110** D3
Westport *Wash., U.S.A.* **110** D2
Westray *Canada* **103** C8
Westray *U.K.* **13** B5
Westree *Canada* **104** C3
Westville *U.S.A.* **110** F6
Westwood *U.S.A.* **108** F3
Wetar *Indonesia* **63** F7
Wetherby *U.K.* **14** D6
Wethersfield *U.S.A.* **115** E12
Wetteren *Belgium* **17** D3
Wetzlar *Germany* **24** E4
Wewoka *U.S.A.* **116** D6
Wexford *Ireland* **12** D5
Wexford □ *Ireland* **12** D5
Wexford Harbour *Ireland* **12** D5
Weyburn *Canada* **103** D8
Weyer Markt *Austria* **26** D7
Weyhe *Germany* **24** C4
Weyib ➤ *Ethiopia* **81** F5
Weymouth *Canada* **105** D6
Weymouth *U.K.* **15** G5
Weymouth *U.S.A.* **115** D14
Weymouth, C. *Australia* **94** A3
Wha Ti *Canada* **100** C8
Whakaari = White I. *N.Z.* **91** B6
Whakatane *N.Z.* **91** B6
Whale ➤ *Canada* **105** A6
Whale Cove *Canada* **103** A10
Whales, B. of *Antarctica* **5** D12
Whalsay *U.K.* **13** A8
Whangamata *N.Z.* **91** B5
Whangamomona *N.Z.* **91** C5
Whanganui △ *N.Z.* **91** C5
Whangarei *N.Z.* **91** A5
Whangarei Harb. *N.Z.* **91** A5
Wharekauri = Chatham
 Is. *Pac. Oc.* **96** M10
Wharfe ➤ *U.K.* **14** D6
Wharfedale *U.K.* **14** C5
Wharton *N.J., U.S.A.* **115** F10
Wharton *Pa., U.S.A.* **114** E6
Wharton *Tex., U.S.A.* **116** G6
Wharton Basin *Ind. Oc.* **96** J2
Wheatland *Calif., U.S.A.* **110** F5
Wheatland *Wyo., U.S.A.* **108** E11
Wheatley *Canada* **114** D2
Wheaton *Md., U.S.A.* **113** F15
Wheaton *Minn., U.S.A.* **112** C5
Wheelbarrow Pk. *U.S.A.* **110** H10
Wheeler *Oreg., U.S.A.* **108** D2
Wheeler *Tex., U.S.A.* **116** D4
Wheeler ➤ *Canada* **105** A6
Wheeler L. *U.S.A.* **117** D11
Wheeler Pk. *N. Mex., U.S.A.*
 109 H11
Wheeler Pk. *Nev., U.S.A.* **108** G6
Wheeler Ridge *U.S.A.* **111** L8
Wheelersburg *U.S.A.* **113** F12
Wheeling *U.S.A.* **114** F4
Whernside *U.K.* **14** C5
Whiddy I. *Ireland* **12** E2
Whiskey Jack L. *Canada* **103** B8
Whiskeytown-Shasta-
 Trinity △ *U.S.A.* **108** F2
Whistleduck Cr. ➤ *Australia* **94** C2

Whistler *Canada* **102** C4
Whitby *Canada* **114** C6
Whitby *U.K.* **14** C7
White ➤ *Ark., U.S.A.* **116** E9
White ➤ *Ind., U.S.A.* **112** F10
White ➤ *S. Dak., U.S.A.* **112** D4
White ➤ *Tex., U.S.A.* **116** E4
White ➤ *Utah, U.S.A.* **108** F9
White ➤ *Vt., U.S.A.* **115** C12
White ➤ *Wash., U.S.A.* **110** C4
White, L. *Australia* **92** D4
White B. *Canada* **105** C8
White Bird *U.S.A.* **108** D5
White Butte *U.S.A.* **112** B2
White City *U.S.A.* **108** E2
White Cliffs *Australia* **95** E3
White Hall *U.S.A.* **112** F8
White Haven *U.S.A.* **115** E9
White Horse, Vale of *U.K.* **15** F6
White I. *N.Z.* **91** B6
White L. *Canada* **115** A8
White L. *U.S.A.* **116** G8
White Mountain Peak
 U.S.A. **109** H4
White Mts. *Calif., U.S.A.* **110** H8
White Mts. *N.H., U.S.A.* **115** B13
White Mts. △ *Australia* **94** C4
White Nile = Nîl el
 Abyad ➤ *Sudan* **81** D3
White Nile Dam =
 Khazzân Jabal al Awliyâ
 Sudan **81** D3
White Otter L. *Canada* **104** C1
White Pass *U.S.A.* **110** D5
White Plains *U.S.A.* **115** E11
White River *Canada* **104** C2
White River *S. Africa* **89** D5
White River *U.S.A.* **112** D3
White Rock *Canada* **110** A4
White Rock *U.S.A.* **109** J10
White Russia = Belarus ■
 Europe **23** B14
White Sands △ *U.S.A.* **109** K10
White Sea = Beloye More
 Russia **8** C25
White Sulphur Springs
 Mont., U.S.A. **108** C8
White Sulphur Springs
 W. Va., U.S.A. **113** G13
White Swan *U.S.A.* **110** D6
White Volta ➤ *Ghana* **83** D4
Whitecliffs *N.Z.* **91** E3
Whitecourt *Canada* **102** C5
Whiteface Mt. *U.S.A.* **115** B11
Whitefield *U.S.A.* **115** B13
Whitefish *U.S.A.* **108** B6
Whitefish B. *U.S.A.* **104** C3
Whitefish L. *Canada* **103** A7
Whitefish Pt. *U.S.A.* **113** B11
Whitegull, L. = Goélands,
 L. aux *Canada* **105** A7
Whitehall *Mich., U.S.A.* **112** D10
Whitehall *Mont., U.S.A.* **108** D7
Whitehall *N.Y., U.S.A.* **115** C11
Whitehall *Wis., U.S.A.* **112** C8
Whitehaven *U.K.* **14** C4
Whitehorse *Canada* **102** A1
Whitemark *Australia* **95** G4
Whiteplains *Liberia* **82** D2
Whiteriver *U.S.A.* **109** K9
Whitesand ➤ *Canada* **102** A5
Whitesands △ *S. Africa* **88** E3
Whitesboro *N.Y., U.S.A.* **115** C9
Whitesboro *Tex., U.S.A.* **116** E6
Whiteshell △ *Canada* **103** D9
Whitesville *U.S.A.* **114** D7
Whiteville *U.S.A.* **117** D15
Whitewater *U.S.A.* **112** D9
Whitewater Baldy *U.S.A.* **109** K9
Whitewater L. *Canada* **104** B2
Whitewood *Australia* **94** C3
Whitewood *Canada* **103** C8
Whithorn *U.K.* **13** G4
Whitianga *N.Z.* **91** B5
Whitman *U.S.A.* **115** D14
Whitney *Canada* **114** A6
Whitney, Mt. *U.S.A.* **110** J8
Whitney Point *U.S.A.* **115** D9
Whitstable *U.K.* **15** F9
Whitsunday I. *Australia* **94** J7
Whitsunday Islands △
 Australia **94** J6
Whitsunday Passage
 Australia **94** J6
Whittier *U.S.A.* **111** M8
Whittlesea *Australia* **95** F4
Wholdaia L. *Canada* **103** A8
Whyalla *Australia* **95** E2
Wiang Kosai △ *Thailand* **64** D2
Wiarton *Canada* **114** B3
Wiawso *Ghana* **82** D4
Wiay *U.K.* **13** D1
Wiązów *Poland* **31** H4
Wibaux *U.S.A.* **108** C11
Wichian Buri *Thailand* **64** E3
Wichita *U.S.A.* **112** G5
Wichita Falls *U.S.A.* **116** E5

Wick *U.K.* **13** C5
Wicked Pt. *Canada* **114** C7
Wickenburg *U.S.A.* **109** K7
Wickepin *Australia* **93** F2
Wickham *Australia* **92** D2
Wickham, C. *Australia* **95** F3
Wickliffe *U.S.A.* **114** E3
Wicklow *Ireland* **12** D5
Wicklow □ *Ireland* **12** D5
Wicklow Hd. *Ireland* **12** D6
Wicklow Mts. *Ireland* **12** C5
Wicklow Mts. △ *Ireland* **12** C5
Widawa *Poland* **31** G5
Widawka ➤ *Poland* **31** G5
Widgeegoara Cr. ➤
 Australia **95** D4
Widgiemooltha *Australia* **93** F3
Widnes *U.K.* **14** D5
Więcbork *Poland* **31** E4
Wiehengebirge =
 Nördlicher Teutoburger
 Wald-Wiehengebirge △
 Germany **24** C4
Wiehl *Germany* **24** E3
Wiek *Germany* **24** A9
Wielbark *Poland* **30** E7
Wieleń *Poland* **31** F3
Wielichowo *Poland* **31** F3
Wieliczka *Poland* **31** J7
Wielkopolski △ *Poland* **31** F3
Wielkopolskie □ *Poland* **31** F4
Wieluń *Poland* **31** G5
Wien *Austria* **27** C9
Wien-Schwechat ✈ (VIE)
 Austria **27** C9
Wiener Neustadt *Austria* **27** D9
Wieprz ➤ *Poland* **31** G8
Wieprza ➤ *Poland* **30** D3
Wieruszów *Poland* **31** G5
Wiesbaden *Germany* **25** E4
Wiesental *Germany* **25** F4
Wiesloch *Germany* **25** F4
Wiesmoor *Germany* **24** B3
Wieżyca *Poland* **30** D5
Wigan *U.K.* **14** D5
Wiggins *Colo., U.S.A.* **108** F11
Wiggins *Miss., U.S.A.* **117** F10
Wight, I. of *U.K.* **15** G6
Wigierski △ *Poland* **30** D10
Wigry, Jezioro *Poland* **30** D10
Wigston *U.K.* **15** E6
Wigton *U.K.* **14** C4
Wigtown *U.K.* **13** G4
Wigtown B. *U.K.* **13** G4
Wil *Switz.* **25** H5
Wilamowice *Poland* **31** J6
Wilber *U.S.A.* **112** E5
Wilberforce *Canada* **114** A6
Wilberforce, C. *Australia* **94** A2
Wilburton *U.S.A.* **116** D7
Wilcannia *Australia* **95** E3
Wilcox *U.S.A.* **114** E6
Wildbad *Germany* **25** G4
Wildeshausen *Germany* **24** C4
Wildeshauser Geest △
 Germany **24** C4
Wildon *Austria* **26** E8
Wildrose *U.S.A.* **111** J9
Wildspitze *Austria* **26** E3
Wilga ➤ *Poland* **31** G8
Wilge ➤ *S. Africa* **89** D4
Wilhelm II Coast *Antarctica* **5** C7
Wilhelmsburg *Austria* **26** C8
Wilhelmshaven *Germany* **24** B4
Wilhelmstal *Namibia* **88** C2
Wilkes-Barre *U.S.A.* **115** E9
Wilkes Land *Antarctica* **5** D9
Wilkie *Canada* **103** C7
Wilkinsburg *U.S.A.* **114** F5
Wilkinson Lakes *Australia* **93** E5
Willandra Creek ➤
 Australia **95** E4
Willapa B. *U.S.A.* **108** C1
Willapa Hills *U.S.A.* **110** D3
Willard *N.Y., U.S.A.* **114** D8
Willard *Ohio, U.S.A.* **114** E2
Willcox *U.S.A.* **109** K9
Willemstad *Neth. Ant.* **121** D6
Willet *U.S.A.* **115** D9
William ➤ *Canada* **103** B7
William 'Bill' Dannelly
 Res. *U.S.A.* **117** E11
William Creek *Australia* **95** D2
Williams *Australia* **93** F2
Williams *Ariz., U.S.A.* **109** J7
Williams *Calif., U.S.A.* **110** F4
Williams Harbour *Canada* **105** B8
Williams Lake *Canada* **102** C4
Williamsburg *Ky., U.S.A.* **113** G11
Williamsburg *Pa., U.S.A.* **114** F6
Williamsburg *Va., U.S.A.* **113** G15
Williamson *N.Y., U.S.A.* **114** C7
Williamson *W. Va., U.S.A.* **113** G12
Williamsport *U.S.A.* **114** E7
Williamston *U.S.A.* **117** D16
Williamstown *Australia* **95** F3
Williamstown *Ky., U.S.A.* **113** F11

Williamstown *Mass., U.S.A.*
 115 D11
Williamstown *N.Y., U.S.A.* **115** C9
Willimantic *U.S.A.* **115** E12
Willingboro *U.S.A.* **113** E16
Williston *S. Africa* **88** E3
Williston *Fla., U.S.A.* **117** G13
Williston *N. Dak., U.S.A.* **112** A2
Williston L. *Canada* **102** B4
Willits *U.S.A.* **108** G2
Willmar *U.S.A.* **112** C6
Willmore Wilderness △
 Canada **102** C5
Willoughby *U.S.A.* **114** E3
Willow Bunch *Canada* **103** D7
Willow L. *Canada* **102** A5
Willow Wall, The *China* **57** C12
Willowick *U.S.A.* **114** E3
Willowlake ➤ *Canada* **102** A4
Willowmore *S. Africa* **88** E3
Willows *U.S.A.* **110** F4
Willowvale = Gatyana
 S. Africa **89** E4
Wills, L. *Australia* **92** D4
Wills Cr. ➤ *Australia* **94** C3
Willsboro *U.S.A.* **115** B11
Willunga *Australia* **95** F2
Wilmette *U.S.A.* **112** D10
Wilmington *Australia* **95** E2
Wilmington *Del., U.S.A.* **113** F16
Wilmington *N.C., U.S.A.* **117** D16
Wilmington *Ohio, U.S.A.* **113** F12
Wilmington *Vt., U.S.A.* **115** D12
Wilmslow *U.K.* **14** D5
Wilpena Cr. ➤ *Australia* **95** E2
Wilsall *U.S.A.* **108** D8
Wilson *N.C., U.S.A.* **117** D16
Wilson *N.Y., U.S.A.* **114** C6
Wilson *Pa., U.S.A.* **115** F9
Wilson ➤ *Australia* **92** C4
Wilson Bluff *Australia* **93** F4
Wilson Inlet *Australia* **93** G2
Wilsons Promontory
 Australia **95** F4
Wilster *Germany* **24** B5
Wilton *U.S.A.* **112** B3
Wilton ➤ *Australia* **94** A1
Wiltshire □ *U.K.* **15** F6
Wiltz *Lux.* **17** E5
Wiluna *Australia* **93** E3
Wimborne Minster *U.K.* **15** G6
Wimmera ➤ *Australia* **95** F3
Wimereux *France* **19** B8
Winam G. *Kenya* **86** C3
Winburg *S. Africa* **88** D4
Winchendon *U.S.A.* **115** D12
Winchester *U.K.* **15** F6
Winchester *Conn., U.S.A.* **115** E11
Winchester *Idaho, U.S.A.* **108** C5
Winchester *Ind., U.S.A.* **113** E11
Winchester *Ky., U.S.A.* **113** G11
Winchester *N.H., U.S.A.* **115** D12
Winchester *Tenn., U.S.A.* **111** J11
Winchester *Tenn., U.S.A.* **117** D11
Winchester *Va., U.S.A.* **113** F14
Wind ➤ *U.S.A.* **108** E9
Wind Cave △ *U.S.A.* **112** D2
Wind River Range *U.S.A.* **108** E9
Windau = Ventspils *Latvia* **30** A8
Windber *U.S.A.* **114** F6
Winder *U.S.A.* **117** D13
Windermere *U.K.* **14** C5
Windhoek *Namibia* **88** C2
Windischgarsten *Austria* **26** D7
Windjana Gorge △ *Australia* **92** C3
Windom *U.S.A.* **112** D6
Windorah *Australia* **94** D3
Window Rock *U.S.A.* **109** J9
Windrush ➤ *U.K.* **15** F6
Windsor *Australia* **95** E5
Windsor *N.S., Canada* **105** D7
Windsor *Ont., Canada* **114** D2
Windsor *U.K.* **15** F7
Windsor *Calif., U.S.A.* **108** G2
Windsor *Colo., U.S.A.* **108** F11
Windsor *Conn., U.S.A.* **115** E12
Windsor *Mo., U.S.A.* **112** F7
Windsor *N.Y., U.S.A.* **115** D9
Windsor *Vt., U.S.A.* **115** C12
Windsor & Maidenhead □
 U.K. **15** F7
Windsorton *S. Africa* **88** D3
Windward Is. *W. Indies* **121** D7
Windward Passage =
 Vientos, Paso de los
 Caribbean **121** C5
Winefred L. *Canada* **103** B6
Winejok *Sudan* **81** F2
Winfield *U.S.A.* **112** G5
Wingate Mts. *Australia* **92** B5
Wingham *Australia* **95** E5
Wingham *Canada* **114** C3
Winisk *Canada* **104** A2
Winisk ➤ *Canada* **104** A2
Winisk L. *Canada* **104** B2
Wink *U.S.A.* **116** F3
Winkler *Canada* **103** D9

Winklern *Austria* **26** E5
Winlock *U.S.A.* **110** D4
Winneba *Ghana* **83** D4
Winnebago, L. *U.S.A.* **112** D9
Winnecke Cr. → *Australia* **92** C5
Winnemucca *U.S.A.* **108** F5
Winnemucca L. *U.S.A.* **108** F4
Winner *U.S.A.* **112** D4
Winnett *U.S.A.* **108** C9
Winnfield *U.S.A.* **116** F8
Winnibigoshish, L. *U.S.A.* **112** B6
Winnipeg *Canada* **103** D9
Winnipeg → *Canada* **103** C9
Winnipeg, L. *Canada* **103** C9
Winnipeg Beach *Canada* **103** C9
Winnipegosis *Canada* **103** C9
Winnipegosis L. *Canada* **103** C9
Winnipesaukee, L. *U.S.A.* **115** C13
Winnisquam L. *U.S.A.* **115** C13
Winnsboro *La., U.S.A.* **116** E9
Winnsboro *S.C., U.S.A.* **117** D14
Winnsboro *Tex., U.S.A.* **116** E7
Winokapau, L. *Canada* **105** B7
Winona *Minn., U.S.A.* **112** C8
Winona *Miss., U.S.A.* **117** E10
Winooski *U.S.A.* **115** B11
Winooski → *U.S.A.* **115** B11
Winschoten *Neths.* **17** A7
Winsen *Germany* **24** B6
Winsford *U.K.* **14** D5
Winslow = Bainbridge
  Island *U.S.A.* **110** C4
Winslow *U.S.A.* **109** J8
Winsted *U.S.A.* **115** E11
Winston-Salem *U.S.A.* **117** C14
Winter Garden *U.S.A.* **117** G14
Winter Haven *U.S.A.* **117** G14
Winter Park *U.S.A.* **117** G14
Winterberg *Germany* **24** D4
Winterhaven *U.S.A.* **111** N12
Winters *U.S.A.* **110** G5
Winterset *U.S.A.* **112** E6
Wintersville *U.S.A.* **114** F4
Winterswijk *Neths.* **17** C6
Winterthur *Switz.* **25** H4
Winthrop *U.S.A.* **108** B3
Winton *Australia* **94** C3
Winton *N.Z.* **91** G2
Wipper → *Germany* **24** D7
Wirrulla *Australia* **95** E1
Wisbech *U.K.* **15** E8
Wisconsin □ *U.S.A.* **112** C9
Wisconsin → *U.S.A.* **112** D8
Wisconsin Rapids *U.S.A.* **112** C9
Wisdom *U.S.A.* **108** D7
Wishaw *U.K.* **13** F5
Wishek *U.S.A.* **112** B4
Wisła *Poland* **31** J5
Wisła → *Poland* **30** D5
Wisłok → *Poland* **31** H9
Wisłoka → *Poland* **31** H8
Wismar *Germany* **24** B7
Wisner *U.S.A.* **112** E5
Wissant *France* **19** B8
Wissembourg *France* **19** C14
Wisznice *Poland* **31** G10
Witbank = eMalahleni
  S. Africa **89** D4
Witdraai *S. Africa* **88** D3
Witham *U.K.* **15** F8
Witham → *U.K.* **14** E7
Withernsea *U.K.* **14** D8
Witjira △ *Australia* **95** D2
Witkowo *Poland* **31** F4
Witless Bay *Canada* **105** C9
Witney *U.K.* **15** F6
Witnica *Poland* **31** F1
Witnossob → *Namibia* **88** D3
Wittdün *Germany* **24** A4
Witten *Germany* **24** D3
Wittenberge *Germany* **24** B7
Wittenburg *Germany* **24** B7
Wittenheim *France* **19** E14
Wittenoom *Australia* **92** D2
Wittingen *Germany* **24** C6
Wittlich *Germany* **25** F2
Wittmund *Germany* **24** B3
Wittow *Germany* **24** A9
Wittstock *Germany* **24** B8
Witu *Kenya* **86** C5
Witvlei *Namibia* **88** C2
Witzenhausen *Germany* **24** D5
Wiwon *N. Korea* **57** D14
Wkra → *Poland* **31** F7
Władysławowo *Poland* **30** D5
Wleń *Poland* **31** G2
Wlingi *Indonesia* **63** H15
Włocławek *Poland* **31** F6
Włodawa *Poland* **31** G10
Włoszczowa *Poland* **31** H6
Woburn *U.S.A.* **115** D13
Wodian *China* **56** H7
Wodonga *Australia* **95** F4
Wodzisław Śląski *Poland* **31** H5
Woerth *France* **19** D14
Woinbogoin *China* **58** A2
Woippy *France* **19** C13

Wojcieszow *Poland* **31** H2
Wokam *Indonesia* **63** F8
Woking *U.K.* **15** F7
Wokingham *U.K.* **15** F7
Wokingham □ *U.K.* **15** F7
Wolbrom *Poland* **31** H6
Wolczyn *Poland* **31** G5
Woldegk *Germany* **24** B9
Wolf → *Canada* **102** A2
Wolf Creek *U.S.A.* **108** C7
Wolf L. *Canada* **102** A2
Wolf Point *U.S.A.* **108** B11
Wolfe I. *Canada* **115** B8
Wolfeboro *U.S.A.* **115** C13
Wolfen *Germany* **24** D8
Wolfenbüttel *Germany* **24** C6
Wolfratshausen *Germany* **25** H7
Wolfsberg *Austria* **26** E7
Wolfsburg *Germany* **24** C6
Wolgast *Germany* **24** A9
Wolhusen *Switz.* **25** H4
Wolin *Poland* **30** E1
Woliński △ *Poland* **30** E1
Wollaston, Is. *Chile* **128** H3
Wollaston L. *Canada* **103** B8
Wollaston Lake *Canada* **103** B8
Wollaston Pen. *Canada* **100** C8
Wollongong *Australia* **95** E5
Wolmaransstad *S. Africa* **88** D4
Wolmirstedt *Germany* **24** C7
Wołomin *Poland* **31** F8
Wołów *Poland* **31** G3
Wolseley *S. Africa* **88** E2
Wolsey *U.S.A.* **112** C4
Wolstenholme, C. *Canada* **98** C12
Wolsztyn *Poland* **31** F3
Wolvega *Neths.* **17** B6
Wolverhampton *U.K.* **15** E5
Wondai *Australia* **95** D5
Wongalarroo L. *Australia* **95** E3
Wongan Hills *Australia* **93** F2
Wonju *S. Korea* **57** F14
Wonosari *Indonesia* **63** G14
Wonosobo *Indonesia* **63** G13
Wonowon *Canada* **102** B4
Wŏnsan *N. Korea* **57** E14
Wonthaggi *Australia* **95** F4
Wood Buffalo △ *Canada* **102** B6
Wood Is. *Australia* **92** C3
Wood L. *Canada* **103** B8
Woodah, I. *Australia* **94** A2
Woodbourne *U.S.A.* **115** E10
Woodbridge *Canada* **114** C5
Woodbridge *U.K.* **15** E9
Woodburn *U.S.A.* **108** D2
Woodenbong *Australia* **95** D5
Woodend *Australia* **95** D5
Woodford *Australia* **95** D5
Woodfords *U.S.A.* **110** G7
Woodlake *U.S.A.* **110** J7
Woodland *Calif., U.S.A.* **110** G5
Woodland *Maine, U.S.A.* **113** C20
Woodland *Pa., U.S.A.* **114** F6
Woodland *Wash., U.S.A.* **110** E4
Woodland Caribou △
  Canada **103** C10
Woodlands *Singapore* **65** d
Woodlands, The *U.S.A.* **116** F7
Woodonga *Australia* **95** F4
Woodridge *Canada* **103** D9
Woodroffe, Mt. *Australia* **93** E5
Woods, L. *Australia* **94** B4
Woods, L. of the *Canada* **103** D10
Woodstock *Australia* **94** B4
Woodstock *N.B., Canada* **105** C6
Woodstock *Ont., Canada* **114** C4
Woodstock *U.K.* **15** F6
Woodstock *Ill., U.S.A.* **112** D9
Woodstock *Vt., U.S.A.* **115** C12
Woodsville *U.S.A.* **115** B13
Woodville *N.Z.* **91** D5
Woodville *Miss., U.S.A.* **116** F9
Woodville *Tex., U.S.A.* **116** F7
Woodward *U.S.A.* **116** C5
Woody → *U.S.A.* **111** K8
Woody → *Canada* **103** C8
Woolacombe *U.K.* **15** F3
Woolamai, C. *Australia* **95** F4
Woolgoolga *Australia* **95** E5
Woomera *Australia* **95** E2
Woonsocket *R.I., U.S.A.* **115** E13
Woonsocket *S. Dak., U.S.A.* **112** C4
Wooramel → *Australia* **93** E1
Wooramel Roadhouse
  Australia **93** E1
Wooroonooran △ *Australia* **94** B4
Wooster *U.S.A.* **114** F3
Worcester *S. Africa* **88** E2
Worcester *U.K.* **15** E5
Worcester *Mass., U.S.A.* **115** D13
Worcester *N.Y., U.S.A.* **115** D10
Worcestershire □ *U.K.* **15** E5
Wörgl *Austria* **26** D5
Workington *U.K.* **14** C4
Worksop *U.K.* **14** D6
Workum *Neths.* **17** B5

Worland *U.S.A.* **108** D10
Wormhout *France* **19** B9
Worms *Germany* **25** F4
Worsley *Canada* **102** B5
Wortham *U.S.A.* **116** F6
Wörther See *Austria* **26** E7
Worthing *Barbados* **121** g
Worthing *U.K.* **15** G7
Worthington *Minn., U.S.A.* **112** D6
Worthington *Pa., U.S.A.* **114** F5
Wosi *Indonesia* **63** E7
Wote *Kenya* **86** C4
Wou-han = Wuhan *China* **59** B10
Wousi = Wuxi *China* **59** B13
Wowoni *Indonesia* **63** E6
Wrangel I. = Vrangelya,
  Ostrov *Russia* **53** B19
Wrangell *U.S.A.* **102** B2
Wrangell Mts. *U.S.A.* **100** C5
Wrath, C. *U.K.* **13** C3
Wray *U.S.A.* **108** F12
Wrekin, The *U.K.* **15** E5
Wrens *U.S.A.* **117** E13
Wrexham *U.K.* **14** D4
Wrexham □ *U.K.* **14** D5
Wriezen *Germany* **24** C10
Wright = Paranas *Phil.* **61** F6
Wright *Fla., U.S.A.* **117** F11
Wright *Wyo., U.S.A.* **108** E11
Wright Pt. *Canada* **114** C3
Wrightson, Mt. *U.S.A.* **109** L8
Wrightwood *U.S.A.* **111** L9
Wrigley *Canada* **100** C7
Wrocław *Poland* **31** G4
Wronki *Poland* **31** F3
Września *Poland* **31** F4
Wschowa *Poland* **31** G3
Wu Jiang → *China* **58** C6
Wu'an *China* **56** F8
Wubin *Australia* **93** F2
Wubu *China* **56** F6
Wuchang *China* **57** B14
Wucheng *China* **56** F9
Wuchuan *Guangdong, China* **59** G8
Wuchuan *Guizhou, China* **58** C7
Wuchuan
  Nei Monggol Zizhiqu, China **56** D6
Wudi *China* **57** F9
Wuding *China* **58** E4
Wuding He → *China* **56** F6
Wudinna *Australia* **95** E2
Wudu *China* **56** H3
Wufeng *China* **59** B8
Wugang *China* **59** D8
Wugong Shan *China* **59** D9
Wuhan *China* **59** B10
Wuhe *China* **57** H9
Wuhsi = Wuxi *China* **59** B13
Wuhu *China* **59** B12
Wujiang *China* **59** B13
Wukari *Nigeria* **83** D6
Wulajie *China* **57** B14
Wulanbulang *China* **56** D6
Wular L. *India* **69** B6
Wulehe *Ghana* **83** D5
Wulian *China* **57** G10
Wuliang Shan *China* **58** E3
Wuliaru *Indonesia* **63** F8
Wuling Shan *China* **58** C7
Wulong *China* **58** C6
Wulumuchi = Ürümqi *China* **52** E9
Wum *Cameroon* **83** D7
Wuming *China* **58** F7
Wun Rog *Sudan* **81** F2
Wundanyi *Kenya* **86** C4
Wuning *China* **59** C10
Wunnummin L. *Canada* **104** B2
Wunsiedel *Germany* **25** E8
Wunstorf *Germany* **24** C5
Wuntho *Burma* **67** H19
Wupatki △ *U.S.A.* **109** J8
Wuping *China* **59** E11
Wuppertal *Germany* **24** D3
Wuppertal *S. Africa* **88** E2
Wuqing *China* **57** E9
Wurtsboro *U.S.A.* **115** E10
Würzburg *Germany* **25** F5
Wurzen *Germany* **24** D8
Wushan *China* **56** G3
Wushishi *Nigeria* **83** D6
Wutach → *Germany* **25** H4
Wutai *China* **56** E7
Wuting = Huimin *China* **57** F9
Wutong *China* **59** E8
Wutonghaolai *China* **57** C11
Wutongqiao *China* **58** C4
Wuwei *Anhui, China* **59** B11
Wuwei *Gansu, China* **60** C5
Wuxi *Jiangsu, China* **59** B13
Wuxi *Sichuan, China* **58** B7
Wuxiang *China* **56** F7
Wuxuan *China* **58** F7
Wuxue *China* **59** C11
Wuyang *China* **56** H7
Wuyi *Hebei, China* **56** F8
Wuyi *Zhejiang, China* **59** C12

Wuyi Shan *China* **59** D11
Wuyishan *China* **59** D12
Wuyo *Nigeria* **83** C7
Wuyuan *Jiangxi, China* **59** C11
Wuyuan
  Nei Monggol Zizhiqu, China **56** D5
Wuzhai *China* **56** E6
Wuzhi Shan *China* **64** C7
Wuzhong *China* **56** E4
Wuzhou *China* **59** F8
Wyaaba Cr. → *Australia* **94** B3
Wyalkatchem *Australia* **93** F2
Wyalusing *U.S.A.* **115** E8
Wyandotte *U.S.A.* **113** D12
Wyandra *Australia* **95** D4
Wyara, L. *Australia* **95** D3
Wycheproof *Australia* **95** F3
Wycliffe Well *Australia* **94** C1
Wye → *U.K.* **15** F5
Wyemandoo *Australia* **93** E2
Wyk *Germany* **24** A4
Wymondham *U.K.* **15** E9
Wymore *U.S.A.* **112** E5
Wyndham *Australia* **92** C4
Wyndham *N.Z.* **91** G2
Wynyard *Australia* **95** G4
Wynyard *Canada* **103** C8
Wyola L. *Australia* **93** E5
Wyoming = Plympton-
  Wyoming *Canada* **114** D2
Wyoming □ *U.S.A.* **108** E10
Wyomissing *U.S.A.* **115** F9
Wyong *Australia* **95** E5
Wyrzysk *Poland* **31** E4
Wysoka *Poland* **31** E4
Wysokie *Poland* **31** H9
Wysokie Mazowieckie
  Poland **31** F9
Wyszków *Poland* **31** F8
Wyszogród *Poland* **31** F7
Wytheville *U.S.A.* **113** G13
Wyżyna Małopolska *Poland* **31** H7

X

Xaafuun *Somali Rep.* **75** E5
Xaafuun, Ras *Somali Rep.* **75** E5
Xaçmaz *Azerbaijan* **35** K9
Xai-Xai *Mozam.* **89** D5
Xainza *China* **60** C3
Xalapa *Mexico* **119** D5
Xangongo *Angola* **88** B2
Xankändi *Azerbaijan* **73** C12
Xanlar *Azerbaijan* **35** K8
Xanten *Germany* **24** D2
Xanthi *Greece* **45** E8
Xanthi □ *Greece* **45** E8
Xanthos *Turkey* **47** E11
Xanxerê *Brazil* **127** B5
Xapuri *Brazil* **124** F5
Xar Moron He → *China* **57** C11
Xarrë *Albania* **44** G2
Xátiva *Spain* **39** G4
Xau, L. *Botswana* **88** C3
Xavantina *Brazil* **127** A5
Xenia *U.S.A.* **113** F12
Xeropotamos → *Cyprus* **49** E11
Xertigny *France* **19** D13
Xhora *S. Africa* **89** E4
Xhumo *Botswana* **88** C3
Xi Jiang → *China* **59** F9
Xi Xian *Henan, China* **59** A10
Xi Xian *Shanxi, China* **56** F6
Xia Xian *China* **56** G6
Xiachengzi *China* **57** B16
Xiachuan Dao *China* **59** G9
Xiaguan *China* **60** D5
Xiajiang *China* **59** D10
Xiajin *China* **56** F9
Xiamen *China* **59** E12
Xi'an *China* **56** G5
Xian Xian *China* **56** E9
Xianfeng *China* **58** C7
Xiang Jiang → *China* **59** C9
Xiangcheng *Henan, China* **56** H8
Xiangcheng *Henan, China* **56** H7
Xiangcheng *Sichuan, China* **58** C2
Xiangdu *China* **58** F6
Xiangfan *China* **59** A9
Xianggang = Hong
  Kong □ *China* **59** F10
Xianghuang Qi *China* **56** C7
Xiangning *China* **56** G6
Xiangquan *China* **56** F7
Xiangquan He = Sutlej →
  Pakistan **68** E4
Xiangshui *China* **57** G10
Xiangtan *China* **59** D9
Xiangxiang *China* **59** D9
Xiangyin *China* **59** C9
Xiangyun *China* **58** E3
Xiangzhou *China* **58** F7
Xianju *China* **59** C13
Xianning *China* **59** C10

Xianshui He → *China* **58** B3
Xiantao *China* **59** B9
Xianyang *China* **56** G5
Xianyou *China* **59** E12
Xiao Hinggan Ling *China* **60** B7
Xiao Xian *China* **56** G9
Xiaofeng *China* **59** B12
Xiaogan *China* **59** B9
Xiaojin *China* **58** B4
Xiaolan *China* **59** F9
Xiaoshan *China* **59** B13
Xiaoyi *China* **56** F6
Xiapu *China* **59** D12
Xiawa *China* **57** C11
Xiayi *China* **56** G9
Xichang *China* **58** D4
Xichong *China* **58** B5
Xichou *China* **58** E5
Xichuan *China* **56** H6
Xide *China* **58** C4
Xiemahe *China* **59** B8
Xieng Khouang *Laos* **64** C4
Xifei He → *China* **56** H9
Xifeng *Gansu, China* **56** G4
Xifeng *Guizhou, China* **58** D6
Xifeng *Liaoning, China* **57** C13
Xifengzhen = Xifeng *China* **56** G4
Xigazê *China* **60** D3
Xihe *China* **56** G3
Xihua *China* **56** H8
Xiliao He → *China* **57** C12
Xilin *China* **58** E5
Xilinhot *China* **56** C9
Xilokastro *Greece* **46** C4
Ximana *Mozam.* **87** F3
Xime *Guinea-Biss.* **82** C2
Ximeng *China* **58** F2
Xin Jiang → *China* **59** C11
Xin Xian = Xinzhou *China* **56** E7
Xinavane *Mozam.* **89** D5
Xinbin *China* **57** D13
Xincai *China* **59** A10
Xinchang *China* **59** C13
Xincheng *Guangxi Zhuangzu,
  China* **58** E7
Xincheng *Jiangxi, China* **59** D10
Xincun *China* **57** E9
Xindu *China* **58** B5
Xinfeng *Guangdong, China* **59** E10
Xinfeng *Jiangxi, China* **59** D11
Xinfeng *Jiangxi, China* **59** D11
Xinfengjiang Skuiku *China* **59** F10
Xing Xian *China* **56** E6
Xing'an *Guangxi Zhuangzu,
  China* **59** E8
Xingan *Jiangxi, China* **59** D10
Xingcheng *China* **57** D11
Xingguo *China* **59** D10
Xinghe *China* **56** D7
Xinghua *China* **57** H10
Xinghua Wan *China* **59** E12
Xinglong *China* **57** D9
Xingning *China* **59** E10
Xingping *China* **56** G5
Xingren *China* **58** E5
Xingshan *China* **59** B8
Xingtai *China* **56** F8
Xingu → *Brazil* **125** D8
Xingwen *China* **58** C5
Xingyang *China* **56** G7
Xinhe *China* **56** F8
Xinhua *China* **59** D8
Xinhuang *China* **58** D7
Xinhui *China* **59** F9
Xining *China* **60** C5
Xinjian *China* **59** C10
Xinjiang *China* **56** G6
Xinjiang Uygur Zizhiqu □
  China **60** B3
Xinjie *China* **58** D3
Xinjin = Pulandian *China* **57** E11
Xinjin *China* **58** B4
Xinkai He → *China* **57** C12
Xinle *China* **56** E8
Xinlitun *China* **57** D12
Xinlong *China* **58** B3
Xinmin *China* **57** D12
Xinning *China* **59** D8
Xinping *China* **58** E3
Xinshao *China* **59** D8
Xintai *China* **57** G9
Xintian *China* **59** E9
Xinxian *China* **59** B10
Xinxiang *China* **56** G7
Xinxing *China* **59** F9
Xinyang *China* **59** A10
Xinye *China* **59** A9
Xinyi *China* **59** F8
Xinyu *China* **59** D10
Xinzhan *China* **57** C14
Xinzheng *China* **56** G7
Xinzhou *Hainan, China* **64** C7
Xinzhou *Hubei, China* **59** B10
Xinzhou *Shanxi, China* **56** E7
Xinzo de Limia *Spain* **36** C3
Xiongyuecheng *China* **57** D12

Xiping *Henan, China* **56** H8
Xiping *Henan, China* **56** H6
Xiping *Zhejiang, China* **59** C12
Xique-Xique *Brazil* **125** F10
Xisha Qundao = Paracel
  Is. *S. China Sea* **62** A4
Xishui *Guizhou, China* **58** C6
Xishui *Hubei, China* **59** B10
Xitole *Guinea-Biss.* **82** C2
Xiu Shui → *China* **59** C10
Xiuning *China* **59** C12
Xiuren *China* **59** E8
Xiushan *China* **58** C7
Xiushui *China* **59** C10
Xiuwen *China* **58** D6
Xiuyan *China* **57** D12
Xixabangma Feng *China* **69** E11
Xixia *China* **56** H6
Xixiang *China* **56** H4
Xixón = Gijón *Spain* **36** B5
Xiyang *China* **56** F7
Xizang Zizhiqu □ *China* **60** C3
Xlendi *Malta* **49** C1
Xochob *Mexico* **119** D7
Xu Jiang → *China* **59** D11
Xuan Loc *Vietnam* **65** G6
Xuan'en *China* **58** C7
Xuanhan *China* **58** B6
Xuanhua *China* **56** D8
Xuanwei *China* **58** C5
Xuanzhou *China* **59** B12
Xuchang *China* **56** G7
Xudat *Azerbaijan* **35** K9
Xuefeng Shan *China* **59** D8
Xuejiaping *China* **59** B8
Xun Jiang → *China* **59** F8
Xun Xian *China* **56** G8
Xundian *China* **58** E4
Xunwu *China* **59** E10
Xunyang *China* **56** H5
Xunyi *China* **56** G5
Xupu *China* **59** D8
Xúquer → *Spain* **39** F4
Xushui *China* **56** E8
Xuwen *China* **59** G8
Xuyen Moc *Vietnam* **65** G6
Xuyong *China* **58** C5
Xuzhou *China* **57** G9
Xylophagou *Cyprus* **49** E12

Y

Ya Xian = Sanya *China* **64** C7
Yaamba *Australia* **94** C5
Ya'an *China* **58** C4
Yaapeet *Australia* **95** F3
Yabassi *Cameroon* **83** E6
Yabelo *Ethiopia* **81** G4
Yabelo △ *Ethiopia* **81** F4
Yablanitsa *Bulgaria* **45** C8
Yablonovyy Khrebet *Russia* **53** D12
Yablonovyy Ra. =
  Yablonovyy Khrebet
  Russia **53** D12
Yabluniv *Ukraine* **29** B9
Yablunytsya *Ukraine* **29** B8
Yabrai Shan *China* **56** E2
Yabrūd *Syria* **74** B5
Yabucoa *Puerto Rico* **121** d
Yacambú △ *Venezuela* **121** E6
Yacheng *China* **64** C7
Yacuiba *Bolivia* **126** A3
Yacuma → *Bolivia* **124** F5
Yadgir *India* **66** L10
Yadkin → *U.S.A.* **117** D14
Yadrin *Russia* **34** C8
Yadua *Fiji* **91** a
Yaeyama-Rettō *Japan* **55** M1
Yagaba *Ghana* **83** C4
Yagasa Cluster *Fiji* **91** a
Yağcılar *Turkey* **47** B10
Yagodnoye *Russia* **53** C15
Yahila *Dem. Rep. of the Congo* **86** D3
Yahk *Canada* **102** D5
Yahotyn *Ukraine* **33** G6
Yahuma
  Dem. Rep. of the Congo **84** D4
Yahyalı *Turkey* **72** C6
Yaita *Japan* **55** F9
Yaiza *Canary Is.* **48** F6
Yajiang *China* **58** B3
Yajua *Nigeria* **83** C7
Yakima *U.S.A.* **108** C3
Yakima → *U.S.A.* **108** C4
Yakishiri-Jima *Japan* **54** B10
Yako *Burkina Faso* **82** C4
Yakobi I. *U.S.A.* **102** B1
Yakoruda *Bulgaria* **44** D7
Yakovlevka *Russia* **54** B6
Yaku-Shima *Japan* **55** J5
Yakumo *Japan* **54** C10
Yakutat *U.S.A.* **100** D6
Yakutia = Sakha □ *Russia* **53** C14
Yakutsk *Russia* **53** C13
Yala *Thailand* **65** J3
Yalboroo *Australia* **94** J6
Yale *U.S.A.* **114** C2

Yalgoo *Australia* **93** E2
Yalgorup △ *Australia* **93** F2
Yalinga *C.A.R.* **84** C4
Yalkabul, Pta. *Mexico* **119** C7
Yalleroi *Australia* **94** C4
Yalobusha → *U.S.A.* **117** E9
Yalong Jiang → *China* **58** D3
Yalova *Turkey* **45** F13
Yalpuh, Ozero *Ukraine* **29** E13
Yalta *Ukraine* **33** K8
Yalu Jiang → *China* **57** E13
Yalvaç *Turkey* **72** C4
Yam Ha Melaḥ = Dead Sea
    Asia **74** D4
Yam Kinneret *Israel* **74** C4
Yamada *Japan* **55** H5
Yamagata *Japan* **54** E10
Yamagata □ *Japan* **54** E10
Yamaguchi *Japan* **55** G5
Yamaguchi □ *Japan* **55** G5
Yamal, Poluostrov *Russia* **52** B8
Yamal Pen. = Yamal,
    Poluostrov *Russia* **52** B8
Yamanashi □ *Japan* **55** G9
Yamanie Falls △ *Australia* **94** B4
Yamato Ridge *Sea of Japan* **54** E7
Yamba *Australia* **95** D5
Yambarran Ra. *Australia* **92** C5
Yambéring *Guinea* **82** C2
Yâmbiô *Sudan* **81** G2
Yambol *Bulgaria* **45** D10
Yame *Japan* **55** H5
Yamethin *Burma* **67** J20
Yamma Yamma, L. *Australia* **95** D3
Yamoussoukro *Ivory C.* **82** D3
Yampa → *U.S.A.* **108** F9
Yampi Sd. *Australia* **92** C3
Yampil *Moldova* **23** D15
Yampol = Yampil *Moldova* **23** D15
Yamrat *Nigeria* **83** C6
Yamrukchal = Botev
    Bulgaria **45** D8
Yamuna → *India* **69** G9
Yamunanagar *India* **68** D7
Yamzho Yumco *China* **60** D4
Yan *Nigeria* **83** C7
Yana → *Russia* **53** B14
Yanagawa *Japan* **55** H5
Yanai *Japan* **55** H6
Yan'an *China* **56** F5
Yanbian *China* **58** D3
Yanbu 'al Baḥr *Si. Arabia* **70** F3
Yanchang *China* **56** F6
Yancheng *Henan, China* **56** H8
Yancheng *Jiangsu, China* **57** H11
Yanchep *Australia* **93** F2
Yanchi *China* **56** F4
Yanchuan *China* **56** F6
Yanco Cr. → *Australia* **95** F4
Yandicoogina *Australia* **92** D2
Yandoon *Burma* **67** L19
Yanfeng *China* **58** E3
Yanfolila *Mali* **82** C3
Yang Xian *China* **56** H4
Yang-yang *S. Korea* **57** E15
Yang-Yang *Senegal* **82** B1
Yangambi
    Dem. Rep. of the Congo **86** B1
Yangbi *China* **58** E2
Yangcheng *China* **56** G7
Yangch'ü = Taiyuan *China* **56** F7
Yangchun *China* **59** F8
Yanggao *China* **56** D7
Yanggu *China* **56** F8
Yangjiang *China* **59** G8
Yangliuqing *China* **57** E9
Yangon = Rangoon *Burma* **67** L20
Yangping *China* **59** B8
Yangpingguan *China* **56** H4
Yangquan *China* **56** F7
Yangshan *China* **59** E9
Yangshuo *China* **59** E8
Yangtse = Chang Jiang →
    China **59** B13
Yangtze Kiang = Chang
    Jiang → *China* **59** B13
Yangudi Rassa △ *Ethiopia* **81** E5
Yangxin *China* **59** C10
Yangyuan *China* **56** D8
Yangzhong *China* **59** A12
Yangzhou *China* **59** A12
Yanhe *China* **58** C7
Yanji *China* **57** C15
Yanjin *China* **58** C5
Yanjing *China* **58** C2
Yankari △ *Nigeria* **83** D7
Yankton *U.S.A.* **112** D5
Yanonge
    Dem. Rep. of the Congo **86** B1
Yanqi *China* **60** B3
Yanqing *China* **56** D8
Yanshan *Hebei, China* **57** E9
Yanshan *Jiangxi, China* **59** C11
Yanshan *Yunnan, China* **58** F5
Yanshou *China* **57** B15
Yantabulla *Australia* **95** D4

Yantai *China* **57** F11
Yantarnyy *Russia* **30** D6
Yanting *China* **58** B5
Yantra → *Bulgaria* **45** C9
Yanuca *Fiji* **91** a
Yanwa *China* **58** D2
Yanyuan *China* **58** D3
Yanzhou *China* **56** G9
Yao Noi, Ko *Thailand* **65** a
Yao Xian *China* **56** G5
Yao Yai, Ko *Thailand* **65** a
Yao'an *China* **58** E3
Yaodu *China* **58** A5
Yaoundé *Cameroon* **83** E7
Yaowan *China* **57** G10
Yap *Pac. Oc.* **96** G5
Yapen *Indonesia* **63** E9
Yapen, Selat *Indonesia* **63** E9
Yapero *Indonesia* **63** E9
Yappar → *Australia* **94** B3
Yaqaga *Fiji* **91** a
Yaqui → *Mexico* **118** B2
Yar-Sale *Russia* **52** C8
Yaraka *Australia* **94** C3
Yaransk *Russia* **34** B8
Yarbasan *Turkey* **47** C10
Yardımcı Burnu *Turkey* **47** E12
Yare → *U.K.* **15** E9
Yaremcha *Ukraine* **29** B9
Yarensk *Russia* **52** C5
Yarfa *Si. Arabia* **80** C4
Yarí → *Colombia* **124** D4
Yarkand = Shache *China* **60** C2
Yarker *Canada* **115** B8
Yarkhun → *Pakistan* **69** A5
Yarlung Zangbo Jiang =
    Brahmaputra → *Asia* **69** H13
Yarmouth *Canada* **105** D6
Yarmūk → *Syria* **74** C4
Yaroslavl *Russia* **32** D10
Yaroslavl □ *Russia* **32** C10
Yarqa, W. → *Egypt* **74** F2
Yarra Yarra Lakes *Australia* **93** E2
Yarram *Australia* **95** F4
Yarraman *Australia* **95** D5
Yarras *Australia* **95** E5
Yartsevo *Sib., Russia* **53** C10
Yartsevo *Smolensk, Russia* **32** E7
Yarumal *Colombia* **124** B3
Yasawa *Fiji* **91** a
Yasawa Group *Fiji* **91** a
Yaselda *Belarus* **23** B14
Yasen *Ukraine* **29** B9
Yashi *Nigeria* **83** C6
Yashikera *Nigeria* **83** D5
Yashkul *Russia* **35** G7
Yasin *Pakistan* **69** A5
Yasinovataya *Ukraine* **33** H9
Yasinski, L. *Canada* **104** B4
Yasinya *Ukraine* **29** B9
Yasothon *Thailand* **64** E5
Yass *Australia* **95** E4
Yāsūj *Iran* **71** D6
Yatağan *Turkey* **47** D10
Yatakala *Niger* **83** C5
Yates Center *U.S.A.* **112** G6
Yathkyed L. *Canada* **103** A9
Yatsushiro *Japan* **55** H5
Yatta Plateau *Kenya* **86** C4
Yauco *Puerto Rico* **121** d
Yavari → *Peru* **124** D4
Yávaros *Mexico* **118** B3
Yavatmal *India* **66** J11
Yavne *Israel* **74** D3
Yavoriv *Ukraine* **31** J10
Yavorov = Yavoriv *Ukraine* **31** J10
Yavuzeli *Turkey* **72** D7
Yawatahama *Japan* **55** H6
Yawri B. *S. Leone* **82** D2
Yaxi *China* **58** D6
Yaxian = Sanya *China* **64** C7
Yazd *Iran* **71** D7
Yazd □ *Iran* **71** D7
Yazd-e Khvāst *Iran* **71** D7
Yazıköy *Turkey* **47** E9
Yazman *Pakistan* **68** E4
Yazoo City *U.S.A.* **117** E9
Ybbs *Austria* **26** C8
Ybycuí △ *Paraguay* **126** B4
Ybytyruzú △ *Paraguay* **127** B4
Ye *Burma* **64** E1
Ye Xian *China* **56** H7
Yebyu *Burma* **64** E2
Yecheon *S. Korea* **57** F15
Yecla *Spain* **39** G3
Yedebub Biheroch
    Bihereseboch na
    Hizboch □ *Ethiopia* **81** F4
Yedintsy = Edineț *Moldova* **29** B12
Yedseram → *Nigeria* **83** C7
Yefremov *Russia* **32** F10
Yeghegnadzor *Armenia* **73** C11
Yegorlyk → *Russia* **35** G5
Yegorlykskaya *Russia* **35** G5
Yegoryevsk *Russia* **32** E10
Yegros *Paraguay* **126** B4
Yehbuah *Indonesia* **63** J17

Yehuda, Midbar *Israel* **74** D4
Yei *Sudan* **81** G3
Yei, Nahr → *Sudan* **81** F3
Yejmiadzin *Armenia* **35** K7
Yekaterinburg *Russia* **52** D7
Yelabuga *Russia* **34** C11
Yelan *Russia* **34** G6
Yelarbon *Australia* **95** D5
Yelatma *Russia* **34** C5
Yelets *Russia* **33** F10
Yélimané *Mali* **82** B2
Yelizavetgrad =
    Kirovohrad *Ukraine* **33** H7
Yell *U.K.* **13** A7
Yell Sd. *U.K.* **13** A7
Yellow = Huang He →
    China **57** F10
Yellow Sea *China* **57** G12
Yellowhead Pass *Canada* **102** C5
Yellowknife *Canada* **102** A6
Yellowknife → *Canada* **102** A6
Yellowstone → *U.S.A.* **108** C12
Yellowstone △ *U.S.A.* **108** D8
Yellowstone L. *U.S.A.* **108** D8
Yelnya *Russia* **32** E7
Yelsk *Belarus* **23** C15
Yelwa *Nigeria* **83** C5
Yemen ■ *Asia* **75** E3
Yen Bai *Vietnam* **58** G5
Yenagoa *Nigeria* **83** E6
Yenakiyeve *Ukraine* **33** H10
Yenakiyevo = Yenakiyeve
    Ukraine **33** H10
Yenangyaung *Burma* **67** J19
Yenbo = Yanbu 'al Baḥr
    Si. Arabia **70** F3
Yenda *Australia* **95** E4
Yende Millimou *Guinea* **82** D2
Yendéré *Burkina Faso* **82** C4
Yendi *Ghana* **83** D4
Yéni *Niger* **83** C5
Yenice *Ankara, Turkey* **72** C5
Yenice *Aydın, Turkey* **47** D10
Yenice *Çanakkale, Turkey* **47** B9
Yenice *Edirne, Turkey* **45** F10
Yenice → *Turkey* **72** D6
Yenifoça *Turkey* **47** C8
Yenihisar *Turkey* **47** D9
Yeniköy *Bursa, Turkey* **45** F13
Yeniköy *Çanakkale, Turkey* **47** B8
Yeniköy *Kütahya, Turkey* **47** C11
Yenipazar *Turkey* **47** D10
Yenişehir *Turkey* **45** F13
Yenisey → *Russia* **52** B9
Yeniseysk *Russia* **53** D10
Yeniseyskiy Zaliv *Russia* **52** B9
Yenne *France* **21** C9
Yenotayevka *Russia* **35** G8
Yenyuka *Russia* **53** D13
Yeo → *U.K.* **15** G5
Yeo, L. *Australia* **93** E3
Yeoju *S. Korea* **57** F14
Yeola *India* **66** J9
Yeong-wol *S. Korea* **57** F15
Yeongcheon *S. Korea* **57** G15
Yeongdeok *S. Korea* **57** F15
Yeongdeungpo *S. Korea* **57** F14
Yeongdong *S. Korea* **57** F14
Yeongju *S. Korea* **57** F15
Yeosu *S. Korea* **57** G14
Yeovil *U.K.* **15** G5
Yepes *Spain* **36** F7
Yeppoon *Australia* **94** C5
Yerbent *Turkmenistan* **52** F6
Yerbogachen *Russia* **53** C11
Yerevan *Armenia* **35** K7
Yerington *U.S.A.* **108** G4
Yerkesik *Turkey* **47** D10
Yerköy *Turkey* **72** C6
Yermak *Kazakhstan* **52** D8
Yermo *U.S.A.* **111** L10
Yerólakkos *Cyprus* **49** D12
Yeropol *Russia* **53** C17
Yeroskipos *Cyprus* **49** E11
Yershov *Russia* **34** E9
Yerushalayim = Jerusalem
    Israel/West Bank **74** D4
Yerville *France* **18** C7
Yes Tor *U.K.* **15** G4
Yesan *S. Korea* **57** F14
Yeşilhisar *Turkey* **72** C6
Yeşilırmak → *Turkey* **72** B7
Yeşilkent *Turkey* **72** D7
Yeşilköy *Turkey* **45** F12
Yeşilova *Turkey* **47** D11
Yeşilyurt *Manisa, Turkey* **47** C10
Yeşilyurt *Muğla, Turkey* **47** D10
Yesnogorsk *Russia* **32** E9
Yeso *U.S.A.* **109** J11
Yessentuki *Russia* **35** H6
Yessey *Russia* **53** C11
Yeste *Spain* **39** G2
Yetman *Australia* **95** D5
Yeu, Î. d' *France* **18** F4
Yevlakh = Yevlax *Azerbaijan* **35** K8
Yevlax *Azerbaijan* **35** K8
Yevpatoriya *Ukraine* **33** K7

Yeya → *Russia* **33** J10
Yeysk *Russia* **33** J10
Yezd = Yazd *Iran* **71** D7
Yezerishche *Belarus* **32** E5
Yhati *Paraguay* **126** B3
Yhú *Paraguay* **127** B4
Yi → *Uruguay* **126** C4
Yi 'Allaq, G. *Egypt* **74** E2
Yi He → *China* **57** G10
Yi Xian *Anhui, China* **59** C11
Yi Xian *Hebei, China* **56** E8
Yi Xian *Liaoning, China* **57** D11
Yialiás → *Cyprus* **49** D12
Yialousa *Cyprus* **49** D13
Yibin *China* **58** C5
Yichang *China* **59** B8
Yicheng *Henan, China* **59** B9
Yicheng *Shanxi, China* **56** G6
Yichuan *China* **56** F6
Yichun *Heilongjiang, China* **60** B7
Yichun *Jiangxi, China* **59** D10
Yidu *China* **57** F10
Yidun *China* **58** B2
Yifag *Ethiopia* **81** E4
Yifeng *China* **59** C10
Yihuang *China* **59** D11
Yijun *China* **56** G5
Yilan *China* **60** B7
Yildiz Dağları *Turkey* **45** E11
Yıldızeli *Turkey* **72** C7
Yiliang *Yunnan, China* **58** D5
Yiliang *Yunnan, China* **58** E4
Yilong *China* **58** B6
Yimen *China* **58** E4
Yimianpo *China* **57** B15
Yinchuan *China* **56** E4
Yindarlgooda, L. *Australia* **93** F3
Ying He → *China* **56** H9
Ying Xian *China* **56** E7
Yingcheng *China* **59** B9
Yingde *China* **59** E9
Yingjiang *China* **58** E1
Yingjing *China* **58** C4
Yingkou *China* **57** D12
Yingshan *Henan, China* **59** B9
Yingshan *Hubei, China* **59** B10
Yingshan *Sichuan, China* **58** B6
Yingshang *China* **59** A11
Yingtan *China* **59** C11
Yining *China* **52** E9
Yinjiang *China* **58** C7
Yinmabin *Burma* **67** H19
Yioúra = Giaros *Greece* **46** D6
Yipinglang *China* **58** E3
Yiyang *Henan, China* **56** G7
Yiyang *Hunan, China* **59** C9
Yiyang *Jiangxi, China* **59** C11
Yizhang *China* **59** E9
Yizheng *China* **59** A12
Yli-Kitka *Finland* **8** C23
Ylikiiminki *Finland* **8** D21
Ylitornio *Finland* **8** C20
Ylivieska *Finland* **8** D21
Yngaren *Sweden* **11** F10
Yoakum *U.S.A.* **116** G6
Yob → *Eritrea* **81** D4
Yobe □ *Nigeria* **83** C7
Yog Pt. *Phil.* **63** B6
Yogan *Togo* **83** D5
Yogyakarta *Indonesia* **63** G14
Yogyakarta □ *Indonesia* **63** G14
Yoho △ *Canada* **102** C5
Yojoa, L. de *Honduras* **120** D2
Yok Don △ *Vietnam* **64** F6
Yokadouma *Cameroon* **84** D2
Yokkaichi *Japan* **55** G8
Yoko *Cameroon* **83** D7
Yokohama *Japan* **55** G9
Yokosuka *Japan* **55** G9
Yokote *Japan* **54** E10
Yola *Nigeria* **83** D7
Yolaina, Cordillera de *Nic.* **120** D3
Yólöten *Turkmenistan* **71** B9
Yom → *Thailand* **64** E3
Yonago *Japan* **55** G6
Yonaguni-Jima *Japan* **55** M1
Yŏnan *N. Korea* **57** F14
Yonezawa *Japan* **54** F10
Yong Peng *Malaysia* **65** M4
Yong Sata *Thailand* **65** J2
Yong'an *China* **59** E11
Yongamp'o *N. Korea* **57** E13
Yongcheng *China* **56** H9
Yongchuan *China* **58** C5
Yongchun *China* **59** E12
Yongde *China* **58** E2
Yongdeng *China* **56** F2
Yongding *China* **59** E11

Yongfeng *China* **59** D10
Yongfu *China* **58** E7
Yonghe *China* **56** F6
Yŏnghŭng *N. Korea* **57** E14
Yongji *China* **56** G6
Yongjia *China* **59** C13
Yongkang *Yunnan, China* **58** E2
Yongkang *Zhejiang, China* **59** C13
Yongnian *China* **56** F8
Yongning *Guangxi Zhuangzu,
    China* **58** F7
Yongning *Ningxia Huizu,
    China* **56** E4
Yongping *China* **58** E2
Yongqing *China* **56** E9
Yongren *China* **58** D3
Yongshan *China* **58** C4
Yongsheng *China* **58** D3
Yongshun *China* **58** C7
Yongtai *China* **59** E12
Yongxin = Jinggangshan
    China **59** D10
Yongxing *China* **59** D9
Yongxiu *China* **59** C10
Yongzhou *China* **59** D8
Yonibana *S. Leone* **82** D2
Yonkers *U.S.A.* **115** F11
Yonne □ *France* **19** E10
Yonne → *France* **19** D9
York *Australia* **93** F2
York *U.K.* **14** D6
York *Ala., U.S.A.* **117** E10
York *Nebr., U.S.A.* **112** E5
York *Pa., U.S.A.* **113** F15
York, C. *Australia* **94** A3
York, City of □ *U.K.* **14** D6
York, Kap *Greenland* **4** B4
York, Vale of *U.K.* **14** C6
York Sd. *Australia* **92** C4
Yorke Pen. *Australia* **95** E2
Yorkshire Dales △ *U.K.* **14** C5
Yorkshire Wolds *U.K.* **14** C7
Yorkton *Canada* **103** C8
Yorkville *U.S.A.* **110** G3
Yoro *Honduras* **120** D2
Yoron-Jima *Japan* **55** L4
Yorosso *Mali* **82** C4
Yos Sudarso, Pulau =
    Dolak, Pulau *Indonesia* **63** F9
Yosemite △ *U.S.A.* **110** H7
Yosemite Village *U.S.A.* **110** H7
Yoshino-Kumano △ *Japan* **55** H8
Yoshkar Ola *Russia* **34** B8
Yotvata *Israel* **74** F4
You Jiang → *China* **58** F6
You Xian *China* **59** D9
Youbou *Canada* **110** D2
Youghal *Ireland* **12** E4
Youghal B. *Ireland* **12** E4
Youkounkoun *Guinea* **82** C2
Young *Australia* **95** E4
Young *Canada* **103** C7
Young *Uruguay* **126** C4
Younghusband, L. *Australia* **95** E2
Younghusband Pen.
    Australia **95** F2
Youngstown *Canada* **103** C6
Youngstown *N.Y., U.S.A.* **114** C5
Youngstown *Ohio, U.S.A.* **114** E4
Youngsville *U.S.A.* **114** E5
Youngwood *U.S.A.* **114** F5
Youxi *China* **59** D12
Youyang *China* **58** C7
Youyu *China* **56** D7
Yozgat *Turkey* **72** C6
Yozgat □ *Turkey* **72** C6
Ypacaraí △ *Paraguay* **126** B4
Ypané → *Paraguay* **126** A4
Yport *France* **18** C7
Ypres = Ieper *Belgium* **17** D2
Yreka *U.S.A.* **108** F2
Yssingeaux *France* **21** C8
Ystad *Sweden* **11** J7
Ysyk-Köl *Kyrgyzstan* **52** E8
Ythan → *U.K.* **13** D7
Ytterhogdal *Sweden* **10** B8
Ytyk-Kyuyel *Russia* **53** C14
Yu Jiang → *China* **58** F7
Yü Shan *Taiwan* **59** F13
Yu Xian = Yuzhou *China* **56** G7
Yu Xian *Hebei, China* **56** E8
Yu Xian *Shanxi, China* **56** E7
Yuan Jiang → *Hunan, China* **59** C8
Yuan Jiang → *Yunnan, China* **58** F4
Yuan'an *China* **59** B8
Yuanjiang *Hunan, China* **59** C9
Yuanli *Taiwan* **59** E13
Yüanli *Taiwan* **59** E13
Yüanlin *Taiwan* **59** F13
Yuanling *China* **59** C8
Yuanmou *China* **58** E3
Yuanqu *China* **56** G6
Yuanyang *Henan, China* **56** G7
Yuanyang *Yunnan, China* **58** F4
Yuba → *U.S.A.* **110** F5
Yuba City *U.S.A.* **110** F5
Yūbari *Japan* **54** C10
Yubdo *Ethiopia* **81** F4

Yūbetsu *Japan* **54** B11
Yubo *Sudan* **81** F2
Yucatán □ *Mexico* **119** C7
Yucatán, Canal de
    Caribbean **120** B2
Yucatán, Península de
    Mexico **98** H11
Yucatan Basin *Cent. Amer.* **119** D7
Yucatan Channel =
    Yucatán, Canal de
    Caribbean **120** B2
Yucca *U.S.A.* **111** L12
Yucca Valley *U.S.A.* **111** L10
Yucheng *China* **56** F9
Yuci *China* **56** F7
Yudu *China* **59** E10
Yuechi *China* **58** B6
Yuendumu *Australia* **92** D5
Yueqing *China* **59** C13
Yueqing Wan *China* **59** D13
Yuexi *Anhui, China* **59** B11
Yuexi *Sichuan, China* **58** C4
Yueyang *China* **59** C9
Yugan *China* **59** C11
Yugoslavia = Serbia ■
    Europe **44** C4
Yuhuan *China* **59** C13
Yúhuan Dao *China* **59** C13
Yujiang *China* **59** C11
Yukhnov *Russia* **32** E8
Yukon *U.S.A.* **116** D6
Yukon → *U.S.A.* **106** a
Yukon Territory □ *Canada* **100** C6
Yüksekova *Turkey* **73** D11
Yukta *Russia* **53** C11
Yukuhashi *Japan* **55** H5
Yulara *Australia* **93** E5
Yule → *Australia* **92** D2
Yuleba *Australia* **95** D4
Yuli *Nigeria* **83** D7
Yüli *Taiwan* **59** F13
Yulin *Guangxi Zhuangzu, China* **59** F8
Yulin *Hainan, China* **64** C7
Yulin *Shaanxi, China* **56** E5
Yuma *Ariz., U.S.A.* **111** N12
Yuma *Colo., U.S.A.* **108** F12
Yuma, B. de *Dom. Rep.* **121** C6
Yumbe *Uganda* **86** B3
Yumbi *Dem. Rep. of the Congo* **86** C2
Yumen *China* **60** C4
Yumurtalık *Turkey* **72** D6
Yun Gui Gaoyuan *China* **58** E3
Yun Ling *China* **58** D2
Yun Xian *Hubei, China* **59** A8
Yun Xian *Yunnan, China* **58** E3
Yuna *Australia* **93** E2
Yunak *Turkey* **72** C4
Yunan *China* **59** F8
Yuncheng *Henan, China* **56** G8
Yuncheng *Shanxi, China* **56** G6
Yunfu *China* **59** F9
Yungas *Bolivia* **124** G5
Yungay *Chile* **126** D1
Yunhe *China* **59** C12
Yunkai Dashan *China* **59** F8
Yunlong *China* **58** E2
Yunmeng *China* **59** B9
Yunnan □ *China* **58** E4
Yunquera de Henares *Spain* **38** E1
Yunt Dağı *Turkey* **47** C9
Yunta *Australia* **95** E2
Yunxi *China* **56** H6
Yunxiao *China* **59** F11
Yupanqui Basin *Pac. Oc.* **97** J17
Yuping *China* **58** D7
Yuqing *China* **58** D6
Yuraygir △ *Australia* **95** D5
Yurga *Russia* **52** D9
Yurimaguas *Peru* **124** E3
Yurkivka *Ukraine* **29** B3
Yurubí △ *Venezuela* **121** D6
Yuryev-Polskiy *Russia* **32** D10
Yuryevets *Russia* **34** B6
Yuscarán *Honduras* **120** D2
Yûsef, Bahr → *Egypt* **80** B3
Yushan *China* **59** C12
Yushanzhen *China* **58** C7
Yushe *China* **56** F7
Yushu *Jilin, China* **57** B14
Yushu *Qinghai, China* **60** C4
Yusufeli *Turkey* **73** B9
Yutai *China* **56** G9
Yutian *China* **57** E9
Yuxarı Qarabağ =
    Nagorno-Karabakh □
    Azerbaijan **73** C12
Yuxi *China* **58** E4
Yuyao *China* **59** B13
Yuzawa *Japan* **54** E10
Yuzha *Russia* **34** B6
Yuzhno-Sakhalinsk *Russia* **53** E15
Yuzhnyy □ *Russia* **35** H5
Yuzhou *China* **56** G7
Yvelines □ *France* **19** D8
Yverdon-les-Bains *Switz.* **25** J2
Yvetot *France* **18** C7
Yzeure *France* **19** F10

Z

Zaanstad *Neths.* 17 B4
Zāb al Kabīr ➤ *Iraq* 73 D10
Zāb aş Şaghīr ➤ *Iraq* 73 E10
Žabalj *Serbia* 28 E5
Žabari *Serbia* 44 B5
Zabarjad *Egypt* 80 C4
Zabaykalsk *Russia* 53 E12
Ząbki *Poland* 31 F8
Ząbkowice Śląskie *Poland* 31 H3
Žabljak *Montenegro* 44 C3
Zabłudów *Poland* 31 F9
Zábol *Iran* 71 D9
Zābol □ *Afghan.* 66 D5
Zābolī *Iran* 71 E9
Zabolotiv *Ukraine* 29 B10
Zabolottya *Ukraine* 31 G11
Zabré *Burkina Faso* 83 C4
Zábřeh *Czech Rep.* 27 B9
Zabrze *Poland* 31 H5
Zabuzhzhya *Ukraine* 31 G10
Zabzuga *Ghana* 83 D5
Zacapa *Guatemala* 120 D2
Zacapu *Mexico* 118 D4
Zacatecas *Mexico* 118 C4
Zacatecas □ *Mexico* 118 C4
Zacatecoluca *El Salv.* 120 D2
Zacharo *Greece* 46 D3
Zachary *U.S.A.* 116 F9
Zachodnio-Pomorskie □
  Poland 30 E2
Zacoalco de Torres *Mexico* 118 C4
Zacualtipán *Mexico* 119 C5
Zadar *Croatia* 41 D12
Zadawa *Nigeria* 83 C7
Zadetkyi Kyun *Burma* 65 G2
Zadonsk *Russia* 33 F10
Zafarqand *Iran* 71 C7
Zafra *Spain* 37 G4
Żagań *Poland* 31 G2
Zagaoua *Chad* 79 E10
Žagarė *Lithuania* 30 B10
Zagazig *Egypt* 80 H7
Zāgheh *Iran* 71 C6
Zagnanado *Benin* 83 D5
Zagora *Greece* 46 B5
Zagorje *Slovenia* 41 B11
Zagórów *Poland* 31 F4
Zagórz *Poland* 31 J9
Zagreb *Croatia* 41 C12
Zagreb ✈ (ZAG) *Croatia* 41 C13
Zagros Mts. = Zāgros,
  Kūhhā-ye *Iran* 71 C6
Zagros, Kūhhā-ye *Iran* 71 C6
Žagubica *Serbia* 44 B5
Zaguinaso *Ivory C.* 82 C3
Zagyva ➤ *Hungary* 28 C5
Zahamena △ *Madag.* 89 B8
Zāhedān *Fārs, Iran* 71 D7
Zāhedān
  Sīstān va Balūchestān, Iran 71 D9
Zahlah *Lebanon* 74 B4
Zahna *Germany* 24 D8
Záhony *Hungary* 28 B7
Zainsk *Russia* 34 C11
Zaïre = Congo ➤ *Africa* 84 F2
Zaječar *Serbia* 44 C6
Zaka *Zimbabwe* 89 C3
Zakamensk *Russia* 53 D11
Zakarpattya □ *Ukraine* 29 B8
Zakataly = Zaqatala
  Azerbaijan 35 K8
Zakhodnaya Dzvina =
  Daugava ➤ *Latvia* 32 D3
Zākhū *Iraq* 73 D10
Zakinthos = Zakynthos
  Greece 46 D2
Zakopane *Poland* 31 J6
Zakroczym *Poland* 31 F7
Zakros *Greece* 49 D8
Zakynthos *Greece* 46 D2
Zakynthos □ *Greece* 46 D2
Zala *Ethiopia* 81 F4
Zala □ *Hungary* 28 D1
Zala ➤ *Hungary* 28 D2
Zalaegerszeg *Hungary* 28 D1
Zalakomár *Hungary* 28 D1
Zalalövő *Hungary* 28 D1
Zalamea de la Serena *Spain* 37 G5
Zalamea la Real *Spain* 37 H4
Zalău *Romania* 28 C8
Žalec *Slovenia* 41 B12
Zaleshchiki = Zalishchyky
  Ukraine 29 B10
Zalesye *Russia* 30 D8
Zalew Wiślany *Poland* 30 D6
Zalewo *Poland* 30 E6
Zalingei *Sudan* 79 F10
Zalishchyky *Ukraine* 29 B10
Zama L. *Canada* 102 B5
Zambeke
  Dem. Rep. of the Congo 86 B2
Zambeze ➤ *Africa* 87 F4
Zambezi = Zambeze ➤
  Africa 87 F4
Zambezi *Zambia* 85 G4
Zambezi △ *Zimbabwe* 87 F2
Zambezia □ *Mozam.* 87 F4
Zambia ■ *Africa* 87 F2
Zamboanga *Phil.* 61 H5
Zambrów *Poland* 31 F9
Zametchino *Russia* 34 D6
Zamfara □ *Nigeria* 83 C6
Zamfara ➤ *Nigeria* 83 C5
Zamora *Mexico* 118 D4
Zamora *Spain* 36 D5
Zamora □ *Spain* 36 D5
Zamość *Poland* 31 H10
Zamtang *China* 58 A3
Zan *Ghana* 83 D4
Záncara ➤ *Spain* 39 F1
Zandvoort *Neths.* 17 B4
Zanesville *U.S.A.* 114 G2
Zangābād *Iran* 70 B5
Zangliveri *Greece* 44 F7
Zangue ➤ *Mozam.* 87 F4
Zanjān *Iran* 73 D13
Zanjān □ *Iran* 71 B6
Zanjān ➤ *Iran* 71 B6
Zannone *Italy* 42 B6
Zante = Zakynthos *Greece* 46 D2
Zanthus *Australia* 93 F3
Zanzibar *Tanzania* 86 D4
Zaouiet El-Kala = Bordj
  Omar Driss *Algeria* 78 C7
Zaouiet Reggâne *Algeria* 78 C6
Zaoyang *China* 59 A9
Zaozhuang *China* 57 G9
Zap Suyu = Zāb al
  Kabīr ➤ *Iraq* 73 D10
Zapadna Morava ➤ *Serbia* 44 C5
Zapadnaya Dvina =
  Daugava ➤ *Latvia* 32 D3
Zapadnaya Dvina *Russia* 32 D7
Západné Beskydy *Europe* 27 B12
Zapadni Rodopi *Bulgaria* 44 E7
Západočeský □ *Czech Rep.* 26 B6
Zapala *Argentina* 128 D2
Zapaleri, Cerro *Bolivia* 126 A2
Zapata *U.S.A.* 116 H5
Zapatón ➤ *Spain* 37 F4
Zapolyarnyy *Russia* 8 B24
Zapopán *Mexico* 118 C4
Zaporizhzhya *Ukraine* 33 J8
Zaporizhzhya □ *Ukraine* 33 J8
Zaporozhye =
  Zaporizhzhya *Ukraine* 33 J8
Zaqatala *Azerbaijan* 35 K8
Zara *Turkey* 72 C7
Zaragoza *Coahuila, Mexico* 118 B4
Zaragoza *Nuevo León, Mexico* 119 C5
Zaragoza *Spain* 38 D4
Zaragoza □ *Spain* 38 D4
Zarand *Kermān, Iran* 71 D8
Zarand *Markazī, Iran* 71 C6
Zărandului, Munţii *Romania* 28 D7
Zaranj *Afghan.* 66 D2
Zarasai *Lithuania* 32 E4
Zárate *Argentina* 126 C4
Zarautz *Spain* 38 B2
Zaraysk *Russia* 32 E10
Zard, Kūh-e *Iran* 71 C6
Zāreh *Iran* 71 C6
Zari *Nigeria* 83 C7
Zaria *Nigeria* 83 C6
Żarki *Poland* 31 H6
Zarko *Greece* 46 B4
Zarneh *Iran* 70 C5
Zărneşti *Romania* 29 E10
Zaros *Greece* 49 D6
Zárów *Poland* 31 H4
Zarqā', Nahr az ➤ *Jordan* 74 C4
Zarrīn *Iran* 71 C7
Zaruma *Ecuador* 124 D3
Zarzis *Tunisia* 79 B8
Żary *Poland* 31 G2
Zarza de Granadilla *Spain* 36 E4
Zas *Spain* 36 B2
Zaskar ➤ *India* 69 B7
Zaskar Mts. *India* 69 C7
Zastavna *Ukraine* 29 B10
Zastron *S. Africa* 88 E4
Žatec *Czech Rep.* 26 A6
Zator *Poland* 31 J6
Zaterechnyy *Russia* 35 H7
Zatyshshya *Ukraine* 29 C14
Zavala *Bos.-H.* 44 D1
Zavāreh *Iran* 71 C7
Zave *Zimbabwe* 89 B5
Zavetnoye *Russia* 35 G6
Zavidovići *Bos.-H.* 28 F3
Zavitinsk *Russia* 53 D13
Zavodovski, I. *Antarctica* 5 B1
Zavolzhsk *Russia* 34 B6
Zavolzhye *Russia* 34 B6
Zawadzkie *Poland* 31 H5
Zawichost *Poland* 31 H8
Zawidów *Poland* 31 G2
Zawiercie *Poland* 31 H6
Zāwiyat al Bayḍā = Al
  Bayḍā *Libya* 79 B10
Zâwyet Shammas *Egypt* 80 A2
Zâwyet Um el Rakham
  Egypt 80 A2
Zâwyet Ungeîla *Egypt* 80 A2
Zāyā *Iraq* 70 C5
Zāyandeh ➤ *Iran* 71 C7
Zaysan *Kazakhstan* 52 E9
Zaysan Köli *Kazakhstan* 52 E9
Zayü *China* 58 C1
Zazafotsy *Madag.* 89 C8
Zbarazh *Ukraine* 23 D13
Zbąszyń *Poland* 31 F2
Zbąszynek *Poland* 31 F2
Zblewo *Poland* 30 E5
Zbruch ➤ 29 B11
Ždar nad Sázavou *Czech Rep.* 26 B8
Zdolbuniv *Ukraine* 23 C14
Ždrelo *Serbia* 44 B5
Zduńska Wola *Poland* 31 G5
Zduny *Poland* 31 G4
Zeballos *Canada* 102 D3
Zebediela *S. Africa* 89 C4
Zebila *Ghana* 83 C4
Zeebrugge *Belgium* 17 C3
Zeehan *Australia* 95 G4
Zeeland *Neths.* 17 C3
Zeeland □ *Neths.* 17 C3
Zeerust *S. Africa* 88 D4
Zefat *Israel* 74 C4
Zege *Ethiopia* 81 E4
Zeggerene, Iracher *Mali* 83 B5
Zégoua *Mali* 82 C3
Zehdenick *Germany* 24 C9
Zeil, Mt. *Australia* 92 D5
Zeila *Somali Rep.* 75 E3
Zeist *Neths.* 17 B5
Zeitz *Germany* 24 D8
Zelena *Ukraine* 29 B9
Zelengora *Bos.-H.* 44 C2
Zelenodolsk *Russia* 34 C9
Zelenogorsk *Russia* 32 B5
Zelenograd *Russia* 32 D9
Zelenogradsk *Russia* 30 D7
Zelenokumsk *Russia* 35 H6
Železná Ruda *Czech Rep.* 26 B6
Železnik *Serbia* 44 B4
Zelienople *U.S.A.* 114 F4
Železovce *Slovak Rep.* 27 C11
Zelina *Croatia* 41 C13
Zell *Baden-W., Germany* 25 H3
Zell *Rhld.-Pfz., Germany* 25 E3
Zell am See *Austria* 26 D5
Zella-Mehlis *Germany* 24 E6
Zelów *Poland* 31 G6
Zeltweg *Austria* 26 D7
Žemaitijos △ *Lithuania* 30 B8
Zémio *C.A.R.* 86 A2
Zempléni-hegység *Hungary* 28 B6
Zemplínska šírava
  Slovak Rep. 27 C15
Zempoala *Mexico* 119 D5
Zemun *Serbia* 44 B4
Zengbé *Cameroon* 83 D7
Zengcheng *China* 59 F9
Zenica *Bos.-H.* 28 F2
Žepče *Bos.-H.* 28 F3
Žeraf, Bahr ez ➤ *Sudan* 81 F3
Zerbst *Germany* 24 D8
Żerków *Poland* 31 F4
Zermatt *Switz.* 25 J3
Zernez *Switz.* 25 J6
Zernograd *Russia* 35 G5
Zerqan *Albania* 44 E4
Zestaponi *Georgia* 35 J6
Zetel *Germany* 24 B3
Zeulenroda *Germany* 24 E7
Zeven *Germany* 24 B5
Zevenaar *Neths.* 17 C6
Zévio *Italy* 40 C5
Zeya *Russia* 53 D13
Zeya ➤ *Russia* 53 D13
Zeytinbaği *Turkey* 45 F12
Zeytindağ *Turkey* 47 C9
Zghartâ *Lebanon* 74 A4
Zgierz *Poland* 31 G6
Zgorzelec *Poland* 31 G2
Zguriţa *Moldova* 29 B13
Zhabinka *Belarus* 31 F11
Zhabokrych *Ukraine* 29 B13
Zhailma *Kazakhstan* 52 D7
Zhambyl = Taraz *Kazakhstan* 52 E8
Zhangaly *Kazakhstan* 35 G10
Zhangaqala *Kazakhstan* 35 F9
Zhangaqazaly *Kazakhstan* 52 E7
Zhangbei *China* 56 D8
Zhangguangcai Ling *China* 57 B15
Zhangjiabian *China* 59
Zhangjiagang *China* 8 B13
Zhangjiakou *China* 56 D8
Zhangping *China* 59 E11
Zhangpu *China* 59 E11
Zhangshu *China* 59 C10
Zhangwu *China* 57 C12
Zhangye *China* 60 C5
Zhangzhou *China* 59 E11
Zhanhua *China* 57 F10
Zhänibek *Kazakhstan* 34 F8
Zhanjiang *China* 59 G8
Zhannetty, Ostrov *Russia* 53 B16
Zhanyi *China* 58 E4
Zhanyu *China* 57 B12
Zhao Xian *China* 56 F8
Zhao'an *China* 59 F11
Zhaocheng *China* 56 F6
Zhaojue *China* 58 C4
Zhaoping *China* 59 E8
Zhaoqing *China* 59 F9
Zhaotong *China* 58 D4
Zhaoyuan *Heilongjiang, China* 57 B13
Zhaoyuan *Shandong, China* 57 F11
Zharkent *Kazakhstan* 52 E9
Zharkovskiy *Russia* 32 E7
Zhashkiv *Ukraine* 23 D16
Zhashui *China* 56 H5
Zhayyq ➤ *Kazakhstan* 6 F16
Zhdanov = Mariupol *Ukraine* 33 J9
Zhdecheng *China* 56 G8
Zhegao *China* 59 B11
Zhejiang □ *China* 59 C13
Zhelezndorozhnyy *Russia* 30 D8
Zheleznogorsk *Russia* 33 F8
Zheleznogorsk-Ilimskiy
  Russia 53 D11
Zheltyye Vody = Zhovti
  Vody *Ukraine* 33 H7
Zhen'an *China* 56 H5
Zhenba *China* 58 A6
Zhenfeng *China* 58 E5
Zheng'an *China* 58 C6
Zhengding *China* 56 E8
Zhenghe *China* 59 D12
Zhengyang *China* 59 A10
Zhengyangguan *China* 59 A11
Zhengzhou *China* 56 G7
Zhenhai *China* 59 C13
Zhenjiang *China* 59 A12
Zhenkang *China* 58 F2
Zhenlai *China* 57 B12
Zhenning *China* 58 D5
Zhenping *Henan, China* 56 H7
Zhenping *Shaanxi, China* 58 B7
Zhenxiong *China* 58 D5
Zhenyuan *Gansu, China* 56 G4
Zhenyuan *Guizhou, China* 58 D7
Zherdevka *Russia* 34 E5
Zherebkove *Ukraine* 29 C14
Zherong *China* 59 D12
Zhetiqara *Kazakhstan* 52 D7
Zhezqazghan *Kazakhstan* 52 E7
Zhicheng *China* 59 B8
Zhidan *China* 56 F5
Zhigansk *Russia* 53 C13
Zhigulevsk *Russia* 34 D9
Zhijiang *Hubei, China* 59 B8
Zhijiang *Hunan, China* 58 D7
Zhijin *China* 58 D5
Zhilinda *Russia* 53 C12
Zhilino *Russia* 30 D8
Zhirnovsk *Russia* 34 E7
Zhitomir = Zhytomyr
  Ukraine 23 C15
Zhizdra *Russia* 32 F8
Zhlobin *Belarus* 23 B16
Zhmerinka = Zhmerynka
  Ukraine 23 D15
Zhmerynka *Ukraine* 23 D15
Zhob *Pakistan* 68 D3
Zhob ➤ *Pakistan* 68 C3
Zhodino = Zhodzina
  Belarus 23 A15
Zhodzina *Belarus* 23 A15
Zhokhova, Ostrov *Russia* 53 B16
Zhongdian *China* 58 D2
Zhongdong *China* 58 F6
Zhongdu *China* 58 E7
Zhongning *China* 56 F3
Zhongshan *Antarctica* 5 C6
Zhongshan *Guangdong, China* 59 F9
Zhongshan
  Guangxi Zhuangzu, China 59 E8
Zhongtiao Shan *China* 56 G6
Zhongwei *China* 56 F3
Zhongxiang *China* 59 B9
Zhongyang *China* 56 F6
Zhorany *Ukraine* 31 G10
Zhoucun *China* 57 F9
Zhouning *China* 59 D12
Zhoushan *China* 59 B14
Zhoushan Dao *China* 59 C14
Zhouzhi *China* 56 G5
Zhovti Vody *Ukraine* 33 H7
Zhovtneve *Lubelskie, Ukraine* 31 H11
Zhovtneve *Mykolayiv, Ukraine* 33 J7
Zhovtnevoye = Zhovtneve
  Ukraine 33 J7
Zhu Jiang ➤ *China* 59 F9
Zhuanghe *China* 57 E12
Zhucheng *China* 57 G10
Zhugqu *China* 56 H3
Zhuhai *China* 59 F9
Zhuji *China* 59 C13
Zhukovka *Russia* 32 F7
Zhumadian *China* 56 H8
Zhuo Xian = Zhuozhou
  China 56 E8
Zhuolu *China* 56 D8
Zhuozhou *China* 56 E8
Zhuozi *China* 56 D7
Zhushan *China* 59 A8
Zhuxi *China* 58 A7
Zhuzhou *China* 59 D9
Zhvanets *Ukraine* 29 B11
Zhytomyr *Ukraine* 23 C15
Zhytomyr □ *Ukraine* 33 G5
Zi Shui ➤ *China* 59 C9
Žiar nad Hronom
  Slovak Rep. 27 C11
Ziārān *Iran* 71 B6
Ziarat *Pakistan* 68 D2
Zibo *China* 57 F10
Zichang *China* 56 F5
Zidarovo *Bulgaria* 45 D11
Zidi = Wandhari *Pakistan* 68 F2
Ziębice *Poland* 31 H4
Zielona Góra *Poland* 31 G2
Zierikzee *Neths.* 17 C3
Ziesar *Germany* 24 C8
Zifta *Egypt* 80 H7
Zigey *Chad* 79 F9
Zigong *China* 58 C5
Ziguinchor *Senegal* 82 C1
Ziguinchor □ *Senegal* 82 C1
Zihuatanejo *Mexico* 118 D4
Zijin *China* 59 F10
Zile *Turkey* 72 B6
Žilina *Slovak Rep.* 27 B11
Žilinský □ *Slovak Rep.* 27 B12
Zillah *Libya* 79 C9
Zillertaler Alpen *Austria* 26 D4
Zima *Russia* 53 D11
Zimapán *Mexico* 119 C5
Zimba *Zambia* 87 F2
Zimbabwe *Zimbabwe* 87 G3
Zimbabwe ■ *Africa* 87 F3
Zimi *S. Leone* 82 D2
Zimnicea *Romania* 29 G10
Zimovniki *Russia* 35 G6
Zinave △ *Mozam.* 89 C5
Zinder *Niger* 83 C6
Zinder □ *Niger* 83 C7
Zinga *Tanzania* 87 D4
Zingaro △ *Italy* 42 D5
Zingst *Germany* 24 A8
Ziniaré *Burkina Faso* 83 C4
Zinnowitz *Germany* 24 A9
Zion △ *U.S.A.* 109 H7
Zirbitzkogel *Austria* 26 D7
Zirc *Hungary* 28 C2
Ziros *Greece* 49 D8
Zirreh, Gowd-e *Afghan.* 66 E3
Zisterdorf *Austria* 27 C9
Zitácuaro *Mexico* 118 D4
Žitava ➤ *Slovak Rep.* 27 C11
Žitište *Serbia* 28 E5
Zitong *China* 58 B5
Zitsa *Greece* 46 B2
Zittau *Germany* 24 E10
Zitundo *Mozam.* 89 D5
Živinice *Bos.-H.* 28 F3
Ziwa Maghariba =
  Kagera □ *Tanzania* 86 C3
Ziway, L. *Ethiopia* 81 F4
Zixi *China* 59 D11
Zixing *China* 59 E9
Ziyang *Shaanxi, China* 56 H5
Ziyang *Sichuan, China* 58 B5
Ziyuan *China* 59 D8
Ziyun *China* 58 E6
Zizhong *China* 58 C5
Zlarin *Croatia* 41 E12
Zlatar *Croatia* 41 B13
Zlatar *Serbia* 44 C3
Zlataritsa *Bulgaria* 45 C9
Zlaté Moravce *Slovak Rep.* 27 C11
Zlatibor *Serbia* 44 C3
Zlatitsa *Bulgaria* 45 D8
Zlatna *Romania* 29 D8
Zlatna Panega *Bulgaria* 45 C8
Zlatni Pyasŭtsi *Bulgaria* 45 C12
Zlatograd *Bulgaria* 45 E9
Zlatoust *Russia* 52 D6
Zletovo *Macedonia* 44 E6
Zlín *Czech Rep.* 27 B10
Zlínský □ *Czech Rep.* 27 B10
Złocieniec *Poland* 30 E3
Złoczew *Poland* 31 G5
Zlot *Serbia* 44 B5
Złotoryja *Poland* 31 G2
Złotów *Poland* 30 E4
Zmeinogorsk *Kazakhstan* 52 D9
Żmigród *Poland* 31 G3
Zmiyiv *Ukraine* 33 H9
Znamenka = Znamyanka
  Ukraine 33 H7
Znamensk *Russia* 30 D8
Znamyanka *Ukraine* 33 H7
Znin *Poland* 31 F4
Znojmo *Czech Rep.* 26 C9
Zobeyrī *Iran* 70 C5
Zobia *Dem. Rep. of the Congo* 86 B2
Zoetermeer *Neths.* 17 B4
Zogang *China* 58 C1
Zogno *Italy* 40 C6
Zogqên *China* 58 A2
Zolochev = Zolochiv
  Ukraine 23 D13
Zolochiv *Ukraine* 23 D13
Zolotonosha *Ukraine* 33 H7
Zolotyy Potik *Ukraine* 29 B10
Zomba *Malawi* 87 F4
Zongo *Dem. Rep. of the Congo* 84 D3
Zonguldak *Turkey* 72 B4
Zonguldak □ *Turkey* 72 B4
Zongyang *China* 59 B11
Zonqor Pt. *Malta* 49 D2
Zonza *France* 21 G13
Zorgo *Burkina Faso* 83 C4
Zorita *Spain* 37 F5
Zorleni *Romania* 29 D12
Zornitsa *Bulgaria* 45 D10
Zorritos *Peru* 124 D2
Zorzor *Liberia* 82 D3
Zossen *Germany* 24 C9
Zou Xiang *China* 56 G9
Zouan-Hounien *Ivory C.* 82 D3
Zouar *Chad* 79 D9
Zouérate = Zouîrât
  Mauritania 78 D3
Zouîrât *Mauritania* 78 D3
Zourika *Niger* 83 B6
Zourma *Burkina Faso* 83 C4
Zoutkamp *Neths.* 17 A6
Zrenjanin *Serbia* 28 E5
Zuarungu *Ghana* 83 C4
Zuba *Nigeria* 83 D6
Zubayr *Yemen* 81 D5
Zubtsov *Russia* 32 D8
Zuénoula *Ivory C.* 82 D3
Zuera *Spain* 38 D4
Zufār *Oman* 75 D5
Zug *Switz.* 25 H4
Zugdidi *Georgia* 35 J5
Zugersee *Switz.* 25 H4
Zugspitze *Germany* 25 H6
Zuid-Holland □ *Neths.* 17 C4
Zuidbeveland *Neths.* 17 C3
Zuidhorn *Neths.* 17 A6
Zújar *Spain* 39 H1
Zújar ➤ *Spain* 37 G5
Żukowo *Poland* 30 D5
Zula *Eritrea* 81 D4
Zülpich *Germany* 24 E2
Zumaia *Spain* 38 B2
Zumárraga *Spain* 38 B2
Zumbo *Mozam.* 87 F3
Zummo *Nigeria* 83 D7
Zumpango *Mexico* 119 D5
Zungeru *Nigeria* 83 D6
Zunhua *China* 57 D9
Zuni Pueblo *U.S.A.* 109 J9
Zunyi *China* 58 D6
Zuo Jiang ➤ *China* 58 F6
Zuozhou *China* 58 F6
Županja *Croatia* 28 E3
Žur *Serbia* 44 D4
Zurbātīyah *Iraq* 73 F12
Zürich *Switz.* 25 H4
Zürich □ *Switz.* 25 H4
Zürichsee *Switz.* 25 H4
Żuromin *Poland* 31 E6
Žut *Croatia* 41 E12
Zutphen *Neths.* 17 B6
Zuurberg △ *S. Africa* 88 E4
Zuwārah *Libya* 79 B8
Zūzan *Iran* 71 C8
Zvenigorodka =
  Zvenyrodka *Ukraine* 33 H6
Zvenyhorodka *Ukraine* 33 H6
Zvezdets *Bulgaria* 45 D11
Zvishavane *Zimbabwe* 87 G3
Zvolen *Slovak Rep.* 27 C12
Zvonce *Serbia* 44 D6
Zvornik *Bos.-H.* 28 F4
Zwedru = Tchien *Liberia* 82 D3
Zweibrücken *Germany* 25 F3
Zwelitsha *S. Africa* 85 L5
Zwenkau *Germany* 24 D8
Zwettl *Austria* 26 C8
Zwickau *Germany* 24 E8
Zwierzyniec *Poland* 31 H9
Zwiesel *Germany* 25 F9
Zwoleń *Poland* 31 G8
Zwolle *Neths.* 17 B6
Zwolle *U.S.A.* 116 F8
Żychlin *Poland* 31 F6
Żyrardów *Poland* 31 F7
Zyryan *Kazakhstan* 52 E9
Zyryanka *Russia* 53 C16
Zyryanovsk = Zyryan
  Kazakhstan 52 E9
Żywiec *Poland* 31 J6
Zyyi *Cyprus* 49 E12

KEY TO EUROPEAN MAP PAGES

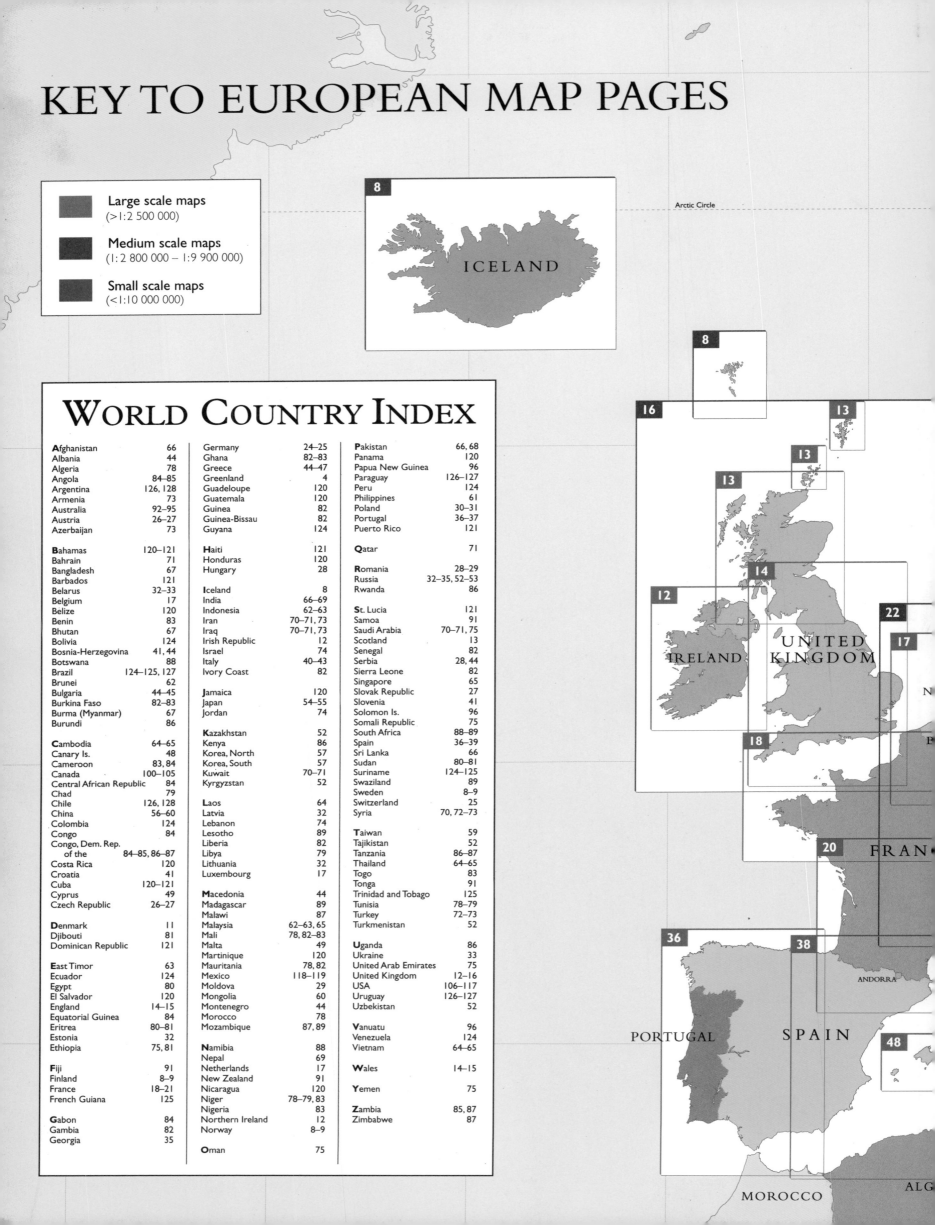

Large scale maps
(>1:2 500 000)

Medium scale maps
(1: 2 800 000 – 1:9 900 000)

Small scale maps
(<1:10 000 000)

8

ICELAND

8

Arctic Circle

16

13

13

13

14

12

22

IRELAND

UNITED KINGDOM

17

18

36

38

20

FRANCE

ANDORRA

PORTUGAL

SPAIN

48

MOROCCO

ALG

WORLD COUNTRY INDEX

Afghanistan	66	**G**ermany	24–25	**P**akistan	66, 68
Albania	44	Ghana	82–83	Panama	120
Algeria	78	Greece	44–47	Papua New Guinea	96
Angola	84–85	Greenland	4	Paraguay	126–127
Argentina	126, 128	Guadeloupe	120	Peru	124
Armenia	73	Guatemala	120	Philippines	61
Australia	92–95	Guinea	82	Poland	30–31
Austria	26–27	Guinea-Bissau	82	Portugal	36–37
Azerbaijan	73	Guyana	124	Puerto Rico	121
Bahamas	120–121	**H**aiti	121	**Q**atar	71
Bahrain	71	Honduras	120		
Bangladesh	67	Hungary	28	**R**omania	28–29
Barbados	121			Russia	32–35, 52–53
Belarus	32–33	**I**celand	8	Rwanda	86
Belgium	17	India	66–69		
Belize	120	Indonesia	62–63	**S**t. Lucia	121
Benin	83	Iran	70–71, 73	Samoa	91
Bhutan	67	Iraq	70–71, 73	Saudi Arabia	70–71, 75
Bolivia	124	Irish Republic	12	Scotland	13
Bosnia-Herzegovina	41, 44	Israel	74	Senegal	82
Botswana	88	Italy	40–43	Serbia	28, 44
Brazil	124–125, 127	Ivory Coast	82	Sierra Leone	82
Brunei	62			Singapore	65
Bulgaria	44–45	**J**amaica	120	Slovak Republic	27
Burkina Faso	82–83	Japan	54–55	Slovenia	41
Burma (Myanmar)	67	Jordan	74	Solomon Is.	96
Burundi	86			Somali Republic	75
		Kazakhstan	52	South Africa	88–89
Cambodia	64–65	Kenya	86	Spain	36–39
Canary Is.	48	Korea, North	57	Sri Lanka	66
Cameroon	83, 84	Korea, South	57	Sudan	80–81
Canada	100–105	Kuwait	70–71	Suriname	124–125
Central African Republic	84	Kyrgyzstan	52	Swaziland	89
Chad	79			Sweden	8–9
Chile	126, 128	**L**aos	64	Switzerland	25
China	56–60	Latvia	32	Syria	70, 72–73
Colombia	124	Lebanon	74		
Congo	84	Lesotho	89	**T**aiwan	59
Congo, Dem. Rep.		Liberia	82	Tajikistan	52
of the	84–85, 86–87	Libya	79	Tanzania	86–87
Costa Rica	120	Lithuania	32	Thailand	64–65
Croatia	41	Luxembourg	17	Togo	83
Cuba	120–121			Tonga	91
Cyprus	49	**M**acedonia	44	Trinidad and Tobago	125
Czech Republic	26–27	Madagascar	89	Tunisia	78–79
		Malawi	87	Turkey	72–73
Denmark	11	Malaysia	62–63, 65	Turkmenistan	52
Djibouti	81	Mali	78, 82–83		
Dominican Republic	121	Malta	49	**U**ganda	86
		Martinique	120	Ukraine	33
East Timor	63	Mauritania	78, 82	United Arab Emirates	75
Ecuador	124	Mexico	118–119	United Kingdom	12–16
Egypt	80	Moldova	29	USA	106–117
El Salvador	120	Mongolia	60	Uruguay	126–127
England	14–15	Montenegro	44	Uzbekistan	52
Equatorial Guinea	84	Morocco	78		
Eritrea	80–81	Mozambique	87, 89	**V**anuatu	96
Estonia	32			Venezuela	124
Ethiopia	75, 81	**N**amibia	88	Vietnam	64–65
		Nepal	69		
Fiji	91	Netherlands	17	**W**ales	14–15
Finland	8–9	New Zealand	91		
France	18–21	Nicaragua	120	**Y**emen	75
French Guiana	125	Niger	78–79, 83		
		Nigeria	83	**Z**ambia	85, 87
Gabon	84	Northern Ireland	12	Zimbabwe	87
Gambia	82	Norway	8–9		
Georgia	35				
		Oman	75		